Corporations

Corporations

Second Edition

JAMES D. COX
Brainerd Currie Professor of Law
Duke University

THOMAS LEE HAZEN
Cary C. Boshamer Distinguished Professor of Law
University of North Carolina at Chapel Hill

1185 Avenue of the Americas, New York, NY 10036
www.aspenpublishers.com

> Permissions
> Aspen Publishers
> 1185 Avenue of the Americas
> New York, NY 10036

Printed in the United States of America.

1 2 3 4 5 6 7 8 9 0

ISBN 0-7355-2598-6 (Student Version)

Library of Congress Cataloging-in-Publication Data

Cox, James D., 1943-
  Corporations / James D. Cox, Thomas Lee Hazen.—2nd ed.
    p. cm.
  Includes bibliographical references and index.
  ISBN 0-7355-3054-8 (3-volume Set)
  1. Corporation law—United States.   I. Hazen, Thomas Lee, 1947-
  II. Title.

KF1414.C69 2002
346.73'066—dc21   2002033208
                                                                  CIP

About Aspen Publishers

Aspen Publishers, headquartered in New York City, is a leading information provider for attorneys, business professionals, and law students. Written by preeminent authorities, our products consist of analytical and practical information covering both U.S. and international topics. We publish in the full range of formats, including updated manuals, books, periodicals, CDs, and online products.

Our proprietary content is complemented by 2,500 legal databases, containing over 11 million documents, available through our Loislaw division. Aspen Publishers also offers a wide range of topical legal and business databases linked to Loislaw's primary material. Our mission is to provide accurate, timely, and authoritative content in easily accessible formats, supported by unmatched customer care.

To order any Aspen Publishers title, go to *www.aspenpublishers.com* or call 1-800-638-8437.

To reinstate your manual update service, call 1-800-638-8437.

For more information on Loislaw products, go to *www.loislaw.com* or call 1-800-364-2512.

For Customer Care issues, e-mail *CustomerCare@aspenpublishers.com*; call 1-800-234-1660; or fax 1-800-901-9075.

Aspen Publishers
A Wolters Kluwer Company

To Bonnie

—JDC

To Lisa, George and Elliott

—TLH

Summary of Contents

Contents

CHAPTER 2

The Evolution of Corporations in America 31

CHAPTER 3

The Incorporation Process 45

Contents

CHAPTER 4

The Scope of the Authorized Business and Duties to Other Constituencies   61

CHAPTER 5

The Promotion of the Corporation   73

CHAPTER 6

Defective Formation of Corporations   89

CHAPTER 7

The Separate Corporate Entity: Privilege and
Its Limitations   99

CHAPTER 8

Powers of Officers and Agents; Criminal Liability of Corporations   117

CHAPTER 9

Functions and Powers of Directors   135

CHAPTER 10

Directors' and Officers' Duties of Care and Loyalty

183

CHAPTER 11

Fiduciary Duties for Executive Compensation, Corporate Opportunities, and Controlling Stockholders

221

CHAPTER 12

Obligations Arising Out of Transactions in Shares

265

Contents

CHAPTER 13

Rights and Powers of Shareholders; Inspection Rights, Voting, and Proxies   327

CHAPTER 14

Close Corporations — 383

Contents

CHAPTER 15

The Derivative Suit   415

CHAPTER 16

Issuance of Shares   479

Contents

CHAPTER 17

Liability for Watered, Bonus, and Underpaid Shares   505

CHAPTER 18

Capital Structure, Preference, and Other Classes of Securities   515

CHAPTER 19

Accounting Statements and Dividend Law   535

CHAPTER 20

Dividend Distributions: Rights, Restrictions, and Liabilities   549

Contents

CHAPTER 21

Purchase and Redemption by a Corporation of Its Own Shares

CHAPTER 25

Amendments to the Corporate Charter   695

CHAPTER 26

Voluntary Dissolution, Administrative
Dissolution, and Winding Up   705

Contents

Preface

This student text is adapted from *Cox & Hazen on Corporations*—a three volume treatise.[1] The first edition of this treatise was selected in 1995 for a national book award by The Association of American Publishers. The first edition and this one were each built upon the solid foundation laid by the late Henry W. Ballantine in his classic single-volume work, *Ballantine on Corporations*. It has been our aim to examine the law of corporations with care and craftsmanship equal to its predecessor. Though corporate law has undergone a sea of change since Ballantine published the last edition of his work, the challenges to the corporate lawyer have not changed over the years. Corporate law is one of the areas most vital to our society, for it regulates the workings of Adam Smith's invisible hand in the allocation of resources among competing uses. Unfortunately, the importance of corporate law is not matched by clarity in its doctrines, principles, and statutes. The field continues to be filled with "trite dogmas, formulas, metaphors, and legal fictions to the fundamental realities and policies of the law."[2]

In this work, we provide a comprehensive analysis of all areas of corporate law and the most significant provisions of the federal securities laws. Contrasting judicial and statutory approaches are examined in both a contemporary commercial context and historical evolution of law on each subject examined. We have avoided a state-by-state review on each topic; instead we devote our energies to capturing and critiquing the significance of the differences in approaches. As evident in each of our chapters, we examine the historical fount of doctrines, their contemporary vitality, and qualifications and weaknesses in their impact. This text is not content to recite the empty metaphors and vague incantations that appear with regrettable frequency in the courts' treatment of important issues of corporate law. We emphasize the financial, political, and social considerations that appear to have guided the courts' dispositions in individual

---

[1] Although the chapter numbers are the same as the multivolume treatise, many section numbers and footnotes have been renumbered.

[2] Preface, Henry W. Ballantine, Ballantine on Corporations iii (rev. ed. 1946).

cases. Simply stated, we seek to provide a helpful and insightful treatment of the law of corporations.

This text is written and edited to provide an understanding of corporate law. Although some leading sources are included, this text is not intended as a research tool. Footnotes from the parent edition have been edited severely. Readers conducting research should consult the three-volume *Cox & Hazen on Corporations*.

Because of the broad impact on the shape of state corporate statutes of the Model Business Corporation Act, close attention is given to the Model Act throughout the text. Major non-Model Act jurisdictions, such as California, Delaware, and New York, are also emphasized in our treatment of statutes and doctrine.

James D. Cox
Thomas Lee Hazen

May 2003

Acknowledgments

We very much appreciate the support and encouragement for this text that we have received from our respective deans. A great debt is also due the numerous students who provided invaluable research on this project. Their numbers are far too large to permit each to be singled out here for fear of inadvertent omissions.

A work such as this does not occur without personal sacrifice. We each thank our families for their patience, understanding, and support.

CHAPTER 1

Forms of Business Association— Definitions and Distinctions

A.   THE CORPORATE FORM OF BUSINESS

§1.01   The Corporation

Much of the industrial and commercial development of the nineteenth and twentieth centuries was made possible by the corporate mechanism. By its use investors may combine their capital and participate in the profits of large- or small-scale business enterprises under a centralized management,[1] with a risk limited to the capital contributed and without peril to their other resources and business. The amount of capital needed for modern business could hardly have been assembled and combined in any other way. The corporate device has indeed raised serious questions as to the undue concentration of economic power.[2]

Long ago it was aptly observed that "A corporation is, after all, but an association of individuals under an assumed name and with a distinct legal entity."[3] What, then, is this corporate entity or personality? It should be clearly understood at the outset that it is entirely a matter of convenience to employ the metaphor or figure of speech by which we call a corporation a legal person. A corporation may more realistically be described as a legal unit, a concern separated off with a legal existence, status, or capacity of its own, a legal device or instrument for carrying on some business enterprise, or some social, charitable, religious, or governmental activities.[4]

Other than the corporation, the forms of business association generally available in this country are (1) the partnership, including the joint venture, (2) the limited partnership, (3) the limited liability company, (4) the joint stock company (sometimes referred to as a "joint stock association"), (5) the Massachusetts or business trust, and (6) in a few states, the "partnership association." These six forms of doing business are distinct from the sole proprietorship in which a single individual owns and operates the business.

§1.02   The Concept of Corporate Entity or Personality

A business corporation is a legal device for carrying on a business enterprise for profit, a legal unit with a status or capacity of its own separate from the share-

---

§1.01   [1] *See* Voeller v. Neilston Warehouse Co., 311 U.S. 531, 537 (1941).

[2] Early concerns for the power of corporations appeared in several classic works. *See* Adolf A. Berle & Gardiner C. Means, The Modern Corporation and Private Property chs. I-III (1932); I. Maurice Wormser, Frankenstein, Inc. (1931); Harold Gill Reuschlein, Federalization—Design for Corporate Reform in a National Economy, 91 U. Pa. L. Rev. 91, 93-96 (1942).

[3] *See, e.g.,* Jordan v. Tashiro, 278 U.S. 123 (1928) (Stone, J.).

[4] Edward H. Warren, Corporate Advantages Without Incorporation 15 (1929) ("A legal unit is whatever has capacity to acquire a legal right or incur a legal obligation. . . . Usually a legal unit which is not a human being is a body of human beings.").

holders or members who own it.[1] In theory the shareholders have only an indirect interest in the assets of the corporation, which interest is manifested in their right to share in profits through dividends and in the distribution of corporate assets on liquidation. The corporation holds property, enters into contracts, executes conveyances, and conducts litigation in a legal capacity separate and distinct from its shareholders.

The famous definition of "corporation" given by Chief Justice Marshall emphasizes the notion that the corporation is a legal entity. "A corporation," Marshall said,

> is an artificial being, invisible, intangible, and existing only in contemplation of law. Being the mere creature of law, it possesses only those properties which the charter of its creation confers upon it, either expressly, or as incidental to its very existence. These are such as are supposed best calculated to effect the object for which it was created. Among the most important are immortality, and, if the expression may be allowed, individuality; properties, by which a perpetual succession of many persons are considered as the same, and may act as a single individual. They enable a corporation to manage its own affairs, and to hold property without the perplexing intricacies, the hazardous and endless necessity, of perpetual conveyances for the purpose of transmitting it from hand to hand. It is chiefly for the purpose of clothing bodies of men, in succession, with these qualities and capacities, that corporations were invented, and are in use. By these means, a perpetual succession of individuals are capable of acting for the promotion of the particular object, like one immortal being.[2]

"Business corporation" has sometimes been defined in terms of an *association* of a number of persons in a business enterprise with the object of economic gain. Thus it has been said: "A corporation is, after all, but an association of individuals under an assumed name and with a distinct legal entity."[3] It should be clearly understood that it is entirely a matter of convenience to employ the metaphor or figure of speech to call the corporation a legal person. A corporation may be more realistically described as a legal unit, a concern separated off with a legal existence, status, or capacity of its own, a legal device or instrument for carrying on some business enterprise or some social, charitable, religious, or governmental activities. Corporation A is a legal person entirely different from individual shareholder X, or, rather, it has a legal capacity that is distinct from X's, even though X organized it, manages it, and owns all or practically all of its shares.

Unlike in an individual enterprise or partnership, in a corporation the maximum loss to shareholders or owners due to the business's debts and torts, with rare exceptions, will not exceed the amount that they have invested in the enterprise. If Y loans money or otherwise extends credit to A Corporation, he must look to the corporate assets for repayment; ordinarily he cannot recover from the

---

§1.02 [1] Edward H. Warren, Corporate Advantages Without Incorporation 15 (1929); Frederic W. Maitland, Collected Papers 307 (1911). *See also* John Dewey, The Historic Background of Corporate Legal Personality, 35 Yale L.J. 655, 656 (1926).

[2] Trustees of Dartmouth College v. Woodward, 17 U.S. (4 Wheat.) 518, 636 (1819).

[3] Hale v. Henkel, 201 U.S. 43, 76 (1906) (Brown, J.).

shareholders or levy on their property.[4] The separateness of the corporation is also generally recognized for tax purposes, the corporation usually being considered a "taxable entity."[5]

The corporation has also been referred to as "a creature of statute." This reflects the fact that a corporation can only be formed by compliance with requirements set forth in the corporation statute of the state in which the corporation is being organized.[6] Incorporation papers setting forth certain basic information, such as the corporation's name, registered agent, and its capital structure, must be prepared and filed with designated public officials.

§1.03   The Corporation and the Constitution

When questions arise concerning the right of corporations to invoke constitutional protections, the Supreme Court resolves the question by examining the nature and purpose of the specific articles, clause, or amendment. Over time, this inquiry has yielded a "corporate personality" for constitutional purposes.[1] Corporations, as artificial persons, are entitled to many, but not all, the protections and guarantees afforded natural persons.

Citizenship. One significant limitation on a corporation's rights under the Constitution is the Supreme Court's refusal to grant it citizenship status for the purposes of the privileges and immunities clause of Article IV, section 2, as well as under the Fourteenth Amendment.[2] As a consequence of being denied citizenship status, states may, as a valid exercise of their police powers, regulate foreign corporations conducting business within their borders, provided the regulations do not impermissibly affect commerce.[3]

On the other hand, a corporation is a citizen for the purposes of determining whether the federal court has jurisdiction based on diversity of citizenship under Article III of the Constitution.[4] The corporation's citizenship for jurisdictional purposes and its presence for venue purposes is now controlled by statute.

Person. Various constitutional provisions afford protection to a "person." The Court interprets this language as including artificial persons such as corporations

---

[4] For a more comprehensive discussion of limited liability and the circumstances in which a court will disregard the separate personality of a corporation and impose liability for the corporation's debts on the shareholder or shareholders, *see* Chapter 7.

[5] Menihan v. Commissioner, 79 F.2d 304 (2d Cir.), *cert. denied*, 296 U.S. 651 (1935).

[6] In most parts of the English-speaking world, a business corporation such as Exxon is called a "company."

§1.03   [1] *See* Dewey, *supra* §1.02 note 1.

[2] Ashbury Hosp. v. Cass County, 326 U.S. 207 (1945).

[3] *See, e.g.,* Alleghany Cotton Co. v. Pittman, 419 U.S. 20 (1974) (state court does not have jurisdiction over corporation incorporated in another state unless there are sufficient intrastate contacts). *Compare* Eli Lilly & Co. v. Sav-on-Drugs, 366 U.S. 276 (1961) (service on foreign corporation upheld where office maintained and 18 employees within state).

[4] Bank of United States v. Deveaux, 9 U.S. (5 Cranch) 61 (1809).

A. The Corporate Form of Business

when the provision does not pertain to a "purely personal guarantee."[5] Thus a corporation is a person for purposes of the Fourth Amendment's protection against unlawful searches and seizures of its property[6] and the Fifth Amendment's protection against double jeopardy.[7] For example, the Court reasoned that, because a corporation's success depends heavily on its goodwill, it should be protected by the Fifth Amendment from a second, damaging criminal trial. The corporation is also a person protected by the due process clauses of the Fifth and Fourteenth Amendments[8] as well as the equal protection clause of the Fourteenth Amendment.[9]

A corporation is not a "person" under the self-incrimination clause of the Fifth Amendment. Because that guaranty is intended to prohibit the use of physical or moral compulsion exerted on the person asserting the privilege, its protection is purely personal in nature and therefore applies only to natural persons.[10]

Corporations, while entitled to many Fourth, Fifth, and Fourteenth Amendment freedoms, do not enjoy the same right of privacy as do individuals.[11] Because a corporation exists solely by the grace of the legislature and "[t]here is a reserved right of the legislature to investigate [a corporation's] contracts and find out whether it has exceeded its powers,"[12] the corporation's books and records carry no personal privacy.[13] This position ensures government the information needed to regulate corporations. While government agencies have a legitimate right to make inquiries to assure the corporation's behavior is consistent with the law and the public interest, the government must be mindful that the Fourth Amendment does protect the corporation from unreasonable searches and seizures.[14]

Liberty. A corporation does not enjoy the full protections of the Fourteenth Amendment's due process guarantees respecting "liberty."[15] The liberties embodied in the Fourteenth Amendment generally are those associated with a natural, not artificial, person. However, in *Grosjean v. American Press Co.*,[16] the Supreme Court held that the Fourteenth Amendment's due process clause accords corporations the protection embodied in the First Amendment.[17] Occasionally the

---

[5] *See* United States v. White, 322 U.S. 694 (1944).

[6] G.M. Leasing Corp. v. United States, 429 U.S. 338 (1977); See v. City of Seattle, 387 U.S. 541 (1967).

[7] *See, e.g.,* United States v. Martin Linen Supply Co., 430 U.S. 564 (1977); Fong Foo v. United States, 369 U.S. 141 (1962).

[8] *See, e.g.,* First Nat'l Bank v. Bellotti, 435 U.S. 735 (1978).

[9] Santa Clara County v. Southern Pac. R.R., 118 U.S. 394, 396 (1886).

[10] *See, e.g.,* United States v. Doe, 465 U.S. 605 (1984) (individual may be entitled to avoid producing document potentially incriminating to him; corporation remains obligated to produce document).

[11] *See, e.g.,* California Bankers Ass'n v. Shultz, 416 U.S. 21, 65-67 (1974); United States v. Morton Salt Co., 338 U.S. 632, 651-652 (1950).

[12] Hale v. Henkel, 201 U.S. 43, 75 (1906).

[13] United States v. White, 322 U.S. 694, 700 (1944).

[14] G.M. Leasing Corp. v. United States, 429 U.S. 338 (1977).

[15] Northwestern Nat'l Life Ins. Co. v. Riggs, 203 U.S. 243 (1906). *Accord:* Hague v. C.I.O., 307 U.S. 496 (1939).

[16] 297 U.S. 233 (1936).

[17] *See also* NAACP v. Button, 371 U.S. 415 (1963) (NAACP accorded standing to assert First Amendment rights distinct from its members); Bowe v. Secretary of Commw., 69 N.E.2d 115 (Mass. 1946) (liberty of press enjoyed and protected by Fourteenth Amendment from abridgment by state).

Court recognizes constitutional protections without having to address the corporation's status. For example, in *First National Bank of Boston v. Bellotti*,[18] the Supreme Court avoided the issue as to whether a corporation is entitled to First Amendment protection by rephrasing the issue. It focused on whether the speech involved itself was constitutionally protected. Reasoning "the Constitution often protects interests broader than those of the party seeking their vindication," the Court there concluded that corporate expenditures to support political activity were constitutionally protected.[19]

Legal Process. In *Ross v. Bernhard*[20] the Court accepted the position that "a corporation's suit to enforce a legal right was an action at common law carrying the right to a jury trial at the time the Seventh Amendment was adopted."[21] Thus the corporation enjoys the right to a jury trial where such right existed at common law. And, relying on the Sixth Amendment, corporations have a constitutional right to effective assistance of counsel.[22] To sue or be sued, however, they must be represented by counsel—that is, a corporation cannot proceed pro se.[23]

§1.04 Non-Tax Advantages of Corporations

The principal non-tax advantages customarily given for doing business in the corporate form are: (1) exemption of shareholders from personal liability; (2) continuity of the organization's existence despite changes in its members; (3) centralized management by a board of directors; (4) free transferability of a participant's interest; (5) access of the business to additional capital; (6) the organization's capacity to act as a legal unit in holding property, contracting, and bringing suit; and (7) standardized methods of organization, management, and finance prescribed by corporation statutes for the protection of shareholders and creditors, including a more or less standardized system of shareholder relations, rights, and remedies.

A primary advantage of the corporation is the shareholders' limited liability.[1] Shareholders are immune from personal liability for corporate debts and torts beyond the amount of their agreed investments in the corporation's stock.

Limited liability may be less of a factor in selecting corporate form today than it once was in light of the growing number of alternative business forms which

---

[18] 435 U.S. 765 (1978).

[19] *Id.* at 776.

[20] 396 U.S. 531 (1970).

[21] *Id.* at 533-534.

[22] *See, e.g.,* United States v. Rad-O-Lite of Philadelphia, Inc., 612 F.2d 740 (3d Cir. 1979).

[23] *See, e.g.,* In re Las Colinas Dev. Corp., 585 F.2d 7 (1st Cir. 1978); United States v. Crosby, 24 F.R.D. 15 (1959) (applying the rule to criminal proceedings). The same is true for a limited liability company. *E.g.,* International Ass'n of Sheet Metal Workers Local 16, 1999 U.S. Dist. LEXIS 9861 (1999); Poore v. Fox Hollow Enterprises, 1994 WL 150872 (Del. Superior Ct. 1994).

§1.04 [1] Limited liability appears to have been established for American corporations by the second or third decade of the nineteenth century. Herbert Hovenkamp, Enterprise and American Law 1836-1937 49 (1991).

A. The Corporate Form of Business

grant limited liability to its owners. For example, the limited partnership,[2] the limited liability partnership,[3] and the limited liability company[4] are forms of doing business where the owners can enjoy limited liability. In addition, even in a general partnership, in most states the partners elect to have the business treated as a limited liability partnership to at least some extent.[5] Most states permit a partnership to elect to become a limited liability partnership and thereby eliminate the partners' personal liability for the negligence of the partnership or of the other partners.[6] A growing number of states,[7] and the 1996 version of the Revised Uniform Partnership Act, provide for full limited liability of the partners with regard to both tort and contract obligations.[8]

A second important advantage gained by incorporation is continuity of existence: Incorporation creates an entity endowed with the capacity to exist either perpetually or for a fixed period, notwithstanding the death or change of its members. When the membership of a partnership changes—for example, when a partner's interest is transferred or when a partner dies—the partnership is dissolved. Unless appropriate provisions have been made in the partnership agreement for the continuation of the business, the enterprise must be liquidated. In contrast, whenever shareholders transfer their shares, the transferees become shareholders in their place; and when shareholders die, their shares pass like other personal property to successors. Neither the separate existence nor the identity of the corporation as a legal unit is affected by these changes. In the colorful language of Blackstone, a corporation is "a person that never dies: in like manner as the River Thames is still the same river, though the parts which compose it are changing every instant."[9]

Because managerial responsibility is lodged with the board of directors and their duly selected officers and agents, the corporation enjoys centralized administration, which as a practical matter is of necessity in a large organization. Although the shareholders elect the directors and in theory have ultimate control over actions taken by the corporation, they do not participate as shareholders in the day-to-day management of corporate affairs.

---

[2] *See* §1.08.

[3] *See* §1.06.

[4] *See* §1.10.

[5] *See* §1.06.

[6] *E.g.,* Del. Stat. Ann. tit. 6 §§1515, 1544 (2001); N.C. Gen. Stat. §59-45(b), (c) (2001). *See* Prefatory Notes to the 1996 Amendments to the Revised Uniform Partnership Act (1996).

[7] *See* Alan R. Bromberg & Larry E. Ribstein, Bromberg & Ribstein on Limited Liability Partnerships and the Revised Uniform Partnership Act §§3.02-3.03 (1997); Prefatory Notes to the 1996 Amendments to the Revised Uniform Partnership Act (1996).

[8] RULPA §306(c) (1996). *See also* RULPA §1001(b) (1996). In addition even limited partnerships can achieve a full limited liability shield through a limited liability limited partnership which insulates the general partnership from unlimited liability that traditionally applied to general partners. *See* Revised Uniform Partnership Act (RUPA) §§306(c), 1001.

[9] Blackstone, Commentaries 468 (1783). Unincorporated joint stock companies and business trusts also issue transferable shares and by contract may continue their existence in spite of membership changes.

In publicly held corporations, free alienation of shares is a distinct advantage of the corporate form of doing business. "A prime requisite for the functioning of the corporation system as a capital-raising device is liquidity for investment. Even with limited liability an investor must still consider the possibility of a change in his own or in corporate circumstances which may affect his investment interest."[10] In a closely held business, however, in which each shareholder often is an active, vital member of the management team and the active participants do not look to outside investors for funds, free transferability of shares may be undesirable.[11]

Great flexibility in financing is available to a corporation. It may issue many different kinds of securities, each with distinct claims and preferences against the corporate income or assets. For instance, a corporation may issue several classes of stock, varieties of bonds, debentures, or notes and hybrid securities having characteristics of both equity securities and debt securities.[12] The great flexibility corporations have in the types of securities they can issue permits corporations to tailor their economic relationships to the demands of particular investors in prevailing market conditions.

Because a corporation is viewed as a legal entity that exists apart from its shareholders, it may sue, be sued, hold property, enter into contracts, and perform most other acts that an individual can perform. Another aspect of the concept of the corporation as a distinct legal person that may prove advantageous is that shareholders, to some extent, can remain anonymous.

At least in large business enterprises, an advantage of corporate organization over some other types of association is the greater standardization of a corporation's organization and operation. Every state statute has detailed provisions on the legal relations of shareholders toward each other and the corporation. Further, an elaborate system of regulation of management and protection of shareholders' and creditors' rights has been established and is constantly under review by the courts.

§1.05 Disadvantages of the Corporate Form

The corporate form of doing business has a number of distinct disadvantages. A single owner or small group of owners starting a new business have little appetite for the more formal procedures of operation that accompany incorporation. A disadvantage of the corporate form is the necessity of compliance with various statutory formalities, which require considerable legal advice and other expert assistance. Examples include the filing of various reports and documents. Further, a corporation experiences greater difficulty in doing business across state lines. A

[10] Henry G. Manne, Our Two Corporation Systems: Law and Economics, 53 Va. L. Rev. 259, 263-264 (1967). *See also* William L. Cary & Melvin A. Eisenberg, Cases and Materials on Corporations 95 (6th ed. 1988).

[11] *See generally* 2 F. Hodge O'Neal & Robert Thompson, O'Neal's Close Corporations: Law and Practice, ch. 7 (1991).

[12] For a discussion of the various kinds of corporate securities, *see* §§18.04-18.14.

corporation domiciled in one state that does business in other states is invariably required to "qualify" in the other states—that is, obtain authorization from each of the other states to transact business. A partnership can generally operate in another state without the formality of qualification.[1] In some states a corporation is prohibited from engaging in specific kinds of activity—for example, only recently did the accounting profession agree to permit its professionals to incorporate. Generally, corporate income is subject to a double tax burden—first, to the corporation and, second, when distributed as dividends, as personal income to the shareholders.[2] In sum, the sentiment is frequently expressed: "When in doubt don't incorporate."[3]

B.   PARTNERSHIPS AND LIMITED LIABILITY COMPANIES

§1.06   Characteristics of the Partnership

An unincorporated association, like a firm, is not generally recognized in American law as a *legal* unit or entity having a separate capacity and rights but, rather, for most purposes it traditionally has been regarded as an aggregation of individuals operating the business as co-owners with individual rights and duties.[1] On some matters, however, such as the continuity of identity of the firm in spite of changes in the personnel or membership, conveyances by and to the firm as if it were a legal unit, and the prior application of the assets of insolvent partnerships to the firm debts in bankruptcy, the Uniform Partnership Act treats the partnership as having to a certain extent a separate identity or individuality, as if the partnership were an independent concern or person.[2] The partnership liabilities may be regarded as primarily the liabilities of a separate legal unit. The obligations of a firm are made payable out of its assets in bankruptcy in priority to the individual debts of the partners. Under statutes, partnerships are often treated as if they

---

§1.05   [1] Qualification by an out-of-state corporation usually involves registration with the Secretary of State. In addition, a registered office must be maintained or a registered agent appointed to receive service of process upon the corporation in the state. *E.g.*, Del. Code Ann. tit. 8, §371 (2001). Some states, however, are beginning to subject out-of-state partnerships to regulations similar to those imposed on out-of-state corporations. *See, e.g.*, N.H. Rev. Stat. Ann. §305-A:1 (1984 & Supp. 1993).

[2] Certain qualifying closely held corporations may elect to avoid double taxation. I.R.C. §§1371-1379 (1988).

[3] *See, e.g.*, George C. Seward & W. John Nauss, Basic Corporate Practice 1 (2d. ed 1977).

§1.06   [1] *See* Donald Weidner, A Perspective to Reconsider Partnership Law, 16 Fla. St. U. L. Rev. 1 (1988); Henry Ballantine, To What Extent Is a Partnership a Legal Entity?, 17 Cal. L. Rev. 625, 703 (1929). The Revised Uniform Partnership Act, which has been adopted in a number of states, takes the more realistic position that a partnership is an entity, separate and distinct from its members. RUPA §201 (1992). The entity concept is discussed *supra* §1.02.

[2] *See* In re Groff, 898 F.2d 1475 (10th Cir. 1990) (partnership is entity distinct from partners); Bartlome v. State Farm Fire & Cas. Co., 256 Cal. Rptr. 719 (Cal. Ct. App. 1989) (California treats partnership as legal entity for purposes of property ownership).

had an entity for purposes of suing and being sued in the firm name.[3] Aside from the rules governing partners' liabilities, the law of partnership is based on contract and agency principles.[4]

The 1990s brought major changes in the law relating to partnerships. The Revised Uniform Partnership Act, which has been adopted in whole or in part in a majority of states, has altered many of the traditional partnership concepts. Perhaps most importantly, the Revised Uniform Partnership Act recognizes a partnership as a separate entity rather than an aggregation of its members. Also, as of 1998, 48 states and the District of Columbia permit partnerships to register as limited liability partnerships and take advantage of at least some limited liability attributes.[5] Most states insulate partners from liability for negligence that they are not involved in, while other states provide a full liability shield for all partnership obligations—both tort and contract—except the partners' own negligence.[6]

The Uniform Partnership Act (UPA) defines "partnership" as "an association of two or more persons to carry on as co-owners a business for profit."[7] The co-ownership element of this definition entails both profit-sharing and sharing in control. An essential characteristic of the partnership is that it is an association for profit. The Uniform Act provides that in most cases receipt of a share of the profits is prima facie evidence of partnership status.[8] The presumption is rebutted by evidence that the party lacks the power to share in control of the business. That is, profit-sharing alone is not sufficient to establish partnership status.[9] This does not require that such control actually be exercised. Control in this context requires more than discharging ministerial tasks; it requires the power to share in significant managerial tasks.[10]

The existence of a partnership does not depend upon a formal written agreement to that effect. For example, the partnership agreement may be oral.[11] Furthermore, a series of understandings may result in a partnership even in the absence of an agreement. The determination of whether a particular business arrangement is a partnership is a highly factual inquiry[12] and is dependent upon

---

[3] *See, e.g.,* New England Herald Dev. Group v. Town of Falmouth, 521 A.2d 693 (Me. 1987); Yuenglin v. Mazur, 328 N.W.2d 624 (Mich. Ct. App. 1982); Decker Coal Co. v. Commonwealth Edison Co., 714 P.2d 155 (Mont. 1986). *Contra* Anderson v. Hall, 755 F. Supp. 2, 4 (D.D.C. 1991) ("partnerships have no legal existence in the District of Columbia, and are not jural entities capable of suing or being sued").

[4] Agency law is discussed *infra* §1.17. *See also* Chapter 8 for discussion of agency in the context of corporate officials.

[5] *See* Elizabeth G. Hester, Registered Limited Liability Partnerships, 69 Aspen Law & Business Corporation Guide 1 (No. 6, March 16, 1998).

[6] *Id.*

[7] Uniform Partnership Act §6(1) (1969) (hereinafter UPA); Revised Uniform Partnership Act §101(6) (hereinafter RUPA).

[8] UPA §§6, 7(4) (1969); RUPA §§101(6), 202(3).

[9] *See* Dalton v. Austin, 432 A.2d 774, 777 (Me. 1981) ("right to participate in control of the business is the essence of co-ownership").

[10] Alan R. Bromberg & Larry E. Ribstein, Bromberg and Ribstein on Partnership §2.14 (2001). Thomas v. Price, 718 F. Supp. 598 (S.D. Tex. 1989), Minute Maid Corp. v. United Foods, Inc., 291 F.2d 577 (5th Cir.), *cert. denied,* 368 U.S. 928 (1961).

[11] *See* Kansallis Fin. Ltd. v. Fern, 40 F.3d 476, 478-479 (1st Cir. 1994) (applying Uniform Partnership Act).

[12] *See, e.g.,* Bass v. Bass, 814 S.W.2d 38, 41 (Tenn. 1991).

B. Partnerships and Limited Liability Companies

not only the written or oral understandings and agreements between the parties but also upon the conduct of the parties and the surrounding circumstances.[13] Each partner has the apparent authority to contract on behalf of the partnership. In the absence of an agreement providing otherwise, all partners have equal rights in the management and conduct of the business, and persons dealing with a partnership are not affected by private agreements between partners. Thus a partner may bind the partnership on a contract within the apparent scope of the partnership business, even though the partnership agreement expressly denies the contracting partner such authority (unless the person with whom the partner dealt has knowledge of the restriction on the partner's authority). All the partners, even those with a proportionately small interest, are liable jointly and severally for loss or injury caused by the tortious or other wrongful act of any partner or employee of the firm who is acting in the ordinary course of the business. Thus innocent partners having only a small interest in the business may be "plunged into the unknown depths of unlimited liability"[14] by contracts made by other persons or torts committed by other persons over whom they have no control.

Partnerships traditionally have had a precarious existence. A partnership is subject to serious risks of dissolution, and to possible liquidation of its assets and termination of its business. Even if a partnership is not a partnership at will but is stated to be for a definite term, any partner may dissolve it at any time in violation of the agreement, subject only to liability for damages for breach of the agreement. A partnership is also dissolved by the death of a partner, by the bankruptcy of a partner, or by a court decree declaring a partner to be insane or guilty of serious misconduct relating to the partnership.[15]

The Revised Uniform Partnership Act is similar in effect except that these events cause the partner's "dissociation" rather than an automatic dissolution of the partnership.[16] A partner's dissociation has several consequences. Dissociation terminates the partner's right to manage or conduct partnership business. Dissociation ends the partner's duty to refrain from competing with the partnership, unless of course the partnership agreement provides otherwise. Dissociation limits the partner's remaining duties of loyalty and care only as to matters or events that occurred before the partner's dissociation.

§1.07   The Joint Venture: A Form of Partnership

Business ventures of limited scope or duration conducted by two or more persons for profit are variously referred to as "joint ventures," "joint adventures," "joint

---

[13] *E.g.*, Hilco Prop. Servs., Inc. v. United States, 929 F. Supp. 526, 537 (D.N.H. 1996).
[14] Henry W. Ballantine, Corporations 7 (rev. ed. 1946).
[15] UPA §§31, 32.
[16] RUPA §§601, 602.

enterprises" and, in some contexts, "syndicates."[1] A "joint venture" has been defined as an association of two or more persons to carry out a *single* business transaction, or a few related transactions, for profit or commercial gain, for which purpose they combine their property, money, efforts, skills, and knowledge.[2] This definition is far from universally accepted; so "joint venture" is "at best a nebulous concept."[3] In broad overview, a joint venture is best distinguished from a partnership in that it has a more limited scope and duration.[4]

Many jurisdictions require the presence of several specific elements to establish a joint venture. The most commonly stated elements of a joint venture are (1) a contract, (2) a common purpose, (3) a community of interest, (4) an equal right of control, and (5) participation in both profits and losses.[5]

§1.08   The Limited Partnership

The limited partnership is a statutorily created method[1] of profit-sharing by passive investors. This form of business organization permits investors to share the profits of a business, with their risk of loss limited to their investment if the investors comply with certain legal formalities. A limited partnership has two classes of partners: (1) one or more general partners, who have complete control, manage the enterprise, and are subject to full liability; and (2) one or more limited partners, who are very similar to firm creditors but are subordinated to creditors if the firm becomes insolvent or is liquidated. The limited partner ordinarily does not take part in the day-to-day control of the business.

The first limited partnership statute in this country was adopted in New York in 1822[2] and was soon replicated in most other industrial states. A safer and more satisfactory form of limited partnership arrived in 1916 with the Uniform Limited Partnership Act, which was drafted by the Commissioners on Uniform State Laws. This statute was enacted by every state.[3] In 1976 the Commissioners on Uniform State Laws approved a Revised Uniform Limited Partnership Act (RULPA) as a recommended replacement. Subsequently, the revised act was adopted in most

§1.07   [1] *See* In re O.W. Limited Partnership, 668 P.2d 56 (Haw. 1983); Smith v. Metropolitan Sanitary Dist. of Greater Chicago, 396 N.E.2d 524 (Ill. 1979).

[2] *E.g.,* Kelley Inv. Co. v. Merrill Lynch, Pierce, Fenner & Smith, 386 F.2d 595 (8th Cir. 1967); State v. Bland, 197 S.W.2d 669 (Mo. 1946); Rust v. Kelly, 741 P.2d 786 (Mont. 1987).

[3] *See* In re Groff, 898 F.2d 1475, 1476 (10th Cir. 1990) ("although its history is not entirely clear, apparently the joint venture concept was developed to extend principles of partnership law to organizations that did not meet the technical requirements of a partnership").

[4] *E.g.,* Pine Products Corp. v. United States, 945 F.2d 1555, 1560 (Fed. Cir. 1991) (joint venture is "a partnership created for a limited purpose").

[5] *See* Sullivan v. Scoular Grain Co., 930 F.2d 798 (10th Cir. 1991).

§1.08   [1] "A limited partnership is strictly a creature of statute. . . ." Hoefer v. Hall, 411 P.2d 230, 232 (N.M. 1965).

[2] N.Y. Laws ch. 244 (1822).

[3] 6 U.L.A. 2 (Supp. 1980).

B. Partnerships and Limited Liability Companies

jurisdictions.[4] The National Conference of Commissioners on Uniform State Laws has been considering additional changes to the Revised Act and has proposed a revision of RULPA which is known as Re-RULPA.[5]

Unlike an ordinary partnership, which can be formed by a mere informal agreement among the participants, a limited partnership is formed only by complying with statutory formalities similar to those required for the creation of a corporation. A verified certificate containing provisions similar to those called for in a corporation's articles of incorporation must be filed with the clerk, recorder, or other designated public official of the county in which the limited partnership's principal place of business is located and sometimes must also be filed in other counties in which it has places of business.[6]

Both the original and revised uniform limited partnership acts limit the liability of persons who attempt to become limited partners. If the statutory requirements for the formation of a limited partnership are *substantially* complied with, or if the persons who attempt to become limited partners in good faith believe themselves to be limited partners, the limited partners enjoy limited liability.[7] Limited partners become subject to liability if they exercise control of the business.[8] As a result of the states having adopted the RULPA, limited partners today have much greater latitude to involve themselves in the partnership without risking their loss of limited liability than they could under the former Uniform Limited Partnership Act.

The 1985 amendments to the Revised Uniform Limited Partnership Act further expanded these safe-harbor activities to include limited partners having the right to approve any matter related to the business of the limited partnership so long as their right to so participate is expressly granted in the limited partnership agreement.[9] Another provision holds that merely being "an officer, director or shareholder" of a corporate general partner of the limited partnership does not constitute taking part in the control of the partnership.[10]

The Revised Uniform Limited Partnership Act also contains a sweeping provision that restricts the class of persons to whom a limited partner is liable to those persons who transact business with the limited partnership reasonably believing, based on the limited partners' conduct, that the limited partner is a general partner.[11] Under this unconditional "creditor-reliance" standard, the creditor's recovery is justified only when limited partners act like the traditional general partners

---

[4] Forty-nine states (all except Louisiana) have adopted some form of the 1976 revised Act. Unif. Ltd. Partnership Act Refs. & Ann., 6A U.L.A. 1 (1995).

[5] When the first reading was scheduled for 2000, it was hoped that Re-RULPA might be adopted by the NCCUSL in 2001.

[6] Under the Revised Act, filings need be made only in the Office of the Secretary of State.

[7] Uniform Limited Partnership Act §2(2) (1969) (hereinafter ULPA); RULPA §201(b) (1976).

[8] ULPA §§7, 11 (1969); RULPA §§303, 304 (1976 with amendments 1985).

[9] RULPA §303(b)(6)(ix).

[10] RULPA §303(b)(1). For a case decided under the earlier ULPA which goes even further, *see* Frigidaire Sales Corp. v. Union Properties, Inc., 544 P.2d 781 (Wash. Ct. App. 1975), *aff'd,* 562 P.2d 244 (Wash. 1977).

[11] *Compare* RULPA (1976), *with* 1985 Amendments to §303(a).

and have failed to let the creditor know that they were acting solely in their limited partner capacity.[12]

The limited liability company has become a more attractive form of business since unlike a traditional limited partnership, all of the participants, including the general managers, enjoy a complete liability shield. A growing number of states have recognized a new variety of limited partnership known as the limited liability limited partnership.[13] This variation permits partners to become general partners and still stand behind a limited liability shield. In a limited liability limited partnership a limited partner may become a general partner without losing his or her limited liability. This permits limited partners to become general partners and have significant say in the day-to-day operations of the partnership business and would likely not be subject to the securities laws for the same reason that a general partnership interest ordinarily is not a security.

§1.09 Tax Considerations in Selecting a Business Form

In broad overview, the partnership is not treated as a tax entity under the federal Internal Revenue Code.[1] The partnership is required to file an information return listing the partners and their share of the partnership income. Each partner's share of the partnership income (whether distributed to the partners or not) is taxed to that partner as personal income. A corporation, however, is usually treated as a taxable unit separate and apart from its shareholders. This commonly results in the same income and same assets being taxed twice, once to the corporation and again to its shareholders. For example, the corporation pays a tax on its income, and dividends received by its shareholders are taxed to the shareholders to the extent they represent distributions from the corporation's earnings and profits. Similarly, the corporation pays state and local property taxes on its assets, and the shareholders often pay property taxes on their shares of stock, which represent among other things their interests in the corporation's assets. Therefore double taxation is a common concern in whether to incorporate a business.

A corporate entity can avoid double taxation by electing to be a Subchapter S corporation. Under the tax laws, an S corporation is similar to a partnership in that the business's income and losses are attributed to its owners (whether dis-

---

[12] *See, e.g.*, Pitman v. Flanagan Lumber Co., 567 So. 2d 1335 (Ala. 1990).

[13] *E.g.*, Ark. Code Ann. §4-43-1111 (2001); Colo. Rev. Stats. Ann. §§7-64-101 *et seq.* (2001); Del. Code Ann. tit. 6 §17-214 (1999 & Supp. 2000); West's Fla. Stats. Ann. §608.402 (2001); Minn. Stats. Ann. §322A.88 (1995 & Supp. 2002); Va. Code §50-73.78 (1998).

§1.09 [1] An important exception to the partnership not being a taxable entity arises in the case of a publicly traded partnership. I.R.C. §7704 (1996). The IRS has established a safe harbor whereby a partnership that is not registered under the federal Securities Act of 1933 and has no more than 100 partners will not be considered a publicly traded partnership.

B. Partnerships and Limited Liability Companies

tributed or not), and the corporation is not a taxable entity. Only a small business corporation may elect to be an S corporation.[2] A "small business corporation" is a corporation with not more than 75 shareholders; it may issue only a single class of stock, which may be owned only by individuals, estates, and certain trusts; and its shares may not be owned by nonresident aliens or certain ineligible corporations, such as financial institutions.[3] The Subchapter S election must be consented to by all the shareholders and must be made no later than by the fifteenth day of the third month of the taxable year in which the election is to take effect. Absent an election, all corporate entities are taxed as C corporations.[4]

In the end, the tax considerations on the type of business to be formed can in isolated cases be quite complex. More generally, however, those forming a small business will be sensitive to non-tax considerations as well, such as shielding its owners from the business's debts. In these situations, the disadvantages of double taxation are ameliorated by the availability of Subchapter S. However, this may come at the irritation of losing some fringe benefits that are available to shareholders of a C corporation.

Formerly, the tax laws imposed severe restrictions on the attributes of entities opting to be taxed other than as a corporation. The IRS, drawing on the guidelines set down by the Supreme Court in *Morrisey v. Commissioner*,[5] identified six factors that were to be considered in deciding whether an association would be taxable as a corporation: (1) associates engaged in a joint venture, (2) the purpose of transacting business and sharing in its gains, (3) continuity of life, (4) centralized management through representatives of its participants, (5) limited liability, and (6) free transferability of interests.[6] An association would not be classified as a corporation unless the association had more corporate characteristics than noncorporate characteristics.[7]

The foregoing six characteristics meant that planners did not have complete freedom in drafting the internal governance and operational rules for noncorporate forms of doing business. All of that changed in 1997 when the IRS replaced the *Morrisey* test with a "check the box" procedure under which an entity may elect to be taxed as a corporation or not.[8] Under the current approach, all that is required at the outset is that a noncorporate form of doing business elect whether or not to be taxed as a corporation. Entities that select noncorporate tax treatment may at a later date elect corporate tax treatment.

---

[2] I.R.C. §1361(a)(1) (2002). After 1996, the number of shareholders of a subchapter S corporation increased to not more than 75.

[3] I.R.C. §§1361(b)(1), (2) (2002). Although only one class of stock is permitted, voting rights within that class may be varied.

[4] The terms "C corporation" and "S corporation" appear only in the world of taxation and distinguish corporations that are governed by the special rules sets forth in Subchapter S from the more generally applicable Subchapter C of the Internal Revenue Code.

[5] 296 U.S. 344 (1935).

[6] *See* Treas. Reg. §301.7701-2(a) (1988).

[7] Treas. Reg. §301.7701-2(a)(3) (1988).

[8] Treas. Reg. §301.7701-3(a).

§1.10 The Limited Liability Company

One of the newest forms of business association is the limited liability company (LLC). The Wyoming legislature in 1977 enacted the first statute authorizing the limited liability company.[1] All states now provide for limited liability companies.[2]

The impetus for the state enactments authorizing the creation of LLCs is securing the federal income tax advantages of partnership status while simultaneously preserving the state law benefits of limited liability for the entity's owners. In 1988, in a key ruling, the Internal Revenue Service (IRS) issued Ruling 88-76 classifying a Wyoming LLC as a partnership for federal income tax purposes.

The limited liability company thus is a relatively new vehicle by which a business's owners can avoid both double taxation and liability for the business's debts. The "interests" of the members of an LLC are not represented by stock; the members hold interests much like partners in a partnership. LLC members have a right to share in profits as spelled out in the LLC operating agreement.[3] Many statutes provide that if the agreement is silent, members share equally in profits. A right to share in profits does not translate into a right to demand a distribution of those profits.[4]

All of the states have now enacted LLC statutes. The National Conference of Commissioners on Uniform Laws circulated its draft of a uniform LLC statute in mid-1994. Notwithstanding the push for uniformity, great variety remains among the states in their limited liability company statutes.

Some limited liability company statutes provide that the existence of an LLC may not exceed 30 years.[5] An LLC's existence may be terminated by dissolution. Dissolution of LLCs is borrowed from partnership law. Early statutes did not address a member's right to dissociate from the entity although some follow the partnership analogy. An LLC's member's interest does not necessarily translate into a right to force a dissolution of the limited liability company.[6] However, the LLC operating agreement may provide that withdrawal is a trigger for dissolution of the LLC.[7]

---

§1.10 [1] *See* Wyo. Stat. §§17-15-101 to 17-15-136 (1977). The current version is Wyo. Stat. §§17-15-101 to 17-15-136 (2001).

[2] *See, e.g.*, Fla. Stat. Ann. §§608.401-608.471 (2001); Mich. Comp. Laws §450-4101-5200 (1990 & Supp. 2002); Va. Code Ann. §13.1-1000-13.1-1073 (Michie 1999 & Supp. 2001). *See also, e.g.*, Charles W. Murdock, Limited Liability Companies in the Decade of the 1990s: Legislative and Case Law Developments and Their Implications for the Future, 56 Bus. Law. 499 (2001).

[3] *Cf.* Christine R. Strong & Susan P. Hamill, Allocations Attributable to Partner Nonrecourse Liabilities: Issues Revealed by LLCs and LLPs, 51 Alabama L. Rev. 603 (2000).

[4] Five Star Concrete, L.L.C. v. Klink, Inc., 693 N.E.2d 583 (Ind. App. 1998) (allocation of income for tax purposes does not create a right to demand distribution of the profits).

[5] *See, e.g.*, Colo. Rev. Stat. §7-80-204(1)(b) (2001); Fla. Stat. ch. 608.407(1)(b) (2001); Nev. Rev. Stat. Ann. §86.161(1)(b) (Michie 1999 & Supp. 2001); Wyo. Stat. §17-15-107(a)(ii) (2001). In contrast, corporate statutes permit perpetual existences, and the RULPA allows the partnership agreement to identify the events of dissolution, which can include "the latest date upon which the limited partnership is to dissolve." RULPA §201(a)(4) (1985).

[6] Lieberman v. Wyoming.com LLC, 11 P.3d 353 (2000) (member had right to withdraw and receive return of his capital contribution but it did not follow that he could force dissolution).

[7] *See* Investcorp, L.P. v. Simpson Investment Co., 893 P.2d 265 (Kan. 1999).

B. Partnerships and Limited Liability Companies

A former common feature of limited liability company statutes were the limitations that accompany transfers of LLC interests. However, limited liability company agreements can readily provide for the free transferability of limited liability company interests without jeopardizing the entity's tax status. Also, more modern LLC statutes readily permit free transferability.

Many statutes provide that absent an agreement to the contrary, limited liability companies are member managed.[8] Under the default provision, which parallels the law of partnership,[9] in member-managed LLCs, each of the members is an agent of the LLC[10] and has the authority to bind it in the ordinary course of business. As an agency relationship, member managed LLCs result in fiduciary duties of its member-manager agents.[11] These fiduciary duties are subject to reasonable limitation in the LLC operating agreement.[12] In the case of nonmember-managed LLCs, the managers will possess the authority established in the agreement. This results in agency principles analogous to those in the corporate structure wherein certain titles, such as general manager, will carry with them certain apparent, implied, and inherent authority. Notwithstanding members' obligations to one another, it has been held that absent a provision in the operating agreement, there is no right to expel an LLC member even for misfeasance in office.[13]

Fiduciary obligations among LLC members presumably include the duties of care and loyalty. Failure to fully disclose conflicts of interest to fellow LLC members can be a breach of the duty of loyalty.[14]

The voting rights of members of limited liability companies are determined by the LLC operating agreement. However, the statutes contain default provisions. Some states, following the partnership model, provide that in the absence of an agreement to the contrary, LLC members have an equal say in the operation of the business.[15] As of 2000, about half of the states had this per capita default rule.[16] Other states impose the default rule based on proportional ownership.[17] As is the case with other forms of doing business, the statute grants LLC members the right to inspect the LLC's books and records.[18]

---

[8] *E.g.,* Del. Stat. Ann. tit. 6 §18-402 (1999 & Supp. 2000).

[9] *See* §1.06.

[10] *See, e.g.,* J.M. Equip. & Transp. v. Gemstone, L.L.C., 1998 Conn. Super. LEXIS 2425 (1998).

[11] *E.g.,* McConnell v. Hunt Sports Enters., 725 N.E.2d 1993 (Ohio Ct. App. 1999) (LLC members like partners owe one another fiduciary duties). *See* §1.06 (duties of partners) and §1.17 (agency principles). *See also, e.g.,* VGS, Inc. v. Castiel, 2000 WL 12773272 (Del. Ch. 2000) (finding breach of fiduciary duty in connection with merger involving LLC).

[12] *See, e.g.,* McConnell v. Hunt Sport Enterprises, 725 N.E.2d 1193 (Ohio App. 1999).

[13] Walker v. Resource Dev. Co., L.L.C., 2000 Del. Ch. LEXIS 127 (2000) (plaintiff whose drinking problem interfered with the performance of his duties could not be expelled).

[14] *E.g.,* VGS, Inc. v. Castiel, 2000 Del. Ch. LEXIS 122 (2000) (setting aside merger for nondisclosures and breach of duty of loyalty). *See also, e.g.,* Cole v. Kershaw, 2000 Del. Ch. LEXIS 117 (2000) (plaintiff could recover damages for merger on terms that were deemed unfair).

[15] *See supra* §1.06.

[16] *See* Melvin Aron Eisenberg, An Introduction to Agency, Partnerships and LLCs 136 (2000).

[17] *Id.*

[18] *See, e.g.,* Del. Stat. Ann. tit. 6 §18-305 (1999 & Supp. 2000).

Again, following the lead of the corporate statutes, most state LLC statutes provide a procedure for derivative suits.[19] Even without express statutory provisions relating to LLCs, analogy can be drawn to the corporate form in recognizing derivative suits within LLCs.[20] These derivative suits permit members to enforce *inter se* the provisions of the LLC operating agreement as well as fiduciary duties that may arise from the LLC relation. Notwithstanding the right to sue derivatively, courts will generally enforce provisions in the operating agreement calling for arbitration of disputes arising thereunder.[21]

Validly formed and properly operated limited liability companies will result in limited liability of the member owners with regard to the obligations of the LLC.[22] Presumably, an abuse of the limited liability company form of doing business could lead to the elimination of limited liability. Just as courts on appropriate facts have pierced the veil of shareholders' limited liability,[23] a limited liability company that is improperly organized or improperly operated can be similarly attacked. As is the case with corporations, it will be the exceptional case in which a court will be willing to pierce the veil of a limited liability company. Among other things, it would have to be proved that the LLC was in fact a sham and really the alter ego of the members[24] or that it was a mere instrumentality of the owners.[25] Failure to follow proper formalities, such as failing to identify the entity as a limited liability can result in the personal liability of the owners.[26] Also, the LLC liability shield will not apply to liabilities arising prior to the formation of the LLC.[27]

As a relatively new form of doing business, there may be questions as to whether laws applying to corporations, partnerships, and other enumerated forms of doing business apply to limited liability companies.[28] In many ways, a limited liability company is essentially a partnership with a legislative grant of limited liability. As such, laws that apply to corporations should apply equally to limited liability companies unless there is an express provision to the contrary or a special reason for according different treatment under the law to partnerships and limited liability companies.[29]

[19] *E.g.,* Uniform Limited Liability Company Act §§1101-1104 (1995).
[20] *See, e.g.,* Taurus Advisory Group Inc. v. Sector Management, Inc., 1996 WL 502187 *2 (Conn. Super. 1996).
[21] *See* Elf Atochem N. Am., Inc. v. Jaffari, 727 A.2d 286, 79 A.L.R. 5th 803 (Del. 1999). *Accord* Plinke v. PNE Media, LLC, 2001 U.S. Dist. LEXIS 4257 (E.D. Pa. 2001).
[22] The limited liability shield does not extend to activities of members unrelated to the business of the LLC. *E.g.,* PB Real Estate v. DEM II Props., 719 A.2d 73 (Conn. Super. 1998).
[23] *See* §§7.02-7.06.
[24] Hollowell v. Orleans Regional Hosp. LLC, 217 F.3d 379 (5th Cir. 2000).
[25] *See, e.g.,* New Horizons Supply Cooperative v. Haack, 590 N.W.2d 282 (Wis. App. 1999) (failure to establish "mere instrumentality" as basis for piercing veil).
[26] *E.g.,* Water, Waste & Land v. Lanham, 955 P.2d 997 (Colo. 1998) (agent held liable for failure to identify entity as an LLC).
[27] Pepsi-Cola Bottling Co. of Salisbury v. Handy, 2000 WL 364199 (Del. Ch. 2000) (fraud predated formation of LLC); Uniform Limited Liability Company Act §303(a).
[28] *See, e.g.,* Meyer v. Oklahoma Alcoholic Beverage Laws Enforcement Commission, 890 P.2d 1361 (Okla. Ct. App. 1995) (although not expressly included in an alcohol control statute, an LLC would be regulated as a separate entity and would not be treated as a partnership).
[29] *E.g.,* Fraser v. Major League Soccer, L.L.C., 97 F. Supp. 2d 130, 134 (D. Mass. 2000).

Because the LLC is a relatively new form of doing business, a number of questions remain to be answered with regard to the LLC. One question is whether law firms and other professionals may use this form of doing business and thereby achieve limited liability. In some states there is express statutory authorization for professional limited liability partnerships (LLPs). It is to be anticipated that the efficacy of professional LLPs (PLLPs) and professional limited liability companies (PLLCs) will be clarified over time. Limited liability statutes are much more diverse than partnership and limited partnership statutes, most of which have uniform acts as models. Thus, there are likely to be more state-by-state variations with LLCs. As discussed in an earlier section,[30] many states now provide the same full liability shield for partners in a registered limited liability partnership. In those states, a partnership desiring limited liability for its partners may find it easier to register as a limited liability partnership than to convert into an LLC even though more and more states have been adopting conversions to facilitate converting one form of business entity into another.[31]

C.   OTHER TYPES OF BUSINESS ASSOCIATIONS

§1.11   The Joint Stock Company

A variant of the partnership form of doing business is the joint stock company. The core of the joint stock company is its articles of association, essentially a private contract among its members. Through the articles of association the participants approach many of the features common to partnerships as well as the corporate characteristics of free transferability of shares, continuity of existence, and centralized management. The principal disadvantage the joint stock company has in common with a common law partnership, even where the joint stock company has been recognized by statute, is that the members do not enjoy limited liability.[1]

Unincorporated joint stock companies have always been recognized as legal in the United States.[2] Most states enacted statutes that permit suits by or against an officer, trustee, or the company itself.[3]

---

[30] *See* §1.06.

[31] *E.g.*, Uniform Limited Liability Company Act art. 9 (1995).

§1.11 [1] *See, e.g.*, Earlsboro Gas Co. v. Vern H. Brown Drilling Co., 52 P.2d 730 (Okla. 1935); Flint v. Culbertson, 309 S.W.2d 269, 270 (Tex. Civ. App.), *reh'g denied*, 159 Tex. 243, 319 S.W.2d 690 (Tex. 1958).

[2] Mason v. American Express Co., 334 F.2d 392 (2d Cir. 1964).

[3] *See, e.g.*, Mass. Ann. Law ch. 182, §6 (1996 & Supp. 2002); Tex. Rev. Civ. Stat. Art. 6133 (West 1970). For cases applying statutes recognizing the joint stock company as an entity for litigation purposes, *see* Mason v. American Express Co., 334 F.2d 392 (2d Cir. 1964) (New York statute); Carl v. Shore, 299 S.W. 860 (Tex. App. Comm'n 1927), *corrected on other grounds and reh'g denied*, 4 S.W.2d 965 (Tex. App. Comm'n 1928).

§1.12 The Business Trust (Massachusetts Trust)

The business trust, often referred to as the "Massachusetts trust" because of its reputed origin in Massachusetts and its frequent use there, is a business organization created by a deed or declaration of trust under which assets suitable for a business enterprise are transferred to trustees to be managed for the benefit and profit of persons holding transferable certificates evidencing the beneficial interests in the trust estate.[1] The trustees have legal title to the property in trust and act as principals for the certificate holders ("shareholders"). Vesting title to the enterprise's assets in trustees and empowering them to act as representatives of the business create a business organization, if not a legal unit.[2] The business trust, therefore, embodies at least three important characteristics of the corporate form of business: limited liability, centralized management, and transferability of ownership. Moreover, continuity of existence is attained by providing for the remaining trustees or the beneficial owners to appoint new trustees as successors in case of vacancies.

The declaration, or deed of trust, somewhat like a corporation's charter or articles of incorporation, establishes the organization, its business purposes, and authorized shares and specifies the powers of the trustees as well as the rights of the certificate holders. The trustees of a business trust perform the same functions as the board of directors of a corporation or joint stock company, although in form they carry on the business in their own names. Trust property is held and conveyed in the names of the trustees, and actions are initiated by and against the trustees. This arrangement gives the enterprise the corporate advantage of centralized management. Incoming shareholders become parties to the trust agreement, or at least claim to be beneficiaries under it. The beneficiaries of the trust are simply passive investors with transferable certificates as shares or units of interest.

One major disadvantage of the business trust is its rather shaky legal status in some jurisdictions. Although a number of state statutes expressly declare that the business trust is a permissible form of association for the conduct of business, and although it would probably be sanctioned by courts in most jurisdictions even in the absence of a statute, the courts in a few states have, in the absence of enabling legislation, treated it like a partnership or joint stock company for purposes of shareholder personal liability.[3]

---

§1.12   [1] *See* F.P.P. Enters. v. United States, 830 F.2d 114, 117 (8th Cir. 1987) (entities failed as business trust because did not carry on business for profit, beneficial interests were not transferable, and trustee did not exercise control over property).

[2] *See* In re Vento Dev. Corp., 560 F.2d 2 (2d Cir. 1977); Lafayette Bank & Trust Co. v. Branchini & Sons Constr. Co., 342 A.2d 916 (Conn. 1975).

[3] *E.g.,* F.D.I.C. v. Slinger, 913 F.2d 7 (1st Cir. 1990) (benefits of business trust status is lost where individual is sole trustee and beneficiary).

C. Other Types of Business Associations

§1.13   Charitable and Other Nonprofit Corporations

Virtually all states have statutes providing for the formation of charitable, educational, literary, scientific, social, fraternal, religious, recreational, and other nonprofit corporations. The nonprofit corporation statutes grew helter-skelter over the years without reference to any statutory model, and at one time they existed in great variety and astonishing combinations.[1] The legislative trend, however, is toward a comprehensive nonprofit corporation statute under which a broad range of nonprofit concerns can be incorporated. Such statutes often exclude some types of organizations from the "nonprofit" category, such as cooperatives, which are conventionally covered by separate incorporation statutes.

A number of jurisdictions have adopted the Revised Model Non-Profit Corporation Act (RMNPCA) drafted by the Corporation, Banking and Business Law section of the American Bar Association. The RMNPCA divides nonprofit corporations into three broad categories: public benefit corporations, which include most types of charitable organizations; mutual benefit corporations, which include entities such as trade associations, social clubs, and other organizations that pursue nonprofit activities that are neither charitable nor religious; and religious corporations. In broad overview, the RMNPCA subjects mutual benefit corporations to the most regulation of the three types of nonprofit corporations. The regulation of mutual benefit corporations approximates that of business corporations. Religious corporations enjoy a good deal of autonomy and noninterference under the RMNPCA.

Although most recent legislation dealing with nonprofit corporations has been entirely separate from legislation relating to business corporations, provisions in the modern nonprofit corporation acts generally parallel those in the business corporation statutes.[2] Thus judicial decisions interpreting and applying a nonprofit statute may be helpful in interpreting and applying a business corporation statute, and vice versa.[3]

Although dividends and profits may not otherwise be distributed to the members of a nonprofit corporation, persons who establish and are members of a nonprofit corporation often expect to benefit personally from its operation. For example, incorporated athletic clubs and music societies provide recreation and entertainment for their members, and incorporated fraternal organizations further the social and benevolent pursuits of their members and often provide group

---

§1.13 [1] Ralph E. Boyer, Nonprofit Corporation Statutes: A Critique and Proposal 1-122 (1957); ABA-ALI Model Non-Profit Corp. Act iv (Rev. 1957). *See also* Howard L. Oleck, Non-Profit Corporations, Associations and Organizations 57-75 (5th ed. 1988).

[2] *See* ABA-ALI, Model Non-Profit Corp. Act vii (rev. ed. 1964).

[3] The Preface to the 1964 version of the Model Nonprofit Corporation Act, after pointing out that the provisions of the Model Nonprofit Corporation Act are closely parallel to the provisions of the Model Business Corporation Act, states: "It follows that decisions under the Model Business Corporation Act, or commentaries on it, which greatly outnumber those in regard to non-profit corporations, should become increasingly helpful in the interpretation and application of the Model Non-Profit Corporation Act itself." *Id.* at viii.

See, e.g., Wells v. League of American Theatres and Producers, Inc., 706 N.Y.S.2d 599, 604 (N.Y. Sup. Ct. 2000) (comparing provisions of New York's Business Corporation Law and Not-For-Profit Corporation Law governing members' rights to inspect corporate records).

insurance, old-age pensions, and funeral benefits. One commentator calls such undertakings "cultural corporations."[4] Incorporated cooperatives, although usually classified as "nonprofit," resemble business corporations even more closely in that they are created for the pecuniary benefit of their members.[5]

A corporation does not cease to be classified as "nonprofit" simply because it seeks to make profits from some of its activities. Many nonprofit organizations engage in profit-making activities. For example, a leading law school once owned and reaped profits from a macaroni factory. The nonprofit status of an enterprise depends not on whether some of its activities are conducted for profit but on what is done with the profits—that is, on whether the profits are devoted to a charitable, religious, or other nonprofit purpose or, on the contrary, are distributed from time to time among the concern's members as returns on their investments.[6]

A nonprofit corporation usually does not take the form of a stock corporation.[7] In other words, it does not issue shares. Instead it may have one or more classes of members, and it may issue certificates evidencing membership. In rare instances a nonprofit corporation is created without either shares or members. If a corporation is to have members, their qualifications and rights are usually set forth in its articles of incorporation or in its bylaws.[8] The non-stock or membership corporation is a suitable way to organize athletic clubs, country clubs, golf clubs, social clubs, fraternal societies, cooperative apartment houses, and other nonprofit enterprises that hold property and conduct a limited amount of incidental business.[9]

Tens of thousands of loose, unincorporated associations of people that carry out various nonprofit activities exist in the United States. Common law does not recognize such organizations as entities so that their members or managers, absent special statutory treatment, run a serious risk of being responsible for the association's activities. In this way, the common law provides a powerful disincentive for volunteerism. An important response to this problem was the promulgation in 1992 of the Uniform Unincorporated Nonprofit Association Act (UUNAA) by the Uniform Law Commissioners. In broad overview, the UUNAA accords entity status to the association in terms of holding and transferring property,

[4] Alfred F. Conard, Corporations in Perspective 142 (1976). This is "to signify what they do for their members and for others whom their activities affect." *Id.*

[5] For example, saving money for its members by purchasing raw materials or obtaining for its members higher prices for farm produce or other products. Many such cooperatives hold and operate large properties and do billions of dollars' worth of business, but not with a view to distributing profits as dividends to members, which is a primary characteristic of business corporations.

[6] *See* Oleck, *supra* note 1, at 5, 212-234. *But see* I.R.C. §§502, 511-513 (1988 & Supp. 1992) (denying tax-exempt status to income from "feeder" corporations and from "unrelated" business activities). *See generally* Stanley Weithorn, 1 Tax Techniques for Foundations and Other Exempt Organizations §14B.01 (1980).

[7] The Model Non-Profit Corporation Act and some other non-profit corporation statutes make no provision for issuance of shares of stock, but in a few states non-profit corporations having shares of stock can be created and do exist. *E.g.*, La. Rev. Stat. §12:210 (1994).

[8] ALI-ABA Model Non-Profit Corp. Act §11 (rev. ed. 1964).

[9] *See* Note, The Legal Framework Governing Operation of Modern Non-Profit Corporations, 47 Iowa L. Rev. 1064 (1962). *See also* In re Pitts' Estate, 22 P.2d 694 (Cal. 1933); Margaret H. Amsler, The Texas Non-Profit Corporation: Past, Present, and Prospective, 10 Baylor L. Rev. 307 (1958).

enjoying standing to sue, and shielding its members and personnel from being responsible for the association's liabilities. The UUNAA also authorizes the appointment of an agent to receive service of process and provides procedures for disposal of an inactive association's property. These benefits are not conditioned by the UUNAA on the association registering with the state or otherwise conforming its organizational or governance structure to any statutory model.

D. TYPES OF CORPORATIONS

§1.14   Publicly Held Corporations and Close Corporations

Perhaps the most significant classifications of business corporations are publicly held corporations (sometimes referred to as "public-issue corporations") and close corporations (often referred to as "closely held corporations"). A publicly held corporation is a business corporation, such as IBM or Microsoft, which have numerous shareholders—perhaps hundreds of thousands scattered all over the world—and whose shares (or some classes of shares) are traded on a national securities exchange or at least are traded regularly in the over-the-counter market maintained by securities dealers.[1] The close corporation, on the other hand, is often defined simply as a corporation with relatively few shareholders.[2] Several statutes determine close corporation status by reference to the number of shareholders the corporation has.[3] Another popular definition describes the close corporation as a corporation whose shares are not generally traded in securities markets.[4]

Adopting an economic approach and focusing on one of the most significant characteristics of many corporations with a small number of shareholders, some authorities have defined the close corporation as one in which "management and ownership are substantially identical."[5] Thus one leading writer defines the close corporation as "one wherein all the outstanding stock (there being no publicly held securities of any other class) is owned by the persons (or members of their

§1.14   [1] The markets for publicly traded securities are highly regulated. *See* Thomas Lee Hazen, Treatise on the Law of Securities Regulation (4th ed. 2002).

[2] For extensive discussion of "close corporation" definitions, *see* 1 F. Hodge O'Neal & Robert Thompson, O'Neal's Close Corporations §§1.02-1.04 (3d ed. 1990). The distinctive needs of the close corporation are discussed in Chapter 14.

[3] *E.g.*, Del. Code Ann. tit. 8, §342(a)(1)-(3) (2001) (fewer than 30 shareholders).

[4] Elvin R. Latty, The Close Corporation and the New North Carolina Business Corporation Act, 34 N.C. L. Rev. 432, 438-439 (1956). In the words of a Massachusetts court, a close corporation is "typified by: (1) a small number of stockholders; (2) no ready market for the corporate stock; and (3) substantial majority stockholder participation in the management, direction and operations of the corporation." Donahue v. Rodd Electrotype Co., 328 N.E.2d 505, 511 (Mass. 1975), noted in 89 Harv. L. Rev. 423 (1975).

[5] Carlos L. Israels & Alan H. Hoffman, Corporate Practice 57 (3d ed. 1974).

immediate families) who are active in the management and conduct of the business."[6] This definition improperly excludes the large number of corporations in which one or more shareholders supply the lion's share or much of the capital for the enterprise but leave the active management of the business to other shareholders, whose holdings may be relatively small.

Although a close corporation is usually a small enterprise, the amount of its assets, the scope of its operations, the number of persons it employs, or the volume of its sales does not determine whether it is "close." Many close corporations have tremendous assets and worldwide operations. For example, Mars, Inc., producer of candies and other foods, and Hallmark Cards, Inc., a leading manufacturer of greeting cards, are close corporations, and until 1955 the vast Ford Motor Company was also. Most of the incorporated enterprises in this country, perhaps 90 percent or more, are close corporations, but publicly held corporations have far greater economic significance. The great bulk of this nation's productive property is controlled by a few hundred giant, publicly held corporations.

Often the number of shareholders in a close corporation gradually increases: Additional shares are issued to friends or relatives of the founding shareholders; shareholders transfer part of their holdings to their children, or a successful close corporation "goes public" by making a public distribution of its shares. Many corporations, of course, are hybrid or intermediate, having characteristics of both publicly held and close corporations. Thus in many situations some shares in the corporation are rather widely distributed, but a majority of the voting shares—enough for effective control of the corporation—are retained by a single individual, a single family, or a relatively small number of people.

§1.15   One-Person Companies; Family Corporations; Subsidiary Corporations

The "closest" of close corporations is the one-person corporation, in which all stock is owned or controlled by a single shareholder,[1] and the family corporation, in which the stock is owned or controlled by members of a family. Perhaps the corporate device was not originally designed for use by individual entrepreneurs or by family businesses in which substantially all the stock is owned or controlled by the head of the family, but, both in England and in this country, one-person companies and family corporations have received judicial sanction[2] and are now widely prevalent.

---

[6] Chester Rohrlich, Organizing Corporate and Other Business Enterprises §2A.02 (5th ed. 1975).

§1.15   [1] The one-person corporation is not to be confused with the corporation sole. For discussion of one-person corporations, *see* Bernard F. Cataldo, Limited Liability With One-Man Companies and Subsidiary Corporations, 18 Law & Contemp. Probs. 473 (1953); Warner Fuller, The Incorporated Individual: A Study of the One-Man Company, 51 Harv. L. Rev. 1373 (1938); Mario Rotondi, Limited Liability of the Individual Trader: One-Man Company or Commercial Foundation, 48 Tulane L. Rev. 989 (1974).

[2] Leventhal v. Atlantic Fin. Corp., 55 N.E.2d 20 (Mass. 1944); Elenkrieg v. Siebrecht, 144 N.E. 519 (N.Y. 1924).

D. Types of Corporations

A wholly-owned subsidiary corporation is a corporation all the shares of which are held by another company, the "parent company." In other words, it is a one-person corporation. A partly owned subsidiary corporation is a corporation in which the parent company owns a majority of the subsidiary's voting shares, or at least enough shares to give the parent effective control of the subsidiary, but in which some of the subsidiary's shares are owned by other holders.[3] Although a partly owned subsidiary is not referred to as a "close corporation," the two types of companies present similar opportunities for the person in control to manipulate the companies' affairs to the prejudice of minority shareholders.

§1.16   The Professional Corporation

Historically, the learned professions were not included in the objects for which corporations could be created.[1] The justification given for this rule was that a professional practice requires personal skills and creates confidential relationships. A corporation, it was reasoned, does not possess the necessary skills and personal qualities.[2]

In recent years, however, a strong movement to permit professionals to incorporate has resulted in every state and the District of Columbia enacting legislation authorizing professionals to use the corporate form or, alternatively, to create an association with corporate characteristics. In most states, in order to avoid conflict with licensing requirements prohibiting the unauthorized practice of a profession,[3] only persons who are qualified members of the particular profession can become shareholders or directors in a professional corporation.[4] Frequently there is a requirement that the expression "professional corporation" or "professional association" or their abbreviations (P.C., P.A.) appear in the corporation's name and on letterheads and other representations to the public.

At one time, the primary purpose of professional corporate legislation was to permit professionals to adopt a business organization that would be treated as a corporation for income tax purposes and thus eligible for tax-advantageous profit-sharing, pension, and stock option plans.[5] Most of the unfavorable treatment of partnerships vis-à-vis corporations was eliminated with Congress's enactment of the Tax Equity and Fiscal Responsibility Act of 1982 (TEFRA).[6] There nevertheless

---

[3] See generally Elvin R. Latty, Subsidiaries and Affiliated Corporations (1936).

§1.16   [1] See 6 William M. Fletcher, Cyclopedia of the Law of Private Corporations §2523 (1989).

[2] See ALI-ABA Model Bus. Corp. Act Ann. §3, Comment at 31 (1966 pocket parts).

[3] See, e.g., People v. Painless Parker Dentist, 275 P. 928 (Colo. 1929); State v. Superior Court, 135 P.2d 839 (Wash. 1943).

[4] See, e.g., Street v. Sugarmen, 202 So. 2d 749 (Fla. 1967); Christian v. Shideler, 382 P.2d 129 (Okla. 1963); In re Rhode Island Bar Ass'n, 263 A.2d 692 (R.I. 1970).

[5] See, e.g., United States v. Empey, 406 F.2d 157 (10th Cir. 1969); Street v. Sugarmen, 202 So. 2d 749 (Fla. 1967). See generally Milton A. Levenfeld, Professional Corporations and Associations, 8 Houston L. Rev. 47 (1970); Stephen B. Scallen, Federal Income Taxation of Professional Associations and Corporations, 49 Minn. L. Rev. 603 (1965); Annot., 4 A.L.R.3d 383 (1965).

[6] See generally Michael S. Sirkin & Stuart A. Sirkin, The Effect of the TEFRA Pension Provisions on Closely Held and Professional Business, 7 Rev. Tax. Indiv. 99 (1983).

still remain some isolated areas where the tax laws continue to favor those doing business as a corporation rather than as a partnership. For example, a professional corporation's retirement plan can purchase life, accident, health, and other insurance for its employee participants and deduct the amounts contributed to the plan, whereas a partnership plan may not.[7]

An increasing motivation for incorporating a professional business is the quest to shield the owners from enterprise liability. The traditional rule that individuals are liable for their own torts applies even in the corporate context. Hence, one's status as a shareholder or employee does not absolve the individual of any liability for one's own malpractice. States, however, vary widely in their treatment of the professional corporation's owners' vicarious liability. Some states provide limited liability to shareholders for both business debts and malpractice claims; others deny limited liability for both types of debts; and some states expose shareholders to limited liability for business debts and recognize limited liability for malpractice claims and vice versa.[8] A few decisions have reached the unusual result of upholding limited liability for all professional corporations except those engaged in the practice of law. This result arises from the typical provision in state constitutions providing that the state's highest court shall have exclusive power over matters relating to the practice of law. Thus, in *First Bank & Trust Co. v. Zagoria*,[9] the Georgia Supreme Court held it violated the state constitution's separation of powers for the legislature to lift the responsibility lawyers have for a partner's malpractice.[10] Other courts have held it was not the intent of the legislature in enacting a professional incorporation statute to alter any liability or relationship between licensed professionals and their clients.[11] In sum, absent a definitive statement of the legislature or state courts, professionals may well find they continue to have unlimited liability for their co-owners' torts, even though they do business through a professional corporation.

As discussed in an earlier section,[12] a number of states have enacted statutes recognizing the limited liability company as a form of business. A few states have indicated that this form may be used as an alternative to the professional corporation. Professional limited liability companies (PLLCs) and professional limited liability partnerships (PLLPs) have become common forms of doing business.

States vary widely in their treatment of professionals who seek to operate through an LLC. It is common among the states to provide that certain professions are not permitted to form LLCs, the main concern being the ability of part-

---

[7] *See generally* Morton A. Harris, Professional Service Organizations in the 1990s, 1991 A.L.I.-A.B.A. Course of Study Qualified Plans, PCs, and Welfare Benefits, C583 ALI-ABA 535 (1991).

[8] *See* Karen M. Maycheck, Shareholder Liability in Professional Legal Corporations: A Survey of the States, 47 U. Pitt. L. Rev. 817 (1986).

[9] 302 S.E.2d 674 (Ga. 1983).

[10] *See generally* David Paas, Professional Corporations and Attorney-Shareholders: The Decline of Limited Liability, 11 J. Corp. L. 371 (1986).

[11] American Nat'l Bank v. Clarke & Van Wagner, 692 P.2d 61, 66-67 (Okla. Ct. App. 1984).

[12] *See* §1.11.

ners to shield their personal assets from any vicarious liability they otherwise would have.[13] Such protection for professionals, however, is sometimes available under modern LLP acts.[14]

§1.17 Agency—Core Concepts

Although not a separate business entity, an agency relationship is central to all forms of business association. The rules of agency determine the legal consequences of acts by individuals with respect to the business associations with which those individuals may be associated. Agency principles are referred to throughout this treatise as they apply to the various issues discussed. What follows here is an overview of agency law.

To begin with, agency is a *fiduciary* relationship which permits one person (the agent) to act on behalf of another (the principal).[1] The existence of an agency relationship depends upon the consent of the principal (actual, apparent, or implied)[2] to allow the agent to act on the principal's behalf, as well as the agent's consent to the relationship.[3] The existence of the relationship can be based on an express agreement or an inference of such an agreement based on the surrounding facts.[4] The existence of the relationship need not be known to third parities,[5] although the principal's actions and words vis-à-vis third parties can by itself create apparent authority.

Within the context of an agency relationship, there are a number of ways in which the principal may be held accountable for the words, acts, or deeds of the agent. The five legal theories for binding a principal are as follows: (1) actual authority[6] (this includes both express and implied authority[7]),

---

[13] *See* Sheldon Banoff, Setting Up a Multistate Professional Practice as an LLC, 2 J. Ltd. Liab. Cos. 66 (1995).

[14] *See, e.g.,* Cal. Corp. Code 15001 *et seq.* (1991 & Supp. 2002).

§1.17 [1] Restatement (Second) of Agency §1(1) (1958). *Cf., e.g.,* A. Gay Jenson Farms Co. v. Cargill, Inc., 309 N.W.2d 285 (Minn. 1981) (finding a loan to in fact be an agency relationship).

[2] The distinctions between actual, apparent, and implied authority are discussed *infra* §8.01.

[3] Restatement (Second) of Agency §1(1) (1958).

[4] *See, e.g.,* A. Gay Jenson Farms Co. v. Cargill, Inc., 309 N.W.2d 285 (Minn. 1981) (commercial loan with significant control over the borrower rendered the borrower an agent of the creditor); Kight v. Sheppard Building Supply, Inc., 537 So. 2d 1355 (Miss. 1989).

[5] An agent who acts on behalf of an undisclosed principal subjects the principal to liability for acts done in the ordinary and usual course of the undisclosed agency relationship. *E.g.,* Morris Oil Co. v. Rainbow Oilfield Trucking Co., 741 P.2d 840 (N.M. 1987); Restatement (Second) of Agency §195 (1958).

[6] Restatement (Second) of Agency §26 (1958). *See, e.g.,* Lind v. Schenley Industries, Inc., 278 F.2d 79, 85 (2d Cir. 1960) ("'Actual authority' means, as the words connote, authority that the principal, expressly or implicitly, gave the agent.").

[7] *E.g.,* Lind v. Schenley Industries, Inc., 278 F.2d 79, 85 (2d Cir. 1960) ("'Implied authority' has been variously defined. It has been held to be actual authority given implicitly by a principal to his agent.").

(2) apparent authority,[8] (3) inherent authority,[9] (4) estoppel,[10] and (5) ratification.[11]

Actual authority refers to any express agreement between the principal and agent as well as any agreement that may be implied from the surrounding circumstances.[12] As defined by the Restatement of Agency, apparent authority is the "authority to do an act that can be created by written or spoken words or other conduct of the principal which, reasonably interpreted, causes the agent to believe that the principal desires him so to act on the principal's account."[13] Express authority is found in written or spoken words. Implied actual authority can be found on the basis of circumstantial evidence.[14]

Apparent authority results from manifestations, not from the principal to the agent but from the principal to the third party, that the agent has authority to perform the act in question.[15] An agent cannot create his or her own apparent authority. There must at least be a manifestation of acquiescence or agreement from the principal. The principal can thus create apparent authority in an agent by allowing an agent to conduct business in a particular way and thereby create the impression that actual authority in fact exists.[16]

Inherent agency power is a concept used by the Restatement of Agency and the courts as a "catch-all"[17] concept to impose liability as a matter of fairness or some other consideration.[18] An agent's authority can also be established using general principles of estoppel.[19] Finally, when an act is without authorization, after-the-fact approval by the principal can operate as a ratification of the previously unauthorized act.[20] Related to the ratification is the concept of affirmance, whereby a principal's acquiescence with knowledge of an agent's unauthorized act can operate as a ratification.

As noted above, agency is a fiduciary relationship and the agent is subject to certain ensuing obligations. For example, unless there is a contrary agreement

[8] Restatement (Second) of Agency §8 (1958). *See, e.g.,* Lind v. Schenley Industries, Inc., 278 F.2d 79, 85 (2d Cir. 1960) ("'Apparent authority' arises when a principal acts in such a manner as to convey the impression to a third party that an agent has certain powers which he may or may not actually possess.").

[9] Restatement (Second) of Agency §8A (1958).

[10] *Id.* §8B.

[11] *Id.* §§81, 84(1).

[12] *See, e.g.,* Trustees of UIU Health & Welfare Fund v. New York Flame Proofing Co., 828 F.2d 79, 83-84 (2d Cir. 1987) (discussing actual authority stemming from membership in multi-employer bargaining group).

[13] Restatement (Second) of Agency §26 (1958).

[14] *E.g.,* Lind v. Schenley Industries, Inc., 278 F.2d 79, 85 (2d Cir. 1960).

[15] Restatement (Second) Agency §8 (1958).

[16] *See, e.g.,* Essco Geometric v. Harvard Industries, 46 F.3d 718 (8th Cir. 1995) (Missouri law); Progress Printing Corp. v. Jane Byrne Political Committee, 601 N.E.2d 1055 (Ill. Ct. App. 1992).

[17] Daniel S. Kleinberger, Agency and Partnership 39-41 (1995).

[18] Restatement (Second) of Agency §8A (1958).

[19] *E.g.,* Trustees of American Foundation of Musicians & Employers Pension Fund v. Steven Scott Enterprises, Inc., 40 F. Supp. 2d 503, 507-511 (S.D.N.Y. 1999) (discussing equitable estoppel and ratification); Yucca Mining & Petroleum Co. v. Howard C. Phillips Oil Co., 365 P.2d 925 (N.M. 1961) (estoppel); Restatement (Second) of Agency §8B (1958) (estoppel).

[20] Restatement (Second) of Agency §82 (1958).

between the principal and agent, the agent is under a duty to act *solely* for the benefit of the principal.[21] This is often referred to as the duty of loyalty.[22] A corollary to this is that unless it is otherwise agreed, an agent may not deal with the principal as an adverse party.[23] In other words, absent full disclosure by the agent and the consent of the principal, the agent cannot sit on both sides of the bargaining table to any transaction.[24] A variation of the agent's duty of loyalty is the rule that unless otherwise agreed, an agent who makes a profit while working for a principal is under a duty to give any profit made by the agent to the principal.[25]

---

[21] Restatement (Second) of Agency §387 (1958).

[22] *See* Chapter 10 for discussion of the duty of loyalty in the corporate context.

[23] Restatement (Second) of Agency §389 (1958).

[24] *See* Restatement (Second) of Agency §390 (1958) (agent acting as adverse party with principal's consent).

[25] Restatement (Second) of Agency §388 (1958). *E.g.*, Tarnowski v. Resop, 51 N.W.2d 801 (Minn. 1952). This rule has played an important role in fashioning the law prohibiting trading in securities while in possession of nonpublic information. *See id.* Comment 4; *infra* Chapter 12.

CHAPTER 2

The Evolution of Corporations in America

A. THE EVOLUTION OF MODERN GENERAL CORPORATION STATUTES

§2.01 Early American Corporations

State legislatures have plenary powers to create corporations. From the post-Revolutionary War period and into the early nineteenth century, American corporations were created by the enactment of special legislative acts[1]—that is, by acts creating a particular corporation, as distinguished from a general law allowing any persons to organize themselves into and be a corporation by complying with prescribed conditions. To incorporate by special act, a private bill had to be introduced in the state legislature, be considered by the legislative committees, pass both houses, and be signed by the governor. Special acts also were used to grant additional privileges to existing corporations or to make changes in their charters.

---

§2.01 [1] E. Merrick Dodd, Jr., The First Half Century of Statutory Regulation of Business Corporations in Massachusetts, in Harvard Legal Essays 65-131 (1934).

Corporations were uncommon prior to the 1800s, and those that existed were specifically chartered by the state to operate banks, insurance companies, and companies to build and operate canals, bridges, and roads.[2] The dominant feature of businesses incorporated in the eighteenth century was their public character.[3] With the charter came the privilege of monopoly status as well as the power to assess members in the locality for any deficiencies or capital requirements. However, as the concept of private property became more and more a part of American society and jurisprudence, the corporation and its members were viewed less and less as simply instruments of the state. For example, the Supreme Court held the Constitution's contract clause prevented the legislature from altering established property rights embodied in the relationship between the corporation and its members.[4] Further evidence of the decline of the public nature of the corporation was the evolution of the law to the view that members could not be assessed without their assent, and courts began to assume that the corporation's members enjoyed limited liability unless they agreed otherwise.[5] Finally, America's embrace of markets and competition was reflected in the courts' construction of the young country's corporate law by the first half of the nineteenth century. For example, the courts began to hold that the grant of a charter did not carry with it monopoly status.[6] Barely a half a century earlier, a major motivating force for incorporation was the monopoly status it conferred for the activity being incorporated.

With the increasing pressures of industrialization, legislatures found themselves deluged with requests for legislation bestowing corporate status. The early reliance on special legislative acts to confer corporate status on individual entities proved not only inefficient but also was rife with the opportunity for favoritism and corruption.[7] Ultimately, states adopted constitutional provisions declaring that, with specified exceptions, the legislature should not pass any special act creating a corporation. These constitutional provisions permitted corporations to be formed only by compliance with general incorporation laws.[8] General incorporation legislation has now developed to the extent that almost any legitimate enterprise can be conducted in corporate form upon compliance with simple statutory formalities. In states that do not have a constitutional prohibition, however, corporations can still be created by special act.

The first American general incorporation act—that is, an act allowing any persons to incorporate by compliance with the terms of the statute, apparently was

---

[2] Lawrence M. Friedman, A History of American Law 188-189 (2d ed. 1985).

[3] Of special note is that the greater number of incorporations were of churches, cities, burroughs, and charities. *Id.*

[4] Trustees of Dartmouth College v. Woodward, 17 U.S. (4 Wheat.) 518 (1819). For an excellent analysis of the continuing implications of the Dartmouth College case, *see* Nelson Ferebee Taylor, Evolution of Corporate Combination Law: Policy Issues and Constitutional Questions, 76 N.C.L. Rev. 687 (1998).

[5] E. Merrick Dodd, Jr., American Business Corporations Until 1860 75-93 (1954).

[6] Morton J. Horwitz, The Transformation of American Law 114-139 (1977).

[7] *Id.* at 195-196.

[8] *See* William L. Cary, Federalism and Corporate Law: Reflections Upon Delaware, 83 Yale L.J. 663, 663-664 (1974).

A. The Evolution of Modern General Corporation Statutes

a statute passed in 1811 in the State of New York. In that year, the New York legislature, seeking to encourage the manufacture of various commodities, enacted a law making incorporation available to organizers of concerns that manufactured specified kinds of products.[9] Corporate existence, however, was limited to 20 years, and the capital of such an enterprise could not exceed $100,000.[10]

Soon after New York's pioneer enactment, other states passed acts authorizing the incorporation of manufacturing companies. The more modern general corporation acts were expansive. They covered almost every kind of lawful business. The trend toward use of general acts permitting incorporation by signing and filing articles of incorporation began immediately after 1835.[11] With the arrival of general incorporation laws, in contrast to incorporation by special act, businessmen could with certainty and efficiency gain the benefits of corporate status for their businesses.

In 1888, the New Jersey legislature authorized corporations organized under the law of that state to purchase and hold shares of stock in other corporations,[12] thus making possible the creation of holding companies with numerous subsidiaries.[13] Delaware and many other states soon followed New Jersey's lead and authorized corporations to hold stock in other corporations. Growth of holding companies and parent-subsidiary relationships among companies resulted in small groups of persons holding large concentrations of economic power.

In 1896, New Jersey enacted what may be regarded as the first permissive modern incorporation act—that is, a statute that conferred broad powers on corporations, empowered promoters of corporations to set up almost any kind of corporate structure they desired, granted broad powers to corporate directors and managers, and provided great protection against liability for corporate directors and managers. Soon, New Jersey was referred to as "the Mother of Trusts."

In 1913, however, reform-minded then-governor Woodrow Wilson caused New Jersey to amend its more permissive provisions. Delaware, which had borrowed most of its corporation law from New Jersey, seized the opportunity to assume leadership in providing and keeping up-to-date a body of permissive corporate laws. At various times, several states—Maine, West Virginia, and later Nevada—have attempted to "out-Delaware Delaware" in an effort to attract incorporation business and, more specifically, tax revenues and fees. These imitators, however, have had little success in displacing Delaware's preeminence in the race for the rechartering business. Still other states have liberalized their statutes to

---

[9] 1811 N.Y. Laws ch. 67, "Act Relative to Incorporations for Manufacturing Purposes." This right to incorporate applied to textile, glass, metal, and paint industries, among others. *See, e.g.,* W. C. Kessler, 48 J. Pol. Econ. 877 (Dec. 1940), as to importance of this New York statute.

[10] E. Merrick Dodd, Jr., American Business Association Law a Hundred Years Ago and Today, in 3 Law: A Century of Progress, 1835-1935, 254, 271, 289 (1937).

[11] *Id.* at 273, 289 (referring to general acts for manufacturing corporations in Pennsylvania (1836), North Carolina (1836), Michigan (1837), and Connecticut (1837)).

[12] 1888 N.J. Laws ch. 269, §1, repealed by 1896 N.J. Laws ch. 190, §10 (*reprinted in* 1 Gen. Stat. of N.J., 1709-1893, at 983). *See* William Randall Compton, Early History of Stock Ownership by Corporations, 9 Geo. Wash. L. Rev. 125 (1940).

[13] Similar provisions now exist in all general business corporation laws.

encourage their local businesses to "stay at home" by incorporating locally rather than organizing in Delaware, New Jersey, or some other permissive jurisdiction.[14]

It can thus be said that, by the end of the nineteenth century, the states had loosened the bonds that once hobbled the corporation's formation and operation. Populist concerns over the concentration of economic powers in large corporations, frequently networked through interlocking ownership or boards of directors, translated into an unending legislative agenda designed to channel or thwart the economic power of corporations.

It is safe to say that the liberalization trend that began toward the end of the nineteenth century continued throughout the twentieth century so that today all states have broadly permissive enabling corporation statutes with very little evidence in any state statute of regulatory or paternalistic provisions. While in some instances the changes were prompted by competition for incorporation fees and the accompanying tax revenues, a more compelling explanation of the trend is the increasing belief among legislators and local drafting groups that corporations are not monolithic in their needs or operations; one set of rules is not appropriate for all corporate entities. Legislatures, especially since the 1960s, have consistently embraced the philosophy of allowing corporations, within the broad framework of local law, to tailor their governance structure to accommodate their own special needs and relationships.

§2.02   Modern Corporation Acts

The first general corporation chartering laws were cumbersome and unartfully drafted. They were overly restrictive in that they imposed burdensome conditions precedent to incorporation and unreasonable limitations on the scope of the corporate franchise. This unfortunate state of affairs led to efforts by legislative drafting committees and committees of concerned business lawyers to formulate clear and precise legislation.

The Model Business Corporation Act first appeared in completed form in 1950. The Model Act continued the liberalizing trend that originated in New Jersey and Delaware[1] and for a long time has been universally viewed as "'enabling,' 'permissive,' and 'liberal' as distinguished from 'regulatory' and 'paternalistic.'"[2] From time to time, other states have competed for the lead in this type of liberalization (which at times has been referred to as "the race to the bottom" although others view it as a "race to the top").[3] The Delaware legislature, however, contin-

---

[14] *See* James Willard Hurst, The Legitimacy of the Business Corporation in the Law of the United States, 1780-1970, 147-150 (1970).

§2.02   [1] *See* §2.01.

[2] Harry G. Henn, Handbook of the Law of Corporations and Other Business Enterprises, 22 n.40 (2d ed. 1970).

[3] William L. Cary, Federalism and Corporate Law: Reflections Upon Delaware, 83 Yale L.J. 663 (1974); Thomas Lee Hazen, Corporate Directors' Accountability: The Race to the Bottom—The Second Lap, 66 N.C. L. Rev. 171 (1987); Roberta Romano, Competition for Corporate Charters and the

ues to be the leader in originating permissive corporate legislation.[4] Delaware's continued popularity among public corporations is documented by the fact that nearly 90 percent of public corporations that change their corporate domicile choose to reincorporate in Delaware.[5] The Model Act was intended not to become a uniform corporation law but rather to serve as a drafting guide for the states. Eventually the Model Act became the pattern for large parts of the corporation statutes in most states (notable exceptions being California, Delaware, and New York). The Committee on Corporate Laws revises the Model Act from time to time, and typically a number of states amend their corporation statutes to adopt the latest revisions.

The first complete revision of the Model Act appears in the Revised Model Business Corporation Act (1984). The Revised Model Act incorporates many simplifying and innovative provisions that the states had experimented with over the years. In addition, the Revised Model Act has through subsequent revisions continued the liberalizing trend that started in Delaware.

Most states, in addition to a general business corporation act, have more specialized general chartering acts governing the formation and regulation of corporations in special fields of business such as banking, building and loan associations, insurance, railroads, and public utilities.[6] Similarly, virtually all states now have a separate act for professional corporations.

Corporation laws deal with such matters as the following: the content of the articles of incorporation; the rights of shareholders; the powers and liabilities of directors; rules governing shareholders' meetings and directors' meetings; restrictions on corporate finance, such as limitations on the withdrawal of funds by way of dividends and share purchases; the keeping and inspection of corporate records; and authorization of organic changes, such as charter amendments, sale of all corporate assets, merger, and consolidation, and dissolution and winding up. Some of these provisions

---

Lesson of Takeover Statutes, 61 Fordham L. Rev. 843, 856-59 (1993); Roberta Romano, The State Competition Debate in Corporate Law, 8 Cardozo L. Rev. 709, 721-722 (1987); Comment, Law for Sale: A Study of the Delaware Corporation Law of 1967, 117 U. Pa. L. Rev. 861 (1969). *See also, e.g.,* Lucian A. Bebchuck & Allen Ferrell, Federalism and Corporate Law: The Race to Protect Managers from Takeovers, 99 Colum. L. Rev. 1171 (1999).

Other commentators have suggested that this is really a race to the top. Daniel R. Fischel, The "Race to the Bottom" Revisited: Reflections on Recent Developments in Delaware's Corporation Law, 76 Nw. U. L. Rev. 913 (1982); Ralph K. Winter, The "Race for the Top" Revisited: A Comment on Eisenberg, 89 Colum. L. Rev. 1526 (1989). *See also, e.g.,* Lucian Arye Bebchuk & Allen Ferrell, Essay: A New Approach to Takeover Law and Regulatory Competition, 87 Va. L. Rev. 111 (2001); William J. Carney, The Political Economy of Competition for Corporate Charters, 26 J. Legal Stud. 303, 313-317 (1997); *infra* §2.03.

[4] *See generally* Ernest L. Folk, The Delaware General Corporation Law, a Commentary and Analysis (1972); Carlos L. Israels & Alan H. Hoffman, Corporation Practice (3d ed. 1974); S. Samuel Arsht & Walter K. Stapleton, Delaware's New General Corporation Law: Substantive Changes, 23 Bus. Law. 75 (1967).

[5] *See* Note, Is Delaware Still a Haven for Incorporation?, 20 Del. J. Corp. L. 965, 999-1002 (1995); Roberta Romano, Law as a Product: Some Pieces of the Incorporation Puzzle, 1 J.L. Econ. & Org. 225, 244 (1985).

[6] *See* Alfred F. Conard, Corporations in Perspective §§5, 6 (1976); Alfred F. Conard, An Overview of the Laws of Corporations, 71 Mich. L. Rev. 621 (1973).

seek to prevent management and majority shareholders from abusing their power to the detriment of minority shareholders and corporate creditors.[7]

§2.03 The "Race of Laxity"

Modern corporation acts became "enabling," "permissive," and "liberal" as a result of state legislative decisions to eliminate or reduce restrictions that earlier incorporation acts had imposed on corporations. Charters granted by the state legislatures and early general incorporation statutes limited the size of corporations, the scope of their business activities, the amount of capital they could assemble by issuing shares, and the size of the indebtedness they could incur by borrowing.

The early restrictions on corporate activities grew out of a suspicion and fear of the corporate mechanism, an attitude manifested in the reported debates of state constitutional conventions before the year 1890.[1] Legislators remembered the unpleasant experiences with large British corporations—the trading companies that colonized and tried to govern the colonies. The American colonies had fought for their independence, in part to free themselves from the control of these large British companies.[2] In an eloquent dissenting opinion in *Louis K. Liggett Company v. Lee*,[3] Justice Brandeis recounted the evolution of state corporation laws and discussed the many restrictions imposed on corporations. In part, Justice Brandeis stated:

> There was a sense of some insidious menace inherent in large aggregations of capital, particularly when held by corporations. So, at first, the corporate privilege was granted sparingly. . . . The later enactment of general incorporation laws does not signify that the apprehension of corporate domination had been overcome. . . . The general laws, which long embodied severe restrictions upon size and upon the scope of corporate activity, were, in part, an expression of the desire for equality of opportunity.
>
> Limitation upon the amount of the authorized capital of business corporations was long universal. The maximum limit frequently varied with the kinds of business to be carried on. . . .
>
> Limitations upon the scope of a business corporation's powers and activity were also long universal. At first, corporations could be formed under the general laws only for a limited number of purposes—usually those which required a relatively large fixed capital, like transportation, banking, and insurance, and mechanical, mining, and manufacturing enterprises. Permission to incorporate for "any lawful purpose" was not common until 1875; and until that time the duration of corporate franchises was generally limited to a period of 20, 30, 40, or 50

---

[7] *See* Chapters 10-11. *See generally* F. Hodge O'Neal & Robert B. Thompson, Oppression of Minority Shareholders (1975).

§2.03   [1] *See, e.g.*, Del Monte Light & Power Co. v. Jordan, 238 P. 710, 713 (Cal. 1925).

[2] Gerard Carl Henderson, The Position of Foreign Corporations in American Constitutional Law 19 (1918).

[3] 288 U.S. 517 (1933).

A. The Evolution of Modern General Corporation Statutes

years. All, or a majority, of the incorporators or directors, or both, were required to be residents of the incorporating state. The powers which the corporation might exercise in carrying out its purposes were sparingly conferred and strictly construed. Severe limitations were imposed on the amount of indebtedness, bonded or otherwise. The power to hold stock in other corporations was not conferred or implied. The holding company was impossible.[4]

In his *Liggett* dissent, Justice Brandeis assailed as highly undesirable the loosening of the restrictions formerly imposed on corporations in this country.

Brandeis's concerns continue to be the subject of debate today over the desirability of our federal system, which allocates control of corporate laws to individual states—or fiefdoms, depending on one's point of view. In a classic work, Professor Cary warned that interstate competition for corporate chartering would lead, as predicted by Gresham's Law, to "bad" corporate law driving out "good" corporation laws.[5] On the other hand, others argue that competition among the states can be seen as necessary to foster an environment for incubating new procedures and mechanisms of corporate governance. Also, diversity of laws among the states allows shareholders and managers to choose the set of rules best suited for their own peculiar position.[6]

Obviously there is a great gulf between these two positions. Those favoring the Cary view believe that ever more permissive corporate laws decrease shareholder wealth by favoring managers over owners. In contrast, those favoring the status quo counsel that permissive statutes actually increase the value of the firm and that Professor Cary and others have overlooked how the markets for capital, the firm's products, and managers constrain any proclivities managers may have to benefit themselves at the expense of shareholders.[7]

There appear to be several weaknesses with the argument that markets have a disciplining effect on managers and state legislatures. First, in order for there to be a realistic threat of a hostile takeover, the corporate laws chosen by managers must produce a substantial decline in the value of the firm. With takeover premiums averaging out at a level of more than 50 percent, the decision—for example, to reincorporate in Delaware—must cause roughly one-third of the firm's value to be lost before there is a realistic threat to the current management's control. Such a decline is not conceivable.

---

[4] Louis K. Liggett Co. v. Lee, 288 U.S. 517, 549-557 (1933) (Brandeis, J., dissenting) (footnotes omitted).

[5] *See* William L. Cary, Federalism and Corporate Law: Reflections Upon Delaware, 83 Yale L.J. 663, 663-664 (1974). He recommended federally imposed minimum standards for state corporate codes. *See also* Thomas Lee Hazen, Corporate Director's Accountability: The Race to the Bottom—The Second Lap, 66 N.C. L. Rev. 171 (1987).

[6] Daniel R. Fischel, The "Race to the Bottom" Revisited: Reflections on Recent Developments in Delaware's Corporation Law, 76 Nw. U. L. Rev. 913, 921-923 (1982). *See also* Stephen J. Choi & Andrew T. Guzman, Choice and Federal Intervention in Corporate Law, 87 Va. L. Rev. 961, 961-963 (2001).

[7] *See, e.g.,* Ralph K. Winter, Jr., State Law, Shareholder Protection, and the Theory of the Corporation, 6 J. Legal. Stud. 251 (1977).

Second, markets are not likely to associate a reincorporation decision necessarily with a value-decreasing motivation. The key to understanding this observation is that reincorporation decisions require the approval of the firm's stockholders, a group not presumed to act against its own interest. We might therefore ask, why would shareholders approve reincorporation in a state whose laws are generally viewed as "lax" or "permissive"? To answer this question we can view a broadly enabling corporate statute like the rain that can fall on the good and the bad alike. The state's corporate laws may facilitate value-increasing mergers and reduce the cost of convening stockholder's meetings while at the same time insulating managerial self-dealing and ineptitude.

A third qualification on the ability of markets to deter overly permissive corporate statutes is that not all firms are vulnerable to market influences. A monopolistic or oligopolistic market structure, perhaps facilitated in some respect by patents and franchises, insulates the firm's managers from competition. Also, the cost of capital is not a concern to managers, who can rely on retention of earnings or nurtured banking relationships for expansion needs. Moreover, state anti-takeover laws and self-help defenses such as poison pills further shield managers from the disciplining influence of a hostile takeover. And a management that has taken care of itself at the stockholders' expense may well not have any concern for the market for managers, but rather only for a retirement spa.

Managers who have initiated reincorporation, most frequently in Delaware, have usually not acted as tramps, pirates, or privateers, preying on their shareholders or customers or other citizens. Their overall objective usually is to reduce the cost, formality, and uncertainty of doing business. Such motivation is a commendable quest for achieving reasonable business arrangements to advance the interests of the stockholders.[8]

With the increasing adoption of the Revised Model Business Corporation Act, whose provisions are nearly as permissive as those of Delaware, there is every reason to expect some decline in the incidence of reincorporations. There will, however, continue to be substantial considerations that will tug public corporations to Delaware.

Professor Romano identifies three factors that explain why Delaware is the situs for over one half of all reincorporations.[9] First, because Delaware depends more than any other state on corporate franchise tax revenues, it is more committed than any other state to remaining an attractive incorporation site. "It cannot afford to lose firms to other states by failing to keep its code up-to-date."[10] Second, Delaware's constitution mandates a two-thirds vote of both state legislative houses to change its corporation statute.[11] This provision makes radical reform in its provisions unlikely. At the same time, the state's dependence on fran-

---

[8] Edward G. Jennings, Federal Incorporation or Licensing of Interstate Corporate Business, 23 Minn. L. Rev. 710, 712 (1939).

[9] Roberta Romano, The State Competition Debate in Corporate Law, 8 Cardozo L. Rev. 709, 721-722 (1987).

[10] Id.

[11] Del. Const. art. IX, §1.

chise revenues assures that the legislature will be responsive to innovations that threaten the state's fiscal health. Finally, Delaware has a corporate legal infrastructure that cannot be easily replicated. Not only does it provide its own specialized Chancery Court staffed with individuals from the corporate bar and a Supreme Court with similar expertise, but its statutes are surrounded by a wealth of legal precedent that assures its corporate law is the most comprehensive body in the land, a consideration that reduces the cost of advising clients. In sum, businesses that quest certainty of result, as well as a sympathetic and experienced ear to the problems of running a public corporation, are assured of finding it in Delaware.

The concentration of most businesses into a relatively few huge incorporated units is not due primarily to lax corporation laws or even to a corporation's privilege to hold shares in other corporations. Whether bigness in business should be curtailed or regulated, and how such controls should be accomplished, are unsettled questions of economic policy, not of corporation law. Various economics issues—for example, whether and the extent to which production, competition, monopoly, labor conditions, profits, and the concentration of wealth should be controlled by government—call for patient, thorough study. This task of regulating corporate bigness and curtailing supposed corporate "evils" should not be confused with the task of establishing modern corporation laws to facilitate incorporation and to define and enforce the rights and duties of shareholders, directors, and officers.[12]

B.   AGENCY PROBLEMS IN THE MODERN CORPORATION

§2.04   Separation of Corporate Ownership from Control

In their classic book on the modern corporation, Adolf Berle and Gardiner Means pointed out that the American corporation is no longer merely a private business tool or device; instead, it has evolved into a dominant institution affecting economic, political, and social conditions in modern society.[1] A large amount of the wealth of individuals has shifted from ownership of actual physical property to ownership of shares of stock representing a set of rights and expectations in an enterprise.

The separation of ownership from control gives rise to various conflicts of interest between passive owners and active managers. In the abstract, managers

---

[12] See Thomas L. Hazen, Corporate Chartering and the Securities Markets: Shareholder Suffrage, Corporate Responsibility and Managerial Accountability, 1978 Wis. L. Rev. 391.

§2.04   [1] Adolf A. Berle & Gardiner C. Means, The Modern Corporation and Private Property, at 44-46, 66-69, 121-125, 250, 352-357 (1932). See also, e.g., Adolf A. Berle, The Twentieth Century Capitalist Revolution 166-169 (1954).

are no different from other individuals when facing an economic choice; so as to maximize their own utility, they can be expected to act like other individuals in exercising discretionary decisions. Utility maximization is an especially interesting problem in the public corporation, where management and ownership are separated. The managers' quest to maximize their utility does not naturally lead to decisions that also maximize the value of the firm.

In a classic article,[2] Ronald Coase developed a powerful model of the firm that explains why firms exist and why they decide to expand. Coase argued that a firm will undertake an activity for itself whenever it is cheaper to do so than to acquire that good or service in the market. A distinct cost of the market is imperfect information about the quality and overall utility of the good or service that others will provide. Further concerns are whether the sellers of goods will be able to produce the desired quantity and make the goods available at competitive prices. Because it is expensive to gather information on these various points and because there may be no economies in relying on the production efforts of others, the firm's managers will decide to provide the good or service itself. The firm thus grows because of its decision to integrate the new activity into the firm's existing operation.

In contrast to Coase's model, Berle and Means take the position that the separation of ownership from management has allowed less economically desirable reasons to distort management's expansion decisions, such as the quest for bigness, as though size itself were a virtue.

The neoclassical economists (sometimes more generally referred to as "the Chicago School") have prodigiously mined the problems posed by separation of ownership from control. Any examination of the issues flowing from the separation of ownership and management should begin by considering the work of Professors Jensen and Meckling,[3] who theorize that managers have strong market-based incentives to contract with shareholders to reduce the managers' misbehavior. In this context the misbehavior need not rise to the level of constituting practices that are fraudulent or even in breach of the manager's fiduciary duties. They can, however, include a range of relatively benign conduct, such as longer lunch hours and directing the corporation's munificence to the manager's alma mater.

The cornerstone of the Jensen and Meckling analysis is that the value of the firm's shares will reflect the investors' perceptions of the amount of the firm's earnings that managers will deflect to themselves or will otherwise act adverse to the firm. Simply stated, conduct that is adverse to the stockholders' interests will depress the market value of the firm. A decline in the value of the firm's shares impacts on the managers to the extent their compensation is based on changes in the firm's value, the managers' ownership of shares in the company, or whether the decline poses a serious threat of a hostile takeover. Managers therefore have an incentive to dampen the investors' perceptions of the likelihood of managerial misbehavior. But how can the managers mollify the investors' con-

---

[2] Ronald H. Coase, The Nature of the Firm, 4 Economica (n.s.) 386 (1937).

[3] Michael C. Jensen & William H. Meckling, Theory of the Firm: Managerial Behavior, Agency Costs and Ownership Structure, 3 J. Fin. Econ. 305 (1976).

B.   Agency Problems in the Modern Corporation

cerns over the dark side of the managers' drive to maximize their own utility? To answer this question one must consider the relative knowledge of the owners and their managers.

Information asymmetries accompany managerial misconduct; that is, managers know the frequency and magnitude of the harm they cause by their misconduct, whereas the outside investors do not. Absent other factors, *ex ante* investors will discount all securities by the average misbehavior committed by all firms' managers, because they otherwise are unable to distinguish *ex ante* among the respective proclivities of a particular firm's managers to misbehave.[4] In general, it would be of little use for managers to proclaim they left their self-interest at the office door, since saints and sinners alike are equally capable of proclaiming their virtue. How then can the firm's managers whose misbehavior is less than the norm effectively convey its message to investors? And why would they wish to do so? What follows is a summary of the neoclassical economists' models within which each of these questions is answered.

A key point in the neoclassical economic view of the firm is that managers must have an incentive compensation arrangement that substantially ties their fortunes to that of the owners. Such an arrangement accomplishes two objectives. First, the typical stock option plan or bonuses based on firm profitability *bonds* the manager to serve the stockholders' interest. Obviously, the strength of the bond is directly proportional to the extent the managers' total compensation packages depends on the changes in the firm's value or profitability. Second, linking the managers' incentives to those of the firm's owners *signals* to the investors the depth of the firm's managers' resolve to maximize the value of the firm.[5] Signaling addresses the information asymmetry problem, so that investors will not discount the firm's securities by the average risk expected for the industry. Consistent with agency theorists' view of the firm is the increasing popularity among public corporations of encouraging or requiring their outside directors to acquire a substantial equity investment in the corporation.[6]

A further step to reduce such discounting is the use of *monitoring* devices designed to police management. Conventional examples of monitoring include that of outside boards of directors and independent accountants. However, monitoring is efficient only to the extent its marginal benefits exceed its marginal cost. Because monitoring can be expected to pose diminishing marginal benefits, it generally prevents only the more extreme managerial departures.

---

[4] The leading authority for this view is George A. Akerlof, The Market for "Lemons": Qualitative Uncertainty and the Market Mechanism, 84 Q.J. Econ. 488 (1970).

[5] Stephen Ross, Disclosure Regulation in Financial Markets: Implications of Modern Finance Theory and Signaling Theory Issues in Financial Regulation 177 (Franklin R. Edwards ed. 1979); A. Michael Spence, Market Signaling 88-95 (1974).

[6] *See* Report of the National Association of Corporate Directors Blue Ribbon Commission on Director Compensation 12 (1995) (recommending that boards of directors establish substantial target stock ownership levels for directors and that director fees be paid in stock or cash. The report also takes the position that benefits such as pension and health care plans for outside directors are likely to make directors less independent because they thereby become more akin to employees in their quest for longevity).

The costs of bonding, signaling, and monitoring, as well as the amount of misbehavior that continues in the face of these steps to deter managerial indiscretions, are collectively referred to as *agency costs*. In view of these mechanisms for reducing agency costs, the neoclassical economists who view the corporation as a "nexus of contracts" reason that what binds the firm together as an entity is not the fiction of its separate existence but the numerous contractual intersections among owners, managers, creditors, and workers through which they define their respective roles, risks, and rights. Under this view, the corporation is reduced to the means for efficient contracting among the owners, managers, creditors, and laborers. Corporate statutes are viewed by these economists as off-the-rack contractual provisions the parties would have embodied in their contract if contracting could occur costlessly. And judges in resolving disputes should similarly confine their analysis.

The neoclassical position is that market forces have minimized the firm's agency costs, and further legal interventions are thus unnecessary and wasteful. In other words, the parties to the corporation are seen as having voluntarily installed those monitoring devices that are cost-efficient (that is, that will prevent greater losses than they themselves cost). Legally mandated reforms are unhelpful because they will result in inefficient expenditures.[7]

Not surprising, there is abundant criticism of this view of the firm. In the end, the neoclassical view of the corporation is vulnerable to the charges that it is both an empty metaphor and tautological:[8] The neoclassical view allows no room for a higher principle or purpose to resolve corporate law questions; disputes are instead resolved according to the presumed intentions of the contracting parties. Thus law is not an engine for societal change and improvement. The neoclassical view has struck many commentators as antithetical even to the basic premises of corporate law.[9]

The nexus-of-contracts interpretation of the firm provides a free-market approach to the problems posed by the separation of ownership from control. In the meantime, the conflicts of interest inherent in the separation of ownership and control continue to create new concerns, such as the broad public alarm about excessive executive compensation and the competitiveness of American industry. Coupled with these concerns are complaints from public interest and consumer groups about the socially undesirable and scandalous conduct that they

---

[7] William A. Klein & John C. Coffee, Jr., Business Organization and Finance Legal and Economic Principles 161 (4th ed. 1990).

[8] William W. Bratton, Jr., The "Nexus of Contracts" Corporation: A Critical Appraisal, 74 Cornell L. Rev. 407, 410 (1989).

[9] Robert C. Clark, Agency Costs versus Fiduciary Duties, in Principals and Agents: The Structure of Business (John W. Pratt & Richard J. Zeckhauger eds. 1985); Victor Brudney, Corporate Governance, Agency Costs, and the Rhetoric of Contract, 85 Colum. L. Rev. 1403 (1985); Melvin A. Eisenberg, The Structure of Corporation Law, 89 Colum. L. Rev. 1461 (1989); Thomas L. Hazen, The Corporate Persona, Contract (and Market) Failure, and Moral Values, 69 N.C. L. Rev. 273 (1991).

For literature suggesting that behavioral aspects of trust should have an impact on corporate law, *see* Margaret M. Blair & Lynn A. Stout, Trust, Trustworthiness, and the Behavioral Foundations of Corporate Law, 149 U. Pa. L. Rev. 1735 (2001). *Compare,* Larry E. Ribstein, Law v. Trust, 81 B.U. L. Rev. 553 (2001).

attribute to corporations. In combination, they continue to spawn a lively debate and action to improve corporate governance mechanisms.

§2.05   Reform Efforts and the American Law Institute's Corporate Governance Project

Undeniably, there is broad-based dissatisfaction with traditional corporate governance procedures.[1] Many of the recommendations have questioned the "race to the bottom" in corporate legal principles, discussed earlier in this chapter, and recommend either the federal chartering of corporations or that the content of state laws be improved through the imposition of federal minimum standards. Others have invoked a structural approach of healing the corporation from within itself. Among the approaches suggested by this group are mandating that corporate boards have a critical mass of "outside" directors, that outside directors be armed with a professional staff to assist them in discharging their responsibilities, that the boardroom become more diversified, with membership including representatives from labor, consumer, or creditor groups, or that there be significant representation of institutional holders on the board of directors. Of these many suggestions, the one that has the greatest currency is expanding the role of outside directors on the boards of publicly traded corporations. Indeed, the most significant corporate development in the last quarter century has been the rapid evolution from the inside to the outside board. The change in the composition of the American boardroom was stimulated by the popular perception within management that outside directors have much to contribute to the vision and strength of the organization. Further impetus for the managers' acceptance of outside directors is the courts' increasing dependence on outside directors as evidence of the propriety of corporate conduct. The most notable corporate law reform project of the past decade, the American Law Institute's Corporate Governance Project, reflects the evolution and thinking of the prominent role that outside directors can and should play in the governance of the American corporation.

The American Law Institute (ALI), after more than a decade of study and fractious debate, adopted in 1992 a voluminous set of principles, recommendations, and commentary entitled the Principles of Corporate Governance: Analysis and Recommendations. A core feature of the project is its heavy reliance on outside directors.

Principles of Corporate Governance is different from earlier ALI projects. It is not merely a restatement of prevailing corporate principles that have developed over time. Many of the ALI's positions have scant support in the states, and in some areas the ALI embraces positions that are a matter of popular practice within corporations but are not legally compelled. It thus has been seen as a reform-minded document, driven by academic theory rather than commercial

---

§2.05   [1] *See generally* Commentaries on Corporate Structure and Governance (Donald E. Schwartz ed. 1979) (a record of four symposiums held in 1977 and 1978, co-sponsored by the American Law Institute, the Section on Corporate Banking and Business Law of the American Bar Association, and ALI-ABA).

practicality, and it has been attacked without quarter by the representatives of the managerial class. As a result of the firestorm of protest that met its early version in 1980, the document underwent important changes that muffled its more innovative contributions. Nevertheless, the document continues to offer authoritative guidance of where the law may go on many important corporate law questions.

In broad overview, Principles of Corporate Governance has detailed provisions on the functions, powers, and rights of directors as well as recommendations that for certain-sized corporations outsiders should compose a majority of the board of directors and that the corporations should also have audit, nominating, and executive compensation committees. The project has sought to bring clarity through rigor to the jurisprudence that surrounds director decision-making. The project therefore has chapters devoted to the duty of care and, more generally, to the business judgment rule, the treatment of conflicts of interest, and the role of directors in hostile attempts to acquire their firm. Finally, there is extensive treatment to all aspects of derivative suit litigation, including the manner for initiating the suit, the corporation's participation in the suit, settlement, damages, and indemnification.

In general, Principles of Corporate Governance carefully distinguishes among what it sets forth as an analysis of the present law, what it asserts the law should be, and what it recommends as good corporate practice though not the law. While its provisions are not likely to be adopted in toto by any state, and it was not drafted with this objective in mind, it surely can be expected to have a distinct impact on the direction of corporate law and good corporate practice. For these reasons, its provisions are examined at appropriate locations throughout this treatise.

CHAPTER 3

The Incorporation Process

A. PRE-INCORPORATION DECISIONS

§3.01 Selection of the Corporate Form

After considering the relevant business and financial exigencies of a formative business, the attorney must weigh the relative advantages and disadvantages of the corporate form and then must give careful thought to the choice of a suitable business form. If the enterprise is to be publicly held, the corporate form is practically foreordained. A real choice exists, however, in a closely held enterprise, and the decision to be made is an important one. This section discusses in broad outline the preliminary considerations involved in determining whether a particular closely held business can be conducted most effectively as a corporation or in some other business form. These comments, it is believed, are sufficient to put the lawyer on notice regarding areas in which a more detailed exploration may be desirable.[1]

Giving advice on how to choose a business form for a closely held enterprise is extremely difficult. Much of the difficulty arises from the limitless variations in the characteristics of businesses and the circumstances of the business participants, and from the probability of constant change in those variables. Thus an organizational form may be adapted to a particular business today, but be unsuited to it tomorrow. These changing needs are not a problem because the entity can transform itself into the type of entity best suited for its contemporary needs. That is, an initial election to be a corporation does not pose insurmountable problems in later adopting the partnership form, and vice versa. Aside from changes in the business or in the situations of the participants, changes in the law can bring about an almost overnight shift in the respective advantages and disadvantages of the various forms. The imposition or repeal of an important tax, such as an excess profits tax, or a substantial change in corporation or individual tax rates clearly can have that effect.[2] What might not be so obvious is that non-tax changes in the law can also be determinative. Traditionally, the choice was between conducting an enterprise as a corporation or as a partnership.

A limited partnership is frequently unsuitable because participants in a closely held enterprise usually want to participate in the management of the business, and limited partners, to retain their limited liability, must refrain from taking part in the control of the business.[3] Furthermore, a limited partnership must have at least one general partner who (except in the case of a limited liability limited partnership) is subject to unlimited liability, and in many businesses no one is willing to become a general partner and assume the risk of liability.[4]

§3.01 [1] On the respective advantages and disadvantages of the various forms of business organizations, *see generally* Chester Rohrlich, Organizing Corporate and Other Business Enterprises §§4.01-5.06 (5th ed. 1990); Leonard Sarner & George F. Shinehouse, Jr., Organizational Problems of Small Businesses 3-23 (1961); Jonathan Sobeloff, Tax and Business Organization Aspects of Small Business, ch. 2 (4th ed. 1974, Supp. 1977); Ray Garrett & Ray Garrett, Jr., Choosing the Form of Business Enterprise, 1954 U. Ill. L.F. 359; George D. Gibson, Selecting the Form of Entity for a Small Business, 18 Bus. Law. 100 (1962); Thomas L. Hazen, The Decision to Incorporate, 58 Neb. L. Rev. 627 (1979); Bauer E. Kramer & Alvin Ziegler, Jr., Choice of Form for the Family Owned Business, 16 Hastings L.J. 509 (1965); Claude M. Maer, Jr. & Richard A. Francis, Whether to Incorporate, 22 Bus. Law. 571 (1967).

[2] The decline in the number of partnerships relative to corporations between 1960 and 1981 has been attributed to the greater tax advantages once associated with being a corporation as well as the states' elimination of restrictions on professionals incorporating. Harry J. Haynsworth, Selecting the Form of a Small Business Entity 5 (1985). Congress's enactment of the Tax Equity and Fiscal Responsibility Act of 1982 (TEFRA) equalized many of these differences so that since its enactment there are fewer tax-based reasons to prefer incorporation. Pub.L. 97-248, Title I, §§116(b), 122(f), (g)(1), 128(a)(2) to (4), 142, 148(a), 96 Stat. 353, 362, 366, 381, 394 (1982).

[3] Uniform Limited Partnership Act §7 (1916); Revised Uniform Limited Partnership Act §303 (1985).

[4] This disadvantage, however, is often minimized by making a corporation the general partner, a form which in itself raises serious questions. *See* Larson v. Commissioner, 66 T.C. 159 (1976); Frigidaire Sales Corp. v. Union Properties, Inc., 562 P.2d 244 (Wash. 1977); Delaney v. Fidelity Lease Ltd., 526 S.W. 2d 543 (Tex. 1975).

A. Pre-Incorporation Decisions

The business trust is not generally a viable alternative to the corporation or partnership, primarily because, in addition to their shaky legal status in some states, business trusts are unfamiliar to most lawyers and entrepreneurs.[5] The joint stock company has the characteristics of a corporation, with the important exception that it does not provide limited liability for the owners.[6] Since a corporation with limited liability can be quickly and easily organized under modern statutes to conduct almost any lawful business, the joint stock company is seldom used.

Beginning in the last quarter of the twentieth century, new forms of business entities developed that have dramatically changed the choice of entity decision. The Wyoming legislature in 1977 enacted the first statute authorizing the limited liability company.[7] The limited liability company form of doing business in essence allows the participants to establish what formerly would have been a general partnership with the unlimited liability of its partners but with a full liability shield. All states now provide for limited liability companies.[8] During the last five years of the twentieth century, another new form of business became recognized. Most states now permit a general partnership to operate under a full liability shield by electing to be organized as a limited liability partnership.[9]

The limited liability company and limited liability partnership are likely to be the entities of choice for many start-up businesses. This is so because the owners will have the protection of limited liability but will not be subject to the burdens of formalities that are necessary to establish and maintain the corporate form.

§3.02 Selecting the State of Incorporation

In selecting the state of incorporation, the attorney makes a decision not only as to the relevant statutory law but also as to the case law that will govern all corporate questions, including the duties of the corporation's officers and directors and the rights of its stockholders. As such, it may be advisable to shop for the jurisdiction that will best suit the organizers' needs.[1] On the other hand, the decision of where to incorporate "should be approached with a strong predisposition to incorporate in the state where the corporation's principal business activity will be

---

[5] See §1.12.

[6] It may be possible, however, to include in a joint stock company, a feature, perhaps desirable in particular circumstances, that is not available in a corporation. See Spraker v. Platt, 143 N.Y.S. 440 (App. Div. 1913) (holding that joint stock company's articles of association may provide for self-perpetuating board of directors).

The joint stock company is taxed as a corporation. I.R.C. §7701(a)(3) (West 2002).

[7] See Wyo. Stat. §§17-15-101 to 17-15-136 (1977). The current version is Wyo. Stat. §§17-15-101 to 17-15-136 (2001).

[8] See, e.g., Fla. Stat. Ann. §§608.401-608.471 (2001); Mich. Comp. Laws §450-4101 to 450-5200 (Supp. 2002); Va. Code Ann. §13.1-1000-13.1-1073 (Michie 1993 & 2002 adv. legis. serv.).

[9] See Alan R. Bromberg & Larry E. Ribstein, Bromberg & Ribstein on Limited Liability Partnerships and the Revised Uniform Partnership Act §1.02(a), (b) (2001).

§3.02 [1] See generally Ray Garrett, Where to Incorporate, 37 Ill. B.J. 386 (1949); Symposium, Where Should the Close Corporation Incorporate?, 52 Nw. U. L. Rev. 361 (1957).

located."[2] This local preference is due to several economic considerations. First, incorporating in a state where it would otherwise not have a sufficient presence to subject the corporation to the state's taxing authority visits upon the corporation an unnecessary tax burden. Moreover, businesses not locally domiciled have to qualify to do business in each state where they operate.[3] Under such qualifications provisions, the "foreign" corporation will be subject to filing requirements, fees, *and taxes*. The corporation also subjects itself to a state's taxing power by incorporating under that state's laws, even though the corporation does not otherwise "do business" in the incorporating state. Thus needless multiple taxes are incurred when a corporation is formed in a state that otherwise lacks a sufficient taxing nexus with the corporation. It follows that foreign incorporation fees and expenses may be wasted if one has to pay substantially the same fees for the privilege of qualifying and conducting business as a foreign corporation in the home state where the business is conducted. A second consideration is whether the corporation's counsel, although otherwise knowledgeable in corporate law, can be expected to provide legal advice as efficiently on the sister state's corporate law.

In contrast to the localized business, when faced with a larger business that is likely to cross state lines, forum-shopping becomes a necessary part of the lawyer's role. As noted earlier,[4] some state statutes take a permissive approach, while others adopt "a more 'regulatory' or 'paternalistic' attitude."[5] While Delaware has generally been regarded as a permissive haven,[6] the overall trend in other states has also been toward more and more permissive statutes.[7] The piecemeal revisions to the Model Business Corporation Act have similarly been permissive.

In selecting the most appropriate corporation domicile, there are several factors to be considered. Although the circumstances of a particular situation will frequently narrow the scope of the inquiry, there are a number of general considerations:[8]

(1) Does the proposed state of incorporation permit the type of business proposed in corporate form?[9]

---

[2] Chester Rohrlich, Organizing Corporate and Other Business Enterprises at 4.01 (5th ed. 1990).

[3] *E.g.*, Del. Code Ann. Tit. 8 §371 (2001); Model Business Corp. Act Chapter 15.

[4] *See supra* note 1 and §2.03.

[5] Alexander H. Frey, Jesse H. Choper, Noyes E. Leech & C. Robert Morris, Jr., Cases and Materials on Corporations 89 (3d ed. 1989).

[6] *See* William L. Cary, Federalism and Corporate Law: Reflections Upon Delaware, 83 Yale L.J. 663 (1974); Pierre S. Dupont, Incorporated in Delaware: The Chief Executive of the Diamond State Explains New Facets of Delaware's Enduring Corporate Appeal, 6 Directors & Boards 12 (1981); Allen M. Terrell, Jr. & Samuel A. Nolen, Recent Developments in Delaware Corporate Law, 7 Del. J. Corp. L. 407 (1982); Comment, Law for Sale: A Study of the Delaware Corporation Law of 1967, 117 U. Pa. L. Rev. 861 (1969).

[7] Daniel R. Fischel, The "Race to the Bottom" Revisited: Reflections on Recent Developments in Delaware's Corporation Law, 76 Nw. U. L. Rev. 913 (1982); Charles W. Murdock, Delaware: The Race to the Bottom—Is an End in Sight?, 9 Loy. U. Chi. L.J. 643 (1978). *See supra* §2.03.

[8] *See* Rohrlich, *supra* note 2.

[9] *See* §4.01 for discussion of corporate powers and purposes.

(2) Does the proposed domicile place restrictions on the residence of incorporators and/or shareholders?[10]
(3) Does the proposed domicile have special rules concerning directors and management norms in general?[11]
(4) What are the rights and liabilities of shareholders?[12]
(5) Do the state's statutes permit the desired capital structure?[13]
(6) Does the proposed domicile have an applicable close corporation statute?[14]
(7) What are the applicable organizational and annual fees and taxes?

§3.03 The Usual Steps in the Formation and Organization of a Corporation

Incorporation procedure varies somewhat from state to state, but most states follow a general pattern of requirements for formation. Failure to comply with the necessary formalities can result in a failure to obtain corporate status, but more frequently such failure poses no serious problems.[1] In any event, the lawyer should be thoroughly familiar with the requirements of the state of incorporation as well as the foreign qualification provisions of all states where business activity is contemplated.

The successive steps usually required or advisable for the incorporation and organization of a business corporation under modern corporation statutes are enumerated below:

(1) Taking preliminary options and making promotion and financing arrangements by the organizers or promoters with the aid of competent legal advice;[2]
(2) Soliciting pre-incorporation subscriptions if desired. In many cases this activity will be subject to meeting the requirements of the securities act laws in each state in which shares will be offered for sale as well as the requirements of the Federal Securities Act of 1933;

---

[10] For example, a number of agricultural states have enacted statutes severely restricting, if not prohibiting, foreign farming corporations. *E.g.*, Iowa Code §§911.1-911.5 (2001). *See* Thomas D. Edmonson & Kenneth R. Krause, State Regulation of Corporate Farming (1978).

[11] *See* Chapters 10 and 11.

[12] *See* Chapter 13.

[13] *See* Chapter 18. This inquiry also includes determination of the dividend rules, which vary from state to state. *See* Chapter 20.

[14] *See generally* F. Hodge O'Neal & Robert B. Thompson, O'Neal's Close Corporations Law and Practice §2.06 (3d ed. 1998 & Supp. 2001).

§3.03 [1] *See* Chapter 6.

[2] Especially in the case of closely held corporate ventures, there is frequently a need for a pre-incorporation agreement between the prospective shareholders. 1 F. Hodge O'Neal & Robert B. Thompson, O'Neal's Close Corporations Law and Practice §2.23 (3d ed. 1998 & Supp. 2001).

(3) Reserving the desired corporate name by application to the secretary of state or other designated state office;[3]

(4) Selecting a registered office and registered agent;[4]

(5) Drafting the articles (certificate) of incorporation;

(6) Executing and acknowledging the execution of the articles of incorporation by the incorporators;

(7) Filing the articles of incorporation with the secretary of state along with any required county filings;

(8) Paying the filing or organization fees to the secretary of state and any required franchise tax;

(9) Holding the first organization meeting of the incorporators or of the subscribers for shares to elect directors if the first directors are not named in the articles;

(10) Convening the first meeting of the directors (generally called an "organization meeting") to complete the corporation's organization by electing officers, adopting bylaws, issuing shares, and taking subscriptions, accepting pre-incorporation subscriptions and contracts, adopting the form of stock certificate, establishing a principal office, fixing the place for regular meetings of the directors, authorizing a depository for corporate funds as well as identifying who has authority to execute checks against the company's account, adopting contracts made by the promoters on behalf of the proposed corporation, authorizing the application for a permit under state blue sky laws to take subscriptions and issue shares, and appointing a resident agent for the service of process;

(11) Obtaining from the secretary of state or other official any permit needed for taking subscriptions and issuing shares as well as all steps to assure compliance with the Federal Securities Act of 1933;

(12) Preparing of minutes of the directors' meeting and opening of corporate books and records;

(13) Paying the minimum paid-in capital, if required, and performing other conditions precedent to engaging in business operations;

(14) Issuing shares;

(15) Qualifying to do business in any state where the corporate business will be conducted.

Some statutes specify a particular step in the proceedings at which the corporation's existence begins. In many states this is when the articles (certificate) of incorporation are filed with the secretary of state or other appropriate state offi-

---

[3] There are statutory procedures for reserving a corporate name. *E.g.,* Model Business Corp. Act §401. There are limitations on permissible corporate names. *E.g.,* Del. Code Ann. tit. 8 §102(a)(1) (2001); Model Business Corp. Act §401. *See* §3.05.

[4] *See* Del. Code Ann. tit. 8 §§131, 132 (2001) (registered office, registered agent); Model Business Corp. Act §§5.01-5.03 (registered office and registered agent).

cer. In a few states, the corporate existence begins when the certificate of incorporation under the state seal is issued by the secretary of state or other official after the articles are filed. Filing copies of the incorporation papers in the offices of the county clerk or recorder is not a condition precedent to corporate existence.[5]

The secretary of state's acceptance or rejection of articles for filing does not create a presumption of the document's validity or invalidity. Generally, the secretary of state should reject the document if it contains illegal or improper provisions. If doubt exists as to the legality of the articles, the secretary of state may submit them to the state's attorney general and his or her staff. Most states allow a direct appeal of the secretary of state's refusal. Under the older view, still found in a few states, review of the secretary of state's refusal occurs through a writ of mandamus.[6]

§3.04   Drafting the Articles of Incorporation

The drafting of the incorporation paper, charter, articles of incorporation, certificate of incorporation, or simply "the articles," as the instrument may be called, is usually the first essential step in the incorporation process (in rare cases the parties may first desire to set forth their understandings in a pre-incorporation agreement). The attorney should carefully review the applicable corporation act, the needs of the business, and the wishes of the organizers; and special emphasis should be given to their plans for controlling, capitalizing, and financing the particular enterprises. For example, it is necessary to examine the statutory requirements for the contents of the articles of incorporation, such as the number, residence, and age of the incorporators (that is, those who are to execute the articles); whether the corporation's initial directors must be set forth in the articles of incorporation; the number of shares that must be subscribed for; and the amount of capital that must be paid in, if any, before commencement of business. Care should also be given to whether under state statute the corporation's name as set forth in the articles of incorporation must include an indication that the business is a separate entity, for example by including "Corporation," "Incorporated," or a suitable abbreviation of corporateness.

The articles of incorporation should set forth all the provisions required by the corporation act, expressing them as nearly as possible in the order and in the exact language found in the statute. The governing corporate statute ordinarily is quite clear in stating what information must be set forth in the articles. Over the years, states have required less and less to be stated in the articles of incorporation so that in most states today the bare minimum contents of the articles can generally be set forth on a single sheet of paper with room to spare. Even though the

---

[5] *But see* Fee Insurance Agency, Inc. v. Snyder, 930 P.2d 1054, 1058-1059 (Kan. 1997) (shareholder liable for corporate debt because the incorporators failed to record a copy of the articles of incorporation with the county register of deeds as required by Kansas Statute §17-6003(c)(5)).

[6] *See* Lloyd v. Ramsay, 183 N.W. 333 (Iowa 1921).

particular requirements vary from state to state, the typical act usually calls for the following:

(1) The corporate name.
(2) The purposes, objects, or general nature of the business authorized.
(3) Information relevant to the service of process on the corporation, such as identifying a registered agent and perhaps the corporation's principal office.
(4) Identification of incorporators and/or initial directors.
(5) The types and amount of stock the corporation is authorized to issue.
(6) The proper execution of the articles of incorporation by the incorporators.

§3.05   Selection and Protection of a Corporate Name

Choosing a corporate name requires great care. It is advisable to inquire of the names available by contacting the secretary of state or other officer with whom the articles of incorporation must be filed.[1] Most states have procedures that not only allow the availability of names to be learned prior to incorporation but also permit an available name to be reserved for a stated period of time, generally 60 to 90 days, after the payment of a nominal fee.[2] The name must contain words or an abbreviation indicating that the business is an entity.[3]

The question of availability of a proposed corporate name is usually determined in the first instance by personnel in the secretary of state's office or other executive department. Under the influence of earlier versions of the Model Business Corporation Act, nearly a majority of the states require that a name not be "the same or deceptively similar." What is deceptively similar is frequently problematic. Because of this concern and the belief that the real concern of the secretary of state's office was limited to avoiding confusing two or more organizations in the *secretary*'s records, the Revised Model Business Corporation Act requires only that the "name must be distinguishable upon the records of the secretary of state."[4]

The bare fact that articles of incorporation have been accepted and filed by the secretary of state is not an adjudication of the right to the name and does not confer an exclusive right to the name chosen as against previous rights of other corporations or partnerships. There is a vast body of law under the general heading of unfair competition, which, among other things, protects the use of a trademark or trade name.[5]

---

§3.05   [1] Model Business Corp. Act §4.02. Former Model Business Corp. Act §9 (1969). *See* 19 William M. Fletcher, Cyclopedia Corporations §2.47 (perm. ed. rev. vol. 1988).

[2] *See, e.g.*, N.Y. Bus. Corp. Law §303(c) (McKinney 1986).

[3] Del. Code Ann. tit. 8 §102(a)(1) (2001).

[4] Model Business Corp. Act §4.01(d).

[5] In addition to federal trademark and trade name protection under the Trademark Act of 1946, which is also referred to as the Lanham Act (15 U.S.C. §§1051 *et seq.* (1997 & Supp. 2002)), there is a large body of relevant case law. *See* J. Thomas McCarthy, McCarthy on Trademarks and Unfair Competition (4th ed. 2002). With regard to the specific question of the corporate name *see id.* ch. 9. *See*

B. The Articles of Incorporation

There is a requirement in most, if not all, states that the name set forth in the articles of incorporation must contain such words as "Company," "Corporation," "Incorporated," "Inc." or "Limited" to indicate its corporate status.[6] Furthermore, there are frequently limitations on filing articles of incorporation setting forth a name including the words "Bank," "Trust," or "Trustee" or related words indicating that the corporation is a bank or trust company, without the certificate of approval of the proper official.[7]

The registered corporate name does not limit the corporation's use of other trade names. Unless there is some express provision to the contrary in a statute, a corporation may assume a name, just as a natural person may, for the purpose of entering into a contract or executing or receiving a conveyance.

B.   THE ARTICLES OF INCORPORATION

§3.06   *Statement of Purposes and Powers in the Articles*

Under the older statutes it was required that a corporation should be formed for some definite enterprise or line of business; a few states even required specification of a single purpose. This requirement reflects the concession theory of the corporation's existence as well as a carry over of the pre-nineteenth century practice of jealously granting charters. When the states require an explicit statement of the corporation's purpose, the drafters usually respond with a lengthy multipurpose clause that assures that the corporation may engage in any lawful activity. Such drafting frequently also assures that the document is unreadable. With the death of the concession theory and an ever-increasing quest for flexibility and economy of words, many states in the 1960s authorized the articles to simply state that the corporation's purpose was "to engage in any lawful business" without any further elaboration.[1] The most resolute response to prolix powers and purposes clauses is found in California, where all sets of filed articles are deemed to include an "all purposes" clause, and any other statements are permitted *only* to *limit* the corporation's powers or purposes.[2] A similar approach is taken by the current version of the Model Act.[3]

Generally, there is no need to limit the purposes to the business actually contemplated, and an "all purposes" clause assures flexibility, certainty, and efficiency.

---

also Rudolf Callmann, Unfair Competition, Trademarks and Monopolies §25.34 (4th ed. 1981 & Supp. 2002) (updated annually).

[6] *See* Del. Code Ann. tit. 8 §102(a) (2001); Model Business Corp. Act §4.01.

[7] *Id. But cf.* Snell v. Engineered Systems & Designs, Inc., 669 A.2d 13 (Del. 1995) (statute prohibiting use of "engineered," by other than licensed engineer, did not impose per se ban).

§3.06   [1] The 1969 version of the Model Act adopted this approach. Model Business Corporation Act §3 (1969).

[2] Cal. Corp. Code §206 (West 1990).

[3] Model Business Corp. Act §3.01(a).

However, the occasion can well arise when a narrow purpose clause is a means for fulfilling the desires of the organizers as well as placing a check on management's ability to change the nature of the business.[4]

The statement of the purposes has as its principal function the affirmative authorization of the management to enter into those contracts and business transactions that may be considered as incidental to the attainment of the purposes. It also imposes implied limitations on their authority by excluding lines of activity that are not so covered.[5] The effect of broad purposes or objects is thus to confer wide discretionary authority on the directors and management as to the kinds of business operations in which they may engage. Dealings that are entirely irrelevant to the purposes are unauthorized. Such dealings are referred to as *"ultra vires."* Statutes do not require repeating in the articles of incorporation the powers that may be enumerated or embodied in the incorporating statute, such as the power to sue, acquire and convey property, make contracts, borrow money, execute bonds and mortgages, sell the entire assets, adopt bylaws, dissolve, merge or consolidate, or amend the articles.[6] Many practitioners, however, for the sake of certainty continue to state in the articles of incorporation many statutory, implied, and incidental powers that might just as well have been left unstated in the articles of incorporation.

§3.07 *Registered Agent and Principal Place of Business*

Nearly every state requires the corporation to select and retain a registered agent to serve process within the state. A registered agent may be an individual or a corporation; in either case the agent must be a resident of the incorporating state. Most states require the articles of incorporation to identify the name and address of the initial registered agent. Thereafter, new agents are added or substituted through a routine filing with the secretary of state.[1] New York's approach is representative of a handful of states that do not require a registered agent; New York designates the secretary of state as the corporation's agent to receive process.[2]

In most states, a registered agent can resign by giving written notice to the secretary of state. On receiving the agent's resignation, the secretary of state forwards a copy of the resignation to the corporation's registered office or principal

---

[4] The doctrine of *ultra vires* may be used to preclude directors and officers from acting beyond their authority. *See* §4.04.

[5] For an extreme use of this principle, *see* Cross v. Midtown Club, Inc., 365 A.2d 1227 (Conn. Super. Ct. 1976), where the court construed the purpose of operating a luncheon club as not giving the directors the power to exclude women.

[6] Former Model Business Corporation Act §4 (1969) listed 16 powers in addition to the catch-all "to have and exercise all powers necessary or convenient to effect its purposes"; Model Business Corporation Act §3.02 (1984) lists 15 powers.

§3.07 [1] *See, e.g.*, Cal. Corp. Code §1502 (West Supp. 2002).

[2] The articles of a New York corporation must designate the secretary of state as an agent to receive service of process on the corporation. N.Y. Bus. Corp. Act §402(a) (McKinney 1986 & Supp. 2002). *See also* N.Y. Bus. Corp. Act §304-306 (McKinney 1986 & Supp. 2002).

office.[3] The reasoning behind the agent submitting his or her resignation to the secretary of state rather than to the corporation is to assure reliability in the central records of the secretary of state's office and reflects as well the frequency in which an agent wishing to extricate himself or herself from continuing to be an agent for a corporation that no longer is operating.

§3.08   Incorporators and Initial Directors

A timing problem arises in the legal mechanics of appointing or electing the first board of directors and adopting bylaws so that the corporation can conduct its business.[1] The link between the inchoate corporation and the completed organization is often the incorporator. Defined functionally, "incorporators" are those who sign the articles of incorporation. They may or may not be subscribers for shares. Most statutes require only a single incorporator.[2] A number of states require that an incorporator be a natural person of at least 18 years of age.[3]

The incorporator's authority under most state statutes transcends executing the articles of incorporation and includes electing the initial directors if they are not identified in the articles of incorporation and any other steps to "complete the organization."[4] Because most states do not require the articles to set forth the names of the initial directors, the question frequently arises as to when it is desirable to do so.

If the initial directors are not identified in the articles of incorporation, until the directors are elected, the incorporators have the power to complete the organization, which includes steps to obtain subscriptions to stock, to fix the issue price of shares, and to adopt bylaws. Because incorporators are frequently only clerks or "dummies" pressed into service to duly execute the articles rather than persons with any economic tie to the firm, one must fully consider in each new incorporation the role the incorporators should play in the entity's formation.

Any meeting of the incorporators or directors must be preceded by notice. Generally three to five days is required under the statutes. However, notice can be waived by all the incorporators or directors either attending the meeting or executing a written waiver of notice. Further flexibility appears in provisions that permit action without a meeting of the incorporators or directors if each incorporator or director, as the case may be, signs a written consent to the action taken.[5]

---

[3] *See, e.g.,* Ind. Code Ann. §23-1-24-3 (Burns 1999); R.I. Gen. Laws §7-1.1-12 (1999); Wash. Rev. Code Ann. §23B.05.030 (West 1994); Model Business Corp. Act §5.03 (1984). Some contemplate the difficulty of locating the corporation by providing that notice should be directed to the corporation's "last known address." *See* Neb. Rev. Stat. §21-2033 (1997).

§3.08   [1] *See* Model Bus. Corp. Act §2.05.

[2] *E.g.,* N.Y. Bus. Corp. Law §401 (McKinney 1986 & Supp. 2002).

[3] Colo. Rev. Stat. 7-102-101 (2001); D.C. Code Ann. §29-101.46 (2001); N.Y. Bus. Corp. Law §401 (McKinney 1986 & Supp. 2002); N.D. Cent. Code §10-19.1-09 (2001); Utah Code Ann. §16-10a-201(2001).

[4] *See, e.g.,* N.Y. Bus. Corp. Law §404(a) (McKinney 1986); Model Business Corp. Act §2.05(a)(2).

[5] *See, e.g.,* Del. Code Ann. tit. 8, §108(c) (2001).

An incorporators' meeting is usually a cut-and-dried affair. The minutes are prepared in advance by the promoters or their attorney and are adopted at the meeting. If required by statute, the incorporators take just enough stock to qualify, generally with the understanding that they are not bound to pay but will later assign their subscriptions to others, who will be bound to pay for the shares. Such meetings seem a useless and empty form.

§3.09 Authorized Shares—Planning the Corporation's Capital Structure

A corporation may issue only the stock that is authorized in its articles of incorporation. The articles of incorporation must therefore set forth both the type of stock and the number of shares of each type of stock authorized. Additionally, in those jurisdictions, such as Delaware, that continue to distinguish between par and no-par shares, the articles of incorporation must specify for each class of stock authorized whether the shares are to be par value or without par value.[1] One consequence of the choice between par and no-par value shares is that in those states where fees paid on incorporation are premised on the type of stock authorized, the fees tend to be higher for no-par incorporations than for par value stock incorporations. This is so because no-par shares either are assigned an arbitrarily high figure—for example, $100 per share—or are taxed by the number of shares authorized, whereas par value shares are taxed only at their aggregate par value. Thus a company authorizing 1000 $1 par value shares has a lower tax than one authorizing 1000 no-par shares. The modern trend, led by the 1977 version of the California General Corporation Law and later by the Revised Model Business Corporation Act, is to treat all stock shares without par value.

Fundamental to drafting the capital section of the articles of incorporation is the principle that all shares of stock authorized have identical rights, privileges, and preferences unless the articles expressly provide otherwise. Thus, if not otherwise provided, all shares enjoy equal rights to participate ratably in dividends when declared by the board of directors, in the net assets of the firm on liquidation, and in voting. Identifying some shares as "Preferred" and others as "Common" or dividing common shares into "Class A" and "Class B" is itself without legal significance because these designations do not themselves embody characteristics that distinguish their rights, privileges, and preferences vis-à-vis those that accompany common shares. Hence, statutes commonly provide that where a corporation's articles of incorporation authorize more than one class of stock, the articles must set forth for each class so authorized their relative rights, privileges, and preferences (as well as their respective qualifications, restrictions, or limitations).[2]

---

§3.09 [1] Par value is examined in greater detail in Chapter 16. It is sufficient to state here that par value essentially establishes in most instances the minimum price at which the shares may be sold.

[2] *See, e.g.,* Del. Code Ann. tit. 8, §102(a)(4) (2001).

B. The Articles of Incorporation

The type and number of shares to authorize for a company to be formed generally are matters of negotiation among the company's principals, but the lawyer plays an important role in attempting to tailor the firm's capital structure to accommodate the economic and control objectives of the parties. For a company whose shares will be held by a handful of owners, there is no reason to authorize more shares than are necessary to meet the parties' agreed-upon proportional ownership interests. On the other hand, if stock is to be sold to the public, an ample number of shares should be authorized to meet the expected demand of that offering. Additional shares should be authorized to meet any prospective option or conversion arrangements.

§3.10 Optional Provisions in the Articles

Under the corporation acts of most states, wide latitude is given to the organizers to include in the articles certain optional provisions and to make certain special variations on the ordinary rules prescribed by statute.[1] Much of what appears in today's broadly enabling corporate statutes are rules for the internal governance that apply in the event the corporation does not specify otherwise. Thus most of the provisions of the Uniform Partnership Act fill in gaps in a partnership agreement, and corporate statutes increasingly set forth procedural rules that apply unless the articles of incorporation or bylaws provide otherwise. Care must be taken by the attorney to identify not only which state statutory provisions can be varied by an act of the corporation but also whether the deviation from the statute must appear in a provision in the articles of incorporation or can appear in either the articles or the bylaws. That is, in some instances the statutes expressly permit variations only in the articles of incorporation.[2] In other instances, the variation may appear in either the articles of incorporation or the bylaws.

The articles of incorporation are not merely a private contract between the incorporators or organizers as to their own individual enterprise. They are much more, *viz.*, the constitution of a continuing statutory business association that consists of a shifting group of associates who are expected to invest their money in the enterprise or take by transfer the places of those who have invested. Future shareholders have no voice in drafting the articles of incorporation that limit and define their rights. Most investors become stockholders without reading the articles of incorporation to ascertain provisions that may deprive shareholders of their customary rights and protections. Special and unusual charter clauses may thus prove traps for unwary investors and give opportunity for abuse and oppression by the management. Grossly unfair or unreasonable provisions will doubtlessly be judicially condemned. There are some limits on the oppressive "contracts" that may have been imposed on a corporation during its infancy by

---

§3.10 [1] 19 W. Fletcher, Cyclopedia of Corporations §2:63 (perm. ed. rev. vol. 1988).
[2] Such is the case, *e.g.*, with preemptive rights. *See* §16.14.

management, who thereby sought to reduce statutory and common law rights and safeguards of future shareholders against fraud.[3]

Under most corporate statutes, certain rules as to corporate organization, meetings, and management are mandatory and cannot be varied by the articles,[4] while other rules apply only in the absence of some variation, which must be stated in the articles[5] (in some cases, the variation may be in either the articles or the bylaws).[6] For example, express permission may be granted to regulate various matters such as voting rights,[7] the quorum of shareholders' and directors' meetings,[8] and the authority to fix the price or consideration at which shares without par value may be issued.[9]

§3.11   The Corporate Charter as a Contract

The term "charter" is frequently used in this country in various senses different from its meaning of royal or executive grant in English law. Sometimes "charter" refers to the articles of incorporation, the organic instrument that sets out the corporate structure under the requirements of a general incorporation act. The term is more often used in a broader sense as indicating the entire corporate constitution, including the articles of incorporation document and the relevant laws under which the corporation is created.[1] Sometimes the term "charter" is used in the sense of "franchise," or right granted by law to exist as a corporation.[2]

[3] Such was the case with the notice provisions of Former Model Business Corp. Act §29. *See, e.g.,* State ex rel. Ross v. Anderson, 67 N.E. 207 (Ind. Ct. App. 1903) (statutory provision for directors to be elected annually by shareholders could not be set aside by organizers in certificate of incorporation).

[4] Model Business Corp. Act §6.02; Former Model Business Corp. Act §§16(f), 33 (1969).

[5] The Revised Model Business Corporation Act is representative of the type of provisions that commonly can be varied only by a contrary requirement in the articles and includes such items as cumulative voting for directors, Model Business Corp. Act §7.28; staggering the terms of directors, *id.* §8.06, restricting the power of stockholders to remove directors, *id.* §8.08, granting preemptive rights, *id.* §6.30, distinguishing the rights among classes of shares, *id.* §§6.01-6.02, and imposing super-voting or quorum requirements for stockholders, *id.* §§7.25-7.27.

[6] The Revised Model Act, for example, permits many variations in its provisions to appear in either the articles or the bylaws: fixing the number of directors, Model Business Corp. Act §8.03; notice for meetings, *id.* §8.22; quorum for board meeting, *id.* §8.24; super-vote for board action, *id.* §8.24; creation of board committees, *id.* §8.25; authorizing certificateless shares, *id.* §6.26; and restricting transfer of shares, *id.* §6.27.

[7] Former Model Business Corp. Act §32 (shareholders); *id.* §40 (directors).

[8] Model Business Corp. Act §§7.25, 8.24. Former Model Business Corp. Act §40 (1969). Even with par value there is great leeway in the directors' power to fix the consideration, *see* §§16.15-16.19.

[9] *See* §16.08.

§3.11   [1] It has been said that a corporation carries its charter wherever it contracts business. Relfe v. Rundle, 103 U.S. 222, 226 (1880).

[2] Helvering v. Northwest Steel Rolling Mills, Inc., 311 U.S. 46, 50-51 (1940); Ohio State Life Ins. Co. v. Clark, 274 F.2d 771, 776 (6th Cir.), *cert. denied,* 363 U.S. 828 (1960); In re Two Crow Ranch, Inc., 494 P.2d 915, 919 (Mont. 1972); Ward Parkway Shops, Inc. v. C.S.W. Consultants, Inc., 542 S.W.2d 308, 312 (Mo. Ct. App. 1976).

B. The Articles of Incorporation

The charter may be regarded as a formal contract made by the organizers with the state under authorization of statute for the benefit of those who shall become shareholders or members. The future parties to the contract are the corporation and the persons who become, from time to time, shareholders or members of the corporation.[3] The incorporators, as such, drop out of the picture as soon as their formal organization functions are performed. The essence of the contract is the corporation's articles of incorporation and the laws of the state of incorporation. The relationships and their corresponding duties and rights that flow through these documents underscore the view, discussed earlier, that the corporation is a "nexus of contracts." The charter is also sometimes said to be a contract among the shareholders. Organizers and promoters may contract to form a corporation, but it is not perceived how the shareholders have any contract *inter se.* Their contract rights are worked out and established through the medium of the corporate entity; those rights include the right to have the business activities confined to the scope of the authorized purposes or the right to vote but, at least conceptually, not as between majority and minority.

§3.12 Corporate Bylaws

The bylaws establish rules for the internal governance of the corporation. Bylaws deal with such matters as how the corporation's internal affairs are to be conducted by its officers, directors, and stockholders. Bylaws also commonly deal with the date of the annual shareholders' meeting, the calling and conducting of shareholders' and directors' meetings, formalities as to proxies and voting, qualifications of directors, executive and other committees of the directors, corporate officers (their duties and spheres of authority), formalities and restrictions as to transfers of shares of stock, execution of papers, reports, and audits, and other internal matters.

Adoption of corporate bylaws is commonly regarded as one of the steps in the organization of the corporation.[1] In broad overview, bylaws must be reasonable, should not conflict with the law of the state of incorporation, and must not limit unduly the rights of shareholders contrary to the policy of the law. Bylaws are subordinate both to the statutes and the charter. Bylaws that conflict with statutes or with the articles of incorporation or with public policy—by requiring unanimous vote of stockholders or directors, for example—are void.[2] Bylaws must be reasonable and must operate equally on all persons of the same class.

The courts exercise a regulating power against provisions deemed contrary to policy. For instance, a bylaws provision that attempts unduly to limit the right of transfer of shares or inspection of the books by shareholders or that requires unanimous voting may be viewed as beyond limits permitted by statute or public

---

[3] *See* F. Hodge O'Neal & Robert B. Thompson, Oppression of Minority Shareholders §9.12 (1985).

§3.12 [1] A bylaw that restricts or alters the voting power of shares as given by statute or by the articles is clearly void. Brooks v. State, 79 A. 790 (Del. 1911).

[2] *See* §§14.08-14.09 regarding restraints or transfer.

policy.[3] In the case of closely held corporations, courts strive to effectuate the intent of the parties and thus may uphold such bylaws as *inter se* contracts between the shareholders.[4] Validation of such restrictions is a reflection of a fundamental change in the way judges and lawyers think about corporations.

The power to approve, amend, or repeal bylaws is primarily vested in the shareholders but may be concurrently delegated to the directors either by statute[5] or charter. The power is sometimes conferred by statute on the incorporators as to the original bylaws.[6] The attorney advising the board of directors that seeks to adopt, amend, or repeal a bylaw provision should carefully consider whether the board can do so without stockholder approval. States vary widely in their approaches to this question. Most states allow board action with respect to the bylaws unless the articles of incorporation provide otherwise.[7] Bylaws may be waived or amended informally.

Statutes commonly specify many matters that may be regulated in the bylaws and sometimes give an option to include provisions on certain matters in either the bylaws or the articles of incorporation.[8] Certain matters, such as preferences of different classes of shares, can as a rule be provided for only in the charter, not in the bylaws.[9]

A majority of the states have provisions patterned on the Revised Model Business Corporation Act authorizing the corporation to adopt "emergency bylaws," when, due to a "catastrophic event" a quorum of the directors cannot be readily assembled to act.[10] The corporation's authority extends only to the period of the emergency and includes only the power to adopt bylaws that address legal requirements that otherwise would prevent convening a meeting under the firm's customary procedures. Thus, during an emergency, the corporation may enact bylaw provisions that relax its quorum requirements or that infuse the board of directors with new members.[11]

---

[3] *E.g.*, Sensabaugh v. Polson Plywood Co., 342 P.2d 1064 (Mont. 1959); E. K. Buck Retail Stores v. Harkert, 62 N.W.2d 288 (Neb. 1954); Clark v. Dodge, 199 N.E. 641 (N.Y. 1936) (agreement by shareholders and directors in close corporation to vote for certain people as officers was permissible despite statutory policy to the contrary).

[4] *See* F. Hodge O'Neal, Molding the Corporate Form to Particularize Business Situations: Optional Charter Clauses, 10 Vand. L. Rev. 1, 20-21 (1956).

[5] Del. Code Ann. tit. 8, §109 (2001); N.Y. Bus. Corp. Law §601(a) (McKinney Supp. 2002). *See also* In re Rye Psych. Hosp. Ctr., Inc., 476 N.Y.S.2d 339, 344 (App. Div. 1984) (since statute does not set forth a particular method by which initial bylaws must be adopted, adoption by incorporators may be established by custom, usage, or acquiescence in course of conduct).

[6] Rogers v. Hill, 289 U.S. 582, 588-589 (1933). *See also* Brumfield v. Consolidated Coach Corp., 40 S.W.2d 356 (Ky. 1931) (bylaws must be adopted by body of stockholders or by board of directors); Trout v. Olson Bros. Mfg. Co., 308 N.W.2d 522 (Neb. 1981) (directors have statutory power to make, alter, and amend bylaws, except that when shareholders make, alter, or amend bylaws, directors may not thereafter change them).

[7] *See, e.g.*, Model Business Corp. Act §§10.20(a).

[8] Gaskill v. Gladys Bell Oil Co., 146 A. 337 (Del. Ch. 1929); Shanghai Power Co. v. Delaware Trust Co., 316 A.2d 589 (Del. Ch. 1974), *modified sub nom.* Judah v. Delaware Trust Co., 378 A.2d 624 (Del. Super. Ct. 1977) (unless preferences clearly spelled out in certificate of incorporation they do not exist).

[9] *See, e.g.*, Judah v. Delaware Trust Co., 378 A.2d 624 (Del. Super. Ct. 1977).

[10] Model Business Corp. Act §2.07.

[11] *See* George D. Gibson, Corporate Management During Nuclear Attack, 17 Bus. Law. 249 (1962).

CHAPTER 4

The Scope of the Authorized Business and Duties to Other Constituencies

A. *ULTRA VIRES* ACTS

§4.01 *Purposes and Powers*

At common law, a corporation had the powers enumerated in its purpose clause as well as the implied powers necessary to the accomplishment of its purpose. If a corporation engaged in conduct not authorized by its express or implied powers, the conduct was deemed *ultra vires* and void. With the decline in the concession theory of corporations and the universal recognition of the serious inequities that accompanied sanctioning *ultra vires* acts, courts over time interpreted corporate powers broadly. Legislatures also addressed these concerns by authorizing a corporation's articles to broadly enable the corporation to engage in "any lawful purpose" and by limiting the relief and sanctions available for *ultra vires* acts.

Corporate purposes and corporate powers, although often confused, are fundamentally different. A purpose clause properly refers to a statement describing the business the corporation is to conduct. The stated purpose or object of a corporation, for instance, may be "to manufacture textiles" or "to conduct a retail shoe business and to buy, sell, and deal in all kinds of shoes." The term "corporate powers," on the other hand, refers to methods the corporation may use to achieve its purpose. The retail shoe company, for instance, must have the power to contract and the power to borrow money.

At an earlier time, purpose clauses were so multifarious, drafted with such absurd particularity of enumeration, that it has been well said that they aimed "not to specify, not to disclose, but to bury beneath a mass of words, the real object or objects of the company with the intent that every conceivable form of activity shall be found included somewhere within its terms."[1]

Even though many corporate statutes still require that a "purpose clause" (or, as it is sometimes called, "specific object clause") be included in a corporation's charter, modern corporate statutes introduce a good deal of economy here by permitting the articles of incorporation simply to authorize the corporation to engage "in any lawful purpose."[2] And states following the Revised Model Business Corporation Act do not even require a statement of the corporation's purpose or object.[3]

A statement in a corporation's charter of its objects or purposes or powers has the practical effect of defining the scope of the authorized corporate enterprise or undertaking. Second, the statement both confers and limits the officers' and directors' authority by impliedly excluding activities that are not in furtherance of the stated purposes.

§4.02 Sources of Corporate Powers

Because the corporation is a creation of state statutes, it is reasonable to inquire as to the source and extent of its powers. Corporations have express and implied powers. The *express powers* are enumerated in the corporation laws of the state of incorporation as well as in the articles of incorporation. At one time it was standard practice to include in the articles of incorporation an extensive list of general powers the corporation was to possess. Even today, attorneys as a matter of habit, but rarely of necessity, sometimes include in the articles of incorporation a lengthy set of "powers" the corporation will have to carry out its purpose or objectives.[1] These powers may include the power to mortgage the corporation's property, guarantee the debt of another, enter into partnerships, and purchase another corporation's stock. Again, this practice derives from an earlier day, in which corporate status was a privilege jealously guarded by the state and the courts so that the inherent powers of corporations were narrowly authorized and recognized.

---

§4.01 [1] Cotman v. Brougham, 1918 A.C. 514, 523.

[2] *See, e.g.*, Michael A. Schaeftler, The Purpose Clause in the Certificate of Incorporation: A Clause in Search of a Purpose, 58 St. John's L. Rev. 476, 482-484 (1984).

[3] Model Bus. Corp. Act Annot. §3.01 at 3-6 (3d ed. 1994).

§4.02 [1] *See* 19 William Fletcher, Cyclopedia of the Law of Private Corporations §2:53 (rev. perm. ed. 1994).

A. *Ultra Vires* Acts

Today, it is rarely necessary to elaborate the corporation's incidental powers because most modern statutes expressly grant such powers.[2]

The doctrine of implied powers is a general rule that corporate management, in the absence of express restrictions, has discretionary authority to enter into contracts and transactions reasonably incidental to its business purposes. For example, a lumber company with the power to invest in securities cannot operate primarily as an investment trust, but it can invest its excess cash in marketable securities.[3] Courts are usually liberal, however, in finding that corporate acts are within the corporation's incidental or implied powers.[4]

Transactions that are outside the express or implied powers of the corporation are commonly known as "*ultra vires* acts," beyond the powers of the corporation. A more realistic view characterizes such activities as being beyond the actual authority of the directors and other representatives of the corporation under the charter contract. The legal effect of a transaction outside the scope of the actual authority of the management is treated later in this chapter.[5]

§4.03 Implied Power—Charitable Contributions and Assistance to Employees

Corporations are regularly solicited to contribute to various charitable enterprises in the communities in which they do business. To refuse such requests entirely would probably excite criticism and injure the goodwill and business of the corporation. Nevertheless, the business of a corporation is primarily to earn a profit for its shareholders. The directors' discretion does not in general extend without limits to humanitarian purposes or to purely philanthropic donations at the expense of the shareholders.[1] Under older decisions, even a small contribution might have involved the management in charges of misappropriation or of exceeding its authority. A pure gift of funds or property by a corporation not created for charitable purposes is generally unauthorized and in violation of the rights of its shareholders unless authorized by statute.[2] Over the years, however,

---

[2] Model Bus. Corp. Act §3.02. The Model Act as revised sets out a list of general powers (*id.*) and a list of emergency powers (*id.* §3.03).

[3] Edward Hines W. Pine Co. v. First Nat'l Bank, 61 F.2d 503, 511 (7th Cir. 1932).

[4] *See, e.g.*, Jacksonville, Mayport & Pablo Ry. & Nav. Co. v. Hooper, 160 U.S. 514 (1896); Sneeden v. City of Marion, 64 F.2d 721, 723 (7th Cir. 1933), *aff'd*, 291 U.S. 262, 269 (1934).

[5] *See* §§4.04-4.05.

§4.03 [1] Dodge v. Ford Motor Co., 170 N.W. 668 (Mich. 1919); Parke v. Daily News Ltd. (1962) Ch. 927; Annot., 3 A.L.R. 433 (1919); E. Merrick Dodd, Jr., For Whom Are Corporate Managers Trustees?, 45 Harv. L. Rev. 1145 (1932); Note, Donations by a Business Corporation as Intra Vires, 31 Colum. L. Rev. 136 (1931).

[2] Rogers v. Hill, 289 U.S. 582, 591-592 (1933) (quoting Rogers v. Hill, 60 F.2d 109, 114 (2d Cir. 1932) (Swan, J., dissenting); "'[T]he majority have no power to give away corporate property against the protest of the minority.'" *See also* Adams v. Smith, 153 So. 2d 221 (Ala. 1963); Fidanque v. American Maracaibo Co., 92 A.2d 311 (Del. Ch. 1952); Moore v. Keystone Macaroni Mfg. Co., 87 A.2d 295 (Pa. 1952).

the courts have become increasingly liberal and have exercised considerable ingenuity in finding a sufficient corporate benefit to sustain contributions for charitable, humanitarian, and educational purposes, though the benefit might be
indirect, long-term, or highly conjectural.[3] Today, this power is made explicit in
corporate statutes.[4] Corporations routinely make sizable charitable contributions.[5]
In 2000, for example, the median for corporate charitable contributions was one
percent of the company's pretax income.[6]

The most eloquent and elucidating opinion on corporate charitable contributions is in *A. P. Smith Manufacturing Company v. Barlow*.[7] At issue was the propriety of a $1500 gift to the trustees of Princeton University. The plaintiff shareholder
challenged the gift as a waste of corporate assets since it resulted in no direct
economic benefit to the corporation. The court first traced the history of corporations, concluding that the corporate entity has always had a role to play as a
responsible societal member.[8] The court validated the gift not only as a donation
to society but also as in furtherance of the free enterprise system on which the corporation's success was dependent.[9]

The *Barlow* case is especially significant because it upheld the gift as a matter
of common law. The holding has won legislative confirmation as evidence by the
Model Business Corporation Act's express recognition of the corporate power
"[t]o make donations for the public welfare or for charitable, scientific or educational purpose."[10] Even under such express statutory authority, however, charitable gifts are subject to challenge if clearly unconnected to the corporation's
present or prospective welfare.

[3] *See generally* Louis O. Kelso, Corporate Benevolence or Welfare Redistribution?, 15 Bus. Law. 259 (1960).
[4] Model Bus. Corp. Act §3.02(13) (1984) ("to make donations for the public welfare or for charitable, scientific, or educational purposes"). *See also id.* §3.02(15) ("to make payments or donations, or to
do any other act, not inconsistent with law, that furthers the business and affairs of the corporation").
[5] *See, e.g.*, R. Franklin Balotti & James J. Hanks, Jr., Giving at the Office: A Reappraisal of Charitable Contributions by Corporations, 54 Bus. Law. 965 (1999).
[6] Amy Kao, Corporate Contributions in 2000, The Conference Board (2001).
[7] 98 A.2d 581 (N.J. 1953), *appeal dismissed*, 346 U.S. 861 (1953).
[8] A. P. Smith Mfg. Co. v. Barlow, 98 A.2d 581, 583-588 (N.J. 1953). Specifically, the court reasoned:

> When the wealth of the nation was primarily in the hands of individuals they discharged
> their responsibilities as citizens by donating freely for charitable purposes. With the trans-
> fer of most of the wealth to corporate hands and the imposition of heavy burdens of indi-
> vidual taxation, they have been unable to keep pace with increased philanthropic sneeds.
> They have therefore, with justification, turned to corporations to assume the modern oblig-
> ations of good citizenship in the same manner as humans do.

Id. at 585-586. Justice Jacobs was obviously sympathetic with the view of Berle and Means with regard
to the impact of the modern corporation. *See* Adolf A. Berle & Gardiner C. Means, The Modern Corporation and Private Property (1932; rev. ed. 1968).
[9] *Barlow, supra*, 98 A.2d at 590.
[10] Model Bus. Corp. Act §3.02(13) (1984); Former Model Bus. Corp. Act §4(m) (1980). For a more
detailed discussion of corporation gift giving, see Nancy J. Knauer, The Paradox of Corporate Giving:
Tax Expenditures, the Nature of the Corporation, and the Social Construction of Charity, 44 DePaul
L. Rev. 1 (1994).

A. *Ultra Vires* Acts

The Delaware counterpart[11] of the Model Business Corporation Act's provision was scrutinized in *Theodora Holding Corporation v. Henderson,*[12] wherein a shareholder challenged a corporate charitable contribution in excess of $525,000. The Delaware Court of Chancery upheld the validity of the contribution, relying on both the state corporation statute and the parameters of permissible charitable deductions as established by the federal tax code.[13]

The Delaware Supreme Court, in *Kelly v. Bell,*[14] reaffirmed the corporation's social responsibility, as the court upheld the corporation's voluntary payments to the county following the repeal of county taxation. The corporation agreed to continue making property tax payments to the county if legislation were passed exempting from taxation all acquisitions of machinery after a specified date. The corporation believed that opposition to the legislation stemmed largely from concerns about the county losing much needed revenues and that its commitment to continue making tax payments would make passage of the exempting legislation more likely. Legislation was enacted that exempted *all* property taxes on machinery, and the corporation continued to make the payments to the county in the amount of its former tax assessments. The court characterized the tax payments as corporate donations. Significantly, the court did not confine its inquiry to the *ultra vires* doctrine but examined the question within the more flexible standards of the business judgment rule. The court upheld the payments because the board of directors had reasonably arrived at a business rationale for continuing to make the payments for a purpose that advanced the corporation's interest.

The court's approach in *Kelly* appears the most sensible and workable approach to questions of *ultra vires* acts because it focuses inquiry on what should be the ultimate question—whether the board of directors acted reasonably in what they believed advanced the corporation's interest.[15]

The general judicial and legislative acceptance of corporate benevolence contrasts sharply with the refusal of the Alabama Supreme Court in *Adams v. Smith*[16] to uphold gifts to the widows of former corporate officers: The court designated the disbursements as an invalid waste of corporate assets. The defendant corporation attempted to support the validity of the payments, notwithstanding the absence of their authorization in either the corporate charter or bylaws, on the ground that they were in furtherance of a valid business purpose,[17] presumably to enable the corporation to continue to attract good executives by demonstrating a concern for the welfare of dependents of executives. The court did not dispute the defendant's argument that such payments would have been valid had

---

[11] Del. Code Ann. tit. 8, §122(9) (1983).

[12] 257 A.2d 398 (Del. Ch. 1969).

[13] I.R.C. §170(b)(2) (2002); I.R.C. §545(b)(2) (2002).

[14] 266 A.2d 878 (Del. 1970).

[15] *Accord, e.g.,* Kahn v. Sullivan, 594 A.2d 48, 58 (Del. 1991). *See also, e.g.,* Nell Minow, Corporate Charity: An Oxymoron?, 54 Bus. Law. 997 (1999).

[16] 153 So. 2d 221 (Ala. 1963). *See also* Rogers v. Hill, 289 U.S. 582 (1933); Heller v. Boylan, 32 N.Y.S.2d 131 (App. Div.), *aff'g* 29 N.Y.S.2d 653 (Sup. Ct. 1941); Moore v. Keystone Macaroni Mfg. Co., 87 A.2d 295 (Pa. 1952).

[17] Adams v. Smith, *supra,* 153 So. 2d at 223-224.

they been made under proper procedure but concluded that the absence of an express contract was fatal to the defense.[18]

Today, both by law and by public sentiment, a greatly enlarged social duty and responsibility of businesses exists for the comfort, health, and well-being of their employees. It is not always sufficient merely to pay the actual wage agreed upon.[19] However, if a bonus or other compensation of directors and executives is so large as to have no relation to the value of the services for which it is given, it may be treated as in reality a gift, which even the majority shareholders have no power to make.[20] An important consideration in all cases is whether the compensation arrangement has been approved by outside directors or by the stockholders.

§4.04   Modern Statutory Treatment of Ultra Vires Acts

The ultra vires doctrine is not dead, but its availability today is severely limited. Modern corporation acts severely restrict the relief or sanctions that once accompanied *ultra vires* acts. By doing so, the statutes reject the view that a corporation lacks the *capacity* to act beyond its purposes or powers, and promote stability and certainty in transactions with corporations. In broad overview, the statutes narrowly authorize the relief, if any, available to (1) the corporation, (2) the corporation's stockholders, and (3) the state for *ultra vires* acts. Because most states have either adopted the Model Business Corporation Act's treatment of *ultra vires* transactions or their statutes closely parallel the Model Act's provisions in this area, it is useful to examine closely the Model Act's approach to *ultra vires* acts.

First, the Model Act-type provisions prevent either the corporation or the other party to an *ultra vires* transaction from raising the defense of *ultra vires,* even though the contract is completely executory on both sides—that is, neither party can avoid the contract solely because it is *ultra vires*.[1] This changes the common law, which allowed either party to set up the *ultra vires* defense in a suit on a completely executory contract.

Second, the Model Act-type provisions authorize suit for damages by or on behalf of the corporation against the corporate executive responsible for the *ultra vires* act.[2] In such a suit, defendants can be expected to shield the decision by arguing their actions are within the business judgment rule.

---

[18] *Id. See, e.g.*, Murrell v. Elder-Beerman Stores Corp., 239 N.E.2d 248 (Ohio C.P. 1968).

[19] Solimine v. Hollander, 16 A.2d 203, 245-247 (N.J. Eq. 1940). In Putnam v. Juvenile Shoe Corp., 269 S.W. 593 (Mo. 1925), the court upheld a bonus consisting of one-third of net profits, noting that such payments tend to stimulate loyalty, faithfulness, and energy and give employees a real interest in the business. *See* Chapter 11.

[20] Rogers v. Hill, 289 U.S. 582, 591 (1933); Adams v. Smith, 153 So. 2d 221 (Ala. 1963); Moore v. Keystone Macaroni Mfg. Co., 87 A.2d 295 (Pa. 1952).

§4.04   [1] Cal. Corp. Code §208 (West 1990 & Supp. 2002); Conn. Gen. Stat. Ann. §33-292 (West 1997); Del. Code Ann. tit. 8, §124 (2001).

[2] *See* Cal. Corp. Code 208 (West 1990 & Supp. 2002); 805 Ill. Comp. Stat. Ann. 5/3.15 (West 1993 & Supp. 2002); N.Y. Bus. Corp. Law §203 (McKinney 1986 & Supp. 2002).

A. *Ultra Vires* Acts

Third, in response to a shareholder suit, "the court may, if all the parties to the contract are parties to the proceeding and if it deems the same to be equitable, set aside and enjoin the performance of such contract."[3] Only rarely, however, have such suits met with success.[4] One noteworthy case is *Blue Cross and Blue Shield of Alabama v. Protective Life Insurance Company*,[5] involving a corporation organized for the purpose of providing health care service plans to subscribers. The corporation intended to acquire a subsidiary to provide life insurance. The court reasoned that the acquisition of a subsidiary to provide life insurance was neither necessary nor incidental to the accomplishment of the corporation's stated purpose. The acquisition was therefore *ultra vires*, and the court enjoined the corporation from acquiring the life insurance company. Shareholders who have themselves participated in *ultra vires* acts cannot attack.[6]

As a means of softening the effects of any injunctive relief, the Model Business Corporation Act provides that in such an action the court may allow the corporation or the other party to the contract compensation for the loss or damage sustained by its action "but anticipated profits to be derived from the performance of the contract shall not be awarded."[7] This provision's major thrust is to compensate the parties for any loss suffered as a consequence of the court enjoining the *ultra vires* activity and as such does not seem to have been well thought through. From whom would the corporation recover damages it suffered from the court's action in enjoining performance of a contract? Recovery from the shareholder bringing the proceedings would discourage such suits and does not appear to be contemplated by the statute, and the case will be rare indeed in which the corporation could justly recover from the other party the losses the corporation suffers from a court's injunction in shareholder-instituted litigation of this kind. Furthermore, awarding damages to the other party appears to disserve both the corporation and the third party. To award damages to the third party, the court must believe the corporation is better off without the *ultra vires* contract even after considering the damages it must pay to the third party. This would appear to be such a rare case that it hardly needs to be contemplated in the statute.

Finally, the Model Business Corporation Act authorizes the state to invoke the corporation's *ultra vires* acts as a grounds for its dissolution.

---

[3] Model Bus. Corp. Act §3.04(b)(1) (1984); Former Model Bus. Corp. Act §7(a) (1969).

[4] In Inter-Continental Corp. v. Moody, 411 S.W.2d 578, 591 (Tex. Civ. App. 1967), the plaintiff was able to intervene in an action to enjoin the payment of a note. However, the note in that case appears to have been the result of a breach of the executive's fiduciary obligation because it was issued in satisfaction of his personal debts. For cases denying injunctive relief where there was no accompanying breach of fiduciary duty, *see* Cushman & Wakefield, Inc. v. Dollar Land Corp., 355 N.Y.S.2d 409 (App. Div. 1974); Diamond Paint Co. of Houston v. Embry, 525 S.W.2d 529 (Tex. Civ. App. 1975); Goodman v. Ladd Estate Co., 427 P.2d 102 (Or. 1967).

[5] 527 So. 2d 125 (Ala. Civ. App. 1987).

[6] *See* Goodman v. Ladd Estate Co., 427 P.2d 102 (Or. 1967).

[7] Del. Code Ann. tit. 8, §124 (2001); Ind. Code Ann. §23-1-22-5 (Michie 1999); N.C. Gen. Stat. §55-3-04 (2000).

B.   THE CORPORATION'S OBJECTIVE VIS-À-VIS OTHER CONSTITUENCIES

§4.05   Other Constituencies Statutes

More than one-half of the states have enacted statutes that allow, and in a few cases even require,[1] the board of directors to take into account the interests of persons or groups other than its stockholders—that is, to consider the interest of other constituencies—when making decisions, especially when the decision relates to a potential change in control.[2] In broad overview, "other-constituencies" statutes authorize the directors to consider the effect of their actions on nonshareholder groups such as employees, creditors, bondholders, suppliers, and communities. Some go further and provide that the directors' judgments may be guided by state or national economic considerations as well as broader societal interests. The overall focus of such provisions is to alter the traditional orientation that corporate decisions are to be adjudged by their impact on stockholder wealth as contrasted with some greater good, such as happier workers and a more vibrant community. The traditional formulation of the directors' fiduciary obligations was summarized nicely by the Delaware Supreme Court as requiring that before directors may take into account other constituencies in arriving at their decision there must "be some rationally related benefit accruing to the stockholders."[3] It was put more strongly by the Michigan Supreme Court in its review of Henry Ford's decision to forgo special dividends so as to reduce the price of automobiles for the public benefit:

> [I]t is not within the lawful powers of the board of directors to shape and conduct the affairs of a corporation for the merely incidental benefit of shareholders and for the primary purpose of benefiting others, and no one will contend that, if the avowed purpose of the defendant directors was to sacrifice the interests of shareholders, it would not be the duty of the courts to interfere.[4]

More recently, the Delaware Supreme Court stated rather crisply that "[a] board may have regard for various constituencies in discharging its responsibilities, provided there are rationally related benefits accruing to the stockholders."[5] These observations are in stark contrast to other constituencies statutes' authorization for the board of directors to consider a wider range of interests that may be

---

§4.05 [1] *See* Conn. Gen. Stat. Ann. §33-756(d) (West 1997 & Supp. 2002).

[2] For a state-by-state compilation of other-constituencies statutes, *see* Steven M. H. Wallman, The Proper Interpretation of Corporate Constituency Statutes and Formulation of Director Duties, 21 Stetson L. Rev. 163, 194-196 (1991).

[3] Revlon Inc. v. MacAndrews & Forbes Holding, Inc., 506 A.2d 173, 176 (Del. Super. Ct. 1986).

[4] Dodge v. Ford Motor Co., 170 N.W. 668, 684 (Mich. 1919).

[5] Revlon, Inc. v. MacAndrew & Forbes Holdings, 506 A.2d 173, 182 (Del. Super. Ct. 1986). *Revlon* thus qualifies the court's earlier dicta that the board of directors may consider the impact of a hostile takeover on "constituencies other than shareholders" when considering whether the bid posed a threat. *See* Unocal Corp. v. Mesa Petroleum Corp., 493 A.2d 946 (Del. 1985).

B. The Corporation's Objective Vis-à-Vis Other Constituencies

impacted by the board's decision. For example, Indiana commands that no one corporate constituency shall be a "dominant or controlling factor" in the board of directors' decisions,[6] and Iowa allows other constituencies' interests to guide the decision where they outweigh the financial interests of the corporation or its shareholders.[7]

For example, consider the breadth of Pennsylvania's statute, which states "directors . . . shall not be required, in considering the best interests of the corporation or the effects of any action, to regard any corporate interest or the interests of any group affected by such action as a dominant or controlling interest or factor."[8] Soon after the statute was enacted, the federal district court held "[i]t was proper for the company to consider the effects the . . . tender offer would have, if successful, on the Company's employees, customers and community."[9] The propriety of the directors' consideration of interests other than the stockholders is nearly unbridled in Pennsylvania because the legislature provided a nearly conclusive presumption of validity for the directors' decision.[10]

The impetus for the states' sudden interest in other-constituencies statutes was the hostile takeovers in the 1980s that frequently led to plant closures, layoffs, and declines in the value of the target corporation's outstanding bonds due to the acquisition being financed by issuing debentures to be paid from the target corporation's future earnings. In essence, other-constituencies statutes are just one of several novel forms of takeover defenses that were developed in the heat of the takeovers that have come to symbolize the "take and break" days of the 1980s. In this context, the state directive or invitation for directors to look beyond the bottom line loses some of its social responsibility zing, especially under most state statutes, where consideration of other constituencies is couched in precatory language.

Minimally, these statutes are vulnerable to the criticism that it removes the bright beacon of wealth maximization as the standard for management's stewardship and replaces it with multiple and sometimes competing standards, thus allowing the directors to choose the constituency by whose interests the directors' action is to be determined.[11] Thus, in the takeover context, the stockholders are benefited by a high takeover premium and disserved if that premium is reduced because the bidder wishes to retain the target company's workforce rather than close inefficient plants.[12] To be sure, these are tragic choices, but ones that are

---

[6] Ind. Code Ann. §23-1-35-1(f) (Michie 1999 & Supp. 2002).

[7] Iowa Code Ann. §491.101B (West Supp. 1999 & Supp. 2002).

[8] 15 Pa. Cons. Stat. Ann. §1715(b) (West 1999 & Supp. 2002).

[9] Baron v. Strawbridge & Clothier, 646 F. Supp. 690, 697 (E.D. Pa. 1986).

[10] *See* 15 Pa. Cons. Stat. Ann. §1715(d) (West 1995 & Supp. 2002). Similarly, Indiana provides a conclusive presumption provided the directors act in "good faith after reasonable investigation." Ind. Code Ann. §23-1-35-1(g) (Michie 1999 & Supp. 2002).

[11] *See* A.B.A. Committee on Corporate Laws, Other Constituencies Statutes: Potential for Confusion, 45 Bus. Law 2253, 2268-2270 (1990).

[12] In this regard, consider §6.02 of the A.L.I. Principles of Corporate Governance: Analysis and Recommendations (1994), which allows nonshareholder interests to be taken into consideration when there is a hostile bid, provided the shareholder interest is not "significantly" disfavored.

judged by the more objective (and some would say neutral) standard of wealth maximization.

Other-constituencies statutes invite not simply a kinder, gentler standard, but the unbridled discretion of management to choose when to favor stockholders and when to favor workers or bondholders. One can surely expect that workers will not be favored when the issue is abolishing inefficient work rules, but protecting those work rules may well be championed by managers facing a hostile bidder who intends to make reductions not only in the factory workforce but in the target management as well.

Others believe that the courts can fine-tune the other-constituencies statutes, with the effect that the statutes require directors' judgments that are Pareto optimal in that no proscribed constituency is worse off and many are better off because of the board of directors' action.[13] This brings to mind the Achilles' heel of other constituencies statutes, which is their inherent indeterminacy because they commit complete discretion to the board of directors without any reliable method to adjudge the appropriateness of its exercise.[14] Thus a committee of the American Bar Association concludes:

> [Constituency statutes may be interpreted] to impose new powers and duties on directors. . . . [T]hey may radically alter some of the basic premises upon which corporation law has been constructed in this country without sufficient attention having been given to all the economic, social, and legal ramifications of such a change in the law.[15]

§4.06 The American Law Institute and Corporate Objectives

Commentators have expressed a good deal of dissatisfaction with the objective of the American corporation.[1] Such commentary provided fuel for the American

---

[13] See Morey W. McDaniel, Stockholders and Stakeholders, 21 Stetson L. Rev. 121 (1991).

[14] For this reason, some commentators have urged that the directors should have the burden of explanation. For example, Professor Mitchell argues that the board of directors should have the burden of explaining why the corporate interest was served whenever a constituency complains it was harmed by the board's action. See Lawrence E. Mitchell, A Theoretical and Practical Framework for Enforcing Corporate Constituency Statutes, 70 Tex. L. Rev. 579, 635-636 (1992). See also Eric W. Orts, Beyond Shareholders: Interpreting Corporate Constituency Statutes, 61 Geo. Wash. L. Rev. 14 (1992) (maintain burden of proof on directors when other constituencies considered in defense to takeover).

[15] A.B.A. Committee on Corporate Laws, Other Constituencies Statutes: Potential for Confusion, 45 Bus. Law. 2253, 2270-2271 (1990). But see Charles Hansen, Other Constituency Statutes: A Search for Perspective, 46 Bus. Law. 1355 (1991) (other constituency statutes are unlikely to have any significant impact on the law of corporate governance).

§4.06 [1] See, e.g., David L. Engel, An Approach to Corporate Social Responsibility, 32 Stan. L. Rev. 1 (1979); Edwin M. Epstein, Societal, Managerial, and Legal Perspectives on Corporate Social Responsibility—Product and Process, 30 Hastings L.J. 1287 (1979); Alfred F. Conard, Response: The Meaning of Corporate Social Responsibility, Variations on a Theme of Edwin M. Epstein, 30 Hastings L.J. 1321 (1979); Friedman, The Social Responsibility of Business Is to Increase Its Profits, N.Y. Times Magazine, Sept. 13, 1978, at 32.

B. The Corporation's Objective Vis-à-Vis Other Constituencies

Law Institute's corporate governance project, particularly section 2.01,[2] which provides:

The Objective and Conduct of the Corporation

(a) Subject to the provisions of Subsection (b) and 6.02 (Action of Directors That Has the Foreseeable Effect of Blocking Unsolicited Tender Offers), a corporation [§1.12] should have as its objective the conduct of business activities with a view to enhancing corporate profit and shareholder gain.

(b) Even if corporate profit and shareholder gain are not thereby enhanced, the corporation, in the conduct of its business:

(1) Is obliged, to the same extent as a natural person, to act within the boundaries set by law;

(2) May take into account ethical considerations that are reasonably regarded as appropriate to the responsible conduct of business; and

(3) May devote a reasonable amount of resources to public welfare, humanitarian, educational, and philanthropic purposes.

Section 2.01 is the type of provision that is intended to provide guidance to corporations, their executives, and the courts on permissible objectives of corporate activities. Central to the proscribed objective is the view that the corporation is an economic institution for which the economic objectives embodied in subsection 2.01(a) apply. Nevertheless, subsection (b) also underscores that in today's world corporations are also viewed as social institutions, so that in some instances (i.e., those proscribed in section 2.01(b)(1)) the corporation's economic objective *must* be constrained by certain social imperatives, and in other situations (i.e., those set forth in section 2.01(b)(2) and (3)) its managers *may* qualify its economic objectives by social considerations.

The debate that surrounds section 2.01 focuses on the necessity of adding subsection (b) to the overall economic objectives that are embodied in subsection (a).[3] The critiques of subsection (b) argue that staying within the bounds of the law as well as the appropriateness of corporate activity being undertaken for ethical or social good could easily be handled by continuing the common law approach of examining the activity to determine whether it is reasonably related to the corporation's economic objective. The common law approach does this through the business judgment rule, which accords a high presumption of propriety to board decisions, so that decisions guided by ethical or social considerations are examined for their plausible relationship to the corporation's economic objectives. As seen earlier in this chapter, this approach is reflected in numerous

[2] ALI 1 Principles of Corporate Governance: Analysis and Recommendations (1994 & Supp. 1998).

[3] *See* M.J. Pritchett, III, Note, Corporate Ethics and Corporate Governance: A Critique of the ALI Statement on Corporate Governance Section 2.01(b), 71 Cal. L. Rev. 994 (1983). For an insightful elaboration of the bases set forth in Section 2.01(b) when management may lawfully engage in activities that do not maximize profits, *see* Melvin A. Eisenberg, Corporate Conduct That Does Not Maximize Shareholder Gain: Legal Conduct, Ethical Conduct, The Penumbra Effect, Reciprocity, The Prisoner's Dilemma, Sheep's Clothing, Social Conduct, and Disclosure, 28 Stetson. L. Rev. 1, (1998).

cases where an activity has been challenged as *ultra vires*. It appears that section 2.01 makes two significant modifications in the common law in this regard.

First, section 2.01 mandates that the corporation must abide by the law, as must a natural person. Under the common law's strict obeisance to the economic objective of the corporation, corporations may disobey the law and remain true to their objectives if the benefits of disobeying the law exceed the cost of compliance and/or apprehension. Section 2.01 rejects such cost-benefit determinations; the ALI commentary permits disobeyance only out of necessity or desuetude.[4] A second modification to the common law arises with those actions covered by section 2.01(b)(2) and (3)—deviations from the profit objective supported by ethical or societal considerations. In place of the economic considerations for judging the propriety of such departures, the ALI substitutes a broad standard of "reasonableness," in which the propriety of a corporation's actions motivated by ethical or societal considerations is tested by such varying considerations as the custom among corporations and the relative nexus between the resources the corporation has committed to the activity and the corporation's business.[5]

Section 2.01 purports to operate solely as a constraint on the corporation, with the likely sanction for a violation being injunctive relief. However, lurking in its shadows is the possibility that responsible directors or officers can be held accountable if their conduct falls outside the protection of the business judgment rule. It would appear, therefore, that directors and officers are well advised to proceed cautiously if their actions fall into one of the narrow sets of circumstances that are driven by ethical or societal concerns but cannot independently be premised on serving the corporation's long-term economic objectives.

---

[4] ALI 1 Principles of Corporate Governance: Analysis and Recommendations §2.01, commentary g (1994 & Supp. 1998).

[5] *Id.* commentary i.

CHAPTER 5

The Promotion
of the Corporation

A. PRE-INCORPORATION CONTRACTS

§5.01 *Functions of Promoters*

Promoters discover business opportunities, prepare plans to take advantage of them, and push those plans to completion. They perform an essential economic function in assembling and coordinating the necessary plan, materials, and personnel for new business enterprises. Although there are many professional promoters, people whose life's work is the conception and organization of business enterprises, most business enterprises are conceived and organized by amateur promoters, people who play the role of promoter only once or twice in a lifetime, usually in connection with a business with which they expect to be permanently identified.

The typical promoter performs many varied services in launching an enterprise, often enlisting the aid of experts, lawyers, bankers, solicitors, and other persons. The various activities of the promoter may be classified as follows: (1) the discovery and investigation of a promising business opportunity; (2) the formulation of business and financial plans; (3) the assembling of the enterprise by negotiating and obtaining some control over the subject matter by options or contracts made on behalf of the proposed corporation or on the promoter's credit; (4) the making of arrangements for financing the enterprise and issuing securities; and (5) the arranging of the promoter's own compensation.[1]

The mere fact that a person becomes an incorporator and signs the articles of incorporation of a proposed corporation does not make that person a promoter.[2] Furthermore, lawyers, bankers, accountants, and others who work with promoters in a professional capacity to bring a business into existence usually are not considered promoters. However, incorporators, attorneys, and others become promoters, and thus subject to promoters' obligations and responsibilities, if they take an active part in launching a new enterprise and if their participation is with a view to sharing in promotion profits.[3]

A promoter often is in a position to sell the enterprise to prospective investors, and thus may seek a speculative profit in securities of the new company. Promoters may further attempt to take advantage of their position and seek unreasonable, undisclosed, and excessive compensation. These "secret profits" are often available to promoters because they are usually in complete control of the enterprise in its early stages. Accordingly, courts have ruled that a promoter owes fiduciary duties to the company and cannot profit unduly at its expense.[4]

§5.02   Pre-Incorporation Contracts: Questions Raised

Under modern statutes, formal incorporation is relatively quick, simple, and inexpensive, but promoters may still find it desirable, and in some instances essential, to make arrangements before incorporation of the business to insure that the corporation will have needed property, funds, patent rights, licenses, services, or key

§5.01   [1] On promoters' compensation, *see generally* Chester Rohrlich, Organizing Corporate and Other Business Enterprises §5.05 (5th ed. 1975); W. J. Brockelbank, The Compensation of Promoters, 23 Or. L. Rev. 195 (1934); Frederick H. Bruenner & Riley C. Gilley, Promoters and Their Profits, 13 Bus. Law. 429 (1958).

[2] *E.g.,* Wheeler & Motter Mercantile Co. v. Lamerton, 8 F.2d 957 (8th Cir. 1925); Benton v. Minneapolis Tailoring & Mfg. Co., 76 N.W. 265 (Minn. 1898).

[3] *See* Oklahoma-Texas Trust v. SEC, 100 F.2d 888 (10th Cir. 1939).

[4] *See, e.g.,* Old Dominion Copper Mining & Smelting Co. v. Bigelow, 203 Mass. 159, 89 N.E. 193 (Mass. 1909), *aff'd on other grounds,* 225 U.S. 111 (1912); Northridge Coop. Section No. 1, Inc. v. 32nd Ave. Constr. Corp., 141 N.E.2d 802 (N.Y. 1957); Frick v. Howard, 126 N.W.2d 619 (Wis. 1964). *See also* Annot., 84 A.L.R.3d 162 (1978).

employees. Thus, before a corporation is formed, its promoters may enter into contracts to obtain or "tie down" the needed assets and personnel.[1]

Frequently these contracts are made in the name of the corporation being formed but not yet in existence. Usually the other contracting party is aware that the corporation has not yet come into being but understands that the promoter is contracting on its behalf and for its benefit. In most instances, no problems develop out of promoters' contracts. The corporation is formed; it is adequately financed, at least for the "short run"; those controlling the corporation after its formation do not question that the contract binds the corporation; both the corporation and the other party to the contract perform their respective obligations under the contract; and no need arises for the other party to the contract to try to subject the promoters to liability.

§5.03 Liability of the Corporation on Pre-Incorporation Contracts

It has long been well established in the law that an agency relationship cannot be recognized without an existing principal.[1] Accordingly, promoters of a corporation are not considered its agents and, apart from statute, they are not recognized as having the power to bind a proposed but not yet formed corporation to contracts made on its behalf.[2] Furthermore, the incorporation of a company will not in itself render that corporation liable on contracts its promoters made on its behalf before incorporation.[3]

§5.04 Theories of Corporate Liability on Promoters' Contracts

American courts have professed difficulty in finding a rational explanation of how a corporation can make itself a party to its promoters' pre-incorporation

---

§5.02 [1] *See, e.g.*, Stanley J. Howe & Assoc. v. Boss, 222 F. Supp. 936 (S.D. Iowa 1963) (contract with architectural firm to perform services for proposed corporation); Perry v. Nevin Hotel Co., 109 N.E.2d 810 (Ill. App. Ct. 1952) (contract with experienced executive to manage designated hotel when it was taken over by promoter or corporation formed by him).

§5.03 [1] Warren Abner Seavey, Agency §34 (1964).

[2] "[P]romoters . . . have no standing in any relation of agency, . . . and, in the absence of any act authorizing them so to do, can enter into no contract, nor transact any business, which shall bind the proposed corporation after it becomes a distinct entity. . . ." Wall v. Niagara Mining & Smelting Co., 59 P. 399, 400 (Utah 1899). *See also, e.g.*, Solomon v. Cedar Acres East, Inc., 317 A.2d 283 (Pa. 1974); Steele v. Litton Indus., 68 Cal. Rptr. 680 (Ct. App. 1968).

[3] *See, e.g.*, In re Vortex Fishing Systems, Inc., 277 F.3d 1057, 1070 (9th Cir. 2002) (applying Montana law). "Two exceptions are made to this rule: (1) corporate liability may be imposed by its articles of incorporation or by a statute which regulates corporate liability in such matters, and (2) liability may be assumed by the corporation by some act after it is in being [ratification]." Ong Hing v. Arizona Harness Raceway, Inc., 459 P.2d 107, 113 (Ariz. Ct. App. 1969). *See also* Air Traffic & Serv. Corp. v. Fay, 196 F.2d 40 (D.C. Cir. 1952).

contracts.[1] A corporation may assume the burdens of a contract by agreement with a promoter on sufficient consideration. But such an assumption of the promoter's obligations under the contract does not give the corporation a right to sue on the contract, a right that it could acquire only by assignment from the promoter or as a third-party beneficiary of the contract.

Five theories have been advanced as to how the liability of the corporation on the promoters' contracts can arise: (1) ratification; (2) adoption; (3) acceptance of a continuing offer; (4) formation of a new contract; and (5) novation.[2]

Adoption is a corporation's assent to a contract that was made in contemplation of the corporation's assuming it after organization. In other words, adoption occurs when a corporation takes the contract rights and obligations of the promoter and makes them its own. Ratification is the corporation's acceptance of an act purportedly made on its behalf by an agent.[3] Strictly speaking, a purported principal must have been in existence at the time of a contract in order to have the capacity to ratify it; therefore ratification is only properly applicable to post-incorporation contracts. Courts, however, often use the term "ratification" loosely to refer to a corporation's acceptance or adoption of a promoter's contract. Adoption and ratification may be shown by any words or acts of responsible corporate officers showing assent or approval, such as by their knowingly accepting benefits of the contract or proceeding to perform obligations imposed on it.[4]

Some courts have drawn a distinction between the effect of ratification and adoption; a ratified contract relates back to the date the promoter made it,[5] whereas an adopted contract becomes binding on the corporation on the date of adoption.[6] However, nothing seems to prevent a corporation from adopting a promoter's contract as of the date it was originally made if the corporation expressly or impliedly agrees to do so.

On what theory does a person who is not a party to a contract become a party by adoption? One theory is that the original promoter's contract is in the nature of a continuing proposal, which the corporation may accept when it comes into existence.[7] Another theory is that a corporation's adoption of a promoter's contract is nothing more than the making of a new contract for new consideration.[8]

---

§5.04 [1] Clifton v. Tomb, 21 F.2d 893 (4th Cir. 1927). *See* Note, Inadequacy of Traditional Concepts in the Treatment of the Promoter, 81 U. Pa. L. Rev. 746 (1933).

[2] *See* Annot., 41 A.L.R.2d 477 (1955); 12 A.L.R. 726 (1939); 49 A.L.R. 673 (1927); 17 A.L.R. 452 (1922). *See also* Restatement (Second) of Agency §326 Comment b (1958).

[3] *See* §8.10 on ratification of unauthorized acts of corporate officers and agents.

[4] *See* §5.05. *See also* Chartrand v. Barney's Club, Inc., 380 F.2d 97 (9th Cir. 1967).

[5] *See* Rees v. Mosaic Technologies, Inc., 742 F.2d 765 (3d Cir. 1984); Stanton v. N.Y. & E. Ry., 22 A. 300 (Conn. 1890).

[6] McArthur v. Times Printing Co., 51 N.W. 216 (Minn. 1892). *See* 23 Minn. L. Rev. 224 (1939).

[7] Kirkup v. Anaconda Amusement Co., 197 P. 1005 (Mont. 1921): "The adoption of such a contract is on the theory that the contract made by the promoters is a continuing offer . . . and that it may be accepted and adopted by the corporation after it is created." *Id.* at 1008.

[8] Kridelbaugh v. Aldrehn Theatres Co., 191 N.W. 803 (Iowa 1923); McArthur v. Times Printing Co., 51 N.W. 216 (Minn. 1892); Neosho Motors Co. v. Smith, 59 S.W.2d 802 (Mo. Ct. App. 1933).

A. Pre-Incorporation Contracts

Still another theory is that whenever the parties to a promoter's contract antici-pate that the corporation when formed will accept the contract and take over its performance, the contract is to be viewed as contemplating a novation, by which the corporation, when it assents after organization, is substituted for the pro-moter.[9] Courts in the past have shown some readiness to take this novation view of a promoter's contract,[10] but more recent decisions have relied on an adoption/ratification theory and have been reluctant to find that such a contract contemplated a novation.[11] Finally, some courts hold corporations liable on pro-moters' contracts under the principle that one who adopts the benefits of an act that another volunteers to perform in the first person's behalf is bound to take the burdens along with the benefits.[12]

§5.05 Adoption and Ratification Theories

In England, courts have held that a promoter's contract made on behalf of a cor-poration before incorporation binds only the promoters, and that the corporation cannot ratify the contract in order to become a party after incorporation. The courts in almost all the American states have repudiated the English doctrine, holding that promoters' contracts made on behalf of a corporation to be formed may be adopted by the corporation when organized, and that the corporation then becomes liable on each contract itself, and not merely for the benefits received.[1]

A corporation's adoption of a contract made by its promoters need not be by formal vote of the shareholders or directors; adoption may be inferred from any conduct on the part of the corporation's shareholders or officers that shows an intention for the corporation to adopt and be bound by the contract. Formal shareholder or director action is required only if it would be necessary for a simi-lar original contract.[2] Thus, if the board of directors or officers of a corporation have the authority to bind it by contract and they accept a contract made on the corporation's behalf by its promoters before incorporation, such recognition amounts to an adoption of the contract, whether the acceptance is expressed orally or in writing or is inferred from conduct.[3]

---

[9] Elements of novation are listed in Haggar v. Olfert, 387 N.W.2d 45, 50 (S.D. 1986).

[10] 2 Samuel Williston, Contracts §306 (3d ed. Jaeger 1959). See Stanley J. Howe & Assoc. v. Boss, 222 F. Supp. 936 (S.D. Iowa 1963).

[11] Hog Heaven Corp. v. Midland Farm Mgmt. Co., 380 N.W.2d 756, 759 (Iowa Ct. App. 1985).

[12] In re Vortex Fishing Systems, Inc., 277 F.3d 1057, 1070 (9th Cir. 2002) (applying Montana law).

§5.05 [1] In re Vortex Fishing Systems, Inc., 277 F.3d 1057, 1070 (9th Cir. 2002); Gardiner v. Equi-table Office Bldg. Corp., 273 F. 441 (2d Cir. 1921).

[2] Fortune Furniture Mfg. Co. v. Mid-South Plastic Fabric Co., 310 So. 2d 725 (Miss. 1975); Bryan v. Northwest Beverages, Inc., 285 N.W. 689 (N.D. 1939); Solomon v. Cedar Acres East, Inc., 317 A.2d 283 (Pa. 1974); Pratt v. Oshkosh Match Co., 62 N.W. 84 (Wis. 1895). See also Air Traffic & Serv. Corp. v. Fay, 196 F.2d 40 (D.C. Cir. 1952).

[3] Stone v. First Wyo. Bank, 625 F.2d 332 (10th Cir. 1980); Wilson v. Harburney Oil Co., 89 F.2d 211 (10th Cir. 1937); United German Silver Co. v. Bronson, 102 A. 647 (Conn. 1917).

Standing alone, the corporation's receipt of benefits flowing from a contract is not sufficient to bind the corporation on the contract. However, most American authorities hold the corporation liable in quantum meruit for the fair value of the benefits it actually receives.[4] For a corporation to be liable in contract, its representatives must have knowledge of the contract at the time they permit the corporation to receive the benefits, or, at a minimum, they must have notice that calls for reasonable inquiry.[5]

As a general rule, the secret knowledge of a mere promoter is not imputed to the corporation.[6] Even where promoters become directors and shareholders of the corporation upon its organization, their knowledge is not imputed to it if they have personal interests antagonistic to the corporation and the circumstances are such that they cannot be expected to reveal their knowledge to other directors and corporate officials.[7] However, where promoters become controlling directors and shareholders, it is reasonable to impute their knowledge to the corporation.[8]

§5.06 The Corporation's Right to Enforce Contracts

Most American courts hold that, if a corporation expressly or impliedly adopts a pre-incorporation contract made for its benefit by its promoters, it makes itself a party to the contract and may sue on it.[1] Some have argued that a corporation cannot claim the benefit of or enforce a promoter's contract made in its name or for its benefit unless it has adopted the contract as its own.[2] The better view is that by bringing an action on the contract, the corporation adopts or ratifies.[3]

---

[4] Omg Hing v. Arizona Harness Raceway, Inc., 459 P.2d 107 (Ariz. Ct. App. 1969); David v. Southern Import Wine Co., 171 So. 180 (La. App. 1936). *See also* Solomon v. Cedar Acres East, Inc., 317 A.2d 283 (Pa. 1974).

[5] Gardiner v. Equitable Office Bldg. Corp., 273 F. 441 (2d Cir. 1921); Steele v. Litton Indus., 68 Cal. Rptr. 680 (Ct. App. 1968); C. & H. Contractors, Inc. v. McKee, 177 So. 2d 851 (Fla. Dist. App. 1965); Illinois Controls, Inc. v. Langham, 639 N.E.2d 771 (Ohio 1994) (offering a thorough description of the circumstances by which the corporation becomes bound on pre-incorporation contracts).

[6] Solomon v. Cedar Acres East, Inc., 317 A.2d 283 (Pa. 1974); Murry v. Monter, 60 P.2d 960 (Utah 1936).

[7] Clifton v. Tomb, 21 F.2d 893 (4th Cir. 1927); Steele v. Litton Indus., 68 Cal. Rptr. 680 (Ct. App. 1968); Commercial Lumber Co. v. Ukiah Lumber Mills, 210 P.2d 276 (Cal. Ct. App. 1949); Abbott v. Limited Mut. Comp. Ins. Co., 85 P.2d 961 (Cal. 1939); Ropes v. Nilan, 119 P. 479 (Mont. 1911).

[8] "As is apparent, one of the essential elements of real assent to a contract is knowledge of its terms, and where the promoters and the corporation are identical, that knowledge is easily inferred. . . ." Ehrich & Bunzl, *supra* §5.01 note 3, at 1036 (most of the cases involved close corporations).

§5.06 [1] Boatright v. Steinite Radio Corp., 46 F.2d 385, 388 (10th Cir. 1931); Speedway Realty Co. v. Grasshoff Realty Corp., 216 N.E.2d 845 (Ind. 1966); Hog Heaven Corp. v. Midland Farm Mgmt. Co., 380 N.W.2d 756, 758 (Iowa Ct. App. 1985).

[2] Macy Corp. v. Ramey, 144 N.E.2d 698 (Ohio C.P. 1957) (promoter withdrawing from agreement before ratification by corporation).

[3] K & J Clayton Holding Corp. v. Keuffel & Esser Co., 272 A.2d 565 (1971) (one way for corporation to adopt promoters' contract is to institute suit thereon); Restatement (Second) of Agency §97 (1958).

A. Pre-Incorporation Contracts

It has been suggested that the corporation might also be allowed to sue as a third-party beneficiary of the promoter's contract. A third-party beneficiary need not be in existence at the time the contract is made.[4] However, a flaw in the third-party beneficiary theory is that the purpose of a promoter's contract is to create mutual obligations after the corporation's formation, with the corporation and the other party becoming bound, rather than merely conferring a naked benefit or right on the corporation. The consideration is usually executory. The better view is that the corporation cannot claim the benefits of the contract without assuming the burden of performance.[5]

§5.07 Liability of Promoters on Pre-Incorporation Contracts

In the absence of an express or implied agreement to the contrary, promoters are generally personally liable on their pre-incorporation contracts even though the contracts are made on behalf of the corporation to be formed. As the Supreme Court of Washington has stated, as a general rule "where a corporation is contemplated but has not yet been organized at the time when a promoter makes a contract for the benefit of the contemplated corporation, the promoter is personally liable on it, even though the contract will also benefit the future corporation."[1] However, cases dealing with a promoter's personal liability on contracts made for the benefit of a proposed corporation present a wide array of factual situations and a number of so-called general rules. The better view is that a promoter's personal liability should depend on the intention of the parties and the form in which the arrangement is cast.[2]

Among the forms a pre-incorporation contractual arrangement might reasonably take are the following:[3]

(1) Promoters may obtain options or offers from third parties for the projected corporation, which it may accept or reject after incorporation. If the promoters enter into an arrangement that expressly excludes their own liability, some courts will view such an arrangement as constituting merely a revocable offer to the projected corporation by the third party

---

[4] Kentucky Tobacco Prods. Co. v. Lucas, 5 F.2d 723, 727 (W.D. Ky. 1925); In re Jacoby, 33 N.Y.S.2d 621, 625 (Sup. Ct. 1942).

[5] See generally 2 Samuel Williston, Contracts §306 (3d ed. Jaeger 1959). In other words, in the face of silence, most promoters' contracts are properly read as implying that corporate adoption of the contract is a condition of performance.

§5.07 [1] Goodman v. Darden, Doman & Stafford Assoc., 670 P.2d 648, 651 (Wash. 1983), quoting Harding v. Will, 500 P.2d 91, 97 (Wash. 1972).

[2] See H. F. Philipsborn & Co. v. Suson, 322 N.E.2d 45 (Ill. 1974) (whether liability will be imposed depends on intent of parties).

[3] See Restatement (Second) of Agency §326, Comment b (1958).

or parties.[4] In such a case, a contract does not arise until the corporation comes into existence and accepts the offer.[5]

(2) Instead of purporting to act on behalf of the corporation, promoters may make a contract in their own names without any provision for it to bind the corporation. Promoters who do this take their chances that the corporation will later assume the contract and indemnify the promoters or otherwise hold them harmless from personal liability.[6]

(3) Promoters may purport to make a contract with the other party in the proposed company's name — that is, on behalf of the proposed company as if they were agents. Under such an arrangement the third party may immediately give or commence performance or may defer performance until the corporation comes into existence and can receive it.[7]

(4) Promoters may make a contract that binds them at the time of contracting, with the stipulation or understanding that if a company is formed it will take their places, and the promoters will be relieved of liability. In other words, the parties may intend an immediate contract between the promoters and the other party but contemplate a novation pursuant to which the corporation will be substituted for the promoters when the corporation is organized and adopts the contract.[8]

(5) Promoters may make a contract that presently binds the promoters, with the stipulation or understanding that if a company is formed and adopts, the promoters thereafter are only secondarily liable as sureties for the performance of the corporation, and will be responsible only if the company becomes judgment-proof or is otherwise unable to fulfill its contractual obligations.

(6) Instead of taking an offer for the corporation to be formed as in (1), which offer a third party can revoke before formation of the corporation and its acceptance, promoters may pay or promise an agreed consideration to the third party for an option in favor of the corporation or one that can be transferred to it. The agreed consideration could be the promoters' promise to use their best efforts to secure the corporation's formation and its adoption of the contract. This arrangement fixes the limits of the promoters' responsibility.[9]

(7) Promoters may make a separate or subsidiary contract under which the third party agrees to contract with the corporation following its forma-

---

[4] R.A.C. Realty Co. v. W.O.U.F. Atlanta Realty Corp., 52 S.E.2d 617 (Ga. 1949); Stewart Realty Co. v. Keller, 193 N.E.2d 179 (Ohio Ct. App. 1962) (if corporation is not formed, contract does not come into existence).

[5] See also Restatement (Second) Contracts §23 (1973).

[6] See O'Rorke v. Geary, 56 A. 541 (Pa. 1903).

[7] Columbia Metal Culvert Co. v. Kaiser Indus. Corp., 526 F.2d 724 (3d Cir. 1975); Surovcik v. D & K Optical, Inc., 702 F. Supp. 1171, 1179 (M.D. Pa. 1988).

[8] See RKO Stanley Warner Theatres, Inc. v. Graziano, 355 A.2d 830 (Pa. 1975) (promoter not released from liability on incorporation; intent of parties was to hold promoter personally liable until corporation was formed and had ratified agreement).

[9] William L. Cary, Cases and Materials on Corporations 89 n.2 (4th ed. unabr. 1969).

tion on specified terms or to hold an offer open which it may accept when organized. The consideration given by the promoters might be, for example, an undertaking to form a corporation and cause it to assent to the main contract or to use their best efforts to organize a corporation and cause it to assent to the contract.

Whenever a promoter entering into a contract on behalf of a projected corporation causes the other contracting party to think the corporation is already in existence and that the promoter is its agent and contracting for it, the promoter may be held liable (1) on the contract, (2) for deceit, (3) for breach of implied warranty of authority from a principal, or (4) for breach of implied warranty of the existence of a principal.[10]

When a promoter makes a contract in the name of a nonexistent corporation, a court may find that either: (1) the parties intended for the promoter to be a party to the contract; (2) the promoter was only to be a party until the corporation is organized and accepts the contract; or (3) the promoter was simply soliciting an offer that the corporation, after formation, could accept or reject.[11] When contracts are ambiguous as to whether the parties intend the promoter to be bound, some jurisdictions allow the use of parol evidence to show the personal liability of the promoter was intended or that the third party was to look only to the corporation.[12] Although most decisions passing on whether a promoter is liable on an ambiguous contract have on one theory or another imposed personal liability on the promoter, a number of the more recent decisions show a greater readiness to interpret nonspecific contracts in a way that shields the promoter from liability, thus reaching a result perhaps more in accord with the intention of the parties.[13]

Absent clear intent on the part of the promoter to be liable on a *post*-incorporation contract, the third party is deemed to have relied on the existing corporation, not on the individual promoter, to pay any claim for services or other performance.[14]

§5.08   Promoters' Liability After Corporation Adopts

When promoters bind themselves personally by a contract on behalf of a proposed corporation, the mere fact of corporate adoption or assumption of the contract does not alone relieve them from liability. Many courts have held that even though the corporation becomes liable, the promoters also remain liable; the third party has the double security of the corporation and the promoters, unless that party

---

[10] *See* Annot., 41 A.L.R.2d 477, 484-485 (1958); 3 Am. Jur. 2d 654-662, Agency §§293-300 (1986).

[11] *See* White & Bollard, Inc. v. Goodenow, 361 P.2d 571, 573-574 (Wash. 1961).

[12] Decker v. Juzwik, 121 N.W.2d 652, 657-658 (Iowa 1963).

[13] *See, e.g.,* Quaker Hill, Inc. v. Parr, 364 P.2d 1056 (Colo. 1961); Isle of Thye Land Co. v. Whisman, 279 A.2d 484 (Md. 1971); Stewart Realty Co. v. Keller, 193 N.E.2d 179 (Ohio Ct. App. 1962).

[14] MacDonald v. Arrowhead Hot Springs Co., 300 P. 105 (Cal. Ct. App. 1931); Restatement (Second) of Agency §320 (1958).

consents to a novation or substitution of the corporation for the promoters.[1] Under a well-settled principle of contract law, without the consent of the other contracting party, one party to a contract cannot relieve herself of her obligations by substituting another person in her place.[2] This double security is a windfall for the other contracting party because had the corporation been in existence at the time of contracting, the other party normally would not have also contracted for the promoter's liability.

The typical promoters' contract might fairly be interpreted as contemplating a novation, and often the other contracting party may be held to have consented in advance to substitute the corporation in the place of the promoters. If all the parties agree at the time a corporation adopts a promoters' contract that the corporation alone will thereafter be liable and that the promoters will be released, there is an express novation. There is in this case sufficient consideration to support the release of the promoters, and no action will lie against the promoters on the contract.[3] Such a novation may also be implied from the conduct of the parties.[4]

B.   PROMOTERS' FIDUCIARY OBLIGATIONS

§5.09   *Promoters' Fiduciary Obligations*

Promoters have such far-reaching control over the enterprise during its formative stages, and even after incorporation, that the law imposes on them fiduciary obligations toward the company and those who contribute its capital. Their fiduciary obligations require them to act in good faith and with the utmost fairness in their promotional activities and dealings. The promoters' fiduciary duties antedate the corporation's formation, arising when the promoters form a clear intention to promote the corporation.[1] In broad overview, the fiduciary duty requires the promoters to act with the utmost good faith in all dealings with the corporation and its shareholders.[2] The fiduciary relationship extends to the promoted corporation, its stockholders, and fellow promoters.[3] Promoters cannot retain inequitable

---

§5.08   [1] Stanley J. Howe & Assoc. v. Boss, 222 F. Supp. 936 (S.D. Iowa 1963) (after corporation was formed, it sent two checks to plaintiff in partial payment).

[2] Mansfield v. Lang, 200 N.E. 110 (Mass. 1936). The other contracting parties may enforce the contract either against the promoters or the corporation, or they can collect part from the corporation and part from the promoters. *See* Wells v. J. A. Fay & Egan Co., 85 S.E. 873 (Ga. 1915); Federal Advertising Corp. v. Hundertmark, 160 A. 40 (N.J. 1932).

[3] Van Vlieden v. Welles, 6 Johns (N.Y.) 85 (1810). *See* Irwin Glass Co., 28 S.W. 668 (Tenn. 1894).

[4] J. H. Lane & Co. v. United Oilcloth Co., 92 N.Y.S. 1061 (App. Div. 1905).

§5.09   [1] Wisconsin Ave. Assoc. v. 2720 Wis. Ave. Coop. Ass'n, 441 A.2d 956, 963 (D.C. 1982).

[2] *See, e.g.,* Whaler Motor Inn., Inc. v. Parsons, 363 N.E.2d 493 (Mass. 1977); Golden v. Oahe Enter., 295 N.W.2d 160 (S.D. 1980); Annot., 84 A.L.R.3d 152 (1978).

[3] Public Inv. Ltd. v. Bandeirante Corp., 740 F.2d 1222 (D.C. Cir. 1984); Topanga Corp. v. Gentile, 58 Cal. Rptr. 713 (Cal. App. 1967) (duty of full disclosure among co-promoters).

B.   Promoters' Fiduciary Obligations

profits from manipulation of corporate purchases and share issues while the enterprise is under their control or influence.

Although the problem of promoter misconduct is now handled chiefly through state and federal securities regulations,[4] the common law still plays a role in appropriate situations. The common law fiduciary relation is still relevant in resolving disputes where overreaching is alleged that cannot be linked directly to deceit practiced on investors. In this context, the common law not only resolves whether a breach has occurred but also guides what remedies should be allowed to the corporation and to individual investors.

Unifying themes across cases invoking the promoters' fiduciary obligations are the mandating of candor and proscribing the promoters' taking unfair advantage of the promoted corporation or its stockholders. Not only do these two themes complement one another, but also the duty of candor in most cases defines what constitutes an undue advantage. Courts that find promoters have breached their fiduciary obligations invariably base their holdings on the promoters' failure to disclose fully all the material facts to either an independent board of directors or to the corporation's outside stockholders,[5] or even to their fellow promoters.[6] This reflects the general prohibition against promoters reaping a secret profit by virtue of their relationship to the corporation. With the approval of an independent body of directors or stockholders and after full disclosure of all material facts to the transaction, the promoters have discharged their fiduciary obligations. When all material facts have not been disclosed, the promoters bear a substantial burden of proving the transaction's entire fairness and the adequacy of the consideration supporting the transaction.[7] Most cases never reach this stage, however, because the promoters have already failed to disclose the wide disparity in value between what they transferred to the corporation and what they received.[8]

The second component of the promoter's fiduciary duty—that no unfair advantage be taken of the corporation or its stockholders—operates in that narrow band of cases where the promoter is the sole stockholder at the time of the transaction. In cases where either an independent board of directors or outside stockholders exist, the responsibility of the promoter is effectively fulfilled by requiring full disclosure of all the facts. Where such independent decision-makers do not exist, courts focus on the relative fairness of the transaction; accordingly any gross disparity in the exchange between the sole promoter and the corporation is treated by the courts as the promoter having taken unfair advantage of his or her position.

---

[4] *See, e.g.*, Miller v. San Sebastian Gold Mines, Inc., 540 F.2d 807 (5th Cir. 1976); Bailes v. Colonial Press, Inc., 444 F.2d 1241 (5th Cir. 1971).

[5] *See, e.g.*, Public Inv. Ltd. v. Bandierante Corp., 740 F.2d 1222 (D.C. Cir. 1984); Wisconsin Ave. Assoc. v. 2720 Wis. Ave. Coop. Ass'n, 441 A.2d 956, 963 (D.C. 1982); Golden v. Oahe Enter., 295 N.W.2d 160 (S.D. 1980).

[6] Topanga Corp. v. Gentile, 58 Cal. Rptr. 713 (Cal. App. 1967).

[7] *See* Public Inv. Ltd. v. Bandeirante Corp., 740 F.2d 1222 (D.C. Cir. 1984).

[8] Golden v. Oahe Enter., 295 N.W.2d 160 (S.D. 1980).

§5.10   Fraudulent Devices Used by Promoters

The principal devices promoters have used to obtain compensation and speculative profits are:

(1) Selling property, greatly overvalued, to the corporation in return for a large part of the corporation's securities.[1] "The most typical promotion situation is presented when a promoter has acquired property at a nominal price which he turns over to a corporation in exchange for a large block of stock which is resold to the public on the basis of the valuation [of the property] made by the promoter-controlled corporation."[2]

(2) Receiving a substantial block of the promoted corporation's shares for no consideration.[3]

(3) Selling to the corporation, at an amount in excess of its cost to the promoter, an option or contract that the promoter holds on certain property, or intercepting part of the purchase price, which the promoter pretends to pay to the owner on behalf of the corporation.

(4) Forming a management corporation, which the promoter controls, and causing the new corporation to make a contract with it that provides management fees and other profitable returns.[4]

(5) Causing the corporation to issue the corporation's securities to the promoter, or to a corporation the promoter controls.[5]

(6) Taking excessive underwriting fees and commissions on the sale of securities.[6]

(7) Misappropriating assets needed to launch the company's operations.[7]

By using these and similar types of abusive promotion schemes promoters are able to divert money to themselves at the expense of the outside investors.

§5.11   The Defense of Full Disclosure

A profit is not secret or unlawful and cannot be successfully challenged if all the parties having an interest in the corporation, including existing and incoming

---

§5.10   [1] *See, e.g.,* San Juan Uranium Corp. v. Wolfe, 241 F.2d 121 (10th Cir. 1957); Topanga Corp. v. Gentile, 58 Cal. Rptr. 713 (Ct. App. 1967).

[2] Brunson MacChesney, The Securities Act and the Promoter, 25 Cal. L. Rev. 66, 71-79 (1936). *See* Public Inv. Ltd. v. Bandeirante Corp., 740 F.2d 1222 (D.C. Cir. 1984).

[3] *See* Froehlich v. Matz, 417 N.E.2d 183 (Ill. App. 1981).

[4] *See* Yacker v. Wiener, 263 A.2d 188 (N.J. Super. Ch. 1970).

[5] *See, e.g.,* Bowers v. Rio Grande Inv. Co., 431 P.2d 478 (Colo. 1967) (enforcing an option agreement); Kingston v. Home Life Ins. Co., 101 A. 989 (Del. Ch. 1917); Golden v. Oahe Enter., 319 N.W.2d 493 (S.D. 1982).

[6] *See, e.g.,* Bovay v. H. M. Byllesby & Co., 38 A.2d 808, 811-814 (Del. 1944); Ludlam v. Riverhead Bond & Mortgage Co., 278 N.Y.S. 487 (App. Div. 1935).

[7] *See, e.g.,* Post v. United States, 407 F.2d 319 (D.C. Cir. 1968); Johnson v. Nychyk, 517 P.2d 1079 (Ariz. App. 1974); Bivens v. Watkins, 437 S.E.2d 132 (S.C. App. 1993).

B. Promoters' Fiduciary Obligations

shareholders, actually know of the profit and assent to it. Accordingly, the promoters' successful defense generally depends on (1) full disclosure of all material facts to an independent board of directors, who approve it[1] or (2) full disclosure of all material facts to all existing shareholders and subscribers for shares, and they assent to it.[2]

Disclosure to the shareholders is of little value unless disclosure is fully made to every shareholder.[3] Promoters who rely on the defense of impartial stockholder approval must be prepared to meet the line of authorities holding that absence of fraud requires the consent of *all* the shareholders. Therefore disclosure to existing shareholders at a meeting, with ratification or approval by a majority, should not be considered sufficient to bind dissenting shareholders if the transaction was fraudulent.[4] It has also been declared that "ratification by stockholders cannot render fair what is unfair to general creditors, for they, too, constitute a part of that community of interest in the corporation which the law seeks to protect."[5] Such a demanding standard requires more than that the promoters are profiting through a resale to the corporation. Fraud does not arise solely because the promoters are profiting; it arises when the price of resale to the corporation is above the property's fair market value.

In the classic case of *Old Dominion Copper Mining & Smelting Company v. Lewisohn,*[6] the U.S. Supreme Court, in an opinion by Justice Holmes, refused to permit recovery by the corporation even where the fraud required bringing in new shareholders, provided full disclosure was made to all the shareholders at the time of the transaction. It was explained that the "plaintiff cannot recover without departing from the fundamental conception . . . that a corporation remains unaffected in its identity by changes in its membership."[7] Although this view is a minority one, some state courts have followed it.[8] Justice Holmes reasoned that, as the only existing shareholders, the promoter and associates were the corporation and had assented to their own profit with full knowledge of the scheme at the time of the transaction. Therefore no wrong was done at that time to anyone, and the rights of the corporation as such were not increased when innocent subscribers subsequently were induced to invest in the corporation. According to this doctrine, the wrong, if any, is the misrepresentation to later investors who acquired

§5.11 [1] *See* Frick v. Howard, 126 N.W.2d 619 (Wis. 1964). An independent board of directors in this context means representatives who are not under the promoter's control or influence.

[2] Tilden v. Barber, 268 F. 587 (D.N.J. 1920); Swafford v. Berry, 382 P.2d 999 (Colo. 1963); Fountainview Assoc. v. Bell, 203 So. 2d 657 (Fla. Dist. Ct. App. 1967), *cert. discharged,* 214 So. 2d 609 (Fla. 1968); Lake Mabel Dev. Corp. v. Bird, 126 So. 356 (Fla. 1930); Old Dominion Copper Mining & Smelting Co. v. Bigelow, 89 N.E. 193 (Mass. 1909); Park City Corp. v. Watchie, 439 P.2d 587 (Or. 1968); Northridge Coop. Section No. 1 v. 32d Ave. Constr. Corp., 161 N.Y.S.2d 404, 141 N.E.2d 802 (N.Y. 1957).

[3] Hughes v. Cadena DeCobre Mining Co., 108 P. 231 (Ariz. 1910) (a single uninformed shareholder was sufficient to deny a finding of corporate assent).

[4] Note, 53 Harv. L. Rev. 1368 (1940); Note 21 Minn. L. Rev. 596. *See* §10.13 with regard to shareholder ratification of directors' fraudulent acts.

[5] United Hotels Co. v. Mealey, 147 F.2d 816, 818 (2d Cir. 1945).

[6] 210 U.S. 206 (1908).

[7] *Id.* at 216.

[8] Hughes v. Cadena DeCobre Mining Co., 108 P. 231 (Ariz. 1910); Lilylands Canal & Reservoir Co. v. Wood, 136 P. 1026 (Colo. 1913); Fountainview Ass'n v. Bell, 203 So. 2d 657 (Fla. Dist. Ct. App. 1967) (preferring majority view but bound by precedent to the contrary).

their shares without knowledge that the corporation's assets had been overvalued by its promoters.

Justice Holmes's opinion in *Lewisohn* is a highly formalistic view of the corporation as well as the nature of fiduciary obligations. This formalism is captured in his conclusion that the sole duty of the promoter is to the few corrupt insiders who for the moment constitute the company. To be sure, *Lewisohn* reduces fiduciary obligations to a consensual basis. This approach is not inappropriate when a truly independent board of directors or body of stockholders exists who can consider the transaction's merits from the perspective of the corporation's and stockholders' interests served thereby. However, where all those within the corporation stand on the same side of the transaction, as they did in *Lewisohn*, they cannot purport to express the interests of future owners as to the worthiness of the property that the promoters seek to transfer to the corporation. Moreover, by definition, the gains the promoters seek from transferring the property to the corporation owned exclusively by the promoters cannot be realized until interests in the corporation are later sold to outsiders. Until those investors appear, the promoters have reaped no secret profit because the transfer is only to themselves. So viewed, on the facts of *Lewisohn*, it is far more logical to recognize the promoters' fiduciary obligation extended until truly independent parties had consented after full disclosure of all material facts. By so holding, courts provide a meaningful prophylaxis for the protection of those who later invest in the corporation.

The leading authority in opposition to the view Justice Holmes advanced is the Massachusetts decision of *Old Dominion Copper Mining & Smelting Company v. Bigelow*,[9] which arose from the same transaction as *Lewisohn*.[10] By reason of their nondisclosure to incoming subscribers, the promoters were able to exact from the plaintiff corporation a secret profit of 50,000 shares of the corporation's stock. Contrary to the United States Supreme Court's ruling, the Massachusetts court held that the promoter was liable to the corporation as well as to the defrauded subscribers individually, where fraud on future subscribers was contemplated as an essential part of the scheme of promotion. Promoters cannot as shareholders or directors absolve themselves in their capacity as promoters from future liability to the corporation for reaping secret profits from dilution of its shares. In *Bigelow*, the corporate assent was invalid because it had no representatives who were able to act independently. The theory of the Massachusetts case was that the fiduciary relationship of a promoter continues until the corporation is completely established.[11] The obligation of faithfulness is coextensive with the plan for completing

---

[9] 89 N.E. 193 (Mass. 1909), *aff'd*, 225 U.S. 111 (1912). *See also* Frick v. Howard, 126 N.W.2d 619 (Wis. 1964); R. D. Weston, Promoters' Liability: Old Dominion v. Bigelow, 30 Harv. L. Rev. 39 (1916).

[10] *See* 89 N.E. at 197.

[11] But no corporate cause of action arises from failure to disclose promoters' profit to future shareholders who purchase their stock after the end of the promotional period. Jeffs v. Utah Power & Light Co., 12 A.2d 592 (Me. 1938); Continental Sec. Co. v. Belmont, 154 N.Y.S. 54 (App. Div. 1915), *aff'd*, 119 N.E. 1036 (N.Y. 1918).

B. Promoters' Fiduciary Obligations

the capitalization of the corporation. Following the lead of *Bigelow*, a majority of courts[12] have recognized in such cases a right of action in the corporation for the benefit of all participants.

---

[12] San Juan Uranium Corp. v. Wolfe, 241 F.2d 121 (10th Cir. 1957); Topanga Corp. v. Gentile, 58 Cal. Rptr. 713 (Ct. App. 1967); Swafford v. Berry, 382 P.2d 999 (Colo. 1963) (complaint dismissed on other grounds).

CHAPTER 6

Defective Formation
of Corporations

§6.01 Problems Arising from Defects in Formation

Although the process of organizing a corporation under today's corporation statutes is a simple one, failure to comply carefully with the statutory formalities for incorporation can result in loss of corporate status with the concomitant personal liability of the associates. Corporations cannot be created like partnerships and joint stock companies solely by mutual agreement of the associates. To reap all the advantages, privileges, and incidents of corporateness depends on substantial compliance with conditions set in a general corporation act.

There are various degrees of noncompliance with the statutory formalities, some of which are of more and others of less importance in affecting corporate status. The defect, shortcoming, or irregularity complained of may or may not be accidental, may or may not affect the merits of a case being litigated, and may or may not have harmed the person who seeks to raise questions of defective incorporation.[1] In determining the consequences attaching to defective organization,

---

§6.01 [1] For empirical studies of the legal effects of defective incorporation, *see* Wayne N. Bradley, Comment, An Empirical Study of Defective Incorporation, 39 Emory L.J. 523 (1990); Alexander Frey, Legal Analysis and the "De Facto" Doctrine, 100 U. Pa. L. Rev. 1153 (1952).

courts typically speak in terms of "de jure corporation," "de facto corporation," and "corporation by estoppel."

Consider the following possibilities: (1) The associates in a business enterprise may brazenly pretend to be incorporated without attempting to take some or any of the required statutory steps or may assume acting as a corporation with knowledge that the steps taken are incomplete.[2] (2) The associates may execute articles of incorporation but, by some inadvertent mischance, may fail to get them filed in any public office. (3) The associates may file the articles of incorporation with a state official, who may reject them. (4) In one of the few states that still require the articles to be filed in two different government offices, they may file the articles in only one of the two prescribed offices. (5) The articles as filed may not be in proper form, may omit required provisions, or may be incorrectly executed or acknowledged by the incorporators. (6) The associates may fail to pay in the minimum required capital in a state in which that is still prescribed as a condition precedent to doing business. (7) The associates may fail to hold an organizational meeting of incorporators, shareholders, or directors, or fail to adopt bylaws or to elect directors and officers.[3] (8) The statute under which the associates attempt to incorporate may be unconstitutional or may not authorize formation of corporations to do the kinds of business the corporation is being organized to conduct. (9) The associates may purport to continue to do business as a corporation after its prescribed term of existence has expired, after revocation of its charter, or after it has been dissolved.

If business associates purport to conduct their enterprise as a corporation but have not complied with statutory requirements for the organization of a corporation, or if the organization is otherwise defective in one or more of the respects just enumerated, will their association be treated as a corporation? Or perhaps the more accurate question is, which of the normal corporate attributes and incidents will the association be recognized as having, under what circumstances, and for what purposes?

Among the diverse problems arising from defects in organization, the following are perhaps the most important: (1) May the association sue as a corporation to enforce a contract if the other party to the contract challenges its capacity to sue or to contract?[4] (2) May the association's creditors and other persons dealing with it sue it as a corporation? And may the association deny its existence as a corporation to defeat litigation brought against it?[5] (3) May the purported corpo-

---

[2] See, e.g., Culkin v. Hillside Restaurant, Inc., 8 A.2d 173 (N.J. Ch. 1939) (organizers deliberately refrained from taking steps required by statute, such as filing certificate of incorporation or paying fees; no recognition of corporate existence).

[3] See Beck v. Stimmel, 177 N.E. 920 (Ohio Ct. App. 1931).

[4] See, e.g., Lenny Bruce Enter. v. Fantasy Records, Inc., 243 N.Y.S.2d 789 (Sup. Ct. 1963) (challenge to purported corporation's legal capacity to sue).

[5] See, e.g., United States v. Theodore, 347 F. Supp. 1070 (D. S.C. 1972), rev'd on other grounds, 479 F.2d 749 (4th Cir. 1973) (suit for production of corporate records; defendants claimed they could not be pursued in their corporate capacity because no articles of incorporation had been filed).

ration receive or make conveyances of property?[6] (4) May the incorporators, subscribers, shareholders, directors, or officers in a seriously defective corporation be held to unlimited personal liability as partners or otherwise? For a debt claim against the business? For a tort committed by an employee of the enterprise? In answering these questions, whether the particular persons charged with liability had knowledge of the defects or actively participated in doing or authorizing the transaction giving rise to the liability may be important considerations.[7] (5) May the association, although defectively formed, enforce pre-incorporation subscriptions?[8] (6) May the association exercise the right of eminent domain?[9] (7) May the purported corporation be dissolved for defective incorporation in an action by the shareholders? In a quo warranto proceeding brought by the attorney general to oust it from the exercise of corporate power and the usurpation of a corporate franchise? (8) May a corporation doing business in a state other than its state of incorporation without qualifying to do business in that state nevertheless obtain de facto status in that state?

The answers given in the mass of judicial decisions that have dealt with these questions present a discouraging and baffling maze. To generalize the results of the decisions is indeed a difficult task.

§6.02   Corporation De Jure

A de jure corporation is recognized as having a corporate existence for all purposes, even as against a direct attack by the state of incorporation.[1] No one, not even the state, can successfully challenge its existence as a corporation. To prove that it is a de jure corporation, it must show not only a valid law under which it might be created, and an attempt to organize under that law, but also compliance with all the mandatory requirements of the law that are conditions precedent to corporate existence.[2]

---

[6] *See* Elson v. Schmidt, 287 N.W. 196 (Neb. 1939) (de facto corporation takes title to personalty as partnership); Kiamesha Dev. Corp. v. Guild Properties, Inc., 151 N.E.2d 214 (N.Y. 1958).

[7] *See, e.g.,* Edward Shoes, Inc. v. Orenstein, 333 F. Supp. 39, 42 (N.D. Ind. 1971) (shareholders purporting to be doing business as corporation under Indiana law will be held personally liable to creditors only if they acted fraudulently or in bad faith).

[8] Capps v. Hastings Prospecting Co., 58 N.W. 956 (Neb. 1894) (subscribers contracted to become shareholders, not partners, in defective corporation). *But see* Alexander Frey, Modern Development in the Law of Preincorporation Subscriptions, 79 U. Pa. L. Rev. 1005, 1013-1015 (1931).

[9] Rogers v. Toccoa Power Co., 131 S.E. 517 (Ga. 1926) (defective corporation without statutory authority to exercise condemnation power).

§6.02   [1] 1 People v. Stockton & V.R.R., 45 Cal. 306 (1873); In re Spring Valley Water Works, 17 Cal. 132 (1860) (failure to comply with "directory" provision does not prevent corporation from being de jure); People v. Ford, 128 N.E. 479 (Ill. 1920) (absence of seal after names of incorporators; irregularities and omissions may be overlooked if they are formal or insubstantial).

[2] *See, e.g.,* People v. Larson, 106 N.E. 947 (Ill. 1914); Attorney General v. Belle Isle Ice Co., 26 N.W. 311 (Mich. 1886).

§6.03   *The De Facto Doctrine*

In the absence of substantial compliance with incorporation requirements, a court may nevertheless treat a defectively organized corporation as a "de facto corporation" and recognize it as having continuity of life, limited liability, and the other corporate attributes. Except in a direct action by the state and perhaps in a few other minor instances, a de facto corporation is treated as though it were de jure. The state in quo warranto proceedings can terminate its life, but no one else can successfully challenge its existence.[1]

Under the de facto doctrine as usually stated, a de facto corporation results if the following essentials are met:

(1) A valid statute under which the corporation could have been formed (or, according to some, an apparently valid statute).

(2) A good faith attempt to comply with the requirements of the statute.

(3) A "colorable compliance" with the statutory requirements—that is, a sufficient compliance to give an appearance of validity to the incorporation.

(4) A use of corporate powers—that is, the transaction of business by the organization as if it were a corporation. This element seems to be of only minor importance.[2] Occasionally, in stating the essentials of the doctrine, a court has omitted the requirement of colorable compliance with the statute, but it is not clear whether this omission is deliberate or inadvertent.[3] On the other hand, courts[4] have sometimes added a fifth requirement—namely:

(5) Good faith in claiming to be a corporation and in doing business as a corporation. Initial good faith may not be sufficient. Later discovery of defects by the associates may thereafter preclude application of the de facto doctrine to their organization.

As discussed in a later section, there is some authority supporting the abolition of the de facto doctrine in states adopting the Revised Model Act; but not all courts agree.[5]

---

§6.03   [1] Thies v. Weible, 254 N.W. 420, 423 (Neb. 1934).

[2] *See, e.g.*, Tulare Irrigation Dist. v. Shepard, 185 U.S. 1 (1902); In re Whatley, 874 F.2d 997 (5th Cir. 1989); Clark-Franklin-Kingston Press, Inc. v. Romans, 529 A.2d 240 (Conn. Ct. App. 1987); Almac, Inc. v. JRH Dev., Inc., 391 N.W.2d 919 (Minn. Ct. App. 1986); DeGeorge v. Yusko, 564 N.Y.S.2d 597 (N.Y. App. Div. 1991).

[3] *See, e.g.*, Municipal Bond & Mortgage Corp. v. Bishop's Harbor Drainage Dist., 182 So. 794 (Fla. 1938); Cranson v. International Bus. Mach. Corp., 200 A.2d 33 (Md. 1964); Paper Prods. Co. v. Doggrell, 261 S.W.2d 127 (Tenn. 1953).

[4] Robertson v. Levy, 197 A.2d 443, 445 (D.C. 1964).

[5] *See* §6.07.

§6.04 Basis of the De Facto Doctrine

The incorporation statutes of various states set forth certain conditions precedent to corporate existence.[1] It may well be asked: Why do courts recognize an organization as being a corporation de facto when it has failed to comply with the legislative conditions precedent?

The recognition of de facto existence promotes the security of business transactions and tends to eliminate quibbling over irregularities. Persons dealing with a corporation will rarely be prejudiced if the company is recognized as a corporation in spite of minor omissions or defects in its formation. A wrongdoer should not be allowed to quibble over incorporation defects to escape liability to the corporation. Similarly, a creditor of a supposed company usually should not be allowed to assert the individual liability of innocent, passive investors on the basis of flaws in the formal steps of incorporation when to do so would be contrary to the investors' expectations and the bargained-for agreement. This would simply give the creditor a windfall.

§6.05 Corporation by Estoppel

Persons may presume to do business as a corporation without having gone far enough in their incorporation attempt to acquire a de facto standing. Nevertheless, under some circumstances and for some purposes, courts sometimes hold either the purported corporation or persons contracting with it estopped to deny its corporate status. The corporation then is often referred to as a "corporation by estoppel."[1] The use of the term "estoppel" in this type of case may be misleading.[2] When a court says that the other parties to a contract are "estopped," this may mean nothing more than that it or they are precluded for some reason from denying the corporate capacity. The word "estopped" does not reveal the reason for the conclusion, as the elements of a true estoppel are lacking in many of the decisions in which the term is used. It might be preferable in some of these decisions to say that the person contracting or dealing with the defective organization is considered to have "admitted" its corporate existence, rather than as being estopped to deny it.

The application of the so-called estoppel doctrine does not mean that the irregular corporation has acquired a corporate status generally and for all purposes. Rather, on the appropriate facts, corporation by estoppel may be used to

---

§6.04 [1] *See* §6.03.

§6.05 [1] *See* Zoning Comm'n v. Lesaynski, 453 A.2d 1144 (Conn. 1982); Harry Rich Corp. v. Feinberg, 518 So. 2d 377 (Fla. Dist. Ct. App. 1987).

[2] As one court explained:

> This term [corporation by estoppel] was a complete misnomer. There was no corporation, the acts of the association having failed even to colorably fulfill the statutory requirements; there was no estoppel in the pure sense of the word because generally there was no holding out followed by reliance on the part of the other party.

Robertson v. Levy, 197 A.2d 443, 445 (D.C. 1964). *See generally* Lowry F. Kline, Comment, Estoppel to Deny Corporate Existence, 31 Tenn. L. Rev. 336 (1964).

bar collateral attacks on corporateness in a particular setting even though the de facto doctrine has been abrogated by statute in the state or is inappropriate given the factual setting.[3] The doctrine is limited in its application to the consequences of a particular transaction done in the corporate name by associates assuming to be a corporation. Estoppel requires a reasonable consideration of the equities of each case and whether the defects or irregularities should be open to inquiry in that particular situation.[4] Just as in the de facto corporation doctrine, procedural convenience, the avoidance of inquiry into irrelevant formalities, and fairness to all parties may favor treating a defective association purporting to be a corporation as though it has certain corporate incidents.

In one situation, all the elements of a true estoppel exist. Associates who hold out their association as a corporate body, and thereby induce persons to deal with it as such, are properly said to be estopped from denying their representation where to do so would prejudice those persons.[5] Thus it has long been established that a person contracting with an association that pretends to be a corporation may sue the associates as a corporation, and the principle of estoppel will prevent the associates from setting up as a defense the falsity of their own representation of corporateness.[6] The representation of corporateness can be to the general public, rather than to a specific party, and still give rise to estoppel.[7] Also, an associate who transacts business in the corporate name is estopped to deny the validity of the corporation for the purpose of holding other associates personally liable on contracts entered into between them in carrying on the firm's business.[8]

In a different type of case—where a defective corporation brings suit against the other party to a contract to enforce the contract—courts often say that the party who has contracted with the supposed corporation is estopped from denying its existence. For example, in the leading case, *Cranson v. International Business Machines Corporation,*[9] a contract creditor was estopped to deny the corporation's

---

[3] At least one court has interpreted the Model Business Corporation Act as having abolished both the corporation by estoppel and the de facto doctrines. *See* Robertson v. Levy, 197 A.2d 443 (D.C. 1964).

[4] *See* Childs v. Philpot, 487 S.W.2d 637 (Ark. 1972); Minich v. Gem State Dev., Inc., 591 P.2d 1078 (Idaho 1979) (to recognize corporation by estoppel would emasculate state requirements for corporations); Lorisa Capital Corp. v. Gallo, 506 N.Y.S.2d 62 (App. Div. 1986) (refusing to allow tax delinquent corporation to assert corporation by estoppel against defaulting party because to do so would subvert tax statute's incentives to pay taxes).

[5] *See* United States v. Harrison, 653 F.2d 359 (8th Cir. 1981) (trustees estopped to deny corporate existence to prevent disclosure to IRS of business records pertaining to family trust where separate tax returns had been filed on behalf of trust entity).

[6] Empire Mfg. Co. v. Stuart, 9 N.W. 527 (Mich. 1881); Gardner v. Minneapolis & St. L. Ry., 76 N.W. 282 (Minn. 1898). *See also* Taylor v. Aldridge, 178 So. 331 (Miss. 1938), noted in 11 Miss. L.J. 325 (1939).

Statutes in some states provide that a corporation cannot set up the want of legal organization as a defense to a claim. *See, e.g.,* Del. Code Ann. tit. 8, §329(a) (1983).

[7] United States v. Theodore, 347 F. Supp. 1070 (D. S.C. 1972) (claim company records were personal records so privilege against self-incrimination applied denied because business had represented itself to public as corporation).

[8] Kingsley v. English, 278 N.W. 154 (Minn. 1938); Dargan v. Graves, 168 S.E.2d 306 (S.C. 1969). *But see* Bradley v. Marshall, 285 A.2d 745 (Vt. 1971).

[9] 200 A.2d 33 (Md. 1964).

existence solely by having carried on all dealings with the defectively formed corporation in that corporation's name.[10] The certificate of incorporation had not been filed with the secretary of state until after the plaintiff had delivered several office machines on account to the business. The business's president and substantial shareholder was unaware of the attorney's oversight in making the tardy filing. In contrast, *Don Swann Sales Corporation v. Echols*,[11] on facts identical to those in *Cranson*, the court, although recognizing that the legislature had intended to preserve the corporation by the estoppel doctrine, refused to recognize the doctrine's application to protect an *individual* purporting to act for a nonexistent corporation. The court relied on a state statute imposing liability on anyone who acts on behalf of a corporation before the secretary of state has issued a certificate of incorporation.

§6.06   Liability of Participants: Active Versus Passive Participation

Should persons having dealt with a defectively organized corporation on a corporate basis be allowed to assert full individual liability against the associates in the business? Numerous decisions hold that associates who deliberately engage in business under the name and pretense of a corporation should be held individually liable if they have not achieved at least a de facto corporate status.[1] The fact that by their pretense they lead outsiders to contract with them as a corporation is said to be no ground of estoppel in their favor. The associates are the principals and co-owners of a business that is carried on by their authorization and for their benefit.

Under this view, if the attempt to comply with the incorporation law does not go far enough to create a corporation de facto, associates who actively participate in the business are held to full liability on contracts authorized or ratified by them, either as partners or as principals.[2] There is said to be no estoppel of one who deals with business associates masquerading under a name that fails to represent a corporation de facto, because the elements of estoppel, viz., action induced by misrepresentation of the party against whom the estoppel is asserted, do not exist.[3]

---

[10] *See also* Harry Rich Corp. v. Feinberg, 518 So. 2d 377 (Fla. Dist. Ct. App. 1987).

[11] 287 S.E.2d 577 (Ga. Ct. App. 1981). *But see* Goodwyne v. Moore, 316 S.E.2d 601 (Ga. Ct. App. 1984) (estoppel applied where articles filed creating corporation to operate bottle shop but promoter unable to secure financing, commenced a salvage business under different name and, after contracting debt that is subject of suit amended earlier, filed articles to reflect new name of corporation).

§6.06   [1] *See, e.g.*, Puro Filter Corp. v. Trembley, 41 N.Y.S.2d 472 (App. Div. 1943); Conway v. Samet, 300 N.Y.S.2d 243 (Sup. Ct. 1969).

[2] *See, e.g.*, Harrill v. Davis, 168 F. 187 (8th Cir. 1909); Clinton Inv. Co. v. Watkins, 536 N.Y.S.2d 270 (N.Y. App. Div. 1989); Minich v. Gem State Dev., Inc., 591 P.2d 1078 (Idaho 1979).

[3] One of the strongest cases on this point is Harrill v. Davis, 168 F. 187 (8th Cir. 1909), holding that four associates, who had actively engaged in the lumber business under a corporate name before filing the articles of incorporation in any public office and who never issued any shares of stock, could not escape individual liability.

§6.07   *Statutes Pertaining to Defective Corporations*

By simplifying the mechanics of incorporation, modern corporation statutes have reduced the number of defective incorporations and thereby the amount of litigation. Furthermore, most modern corporation acts contain provisions designed to clear up some of the problems of defective organization. Such provisions either dictate the moment in the incorporation process that a corporation comes into existence by providing that the filing of the articles of incorporation or the issuance of a certificate of incorporation by the secretary of state is either presumptive evidence or "conclusive evidence" or "conclusive proof" that all conditions precedent to incorporation have been met or they specify the consequences of particular defects in the organization process, as well as forbidding collateral attack on incorporation in certain types of cases. The effect of some of these provisions on traditional doctrines such as de facto incorporation and corporation by estoppel is far from clear.

In many jurisdictions, the corporation statute states that a corporation comes into existence either when its articles of incorporation are filed or when the secretary of state issues a certificate of incorporation,[1] and in addition provides that either acceptance and filing of articles of incorporation by the secretary of state or the secretary's issuance of a certificate of incorporation shall be "conclusive evidence," except against the state, that all conditions precedent to incorporation have been performed.

Statutes containing "conclusive evidence" or "conclusive proof" language seemingly do away with the necessity of litigating some of the questions that might arise under the de facto doctrine, such as what effect defects in the incorporation papers or their execution have and what amounts to sufficient use of corporate powers. In a "conclusive evidence" or "conclusive proof" jurisdiction, de facto questions can arise only if the articles are not filed or the certificate is not issued, or if a corporation of some other state is involved. On the other hand, in states with statutes providing that a certified copy of the articles is only "prima facie evidence" or "evidence" of corporate existence, presumably only the burden of proof or the amount of proof is changed, and the traditional questions as to colorable compliance, use of the franchise, and the need of dealings on a corporate basis may still be raised.

In addition to adopting the Model Act provision on when corporate existence commences, some states have enacted a provision from the 1950 and 1969 versions of the Model Act, which stated: "All persons who assume to act as a corporation without authority so to do shall be jointly and severally liable for all debts and liabilities incurred or arising as a result thereof."[2] The District of Columbia

---

§6.07   [1] *See* §6.02.

[2] Former Model Bus. Corp. Act §146 (1969). *Cf.* Model Bus. Corp. Act §2.04 (1984). *See, e.g.*, Colo. Rev. Stat. §§7-2-104, 7-3-104 (1973) (repealed effective 1999); D.C. Code §§29-101.49, 29-301.100 (2001); 805 ILCS 5/2.15, 3.20 (West 1993 & Supp. 2002); Iowa Code §§490.203, 490.204 (1999 & Supp. 2002); Or. Rev. Stat. §§60.024, 60.054 (1997).

In Timberline Equip. Co. v. Davenport, 514 P.2d 1109 (Or. 1973), the court found the language of Former Model Bus. Corp. Act §146 ambiguous as to who would qualify as a "person who assume[s]

Court of Appeals held that the impact of this provision and the corporate commencement section, taken together, is "to eliminate the concepts of estoppel and de facto corporateness."[3] The court reasoned that one purpose of modern corporation statutes is to eliminate problems and confusion inherent in the de jure, de facto, and estoppel concepts. It concluded that under the District of Columbia equivalent of the Model Act there is no corporation de jure, de facto, or by estoppel before a certificate of incorporation is issued[4] and, further, that individuals assuming to act as a corporation before a certificate of incorporation has been issued will be held jointly and severally liable.[5]

In the Maryland case of *Cranson v. International Business Machines,*[6] because of an attorney's oversight the articles of incorporation had not been filed. A creditor of the company sought to hold its president personally liable on the ground that failure to file the articles precluded corporate existence. Although the court did not find it necessary to decide whether the failure to file absolutely ruled out a de facto corporation,[7] the court held that the plaintiff was "estopped" from denying the corporation's existence. At the time of this decision, Maryland had a statutory section similar to the Model Act provision on when corporate existence commences.[8] The approach of the Maryland court seems highly preferable to the mechanistic, nothing-or-all (nothing before certificate issues; unassailable de jure corporation afterward) rule adopted in the District of Columbia.[9]

Statutes in a number of states forbid collateral attack on incorporation. The Delaware statute, for example, provides that "no corporation of this State and no person sued by any such corporation shall be permitted to assert the want of legal organization as a defense to any claim."[10] A provision of this kind seems to be merely declaratory of the common law and does not supersede the usual rules as to de facto corporations and corporations by estoppel.[11]

---

to act as a corporation." The court concluded that anyone having an investment in the organization who actively participates in policy and operational decisions of the organization (not necessarily just those who participate in decisions or acts connected with the obligation on which suit is brought) could be held liable.

[3] Robertson v. Levy, 197 A.2d 443, 447 (D.C. 1964).

[4] 197 A.2d at 446.

[5] 197 A.2d at 447. DBA/Delaware Sys. Corp. v. Greenfield, 636 A.2d 1318 (R.I. 1994) (promoters liable on pre-incorporation contract because statute interpreted to remove defense of de facto corporation).

[6] 20 A.2d 33 (Md. 1964).

[7] *See* Vincent Drug Co. v. Utah State Tax Comm'n, 407 P.2d 683 (Utah 1965) (Model Act does not preclude de facto corporation concept); Sunman-Dearborn Community Sch. Corp. v. Kral-Zepf-Freitag & Assocs., 338 N.E.2d 707 (Ind. Ct. App. 1975) (same). *But see* Edward Shoes, Inc. v. Orenstein, 333 F. Supp. 39, 42 (N.D. Ind. 1971) (Indiana statute preempts the common law of de facto corporation and "is now the sole source of shareholder liability in Indiana"). *See generally* Paul J. Galanti, Survey—Business Associations, 10 Ind. L. Rev. 57, 80-85 (1976).

[8] Md. Corp. & Assns. Code Ann. §2-102(b) (1999), formerly Md. Code Ann. art. 23, §131(b) (1966).

[9] *See* Dargan v. Graves, 168 S.E.2d 306 (S.C. 1969) (recognizing estoppel); Sunman-Dearborn Community Sch. Corp. v. Kral-Zepf-Freitag & Assocs., 383 N.E.2d 707 (Ind. Ct. App. 1975) (same).

[10] Del. Code Ann. tit. 8, §329(a) (2001). *See also* Kan. Stat. Ann. §17-7104 (1995).

[11] Davis v. Stevens, 104 F. 235, 238 (S.D. 1900). In fact, the Delaware statute itself states that. Del. Code Ann. tit. 8, §329(b) (2001). *See also* Kan. Stat. Ann. §17-7104 (1995).

CHAPTER 7

The Separate
Corporate Entity:
Privilege and Its Limitations

A. THE ENTITY CONCEPT AND
LIMITED LIABILITY

§7.01 The Corporate Entity

Recognition of a corporate personality generally is considered to be the most distinct attribute of the corporation.[1] To speak of a corporation as "a legal person" is

---

§7.01 [1] *See* Anderson v. Abbott, 321 U.S. 349, 361 (1943).

a convenient figure of speech used to describe the corporation as a legal unit, a separate concern with a capacity, like a person's, to hold property and make contracts, to sue and be sued, and to continue to exist notwithstanding changes of its shareholders or members.

If *A, B,* and *C* are incorporated into the A, B & C Co., the entity in its corporate capacity is the holder of the rights and liabilities arising from the transactions of the company. The property or rights acquired, or the liabilities incurred on behalf of the corporation, are treated as the property rights and liabilities of the corporate legal person distinct from those of the shareholders who comprise it.[2] A contract entered into by the shareholders of a corporation is not the contract of the corporation unless adopted by authority of its directors. Thus, if a sole shareholder borrows money on a personal note secured by shares of stock for the company's use and benefit even though the money is used to pay off corporate bills, the corporation is not liable on the note when credit was extended to the sole shareholder.[3] A corporation and its shareholders are not liable on each other's contracts. Shareholders' immunity from corporate obligations is one of the most important incidents and advantages of the separate legal entity and serves a useful purpose in business life.[4] Under some circumstances, however, sufficient equity may be shown to disregard the distinct legal personality and thereby pierce the corporate veil.[5]

§7.02   *Limited Liability Reconsidered*

No principle is more engrained in corporate law than that shareholders enjoy limited liability. Indeed, limited shareholder liability is not simply a principle of corporate law, but a cornerstone of capitalism. Because of limited liability, a good deal of the enterprise's risks are shifted from owners to third parties. It is the tort or contractual claimant, not the corporation's shareholders, that bear the loss whenever the corporation's resources are insufficient to satisfy the claim. As seen before, limited liability became well established in this country by the middle of the nineteenth century.[1]

A rich debate has recently ensued among economists and legal commentators (although not by any means divided along those lines) as to the desirability of

[2] In Donnell v. Herring-Hall-Marvin Safe Co., 208 U.S. 267, 273 (1908), Justice Holmes observed: "A leading purpose of [corporation] statutes and of those who act under them is to interpose a nonconductor, through which, in matters of contract, it is impossible to see the men behind."

[3] *E.g.,* In re John Koke Co., 38 F.2d 232 (9th Cir.), *cert. denied,* 282 U.S. 840 (1930); Wiebker v. Richard & Sons, 266 N.W.2d 326 (Wis. 1978). *Cf.* In re Marriage of Murray, 213 N.W.2d 657 (Iowa 1973) (losses incurred by one-person corporation not deductible from personal income of sole shareholder in calculating taxable income). This rule is limited to cases of valid use of the corporate privilege and will not shield the shareholder who merely uses the corporate form as a sham "alter ego." *See* §§7.03-7.06.

[4] *See generally* 1 William M. Fletcher Cyclopedia of Corporations §29 (1983).

[5] *See* §§7.05-7.06.

§7.02   [1] *See* §2.01. Interestingly, California provided for unlimited liability until 1931. *See generally* Harold Marsh, California Corporation Law §15.13 (2d ed. 1985).

A. The Entity Concept and Limited Liability

a limited liability rule.[2] Among the advantages cited in support for limited liability is that it stimulates investment by placing a known cap on the loss any investors can expect to incur. Limited liability therefore encourages risk-taking activity by both managers and investors: managers may more easily raise the funds from investors whose risk in any one venture is limited by the amount invested and whose overall risk is lowered through diversification.[3]

Limited liability also promotes efficiency because it facilitates even greater divisions of labor than would otherwise exist.[4] Investors may commit to others the more specialized tasks of managing a particular business so that investors may pursue full-time the vocation for which they are better suited; thus limited liability not only spawns the large public corporations that are characterized by the division of ownership and management, but also nurtures the creation of a large managerial class. Additionally, it is argued that to abandon limited liability would increase the agency costs, because shareholders would seek even greater bonding and monitoring activities to assure that their managers' goals with respect to risk exposure are congruent with those of the owners.

It has also been argued that abandonment to limited liability will discourage investment in large corporations by large, wealthy investors.[5] Certainly one must recognize that as the corporation increases in size the potential of the claims it may produce grows exponentially and that in a world without limited liability the likely target for any unsatisfied claim would be the financial institutions that typically hold the largest ownership blocks in public corporations. In this regard, it can be seen that one effect of limited liability is that it nurtures diversification—that is, portfolio investment strategies. If there were unlimited liability, one large claim by the unsatisfied creditors of a company held in an investor's portfolio could well wipe out the investor. This fear could cause investors to reasonably determine that investing in fewer rather than more companies, basically a nondiversification strategy, is wise because to hold more stocks actually increases the risk of personal liability.[6] The virtue of limited liability is also its vice; limited liability encourages corporations to engage in riskier or more damaging endeavors because owners are allowed to externalize the enterprise's costs (that is, they shift

---

[2] *See, e.g.,* Kenneth Arrow, Essays on the Theory of Risk Bearing 139-143 (1971); Richard Posner, Economic Analysis of Law §14.3 (4th ed. 1992); Robert C. Clark, The Regulation of Financial Holding Companies, 92 Harv. L. Rev. 789, 825-836 (1975); Frank Easterbrook & Daniel Fischel, Limited Liability and the Corporation, 52 U. Chi. L. Rev. 89 (1985); Henry Hansmann & R. Kraakman, Toward Unlimited Shareholder Liability for Corporate Torts, 100 Yale L.J. 1879 (1991); David W. Leebron, Limited Liability, Tort Victims, and Creditors, 91 Colum. L. Rev. 1565 (1991).

[3] Because a disproportionate amount of the close corporation's owner's total wealth is likely to be invested in the corporation, its owner has less chance to diversify, so that limited liability assumes even more importance than it does for the public corporation's stockholders. *See* David W. Leebron, Limited Liability, Tort Victims, and Creditors, 91 Colum. L. Rev. 1565, 1626-1636 (1991).

[4] Frank Easterbrook & Daniel Fischel, Limited Liability and the Corporation, 52 U. Chi. L. Rev. 89, 93-94 (1985).

[5] *See* Henry Manne, Our Two Corporation Systems: Law and Economics, 53 Va. L. Rev. 259, 262 (1967).

[6] *See* David W. Leebron, Limited Liability, Tort Victims, and Creditors, 91 Colum. L. Rev. 1565, 1597 (1991).

to third parties the costs created by the enterprise beyond its net worth and insurance).

Tort claimants are particularly vulnerable in the damaging wake created by limited liability because they generally lack victims' insurance or other means to spread the risk externalized on to them. Some have further argued that limited liability erodes both the deterrent and compensatory objectives of tort law.[7] More sophisticated claimants, such as bondholders and large creditors, however, may contract around limited liability rules to reduce their risk and may also have a greater capacity to spread their risk, such as through diversification of their lending or the rate of interest charged for loans. The concerns for the impact that a limited liability rule has on spreading risk provides an interesting juxtaposition with how responsibility for torts is addressed in other contexts. Much of our approach to who should be responsible for torts is based on judgments regarding who can more efficiently bear the cost of the activity. A similar inquiry in a context where the corporation is the tortfeasor may well reveal that the shareholders are the most efficient risk bearers, especially if liability is shared on a strict pro rata basis among stockholders.[8]

The above would suggest that the most appealing cases for disregarding the corporation's separate entity and imposing liability on the shareholders would be cases involving tort claimants. As is seen below, this is not the case. Professor Robert Thompson conducted an extensive empirical study of 1600 corporate piercing-the-veil cases.[9] Among his study findings are the following:[10]

Context	Total Cases	Piercing Cases	Cases Not Piercing	% Piercing
Contract	779	327	452	41.98
Tort	226	70	156	30.97
Criminal	15	10	5	66.67
Statute	552	224	328	40.58

[7] See Christopher Stone, The Place of Enterprise Liability in the Control of Corporate Conduct, 90 Yale L.J. 1 (1980). Dean Clark has suggested several methods of introducing greater fairness into a liability system. See Robert C. Clark, Duties of the Corporate Debtor to Its Creditors, 90 Harv. L. Rev. 505, 540-553 (1977).

[8] See David W. Leebron, Limited Liability, Tort Victims, and Creditors, 91 Colum. L. Rev. 1565, 1595 (1991).

[9] Robert Thompson, Piercing the Corporate Veil: An Empirical Study, 76 Cornell L. Rev. 1036 (1991).

[10] Id. at 1058. Professor Thompson has examined his sample further. See Robert B. Thompson, The Limits of Liability in the New Limited Liability Entities, 32 Wake Forest L. Rev. 1, 9-11 (1997) (piercing has occurred only within corporate groups or in close corporations with fewer than ten shareholders; most successful piercing cases involve active manager-shareholders or corporate groups in which the parent corporation named managers of the subsidiary). In the latest extension of his sample to 3,800 cases, Professor Thomson concludes courts are less likely to pierce corporate veils in cases involving tort as compared with contract liability. Robert B. Thompson, Piercing the Veil Within Corporate Groups: Corporate Shareholders as Mere Investors, 13 Conn. J. Int'l Law 379 (1999).

B. Bases for Disregarding the Corporate Entity

The differences in the above contexts in which the issue of piercing the corporate veil arises underscores several important considerations in this area. First, the interest to be served is not the same in each context, so that one should expect to find a greater willingness in some areas to pierce than in others. For example, statutory applications fulfill the legislative policy of regulating all aspects of an economic unit rather than a division that has been discretely carved out of that unit by the entire unit's owners. Second, the consequences of piercing the veil are not the same in all contexts. For example, many of the statutory applications of the doctrine do not involve visiting upon the pierced corporation's owners substantial damages; courts in this context can be expected to be less sympathetic to the defendant than in a case where the consequence of piercing the veil is to cause the corporation's owners to dig deep into their pockets. A third consideration is that the contractual context is far more likely to present the type of facts that make a more appealing case for piercing the veil than does a case involving an unsatisfied tort claimant. What is so surprising is that the above widely varying results have occurred under a doctrine whose content the courts purport to apply evenly in all veil-piercing contexts.

The expanding obligations of bank holding companies is one area of regulation that can be rationalized along the lines of those who argue that the abandonment of limited liability will lead to greater efficiency by forcing corporations to internalize their full costs. During the last part of the twentieth century, the regulatory burdens and accompanying sanctions of bank holding companies expanded as a means to address irresponsible risk taking in their subsidiary banks. This regulatory approach can be seen as a discrete intrusion on the doctrine of limited liability that is justified as a means to address the better access to information that the holding company has than would government regulators and as a means of reducing the moral hazard problem that otherwise accompanies limited liability.[11]

B. BASES FOR DISREGARDING THE CORPORATE ENTITY

§7.03 Approaches Used to Disregard the Corporate Entity

In general, a corporation may exist and act as an entity or legal unit separate and apart from its shareholders. In many cases, however, the courts place limitations on this privilege. These limitations usually are expressed in terms of "disregarding the corporate fiction," "piercing the corporate veil," or "looking at the substance of the business operation rather than at its form."[1]

---

[11] *See* Howell Jackson, The Expanding Obligations of Financial Holding Companies, 107 Harv. L. Rev. 507, 565-566, 570-571 (1994).

§7.03   [1] *See, e.g.,* Establissement Tomis v. Shearson Hayden Stone, Inc., 459 F. Supp. 1355, 1365 (S.D.N.Y. 1978); Minton v. Cavaney, 364 P.2d 473 (Cal. 1961); Yacker v. Weiner, 263 A.2d 188 (N. J. Super. Ct. Ch. Div. 1970), *aff'd,* 277 A.2d 417 (N.J. Super. Ct. App. Div. 1971).

The disregard of the corporate entity occurs in a variety of settings, the most common being to impose personal liability on the corporation's stockholders. If the corporation is insolvent, its unsatisfied creditors, including any tort claimants, can be expected to pursue all reasonable avenues to reach the personal assets of its shareholders by arguing that the corporation is not truly a separate entity. Sometimes it is important to determine whether the real party in interest is the corporation or an individual. For example, state usury laws frequently apply if the borrower is an individual but not if the borrower is a corporation. Cases have therefore posed the question whether the corporate entity should be disregarded for the purpose of applying the state usury law. Another illustration where holding a statute had been violated turned on whether to disregard the separate identity of a corporation arose in *Sundaco, Inc. v. State*,[2] where, to circumvent a state law mandating that businesses close on alternate weekends, a subsidiary corporation was formed to operate the business on the weekends that the business was not being operated by its parent.

If the separate corporate capacity is used dishonestly, such as to evade obligations or statutory restrictions, the courts will intervene to prevent the abuse.[3] The figurative terminology and formulae invoked by the judges to disregard legal fictions often obscure the real issues presented.[4] Concepts such as "alter ego" and "instrumentality" do not provide general formulae applicable in all cases; each set of circumstances must be considered by the court on its merits.[5] The facts presented must demonstrate some misuse of the corporate privilege or establish a need to limit it in order to do justice.[6] Disregard of the separate corporate entity privilege for one purpose does not mean necessarily that it will be disregarded for other purposes.[7] The absence of clear-cut rules and the reliance on the equities of each fact situation make it difficult to generalize as to the factors that will lead a court to find individual shareholder liability.[8] Thus drawing the line between a proper use of corporate form in order to avoid personal liability and an abuse of corporate form to defraud a corporation's creditor is sometimes quite difficult.

There are three primary variants within the "piercing the corporate veil" jurisprudence—(1) the "instrumentality" doctrine, (2) the "alter ego" doctrine, and (3) the "identity" doctrine.[9] The instrumentality doctrine's overall approach

[2] 463 S.W.2d 528 (Tex. Civ. App. 1970).

[3] *See, e.g.,* Attorney General v. M.C.K., Inc., 736 N.E.2d 373, 380 (Mass. 2000) (doctrine of corporate disregard may be used to carry out legislative intent and thereby avoid evasion of statutes).

[4] *See* Robert W. Hamilton, The Corporate Entity, 49 Tex. L. Rev. 979, 983 (1971).

[5] *E.g.,* Dewitt Truck Brokers, Inc. v. W. Ray Flemming Fruit Co., 540 F.2d 681 (4th Cir. 1976) (South Carolina law); Swanson v. Levy, 509 F.2d 859, 861-862 (9th Cir. 1975) (California law).

[6] Pepper v. Litton, 308 U.S. 295, 310 (1939); Federal Deposit Ins. Corp. v. Allen, 584 F. Supp. 386 (E.D. Tenn. 1984); McKissick v. Auto-Owners Ins. Co., 429 So. 2d 1030 (Ala. 1983); Minton v. Cavaney, 364 P.2d 473 (Cal. 1961).

[7] Cooperman v. Unemployment Appeals Bd., 122 Cal. Rptr. 127, 132 (Ct. App. 1975); Norman v. Murray First Thrift & Loan Co., 596 P.2d 1029 (Utah 1979).

[8] *See* §7.02.

[9] Phillip I. Blumberg, The Law of Corporate Groups: Tort, Contract, and Other Common Law Problems in the Substantive Law of Parent and Subsidiary Corporation 111 (1987). Blumberg's treatise is the most comprehensive treatment of the liability aspects of piercing the corporate veil. For an equally definitive treatment of veil-piercing questions under various federal statutes, *see* Phillip I.

B. Bases for Disregarding the Corporate Entity

focuses on the presence of three factors, as reflected in the frequently cited language of its leading case, *Lowendahl v. Baltimore & Ohio Railroad:*[10]

(1) Control, not merely majority or complete stock control, but complete domination, not only of finances, but of policy and business practices in respect to the transaction attacked so that the corporate entity had at the time no separate mind, will, or existence of its own; and

(2) Such control must have been used by the defendant to commit fraud or wrong, to perpetuate the violation of a statutory or other positive legal duty, or a dishonest and unjust act in contravention of the plaintiff's legal rights; and

(3) The aforesaid control and breach of duty must proximately cause the injury or unjust loss complained of.[11]

The "alter ego" doctrine is stated with a far greater economy of words but with much less precision than the statement of instrumentality doctrine. The alter ego doctrine holds that it is appropriate to pierce the veil when (1) a unity of ownership and interests exists between the corporation and its controlling stockholder such that the corporation has ceased to exist as a separate entity and the corporation has been relegated to the status of the controlling stockholder's alter ego and (2) to recognize the corporation and its controlling stockholder as separate entities would be sanctioning fraud or would lead to an inequitable result.[12]

The leading case for the "identity" doctrine is *Zaist v. Olson,*[13] where the court states:

> If plaintiff can show that there was such a unity of interest and ownership that the independence of the corporations had in effect ceased or had never begun, an adherence to the fiction of separate identity would serve only to defeat justice and equity by permitting the economic entity to escape liability arising out of an operation of one corporation for the benefit of the whole enterprise.[14]

Although stock ownership is a significant factor under the "identity" approach, a court may impose personal liability on a controlling person even if he or she is not a shareholder.[15]

On close scrutiny, none of the three above variants of "piercing the veil" offers precision or a characteristic that distinguishes it from the other two variants.

Blumberg, The Law of Corporate Groups: Problems of Parent and Subsidiary Corporations Under Statutory Law of General Application (1989).

[10] 287 N.Y.S. 62 (App. Div.), *aff'd,* 6 N.E.2d 56 (N.Y. 1936).

[11] *Id.* at 76. *See, e.g.,* 66, Inc. v. Crestwood Commons Redevelopment Corp., 998 S.W.2d 32, 40 (Mo. 1999) (*en banc*); Hyland Meat Co., Inc. v. Tsagarakis, 609 N.Y.S.2d 625 (2d Dept. App. Div. 1994) (piercing veil based on exercise of dominion and control).

[12] *See* Doe v. Unocal Corp., 248 F.3d 915, 926 (9th Cir. 2001); Pearson v. Component Technology Corp., 247 F.3d 471, 485 (3d Cir. 2001). Flynt Distrib. Co. v. Harvey, 734 F.2d 1389, 1393 (9th Cir. 1984).

[13] 227 A.2d 552 (1967).

[14] *Id.* at 558. *See also* McFarland v. Brier, 769 A.2d 605, 613 (R.I. 2000).

[15] McCormick v. City of Dillingham, 16 P.3d 735, 744 (Alaska 2001); LFC Marketing Group, Inc. v. Loomis, 8 P.3d 841, 847 (Nev. 2000).

In practice, they are virtually indistinguishable from one another, and the outcome of the cases does not appear to depend on which standard is applied.[16] As commentators have frequently noted, the results in cases appear guided not so much by the doctrine invoked[17] as by the "mist of metaphors."[18]

§7.04 Lack of Formality and Confusion of Affairs as Bases for Piercing the Corporate Veil

When the dominant shareholders treat the corporate business and property as their own and the affairs of the corporation and the shareholders are confused or intermingled, the separate corporate entity no longer can be respected. If the shareholders themselves disregard the separateness of the corporation, the courts also will disregard it so far as necessary to protect individual and corporate creditors.[1]

When the same facts arise in the parent-subsidiary context, courts frequently characterize the parent's control as that of treating the subsidiary as though it is merely a department of the parent company.[2] Similarly, a court may disregard separate entities when related corporations under common control fail to observe the formal barriers between them.[3]

A frequent factor supporting a finding of confusion is the failure to comply with corporate formalities in the conduct of the corporation's business.[4] Lapses in corporate formalities that are emphasized in veil-piercing cases are: failing to hold stockholders' or directors' meetings;[5] directing receipts to the controlling stockholder's bank account and using a single endorsement stamp for all affiliated companies;[6] the parent company's board of directors establishing salaries, appointing auditors, and declaring dividends of its subsidiary.[7]

---

[16] Phillip I. Blumberg, The Law of Corporate Groups: Tort, Contract, and Other Common Law Problems in the Substantive Law of Parent and Subsidiary Corporation 120 (1987). *See also* Pearson v. Component Technology Corp., 247 F.3d 471, 484 n.2 (3d Cir. 2001) (noting that courts rarely distinguish among these three tests, which generally are similar).

[17] *See, e.g.*, Elvin R. Latty, Subsidiaries and Affiliated Corporations 157-158 (1936); Robert W. Hamilton, The Corporate Entity, 49 Tex. L. Rev. 979 (1971).

[18] Berkey v. Third Ave. Ry., 155 N.E. 58, 61 (1926) (J. Cardozo).

§7.04 [1] *E.g.*, United States v. Pisani, 646 F.2d 83 (3d Cir. 1981); Bucyrus-Erie Co. v. General Prods. Corp., 643 F.2d 413 (6th Cir. 1981); United States v. Thomas, 515 F. Supp. 1351 (W.D. Tex. 1981).

[2] Consolidated Rock Prods. Co. v. Du Bois, 312 U.S. 510 (1941); Bendix Home Sys. v. Hurston Enter., 566 F.2d 1039 (5th Cir. 1978); Henry W. Ballantine, Separate Entity of Parent and Subsidiary Corporations, 14 Cal. L. Rev. 12 (1925). *See infra* §7.08.

[3] *See* Attorney General v. M.C.K., Inc., 736 N.E.2d 373, 382 (Mass. 2000).

[4] *See, e.g.*, Walter E. Heller & Co. v. Video Innovations, Inc., 730 F.2d 50, 53 (2d Cir. 1984); Brown v. Benton Creosoting Co., 147 So. 2d 89 (La. Ct. App. 1963).

[5] *See, e.g.*, Iron City Sand & Gravel v. West Fork Towing Corp., 298 F. Supp. 1091, 1098 (N.D. W. Va. 1969).

[6] *See* Brown v. Benton Creosoting Co., 147 So. 2d 89, 93 (La. Ct. App. 1963).

[7] *See, e.g.*, Gentry v. Credit Plan Corp., 528 S.W.2d 571 (Tex. 1975).

B. Bases for Disregarding the Corporate Entity

Disregard of corporate formalities, however, does not appear sufficient by itself to pierce the corporate veil.[8] Some have even sought to restrict this factor further by requiring a causal relationship between the failure to observe corporate formalities and the fraud or inequitable result that would follow if the veil were not pierced.[9] The mere fact that the business's affairs have been carried out with strict obeisance to corporate formalities, however, does not immunize the corporation from having its separate entity disregarded if other factors justify piercing the corporate veil.[10] The want of corporate formalities is but one consideration, and courts customarily require some suggestion of fraud, illegality, or unfairness that will result if the veil is not disregarded.[11] A disregard of form standing by itself, thus, will not be enough to pierce the corporate veil.[12]

A related consideration is whether there has been mingling of business or assets of the controlling stockholder and the corporation or among affiliated corporations.[13] Cases that have pierced the veil because of mingling of assets and affairs customarily involve facts suggesting there has been such control exercised over the corporation's assets by its dominant stockholder that the stockholder has essentially ignored the corporation as a distinct entity.[14]

There are several rationales that can be suggested as to why mingling or a lack of obeisance to corporate formalities should lead to the corporation's separate entity being disregarded. One theory is that logic compels treating the dominated corporation and its controlling stockholder as inseparable because the dominant stockholder has chosen to ignore the corporation as a distinct entity. This reasoning does not itself answer why such draconian results should follow from the fact that the dominant shareholder has caused the corporation to conduct its business informally. One would expect some greater purpose should underlie the imposition of personal liability on the dominant stockholder than the rather hollow purpose of assuring the corporation's separate personality is preserved through a respect for formal operations.

---

[8] Solomon v. Western Hills Dev. Co., 312 N.W.2d 428, 434 (Mich. Ct. App. 1981).

[9] See Transamerica Cash Reserve, Inc. v. Dixie Power & Water, 789 P.2d 24 (Utah 1990).

[10] See, e.g., United States v. Jon-T Chem., Inc., 768 F.2d 686 (5th Cir. 1985).

[11] See, e.g., Pepsi-Cola Metro. Bottling Co. v. Checkers, Inc., 754 F.2d 10 (1st Cir. 1985); K-Mart Corp. v. Knitjoy Mfg., 542 F. Supp. 1189, 1192 (E.D. Mich. 1982); Falcone v. Night Watchman, Inc., 526 A.2d 550 (Conn. Ct. App. 1987); Soloman v. Western Hills Dev. Co., 312 N.W. 2d 428, 434 (Mich. Ct. App. 1981); ADT Security Sys. Mid-South, Inc. v. Central Distribution, Inc., 1994 WL 43872 (Minn. Ct. App. 1994) (piercing veil where sole shareholder's misuse of corporate form amounted to constructive fraud).

[12] See, e.g., Rogerson Hiller Corp. v. Port of Port Angeles, 982 P.2d 131, 134 (Wash. App. 1999).

[13] It is not uncommon to find both a want of formalities and commingling in the same facts. See, e.g., Bergen v. F/V St. Patrick, 816 F.2d 1345, 1352 (9th Cir. 1987); United States v. Jon-T Chem., Inc., 768 F.2d 686, 695 (5th Cir. 1985); Brown v. Benton Creosoting Co., 147 So. 2d 89, 93 (La. Ct. App. 1963); Dumas v. InfoSafe Corp., 463 S.E.2d 641 (S.C. Ct. App. 1995).

[14] See, e.g., Pepsi-Cola Metro. Bottling Co. v. Checkers, Inc., 754 F.2d 10, 14 15 (1st Cir. 1985); America Pioneer Life Ins. Co. v. Sandlin, 470 So. 2d 657, 668 (Ala. 1985); Sawyer Realty Group v. Jarvis Corp., 415 N.E.2d 560 (Ill. App. Ct. 1980); AMFAC Mech. Supply Co. v. Federer, 645 P.2d 73, 78-79 (Wyo. 1982). Theberge v. Dabro, Inc., 684 A.2d 1298 (Me. 1996) (breakdown in formalities so serious that trial court could well conclude that corporation was but a shell dominated by the defendant; further confusion arose by the fact defendant's agent represented he would be responsible for the company's debts).

Veil piercing for lack of corporate formalities and the mingling of affairs and assets are most appropriate where the facts are sufficiently strong to create a serious doubt whether creditors have been prejudiced by the transfer of corporate assets without sufficient consideration. This is most easily established in cases where there has been mingling of affairs or assets. A breach of corporate formalities should also be sufficient where the breach is so pervasive as to raise grave concerns that it is not possible to determine whether the corporate assets had ever been transferred to its stockholders without fair consideration or the lack of formalities may have caused a sufficient misimpression of personal rather than corporate responsibility for the debts contracted.

§7.05 Dominating the Corporation's Affairs as the Basis for Piercing the Corporate Veil

A frequent consideration in veil-piercing cases is whether the controlling stockholder has so dominated the affairs of the corporation that the corporation has no existence of its own. Usually there is the additional requirement that fraud, illegality, or gross unfairness will result if the corporate existence is not disregarded.[1]

Domination is far more frequently a consideration in the parent-subsidiary context than in cases in which the veil is being pierced to reach an individual stockholder.[2] The lesser role of domination in veil-piercing cases involving individual-close corporations is a sensible recognition that it defies even metaphysics to expect such a corporate entity to have a mind or soul distinct from its controlling stockholder. In contrast, even though it is equally unrealistic to expect a subsidiary to act independently of its parent corporation's strategies and wishes, both parent and subsidiary corporations can be expected to at least formalistically separate their decision-making so as to avoid creating the false impression that the subsidiary is but a branch or division of the parent corporation.[3] Such an impression assumes significance because it misrepresents the status of the subsidiary to third parties, and also suggests a mingling of assets and affairs of the two entities such that there may be fraud on creditors lurking in the background. There also may be facts supporting the conclusion that the subsidiary has no independent profit objective such that creditors are presented with a corporate debtor that has only down-side risks.

Professor Blumberg identifies four factors that are frequently emphasized in parent-subsidiary veil-piercing cases finding undue domination of the subsidiary's affairs:

(1) the parent's participation in day-to-day operations;
(2) the parent's determination of important policy decisions;

§7.05 [1] *See, e.g.*, MAG Portfolio Consult, GMBH v. Merlin Biomed Group LLC, 268 F.3d 58, 63 (2d Cir. 2001) (applying New York law); Williams v. McAllister Bros., 534 F.2d 19, 21 (2d Cir. 1976).

[2] *See, e.g.*, William J. Rands, Domination of a Subsidiary by a Parent, 32 Ind. L. Rev. 421 (1999).

[3] However, mere references in the parent's annual report to subsidiaries or chains of subsidiaries as "divisions" of the parent company do not establish the existence of an alter ego relationship. Doe v. Unocal Corp., 248 F.3d 915, 928 (9th Cir. 2001).

B.   Bases for Disregarding the Corporate Entity

(3) the parent's determination of the subsidiary's business decisions, bypassing the subsidiary's directors and officers;

(4) the parent's issuance of instructions to the subsidiary's personnel or use of its own personnel in the conduct of the subsidiary's affairs.[4]

§7.06   Inadequate Capitalization as a Factor for Piercing the Veil

Inadequate capitalization is frequently a factor considered by courts in veil-piercing cases.[1] This consideration most frequently appears in tort cases involving close corporations and in the parent-subsidiary context.[2] *Minton v. Cavney*[3] is the leading case for a seemingly aggressive use of inadequate capitalization as a grounds to pierce the corporate veil. Plaintiff had secured a $10,000 tort judgment against the corporation for the death of her daughter, who had drowned in the corporation's swimming pool. The corporation operated a public swimming pool in a facility it leased and had received no consideration for its stock. Justice Roger Traynor reasoned that there had been "no attempt to provide adequate capitalization," reasoning the corporation's "capital was 'trifling compared with the business to be done and the risks of loss.' "[4] The court therefore upheld the complaint against a shareholder with a one-third interest who was also an officer and director of the corporation.

Minton stands alone as a case that pierced the veil solely for inadequate capitalization. Subsequent cases have relegated inadequate capitalization to one of many factors courts can consider to determine whether to disregard the corporate entity.[5] Even in *Automotriz del Golfo de California v. Resnick,*[6] the case heavily relied on by *Minton,* there were factors in addition to the court's finding that $5,000 capital was inadequate for a business whose monthly gross receipts were $100,000-$150,000. *Minton* can therefore be seen as a case where it was not simply a matter of capital inadequacy but where there was no attempt to provide any

---

[4] Phillip I. Blumberg, The Law of Corporate Groups: Problems of Parent and Subsidiary Corporations Under Statutory Law of General Application 188 (1989).

§7.06 [1] *See, e.g.,* Refco, Inc. v. Farm Prod. Ass'n, 844 F.2d 525 (8th Cir. 1988); Eastridge Dev. Co. v. Halpert Assocs., 853 F.2d 772 (10th Cir. 1988).

[2] *See* Phillip I. Blumberg, The Law of Corporate Groups: Problems of Parent and Subsidiary Corporations Under Statutory Law of General Application 202 (1989).

[3] 364 P.2d 473 (Cal. 1961). *See also* Western Rock Co. v. Davis, 432 S.W.2d 555 (Tex. Civ. App. 1968) (court disregarded entity of insufficiently capitalized corporation it found to have been created to shield defendants from liability).

[4] 364 P.2d at 475, quoting Automotriz del Golfo de Cal. v. Resnick, 306 P.2d 1, 4 (Cal. 1957).

[5] *See, e.g.,* Bendix Home Systems v. Hurston Enter., 566 F.2d 1039 (5th Cir. 1978).

[6] 306 P.2d 1 (1957). *But see* Slottow v. American Casualty Co. of Reading, Penn., 10 F.3d 1355, 1360 (9th Cir. 1993) (in California, inadequate capitalization alone may be enough to hold the parent liable for its subsidiary's debts).

capitalization. This view brings it closer to the cases that have pierced the veil when the facts suggest the corporation is a sham.[7]

In a leading case, the New York Court of Appeals in *Walkovszky v. Carlton*[8] refused to apply the "thin capitalization" theory of piercing the corporate veil. The individual defendant was the sole shareholder of ten corporations, each of which owned two taxicabs and carried only the minimum amount of automobile insurance allowed by the law. The plaintiff was injured due to the negligence of one of defendant's drivers. The court, despite a vigorous dissent, deferred to the legislature in holding that by maintaining the statutory minimum insurance the corporation was not too thinly capitalized. The only basis for piercing the corporate veil would be on a showing that there was such an intermingling of assets as to constitute an abuse of the corporate privilege.[9]

On close inspection, the role of inadequate capitalization is best left as a surrogate for the promoter's possible bad faith as that factor may relate on the overall equities of disregarding the corporate entity.[10] Consider in this regard that the inadequacy of the firm's capital is to be measured at the time of the corporation's inception.[11] Capital must then have been sufficient to meet the prospective risks of the business in which the corporation is to engage.

Testing capital adequacy at the corporation's inception and evaluating its amount strictly in terms of the magnitude of future business risks introduce a good deal of ambiguity and unreasonableness into the equation. Are the risks to be perceived only those that are normal for a business, or do they include a highly unusual tort claim that greatly exceeds the firm's liability insurance?[12] Does the test demand that the total amount the shareholders invest must literally equal the present value of all future liabilities of the firm or does it entail some lesser amount that is simply necessary to launch the firm such that its future cash flows will meet its normal operating expenses? The former is clearly an unreasonable demand because no company can be expected to endow its future operating expenses and liabilities as a precondition to opening its doors. As for gauging capital adequacy in terms of massing assets sufficient to generate a positive cash flow, it must be borne in mind that the mere fact a business fails in terms that it produced a negative, rather than a positive, cash flow is custom-

---

[7] *See, e.g.*, Wesco Mfg. v. Tropical Attractions of Palm Beach, Inc., 833 F.2d 1484 (11th Cir. 1987); Hart v. Steel Products, Inc., 660 N.E.2d 1270 (Ind. Ct. App. 1996).

[8] 223 N.E.2d 6 (N.Y. 1966).

[9] The plaintiff subsequently amended her complaint to comport with this alter-ego rationale, and the cause of action was sustained. Walkovszky v. Carlton, 287 N.Y.S.2d 546 (App. Div.), *aff'd*, 244 N.E.2d 55 (N.Y. 1968). *See also, e.g.*, Miller v. Brass Rail Tavern, Inc., 702 A.2d 1072 (Pa. Super. 1997) (affirming trial court's refusal to pierce veil notwithstanding some evidence of thin capitalization and intermingling of funds; upon discovery the intermingling was corrected and the funds reimbursed).

[10] *See, e.g.*, Sansone v. Moseley, 912 S.W.2d 666, 669 (Mo. Ct. App. 1995) (veil pierced for inadequate capitalization when company was created to conceal assets from creditors).

[11] *See, e.g.*, Pierson v. Jones, 625 P.2d 1085 (Idaho 1981); 66, Inc. v. Crestwood Commons Redevelopment Corp., 998 S.W.2d 32, 41 (Mo. 1999) (*en banc*).

[12] On the question whether liability insurance can serve as a substitute for capital, *see* Walkovszky v. Carlton, 223 N.E.2d 6 (N.Y. 1966).

arily explained by a good many factors other than the relative amount invested in the firm. And to require an investment that assures a positive cash flow surely will have a chilling effect on entrepreneurial activity because a central risk of any business venture is that it will not, because of competition and other market forces, be able to generate a cash flow sufficient to support itself. It would therefore appear that inadequate capitalization has correctly assumed a limited role in veil-piercing cases, that of being a surrogate for the probable bad faith of the firm's promoters.

§7.07   Definitions: "Parent Company," "Holding Company," "Subsidiary," and "Affiliate"

Subsidiary and affiliated corporations have become important instruments of large-scale business. The same shareholder or group of shareholders may form or acquire various affiliated corporations for use as related branches of an enterprise under the unified management of common directors and officers. Much the same result is accomplished by subincorporation, when a parent or holding company reincorporates itself and splits its personality into several branches of the business.

A corporation with the power to elect a majority of the directors of another corporation and thus exercise working control is a parent company with reference to the corporation so controlled.[1] The parent company may have this power directly by virtue of its controlling equity interest or indirectly through another corporation or series of corporations. The term "holding company"[2] is used most frequently to refer to a corporation created specifically to acquire and hold shares in other corporations for investment purposes, with or without actual control. However, the term sometimes is used interchangeably with "parent company" when the corporation has sufficient equity interest in, or power of control over, another corporation to elect its directors and influence its management.[3]

A corporation subject to control by a parent or holding company is a "subsidiary"[4] of the controlling company, even when it may in turn be the parent or holding company of a third corporation. Corporations related to each other by common control of voting stock and operated as parts of a system or enterprise are "affiliates."

---

§7.07   [1] A "parent corporation" is one that has working control through stock ownership of its subsidiary corporations. Culcal Stylco, Inc. v. Vornado, Inc., 103 Cal. Rptr. 419, 421 (Ct. App. 1972).

[2] *See, e.g.,* 12 U.S.C. §1841(a)(1) (2000) ("'bank holding company' means any company which has control over any bank"). *See also, e.g.,* 15 U.S.C. §79b(a)(7)(A) (2000) (definition of public utility holding company).

[3] *E.g.,* Kelley, Glover & Vale, Inc. v. Heitman, 44 N.E. 2d 981 (Ind. 1943), *cert. denied,* 319 U.S. 762 (1943).

[4] When a parent owns all of the shares of another company, this is sometimes referred to as a wholly-owned subsidiary.

111

§7.08 Disregarding the Separate Entity in the Parent-Subsidiary Context

Problems regarding the corporate entity frequently arise within the context of parent and subsidiary or between affiliated corporations. The same principles apply here as to individual shareholders and their corporations.[1] There is no general formula that furnishes an objective test to determine shareholder liability for the torts or contracts of controlled corporations. Courts exercise their discretion to prevent abuses and regulate the privilege of separate corporate capacities, and in doing so they weigh various factors in deciding the question.[2] At the same time courts will not ordinarily disregard the separation of corporate entities in the absence of a showing that injustice or unfairness would otherwise result.[3]

§7.09 The Corporation's Separate Entity Under State and Federal Statutes

As seen earlier,[1] a significant number of cases regarding the piercing of the corporate veil are those arising in disputes involving the application of a state or federal statute. The greater frequency of veil-piercing in statutory contexts rather than in the contract claim contexts is due to the different objectives served in the statutory contexts—invariably the objective and policy of state and federal statutes invite a more liberal application of veil-piercing considerations.[2] Furthermore,

---

§7.08 [1] *See* Annot., 38 A.L.R.3d 1102 (1971); 7 A.L.R.3d 1343 (1966). It can be argued that courts should be willing to pierce through multiple levels of corporate veils because even in doing so, personal liability of the shareholders remains unscathed. This is a shortsighted view because, for example, when dealing with several corporate entities, each may have its own set of innocent creditors who may suffer from the piercing.

[2] *See* Dewitt Truck Brokers, Inc. v. W. Ray Flemming Fruit Co., 540 F.2d 681 (4th Cir. 1976) (court lists seven factors to be considered in decision whether to pierce corporate veil; inquiry is highly fact-oriented); Sabine Towing & Transp. Co. v. Merit Ventures, Inc., 575 F. Supp. 1442 (E.D. Tex. 1983) (court lists 15 factors to be considered in a decision whether to pierce corporate veil); Eagle Air Inc. v. Corron & Black/Dawson & Co., 648 P.2d 1000 (Alaska 1982) (court lists 11 factors to be considered in decision whether to pierce veil in parent-subsidiary context). *Cf.* the eight-factor test that has been applied to establish the liability of individual shareholders, Amoco Chem. Corp. v. Bach, 567 P.2d 1337, 1341-1342 (Kan. 1977).

[3] *E.g.*, Fletcher v. Atex, Inc., 68 F.3d 1451, 1461 (2d Cir. 1995). For the suggestion that domination and control can substitute for a showing of unfairness, see, *e.g.*, Thomson-CSF, S.A. v. American Arbitration Association, 64 F.3d 773, 777 (2d Cir. 1995); Carte Blanche (Singapore) Pte., Ltd. V. Diners Club International, Inc., 2 F.3d 24, 26 (2c Cir. 1993). *But see, e.g.*, Craig v. Lake Asbestos of Quebec, Ltd., 843 F.2d 145 (3d Cir. 1988) (there was an insufficient showing of control to warrant piercing of the parent/subsidiary veil).

§7.09 [1] *See* table in §7.02.

[2] An exhaustive study of this subject appears in Phillip I. Blumberg, The Law of Corporate Groups: Problems of Parent and Subsidiary Corporations Under Statutory Law of General Application (1989). *See also* Phillip I. Blumberg, The Increasing Recognition of Enterprise Principles in Determining Parent and Subsidiary Corporation Liabilities, 28 Conn. L. Rev. 295 (1996).

federal courts are more likely to pierce the veil in order to effectuate federal policy and thereby prevent state corporate laws from being used to frustrate the federal objectives.[3] Courts do not purport to invoke different standards for piercing the veil in the context of interpreting state or federal statutes than they use in cases involving creditors who seek payment. The greater willingness to pierce the veil in the statutory context reflects in part that the consequences are not nearly as severe as in veil-piercing cases where the object is to impose liability on the dominant stockholder for all the insolvent corporation's debts. Also, there are numerous related questions in the statutory context that call for expanding responsibility beyond a single corporate actor so as to include perhaps its sister corporations, its parent corporation, or even an individual controlling stockholder. Such expansion can occur by either piercing the corporate veil or by holding that the act's language reaches controlling stockholders or controlled companies regardless of whether the facts support piercing the veil.

C.   EQUITABLE SUBORDINATION

§7.10   Equitable Subordination of Controlling Stockholders' Loans and Guaranties

Shareholders make loans to their corporation for a number of legitimate reasons.[1] Because a corporation is treated as an entity distinct from its stockholders, the stockholder-lender enjoys a priority equal to that of outside creditors. Even claims of a sole shareholder, whether an individual or a corporation, can compete with outside creditors for bona fide advances.[2] In contrast, partners' loans in liquidation are paid only after all outside creditors have been satisfied.

The courts, however, scrutinize a controlling stockholder's claim to determine whether the "advance" should be treated as a loan or as a capital investment and also to judge whether it would be inequitable to accord that claim a priority equal to that enjoyed by outside creditors.[3] There are, therefore, two distinct

---

[3] Pearson v. Component Technology Corp., 247 F.3d 471, 484 n.2 (3d Cir. 2001).

§7.10   [1] For a discussion of the tax advantages of low equity capitalization and the dangers of "thin capitalization," see 1 F. Hodge O'Neal & Robert B. Thompson, O'Neal's Close Corporations, Law and Practice §§2.14-2.17 (3d ed. 1998); Samuel D. Cheris, Note, Stockholder Loans and the Debt-Equity Distinction, 22 Stan. L. Rev. 847, 851-853 (1970) (discussing capital structure planning).

[2] For a review of factors considered in determining if a loan is truly a loan, see O'Neal & Thompson, supra note 1 §2.16; David P. Hariton, Distinguishing Between Equity and Debt in the New Financial Environment, 49 Tax L. Rev. 499 (1994).

[3] See, e.g., In re Multiponics, Inc., 436 F. Supp. 1065 (E.D. La. 1977); Tanzi v. Fiberglass Swimming Pools, Inc., 414 A.2d 484 (R.I. 1980). See generally Robert C. Clark, The Duties of the Corporate Debtor

questions: Are the advances to be treated as loans; and, assuming the advances are bona fide loans, do equitable considerations compel that the controlling stockholder's loans be subordinated to other claimants in the bankruptcy or receivership proceedings?

Whether an advance is viewed as a bona fide loan generally depends on whether it bears the indicia common to loans. In deciding whether advances are loans or capital, substance very much governs over form.[4] In broad overview, the litmus is whether from the totality of the circumstances the advances were made when no other disinterested lender would have extended credit. Courts thus examine the relative riskiness of the enterprise as well as whether the lending stockholder has acted as a third-party lender by demanding the protection and terms a third party would have sought under the circumstances. Advances have been treated as capital where the stockholder has agreed to subordinate its loans to the much smaller loans made by banks,[5] where the firm's initial capital is inadequate,[6] when the debt appears to be held proportionally among the stockholders,[7] where investors have shifted a portion of their capital investment to loans in the face of bankruptcy,[8] and where the debt-to-equity ratio was believed too high.[9] One has legitimate cause for concern whether such considerations are too crude to separate reliably legitimate lending practices from investments of capital.

Even though debt is bona fide, it may nonetheless be subordinated to the demands for payment by other claimants.[10] Equitable subordination of stockholder's debt is frequently referred to as the "Deep Rock" doctrine, the reference being to the subsidiary in *Taylor v. Standard Gas & Electric Company*,[11] the leading case on the subject.

---

to Its Creditors, 90 Harv. L. Rev. 505 (1977); Asa S. Herzog & Joel B. Zweibel, The Equitable Subordination of Claims in Bankruptcy, 15 Vand. L. Rev. 83, 90-93 (1961); Kathleen Kinney, Note, Equitable Subordination of Shareholder Debt to Trade Creditors: A Reexamination, 61 B.U. L. Rev. 433 (1981).

[4] This approach was first enunciated in Pepper v. Litton, 308 U.S. 295 (1939).

[5] Diasonics, Inc. v. Ingalls, 121 B.R. 626 (Bankr. N.D. Fla. 1990).

[6] *See, e.g.*, In re Multiponics, Inc., 622 F.2d 709 (5th Cir. 1980).

[7] L. & M. Realty Corp. v. Leo, 249 F.2d 668 (4th Cir. 1957).

[8] In Costello v. Fazio, 256 F.2d 903 (9th Cir. 1958), on incorporation of a failing partnership, three partners each received $2,000 in the corporation's stock, and the balance of partnership equity by other two partners was represented by notes-payable if the corporation was profitable. The court held that the capital was clearly inadequate, but could also have considered the debt was not truly debt.

[9] The higher the ratio, the easier the case. Thus a ratio of 80:1 permits classification as capital without additional showing. *See* In re Fett Roofing & Sheet Metal Co., 438 F. Supp. 726 (E.D. Va. 1977), but a ratio in the low teens requires other factors to support reclassification. *See* In re Mobile Steel Co., 563 F.2d 692 (5th Cir. 1977).

[10] In the typical bankruptcy or receivership setting where such disputes arise, there is no difference in result between subordinating the debt and recharacterizing it as capital: In either case, the controlling stockholder is paid nothing for the claim because the debtor corporation's estate was insufficient to satisfy all its creditors.

[11] 306 U.S. 307 (1939).

C. Equitable Subordination

The doctrine of equitable subordination is distinct from the analysis followed in veil-piercing cases. In veil-piercing cases, there is an overall concern as to whether the controlling stockholder has respected the corporation as a distinct entity. In cases involving equitable subordination, the focus is whether the controlling stockholder has behaved unfairly to the detriment of the corporation's creditors or even other stockholders. In *Taylor*, the parent company's unfair behavior was failing to adequately capitalize the subsidiary, which operated on the precipice of bankruptcy, extracting above-market rates of interest on intercompany loans, and causing the subsidiary to pay dividends when it was short of cash. Section 510(c) of the Bankruptcy Code codifies the previous law by providing that the bankruptcy court "may . . . under principles of equitable subordination, subordinate . . . all or part of an allowed claim to all or part of another allowed claim."[12]

Courts express in various ways the grounds for subordinating the stockholder's loans. A most widely cited version is that set forth in *In re Mobile Steel Company*:[13]

(1) The claimant must have engaged in some type of inequitable conduct.
(2) The misconduct must have resulted in injury to the creditors of the bankrupt or conferred an unfair advantage on the claimant.
(3) Equitable subordination of the claim must not be inconsistent with the provisions of the Bankruptcy Act.[14]

While inadequate capitalization is frequently a factor raised in deciding to subordinate the controlling stockholder's loans,[15] it is by no means clear whether capital inadequacy alone is sufficient cause for subordination.[16] Other factors that lead to subordination include control of the subsidiary's dividend policy to bleed and innervate the corporation,[17] imposition on controlled corporation of excessive management or consulting fees,[18] intertwining of the parent's and subsidiary's affairs,[19] and intercompany transactions on terms unfavorable to the subsidiary.[20]

---

[12] 11 U.S.C. §510(c) (2000).

[13] 563 F.2d 692, 699-700 (5th Cir. 1977). Others are more succinct. *See, e.g.,* Wegner v. Grunewaldt, 821 F.2d 1317, 1323 (8th Cir. 1987).

[14] 563 F.2d 692, 700 (5th Cir. 1977) (citations omitted). *See also* In re Fabricators, Inc., 926 F.2d 1458 (5th Cir. 1991).

[15] *See* In re Fabricators, Inc., 926 F.2d 1458 (5th Cir. 1991); In re Loewer's Gambrinus Brewery Co., 167 F.2d 318, 320 (2d 1948) (unfair to allow one who has failed to provide adequate capital to have potential for large upside gain to then share proportionally with outside lenders who have bargained for lower return to be shared only by those having similar expectations) (Hand, J.).

[16] *See, e.g.,* In re Branding Iron Steak House, 536 F.2d 299 (9th Cir. 1976); In re Brunner Air Compressor Corp., 287 F. Supp. 256 (N.D.N.Y. 1982). For the argument that capital inadequacy alone should cause subordination, *see* Asa S. Herzog & Joel B. Zweibel, The Equitable Subordination of Claims in Bankruptcy, 15 Vand. L. Rev. 83, 93-94 (1961).

[17] In re Tri-State Bldg. Materials Co., 279 F. Supp. 1020 (D.S.D. 1968).

[18] In re American Apparel, Inc., 55 B.R. 160 (Bankr. E.D. Pa. 1985). This factor was also present in Taylor v. Standard Gas & Elec. Co., 306 U.S. 307, 316-320 (1939).

[19] Henry v. Dolley, 99 F.2d 94 (10th Cir. 1938).

[20] Bankers Life & Cas. Co. v. Kirtley, 338 F.2d 1006 (8th Cir. 1964) (parent purchased subsidiary's stock); In re Inland Gas Corp., 187 F.2d 813 (6th Cir. 1951) (purchase by subsidiary of its bonds from parent); In re Multiponics, Inc., 622 F.2d 709 (5th Cir. 1980).

CHAPTER 8

Powers of Officers and Agents; Criminal Liability of Corporations

A. CORPORATE OFFICERS

§8.01 A Summary of Rules Regarding the Agent's Authority

The officers of a corporation are in legal theory the agents of the corporation. The more important corporate officers are usually selected by the board of directors, and the actions of all corporate officers and agents are subject to the supervision and control of the board of directors.

The rules of agency law governing an agent's capacity or ability to bind a principal by contract, conveyance, or other act purportedly on the principal's behalf, as well as the agent's capacity to subject the principal to tort liability, are as applicable to corporate principals as to individual principals. Thus a corporation is bound by an agent's act if the agent has either authority or apparent authority to perform the act on the corporation's behalf.[1] Further, although language in many judicial decisions suggests that a principal is not bound by an agent's acts if the agent has neither actual authority nor apparent authority, the modern view is that a principal, including a corporate principal, may be bound in situations in which the agent has neither actual nor apparent authority if the agent possesses what is referred to as "inherent agency powers."[2] In addition, an individual or a corporate principal that ratifies a contract or transaction made for the principal by a person purporting to act on the principal's behalf usually becomes bound by the contract or transaction.[3] Finally, a corporate principal, just like an individual principal, even if not bound under agency rules, nevertheless "may be liable to a third person on account of a transaction with an agent, because of the principles of estoppel, restitution or negotiability."[4]

In the past the courts and writers have often used the terms "authority," "express authority," "implied authority," and "apparent authority" loosely and interchangeably and with varying meanings. The Restatement of Agency, however, carefully distinguished these terms,[5] and the Restatement distinctions are now generally accepted by the courts. According to the Restatement, an agent is "authorized" when the principal has manifested to the agent his or her consent for the agent to act on the principal's behalf. "Authority," according to the Restatement, "is the power of the agent to affect the legal relations of the principal by acts done in accordance with the principal's manifestations of consent to him,"[6] and "authority to do an act can be created by written or spoken words or other conduct of the principal which, reasonably interpreted, causes the agent to believe that the principal desires him so to act on the principal's account."[7]

To the extent that the principal specifies the agent's task, the agent can be said to have "express authority." Much authority, however, is created by implication; it is inferred from custom, the relations of the parties, or from general words of the principal to the agent such as "You are to be my sales manager," a statement that of course indicates that the agent is authorized to perform those acts which

§8.01   [1] Restatement (Second) of Agency §§140(a)-140(b), 144, 159 (1958).

[2] Restatement (Second) of Agency §§8A, 140(c), 161, 194 (1958); Warren Abner Seavey, Studies in Agency 181-202 (1949), reprinted from 1 Okla. L. Rev. 1 (1948). See also, e.g., Restatement (Second) of Agency §161, Comment b (1958).

[3] Restatement (Second) of Agency §143 (1958).

[4] Id. §141.

[5] Id. §7 (especially Comment c), §8. See, e.g., Scientific Holding Co. v. Plessy, Inc., 510 F.2d 15 (2d Cir. 1974) (lack of board approval precluded a finding of authority but corporation was bound by principles of estoppel).

[6] Restatement (Second) of Agency §7 (1958).

[7] Id. §26. Generally the authority of an officer or agent to bind his corporation is a question of fact to be determined by a jury. Czarneck v. Plastics Liquidating Co., 425 A.2d 1289 (Conn. 1979); Simon v. H. K. Porter Co., 180 A.2d 227, 229 (Pa. 1962); Daniel Boone Complex, Inc. v. Furst, 258 S.E.2d 379 (N.C. Ct. App. 1979); Aimonetto v. Rapid Gas, Inc., 126 N.W.2d 116 (S.D. 1964).

A. Corporate Officers

sales managers in that type of business customarily perform. An agent has implied authority to do whatever acts "are incidental to or are necessary, usual and proper to accomplish or perform" the task the principal has assigned to the agent.[8]

"Apparent authority," as distinguished from "implied authority," results from manifestations, not from the principal to the agent but from the principal to the third party, that the agent has authority to perform the act in question.[9] The difference between actual authority (express or implied) and apparent authority can be seen from the following triangle.

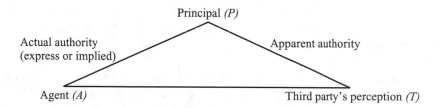

Principal *(P)*

Actual authority (express or implied)   Apparent authority

Agent *(A)*   Third party's perception *(T)*

Manifestations routed down the side of the triangle from *P* to *A* result in "authority." The agent is told by these manifestations what the principal consents to the agent doing on the principal's behalf. Often the manifestations from the principal to the agent do not spell out in so many words the acts that the agent is authorized to perform; the agent may not be given "express authority" to do a particular act, such as to employ ten workers to install specified machinery in a particular plant. The authority to do that act may have to be inferred or implied from either the title or position the principal has given to the agent or the nature and scope of the task the principal has assigned to the agent. The authority is then referred to as "implied authority." If the agent reasonably believes from the principal's manifestations, interpreted in the setting in which they were made, that the principal wants the agent to perform an act on the principal's behalf, the agent is authorized to perform that act and has the same power to affect the principal's legal relations by performing the act as an agent who has been given express authority to perform it.

On the other hand, "apparent authority"—sometimes labeled "ostensible authority"—results from manifestations such as those routed down the side of the triangle from *P* to *T.* By these manifestations the principal is telling another party what authority the agent has to act on behalf of the principal. These manifestations create an appearance of authority, which may or may not accurately reflect the authority actually given. Nevertheless, the agent with apparent authority has the power to bind the principal to the third party. A manifestation that creates apparent authority in an agent can be either a direct communication to a third party or a communication to the public in general, such as by advertisement.[10]

---

[8] Aimonetto v. Rapid Gas, Inc., 126 N.W.2d 116, 120 (S.D. 1964).

[9] Apparent authority is thus distinct from express or implied authority. Lee v. Jenkins Bros., 268 F.2d 357, 365 (2d Cir.), *cert. denied,* 361 U.S. 913 (1959); Restatement (Second) Agency §8 (1958).

[10] The principal's communications to a third party may or may not specify in so many words the act or acts that the agent is authorized to perform.

Apparent authority ordinarily cannot be created by the agent's own words or actions, such as by falsely representing to a third party that the agent is authorized.[11] The principal nevertheless can authorize the agent to state that the agent has authority (even though the principal may have expressly told the agent that he does not have authority and is not to do the act), and in such a case the agent's statement to a third party that he has authority will create an apparent authority, because the authorized statement by the agent on behalf of the principal is in law treated the same as a statement or manifestation by the principal to the third party.[12] Correlatively, an agent is not liable on a contract where the surrounding circumstances reasonably demonstrate the agent was acting in a purely representative capacity.[13] However, federal or state statute may, in appropriate instances, impose liability on anyone taking delivery of goods, even though that person clearly is acting in a representative capacity.[14]

A principal's acquiescence in an agent's performance of unauthorized acts may create authority in the agent insofar as the agent thereafter reasonably believes that the principal consents to performance of similar acts in the future. The principal's acquiescence may also create apparent authority in the agent, because a third party aware of the agent's performance of the acts may reasonably believe from the principal's manifestations (apparent acquiescence) that the agent is authorized to perform such acts on the principal's behalf.[15] This apparent authority may continue even though the principal later, but without the third party's knowledge, expressly orders the agent not to perform acts of that kind again. Furthermore, acquiescence by the principal may be held to constitute ratification of an unauthorized act. In this area the concept of apparent authority and the doctrine of estoppel tend to intertwine.[16]

§8.02   *Corporate Officers and Their Sources of Power*

The chief executive officer, president, vice president, treasurer, and secretary are the traditional officers of the corporation, and these are the officers that were most often mentioned in the corporation statutes.[1] The modern trend is not to be wed to specific statutory nomenclature.[2]

Although most officer functions have remained relatively constant over time, the roles, duties, and titles in corporate management are constantly changing. Many corporations, especially the large publicly held corporations, now have

---

[11] Restatement (Second) of Agency §168 (1958). *See, e.g.,* Har-Bel Coal Co. v. Asher Coal Mining Co., 414 S.W.2d 128, 130 (Ky. 1966).

[12] *Cf.* Restatement (Second) of Agency §169 (1958).

[13] *See* Curtis G. Testerman Co. v. Buck, 667 A.2d 649 (Md. Ct. App. 1995).

[14] *See, e.g.,* Wheaton Van Lines, Inc. v. Gahagan, 669 A.2d 745 (Me. 1996) (Interstate Commerce Act imposes liability on a person identified as consignee on bill of lading when goods are delivered to such person).

[15] *See* Foote & Davies, Inc. v. Arnold Craven, Inc., 324 S.E.2d 889 (N.C. 1985).

[16] Restatement (Second) of Agency §§82-104, 143 (1958).

§8.02   [1] *E.g.,* Former Model Bus. Corp. Act §50 (1969).

[2] *E.g.,* Model Business Corp. Act §8.40(a).

A. Corporate Officers

other executives and agents who are denominated "officers." For example, the title of "chief executive officer" ("CEO") was rarely used 50 years ago, and the title of "president" was reserved for the head corporate officer. Today, presidents are frequently subordinate to the CEO. Many of the older cases use "president" to describe today's CEO but what is said in those cases for the president applies with equal force to the CEO position. However, it must be borne in mind that when both positions exist within a single corporation, the CEO's power is superior and broader than that of the president. The president in such a situation is likely to be more of a chief operating officer ("COO"). In many respects, the COO resembles the position of general manager[3] that may exist in small business or within corporate divisions.

A large corporation may have a number of vice presidents, assistant vice presidents, assistant secretaries, assistant treasurers, and so on. A number of modern corporation statutes provide flexibility by permitting officer titles and duties to be stated in the bylaws or determined by the board of directors.[4] As the number of vice presidents in corporations has proliferated, super vice presidencies under such titles as "executive vice president" or "senior vice president" have been created in an effort to retain distinctive titles. Most large corporations have a "chairman of the board," and in fact in a considerable number of companies that is the title given the chief executive officer.

The source of the authority of an officer or agent to bind a corporation on a contract or to act for the corporation in a conveyance of property or other transaction is an action by the board of directors conferring on the officer the authority to act.[5] The board of directors of necessity is the authority because corporate statutes customarily state that "[a]ll corporate powers shall be exercised by or under the authority of, and the business and affairs of the corporation managed by or under the direction of, its board of directors."[6] As will be examined more closely later,[7] there are limits on delegations of the board's discretionary powers. For example, it is impermissible for the board of directors to grant carte blanche power to the president and secretary to sell all the company's real estate; such a grant is valid if limited to fixing the sales price but not to other matters, such as the timing and manner of payment.[8]

§8.03   Selection of Officers

The board of directors usually selects a corporation's principal officers. Applicable statutes, however, vary considerably. In some states the corporation statute

---

[3] *See* §8.10.

[4] *See, e.g.,* 805 ILCS 5/8.50 (Smith-Hurd 1993); Model Business Corp. Act §§8.40, 8.41.

[5] *See, e.g.,* Evanston Bank v. Conticommodity Services, Inc., 623 F. Supp. 1014, 1030 (N.D. Ill. 1985) ("To find that the bank authorized Thomas' acts, his authority must be legally traceable, directly or indirectly, to the bank's board of directors").

[6] Model Business Corp. Act §8.01(b).

[7] *See* §9.15.

[8] *See* Clarke Memorial College v. Monaghan Land Co., 257 A.2d 234 (Del. Ch. 1969).

expressly designates the board of directors as the body to elect or appoint officers.[1] In other states, the statutes are more flexible because they provide that the officers will be selected in the manner provided in the bylaws,[2] or that the officers shall be elected by the board unless the bylaws provide otherwise.[3]

Corporation statutes commonly state that the same person may hold more than one corporate office. The 1969 Model Business Corporation Act, for instance, provided that "any two or more offices may be held by the same person, except the offices of president and secretary."[4] The California and Delaware statutes state that any two offices may be held by the same person unless otherwise provided in the corporation's charter or bylaws.[5] The current version of the Model Act is similar.[6]

§8.04   Removal or Resignation of Officers or Agents

The board of directors can remove an officer, with or without cause, even though the corporation has entered into an employment contract and the term has not expired.[1] The corporation, however, may be liable to the officer for damages for breach of an employment contract if the officer is removed without cause before his contract term expires.[2] In many states the corporation statute provides that the board's power of removal does not destroy any rights the removed officer may have under an employment contract, shareholders agreement, or other contract.[3] In general, courts have not challenged the removal of officers by boards of directors unless the directors have clearly abused their discretion as to what is in the corporation's best interest.[4]

---

§8.03   [1] *E.g.,* Former Model Bus. Corp. Act §50 (1969) (president, vice president, secretary, and treasurer); Minn. Stat. Ann. §302A.311 (West 1985); Ohio Rev. Code Ann. §1701.64(A) (Anderson 2001).

[2] *E.g.,* Del. Code Ann. tit. 8, §142 (2001); 805 ILCS §5/8.50 (Smith-Hurd 1993) ("[officers] may be elected or appointed by the board of directors or chosen in such other manner as may be prescribed in the bylaws"). *See also* Model Bus. Corp. Act §8.40(b) (1984) ("[t]he board of directors may elect individuals to fill one or more offices of the corporation").

[3] *E.g.,* Cal. Corp. Code §312(b) (West 1999); Md. Code Ann., Corps. & Assns. §2-413 (1993); Mich. Comp. Laws §450.1531(1) (West 1990).

[4] Former Model Business Corp. Act §50 (1969). *Accord,* N.Y. Bus. Corp. Law §715(e) (McKinney Supp. 2002).

[5] Cal. Corp. Code Ann. §312 (West 1990); Del. Code Ann. tit. 8, §142(a) (2001).

[6] Model Business Corp. Act §8.40(d).

§8.04   [1] United Prod. & Consumers Coop. v. Held, 225 F.2d 615 (9th Cir. 1955) (bylaw stated officers hold office at pleasure of board).

[2] Despite a bylaw provision authorizing the board of directors to remove officers "at will" or "at pleasure," a corporation is liable for damages when its board removes an officer without cause before the expiration of the term fixed in an employment contract. United Prod. & Consumers Coop. v. Held, 225 F.2d 615 (9th Cir. 1955); Realty Acceptance Corp. v. Montgomery, 51 F.2d 636 (3d Cir. 1930); Hernandez v. Banco de las Americas, 570 P.2d 494 (Ariz. 1977).

[3] Statutes frequently clearly state that election or appointment of an officer does not itself create contract rights. *See, e.g.,* 805 ILCS 5/8.55 (Smith-Hurd 1993); N.Y. Bus. Corp. Law §716(b) (McKinney Supp. 2002); 15 Pa. Cons. Stat. Ann. §1733 (1995); Model Business Corp. Act §8.44(b) (1984).

[4] Franklin v. Texas Int'l Petroleum Corp., 324 F. Supp. 808 (W.D. La. 1971); Lager v. Su Su Fashions, Inc., 199 N.Y.S.2d 169 (App. Div. 1960); Ehrlich v. Alper, 145 N.Y.S.2d 252 (Sup. Ct. 1955), *aff'd mem.,* 149 N.Y.S.2d 562 (App. Div. 1956); Freeman v. King Pontiac Co., 114 S.E.2d 478 (S.C. 1960); Terry v. Zachary, 272 S.W.2d 157 (Tex. Civ. App. 1954).

B. AUTHORITY OF OFFICERS AND DIRECTORS

§8.05   The Chief Executive Officer's and President's Authority

For most of the history of American corporations, the corporation's chief executive officer was its president who simply carried the title of president. Over time corporations, especially publicly held corporations, changed the titles of their officers. The chief executive officer ("CEO") became the official title. Many CEOs have both titles of president and chief executive officer. Other companies have reserved the title of president for the general manager[1] or chief operating officer ("COO"). Smaller corporations are more likely to retain the traditional nomenclature of president.

Under the traditional governance norms a corporation's CEO or president may be given the authority by the corporation's charter, bylaws,[2] resolutions of the directors, or the board's acquiescence to make particular contracts, including the power to hire employees,[3] to borrow money,[4] or to execute conveyances and mortgages and do other acts. The CEO or president may be expressly given general authority to supervise and manage the business of the corporation, or a particular part of it. In such a case the president's authority extends impliedly to any contract or other act that is incident to the ordinary business of the corporation, or to that part with which he or she is entrusted; thus there is no need for special authority for the particular acts within the ordinary business of the corporation or that part of its operations to be expressly granted.[5] Furthermore, in the absence of express authority a corporation may be estopped to deny the authority of its president where it has created apparent authority in the president to make contracts or do other acts, as when a corporation allows its managing officers generally or habitually to make contracts or perform acts of that type.[6] The president's

---

§8.05   [1] *See* §8.10 for discussion of the authority of general managers.

[2] *See* Squaw Mountain Cattle Co. v. Bowen, 804 P.2d 1292, 1295 (Wyo. 1991). Ordinarily a corporation's charter does little or nothing toward defining the scope of the president's authority. *See* Note, 50 Yale L.J. 348 (1940).

The bylaws tend to be more specific. *Compare* 1A Fletcher, Corporation Forms Annotated §1204, art. IV, §5 (4th ed. 1993) (hereinafter Fletcher, Corporation Forms) (designed for the Model Act) *with id.* §1212.1, art. V, §3 (designed for Pennsylvania corporations).

[3] Diston v. EnviroPak Medical Products, 893 P.2d 1071 (Utah App. 1995) (president had apparent authority to hire employees); Lee v. Jenkins Bros., 268 F.2d 357, 365 (2d Cir.), *cert. denied*, 361 U.S. 913 (1959) (apparent authority of corporate president was question of fact).

[4] *Cf.* Schmidt v. Farm Credit Services, 977 F.2d 511 (10th Cir. 1992) (question of fact whether third party knew that corporate president was planning to personally appropriate funds rather than borrow them for his corporation's benefit).

[5] Meyer v. Glenmoor Homes, Inc., 54 Cal. Rptr. 786 (Ct. App. 1966), *reh'g denied*, 55 Cal. Rptr. 502 (Ct. App. 1966); Crumment v. Fresno Glazed Cement Pipe Co., 185 P. 388 (Cal. 1919); Missouri Valley Steel Co. v. New Amsterdam Casualty Co., 148 N.W.2d 126 (Minn. 1966); Federal Deposit Ins. Corp. v. Beakley Corp., 12 A.2d 700 (N.J. 1940); P. Curtis Ko Eune Co. v. Manayunk Yarn Mfg. Co., 103 A. 720 (Pa. 1918).

[6] Schmidt v. Farm Credit Servs., Inc., 977 F.2d 511 (10th Cir. 1992). Lettieri v. American Sav. Bank, 437 A.2d 822 (Conn. 1980); Joseph Greenspon's Sons Iron & Steel Co. v. Pecos Valley Gas Co., 156 A. 350 (Del. Super. Ct. 1931); Murphy v. W. H. & F. W. Cane, Inc., 822 A. 854 (N.J. 1912); Chambers

implied, apparent, or inherent authority is limited to carrying on the corporation's ordinary business and does not extend to extraordinary transactions.[7] In any particular case, the scope of the CEO's authority necessarily boils down to a question of fact.[8]

The decisions of the courts are in conflict regarding a corporate president's power, in the absence of any express or implied conferring of authority, to act on behalf of the corporation.[9] Even in the same jurisdiction courts have vacillated on this question.[10] The president of a corporation, as its executive head, is often expressly or impliedly given supervision and control of its business. In view of this general practice, some courts have adopted a doctrine of "inherent authority"—namely, that the president of a business corporation, solely by virtue of the office, may bind the corporation by contract and by other acts in the usual course of its business.[11] Other courts recognize a "presumptive authority," taking the position that contracts entered into or acts performed by the president of a corporation in the ordinary course of the corporation's business are presumed to be within his or her authority until the contrary is proven.[12] The presumption is limited, however, to acts in the ordinary course of business and does not extend to all matters that can be authorized by the board of directors.[13]

---

v. Lancaster, 54 N.E. 707 (N.Y. 1899); Oakes v. Cattaraugus Water Co., 38 N.E. 461 (N.Y. 1894); Templeton v. Nocona Hills Homeowners Ass'n, 555 S.W.2d 534 (Tex. Civ. App. 1977).

[7] *See, e.g.,* Bresnahan v. Lighthouse Mission, Inc., 496 S.E.2d 351 (Ga. App. 1998) (president's authority did not extend to sale of real estate that did not fall within purview of corporation's ordinary business).

[8] *See, e.g.,* Wojcik v. Lewis, 419 S.E.2d 135 (Ga. App. 1992) (issue of fact raised as to whether chairman of board was acting in personal rather than corporate capacity in granting an employment contract). *See also, e.g.,* Lee v. Jenkins Bros., 268 F.2d 357, 370 (2d Cir. 1959), *cert. denied,* 361 U.S. 913 (1959).

[9] Note, Inherent Power as a Basis of a Corporate Officer's Authority to Contract, 57 Colum. L. Rev. 868 (1957). *See generally* Annot., 96 A.L.R.2d 549 (1964); 65 A.L.R.2d 1321 (1959); 53 A.L.R.2d 1421 (1957); 10 A.L.R.2d 701 (1950); 5 A.L.R. 1485 (1920).

[10] *See generally* Note, 50 Yale L.J. 348 (1940).

[11] In re Lee Ready Mix & Supply Co., 437 F.2d 497 (6th Cir. 1971); DuSesoi v. United Refining Co., 540 F. Supp. 1260 (1982) ("Under both Texas and Pennsylvania law the President of a corporation has the authority to bind that corporation contractually").

But see Lee v. Jenkins Bros., 268 F.2d 357, 366 (2d Cir.), *cert. denied,* 361 U.S. 913 (1959) (liberally construing term "usual" so as to find president's granting of lifetime employment contracts within scope of power); Yucca Mining & Petroleum Co. v. Howard C. Phillips Oil Co., 365 P.2d 925, 929 (N.M. 1961) (The pace of modern business life was too swift to insist on the approval by the board of directors of every transaction that was in any way "unusual.").

The holdings on the subject of what are "ordinary" contracts and what are "extraordinary" contracts are highly inconsistent. The party asserting that a corporation's president has the power to execute a particular contract and bind the corporation has the burden of proving that the contract is "ordinary." Templeton v. Nocona Hills Owners Ass'n, 555 S.W.2d 534 (Tex. Civ. App. 1977).

[12] Adams v. Barron G. Collier, Inc., 73 F.2d 975 (8th Cir. 1934); (president has prima facie the power "to do any act which the directors could authorize or ratify").

[13] Southwest Forest Indus. v. Sharfstein, 483 F.2d 915 (9th Cir. 1972); Pettitt v. Doeskin Prods., Inc., 270 F.2d 95 (2d Cir. 1959), *cert. denied,* 362 U.S. 910 (1960); Schwartz v. United Merchants & Mfgrs. Inc., 72 F.2d 256 (2d Cir. 1934); Lieberman v. Princeway Realty Corp., 195 N.E.2d 57 (N.Y. 1963) (promise to pay bonus of $25,000 found to be so unusual as not to bind corporation).

See also, e.g., Management Technologies, Inc. v. Morris, 961 F. Supp. 640, 648 (S.D.N.Y. 1997) (it did not fall within ordinary business for chief executive officer of parent to institute insolvency proceedings of two subsidiaries; however "the law of agency teaches that corporate officers, acting in

B. Authority of Officers and Directors

According to a third group of courts,[14] the president's power to act for the corporation is limited to authority conferred by the corporation's charter or bylaws or by action of its board of directors. Nevertheless, even where the strict rule prevails, the president or other officer may of course be given authority to represent the corporation and to contract for it (1) by the corporation's articles or bylaws; (2) by a resolution of the board of directors; or (3) by acquiescence of the directors or shareholders in the known exercise or assumption of power.[15]

§8.06   *Authority of the Chairman of the Board*

Many corporations have an office titled "chairman of the board."[1] The functions of the chairman of the board vary widely from company to company. In some companies the chairman of the board has no other duty than presiding at meetings of the board, a responsibility that of course is not executive in nature. In other companies the chairman of the board provides advice and counsel to the president or the board of directors.[2] In still other companies the chairman is the chief executive officer or general manager, with vast responsibility and power.[3] Whenever a company's chief executive officer is titled "chairman of the board," the title of "president" is often conferred on the company's chief executive officer. The same person may be both chairman of the board and president. Such appointments create the apparent authority to bind the corporation on transactions within the ordinary course of its business.[4] The same authority applies to one appointed as a managing director.[5]

The title of chairman of the board and chief executive officer, when held by a single person, identifies the center of actual power within the organization. Recently there has been much discussion whether the governance of the public

---

good faith and with reasonable discretion, implicitly are empowered to protect the corporation where emergency or necessity requires action beyond their usual or regular authority").

[14] Buxton v. Diversified Resources Corp., 634 F.2d 1313 (10th Cir. 1980); *cert. denied,* 454 U.S. 821 (1981); Belcher v. Birmingham Trust Nat'l Bank, 348 F. Supp. 61, 122 (N.D. Ark. 1968); Black v. Harrison Home Co., 99 P. 494 (Cal. 1909).

[15] *See* Juergens v. Venture Capital Corp., 295 N.E.2d 398 (Mass. App. Ct. 1973) (finding a combination of apparent authority and ratification); People v. Jasman, 284 N.W.2d 496, 499 (Mich. App. Ct. 1979).

§8.06   [1] California law requires a corporation to have a chairman of the board or a president or both. Cal. Corp. Code §312(a) (West 1990). Some corporation statutes recognize that corporations may have an officer titled "chairman of the board" but do not require such an officer. *See, e.g.,* Mo. Ann. Stat. §351.360(3) (Vernon 2001).

[2] *See* Whitley v. Whitley Constr. Co., 175 S.E.2d 128 (Ga. 1970).

[3] *See* Cal. Corp. Code §312(a) (West 1990) ("The president, or if there is no president, the chairman of the board, is the general manager and chief executive officer of the corporation, unless otherwise provided in the articles or bylaws"); Mo. Ann. Stat. §351.360(3) (Vernon 2001) (chairman of the board may do any of the acts required or permitted to be done by president if designated chief executive officer by board or bylaws).

[4] *See, e.g.,* American Express Co. v. Lopez, 340 N.Y.S.2d 82, 84 (Civ. Ct. 1973); FDIC v. Texas Bank of Garland, 783 S.W.2d 604 (Tex. 1989).

[5] *See* Covington Hous. Dev. v. City of Covington, 381 F. Supp. 427 (E.D. Ky. 1974).

corporation would be improved by separating the two positions and assigning to an outside director the role of chairmanship of the board of directors so as to provide something of a counterweight to the inertial flow of power to the chief executive officer.

As many people dealing with a corporation are likely to consider a person with the title of "chairman of the board" to be a principal corporate officer, one of the corporation's "senior citizens" with authority to enter into important transactions, the courts should hold that a board chairman, even in the absence of an additional title such as "president" or "general manager," has by virtue of the position and title very broad power (whether classified as implied, inherent, or apparent authority) to act for the corporation.[6] The courts nevertheless are hesitant to accord autonomous power to the chairman of the board. Therefore, even though a corporation's bylaws provide that the president is to exercise general management responsibilities "subject to the direction of the chairman and the board," a court has held that the chairman lacked the authority to strip the president of his authority.[7] Such a result is consistent with the well-established principle that only as a deliberative body, not as individuals, does the board have corporate power.[8]

§8.07   The Vice President's Authority

A corporation's vice president is generally held to have no authority merely by virtue of the office to dispose of the corporation's property or to bind the corporation by notes or other contracts.[1] A vice president, however, is sometimes entrusted with management of the business or a particular part of it, and in such a case he or she may bind the corporation by a contract within the scope of express or apparent authority.[2]

Even the more liberal courts, however, have held that a vice president does not have power to act on behalf of the corporation in highly important and unusual transactions in the absence of specific authorization in the bylaws or a resolution of the board of directors.[3]

---

[6] See City Nat'l Bank v. Basic Food Indus., 520 F.2d 336 (5th Cir. 1975); American Express Co. v. Lopez, 340 N.Y.S.2d 82 (Civ. Ct. 1973).

[7] See Delaney v. Georgia-Pacific Corp., 564 P.2d 277, 288 (Or. 1977).

[8] See Star Corp. v. General Screw Prod. Co., 501 S.W.2d 374, 380 (Tex. Civ. App. 1973).

§8.07   [1] Royal Mfg. Co. v. Denard & Moore Constr. Co., 224 S.E.2d 770 (Ga. Ct. App. 1976); Interstate Nat'l Bank v. Koster, 282 P. 895, 812 (Kan. 1930).

[2] Townsend v. Daniel, Mann, Johnson & Mendenhall, 196 F.3d 1140 (10th Cir. 1999); Thomas Register of American Manufacturers, Inc. v. Proto Systems of Electronic Packaging, Inc., 471 S.E.2d 235 (Ga. App. 1996).

[3] Colish v. Brandywine Raceway Ass'n, 119 A.2d 887 (Del. 1955) (no implied authority to consummate such extraordinary transaction as employing architect to design new plant); Jennings v. Pittsburgh Mercantile Co., 202 A.2d 51 (Pa. 1964) (officer, who was both vice president and treasurer-comptroller, did not have apparent authority to accept offer of sale-and-leaseback of all corporation's real estate).

B. Authority of Officers and Directors

§8.08 The Secretary's Authority

The principal duties of a corporation's secretary are to make and keep the corporate records and to properly record votes, resolutions, and proceedings of the shareholders and directors as well as other matters that should be entered on corporate records.[1] The secretary's certification of a corporate resolution or the content of a corporate record is conclusive in favor of a person reasonably relying thereon.[2]

The secretary traditionally has been thought of as "merely a ministerial officer who keeps the books and minutes of the stockholders' and directors' meetings and has charge of the seal of the company."[3] Accordingly, the secretary has no authority merely by virtue of the office to make contracts on behalf of the corporation or to bind it by other acts.[4]

In a modern corporation, however, the secretary is generally more than a functionary with purely ministerial duties. The secretary is often a lawyer by profession and, not uncommonly, is also a director.

§8.09 The Treasurer's Authority; the Comptroller's Duties

The treasurer of a corporation is the proper officer to receive and keep the moneys of the corporation, and to disburse them as he or she may be authorized.[1] As is the case with the corporate secretary, the treasurer is frequently referred to as a "ministerial" position.[2] As a general rule, a corporation's treasurer has no implied authority, merely by virtue of the office, to bind the corporation by contracts or other acts made or done in its name, or to dispose of its assets except as authorized by the directors or other managing officers.[3]

Just like any other corporate officer, the treasurer may be entrusted with the general management of the corporation's business or a particular part of it; in such a case he or she has the same authority, in the absence of restrictions, as any other manager.[4] Even if the treasurer is not given broad general management

---

§8.08 [1] *See* Field v. Oberwortmann, 148 N.E.2d 600 (Ill. App. Ct. 1958), *cert. denied,* 358 U.S. 833 (1958).

[2] *See, e.g.,* McMan Oil & Gas Co. v. Hurley, 24 F.2d 776 (5th Cir. 1928).

[3] *See* Meyer v. Glenmoor Homes, Inc., 54 Cal. Rptr. 786, 801 (Cal. Ct. App. 1966), *reh'g denied,* 55 Cal. Rptr. 502 (Ct. App. 1966).

[4] Emmerglick v. Philip Wolf, Inc., 138 F.2d 661 (2d Cir. 1943) (secretary "is merely a ministerial officer" and therefore execution of affidavit by corporation's secretary cannot be deemed execution by corporation).

§8.09 [1] Clark v. Minage, 65 So. 832 (Ala. 1914); Blackwell v. Saddleback Lumber Co., 151 A. 534 (Me. 1930); Lydia E. Pinkham Medicine Co. v. Gove, 20 N.E.2d 482, 488 (Mass. 1939).

[2] *E.g.,* Ideal Foods, Inc. v. Action Leasing Corp., 413 So.2d 416 (Fla. Dist. Ct. App. 1982).

[3] Ideal Foods, Inc. v. Action Leasing Corp., 413 So.2d 416 (Fla. Dist. Ct. App. 1982) (no authority to bind corporation to third party unless expressly or impliedly authorized).

[4] Vaught v. Charleston Nat'l Bank, 62 F.2d 817 (10th Cir. 1933). *See also* Former Model Bus. Corp. Act §50 (1969); Model Bus. Corp. Act §8.41 (1984).

powers, the directors or corporate executive officers, by acquiescence in the treasurer's actions or by otherwise leading other persons reasonably to believe that he or she has authority to act for the corporation in particular kinds of transactions, may create an apparent authority to enter into such transactions on the corporation's behalf.[5]

The comptroller or, as this officer is sometimes called, the "controller," is the chief accounting officer.[6] The comptroller's duties are to keep, or cause to be kept, all the corporation's books of accounts and accounting records and to prepare, or have prepared, appropriate financial statements for submission to the board of directors, the board's executive committee, appropriate corporate officers, and the shareholders.[7]

§8.10 Ratification of Unauthorized Contracts or Transactions

A corporation can ratify a contract or other act of a corporate officer or agent that was unauthorized if the act is legal and the corporation has the legal capacity to perform it.[1] In general, whoever could have originally authorized a transaction on behalf of a corporation can ratify it. Thus, an unauthorized act of a corporate officer or agent can be ratified for the corporation by its board of directors, its shareholders, or one or more of its officers, depending on which of these has the power to authorize the kind of act in question.[2]

Ratification need not be by formal vote or even by parol assent; as in the case of ratification by a natural person, it may be implied from the acts of the shareholders or officers having authority to ratify, in accepting the benefits with knowledge of the facts or otherwise treating or recognizing the contract or act as binding. Under some circumstances ratification may be implied from a mere failure to repudiate or disaffirm.[3] Where the board of directors has the power to ratify, some courts say that knowledgeable acquiescence by the entire board is

---

[5] Kilpatrick Bros. v. International Bus. Mach. Corp., 464 F.2d 1080 (10th Cir. 1972); Blake v. Domestic Mfg. Co., 39 A. 241, 258 (N.J. Ch. 1897); Manheim Dairy Co. v. Little Falls Nat'l Bank, 54 N.Y.S.2d 345 (Sup. Ct. 1945); Kimball v. Kimball Bros., 56 N.E.2d 60 (Ohio 1944).

[6] Corporation statutes do not mention the comptroller. *See, e.g.*, Model Business Corp. Act §8.40; Former Model Business Corp. Act §50 (1969).

[7] *See* Jennings v. Ruidoso Racing Ass'n, 441 P.2d 42 (N.M. 1968); G. Kibby Munson, The Duties of the Controller as a Corporate Officer, 20 A.B.A.J. 57 (1934); Henry C. Knight, The Corporate Controller's Difficult Job, 153 J. Acct. 87-91 (1982).

§8.10 [1] Home Tel. Co. v. Darley, 355 F. Supp. 992, 1000 (N.D. Miss. 1973), *aff'd*, 489 F.2d 1403 (5th Cir. 1974).

[2] Lewis v. Dansker, 357 F. Supp. 636, 644 (S.D.N.Y. 1973) (shareholders may only ratify corporate agent's unauthorized actions if shareholders could have originally authorized such acts); Kaufman v. Henry, 520 S.W.2d 152, 155 (Mo. Ct. App. 1975) (a simple majority of shareholders cannot ratify what they could not have authorized in the first place).

[3] *See, e.g.*, 3 A's Towing Co. v. P & A Well Serv., Inc., 642 F.2d 756 (5th Cir. 1981).

necessary to constitute ratification, while other courts say knowledgeable acquiescence by a majority of the directors is sufficient.[4]

The party alleging ratification has the burden of proving it.[5] When ratification is established, it relates back to the time the unauthorized act occurred and is legally equivalent to original authority.[6]

§8.11   Constructive Knowledge of the Corporation

"A corporation cannot see or know anything except by the eyes or intelligence of its officers."[1] It is well settled that if an officer or agent of a corporation acquires or possesses knowledge in the course of her employment as to matters that are within the scope of her authority, this knowledge is imputed to the corporation.[2] Conversely, knowledge acquired by a corporate officer or agent in relation to a matter that is not within the scope of her authority is usually not imputed to the corporation.[3] If duties do not require transmittal of knowledge to other corporate representatives acting in transactions in which the agent is not involved, the corporation's rights and liabilities arising out of those transactions are not affected by the agent's knowledge.

Courts generally base the doctrine that a principal is chargeable with knowledge of facts known to an agent on the agent's duty to communicate his knowledge to the principal and the presumption that this duty has been performed; the presumption is usually treated as conclusive. According to many courts, such a presumption does not arise if the agent is acting out of self-interest or his interest is adverse to that of the principal. Therefore, whenever a director or other officer has an interest adverse to the corporation, his knowledge relevant to the transaction is generally not imputed to the corporation.[4]

---

[1] *Compare, e.g.*, Hurley v. Ornsteen, 42 N.E.2d 273 (Mass. 1942) (except in rare circumstances, knowledge and acquiescence by all the directors is necessary) *with* Mickshaw v. Coca Cola Bottling Co., 70 A.2d 467 (Pa. Super. Ct. 1950) (majority of directors is sufficient).

[5] Home Tel. Co. v. Darley, 355 F. Supp. 992, 1000-1001 (N.D. Miss. 1973), *aff'd*, 489 F.2d 1403 (5th Cir. 1947); Phoenix W. Holding Corp. v. Gleeson, 500 P.2d 320 (Ariz. Ct. App. 1972).

[6] 3 A's Towing Co. v. P & A Well Serv., Inc., 642 F.2d 756 (5th Cir. 1981); Michelson v. Duncan, 386 A.2d 1144, 1151 (Del. Ch. 1978); Frick v. Rockwell City Canning Co., 181 N.W. 475 (Iowa 1921).

§8.11   [1] Factor's & Traders' Ins. Co. v. Marine Dry Dock & Shipyard Co., 31 La. Ann. 149, 151 (1879).

[2] Volkswagen of Am., Inc. v. Robertson, 713 F.2d 1151, 1163 (5th Cir. 1983); In re Pubs, Inc., 618 F.2d 432, 438 (7th Cir. 1980).

[3] England v. American Southern Ins. Co., 380 F.2d 137, 140 (4th Cir. 1967) (notice to agent not ascribable to principal unless "'in regard to matter coming within the sphere of the agent's duty'").

[4] American Nat'l Bank v. Miller, 229 U.S. 517 (1913); First Nat'l Bank v. Transamerica Ins. Co., 514 F.2d 981, 986 (8th Cir. 1975); Dihlon v. Berg, 326 F. Supp. 1214, 1224 (D. Del. 1971), *aff'd*, 453 F.2d 876 (3d Cir. 1971).

§8.12 Formal Evidence of an Officer's Authority

In highly important matters, such as the execution of conveyances, mortgages, and long-term contracts, a person dealing with a corporation should insist on evidence of the agent's authority in the form of a certified copy under the corporate seal of a resolution of the board of directors.[1] A certified copy of a duly adopted bylaw is also satisfactory evidence of authority.

In the absence of a contrary charter or bylaw provision, the secretary is the custodian of the corporate seal,[2] and the proper person to affix the seal to an instrument is the secretary or assistant secretary.[3] The affixing of the corporate seal to an instrument is generally held to be prima facie evidence of the corporation's approval of the transaction and of the authority of the officer or officers who signed the instrument. The burden of showing lack of authority is then on the party attacking the instrument.[4]

C. CRIMINAL LIABILITY

§8.13 Criminal Liability of Corporations

The extent of corporate criminal liability has been in dispute since early days. It was formerly doubted whether a corporation could be prosecuted for any crime. The early cases declared that a corporation could not commit a crime for want of the requisite mens rea or intent,[1] but today "it is almost universally conceded that a corporation may be criminally liable for actions or omissions of its agents in its behalf." While a corporation cannot be imprisoned, it may be fined, and the fine may be enforced against its property, its charter may be forfeited because of its misuse or abuse, or other sanctions may be imposed as a condition of probation. One criticism is that these punishments are in reality inflicted on the shareholders for the acts of others out of corporate assets by the prosecution and fining of the corporation.

A large number of regulatory statutes—both federal and state—now expressly subject corporations to criminal liability for offenses defined in the statutes,[2] and corporations have often been convicted of violating this kind of reg-

---

§8.12 [1] Director action, both formal and informal, is discussed in §§9.05-9.06.

[2] Stovell v. Alert Gold Mining Co., 87 P. 1071 (Colo. 1906); New Jersey Bank v. Azco Realty Co., 372 A.2d 356, 359 (N.J. Super. Ct. 1977).

[3] Meyer v. Glenmoor Homes, Inc., 54 Cal. Rptr. 786 (Ct. App. 1966), *reh'g. denied*, 55 Cal. Rptr. 502 (Ct. App. 1966). For more detailed discussion of the corporate secretary's authority, *see supra* §8.09.

[4] Meyer v. Glenmoor Homes, Inc., 54 Cal. Rptr. 786, 792-793 (Ct. App. 1966), *reh'g denied*, 55 Cal. Rptr. 502 (Ct. App. 1966); Associates Discount Corp. v. Tobb Co., 50 Cal. Rptr. 738 (Ct. App. 1966).

§8.13 [1] 1 W. Blackstone, Commentaries 476. *See* Anonymous, 88 Eng. Rep. 1518 (K.B. 1701).

[2] *See, e.g.,* Federal Food, Drug and Cosmetic Act, 52 Stat. 1040, 21 U.S.C. 321(e) (1970); N.Y. Evntl. Conserv. Law §3302 (24) (Supp. 1976-77).

C. Criminal Liability

ulatory legislation. Instances include violation of a statute punishing usury,[3] violation of statute punishing contractors for exacting from laborers more than a stated maximum number of hours per day,[4] violation of a law regulating child labor,[5] violation of a labor-management relations act,[6] peddling by an agent without a license,[7] violation of the weights and measures law by giving short weight on a sale of ice,[8] violating a price regulation,[9] violation of the antitrust laws,[10] violation of federal campaign contribution statutes,[11] as well as violation of the securities laws.[12] There is a lively debate whether such regulatory matters are appropriate for, and effectively addressed within, the criminal arena rather than the procedurally more flexible civil prosecution.[13]

In some of the legislatively defined offenses the employer is subjected to criminal sanctions for acts of employees without regard to any fault or culpability on his part, even though he may have given his employees instructions to comply with the law.[14] By definition, mens rea on the part of the corporation or its agents is not an element of the offense proscribed by a strict liability statute. The criminal penalties often form an integral part of regulatory practice and may be based on pragmatic experience indicating their usefulness. In many cases, however, criminal penalties seem to have been added to legislation hastily and without adequate consideration of their necessity or usefulness.

§8.14   Criminal Liability of Officers and Directors

Corporate officers and directors are individually liable for the crimes they commit as well as the crimes the corporation commits in which it has participated and

---

[3] State v. Security Bank, 2 So. 2d 538, 51 N.W. 337 (1892).

[4] United States v. John Kelso Co., 86 F. 304 (N.D. Cal. 1898).

[5] People v. Sheffield Farms-Slawson-Decker Co., 225 N.Y. 25, 121 N.E. 474 (1918).

[6] Korholz v. United States, 269 F.2d 897 (10th Cir.), *cert. denied,* 361 U.S. 929 (1959) (the corporation, its president, and a union official were all convicted).

[7] Standard Oil Co. v. Commonwealth, 107 Ky. 606, 55 S.W. 8 (1900) (but defendant found not guilty); New Jersey Good Humor, Inc. v. Board of Comm'rs. 123 N.J.L. 21, 7 A.2d 824 (1939).

[8] State v. People's Ice Co., 124 Minn. 307, 144 N.W. 962 (1914).

[9] United States v. Armour & Co., 168 F.2d 342 (3d Cir. 1948); United States v. George F. Fish, Inc., 154 F.2d 798 (2d Cir. 1946), *cert. denied,* 328 U.S. 869 (1946). State v. Dried Milk Prods. Co-op., 16 Wis. 2d 357, 114 N.W.2d 412 (1962) (employer must at his peril *see* that statute is not violated by his employees).

[10] United States v. General Motors Corp., 121 F.2d 376, 411 (7th Cir.), *cert. denied,* 314 U.S. 619 (1941), noted in 40 Colum. L. Rev. 554 (1940); United States v. Arcos Corp., 234 F. Supp. 355 (N.D. Ohio 1964).

[11] 2 U.S.C. §441b (1982).

[12] *See* Matthews, Criminal Prosecutions Under The Federal Securities Laws and Related Statutes: The Nature and Development of SEC Criminal Cases, 39 Geo. Wash. L. Rev. 901 (1971).

[13] *See* V.S. Khanna, Corporate Criminal Liability: What Purpose Does It Serve?, 109 Harv. L. Rev. 1477 (1996).

[14] United States v. Hilton Hotels Corp., 467 F.2d 1000 (9th Cir. 1972), *cert. denied sub nom.* Western Int. Hotels v. United States, 409 U.S. 1125 (1973).

meets the requisite mens rea for the offense.[1] The individual does not have a defense that she committed the crime to further the corporation's interests.[2] Conscious avoidance can be the equivalent to the officer acting with knowledge.[3] Because mens rea has been a staple of English common law,[4] officers and directors in most instances are not vicariously responsible under the criminal law for the violations of their subordinates.[5] However, with the enactment of strict liability criminal provisions in public welfare and regulatory statutes, the traditional bases for criminalizing conduct shifted from punishment of misbehavior to protection of the public from harm. This shift in emphasis has given rise to the "responsible corporate officer" doctrine whereby a corporate official can be criminally responsible without proof of his knowledge of a violation. The doctrine, however, is limited to violation of certain "public welfare" or "regulatory" statutes encompassing a strict liability standard.

The responsible corporate officer doctrine traces its genesis to two Supreme Court decisions, the most significant being *United States v. Park*.[6] Park was president and CEO of a national food chain whose warehouse was found to have evidence of rodents. He was prosecuted under the Food, Drug and Cosmetic Act's provision that imposed strict liability for adulterated products. The Supreme Court affirmed a jury instruction that he violated the act if the jury found he "had a responsible relation" to the violation.[7]

The most important limitation on the scope of the responsible corporate officer doctrine is found in *Park*'s facts. A predicate to the Court's holding was its emphasis that the violation was of a "public welfare" statute.[8] Moreover, the offense was a misdemeanor punishable by a very small fine.[9] These factors should have a significant influence in restricting application of the doctrine beyond the

§8.14   [1] *See, e.g.,* United States v. Sherpix, Inc., 512 F.2d 1361 (D.C. Cir. 1975); State v. Santa Rosa Sales & Mktg., 475 N.W.2d 210 (Iowa 1991); Rosenzweig v. Morton, 737 A.2d 650 (N.H. 1999).

[2] *See, e.g.,* Pugh v. State, 536 So. 2d 99 (Ala. Crim. App. 1986); State v. Williams, 324 N.W.2d 154 (Minn. 1982); Bourgeois v. Commonwealth, 227 S.E.2d 714 (Va. 1976).

[3] *See, e.g.,* United States v. Gold, 743 F.2d 800 (11th Cir. 1984).

[4] For an elegant and thorough review of the history of mens rea, *see* United States v. Cordoba-Hincapie, 825 F. Supp. 485, 489-496 (E.D.N.Y. 1993) (J. Weinstein).

[5] 19 Am. Jur. 2d 1391.

[6] 421 U.S. 658 (1975). The other, United States v. Dotterweich, 320 U.S. 277 (1943), is less important because its actual holding was limited to whether individuals were included within the statutory proscription of "persons." Its contribution to the subject is that in reaching its conclusion that they are, the court held that defendants include those who had a "responsible share in the furtherance of the activity." *Id.* at 284.

[7] 421 U.S. at 666 n.9.

[8] In United States v. X-Citement Video, Inc., 513 U.S. 64 (1994), the Supreme Court held there is a presumption that Congress intended a scienter requirement, notwithstanding the public welfare qualities of the statute. But the case contained language supporting use of a "responsible corporate officer" approach in copyright infringement cases. *See* Gershwin Publ. Corp. v. Columbia Artists Mgmt., 443 F.2d 1159 (2nd Cir. 1971); Feder v. Videotrip Corp., 697 F. Supp. 1165 (D. Colo. 1988).

[9] The fine for each violation (there were five in *Park*) was $50. 421 U.S. at 666.

C. Criminal Liability

food, health, and safety area.[10] The doctrine has been invoked in tax matters[11] and has been followed in many state court decisions.[12]

In 2002, there was a flurry of criminal indictments in the wake of the Enron, Worldcom, and Tyco calamities. The specter of widespread corporate fraud led to the Sarbanes-Oxley Act of 2002,[13] which provided for enhanced criminal penalties for corporate officials of public companies who defraud their shareholders.[14]

---

[10] *See, e.g.,* U.S. v. MacDonald & Watson Waste Oil Co., 933 F.2d 35 (1st Cir. 1991) (responsible officer doctrine does not apply to felony prosecution involving specific intent).The environmental area is an area of intense efforts to apply the doctrine, with only limited success. *See* Cynthia H. Finn, Comment, The Responsible Corporate Officer, Criminal Liability, and Mens Rea: Limitations on the RCO Doctrine, 46 Am. U. L. Rev. 543, 562-569 (1996).

[11] *See* Purcell v. United States, 1 F.3d 932, 936 (9th Cir. 1993).

[12] *See* State v. Kailua Auto Wreckers, 615 P.2d 730 (Haw. 1980) (spouse who was figurehead president deemed a responsible party for environmental violations); State v. Standard Tank Cleansing Corp., 665 A.2d 753 (N.J. Super. Ct. App. Div. 1995); State v. Rollfink, 475 N.W.2d 575 (Wis. 1991). *Contra* T.V. Spano Bldg. Corp. v. Department of Natural Res. & Envtl. Control, 628 A.2d 53 (Del. 1993) (officer must be actively involved in wrongdoing); Longenecker v. Commonwealth, 596 A.2d 1261 (Pa. Cmwlth. 1991) (same).

[13] Pub. Law 107-204, (July 30, 2002).

[14] Id. tit. VIII, IX, §§801-807, 901-906. For discussion of the enhanced criminal penalties and the Act's requirement that the chief executive officer and chief financial officer personally certify the accuracy of the corporation's financial filings, *see* 2 Thomas Lee Hazen, Treatise on the Law of Securities Regulation §9.3[2] (2003 Pocket Part).

CHAPTER 9

Functions and Powers of Directors

A.   THE BOARD OF DIRECTORS

§9.01   The Traditional Pattern
of Corporate Governance

The traditional corporate pattern is triangular, with the shareholders at the base. The shareholders, who are generally viewed as the ultimate or residual owners of the business, select the personnel at the next level—namely, the board of directors.[1] According to accepted wisdom, the board of directors appoints the chief executive officer and other corporate officers, determines corporate policies, oversees the officers' work, and in general manages the corporation or supervises the management of its affairs. The directors' control of a corporation is limited by statutory requirements that shareholder approval be obtained for fundamental corporate acts such as charter amendments, consolidations, mergers, voluntary dissolution, and sale or lease of all or substantially all corporate assets.

The principal corporate officers, or executives, are at the top of the corporate triangle. These officers execute policies that supposedly have been fixed by the board of directors. The corporation's executives and operating management are said to derive their authority and legitimacy from the board.[2]

In legal theory, the directors are supreme during their term of office. Majority rule is the traditional governing principle, and the holders of a majority of the voting shares certainly has the ultimate power to control the corporation.[3] The holders of a majority of the voting shares elect the directors, or most of them.[4] In turn, the board of directors usually acts by majority vote of directors present and voting.

§9.02   Continuing Efforts to Strengthen the Monitoring
Role of the Board of Directors

How and why corporate governance has evolved for the public corporation in the United States is best illustrated by the contrasting approaches in two leading decisions in Delaware. In a 1963 decision, the Delaware Supreme Court in *Graham v. Allis-Chalmers Manufacturing Co.,*[1] dismissed a derivative action against the directors of a large publicly held corporation that sought to recover from the directors

---

§9.01   [1] This may be by a straight majority vote or under a system of cumulative voting for directors. *See* §§13.10, 13.14, 13.23.

[2] The powers of officers and agents are discussed in Chapter 8.

[3] In many publicly held corporations, however, shares are so widely distributed, perhaps with no person holding or controlling over a fraction of 1 percent of shares outstanding, that the shareholders cannot organize into effective political or decision-making units. The consequence is that real control is severed from ownership, and the chief executive officer or a group of the corporation's principal executives actually control the corporation.

[4] *See* MBCA §§7.21, 8.03 (1984); Former MBCA §§33, 36 (1969). *See also* §13.14.

§9.02   [1] 188 A.2d 125 (Del. 1963).

A. The Board of Directors

losses the corporation suffered as a consequence of illegal price fixing by subordinates in one of the numerous divisions within the highly decentralized management structure of the large public corporation. The plaintiff argued the directors were remiss in not installing surveillance and compliance programs that would have prevented the antitrust violation. The Court dismissed the action, reasoning:

> [T]he question of whether a corporate director has become liable for losses to the corporation through neglect is determined by the circumstances. If he has recklessly reposed confidence in an obviously untrustworthy employee, has refused or neglected cavalierly to perform his duty as a director, or has ignored either willfully or through inattention obvious danger signs of employee wrongdoing, the law will cast the burden of liability upon him. This is not the case at bar. . . .
>
> [A]bsent cause for suspicion there is no duty upon the directors to install and operate a coporate system of espionage to ferret out wrongdoing which they have no reason to suspect exists.[2]

Thirty-three years later, the highly respected Chancellor of the Delaware Court of Chancery opined:

> [I]t would, in my opinion, be a mistake to conclude that our Supreme Court's statement in *Graham* concerning "espionage" means that corporate boards may satisfy their obligation to be reasonably informed concerning the corporation, without assuring themselves that information and reporting systems exist in the organization that are reasonably designed to provide senior management and the board itself timely, accurate information sufficient to allow management and the board, each within its scope, to reach informed judgments concerning both the corporation's compliance with law and its business performance. . . .
>
> Thus, I am of the view that a director's obligation includes a duty to attempt in good faith to assure that a corporate information and reporting system, which the board concludes is adequate, exists, and that failure to do so under some circumstances may, in theory at least, render a director liable for losses caused by non-compliance with applicable legal standards.[3]

The contrasting approaches illustrate the movement from the view that the board of directors is a "super management" body that reviews and approves corporate strategies to today's widely held view that the board's essential function is to monitor the officer's stewardship. That movement did not occur without intense debate. It is a debate that continues to inform the expectations, and hence, demands placed upon the modern board of directors.

Thus the debate shifted from evidence of weaknesses in corporate governance to its cure. Former Supreme Court Justice Arthur J. Goldberg popularized

---

[2] *Id.* at 130.

[3] *In re* Carcmark International Inc. Derivative Litigation, 698 A.2d 959 (Del. Ch. 1996). The case involved a derivative suit seeking damages for the directors' failure to prevent subordinates from engaging in illegal referral payments to physicians. Before trial, the case was settled and Chancellor William T. Allen's opinion was in connection with his approval of the settlement.

a role for a body of "overseers" composed entirely of outside directors who, with the assistance of a staff of experts (auditors, lawyers, financiers, and scientific experts), would evaluate management performance and yield reports to the stockholders.[4] A prominent California lawyer, reflecting Justice Goldberg's view for an increased role for non-management directors, also called for "the increased focus on due diligence requirements for individual directors."[5] Professor Christopher Stone, using insights from organization behavior literature, suggested a number of structural changes within the corporate hierarchy, such as officers who would have responsibility and authority with respect to environmental and product safety.[6] Dean Bayless Manning called for improving the flow of information to the board and the stockholders so that management's performance and leadership could be objectively evaluated.[7] And, consumer gadfly Ralph Nader and others reasoned that large public corporations have too significant an impact upon the nation for their governance practices to be a matter solely of state law; they accordingly called for the federal chartering of the larger and more powerful corporations.[8] Even the SEC entered the debate with its own proposals for improving corporate governance.[9]

The most enduring criticism of the hundreds of commentators is that of Professor William Cary, who called for federally imposed "minimum standards" for conduct by public corporations.[10] Though the object of his criticism is the law and courts of Delaware, the fount of that criticism is the internal affairs doctrine, the most significant of all legal principles. The internal affairs doctrine is essentially a choice of law rule; it holds that questions regarding the relations among shareholders, directors, and officers are governed by the law of the state of incorporation.[11] The emphasis here on the state reflects not only the federal system of

---

[4] Arthur J. Goldberg, Debate on Outside Directors, N.Y. Times, Oct. 29, 1972, §3, at 1, col. 3. ("The board is relegated to an advisory and legitimizing function that is substantially different from the role of policy maker and guardian of shareholder and public interest contemplated by the law of corporations.").

[5] *See* Marshall L. Small, The Evolving Role of the Director in Corporate Governance, 30 Hastings L. J. 1353, 1355-1362 (1979). *See also* Thomas L. Hazen, Corporate Chartering and the Securities Markets: Shareholder Suffrage, Corporate Responsibility and Managerial Accountability, 1978 Wis. L. Rev. 391.

[6] *See* Christopher D. Stone, Where the Law Ends: The Social Control of Corporation Behavior (1975).

[7] Bayless Manning, Thinking Straight About Corporate Law Reform, 41 Law & Contemp. Prob. 3, 27-28 (Summer 1977).

[8] Ralph Nader, Mark Green & Joel Seligman, Taming the Giant Corporation (1976). *See also* Donald E. Schwartz, A Case for Federal Chartering of Corporations, 31 Bus. Law. 1125 (1976).

[9] *See* SEC Rule Proposals Concerning Shareholder Democracy and Corporate Governance, SEC Securities Exchange Act Rel. No. 34-14970 (July 18, 1978) in [1978 Transfer Binder] Fed. Sec. L. Rep. (CCH) ¶81,645. The proposals led to heightened disclosure regarding the structure, composition and function of the board of directors and committees of the board. *See* SEC Securities Exchange Act Rel. No. 34-15384 (Dec. 6, 1978) [1978 Transfer Binder] Fed. Sec. L. Rep. (CCH) ¶81,766.

[10] William L. Cary, Federalism and Corporate Law: Reflections Upon Delaware, 83 Yale L.J., 663 (1974).

[11] The internal affairs doctrine is not, however, without qualification. By statute, certain provisions of the corporate law of California and New York apply to certain corporations with a substantial presence in the host state, even though incorporated in another state. *See* Norwood P. Beveridge, Jr., The Internal Affairs Doctrine: The Proper Law of a Corporation, 44 Bus. Law. 693 (1989) (discussing few instances in which host states have applied their law rather than the state of incorporation). *See* §2.02.

A. The Board of Directors

government in the United States, but also the inertial forces of history whereby matters of corporate law have been a matter of state, not federal, law. And, unlike the continental "law of the seat" approach,[12] there is no requirement in the United States that incorporation be in a state where the company has its principal place of business or, for that matter, any business. Not only the state of incorporation is a matter of choice; to the extent that material differences exist in corporate governance procedures, there is also freedom to choose the level of rigor of applicable corporate governance rules.[13] And, it should be noted that the choice is one made by management.[14] Cary's article introduced into the debate on corporate governance the question whether the result of such choice was a "race to laxity," in which all states were competing for corporate charters by sacrificing protection of stockholders by amending their statutes to provide ever increasing levels of discretion to managers.

In the race for corporate charters, Delaware remains supreme. Over forty percent of the corporations listed on the New York Stock Exchange are incorporated in Delaware. Delaware's supremacy is easily understood. Indeed, it enjoys an unerodible advantage over other states.[15] First, it has the largest body of precedent interpreting a corporate statute. To the extent businesspeople like certainty, Delaware provides it. Though its present code bears the date of its enactment in 1967, it carried forward significant portions of the earlier law so that pre-1967 decisions continue to illuminate the Delaware statute. Second, Delaware's corporate law cannot be easily amended because the state constitution conditions any change in the corporate law upon a two-thirds vote of the legislature.[16] This stability of the legal landscape provides further certainty. Third, Delaware populates its judiciary with those experienced in the trenches of practicing corporate law. Though they have not themselves been captains of industry, members of the Supreme Court and the Court of Chancery have counseled many who were. Fourth, Delaware's Court of Chancery is not only experienced in handling numerous corporate matters, but its procedures facilitate the litigants' securing a hearing and resolution in the most time-bounded disputes, especially issues that arise in the context of takeovers. And finally, though perhaps not uniformly the most

---

[12] *See* Sørensen, Karsten Engsig, "Prospect for European Company Law After the Judgment of the European Court of Justice in *Centros Ltd.*," in Dashwood, Alan and Ward, Agegla (eds.), The Cambridge Yearbook of European Legal Studies 203 (1999).

[13] For a market-oriented argument in favor of such choice, *see, e.g.,* Roberto Romano, The State Competition Debate in Corporate Law, 8 Cardozo L. Rev. 709 (1987); Ralph Winter, State Law, Shareholder Protection and the Theory of the Corporation, 6 J. Legal Stud. 251 (1977). For a review of the empirical studies of the relative wealth effects of the corporate law that applies to a entity, *see* Elliott Weiss & Lawrence J. White, Of Econometrics and Indeterminancy: A Study of Investors' Reactions to "Changes" in Corporate Law, 75 Cal. L. Rev. 551 (1987).

[14] To be sure, when an existing corporation reincorporates in another state the procedure customarily involves a merger of the existing company with one formed under the new domicile's laws; this transaction requires a vote of the stockholders. However, there is no evidence of successful resistance to management's recommendation that the company reincorporate.

[15] *See generally* Douglas Branson, Indeterminancy: The Final Ingredient in an Interest Group Analysis of a Corporate Law, 43 Vand. L. Rev. 85 (1990); Jonathan Macey and Geoffrey Miller, Toward an Interest-Group Theory of Delaware Corporate Law, 65 Tex. L. Rev. 469 (1987).

[16] Del. Const., Art. IX, §1.

permissive and broadly enabling of all corporate statutes, any differences from the statutes of states are at the margins.[17] Overall, Delaware's success in attracting corporate charters is most understandable.

Through out all the commentary in the 1970s there was the theme that the board of directors needed to be more independent of management. The crispest insights into this call were provided by Professor Mel Eisenberg and were ultimately memorialized into an influential book.[18] He wisely advised that the issue was not just that of independence, although independence is a necessary condition. The issue ultimately was melding the outside director to a task that she or he is capable of discharging. Even when outside directors constitute a majority of the board of directors, they face important constraints on time, information, and staff to permit them to perform as super policymakers or managers. Professor Eisenberg suggests that the appropriate aspiration for outside directors be changed to that of evaluating management's stewardship, removing poorly performing managers, and developing and enacting succession plans.[19]

As the above quote from *Caremark* indicates, the rest is history.[20] Between the 1960s to the mid 1980s a tremendous change in the composition of the American boardroom occurred. Where in 1960 approximately 63 percent of the corporations could report that a majority of their directors were outsiders, by 1989 the percentage had climbed to 86 percent.[21] More generally, the trend that began three decades ago has resulted in (1) boards of directors of publicly held corporations having a higher percentage of independent outside directors; (2) independent outside directors now serve on key committees and on some committees, for example audit and compensation committees, are a majority; (3) director fees have generally increased over time; (4) outside directors are devoting more time to corporate affairs; (5) there is evidence that outside directors are developing greater expertise in the work of the committees on which they serve; and (6) independent outside directors are more engaged in determining policy and monitoring the performance of executives.[22]

[17] *See* William J. Carney, The Production of Corporate Law, 71 So. Cal. L. Rev. 715 (1998).

[18] *See* Melvin A. Eisenberg, The Structure of the Corporation: A Legal Analysis (1976). The points on this issue are more fully developed in Melvin A. Eisenberg, Legal Models of Management Structure in the Modern Corporation: Officers, Directors, and Accountants, 63 Cal. L. Rev. 375 (1975).

[19] Eisenberg, *supra* note 18, at 159-168.

[20] Even some conservative, board-oriented organizations encourage corporations to enlarge the number of outside directors on the board of public companies and to give such directors a more prominent role. *See, e.g.,* The Role and Composition of the Board of Directors of the Large Publicly Owned Corporation: Statement of the Business Roundtable, reprinted in 33 Bus. Law. 2083, 2092-2112 (1978); Corporate Director's Guidebook, prepared by the Committee on Corporate Laws, Section of Business Law, American Bar Assoc. as published in 56 Bus. Law. 1571 (2001).

[21] *See* Jeremy Bacon, Membership and Organization of Corporate Boards, tbl. 6 at 8 (N.Y. Conf. Bd. 1990).

[22] *See, e.g.,* Myles M. Mace, 54 Harv. Bus. Rev. 40, 46 (Sep.-Oct. 1976); Lorsch, Jay W., and Elizabeth MacIver, Pawns or Potentate: The Reality of America's Corporate Boards, (1989). This said, there remains the question of just how frequently the outside directors will rebuff opportunistic overreaching by managers or whether they will act to replace underperforming managers as quickly as they should. For the view that the independence of outside directors is likely overstated, *see* Victor Brudney, The Independent Director—Heavenly City or Potemkin Village?, 73 Cal. L. Rev. 1671 (1982).

A. The Board of Directors

Through most of the 1980s, the major forum, and even focal point, of debate on corporate governance was not the epic tales that were to be told in the heyday of takeover contests, but rather the American Law Institute's Corporate Governance Project. Historically, the ALI produced thoughtful restatements of the law whose black letter law and supporting commentary nurtured efforts for greater uniformity among the states, frequently recognizing that the better approaches were not those followed by a minority of the states. The project's reporters, led by Professor Mel Eisenberg, professed (1) to restate the law where judicial authority was deemed satisfactory under modern standards and (2) proffer recommendations where no judicial authority existed or where judicial decisions were unsatisfactory by modern standards.[23] This said, the project's critics believed there was too much reform, certainly in the early drafts of the Corporate Governance Project, so that throughout the project was never seen as the more traditional restatement of the law. This caused it to become the most controversial of all ALI projects and, equally visible, to drop any reference to "restatement" from its title.[24] But the primary theme that public corporations[25] are to have independent directors who are to adhere to an active, monitoring model survived the more than decade long assaults on the project.[26] The membership of the American Law Institute approved the final draft in May 1992.

The overarching principle of the ALI is its recognition of the board of directors as a corporate organ that can and should perform a monitoring function, and among other things, to address potential overreaching by management, to replace management if it is not meeting established corporate goals, and to prevent the commission of illegal acts.[27] Significantly, the ALI Project, in addition to calling for an independent audit committee, recommends that large public corporations also have nominating and compensation committees. The project also strengthens the role that independent directors are to play in policing conflicts of interest, usurpation of corporate opportunities, and the conduct of derivative suits.

---

[23] See James S. Mofsky & Robert D. Rubin, Introduction: A Symposium on the ALI Corporate Governance Project, 37 U. Miami L. Rev. 169, 170 (1983).

[24] The project's first formal name was Principles of Corporate Governance and Structure: Restatement and Recommendations (Tent. Draft No. 1 1982), but as finally approved dropped reference to "restatement" to become Principles of Corporate Governance: Analysis and Recommendations (1992) [hereinafter A.L.I. Project].

[25] The project calls for large public corporations to have an audit commitee composed of at least three outside directors. See A.L.I. Project §3.05. However, an independent board for such corporations is not mandated, but merely recommended "as a matter of corporate practice." See id. at §3A.01. A "large public corporation" is defined as one with 2000 or more record shareholders with assets of $100 million or more. See id. at §1.24.

[26] It should be noted that by the time first drafts of the Corporate Governance Project were being circulated that, at least on paper, the vast majority of large American public corporations had significant outside director representation on their boards and there was evidence to believe they discharged the functions ultimately called for by section 3.02 of the project. See [1981-82 Transfer Binder] Fed. Sec. L. Rep. (CCH) ¶24,119 (Feb. 5, 1981). See also Ira S. Levine, Comment, The Proposed Restatement of Corporate Governance: Is Reform Really Necessary?, 11 Pepperdine L. Rev. 499, 517 (1983-84).

[27] A.L.I. Project, supra note 24, §3.02.

Among the most recent trends among American boardrooms is the movement toward encouraging, and in some instances requiring, the outside director to have a substantial equity position in the corporation on whose board the director serves. The call is to reduce the customary perquisites enjoyed by the outside director, and particularly providing health and retirement benefits and providing for the director to devote some of his director's fees to the purchase of shares in the company. The obvious objective is to more closely align the outside director with the firm's owners.[28] Another trend has been reexamining certain matters bearing directly on the commitment of outside directors to monitor management as well as internal procedures that nurture a viable monitoring role. In 1996 a Blue Ribbon Commission suggested a number of practices for public corporations that would enhance the effectiveness of their outside directors.[29] Among the Commission's recommendations were the call that directors not serve on more than six boards, that there be procedures for independent review of the CEO's and directors' effectiveness, that there be created a board governance committee, an outside director be designated to chair the board, and that there be periodic executive sessions for outside directors.

There is a good deal of intuitive appeal to firming up the bonds between the outside directors and the shareholders. Pursuing strategies to this end is likely to be the area of great attention in the next few years. Several considerations point toward this being a politically viable option. As we are well aware, approximately one-half of all equity investments are held by financial institutions, the most significant group being public and private pension plans.[30] With such institutionalization of ownership, the refrain of Berle and Means[31] that the seriousness of the problem posed by the separation of ownership from management is exacerbated by owners being both numerous and that their holdings are relatively small is only partially true. And, more is involved than simply the institutionalization of share holdings. Because a significant percentage of such institutional holdings are indexed, their holders effectively cannot exit from underperforming or overreaching managers by disposing their shares. Thus, in theory, a significant portion of publicly traded shares are held by investors who not only are sophisticated (or are advised by those that are), but also, by reason of the absolute size of their holdings and the absence in many instances of the possibility of exit, have financial

---

[28] See Report of the National Association of Corporate Directors Blue Ribbon Commission on Director Compensation 12 (1995). Charles M. Elson, Director Compensation and the Management-Captured Board—The History of a Symptom and a Cure, 50 SMU L. Rev. 127 (1996) (setting forth the reasons equity-based compensation for directors best aligns the interests of outside directors with that of the firm's owners). For a review of empirical evidence that outside directors discharge their functions better if they have a substantial equity interest in the firm, see Charles M. Elson, The Duty of Care, Compensation, and Stock Ownership, 62 U. Cin. L. Rev. 649, 684 (1995). See also Sanja Bhagat et al., Director Ownership, Corporate Performance, and Management Turnover, 54 Bus. Law. 885, 909 (1999) (finding direct relationship between likelihood of management being replaced and dollar value of director's holding in the firm when there has been poor financial performance).

[29] See Report of the NACD Blue Ribbon Commission on Director Professionalism (1996).

[30] See NYSE Fact Book for the Year 2000, 61 (50.8% of equity shares are held by financial institutions at the end of the third quarter of 2000).

[31] The reference is to the classic work, Adolf A. Berle & Gardiner C. Means, The Modern Corporation and Private Property (1933).

A. The Board of Directors

incentives that are best served by their portfolio companies' managers performing well.[32] So viewed, there will likely be on-going discussions of mechanisms that can be used to assure representation of some institutional holders on the board of public companies.[33] One ingenious, but effective suggestion is to restore the prominent role that cumulative voting once had with the American *public* corporation. In a careful study of the cumulative voting, Professor Jeff Gordon finds that the number of states mandating cumulative voting peaked in 1956, but fell into disuse because of the fear that it encouraged proxy contests and would facilitate hostile takeovers.[34] He envisons restoring cumulative voting to the public corporation as a means for institutional holders to secure a voice on the board.[35]

Prior to 1992, the SEC's regulations for proxies stilled the voice of financial institutions.[36] By broadly defining proxies to include any communication that would encourage or discourage a holder in how to vote, and subjecting each such solicitation to nontrivial regulation, institutions faced excessive coordination costs with respect to not only pursuing common objectives, but also simply learning whether they indeed had common objectives or concerns with respect to their portfolio companies. Important steps were taken in 1992 by the SEC to facilitate the institutions in exercising their collective voice within the boardroom.[37] The SEC amended its rules with the overall effect of reducing the restrictions on stockholder communication among themselves. For example, new Rule 14a-2(b)(1) exempts from the filing and format requirements communications by a person who is not seeking proxies and does not have certain specified types of "substantial interest" in the subject matter.[38] Further, new Rule 14a-1(l)(2)(iv) permits

[32] *See generally* Albert Hirshman, Exit, Voice, and Loyalty (1970) (when exit costs are significant, a rational actor will seek to address the cause for exit by involving himself more in the organization's decision making).

[33] For a proposal in this regard, see Ronald J. Gilson & Reinier Kraakman, Reinventing the Outside Director: An Agenda for Institutional Investors, 43 Stan. L. Rev. 863 (1991). *See also* Ed Rock, The Logic and (Uncertain) Significance of Institutional Shareholder Activism, 79 Geo. L. Rev. 445 (1991) (questioning cause for optimism that institutions will be effective check on management in light that many shareholder proposals regarding removal of antitakeover provisions fail to secure a majority vote while management antitakeover proposals are supported by the stockholders).

[34] *See* Jeffrey N. Gordon, Institutions as Relational Investors: A New Look at Cumulative Voting, 94 Colum. L. Rev. 124 (1994).

[35] This is not to suggest that financial institutions are monolithic. Certainly wide variance exist in the culture among types of institutions. *See* O'Barr, Wm. M. & Conley, John M., Fortune and Folly: The Wealth and Power of Institutional Investing (1992). Private pension funds or common trusts of banks, due to their conflicts of interest, are not as likely to seek a position on their portfolio company's board as would a public pension fund. *See* John C. Coffee, Jr., The SEC and the Institutional Investor: A Half-Time Report, 15 Cardozo L. Rev. 837, 864 (1994) ("proxy activism that could produce gains to the pension fund's beneficiaries may yet result in a net loss to the fund manager"); Melvin Aron Eisenberg, Corporations 158-161 (8th ed. 2000).

[36] *See* Bernard Black, Shareholder Passivity Reexamined, 89 Mich. L. Rev. 520 (1990).

[37] *See* Securities Exchange Act Release No. 34-31326 (Oct. 16, 1992).

[38] This provision is not available, for example, to officers, directors, director nominees, or a person who has in its Williams Act filing disclosed an intent to control the issuer. A holder of more than $5 million of the company's shares must nevertheless file the communication with the SEC within three days of its circulation.

holders to announce how they will vote on any matter. Under these rules, holders, and particularly financial institutions, can more easily coordinate their actions to maximize their influence at stockholders meetings because they no longer face costly and burdensome prefiling and format requirements.[39]

In the wake of growing concern about the prevalence of "earnings management," restatements of reported income, and massive accounting frauds by public companies, then Chairman of the SEC, Arthur Levitt, in 1998 called for "nothing less than a fundamental cultural change on the part of corporate management as well as the whole financial community."[40] Front and center in this reform initiative were changes that the SEC, with the aid of a Blue Ribbon Committee, brought about for audit committees of corporations listed on the NYSE, AMEX, and Nasdaq. Informing the thrust of the changes for the audit committee was a 1999 study of companies charged by the SEC with financial fraud from 1987 to 1997, which found, among other factors, that 25 percent of the surveyed companies did not have an audit committee, that of those that did have audit committees nearly one-third of the committee members' independence was compromised by close relationship with, or actual participation in, the firm's management, and that 65 percent of the committee members lacked accounting or financial expertise.[41] Though some of the recommendations of the Blue Ribbon Committee[42] were ultimately modified, most of its proposals were embraced by the financial community and are now part of the listing requirements of the the the NYSE, AMEX, and Nasdaq.[43]

The core conisderations of each organization's listing requirements pertaining to audit committees are substantially identical: listed firms are to have an audit committee of three "independent" directors; independence requires, among other features, that the member have not been an employee within three years or received (excluding board fees) compensation greater than $60,000 (the NYSE expresses this more generally in terms of a relationship that will impede independence); each member must be financially literate; one member must have financial sophistication, such as employment experience in finance or accounting; and the committee must have a written charter.[44]

---

[39] However, their communication remains a "proxy solicitation" that is subject to Rule 14a-9's prohibition against material omissions or misstatements in a proxy solicitation.

[40] Arthur Levitt, Chairman, SEC, Address to the NYU Center for Law and Business (Sept. 28, 1998), quoted in Edward Brodsky, New Rules for Audit Committees and Quarterly Statements, 223 NYLJ 3 (Apr. 12, 2000).

[41] See Mark S. Beasley et al., Fraudulent Financial Reporting 1987-97, An Analysis of U.S. Companies (COSO 1999).

[42] See Report and Recommendations of the Blue Ribbon Committee on Improving the Effectiveness of Corporate Audit Committees, reprinted in 54 Bus. Law. 1067 (1999).

[43] The SEC's actions occurred on two fronts. First, it approved amendments to the listing requirements adopted by the NYSE, AMEX and Nasdaq to embrace the reforms for audit committees. See SEC Release No. 34-42231 (Dec. 1, 1999). Second, it amended its own disclosure requirements for Regulation S-K. See SEC Release No. 34-422266 (Dec. 14, 1999).

[44] The charter must, among other matters, specify the scope of the committee's responsibilities, the outside auditor's responsibilities to the board and the audit committee, and the audit committee's responsibility in the selection and oversight of the auditor.

A. The Board of Directors

The SEC's disclosure requirements reinforced the listing requirements for audit committees. The audit committee must disclose whether it has recommended to the board that the audited financial statements be included in the company's annual report on Form 10-K or 10-KSB (for qualified small business issuers).[45] Moreover, the audit committee must acknowledge whether it has had discussions with management and the independent accountants, and whether those discussions were the basis for its recommendations regarding the inclusion of the financial reports.[46] The significance of this is it draws the audit committee members closer to the information contained in any included financial report, thus making it easier to establish they are primary participants with respect to any misrepresentation that may be committed in the financial statements. This may not be that significant a development since all directors must sign the Form 10-Q that is filed with the SEC and at least one circuit has held this is sufficient to make each director a primary participant in any resulting suit under the antifraud provision.[47] A further disclosure requirement is that each proxy statement must disclose whether the company has an audit committee, and once every three years the proxy statement must disclose the responsibilities and duties of the audit committee as embodied in its charter.[48]

The most recent developments for corporate governance began with the collapse in the fall of 2001 of Enron Corporation, a company that was the sixth largest American corporation and which had been ranked the most innovative for five straight years by Fortune 500 executives. Within a few weeks its stock plummeted from a trading in the high $40's to being nearly worthless when it filed for bankruptcy in early November 2001. Enron's final achievement was its becoming the largest bankruptcy every filed; an honor it held only briefly, being dwarfed by the bankruptcy of WorldCom in 2002, another failure that was linked to serious financial fraud by senior executives.[49] Enron, WorldCom, and no fewer than a dozen other large public companies shocked the public conscience, not because they failed, but because of the revelations of extensive reporting frauds, overreaching, and wasteful misbehavior by their most senior executives. Certainly there were multiple failures in the role of each company's outside directors, their certified public accountants, and others. The collapse of Enron et al. came when

---

[45] *See* Item 306(a)(4) of Regulation S-K, 17 C.F.R. §228.306(a)(4) (2001).

[46] *Id.* This acknowledgment and recommendation are to include the printed names of each member of the audit committee.

[47] *See* Howard v. Everex Sys. Inc., 228 F.3d 1057 (9th Cir. 2000). There continues to be the substantial requirement that the director's commission of the misrepresentation was with scienter. Ernst & Ernst v. Hochfelder, 425 U.S. 185 (1976). Of importance here is that the disclosures are not treated as part of the proxy statement and, therefore, escape the more plaintiff-friendly liability standards for misrepresentations for actions under Section 14(a) and Rule 14a-9 or section 18 of the Exchange Act. *See* Rule 14a-101(e)(v), 17 C.F.R. §240.14a-101(e)(v) (2002).

[48] *See* Regulation Rule 14a-101(e)(ii) & (iii), 17 C.F.R. §240.14a-101(e)(ii) & (iii) (2002).

[49] For discussions of Enron and the causes of its collapse, *see, e.g.,* William Bratton, Enron and the Dark Side of Shareholder Value, 76 Tulane L. Rev. 1275 (2002); John C. Coffee, Jr., Understanding Enron: "It's About Gatekeepers, Stupid," 57 Bus. Law. 1403 (2002); Jeffrey N. Gordon, What Enron Means for the Management and Control of Modern Business Corporations: Some Initial Reactions, 69 U. Chi. L. Rev. 1233 (2002).

investors were witnessing a meltdown in market capitalization on Wall Street of approximately 4 trillion dollars. The national mood was not to turn a blind eye to the problems of the American corporation.

The first wave of regulatory responses came from the New York Stock Exchange and Nasdaq, both of which strengthened their corporate governance requirements for listed companies by mandating at least a majority of the board be independent (this requirement does not apply to so-called controlled companies where there is a definite controlling stockholder). Not surprisingly, a central focus of their efforts was the audit committee. Both bodies require listed companies to have a majority of their board of directors to meet the new tightened standard for independence and that the audit committee must be comprised solely of independent directors. The nominating and compensation committees of NYSE listed companies must also be comprised only of independent directors. Nasdaq instead permits nominating committees to have one non-independent member (if disclosed) or nominations can instead be approved by a majority of the independent directors. The NYSE's new requirements provides that the board is to determine whether a director has a "material relationship" that would prevent a director from being independent; the NYSE does not further define specifically what such a relationship would be but asks that the board consider "all relevant facts and circumstances."[50] Nasdaq specifies that a director would not be independent if he or she, or a family member, received payments in excess of $60,000. Both the NYSE and Nasdaq further require that all non-management directors meet regularly in executive sessions. And, subject to certain limitations, shareholders must be allowed to vote on all equity-based compensation plans. Finally, the NYSE mandates that companies adopt corporate governance guidelines, and both the NYSE and Nasdaq require codes of conduct with prompt publication of any waiver of their requirements for senior executive officers. The NYSE requires the CEO to annually certify to the Exchange that the company complies with the governance provisions for listing. Nasdaq enters the field of conflict of interest transactions by requiring the audit committee to approve all related party transactions.

Congress too entered the fray, passing in July 2002 the far-reaching Sarbanes-Oxley Act that, among other features, amended the Securities Act of 1933 and the Securities Exchange Act of 1934. In response to the common practice of auditors to provide substantial non-audit services to their audit clients, Section 10A of the Exchange Act was amended to bar auditors from providing certain non-audit services.[51] The amendments also seek to centralize the company-auditor relationship with the audit committee by requiring that all services provided by the auditor be approved by the audit committee, subject to a 5 percent de minimus exemption.[52] And, the auditor is required to make timely reports to the audit committee of all critical accounting policies, alternative treatments that have been discussed, and

---

[50] The NYSE does provide for a five-year cooling off period and Nasdaq has a three-year period in the case of former employees before they can be deemed independent.

[51] 15 U.S.C. §78j-1 (g).

[52] 15 U.S.C. §78j-1(i).

A. The Board of Directors

other material communications with managment.[53] Issuers must disclose whether its audit committee has a "financial expert," thus putting pressure on companies to assure that at least one member of the audit committee meets this indirect requirement. Finally, audit partners are to rotate every five years,[54] thereby hopefully avoiding too cozy a relationship from forming between the issuer and the engagement partner. Sarbanes-Oxley also has extensive provisions for the audit committee, calling for the committee to be comprised totally of independent directors (meaning at least one can receive fees other that director fees from the corporation or otherwise be deemed an "affiliate") and the audit committee must establish a process for addressing complaints or reports of accounting irregularities.[55]

Perhaps the most radical step for Sarbanes-Oxley was its entering into an area that heretofore was exclusively the domain of the states. The Act amends section 13 of the Securities Exchange Act to bar reporting companies from making personal loans to directors or officers.[56] The initial issues posed by this bar is what impact it would have on a wide range of standard practices such as advancing relocation expenses, litigation expenses per state indemnification statutes, and stock option plans that envision cashless exercise by their holder.

The Act duplicated efforts already under way at the SEC by mandating the chief executive officer and the chief financial officer to certify that the periodic reports filed with the SEC (1) have been reviewed, (2) to the certifying officer's knowledge the report "does not contain any untrue statement of material fact," and (3) to the certifying officer's knowledge "the report fairly presents in all material respects the financial condition and results of operations of the issuer."[57] The sobering experience of periodically having to so attest may well introduce a bit of conservatism into the dynamics between senior management and the outside auditor that heretofore has been missing.

The new requirements for audit committees have yet to be tested by the forces of time. They were greeted with some skepticism from the time they were first proposed. The wise observation is that good dedicated individuals are what protect investors, not regulatory hoops.[58] Furthermore, there is legitimate concern that the new requirements, by more closely involving audit committee members with the firm's financial reports, necessarily places a large litigation bull's-eye on each of the committee's members. Certainly fears that increased involvement by the audit committee members will lead to their having greater exposure to liability finds some support in the cases that predated the new audit committee requirements. Courts have consistently dismissed on the pleadings actions by

---

[53] 15 U.S.C. §78j-1(k).

[54] 15 U.S.C. §78j-1(j).

[55] 15 U.S.C. §78j-1(m).

[56] 15 U.S.C. §78m(k).

[57] 15 U.S.C. §§78n & 78(d).

[58] *See, e.g.,* John F. Olson, How to Really Make Audit Committees More Effective, 54 Bus. Law. 1097 (1999) (good audit committees have a broader mission than that called for by the Blue Ribbon committee and are staffed by independent directors with backgrounds that will enable them to understand the company's business).

audit committee members where the pleadings did not allege audit committee members played a role in the dissemination of the misleading financial statements.[59] But, when audit committee members have reviewed the information that is alleged to be materially misleading, and the circumstances suggest they should have been aware that the information deviated from their own knowledge of the firm's financial position and performance, the plaintiff's complaint has withstood the defendant's motion to dismiss.[60] At the same time, for three decades, the response of American corporate governance to weaknesses in corporate practices has been to strengthen the role of the independent director. So was the case with the recent reforms for the audit committee. The reforms strengthen the committee through threshold requirements of independence and affirmative obligations to put each committee member's name on the line that says he or she has reviewed the financial information to be filed with the SEC. Liability exposure is no doubt a necessary correlative to assuring these tasks are properly performed.

§9.03   Changes in the Statutory Description of Functions of the Board of Directors

Representative of early statutory expressions of the board's power are the early versions of the Model Business Corporation Act that provided simply that "the business and affairs of a corporation shall be *managed* by a board of directors."[1] As discussed in the preceding section, boards as a practical matter do not manage the company's affairs; this is a task commended to its officers, even within the closely held corporation. To reflect this reality, in 1974 the Model Act's language was amended to provide that corporate power was exercised "by or under the authority" of the board and that the corporation's affairs would be managed "under the direction" of the board.[2] This is the pattern of most modern statutes. Hopefully, among the effects of the modern expression of the board's role is to dissuade courts from otherwise harboring the view that the board of directors is to involve itself in the day-to-day management of the corporation or imposing liability for failure to exercise close supervision over the firm's executives.

Another change in the expression of the board's power is the invitation for corporation's to deviate from the statutory norm of a centralized management. This invitation appears in conjunction with language that provides that corporate powers and management occur pursuant to the authority or direction of the

---

[59] *See, e.g.,* Haltman v. Aura Systems, Inc., 844 F. Supp. 544 (C.D. Cal. 1993); Bomarko, Inc. v. Hemodynamics, 848 F. Supp. 1335 (W.D. Mich. 1993); *and* In re Livent, Inc. Sec. Lit., 78 F. Supp. 194 (S.D.N.Y. 1999).

[60] *See* In re JWP Inc. Sec. Lit., 928 F. Supp. 1239 (S.D.N.Y. 1996); Tischler v. Baltimore Bancorp., 801 F. Supp. 1493 (D. Md. 1992).

§9.03   [1] *See* Model Business Corporation Act §33 (1950) & (1960) (emphasis added).

[2] *See* Model Business Corporation Act Ann. §8.01 (3d ed. 1994) (Historical Background). *See also* Cal. Corp. Code §300 (West 1990); Del. Code Ann., tit. 8, §141(a) (2001); Kan. Stat. Ann. §17-6301 (1995); N.Y. Bus. Corp. Law §701 (McKinney 1986); Utah Code Ann. §16-10a-732 (2001).

A. The Board of Directors

board, "except as otherwise provided in the articles of incorporation."[3] The statute's broad invitation recognizes the validity of transferring to the shareholders (and likely a third party, such as a creditor) powers or authority customarily exercised by the board of directors. Because the exact scope of such a transfer has not been litigated, it remains to be seen whether a court might nonetheless impose important limits on the ability of the shareholders to transfer fundamental board powers to themselves. One potential area of conflict arises from the consistent practice of corporate statutes to require board approval as a condition to the stockholders considering certain transactions, such as the amendment of the articles, a merger, or a sale of substantially all the firm's assets.[4] Because the clear reading of the statute calls for board approval, not the approval of someone who has the authority to act for the board, there is a reasonable basis to doubt that a special provision in the articles of incorporation can change this part of the normative structure of the corporation.[5]

§9.04 Authority and Powers of the Directors

A corporation's board of directors is legally the supreme authority in matters of the corporation's regular business management.[1] Most corporate statutes provide that the corporate business is managed by or under the direction of the board of directors.[2] The basic management function of directors, as traditionally defined, can be summarized as including: (1) setting the course of the enterprise by determining the company's general objectives, goals, and philosophies; (2) selecting the chief executive and senior officers and seeing that able young executives are developed; (3) determining executive compensation, pension, and retirement policies; (4) delegating to the chief executive and subordinate executives authority for administrative action; (5) providing advice, counsel, and assistance to corporate officers; (6) fixing policies relating to such matters as pricing, labor relations, expansion, and new products; (7) determining the dividend payments,

---

[3] *See, e.g.,* Mich. Comp. Stat. Ann. §450.1501 (West 1990); Del. Code Ann., tit. 8, §141(a) (2001).

[4] *See, e.g.,* Del. Code Ann., tit. 8, §271 (2001); Former MBCA §12.02 (1984).

[5] In Jackson v. Turnbull, 1994 Del. Ch. Lexis 25, *aff'd,* 1994 Del. Ch. Lexis 382, the court held the board of directors violated section 251(b) of the Delaware General Corporation Law by delegating to a third party the responsibility for determining the price at which a merger was to occur.

§9.04 [1] Schein v. Caesar's World, Inc., 491 F.2d 17 (5th Cir.), *cert. denied,* 419 U.S. 838 (1974); In re Raljoed Realty Co., 277 F. Supp. 225 (S.D.N.Y.), *aff'd,* 387 F.2d 948 (2d Cir. 1967); Yarnall Warehouse & Transfer, Inc. v. Three Ivory Bros. Moving Co., 226 So. 2d 887 (Fla. Dist. Ct. App. 1969); Hanson v. Ontario Milk Producers Coop., 294 N.Y.S.2d 936 (Sup. Ct. 1968); Templeton v. Nocona Hills Owners Ass'n, 555 N.W.2d 534 (Tex. Civ. App. 1977).

[2] Many states have varied this formula by permitting restrictions on board authority in the articles or elsewhere. *E.g.,* Former MBCA §35 (1969, as amended). *Accord,* MBCA §8.01 (1984). *See* §9.13.

financing, and capital changes; (8) monitoring the company's progress, exercising vigilance for its welfare, and taking appropriate action in light of its progress; (9) submitting for shareholder action proposals requiring their approval; and (10) creating adequate machinery for conducting the board's business.

The board of directors has the power to select corporate officers[3] and to determine their compensation.[4] Perhaps the single most important board function is choosing the company's chief executive officer. The board has authority to direct the use of the corporation's property in the operation of its business.[5] It can sell or otherwise dispose of corporate assets,[6] including real estate,[7] in the normal course of business. The board has the power and responsibility to determine whether the financial condition of the company is such as to warrant the declaration and payment of dividends.[8] It can create and control a corporate pension plan;[9] apply the funds of the corporation to the payment of its debts and agree with creditors on an extension of debts;[10] authorize an assignment of all the corporation's property for the benefit of its creditors or the filing of a voluntary petition in bankruptcy;[11] determine whether the corporation will sue to rectify corporate injuries;[12] and waive the corporation's rights to attorney's fees.[13]

The board of directors, not the shareholders, has the original and supreme authority to make corporate contracts. Thus the board can borrow money needed for corporate business, execute or authorize the execution of negotiable notes or bonds to secure borrowing,[14] pledge or mortgage real or, personal corporate

---

[3] Stott v. Stott Realty Co., 224 N.W. 623 (Mich. 1929) (directors also have power to remove the officers); Nelms v. A. & A. Liquor Stores, Inc., 445 S.W.2d 256 (Tex. Civ. App. 1969).

[4] Cox v. First Nat'l Bank, 52 P.2d 524 (Cal. Ct. App. 1935); Wilderman v. Wilderman, 315 A.2d 610 (Del. Ch. 1974); Murrell v. Elder-Beerman Stores Corp., 239 N.E.2d 248 (Ohio C.P. 1968).

[5] Continental Sec. Co. v. Belmont, 99 N.E. 138 (N.Y. 1912).

[6] Hayes v. Johnson, 299 So. 2d 566 (La. Ct. App. 1974) (articles of incorporation granted power to board); Greenbaum v. American Metal Climax, Inc., 278 N.Y.S.2d 123 (App. Div. 1967) (directors also have power to decide not to exercise option to repurchase former corporate assets).

[7] Jeppi v. Brockman Holding Co., 206 P.2d 847 (Cal. 1949); Hendren v. Neeper, 213 S.W. 839 (Mo. 1919). See Lucey v. Hero Int'l Corp., 281 N.E.2d 266 (Mass. 1972).

[8] Liebman v. Auto Strop Co., 150 N.E. 505 (N.Y. 1926); M. Mortimer Feuer, Personal Liabilities of Corporate Officers and Directors, 116-121 (2d ed. 1974). See also Sinclair Oil Corp. v. Levien, 280 A.2d 717 (Del. 1971). Corporate dividends are discussed in Chapter 20.

[9] Delaney v. St. Louis Union Trust Co., 518 S.W.2d 704, 708 (Mo. Ct. App. 1974).

[10] Puma v. Marriott, 283 A.2d 693 (Del. Ch. 1971); Rocket Mining Corp. v. Gill, 483 P.2d 897 (Utah 1971). See First Nat'l Bank v. Pine Belt Producers Coop., 363 So. 2d 1201, 1207 (La. Ct. App. 1978).

[11] Royal Indem. Co. v. American Bond & Mortg. Co., 289 U.S. 165 (1933); In re DeCamp Glass Casket Co., 272 F. 558 (6th Cir. 1921); Note, 50 Harv. L. Rev. 662 (1937).

[12] Burks v. Lasker, 441 U.S. 471 (1979). Cf. Nussbacher v. Continental Ill. Nat'l Bank & Trust Co., 518 F.2d 873 (7th Cir. 1975), rev'g 61 F.R.D. 399, 402 (N.D. Ill. 1973), cert. denied, 424 U.S. 928 (1976). See infra §15.04.

[13] Tasby v. Estes, 416 F. Supp. 644 (N.D. Tex. 1976).

[14] H. Watson Dev. Co. v. Bank & Trust Co., 374 N.E.2d 767 (Ill. App. Ct. 1978); Saltmarsh v. Spaulding, 17 N.E. 316 (Mass. 1888).

A. The Board of Directors

property, secure debts lawfully contracted,[15] enter a guaranty contract,[16] enter leases,[17] and execute compromise agreements.[18]

The directors' authority generally is restricted to the management of the corporation's business affairs. Without shareholder approval, they cannot effect fundamental changes in the corporation's charter or organization or dissolve the corporation, since such actions do not relate to ordinary business.[19]

There is one area—the making and amending of bylaws—where the board's power as directors, vis-à-vis the power of the shareholders, has increased in recent years. The power to make bylaws was traditionally with the shareholders as an incident of their ownership of the business.[20] On the other hand, virtually all current statutes grant the directors the power to adopt, amend, and repeal bylaws or provide a method by which they can be given such power, such as by appropriate provision in the articles of incorporation.[21] In fact, originally the Model Business Corporation Act[22] empowered the directors or the incorporators to adopt the initial bylaws and further stated that only the directors shall possess the power to amend or repeal the bylaws, except to the extent that such power is reserved exclusively to the shareholders by the articles of incorporation.[23]

Directors, as a practical matter, often have almost exclusive control over the corporation's issuance of additional stock. Shareholder approval is required to amend the corporation's charter to increase the kind or amount of stock authorized to be issued. Modern statutes do not require that all authorized stock be issued at once, and the widespread practice is to authorize in the original charter or by charter amendments large amounts of stock in excess of that expected to be issued in the near future.[24]

[15] In re Lee Ready Mix & Supply Co., 437 F.2d 497, 499 (6th Cir. 1971), noted in 18 Wayne L. Rev. 904 (1972); Saltmarsh v. Spaulding, 17 N.E. 316 (Mass. 1888). *See also* Sailer v. Land-Livestock-Recreation, Inc., 522 P.2d 214 (Or. 1974); N.Y. Bus. Corp. Law §911 (McKinney 1986 Supp.); Former MBCA §78 (1969); MBCA §12.01 (1984).

[16] Westinghouse Credit Corp. v. Hydroswift Corp., 528 P.2d 156, 157 (Utah 1974).

[17] Ohio Drill & Tool Co. v. Johnson, 361 F. Supp. 255, 263 (S.D. Ohio 1973), *vacated in part and remanded,* 498 F.2d 186 (6th Cir. 1974).

[18] Schein v. Caesar's World, Inc., 491 F.2d 17 (15th Cir.), *cert. denied,* 419 U.S. 838 (1974).

[19] Chicago City Ry. v. Allerton, 85 U.S. (18 Wall.) 233 (1874); Duvall v. Moore, 276 F. Supp. 674 (N.D. Iowa 1967); Gimbel v. Signal Co., 316 A.2d 599 (Del. Ch.), *aff'd per curiam,* 316 A.2d 619 (Del. 1974); Hodge v. Cuba Co., 60 A.2d 88, 93 (N.J. Ch. 1948); Feuer, *supra* note 8, at 26.

[20] Rogers v. Hill, 289 U.S. 582, 588-589 (1933); North Milwaukee Town-Site Co., No. 2 v. Bishop, 79 N.W. 785 (Wis. 1899) (power to make bylaws rests primarily with the shareholders; directors have the power only if it is granted by law, the articles of incorporation, or appropriate action of the shareholders).

[21] *See, e.g.,* Former MBCA §25 (2001). *But see* MBCA §§22.06, 10.20 (1984) (shareholder may freely amend bylaws even if adopted by board), Former MBCA §27 (same); Del. Code Ann. tit. 8, §109 (1991); N.J. Stat. Ann. §14A:2-9 (West 1969); Tex. Bus. Corp. Act Ann. art. 2.23(B) (Cum. Supp. 2000).

[22] Former MBCA §27 (1969); MBCA §§2.06, 10.20 (1984).

[23] *See infra* §9.11. Under an earlier version that is currently in force in a number of states, the directors' power is subject to repeal or amendment by the shareholders. *See supra* §3.12. A few statutes will set specific limitations on the directors' power to make or amend bylaws. For example, Nebraska gives the shareholders the power to establish bylaws that cannot be amended or repealed by the directors. Neb. Rev. Stat. §21-20,125(1)(a) (1999). *See also* N.Y. Bus. Corp. Law §601(a) (McKinney 1986).

[24] The authorization and issuance of shares are discussed in Chapter 16.

B.   FORMALITIES FOR ACTION BY THE BOARD OF DIRECTORS

§9.05   Necessity for Board Action in a Lawfully Convened Meeting

The authority to manage the affairs of the corporation is vested in the directors not individually but as a board.[1] The traditional rule, as usually stated, is that directors cannot act individually to bind the corporation but must act as a board at a legally convened meeting. As will be seen, statutes frequently authorize important exceptions to this rule, and courts have upheld informal director approval where it is equitable to bend the requirements that the board act as a deliberative body.

Many cases have held that if directors act or give their consent separately or if they act at other than a legal meeting, their action is not that of the corporation, even though all may consent, and, in the absence of statute, ratification, or estoppel, the corporation is not bound.[2] These holdings proceed on the theory that the directors must meet and counsel with each other, and that any determination affecting the corporation shall only be arrived at after a consultation at a meeting of the board on notice to all and attended by at least a quorum of its members.[3] The shareholders are entitled to the directors' combined wisdom, knowledge, and business foresight, which give efficiency and safety to corporate management.

Modern technology has modified the concept of a board meeting. A number of corporation statutes now specifically provide that meetings of directors can be validly held by conference telephone or similar communications methods.[4] Even in the absence of statutory authorization, a meeting of this kind should be held to be a valid formal meeting, as the directors have full opportunity to consult and counsel with each other.

Courts in many instances have upheld the directors' approval, even though the directors' approval was not the product of a meeting convened in accordance with the statutes or bylaws.[5] For example:

    (1) Considerable judicial support exists for the proposition that even in the absence of a statute, the separate consent of all the directors is sufficient

---

§9.05   [1] *See, e.g.,* Amer. Bank & Trust Co. v. Freeman, 560 S.W.2d 444 (Tex. App. 1977) (individual director without authorization from the board cannot bind corporation on a promise to secure plaintiff's election to the board).

[2] Hotaling v. Hotaling, 193 Cal. 11 (1867); First Nat'l Bank v. Drake, 11 P. 445 (Kan. 1886); Baldwin v. Canfield, 1 N.W. 261 (Minn. 1879).

[3] In re Rye Psychiatric Hosp. Ctr. v. Schoenholtz, 476 N.Y.S.2d 339 (App. Div. 1984).

[4] Model Bus. Corp. Act §8.20 (1984). Delaware is even more attuned to changes in technology. It has eliminated the requirement that "other" communications equipment be "similar" to a conference telephone, as long as all the directors can hear each other. Del. Code Ann. tit. 8, §141(i) (2001).

[5] *See generally* Matthew N. Perlstein, Note, Corporations: When Informal Action by Corporate Directors Will Be Permitted to Bind the Corporation, 53 B.U. L. Rev. 101 (1973).

B. Formalities for Action by the Board of Directors

to bind the corporation without a formal meeting as a board,[6] and some support exists for the proposition that consent of a majority of the board, although acting separately, will suffice.[7]

(2) Courts tend not to apply the strict rule requiring a formal meeting if the shareholders have acquiesced in the directors' custom and usage of acting separately and not as a board.[8]

(3) If the directors own all of a corporation's shares, a conveyance, mortgage, or contract authorized by them, although not assembled at a meeting, is valid.[9] Courts have repeatedly departed from the traditional rule in order to sustain action taken by owner-directors in family and close corporations.[10]

(4) The shareholders may waive the necessity of a board meeting and thereby authorize acts to be done by agents of the corporation or ratify acts already done and thus bind the corporation. The shareholders are the residuary owners, and the rule requiring directors' meetings be held to authorize acts is for the shareholders' benefit.[11] Where, by acquiescence, the shareholders vest the executive officers with the powers of the directors as the usual method of doing business and the board is inactive, the acts of such officers, although not authorized by a vote of either shareholders or directors, generally will bind the corporation.[12]

---

[6] National State Bank v. Sandford Fork & Tool Co., 60 N.E. 699 (Ind. 1901); Daly v. Opelousas Ins. Agency, 181 La. 89, 158 So. 631 (1935) (contract signed by respective directors at their office or home); Winchell v. Plywood Corp., 85 N.E.2d 313 (Mass. 1949) (majority of board participated in corporate act and other directors acquiesced with knowledge or otherwise adopted it); Hurley v. Ornsteen, 42 N.E.2d 273 (Mass. 1942); Baker v. Smith, 102 A. 721 (R.I. 1916) (informal conferences); Stablein v. Hutterische Gemeinde, 189 N.W. 312 (S.D. 1922); Magowan v. Groneweg, 91 N.W. 335 (S.D. 1902).

[7] Forest City Box Co. v. Barney, 14 F.2d 590 (8th Cir. 1926); Holy Cross Gold Mining & Milling Co. v. Goodwin, 223 P. 58 (Colo. 1924); Buckley v. Jennings, 114 A. 40, 41 (Vt. 1921). *But see* Hurley v. Ornsteen, 42 N.E.2d 273 (Mass. 1942); Mosell Realty Corp. v. Schofield, 33 S.E.2d 774 (Va. 1945).

[8] Garmany v. Lawton, 53 S.E. 669 (Ga. 1906); Kozy Theatre Co. v. Love, 231 S.W. 249 (Ky. 1921); Gross Iron Ore Co. v. Paulle, 156 N.W. 268 (Minn. 1916); Baker v. Smith, 102 A. 721 (R.I. 1916); Bank of Middlebury v. Rutland & W. R.R., 30 Vt. 159 (1858); First Trust Co. v. Miller, 151 N.W. 813 (Wis. 1915).

[9] Jordan v. Collins, 18 So. 137 (Ala. 1895). *See also* Gerald v. Empire Sq. Realty Co., 187 N.Y.S. 306 (App. Div. 1921); First Nat'l Bank v. Frazier, 22 P.2d 325 (Or. 1933); Vawter v. Rouge River Valley Canning Co., 262 P. 851 (Or. 1928); Steeple v. Max Kuner Co., 208 P. 44 (Wash. 1922).

[10] *See, e.g.,* Haff v. Long Island Fuel Corp., 251 N.Y.S. 67, 71 (App. Div. 1931). *See also* American Cas. Co. v. Dakota Tractor & Equip. Co., 234 F. Supp. 606, 611 (D.N.D. 1964); Sharon Herald Co. v. Granger, 97 F. Supp. 295, 301 (W.D. Pa. 1951), *aff'd,* 195 F.2d 890 (3d Cir. 1952); Simonson v. Helburn, 97 N.Y.S.2d 406, 413 (Sup. Ct. 1950). *See generally* 1 & 2 F. Hodge O'Neal & Robert B. Thompson, O'Neal's Close Corporations: Law and Practice §§3.62, 8.03.

[11] Merchants' & Farmers' Bank v. Harris Lumber Co., 146 S.W. 508 (Ark. 1912); Morisette v. Howard, 63 P. 756 (Kan. 1901); Fitzpatrick v. O'Neill, 118 P. 273 (Mont. 1911).

[12] Galbraith v. First Nat'l Bank, 221 F. 386 (8th Cir. 1915); Cunningham v. German Ins. Bank, 101 F. 977 (6th Cir. 1900); Lahnston v. Second Chance Ranch Co., 968 P.2d 32 (Wyo. 1998) (minority owner of two person corporation, because he acquiesced with knowledge, had impliedly ratified loans to corporation made by majority owner); Garmany v. Lawton, 53 S.E. 669 (Ga. 1906); Gross Iron Ore Co. v. Paulle, 156 N.W. 268 (Minn. 1916); Barkin Constr. Co. v. Goodman, 116 N.E. 770, 772 (N.Y. 1917) ("In the daily conduct of its affairs there was no one except the secretary who assumed to speak for it. If he was not the manager, the company had none.").

(5) A corporation may be estopped, as against an innocent third person, to deny the validity of a mortgage or other act done or authorized by the directors separately, or otherwise than at a legal meeting, by long acquiescence or voluntary receipt or retention of benefits with either actual or presumed knowledge.[13]

(6) Many cases hold that where a single shareholder owns substantially all the shares of stock, she may bind the corporation by her acts without a resolution of the board of directors.[14] This is usually based on the ground of disregarding the separate corporate entity but may better be explained as a liberalized agency doctrine and a dispensing with the formalities of usual corporate procedure where they can serve no useful purpose.

(7) Ratification by vote or acquiescence of the shareholders, on full disclosure of the circumstances, is generally held effective to validate irregular or voidable acts of the directors.[15] A few cases hold that the shareholders cannot ratify any irregular or invalid act of the board that they, as shareholders, could not authorize.[16] But even when an effective ratification does not take place, the corporation may be "estopped" by the receipt or retention of benefits to deny its liability.[17]

§9.06   *Statutes Authorizing Informal Board Action*

In many states the corporation statutes now depart from the traditional requirement of formal board meetings and permit directors to act informally and without a meeting by signing a written consent.[1]

---

[13] Wood Estate Co. v. Chanslor, 286 P. 1001 (Cal. 1930); Luitwieler v. Luitwieler Pumping Engine Co., 228 P. 398 (Cal. Ct. App. 1924); Berman v. Minneapolis Photo Engraving Co., 43 N.H. 343 (1861); Jourdan v. Long Island R.R., 22 N.E. 153 (N.Y. 1889).

[14] Wenban Estate, Inc. v. Hewlett, 227 P. 273 (Cal. 1924), noted in 13 Cal. L. Rev. 235 (1925). Acts of sole shareholder bound corporation, though not done in the corporate name or by authority of the board of directors. *See* Ritz Realty Corp. v. Eypper & Beckmann, Inc., 138 A. 900 (N.J. Ch. 1927), *aff'd mem.*, 141 A. 921 (N.J. 1928), noted in 26 Mich. L. Rev. 812 (1928).

[15] Morisette v. Howard, 63 P. 756 (Kan. 1901); Myhre v. Myhre, 554 P.2d 276, 282 (Mont. 1976); Poweroil Mfg. Co. v. Carstensen, 419 P.2d 793 (Wash. 1966). But consent of the shareholders obtained without full disclosure does not excuse or ratify a fraud. First Trust & Sav. Bank v. Iowa-Wis. Bridge Co., 98 F.2d 416, 427 (8th Cir. 1938). Nor does consent of a majority of the shareholders, even with knowledge, ratify fraud. Parish v. Maryland & Va. Milk Producers Ass'n, 242 A.2d 512 (Md. 1958), *cert. denied*, 404 U.S. 940 (1971). A shareholder who with knowledge of the material facts consented or acquiesced in the transaction of which he complains ordinarily cannot attack the transaction on behalf of the corporation. Ramacciotti v. Joe Simpkins, Inc., 427 S.W.2d 425 (Mo. 1968).

[16] Curtin v. Salmon River Hydraulic Gold Mining & Ditch Co., 62 P. 552, 555 (Cal. 1900); Blood v. La Serena Land & Water Co., 41 P. 1017 (Cal. 1895), *rev'd on reh'g*, 45 P. 252 (Cal. 1896).

[17] New Blue Point Mining Co. v. Weissbein, 244 P. 325 (Cal. 1926); Curtin v. Salmon River Hydraulic Gold Mining & Ditch Co., 74 P. 851 (Cal. 1903).

§9.06 [1] Model Bus. Corp. Act §8.21(a) (1984). *See, e.g.*, Colo. Rev. Stat. §7-5-108-202 (2000); Del. Code Ann. tit. 8, §141(f) (2001).

B. Formalities for Action by the Board of Directors

Under these statutes, *all* the directors must sign for the written consent to be effective.[2] To some extent, the unanimity requirement "precludes the stifling of opposing argument"[3] in that a single director can force a meeting at which she will have an opportunity to reason with her colleagues. The written consent is effective when the last director executes her consent, unless a different date is specified.[4]

§9.07 The Notice Requirement for Board Meetings

Subject to the exceptions noted in the preceding sections, directors must act as a board at a legal meeting, regular or special, at which a quorum is present.[1] As a general proposition, all directors must be properly notified of board meetings.[2]

A distinction is made between regular and special meetings. Unless otherwise provided by statute, the charter, or bylaws, if the time and place of regular meetings of the board of directors are fixed in the corporation's charter or bylaws, by resolution of the board or by usage, such meetings may be held without additional notice.[3] It is common practice, however, to send a courtesy notice or reminder to the directors. The great weight of authority is that every director must be given notice of a special meeting of the board.[4] A special meeting held without due notice to all directors is illegal and, though a quorum may be present, action taken at such a meeting is invalid.[5]

Most current statutes provide that the bylaws may prescribe what shall constitute notice of a meeting of the board of directors.[6] Some jurisdictions specify what notice must be given in the absence of a bylaw provision.[7] The bylaws

---

[2] Tenn. Code Ann. §48-18-202 (LEXIS 2002) requires that decision to act without a meeting be unanimous; action taken needs same number of votes it would in a meeting.

[3] 1 Former MBCA Ann. §44, Comment ¶2 (2d ed. 1971).

[4] Herkowitz v. Pilot House Motor Inns, Inc., 806 S.W.2d 531 (Tenn. Ct. App. 1990).

§9.07 [1] For example, an action of one of two directors in terminating the other's employment was declared invalid because the corporation did not have a validly constituted board of directors, as required by N.Y. Bus. Corp. Law §702 (McKinney 1986) (minimum of three directors generally required). *See* Lehman v. Piantkowski, 460 N.Y.S.2d 817 (App. Div. 1983), *aff'd*, 460 N.E.2d 1091 (N.Y. 1984).

[2] *See* Rare Earth, Inc. v. Hoorelbeke, 401 F. Supp. 26 (S.D.N.Y. 1975); Schroder v. Scotten, Dillon Co., 299 A.2d 431 (Del. Ch. 1972); Geiselmann v. Stegeman, 443 S.W.2d 127 (Mo. 1969); State ex rel. Heikkenen v. Kylmanen, 231 N.W. 197 (Minn. 1930); Piedmont Press Ass'n v. Record Pub. Co., 152 S.E. 721 (S.C. 1930); Lycette v. Green River Gorge, 153 P.2d 873 (Wash. 1944).

[3] White v. Penelas Mining Co., 105 F.2d 726 (9th Cir. 1939). Many statutes expressly authorize regular meetings of the board to be held without notice if the bylaws or the board of directors fix the time and place of such meetings.

[4] Rare Earth, Inc. v. Hoorelbeke, 401 F. Supp. 26, 32 (S.D.N.Y. 1975) (Michigan law).

[5] *See* Whitman v. Fuqua, 549 F. Supp. 315 (W.D. Pa. 1982) (meeting called without notice and purpose given was without authority in law and any action taken was invalid or *ultra vires*).

[6] *E.g.*, N.Y. Bus. Corp. Law §711(b) (McKinney 1986); Former MBCA §43 (1969); MBCA §8.22 (1984). Delaware, however, does not have a statute on notice of directors' meetings.

[7] Connecticut requires that each director be notified orally or in writing two days in advance of a special meeting. Conn. Gen. Stat. Ann. §33-750(b) (1997). *See also* Cal. Corp. Code §307(a)(2) (West 1990) (48 hours' notice delivered personally or four days' written notice by mail); Ga. Code Ann. §14-2-822(b) (1994) (two days' written or oral notice).

customarily specify how many days in advance of a meeting notice must be given. In the absence of a bylaw authorizing other means of giving notice,[8] the notice of a directors' meeting must be a personal notice,[9] unless, by custom, notice by mail or otherwise is authorized[10] or unless some of the directors are absent and notice cannot be given to them except by mail or telegram.[11] The notice must be given a reasonable length of time before the hour or day fixed for the meeting.[12] Bylaws may also call for specificity regarding the nature of the business to be conducted.[13]

In the absence of a contrary provision in the charter or bylaws, general notice of the time and place of a directors' meeting, even though it does not specify the business to be transacted, is sufficient, at least to authorize the transaction of the corporation's ordinary business affairs.[14] Many corporation statutes broadly state that neither the business to be transacted at a meeting of the board, whether regular or special, nor the purpose of the meeting need be specified in the notice unless required by the bylaws, thus apparently eliminating any necessity of reference even to extraordinary business to be transacted at a meeting.[15] In the absence of such broad statutory permission, it is doubtful that extraordinary business may be transacted if not specified in the notice.[16]

If a director has notice of a meeting and fails to attend, he waives his rights.[17] A director has constructive notice when he purposely refuses to accept a regis-

---

[8] *See, e.g.,* Johnson v. Busby, 278 F. Supp. 235 (N.D. Ga. 1967) (by telephone); Schroder v. Scotten, Dillon Co., 299 A.2d 431 (Del. Ch. 1972) (registered mail); Conn. Gen. Stat. Ann. §33-750(b) (1997) (oral notification permissible); Ga. Code Ann. §14-2-822 (1994) (oral or written notice).

[9] Harding v. Vandewater, 40 Cal. 77 (1870); Bank of Little Rock v. McCarthy, 18 S.W. 759 (Ark. 1892). Notice by mail is sufficient if it is shown to have been received. Ashley Wire Co. v. Illinois Steel Co., 45 N.E. 410 (Ill. 1896); People ex rel. Swinburne v. Albany Med. Col., 26 Hun. (33 Sup. Ct.) 348, *aff'd,* 89 N.Y. 635 (1882). It has been held that, when notice is sent by mail, its receipt will be presumed, in the absence of proof to the contrary. Stockton Combined Harvester & Agric. Works v. Houser, 41 P. 809 (Cal. 1895).

[10] Stockton Combined Harvester & Agric. Works v. Houser, 41 P. 809 (Cal. 1895); Williams v. German Mut. Ins. Co., 68 Ill. 387 (1873).

[11] Chase v. Tuttle, 12 A. 874 (Conn. 1888).

[12] Hayes v. Canada, Atlantic & Plant S.S. Co., 181 F. 289 (1st Cir. 1910); Mercantile Library Hall Co. v. Pittsburgh Library Ass'n, 33 A. 744 (Pa. 1896); *cf.* In re Argus Co., 34 N.E. 388 (N.Y. 1893). The current Model Business Corporation Act has extensive rules regarding the effective date of notice and the manner of giving notice. *See* MBCA §1.41 (1984).

[13] *See* Valerino v. Little, 490 A.2d 756 (Md. Ct. Spec. App. 1985) (bylaw provision calling for notice "in detail" of agenda for special meeting was not satisfied by notice that stated meeting's purpose was to consider "purchase and sale" of capital stock when the issue was the approval of issuing new shares).

[14] In re Argus Co., *supra* note 12.

[15] *E.g.,* N.Y. Bus. Corp. Law §711(b) (McKinney 1986); 2 Former MBCA Ann. §8.22 (3d ed. 1994). A few states have a statute requiring that the purpose of a special meeting be included in the notice. Alaska Stat. 10.06.470(b) (1996) requires purpose of special meeting in notice unless otherwise in bylaws. *But see* Mass. Ann. Laws ch. 156B, §56 (Law. Co-op. 1979) (purpose need not be set forth in notice).

[16] *See* Mercantile Library Hall Co. v. Pittsburgh Library Ass'n, 33 A. 744 (Pa. 1896). Especially where a notice states that the meeting is called for a particular purpose or for ordinary business, extraordinary business outside of such purpose cannot be transacted unless all the directors are present. Fay v. Charles Michel & Sons, 147 N.Y.L.J. 15 (Sup. Ct. 1962).

[17] Potter v. Patee, 493 S.W.2d 58, 64 (Mo. Ct. App. 1973); Avien, Inc. v. Weiss, 269 N.Y.S.2d 836 (Sup. Ct. 1966). *See* Holcombe v. Trenton White City Co., 82 A. 618, 624 (N.J. Ch. 1912), *aff'd mem.,* 91 A. 1069 (N.J. 1913).

tered letter giving notice of the meeting.[18] Similarly, a director may waive notice by signing a written waiver of notice before the meeting. A waiver of notice by an absent director subsequent to a meeting has been held invalid by some courts[19] and valid by others.[20]

§9.08 Directors' Meetings: Place, Call, Quorum, Votes, Disqualification by Interest

The time and place of board meetings is usually fixed by the bylaws or by procedures set up therein; however, if no provision on these matters is included in the bylaws, the board of directors may determine the time and place.[1] Most current corporation statutes provide that directors may hold both regular and special board meetings outside the state of incorporation.[2]

A majority of the entire board of directors constitutes a quorum[3] for the purpose of transacting business unless a greater or lesser number is required by statute, the corporation's charter, or its bylaws.[4] The quorum remains the same even though vacancies occur on the board.[5]

Unless authorized by statute, charter, or bylaw, less than a majority of the full number of directors cannot meet and bind the corporation by any act or resolution.[6] All they can do is adjourn.[7] Action at a meeting of directors that was invalid

---

[18] Schroeder v. Scotten Dillon Co., 299 A.2d 431 (Del. Ch. 1972).

[19] United States v. Interstate R.R., 14 F.2d 328 (W.D. Va. 1926); Lippman v. Kehoe Stenograph Co., 95 A. 895 (Del. Ch. 1915); Moffatt v. Niemitz, 139 A. 798 (N.J. Ch. 1928).

[20] Stafford Springs St. Ry. v. Middle River Mfg. Co., 66 A. 775 (Conn. 1907); Daly v. Opelousas Ins. Agency, 158 So. 631 (La. 1935). See 27 Colum. L. Rev. 323 (1927); 12 Minn. L. Rev. 756 (1928).

§9.08 [1] Bylaws typically specify that regular board meetings be held on a specified day each month.

[2] See, e.g., Former MBCA §43 (1969); MBCA §8.20 (1984); Cal. Corp. Code §307(a)(5) (West 1990) (unless otherwise provided in charter or bylaws); N.Y. Bus. Corp. Law §710 (McKinney 1986) (same).

[3] The term "quorum" refers to the number of members of a body that, when properly assembled, is legally competent to transact business.

[4] In re Webster Loose Leaf Filing Co., 240 F. 779, 784 (D.N.J. 1916); Sargent v. Webster, 54 Mass. (13 Met.) 497 (1847); Ex parte Willocks, 7 Cow. 402 (N.Y. 1827); James E. Lyons, Comment, The Validity or Invalidity of Corporate Directors' Action and the Quorum Requirements, 15 U. Kan. L. Rev. 366 (1967).

[5] Currie v. Mason, 33 F. Supp. 454, 456-457 (W.D. La. 1940); Cirrincione v. Polizzi, 220 N.Y.S.2d 741 (App. Div. 1961).

[6] In re Rye Psychiatric Hosp. Ctr. v. Schoenholtz, 476 N.Y.S.2d 339 (App. Div.), appeal dismissed, 480 N.Y.S.2d 206 (Ct. App. 1984) (three of six shareholders attending special meetings constituted a quorum only for purpose of electing directors and not for any other business). See Olincy v. Merle Norman Cosmetics, Inc., 19 Cal. Rptr. 387 (Ct. App. 1962) (action attempted to be taken without quorum is void).

Consider the inability of two of three directors to convene a meeting where bylaws authorized the board or the president to convene special meetings and the president, who was the third director, refused to convene a meeting. See American Ctr. for Educ. v. Cavnar, 102 Cal. Rptr. 575 (Ct. App. 1972) (not a valid call if by only two of directors).

[7] A meeting without notice or a quorum is invalid. Rare Earth, Inc. v. Hoorelbeke, 401 F. Supp. 26, 31-32 (S.D.N.Y. 1975).

because of the absence of a quorum may be subsequently ratified at a legal directors' meeting or by the shareholders, at least if they could have authorized the action in the first instance.[8]

The attending directors must be personally present and act for themselves. Votes at a directors' meeting cannot be by proxy unless that privilege is conferred by charter or bylaw provision.[9] Although the rule is not settled in most jurisdictions, a meeting at which a quorum is initially present should be able to continue to transact business, notwithstanding the withdrawal of directors, at least if any action taken is approved by a majority of the required quorum for the meeting.[10]

Modern corporation statutes typically provide that a majority of the number of directors fixed in the bylaws or otherwise will constitute a quorum and that the act of a majority of the directors present at a meeting at which a quorum is present shall be the act of the board. Nevertheless, the statutes permit charter provisions requiring a higher quorum or a greater vote[11] or, more liberally, permit such provisions in either charter or bylaws[12] or, even more liberally, in the charter, bylaws, or a shareholder's agreement.[13] Some statutes permit the quorum to be fixed by charter or bylaw provision at *less* than a majority of the entire board but not less than one-third.[14]

§9.09   The Virtual Board: Melding Electronic Media to the Conduct of Board Meetings

As seen earlier,[1] all states permit a director to participate telephonically in a meeting of the board; this permission is generally conditioned upon prior consent on the part of the corporation, such as authorization in its bylaws, and, furthermore, that each director present, physically or telephonically, be able to hear and speak with each of the other participating directors. As breathtaking as this development

---

[8] Michelson v. Duncan, 407 A.2d 211, 219 (Del. 1979); Morisette v. Howard, 63 P. 756 (Kan. 1901).

[9] Perry v. Tuscaloosa Cotton-Seed Oil-Mill Co., 9 So. 217, 219 (Ala. 1891); Greenburg v. Harrison, 124 A.2d 216 (Conn. 1956).

[10] *See* In re Orfa Corp., 115 B.R. 799, 804 (E.D. Pa. 1990).

[11] *See, e.g.,* Former MBCA §40 (1969); *Accord,* MBCA §8.24 (1984); Cal. Corp. Code §307(a)(7)-(8) (West 1990); N.Y. Bus. Corp. Law §§707-709 (McKinney 1986). Bylaws or shareholders' agreements purporting to establish high quorum or high vote requirements have been held ineffective. Frantz Mfg.Co. v. EAC Ind., 501 A.2d 401 (Del. 1985); Model, Roland & Co. v. Industrial Acoustics Co., 209 N.E.2d 553 (N.Y. 1965). There is a division of authority as to whether newly created but unfilled positions are to be considered in determining what is a quorum. *See* Rocket Mining Corp. v. Gill, 483 P.2d 897 (Utah 1971) (should not count); Bruch v. National Guar. Credit Corp., 116 A.2d 738, 740 (Del. Ch. 1921) (consider vacancies); Avien, Inc. v. Weiss, 269 N.Y.S.2d 836 (Sup. Ct. 1966) (vacancies should be considered).

[12] *E.g.,* Former MBCA §40 (1969); MBCA §8.24 (1984).

[13] *See* 1 O'Neal & Thompson, O'Neal's Close Corporations, *supra* §9.05 note 10, §1.14.

[14] *E.g.,* Del. Code Ann. tit. 8, §141(b) (2001). *See also* Everett v. Riverside Hose Co. No. 4, 261 F. Supp. 463 (S.D.N.Y. 1966); Kerbs v. California E. Airways, Inc., 90 A.2d 652 (Del. 1952).

§9.09   [1] *See* §9.05.

B. Formalities for Action by the Board of Directors

was a few years ago, it now appears primitive compared with the steps a majority of the states have recently taken to incorporate new communication technologies into their corporate governance procedures. Not surprisingly, the trend to expressly embrace new electronic media began with California's 1995 amendment of its Corporations Code to permit notice of board meetings to be given via "electronic mail or other electronic means"[2] and further provided that members of the board could participate in meetings through "electronic video screen communication, or other communications equipment" so long as each member is able to communicate with all others "concurrently."[3] Without such technical reference, the more general, traditional statutory authorization for remote participation so long as each participating director can "hear each other during the meeting"[4] certainly reaches all imaginable media that transmits the directors' voices. The California-like statute broad ns the range of permissible communications to written, not voice, transmissions, provided the technology used meets the requirement that they occur concurrently.

Most state statutes authorize notice of directors' meetings to be imparted through a broad range of media, including mail, telephone, facsimile, or "other form of wire or wireless communication."[5] A few states broadly defer to the company's bylaws to set forth the manner of giving notice for directors' meetings.[6] Only a handful of states continue to rely upon a paper-based system for notice of directors' meetings by requiring notice to take some tangible form.[7] A common scheme among liberal-notice states is to provide a wider range of media for imparting any required notice to directors than is authorized for any notice required to be directed to the stockholders.

Overall, the Internet and the chip have not changed the fundamental postulates for the board. State statutes that embrace newly developed technologies continue to view the board as a deliberative body. Even the most forward-looking statutes continue the requirement that each participating director be able simultaneously, or certainly without undue delay, to engage his or her fellow director on the topic before the board.

---

[2] Cal. Corp. Code §307(2) (West Supp. 2001).

[3] *Id.* at 307(6) (added in 1997). Consider here Wisconsin's approach, authorizing director participation provided "directors can immediately transmit or receive messages from all other participating directors," Wis. Stat. Ann. §180.0820(2) (West 1992).

[4] *See, e.g.,* Colo. Rev. Stat. §7-108-201(2) (2000); 805 Ill. Comp. Stat. Ann. 5/7.15(d) (West 1993); Mass. Gen. Laws Ann. ch. 156B, §59 (West 1996); N.J.S.A. §14A:6-10 (West Supp. 2001); N.Y. Bus. Corp. L. §708(c) (McKinney Supp. 2002); Tenn. Code Ann. §48-11-201(b) (1995); Va. Code Ann. §13.1-686(b) (Michie 1999).

[5] *See, e.g.,* Ala. Code §10-2B-1.41(b) (Michie 1999); Colo. Rev. Stat. §7-101-402(2) (2000); Ind. Code Ann. §23-1-20-29 (Michie 1999); 2 Or. Rev. St. §60.034(2) 1999); Va. Code Ann. §13.1-610(b) (Michie 1999). *But see* Ala. Code §10-2B-7.05(a) (Michie 1999) (notice to stockholders must be in writing).

[6] *See, e.g.,* 805 Ill. Comp. Stat. Ann. 5/7.15 (West 1993); Me. Rev. Stat. Ann.tit. 13 A §709(2) (West 1981); Mass. Gen. Laws Ann. ch. 158, §34 (West 1996).

[7] *See, e.g.,* Kan. Stat. Ann. §17-6008(b) (1995); Ohio Rev. Code Ann., tit. 17, §1701.61(c) (Baldwin Supp. 2001).

§9.10   *Governance and Authority Within the LLC*

Determining the governance and management within an LLC is a matter of choice which is exercised in the shadow of the default rule set forth in the governing statute. By far the most common approach among the states is that the LLC is member managed, unless otherwise provided in the articles of organization[1] (a few states permit this designation in the operating agreement).[2] Only a few state's default rule embraces manager-operated firms, unless provided otherwise.[3] Some states expressly recognize that even if the members opt generally for centralized management, that their operating agreement, or even the articles of organization, can provide that as to certain matters, or even broad categories of issues, members not managers have the authority to act.[4] Because the choice of governance is essentially elected, it is logical to assume that even without express statutory recognition that the operating agreement or articles of organization may validly divide authority between the members and managers so that the election need not totally favor manager- or member-management. Such a division, however, may not under certain circumstances be enforceable against third parties who contract with, for example, managers in the reasonable belief that they enjoy the authority to act when in fact the operating agreement provides otherwise.

When the LLC is manager-managed, a decision of the managers may, depending on the statute, require more than a majority of the managers present at a meeting. Some states expressly provide that, in the absence of a contrary provision in the articles of organization, when the company is manager-managed any decision by the managers affecting its business affairs must be by a majority of the managers (not simply a majority of the quorum).[5] Indeed, because LLC statutes typically do not set forth, as do corporate statutes, notice, quorum or even voting requirements that are to apply to manager-operated firms, the operating agreement should address each of these. That is, it is rare among LLC statutes to find default rules regarding the procedures that are to apply for action by managers in manager-operated firms.[6]

Another subject that should be addressed in the operating agreement is the members' power to remove a manager before her term has expired. Few states provide for the managers to be removed by the members.[7] Even in the absence of

---

§9.10   [1] *See, e.g.,* Cal. Corp. Code §17150 (West. Supp. 2002); Ind. Stat. Ann. §23-18-4-1 (Burns 1999); 15 Pa. Stat. Ann., §8941 (Purdons 1995); Wis. Stat. Ann. §183.0401 (West Supp. 2001). For a complete compilation of this statutory patterns, *see* Larry E. Ribstein & Robert R. Keatinge, 1 Ribstein and Keatinge on Limited Liability Companies App. 8-1 *et seq.* (1997).

[2] *See, e.g.,* N.J. Stat. Ann. §42:2B-27 (West Supp. 2002).

[3] *See* Minn. Stat. Ann. §322B.606 (West 1995) (managed by a board of governors, unless otherwise set forth in the operating agreement); Tex Rev. Civ. Stat. tit. 32, art. 1528n §2.12 (Vernons 1997) (unless provided otherwise in the articles of organization).

[4] For such express statutory recognition, *see* Minn. Stat. Ann. §322B.37 & 606 (West Supp. 2002).

[5] *See* Conn. Stat. Ann. §34-142 (West 1997).

[6] For the exception, *see* Tex. Civ. Stat. tit. 32, art. 1528n §2.23 (Vernon's 1997).

[7] *See, e.g.,* Cal. Corp. Code §17152(b) (West Supp. 2002) (removal by majority of interested of members); Colo. Rev. Stat. Ann. §7-80-405 (West 2001) (members may remove with or without cause by vote of majority of members at a meeting expressly called for that purpose); Tex. Civ. Stat. tit. 32, art.

B. Formalities for Action by the Board of Directors

express statutory recognition, removal by the members should be valid. Certainly the analogy to the inherent rights of stockholders to remove a director for cause is a compelling one. But the broad embrace in most LLC statutes of free and open contracting, in which members have broad authority to opt for a form of governance structure they prefer, argues strongly for the position that members enjoy inherent rights to remove their managers that are broader than those recognized at common law for shareholders.

LLC statutes customarily list types of transactions that require the approval of the members, even when a firm is manager-managed.[8] Thus, the LLC statutes carry forward the philosophy of corporate statutes that certain transactions are so fundamental, or related to the individual member's investment, that it should not occur without providing each member with an opportunity to vote on the transaction. Care must be taken in drafting the articles of organization and operating agreement because many statutes provide that absent a contrary provision in the articles of organization (and sometimes the operating agreement) such fundamental changes require the consent of all the members, not merely a majority in interest. A further consideration here is when drafting to authorize less than unanimous approval by the members is whether a call for "majority approval" is meant to mean a majority of the members or a majority by interest among the members.

A final wrinkle in the manager-managed LLC is the agency authority of individual managers when there are two or more managers. When the LLC is manager-managed, the governing LLC statute provides that only managers have the authority to bind the firm. Most states recognize the authority of any manager to bind the firm, even when there are multiple managers.[9]

When the LLC is member-managed, the operating agreement should give due attention to governance procedures, such as notice and quorum for member meetings as well as the vote that is required. The default rule of many states is that members vote per capita, rather than by interest.[10] Most LLC statutes permit voting power to be allocated among the members, or even classes of members, as the articles of organization or organization agreement may provide. The members can also provide in the articles of organization or operating agreement for super-majority vote; and, in any case, the careful lawyer needs to be aware that many statutes require unanimous approval of the members

---

1528n §2.13 (Vernon's 1997) (when authorized in the "regulation," the permissible content of which is set forth in §2.09, *id.*).

[8] *See, e.g.,* Ariz. Rev. Stat. Ann. §29-681 (West 1998); 11 Ga. Code Ann. §14-11-308(b) (Michie 1994); Mich. Comp. Laws Ann. §450.4502 (3) (West Supp. 2001); N.Y. Limited Liability Comp. L. §402(c) (McKinney Pamp. 2002); Wash. Rev. Code Ann. §25.15.120 (Supp. 2002).

[9] *See, e.g.,* Del. Code. Ann. tit. 6, §18-402 (1999) ("each member or manager has the authority to bind the . . . company"); 808 Ill. Comp. Stat. §180/13-5(b)(1) (West Supp. 2002) ("each manager is an agent of the company"); and N.Y. Ltd. Liability Comp. L. §412(b)(2) (McKinney Pamp. 2002) (same); and Tex. Rev. Civ. Stat. tit. 32, art. 1528n §2.21 B (Vernon's 1997) (each member is an agent of the company subject to regulations or resolution adopted by the managers).

[10] *See, e.g.,* Ariz. Rev. Stat. §29-681 D 1 (1998); 805 Ill. Comp. Stat. §180/15-1(a) (Supp. 2000); Mo. Rev. Stat. §347.079 (4) (West 2001); and 15 Pa. Comp. Stat. Ann. §8942(a) (Purdon Supp. 2002).

unless a lower vote is set forth in the articles of organization or operating agreement.

When the LLC is member-managed, the typical default rule follows the partnership analogy to the effect that each member has the inherent authority to bind the company on any matter within the ordinary scope of its business.[11] When a member acts outside the scope of her actual authority with respect to a transaction within the usual course of the LLC's affairs, and the third person is not aware of the limitation on the member's authority, traditional agency principles arise to bind the company on the transaction with the third person.

C.   REMOVAL OF DIRECTORS

§9.11   The Power of Shareholders to Control the Acts of Directors

Directors are not the servants of a majority of the shareholders. One of the basic advantages of the corporate form of doing business, found also in unincorporated joint stock companies and business trusts, is that the collective interests of the owners (shareholders) are represented by the centralized management of a board of directors. The directors control and supervise the conduct of the business. Individual shareholders generally have little direct voice in determining the corporation's business policies.

Each shareholder has a right to have the corporation's affairs managed by its board of directors. This right is derived from the statute under which the corporation is organized and from the corporation's charter and bylaws. Statutory, charter, and bylaw provisions for management by the directors are viewed as part of a control among the shareholders. Consequently, a majority of the shareholders cannot deprive the minority of their right to the directors' judgment and discretion.

The shareholders' participation in a corporate decision is usually "in the form of an assent, request, or recommendation."[1] Traditionally they have only limited powers of initiative. Even fundamental corporate action that requires a favorable shareholder vote, such as a charter amendment, merger, consolidation, voluntary dissolution, or sale of substantially all corporate assets other than in the usual course of business is, in practice, usually initiated by the directors, and, in any case, reaches the stockholders *only after* approval by the board of directors. Indeed, most statutes expressly require board approval of such action before sub-

---

[11] *See, e.g.*, Cal. Corp. Code §17157(a) (West 1990); Del. Code Ann., tit. 6, §402 (1999); Md. Code Ann. §4A-401(a) (1990); N.Y. Ltd. Liability Comp. Law §412(a) (McKinney Pamp. 2002); and Wis. Stat. §183.0301(1)(a) (West Supp. 2001).

§9.11   [1] Continental Sec. Co. v. Belmont, 99 N.E. 138, 141 (N.Y. 1912).

C. Removal of Directors

mission to the shareholders.[2] The shareholders may act as a ratifying or approving body and thereby validate an unauthorized act or voidable corporate contract.[3]

It would be wrong to conclude that shareholders have no capacity to act affirmatively to change corporate policies or practices. A good illustration of effective shareholder initiative is provided by the leading New York case of *Auer v. Dressel.*[4] The corporation's charter provided for eleven directors; the class A shareholders elected nine, and the common shareholders elected two. The directors removed and replaced the corporation's president. A majority of the class A shareholders were displeased with that action and duly invoked a bylaw that imposed a duty on the president to call a meeting when requested in writing by holders of a majority of shares entitled to vote. Among the objectives for the meeting were: (1) to adopt a resolution endorsing the administration of the old president and demanding that he be reinstated; (2) to consider a proposal to amend the charter and bylaws to provide that vacancies in the board of directors caused by shareholder removal of a director or by resignation of a director against whom charges had been preferred, could be filled with the unexpired term only by the shareholders of the class represented by the director; and (3) to hear charges preferred against four of the directors, vote on their removal, and select successors if needed. The court held that all of the reasons advanced were proper purposes for holding a shareholder meeting. Although the shareholders, by endorsing the administration of the old president, would not be able directly to effect a change in officers, they were entitled to express themselves and thus alert the directors who would stand for election at the next annual meeting.[5]

There is a good deal of uncertainty whether the stockholders can adopt bylaw provisions that restrain the authority of the board of directors. The source of this uncertainty is the uneasy fit of two standard provisions of corporate statutes.[6] First is the broad grant of authority to the board of directors to manage or direct the

---

[2] *See, e.g.*, Former MBCA §59 (1969) (amendment of articles); MBCA §10.03 (1984); Former MBCA §71 (1969) (merger); MBCA §11.02 (1984); Former MBCA §79 (1969) (sale of assets other than in regular course of business); MBCA §12.02 (1984); Former MBCA §84 (1969) (voluntary dissolution by act of corporation); MBCA §14.02 (1984); Del. Code Ann. tit. 8, §251(b)-(c) (2001) (merger); Fla. Stat. Ann. §607.1102 (West 1993) (consolidation). N.C. Gen. Stat. §§55-10-01-55-10-03 (2000) do not permit shareholder initiative as §55-100(b)(1) (1982) used to; the 1982 statute has no equivalent today. *See also* Chapter 13.

[3] *See, e.g.*, Goldboss v. Reimann, 55 F. Supp. 811, 819 (S.D.N.Y. 1943), *aff'd mem.*, 143 F.2d 594 (2d Cir. 1944); Diston v. Loucks, 62 N.Y.S.2d 138, 146 (Sup. Ct. 1941), *aff'd mem.*, 35 N.Y.S.2d 715 (App. Div. 1942); Talbot v. Harrison, 270 N.Y.S. 171 (Sup. Ct. 1932), *aff'd mem.*, 268 N.Y.S. 875 (App. Div. 1933); Nursing Home Bldg. Corp. v. DeHart, 535 P.2d 137 (Wash. Ct. App. 1975).

[4] 118 N.E.2d 590 (N.Y. 1954).

[5] 118 N.E.2d at 593. The court stated further that shareholders who have the power to elect directors have the inherent power to remove them for cause and that the shareholders can amend corporate bylaws to provide that they will elect successors of such directors as shall be removed or such directors as shall resign pending hearing. *Id.* Cf. New Iberia Bancorp, Inc. v. Schwing, 664 So. 2d 784 (La. Ct. App. 1996) (upholding right of stockholders to consider proposal that a shareholder committee be established to consider possible merger or sale of the firm). *See also infra* §9.12.

[6] For the view that harmonizing the statutory provisions is not a priority in this area, *see* Jeffrey N. Gordon, "Just Say Never?" Poison Pills, Deadhand Pills, and Shareholder-Adopted Bylaws: An Essay for Warren Buffett, 19 Cardozo L. Rev. 511, 547 (1997).

corporation's affairs, except as may be otherwise provided in this statute or the articles of incorporation.[7] Second, statutes authorize bylaws not inconsistent with law or the articles of incorporation, and empower the stockholders to adopt, amend and repeal the bylaws.[8]

> At some point the broad shareholder power to adopt or amend corporate by-laws must yield to the board's plenary authority to manage the business and affairs of the corporation. . . . The difficulty of pinpointing where a proposal falls on this spectrum of sometimes overlapping authority is exacerbated by the absence of state-law precedent demarcating this boundary.[9]

Just how much restraint can a shareholder-adopted bylaw impose on the broad command that the affairs of the corporation are to be managed by or under the direction of the board of directors? Should the qualification on the board's authority found in the reference to except "as otherwise provided in this statute" incorporate limitations that can be imposed by the bylaws? Professor Lawrence Hamermesh argues that the exception refers only to statutory provisions that deal specifically with the allocation of power between stockholders and the board of directors, such as provisions requiring stockholder approval of mergers or the authority of court appointed trustees or custodians; more generally, he advises the corporate statute must be interpreted in light of the contemporary view of the strong board with limited involvement by the stockholders in the conduct of company affairs.[10] On the other hand, Professor John Coffee argues stockholders can through their amendment of the bylaws introduce significant, albeit reasonable, departures from the traditional model of the board primacy:

> [T]he bylaws are the appropriate location for constraints that limit the exercise of corporate power, including by the directors. The key distinction then seems to be between affirmative instructions to take specific actions (which generally seem impermissible) and negative constraints that affect the allocation of power between the board and the shareholders (which generally seem permissible).[11]

[7] *See, e.g.,* Del. Code Ann., tit. 8 §141(a) (2001); N.Y. Bus. Corp. Law §701(a) (McKinney 1986); M.B.C.A. §8.02(b) (1984).

[8] *See, e.g.,* Del. Code Ann., tit. 8 §109(a)(b) (2001); N.Y. Bus. Corp. Law §601 (McKinney 1986); M.B.C.A. §10.20 (1984).

[9] Randall S. Thomas & Catherine T. Dixon, Aranow & Einhorn on Proxy Contests for Corporate Control §160.5 (3d ed. 1998).

[10] Lawrence A. Hamermesh, Corporate Democracy and Stockholder-Adopted By-Laws: Taking Back the Street, 73 Tulane L. Rev. 409, 431 & 452 (1998). *See also* Charles F. Richards, Jr. & Robert J. Stearn, Jr., Shareholder By-Laws Requiring Boards of Directors to Dismantle Rights Plans Are Unlikely to Survive Scrutiny Under Delaware Law, 54 Bus. Law. 607, 625 (1999).

[11] John C. Coffee, Jr., The Bylaw Battlefield: Can Institutions Change the Outcome of Corporate Control Contests?, 51 U. Miami L. Rev. 605, 608 (1997). Professor Coffee believes bright-line tests for legitimacy could be based on consideration whether the bylaw involved ordinary versus fundamental issues, constituted affirmative or negative instructions to the board, deals with procedural or substantive matters, and can be seen as related to corporate governance or business decisions. *Id.* at 613-614. For a reply to these categories, *see* Hamermesh, *supra* note 10, at 433-442.

C. Removal of Directors

Not surprisingly, this issue has surfaced in the context of management's steps to prevent a takeover, a subject in which managers frequently are not of the same mind as the company's stockholders. In *International Brotherhood of Teamsters General Fund v. Fleming Companies,*[12] the shareholders proposed a bylaw which would restrict the board of directors from implementing a rights plan (poison pill) that would impede a hostile takeover of the firm. The Oklahoma Supreme Court upheld the shareholders' power to propose the restriction on the directors, reasoning that a rights plan is similar to stock option plans whose approval or content are appropriate for shareholder action. If the court's analogy to the stockholders' power with respect to stock options is not central to its decision, then *Fleming*'s holding is even more profound. *Sans* the analogy to options, there would appear to be few limits upon the stockholders's power to adopt bylaws that either limit the discretionary authority of the board of directors or, as was part of the proposed bylaw in *Fleming,* mandating that the board pursue a specific course of action (in *Fleming,* to redeem the outstanding rights). To date, *Fleming* represents the only decision evaluating the power of the shareholders through a bylaw to constrain the discretion enjoyed by the board of directors. The fanfare that has surrounded *Fleming* is likely to assure that there will soon be other decisions on this point as institutional investors push proposals that reduce the discretion enjoyed by the board of directors.

The statutory provisions that served as the backdrop for the contest in *Fleming* are consistent with those found in most states. Nevertheless, as reflected in the differing views of Professors Hamermesh and Coffee, discussed above, the area depends heavily upon one's overall approach to governance issues so that a court favoring a strong board can easily and quite reasonably reach a result different from that arrived at in *Fleming.*

A further question is whether the stockholders can provide that the bylaw they have adopted cannot be amended or repealed by the board. This is directly answered in the Model Act which allows the adopting shareholder to place a bylaw beyond the reach of the board of directors.[13] The cases suggest that such a limitation would not be valid when a provision of the articles of incorporation confers broad authority on the board with respect to the bylaws.[14]

§9.12   Board Vacancies

A vacancy on the board can arise through the resignation, death, or removal of a director. Newly authorized directorships not yet filled are customarily considered

---

[12] 975 P.2d 907 (Okla. 1999).

[13] *See* Former MBCA §10.20(a)(2) (1984).

[14] *See, e.g.,* Centaur Partners, IV v. National Intergroup, Inc., 582 A.2d 923, 929 (Del. 1990); Whitman v. New Hampshire Elec. Corp., 459 A.2d 224, 225-26 (N.H. 1983). *Contra* Petition of Buckley, 50 N.Y.S. 2d 54, 55-56 (N.Y. Sup. Ct. 1944). Note in this regard that the New York statute expressly permits shareholders to amend or repeal any board adopted bylaw, but conspicuously does not authorize the board to amend or repeal a shareholder adopted bylaw. *See* N.Y. Bus. Corp. Law §601(a) (McKinney 1986).

creating a "vacancy" on the board. A few corporate statutes specify what constitutes a vacancy, and all states have provisions dealing with how any vacancy is to be filled.[1]

In broad overview, all states variously authorize either the shareholders or the board to fill vacancies on the board.[2] Obviously, once either of these bodies has acted to fill a vacancy the vacancy no longer exists and, hence, there no longer is authority for the other body to appoint someone to fill the formerly vacant seat. When a vacancy arises there can be a question regarding what constitutes a quorum for the board. The first step in addressing this question is the language of the quorum requirement; if it does not set a specific number for a quorum, does it specify a certain percentage of the "authorized" or the number "in office"? The Utah court provided an expedient answer to the quorum issue in resolving the validity of board action taken by a vote of three to one after the articles had been amended expanding the board from four to seven, but before the three new directorships had been filled. The quorum requirement was a majority of the directors. The court held that the unfilled directorships were not to be counted in determining a quorum.[3] This question is directly dealt with in the great majority of the state statutes because they expressly authorize the majority of the directors to fill a vacancy, even though they are less than a quorum.[4] Those states following the Model Business Corporation Act restrict the board's authority to act by a vote of a majority of its remaining members to instances in which "the directors remaining in office constitute fewer than a quorum."[5] The Model Act's provision is consistent with the holding in *Tomlinson v. Loew's Inc.*,[6] arising from a proxy contest for control of MGM. One provision of the company's bylaws provided that the board could act only through a majority vote at a meeting with a quorum present; another bylaw provision provided directors in office could fill a vacancy "although less than a quorum." The court held the latter provision applied only when it was not possible to convene a quorum; it accordingly held that the new directors appointed at a meeting without a quorum were not validly selected since it was

---

§9.12   [1] *See, e.g.,* In Grossman v. Liberty Leasing Co., 295 A.2d 749 (Del. Ch. 1972), relying in part on the legislature having eliminated any statutory distinctions among types of vacancies, the court upheld the power of the board to fill a seat that had not, in response to a recommendation by the board of directors, been filled for two years by the shareholders.

[2] *See, e.g.,* Conn. Bus. Corp. Act §33-744 (West 1997); Idaho Code §30-1-810 (1999); Or. Rev. Stat. §60-331 (2001); & Va. Code §13.1-682 (1999). *See also* Former MBCA §8.10.Only a few condition the board's authority to fill a vacancy such as requiring the articles to authorize the board to fill a vacancy arising from a director's removal, Tenn. Code Ann. §48-18-110 (LEXIS 2002), or expansion of the board, D.C. Code Ann. §29-335 (West 2001).

A provision in the bylaws that calls for shareholders to elect directors at the *annual* meeting should not be interpreted as barring shareholders from electing at a *special* meeting those to fill seats that have been newly created. *See* Burr v. Burr Corp., 291 A.2d 409 (Del. Ch. 1972).

[3] *See* Rocket Mining Corp. v. Gill, 483 P.2d 897 (1971). *See also* Blish v. Thompson Automatic Arms. Corp., 64 A.2d 581 (Del. 1948); *and* Robertson v. Hartman, 57 P.2d 1310 (1936).

[4] *See, e.g.,* Del. Code Ann. tit. 8, §223 (2001); Ind. Code Ann. §23-1-33-9 (Burns 1999); N.J. Stat. Ann. §14A:6-5 (West Supp. 2002); *and* R.I. Gen. Laws §7-1.1-36 (1999).

[5] *See* Former MBCA §8.10(a)(3) (1984).

[6] 134 A.2d 518 (1957).

under the circumstances possible to convene a quorum.[7] Thus, two of three remaining directors acted properly to fill a vacancy on the five-person board pursuant to a bylaw provision authoring "directors in office" to appoint a "successor or successors," even though the articles of incorporation and bylaws had a general provision requiring seventy-five percent of the directors to be present for a quorum.[8]

§9.13 Removal of Directors by Shareholders

Shareholders have the inherent power to remove a director for cause, even in the absence of a statute or a clause in the corporation's charter or bylaws providing for such a removal.[1] Even though a shareholders' agreement provides that a particular director shall be maintained in office, the shareholders usually may remove the director for cause, because the agreement is subject to an implied condition that the director faithfully perform the duties of the office.[2] The inherent right of the shareholders to remove a director for cause, however, can only be exercised by shareholders controlling a majority of the votes or, if the corporation's charter requires a higher vote for shareholder action, such number greater than a majority as is provided in the charter.[3]

A proceeding to remove a director for cause need not be conducted with the same formality a judicial proceeding, but the accused director must be served with the specific charges, be given adequate notice, and be afforded full opportunity to meet the accusations.[4] In a publicly held corporation, where only a fraction

---

[7] But, when a statute expressly authorizes a majority of the remaining directors to fill a vacancy, then action to fill vacancies by two of three remaining directors of a board of five under statutes such as the former Model Act provisions that expressly provide for a vacancy to be filled by a majority of the directors even though less than a quorum. *See* Avien, Inc. v. Weiss, 269 N.Y.S.2d 836 (Sup. Ct. 1966).

[8] *See* Jacobson v. Moskowitz, 261N.E.2d 613 (N.Y. 1970).

§9.13 [1] Pardue v. Citizens Bank & Trust Co., 247 So. 2d 368 (Ala. 1971); Grace v. Grace Inst., 226 N.E.2d 531 (N.Y. 1967); In re Burkin, 136 N.E.2d 862 (N.Y. 1956) (referring to this power as the power of "amotion"); Auer v. Dressel, 118 N.E.2d 590, 593 (N.Y. 1954) (although charter gives directors power to remove directors for cause, shareholders retain their power); In re Koch, 178 N.E. 545, 545-556 (N.Y. 1931); Rodyk v. Ukrainian Autocephalic Orthodox Church of St. Volodomir, Inc., 296 N.Y.S.2d 496 (App. Div. 1968), *aff'd mem.*, 278 N.E.2d 917 (N.Y. 1972). *See also* Campbell v. Loew's, Inc., 134 A.2d 852 (Del. Ch. 1957).

Shareholders in fact have the power to vote to remove the entire board at once, which may be desirable to avoid an otherwise antagonistic board from filling the vacancies created if only selected directors have been removed. *See* Scott County Tobacco Warehouse, Inc. v. Harris, 201 S.E.2d 780 (Va. 1974).

[2] *See* Springut v. Don & Bob Restaurants of Am., Inc., 394 N.Y.S.2d 971 (App. Div. 1977). The question of whether a corporation's shareholders can by appropriate charter or bylaw provision deprive themselves of their inherent power to remove directors for cause was left open in Campbell v. Loew's, Inc., 134 A.2d 852, 858 (Del. Ch. 1957).

[3] *See* Springut v. Don & Bob Restaurants of Am., Inc., 394 N.Y.S.2d 971 (App. Div. 1977); In re Burkin, 136 N.E.2d 862 (N.Y. 1956) (where unanimity was required to remove, court stayed arbitration instituted by one faction on issue of removal for cause when shareholder vote for removal was divided).

[4] Schirmer v. Bear, 672 N.E.2d 1171 (Ill. App. Ct. 1996); Brenner v. Hart Systems, Inc., 493 N.Y.S.2d 881 (N.Y. App. Div. 1985); Cooke v. Teleprompter Corp., 334 F. Supp. 467 (S.D.N.Y. 1971); Campbell v. Loew's, Inc., 134 A.2d 852 (Del. Ch. 1957).

of the shareholders attend meetings in person, an accused director must be afforded an opportunity to communicate with the shareholders. In a leading Delaware case,[5] the chancellor provided a fair hearing by requiring that the accused directors be given an opportunity, at the corporation's expense, to present their defense to the shareholders in the form of a statement that would "accompany or precede the initial solicitation of the proxies seeking authority to vote for the removal of such director for cause."

Whether cause exists for the removal of a director or directors is subject to judicial review.[6] As a general proposition, a director must be guilty of some abuse of trust or malfeasance or nonfeasance in office to justify dismissal.[7] Thus a director's disagreement with shareholders on corporate policy or a mistake by a director is not grounds for dismissal.[8] A desire to take over control of the corporation or failure to cooperate with the president has been held insufficient cause for director removal.[9] On the other hand, improper withdrawal of funds and payment of salaries, commissions, and management fees have been held to constitute an abuse of trust and thus cause for dismissal.[10] Other improprieties that have been held to constitute sufficient cause include a director's allowing the payment of rebates contrary to the board's orders[11] and a director's organizing a competing company or accepting employment with a competing company.[12]

In the absence of a controlling statute or valid charter or bylaw provision, courts have generally held that the shareholders do not have the power to remove a director without cause; consequently, a director who is serving the corporation faithfully is privileged to continue in office until the end of the term despite the opposition of a majority of the shareholders.[13] In most states, clear statutory or judicial support exists for the use of a charter or bylaw provision for removal without cause, and such provisions are common.[14]

[5] Campbell v. Loew's, Inc., 134 A.2d 852, 861-862 (Del. Ch. 1957), noted in 71 Harv. L. Rev. 1154 (1958).

[6] See, e.g., Grace v. Grace Inst., 226 N.E.2d 531 (N.Y. 1967) (court reluctant to interfere with judgment for or against removal of those running corporation when evidence exists to support each judgment); In re Koch, 178 N.E. 545 (N.Y. 1931).

[7] See generally 2 William M. Fletcher, Cyclopedia of the Law of Private Corporations §356 (perm. ed. rev. vol. 1990) (hereinafter, Fletcher, Cyclopedia).

[8] See Abreu v. Unica Ind. Sales, Inc., 586 N.E.2d 661 (Ill. App. Ct. 1991) (dealing with cause for removal by a court); Fox v. Cody, 252 N.Y.S. 395 (Sup. Ct. 1930).

[9] Campbell v. Loew's, Inc., 134 A.2d 852, 860-861 (Del. Ch. 1957). See also Markovitz v. Markovitz, 8 A.2d 46 (Pa. 1939).

[10] People v. Singer, 85 N.Y.S.2d 727 (Sup. Ct. 1949) (action by attorney general).

[11] Koppitz-Melchers, Inc. v. Koppitz, 24 N.W.2d 220 (Mich. 1946).

[12] Eckhaus v. Ma, 635 F. Supp. 873 (S.D.N.Y. 1986); Fells v. Katz, 175 N.E. 516 (N.Y. 1931).

[13] E.g., Toledo Traction, Light & Power Co. v. Smith, 205 F. 643 (N.D. Ohio 1913); Frank v. Anthony, 107 So. 2d 136 (Fla. Dist. Ct. App. 1958), noted in 12 U. Fla. L. Rev. 232 (1959), 8 U. Kan. L. Rev. 154 (1959); Abberger v. Kulp, 281 N.Y.S. 373, 376 (Sup. Ct. 1935).

[14] E.g., People ex rel. Manice v. Powell, 94 N.E. 634, 637 (N.Y. 1911). Some states require a charter or bylaw provision to authorize removal without cause. See, e.g., N.Y. Bus. Corp. Law §706(b) (McKinney 1986); MBCA §8.09. See 1 O'Neal & Thompson, O'Neal's Close Corporations, supra §9.05 note 10, §3.59.

C. Removal of Directors

A large number of corporation statutes now specifically grant power to a majority of the shareholders to remove directors without cause or specifically authorize charter or bylaw provisions granting such power.[15] The Model Business Corporation Act, for example, states in part:

> The shareholders may remove one or more directors with or without cause unless the articles of incorporation provide that directors may be removed only for cause.[16]

Under a statute of this kind, "the right of removal hinges not upon the propriety of a director's conduct but upon the bare question of whether the shareholders desire to retain him as a representative on the board for whatever reason."[17]

In a corporation with a number of classes of shares, with each class electing a specified number of directors, the issue may arise as to whether directors elected by a particular class of stock can be removed by a vote of the shareholders generally or only by a vote of holders of the class of shares that elected the directors. The better view is that shareholders of a specific class should have exclusive power to remove the directors whom they elect,[18] although the case law bearing on this point is sparse and inconclusive.[19] Many corporation statutes now specifically protect directors elected by a particular class of shares under a system of class voting against removal by the votes of holders of other classes of shares.[20]

Cumulative voting rights also need protection against shareholder removal of directors elected by minority shareholders. To permit majority shareholders to remove, without cause, the directors elected by minority shareholders under cumulative voting would obviously be unfair to the minority.[21] Most modern statutes empowering shareholders to remove directors contain a clause designed to protect cumulative voting rights.[22] A surprising decision held that the articles of

---

[15] *See, e.g.*, Del. Code Ann. tit. 8, §141(k) (2001); Mich. Comp. Laws Ann. §450.1511(1) (West 1990); N.Y. Bus. Corp. Law §706(b)-(c) (McKinney 1986); Former MBCA §39 (1969); MBCA §8.08 (1984).

[16] MBCA §8.08(a) (1984). *Accord* Former MBCA §39 (1969).

[17] Former MBCA Ann. §39, Comment ¶2 (2d ed. 1971).

[18] *See* Ernest E. Folk, The Delaware General Corporation Law §141, p. 59 (1972).

[19] *See* Auer v. Dressel, 118 N.E.2d 590 (N.Y. 1954), discussed *supra* §9.11.

[20] Cal. Corp. Code §303(a)(2) (West 1990) (removal without cause); Del. Code Ann. tit. 8, §141(k) (2001) (removal without cause); Mont. Code Ann. §35-1-424(2) (1993); N.Y. Bus. Corp. Law §706(c)(2) (McKinney 1986) (removal with or without cause); N.D. Cent. Code §10-19.1-41(3) (1995) (with or without cause); Ohio Rev. Code Ann. §1701.58 (West 1993); Former MBCA §39 (1969) (query whether statute covers removal with cause); MBCA §8.08 (1984) (with or without cause).

The Delaware statute, which seemingly shields directors only against removal without cause, leaves directors elected by a particular class vulnerable to being charged with misconduct and tried by a different and perhaps less friendly forum than the shareholders who elected them.

[21] As to the effect on cumulative voting rights of power to remove directors, *see* Note, 22 U. Chi. L. Rev. 751 (1955). *See also* In re Rogers Imports, Inc., 116 N.Y.S.2d 106 (Sup. Ct. 1952) (later amendment to articles of incorporation to authorize cumulative voting invalidated existing bylaw provision allowing removal without cause by majority).

[22] *See, e.g.*, Cal. Corp. Code §303(a)(1) (West 1990); Del. Code Ann. tit. 8, §141(k)(2) (2001); N.Y. Bus. Corp. Law §706(c)(1) (McKinney 1986); N.C. Gen. Stat. §55-8-08 (2000); Ohio Rev. Code Ann. §1701.58(2)(c) (West 1993); Former MBCA §39 (1969); MBCA §8.08 (1984).

incorporation and bylaws could not provide a greater vote to remove a director than the two-thirds vote set forth in the state statute.[23]

A novel question is whether removal without cause is inconsistent with a provision of the articles of incorporation that calls for directors to serve staggered three-year terms.[24] The Delaware Chancery Court held that a bylaw provision providing for removal without cause was invalid in the face of the articles mandating staggered director terms, reasoning that otherwise the bylaws would frustrate the purpose sought by having the directors serve three-year terms.[25] The decision quite likely would have gone the other way if the authority to remove the directors without cause had been included in the articles of incorporation rather than in the bylaws.

§9.14   Removal of Directors by Action of the Board of Directors

In the absence of authorization by statute or charter or bylaw, the directors do not have the power to remove one of their members even for cause.[1] Charter and bylaw provisions empowering a board of directors to remove a director for cause probably are valid in most states under statutes broadly authorizing optional charter and special bylaw provisions.[2] A few statutes specify that a charter or bylaw provision adopted by the shareholders may empower the board of directors to remove a director for cause.[3]

§9.15   Judicial Removal of Directors

Modern court decisions are fairly consistent in holding that, absent statutory authorization, there is no judicial power to remove legally elected directors, even

---

[23] *See* Georgia-Pacific Corp. v. Great Northern Nekoosa Corp., 731 F. Supp. 38 (D. Me. 1990) (citing commentary to Maine statute that "if shareholders have acquired sufficient votes to command a two-thirds majority, they should be able to put in their own board of directors, as a matter of right."). The decision may well be understood as guided by its circumstances, a battle for control, and the court wishing to preserve as best its could a level playing field among the combatants.

[24] For a defense of the benefits of a classified board, greater director independence improved long-term planning and increased stability, *see* Richard H. Koppes, Lyle G. Ganske & Charles T. Haag, Corporate Governance Out of Focus: The Debate Over Classified Boards, 54 Bus. Law. 1023 (1999).

[25] Essential Enter. Corp. v. Automatic Steel Prods., Inc., 159 A.2d 288 (Del. Ch. 1960).

§9.14   [1] Dillon v. Berg, 326 F. Supp. 1214, 1225 (D. Del.), *aff'd per curiam on other grounds,* 453 F.2d 876 (3d Cir. 1971) discussed in 29 Wash. & Lee L. Rev. 181 (1972).

[2] *See* 1 O'Neal & Thompson, O'Neal's Close Corporations, *supra* §9.05 note 10, §§3.40-3.74. The validity of a charter or bylaw provision empowering the board to remove a director without cause is more doubtful. *Id.* §§3.50-3.53. *See* Dillon v. Berg, 326 F. Supp. 1214, 1225 (D. Del.), *aff'd per curiam on other grounds,* 453 F.2d 876 (3d Cir. 1971).

[3] *See, e.g.,* N.J. Stat. Ann. §14A:6-62(d)(3) (Supp. 2000); N.Y. Bus. Corp. Law §706(a) (McKinney 1986) (except when there is cumulative voting).

on a showing of directors' dishonesty or inability to perform their duties.[1] These holdings are in stark contrast to the result reached during the early formative period of corporate law, when courts were willing to invoke their well-established equity powers to remove trustees for substantial cause, such as misappropriation, long continued absence, and antagonism of interest.[2]

The language of Section 8.09 of the Model Act illustrates the high threshold for misbehavior required for a director's removal by the court:

> (a) The [name of the court] . . . may remove a director . . . if the court finds that (1) the director engaged in fraudulent or dishonest conduct, or gross abuse of authority or discretion, with respect to the corporation and (2) removal is in the best interest of the corporation.

The showing required is set high in recognition of the primacy of stockholder suffrage rights that elected the director to office. The exercise of stockholders' voting power should not easily be undone by a court. At the same time, access to a court is an important safety valve in those instances in which traditional internal governance procedures cannot reasonably be expected to protect the corporation or its stockholders from the on-going misbehavior by a director.

D.   COMMITTEES OF THE BOARD OF DIRECTORS

§9.16   Committees of the Board of Directors

Boards of directors of publicly held corporations have long used committees to structure their control and supervision of corporate operations. The committee system permits a board to operate more effectively and expeditiously. Committees can study assigned problems in much greater depth than is possible for the full board;[1] they can develop and utilize specialized knowledge and experience; and they can provide a sharper and more intensive focus on particular business issues and activities.[2] Indeed, the boards of the large, publicly held corporations could not function effectively without committees.

---

§9.15 [1] Ross Sys. Corp. v. Ross, No. Civ. A. 10378, 1993 WL 49778 (Del. Ch. 1993); Harkey v. Mobley, 552 S.W.2d 79 (Mo. Ct. App. 1977); Griffin v. St. Louis Vine & Fruit Growers' Ass'n, 4 Mo. App. 596 (1877); In re Burkin, 136 N.E.2d 862 (N.Y. 1956); Cella v. Davidson, 156 A. 99 (Pa. 1931); Annot., 124 A.L.R. 364 (1940).

[2] See George G. Bogert, The Law of Trusts and Trustees §527 (2d rev. ed. 1978); Restatement (Second) of Trusts §107 (1959).

§9.16 [1] See, e.g., Gaillard v. Natomas Co., 256 Cal. Rptr. 702 (Cal. Ct. App. 1989) (use of committees is intended to enhance level of scrutiny).

[2] See The Role and Composition of the Board of Directors of the Large Publicly Owned Corporation: Statement of the Business Roundtable, reprinted in 33 Bus. Law. 2083, 2109 (1978).

Committees also permit governance of the firm to be improved by parceling out responsibilities among directors in ways that more closely address concerns for good corporate practices. The ALI's Principles of Corporate Governance strongest recommendation in this area is that state statutes should include a provision requiring that "large publicly held corporations"[3] should have an audit committee of at least three disinterested members.[4] All the other ALI provisions concerned with the board's structure and its committees are mild suggestions directed exclusively to corporations and their counselors, not to courts and legislatures. The recommendations in this regard are not normative, so noncompliance is not the basis of liability. For example, the ALI recommends that a majority of the board of directors of large publicly held corporations not have a significant financial relationship to the company's senior executives,[5] and other publicly held corporations should have at least three disinterested directors.[6] An audit committee[7] and a nominating committee[8] are each recommended for all public corporations, and a compensation committee is recommended for large publicly held corporations.[9]

Executive Committee. Historically, the "executive committee"[10] has been the most important and the most widely prevalent committee. The bylaws of most publicly held corporations provide for an executive committee and define its powers, usually in broad and general terms. The bylaws or board resolution setting up an executive committee typically vests the committee with "the powers of the board" or "the full powers of the board."[11]

Executive committees once were expected to act only between meetings of the board. The present practice in many corporations is for the executive committee not only to act between meetings of the full board but also to review, before presentation to the full board, virtually all matters going before the board for action, including major policy decisions and long-range planning.

Almost invariably, executive committees are controlled by a small number of key "inside" (management) directors. A typical executive committee, for example, might be composed of the chief executive officer, one or two inside directors, and an outside director.[12] There is little doubt that the use of an executive committee

---

[3] The ALI defines this term to mean a corporation having 2000 shareholders and $100 million in assets. ALI, Principles of Corporate Governance Analysis and Recommendations §1.24 (1992).

[4] *Id.* §3.05. A director is disinterested if the director has not been employed by the company during the preceding two years and has no significant relationship with the company's senior executives.

[5] *Id.* §3A.01(a).

[6] *Id.* §3A.01(b).

[7] *Id.* §3A.02.

[8] *Id.* §3A.04.

[9] *Id.* §3A.05.

[10] *See generally* Nancy F. Halliday, Note, Corporation Executive Committees, 16 Clev.-Mar. L. Rev. 167 (1967); Note, Executive Committee—Creation, Procedures, and Authority, 1967 Wash. U. L.Q. 42.

[11] For specimen bylaw provisions, *see* 1A William M. Fletcher, Corporation Forms Annotated, §§1294-1297.36 (4th ed. 1999).

[12] *See* Avery S. Cohen, The Outside Director—Selection, Responsibilities, and Contributions to the Public Corporation, 34 Wash. & Lee L. Rev. 837, 854 (1997) (recommending that "executive com-

D. Committees of the Board of Directors

composed entirely or largely of management directors raises a serious question regarding the role of the full board of directors. However, a broadly empowered executive committee composed of entirely inside directors is not necessarily inconsistent with the outside directors serving an aggressive monitoring role of management's stewardship. In such a context, one needs to bear in mind that there is a difference between management and monitoring, and in the public corporation it is the latter role that is commended to outside directors. That role does not require that outside directors be involved in the formulation and execution of corporate decisions. One must, however, be concerned that an executive committee not be the tool to exclude directors representing minority interests from real participation in board decisions.[13]

Executive committees have often been aggressive in exercising powers allegedly granted them. Occasionally, they have even tried to usurp the powers of the full board. Courts have usually condemned such attempts to seize complete control of a corporation and exclude the other directors from their management powers.[14]

Audit Committee. The role of the audit committee has long been an evolving one.[15] There has long been considerable divergence of opinion on what the duties and objectives of such a committee are or should be; these differences continue today. It has been observed that "[t]he primary purpose and function of the Audit Committee, as originally conceived and, in most cases, as currently intended, is limited to providing an opportunity for direct communication with the Board of Directors by the corporation's independent auditors, thereby tending to strengthen their independence and objectivity."[16]

---

mittees draw a majority of their membership from among the outside directors, to serve the same function, in essence, as is served by those directors on the board as a whole.").

[13] This is achieved by reaching decisions at the committee level and then formally convening the full board to summarily approve the committee's recommendations.

For other practices sometimes used by majority shareholders to circumvent cumulative voting rights of minority shareholders, *see* F. Hodge O'Neal & Robert B. Thompson, O'Neal's Oppression of Minority Shareholders §6.03 (2d ed. 1985).

[14] *E.g.*, Robinson v. Benbow, 298 F. 561, 570 (4th Cir. 1924); Hayes v. Canada, Atl. & Plant S.S. Co., 181 F. 289 (1st Cir. 1910); Maryland Trust Co. v. National Mechanics' Bank, 63 A. 70 (Md. 1906); Commercial Wood & Cement Co. v. Northampton Portland Cement Co., 82 N.E. 730 (N.Y. 1907). *But cf.* McNeil v. Boston Chamber of Commerce, 28 N.E. 245 (Mass. 1891) (action of committee with apparent authority binds corporation even though committee does not have actual authority; apparent authority can be derived from course of action of directors).

[15] *See* SEC Rule Proposals Concerning Shareholder Democracy and Corporate Governance, SEC Securities Exchange Act Release No. 34-14970, [1978 Transfer Binder] Fed. Sec. L. Rep. (CCH) ¶81,645 (July 18, 1978); Edward F. Greene & Bernard B. Falk, The Audit Committee—A Measured Contribution to Corporate Governance: A Realistic Reappraisal of Its Objectives and Functions, 34 Bus. Law. 1229 (1979); Charles B. Tomm, Director and Audit Committee Responsibilities Relating to Prerequisites, 36 Wash. & Lee L. Rev. 83, 96-98, 104 (1979).

[16] The Overview Committee of the Board of Directors: A Report by the Committee on Corporate Laws, 34 Bus. Law. 1837, 1861 (1979) (hereinafter Overview Committee). *Compare* Greene & Falk, *supra* note 15, at 1240: "The primary objective of the Audit Committee should be to ascertain that various processes, controls and procedures confirming or reviewing financial and possibly certain other information relating to the company are conducted by the designated persons in an adequate and appropriate manner."

Compensation Committee. The compensation committee is becoming increasingly common. It approves or recommends to the full board compensation arrangements for the company's senior management and any compensation plans in which the directors or officers are eligible to participate.[17] The compensation committee should be composed exclusively of non-management directors to assure an impartial and independent judgment on the fairness of management compensation.[18] In 1992, the SEC amended the reporting requirements for public corporations so that today a graphic representation of the senior executives' total compensation must be matched against data tracking the company's overall financial performance. The obvious impact of the disclosure rules is to heighten the directors' sense of obligation when establishing executive compensation. An unintended consequence of the new disclosure is to introduce to executive compensation a phenomenon previously enjoyed only in Lake Wobegon, a mythical community where everyone is above average. An observed consequence of the 1992 disclosures is more rapid ratcheting upwards of the executive's compensation, lest they be below the median for their industry.[19]

Nominating Committee. The nominating committee or, more rarely, the "committee on succession," has greater potential for improving corporate governance. This committee selects, or recommends to the full board, candidates for election to the board. The committee's responsibility should include passing on the performance of incumbent directors and determining whether they should be retained. In some corporations, the nominating committee recommends to the full board the membership of board committees and, even more importantly, the choice of successor to top management posts. The nominating committee might also develop and submit to the full board for approval the criteria for board membership.[20] While a minority view holds that a corporation's chief executive officer should be a member of the nominating committee, the better view, and the one gaining increasing acceptance, is that the committee should be composed exclusively of independent, non-management directors. The benefits of assuring the nominating committee's independence from its CEO has strong empirical support.

[17] "Its chief function is to monitor compensation arrangements with a view to insuring that the corporation is attracting and retaining highly qualified management, through competitive salary and benefit programs, and encouraging extraordinary effort through incentive rewards." Overview Committee, *supra* note 16, at 1848. Executive compensation is discussed in §§11.01-11.05.

[18] For a decision holding it is inappropriate to grant the committee members' motion for summary judgment to a challenge to golden parachutes approved by the committee's independent members, *see* Gaillard v. Natomas Co., 256 Cal. Rptr. 702 (Cal. Ct. App. 1989) (the possibility of facts removing the committee's decision from the business judgment rule's protection was present because the golden parachutes were initiated and approved after management had approved the merger).

[19] *See* Randall S. Thomas & Kenneth J. Martin, The Effect of Shareholder Proposals on Executive Compensation, 67 Cinn. L. Rev. 1021 (1999).

[20] *See* Overview Committee, *supra,* note 16, at 1845. Other possible responsibilities include the following: periodic review to determine the optimum size of the board; recommendations as to the kinds of committees the board should have and the structure and functions of those committees; and review of the quality, currency, and adequacy of information furnished the directors. *Id.* at 1846-1847.

D. Committees of the Board of Directors

§9.17 Limitations on Delegation of Board Powers to Committees

Under both common law and statutes, as well as under charter or bylaw provisions, questions arise as to the extent to which the board of directors can delegate its powers to a committee. Does the power to delegate extend to delegation of acts requiring the exercise of judgment and discretion? Is this power limited to delegating authority to act in ordinary business transactions? Or does it extend to important decisions, such as approving a merger and recommending it to the shareholders, adopting a pension or profit-sharing plan, declaring dividends, selecting the company's principal executive officers, fixing the officers' compensation, removing officers, and amending the bylaws?[1]

Some of the earlier cases held that the board could delegate "ministerial" duties to a committee but could not grant authority to a committee to determine matters involving high judgment or discretion or to inaugurate reversals of or departures from fundamental corporate policies.[2] Most modern statutes first state that a committee of the board "shall have and may exercise all the authority of the board" to the extent provided in a resolution of the board or in the corporation's charter or bylaws, but then carve out exceptions by specifying extraordinary acts that cannot be delegated.[3] Many statutes do not permit delegation to a committee of the power to act on fundamental corporate changes, such as approving a charter amendment, adopting a plan of merger or consolidation, recommending to the shareholders the sale, lease, or other disposition of all or substantially all of the corporation's assets, or recommending a voluntary dissolution.[4] Other nondelegable duties in a substantial number of states include filling vacancies on the board or board committees, electing or removing officers, altering resolutions of the full board, declaring dividends or distributing corporate assets, and issuing or retiring shares of stock.[5]

§9.18 Responsibility of Noncommittee Directors for Committee Actions

Directors can delegate power to act, but they cannot shed responsibility for oversight and supervision.[1] They cannot abdicate their responsibilities by delegation

---

§9.17 [1] *See* Hayes v. Canada, Atl. & Plant S.S. Co., 181 F. 289 (1st Cir. 1910); Commercial Wood & Cement Co. v. Northampton Portland Cement Co., 82 N.E. 730 (N.Y. 1907); Fensterer v. Pressure Lighting Co., 149 N.Y.S. 49 (City Ct. 1914). *See generally* Comment, 42 Mich. L. Rev. 133 (1943); Note, 5 Ark. L. Rev. 486 (1952); Note, 35 Ky. L.J. 156 (1947) (executive committees).

[2] *E.g.,* Fensterer v. Pressure Lighting Co., 149 N.Y.S. 49, 53 (City Ct. 1914). For early cases stating that directors could not delegate their discretionary powers, *see* E. Merrick Dodd, Jr., American Business Corporations Until 1860, at 193 (1954).

[3] *E.g.,* Former MBCA §42 (1969); *Accord,* MBCA §8.25 (1984); Del. Code Ann. tit. 8, §141(c) (2001); N.Y. Bus. Corp. Law §712(a) (McKinney 1986).

[4] See the discussion of the various state statutes in 2 Former MBCA Annot. §8.25 at 8-156 to 8-158 (3d ed. 1994).

[5] *Id.*

§9.18 [1] *See* De Met's, Inc. v. Insull, 122 F.2d 755 (7th Cir. 1941), *cert. denied,* 315 U.S. 806 (1942); Williams v. McKay, 18 A. 824 (N.J. Ch. 1889).

of authority and thereby immunize themselves from liability. Delegation of the entire supervision and control of a corporation to an executive committee has been held to be inconsistent with the duty imposed on directors by statute or corporate charter to manage the corporation's business and affairs or to supervise that management.[2] As a matter of good corporate practice, there should be formal action by the full board on all matters of major or fundamental corporate policy.[3]

Most corporation statutes contain provisions designed to emphasize the board's continuing duty of supervision and consequent responsibility in the important areas of corporate activity. Some statutes specify that the board's designation of a committee and the delegation of authority to it "shall not operate to relieve the board of directors, or any member thereof, of any responsibility imposed by law."[4] Nevertheless, when action by the full board of directors is taken in a matter after a report or recommendation by a committee, the directors may rely on the committee unless there is reason to believe such reliance would be misplaced.[5] Similarly, directors are not under an affirmative duty to investigate the activities or decisions of a committee unless the circumstances are such that a reasonable person would believe investigation was warranted.[6]

E. ARRANGEMENTS THAT ENCROACH ON THE BOARD'S POWERS

§9.19 Management Agreements and Other Corporate Contracts Delegating Control

Corporations sometimes execute agreements entrusting management or control over certain aspects of corporate operation to a creditor or to some other individual or corporation. In a management agreement,[1] the corporation is one of the

---

[2] See Williams v. McKay, 18 A. 824 (N.J. Ch. 1889); Kavanaugh v. Gould, 131 N.Y.S. 1059 (App. Div. 1911), aff'd mem., 153 N.Y.S. 1122 (App. Div. 1915), rev'd, 119 N.E. 237 (N.Y. 1918).

[3] The Securities and Exchange Commission has indicated that the board of directors should not leave the major corporate decisions solely to an executive committee. See Report of Sterling Homex Corp. Investigation, [1975-1976 Transfer Binder] Fed. Sec. L. Rep. (CCH) ¶80,219 (1975).

[4] See, e.g., Ga. Code Ann. §14-2-825 (1989).

[5] See MBCA §8.30; 1 ALI, Principles of Corporate Governance: Analysis and Recommendations §4.03 (1994).

[6] Overview Committee, supra §9.16 note 16, at 1841-1842. Noncommittee members must use care in "the delegation to and supervision over the committee," which may be facilitated, in the usual case, "by review of minutes and receipt of other reports concerning committee activities." Comment to MBCA §8.25 (1984).

§9.19 [1] If a contract attempts to vest the entire management of the corporation or even substantial management powers in another corporation or an individual, especially if a substantial fee is to be paid for these management services, the contract is usually referred to as a "management agreement." A common example of this relationship is found in investment companies (e.g., mutual funds), where the investment management is contracted out to investment advisors. See Thomas L. Hazen, Treatise on the Law of Securities Regulation §§20.2, 20.9 (4th ed. 2001).

principal contracting parties, and by agreement the corporation *itself* undertakes to vest its management in the other contracting party. The difference between an internal arrangement delegating authority to a committee or some of the corporation's officers[2] and a management agreement is that the former is always subject to the supervision and overriding power of the board of directors, which usually can modify or terminate the authority of a committee or an officer at any time, while a management agreement does not leave ultimate power in the board.

The decisions indicate that in general a management contract may be subject to attack on two grounds:[3] (1) violation of a statute providing that the affairs of a corporation shall be managed by its board of directors;[4] and (2) the directors, in view of their limited term of office, do not have the capacity to enter into long-term contracts on basic policy or management matters binding future boards for long or indefinite periods.[5] Insofar as a challenge to a management contract is based on the first ground, the authorities dealing with the supposed conflict between shareholders' agreements and the statutory norm conferring management powers on directors appear to be equally applicable to management contracts.[6]

The validity of a contract by which a corporation vests control of its affairs in another person or entity seems to depend on the relative quantity of the powers that are delegated, on the length of time for which the powers are to be held,[7] and perhaps on the purpose of the contract or the situation out of which it arises.[8] Simply stated, when the board's authority is relatively unfettered to withdraw from the arrangement and substitute its judgment for that of the third party, the delegation it can validly make is much greater than the powers it can cede to another when

---

[2] *See, e.g.,* Schoonejongen v. Curtiss-Wright Corp., 143 F.3d 120 (3d Cir. 1998) (upholding delegation to an officer of retirement plan matters, including amendments thereto). *See also, supra* §9.18.

[3] A management agreement for the control of a public utility or other special type of corporation may contravene federal or state legislation. *See, e.g.,* Investment Company Act of 1940, 54 Stat. 812, 15 U.S.C. §80a-15 (2000); Public Utility Holding Company Act of 1935, 49 Stat. 825, 15 U.S.C. §79m (1988); Wis. Stat. Ann. §182.0135 (West 1992).

[4] Marvin v. Solventol Chem. Prods., Inc., 298 N.W. 782 (Mich. 1941); Long Park, Inc. v. Trenton-New Brunswick Theatres Co., 77 N.E.2d 633 (N.Y. 1948). *See also* Mohawk Ins. Co. v. Bankers Trust Co., 234 N.Y.S.2d 240, 242 (Sup. Ct. 1962).

[5] *See* General Paint Corp. v. Kramer, 57 F.2d 698 (10th Cir. 1932); Beaton v. Continental Southland Sav. & Loan Ass'n, 101 S.W.2d 905 (Tex. Civ. App. 1937).

[6] *See, e.g.,* Walton Motor Sales, Inc. v. Ross, 736 F.2d 1449 (11th Cir. 1984) (upholding shareholders agreement conferring significant management powers upon a creditor); Fournier v. Fournier, 479 A.2d 708 (R.I. 1984) (upholding shareholder agreement that provided that a shareholder "shall act as general manager of the Corporation with full authority to hire, approve sales and contribute to policy decisions affecting" the corporation).

[7] *See* McKinney v. Gannett Co., 817 F.2d 659 (10th Cir. 1987); Sherman & Ellis, Inc. v. Indiana Mut. Cas. Co., 41 F.2d 588 (7th Cir.), *cert. denied,* 282 U.S. 893 (1930); Jones v. Williams, 40 S.W. 353 (Mo. 1897); Fournier v. Fournier, 479 A.2d 708 (R.I. 1984).

[8] *See, e.g.,* Grimes v. Donald, 673 A.2d 1207 (Del. 1996) (giving CEO unilateral right to terminate employment if directors interfered too much in management was not an abdication of directors' duty to manage).

its ability to withdraw from the arrangement is significantly restricted.[9] To illustrate this, consider *Grimes v. Donald*,[10] which provided that the chief executive officer would, among other benefits, be paid $20 million and receive handsome retirement benefits, if he should conclude there was "unreasonable interference" by the board of his management of the company. The Delaware Supreme Court held as a matter of law the contract was not void on the ground it constituted an impermissible abdication of the board's power over the company's affairs. The court reasoned that the sum payable to the executive was not so significant, given the size of the company, that its payment would preclude the board from exercising its responsibilities for overseeing the firm's affairs. The court further reasoned that judgments regarding the extent the board can restrict its future freedom are ones best commended to the business judgment of the board. In contrast, contracts delegating substantially all management powers to outsiders for indefinite or extended periods of time are usually held invalid. Thus a contract between two insurance companies that gave one the "underwriting and executive management" of the other for a period of 20 years was struck down.[11] From the terms of the agreement and the length of time it was to remain in effect, the court concluded that "not only managerial powers were delegated, but the entire policy" of one company was to be fixed and determined by the other.[12] Similarly, an agreement by a corporation giving the purchaser of some of its five-year convertible bonds the power to designate a comptroller for the corporation and providing that the comptroller would have complete charge of all finances of the company and that no expenditures should be made or authorized without his prior approval was declared against public policy and unenforceable.[13] On the other hand, corporations have been permitted to delegate to outsiders at least for a limited period some of the functions usually performed by its directors and officers. For instance, an agreement employing an executive for a period of five years and giving him the position of editor and manager of a large daily newspaper, with power to determine editorial policy, has been held to be permissible.[14] A management contract will be upheld where authorized by a separate provision of the state's general corporation law.[15]

[9] Thus, the delegation to a management company of complete authority over the company's investments was valid because the company reserved the right to cancel the arrangement upon notice. *See* Canal Capital Corp. v. French, 1992 Del. Ch. Lexis 133 (July 2, 1992).

[10] 673 A.2d 1207 (Del. 1996).

[11] Sherman & Ellis, Inc. v. Indiana Mut. Cas. Co., 41 F.2d 588 (7th Cir), *cert. denied*, 282 U.S. 893 (1930). *Accord*, Kennerson v. Burbank Amusement Co., 260 P.2d 823 (Cal. Ct. App. 1953) (voided without discussing the length of the delegation); Boston Athletic Ass'n v. International Marathons, Inc., 467 N.E.2d 58 (Mass. 1984).

[12] Sherman & Ellis, Inc. v. Indiana Mut. Cas. Co., 41 F.2d 588, 591 (7th Cir.), *cert. denied*, 282 U.S. 893 (1930).

[13] Marvin v. Solventol Chem. Prods., Inc., 298 N.W. 782 (Mich. 1941). *But cf.* In re Chicago & N.W. Ry., 35 F. Supp. 230, 249 (N.D. Ill. 1940), *aff'd*, 126 F.2d 351 (7th Cir. 1947) (recognizing that lender "may lawfully require the creation of a finance committee and a voting trust as further security . . .").

[14] Jones v. Williams, 39 S.W. 486, 40 S.W. 353 (Mo. 1897). *See also* Pohn v. Diversified Indus., 403 F. Supp. 413 (N.D. Ill. 1975); Dyer Bros. Golden W. Iron Works v. Central Iron Works, 189 P. 445 (Cal. 1920).

[15] *See, e.g.*, Cal. Gen. Corp. Code §300(a) (West 1990) ("The board may delegate the management of day-to-day operations of the business of the corporation to a management company.").

E. Arrangements That Encroach on the Board's Powers

§9.20 Long-Term Employment Contracts

Corporations often contract with an executive or other key employees,[1] promising employment for life, "permanent employment," for an unusually long term, such as 25 years, or assuring employment as long as the employee holds stock in the corporation. Under a view that must be viewed as dated, and hence, badly out of step with today's business climate, such long-term contracts were of doubtful validity.[2] The rationale behind these early decisions was that (1) the corporation statutes give the board power to manage corporate affairs and one board cannot properly take away from future boards part of that statutorily granted power by "freezing in" the company's agents and employees; and (2) the statutes, by providing for the periodic election of directors by the shareholders, contemplate that the shareholder can elect new directors and through the new directors effectuate a complete change of corporate management, a power that would be frustrated if corporate officers and other key personnel could not be removed from their positions.[3] Today, a successful assault upon the validity of a long-term employment contract is made upon contract, not corporate principles. That is, a considerable number of modern decisions sustain long-term, and even lifetime, employment contracts without mentioning their impinging upon the authority of a future board of directors.[4]

---

§9.20 [1] Executive compensation is discussed *infra* §§11.01-11.05. *See also* 1 O'Neal & Thompson, O'Neal's Close Corprations, *supra* §9.05 note 10, §§6.06-6.09.

[2] *See generally* Annot., 135 A.L.R. 646 (1941), 35 A.L.R. 1432 (1925); Wayne Carroll, Comment, Conflicts Between By-Laws, Charter or Statutes and Long-Term Employment Contracts, 45 Ky. L.J. 544 (1957).

[3] Beers v. New York Life Ins. Co., 20 N.Y.S. 788, 792-793 (Sup. Ct. 1892):

> If they [the directors] can employ a man to do nothing in a so-called "advisory capacity" as long as he shall live, there is no reason why they could not employ every clerk, accountant, messenger boy, or other employee for the same length of time, and thus take the management of the business of the corporation out of the hands of the owners of its assets, viz., the policy holders, with whom the policy of the law supposes the ultimate authority lies.

Today's more flexible attitude toward employment arrangements is illustrated by Grimes v. Donald, 673 A.2d 1207 (Del. 1996), where the Delaware Supreme Court upheld a contract that permitted an officer to terminate his employment and receive $20 million in liquidated damages if the board of directors interfered with his management. The court reasoned (1) that this was not such a substantial sum as to discourage the board's interference if conditions required and (2) that corporations must have the discretion to retain managers on such terms as their boards of directors believe are in the corporation's interest. *Id.* at 1214-1215.

[4] Baltimore & O. R. C. v. Foar, 84 F.2d 67 (7th Cir. 1936); Riefkin v. E. I. Du Pont de Nemours & Co., 290 F. 286 (D.C. Cir. 1923); Osborne v. Locke Steel Chain Co., 218 A.2d 526 (Conn. 1966).

Company bylaws may prohibit the terms of officers beyond a certain time period such that an officer's employment contract specifying a longer term will not assure the officer can continue to serve as an officer. However, the officer's removal will nonetheless subject the corporation to a claim of breaching that contract. *See* Pioneer Specialties, Inc. v. Nelson, 339 S.W.2d 199 (Tex. 1960). *Cf.* Streett v. Laclede-Christy Co., 409 S.W.2d 691 (Mo. 1966). However, stockholder ratification of the employment contract is an implicit amendment of the bylaw limitation. Magnus v. Magnus Organ Corp., 177 A.2d 55 (N.J. Super. 1962).

At least one jurisdiction has a statute that expressly authorizes corporations to enter into long-term employment contracts. Tex. Bus. Corp. Act Ann. art. §2.02A(12) (1995). *See also* Md. Code Ann.,

There is no apparent reason for a corporate employer to have less power than an individual to enter into long-term contracts. If the corporation is not permitted to enter into long-term contracts, the directors may not be able to enter into contracts that, in their sound judgment, are in the corporation's best interest, including employment contracts designed to obtain needed key personnel.

The commercial justifications for long-term employment arrangements can easily be understood. Moreover, any blanket prohibition of long-term employment contracts would merely bring about a result similar to that which occurs when you squeeze a balloon. The restraint in one area merely causes the expansion of the compressed air's force to another area of the balloon. There are numerous alternatives available to the firm to attract key employees: a grant of stock options, a promise of substantial compensation upon severance, early vesting retirement benefits, etc. So viewed, the natural question is why should the law single out one approach for attack on principles of governance and defer to the board's business judgment with respect to all other approaches.[5] This reasoning appears to explain why the lens through which long-term contracts are examined is that of contract and not corporate law.

The first consideration for the validity of a long-term employment contract is whether it satisfies the applicable statute of frauds.[6] Many states also require that the employee's promise should be supported by consideration independent of her promise to competently perform the work called for in the contract.[7] This requirement appears inconsistent with a fundamental tenet of contract law, namely that a binding contract requires not *adequate* consideration, but consideration. A far wiser approach is not to require that the employee provide independent consideration in exchange for the promise of long-term employment.[8] Instead, we should treat the presence or absence of such consideration as evidence bearing upon the existence of an express or implied promise of such employment. That is, the expressions "for life," "for as long as the employee chooses" and "permanent" may be used in a casual sense, may even be understood by the parties to have been effusive puffery, so that the agreement in fact called

---

Corps. & Ass'ns §4-401(a) (1993) (authorizing all the shareholders of a close corporation to enter into an agreement that includes "the terms and conditions of the employment of any officer or employee . . . without regard to the period of his employment").

[5] For a case where the business judgment rule protected the board awarding millions of dollars in severance benefits if the executive should leave because he believed the board was interfering with his management, *see* Grimes v. Donald, 673 A.2d 1207 (Del. 1996).

[6] *See, e.g.,* Merlo v. United Way of America, 43 F. 3d 96 (4th Cir. 1994) (employment contract extending beyond one year required by Florida law to be in writing); McInerney v. Charter Golf, Inc., 680 N.E.2d 1347 (Ill. 1997) (partial performance does not remove this contract from statute of frauds).

[7] *See, e.g.,* Deus v. Allstate Ins. Co., 15 F.3d 506 (5th Cir. 1994) (independent consideration includes employee winding up an existing business, transferring a secret formula, or settling a personal claim in exchange for the promise of lifetime employment); Merlo v. United Way of America, 43 F.3d 96 (4th Cir. 1994) (such consideration should be other than relinquishing another position).

[8] For a case rejecting the necessity of independent consideration, *see* McInerney v. Charter Golf, Inc., 680 N.E. 1347 (Ill. 1997) (recognizing bargained for consideration was that employer gave up right to terminate at will in exchange for employee passing up a lucrative job offer from a third person).

E. Arrangements That Encroach on the Board's Powers

for employment for an indefinite term so that it was terminable by the will of either party. So viewed, the presumption of being an at will employment contract can be overcome by proof the parties expressly or impliedly agreed the employee could only be terminated for cause *or* the contract was supported by consideration independent of the services to be performed.[9]

The further issue is the authority of the officer to enter into the long-term arrangement. Such a contract is rightfully seen as typically beyond the inherent authority of the chief executive officer. Thus, in *Boothby v. Texon, Inc.*,[10] the employee was successful in establishing the validity of a promise of "permanent employment" by the company's president by proving that the president acted with the implied authority of the board of directors. This was established by evidence that the board was informed by the president that "job security" was the issue that most concerned the employee and at a meeting of the board its chair instructed the president to do whatever was necessary to get the employee to join the corporation. A final consideration is that the employment contract should be tied to some test of competency.[11]

---

[9] *See* Cunico v. Bowie, 133 F.3d 926 (9th Cir. 1997); S & W Agency, Inc. v. Foremost Ins. Co., 51 F. Supp. 959 (N.D. Iowa 1998) (lifetime employment is extraordinary arrangement requiring strong proof of parties' intent).

[10] 608 N.E.2d 1028 (Mass. 1993).

[11] *See, e.g.*, McInerney v. Charter Golf, Inc., 680 N.E.2d 1347 (Ill. 1997) (may be discharged for dishonesty or disability); Boothby v. Texon, Inc., 608 N.E.2d 1028 (Mass. 1993) (fails to perform satisfactorily).

CHAPTER 10

Directors' and Officers' Duties of Care and Loyalty

A. DILIGENCE, SKILL, AND CARE; LIABILITY FOR NEGLIGENCE IN MANAGEMENT

§10.01 Liability for Imprudence and Honest Errors of Judgment: The "Business Judgment Rule"

What is the liability of directors for incompetence? Although directors are commonly said to be responsible both for reasonable care and for prudence, the formula is continually repeated that directors are not liable for losses due to imprudence or honest errors of judgment.[1] This formula is frequently referred to as the "business judgment rule."[2] Taken in its most cynical light, the business judgment rule means that management's position is vindicated.[3]

> Courts do not measure, weigh, or quantify directors' judgments. We do not even decide if they are reasonable in this context. Due care in the decision-making context is *process* due care only. Irrationality is the outer limit of the business judgment rule. Irrationality may be the functional equivalent of the waste test or it may tend to show that the decision is not made in good faith, which is a key ingredient of the business judgment rule.[4]

The above description of the business judgment rule is best understood by distinguishing between the duty of care and the business judgment rule. The former can be seen as embracing a standard for officer and director conduct, whereas the latter embodies a standard of judicial review.[5] The twin features of the business judgment rule's application to a decision of the directors is that the directors will not be liable for any losses proximately caused by that decision and the court will not substitute its judgment or that of the plaintiff for the decision made by the directors. We can therefore understand judicial incantations regarding the care obligations of directors and officers as aspirational, even normative. However, whether the officer's or director's departure from an understood norm results in

---

§10.01 [1] In re Reading Co., 711 F.2d 509 (3d Cir. 1983); Lewis v. Curtis, 671 F.2d 779 (3d Cir. 1982).

[2] *E.g.*, Burks v. Lasker, 441 U.S. 471 (1979); Abbey v. Control Data Corp., 603 F.2d 724 (8th Cir. 1979), *cert. denied*, 444 U.S. 1017 (1980); Auerbach v. Bennett, 393 N.E.2d 994 (N.Y. 1979).

[3] As one commentator has put it, when the court finds no breach of a duty of care "[t]he court in effect [is] applying the business judgment rule." *See* Harry G. Henn, Corporations: Cases and Materials 587 (1974).

[4] Brehm v. Eisner, 746 A.2d 244, 264 (Del. 2000) (emphasis original).

[5] *See* Melvin Aron Eisenberg, The Divergence of Standards of Conduct and Standards of Review in Corporate Law, 62 Fordham L. Rev. 437 (1993). Thus, section 8.30(b) of the Model Business Corporation Act sets forth a standard of care for directors, but a breach of that standard assumes legal significance only if the director's decision is not protected pursuant to the review standards set forth in section 8.31. *See* Model Business Corporation Act §8.31 Official Comment (1984). For an example of a court distinguishing between the business judgment "rule" and the business judgment "doctrine," with the effect that the former was viewed to shield the directors from liability for their decisions and the latter protects the transaction from further scrutiny, *see* Gries Sports Enters., Inc. v. Cleveland Browns Football Co., 496 N.E.2d 959, 964 (Ohio 1986).

A. Diligence, Skill, and Care; Liability for Negligence in Management

liability (or the court substituting its judgment for that of the corporate decision maker) depends on how her conduct is assessed under the review standard embraced in the business judgment rule.[6]

In general, courts will not undertake to review the expediency of contracts or other business transactions authorized by the directors. Directors have a large degree of discretion. Questions of value and policy have been said to be part of the directors' business judgment, although their errors may be so gross as to show their unfitness to manage corporate affairs.[7] According to the better view, the business judgment rule presupposes that reasonable diligence and care have been exercised.[8] But are there not, in addition, some limits on the immunity for losses due to honest errors resulting from a director's lack of intelligence, foresight, and business sense? Hasty action by an ill-informed board will not be insulated by the business judgment rule.[9] However, directors and officers do not operate in a world that permits them to have all the information they would prefer to have before they act. "The need to make judgments with only imperfect information available, and other elements of risk taking, are often inherent in business decisionmaking."[10]

The evolution in publicly held corporations of a class of directors who are compensated well and devote substantial time to the affairs of each corporation on whose board they serve, coupled with heavy investor reliance on director competence and diligence, arguably justifies imposing professional-like standards of competence on directors.

Nevertheless, the courts and the legislatures (or, perhaps more accurately, the leaders of the corporate bar who draft statutory standards for directors)[11]

---

[6] *See generally* Joy v. North, 692 F.2d 880, 885 (2d Cir. 1982) (in contrast to actors in common tort cases, corporate officers or directors are rarely responsible for their mistakes in judgment).

[7] Everett v. Phillips, 42 N.E.2d 18, 20 (N.Y. 1942). *See also* Helfman v. American Light & Traction Co., 187 A. 540 (N.J. Ch. 1936); Chelrob, Inc. v. Barrett, 57 N.E.2d 825, 833 (N.Y. 1944); Pollitz v. Wabash R.R., 100 N.E. 721 (N.Y. 1912); Holmes v. St. Joseph Lead Co., 147 N.Y.S. 104 (Sup. Ct. 1914) (Cardozo, J.).

[8] FDIC v. Stahl, 89 F.3d 1510 (11th Cir. 1996) (business judgment rule assumes that the directors have been diligent and careful; plaintiffs need not establish gross negligence, ordinary negligence is sufficient); Lewis v. Curtis, 671 F.2d 779 (3d Cir.), *cert. denied,* 459 U.S. 880 (1982); Otis & Co. v. Pennsylvania R.R., 61 F. Supp. 905, 911 (E.D. Pa. 1945), *aff'd per curiam,* 155 F.2d 522 (3d Cir. 1946); Stamp v. Batastini, 636 N.E.2d 616 (Ill. App. Ct. 1993); Casey v. Woodruff, 49 N.Y.S.2d 625, 642-643 (Sup. Ct. 1944).

[9] Smith v. Van Gorkom, 488 A.2d 858 (Del. 1985). At the same time, the circumstances may well cause the board to proceed quickly, even when it is aware that the board does not have all the information it would like to have, but which the particularly factual exigencies prevent the board from acquiring. *See* A.L.I., 1 Principles of Corporate Governance: Analysis and Recommendations §4.01(c), Comment e at 178 (1992).

[10] A.L.I., 1 Principles of Corporate Governance: Analysis and Recommendations §4.01(c), Comment f at 182.

[11] *See* Report of Committee on Corporate Laws: Changes in the Model Business Corporation Act, 30 Bus. Law. 501, 505 (1975) (hereinafter Report of Committee on Corporate Laws). *See also* Corporate Director's Guidebook (3d ed. 2001), prepared by the Committee on Corporate Laws, Section of Corporation, Banking and Business Law, American Bar Association, as published in 56 Bus. Law. 1571 (2001) (hereinafter Corporate Director's Guidebook). *See also* Model Business Corporation Act Ann. §§35 & 2, first paragraph (Comment), at p.257 (1977 Supp.) (hereinafter Former MBCA).

apparently are not yet ready to recognize the professional status of directors in publicly held corporations and impose truly professional standards of competence on them.

§10.02   Standard of Care and Diligence

There has been some difference in the language used by the legislatures and the courts to designate the standard of care and diligence required of the directors of a corporation in the management or supervision of its affairs. It is difficult, however, to tell whether the differing standards, which have been referred to as "semantic,"[1] make much difference in practical application. The particular statute's precise formulation of the director's duty of care does not assume great importance in the court's judgment whether the director has breached her duty.[2]

In New York an early theoretical standard was declared to be the care and diligence that an ordinarily prudent man would exercise in the management of his own affairs.[3] The fairer and more satisfactory rule is that degree of care and diligence that an ordinarily prudent director can reasonably be expected to exercise in a like position under similar circumstances. This standard was adopted by the Model Act, and a great number of states have followed suit.[4] However, in 1997, the Revised Model Act provision was changed so as to eliminate reference to this negligence-type standard. Instead, the 1997 version merely provides that "Each member of the board of directors, when discharging the duties of a director, shall act (1) in good faith, and (2) in a manner the director reasonably believes to be in the best interests of the corporation."[5] The conflict of standards, however, may be more apparent than real; in practical application such vague abstractions are meaningless, and a judge and jury will necessarily formulate their own measuring rods according to their own standards.[6] For example, the changes to the Model Act still refer to "director reasonably believes to be in the best interests of the corporation,"[7] which still captures the negligence concept of how a reasonable director would act under like circumstances. It would be most unfortunate should this change in wording result in lowering director accountability for breaches of the duty of care. The 1997 revisions to the Model Act also brought in a new section dealing with the standards of liability for directors.[8]

---

§10.02   [1] Richard W. Jennings & Richard M. Buxbaum, Corporations; Cases and Materials 178 (5th ed. 1979).

[2] *See* Edward Brodsky & M. Patricia Adamski, The Law of Corporate Officers and Directors: Rights, Duties and Liabilities §2.04 (1984).

[3] Hun v. Cary, 82 N.Y. 65 (1880). More recently, a New York court concluded that the business judgment rule applies when "reasonable diligence" has been exercised. Casey v. Woodruff, 49 N.Y.S.2d 625, 643 (N.Y. App. Div. 1944).

[4] Former MBCA §35 (1980).

[5] MBCA §8.30(a) (1997). *See* Committee on Corporate Laws, Changes in the Model Business Corporation Act—Amendments Pertaining to Electronic Filings/Standards of Conduct and Standards of Liability for Directors, 53 Bus. Law. 157 (1997).

[6] *See* Richard H. Dyson, The Director's Liability for Negligence, 40 Ind. L.J. 341, 371 (1965).

[7] MBCA §8.30(a) (1997).

[8] MBCA §8.31 (1997).

A. Diligence, Skill, and Care; Liability for Negligence in Management

§10.03   The Directors' Obligation to Be Attentive

A directorship, although conferring prestige and power, comes with the heavy demand that the director regularly attend board meetings and otherwise be attentive to the corporation's affairs. The precise commands of these obligations are gleaned from the few cases that have considered the fate of directors held to have shirked their responsibility. The obligation to attend meetings on a regular basis is breached by the director who is habitually absent.[1] Moreover, there is not one standard for a nonresident director who is retired and another for active resident directors.[2] But the duty of attentiveness commands more than regular attendance at meetings. In the early case of *Barnes v. Andrews,*[3] the court held that Andrews, an outside director whose tenure was less than nine months, breached his duty to inform himself adequately about the newly created company's operations. Even though the firm had raised a substantial amount of capital through a public offering, possessed a well-equipped and -staffed factory, and produced enough parts for starter motors, the firm was experiencing dramatic delays in assembling starter motors. The company ultimately failed. The court held Andrews breached his duty by failing to inform himself adequately about the firm's performance and position.

Barnes's holding is all the more striking because of an absence of any facts or circumstances known to Andrews that would have imparted reasonable notice to him that the firm was experiencing problems. Since *Barnes* was decided, a good deal of change has occurred in the boardroom of America's public corporations.

There is a collective view in business, government, and academia that we must discard the predominance of the inside board of directors and replace them with substantial monitoring obligations for outside directors.[4] This view is reflected in the reasoning of cases such as *Francis v. United Jersey Bank,*[5] where a director who was unfamiliar with the rudiments of the corporation's business, never read annual reports, and visited the corporation's offices only once during her five-year tenure on the board (during most of which she was in poor physical health), was held liable for the embezzlements committed by her two sons, who were the corporation's officers and remaining directors. *Francis* expresses the prevailing view regarding the director's duty of attentiveness:

> Directors are under a continuing obligation to keep informed about the activities of the corporation. . . . [D]irectors may not shut their eyes to corporate misconduct and then claim that because they did not see the misconduct, they did not have a duty to look. The sentinel asleep at his post contributes nothing to the enterprise he is charged to protect.

---

§10.03   [1] *See, e.g.,* Bowerman v. Hamner, 250 U.S. 504, 513 (1919); Hoye v. Meek, 795 F.2d 893, 896 (10th Cir. 1986).

[2] *Id.*

[3] 298 F.2d 614 (D. N.Y. 1924). *Compare* Cede & Co. v. Technicolor, Inc., 634 A.2d 345 (1993).

[4] *See* James D. Cox & Nis Jul Clausen, The Monitoring Duties of Directors Under the EC Directives: A View from the United States Experience, 2 Duke J. Comp. & Int'l L. 29, 31-44 (1992).

[5] 432 A.2d 814 (N.J. 1981).

> Directorial management does not require a detailed inspection of day-to-day
> activities, but rather a general monitoring of corporate affairs and policies.[6]

Francis also reflects the prevailing view that directors are not excused because of intellectual or physical incapacity from their obligation to inform themselves on a regular basis on the financial and operational status of the business.[7] But does the obligation to be attentive command more than regular attendance of meetings? Neither *Barnes* nor *Francis* emphasizes the number of meetings missed, but instead focuses on the necessity for the director to stay abreast of the corporation's financial position, progress, and performance.[8] For example, in *Barnes* Judge Learned Hand describes how Andrews, even though a regular commuter into Manhattan each day with the company's president, failed to learn of the company's production problems. And in *Francis* the court stressed that any review of the company's financial statements would have readily revealed the officer's embezzlements.

There indeed are a good many cases imposing the responsibility on directors to investigate and check the possible wrongdoing of co-directors, officers, and subordinates.[9] Where suspicions are aroused, or should be aroused, it is the director's duty to make the necessary inquiries; ignorance is no basis for escaping liability.[10] And the director's obligation does not end with a reasonable investigation but carries forward the duty to act reasonably in light of the information gained thereby. However, absent such reasonable suspicion, the director or officer acts reasonably in relying upon others, whether they be officers, employees or outside consultants.[11]

A somewhat different question is whether directors are under an obligation to install systems designed to discourage and detect the fraudulent, illegal, or criminal activities of subordinates. An early decision on the obligation of directors to monitor the activities of subordinates for the purpose of discouraging or detecting illegal activities is *Graham v. Allis-Chalmers Manufacturing Company.*[12] In *Allis-Chalmers* a derivative suit was brought against the company's directors to recover damages the company suffered because its employees engaged in massive bid-

---

[6] *Id.* at 822. *See also* Hoye v. Meek, 795 F.2d 893, 895 (10th Cir. 1986) (liability imposed on chairman whose attendance at board meetings was irregular); Senn v. Northwest Underwriters, Inc., 875 P.2d 637 (Wash. App. Ct. 1994).

[7] *Contra,* Berman v. LeBeau InterAm., Inc., 509 F. Supp. 156, 161 (S.D.N.Y.), *aff'd mem.,* 679 F.2d 879 (2d Cir. 1981) (director who was "virtual figurehead" not liable); Allied Freightways, Inc. v. Cholfin, 91 N.E.2d 765, 768 (Mass. 1950) ("an ordinary housewife with no business experience").

[8] *See also* Brane v. Roth, 590 N.E.2d 587 (Ind. Ct. App. 1992) (directors of cooperative breached duty by retaining inexperienced manager and failing to reasonably supervise manager to assure adequate hedging against possible declines in price of grain).

[9] *See, e.g.,* Michelsen v. Penney, 135 F.2d 409, 419 (2d Cir. 1943); Gamble v. Brown, 29 F.2d 366 (4th Cir. 1928), *cert. denied,* 279 U.S. 839 (1929) (bank directors breached duty by relying wholly on integrity of president or cashier without causing reasonable audits and examinations to be made or examining reports of bank examiners); Atherton v. Anderson, 99 F.2d 883 (6th Cir. 1938); Weigand v. Union Nat'l Bank, 610 P.2d 572 (Kan. 1982) (officer-director could not rely on president's misrepresentation of corporation's financial strength to escape liability when he had access to and duty to inspect corporate books).

[10] Hoye v. Meek, 795 F.2d 893, 896 (10th Cir. 1986).

[11] *See, e.g.,* Dellastatious v. Williams F.3d (4th Cir. 2001).

[12] 188 A.2d 125 (Del. 1963).

rigging with competitors, a flagrant violation of the antitrust laws. One theory of the plaintiff's action was that the directors had acted unreasonably in failing to establish a system to detect and prevent the bid-rigging. The Delaware Supreme Court dismissed the suit, reasoning that within a large multinational firm such as Allis-Chalmers, with over 30,000 employees, it is unreasonable to require the directors to undertake an active investigation of each division of the firm absent their being on adequate notice of any wrongdoing.[13] The court held the directors acted reasonably in relying on the reports and summaries of operations, which they had no reason to believe were untrustworthy.[14] More important, the court held the Allis-Chalmers directors had no responsibility to establish and maintain a system of surveillance unless there was suspicion of wrongdoing.[15]

One finds a good deal of dissonance between the *Allis-Chalmers* holding and the reasoning quoted above from *Francis v. United Jersey Bank*. The difference may likely be explained by their placement in time. *Francis* is far more consistent with the perceived role of today's outside directors as monitors. Moreover, since *Allis-Chalmers* was decided, there is a solid perception that it is good corporate practice for public corporations to design and implement legal compliance systems such as those argued for in *Allis-Chalmers*.[16] In the widely celebrated decision *In re Caremark International Derivative Litigation*,[17] involving approval of a settlement of a derivative suit alleging directors failed to properly oversee employees who engaged in felonious payments for patient referrals, Chancellor Allen opined that:

> [I]t would be . . . mistake to conclude that . . . corporate boards may satisfy their obligation to be reasonably informed concerning the corporation, without assuring themselves that information and reporting systems exist in the organization that are reasonably designed to provide to senior management and to the board itself timely, accurate information sufficient to allow management and the board, each within its scope, to reach informed judgments, concerning both the corporation's compliance with law and its business performance. . . .
>
> Thus, I am of the view that a director's obligation includes a duty to attempt in good faith to assure that a corporate information and reporting system, which the board concludes is adequate, exists, and that failure to do so under some circumstances may, in theory at least, render a director liable for losses caused by non-compliance with applicable legal standards.[18]

Though dicta in the matter before Chancellor Allen in *Caremark*, the above appears to accurately reflect the likely result that would be reached today should

---

[13] The court rejected the plaintiff's argument that antitrust consent decrees 19 years earlier imparted such notice, reasoning in part that the current board of directors were not aware of those decrees. *Id.* at 129-130.

[14] *Id.* at 130.

[15] *Id. Cf.* the internal controls reporting obligation of public companies under federal law. *See* 15 U.S.C. §78m(b)(2) (1988).

[16] *See* Corporate Director's Guidebook, *supra* §10.01 note 11, at 1274; A.B.A., Section on Corporation, Banking and Business Law, The Role and Composition of the Board of Directors of the Large Publicly Owned Corporation, 33 Bus. Law. 2083, 2101 (1978).

[17] 698 A.2d 959 (Del. Ch. 1996).

[18] *Id.* at 970.

the question be posed. Because the duty of care is an objective one, the practices prevalent within an industry and across types of corporations are normative in assessing whether a board of directors has acted properly under the circumstances. The prevalence of compliance programs across all types of companies and industries make the absence of such a program in a particular company appear to be a dangerous departure from custom. Accordingly, there is ample reason to doubt the continuing force of *Allis-Chalmers*'s sweeping rejection of the responsibility of directors to install a compliance system.[19]

§10.04   Directors' Actions Should Be the Product of Reasonable Investigation and Consideration

Lawyers are well acquainted with the connection between reasonable processes and the quality of decision-making. Not only does procedural due process enhance the validity of a decision but the discipline yields a better decision. These benefits are the object of the courts' preoccupation with whether directors' decisions are the product of a reasonable investigation and consideration of facts and issues surrounding any matter before the board.[1] A director is reasonably informed if the director considers the *material* facts that are *reasonably available*; there is no need to pursue immaterial facts or information that could not be acquired reasonably under the circumstances.[2]

Any doubt about the force of this judicial preoccupation is removed by the Delaware Supreme Court's landmark decision in *Smith v. Van Gorkom*,[3] where the court held the directors breached their duty of care in approving the sale of Trans Union Corporation. The sale was approved by the board of directors at a meeting that lasted only two hours. The presentation was completely oral, no written drafts of the acquisition agreement were circulated, and Van Gorkom (Trans Union's president) did not disclose that the sales price was proposed not by the buyer but rather by Van Gorkom. The board was not told that the selling price of $55 per share reflected the price Trans Union's own cash flow would justify if the purchase were a management buyout. Thus, the selling price did not indicate in any way the significant synergies of any profitable firm acquiring Trans Union.[4] Furthermore,

---

[19] Two leading Delaware practitioners (one now Chief Justice of the Delaware Superior Court) conclude that *Allis-Chalmers* would likely be decided differently today because of the changed perception of the role of outside directors. E. Norman Veasey & William E. Manning, Codified Standard—Safe Harbor or Uncharted Reef? An Analysis of the Model Act Standard of Care with Delaware Law, 35 Bus. Law. 919 (1980).

§10.04   [1] *See generally* Corporate Director's Guidebook, *supra* §10.01 note 11.

[2] Brehm v. Eisner, 746 A.2d 244, 259 (Del. 2000).

[3] 488 A.2d 858 (Del. 1985).

[4] The major source of any synergies was the large amount of unused investment tax credits that Trans Union had accumulated as a major purchaser of rail cars. The case facts clearly reflect that Trans Union had for many years been unable to realize any benefits from the ever-increasing amount of investment tax credits because its taxes were substantially reduced by the accelerated depreciation charges taken on its assets.

A. Diligence, Skill, and Care; Liability for Negligence in Management

there was no evidence in the record of the directors questioning Van Gorkom on the sale. Indeed, the case reflects the board's uncritical acceptance of the senior management's recommendation. Several facts were in evidence that supported the directors' quick approval of the sale. For example, the selling price represented nearly a 50 percent premium over the prevailing market price for Trans Union stock; furthermore, the buyer's offer was open for only 48 hours. These factors appear to explain why the directors so quickly approved the sale and in doing so they did not consult any outside financial consultants regarding the sale. Despite these factors that appeared to call for the board to act quickly, the Delaware Supreme Court held that the directors failed to inform themselves adequately and therefore acted with "gross negligence" in approving Trans Union's sale.[5] The court chastised the directors for failing to inquire how the sales price was determined and for failing to inform themselves of the intrinsic value of the firm.[6] *Smith v. Van Gorkom* does not hold that the directors approved the sale of their firm at too low a price; its holding is that the corporation was deprived of a reasonable determination of the sales price by its directors. The case was therefore remanded for determination of whether any damages in fact befell the stockholders because of the faulty deliberations by the board of directors.[7]

Smith v. Van Gorkom illustrates the *process* component of the duty of care, as contrasted with the substantive component that is discussed later in connection with the rational basis requirement of the duty of care. To meet the duty of care's concern for process, whenever practicable, it is good corporate practice to circulate in advance of the board meeting an agenda of such information as is useful to the board to understand the items to be discussed at the upcoming meeting. Such advance circulation, however, is not a prerequisite for the directors to be deemed to have acted reasonably. Director decisions are within the protection of the business judgment rule, even when made at meetings convened without an agenda or when material has not been circulated earlier, provided the facts otherwise reflect that the board was informed and adequately deliberated the matter.[8]

Just what is required for the board to act reasonably to inform itself varies with the facts. Some decisions and some circumstances may call for less information, and less consideration, than others.

[5] 488 A.2d at 874.

[6] *Id. See* Hanson Trust PLC v. SCM Corp., 781 F.2d 264, 275 (2d Cir. 1986); Sealy Mattress Co. of N.J. v. Sealy, Inc., [1987 Transfer Binder] Fed. Sec. L. Rep. (CCH) ¶93,331 (Del. Ch. 1987); Plaza Sec. Co. v. Fruehauf Corp., 643 F. Supp. 1535, 1540 (E.D. Mich. 1986), *aff'd*, Edelman v. Fruehauf Corp., 798 F.2d 882 (6th Cir. 1986). *See also* Meyers v. Moody, 693 F.2d 1196, 1209 (5th Cir. 1982), *cert. denied*, 464 U.S. 920 (1983); Doyle v. Union Ins., 277 N.W.2d 36 (Neb. 1979).

[7] The case was settled for $23.5 million, with $10 million coming from the corporation's directors' and officers' liability policy and most of the remainder from the buyer. Bayless Manning, Reflections and Practical Tips on Life in the Boardroom After *Van Gorkom*, 41 Bus. Law. 1 (1985).

[8] Unocal Corp. v. Mesa Petroleum Co., 493 A.2d 946 (Del. 1985) (consultations over 11 hours with legal and financial advisors); Bennett v. Propp, 187 A.2d 405 (Del. 1962).

In addition to sparking a good deal of commentary[9] and adding to the demand for consultants such as investment bankers, *Smith v. Van Gorkom* reinforces the importance of the board's counselor to assure that the directors act in as deliberate and thorough manner as is possible under the circumstances. Courts repeatedly accord greater weight to the actions of directors who are informed by outside experts and consultants.[10] Similarly, a board's delegation to or reliance upon a committee of directors charged with responsibility to handle a matter is a reasonable practice.[11] The consultants need not be from outside the organization; reliance on officers and employees within the organization is appropriate, provided the directors are not on notice of any facts suggesting such reliance is unjustified.[12] Many corporate statutes expressly provide that directors in discharging their duties may rely on information, opinions, and reports of consultants, experts, subordinates, and committees.[13]

The ability of directors to rely on information, opinions, and reports prepared by others is not an open invitation to shirk their responsibilities. Minimally, their duty to act in good faith requires the directors to have read the report or attended the meeting at which the information or opinion was orally presented, or to have otherwise taken reasonable steps to familiarize themselves with its contents.[14] There is also the qualification that the directors have some reason to believe the matter is within the competence or expertise of the consultant, subordinate, or committee on whom they are relying.[15] Thus the directors are not enti-

[9] *See, e.g.*, Dierdre A. Burgman & Paul N. Cox, Corporate Directors, Corporate Realities and Deliberative Process: An Analysis of the Trans Union Case, 11 J. Corp. L. 311 (1986); Daniel R. Fischel, The Business Judgment Rule and the Trans Union Case, 40 Bus. Law. 1437 (1984); Manning, *supra* note 7.

[10] *See, e.g.*, Treadway Co. v. Care Corp., 638 F.2d 357 (2d Cir. 1980); Enterra Corp. v. SGS Assocs., 600 F. Supp. 678 (E.D. Pa. 1985); Harriman v. E. I. du Pont de Nemours & Co., 372 F. Supp. 101 (D. Del. 1975); Pogostin v. Rice, 480 A.2d 619 (Del. 1984); Puma v. Marriott, 283 A.2d 693, 694 (Del. Ch. 1971). However, courts properly disregard outside experts where they are little more than an empty ritual. *See* Weinberger v. UOP, Inc., 457 A.2d 701, 707 (Del. 1983) (investment banker drafted fairness opinion for which price had been left blank until just before board meeting); Joseph v. Shell Oil Co., 482 A.2d 335, 341 (Del. Ch. 1984) (investment banker's fairness opinion regarding acquisition was prepared without considering value of probable oil reserves and was prepared in less than eight days although intrinsic value of oil company was believed extremely complex); Gilbert v. Burnside, 216 N.Y.S.2d 430 (App. Div. 1961), *aff'd*, 183 N.E.2d 325 (N.Y. 1962). For criticism that decisions such as Smith v. Van Gorkom wrongly encourage directors to retain outside advisors who may only legitimize the decisions of directors already "captured" by managers, *see* Charles M. Elson, The Duty of Care, Compensation, and Stock Ownership, 63 U. Cin. L. Rev. 649, 684 (1995).

[11] Pogostin v. Rice, 480 A.2d 619 (Del. 1984).

[12] It is on this point that the circumstances that separate the inside from the outside director are significant. For example, in the leading case, Bates v. Dresser, 251 U.S. 524 (1920), Justice Holmes held that a teller's flashy lifestyle should have prompted the bank's president to inquire whether shrinkages in the bank's deposits were the result of the teller's embezzlements. *Id.* at 530. The bank's outside directors, however, not being similarly on notice, were entitled to rely on the reassurances of the president and the government examiner that nothing was amiss. *Id.* at 529. *See also* Rowen v. LeMars Mut. Ins. Co., 282 N.W. 639, 652 (Iowa 1979).

[13] *See, e.g.*, Cal. Corp. Code §309(b) (West 1990); Del. Code Ann. tit. 8, §141(c) (2001); N.Y. Bus. Corp. Law §717 (McKinney 1986); MBCA §8.30(b) (1984). *See, e.g.*, Theriot v. Bourg, 691 So. 2d 213 (La. Ct. App. 1997) (affirming finding that reliance on ill-prepared advisors satisfied the business judgment rule).

[14] MBCA §8.30(b), Official Comment (1984).

[15] *See, e.g.*, MBCA §8.30(b).

A. Diligence, Skill, and Care; Liability for Negligence in Management

tled to rely on an attorney's advice that pertains mainly to factual questions for which the attorney is no better equipped to opine than the directors.[16] On the other hand, directors act reasonably in relying on their attorney's advice on either purely legal, as well as a matter that involves a mixture of law and facts, unless the advice is patently incorrect.[17] There is always the substantial qualification that a director may not rely on a consultant's, subordinate's, or committee's report if a director is on notice that such reliance is not warranted.[18] Directors breach their duty of care if they fail to question facts or opinions expressed in a report where the circumstances call for further elucidation or challenge.[19]

Directors' knowledge of the facts raising their suspicions can occur as a result of information gained through their non-director status.[20] Thus, the Second Circuit held in *Hanson Trust PLC v. ML SCM Acquisition, Inc.*[21] that the directors breached their duty of care by uncritically accepting their investment banker's opinion respecting the fair value of a product line without probing how such value was determined; had they made such an inquiry the board would have learned that the advisor had failed to calculate a range of values in determining the fairness of the price.[22] Also, reliance is not reasonable when the expert's advice is clearly inconsistent with all other facts before the directors.[23] Directors do not act reasonably in informing themselves as to a transaction's benefits by relying solely on the representations of a person known to have a financial interest in the transaction.[24]

An important qualification on the directors' ability to rely with impunity on the reports of others appears in a critical passage of *Smith v. Van Gorkom:*

> Under 8 Del. C. 141(e), directors are fully protected in relying in good faith on reports made by officers. . . . However, there is no evidence that any "report" . . . was presented to the Board. . . . Van Gorkom's oral presentation of his understanding of the terms of the proposed Merger Agreement, which he had not seen,

---

[16] Douglas W. Hawes & Thomas J. Sherrard, Reliance on Advice of Counsel as a Defense in Corporate and Securities Cases, 62 Va. L. Rev. 1, 148 (1976).

[17] *Id.* at 43-47. *See also* Dellastatious v. Williams, 242 F.3d 191 (4th Cir. 2001) (outside directors not liable for misrepresentations appearing in private placement memorandum because they justifiably relied upon officers and counsel who prepared the document and were much more familiar with the matters that were misrepresented therein).

[18] Gould v. American Hawaiian S.S. Co., 351 F. Supp. 853, 865 (D. Del. 1972), *rev'd and remanded on other grounds,* 535 F.2d 761 (3d Cir. 1976). It may well be more accurate to view the director's reliance on another's report as part of the totality of the circumstances in measuring the reasonableness of the directors' actions.

[19] Spirit v. Bechtel, 232 F.2d 241 (2d Cir. 1956); Speer v. Dighton Grain, Inc., 624 P.2d 952 (Kan. 1981) (accountant's report reflected mismanagement afoot).

[20] *See* Rowen v. LeMars Mut. Ins. Co., 282 N.W.2d 639, 655 (Iowa 1979).

[21] 781 F.2d 264 (2d Cir. 1986).

[22] *Id.* at 275. In his concurring opinion, *id.* at 284, Judge Oakes reasoned:

> To obtain the benefit of the business judgment rule, then, the directors must make certain that they are fully informed, and, to the extent that they are relying on advisers, that the advisers are fully informed and in turn fully inform the directors.

[23] Harriss v. Pearsall, 190 N.Y.S.2d 61 (Sup. Ct. 1921).

[24] *See* Fitzpatrick v. Federal Deposit Ins. Corp., 765 F.2d 569, 577 (6th Cir. 1985).

and Roman's brief oral statement of his preliminary study regarding the feasibility of a leveraged buy-out of Trans Union do not qualify as 141(e) "reports" for these reasons: The former lacked substance because Van Gorkom was basically uninformed as to the essential provisions of the very document about which he was talking. Roman's statement was irrelevant to the issues before the Board since it did not purport to be a valuation study.[25]

Smith therefore adds to the qualification that the directors not be aware of cause for believing reliance on an officer is unjustified. What Smith thus provides is the further requirement that the subordinate's presentation pertain to the very issue before the board (Roman's fairness opinion did not), and the officer must herself be adequately informed regarding the matter addressed. Certainly the latter is far more troubling, because if Smith is taken literally, it would deny the protections of the business judgment rule to directors who were otherwise unaware that the officer was not adequately informed on the topic. This clearly is a major departure from established principles[26] and appears inconsistent with provisions that permit directors to rely unless they are on notice of circumstances that make such reliance unjustified. It would appear a far better approach in Smith if the court had instead denied the directors' the ability to raise as a defense for failing to be adequately informed that they had relied upon Van Gorkom's and Roman's presentation by the court holding instead that his report did not deal with the substantive fairness of the price. Viewed in this way, it could fairly be said that the board had received no information on which to base its decision.[27]

§10.05   Directors' Decisions Should Embody a Rational Basis for Action

The duty of care has both procedural and substantive requirements. The requirements that the directors be attentive and reasonably informed are procedural in nature; the substantive requirement is that their decision have a "rational basis" or, as it is sometimes expressed, be "reasonable."[1] At first glance this requirement would appear to invite a good deal of second-guessing and intrusion by the courts and disappointed stockholders. But public policy considerations, discussed earlier, have caused the courts not to apply these standards rigorously but instead to

[25] Smith v. Van Gorkom, 488 A.2d 858, 874-875 (Del. 1985).

[26] See Fitzpatrick v. Federal Deposit Ins. Corp., 765 F.2d 569, 577 (6th Cir. 1985) (duty to inquire into reasonableness of subordinate's investigation does not arise until directors are already on inquiry notice).

[27] Panter v. Marshall Field & Co., 486 F. Supp. 1168, 1180, 1194 (N.D. Ill. 1980), aff'd, 646 F.2d 271 (7th Cir.), cert. denied, 454 U.S. 1092 (1981); Elfenbein v. American Fin. Corp., 487 F. Supp. 619 (S.D.N.Y. 1980); Warshaw v. Calhoun, 221 A.2d 487, 494 (Del. 1966); Muschel v. Western Union Corp., 310 A.2d 904, 908-909 (Del. Ch. 1973).

§10.05   [1] Meyers v. Moody, 693 F.2d 1196, 1211 (5th Cir. 1982); McDonnell v. American Leduc Petroleum, Ltd., 491 F.2d 380, 384 (2d Cir. 1974); Romanik v. Lurie Home Supply Ctr., 435 N.E.2d 712 (Ill. App. Ct. 1982).

A. Diligence, Skill, and Care; Liability for Negligence in Management

afford directors and officers great latitude in their actions and decision-making.[2] In its most rigorous form, the duty of care requires only that managers have a reasonable basis for their decisions, despite the availability of more compelling alternative choices available to them. One court has held for the standard to be violated, the directors' decision must be "so unwise or unreasonable as to fall outside the permissible bounds of the directors' sound discretion."[3]

To illustrate the wide latitude accorded directors under the rational basis standard, consider the leading case of *Kamin v. American Express Company*.[4] A derivative suit was brought against the directors of American Express Company questioning their decision to distribute as a dividend in kind nearly 2 million shares of Donaldson, Lufken, and Jenrette (DL&J) stock that American Express had acquired for investment at a cost of $29.9 million. The directors decided to distribute the shares as a dividend rather than to realize a $25 million loss by selling the DL&J shares in the market. The derivative suit plaintiff asserted this was a waste of the nearly $8 million American Express would have realized in tax savings had the shares been sold and the loss reported on its tax return. By distributing the DL&J shares to its stockholders, American Express avoided recognizing the loss on either its tax return or income statement.[5] The board of directors rationalized its decision as an attempt to avoid depressing American Express' stock price by reporting a $25 million loss on its income statement, which would have been required if the shares had been sold. As it was, the loss on the DL&J shares was merely reported as a deduction to stockholders' equity on the company's balance sheet. Certainly those who believe capital markets are efficient have good cause to question whether astute investors would overlook the true economic significance of the board's decision. Indeed, a compelling case can be made that the *wiser* course was that advocated in the derivative suit, especially since American Express did not deny that its financial statements would have to give some prominence to removing the DL&J shares from among its assets. Nevertheless, the court held that the directors acted reasonably under the circumstances and dismissed the case.

Kamin clearly underscores that the "rational basis" or "reasonableness" standard does not require directors to reach the best or even optimal result. It is sufficient that the decision have the appearance of being a reasoned response to a situation. Thus, entering into a multi-million dollar settlement with a terminated

---

[2] *See, e.g.*, Hills Stores Co. v. Bozic, 769 A.2d 88 (Del. Ch. 2000) (directors' decision to reject bid for control upheld, even though as a consequence it triggered contractual rights of officers for substantial severance award).

[3] Cramer v. General Tel. & Elecs. Corp., 582 F.2d 259, 275 (2d Cir. 1978), *cert. denied*, 439 U.S. 1129 (1979). *See* Brehm v. Eisner, 746 A.2d 244, 264 (Del. 2000) ("irrationality may be the functional equivalent of the waste test"); Giblin v. Murphy, 469 N.Y.S.2d 211 (App. Div. 1983) (rapid failure in wake of several questionable decisions by new management supported award for reckless and negligent management).

[4] 383 N.Y.S.2d 807 (Sup. Ct.), *aff'd*, 387 N.Y.S.2d 993 (App. Div. 1976).

[5] Moreover, the American Express stockholders would not be able to recognize the loss because their basis in the shares they received was the fair market value of the shares on the date the DL&J were distributed. Thus the real gainer in the transaction was the U.S. government.

executive is not waste where alternative was to incur uncertainty whether the executive could be fired and paid less.[6] To be sure, the result is a standard unlikely to command much respect in business schools and executive education programs, where the emphasis is on the optimal or even right response. On the other hand, a more demanding standard would most clearly result in less risk-taking by directors.

§10.06   *Knowing Violations of a Criminal Statute*

As has been seen, the commentators have offered many suggested approaches to conform the corporation's behavior to desirable social goals. The cry that corporations must act in a socially responsible manner is in fact an invitation to corporations to act beyond the commands of the law. That is, the call to act in a socially responsible manner seeks more than staying within the bounds of the law by, for example, assuring that their effluents into the air and rivers not violate state or local directives. Corporations are socially responsible when their internal goal is to surpass the minimum standard of acceptable behavior embodied in state and federal directives. A socially responsible corporation thus is one that avoids walking close to the line.

But what corporate-law-based punishment awaits the corporation directors or officers who cross the line by knowingly engaging in a criminal act? For example, what is the liability of directors who knowingly flaunt pollution requirements by failing to install the expensive scrubbers in their plant's chimneys that are mandated by federal law if the corporation is ultimately fined $75,000? Assume, however, that the delay in complying with the law allows the corporation to operate more efficiently, so that over the course of its noncompliance the violation yielded a net savings of $1 million—does corporate law provide its own disciplining force to discourage such conduct, or does crime pay?

Two early decisions appear to remove the protections of the business judgment rule entirely on proof of a knowing violation of a criminal statute. In *Roth v. Robertson*[1] the manager of an amusement park paid hush money to individuals who threatened to prevent the park from operating in violation of the state's Sunday closing laws. Even though the corporation received a large percentage of its total revenues from Sunday operations, the court upheld a jury award of $800, the amount of the hush money payments. The court partially based its holding on the payments being a violation of the state's criminal statutes. Another early leading case is *Abrams v. Allen*,[2] where the criminal violation was the corporation's board of directors' approval of the dismantling of plants for the purpose of intimidating union organizing efforts. One of four possible theories of recovery embraced by the court was the illegality of the board's actions.

---

[6] *See* Brehm v. Eisner, 746 A.2d 244, 266 (Del. 2000).

§10.06   [1] 118 N.Y.S. 351 (Sup. Ct. 1909).

[2] 74 N.E.2d 305 (N.Y. 1947).

A. Diligence, Skill, and Care; Liability for Negligence in Management

The contemporary view of the impact a knowing violation of a criminal statute has on the availability of the business judgment rule is reflected in *Miller v. American Telephone & Telegraph Company*,[3] a derivative suit seeking to recover a $1.5 million phone bill of the Democratic National Committee, which the AT&T directors forgave. The plaintiff attacked the directors' decision as an unlawful political contribution. Reasoning that "directors must be restrained from engaging in activities which are against public policy,"[4] the *Miller* court, relying on *Roth* and *Abrams*, concludes that the business judgment rule's presumption of propriety does not extend to directors who knowingly violate a criminal statute.[5] However, finding a knowing violation did not record an automatic award for the derivative suit plaintiff. *Miller*, a diversity action, was bound by New York law, which since *Roth* and *Abrams* has evolved to require the plaintiff to prove not only that the directors have knowingly violated a criminal statute but also that the corporation has suffered a *net loss* through the acts challenged.[6] Thus, if the overall gains of the violation exceed the losses directly associated with the violation, such as fines and attorneys' fees, there is no liability on the part of the responsible directors or officers. Stated more bluntly, purely from the perspective of corporate law, crime may well pay. As one of the authors has written:

> This limitation prevents the derivative suit from serving as a vehicle for redressing social harms committed by the corporation's managers. However offensive the conclusion that within the derivative suit context "crime pays," the net loss requirement may signal no more than the fact the derivative suit is otherwise a poor medium for enforcing societal directives not devoted exclusively to the corporation's efficient performance. The state's concern for pure air and water, safe consumer products, and fair employment practices implicates protections for a more diverse group than the class of shareholders with standing to maintain a derivative suit. When the deterrence question is instead focused upon a threatened harm to the shareholders themselves, there is a stronger basis to permit some recovery out of prophylactic considerations to remind the directors and officers that their ultimate responsibilities are to the shareholders.[7]

Overall, courts should broaden their costs and benefits inquiry to consider their holdings' likely impact on the corporation and corporate norms generally. Such

---

[3] 507 F.2d 759, 762-763 (3d Cir. 1974).

[4] *Id.* at 763.

[5] *Id.* at 762.

[6] *See, e.g.*, Smiles v. Elfred, 149 N.Y.L.J., Feb. 20, 1963, at 14, col. 6 (N.Y. Sup. Ct. 1963); Bordon v. Cohen, 231 N.Y.S.2d 902 (Sup. Ct. 1962); Clayton v. Farish, 73 N.Y.S.2d 727 (Sup. Ct. 1947). *See generally* Wesley E. Forte, Liabilities of Corporate Officers for Violations of Fiduciary Duties Concerning Antitrust Laws, 40 Ind. L.J. 313, 333-339 (1965); Note, Pleading and Proof of Damages in Stockholders' Derivative Actions Based on Antitrust Convictions, 64 Colum. L. Rev. 174, 179 (1964). *Roth* may be read to have impliedly based its decision on there being an overall loss to the corporation as a consequence of the violation by its conditioning liability on proof that the directors caused a "loss to the corporation." 118 N.Y.S. at 353. In *Abrams*, the plaintiff alleged that the corporation suffered a financial loss because of the plant closings. 74 N.E.2d at 306.

[7] James D. Cox, Compensation, Deterrence, and the Market as Boundaries for Derivative Suit Procedures, 52 Geo. Wash. L. Rev. 745, 765 (1984).

an approach is desirable where the particular criminal statute was for the protection of stockholders or other corporate interests.[8] A broad inquiry into the potential benefits of a successful derivative suit may well reveal there is no genuine conflict between the compensatory and deterrent objectives of such suits.

The American Law Institute's Principles of Corporate Governance is resolute in dealing with directors and officers who knowingly participate in illegal conduct. Their violations are outside the protections of the business judgment rule[9] and are not within the permissible bounds of a charter provision that otherwise can immunize directors from liability for damages.[10] And when the conduct is the subject of a derivative suit, the recommendation of the board or committee that the suit be dismissed is subject to a higher level of review by the court than are care violations and most categories of overreaching behavior.[11] More generally, the ALI incorporates into its broad duty of care the obligation that directors and officers act within the bounds of the law.[12]

The great hurdle in any suit not premised on the directors' knowing violation of a criminal statute but rather on their negligence in failing to detect the violations of subordinates is the problem of causation. No law compliance program is foolproof, and many violations by subordinates are likely to go undetected even under the most aggressive compliance systems. This poses a serious problem to the plaintiff who seeks to impose liability on the directors on the theory that the directors' failure to install *any* compliance program is a breach of the directors' duty of care. Because the plaintiff has the burden of proving not only that the directors breached their duty of care but also that their breach proximately harmed the corporation, the plaintiff generally will have great difficulty establishing a causal relationship between the absence of a compliance system and the injury to the corporation flowing from the violation.[13] The court may well conclude that the directors' failure to install any law compliance system constitutes only a technical breach, much as Andrew's failure to inform himself was so held in *Barnes v. Andrews,* discussed earlier. Thus the causation requirement lifts some of the pressure of personal liability from the directors' shoulders to aggressively pursue law compliance systems. Because the ALI does not have its own provision on causality, its various provisions dealing with directors' obligations to assure compliance with the law are accordingly weakened.

§10.07   Statutory Developments Limiting Directors' Liability for Duty-of-Care Violations

In 1986, the Delaware legislature amended its general corporation law to allow the charters of Delaware corporations to include provisions that limit the liability of

---

[8] *Id.* at 776.
[9] ALI Principles of Corporate Governance: Analysis and Recommendations §4.01 (1994).
[10] *Id.* §7.19(1).
[11] *Id.* §7.10(a)(2).
[12] *Id.* §§2.01(b)(1) and 4.01(a) and commentary at pp. 195-197.
[13] *See* §10.03.

A. Diligence, Skill, and Care; Liability for Negligence in Management

directors for damages arising from breaches of their duty of care.[1] Following Delaware's lead, numerous states have since enacted similar statutory provisions.[2] The standard format of such exoneration statutes is that they authorize the articles of incorporation to include a provision eliminating or limiting the liability of a director, except for certain types of breaches. For example, section 102(b)(7) of the Delaware general corporation statute provides:

> A provision eliminating or limiting the personal liability of a director to the corporation or its stockholders for monetary damages for breach of fiduciary duty as a director . . . [except] (i) for any breach of the director's duty of loyalty to the corporation or its stockholders; (ii) for acts or omissions not in good faith or which involve intentional misconduct or knowing violation of law; (iii) . . . [for unlawful distributions]; (iv) for any transaction from which the director derived an improper personal benefit.

The above excepted categories are typical of those found in other state statutes.[3] Three important facets of the exoneration statutes narrow their impact. First, its protection is limited only to breaches committed as a director. Thus, if a person serves as both a director and an officer and breaches duties in both capacities,[4] he would not be protected by such a provision for any violations of care committed as an officer.[5] Second, the provision's protections are limited to actions for damages. Equitable actions, such as for injunctive relief or rescission, are unaffected by the charter limitation on damages. Finally, the directors remain responsible for damages they cause to third parties; the charter provision protects the directors only from liability to the corporation or its shareholders. The typical exoneration statute is in the nature of an affirmative defense so that the burden is upon the person seeking the protection of the exculpatory provision to demonstrate the conduct fell within that provision.[6]

Other states have taken a different approach by stating affirmatively the types of actions for which directors can be held personally liable. This is something of a reversal of the exoneration statutes described above: rather than authorizing charter provisions that can eliminate or limit director liability, which the individual

---

§10.07 [1] *See* Del. Code Ann. tit. 8, §102(b)(7) (2001).

[2] *See generally* Deborah A. DeMott, Limiting Directors' Liability, 66 Wash. U. L.Q. 295, 297-310 (1988). For a discussion of other legislative responses, *see* Thomas L. Hazen, Corporate Directors' Accountability: The Race to the Bottom—The Second Lap, 66 N.C. L. Rev. 1171 (1987).

[3] Notable differences include California's statute, whose section affects actions "brought by or in the right of the corporation," so that they are not applicable to actions brought directly by shareholders. *See* Cal. Corp. Code §204(10) (West 1990). South Dakota extends its protections to actions by depositors and policyholders. *See* S.D. Codified Laws Ann. §47-2-58.8 (Lexis 2000). Some states extend their protection to officers as well. *See, e.g.,* La. Rev. Stat. Ann. §12.24(C)(4) (West 1994). *See generally* DeMott, *supra* note 2.

[4] *See* Smith v. Van Gorkom, 488 A.2d 858 (Del. 1985) (misconduct by Van Gorkom, who was both director and CEO).

[5] Section 102(b)(7) shields the directors from damages whether they arrive in law or equity for rescission. Arnold v. Society for Savings Bancorp, Inc., 678 A.2d 533, 540 (Del. 1996).

[6] *See* Emerald Partners v. Berlin, 726 A.2d 1215, 1224 (Del. 1999) (*dicta* because complaint only alleged a violation of the duty of care); In re Lukens Inc. Shareholder Lit., 757 A.2d 720, 733-734 (Del. Ch. 1999) (same).

corporation can elect, this state statute accords the exemption to its state's corporations without any election on the corporation's part.[7] Thus Florida provides that directors are personally liable only for certain violations of criminal statutes, receiving an improper personal benefit, unlawful distributions, consciously disregarding the corporation's interest, and willful misconduct.[8]

There is an interesting interplay between the exoneration statute and the court's review of a tranaction alleged to pose a conflict of interest. In *Emerald Partners v. Berlin*,[9] the Delaware Chancery court dismissed the plaintiff's suit against the three directors based upon allegations that a merger of the corporation with thirteen companies owned by the controlling stockholder was unfair to the minority stockholders. The Chancery Court justified the dismissal upon its belief the defendant directors had established their defense under the company's exoneration provision but showing they had received no benefit from the transaction not enjoyed by other stockholders and had acted independently of the controlling stockholder. The Delaware Supreme Court reversed the dismissal, holding that the lower court had proceeded improperly by considering the exoneration provision before first determining whether the merger met the "entire fairness" standard.[10] Thus, *Emerald Partners* requires that in cases where the complaint properly pleads a conflict-of-interest transaction, breach of duty of loyalty, or otherwise a failure to act in good faith that the court must first determine whether the transaction meets the entire fairness standard. If it does not, the court then is to assess the role the directors played in this failure and more particularly whether their lapse was a result of conduct exonerated by the charter provision. This approach is likely to lead not only to closer scrutiny of the transaction but also to the individual director's engagement with the challenged transaction. Under the Delaware entire fairness standard the court evaluates not just the price but the manner in which the transaction was considered. This would appear to result in closer attention to the director's involvement at each stage of the approval process than if the review focused only upon the grounds set forth in the state exoneration statute that removed its protection for the director.

A final variation on statutory responses to director liability is that embraced in Virginia, which in 1987 amended its general corporation law to impose a specific cap on damages that are recoverable from officers and directors in any action brought by or on behalf of the corporation. The specific cap is the *lesser* of (1) the monetary amount stated, if any, in the corporation's articles or bylaws (which must have been adopted by the stockholders) or (2) the greater of $100,000 or the cash compensation received by the officer or director in the 12 months preceding the action or omission charged.[11] A similar cap is suggested by the American Law Insti-

---

[7] *See, e.g.*, Ohio Rev. Code Ann. §§1701.59 D (West Supp. 2001); Wis. Stat. Ann. §180.0828 (West 2002).

[8] Fla. Stat. Ann. §607.0831(1) (West 2001). The last offense gives rise to liability only if the action is by the corporation or shareholder. A fifth category of director personal liability arises for reckless or wanton misconduct, omissions committed in bad faith, or wanton and willful disregard of human rights, safety, or property when the action is brought by a plaintiff other than the corporation or its stockholders.

[9] 787 A.2d 85 (Del. 2001).

[10] *Id.* at 97.

[11] Va. Code §13.1-692.1 (1999). One can more easily justify caps on liability for the director's breach of a duty of care, but not for the more purposeful breach of the duty of loyalty. Virginia's embrace of

tute, except the American Law Institute's approach allows the corporation to opt into the cap, whereas the Virginia statute mandates the cap for all corporations and permits the charter or bylaw merely to prescribe a *lower* cap than would otherwise apply.

The overall effect of such charter provisions is to focus attention on the transaction itself through a prayer for injunctive relief, rather than focusing on the personal liability of the directors. While appearing to be a major retreat from directors' responsibilities, the irony of charter provisions such as Delaware's is that they may actually stimulate an increase in the amount of litigation that questions director judgment. When the object of a suit is damages for the losses related to the directors' breaching their duty of care, there is the ever-present disquiet that the sanction for the breach is disproportionate to the directors' fault. The draconian nature of the suit therefore has caused the courts to insulate the directors through heightened procedural and substantive rules.[12] A charter provision shielding directors from liability for breaches of care may well encourage the courts to scrutinize directors' decisions more closely without fear that substituting the court's judgment for that of the directors will also visit a draconian remedy on the individual director. The object of such a suit is an injunction or rescission.

Moreover, the elimination of a damage recovery does not reduce the incentive for care-based suits, because plaintiffs' attorneys' fees still are awarded on proof that the directors breached their duty of care so that equitable relief is appropriate.[13] Thus the overall impact of the very popular exoneration provisions may well be that of encouraging plaintiffs to sue earlier and more frequently for protective equitable relief as well as lessening modestly the historical reluctance of courts to closely scrutinize director decisions. If this in fact is the impact of the provisions, we will have witnessed their having an impact quite different from their intended purpose, for their ultimate beneficiary will be the derivative suit plaintiffs, not the directors. At the same time, this result is not necessarily a bad one if the effect of the courts' activism is to use their equitable powers to protect corporations and stockholders from poorly conceived policies, practices, and transactions.

§10.08   Executive Officers; Supervision of Subordinates

The president, cashier, or general manager may come under even greater responsibility for the fraud or neglect of subordinates than do directors.[1] Thus, where it

---

caps is puzzling since a parallel provision of the Virginia general corporation statute rejects the "reasonable person" standard as part of the director's fiduciary obligations so that any inquiry into improper action by a director focuses exclusively upon the director's "good faith." *See* Va. Code §13.1-690 (1999); WLR Foods, Inc. v. Tyson Foods, Inc., 65 F.3d 1172 (4th Cir. 1995) (exclusive fiduciary standard in Virginia is the duty of loyalty).

[12] *See* Kenneth Scott, Corporation Law and the American Law Institute Corporate Governance Project, 35 Stan. L. Rev. 927 (1983); John C. Coffee, Jr. & Donald Schwartz, The Survival of the Derivative Suit: An Evaluation and a Proposal for Legislative Reform, 81 Colum. L. Rev. 261 (1981). More generally, *see* Reinier H. Kraakman, Gatekeepers: The Anatomy of a Third-Party Enforcement Strategy, 2 J. Law, Econ. & Organization 53 (1986) (low sanctions needed when small likelihood that monitors will act corruptly).

[13] Tandycrafts, Inc. v. Initio Partners, 562 A.2d 1162, 1164 (Del. 1989).

§10.08   [1] *Cf.* United States v. Park, 421 U.S. 658 (1975) (upholding conviction of president where unsanitary conditions existed at one of twelve warehouses; corporation had 36,000 employees and

is the duty of the president of a corporation to supervise its affairs and to take and keep bonds from subordinate officers, and the president negligently fails to take the required bond from an officer who is entrusted with funds and becomes a defaulter, it is the president who is liable to the corporation for the loss.[2]

In a leading Supreme Court case[3] a bookkeeper of a small national bank on a salary of $12 per week defrauded the bank during a series of years of over $300,000, aggregating more than the bank's capital and more than the normal average of its deposits. This was accomplished in a novel and ingenious way by falsifying the deposit ledger and making false charges against deposits, thereby diminishing the apparent liability to depositors. The fraud could have been discovered by the cashier had he examined checks as they came from the clearing-house, or had he compared the deposit ledger with the depositors' pass books. But he negligently placed too much trust in the bookkeeper. The directors, serving gratuitously, were held not negligent in accepting the cashier's statements of liabilities and were not bound to inspect the depositors' ledger or call in the pass books and compare them with it. The president, who had received certain warnings that the bookkeeper was living fast and dealing in stocks, was held to have been negligent in failing to make an examination, especially as he was in control of the bank's affairs, with immediate access to the depositors' ledger.[4] More recently the Supreme Court upheld the criminal conviction of the president of a 36,000-employee concern with 870 retail outlets where the president's failure to supervise resulted in one of the company's 12 warehouses being in violation of federal sanitary standards.[5]

B.   DEALINGS BETWEEN DIRECTORS AND THEIR CORPORATIONS — CONFLICTS OF INTEREST

§10.09   The Scope of the Officers' and Directors' Duty of Loyalty

Mapping the scope of the directors' or officers' fiduciary obligations is not easy. The nature of the challenge is concisely stated in the now classic observation by Supreme Court Justice Felix Frankfurter in *Securities and Exchange Commission v. Chenery Corp.*: "[T]o say that a man is a fiduciary only begins the analysis; it gives

---

874 retail outlets). The duty of supervision is necessarily dependent on the corporation's governance structure. *See supra* §§9.01-9.04; Richard M. Buxbaum, The Internal Division of Powers on Corporate Governance, 73 Cal. L. Rev. 1671 (1985).

[2] Pontchartrain R.R. v. Paulding, 11 La. 30 (1837).

[3] Bates v. Dresser, 251 U.S. 524 (1920).

[4] *Cf.* Bates v. Seeds, 272 N.W. 515 (Iowa 1937); 3A William M. Fletcher, Cyclopedia of Corporations §§1070-1080 (1994 rev. ed.).

[5] United States v. Park, 421 U.S. 658 (1975).

B. Dealings Between Directors and Their Corporations

direction to further inquiry. To whom is he a fiduciary? What obligations does he owe as a fiduciary? In what respect has he failed to discharge these obligations?"[1] In the early formative years of corporate law, it was assumed that the rules governing directors and officers should conform to the strict rules governing trustees and agents. Hence, courts frequently referred to directors as both trustees and agents with the effect of holding directors to the same strict rules of disqualification to contract with their principal the corporation.[2] However, the functions performed, and hence the obligations implicit to fulfill the fiduciary's undertakings, are not the same for trustees, guardians, executors, administrators, agents, partners, promoters, directors and officers.[3] The differences in the expressed tasks, and the undertakings implicit for their accomplishment, necessarily weaken the analogy between, on the one hand, trustees and, on the other hand, corporate directors or officers. Nevertheless, an aspect of the relationship of directors and officers to the corporation is a fiduciary relationship, and the corporation's owners are the beneficiaries of the duties owed by the officers and directors. The rhetoric of the director or officers as a trustee, therefore, continues to appear in today's decisions, although the guidance that courts invoke to determine the content of the officer's or director's fiduciary obligation is gleaned not by reference to the law of trusts but to the extensive body of corporate fiduciary case law.

The preceding sections of this chapter have closely examined the many facets of the duty of care. Directors and officers must also comply with their duty of loyalty[4] if they are to enjoy the protective benefits of the business judgment rule. The divide between the duty of care and loyalty is not a sharp one, and the courts frequently blur the distinction between these twin obligations.[5] As seen in the preceding material of this chapter, there are many dimensions to the duty of care. In broad overview, the duty of care is about process by which officers and directors

§10.09 [1] 318 U.S. 80, 85-86 (1942).

[2] *See, e.g.*, North Confidence Mining & Dev. Co. v. Fitch, 208 P. 328 (Cal. Ct. App. 1922); Stack v. Welder, 31 P.2d 436 (Cal. Ct. App. 1934); Gates v. Plainfield Trust Co., 191 A.304, 318 (N.J. Ch. 1937), *aff'd*, 194 A. 65 (N.J. 1937). As to agents, *see* Restatement (Second) Agency §§389-393 (1958). One can even find in the Supreme Court's rhetoric the analogy to the law of trusts when setting forth the obligations of corporate directors. *See, e.g.*, Pepper v. Litton, 308 U.S. 295, 311 (1939) ("He who is in such a fiduciary position cannot serve himself first and his cestuis second. . . . He cannot use his power for his personal advantage and to the detriment of the stockholders and creditors no matter how absolute in terms that power may be and how meticulous he is to satisfy technical requirements.").

[3] *See* Austin Wakeman Scott, The Trustee's Duty of Loyalty, 49 Harv. L. Rev. 521 (1936). *But see* Bovay v. H.M. Byllesby & Co., 38 A.2d 808 (Del. 1944).

[4] The duty of loyalty is equated to the "good faith" requirement that appears in statutes and in court opinions dealing with the obligations of directors and officers. *See, e.g.,* Gaylord Container Shareholders Litig., 753 A.2d 462, 475-476 n.41 (Del. Ch. 2000).

[5] *See* Mills Acquisition Co. v. MacMillan, Inc., 559 A.2d 1261, 1284 n.32 (Del. 1989) (disinterested directors who abandon their oversight responsibilities in context of takeover breach their duties of care and loyalty); Lawrence A. Cunningham & Charles M. Yablon, Delaware Fiduciary Duty Law After QVC and *Technicolor*: A Unified Standard and the End of *Revlon* Duties?, 49 Bus. Law. 1594, 1625 (1994).

are to reach decisions and, more generally, fulfill their monitoring obligations. Hence the material earlier in this chapter focused upon the obligations to be attentive, make reasonable inquiry and have a rational basis for decision making. In contrast, loyalty is not about the decision making process or, for that matter, monitoring. The duty of loyalty is about the director's or officer's motives, purposes, and the goals that are necessary if his action is to enjoy the protective benefits of the business judgment rule.

The duty of loyalty most certainly includes officer or director self-dealing contracts and transactions which more generally are referred to as conflict-of-interest transactions. But an officer or director can be disloyal to her corporation in many more ways than merely transacting business with the corporation. Material elsewhere in this treatise reviews many instances in which special doctrines have evolved in situations that raise concern for the director's or officer's loyalty. A prime example of such a situation is the directors' defense of control where the courts uniformly remove the actions of the board of directors from the protective presumption of the business judgment rule for fear that the directors may be acting to protect their personal self-interest and not serving the interests of the corporation or its stockholders.[6] An even more blatant form of loyalty breach arises when the officer or director has usurped a corporate opportunity.[7] Interestingly, in special instances, loyalty violations can even arise when the directors or officers are acting in their good faith belief they are advancing the corporation's interest.[8] Thus, most certainly the duty of loyalty includes more than either self-dealing or usurping corporate opportunities.

An important question regarding the scope of the duty of loyalty is whether it requires more than the absence of self-interest, personal gain, and the like on the part of a director or officer. Or, does the duty of loyalty move beyond such minimalist considerations to require the fiduciary to act positively to advance the corporation's interests? That is, does the duty of loyalty have both negative and positive descriptions for how officers and directors are to behave?[9] For example, the American Law Institute's Corporate Governance Project sweeps the duty of loyalty into its obligation for "fair dealing," which prescribes a course of behavior when an officer, director, or controlling stockholder is financially interested in a matter.[10] Pronouncements of the Delaware Supreme Court can be seen as embodying a more expansive view of the duty of loyalty. For example, in a leading case on the disclosure obligations of officers and directors, the court analogized the duty to a "compass" that is to serve as constant guide for the fiduciary when

[6] See §23.06.

[7] See §11.08.

[8] See Blasius Indus. v. Atlas Corp., 564 A.2d 651, 663 (Del. Ch. 1988) (even though acting in the good faith belief they are serving the corporation's interest, management must demonstrate a compelling justification for action taken for purpose of thwarting the on-going efforts of a stockholder to exercise its rights of corporate suffrage).

[9] See Lyman Johnson, Enron: Loyalty Discourse in Corporate Law, 28 J. Comp. Law (forthcoming 2003).

[10] See generally Melvin A. Eisenberg, Corporate Law and Social Norms, 99 Colum. L. Rev. 1253, 1265 & 1273 (1999).

B.   Dealings Between Directors and Their Corporations

acting for the corporation.[11] And, in a leading corporate opportunity case, *Guth v. Loft, Inc.,*[12] the court observed that the directors have a duty "affirmatively to protect the interests of the corporation committed to his charge."[13] To so view the duty of loyalty places the obligations of directors and officers on a footing equal to that of contemporary standards for fiduciaries generally where the obligation is not simply to subordinate self-interested behavior, but also to "act exclusively for the benefit of the other party."[14] So viewed, the duty of loyalty is not merely regulatory, but has a strong moral element.

Those who prefer to view the corporation as a web of contract have little regard for the duty of loyalty being morally based. Instead, adherents of such a contractual view of the corporation argue that the source of officer and director obligations is what the parties would have agreed to ex ante.[15] Even with such a simplified view of the corporate enterprise, it is not clear that owners and their officers and directors would not have embodied in their contract a broad duty of loyalty. Indeed, the information asymmetries that abound when passive owners commit funds to the stewardship of others should minimally give rise to a strong presumption that the stewards were to always act exclusively to benefit the firm and its owners. The difference in the result is that the meaning of the duty of loyalty pursuant to the contractual view is driven exclusively by self-interest of the economic actors, whereas for non-contractarians the content is moral in nature having its roots in the social values of our culture.[16] What may be at risk in making a choice between these two views is that a view anchored so firmly in the methodology of economics, as is the case with the contractual view, may well blind or divert the inquiry from a richer perspective that gives regard to a wider range of social inputs.

An example of a breach of the director's duty of loyalty arises when the director, even though financially disinterested, knowingly fails to warn his fellow directors of material facts relevant to a transaction before the board.[17]

---

[11] *See* Malone v. Brincat, 722 A.2d 5, 10 (Del. 1998).

[12] 5 A.2d 503 (Del. 1939).

[13] *Id.* at 510. The court, after recognizing this broad responsibility then proceeded to find that this carried with it the additional obligations "to refrain from doing anything that would work injury to the corporation, or to deprive it of profit or advantage which his skill and ability might properly bring to it." *Id. See also* Model Bus. Corp. Act. Ann. §8.60 commentary (in determining whether a transaction is fair to the corporation, the court should be persuaded the transaction *furthers* the corporation's interest) and A.L.I. Principles of Corporate Governance: Analysis and Recommendations 219 (1992) (for director of conflict-of-interest transactions the decision maker must be satisfied the transaction is "affirmatively will be in the corporation's best interests").

[14] *See* Gregory S. Alexander, A Cognitive Theory of Fiduciary Relationships, 85 Cornell L. Rev. 767, 776 (2000).

[15] *See, e.g.,* Frank H. Easterbrook & Daniel R. Fischel, Contract and Fiduciary Duty, 36 J. L. & Econ. 425 (1993).

[16] Consider here the insight of former Chancellor William Allen: "[C]orporation law exists, not as an isolated body of rules and principles, but rather in a historical setting and as part of a larger body of law premised upon shared values." City Capital Associates Limited Partnership v. Interco, Inc., 551 A.2d 787, 800 (Del. Ch. 1988).

[17] *See, e.g.,* Berkman v. Rust Craft Greeting Cards, Inc., 454 F. Supp. 787 (S.D.N.Y. 1978) (some of the directors failed to disclose to their fellow directors their knowledge that the investment banker

§10.10   Interested Officer and Director Transactions: Defined and Historical Treatment

A few early American decisions adopted the inflexible English rule of disqualification whereby directors were forbidden to enter into contracts in which they have a personal interest that conflicts with their fiduciary duty of loyalty to the corporation. Under this view, unless there had been shareholder ratification, any contract with a director is voidable at the election of the corporation, regardless of whether it is fair and honest.[1] The theory of disqualification was that the corporation is entitled to the advice of each of its directors, and that directors may not abdicate their duty to the corporation and bargain with it in their own interest as a stranger, even if the corporation is represented by an independent majority of its directors.[2] It is argued that there cannot be real bargaining where the same person is acting on both sides of the transaction.[3] This rule of voidability is thus firmly grounded on the agency concept of representation.

Today, all American jurisdictions have found it impractical to disqualify directors or officers from contracting with their corporation. The earlier fear that a cor-

---

whose fairness opinion the board would rely upon had a material financial interest in the outcome of the transaction). In an early decision, Globe Woolen Company v. Utica Gas & Electric Company, 121 N.E. 378 (N.Y. 1918), Judge Cardozo examined the director's duty of loyalty in terms of failing to bring to the board's attention the one-sided nature of a contract with a company in which the director was deeply involved. Rather than emphasizing the pure conflict-of-interest nature of the transaction, Judge Cardozo focused on the broader obligation to protect the interest of the corporation from a potentially harmful contract. In *Globe Woolen Company,* the plaintiff corporation sued to compel specific performance of contracts to supply electric current to its mills. The defendant corporation answered that the contracts were made under the dominating influence of a common director and were unfair and oppressive. Maynard, the plaintiff's chief stockholder, resident, and member of its board of directors, was also a director of the defendant and chairman of its executive committee, holding a single share to qualify him for office. Maynard presided at the defendant's executive committee at which the contract was ratified, but he did not vote. It was held that the contract was voidable at the defendant's election. Judge Cardozo said:

> The trustee is free to stand aloof, while others act, if all is equitable and fair. He cannot rid himself of the duty to warn and to denounce, if there is improvidence or oppression, either apparent on the surface or lurking beneath the surface, but visible to his practiced eye. . . . There slumbered within these contracts a potency of profit which the plaintiff neither ignored in their making nor forgot in their enforcement. . . . [T]he refusal to vote does not nullify, of course, an influence and predominance exerted without a vote. *Id.* at 380.

§10.10   [1] Morgan v. King, 63 P. 416 (Colo. 1900); Pearson v. Concord R. Corp., 62 N.H. 537 (1883); Cuthbert v. McNeill, 13 A.2d 667 (N.J. Eq. 1940); Regal (Hastings) Ltd. v. Gulliver, A.C. [1942] 1 All. E. R. 378 (H.L.); Notes, 58 L.Q. Rev. 434 (1942).

[2] Rothenburg v. Franklin Washington Trust Co., 13 A.2d 667, 672 (N.J. Ch. 1940). It cannot be ascertained what amount of influence any particular director exerts in favor of any matter in which he has an interest coming before his board. Although not voting, he may by argument or discussion induce votes from his fellow members, as well as by friendship, association, or confidence, or by knowledge that although he refrains from voting he desires favorable action by others.

[3] *See generally* Snead v. United States Trucking Corp., 380 So. 2d 1075 (Fla. Dist. Ct. App. 1980) (deal not at arm's length when officer-director-stockholder of one corporation contracted with second corporation of which he was salaried employee).

porate fiduciary's dealings with the corporation was rife with the possibility of dishonesty or unfairness has given way to the belief that there are commercial advantages to such transactions and that regulation, rather than strict prohibition, is the approach with the greatest social welfare.[4] In most jurisdictions, interested directors may be counted toward the quorum necessary for the board to take action on the transaction in which the directors have an interest.[5] And in broad overview, the approach in all states is that a corporation's contract with its director or officer is not voidable if approved by a disinterested body of directors or stockholders, or if the contracting director or officer successfully bears the burden of showing the fairness of the transaction.[6] As discussed below, this rule is now declared by most corporation statutes.[7]

§10.11   Burden of Proof of Fairness in Fiduciary Contracts

It has long been the prevailing rule that directors or officers seeking the benefits of a contract or transaction with their corporation have the burden of showing that the transaction meets the requirements of state conflict-of-interest provision. This is the case whether the suit is by the corporation to rescind or by the director or officer to enforce the contract.[1] However, proof that the transaction was approved by disinterested directors after full disclosure shifts the burden back to the complaining stockholder.[2] Similarly, approval of the transaction by the shareholders[3] or an independent committee will shift the burden back to the person challenging the transaction. However, when the committee lacks independence, the defendants retain the burden of proving the transaction's fairness.[4]

---

[4] 3 Fletcher, *supra* §10.08 note 4, §931; 12 Samuel Williston, Contracts §1533 (3d ed. 1970); Harold Marsh, Are Directors Trustees?, 22 Bus. Law. 35, 36-45 (1966).

[5] *See, e.g.,* Karris v. Water Tower Trust & Sav. Bank, 389 N.E.2d 1359 (Ill. App. Ct. 1979); American Discount Corp. v. Katz, 206 N.E.2d (Mass. 1965); Davis v. Heath Dev. Co., 558 P.2d 594 (Utah 1976); Rocket Mining Corp. v. Gill, 483 P.2d 897 (Utah 1971).

[6] Pepper v. Litton, 308 U.S. 295 (1939); Norlin Corp. v. Rooney, Pace, Inc., 744 F.2d 255 (2d Cir. 1984); Gearhart Indus. v. Smith Int'l, 741 F.2d 707, 720 (5th Cir. 1984); Drobbin v. Nicolet Instrument Corp., 631 F. Supp. 860, 880 (S.D.N.Y. 1986); Bellis v. Thal, 373 F. Supp. 120 (E.D. Pa. 1974), *aff'd,* 510 F.2d 969 (3d Cir. 1975); American Timber & Trading Co. v. Niedermeyer, 558 P.2d 1211 (Or. 1976). *See also, e.g.,* Sammis v. Stafford, 48 Cal. App. 4th 1935, 56 Cal. Rptr. 2d 589 (Cal. App. 4th Dist. 1996) (defendant met the burden of establishing that the challenged transaction was "just and reasonable").

[7] *See* Former MBCA §41 (1969); *accord,* MBCA §8.31 (1984).

§10.11   [1] *See, e.g.,* Pepper v. Litton, 308 U.S. 295, 306 (1939).

[2] Weiss v. Kay Jewelry Stores, 470 F.2d 1259 (D.C. Cir. 1972); Gottlieb v. Heyden Chem. Corp., 91 A.2d 57 (Del. 1952). *See* Demoulas v. Demoulas Super Markets, Inc., 677 N.E.2d 159, 181 (Mass. 1997) (absent disinterested approval after full disclosure, the interested director has the burden of proving fairness).

[3] Solomon v. Armstrong, 747 A.2d 1098, 1117 (Del. Ch. 1999), *aff'd,* 746 A.2d 277 (Del. 2000).

[4] Kahn v. Tremont Corp., 694 A.2d 422 (Del. 1997) (lower court erred in shifting the burden of proof to plaintiffs challenging corporation's stock purchase from a related company).

§10.12   Statutory Treatment of Transactions with Interested Officers and Directors

A provision of the California general corporation law,[1] adopted in 1931, changed the former rule as to the disqualification of directors or officers to represent their corporation. Under that statute, if financially interested directors have to be counted to make up a quorum or majority to authorize a transaction, such transactions would no longer be voidable at the option of the corporation solely because of such director's participation, provided one of three alternative safeguards or conditions is met: (1) ratification by an independent majority of directors, (2) approval or ratification by the shareholders, or (3) a showing that the contract is just and reasonable as to the corporation. The statute thus set forth procedures for contracts between a corporation and its officers or directors, as well as between corporations that have some overlap of directors or officers.

Following the lead of the California statute, the 1950, 1969, and 1984 versions of the Model Business Corporation Act embraced the same three alternative safe harbors as were adopted in the path-breaking California provision.[2] Thus, under Section 8.31 of the 1984 Model Act, an interested director may be counted in the quorum, and a particular contract or transaction is not void or voidable "because of such relationship or interest." The statute does not provide per se validation of all contracts where the statutory procedure has been followed and thus does not preclude further scrutiny.[3] The Model Act deals only with director conflict-of-interest transactions. Conflict-of-interest transactions involving non-director officers or employees are dealt with under the general principles of fiduciary obligations and the law of agency. All states except Massachusetts and South Dakota have conflict-of-interest statutes that mirror the approach first taken in California; most of the states have patterned their statutes after the pre-1988 versions of the Model Act.[4] Section 8.31 provides somewhat detailed descriptions of what constitutes an "indirect" conflict-of-interest as well as the voting requirements for *impartial* director or shareholder approval; this section, like earlier vintages of the Model Act, is general, even sometimes vague, in its requirements and scope. Because generality and vagueness necessarily rob transactions of predictability, the 1988 revision of the Model Business Corporations Act substitutes new sections 8.60-8.62. The overall philosophy of the 1988 amendments is to

---

§10.12   [1] *See* Henry W. Ballantine & Graham L. Sterling, California Corporation Laws 98-102 (1938). For a more recent version of the California statute, *see* Cal. Corp. Code §310 (West 1990). California §310(a) is a legislative step forward. It provides for validation of "interested" transactions by disinterested director ratification plus a showing that the transaction was fair and reasonable or by disinterested shareholder ratification in good faith and after having been informed of the director's interest. There is no statutory fairness requirement in the latter case.

[2] Former MBCA §41 (1969); *accord*, MBCA §8.31 (1984).

[3] *See* Remillard Brick Co. v. Remillard-Dandini Co., 241 P.2d 66, 72 (Cal. Ct. App. 1952), where the court held that notwithstanding compliance with statutory formalities, the contract if "unfair and unreasonable to the corporation may be avoided." *See* Alison Grey Anderson, Conflicts of Interest: Efficiency, Fairness and Corporate Structure, 25 UCLA L. Rev. 738 (1978).

[4] Model Bus. Corp. Act Ann. §8.61 at 8:43 (3d ed. 1994).

B. Dealings Between Directors and Their Corporations

adopt a bright-line test and to make the provisions' proscription exclusive (circumstances falling outside the statutory definition of conflicting interests cannot be challenged on the basis of the transaction involves a conflict of interest, although challenges on other grounds are not foreclosed). The most distinguishing characteristics of the 1988 amendments are the level of detail with which they define "conflicting interests"[5] and specify when judicial intervention is appropriate. The 1988 amendments have met with modest success in the state legislatures as twelve states have patterned their conflict-of-interest statutes after the 1988 amendments; most states have patterned their conflict-of-interest provisions on the 1984 versions of the Revised Model Business Corporations Act.[6]

Scope of Conflict-of-Interest Statutes. In broad overview, conflict-of-interest statutes pose three distinct questions to the practitioner. The first is whether a given transaction falls within the statute's coverage.[7] For example, is a subsidiary's declaration of a dividend in response to the influence of its parent a conflict-of-interest transaction? One may consider that declaring a dividend entails creating a "contract or transaction" between the subsidiary and its parent, on whose board many of the subsidiary's directors are also directors, especially since the declaration of a dividend establishes a distinct contractual relationship between the corporation and the stockholders entitled to the dividend. The Delaware Supreme Court, however, has held that, because a dividend is proportional to all the company's stockholders, it is not a conflict-of-interest transaction.[8] The 1984 Model Business Corporation Act strives to provide greater specificity to this question by providing two distinct bases for conflicts of interest: a direct conflict of interest, for which no separate definition is provided, and an *in*direct conflict of interest, for which an elaborate proscription of the types of relationships between the corporation and an entity with whom it contracts that will trigger the statute's application.

However, even the Model Business Corporation Act does not deal with the more problematic inquiry as to the meaning of a "contract or transaction."[9] Thus,

---

[5] Professor Branson in a careful review of the 1988 amendments quite properly concludes they define too narrowly what is a conflict of interest and seriously erode the fiduciary obligation of directors. Douglas M. Branson, Assault on Another Citadel: Attempts to Curtail the Fiduciary Standard of Loyalty Applicable to Corporate Directors, 57 Fordham L. Rev. 375 (1988).

[6] *See, e.g.,* Alabama, Ala. Code Ann. §10-2B-8.60-8.63 (1998); Georgia, Ga. Code Ann. §14-2-860-863 (1994); Mississippi, Miss. Code Ann. §79-4-8.60-63 (Supp. 1994); Montana, Mont. Code Ann. §35-1-464 (1999); Utah, Utah Code Ann. §16-109-850-10a-853 (Supp. 1994); Vermont, Vt. Stat. Ann. tit. 11A §§8.60-8.63 (1993); and Washington, Wash. Rev. Code Ann. §23B.08.730 (West 1994), have adopted the 1988 Amendments.

[7] When all the directors, being served as defendants in a suit, voted to advance themselves funds to cover their litigation expenses as authorized by the indemnification provisions of the corporate statute, the courts are split whether the board's action is to be assesses solely by the requirements of the indemnification statute or must also satisfy the fairness requirements of the conflict-of-interest provision.

[8] Sinclair Oil Corp. v. Levien, 280 A.2d 717 (Del. 1971).

[9] The 1988 Model Act "conflicting interest" provisions apply to "transactions" which the commentary describes as "negotiations or a consensual bilateral arrangement between the corporation and another party or parties that concern their respective and differing economic rights or interests—not simply a unilateral action by the corporation, but rather a 'deal.'" Model Bus. Corp. Act Annot. §8.60 Comment 2 at 8-373.

a finder's fee that an officer can earn upon a sale of the company to a third party was held within a conflict-of-interest transaction.[10] The question whether a given contract or transaction falls within a state's conflict-of-interest statute is not purely an academic question. As will be seen below, two distinct philosophies can be attributed to the purpose of conflict-of-interest statutes, one being that compliance with the statute immunizes the transaction from attack on any grounds. Under this view, the conflict-of-interest statute has a broad regulatory purpose. So viewed, one seeking to assure no successful attack can be brought against the transaction on grounds that it is unfair or unreasonable can approach the conflict-of-interest statute's alternative validating mechanisms as desirable and useful safe harbors to shield the transaction from further challenge or scrutiny. On the other hand, a second view of conflict-of-interest statutes is that they serve only as a procedural mechanism to overcoming the automatic voidability that existed at common law. Under this approach, satisfaction of one of the conflict-of-interest provisions merely removes any adverse inference that otherwise would be drawn from the director's interest in the transaction. This narrower construction of the statute's scope means the transaction may still be examined under the broader and less predictable standards of the director's or officer's fiduciary obligations; this approach is thus less attractive to the lawyer who wishes certainty and predictability when planning a transaction.

Methods of Satisfying the Statute. The second practical question posed by state conflict-of-interest statutes is how to comply with the statute's requirements. The typical conflict-of-interest statute sets forth three *alternative* mechanisms for validating a conflict-of-interest transaction: impartial director approval, impartial shareholder approval, or proof of the transaction's fairness. From the view of counseling a client, the least attractive of the three options is relying on proof of the transaction's fairness or reasonableness to the corporation. Courts uniformly place the burden of establishing fairness on the interested director or officer.[11] Fairness typically requires that the transaction reflect terms one would expect in an arm's length transaction, which means generally that a self-dealing fiduciary must treat his corporation's interest as his own.[12] The fiduciary should neither take any advantage from his position on both sides of the transaction nor act in conflict with the corporation's interest to even the slightest extent.[13] Moreover, fairness is more encompassing than the adequacy of consideration; it includes the entirety of the transaction.[14] An important factor in any such fairness inquiry is the

[10] *See, e.g.*, Ryan v. Tad's Enterprises, Inc., 709 A.2d 682 (Del. Ch. 1996) (consulting agreement secured by dominant stockholders in their sale of restaurant business was linked to their purchase of the two remaining divisions); Dunaway v. Parker, 453 S.E.2d 43 (Ga. Ct. App. 1994).

[11] *See, e.g.*, Cascade West Assocs. Ltd. P'ship v. PRC, Inc., 1995 WL 105858 (Va. 1995) (because directors are akin to trustees, they must meet burden of proof pursuant to the clear and convincing evidence standard); Lynch v. Patterson, 701 P.2d 1126 (Wyo. 1985).

[12] Noe v. Roussel, 310 So. 2d 806 (La. 1975); Harris Trust & Sav. Bank v. Joanna-Western Mills Co., 368 N.E.2d 629 (Ill. App. Ct. 1977) (transaction should be one that commended itself to a wholly independent board).

[13] Noe v. Roussel, 310 So. 2d 806 (La. 1975).

[14] Johnson v. Witkowski, 573 N.E.2d 513, 521 (Mass. App. Ct. 1991); Voss Oil Co. v. Voss, 367 P.2d 977 (Wyo. 1962) (fairness test also includes inquiry into degree of disclosure interested director has made).

B. Dealings Between Directors and Their Corporations

actual consideration paid compared with an independent appraisal of the property's fair market value.[15] Thus, the fairness of a lease transaction was considered in light of evidence of the market price of similar leases, the corporation's need for the property, the absence of any evidence that a better deal was possible with a noninterested party, the possibility that the interested party was diverting gain to himself, and whether full disclosure to the disinterested directors and shareholders was made.[16]

As between the two other validating mechanisms—impartial approval by the shareholders and impartial approval by the directors—the latter is certainly the more efficient. One needs to take care when seeking ratification of a completed conflict-of-interest transaction as to whether the applicable statute permits the disinterested directors to *ratify* a consummated conflict-of-interest transaction or merely to *approve* a yet to be consummated conflict-of-interest transaction.[17] It is generally recognized and so expressed in most conflict-of-interest statutes that the shareholders have the inherent power to both approve and ratify conflict-of-interest transactions. Central to the power of the disinterested directors or stockholders to approve or ratify a conflict-of-interest transaction is that their approval be impartial, in good faith, and follow full disclosure of the material facts as to the director's or officer's interest as well as to the transaction itself. Each of these requirements is examined in the following paragraphs.

Many state statutes adhere to the 1984 Model Business Corporation Act's scheme of providing detailed rules for ascertaining whether the approving or ratifying body, whether stockholders or directors, is impartial—that is, disinterested. For example, the Model Business Corporation Act requires that approval be by a majority of the voting shares not owned or under the control of the interested party. In states whose statutes do not so limit the shares that can approve or ratify a conflict-of-interest transaction, the result similar to that achieved in the Model Business Corporation Act can be achieved by a reasonable construction of the "good faith" approval requirement so that good faith minimally requires impartiality on the part of the decisionmaker.[18]

---

[15] 573 N.E.2d at 521-522. A sale for less than appraised value though may still be fair. In Spruiell v. Ludwig, 568 So. 2d 133, 143 (La. Ct. App. 1990), the court upheld the transaction on the fairness of the entirety of the transaction even though corporation sold property to its director at an option price that was 60 percent of its appraised value. The court considered the option as a reward for the director's contributions to the formation and success of the company. It was also important that the noninterested directors acted in good faith.

[16] *See, e.g.,* Pittsburgh Terminal Corp. v. Baltimore and Ohio R.R., 875 F.2d 549 (6th Cir. 1989) (dominant consideration is fairness of the price and that there is no further requirement of "fair dealing" as occurs under the Delaware jurisprudence); Oberly v. Kirby, 592 A.2d 445 (Del. 1991) (fairness satisfied by evidence of lengthy bargaining, value approached midpoint of both sides, and absence of viable alternatives). Ryan v. Tad's Enterprises, Inc., 709 A.2d 682 (Del. Ch. 1996) (no steps taken to neutralize majority holder's conflict of interest and the evidence failed to reflect indicia of arm's-length dealings).

[17] Richard M. Buxbaum, Conflict-of-Interest Statutes and the Need for a Demand on Directors in Derivative Actions, 68 Cal. L. Rev. 1122 (1980) (distinction being that directors are less likely to feel freedom to fully consider and reject a transaction that is consummated than one that remains executory).

[18] Even upon approval of a majority of the disinterested shares, the transaction can still be reviewed under a waste standard meaning "an exchange to which no reasonable person not acting under compulsion and in good faith could agree" that the transaction is fair. *See* Lewis v. Vogelstein, 699 A.2d 327 (Del. Ch. 1997).

Special care must be taken with respect to the type of vote required to satisfy a state's conflict-of-interest statute via impartial director approval. Different patterns exist among the states. Delaware, for example, requires that the approval be "by a majority of the disinterested directors."[19] On the other hand, some states merely condition approval being by votes normally sufficient after disregarding the votes of the interested directors.[20] Thus, consider the vote necessary at a meeting attended by a corporation's seven authorized directors and approval is sought for a transaction in which four of the directors are interested. The Delaware conflict-of-interest provision would be satisfied if at least two of the disinterested directors vote favorably.[21] But in a state that merely disregards the votes, but not the physical presence of the interested directors, the transaction would not be approved. A common mechanism for overcoming any problems in securing a proper vote at the board of directors is for the board to exercise its powers under the charter or bylaws to create a committee of disinterested directors and to assign to that committee the responsibility to approve or ratify the conflict-of-interest transaction.[22]

Whether authorization or ratification is by the board of directors or by the stockholders, it is subject to the statute's requirement that the decisionmaker have acted in "good faith." As seen earlier in this chapter, good faith implicates the motives or intentions of the approving or ratifying body.[23] As is true in any area of the law that turns on a person's intentions or motives, good faith is established circumstantially. In this regard, impartiality in terms of the voting directors or shareholders not having a financial interest served by the contract or transaction (except to the extent it is beneficial to the corporation itself) is the best measure of whether their approval or ratification is in good faith. Minimally, therefore, good faith requires impartiality. Thus a shareholder who controlled 99 percent of the corporation's stock and was himself an interested party in the transaction was held not to have acted in good faith in approving that transaction.[24] Lack of good faith was established by the self-interested dominating director convening a special board meeting without notice to ratify the conflict-of-interest transaction.[25] Substantial prior business relations with the interested party or apathy, such as

---

[19] Del. Code Ann., tit. 8 §144 (2001).

[20] See Weiss Med. Complex v. Kim, 408 N.E. 2d 959 (Ill. App. Ct. 1980) (quorum not present when four of seven directors had a personal interest in a matter); Possis Corp. v. Continental Mach., Inc., 425 N.W.2d 286 (Minn. Ct. App. 1988) (affirmative vote "of a majority of the directors present" does not mean noninterested directors present).

[21] See Rapoport v. Schneider, 278 N.E.2d 642 (N.Y. 1972) (5-to-1 vote deemed approval of transaction when three of yes votes were interested).

[22] But the committee must act in good faith which requires minimally its independence from the interested party. See Kahn v. Tremont Corp., 694 A.2d 422 (Del. 1997) (independence suggestive of real bargaining power was found absent because two of the three committee members did not actively participate in the committee's work, deferring to the committee's chairman who had significant prior business relationships with the interested party).

[23] See §10.09.

[24] Rivercity v. American Can Co., 600 F. Supp. 908, 921 (E.D. La. 1984).

[25] Groves v. Rosemound Improvement Ass'n, 490 So. 2d 348, 350-351 (La. Ct. App. 1986).

B. Dealings Between Directors and Their Corporations

rarely attending meetings at which the transaction was discussed, are each inconsistent with the good faith requirement.[26] Evidence of an ulterior motive hostile to the corporation's best interest also established a lack of good faith.[27] Furthermore, neither the directors nor the stockholders can by a majority vote ratify a fraudulent or wasteful transaction.[28]

Disclosure can well be viewed as the sine qua non of conflict-of-interest statutes. Not only have courts equated the absence of disclosure with inherent unfairness,[29] but also the efficacy of impartial director or shareholder approval is necessarily dependent on the reviewing body's knowledge of all material facts.[30] It is that body's independent and thoughtful approval after deliberating on all the facts that is intended by the conflict-of-interest statute to protect the corporation from the director's or officer's conflict of interest. Disclosure requires that the interested director or officer bring to the approving or ratifying body of directors or shareholders all facts material to the transaction, not merely that the transaction involves self-dealing by the director or officer.

The central consideration for effective approval by the stockholders is the fullness of disclosure of the director's or officer's interest as well as the material facts of the transaction and the independence of the approval. Impartial approval is absent if a majority of the votes favoring the transaction are held or controlled by the interested director or officer.[31] It is possible that the stockholder approval can occur informally, by open acquiescence or accepting the benefits of the transaction, provided there is strong evidence that the holders of a majority of the shares were aware of the material facts bearing on the transaction.[32]

[26] See Kahn v. Tremont Corp., 694 A.2d 422 (Del. 1997). Helpful in considering the directors' impartiality is guidance from the derivative suit in which the courts are regularly called upon to determine whether the plaintiff can proceed with the suit without making a demand upon the board of directors. Courts have excused the demand where the plaintiff has successfully pled facts showing family relationships or business relationships raise a reasonable doubt regarding the directors' impartiality. See, e.g., Rales v. Blasband, 634 A.2d 927 (Del. 1993) (Sherman, a director of Company A, was deemed not impartial because derivative suit defendants were the board chair and executive committee chair of Company B for which Sherman was president).

[27] See Nord v. Eastside Ass'n, 664 P.2d 4, 6 (Wash. Ct. App. 1983).

[28] See, e.g., Wolf v. Frank, 477 F.2d 467 (5th Cir. 1973) (all disinterested directors cannot ratify fraud on part of other directors); Lewis v. Vogelstein, 699 A.2d 327 (Del. Ch. 1997) (wasteful options granted directors cannot be ratified by mere majority vote of stockholders).

[29] See, e.g., Dynan v. Fritz, 508 N.E.2d 1371 (Mass. 1987) (an independent ground to avoid the contract is failure to make full disclosure); State ex rel. Hayes Oyster Co. v. Keypoint Oyster Co., 391 P.2d 979 (Wash. 1964); Voss Oil Co. v. Voss, 367 P.2d 977 (Wyo. 1962).

[30] See, e.g., Dollar Time Group, Inc. v. Sasson, 223 B.R. 237 (Bankr. S.D. Fla. 1998); Dunaway v. Parker, 453 S.E. 2d 43 (Ga. Ct. App. 1994); Geller v. Allied-Lyons PLC, 674 N.E. 2d 1334 (Mass. App. Ct. 1997); General Dynamics v. Torres, 915 S.W. 2d 45 (Tex. App. 1995). For a case unwilling to impute to the "ratifying" directors information in the company's files, see Harris Trust & Sav. Bk. V. Joanna-Western Mills Co., 368 N.E. 2d 629 (Ill. Ct. App. 1977).

[31] See, e.g., Pappas v. Moss, 393 F.2d 865 (3d Cir. 1968) (burden not shifted by shareholder approval when interested party held a majority of the shares); Oberhelman v. Barnes Inv. Corp., 690 P.2d 1343 (Kan. 1984) (same).

[32] See Robert A. Washsler, Inc. v. Florafax Int'l, Inc., 778 F.2d 547 (10th Cir. 1985).

Effect of Compliance with Statute. The final question posed by conflict-of-interest statutes is the effect of complying with one of its alternative validation provisions. The preamble to most conflict-of-interest statutes provides that the contract or transaction will not be voidable solely because of the director's or officer's interest if one of the three validating alternatives is satisfied. Some courts interpret this language literally so that the effect of, for example, good faith independent stockholder approval is that such approval shields the transaction from being rescinded *solely* because it involves a conflict of interest.[33] Thus, under this approach, the effect of a transaction having satisfied one of the conflict-of-interest statute's three authorizing provisions is that such satisfaction removes any adverse inference that otherwise would be drawn because of the director's interest. As a correlative proposition, satisfaction of the statute's authorizing provisions shifts the burden of proof back to the objecting stockholder.[34] The result of such an interpretation is to allow the transaction to be questioned as beyond the protection of the business judgment rule because it was wasteful or not in the corporation's best interests. In such a suit, the plaintiff would bear the burden of proof.[35] Thus, under this view of compliance with the conflict-of-interest statute, the impact of the statute is primarily returning the burden of proof to the one challenging the transaction. If there had not been impartial director or stockholder approval, the burden of proving fairness to the corporation would have been on the director or officer with the conflict of interest.[36]

A different and more sweeping view of satisfying any of the conflict-of-interest statute's validating mechanisms is that it removes the transaction from any further scrutiny. That is, the requirements within the validating mechanisms of the statute that are relied on become the exclusive focus of any judicial attack. Thus, once the court is satisfied that the shareholders have independently and in good faith approved a self-dealing transaction after full disclosure of all material facts, the inquiry is closed.[37] Under this view, proof of the transaction's overall unfairness is pushed aside by deference to the will of the independent approving body

---

[33] *See, e.g.,* Fliegler v. Lawrence, 361 A.2d 218 (Del. 1976).

[34] *See, e.g.,* Palumbo v. Deposit Bank, 758 F.2d 113 (3d Cir. 1985); Cohen v. Ayers, 596 F.2d 733 (7th Cir. 1979); Rosenfield v. Metals Selling Corp., 643 A.2d 1253 (Conn. 1994); Fliegler v. Lawrence, 361 A.2d 218 (Del. 1976); Lewis v. Vogelstein, 699 A.2d 327 (Del. Ch. 1997); Weiss Med. Complex v. Kim, 408 N.E. 2d 959 (Ill. App. Ct. 1980). *See also* Marciano v. Nakash, 535 A.2d 400 (Del. 1987). However, a leading case held the burden did not shift when the bulk of the approving votes were those by the interested shareholder. Fliegler v. Lawrence, *supra.*

A questionable result was reached in Miller v. Magline, Inc., 256 N.W. 2d 761 (Mich. Ct. App. 1977), where the directors approved in serial fashion their salaries as officers, with no director voting when his salary was before the other directors. The court held the statute's requirements had been met so that the burden of proving the compensation was excessive was on the plaintiff. The overall thrust of the plaintiff's case was that they, no longer being officers, shared less in the corporation's good fortune than those who were officers and drew salaries that reduced the amount of dividends that could be declared.

[35] *See, e.g.,* Melrose v. Capitol City Motor Lodge, Inc., 705 N.E. 2d 985 (Ind. 1998).

[36] *See, e.g.,* Pittsburgh Terminal Corp. v. Baltimore and Ohio R.R., 875 F. 2d 549 (6th Cir. 1989); Byelick v. Vivadelli, 79 F. Supp. 2d 610 (E.D. Va. 1999); Rosenfield v. Metals Selling Corp., 643 A.2d 1253 (Conn. 1994).

[37] *See* Camden v. Kaufman, 613 N.W. 2d 335 (Mich. Ct. App. 2000).

acting in good faith. Such a perspective appears to comport with a sound view of the role of the reviewing court. A court should avoid second-guessing the diligent and fair deliberations of the independent stockholders or directors. However, there is ample authority to the contrary. Courts have been much influenced in this area by a leading conflict-of-interest case, *Remillard Brick Co. v. Remillard-Dandini Company*,[38] which held that bare technical compliance with the validating provisions of the California conflict-of-interest statute did not remove the transaction from having to be inherently fair to the corporation. *Remillard Brick Co.* has been consistently relied on as standing for the proposition that good faith impartial approval after full disclosure does not obviate the need for the transaction to also be fair to the corporation. While this view is consistent with the *language* used by *Remillard Brick Co.*, the facts of the case are considerably narrower: the defendants held proxies for most of the voting shares of the company and voted those shares in approval of an arrangement that would allow the defendants to divert much of the company's sales to themselves. The court could easily have found that the approval expressed by the defendants was not granted in "good faith," as expressly required by the statute. Instead, the court assumed the statute was complied with, albeit technically, and proceeded to add its own veneer by requiring that the transaction be fair. Ever since *Remillard Brick Co.*, there has been a good deal of confusion as to the substantive effects of satisfying a conflict-of-interest statute's provisions pertaining to impartial director or shareholder approval.

§10.13   The Power of the Shareholders to Ratify

A fundamental principle of corporate law is that waste, gifts, fraud, and ultra vires acts cannot be approved by a mere majority vote; unanimity is the only means to ratify waste.[1] The presence of waste thus is a major qualification of the fundamental principle of majority rule within the corporation. The analogy to constitutional law is apt in such a case. Just as the Bill of Rights protects the minority from the tyranny or misdirection of the mob, so it is that a requirement of unanimity protects the minority from opportunism or improvidence sought by the

---

[38] 241 P.2d 66 (Cal. Ct. App. 1952).

§10.13   [1] *See* Michelson v. Duncan, 407 A.2d 211, 219 (Del. 1979); Weiss Med. Complex v. Kim, 408 N.E.2d 959 (Ill. App. Ct. 1980) (where four of seven directors had personal interest in matter, no quorum existed; board's action thus voidable but could have been ratified by shareholders). *See also* Solomon v. Armstrong, 747 A.2d 1098, 1117 (Del. Ch. 1999), *aff'd*, 746 A.2d 277 (Del. 2000) (informed shareholder ratification shifts burden of proof of entire fairness to plaintiffs but does not extinguish their claim); Schreiber v. Bryan, 396 A.2d 512 (Del. Ch. 1978) (waste of corporate assets is subject only to unanimous shareholder ratification); Aronoff v. Albanese, 446 N.Y.S.2d 368 (App. Div. 1982) (gift or waste of corporate assets not ratifiable by majority shareholder vote).

In view of majority shareholder's fiduciary duty to minority where minority's approval of proposed merger has been achieved by misleading proxy statement, action for fraud is not barred. *See, e.g.*, Harman v. Masoneilan Int'l, 442 A.2d 487 (Del. 1982).

majority.[2] It is just such thinking that qualifies the operation of conflict-of-interest statutes, discussed in the preceding section, where the statute's bare language would appear to authorize informed stockholder ratification as a means for validating a self-dealing transactions. As seen there, the effect of such approval is merely to restore the presumption of the business judgment rule so that the transaction can still be subject for challenge on the grounds of waste. Placing the burden on the minority in such a case overcomes concern for the tyranny of the minority.[3]

A heuristic the courts sometimes use in determining what conduct may not be ratified by the majority is whether the complaint implicates the directors' or officers' duty of care or does it raise the specter of a duty of loyalty violation. The approval of an informed majority extinguishes the shareholder's duty of care claim.[4] This result would appear best understood if limited to questions of the process the directors or officers pursued in their consideration and approval of the transaction. Majority approval should not, however, prevent the plaintiff from the option of his bearing the substantial burden of proof that the transaction is so one-sided as to constitute waste.

To be valid, ratification must be after full disclosure of all material facts.[5] If shares owned or controlled by the interested party are needed to satisfy the majority approval, the better view is that the transaction should be proven to be fair to the corporation.[6] However, absent a fraud on creditors the sole stockholder's approval of her one-sided self-dealing transactions prevented the company's bankruptcy trustee from later seeking to recover for the damages the corporation suffered on the earlier transactions.[7] A purported ratification should not take the form of a blanket or whitewash resolution of approval of everything done by the directors for the past year or more, given by proxies solicited by the management of the corporation for the occasion.

---

[2] See Melvin A. Eisenberg, The Structure of the Corporation: A Legal Analysis 392-5 (1976); Douglas M. Branson, Assault on Another Citadel: Attempts to Curtail the Fiduciary Standard of Loyalty Applicable to Corporate Directors, 57 Fordham L. Rev. 375 (1988).

[3] For the contrary view, namely, that informed majority ratification should remove the transaction from any further scrutiny, see Mary A. Jacobson, Interested Director Transactions and the (Equivocal) Effects of Shareholder Ratification, 21 Del. J. Corp. L. 981, 1021 (1996).

[4] See, e.g., In re Wheelabrator Technologies, Inc. Shareholder Litigation, 663 A.2d 1194 (Del. Ch. 1995) (plaintiff can continue to pursue duty of loyalty claim); Solomon v. Amrstrong, 128 N.E.2d 429 (Ohio 1995) (suit dismissed upon majority approval, absent showing of self dealing or vote the product of coercion).

The Delaware Supreme Court has stated it retains an open mind whether duty of loyalty claims can be ratified by the majority, see Williams v. Geier, 671 A.2d 1368, 1379 n.23 (Del. 1996).

[5] Robert A. Wachsler, Inc. v. Florafax Int'l, Inc., 778 F.2d 547 (10th Cir. 1985) (Delaware conflict-of-interest statute requires vote or acquiescence by majority shareholders after full disclosure).

[6] See Stevens ex rel. Parkview Corp. v. Richardson, 755 P.2d 389, 395 (Alaska 1988); Fliegler v. Lawrence, 361 A.2d 218 (Del. 1976); Oberhelman v. Barnes Inv. Corp., 690 P.2d 1343 (Kan. 1984).

[7] See Dannen v. Scafidi, 393 N.E.2d 1246 (Ill. Ct. App. 1979).

B. Dealings Between Directors and Their Corporations

§10.14 Actions Against Directors and Officers for Mismanagement: Corporate, Individual, and Creditor Grounds to Complain

When directors or officers are guilty of mismanagement or negligence in conducting corporate affairs, the right of action is primarily in the corporation or, in the case of insolvency, in the corporation's receiver or trustee in bankruptcy.[1] It is generally held that the corporation or its receiver may sue the delinquent officers to avoid multiplicity of suits against several officers and to do complete justice in one proceeding.[2] Creditors cannot sue individually for any loss suffered as a consequence of a director's or officer's breach of a duty to the corporation.[3] Individual shareholders cannot sue in their own right for impairment of the value of their shares by mismanagement of directors, but under certain conditions they may sue in a derivative or shareholders' suit for the benefit of the corporation, making the corporation and the guilty officers parties-defendants.[4]

To permit shareholders to sue separately for impairment of the value of their shares by wrongs done to the corporation would ordinarily result in confusion and wasteful multiplicity of actions and, further, would not protect the prior rights of creditors to corporate assets. Directors are liable to those who are injured by the directors' own tortious conduct regardless of whether the corporation is also liable.[5]

It is broadly recognized that the directors of a financially healthy corporation owe their fiduciary obligations to the corporation and its shareholders;[6] creditors' rights are accordingly limited to the fair construction of a creditor's contract with the corporation.[7]

There is a developing body of law that suggests directors do owe a fiduciary duty to creditors when the corporation is insolvent or is approaching insolvency.[8]

---

§10.14 [1] *See, e.g.,* Ross v. Bernhard, 396 U.S. 531, 534-535 (1970); Speer v. Dighton Grain, Inc., 624 P.2d 952 (Kan. 1981) (creditors of insolvent corporation may not sue directors and officers for mismanagement of corporate affairs; right reserved for corporation itself).

On the possibility that officers or directors may also be liable to the firm's accountants when each have been linked to misleading financial statements and other fraudulent practices, *see* Michael R. Young, The Liability of Corporate Officials to Their Outside Auditor for Financial Statement Fraud, 64 Fordham L. Rev. 2155 (1996).

[2] Meyers v. Moody, 693 F.2d 1196 (5th Cir. 1982); Baker v. Allen, 197 N.E. 521, 524 (Mass. 1935).

[3] Speer v. Dighton Grain, Inc., 624 P.2d 952 (Kan. 1981).

[4] Shareholder litigation is discussed in Chapter 15. For the distinction between direct or class and derivative suits, *see infra* §15.02.

[5] *See* Frances T. v. Village Green Owners Ass'n, 229 Cal. Rptr. 456 (Cal. 1986) (directors of nonprofit corporation who have met minimum standard of care owed to corporation are not protected by business judgment rule from liability to third parties if directors have engaged in tortious conduct).

[6] *See, e.g.,* Simons v. Cogan, 549 A.2d 300 (Del. 1988).

[7] *See infra* §18.15 with respect to the duties owed to preferred stockholders who are treated similarly to creditors.

[8] *See, e.g.,* Rapids Constr. Co. v. Malone, 139 F.3d 892 (4th Cir. 1998) (shareholders of financially shaky corporation breached fiduciary duty to creditors when they caused corporation to engage in stock repurchase; applying Virginia law). For the view that corporations are *always* in the vicinity of

In 1991, this infant area of the law was given greater attention by Chancellor Allen in *Credit Lyonnaise Bank Nederland, N.V. v. Pathe Communications Corporation*,[9] involving a question of whether the board of directors of a corporation in financial distress acted properly in rejecting pressure from its controlling shareholder to engage in certain asset sales. In upholding the directors' actions, the Chancellor reasoned:

> At least where a corporation is operating in the vicinity of insolvency, a board of directors is not merely the agent of the residual risk bearers, but owes its duty to the corporate enterprise. . . . [T]he board . . . had an obligation to the community of interest that sustained the corporation, to exercise judgment in an informed, good faith effort to maximize the corporation's long-term wealth creating capacity.[10]

The Chancellor, however, could have easily premised his decision on a finding that an elaborate corporate governance contract entered into between the controlling shareholder and the corporation's major lender would have been violated had the board of directors acceded to the wishes of its controlling stockholder.

The cases in which creditors have successfully invoked fiduciary obligations owed to them arise in decisions involving closely held corporations and the directors or those in control of the corporation that have been engaged in self-dealing.[11] More specifically, the cases are a variety of fraud on creditors that arises in distinct types of transactions:

> [T]he courts seem to have adopted the narrow version of directors' obligations. All of the decisions in which the courts have allowed creditors to recover for breach of fiduciary duty have involved directors of an insolvent corporation diverting corporate assets for the benefit of insiders or preferred creditors. These cases fall into five general categories: (1) withdrawing assets from the insolvent corporation as alleged payment of claims that the directors had against the corporation, such as loans to the company or unpaid commissions; (2) using corporate funds to pay off the company's loans that the directors had personally guaranteed; (3) engaging in transactions, usually without fair consideration to the company, for the benefit of its parent corporation or related entities; (4) pocketing the proceeds of a sale of all corporate assets to a third party or otherwise transferring property to a related entity, leaving the former corporation insolvent; and (5) other forms of self-dealing in which the directors use assets of the insolvent firm for their own benefit, such as pledging stock owned by the corporation as collateral to finance the directors' personal stock purchases.[12]

---

insolvency, *see* Thomas A. Smith, The Efficient Norm for Corporate Law: Neotraditional Interpretation of Fiduciary Duty, 98 Mich. L. Rev. 214 (1999).

[9] 1991 Del. Ch. LEXIS 215.

[10] *Id.* at 226. For well-reasoned arguments in support of the Chancellor's view that directors of a bankrupt or near-bankrupt company owe creditors a fiduciary obligation, *see* Steven L. Schwartz, Rethinking a Corporation's Obligations to Creditors, 17 Cardozo L. Rev. 647 (1996).

[11] Rapids Constr. Co. v. Malone, 139 F.3d 892 (4th Cir. 1998) (repurchase of shares breached fiduciary duty to creditors; applying Virginia law). *See* Laura Lin, Shift of Fiduciary Duty Upon Corporate Insolvency: Proper Scope of Directors' Duty to Creditors, 46 Vand. L. Rev. 1485, 1518 (1993).

[12] *Id.* at 1513-1518. *See also* St. James Capital Corp. v. Pallet Recycling Associates of North America, Inc., 589 N.W.2d 511 (Minn. Ct. App. 1999) (duty owed to creditors by officers and directors limited to avoidance of self-dealing or preferential transfers); Whitley v. Carolina Clinic, Inc., 455 S.E.2d 896, 900 (N.C. Ct. App. 1995) (directors' "fiduciary obligation" to creditors not to make preferential transfers is not triggered unless insolvent in the equity sense).

B. Dealings Between Directors and Their Corporations

The major advantage to creditors of pursuing the directors on the theory that they have breached a fiduciary obligation owed to creditors is that the creditors can potentially recover a greater amount than can be recovered under the more traditional fraudulent-conveyance or preferential-transfer claim, where only the amount of the transfer can be recovered.

§10.15 Disclosure Obligations Based Upon Fiduciary Principles

A rapidly developing area of fiduciary responsibility is the disclosure duty owed shareholders by directors, officers, and controlling shareholders.[1] Though there has long been a developed body of state law pertaining to directors' and officers' disclosure obligations when trading in their company's shares on the basis of material non-public confidential corporate information,[2] only recently has there been the recognition of broader disclosure obligations for company fiduciaries. In the seminal case, *Lynch v. Vickers Energy Corp.*,[3] the Delaware Supreme Court held that directors owe shareholders a duty of "complete candor," so that the objective was "completeness and not adequacy."[4] From this broad language, Delaware courts have imposed a duty of full disclosure on directors[5] and controlling shareholders.[6] The duty is most readily applied when shareholder approval has been sought through proxy materials that omit or misstate material facts.[7] However, the emerging disclosure doctrine has now been recognized for misleading information in SEC filings in connection with a firm's takeover,[8] in the notice of a stockholders' meeting for a close corporation where no proxy was solicited,[9] and for misrepresentations that were not in connection with any transaction that would

§10.15 [1] *See generally* Lawrence A. Hamermesh, Calling Off the Lynch Mob: The Corporate Director's Fiduciary Disclosure Duty, 49 Vand. L. Rev. 1087 (1996). A claim for breach of the fiduciary duty of disclosure implicates only the duty of care when the violation occurs as a result of a good faith, but nevertheless erroneous, judgment about the proper scope or content of the required disclosure. However, if a disclosure violation is made in bad faith or is knowing or intentional, it implicates the duty of loyalty. O'Reilly v. Transworld Healthcare, Inc., 745 A.2d 902, 914-915 (Del. Ch. 1999).

[2] *See* §12.06.

[3] 383 A.2d 278 (Del. 1977).

[4] *Id.* at 281.

[5] *See, e.g.,* Arnold v. Society for Savings Bancorp., 650 A.2d 1270 (Del. 1994).

[6] *See, e.g.,* Weinberger v. UOP, Inc., 457 A.2d 701, 711-712 (Del. 1983).

[7] Lacos Land Co. v. Arden Group, Inc., 517 A.2d 271 (Del. Ch. 1986). *Cf.* Skeen v. Jo-Ann Stores, Inc., 750 A.2d 1170, 1174 (Del. 2000) (omitted facts are not material simply because they might be helpful; court rejected claims of minority stockholders who were cashed out in merger that information statement did not contain enough financial information for them to decide whether to accept merger consideration or seek appraisal); Jackson Nat'l Life Ins. Co. v. Kennedy, 741 A.2d 377, 388 (Del. Ch. 1999) (since neither corporation statute nor certificate of incorporation provided preferred stockholder with right to vote on corporation's sale of assets, president had no fiduciary obligation to disclose transaction to preferred stockholder).

[8] Weinberger v. Rio Grande Ind., Inc., 519 A.2d 116 (Del. Ch. 1986).

[9] Stroud v. Grace, 606 A.2d 75 (Del. 1992).

call for shareholder action.[10] Directors who breach the duty are liable for damages that the shareholders suffer as a consequence of their breach, even though they did not benefit personally because of their omission or misstatement.[11] By far the most significant expansion of *Lynch* was made in *Malone v. Brinkat*,[12] which held that directors and officers breached their duty of candor by knowingly releasing false financial information regarding the company's performance and financial position. The significance of *Malone* is that the court expressly held that *Lynch's* duty of candor applied even when shareholders were not being asked to vote or otherwise approve a matter.

Though these fiduciary-based disclosure obligations are growing rapidly in Delaware, there is little litigation on this subject in other states. In 1998, Congress enacted the Uniform Standards Act to preempt the state court's jurisdiction over securities class actions.[13] However, among the exceptions it provided was the so-called Delaware carve-out that preserves state court jurisdiction to hear claims of disclosure violations premised upon state law fiduciary obligations.[14] Thus, the rapidly expanding disclosure obligations founded on state law fiduciary principles will not likely be slowed by the recent federal legislation.

[10] Malone v. Brincat, 722 A.2d 5 (Del. 1998). Claims based on disclosure violations arising out of communications that do not contemplate stockholder action must be supported by a well-pleaded complaint with allegations sufficient to warrant the remedy sought, regardless of whether the requested remedies are for nominal damages, compensatory damages, or some other type of relief. O'Reilly v. Transworld Healthcare, Inc., 745 A.2d 902, 919-920 (Del. Ch. 1999).

[11] Zirn v. VLI Corp., 621 A.2d 773 (Del. 1993), *aff'd* 681 A.2d 1050 (Del. 1996). The *Zirn* court concluded that the directors were not protected by the exculpatory provision in the company's charter, reasoning that any breach of the directors' disclosure duty was a breach of their duty of loyalty, which is beyond the type of conduct Delaware law permits to be included in such an exculpatory provision. *Id.* at 783. In Arnold v. Society for Savings Bancorp, 650 A.2d 1270, 1277 (Del. 1994), the court, providing a close reading of the Delaware statute that authorizes such exculpatory provisions, held that disclosure breaches were covered by the exculpatory provision in the company's articles of incorporation. *See also* O'Reilly v. Transworld Healthcare, Inc., 745 A.2d 902, 914 (Del. Ch. 1998) (when certificate of incorporation contains exculpatory provision, claims against directors can be dismissed only if complaint fails to plead sufficiently that directors' conduct falls into at least one statutory exception under which directors are not protected).

[12] 722 A.2d 5 (Del. 1999).

[13] SLUSA is discussed *infra* §12.08. States may also choose to dismiss the action on the traditional considerations of forum non conveniens. *See* Friedman v. Alcatel Alsthom, 752 A.2d 544 (Del. Ch. 1999).

[14] *See, e.g.*, Gibson v. P.S. Group Holdings, Inc., 2000 WL 777818 (S.D. Cal. 2000) (holding removal to federal court under SLUSA conflicted with the Delaware carve out provision); Gordon v. Buntrock, 2000 WL 556763 (N.D. Ill. 2000) (same); Pauline Lalodriz v. USA Networks, Inc., 68 F. Supp. 2d 285 (S.D.N.Y. 1999) (approving *Malone* and holding SLUSA did not bar the action).

CHAPTER 11

Fiduciary Duties for Executive Compensation, Corporate Opportunities, and Controlling Stockholders

A.   EXECUTIVE COMPENSATION

§11.01   Contracts for Compensation of Directors and Officers

No matter is more delicate or important in a corporation, whether it be closely held or publicly held, than the compensation arrangement between the corporation and its executives. A well-designed and thoughtful compensation arrangement provides incentives for managers to reduce the agency costs that are inherent in a public corporation, and in a close corporation it serves as a significant component of how the stockholders will divide the company's cash flows among themselves. Just as there are perplexing planning problems concerning how best to provide rewards and incentives to managers,[1] there are equally challenging jurisprudential questions of the proper role of the courts when asked to judge the propriety of a particular compensation arrangement.[2]

Courts traditionally have been reluctant to imply contracts for director compensation. It has long been a presumption at common law that directors serve without pay. They cannot recover on an implied contract for the reasonable value of their services because both custom and their fiduciary relationship repel any implication that official services are to be paid for.[3] This presumption also applies to executive officers such as president, vice president, secretary, and treasurer, who are not entitled to recover compensation for performing the ordinary duties of their office as directors in the absence of an express agreement.[4] Similarly, no claim will lie in an action for quantum meruit.[5]

In the absence of a statute[6] or a delegation of authority, the fees for compensation of the directors for their ordinary duties must be fixed by the shareholders or by a provision in the bylaws.[7] However, the clear statutory trend is to

---

§11.01   [1] See Subcommittee on Executive Compensation of the ABA Section on Corporation, Banking and Business Law, Executive Compensation: A 1987 Road Map for the Corporate Advisor, 43 Bus. Law. 185 (1987). See also Report of the National Association of Corporate Directors Blue Ribbon Commission on Director Compensation 12 (1995) (recommending that the board establish a substantial target of stock ownership for directors and that director fees be paid in stock or cash; also, the report expresses the view that benefits such as pension and health plans are likely to make directors less independent because they are more like employees who seek longevity).

[2] See Detlev F. Vagts, Challenges to Executive Compensation: For the Markets or the Courts?, 8 J. Corp. L. 231 (1983).

[3] Corinne Mill, Canal & Stock Co. v. Toponce, 152 U.S. 405 (1894); Vernars v. Young, 539 F.2d 966 (3d Cir. 1976); Savage v. Lorraine Corp., 217 F.2d 378 (9th Cir. 1954).

[4] Savage v. Lorraine Corp., 217 F.2d 378 (9th Cir. 1954) (director-president); Upright v. Brown, 98 F.2d 802 (2d Cir. 1938) (director-treasurer); Aries Ventures Ltd. v. Axa Fin. S.A., 729 F. Supp. 289 (S.D.N.Y. 1990).

[5] Air Traffic & Serv. Corp. v. Fay, 196 F.2d 40 (D.C. Cir. 1952); Portman v. American Home Prods. Co., 98 F. Supp. 494 (S.D.N.Y. 1951); Kilpatrick v. Penrose Ferry Bridge Co., 49 Pa. 118 (1865).

[6] See McDonald v. Sealift Terminals, Inc., 505 So. 2d 675 (Fla. Ct. App. 1987).

[7] Palmer v. Scheftel, 170 N.Y.S. 588, 590 (N.Y. App. Div. 1918).

A. Executive Compensation

authorize the board of directors to set the compensation for directors.[8] Even where no statutory authority exists, the charter or the shareholders frequently authorize directors to fix their own fees or salaries[9] and, as such, the presumptions of the business judgment rule apply to even sizable awards to the directors.[10] Substantial fees are frequently provided for attendance at directors' meetings or at meetings of committees of the board of large corporations.

Typically, the compensation of officers is established yearly by a resolution of the board of directors, although it is not uncommon for executive compensation to be set forth in the bylaws[11] or approved by the stockholders. When a person is selected to be an officer or employee under circumstances indicating an expectation of payment but without any express contract, the law will imply a promise on the part of the corporation to pay a reasonable compensation.[12] It has long been recognized that officers involved in the active management of the company are entitled to reasonable compensation for services as managers even if no compensation had been previously fixed, because such onerous managerial services could not be expected to be performed for nothing.[13]

By the great weight of authority, the presumption against an implied contract of compensation for the directors and officers of a corporation does not apply to unusual or extraordinary services—that is, services that are not properly incidental to their office and are rendered outside of their regular duties. If directors or other officers perform such services at the request of the board of directors with the understanding that they are to be paid for, the law will, in the absence of any special agreement, imply a promise to pay what they are reasonably worth.[14] Thus

---

[8] Former Model Bus. Corp. Act §4(k) (1969) (officers and agents); *id.* §35 ("The board of directors shall have the authority to fix the compensation of directors unless otherwise provided in the articles of incorporation."). *Accord* Model Bus. Corp. Act §§3.02(11), 8.11 (1984) (hereinafter MBCA).

In Marx v. Akers, 666 N.E.2d 1034 (N.Y. 1996), a derivative suit challenging the board's decision to more than double each director's annual compensation, the court dismissed the suit. The court reasoned the directors acting pursuant to their statutory authority to set their own compensation that the only basis for excusing a demand in such a suit would be that the compensation was so egregious on its face as to be beyond the protection of the business judgment rule.

[9] National Oil Co. v. Reeves, 310 S.W.2d 242 (Ark. 1958); Godley v. Crandall & Godley Co., 105 N.E. 818 (N.Y. 1914).

[10] *See, e.g.,* In re 3 Com Corp. Shareholder Litigation, 1999 WL 1009210 (Del. Ch. Oct. 25, 1999) (no waste plead for stockholder approved plan whereby each director received options valued at $650,000 pursuant to stockholder approved plan).

[11] In Schraft v. Leis, 686 P.2d 865 (Kan. 1984), bylaws required officers' salaries to be approved by the board of directors but court held that agreement between sole owners of company as to salary constituted implied ratification of establishing salaries in manner not authorized in bylaws.

[12] Rocky Mtn. Powder Co. v. Hamlin, 310 P.2d 404 (Nev. 1957) (sales manager not a director or officer); Smith v. Long Island R.R., 6 N.E. 397 (N.Y. 1886) (secretary not a director or officer).

[13] Bellehurst Syndicate v. Commissioner, 83 F.2d 801, 803 (9th Cir. 1936); National Loan & Inv. Co. v. Rockland Co., 94 F. 335 (8th Cir. 1899); Navco Hardwood Co. v. Bass, 108 So. 452, 454 (Ala. 1925) (superintendent or general manager who devoted practically his entire time to the business).

[14] Corinne Mill, Canal & Stock Co. v. Toponce, 152 U.S. 405 (1894); Neidert v. Neidert, 637 S.W.2d 296 (Mo. Ct. App. 1982); Rocky Mtn. Powder Co. v. Hamlin, 310 P.2d 404 (Nev. 1957); Rector v. Director of Dept. Employment Sec., 390 A.2d 370 (R.I. 1978).

the president of a company who acted as the general contractor for the construction of an office building was not entitled to be compensated additionally for the services he rendered as the general contractor where the costs of constructing the building exceeded the funds available and he took on the additional responsibilities to cut costs. Furthermore, the president had not been asked by the stockholders to assume the role of general contractor.[15]

§11.02   Methods of Paying Executive Compensation

Traditionally, there have been three basic ways of compensating the corporate executive: (1) salary, (2) bonuses, and (3) a pension or other deferred compensation. As a result of increased sophistication in planning, the variations of the three basic forms of compensation defy exhaustive categorization.[1] The growing use of compensation "packages" arises out of a desire to attract and hold top-flight personnel, provide them with incentives for greater effort and dedication, and fully utilize tax advantages offered by some forms of compensation. Tailoring the most advantageous compensation plan requires careful consideration of the securities law, tax consequences,[2] and the Federal Employment Retirement Income Security Act (ERISA).[3] There is a widespread use in publicly held corporations, and in the large close corporations for that matter, of various kinds of contingent or deferred compensation[4]—cash bonuses, stock bonuses, stock options, stock purchase plans, profit-sharing plans, pension programs, allowances to surviving spouses and dependents, medical and dental payment plans, and other kinds of employee benefits.[5]

Stock options are a highly popular form of executive compensation in the United States.[6] The granting of stock options does not require a present expendi-

---

[15] Roach v. Bynum, 403 So. 2d 187 (Ala. 1981).

§11.02   [1] For an historical analysis of executive compensation via stock ownership, *see* Clifford G. Holderness, Randall S. Kroszner & Dennis P. Sheehan, Were the Good Old Days That Good? Changes in Managerial Stock Ownership Since the Great Depression, Working Paper No. 6550, (Nat'l Bureau Econ. Res. 1998).

[2] *See, e.g.*, Susan J. Stabile, Is There a Role of Tax Law in Policing Executive Compensation?, 72 St. John's L. Rev. 81 (1998).

[3] Pub. L. No. 93-406, 88 Stat. 829 (1974).

[4] For the view that compensation based on longer-term performance yields positive benefits to the corporation, *see* John F. Boschen & Kimberly J. Smith, You Can Pay Me Now and You Can Pay Me Later: The Dynamic Response of Executive Compensation to Firm Performance, 68 J. Bus. L. 577 (1995).

[5] *See generally* Steve Balsam, An Introduction to Executive Compensation (2002) (practitioner's guide with rich use of examples); Bruce R. Ellig, The Complete Guide to Executive Compensation (2001) (reviews key developments for past two decades as well as current issues for design of plans); B.B. Overton & Susan E. Stoffer Executive Compensation Answer Book (5th ed. 2001) (addressing wide range of issue for design of plans to recruit and retain executives).

[6] The average CEO stock option grant increased 700 percent between 1980 and 1994 (rising from $155,000 to $1.2 million). *See* Brian J. Hall, A Better Way to Pay CEOs?, in Executive Compensation and Shareholder Value Theory and Evidence 35 (J. Carpenter & D. Yermack eds. 1999).

ture of corporate funds, which may be badly needed for business operations or for expansion. Executives find stock options attractive because of their speculative appeal in offering a chance for really large financial gain. Further, under some circumstances, stock options carry substantial tax advantages for executives.[7] When the options are exercised, the proportionate interests of existing shareholders in the company will be diluted, but presumably by that time the employees exercising the options will have proved their worth and have benefitted the shareholders by contributing to an increase in the value of the corporation's shares.

§11.03 *Compensation for Past Services*

A decision by the directors to pay a bonus or to increase the compensation of an officer or employee for past services (i.e., for services already rendered) was formerly invalid. Such a payment was regarded as a gift and thus a misapplication of corporate funds.[1] The rule against compensation for past services does not apply, however, where the services were rendered with a formal or informal understanding that the fixed salary was only a minimum compensation and that additional allowances or compensation, although indefinite, would be paid.[2] The compensation in such a case can be seen as not in fact being for past services and the courts accordingly permit the directors to pay additional compensation in the exercise of reasonable discretion after the services have been performed or the contract for fixed compensation has been entered into.[3]

In recent years, with respect to payments based on past services, there has been a significant retreat from formalistic attitudes and movement toward a rule of reasonableness.[4] In some states statutes expressly grant authority to provide bonuses and retroactive pension plans.[5]

---

[7] Dixon v. Pro Image Inc., 987 P.2d 48, 57 (Utah 1999) (when stock option provision does not indicate whether parties contemplated registered or unregistered stock, court should not presume that parties contracted for unregistered stock; rather, extrinsic evidence is necessary to ascertain parties' intentions).

§11.03 [1] *See, e.g.,* Hurt v. Cotton States Fertilizer Co., 159 F.2d 52 (5th Cir.), *cert. denied,* 331 U.S. 828 (1947).

For a discussion of problems raised when a corporation makes payments to a deceased officer's spouse not called for by a contract with the deceased, *see* Belcher v. Birmingham Trust Nat'l Bank, 348 F. Supp. 61 (N.D. Ala. 1968); Adams v. Smith, 153 So. 2d 221 (Ala. 1963).

[2] *See, e.g.,* Blish v. Thompson Automatic Arms Corp., 64 A.2d 581, 606-607 (Del. 1948) (exception to retroactive compensation arises when the payment is pursuant to an earlier implied contract or the amount is not unreasonable in view of the services rendered).

[3] *See, e.g.,* Estate of Bogley v. United States, 514 F.2d 1027 (Ct. Cl. 1975); McQuillen v. National Cash Register Co., 112 F.2d 877, 884 (4th Cir.), *cert. denied,* 311 U.S. 695 (1940).

[4] *See* Wolf v. Fried, 373 A.2d 734, 736 (Pa. 1977) (board's judgment that manager was "unique and knowledgeable" and worthy of additional compensation is evidence there was adequate consideration supporting additional pay).

[5] Wis. Stat. Ann. §180.0302(12) (West 1992); Va. Code Ann. §13.1-627(11) (Michie 1999). *Cf.* Former MBCA §41 (1969) (a corporation has power to "pay pensions and establish pension plans, pension trusts, . . . stock bonus plans . . . and other incentive plans for any or all of its directors, officers and employees").

§11.04   Judicial Review of Fairness of Executive Compensation: Self-Dealing

Most states have enacted conflict-of-interest statutes[1] that are sufficiently broad to include board-of-director action establishing the compensation of one of its members. Close judicial scrutiny customarily occurs when those receiving the compensation are the same individuals approving the compensation.[2] Conflict-of-interest statutes set forth steps that, if satisfied, invoke the protection of the business judgment rule for executive compensation. In broad overview, the steps require good faith impartial approval by the directors or shareholders after full disclosure of all material facts. Where such a statute does not exist, the courts similarly consider the circumstances of the directors' or stockholders' approval of the interested director's executive compensation.[3]

Sometimes an attempt is made to give the illusion of a disinterested quorum and majority by having the directors vote on compensation for each office separately, with each director abstaining from voting on her own compensation but voting on the compensation of her co-directors. It has generally been held that where the directors have the common object of procuring a salary or a salary increase for each of them as officers, the device of passing a separate resolution for each instead of one joint resolution for all will not be effective to validate the salary increases. The mutual back-scratching or reciprocal voting voids the action as to each.[4]

Many companies provide "golden parachutes" for their most senior executives. The large payment in the event of a change in control that the arrangement provides is designed to assure greater neutrality on the part of managers when assessing the merits of an offer from the firm's suitor and to secure their services through the uncertainty created by the bid for control. Because the objective of the golden parachute is upon the officers' conduct before the change in control occurs, it is understandable that the courts have not conditioned the validity of a golden parachute upon any requirement that the manager exercise reasonable efforts to find comparable compensated employment.[5] A further concern for

---

§11.04   [1] *See, e.g.*, Giannotti v. Hamway, 387 S.E.2d 725, 731 (Va. 1990) (in absence of showing of fraud or bad faith, presumption of propriety applies). *See also* Former MBCA §41 (1969); Cal. Corp. Code §310 (West 1990); Del. Code Ann. tit. 8, §144 (2001).

[2] *See, e.g.*, Morrissey v. Curran, 650 F.2d 1267 (2d Cir. 1981). However, even when the burden is placed on the board, the compensation plan is not doomed to failure. *See* Hanrahan v. Kruidenier, 473 N.W.2d 184 (Iowa 1991) (award of bonuses upheld despite basis to question board's loyalty and care).

[3] *See, e.g.*, Moran v. Edson, 493 F.2d 400 (3d Cir. 1974); McDonald v. Sealift Terminals, Inc., 505 So. 2d 675 (Fla. Dist. Ct. App. 1987); Landstreet v. Meyer, 29 So. 2d 653 (Miss. 1947).

Informed stockholder ratification generally shifts the burden of proof to the plaintiff. *See* Michelson v. Duncan, 407 A.2d 211, 224 (Del. 1979).

[4] Angelus Sec. Corp. v. Ball, 67 P.2d 152 (Cal. Ct. App. 1937); Davids v. Davids, 120 N.Y.S. 350 (App. Div. 1909); Wonderful Group Mining Co. v. Rand, 191 P. 631 (Wash. 1920); Stoiber v. Miller Brewing Co., 42 N.W.2d 144 (Wis. 1950), noted in 38 Cal. L. Rev. 906 (1950).

[5] *See* Royal Crown Companies, Inc. v. McMahon, 359 S.E.2d 379 (Ga. App. 1987); Koenings v. Joseph Schlitz Brewing Co., 377 N.W.2d 593 (Wis. 1985) (viewing payment as a type of liquidated damage).

golden parachutes is whether they will be seen as violating the "all holders" and "best price" rules that apply to tender offer involving a company registered with the SEC.[6] In essence, courts have reasoned that payments to officers in the context of a takeover may be deemed additional consideration paid for shares that should have also been offered to all the company's stockholders.[7] The cases follow the reasoning of *Epstein v. MCA, Inc.*,[8] that at $21 million payment to an executive to secure his support of a takeover offer *might* be considered as being made during the tender offer, even if agreed to before the tender offer commenced and paid after its conclusion.

§11.05 Judicial Review of Executive Compensation: Equitable Limits

Directors have wide business discretion in fixing executive compensation.[1] However, in appropriate cases, for a suit of a shareholder attacking executive compensation as excessive, courts will review the fairness and reasonableness of compensation of executives and shareholder-employees.[2] A majority shareholder cannot give away the corporate funds in the guise of compensation as against the interest of a dissenting minority or in fraud of creditors.[3] Similarly, even if there are no injured shareholders or creditors, exorbitant compensation withdrawals by corporate officers may be classified in part as dividends and as an attempt to evade taxes. However, judicial reversal of executive compensation decisions in public corporations is rare.[4]

A striking factor among the reported decisions holding that a particular executive compensation arrangement is wasteful or excessive is that they universally involve close corporations. There are several reasons why public corporations are not represented among the decisions upsetting executive compensation arrangements. The first explanation is procedural. As will be seen later in Chapter 15, a

---

[6] These rules are part of the Williams Act Amendments to the Securities Exchange Act of 1934 and are discussed in §24.04.

[7] *See* Millionerrors Inv. Club v. General Elec. Co., 2000 WL 1288333 (W.D. Pa. Mar. 21, 2000); Katt v. Titan Acquisition, Ltd., 133 F. Supp. 2d 632 (M.D. Tenn. 2000). *Contra* McMichael v. United States Filter Corp., 2001 U.S. Dist. Lexis 3918 (Feb. 22, 2001) (payments pursuant to preexisting golden parachute agreement are not extra payment within the tender offer).

[8] 50 F.3d 644 (9th Cir. 1995). *Contra* Lerro v. Quaker Oats Co., 84 F.3d 239 (7th Cir. 1996) (contract signed before tender offer's commencement is not within the tender offer).

§11.05 [1] *See, e.g.,* Cramer v. General Tel. & Elec. Corp., 582 F.2d 259 (3d Cir. 1978), *cert. denied,* 439 U.S. 1129 (1979); Klaus v. Hi-Shear Corp., 528 F.2d 225 (9th Cir. 1975); Miller v. American Tel. & Tel. Co., 507 F.2d 759 (3d Cir. 1974).

[2] Galler v. Galler, 316 N.E.2d 114 (Ill. App. Ct. 1974).

[3] *See, e.g.,* Rogers v. Hill, 289 U.S. 582 (1933); Delta Star, Inc. v. Patton, 76 F. Supp. 3d 617 (W.D. Pa. 1999) (president and chairman set salaries, including for himself, without consulting the board of directors); Michelson v. Duncan, 407 A.2d 211 (Del. 1979).

[4] *See generally* Randall S. Thomas & Kenneth J. Martin, Litigating Challenges to Executive Pay. An Exercise in Futility, 79 Wash. U.L.Q. 569 (2001) (reporting findings that plaintiffs do win more often than is commonly understood, and especially with respect to challenges of compensation paid in a close corporation).

precondition to any successful derivative suit is convincing the court that the plaintiff need not make a demand on the board of directors. It is far more likely that there will be outside directors in the public corporation and that their presence will erect an unsurpassable barrier in the plaintiff's quest to challenge executive compensation. Thus, in a leading derivative suit case,[5] the plaintiff challenged the decision to award its aged controlling stockholder a salary of $100,000 per year regardless of whether he performed any service to the corporation. The derivative suit was dismissed because the plaintiff failed to persuade the court that the company's outside directors lacked sufficient independence to respond impartially to the plaintiff's demand. Thus, in a widely watched matter, the Delaware Supreme Court affirmed the dismissal of a derivative suit challenging a severance package valued at approximately $140 million, which not surprisingly the court viewed as "exceedingly lucrative" compensation.[6] The court strongly embraced the view that the size and structure of executive compensation are inherently matters of the directors' judgment, unless they act "irrationally."[7]

A second consideration that reduces the viability of a challenge to executive compensation in public corporations is also related to the presence of outside directors. A major concern is whether the arrangement is protected by the business judgment rule. Courts are loath to substitute their judgment for that of the directors in such matters, particularly if the decision carries the imprimatur of a critical mass of independent directors. To this end, compensation decisions are routinely submitted to the outside directors for their separate approval, and compensation plans involving stock options and special bonus arrangements are more frequently approved by the stockholders. Such independent approvals dampen the derivative suit attorney's interest in trying to convince the court that it should substitute its judgment for that of the outside directors, or perhaps that of the stockholders. As a result, the modern cases setting aside executive compensation arrangements arise in the close corporation setting, where such impartial approval is absent.

The courts have had great difficulty in formulating definitive standards to determine the propriety of the amount of compensation paid corporate executives. One court or another has said that controlling shareholders may not take advantage of their control to vote themselves excessive salaries or to cause excessive salaries to be voted to them by directors they control;[8] that directors must act honestly and reasonably in fixing executive compensation;[9] that directors may not "waste" the corporation's assets by granting excessive compensation;[10] that com-

---

[5] Aronson v. Lewis, 473 A.2d 805 (Del. 1984).

[6] Brehm v. Eisner, 746 A.2d 244, 249 (Del. 2000).

[7] *Id.* at 263.

[8] 5A William M. Fletcher, Cyclopedia of the Law of Private Corporations §2132 (rev. perm. ed. 1995).

[9] 5A Fletcher, *supra* note 8, §2132. *See also* Barrett v. Smith, 242 N.W. 392, 394 (Minn. 1932) (salaries of corporate officers may be so high as to evidence fraud and oppression of minority).

[10] Brehm v. Eisner, 746 A.2d 244, 263-264 (Del. 2000) (although executive compensation is inherently matter of board's business judgment, directors may not irrationally squander or give away corporate assets); Baker v. Cohn, 42 N.Y.S.2d 159 (Sup. Ct. 1942), *modified,* 40 N.Y.S.2d 623 (App. Div. 1943), *aff'd,* 54 N.E.2d 689 (N.Y. 1944).

A. Executive Compensation

pensation must bear a reasonable relation to the value of the services rendered[11] and to the ability of the corporation to pay;[12] and that courts of equity will review the fairness and reasonableness of compensation.[13]

Whether executive compensation is excessive is a fact question.[14] Courts proffer a variety of tests for judging whether the challenged compensation arrangement should be struck down, using such expressions as "fraud," "bad faith," "oppression," "excessive and unreasonable," or "a waste of corporate assets."[15] Such labels at best communicate a sense that when viewed in its totality the compensation arrangement departs substantially from what one can view as normative. A wide range of factors[16] are weighed by courts reviewing executive compensation: the executive's qualifications,[17] the nature, extent, and scope of the executive's work, the size and complexities of the business, economic conditions of the company, industry, and country, comparison of salaries to those of similarly situated executives[18] as well as to the company's dividends, past compensation of the executive, the time devoted to the job, the success of the company, if any, during the executive's tenure,[19] and whether the Internal Revenue Service has disallowed the salary.

Particularly important in weighing these factors is whether the executive compensation has received the impartial approval of the directors or the stockholders. In an attack on allegedly exorbitant compensation, the scope of review depends on whether the recipient officers or directors have participated in fixing the compensation. Where the person compensated does not fix the compensation and the amount is set by directors without any adverse interest or influence that would prevent the exercise of a fair judgment, judicial review is very limited.[20] It is considered outside the proper judicial function to go into the business question of the fairness or reasonableness of the compensation as determined by the board of directors. In contrast, if there is self-dealing because the directors stand to gain from their actions, the business judgment rule is not available, and the burden

---

[11] Security-First Nat'l Bank v. Lutz, 322 F.2d 348, 354 (9th Cir. 1963) (executives entitled to receive as salary for services to corporation what those services reasonably worth).

[12] Glenmore Distilleries Co. v. Seideman, 267 F. Supp. 915 (E.D.N.Y. 1967).

[13] Stratis v. Andreson, 150 N.E. 832 (Mass. 1926); Worley v. Dunkle, 161, 62 A.2d 699 (N.J. Super. Ct. 1948).

[14] Pacific Grains Inc. v. Commissioner, 399 F.2d 603 (9th Cir. 1968); Goldman v. Jameson, 275 So. 2d 108 (Ala. 1973); Smith v. Dunlap, 111 So. 2d 1 (Ala. 1959); Michelson v. Duncan, 407 A.2d 211 (Del. 1979); Black v. Parker Mfg. Co., 106 N.E.2d 544 (Mass. 1952).

The authorities disagree on whether an executive whose compensation is challenged has the burden of proving its reasonableness or the challenger has the burden of proving its unreasonableness. Most decisions indicate that the presence or absence of self-dealing is the determinative factor.

[15] E.g., McQuillen v. National Cash Register Co., 112 F.2d 877, 883 (4th Cir.), cert. denied, 311 U.S. 695 (1940).

[16] See, e.g., Wilderman v. Wilderman, 315 A.2d 610 (Del. Ch. 1974); Fendelman v. Fenco Handbag Mfg. Co., 482 S.W.2d 461 (Mo. 1972); Ruetz v. Topping, 453 S.W.2d 624 (Mo. Ct. App. 1970).

[17] See, e.g., Neidert v. Neidert, 637 S.W.2d 296 (Mo. Ct. App. 1982).

[18] See Murphy v. Washington Am. League Base Ball Club, 324 F.2d 394 (D.C. Cir. 1963).

[19] Hurt v. Cotton States Fertilizer Co., 159 F.2d 52 (5th Cir.), cert. denied, 331 U.S. 828 (1947); Wilderman v. Wilderman, 315 A.2d 610 (Del. Ch. 1974) (listing eight factors including IRS determination of permissible salary deduction).

[20] See, e.g., Cohen v. Ayers, 596 F.2d 733 (7th Cir. 1979).

shifts to those receiving the compensation to show good faith and overall fairness to the corporation.[21]

A major portion of an executive compensation package frequently takes the form of a bonus or profit-sharing arrangement, and today more typically pursuant to stock options. Bonus and profit-sharing arrangements are of various types, such as an individual cash or stock bonus based on a percentage of the company's annual earnings, an employees' stock purchase plan, or an interest in a bonus or management fund in which a number of important executives may share. To afford the managers of large companies as well as other key employees some share of the profits is generally considered a good business policy. Certainly by linking the employee's pay, or at least an important component of it, to future increases in the value of the firm, addresses directly the separation of ownership from management problem. However, equity-based compensation while portending significant rewards to the manager also carries with it great costs to the firm.[22] In some smaller companies, however, an undue share of the income is sometimes paid to the principal owners by way of compensation, and little or nothing is paid in dividends. Even in publicly held companies a substantial percentage of the earnings is frequently paid to the executive group. A fundamental issue is raised as to the real relationship between management and the shareholders of publicly held corporations. Should directors be regarded as fiduciaries, representatives of the owners, or managers of the enterprise for the sole benefit of the shareholders? Or should they be viewed as managing partners, conducting the business partly for themselves as well as for the benefit of the passive and silent partners, the shareholders, who contribute the capital for an uncertain return, a contingent share of the profits, when and as fixed by management?[23]

The most famous compensation litigation came before the United States Supreme Court in *Rogers v. Hill*.[24] The case challenged the emoluments of the American Tobacco Company's president and executives, who received large fixed salaries and in addition participated in company profits through a huge annual bonus and certain profitable stock subscription plans.[25] The annual bonus, which

[21] *Id. See* Delta Star, Inc. v. Patton, 76 F. Supp. 3d 617 (W.D. Pa. 1999) (president set his own salary and that of others without consulting his board of directors); Steiner v. Meyerson, 1995 LEXIS 95 (Del. Ch. 1995) (yearly director compensation of $20,000 not clearly waste, but defendant's motion for summary judgment could not be granted because the court could not conclude that under all circumstances this amount met the "intrinsic fairness" standard).

[22] *See* Calvin H. Johnson, Stock Compensation: The Most Expensive Way to Pay Future Cash, 52 SMU L. Rev. 423 (1999) (demonstrating that deferred compensation is better for the employee and less expensive to the corporation, when an appropriate discount rate and tax effects are considered, than grant of stock options).

[23] *See* Ferdinand Pecora, Wall Street Under Oath, 113-120, 143-146, particularly at 119 (1939); George T. Washington & Henry V. Rothschild, Compensating the Corporate Executive ch. 19 (3d ed. 1962).

[24] 289 U.S. 582 (1933). See also its companion case, Rogers v. Guaranty Trust Co., 288 F. Supp. 123 (1933).

[25] Rogers v. Hill, 289 U.S. 582, 590 (1933); Rogers v. Guaranty Trust Co., 288 U.S. 123 (1933); Heller v. Boylan, 29 N.Y.S.2d 653, 660, 669, 675, 701 (Sup. Ct. 1941), *aff'd*, 32 N.Y.S.2d 131 (App. Div. 1941). *See* 2 Washington & Rothschild, *supra* note 23, at 880-889.

A. Executive Compensation

was calculated as 10 percent of any increase in earnings over the company's earnings of 1910, was to be paid to the president and five vice presidents annually. The market price for stock allotted to the directors voting for the stock allotment plan of 1919 (the president not voting) was nearly $2,000,000 greater than the allotment price; the plan was never submitted to the stockholders for their approval.[26] In June 1930, the directors of the company proposed another and further stock subscription plan for officers and employees that was embodied in a bylaw submitted to and approved by the requisite vote of the shareholders as required by the New Jersey statute. Under this plan the directors in 1931 authorized the sale of some 56,000 shares of stock at the par value of $25 per share, which had a current market price of $112. "Of this number, 32,370, more than half, were allotted to the directors, of which 13,440 were allotted to the president. The remaining 24,342 shares were allotted in relatively small amounts to 525 employees."[27] On the day of the allotment, the market price, $112 per share, was more than four times the subscription price. The value of the rights granted to Mr. Hill, the president, in 1919 was estimated at $705,000, and his 1931 grant at $1,169,000; this was in addition to his other compensation of over $1,000,000. Rogers, a minority shareholder, instituted six suits against the company, its directors, and officers, two of which ultimately came before the United States Supreme Court. One suit attacked the bonus payments, the other, the stock subscription privilege. The bonus case was lost before the Second Circuit Court, with Judge Swan dissenting. The Supreme Court, however, reversed:

> Much weight is to be given to the action of the stockholders, and the by-law is supported by the presumption of regularity and continuity. But the rule prescribed by it cannot, against the protest of a shareholder, be used to justify payments of sums as salaries so large as in substance and effect to amount to spoliation or waste of corporate property. The dissenting opinion of Judge Swan indicates the applicable rule, "If a bonus payment has no relation to the value of services for which it is given, it is in reality a gift in part, and the majority stockholders have no power to give away corporate property against the protest of the minority." 60 F.2d 109, 113. The facts alleged by plaintiff are sufficient to require the District Court, upon a consideration of all the relevant facts brought forward by the parties, to determine whether and to what extent payments to the individual defendants under the by-laws constitute misuse and waste of the money of the corporation.[28]

Rogers v. Hill represents one of the few successful challenges to executive compensation arrangements within a publicly held corporation based exclusively on its excessiveness. The case provides, however, little guidance as to how excessiveness is to be determined. Cases involving public corporations decided after *Rogers v. Hill*, as discussed below, emphasize the process by which the bonus or profit-

---

[26] Penn v. Robertson, 115 F.2d 167, 170 (4th Cir. 1940).

[27] Rogers v. Guaranty Trust Co., 288 U.S. 123, 134 (1933) (Stone, J., dissenting).

[28] Rogers v. Hill, 289 U.S. 582, 591-592 (1933). *See* Note, American Tobacco Co. Bonus Plans: Legal Control of Executive Remuneration, 46 Harv. L. Rev. 828 (1933); Comment, Profit Sharing for Executives and Employees: The *American Tobacco Co.* Case, 42 Yale L.J. 419 (1932); Note, 32 Mich. L. Rev. 672, 675 (1934).

sharing arrangement was approved over the more indefinite question of whether the amounts actually awarded are excessive.

Over the years the Delaware Supreme Court has been an important influence on the standards to be used in assessing bonus and profit-sharing arrangements. In the leading case concerning stock options, *Beard v. Elster*,[29] the court summarized the tests to be employed as follows:

> All stock option plans must be tested against the requirements that they contain conditions, or that surrounding circumstances are such, that the corporation may reasonably expect to receive the contemplated benefit from the grant of the options. Furthermore, there must be a reasonable relationship between the value of the benefits passing to the corporation and the value of the options granted.[30]

Applying the above, *Beard* upheld lucrative stock options granted to officers and supervisory personnel emphasizing that the option plan had been approved by the disinterested directors, that the terms of the plan required that the optionee must be an employee when the option is exercised, and that most of the beneficiaries of the option plan had remained in the company's employ after the plan had been adopted.

On closer analysis, the above tests provide very little specificity. This observation is best understood by considering the weak distinctions *Beard* offered to set its decision apart from two earlier cases, *Kerbs v. California Eastern Airways*[31] and *Gottlieb v. Heyden Chemical Corporation*,[32] where the court refused to protect stock option plans. *Beard* distinguished its earlier reversal of a stock option plan in *Kerbs* because Kerbs's plan allowed employees to exercise their options anytime within six months *of having worked* for the company. This is not itself a satisfactory distinction between the two plans' terms. The stock option plan's terms in *Beard* did not themselves assure that an employee would remain with the company after being granted the right to exercise her options. That plan required only that the officer be in the company's employ when the option was exercised. It was entirely possible under the terms of the plan for the employee to exercise the options, resign, and begin work with a competitor.[33]

The second *Beard* test—namely, that there be a reasonable relationship between the gains the employee reaps on the exercise of the option and the value the corporation receives from that employee's continued service—is at best problematic. The gain to the employee is the difference between the exercise price and the stock's value on the date of exercise. This amount can be quite significant and can be attributed to a good many exogenous events unrelated to that employee's

---

[29] 160 A.2d 731 (Del. 1960).

[30] Beard v. Elster, 160 A.2d 731, 737 (Del. 1960).

[31] 90 A.2d 652 (Del. 1952).

[32] 90 A.2d 660 (Del. 1952).

[33] A liberal, *ex post*-view of this inquiry was taken in Newberger v. Rifkind, 104 Cal. Rptr. 663, 665 (Cal. 1972), where the court reasoned that consideration is given for an option by the employee's continuous service to the company.

A. Executive Compensation

worth.[34] The *Beard* court reasoned that its earlier holding against the stock option plan in *Gottlieb* was justified because there had not been in that case any "independent appraisal of the value of the services to be retained by means of the options and the value of the options granted."[35] The *Beard* court thus deferred not to its determination of reasonableness but to that of the independent directors.

Beard reveals that the truly significant test for stock options and profit-sharing arrangements, and executive compensation generally, is not the content that the courts give to the tests or standards they articulate; the dominant consideration is the *process* by which the corporate decision-maker arrives at the executive compensation package that is awarded. The most important consideration, indeed the sole consideration in the public corporation, is good faith impartial approval by the directors and/or the stockholders. As *Beard* itself illustrates, even a plan that potentially fails solely by its terms to assure the officer's continued service, because the officer could exercise the option and then resign from the company, is saved because the approving directors were not themselves the beneficiaries of the stock option plan and otherwise acted in good faith and with reasonable care. However, the awards approved by the board of directors or compensation committee must be consistent with the constraints embodied in the plan.[36]

Good faith ratification by the stockholders after full disclosure also invokes the same presumptions, even if the approving directors lack authority to approve or modify a stock option plan.[37] When a plan receives the impartial approval of the directors or stockholders, the burden of proof is on the challenging party to prove the stock option or profit-sharing plan constitutes waste.[38] Not since *Rogers v. Hill* has there been a reported case involving a public corporation where executive compensation in a public corporation was struck down solely on the basis of being excessive.[39] However, in *Lewis v. Vogelstein*,[40] the derivative suit challenged the directors awarding themselves with highly valuable options that could be exercised immediately. Even though the option plan had been ratified by disinterested, informed stockholders, the court rejected the defendants' motion to dismiss, and set the matter for trial. Defining waste as arising when the "exchange of corporate assets for consideration so disproportionately small as to lie beyond the range at which any reasonable person might be willing to trade,"[41] the court believed it could not rule as a matter of law that facts that could be introduced at the trial may not persuade the reasonable person that under the circumstances the options constituted waste.[42]

---

[34] *See* Berkwitz v. Humphrey, 163 F. Supp. 78 (N.D. Ohio 1958) (no reasonable relationship between market gains and officer's contribution); *contra,* Lieberman v. Becker, 155 A.2d 596 (Del. 1959).

[35] 90 A.2d at 737.

[36] *See* Sanders v. Wang, 1999 WL 1044880 (Del. Ch. Nov. 8, 1999) (awards by the board may not exceed number of shares authorized for the plan).

[37] *See* Michelson v. Duncan, 407 A.2d 211 (Del. 1979).

[38] *Id.*

[39] *See generally* Douglas C. Michael, The Corporate Officer's Independent Duty as a Tonic for the Anemic Law of Executive Compensation, 17 J. Corp. L. 785 (1992).

[40] 699 A.2d 327 (Del. Ch. 1997).

[41] *Id.* at 336.

[42] *Id.* at 339.

Quite aside from the fiduciary standards that apply to directors and officers establishing executive compensation are the fiduciary obligations corporations subject to ERISA have under section 404 of the act. Among the obligations imposed on the company is that it may not commit material misrepresentations to plan participants respecting planned changes in employee pension benefits.[43] This duty begins at least when benefit changes are being considered by those with authority to implement the pension benefit changes.[44]

§11.06   Executive Compensation and the Internal Revenue Code

Because a corporation can deduct salary payments, whereas dividends are paid out of after-tax dollars,[1] there is a powerful tax incentive to pay as much as possible in salary. This is an especially critical factor when dealing with closely held enterprises because of the close identity of ownership and management. Accordingly, there are a good many cases in which the Internal Revenue Service challenges compensation as a disguised dividend.[2] In such cases, excessive compensation, if found, results in the excess payment being treated as a dividend so that the corporation is denied a deduction for that disallowed amount. The traditional approach to determining under the IRC whether compensation is excessive is the multi-factor test. Under this approach, the court weighs a number of considerations, with no single factor being dispositive. Factors include (1) the employee's role, position and qualifications in the corporation, (2) duties of, and hours devoted to company, by the employee, (3) comparison of challenged compensation with that of similar companies, (4) character and financial condition of the company including return on investment and changes in market value of firm, (5) dividend record of the company, and (6) the consistency with which the compensation has been paid.[3] An emerging approach is the so-called "independent investor test," whereby a salary is presumptively reasonable when it is paid by a company whose owners are enjoying a desirable rate of return.[4] Applying this test, a court upheld compensation of $1.3 million in the face

---

[43] See Fischer v. Philadelphia Elec. Co., 994 F.2d 130 (3d Cir. 1993).

[44] See Fischer v. Philadelphia Elec. Co., 96 F.3d 1533, 1537 (3d Cir. 1996). But see Pocchia v. NYNEX Corp., 81 F.3d 275, 278 (2d Cir. 1996) (fiduciary not required to voluntarily disclose changes in a benefit plan before they are adopted).

§11.06   [1] See I.R.C. §162(a)(1) (2000); Treas. Reg. §1.162-7(a) (2002).

[2] For an illustrative case on the taxation issue see Rapco Inc. v. Commissioner, 85 F.3d 950, 955 (2d Cir. 1996) (salary of $900,000 to 95 percent owner disallowed where it was not supported by expert testimony, ignored the bylaw's bonus compensation scheme, and was set by its recipient).

[3] See, e.g., Eberl's Claim Service, Inc. v. Commissioner, 249 F.3d 994 (10th Cir. 2001); Lablegraphics, Inc. v. Commissioner, 221 F.3d 1091 (9th Cir. 2000) (deduction denied for fourfold increase in one year's compensation); Alpha Medical, Inc. v. Commissioner, 172 F.3d 942 (6th Cir. 1999); ($4 million payment upheld where justified to overcome undercompensation of prior years); Dexsil Corp. v. Commissioner, 147 F.3d 96 (2nd Cir. 1998).

[4] See, e.g., Exacto Spring Corp. v. Commissioner, 196 F.3d 833 (7th Cir. 1999). One court has opined this test is but one consideration in the multi-factor approach. See Dexsil Corp. v. Commissioner, 147 F.3d

of expert evidence that investors would expect a 13% return on their investment and were in fact enjoying a 50 percent return.[5]

An important limitation on senior executive compensation was the addition in 1993 of section 162(m) of the Internal Revenue Code, which denies a federal income tax deduction for all taxable years commencing after January 1, 1994, to publicly held corporations for compensation in excess of $1 million per year to any of the corporation's top five officers.[6] An important exemption to this provision applies to "performance-based compensation" arrangements.[7] This exemption applies when compensation is awarded pursuant to a predetermined compensation arrangement that contains objective performance goals established by a committee of outside directors and approved by the shareholders after full disclosure of the arrangement's material terms. Also beyond the scope of section 162(m) is deferred compensation that is paid to a person who is no longer one of the five top officers of the corporation. In applying this provision to stock options and other contingent compensation arrangements, the tax consequences are determined on the date of exercise, not on the date the option is granted. There is no evidence that section 162(m) has retarded the rate of increase in executive compensation.[8]

A further attempt to restrict excessive awards appears in section 280G.[9] This provision applies when excessive compensation is paid to executives conditional upon a change of control. The provision defines excessive compensation as being three times the executives annual compensation. If the provision applies, not only is the corporation denied a deduction, but the recipient incurs a 20 percent excise tax. The clear intent of Section 280G is to reach "excessive" golden parachute arrangements; however, a strategy that is sometimes followed is merely to "gross up" the recipient's award to cover the anticipated tax effects and to forego the deduction.

§11.07   Regulating Executive Compensation Through Improved Governance and Disclosure

In recent years, the amount of compensation garnered by executives of publicly held corporations has become a public issue eliciting cries within the Congress

---

96 (2nd Cir. 1998). *See generally* L.R. Dutton, The Independent Investor Test: The Latest Test in the Search for Reasonable Compensation Is Blurred in the Second Circuit, 45 Wayne L. Rev. 1953 (2000).

[5] Exacto Spring Corp. v. Commissioner, 196 F.3d 833 (7th Cir. 1999).

[6] I.R.C. §162(m) (2000). *But see* Note, Rethinking Section 162(m)'s Limitation on the Deduction of Executive Compensation: A Review and a Commentary, 15 Va. Tax Rev. 371 (1995). The IRS has issued regulations defining such terms as the meaning of "pre-established goal," "outside director," and the "substantially uncertain" requirement. *See* Treas. Reg. §1.162-27(e) (1995).

[7] *See generally* Joseph Antenucci & Peter Woodlock, Types of Compensation Qualified As "Performance Based" Under Code Section 162(m), 76 Taxes 27 (Sept. 1998).

[8] *See* Susan J. Stabile, Is There a Role for Tax Law in Policing Executive Compensation?, 72 St. John's L. Rev. 91,89 (1998) (reporting that executive pay grew 29 percent faster in the year after the enactment of section 162(m) than was the rate of growth in the previous 14 years).

[9] I.R.C. §280G. *See generally* Bruce A. Wolk, The Golden Parachute Provisions: Time for Repeal?, 21 Va. Tax. Rev. 125 (2001) (examining various ways corporations have developed to escape provision's effect and the deficiencies/"loopholes" within provision).

demanding either capping of executive compensation or subjecting the compensation to severe tax consequences. Two important corporate responses to this national malaise is the increasing use of compensation committees and enhanced mandatory disclosure rules for public corporations.

Nearly all sizable public corporations today have compensation committees.[1] The provisions of the American Law Institute embody a prevalent sphere of authority for the compensation committee:

> (b) The compensation committee should:
> (1) Review and recommend to the board, or determine, the annual salary, bonus, stock options, and other benefits, direct and indirect, of the senior executives.
> (2) Review new executive compensation programs; review on a periodic basis the operation of the corporation's executive compensation programs to determine whether they are properly coordinated; establish and periodically review policies for the administration of executive compensation programs; and take steps to modify any executive compensation programs that yield payments and benefits that are not reasonably related to executive performance.[2]

The great virtue of a compensation committee is the independence of judgment its members can bring to compensation questions. This of course demands that its membership be composed of outside directors and that the committee has broad authority to establish, review, and modify the compensation of senior executives. Nevertheless, there is a certain disquiet that executive compensation could have soared to such prominence in the national consciousness during a time when most public corporations have had compensation committees. Until studies are made of the actual operation of compensation committees, there will continue to be some doubt as to whether they are an effective fulcrum for balancing the interests of the stockholders against the managers' quest for ever-increasing compensation.

The SEC confronted the issue of executive compensation by adopting new disclosure guidelines for the express purpose of providing a clearer presentation of senior executive compensation.[3] There is also the important collateral and moderating influence that arises with any revealing disclosure requirements such as are now required by the SEC. In this respect, recall Brandeis's wise observation: "Sunlight is said to be the best of disinfectants; electric light the most efficient policeman."[4] Among the executive compensation disclosures required is that the board of directors or compensation committee discuss the relationship of corporate performance to executive compensation with respect to the compensation awarded for the last fiscal year.[5] Even more detailed discussion is required with

---

§11.07   [1] *See, e.g.*, Heidrick & Struggles, The Changing Board Table 11, 13 (93 percent of surveyed corporations in 1989 had compensation committees). Even as early as 1981 some 72 percent of the proxies surveyed by the SEC revealed the presence of a compensation committee. SEC Staff Report, Corporate Accountability 612-614 (1981).

[2] ALI Principles of Corporate Governance: Restatement and Recommendations §3A.05(b) (1992).

[3] *See* Executive Compensation Disclosure, Securities Act Release No. 6962 [1992 Transfer Binder] Fed. Sec. L. Rep. (CCH) ¶85,056 (Oct. 16, 1992).

[4] Louis D. Brandeis, Other People's Money 92 (Stokes 1932).

[5] Item 402(k)(1) of Regulation S-K, 17 C.F.R. 229.402(k)(1) (2002).

respect to the relationship of the chief executive officer's compensation to the company's financial performance.[6] The SEC requires a line-graph plotting for five years of the relationship of executive compensation to overall corporate performance as embodied in a measure of cumulative total shareholder return, which itself is contrasted with an acceptable stock index. Matters that may compromise the directors' independence must also be disclosed.[7] The disclosures are required to identify the directors or committee members who had responsibility for making the disclosures mandated by the executive compensation disclosure rules.[8]

B.   CORPORATE OPPORTUNITIES

§11.08   *Misappropriation of Corporate Opportunities: Disloyal Diversion of Business*

Directors and officers as insiders cannot utilize their strategic position for their own preferment or use their powers and opportunities for their own advantage to the exclusion or detriment of the interests they are to represent. Thus directors and officers as corporate insiders cannot utilize their strategic position or their powers and opportunities for their personal advantage to the detriment of other corporate constituencies.[1] They cannot sell their votes or their influence in the management of the corporation. A few cases have employed the corporate opportunity doctrine-type analysis to shareholders.[2] There appears little reason why the test should be limited to fiduciaries who are directors or officers; the policy considerations underlying proscribing some opportunities as belonging to the firm are applicable to all who have a fiduciary relationship to the firm.[3] A fiduciary cannot profit personally from information and knowledge that they have acquired in confidence in their corporate capacity, even though the corporation suffers no injury.[4]

---

[6] *See, e.g.,* Item 402(a)(4) and Item 402(k)(2) of Regulation S-K, 17 C.F.R. 229.402(a)(4) & (k)(2) (2002).

[7] *See* Item 402(j)(3) of Regulation S-K, 17 C.F.R. 228.402(j)(3) (2002).

[8] Item 402(k)(3), Regulation S-K 228.402(k)(3) (2002).

§11.08   [1] *See, e.g.,* Pepper v. Litton, 308 U.S. 295 (1939); Gulledge v. Frosty Land Foods Int'l, 414 So. 2d 60 (Ala. 1982); Miller v. Miller, 222 N.W.2d 71, 78 (Minn. 1974).

[2] *See, e.g.,* Thorpe by Castleman v. CERBCO, Inc., 676 A.2d 436 (Del. 1996); Lyon v. Campbell, 707 A.2d 850, 864 (Md. App. 1998); A. Teixeira & Co., Inc. v. Teixeira, 699 A.2d 1383 (R.I. 1997) (members of close corporation are analogous to partners in a partnership and hence, as fiduciaries, owe duty not to usurp opportunities).

[3] *See* United Teachers' Assoc. Ins. Co. v. MacKeen & Bailey, Inc., 99 F.3d 645 (5th Cir. 1996) (actuary retained by the firm deemed a fiduciary who usurped opportunity to acquire another firm); Delta Envtl., Inc. v. McGrew, 56 F. Supp. 2d 716 (S.D. Miss. 1999) (regional sales manager subject to doctrine); Hill v. Southeastern Floor Covering, 596 So. 2d 874 (Miss. 1992) (general manager subject to doctrine); Community Nat'l Bank v. Medical Benefit Administrators, LLC, 626 N.W.2d 340 (Wis. Ct. App. 2001) (bankruptcy referee subject held to usurp bankrupt company's opportunity).

[4] *E.g.,* Weigle v. Shapiro, 608 F.2d 268 (7th Cir. 1979); Gulledge v. Frosty Land Foods Int'l, 414 So. 2d 60 (Ala. 1982).

Of special concern, and the focus of this section, is that directors and officers not acquire for themselves property or business opportunities that are an opportunity or advantage that belongs to the corporation. In broad overview, corporations have a prior claim vis-à-vis their directors, officers, and agents to opportunities for business and profit that may be regarded as sufficiently incident or connected to the corporation's business, or the director's and officer's acquisition of the opportunity is otherwise accomplished through disloyalty and unfairness to the corporation. What opportunities are so related to the corporation's business, or the behavior that is disloyal or unfair to the corporation, is answered only in the context of the circumstances of the particular case and sometimes depends on the particular test followed by the jurisdiction. In making this determination, the facts and circumstances when the fiduciary acquired the opportunity are considered and not those that exist thereafter.

There are several widely differing tests applied by the courts. While the discussion that follows examines each of the prevalent tests, a word of caution is in order. Courts rarely articulate a specific test[5] and apply it strictly. Instead, courts examine a number of factors common to two or more of the tests described below. And, even when purporting to apply a specific test, the factors of each test are so general that the outcome is more sensitive to the egregiousness of the director's or officer's behavior than to the particular test the court applies. Overall, this area of the law is very fact-specific, and a good deal of uncertainty exists as to what constitutes a usurpation of a corporate opportunity (sometimes also referred to as the taking of a corporate advantage).

"Interest or Expectancy" Test. A few cases impose the "interest or expectancy" test first announced in *Lagarde v. Anniston Lime & Stone Company,*[6] where the company had unsuccessfully negotiated with *M* for the purchase of an outstanding one-third interest in a stone quarry in which it already had a one-third interest and a lease on the remaining one-third from *C.* The quarry was located near other lands that the company was operating. The two defendants, directors and officers, were held not liable for acquiring *M's* interest for themselves on information gained by their official position, but they were held liable for breach of duty as to the purchase of *C's* interest, which had already been under contract and lease to the company such that the company then had an "interest or expectancy" in the property. The court said: "Good faith to the corporation does not require of its officers that they steer from their own to the corporation's benefit enterprises or investments which, though capable of profit to the corporation, have in no way become subjects of their trust or duty."[7]

---

[5] *See, e.g.,* Rapistan Corp. v. Michaels, 511 N.W.2d 918 (Mich. Ct. App. 1994) (wrongful usurpation of corporate opportunity arises when (1) the opportunity is essential to the corporation, (2) the corporation has an interest or expectancy, or (3) fiduciary has used corporate assets to acquire or develop).

[6] 28 So. 199 (Ala. 1899). *See also* Solimine v. Hollander, 16 A.2d 203 (N.J. Eq. 1940); Tierney v. United Pocahontas Coal Co., 102 S.E. 249 (W. Va. 1920). Alabama now embraces a more sweeping inquiry. *See* Morad v. Coupounas, 361 So. 2d 6 (Ala. 1978).

[7] 28 So. at 201.

B. Corporate Opportunities

The court's treatment of the purchase from *M* is questionable because this interest was important to the corporation, and if the company had not abandoned its efforts to acquire this interest, the court clearly should have reached a different result.[8] In any case, *Lagarde* established the "interest or expectancy" test, whereby an officer or director is deemed to usurp a corporate opportunity only where the corporation has an existing interest in the property or an expectancy growing out of an existing right. For example, a corporation was deemed to have an interest or expectancy in a contract with a customer with whom it had an ongoing relationship such that when its former officer contracted with that customer to provide the same services, it was deemed a usurpation of the corporation's opportunity.[9] And, the corporation had an interest in land adjacent to the corporation's existing property, which the stockholders had frequently discussed acquiring at their meetings.[10]

A consideration frequently invoked in connection with the "interest or expectancy" inquiry is whether the opportunity is "essential" to the corporation's operation or existence.[11]

"Line of Business" Test. In contrast to the narrowness of the "interest or expectancy" test is the "line of business" test, which treats as belonging to the corporation an opportunity that is related to or is in the company's line of activities and is an activity that the company could reasonably be expected to enter.[12] In the leading line-of-business case, *Guth v. Loft, Inc.,*[13] Guth was the president of Loft, Inc., which was engaged in the manufacture and sale of beverages and candy. Guth bought the Pepsi-Cola secret formula and trademark from a bankrupt corporation and, with *M*, organized a new corporation with the aid of money from Loft. Guth used Loft's capital, plant facilities, materials, credit, and employees to perfect the mixture, and the product was sold to Loft for distribution at cost plus 10 percent. The Delaware court held that Guth had appropriated a business opportunity that belonged in equity to Loft, Inc., and had made profits to which Loft was entitled.[14] The opportunity was so closely associated with the existing business activities of Loft and so important to those activities as to bring it within

---

[8] Warner Fuller, Restrictions Imposed by the Directorship Status on the Personal Business Activities of Directors, 26 Wash. U. L.Q. 189, 205 (1941); Note, 54 Harv. L. Rev. 1191, 1195 (1941).

[9] Southeast Consultants, Inc. v. McCrary Engg. Corp., 273 S.E.2d 112 (Ga. 1980).

[10] Farber v. Servan Land Co., 662 F.2d 371 (5th Cir. 1981).

[11] *See, e.g.,* Broz v. Cellular Information Systems, Inc., 673 A.2d 148 (Del. 1996); Rapistan Corp. v. Michaels, 511 N.W.2d 918 (Mich. Ct. App. 1994) (dismissing on the ground, in part, that the opportunity "was not indispensably necessary to the conduct of the business").

[12] *See, e.g.,* Levy v. Markal Sales Corp., 643 N.E.2d 1206 (Ill. App. Ct. 1994).

[13] Guth v. Loft, Inc., 5 A.2d 503 (Del. 1939).

[14] *Id.* at 510:

> The rule, inveterate and uncompromising in its rigidity, does not rest upon the narrow ground of injury or damage to the corporation resulting from a betrayal of confidence, but upon a broader foundation of a wise public policy that, for the purpose of removing all temptation, extinguishes all possibility of profit flowing from a breach of the confidence imposed by the fiduciary relation. Given the relation between the parties, a certain result follows; and a constructive trust is the remedial device through which precedence of self is compelled to give way to the stern demands of loyalty.

the scope of Guth's fiduciary duty, even if Guth had not used Loft's facilities and resources to engage in a competing business.[15]

What is within a corporation's line of business is not always easy to identify *ex ante*. Though the test is broader than the interest or expectancy test, courts can still have a very narrow view of what is within a firm's line of business.[16] Furthermore, fine factual distinctions abound even under the broader line of business test. Thus an opportunity to earn a large profit quickly by purchasing a parcel of land should be considered within the line of business of a company that generally develops land but rarely itself speculates in land.[17] The question would be much closer, however, if the company only developed land and never speculated in land. Of course, the corporation may have in its articles, bylaws, or a resolution of its board of directors a provision that unequivocally identifies the types of business or activity in which the company does not have an interest and that are fair game for its directors or even officers.[18] Such an approach is expressly authorized by the American Law Institute's Corporate Governance Project,[19] which otherwise applies a line-of-business approach to opportunities acquired by senior executive officers. There is another route built on the view that the corporation is but a web of contracts. This school has provided the impetus for statutes authorizing provisions to be included in the corporation's articles of incorporation that prescribe what will not be deemed corporate opportunities.[20]

"Multifactor Analysis." A majority of the cases determine whether the director or officer has usurped a corporate opportunity by weighing a range of factors.

For another classic formulation of the doctrine, *see* Litwin v. Allen, 25 N.Y.S.2d 667, 685-686 (Sup. Ct. 1940).

[15] 5 A.2d at 514:

> Where a corporation is engaged in a certain business, and an opportunity is presented to it embracing an activity as to which it has fundamental knowledge, practical experience and ability to pursue, which, logically and naturally, is adaptable to its business having regard for its financial position, and is one that is consonant with its reasonable needs and aspirations for expansion, it may properly be said that the opportunity is in the line of the corporation's business.

Recently, Delaware recognized the ambiguity in the meaning of the "reasonable needs and aspirations" language; however, the court resolved this question by relying on the testimony of several sitting directors that the business opportunity would not have been of interest to the corporation. *See* Broz v. Cellular Info. Systems, Inc., 673 A.2d 148, 156 n.7 (Del. 1996).

[16] *See, e.g.,* Account, Inc. v. Automated Prescription Sys., Inc., 651 So. 2d 308 (La. Ct. App. 1995) (developing a modified version of a device that company was negotiating to acquire not within the same line of business); ICOM Sys., Inc. v. Davies, 990 S.W.2d 408 (Tex. App. 1999) (interactive software developed to on-line garden supply business not in same line of business as company created to market interactive software whose only product pertained to scheduling tee times for golf courses).

[17] *See* Imperial Group (Texas), Inc. v. Scholnick, 709 S.W.2d 358 (Tex. Ct. App. 1986).

[18] *See* American Inv. Co. v. Lichtenstein, 134 F. Supp. 857 (E.D. Mo. 1955).

[19] ALI Principles of Corporate Governance, *supra* §11.07 note 2, §5.09. For a insightful analysis of the efficiency of such ex ante waivers by the corporation, *see* Richard A. Epstein, Contract and Trust in Corporate Law: The Case of Corporate Opportunity, 21 Del. J. Corp. L. 5 (1996).

[20] *See, e.g.,* Del. Code Ann. tit. 8 §122(17) 2001; ALI, 1 Principles of Corporate Governance: Analysis and Recommendations §5.09 (1992).

B. Corporate Opportunities

Even Delaware, which purports to apply a combined line of business and interest or expectancy test, acknowledges that *Guth* enunciates factors that need to be taken into account by the reviewing court in balancing the equities of the individual case.[21] Among the factors or circumstances having significance in distinguishing between corporate opportunities that impose a "mandate" or duty to act for the corporation and those opportunities that are open to appropriation by corporate officers are: (1) Is the opportunity to acquire real estate, patents, etc., of special and unique value, or needed for the corporate business and its expansion? (2) Did the discovery or information come to the officer by reason of his official position? (3) Was the company in the market, negotiating for, or seeking such opportunity or advantage, and, if so, has it abandoned its efforts in this regard? (4) Was the officer especially charged with the duty of acquiring such opportunities for his enterprise? (5) Did the officer use corporate funds or facilities in acquiring or developing it? (6) Does taking the opportunity place the director in an adverse and hostile position to his corporation? (7) Did the officer intend to resell the opportunity to the corporation? (8) Was the corporation in a favorable position to take advantage of the opportunity, or was it financially or otherwise unable to do so? Such factors are among those that must be weighed and balanced, but it is not possible for the most part to lay down any hard and fast rules as to their effect in imposing a mandate, and variable results have been reached. The multifactor approach is the least rigorous of the tests and therefore provides the least certainty to the director or officer considering *ex ante* whether she can acquire a business opportunity or whether it must first be offered to the corporation.[22]

The ALI Approach. The American Law Institute's Corporate Governance Project may have a considerable impact on future judicial decisions on corporate

---

[21] Broz v. Cellular Information Systems, Inc., 673 A.2d 148, 155 (Del. 1996). Delaware law allows a corporation to renounce its interest or expectancy in specified business opportunities or categories of business opportunities, either in its certificate of incorporation or by action of the board of directors. Thus, a corporation can determine in advance whether certain business opportunities belong to the corporation, rather than addressing them as they arise. *See* Del. Code Ann. tit. 8, §122(17) (2001).

[22] In Miller v. Miller, 222 N.W.2d 71 (Minn. 1974), the Minnesota Supreme Court attempted to introduce some rigor to the equitable-factors test by combining it with the line-of-business test in a two-step approach. The first question is whether the business opportunity is a corporate opportunity—that is, whether it is of sufficient importance and is so closely related to the existing or prospective activity of the corporation as to warrant judicial sanctions against its personal acquisition. The Georgia Supreme Court feared the line-of-business standard for *Miller*'s first step may preclude former officers from competing with their former employers. It therefore modified *Miller* by adopting for the first step the "interest or expectancy" test. *See* Southeast Consultants, Inc. v. McCrary Engg. Corp., 273 S.E.2d 112, 117 (Ga. 1980). This question is one of fact, with the burden of proof resting on the party attacking the acquisition. The second question, if the opportunity is found to be a corporate opportunity, is whether the officer or director violates his duty of loyalty and fair dealing in acquiring the opportunity; if not, he is not liable. This second step involves close scrutiny of equitable considerations, and the burden of proof is on the officer or director who appropriates the opportunity. Distinguished commentators have condemned this two-step process as creating confusion in the thinking of those who use it. *See* Victor Brudney & Robert C. Clark, Look at Corporate Opportunities, 94 Harv. L. Rev. 997, 998 n.1 (1981).

opportunity. The Supreme Courts of Maine, Massachusetts, and Oregon have already adopted the definition of "corporate opportunity" as it appeared in a tentative draft of the Governance Project, even though that definition was subject to being revised by the American Law Institute.[23] The American Law Institute defines "corporate opportunity" as follows:

> (1) Any opportunity to engage in a business activity of which a director or senior executive becomes aware, either
>> (A) in connection with the performance of functions as a director or senior executive, or under circumstances that should reasonably lead the director or senior executive to believe that the person offering the opportunity expects it to be offered to the corporation;[24] or
>> (B) through the use of corporate information or property, if the resulting opportunity is one that the director or senior executive should reasonably be expected to believe would be of interest to the corporation; or
> (2) Any opportunity to engage in a business activity of which a senior executive becomes aware and knows is closely related to a business in which the corporation is engaged or expects to engage.[25]

The American Law Institute provides a much broader proscription of business opportunities for senior executive officers than for outside directors, essentially applying a line-of-business test to opportunities before the senior executive officer. The American Law Institute also casts aside the multifactor approach, opting for the more certain inquiries of the circumstances surrounding the fiduciary learning of the opportunity or its acquisition as well as, in the case of senior executive officers, its relationship to a present or contemplated business of the corporation. Although there is not much precedent to support its position, the American Law Institute separately proscribes the fiduciary obligation of controlling stockholders.[26] Finally, the American Law Institute eliminates the possible

[23] See Northeast Harbor Golf Club, Inc. v. Harris, 661 A.2d 1146 (Me. 1995); Demoulas v. Demoulas Super Markets, Inc., 677 N.E.2d 159 (Mass. 1997) (liberally citing to the ALI and essentially adhering to an approach parallel to that of the ALI); Klinicki v. Lundgren, 695 P.2d 906 (Or. 1985).

[24] This is the crucial factor in Northeast Harbor Golf Club, Inc. v. Harris, 661 A.2d 1146 (Me. 1995), where the court appears to emphasize more the intent of the broker offering the opportunity than the reasonable belief of the purchasing company official.

[25] ALI, Principles of Corporate Governance, supra §11.07 note 2, §5.05(b), as quoted in 695 P.2d at 917-918. Thus, in adopting the ALI approach, the case was remanded to determine how a golf club's president learned of the opportunity to acquire land adjacent to the course. See Northeast Harbor Golf Club, Inc. v. Harris, 661 A.2d 1146 (Me. 1995).

[26] ALI, Principles of Corporate Governance, supra §11.07 n.2, §512. As to controlling stockholders, "corporate opportunity" is defined in terms of the property having been "developed or received by the corporation," or having come to the controlling stockholder because of his relationship to the company, or is of the type that was held out to the stockholder as being an activity within the scope of the company's business. Id. §5.12(b)(1)(2). The absence of case law on whether controlling shareholders can usurp a corporate opportunity may be partly a semantic distinction. See Thorpe v. CERBCO, Inc., 676 A.2d 436 (Del. 1996) (controlling shareholders not liable for having usurped a corporate opportunity by diverting an offer to buy the corporation so that they instead sold their majority interest in the corporation; however, they would be liable for any damages caused by their breach of duty of loyalty).

B. Corporate Opportunities

defenses of incapacity or inability, financial or otherwise, of the corporation to embrace the opportunity.[27] If the activity falls within the ALI's proscription of a corporate opportunity, the sole defense is that the board or stockholders have rejected the opportunity. The truly significant contribution of the Corporate Governance Project's section 5.05 is that it causes the director or senior executive officer to *first* obtain disinterested approval of the board of directors. More significantly, the directors are allowed to approve the director's or senior executive officer's acquisition of the business opportunity only in advance of its acquisition; their approval after the acquisition is given no operative effect under the provision.[28] Absent such approval, the only option is the more cumbersome and expensive process of obtaining shareholder approval or the less predictable burden of proving no unfairness to the corporation.[29]

Opportunities in Close Corporations. In the close corporation context, there is growing support for greater flexibility in resolving whether a director or officer has usurped a corporate opportunity:

> A more flexible approach, however, is dictated when dealing with a small corporation which is generally contractual in nature. . . . [T]he small number of players in a private venture result in better communication between the members. Additionally, agreements are entered into which are tailored to particular situations and objectives.[30]

Factors in a close corporation setting that shape the conclusion that no corporate opportunity was usurped are the co-owners' awareness when the corporation was formed that their defendant-fiduciary actively engaged in similar outside activities[31] and whether the opportunity appeared within the parties' reasonable expectation.[32]

---

[27] *See* Klinicki v. Lundgren, 695 P.2d 906 (Or. 1985). Without citing the ALI, the same result was reached in Imperial Group (Texas), Inc. v. Scholnick, 709 S.W.2d 358 (Tex. Ct. App. 1986). *See also, e.g.,* Demoulas v. Demoulas Super Markets, Inc., 677 N.E.2d 159, 181 (Mass. 1997) ("[O]pportunities must be presented to the corporation without regard to possible impediments . . . so that the corporation may consider whether and how to address these obstacles.").

[28] ALI, Principles of Corporate Governance, *supra* §11.07 note 2, §5.05(a)(1). Subsection (e) does allow approval after the fact by the directors where the director or senior executive officer failed to get earlier approval because of a good faith belief the business activity was not a corporate opportunity.

[29] *Id.* §§5.05(a)(3)(C), 5.05(c). Courts also place the burden of proving no usurpation of a corporate opportunity on the officer or director. *See* Independent Distributors, Inc. v. Katz, 637 A.2d 886 (Md. App. Ct. 1994).

[30] Leavitt v. Leisure Sports, Inc., 734 P.2d 1221, 1225 (Nev. 1987).

[31] *See* Pitman v. Aran, 935 F. Supp. 637 (D. Md. 1996).

[32] Graham v. Mimms, 444 N.E.2d 549 (Ill. App. Ct. 1982). In their thoughtful article, Professors Brudney and Clark suggest that the appropriate basis for defining corporate opportunities in close corporations is to consider the reasonable expectations of the parties. *See* Victor Brudney & Robert C. Clark, A New Look at Corporate Opportunities, 94 Harv. L. Rev. 1010 (1981). Thus, in cases not involving the use of the corporation's assets to either acquire or develop the opportunity, they suggest, *id.* at 1011, the following should govern the taking of business opportunities:

> (1) If the disputed opportunity is functionally related to the corporation's business, then, whether or not it is "necessary" or of "special value," individual participants may not take it.

Absent strong evidence of prejudice to creditors, there is little reason to hold that the sole shareholder can usurp a corporate opportunity.[33]

Defenses. Directors and officers commonly defend their acquisition of a business opportunity on the grounds that, because of financial distress, or legal restrictions, or otherwise, the corporation was unable itself to acquire the opportunity.[34] In a leading case,[35] the United States Court of Appeals, Second Circuit, invalidated the directors' formation of a syndicate to purchase controlling interests in certain radio patents that the corporation had an option to purchase. The defense was that the corporation was financially unable to take advantage of the opportunity, but it was not clearly shown that greater efforts on their part would not have enabled the corporation to obtain the necessary funds. Judge Swan, in his opinion, said:

> While these facts raise some question whether [the corporation] actually lacked the funds or credit necessary for carrying out its contract, we do not feel justified in reversing the District Court's finding that it did. Nevertheless, they tend to show the wisdom of a rigid rule forbidding directors of a solvent corporation contract on the plea of the corporation's financial inability to perform. If the directors are uncertain whether the corporation can make the outlays, they need not embark it upon the venture; and if they do, they may not substitute themselves for the corporation any place along the line and divert possible benefits into their pockets.[36]

Not all courts would feel impelled to adopt such a rule of "uncompromising rigidity" as to inability.[37] In a later Delaware case,[38] for example, the court rejected a

---

(2) If the corporation has an "interest" or "expectancy" in the opportunity, individual participants may not take it.

(3) If the participants consent in advance or contemporaneously to diversion of the new project, an individual participant may take it, even though the taking would otherwise run afoul of (1) or (2); provided, however, that nothing less than express contemporaneous consent will permit the taking of functionally related opportunities whose acceptance is "necessary" to prevent loss or injury to the corporation.

(4) If the new project is not covered by the preceding rules, it may be taken by some individual participants without sharing with the others and without the consent of the others.

[33] *See* In re Safety Intl., Inc., 775 F.2d 660 (5th Cir. 1985) (invoking a theory of ratification); In re Tufts Electronics, Inc., 746 F.2d 915 (1st Cir. 1984) (corporate opportunity is a rule of disclosure); Pittman v. American Metal Forming Corp., 649 A.2d 356 (Md. App. Ct. 1994).

[34] *See, e.g.,* Lange v. Lange, 520 N.W.2d 113 (Iowa 1994); Collie v. Becknell, 762 P.2d 727 (Colo. Ct. App. 1988) (defendant estopped to raise company's incapacity because his actions caused the company's financial inability); Lussier v. Mau-Van Dev., Inc., 667 P.2d 804 (Haw. Ct. App. 1983) (whether corporation financially able to undertake activity is first step in defining whether there is corporate opportunity).

[35] Irving Trust Co. v. Deutsch, 73 F.2d 121 (2d Cir. 1930), *cert. denied,* 294 U.S. 708 (1935).

[36] *Id.* at 124. *See also* Levy v. Markal Sales Corp., 643 N.E.2d 1206 (Ill. Ct. App. 1994).

[37] Hauben v. Morris, 5 N.Y.S.2d 721, 730 (App. Div. 1938), *aff'd,* 22 N.E.2d 482 (N.Y. 1939); Klinicki v. Lundgren, 678 P.2d 1250 (Or. Ct. App. 1984) (following *Irving Trust, supra* note 35).

[38] Schreiber v. Bryan, 396 A.2d 512 (Del. Ch. 1978); A. Teixeira & Co., Inc. v. Teixeira, 699 A.2d 1383 (R.I. 1997) (successful defense premised upon lack of financial capacity). For a case holding that lack of financial capacity cannot be raised when the firm's insolvency was caused by the misconduct of the usurping fiduciary, *see* Aqua-Culture Techs., Ltd. v. Holly, 677 So. 2d 171 (Miss. 1996).

rigid rule but held that the burden of proving financial inability rested with the defendant officers and directors.

The approach taken by the Massachusetts Supreme Court appears to be most appropriate:

> [T]o ensure fairness . . . , opportunities must be presented to the corporation without regard to possible impediments, and material facts must be fully disclosed, so that the corporation may consider whether and how to address these obstacles.[39]

The above quote supports the view that the better choice is to place the burden of proving financial inability or legal incapacity and the like on the defendant. Recall that the fiduciary has had the chance to present the opportunity to his corporation before taking it for himself. Had this occurred, it would certainly have put the corporation to the test of whether it had a desire to acquire the opportunity as well as the financial and legal capacity to acquire it. Having not taken that course because the fiduciary believed it would have been a useless exercise, it is only appropriate that the fiduciary should later have the burden of proving such futility.

The third party's purported refusal to contract or deal with the corporation does not relieve the director or officer of presenting the opportunity to the corporation.[40] Unless the third party's refusal has at least first been disclosed to the corporation, there is no adequate means to test the assertion the corporation could not have acquired the opportunity had its directors or stockholders desired to take the plunge.[41] Similarly unsuccessful is the bald assertion that the corporation would not have acquired the opportunity if it had been given the chance. As one court reasoned, "if an opportunity is within the scope of a corporation's business, then the only acceptable method of determining whether a corporation would take advantage of the opportunity is by complete disclosure of the opportunity to it. To permit an after-the-fact determination as to whether [plaintiff] would have purchased the [opportunity] under the facts before us would abrogate the full disclosure rule."[42]

The overall thrust of proscribing the fiduciary's usurpation of a corporate opportunity is to avoid self-seeking behavior to prevail over the fiduciary's loyalty to the corporation.[43] Some business opportunities, however, may be regarded as coming to the officer in his individual capacity or under circumstances free from any prior corporate claim. If the opportunity genuinely came to the director or officer in her individual, nonfiduciary capacity she will not be under a duty to act

[39] Demoulas v. Demoulas Super Markets, Inc., 677 N.E.2d 159, 181 (Mass. 1997) (the defense to creating separate retail company without the plaintiff's participation was that state law limited the number of licenses for beer and wine that could be held by a single entity).

[40] Energy Resources Corp. v. Porter, 438 N.E.2d 391 (Mass. App. Ct. 1982); Production Finishing Corp. v. Shields, 405 N.W.2d 171 (Mich. Ct. App. 1987).

[41] Energy Resources Corp. v. Porter, 438 N.E.2d 391 (Mass. App. Ct. 1982).

[42] Imperial Group (Texas), Inc. v. Scholnick, 709 S.W.2d 358, 363 (Tex. Ct. App. 1986). Similarly, legal impediments may be overcome after the board requests assistance of its counsel. See Kerrigan v. Unity Sav. Assoc., 317 N.E.2d 39 (Ill. 1974).

[43] See Science Accessories v. Summagraphics, 425 A.2d 957 (Del. 1980); Demoulas v. Demoulas Super Markets, Inc., 677 N.E.2d 159, 180 (Mass. 1997).

or contract as a representative of the corporation. This is an important consideration in defending against the charge that her acquisition of the opportunity was a breach of fiduciary duty. Indeed, this is one of two grounds under the ALI approach for proscribing corporate opportunities by non-senior management personnel.[44] For this defense to be successful there should not be countervailing considerations, such as the wrongful use of the corporation's assets or personnel to acquire or nurture the opportunity or that the business opportunity was necessary to the corporation.[45] It should not be a defense that the director or officer was not such when the opportunity was acquired if he learned of the opportunity while an officer or director. Resigning from the position does not rid a person of a fiduciary obligation to turn over opportunities discovered while a director or officer.[46]

The ultimate defense is that the board of directors or stockholders have rejected the business opportunity or otherwise have approved or ratified the director's or officer's acquisition of the opportunity. Mere hesitation in response to the third party's terms does not alone amount to a rejection such that the fiduciary may then acquire the opportunity.[47] The approval or ratification need not be formal; it can occur informally by the disinterested directors or stockholders acquiescing in the director's or officer's acquisition of the opportunity.[48] However, the defense of rejection, approval, or ratification is conditioned on *full disclosure* of all material facts to the rejecting, approving, or ratifying body.[49] Disclosure to a lower-level employee does not satisfy the fiduciary's obligation to disclose relevant information to the corporation.[50] Absent such disclosure, the fiduciary has the burden of proving that acquiring the opportunity has not harmed the corporation.[51]

---

[44] *See, e.g.*, Northeast Harbor Golf Club, Inc. v. Harris, 661 A.2d 1146 (Me. 1995).

[45] Red Top Cab Co. v. Hanchett, 48 F.2d 236 (N.D. Cal. 1931); Broz v. Cellular Info. Systems, Inc., 673 A.2d 148 (Del. 1996) (the interest is that of the corporation on whose board the outside director served and not that of its prospective acquiror); Lussier v. Mau-Van Dev., Inc., 667 P.2d 804 (Haw. Ct. App. 1983); Comedy Cottage, Inc. v. Berk, 495 N.E.2d 1006 (Ill. App. Ct. 1986) (usurped opportunity when learned lease would be terminated, managers resigned and bid against former employer for new lease).

[46] Comedy Cottage, Inc. v. Berk, 495 N.E.2d 1006 (Ill. App. Ct. 1986); Schildberg Rock Prods. Co. v. Brooks, 140 N.W.2d 132 (Iowa 1966).

[47] CST, Inc. v. Mark, 520 A.2d 469 (Pa. Super. Ct. 1987).

[48] Approval by controlling stockholder of opportunity appropriated by his son was deemed not to be sufficient ratification in Ostrowski v. Avery, 703 A.2d 117 (Conn. 1997). *See also* Broz v. Cellular Information Systems, Inc., 673 A.2d 148 (Del. 1996) (opportunity acquired after conversations with some of the directors who opined the opportunity was not appropriate for the corporation); Yiannatsis v. Stephanis, 653 A.2d 275, 279 (Del. 1995) (absence of fair presentation before the board negates defense of rejection of opportunity by the board); I.P. Homeowners, Inc. v. Radtke, 558 N.W.2d 582 (Neb. Ct. App. 1997) (consent of one of three corporate representatives not a defense); Suburban Motors, Inc. v. Forester, 396 N.W.2d 351 (Wis. Ct. App. 1986).

[49] [50] *See, e.g.*, Ostrowski v. Avery, 703 A.2d 117 (Conn. 1997); Yiannatsis v. Stephanis, 653 A.2d 275 (Del. 1995); Demoulas v. Demoulas Super Markets, Inc., 677 N.E.2d 159, 181 (Mass. 1997); Hanover Ins. Co. v. Sutton, 705 N.E.2d 279 (Mass. Ct. App. 1999) (disclosing that officer had created a company to engage in business but not that he was operating the business through the newly established company was deficient); Energy Resources Corp. v. Porter, 438 N.E.2d 391 (Mass. App. Ct. 1982); Production Finishing Corp. v. Shields, 405 N.W.2d 171 (Mich. Ct. App. 1987).

[50] Production Finishing Corp. v. Shields, *supra*.

[51] *See, e.g.*, Ostrowski v. Avery, 703 A.2d 117 (Conn. 1997).

B. Corporate Opportunities

Remedies. Where there has been a usurpation of a corporate opportunity, the corporation may elect to claim the benefits of the transaction.[52] The property the officer or director has acquired in violation of his fiduciary duty is held in constructive trust for the corporation.[53] Even if the defendant lost money on the usurped opportunity, the corporation is entitled to recover damages from the defendant for the profits it would have made.[54]

§11.09   Forbidden Profits; Gains by Abuse of Official Position

Directors and officers are fiduciary representatives and as such are not allowed to obtain or retain a commission, bonus, gift, or personal profit or advantage "on the side" for their official action, as in connection with a purchase, sale, lease, loan, or contract by the corporation.[1] Accordingly, they may not keep such rewards without the knowledge and consent of the corporation.[2] A director or officer who has used corporate property or her position to profit personally cannot avoid disgorgement of the ill-gotten gains by invoking that she acted in good faith.[3] Similarly, the officers and directors may not permit any secret profit to be obtained by others.[4]

The rule against insider secret profits by directors and officers is similar to that which applies to agents generally. If an agent receives anything for his acts as such without the knowledge and consent of his principal, he is subject to liability to deliver it or its value or proceeds to the principal.[5] In a famous federal case,[6] *T,*

---

[52] *See, e.g.,* Science Accessories Corp. v. Summagraphics Corp., 425 A.2d 957 (Del. 1980); United Seal & Rubber Co. v. Bunting, 285 S.E.2d 721 (Ga. 1982); Southeast Consultants, Inc. v. McCrary Engg. Corp., 273 S.E.2d 112 (Ga. 1980); Graham v. Mimms, 444 N.E.2d 549 (Ill. App. Ct. 1982); Poling Transp. Corp. v. A & P Tanker Corp., 443 N.Y.S.2d 895 (App. Div. 1981).

[53] *See* Restatement of Restitution §§194, 195 (1937). *See, e.g.,* I.P. Homeowners, Inc. v. Radtke, 558 N.W.2d 582 (Neb. Ct. App. 1997); Billman v. State Deposit Ins. Fund Corp., 585 A.2d 238 (Md. Ct. Spec. App. 1991); Demoulas v. Demoulas Super Markets, Inc., 677 N.E.2d 159, 195 (Mass. 1997).

[54] *See* CST, Inc. v. Mark, 520 A.2d 469 (Pa. Super. Ct. 1987).

§11.09 [1] Delano v. Kitch, 542 F.2d 550 (10th Cir. 1976) (bare disclosure of commission received by director on sale of stock is not sufficient under Kansas law); City Fed'l Sav. & Loan Assoc. v. Crowley, 393 F. Supp. 644 (E.D. Wis. 1975); (secret payment to facilitate award of loan by employer).

[2] Delano v. Kitch, 663 F.2d 990 (10th Cir. 1981); Leavy v. Amer. Federal Savings Bank, 764 A.2d 366 (Md. Ct. App. 2000).

[3] *See, e.g.,* Wilshire Oil Co. of Texas v. Riffe, 381 F.2d 646, 651 (10th Cir. 1967).

[4] *See generally* Berkman v. Rust Craft Greeting Cards, Inc., 454 F. Supp. 787 (S.D.N.Y. 1978) (failure of a some directors to disclose to other board members that investment banker held an interest in firm's acquisition partner).

[5] Restatement (Second) of Agency §§388, 403 (1958); Restatement of Restitution §§190, 197 (1937). Sara Lee Corp. v. Carter, 500 S.E.2d 732 (N.C. Ct. App.), *rev'd on other grounds,* 519 S.E.2d 308 (N.C. 1998) (purchasing agent was the secret vendor for computer equipment acquired by employer). "Is it right that the wolf should give a sop to the watchdog without his master's leave?" Archer's Case, [1892] 1 Ch. Div. 322 (CA).

[6] Fleishhacker v. Blum, 21 F. Supp. 527 (N.D. Cal. 1937), *aff'd in part, rev'd in part,* 109 F.2d 543 (9th Cir.), *cert. denied,* 311 U.S. 665 (1940). *See* Note, 39 Mich. L. Rev. 314 (1940). *But cf.* Bay City Lumber Co. v. Anderson, 111 P.2d 771 (Wash. 1941).

in order to obtain funds with which to bid at a government sale of steel, offered *D*, president and a director of the *A* bank, a one-half interest in the venture. *D* caused the bank to make large loans to the *Y* corporation which had been organized by *T* to finance the steel transaction. The loans were approved by the bank's loan committee on *D*'s recommendation. They were good loans and were repaid promptly. *D* received from the steel venture $75,000 in salary, $73,000 in dividends, and $200,000 on the sale of his shares. After the bank directors refused to sue, the plaintiff shareholder sued on behalf of the bank to recover the profits received by *D*. The court held that *D* was liable to the bank for the profits so received because of his official relation to the bank. It was immaterial that the bank suffered no actual loss. Compensation paid by third persons to a corporate officer for a loan made by the corporation is properly regarded as part of the consideration for the loan or as a commission given for the officer's supposed influence in obtaining the loan.

A director of a corporation cannot remain silent when she knows that a fraud is being attempted against her corporation (and ultimately against its shareholders). It is her duty to acquaint the other officers of the corporation with the facts and to use every effort to prevent the consummation of the fraud. If by passive acquiescence he permits any part of the assets of the corporation to be fraudulently diverted or secret profits to be obtained, she is guilty of neglect of duty to the corporation, for which she is liable in damages notwithstanding the fact that she did not herself profit financially thereby.[7]

Section 504 of the American Law Institute comprehensively addresses the use of corporation property and information by directors and senior executives.[8] In broad overview, the ALI proscribes the use of corporate position, property, or information without proof of harm to the corporation, except when non-proprietary information is used (for other than a transaction in securities) in which case proof of harm to the corporation is required.[9] Under the ALI's formulation, the officer or director can defend the charges by proving authorization or ratification by disinterested directors or shareholders after full disclosure.[10]

---

[7] Reid v. Robinson, 220 P. 676, 681 (Cal. Ct. App. 1923); General Rubber Co. v. Benedict, 109 N.E. 96 (N.Y. 1915). *See* Globe Woolen Co. v. Utica Gas & Elec. Co., 121 N.E. 378 (N.Y. 1918).

[8] 1 ALI, Principles of Corporate Governance: Analysis and Recommendations §5.04 (1992).

[9] *Id.* §5.04(a)(3). To illustrate:

> A, a senior executive of X Corporation, negotiates on X Corporation's behalf a long-term contract with Y Corporation pursuant to which X Corporation will purchase a significant portion of Y Corporation's output. The contract will require Y Corporation to build a new plant. As a result of the negotiations, A learns the proposed location of Y Corporation's new plant, and purchases land in the vicinity of the plant site with the expectation of selling the land at a profit to third parties after Y Corporation's plant is built. A's purchase does not harm X Corporation, A has not breached a duty to X Corporation under §5.04.

Id. Example 15 at 273.

[10] *Id.* §5.04(a)(4).

B. Corporate Opportunities

§11.10 The Duty of Employees Not to Compete

Employees (including officers) are precluded from actively competing with their employer during the course of their employment, even though they are not subject to a covenant not to compete.[1] The application of this universal principle occurs within the conflicting tugs of two important commercial considerations. On the one hand, our society prizes entrepreneurial activity and generally nurtures free and vigorous competition. It is with this spirit that fiduciaries are allowed to make important preparations to compete while still in their company's employ and also are allowed within broad limits to leave with skills and knowledge acquired from the company. On the other hand, there is the strong view that it is unfair for the employing company to compete with the very individuals in whom it then places trust and responsibility for serving its best interests.

To what extent may an employee prepare to compete with his employer? Within the broad principles discussed below, the answer to this question is heavily dependent on the facts of the individual case.[2] Most courts recognize the right of an employee while still an employee to incorporate a rival corporation and procure land, buildings, and equipment for its future operation.[3] Obviously, there is a concern that the employee not usurp any opportunity belonging to the employer company when acquiring assets for the employee's own business.[4] Indeed, many cases that appear to raise questions of an employee competing with her employer are instead examined through the usurpation of corporate opportunity window examined in the preceding section.[5] The employee is not allowed to venture beyond the formation and outfitting while an employee; once the employee terminates his relationship with the employer, however, he may actively compete.[6] Setting up any prospective business involves recruiting employees, and there has been a good deal of litigation whether a departing officer has breached his fiduciary duty by recruiting his employer's employees to work for him in the business to be established. Absent evidence of an intent to cripple the current employer by raiding its key employees, some jurisdictions permit informing fellow

---

§11.10 [1] See, e.g., Maryland Metals, Inc. v. Metzner, 382 A.2d 564, 568 (Md. 1978). Unless, of course, the employer consents.

[2] See Bancroft-Whitney Co. v. Glen, 411 P.2d 921, 935 (Cal. 1966); Maryland Metals, Inc. v. Metzner, 382 A.2d 564, 570 (Md. 1978).

[3] See Raines v. Toney, 313 Sw.2d 802, 809 (Ark. 1958); Lawter Int'l, Inc. v. Carroll, 451 N.E.2d 1338, 1349 (Ill. App. Ct. 1983); Professional Balance Co. v. Fulton & Assoc. Balance, 1999 WL 436568 (Ohio Ct. App. 1999).

[4] See Chelsea Indus. v. Gaffney, 449 N.E.2d 320 (Mass. 1983).

[5] See, e.g., Am. Fed. Group, Ltd. v. Rothenberg, 136 F.3d 897 (2d Cir. 1998) (solicited customers of firm); United Teachers' Association, Ins. Co. v. MacKeen & Bailey, Inc., 99 F.3d 645 (5th Cir. 1996); Prodan v. Hemeyer, 610 N.E.2d 600 (Ohio App. Ct. 1992) (solicited customers of the firm).

[6] Vernon Library Supplies, Inc. v. Ard, 550 S.2d 108 (Ga. Ct. App. 2001); Maryland Metals, Inc. v. Metzner, 382 A.2d 564, 568 (Md. 1978).

workers of an intent to start a competing firm and even permit mild forms of solicitation of co-workers.[7] There are, however, more restrictive jurisdictions that proscribe an employee soliciting co-workers to join him in a competing enterprise
before he has severed his own employment relationship with the employer.[8]

Even though employees cannot solicit their employer's customers as long as
they are employees, they can advise the customers of their intent to leave and
start a competing business.[9] The corporation has a right to be free from interference with its customers from those employed by the corporation.[10] The line
between solicitation and advising is not always a bright one. The question turns
upon just how specific the communication is so that the more general the communication the more it appears to be mere preparation to leave and not to compete as such. Merely informing customers of an intent to leave and of a desire
for their business in the future does not constitute solicitation.[11] However, pressing the customer for business[12] and *a fortiorari* filling customer orders while still
an employee[13] are impermissible solicitations. In *C-E-I-R, Inc. v. Computer Dynamics Corporation*,[14] the court observed that the statement that the "defendants
hoped that when they got organized and got in business they'd have an opportunity to compete for the [customer's] business" taken alone was not solicitation, but when repeated and combined with other factors in the case the
defendants engaged in solicitation.

Normally, once the employee leaves the corporation, she can solicit its customers.[15] However, if the customer list is confidential or amounts to a trade secret,
the former employee cannot use the information to approach customers.[16] As will
be seen later, customer lists may become a trade secret when they are unusually

---

[7] The easiest case for finding no breach is when co-workers approach the defendant to inquire if
they can also join the new venture. *See* The McCallister Co. v. Lynn Kastella, 825 P.2d 980 (Ariz. Ct.
App. 1992). For support permitting solicitation of employees, *see* Cudahy Co. v. American Labs., Inc.,
313 F. Supp. 1339, 1347 (D. Neb. 1970); The McCallister Co. v. Ynn Kastella, 825 P.2d 980 (Ariz. Ct.
App.); Professional Balance Co. v. Fulton & Assoc. Balance Co., 1999 WL 436568 (Ohio Ct. App.
1999); Restatement of Agency (Second) §393, Comment e (1958).

[8] *See* Fish v. Adams, 401 So. 2d 843, 845 (Fla. Ct. App. 1981); ABC Trans National Transp., Inc. v.
Aeronautics Forwarders, Inc., 379 N.E.2d 1228, 1237 (Ill. App. Ct. 1978); Porth v. Iowa Dept. of Job
Service, 372 N.W.2d 269, 273 (Iowa 1985).

[9] The McCallister Co. v. Lynn Kastella, 825 P.2d 980 (Ariz. Ct. App. 1992); Jet Courier Service v.
Mulei, 771 P.2d 486 (Colo. 1989); Nilan's Alley, Inc. v. Ginsburg, 430 S.E.2d 368 (Ga. Ct. App. 1993);
Ellis & Marshall Assocs. v. Marshall, 306 N.E.2d 712, 717 (Ill. App. Ct. 1973).

[10] *See* ABC Trans Nat'l Transp., Inc. v. Aeronautics Forwarders, Inc., 379 N.E.2d 1228, 1239 (Ill.
App. Ct. 1978).

[11] Ellis & Marshall Assocs. v. Marshall, 306 N.E.2d 712, 714 (Ill. App. Ct. 1973).

[12] Duane Jones Co. v. Burke, 117 N.E.2d 237 (N.Y. 1954); Knott's Wholesale Foods, Inc. v. Azbell,
1996 WL 697943 (Tenn. Ct. App. 1996).

[13] Cross Wood Prods., Inc. v. Suter, 422 N.E.2d 953 (Ill. App. Ct. 1981).

[14] 183 A.2d 374, 377 (Md. 1962).

[15] *See* J. Bar, Inc. v. Joanna Johnson, 822 P.2d 849, 861 (Wy. 1991) (former 50 percent owner who
was squeezed out of the business can commence a competing business).

[16] Raines v. Toney, 313 S.W.2d 802, 809 (Ark. 1958). Criminal sanctions are now available under the
Economic Espionage Act of 1996, 18 U.S.C. §1831 *et seq.* (1994), for the misappropriation of trade
secrets.

B. Corporate Opportunities

sensitive, are not generally known in the trade, or were built after great effort and expense by the plaintiff. For example, when the defendant who was a former employee of the plaintiff's home cleaning business used the list of plaintiff's customers to secure clients for his business, the court held that the list could not be used because the plaintiff had developed it after great effort and expense.[17] After all, it was not common knowledge which houses out of all those in the city would desire a cleaning service. On the other hand, if the names can be ascertained from a phone book or industry listing, there generally is no protection afforded to the list. Thus, when a plaintiff dairy sought to enjoin a former employee from soliciting the dairy's customers, the court reasoned that it was a small town and everyone drank milk. The court refused to issue the injunction.[18]

Even if the customer list is not a trade secret, the list may still be a protected property right of the defendant's former employer. For example, if the employee copied, physically removed, or intently studied the list, the employee's subsequent use of the list will be enjoined on the theory the list had been converted.[19] But if only "casual memory" is involved, no breach exists if the customers are solicited soon after the employee resigns.[20] As a rule of thumb, the smaller the list, the lower the percentage solicited, or the more widely known are the customers all make less likely the finding of a breach.

The fiduciary may not use the corporation's facilities to compete or prepare to compete,[21] and it is a breach to use corporate trips to evaluate prospective sites for a competing factory or to learn how to design and build a factory similar to the current employer's factory.[22]

Courts deciding whether a director, officer, or employee has unfairly competed frequently do so on the basis of the fiduciary having misappropriated his employer's trade secret. A trade secret is "a plan or process, tool, mechanism or compound known to its owner and those of his employees to whom it is necessary to confide it. In order for the business information to be a trade secret, it must have value to the business; it must take a form different from ordinarily acquired general information."[23] Some factors used to determine if something is a trade secret are: (1) the extent to which the information is known outside the business; (2) the extent to which it is known by employees and others involved in the business; (3) the extent of measures taken by the owner to guard the secrecy of the information; (4) the value of the information to the owner and to its competitor; (5) the amount of effort or money expended in developing the information; and (6) the ease or difficulty with which the information can be properly acquired or

---

[17] Town & Country House & Home Serv. v. Newberry, 147 N.E.2d 724 (N.Y. 1958).

[18] Abdallah v. Crandall, 76 N.Y.S.2d 403 (App. Div. 1948).

[19] See Leo Silfen, Inc. v. Cream, 278 N.E.2d 636 (N.Y. 1972) (no violation because only 47 of 1100 customers were solicited).

[20] Id. at 641.

[21] Science Accessories v. Summagraphics, 425 A.2d 957, 965 (Del. 1980) (company resources used during company time to develop working model to be used to compete with employer).

[22] Chelsea Indus. v. Gaffney, 449 N.E.2d 320, 323 (Mass. 1983).

[23] Bimba Mfg. Co. v. Starz Cylinder Co., 256 N.E.2d 357, 363 (Ill. App. Ct. 1969).

duplicated by others.[24] Public disclosure of the information destroys its confidentiality and hence the information's protection in equity.[25]

When misconduct is found, courts have applied a variety of sanctions and remedies. The employee may be enjoined[26] and a constructive trust imposed on the competing business and profits therefrom.[27] Courts also invoke their equitable powers to substitute the former employer as a party to a contract that the employee wrongfully caused the former employer to lose.[28] The employee can also be required to return any compensation he received from the employer during the period of his breach.[29] In addition, any consequential damages suffered by the employer can be recovered from the employee.[30]

C.   CONTROLLING STOCKHOLDER'S FIDUCIARY OBLIGATIONS

§11.11   *Fiduciary Duties of Majority Shareholders to the Minority*

Courts and legal scholars have given much attention to the scope of the controlling stockholder's[1] fiduciary duty to the corporation and its minority shareholders.[2] Typically, the duty is breached because of the effects of a corporate activity

---

[24] *See* Restatement of Torts §757, Comment (1939). This topic is no longer covered in the torts restatement but in the unfair competition restatement. *See also* ALI, Restatement of the Law of Unfair Competition 39 Comment d (1993); Uniform Trade Secrets Act §1(4), 14 U.L.A. 433 (1990).

[25] Bimba Mfg. Co. v. Starz Cylinder Co., 256 N.E.2d 357, 364 (Ill. App. Ct. 1969).

[26] C-E-I-R, Inc. v. Computer Dynamics Corp., 183 A.2d 374 (Md. 1962); Lawter Int'l, Inc. v. Carroll, 451 N.E.2d 1338, 1347 (Ill. App. Ct. 1983).

[27] *See* 3 Fletcher, *supra* §11.05 note 8, §856 (rev. ed. 2002). *See, e.g.,* Des Moines Terminal Co. v. Des Moines Union Ry., 52 F.2d 616, 633 (8th Cir. 1931) (competing company's profits held in trust for exclusive and perpetual use of the former employer company).

[28] Sialkot Importing Corp. v. Berlin, 68 N.E.2d 501 (N.Y. 1946).

[29] Cameco Inc. v. Gedicke, 724 A.2d 783 (N.J. 1999); Chelsea Indus. v. Gaffney, 449 N.E.2d 320, 329 (Mass. 1983).

[30] *Id.* For the view that the corporation's recovery of its employee's ill-gotten gains does not depend upon actual proof of loss by the employer-corporation, *see* Jet Courier Service, Inc. v. Mulei, 771 P.2d 486, 497 (Colo. 1989).

§11.11   [1] In corporate law, "controlling interest" refers to dominant ownership of a corporation's stock. Dixon v. Pro Image Inc., 987 P.2d 48, 54 (Utah 1999). It is not necessary to own a majority of the voting shares to be a controlling stockholder. Thus, for example, allegations that the defendant owned 20.6 percent of the stock and no other person owned more than 5 percent was enough to support a claim the defendant was bound by fiduciary duty as a controlling stockholder. Traub v. Barber, 45 N.Y.S.2d 575 (App. Div. 1982). *See also* Locati v. Johnson, 980 P.2d 173, 175 (Or. Ct. App. 1999) (one 50 percent owner can be a controlling stockholder with fiduciary obligations to the other 50 percent owner), *citing* Delaney v. Georgia-Pacific Corp., 564 P.2d 277 (Or. 1977).

[2] *See* Thomas L. Hazen, Transfers of Corporate Control and Duties of Controlling Shareholders— Common Law, Tender Offers, Investment Companies—and a Proposal for Reform, 125 U. Pa. L. Rev. 1023, 1027 (1975).

C. Controlling Stockholder's Fiduciary Obligations

instituted in response to the controlling stockholder's influence.[3] Unlike the directors' and officers' fiduciary obligations, where the breach can be found for nonfeasance as well as misfeasance, cases finding breaches by controlling stockholders involve affirmative action that can be traced to the controlling stockholder. Thus, it can be said that the controlling stockholder's fiduciary duty does not require that the controlling stockholder act as a guardian charged with the duty to act affirmatively by encouraging or driving the corporation to take action that will increase the value of the shares.[4]

The basis for the controlling stockholder's fiduciary obligation is the sound policy that, just as directors are bound by certain fiduciary obligations, one who has the potential to control the board's actions should be subject to an obligation as rigorous as those applied to the directors. Quite separate is the belief that control in a corporation, whether publicly or closely held, carries with it the potential that the controlling stockholder may choose to exercise control to reap disproportionate benefits at the expense of the corporation or noncontrolling shareholders such that protection of their interests is desirable. That protection arises by imposing the fiduciary standards on the controlling stockholder exercising the controlling influence. The overall objective of the controlling stockholder's fiduciary obligation is not to bar the controlling stockholder from acting in his own self-interest but to assure that when so acting the interests of the corporation are also served.[5]

In the public corporation, the threshold question is invariably whether the challenged activity or transaction is to be judged by the business judgment rule or the "inherent fairness" test. This is essentially a question of whether the activity or transaction is to be viewed somewhat neutrally so that it carries a presumption of propriety, or whether the court will approach the activity or transaction skeptically by placing the burden of proving its overall fairness on the controlling stockholder. The leading case emphasizing this dichotomy is *Sinclair Oil Corporation v. Levien*,[6] where, under the influence of its parent, the subsidiary corporation over a seven-year period had paid $38 million more in dividends than it had earned. The plaintiff argued that the subsidiary's dividend policy was guided exclusively by the parent's need for cash and resulted in the subsidiary company's oil exploration activities contracting at a time that the parent company's exploration activities were dramatically expanding. The Delaware Supreme Court held the

---

[3] *See, e.g.,* Crowley v. Communications for Hosps., Inc., 573 N.E.2d 996 (Mass. App. Ct.), *review denied,* 577 N.E.2d 309 (Mass. 1991).

[4] *See, e.g.,* Jones v. H. F. Ahmanson & Co., 460 P.2d 464 (Cal. 1969) (controlling stockholder under no duty to have caused company to split company's shares so all shares were more marketable, but when did act to increase marketability had a duty to assure equal treatment for all shareholders).

[5] *See, e.g.,* Chiles v. Robertson, 767 P.2d 903, 912 (Or. Ct. App. 1989) ("The fiduciary best fulfills its duties if it approaches them with the attitude of seeking the beneficiary's interests rather than the personal interests of the fiduciary. . . ."). *See* Ferber v. American Lamp Corp., 469 A.2d 1046 (Pa. 1983). *Cf.* Sager Spuck Statewide Supply Co., Inc. v. Meyer, 710 N.Y.S.2d 429, 433 (N.Y. App. Div. 2000) (preferred stockholder owed no fiduciary duty to corporation, since he did not participate in management and control of corporation, and his relationship with common stockholders was not akin to that between partners).

[6] 280 A.2d 717 (Del. 1971).

Chancellor erred in placing on the parent the burden of proving the dividend pol-icy's intrinsic fairness. The Supreme Court held that the burden of proving intrin-sic fairness is imposed only when there is self-dealing: "Self-dealing occurs when the parent, by virtue of its domination of the subsidiary causes the subsidiary to act in such a way that the parent receives something from the subsidiary to the exclusion of, *and* detriment to, the minority stockholders of the subsidiary."[7] The plaintiff has the burden of proving self-dealing.[8]

Sinclair Oil held that because all stockholders shared proportionately in the dividend declarations there was no self-dealing, and hence the dividend policy car-ried the presumptions of the business judgment rule. Only if the plaintiff could have borne the difficult burden of establishing that the dividends were the prod-uct of an improper motive or waste would the parent have been required to prove the subsidiary's dividend policy was intrinsically fair.[9] The plaintiff in *Sinclair Oil* also questioned the parent causing the subsidiary to modify to the parent's advan-tage contracts that obligated the parent to purchase specified quantities of oil at established prices. Because the parent's contracting with the subsidiary fit within the above definition of self-dealing, the court held the parent had the burden of proving the contracts' modification was intrinsically fair.

Sinclair Oil's standard of self-dealing purports to be a test of who should bear the burden of proof in actions challenging transactions undertaken in response to the controlling stockholder's influence. On close inspection one may reason-ably question whether the Delaware Supreme Court's standard of self-dealing involves more than deciding who bears the burden of proof. It would appear an extremely rare case where the controlling stockholder will be able to establish the transaction's intrinsic fairness after the court has concluded that the same trans-action had allowed the controlling stockholder to receive a benefit "to the exclu-sion of, and detriment to, the minority stockholders."[10] It may therefore be more appropriate to view *Sinclair Oil*'s test of self-dealing as a test of who prevails in the suit.

Erosion of *Sinclair Oil* at the expense of minority holders occurs in *Thorpe by Castleman v. CERBCO, Inc.,*[11] where the controlling stockholder responded to a third person's offer to acquire the assets of a controlled subsidiary by selling its control in the holding company. The court held that, even though there was a breach of the controlling stockholder's fiduciary obligation by his usurping the opportunity to sell the subsidiary, the damages from the breach were *not* the amount of the purchaser price that would have been allocated to the minority. The court reasoned that since the controlling stockholder could block any sale, damages must be restricted to expenses the controlled company incurred to facil-itate the transfer of control to the third party as well as the earnest money the con-

[7] 280 A.2d at 720 (emphasis added).
[8] Gabelli & Co. Profit Sharing Plan v. Liggett Group, Inc., 444 A.2d 261 (Del. Ch. 1982).
[9] The court suggests such would have been established if plaintiff could prove that business oppor-tunity embraced by the parent would otherwise have gone to the subsidiary.
[10] 280 A.2d at 720.
[11] 676 A.2d 436 (Del. 1996).

C. Controlling Stockholder's Fiduciary Obligations

trolling stockholder received.[12] Thus, the defendant's control over the enterprise could be used defensively to reduce the minority's recovery for losses they suffered as a result of the abuse of control.

Outside of Delaware, courts adhere to the dichotomy between a presumption of propriety (that is, the business judgment rule) and imposing the burden of proving fairness (that is, the intrinsic fairness standard) but do not have the same rigorous and narrow test for their application as embodied in *Sinclair Oil*. Evidence of disproportionate gains to the controlling stockholder is prima facie evidence of a breach.[13] For example, the California Supreme Court set forth the controlling stockholder's obligation when exercising influence over the corporation's affairs, requiring that they exercise their power to benefit the shareholders proportionately and in a manner that is not in conflict with the proper conduct of the corporation's business.[14] Many jurisdictions therefore choose not to follow *Sinclair Oil*'s requirement that the controlling stockholder's influence must produce both an exclusive benefit to itself as well as a corresponding detriment to the corporation or its noncontrolling stockholders.

In broad overview, transactions shown to produce disproportionate gains to the controlling stockholders are typically judged by a standard of fairness, and the burden of proof is on the controlling stockholder. Thus, the burden of establishing the fairness of the transaction is placed upon the controlling stockholder when it is transacting business with the corporation and when the plaintiff has made a threshold showing that the transaction disproportionately benefits the controlling stockholder.[15] "Fairness" is articulated in many different ways, such as bearing the qualities one would expect in "arms-length bargaining,"[16] or having terms within the "expectations" of the stockholders,[17] or bearing indicia of "objective fairness." As is apparent, none of these standards portends exactness, so the results in individual cases are difficult to predict *ex ante,* and the cases frequently appear in conflict.

The greatest variance across jurisdictions appears in disputes on matters that are inherent and peculiar to parent-subsidiary corporations.[18] The environment

---

[12] *Id.* at 444.

[13] *See, e.g.,* Chiles v. Robertson, 767 P.2d 903 (Or. Ct. App. 1989) (relying upon Sections 5.04 and 5.11 of the ALI Principles of Corporate Governance: Analysis and Recommendations (1992), holds the duty is owed to "use their power to control the corporation in a way that would benefit all shareholders proportionately"); Iavarone v. Raymond Keyes Assoc., 733 F. Supp. 727 (S.D.N.Y. 1990); Smith v. Tele-Communications, Inc., 184 Cal. Rptr. 571 (Ct. App. 1982).

[14] *See* Jones v. H. F. Ahmanson & Co., 460 P.2d 464 (Cal. 1969).

[15] *See* Locati v. Johnson, 980 P.2d 173 (Or. Ct. App. 1999). *Sinclair* thus holds that the burden of proving fairness arises only in self-dealing transactions which it defines as a transaction whose effects are not visited proportionally upon the control and noncontrol stockholders.

[16] *See* Odyssey Partners Ltd. Partnership v. Fleming Corp., 735 A.2d 386 (Del. Ch. 1999) (need not bid a "fair" price at foreclosure sale at which other possible bidders were present, even though foreclosure proceeding initiated by the controlling stockholder); Pepper v. Litton, 308 U.S. 295 (1939).

[17] Case v. New York Central R.R., 204 N.E.2d 643 (N.Y. 1965).

[18] *See* Chanoch Schreiber & Aaron Yoran, Allocating the Tax Savings Derived from Filing Consolidated Corporate Tax Returns, 29 Baylor L. Rev. 243 (1977); Note, Corporate Fiduciary Doctrine in the Context of Parent-Subsidiary Relations, 74 Yale L.J. 338 (1964).

of parent-subsidiary corporations is rife with instances where for tax or other regulatory purposes the activities of the parent and subsidiary may be combined. When their joint treatment yields a common benefit, the question frequently arises how that benefit is to be allocated. For example, in *Case v. New York Central Railroad*,[19] the parent filed a consolidated return with its 80 percent owned subsidiary whereby the parent's losses offset the subsidiary's gains, producing a net tax savings to the subsidiary of $3,825,717.43. Pursuant to a preexisting agreement between the two corporations, 97 percent of the tax savings was paid by the subsidiary to the parent. The court found no advantage was gained by the parent corporation at the expense of subsidiary. The court emphasized that the division of the tax savings was pursuant to the preexisting agreement,[20] that the arrangement did produce a benefit of reducing the subsidiary's taxes that it would not have enjoyed but for the agreement, and that the parent's losses were a valuable factor in producing the tax savings. In sum, the arrangement was upheld because the subsidiary was no worse off than it would have been had there been no consolidation.[21]

There is no easy reference point to decide what would be a fair sharing in benefits that can occur only in control relationships. Certainly it is too abstract to judge such transactions by what would occur in arm's-length dealings, because the filing of consolidated tax returns by definition does not involve arm's-length transactions.[22] Moreover, reference to what allocations occur in other parent-subsidiary relationships will only invoke a standard that itself is likely to embody dominance and control. California appears to provide the most certainty by holding that fairness requires the benefit be shared proportionately.[23] There is a good deal of appeal to the view that if the controlling stockholder garners more than its proportionate share, it should at least have the burden of proving circumstances justifying why the allocation was fair to the controlled company.

Much like what occurs when directors contract with their corporation, contracts between the corporation and its controlling stockholder invoke critical review. Absent disinterested approval or ratification, the controlling stockholder has the burden of proving the transaction's overall fairness to the corporation.[24] It is well recognized that disinterested minority shareholder approval of a transaction between the controlling stockholder and the corporation places the bur-

---

[19] 204 N.E.2d 643 (N.Y. 1965).

[20] *See also* In re Reading Co., 711 F.2d 509 (3d Cir. 1983).

[21] In a more demanding jurisdiction, more is required than not being worse off because of the agreement. In Alliegro v. Pan Am. Bank, 136 So. 2d 656 (Fla. Dist. Ct. App. 1962), the allocation arrangement whereby the tax savings were allocated to the loss company was held an improper arrangement unless ratified by the stockholders.

[22] Myerson v. El Paso Natural Gas Co., 246 A.2d 789, 794 (Del. Ch. 1967) (allocation of entire tax savings to the parent upheld where court found nature of the issues so problematic that the wisest policy is to commit the allocation to the business judgment rule unless the plaintiff established "gross and palpable overreaching").

[23] Smith v. Tele-Communications, Inc., 184 Cal. Rptr. 571 (Cal. Ct. App. 1982).

[24] Efron v. Kalmanovitz, 38 Cal. Rptr. 148 (Ct. App. 1964); Sterling v. Mayflower Hotel Corp., 93 A.2d 107 (Del. 1952).

C. Controlling Stockholder's Fiduciary Obligations

den on the challenging party to prove the transaction's unfairness.[25] There is authority that the same presumption of propriety can attach if the independent body of directors approves the transaction.[26]

The American Law Institute's Corporate Governance Project deals specifically with transactions between the corporation and its controlling stockholder,[27] the controlling stockholder's use of corporate assets, information, and influence,[28] and the controlling stockholder's usurpation of a corporate opportunity.[29] In broad overview, the scheme of the American Law Institute places the burden of proving fairness on the controlling stockholder with respect to any challenge to a transaction between the corporation and its controlling stockholder and allegations that the controlling stockholder has usurped a corporate opportunity[30] unless the particular transaction has received disinterested director approval, shareholder approval, or ratification. When the controlling stockholder uses corporate assets or information or otherwise exercises influence over the corporation with the effect of securing an economic benefit, the American Law Institute demands either that value be given to the corporation or that any benefit the controlling shareholder secures is proportionally available to other shareholders similarly situated.[31] In sum, the American Law Institute follows a course that is more protective of stockholder rights on these questions than does Delaware but is well within the approach that appears to apply in most jurisdictions.

In the close corporation setting, the breach can be established on more personal basis, such as by proving that the controlling stockholder had an abrasive or intimidating manner toward the minority stockholders[32] or that the controlling

---

[25] See, e.g., Rosenblatt v. Getty Oil Co., 493 A.2d 929 (Del. 1985); Schreiber v. Carney, 447 A.2d 17 (Del. Ch. 1982); cf. Efron v. Kalmanovitz, 38 Cal. Rptr. 148 (Ct. App. 1964) (absent disinterested stockholder approval, controlling stockholder has burden of proving fairness when contracting with the corporation).

[26] See, e.g., Odyssey Partners v. Fleming Corp., 735 A.2d 386 (Del. Ch. 1999) (noting director fees of $24,000 per year not so great as to compromise independence and a director who formerly was employee of, and who had a consulting arrangement with, controlling stockholder deemed independent where his membership on board was requested by directors who were clearly independent). Weinberger v. UOP, Inc., 457 A.2d 701, 709 n.7 (Del. 1983); Puma v. Marriott, 283 A.2d 693 (Del. Ch. 1971).

[27] ALI Principles of Corporate Governance, supra §11.07 note 2, §5.10.

[28] Id. at §5.11.

[29] Id. at §5.12.

[30] With respect to a controlling stockholder, "corporate opportunity" is defined in terms of whether it was developed or received by the corporation, came to the controlling stockholder *primarily* because of the stockholder's relationship to the corporation, or is business activity the controlling stockholder has represented to the shareholders as being of the type that will be within the corporation's scope of business. Id. §5.12(b). See Thorpe v. CERBCO, Inc., 676 A.2d 436 (Del. 1996) (controlling stockholders were entitled to obtain a control premium for their shares and in that sense compete with their corporation, but only after disclosing to the corporation that they had received a bid to purchase the corporation).

[31] ALI Principles of Corporate Governance, supra §11.07 note 2, at §5.11(a)(1) & (2).

[32] See, e.g., Evans v. Blesi, 345 N.W.2d 775 (Minn. Ct. App. 1984).

stockholder foreclosed the minority from the opportunity to participate in meetings or receive information about corporate transactions.[33] In the closely held corporation the controlling stockholder's fiduciary obligation is increasingly viewed as being akin to the obligation that partners owe to one another.[34] The close corporation's controlling stockholder owes a duty of "utmost good faith and fairness" to the controlled corporation and its stockholders.[35] To be sure, such a standard is inherently devoid of specifics but nevertheless embodies a tone that carries with it the view that challenges transactions between the controlling stockholder and the corporation, or merely the exercise of influence over corporate activities; each will be subjected to close review for overall fairness and proper motivation.[36]

§11.12 Unequal Treatment Among Different Classes of Securities or Holders of Same Class of Security[1]

Disputes regarding the controlling stockholder's obligations sometimes occur in the context of the conflicting rights between different classes of stock where the focus of the dispute is the power of one class (that is, that held by the controlling stockholder) over the rights of another class of stock (that is, the class held by the minority shareholders) and also among holders of the same class of security where disparate treatment among holders arises as a result of actions by those in control of company. In this context, courts frequently support fiduciary obligations by officers, directors, and controlling stockholders to all classes of stockholders, preferred as well as common.[2] The leading decision involving duties of the controlling shareholder qua shareholder is the Third Circuit's decision in *Zahn v. Transamerica Corporation.*[3] The essence of the complaint was that Transamerica, as

[33] *See, e.g.*, Duncan v. Lichtenberger, 671 S.W.2d 948 (Tex. Ct. App. 1984). No breach of the controlling stockholder's duty was found where an amendment was passed establishing "tenure voting" that solidified the controlling position of the present majority shareholders. *See* Williams v. Geier, 671 A.2d 1368 (Del. 1996). *See also* Lacos Land Co. v. Arden Group, Inc., 517 A.2d 271 (Del. Ch. 1986).

[34] Estate of Schroer v. Stamco Supply Inc., 482 N.E.2d 975 (Ohio Ct. App. 1984). The courts sometimes premise the existence of the duty on the trust and confidence a shareholder places in another. *See* In re Estate of Mihm, 497 A.2d 612 (Pa. 1985). *Contra* Riblet Products Corp. v. Nagy, 683 A.2d 37 (Del. 1996) (fiduciary duty is not implicated where minority shareholder sues for wrongful dismissal from employment because no fiduciary duty was owed the plaintiff qua employee but only qua stockholder).

[35] Crowley v. Communications for Hosps., Inc., 573 N.E.2d 996 (Mass. App. Ct.), *review denied*, 577 N.E.2d 309 (Mass. 1991); Krukemeier v. Krukemeier Mach. & Tool Co., 551 N.E.2d 885 (Ind. Ct. App. 1990).

[36] *E.g.*, Knaebel v. Heiner, 663 P.2d 551 (Alaska 1983); Linge v. Ralston Purina Co., 293 N.W.2d 191, 194 (Iowa 1980); Donahue v. Rodd Electrotype Co., 328 N.E.2d 505 (Mass. 1975). *Cf.* Meinhard v. Salmon, 164 N.E. 545, 546 (N.Y. 1928) (duty as between partners).

§11.12 [1] Material in this section has been adapted from James D. Cox, Equal Treatment For Shareholders: An Essay, 19 Cardozo L. Rev. 615 (1997).

[2] *See, e.g.*, Eisenberg v. Chicago Milwaukee Corp., 537 A.2d 1051, 1062 (Del. Ch. 1987); Jackson Nat'l Life Ins. Co. v. Kennedy, 741 A.2d 377 (Del. Ch. 1999). *See also* §18.15.

[3] 162 F.2d 36 (3d Cir. 1947). *See also, e.g.*, Mansfield Hardwood Lumber Co. v. Johnson, 268 F.2d 317 (5th Cir.), *cert. denied*, 361 U.S. 885 (1959); Judah v. Delaware Trust Co., 378 A.2d 624 (Del. 1977).

the controlling shareholder of the Axton-Fisher Tobacco Company, breached its fiduciary duty to minority shareholders in executing its plan to liquidate Axton-Fisher.[4] The controversy pitted Transamerica, who owned virtually all the Class B common shares, against the holders of the Class A common shares. The Class A common shares were convertible into Class B shares, could be redeemed at $60 (plus any dividends in arrears), by the board after notice, and on liquidation was entitled to receive twice as much as the Class B common shares. Transamerica owned virtually all the Class B common shares and through their greater voting power elected Axton-Fisher's board of directors. Transamerica, with full knowledge of the increased value of Axton-Fisher's inventory of tobacco, proceeded toward a two-step liquidation that took advantage of the Class A shareholders' ignorance of the increased asset value. Transamerica caused the Axton-Fisher board to redeem its Class A shares at a price much lower than their liquidation value and then proceeded to liquidate Axton-Fisher.[5] The notice to the Class A common shareholders of its intent to redeem their shares at $60 per share (plus an additional $20.80 in accrued dividends) did not disclose the board's intention to liquidate Axton-Fisher or the liquidation value of Axton-Fisher.

The Third Circuit held that there was an "unmistakable fiduciary duty of those in control of the corporation."[6] However, the opinion speaks rather vaguely as to why Transamerica breached its fiduciary duty to the holders of the Class A common shares. The opinion strongly suggests that Transamerica breached its duty by causing Axton-Fisher's board of directors to redeem the Class A common shares on the eve of the company's liquidation. If this were in fact the court's holding, it would conflict with the contractual right of Axton-Fisher to redeem the Class A common shares at a set price.

The objective of any redemption provision is to allow those in control of the corporation—i.e., Transamerica—to eliminate an expensive financial appendage—i.e., the Class A common shares—when it is in the best interests of the residual owners of the firm—i.e., the Class B common shares—Transamerica. A far wiser approach in such a case is not to condemn the exercise of one class's contractual rights over another class but to examine the totality of their contractual arrangement to discern whether the exercise is consistent with the relationship they have woven through their relative rights, preferences, and privileges. The resolution of the controlling stockholder's fiduciary obligation to another class of shareholders by reference to their relative rights in the corporation's articles of incorporation is but an application of the more general approach of allowing stockholders the freedom to contract among themselves as to the standards

---

[4] Transamerica owned virtually all of the Axton-Fisher Class B common stock that had full voting rights. The plaintiffs' Class A shares, in addition to having cumulative dividend and conditional voting rights, were callable at $60 per share plus accrued dividends and were convertible into Class B shares on a one-for-one basis. The Class A shares also contained a liquidation preference and were entitled to receive twice as much as Class B out of the common fund. 162 F.2d at 38-39.

[5] For an analysis of the extent of the plaintiffs' injury and the proper measure of damages, *see* Speed v. Transamerica Corp., 135 F. Supp. 176, 186-194 (D. Del. 1955), *modified on other grounds*, 235 F.2d 369 (3d Cir. 1956).

[6] 162 F.2d at 42.

they believe appropriate for their relationship. In both close and public corporations the controlling stockholder does not breach his fiduciary obligation to the other stockholders by engaging in conduct that, though harmful to the noncontrolling stockholder, is nevertheless consistent with the terms of the parties' agreement.[7]

Thus in *In re Reading*[8] the Third Circuit upheld the controlling stockholder being able to acquire services from the corporation at below market rate pursuant to an agreement among all the stockholders, even though the complaining minority stockholder's business had changed such that it could no longer make use of the corporation's services. The court held that as long as the discount was authorized by the stockholders' agreement, the controlling stockholder was not required to recognize the change in circumstances for the minority stockholder.[9] Similarly, the Third Circuit in *Zahn* could easily have concluded that Transamerica's breach was not its causing Axton-Fisher's board to redeem the Class A common shares or liquidating Axton-Fisher; rather, the breach was failing to disclose the liquidation value of Axton-Fisher. Armed with such information, and facing a pending redemption of their shares, the holders of Class A common shares would exercise their right to convert into the Class B common shares, where they would reap more than the $80.80, to be received solely through the redemption of their Class A common shares. That is, the very purpose behind the Class A common shares having a right to convert into Class B common shares, as well as a waiting period between the board's announced intention to redeem the Class A common shares and the actual redemption can easily be seen as having the intent of facilitating the conversion of the Class A common shares into the Class B common shares.[10]

Accordingly, in subsequent proceedings the Third Circuit held that the call of the Class A common shares was valid even though it was driven by the desire to benefit one class of shares over another such that the proper measure of damages was what the Class A stockholders would have received had they converted their shares into Class B common shares.[11] Courts frequently find in such contractual settings an implied condition that the board of directors will give adequate notice to the minority holders so they can exercise their right to convert.[12] Claims of unfair treatment can also arise among shareholders of the same class of security or between different classes of securities where there is no dominant stockholder.

___

[7] *See, e.g.*, Evangelista v. Holland, 537 N.E.2d 589 (Mass. App. Ct. 1989); Case v. New York Central R.R., 204 N.E.2d 643 (N.Y. 1965). For an insightful analysis of why this approach is called for in mediating tensions between common and preferred holders, and can be useful in curbing opportunistic behavior by the controlling stockholder or managers vis-à-vis the holders of a senior class of securities, *see* Victor Brudney, Contract and Fiduciary Duty in Corporate Law, 38 B.C.L. Rev. 595 (1997).

[8] 711 F.2d 509 (3d Cir. 1983).

[9] *Id.* at 520.

[10] One may question what then is the purpose behind allowing the Class A common shares to receive twice as much on liquidation as the Class B common shares? This provision assumes significance where the liquidation is involuntary—e.g., bankruptcy, and not at the request of the controlling stockholder.

[11] Speed v. Transamerica Corp., 235 F.2d 369 (3d Cir. 1956).

[12] *See, e.g.*, Van Gemert v. Boeing Co., 520 F.2d 1373 (2d Cir. 1975).

C. Controlling Stockholder's Fiduciary Obligations

What is "fair" is always an intriguing question. In the corporate context, fairness is not a point, but a spectrum of values. Inquiries in this context therefore seek to determine whether the transaction falls within that spectrum. When the question is the rights among stockholders, particularly those of the same class, there is some authority that there are spectrums within spectrums. For example, in *Nixon v. Blackwell*,[13] the Delaware Supreme Court reversed the Chancery Court's holding that the non-employee holders of Class B stock were entitled to liquidity equal to that which the employee holders of Class B stock enjoyed. More than half of the Class B shares were held by an employee stock ownership plan ("ESOP"). Employees being terminated and those retiring were granted the option to receive their interest in the ESOP in Class B shares or cash; senior officers and directors owned Class A shares and, by agreement, could exchange those shares for Class B shares upon the officer's or director's retirement or death.[14] To facilitate repurchase of Class B shares held by former officers or directors, the corporation purchased "key man" insurance to fund purchases that were triggered by the holder's death.[15] Because a comparable repurchase option was not extended to non-employee Class B stockholders, they sued, alleging they were improperly excluded from the company's share repurchase program.

The *Nixon* case involved self-dealing because directors, as prospective holders of Class B shares, unlike the plaintiffs, enjoyed their shares being redeemed by the corporation with funds provided by insurance policies purchased by the corporation. Nevertheless, Chief Justice Veasey rejected the plaintiff's call for equal treatment, reasoning that "[t]o hold that fairness necessarily requires precise equality is to beg the question."[16] "[S]tockholders," he explained, "need not always be treated equally for all purposes."[17] Nixon answered the question of fair treatment for the non-employee Class B holders by identifying a corporate benefit with the

---

[13] 626 A.2d 1366 (Del. 1993).

[14] *Id.* at 1371.

[15] *Id.* at 1372.

[16] *Id.* at 1377.

[17] *Id.* at 1376. On this point, the court was greatly influenced by the reasoning of Judge Easterbrook and Professor Fischel:

> Many scholars, though few courts, conclude that one aspect of fiduciary duty is the equal treatment of investors. Their argument takes the following form: fiduciary principles require fair conduct; equal treatment is fair conduct; hence, fiduciary principles require equal treatment. The conclusion does not follow. The argument depends on an equivalence between *equal* and fair treatment. To say that fiduciary principles require equal treatment is to beg the question whether investors would contract for equal or even equivalent treatment.

Frank H. Easterbrook & Daniel R. Fischel, The Economic Structure of Corporate Law 110 (1991) (emphasis original). The above thesis is advanced by Easterbrook and Fischel in the context of their discussion of fiduciary obligations in *close* corporations and is predicated upon their view that, because individuals bring to the corporation very different backgrounds, talents, and motives, transactions that maximize wealth for the stockholders may require disproportionate sharing of gains so as to provide those in control with sufficient rewards for their risky entrepreneurial activities. Though this may well form the reasonable expectations of the parties, and thus inform the content of fiduciary obligations in specific close-corporation issues, this reasoning would seem less compelling in the context of the *public* corporation.

corporation's repurchase of retiring employees' shares—to prevent the shares from passing into the hands of members of the founder's family or descendants of employees.[18] The court believed the arrangement was consistent with the intent underlying the original creation of the Class B stock; the Class B shares were to be held by passive investors with no active voice in the corporation.[19]

One can easily get lost in a vast semantical battle under *Nixon*'s approach to fairness, where qualities unrelated to the share terms are considered in evaluating how value is to be distributed among the owners. For example, no one disputes the fact that parties receiving the same, i.e., equal, amount for their shares have each been treated fairly. If one looks beyond a person's status as a shareholder, however, to some other endowment she carries to the transaction, such as longevity, loyalty, or some element of sacrifice for the corporate good, one may argue that the failure to compensate such shareholder for those intangible qualities results in that person's unfair treatment. In this case, equal payment for all shares is unfair because it fails to respect the additional value some holders add to their shares.

Correlatively, if the person who brings additional endowments to the corporation receives a higher price than those who do not, those receiving the lesser amount are not being treated unfairly. Under this type of analysis, the semantical question turns on the context in which "fairness" is being assessed. Should it be evaluated only with respect to the rights of a share, or should it include the characteristics of the shareholder herself? If the latter theory prevails, the fairness approach advocated by *Nixon* appears to be correct.

Fiduciary duties in the corporate context exist to fill gaps where the parties have not otherwise set forth their rights and relationships. Fiduciary duties are therefore similar to corporate statutes in that they provide convenient off-the-rack rules to simplify the process of contracting, and permit deviations from corporate provisions when the interests of third parties (most notably, creditors) will not be harmed. Though there is much concern and uncertainty regarding the duty owed minority stockholders, the burdens of the directors' and controlling stockholders' fiduciary duties are not great. The commands of corporate fiduciary duties provide a fairly low threshold for what constitutes appropriate behavior in the corporation. Indeed, the most notable feature of corporate fiduciary duty law is the lack of rigor found in its prescriptions.

Far more important than the broad standards by which the courts purport to judge defendants' behavior is whether the court will deprive the challenged transaction of the deferential presumptions dictated by the business judgment rule.[20] The all-important burden of persuasion follows from whether the defendants' conduct falls within the business judgement rule. So viewed, the single most important issue in considering the content of fiduciary duty obligations among stockholders is the threshold consideration whether the challenged transaction

[18] 626 A.2d at 1377, 1379.
[19] *Id.* at 1379.
[20] *See* Cede & Co. v. Technicolor, 634 A.2d 345 (Del. 1993).

C. Controlling Stockholder's Fiduciary Obligations

enjoys the presumption of propriety.[21] In this context, the question of the content of the fiduciary duty among stockholders is answered by inquiring into what assumptions we should make regarding the rights, privileges, and preferences among stockholders who have not otherwise chosen to deviate from the recognized norm. Armed with this standard, courts can then take the next step of determining what showing is necessary to consider whether the parties before it have chosen to depart from that norm. This is precisely the course followed by Justice Traynor in *Jones v. H.F. Ahmanson & Co.*[22]

In *Jones*, the defendants transferred their Association common stock (which represented 85 percent of all outstanding shares) to United Financial, a holding company they had created. For each share exchanged, they received 250 United shares and $927.50 cash. The minority were not provided an opportunity to participate in the exchange. They prevailed in their suit charging that their exclusion was wrongful and effectively destroyed the marketability of their shares. Justice Traynor, reasoning that "whenever control is material" there is a comprehensive rule of good faith and inherent fairness to the minority.[23] After several such incantations of the majority's fiduciary obligations to act in good faith toward the minority, *Jones* applies the standard of equal treatment for the minority, unless the majority invokes a *compelling justification* for deviating from the norm.[24] That is, the most important point for the court was that the minority shareholders were excluded and that there was a consequential disproportionate gain on the part of the majority holders.

---

[21] *See* Levien v. Sinclair Oil Corp., 261 A.2d 911 (Del. Ch. 1969), *rev'd*, Sinclair Oil Corp. v. Levien, 280 A.2d 717 (Del. 1971), discussed in text in §11.11.

[22] 460 P.2d 464 (Cal. 1969).

[23] *Id.* at 474.

[24] *Id.* at 476.

CHAPTER 12

Obligations Arising Out of Transactions in Shares

I.   STATE LAW

A.   SALE OF CONTROL AND CORPORATE OFFICE

§12.01   *The Sale of Corporate Control*

A purchaser of a controlling interest in a corporation often pays a premium above the prevailing market price for the stock.[1] Legal scholars, the judiciary, and, more recently, Congress have examined the extent to which these premiums are unfair to the remaining shareholders and to the corporation. Significant scholarly energy has been devoted to the sale of corporate control and the appropriate treatment of the resulting premium, with a view toward providing unifying principles to aid courts in their analysis of control transfers.[2]

In 1932, Professor Berle developed the "corporate asset" theory of control.[3] The essence of this theory is that the premium above the per share market price realized by the seller in return for a controlling block of stock is a corporate asset because it "arises out of the ability which the holder has to dominate property which in equity belongs to others."[4] It follows that the entire premium "if it goes anywhere, must go into the corporate treasury."[5] A major objection to Professor Berle's approach is that the price paid for a controlling block will necessarily be higher than the previous prevailing per share price because the control purchaser creates an increased demand that, combined with a constant supply, results in an

---

§12.01   [1] How many shares constitute a "controlling" interest must often be determined by a factual inquiry in the particular case. *See, e.g.,* Kings County Dev. Co. v. Buell, 709 F.2d 1516 (9th Cir. 1983) (court held that sale of 14 percent of corporation's outstanding stock to purchaser who already owned 20 percent was not a sale of control); Fischbein v. First Chicago Corp., 161 F.3d 1104 (7th Cir. 1998) (interpreting a "change in control" clause of stock option after a merger of equals, the court concluded no change occurred even though corporation was not the surviving corporation since its former owners and directors would be a majority in the combined companies).

[2] John C. Coffee, Transfers of Control and the Quest for Efficiency: Can Delaware Law Encourage Efficient Transactions While Chilling Inefficient Ones?, 21 Del. J. Corp. L. 359 (1996); Benjamin Hermalin & Alan Schwartz, Buyouts in Large Companies, 25 J. Legal Studies 351 (1996); Lucian A. Bebchuk, Efficient and Inefficient Sales of Corporate Control, 1994 Q.J. Econ. 957; Marcel Kahan, Sales of Corporate Control, 9 J. L. Econ. & Org. 368 (1993); Einer Elhauge, The Triggering Function of Sale of Control Doctrine, 59 U. Chi. L. Rev. 1465 (1992); Saul X. Levmore, A Primer on the Sale of Corporate Control, 65 Tex. L. Rev. 1061 (1987); Thomas L. Hazen, Transfers of Corporate Control and Duties of Controlling Shareholders—Common Law, Tender Offers, Investment Companies—And a Proposal for Reform, 125 U. Pa. L. Rev. 1023 (1977).

[3] Adolf A. Berle & Gardiner C. Means, The Modern Corporation and Private Property 207-252 (rev. ed. 1968).

[4] Berle & Means, *supra* note 3, at 216.

[5] Berle & Means, *supra* note 3, at 216-217. More recently, in a series of articles now consolidated in a book, Professor Bayne takes the position that control, while not a corporate asset, is nevertheless to be held in trust such that any separate payment for control is akin to a bribe. *See* David C. Bayne, The Philosophy of Corporate Control (1986).

A. Sale of Control and Corporate Office

upward pressure on the price. Another reason suggested for rejecting a per se prohibition on control premiums is that the ability to exercise control as a vehicle for making the enterprise more valuable is a cognizable property right attaching to a controlling interest rather than a corporate asset.

Another school of thought counsels that the obligation of the controlling stockholder is to assure an equal sharing of the premium among the noncontrol shares as well as the control shares. Under this approach, all stockholders must have an equal opportunity to sell the same portion of shares as the controlling stockholder. Thus, if the existing control stockholder owns 51 percent of the shares and the purchaser wishes to acquire 51 percent, the existing control stockholder may sell only 51 percent of her shares, and the noncontrol stockholders must also have the opportunity to each sell 51 percent of their shares at the same price as that offered to the existing control stockholder. This theory has a parallel in a fundamental principle of corporate law that all shares of the same class are to be treated equally.[6] For example, any discrimination in a merger in the amount paid for shares is unlawful such that the higher amount must be paid to all holders.[7]

Within the equal sharing approach are powerful incentives for the existing control stockholder to closely examine the worthiness of the purchaser of control whenever the new purchaser wishes to acquire less than all the outstanding shares. This vigilance arises under the equal opportunity approach because when the new purchaser acquires less than all the outstanding shares, the former controlling stockholder becomes a minority stockholder such that her holdings are a risk should the new purchaser of control prove to be harmful to the corporation or the minority stockholders. A negative aspect of the equal opportunity approach is that its adoption tends to reduce the frequency of transfers of control because the existing control stockholders do not wish to become minority stockholders but instead prefer the purchase of all their shares.

Under the equal opportunity approach, however, the purchase of all the existing control person's shares can occur only when the purchaser of control is willing to acquire all the company's voting stock. This necessarily raises the cost of the acquisition. A natural economic corollary is that the equal opportunity approach will result in fewer transfers of control. It is wise to view transfers of control, especially at a premium, as desirable because on average the company's resources will be put to a greater use; the very sources of the premium are the financial or operating synergies the purchaser of control contemplates from the acquisition. There is strong empirical support for the view that the value of the noncontrolling stockholders' shares increases following a transfer of control.

---

[6] *See, e.g.,* In re Sealand Corp., 642 A.2d 792, 800 n.10 (Del. Ch. 1993) ("all shares of the same type, series, or class are, by definition, equal"); Bank of N.Y. Co. v. Irving Bank Corp., 536 N.Y.S.2d 923, 925 (N.Y. 1988) (same).

[7] *See* Beaumont v. American Can Co., 538 N.Y.S.2d 136, 137 (N.Y. Sup. Ct. 1988).

While the sale of control provokes a good deal of academic debate, the courts have not embraced any of the above schools of thought and have taken a more ad hoc approach to the facts of a particular case.

Courts generally hold that any premium paid to acquire controlling stock is merely a reflection of the greater value of that stock due to its control potential, and as such it is a natural consequence of stock ownership and cannot be considered a corporate asset. More generally, every stockholder, including the controlling stockholder, is at liberty to dispose of her shares at any price as long as there is no cause to believe or suspect the sale will proximately harm the corporation or its stockholders, or will necessarily interfere or mislead the other stockholders in exercising their same right to sell.[8]

§12.02   *Fiduciary Duties of Sellers of Corporate Control*

Numerous courts have held that a seller of control may become liable in certain circumstances for the harm to the corporation caused by the purchaser. Clearly, however, the liability is far from absolute.[1] In the leading case, *Insuranshares Corporation v. Northern Fiscal Corporation,*[2] after the transfer of a controlling interest, the purchasers proceeded to loot the corporation. The district court held the control sellers liable and reasoned that, at a minimum, the transferor of a controlling block of shares owes a duty to the corporation to protect it when "the circumstances surrounding the proposed transfer are such as to awaken suspicion and put a *prudent* man on his guard—unless a *reasonably adequate* investigation discloses such facts as would convince a *reasonable person* that no fraud is intended or likely to result."[3] When the circumstances do awaken suspicion in the reasonably prudent person, the seller of control has a duty to make such inquiry as a reasonably prudent person would make.[4] Liability does not attach, however, merely for the exercise of poor business judgment.[5] A minority view requires proof that the

---

[8] *See* Doleman v. Meiji Mut. Life Ins. Co., 727 F.2d 1480 (9th Cir. 1984); Delano v. Kitch, 663 F.2d 990 (10th Cir. 1981); Roby v. Dunnett, 88 F.2d 68, 69 (10th Cir. 1937); Frantz Mfg. Co. v. EAC Indus., 501 A.2d 401, 408 (Del. 1985); Zetlin v. Hanson Holdings, Inc., 397 N.E. 2d 387 (N.Y. 1979).

§12.02   [1] *E.g.,* Clagett v. Hutchinson, 583 F.2d 1259 (4th Cir. 1978).

[2] 35 F. Supp. 22 (E.D. Pa. 1940).

[3] *Id.* at 25 (emphasis supplied). Rather than emphasizing the existence of a special relationship between the parties, the tenor of the decision lies in its use of the negligence rubric by pointing to constructive notice as creating the defendant's duty to act in a certain manner and with a certain degree of care. For a broad statement of this duty, *see* Estate of Hooper v. Virgin Islands, 427 F.2d 45, 47 (3d Cir. 1970).

[4] Harman v. Willbern, 374 F. Supp. 1149 (D. Kan. 1974), *aff'd,* 520 F.2d 1333 (10th Cir. 1975); DeBraun v. First W. Bank & Trust Co., 120 Cal. Rptr. 354 (Cal. Ct. App. 1975); Harris v. Carter, 582 A.2d 222 (Del. Ch. 1990) (seller of control where there is reasonable suspicion and who inquires further is liable if he commits gross negligence in conduct of the inquiry); Pitterich v. Styling Technology Corp., 2000 Pa. D. & C. Lexis 183 (Pa. Com. Pl. 2000).

[5] Harman v. Willbern, 374 F. Supp. 1149, 1161-1163 (D. Kan. 1974), *aff'd,* 520 F.2d 1333 (10th Cir. 1975); Shoaf v. Warlick, 380 S.E. 2d 865 (S.C. Ct. App. 1989).

controlling stockholder had actual knowledge, not inquiry notice.[6] The weakness of requiring actual knowledge is that the standard encourages the seller to place his head in the sand when negotiating with his buyer.[7] On the other hand, the minority shareholders owe no fiduciary obligation to their fellow minority holders.[8]

The circumstances awakening suspicion in *Insuranshares Corporation* were as follows: (1) the sellers' probable knowledge that the purchase would be financed by a pledge of the corporation's assets; (2) the corporation president's clear disposition to allow a sale to be financed by pledging those assets; (3) the sellers' awareness of the purchasers' plan to have a large part of the corporation's assets converted into cash prior to the sale; (4) the inflated price or premium paid for control, especially given the nature of the business, which was an investment trust with no physical assets but only the ready equivalent of cash in the form of marketable securities; (5) warnings from the sellers' attorneys as to their potential liabilities for dealing with little-known purchasers; and (6) the fact that the corporation had been looted five years before by a different group, who had gained control by using the same method of financing.[9]

The cases illustrate the highly factual nature of a court's determination in sale of control litigation. This orientation is embraced by the American Law Institute, whose provision makes the controlling stockholders' fiduciary obligation depend in part on the transfer not occurring when "it is apparent from the circumstances that the purchaser is likely" to violate the purchaser's fiduciary obligations so as to acquire a substantial financial benefit for himself.[10]

Looting and mismanagement by the purchaser of control are classic types of misbehavior that form the backdrop for inquiring whether the seller's suspicions were sufficiently piqued for there to have been a breach in disposing of control. Many cases do not involve looting or mismanagement by the new controlling stockholder but rather the diversion of a potential premium from the noncontrolling stockholders by the former controlling stockholder. This occurs when the purchaser offers to acquire at a substantial premium an asset of the company[11] or

---

[6] The leading case for this view is Levy v. American Beverage Corp., 38 N.Y.S.2d 517, 526 (App. Div. 1942). Later New York cases have abandoned *Levy*.

[7] *See* Swinney v. Keebler Co., 329 F. Supp. 216, 233 (D. S.C. 1971), *aff'd*, 480 F.2d 573, 577 (4th Cir. 1973).

[8] *See, e.g.,* Priddy v. B. Edelman, 883 F.2d 438 (6th Cir. 1989); Gilbert v. El Paso Co., 490 A.2d 1050, 1055 (Del. Ch. 1984).

[9] 480 F.2d at 577. *See also* DeBaun v. First W. Bank & Trust Co., 120 Cal. Rptr. 354 (Ct. App. 1975). Compare, *e.g.,* Swinney v. Keebler Co., 480 F.2d 573 (4th Cir. 1973). *But see* DeBaun v. First W. Bank & Trust Co., 120 Cal. Rptr. 354 (Ct. App. 1975).

[10] ALI, Principles of Corporate Governance: Analysis and Recommendations §5.16(b) (1994) (hereinafter ALI, Principles of Corporate Governance). For the other requirement the controlling stockholder must meet when disposing of control, *see infra* note 13.

[11] *See, e.g.,* Dunnett v. Arn, 71 F.2d 912 (10th Cir. 1934) (officers who owned controlling block of stock sold their shares at price not available to noncontrol shares after earlier refusing to sell company assets to purchaser of shares); Commonwealth Title Ins. & Trust Co. v. Seltzer, 76 A. 77 (Pa. 1910) (control block sold in response to offer to purchase main asset of corporation).

all the shares of the company[12] and the controlling stockholder diverts most or all of the premium to himself by converting the offer for the asset or all the shares to a transaction in which the controlling stockholder sells only his shares to the third party at a substantial premium. In these situations, the courts embrace the idea that the fiduciary obligation of controlling stockholders is not to divert or appropriate for themselves an offer or opportunity that a third-party purchaser is prepared to extend that would benefit all the stockholders proportionally. The language of the American Law Institute's provisions is broad enough to proscribe the controlling stockholder's appropriation of the corporation's opportunity to sell its asset at a premium,[13] but these provisions appear to proscribe the conversion of an offer for all the stockholders' shares only if the controlling stockholder secretly acquires shares from the noncontrolling shareholders as part of his disposition of a control block to a third party.[14]

No case has held, however, that the controlling stockholder breaches its duty by failing actively to initiate transactions that are likely to yield a premium for the noncontrolling stockholders' shares.[15] The controlling stockholder's fiduciary duty with respect to dispositions of control is breached by commission, not omission. One of the most unusual factual settings where this was demonstrated was in *Jones v. H. F. Ahmanson & Company*,[16] where Chief Justice Roger Traynor invoked an equal-opportunity approach, discussed earlier.[17] The case is unique because the opportunity diverted in *Jones* was created by the controlling stockholder rather than by a third party. In *Jones* the individual defendants together held 85 percent of the stock in the United Savings and Loan Association (Association), a closely held corporation whose stock was rarely marketed beyond the original shareholders. Wanting to take advantage of a bullish market for savings and loan stock, the defendants decided to undertake a public offering. The individual defendants formed United Financial as a holding company for their shares in the savings and loan association, and then caused United Financial to make a public offering of its shares. The minority shareholders, who were not allowed to place their stock in the holding company and participate in the offering, filed suit, claiming that the formation of the holding company and the subsequent public offering constituted a breach of the majority's fiduciary duty to the minority shareholders, as the minority shareholders were denied their share of the benefits resulting from the creation of a public market. Chief Justice Traynor, writing for the court, used broad language in upholding the plaintiffs' complaint: "[T]he comprehensive rule of good faith and inherent fairness to the minority in any transaction where

---

[12] Brown v. Halpert, 76 Cal. Rptr. 781 (Ct. App. 1969); Thorpe v. CERBCO, Inc., 676 A.2d 436 (Del. 1996).

[13] ALI, Principles of Corporate Governance, *supra* note 10, §5.12(b)(1).

[14] *Id.* at §5.16(a).

[15] There is no duty to obtain a premium for the minority's shares, even if the controlling stockholder successfully negotiates for a few of the minority to dispose of their shares at the same premium that the controlling stockholder receives. *See* Martin v. Marlin, 529 So. 2d 1174, 1179 (Fl. Dist. Ct. App. 1988).

[16] 460 P.2d 464 (Cal. 1969).

[17] *See* §§11.12, 12.01.

A. Sale of Control and Corporate Office

control of the corporation is material properly governs controlling shareholders in this state."[18] The court accordingly held that the minority shareholders of the savings and loan association were entitled to damages on the basis of what they would have received had they been invited to participate on an equal basis in the formation of the holding company and the subsequent public offering.[19]

Two interesting and distinctive facts in *Jones* were the absence of any finding that the minority stockholders were worse off after United Financial was created by the defendants[20] and that *Jones* is not a true sale-of-control case because the defendants continued to control Association through their control of United Financial. *Jones* is a rare example of a court awarding damages without finding the noncontrolling stockholders or the corporation were worse off after the transaction. The decision appears to be guided by the court's belief that any disproportionate gain the controlling stockholder garners through its controlling position should be proscribed.[21]

When there has been a breach of duty in the transfer of control, the more frequently invoked remedy is to require the vendor of control to disgorge the control premium.[22] The best illustration of this is the classic decision of *Perlman v. Feldman*,[23] where a controlling block of stock to Newport, a producer of steel, had been sold at a premium to Wilport, a consortium of steel users. The court viewed the premium as a bonus for transfer of the ability to control Newport's steel allocation—an especially valuable asset during the war-time shortage.[24] The court therefore ordered that the control premium be disgorged.[25]

The holding is especially interesting in the absence of any finding that Newport had been harmed by Wilport; there was no evidence that Wilport caused Newport to sell its production to Wilport at less than market prices or that Newport's long-term interests were sacrificed to serve the short-term needs of Wilport. For these reasons *Perlman* remains a provocative decision. It should be observed

[18] *Id.* at 474 (emphasis supplied; footnote omitted).

[19] The *Ahmanson* decision was heralded as breaking new ground in even its most narrow reading by "chang[ing] the generally accepted theory of stockholders' fiduciary responsibility." 83 Harv. L. Rev. 1904, 1906 (1970).

[20] There was even reason to conclude the minority were better off after United Financial was created because following its creation they were offered $2,400 for their Association shares, which was greater than the nonmarketable value before United Financial was created.

[21] *See supra* §11.12.

[22] *See, e.g.*, Perlman v. Feldman, 219 F.2d 173, *cert. denied*, 349 U.S. 952 (1955), where it was necessary to also determine the fair value of the shares without their "appurtenant control" over the company's production and marketing. *See* Perlman v. Feldman, 154 F. Supp. 436 (D. Conn. 1957).

[23] 219 F.2d 173 (2d Cir.), *cert. denied*, 349 U.S. 952 (1955).

[24] *Id.* at 178.

[25] On remand, the district court found the enterprise value of the corporation, based on its book value and earnings potential, to be $14.67 per share. This amount was then subtracted from the $20 received by Feldman and his fellow sellers, giving rise to a total premium of $2,126,280. The complaining stockholders, who held 63 percent of the stock, were granted a judgment of $1,339,769, their proportionate amount of the control premium. Perlman v. Feldman, 154 F. Supp. 436 (D. Conn. 1957). This amount was paid directly to the noncontrolling stockholders to assure that Wilport was not benefited, but the defendants were allowed to retain their pro rata share of the premium. *Id.* at 446-447.

that compelling the *Perlman* defendants to disgorge their premium could best be justified on prophylactic considerations: the court reasoned that the defendants had committed at least a technical breach of their fiduciary duties by transferring control to a buyer, about whom there was genuine suspicion that the buyer may well not have been committed to nurturing and protecting the long-term interests of Newport. It is hard to believe, for example, that the court would have required the premium to be disgorged if the defendants had sold control to General Foods or to another buyer who was not an end user of steel. But having sold their shares to an end user of the company's product during a time in which that product was in very short supply and not having inquired as to the future treatment of Newport or its noncontrolling stockholders, there is every reason to find the selling defendants had committed a technical breach of their fiduciary obligations.

It is also possible to recover for any assets or profits lost because of the misbehavior of the new controlling stockholder.[26] The purchaser of control is liable for his vendor's breach on a theory of civil conspiracy.[27]

§12.03   *Resignation of Directors in Connection with the Sale of Control*

In general, a director or other officer, even though elected for a fixed term, may resign at any time with definite notice. Unless a future date or acceptance by the corporation is specified, resignation takes effect at once, and no acceptance is necessary.[1] There are occasions, however, when directors and officers are not free to quit with impunity. It continues to be true today that directors cannot accept payment in any form or guise for their resignations and delivery of control or for the substitution of others in their place, and they are accountable for any monies so received.[2]

The English case of *Gaskell v. Chambers*[3] is the forerunner of the modern-day control premium cases. In *Gaskell*, the premium was in the form of direct compensation to the directors for "the loss of their offices."[4] The court held that the plaintiffs had presented a prima facie case for an accounting of profits and issued an interlocutory order directing the defendants to give up that portion of the purchase price attributable to the sale of their seats on the board of directors.

---

[26] *See* DeBaun v. First W. Bank & Trust Co., 120 Cal. Rptr. 354, 362 (Ct. App. 1975).

[27] Doleman v. Meiji Mut. Life Ins. Co., 727 F.2d 1480 (9th Cir. 1984) (no duty owned directly by purchaser of control for misconduct in transfer of control).

§12.03   [1] DuBois v. Century Cement Prods. Co., 183 A. 188 (N.J. 1936); Western Pattern & Mfg. Co. v. American Metal Shoe Co., 184 N.W. 535 (Wis. 1921).

[2] Mitchell v. Dilbeck, 74 P.2d 233 (Cal. 1937); McClure v. Law, 55 N.E. 388 (N.Y. 1899), *aff'g* 47 N.Y.S. 84 (App. Div. 1897); Gerdes v. Reynolds, 28 N.Y.S.2d 622, 651 (N.Y. Sup. Ct.), s.c., 30 N.Y.S.2d 755 (Sup. Ct. 1941).

[3] 53 Eng. Rep. 937 (Ch. 1858). *Cf.* Snugden v. Crossland, 65 Eng. Rep. 620 (Ch. 1856) (sale of trusteeship revoked).

[4] 53 Eng. Rep. at 937. *See also* Gerdes v. Reynolds, 28 N.Y.S.2d 622 (N.Y. Sup. Ct. 1941).

A. Sale of Control and Corporate Office

The seller of a block of shares may lawfully arrange for sitting directors to resign seriatim and for the nominees of her purchaser to be appointed to the board vacancies created by the resignations, provided the block so transferred represents working control. To be sure, it is always possible for one who purchases control between the annual election of directors to simply wait until the next annual meeting or to seek a special meeting at which the new controlling stockholder's nominees can be elected. This rarely occurs because the new holder of control wishes her influence to be felt immediately. There are sound policy reasons supporting this desire:

> The easy and immediate transfer of corporate control to new interests is ordinarily beneficial to the economy and it seems inevitable that such transactions would be discouraged if the purchaser of a majority stock interest were required to wait some period before his purchase of control could become effective. Conversely, it would greatly hamper the efforts of any existing majority group to dispose of its interests if it could not assure the purchaser of immediate control over corporation operations. I can see no reason why a purchaser of majority control should not ordinarily be permitted to make this control effective from the moment of the transfer of stock.[5]

The above quoted justification is equally sound for a block that represents working control even though it represents less than a majority of the shares.[6] Just such a situation was presented in *Essex Universal Corporation v. Yates*,[7] where the defendant contracted to sell at a premium to the plaintiff more than 28.3 percent of the outstanding shares of Republic Theaters. One clause in the sale agreement provided that the defendant, who was also president and chairman of Republic's board, would resign his offices. The defendant raised the invalidity of the resignation clause and the premium as a defense to the plaintiff's action for breach of

---

[5] Essex Universal Corp. v. Yates, 305 F.2d 572, 578-579 (2d Cir. 1962).

[6] *See, e.g.*, In re Caplan, 246 N.Y.S.2d 913, 915 (N.Y. App. Div.), *aff'd*, 249 N.Y.S.2d 877 (N.Y. 1964). This is true even when those resigning their offices, in connection with the transfer of shares that conferred control upon their buyer, have sold their rights to a proxy/option agreement and in combination agreed to resign as directors and officers. *See* Martin v. Marlin, 529 So. 2d 1174, 1179 (Fl. Dist. Ct. App. 1988).

[7] 305 F.2d 572 (2d Cir. 1962). *See also, e.g.*, Honigman v. Green Giant Co., 309 F.2d 667 (8th Cir. 1962), *cert. denied*, 372 U.S. 941 (1963), where the court refused to disturb an internal recapitalization under which the defendants, as owners of all the voting stock, received a premium as compared to the exchange rate for the complaining, nonvoting shareholders. The plan had been approved by over 90 percent of the nonvoting shares. The court first held that the plaintiff failed to demonstrate Minnesota's adoption of the Berle approach; second, it relied on the subsequent ratification by the holders of nonvoting stock. Professor Berle observed:

> The Green Giant decision held only that under the law of Minnesota, through due corporation procedure for recapitalization, *stockholders* may vote to compensate the holders of voting control for giving it up. It does not, and does not purport to, settle the question whether the holders of control can sell their control without liability to account to the corporation or their fellow stockholders.

Adolf A. Berle, The Price of Power: Sale of Corporate Control, 50 Cornell L.Q. 628, 637 (1965).

the contract. Relying largely on an early New York case, writing separately,[8] Judges Lumbard and Friendly in *Essex Universal Corporation* agreed that directors' agreements to resign were not invalid if they accompanied the transfer of a block that had effective working control, meaning the power to see that a majority of directors were the nominees of the holder of that block of shares.[9]

Thus a provision calling for directors to resign seriatim, with their replacements being the nominees of the purchasing party, is easily upheld when the block of shares transferred constitutes a majority of the voting shares. However, control frequently is exercised by a minority block of shares, especially in public corporations, so that there is not always numerical certainty whether the transferred block will indeed represent voting control in the hands of its purchaser.[10] Courts have had little problem holding that the premium paid for shares representing only 3 percent[11] or 4 percent[12] was in payment for the directors' resignations and not for working control. When, however, the new nominees were reelected at the first stockholders' meeting following their appointment, the court held there was no wrongful sale of a corporate office, even though the block of shares transferred represented only 10 percent of the voting power.[13]

§12.04   Statutory Provisions Affecting Control Transactions

Several states have provisions that empower a stockholder to petition for an election of the directors whenever a majority of the sitting directors have been appointed rather than elected by the stockholders.[1] Such provisions can provide a mechanism for testing whether seriatim resignations and appointments in fact are coupled with a block of shares that represents working control.[2] The true significance of such provisions is that they provide the means for stockholders to reestablish their bond to the board. As a practical matter, such provisions are likely to be invoked only when there is no clear group that represents working control, so that the election can be seen as reestablishing the board as the stockholders' representatives.

Section 14(f) of the Securities Exchange Act of 1934 requires extensive disclosures of the new directors' backgrounds whenever a majority of the board of directors is appointed as a consequence of an arrangement with a person required to make the filings required by the Williams Act amendments to the Securities

---

[8] Barnes v. Brown, 80 N.Y. 527 (1880).

[9] Judge Lumbard in *Essex Universal* added the additional requirement that this power be established on the assumption that management was neutral in the solicitation of the stockholders' votes.

[10] In Insuranshares Corp. v. Northern Fiscal Corp., 35 F. Supp. 22 (E.D. Pa. 1940), the court held 27 percent ownership, when coupled with board membership and incumbency as an officer, represented working control.

[11] In re Caplan, 246 N.Y.S.2d 913 (App. Div.), *aff'd,* 249 N.Y.S.2d 877 (N.Y. 1964).

[12] Brecher v. Gregg, 392 N.Y.S.2d 776 (Sup. Ct. 1975).

[13] Carter v. Muscat, 251 N.Y.S.2d 378 (App. Div. 1964).

§12.04   [1] Cal. Corp. Code §305(c) (West 1990); Del. Code Ann. tit. 8, §223 (2001).

[2] *See* Carter v. Muscat, 251 N.Y.S.2d 378 (App. Div. 1964).

A. Sale of Control and Corporate Office

Exchange Act by virtue of its purchases of, or tender offer for, a corporation's shares.[3] The information must be circulated to all voting stockholders not less than ten days before the directors are to take office.

§12.05 Other Share Transfers That Trigger Fiduciary Obligations — Greenmail and Equal Opportunity Concerns

"Greenmail" has been defined as the purchase at a premium price of a takeover bidder's or dissident's stock that is not available to other stockholders.[1] Several studies have found that the payment of greenmail causes a net decline in the value of the corporation, a decline that can be attributed to the above-market price paid for the shares as well as providing the unmistakable message that the board of directors does not welcome bids for control of the firm. A traditional analysis examines the board's payment of greenmail for evidence the directors have acted unreasonably or in bad faith and places a slightly higher burden on those directors with a direct financial interest served by the preservation of the status quo.[2] The fact that a board's decision to pay greenmail is made in haste and with little evidence that there has been a genuine threat posed by the dissident shareholder provide powerful circumstantial evidence that the true motive of the directors in paying greenmail is to preserve their control.[3] On the other hand, evidence that the dissidents pose a threat to the corporation or its stockholders overcomes any suggestion that the greenmail payment was prompted solely by managerial self-interest.[4] A few states have enacted anti-greenmail provisions that, for example, condition repurchase of shares above a certain percentage upon stockholder approval.[5] Since 1987, greenmail payments have become much less attractive because section 5881 of the Internal Revenue Code of 1986 imposes a 50 percent excise tax of the gain on the shares' resale to the corporation. For the purpose of this provision, "greenmail" is defined as (1) the payment of any consideration by a corporation to acquire its shares from a stockholder when the shares have been held for less than two years; (2) within two years of their purchase the stockholder or those associated with the stockholder made or threatened to make a tender offer for the company's shares; and (3) the buyback offer is not made to all the stockholders. A few states have prohibited greenmail payments unless approved by the stockholders.[6]

---

[3] The Williams Act is triggered when market purchases or a tender offer will bring one's ownership of a class of a reporting company's equity securities above 5 percent. *See generally* David Ratner, Section 14(f): A New Approach to Transfers of Control, 54 Cornell L.Q. 65 (1968).

§12.05 [1] Unocal Corp. v. Mesa Petroleum Co., 493 A.2d 946 (Del. 1985).

[2] *See, e.g.,* Cheff v. Mathes, 199 A.2d 540 (Del. 1964).

[3] *See* Heckman v. Ahmanson, 214 Cal. Rptr. 177 (Ct. App. 1985).

[4] *See* Polk v. Texaco Petroleum Co., 507 A.2d 531 (Del. 1986).

[5] *See, e.g.,* Minn. Stat. Ann. §302A.553(3) (West Supp. 2002); Ariz. Rev. Stat. Ann. §10-2704 (West 1996).

[6] *See, e.g.,* Minn. Stat. Ann. §302A.553(3) (West Supp. 2002); Ariz. Rev. Stat. Ann. §10-2704 (West 1996).

Hostile takeovers are a phenomenon only of publicly traded corporations; greenmail does not arise in closely held corporations. When a close corporation purchases shares at a premium, the corporation has a very different and unique concern: whether all the stockholders should have an opportunity to sell their shares to the corporation at the same price. In a leading case, *Donahue v. Rodd Electrotype Company,*[7] a close corporation purchased shares from one of the controlling stockholders without offering to purchase the minority's holdings at the same price. The court analogized the relationship among owners of a close corporation to the relationship among participants in a partnership. The court thus applied the strict partnership standard, which requires "utmost good faith and loyalty" rather than the "less stringent standard of fiduciary duty" for public corporations.[8] It may be possible to extrapolate from *Donahue* the view that control premiums are a *per se* breach in close corporations.[9] However, the facts of the case are much narrower than its rhetoric. In *Donahue* there was no stated business reason for the corporation's purchase of its controlling stockholder's shares or the board's decision not to extend the offer to the noncontrolling stockholders. The case was simply about a grab for company assets by the company's dominant stockholder and those he had elected to the board. Moreover, because a characteristic of close corporations is the relative illiquidity of its owners' shares, there is every reason to require special justification for excluding noncontrol shares from a deep and rich market for the company's shares when that market is the corporation itself. *Donahue,* however, continues to be relied on for the broad proposition that the minority must be given an equal opportunity to dispose of their shares in the same manner as the controlling stockholder when the close corporation is the purchaser.

As discussed in an earlier chapter,[10] transactions between a director and the corporation will be subject to a fairness scrutiny. Transactions in shares between a controlling shareholder and the corporation will be subject to a similar intrinsic fairness requirement.[11]

B.   INSIDER TRADING

§12.06   *The Insider Trading Debate*

No area of corporate law has sparked more controversy than the question of whether insider trading is unlawful. In a classic work, Henry Manne, relying upon

[7] 328 N.E.2d 505 (Mass. 1975), noted in 61 Cornell L. Rev. 986; 89 Harv. L. Rev. 423 (1975).
[8] 328 N.E.2d at 521.
[9] *See* Hazen, *supra* §12.01 note 2, at 1039-1041.
[10] *See* §§10.09-10.14.
[11] Kahn v. Tremont Corp., 694 A.2d 422 (Del. 1997) (existence of special negotiating committee did not relieve the burden of proving intrinsic fairness where one of the committee members had commercial ties to the controlling shareholder).

B.   Insider Trading

fundamental economic principles, found several justifications for insider trading.[1] He reasoned that insider trading promotes stock price changes and stimulates managerial performance.[2] The connection between insider trading and stock price changes lies in the fact that corporations frequently possess material nonpublic information but cannot promptly publicly disclose the information because premature disclosure will be harmful to the corporation's interests. For example, in *SEC v. Texas GW Sulphur Co.*,[3] a large discovery of copper and zinc near Timmins, Ontario was not disclosed for five months so that the corporation could quietly and cheaply acquire neighboring land. Extensive insider trading occurred in the months between the discovery and the ultimate disclosure; Manne believed such trading was socially useful as it discreetly moved the price of Texas Gulf Sulphur (TGS) shares to their appropriate market price. The rejoinder to this argument comes from those who sold to the TGS insiders and see insider trading as a poor second choice to the insiders either disclosing their information or abstaining from trading. Those who sold TGS shares to insiders received a much lower price for their shares than they would have received had there been full disclosure of the material nonpublic information.

Manne's second argument, that insider trading provides powerful economic incentives for managers to serve the corporate interest, treats insider trading much like a stock option. That is, managers are more likely to engage in useful and rewarding entrepreneurial activity if they are aware they can reap a substantial reward for themselves if their actions produce gains to the firm. Thus, the TGS managers are more likely to aggressively and skillfully guide the exploration for minerals in Timmins, Ontario if they are aware that they can reap substantial gains for themselves by purchasing TGS common shares on their private knowledge that such exploration has yielded a great ore discovery. Hence, insider trading is a means of rewarding the efforts of managers. Professors Fischel and Carlton have even extended this argument to cases where the managers' actions produce a failure rather than a success.[4] They argue that managers should be free to gain from events that decrease as well as increase the value of the firm. Permitting managers to profit on bad news, they argue, is necessary to overcome the managers' aversion to risk; the manager will be more willing to embrace risky ventures if she is aware that should that venture fail she nevertheless will be able to turn the failure into a personal gain.[5] A rejoinder to this "heads I win, tails you lose" view of managerial incentives is the complaint that insider trading will have the effect not simply of making managers risk preferring but risk neutral, such that concern arises whether the managers' insider trading agenda or the corporation's long-term economic interests will predominate in the thinking of managers.[6]

§12.06   [1] Henry Manne, Insider Trading and the Stock Market (1966).

[2] *Id.* at 78-104.

[3] 401 F.2d 833 (2d Cir. 1968), *cert. denied,* 404 U.S. 1005 (1971).

[4] Dennis W. Carlton & Daniel R. Fischel, The Regulation of Insider Trading, 35 Stan. L. Rev. 857 (1983).

[5] *Id.* at 873-876.

[6] *See* James D. Cox, Insider Trading and Contracting: A Critical Response to the "Chicago School," 1986 Duke L.J. 628, 649-653.

The arguments against insider trading, and, therefore, in favor of its contin-ued prohibition focuses on the possible abuses and ill-effects that are likely to fol-low if there were a laissez faire attitude toward insider trading. The most basic complaint against insider trading is that it is unfair for some traders to have mate-rial nonpublic information and others not to have such access, especially when those that do have such access gain it by virtue of their employment. There are many components to the unfairness argument. One is the egalitarian-based notion that there should be "parity" among investors in terms of the information each has access to. It must be observed both that the Supreme Court has rejected the notion that insider trading regulation is premised on the quest for all investors to have the same access to information,[7] and that there are many instances in which the law condones a party's purchasing or selling shares on the basis of infor-mation not available to other investors. A classic example arises in the context of hostile corporate takeovers. The suitor of the target corporation customarily acquires through open market purchases a substantial block of the target corpo-ration's shares, before announcing its public bid to acquire more shares at a price substantially above the earlier market price. The Williams Act amendments to the Securities Exchange Act of 1934, which regulate tender offers, allows this practice, because a public disclosure of the intent to make a bid for the target corporation is not required until 10 days after the bidder has become the owner of more than five percent of the target's shares. An unqualified embrace that all investors should have access to the same information would dampen some of the incentive to create economically valuable information. For example, if the bidder were required to announce in advance of any purchase that it planned to acquire the target company at an above market price this would remove some of the gains the bidder expected to garner through the acquisition and thereby reduce the attrac-tiveness of making the acquisition at all.[8] A refinement of the fairness argument focuses not on the quest for parity among investors, but on the unfairness of allow-ing someone who did not produce the material nonpublic information to trade on that information. Thus, we may well applaud, or at least condone, the bidder secretly entering the market to purchase the target's shares before triggering the level of ownership that requires a Williams Act announcement, and at the same time condemn the bidder's lawyers, investment bankers, or employees purchasing the target shares on their secret, knowledge of their employer's intent to make a public bid for the target. The distinction between the two groups of traders—the bidder and those it employs—is that the bidder is the creator and, hence, the owner of the information on which the trading occurs. The justifications for allow-ing the bidder to trade on its intent to launch an above market bid for the target corporation do not exist, unless one accepts the earlier arguments of Henry Manne.

Another argument that has been invoked to justify insider trading regulation is that if insider trading were legal the company's officers and directors and other

---

[7] Chiarella v. United States, 445 U.S. 222, 233-234 (1980).

[8] *See* Victor Brudney, Insiders, Outsiders, and Informational Advantages Under the Federal Securi-ties Laws, 93 Harv. L. Rev. 322 (1979).

corporate insiders would have powerful incentives to delay the release of material nonpublic information. If insiders could trade on material nonpublic information, the argument goes, they may delay the release of corporation information until they, and their various tippees, have reaped full advantage of their privileged knowledge of the information.[9] Furthermore, insiders may not be content to await the occurrence of really significant economic events that are likely to produce a surge in the stock's price. They may contrive events or disclosures or otherwise manipulate the stock's price to serve their insider trading agenda. Thus, insider trading regulation has been justified as an important prophylactic against tardy disclosure practices or manipulative acts that are harmful to investors.

The broadest justification for insider trading regulation, even broader than the fairness argument, is that if insider trading were lawful the integrity of American capital markets would be severely weakened such that investors are either unwilling to invest in stocks or will demand a higher return. The cause for such a weakening of the market's integrity lies in a perceived linkage between insider trading activity and accuracy and timeliness of corporate disclosures. As discussed in the preceding paragraph, if allowed to trade on material nonpublic information, managers may be tempted to delay the release of significant information or to distort announcements so as to enable the managers to reap larger rewards by trading on their knowledge of the true facts. Investors confronted with such an environment may choose either to withdraw from the markets—they can leave their spare funds in treasury bonds or hidden in their mattresses—or demand a somewhat higher return to compensate them for the special market and disclosure risks that arise because of the possibility of insider trading. With not only the prohibition of insider trading but the aggressive detection and enforcement mechanisms that exist in American capital markets, investors are attracted to American markets and the cost to firms raising capital in those markets is reduced.

§12.07   Common Law Fiduciary Duty of Directors and Officers When Trading in Their Corporation's Shares

The courts are in conflict as to how far and when directors and officers come under a fiduciary duty to disclose inside information to individual shareholders before purchasing their shares. There is a growing tendency to hold officials responsible for taking unfair advantage of the ignorance of selling shareholders by failing to disclose to them non-public corporate information affecting the value of the shares.[1] Nonetheless, the common law has had some difficulty, however, in

---

[9] *See* Cox, *supra* note 6 at 635-637.

§12.07 [1] Though the violation is premised on the defendant's position, such as being an officer or director, with the company, the violation itself is not an act committed in the defendant's capacity as, for example, an officer or director, but in her individual capacity. As such the conduct is properly seen as being outside the standard coverage of the liability policy for "acts performed in the capacity

consistently imposing liability on unscrupulous directors and officers dealing in a faceless market behind the screen of a stock exchange.

What Is Insider Trading? The insider trading problem can be pointed up by the following example. *D,* a director and president of the C Oil Company, knows by virtue of his official position that the corporation, after long efforts, has discovered oil on its land, increasing the value of its assets and its shares many-fold. This discovery is carefully concealed by the management so that the directors themselves can acquire adjoining lands and they and other insiders can buy up as many shares of the company's stock as possible. The shares are listed on a local stock exchange. *D* locates *P,* who is not an insider, and buys certain shares from her privately at the market price, which *D* knows is much less than their actual value. *P* asks no questions, and *D* volunteers no hint of any unusual development. *D* also purchases additional shares from *P* through brokers on the stock exchange before any report of the discovery has been made to the shareholders. Soon the news of the discovery becomes public, and the shares at once quadruple in value. *P,* who would not have sold if she had been informed of the discovery, seeks to have the sales that she made to *D* rescinded or to hold *D* accountable for the profits that *D* gained by his nondisclosure.[2]

Corporate officers and directors when trading in their corporation's shares must refrain from any designed or active misrepresentation by word or act. Pursuant to a view that was once the weight of authority, directors and officers are deemed not to stand in a fiduciary relationship to their opposite traders when trading in their corporation's shares, because individual dealing in shares is not corporate business. Formally, the director's or officer's fiduciary relationship is, under this view, seen as being with the corporation and not its shareholders and certainly not with someone who will not become a shareholder until the challenged transaction is completed. Absent a fiduciary duty to the insider's opposite trader there is no basis upon which to premise a duty to disclose material non-public information known to the insider. On the other hand, a director who acts for the *corporation purchasing its own stock* does have a fiduciary relationship to the selling shareholder.[3]

Early Laissez-Faire Approval. Under the not-a-fiduciary view, corporate insiders are free to trade at arm's length, provided they do not commit a deliberate active fraud for the purpose of procuring the sellers' stock.[4] The not-a-fiduciary cases thus hold that officers and directors need not disclose to selling shareholders important corporate information that they possess—at least not in the

---

of an officer or director." *See, e.g.,* Cincinnati Ins. Co. v. Irwin Co., 2000 WL 1867297 (Ohio Ct. App. Dec. 22, 2000).

[2] An analogous situation arose in the SEC v. Texas Gulf Sulphur Co., 401 F.2d 833 (2d Cir. 1968), *cert. denied,* 394 U.S. 976 (1969), where the defendant insiders had advance knowledge of ore discoveries. This classic insider trading case, decided under the federal securities laws, is discussed *infra* §12.10.

[3] Fleetwood Corp. v. Mirich, 404 N.E.2d 38 (Ind. Ct. App. 1988).

[4] Sometimes, however, when officers or directors fail to disclose information that is significant to the transaction, there is a distinct likelihood their omission will be treated as a *tacit* misrepresentation of the facts. *See* Jim Short Ford Sales, Inc. v. Washington, 384 So. 2d 83, 86-87 (Ala. 1980); Rzepka v. Farm Estates, Inc., 269 N.E.2d 270 (Mich. App. Ct. 1978).

B. Insider Trading

absence of inquiry.[5] As any action by sellers had to be grounded on common law fraud, it was not only active misrepresentation that was required, but also proof of reliance upon the misrepresentation by the selling shareholders thereon in parting with their shares.[6]

The not-a-fiduciary rule unjustly favors unscrupulous and scheming officers and directors who are seeking to take advantage of their positions and official knowledge and are dishonestly concealing favorable information in order to deprive shareholders of the benefit of their holdings. It is a rule of unconscionable laxity that has been condemned by most text writers and commentators as well as by an increasingly large number of the courts. More frequently courts hold that a corporate officer or director is subject to a fiduciary duty to disclose to a shareholder from whom he is purchasing stock any corporate information that materially affects the value of the shares and puts the shareholder at an unfair disadvantage.[7] As will be discussed more fully below, this "modern rule" has continued to gain increasing acceptance and, at least in a qualified form, is generally followed today.[8]

"Special Facts" Doctrine. Not all courts have found it necessary to choose between the rule that officers and directors are always subject to a strict fiduciary duty to the shareholders to volunteer all information and the view that they are always free to trade in their corporation's shares without revealing non-public information. The tendency has been to break down the harsh not-a-fiduciary rule by recognizing exceptions to it in "special facts" or "special circumstances" that give rise to a duty to make disclosure. Circumstances or developments that have been held to constitute "special circumstances" include knowledge by officers or directors of important transactions, such as prospective mergers, probable sales of the entire assets or business, agreements by third parties to buy large blocks of stock at a high price, and impending declarations of unusual dividends.[9] Under such circumstances, it clearly is reasonable to require officials to refrain from taking advantage of the ignorance of the shareholders whom they are supposed to represent and protect. The New York courts, once leaders in maintaining the older position, after first giving cautious recognition of the possibility of imposing an affirmative fiduciary duty of disclosure if the special circumstances are sufficiently strong,[10] now counts among their jurisprudence a far-reaching decision recognizing a strict fiduciary duty.[11]

---

[5] *See, e.g.,* Hardy v. South Bend Sash & Door Co., 603 N.E.2d 895 (Ind. Ct. App. 1992).

[6] *E.g.,* Dupont v. Dupont, 242 F. 98, 136 (D. Del.), *cert. denied,* 250 U.S. 642 (1917).

[7] *See* Oliver v. Oliver, 45 S.E. 232 (Ga. 1903); Dawson v. National Life Ins. Co., 157 N.W. 929 (Iowa 1916): "There is something wrong in any rule which will enable a director legally by his position to obtain for himself alone profits all have won."

[8] *E.g.,* Fisher v. Pennsylvania Life Co., 138 Cal. Rptr. 181 (Ct. App. 1977); Brophy v. Cities Serv. Co., 70 A.2d 5 (Del. Ch. 1969); Blakesley v. Johnson, 608 P.2d 908 (Kan. 1980); Ragsdale v. Kennedy, 209 S.E.2d 494 (N.C. 1974). *Cf.* Diamond v. Oreamuno, 248 N.E.2d 910 (N.Y. 1969).

[9] Lesnik v. Public Indus. Corp., 144 F.2d 968, 977 (2d Cir. 1944); Brophy v. Cities Serv. Co., 70 A.2d 5 (Del. Ch. 1949); Fox v. Cosgriff, 159 P.2d 224, 229 (Idaho 1945); Blakesley v. Johnson, 608 P.2d 908 (Kan. 1980).

[10] Fischer v. Guaranty Trust Co., 18 N.Y.S.2d 328, 333, 334 (App. Div. 1940). *See* Lesnik v. Public Indus. Corp., 144 F.2d 968, 977 (2d Cir. 1944); Goodwin v. Agassiz, 186 N.E. 659 (Mass. 1933).

[11] Diamond v. Oreamuno, 248 N.E.2d 910 (N.Y. 1969).

The "special circumstances" or "special facts" doctrine was applied by the U.S. Supreme Court in a pre-*Erie* decision in the leading case of *Strong v. Repide*.[12] The defendant in that case was the general manager, one of the five directors, and the owner of three-fourths of the shares of a land corporation in the Philippine Islands. He was also the chief negotiator for the sale of the company's lands to the U.S. government and knew of the probable sale of the land at a price that would greatly enhance the value of the shares. Concealing his identity, the defendant obtained the plaintiff's shares through a broker for about one-tenth of what the shares were worth. The Court granted rescission of the sale, holding that the defendant had a duty to disclose to the plaintiff the special facts and circumstances affecting the value of the shares. The defendant's dishonest concealment of his identity as the purchaser was also an element showing bad faith.[13]

Under the "special facts" doctrine, uncertainties exist as to what developments are sufficiently important to call for disclosure of information if the selling shareholder makes no inquiry about developments that affect the value of the shares.[14] Some courts say that an officer or director need not volunteer information as to the prospects of the company or the probability of dividends, but that the official must give truthful answers to such questions as the shareholder asks. At common law, if the official undertakes to inform the selling shareholder, he must speak fully and truthfully and is liable for misleading the seller even by expressions of his opinion.[15] It would seem, however, that the official should also be obliged to speak fully if he seeks out the shareholder and is active in inducing the sale or if he knows of overtures to purchase the corporate property or shares or any other matter that ought in all fairness to be disclosed.[16] Under SEC Rule 10b-5[17] and the federal securities acts' antifraud provisions generally, the test of materiality for both misstatements and omissions is whether the reasonable investor would have considered the fact important if the defendant had disclosed the information to him.[18]

In a leading Kansas case for more demanding disclosure by corporate insiders, *Hotchkiss v. Fisher*,[19] the plaintiff wished to sell her shares if no dividend could

---

[12] 213 U.S. 419 (1909).

[13] For other decisions adopting the special facts doctrine, *see, e.g.*, Fisher v. Pennsylvania Life Co., 138 Cal. Rptr. 464 (Cal. Ct. App. 1977); Lank v. Steiner, 224 A.2d 242 (Del. Ch. 1962); Miller v. Miller, S.W.2d 941 (Tex. Ct. App. 1985); Bailey v. Vaughan, 359 S.E.2d 599 (W. Va. 1987).

[14] Van Schaack v. Van Schaack Holdings, Ltd., 867 P.2d 892, 899 (Colo. 1994) (officer in close corporation had a duty to disclose material facts when purchasing shares from a stockholder and duty breached by his failure to disclose Denver airport would be relocated onto a portion of land owned by the corporation); Waller v. Hodge, 283 S.W. 1047, 1050 (Ky. 1926); Fischer v. Guaranty Trust Co., 18 N.Y.S.2d 328, 333, 334 (App. Div. 1940). *See generally* Wm. K.S. Wang & Marc I. Steinberg, Insider Trading, ch. 16 (1996).

[15] Ragsdale v. Kennedy, 209 S.E.2d 494 (N.C. 1974); Poole v. Camden, 92 S.E. 454 (W. Va. 1916); Schroeder v. Carroll, 212 N.W. 299 (Wis. 1927).

[16] *See* Hayes v. Kelley, 112 F.2d 897, 901 (9th Cir. 1940).

[17] 17 C.F.R. §240.10b-5 (2002), discussed *infra*.

[18] *See* TSC Indus. v. Northway, Inc., 426 U.S. 438, 449 (1976) (decided under federal proxy rules).

[19] 16 P.2d 531 (Kan. 1932), noted in 46 Harv. L. Rev. 847 (1933), s.c., 31 P.2d 37 (Kan. 1934). *Hotchkiss* has been said to reflect a "strict accountability" rule. Amen v. Black, 234 F.2d 12 (10th Cir. 1956). *See also* Blakesley v. Johnson, 608 P.2d 908 (Kan. 1980).

reasonably be expected in the near future. She sought the advice of *D*, the corporation's president and a director. He declined to express an opinion on whether dividends would be declared at the upcoming meeting of the directors but furnished the plaintiff with copies of the corporation's last financial statements. *D* purchased the plaintiff's shares for $1.25 per share. A week or so later the directors declared a dividend of $1.00 a share. The shareholder sued for damages. The court imposed a strict fiduciary rule, holding it was not sufficient to protect the officer based on the fact that he had truthfully answered the questions the plaintiff had asked. *D* was obligated to point out the significance of the data on the financial statements and volunteer any information that he had bearing on the likelihood of a dividend declaration, such as large earning capacity, large surplus, and liquid assets. The American Law Institutes adopts the approach taken by *Hotchkiss*.[20]

There is a problem as to purchases of listed shares by directors and officers through the medium of a stock exchange, as is pointed out in the leading Massachusetts decision of *Goodwin v. Agassiz*.[21] Purchases and sales of shares of stock through brokers on a stock exchange are commonly impersonal affairs. Because the buyer and seller are anonymous, it is not practicable for an officer or director to make a personal disclosure to the buyer or for the buyer to request such a disclosure. *Goodwin* therefore held that given the impersonal nature of the trade between the plaintiff and the defendant, insiders owe no fiduciary duty to disclose their private knowledge of material information about the company. The formalism of the *Goodwin* court's reasoning leaves much to be desired. Any disclosure complications should not confer complete immunity on an officer or director who purchases his company's shares through a stock exchange. If the officer or director is one of the corporate officials implicated in a dishonest or willful failure to report to the shareholders information they need for their guidance, particularly if the nondisclosure is for the very purpose of buying shares for or taking other advantage of outside shareholders or the corporation, he may well be held accountable to the selling shareholders. Dishonest officers or directors should not find absolution from retributive justice by concealing their identity from their victims under the mask of the stock exchange.[22]

Corporate Recovery of Ill-Gotten Gains. The preceding discussion has focused on the duty of candor that officers and directors owe to their sellers or buyers when trading on non-public information. A very distinct duty question is whether the fiduciary breaches his duty *to his corporate employer* when he trades on material non-public information acquired by virtue of his relationship to the corporation.

---

[20] *See* 2 A.L.I., Principles of Corporate Governance: Analysis and Recommendations §5.04(a) (1992).

[21] 186 N.E. 659 (Mass. 1933), noted in 47 Harv. L. Rev. 353 (1933).

[22] *See* Adolf A. Berle, Studies in Corporation Finance, ch. 9, at 177, 184-185 (1928); Adolf A. Berle, Publicity of Accounts and Directors' Purchases of Stock, 25 Mich. L. Rev. 827, 835, 836 (1927); Comment, Duty of Director to Stockholder in Stock Exchange Sales, 32 Mich. L. Rev. 678 (1934); Note, 19 Cornell L.Q. 103 (1933). *But cf.* I. Beverley Lake, The Use for Personal Profit of Knowledge Gained While a Director, 9 Miss. L.J. 427, 453 (1937).

This question was addressed in an early Delaware decision[23] involving a "confidential secretary" who had advance knowledge of a corporation's plans to purchase its own stock on the open market. Armed with this knowledge, the secretary purchased stock on his own account, which he resold at a profit when the information became public. The court allowed the corporation to recover the secretary's profit and explicitly stated that no loss or damage to the corporation by the secretary's trading needed to be alleged.[24] The court reasoned that the fiduciary duty the secretary owed the corporation and the agency doctrine that a principal is entitled to recover from an agent the profits ("fruits") arising out of the agency. The *sine qua non* of a fiduciary's breach in all cases is that the fiduciary traded on the basis[25] of material non-public information[26] that was acquired through a relationship of trust and confidence with the corporation.[27] The fiduciary obligation so recognized is broad enough to include trading in another corporation's shares as long as the information used in so trading was acquired through the defendant's relationship to the plaintiff corporation.[28] The key to understanding the corporation's recovery of its fiduciary's insider trading profits is that the fiduciary has acted in a manner inconsistent with the trust placed in him by the corporation that the information be used for corporate and not private purposes. Or, stated somewhat differently, disgorgement to the corporation is a necessary disincentive to the fiduciary not to compromise the relationship of trust by extracting non-consented-to benefits from the relationship. Note that the source of the fiduciary obligation is not just the defendant's position in the company, but the access that position provides him to confidential corporate information. Once the defendant has achieved access to such information he should be bound not to compromise either its confidentiality or the trust placed in him by trading on the basis of that information.

In a leading case, *Diamond v. Oreamuno*,[29] the New York Court of Appeals held that the corporation may recover the insider trading profits of two senior officers who traded on material non-public information they acquired through their corporate positions. The court held the corporation could recover the ill-gotten gains of its fiduciaries without proof the corporation had been harmed by the insider trading (although the court did acknowledge the likelihood of a reputational injury is likely to be suffered by any corporation whose high-ranking officers abuse their positions by trading on inside information). In contrast, there is no breach of duty, however, when the board of directors has authorized a selective disclosure

[23] Brophy v. Cities Serv. Co., 70 A.2d 5 (Del. Ch. 1949). *See generally* Douglas M. Branson, Choosing the Appropriate Default Rule—Insider Trading Under State Law, 45 Ala. L. Rev. 753 (1994).

[24] In so ruling, the court relied on Restatement of Restitution §200 comment a (1937) and Austin Wakeman Scott, The Law of Trusts §505.1 (1939).

[25] *See* Polin v. Conductron, 552 F.2d 797 (8th Cir. 1977) (sold not because of content of information but because needed cash for new business).

[26] *See, e.g.*, Thomas v. Boblin Indus., 520 F.2d 1393 (3d Cir. 1975) (information of company's problems publicly available); Katz Corp. v. T. H. Canty & Co., 362 A.2d 975 (Conn. 1975) (information had been disclosed).

[27] *See* Walton v. Morgan Stanley & Co., 623 F.2d 796 (2d Cir. 1980).

[28] *See, e.g.*, Cambridge Fund v. Abella, 501 F. Supp. 598 (S.D.N.Y. 1980); Gottlieb v. McKee, 107 A.2d 240 (Del. 1954).

[29] 248 N.E.2d 919 (N.Y. 1969).

B. Insider Trading

of material non-public information for the purpose of encouraging a third party to purchase the company's securities.[30]

Not all courts, however, interpret the corporation's rights to recover its fiduciary's insider trading profits. For example, the Florida Supreme Court held in *Schein v. Chasen*[31] that the corporation may recover its directors' and officers' profits made through trading on inside information obtained through their corporate positions only if the corporation is able to prove it was harmed because of its fiduciary's trading. The result in *Schein* thus rejects the position taken in cases such as *Diamond* that disgorgement is needed as a necessary prophylaxis to deter breaches that *could possibly* harm the corporation. A very different approach was taken by the federal court in *Freeman v. Decio*,[32] which held that under the law of the state of the corporation's formation, Indiana, the corporation may recover the insider trading profits of its fiduciaries only when the fiduciary's trading can be seen as being in competition with the corporation's power secretly to use that information to its own advantage. Under this approach, executives who, similar to the facts of *Diamond*, sell their shares on their secret knowledge that the corporation's income had declined substantially would likely not be liable to the corporation for their profits (i.e., the difference between the price at which the shares were sold and the lower shares' price following disclosure of the decline in the corporation's income) since it is difficult to envision how the corporation could have used such information to its advantage. Moreover, the Second Circuit opined that New Jersey likely would not recognize a corporate recover of its insider's profits absent injury to the corporation.[33]

As a practical matter, the state insider trading law is today largely eclipsed by the extensive development of insider trading regulation that has occurred under the federal securities laws.[34] The same can be said of state Blue Sky laws application to insider trading.[35] Commentators have noted, for example, that state common law has been "overshadowed if not superseded" by Section 10(b) of the Securities Exchange Act of 1934.[36]

---

[30] *See* Frigitemp Corp. v. Financial Dynamics Fund, Inc., 524 F.2d 275 (2d Cir. 1975).

[31] 313 So. 2d 739 (Fla. 1975). *Schein* has an interesting procedural history. Suit was initiated in the federal court where on appeal the Second Circuit allowed recovery, relying on *Diamond*. Schein v. Chasen, 478 F.2d 817 (2d Cir. 1973). This decision was vacated by the Supreme Court on the ground the Second Circuit gave insufficient consideration to certifying to the Florida Supreme Court, the corporation's domicile, the question whether disgorgement would be required under Florida law. *See* Lehman Bros. v. Schein, 416 U.S. 386 (1974).

[32] 584 F.2d 186 (7th Cir. 1978).

[33] *See* Frankel v. Slotkin, 984 F.2d 1328, 1337 (2d Cir. 1993). An additional basis for possible dismissal of the corporate recovery absent proof of harm to the corporation is fear of subjecting the defendant to duplicate recoveries. *See* In re Symbol Technologies Sec. Lit., 762 F. Supp. 510, 518 (E.D.N.Y. 1991). If the corporate recovery is driven solely by the desire to remove the ill-gotten gains of the breach, dismissal appears to be the correct result for the court to reach.

[34] *See* §§12.08-12.12.

[35] *See, e.g.*, Cal. Corp. Code §§25402, 25502, 25502.5 (West 2001); New York Gen. Bus. Law §352-c (McKinney 1986) (the Martin Act however does not provide injured investors with a private cause of action per CPC Intl. Inc. v. McKesson Corp., 514 N.E.2d 116, 118-19 (N.Y. 1987); Uniform Securities Act §410(h) (1956) (parallels language of Rule 10b-5 of the Securities Exchange Act).

[36] William L. Cary & Melvin A. Eisenberg, Corporations Cases & Materials 714 (5th unab. ed. 1980).

II. FEDERAL LAW

A. SHORT-SWING PROFITS

§12.08   Short-Swing Profits Under Section 16
of the Securities Exchange Act

Directors and officers of publicly traded companies are not ordinarily held accountable to the corporation for profits made in the purchase and sale of its shares unless they have taken unfair advantage of information that equitably belonged to the corporation.[1] To prevent the unfair use of inside information for the purpose of speculation, Congress has provided in section 16 of the Securities Exchange Act of 1934 (as amended),[2] that every person who is a director, officer, or beneficial owner of more than 10 percent of any class of "equity security" that is registered pursuant to section 12 of that Act[3] must file a statement and report each month the changes of ownership that have occurred during that month as to such securities. Any profit realized from any "purchase and sale" or "sale and purchases" of any such equity security within a period of less than six months is recoverable by the issuer without the need of proving unfair use of official information.[4] Section 16 is intended to be a prophylaxis for such trading.[5] The remedy provided in Section 16 in no way restricts the sanction or recovery that can be obtained pursuant to state law or other provisions of the federal securities law.

Under the early cases, the federal courts consistently interpreted 16(b) to require an objective and mechanical application. The statute continues to be read literally, without a pragmatic eye toward its purpose, except when the transaction is other than a standard securities transaction. When the transaction is of an extraordinary nature in the sense that it does not, for example, fall literally within the common definition of "sale" or "purchase," the courts apply a subjective, pragmatic test pursuant to which they inquire whether the circumstances were such

---

§12.08   [1] *E.g.,* Weigel v. Shapiro, 608 F.2d 268 (7th Cir. 1979); Bisbee v. Midland Linseed Prods. Co., 19 F.2d 24 (8th Cir.), *cert. denied,* 275 U.S. 564 (1927).

[2] 15 U.S.C. §§78p(a), 78p(b) (2000). *See generally* Donald C. Cook & Myer Feldman, Insider Trading Under the Securities Exchange Act, 66 Harv. L. Rev. 385, 612 (1953); Thomas L. Hazen, The New Pragmatism Under Section 16(b) of the Securities Exchange Act, 54 N.C. L. Rev. 1 (1975).

[3] The Securities Exchange Act, as amended, requires that an issuer register its securities pursuant to section 12 of that act if the issuer is listed on a national exchange or has total assets exceeding $10 million and a class of equity security held of record by 500 or more persons. The Securities and Exchange Commission has promulgated a number of exemptions to registration under the section to alleviate the burdens imposed on small business. *See* Exchange Act Rule 12g-1, 17 C.F.R. §240.12g-1 (2002).

[4] 15 U.S.C. §78p(b) (2000).

[5] For a more modern and perhaps revisionist's view of what Congress may have been about when it enacted Section 16(b), *see* Okamato, Rereading Section 16(b) of the Securities Exchange Act, 27 Ga. L. Rev. 183 (1992); Steve Thel, The Genious of Section 16: Regulating the Management of Publicly Held Corporations, 42 Hastings L.J. 393 (1991).

that the defendant might have had access to inside information when she traded.[6] The courts have thus employed a more subjective analysis in such non-cash non-garden variety transactions as mergers, share exchanges, and exercises of stock options. Similarly, a case-by-case analysis has also been used when trying to determine whether someone who is denominated an officer in fact should be given officer status within the context of section 16(b)'s prophylactic provisions. In such cases, before applying 16(b) liability, the courts have looked to the potential for speculative abuse. Section 16(b) was aimed at a particular type of abuse—namely, those instances in which an insider could make a sure-thing short-swing profit by entering into transactions in anticipation of price changes that would lead to a profit at the second stage of the short-swing transaction. In other words, the section was aimed at discouraging insiders from speculating in their own company's stock especially when such speculation is based on special knowledge of facts soon to be made public. Notwithstanding the section's apparent objectivity and supposed ease of application, a number of section 16(b) issues have resulted in protracted litigation. Thus the statute falls far short of providing a predictable rule of thumb.[7]

Section 16(b)'s provisions are enforceable solely by means of private litigation, pursuant to the section's self-contained cause of action, a hybrid cause of action that lies somewhere between a derivative suit and a direct action. There is exclusive federal jurisdiction over such suits. The plaintiff shareholder must demand that the corporation sue, and the corporation can bring suit. However, if the corporation fails to respond within 60 days, the shareholder can initiate the suit with any recovery going to the corporation. Unlike the standard derivative suit, a good faith determination by the board of directors that the suit should not be prosecuted cannot bar the shareholder from maintaining the suit to recover short-swing profits. Moreover, the section does not contain a requirement that the plaintiff have been a shareholder at the time of the trading transactions in question.[8] Since the suit can be either at equity or in law, the plaintiff has a choice of whether or not to have a jury trial.[9]

One of the more perplexing 16(b) issues has revolved around the statutory definitions of "purchase" and "sale." For example, an early case[10] held that the exercise of conversion rights[11] constituted a 16(b) purchase. Two courts of appeal

---

[6] *See* 2 Louis Loss & Joel Seligman, Securities Regulation 1040-1045 (3d ed. 1989); Hazen, *supra* note 2; Lewis D. Lowenfels, Section 16(b): A New Trend in Regulating Insider Trading, 54 Cornell L. Rev. 45 (1968).

[7] *See* Hazen, *supra* note 2; Note, Exceptions to Liability Under Section 16(b): A Systematic Approach, 87 Yale L.J. 1430 (1978). The most striking example is found in Gold v. Sloan, 486 F.2d 340 (4th Cir. 1973), *cert. denied,* 419 U.S. 873 (1974), where the same transaction resulted in section 16(b) liability as to some statutory insiders but not as to others.

[8] In contrast, such a contemporaneous ownership rule generally applies to shareholder derivative suits—*e.g.,* Fed. R. Civ. P. 23.1. *See* Chapter 15.

[9] Arbetman v. Playford & Alaska Airlines, Inc., 83 F. Supp. 335 (S.D.N.Y. 1949); Dottenheim v. Emerson Elec. Mfg. Co., 7 F.R.D. 343 (E.D.N.Y. 1947).

[10] Park & Tilford, Inc. v. Schulte, 160 F.2d 984 (2d Cir.), *cert. denied,* 332 U.S. 871 (1947).

[11] Either preferred stock or debentures may contain conversion rights that allow the security holder at her option to "convert" her holdings into the underlying security pursuant to a predetermined formula.

subsequently took the contrary position and held 16(b) inapplicable.[12] The question of the status of conversions remained in doubt[13] until the adoption of SEC Rule 16b-9, which provides that generally a conversion constitutes neither a sale nor a purchase.[14]

In *Kern County Land Company v. Occidental Petroleum Corporation*,[15] the Court eschewed an objective approach and opted for a pragmatic analysis.[16] In *Kern County*, the management of the target company opposed a takeover by Occidental Petroleum and reacted with a defensive merger with Tenneco Corporation. As a result of the merger, Occidental was to receive Tenneco preferred stock. Occidental, not wanting to own an interest in one of its competitors, issued to Tenneco an option to repurchase the Tenneco preferred. More than six months after both the purchase by Occidental of the Old Kern stock and Occidental's acquisition via the exchange of the Tenneco stock, Tenneco exercised the option.

Kern County asserted that 16(b) required Occidental to disgorge its short-swing profits. The court thus had to decide (1) whether Occidental's disposition of the Kern stock in exchange for the Tenneco preferred was a sale and (2) whether the subsequent option arrangement resulted in a sale within six months of the purchase. The district court held that Occidental's acquisition of Tenneco stock pursuant to the Old Kern-Tenneco merger was a section 16(b) "sale" within six months of its purchase pursuant to the original tender offer and, further, that the subsequent option agreement was a second "sale" also within the reach of section 16(b).[17] On appeal, the Second Circuit reversed, reasoning that the exchange pursuant to the merger could not properly be classified as a 16(b) "sale" because there had been no potential for speculative abuse, and the court also found that the option did not violate section 16(b).[18] The Supreme Court followed the court of appeals and took a pragmatic approach:

> In deciding whether borderline [unorthodox] transactions are within the reach of the statute, the courts have come to inquire whether the transaction may serve as a vehicle for the evil which Congress sought to prevent—the realization of short-swing profits based upon access to inside information—thereby endeavor-

[12] Petteys v. Butler, 367 F.2d 528 (8th Cir. 1966), *cert. denied*, 385 U.S. 1006 (1967); Feraiolo v. Newman, 259 F.2d 342 (6th Cir. 1958), *cert. denied*, 359 U.S. 927 (1959). Potter Stewart's opinion in the *Feraiolo* case has been identified as the first of the so-called pragmatic decisions. *See supra* note 7.

[13] *See* Blau v. Lamb, 363 F.2d 507 (2d Cir.), *cert. denied*, 385 U.S. 1002 (1967) (conversion not a sale); Heli-Coil v. Webster, 352 F.2d 156 (3d Cir. 1965) (conversion is sale of convertible security and purchase of underlying security); Blau v. Max Factor & Co., 342 F.2d 304 (9th Cir.), *cert. denied*, 382 U.S. 982 (1965) (conversion not a purchase).

[14] 17 C.F.R. §240.16b-9 (2002). *See* Sidney F. Davis, Conversions as Purchases and Sales under Section 16(b) of the Securities Exchange Act of 1934, 24 Bus. Law. 1109 (1969).

[15] 411 U.S. 582 (1973).

[16] *See generally* Thomas L. Hazen, The New Pragmatism Under Section 16(b) of the Securities Exchange Act, 54 N.C.L. Rev. 1 (1975).

[17] Abrams v. Occidental Petroleum Corp., 323 F. Supp. 570, 579-580 (S.D.N.Y. 1980).

[18] It also rejected the alternative of classifying the option agreement as a "sale" because Occidental's obligation to dispose of the shares had not been fixed until Tenneco exercised the option more than six months later.

ing to implement congressional objectives without extending the reach of the statute beyond its intended limits.[19]

The sale or purchase occurs when the seller's or purchaser's obligations become fixed, which is customarily when the price and number of shares are determined.[20]

Following the Supreme Court's lead, the trend toward pragmatism has continued to flourish in defining "purchase" and "sale" in unorthodox transactions. One court has gone so far as to apply 16(b) to certain statutory insiders but not to others in the same transaction.[21] Thus, for example, in the context of a negotiated merger, a director of one of the constituent companies who was actively involved in the merger negotiations was held to have been subject to section 16(b)'s disgorgement provisions, while an outside director was not.[22] The court reasoned that the outside director, who did not participate in the merger negotiations, did not have access to the type of information that could be the basis of the type of "sure thing" speculation that section 16(b) was designed to prevent.

Another significant 16(b) issue is the question of who is a statutory insider. For example, where a corporation appoints or deputizes one of its officers or directors to sit on another corporation's board, that individual's insider status may be attributed to the deputizing body.[23] Similarly, notwithstanding the maintenance of separate brokerage accounts and different investment advisers, a spouse's sale may be matched with an insider's purchase to find a 16(b) profit.[24] Similarly, questions arise about what constitutes a "class" of securities for the purpose of calculating whether the defendant is an owner of more than 10 percent of a class.[25]

The SEC has invoked its rule-making power to clarify the meaning of "beneficial ownership." The rules are directed at those persons who can exercise sufficient control over the company's management to justify presuming access to inside information.[26] The tests of beneficial ownership the SEC uses for

---

[19] 411 U.S. at 594-595 (footnote omitted). The Court acknowledged some continued adherence to the objective approach of *Park & Tilford* and *Heli-Coil* (*see supra* notes 10, 13) but concluded that "[b]y far the greater weight of authority is to the effect that a 'pragmatic' approach to 16(b) will best serve the statutory goals." *Id.* at 594 n.26.

[20] Magma Power Co. v. Dow Chemical Co., 136 F.3d 316 (2d Cir. 1998) (shares purchased when option acquired that set forth price and amount of shares and not later when option exercised).

[21] Gold v. Sloan, 486 F.2d 340 (4th Cir. 1973), noted in 42 Fordham L. Rev. 852 (1974).

[22] *Id.*

[23] Feder v. Martin Marietta Corp., 406 F.2d 260 (2d Cir. 1969). *See also, e.g.*, Blau v. Lehman, 368 U.S. 403 (1962) (partnership); Popkin v. Dingman, 366 F. Supp. 534 (S.D.N.Y. 1973). *See* Carroll L. Wagner, Jr., Deputization under Section 16(b): The Implications of *Feder v. Martin Marietta Corporation*, 78 Yale L.J. 1151 (1969).

[24] Whiting v. Dow Chem. Co., 523 F.2d 680 (2d Cir. 1975).

[25] *See, e.g.*, Morales v. Freund, 163 F.3d 763 (2d Cir. 1999) (class A preferred shares were separate class where their vote would have been sufficient to block company's reorganization).

[26] The SEC observed that, as is the case with the 5 percent reporting requirements of the Williams Act (§13(d), 15 U.S.C. §78m(d)) (2000), "[s]ection 16, as applied to ten percent holders, is intended to reach those persons who can be presumed to have access to inside information because they can influence or control the issuer as a result of their equity ownership." Sec. Exch. Act Rel. No. 34-28869 [1990-1991 Transfer Binder] Fed. Sec. L. Rep. (CCH) ¶84,709 (Feb. 8, 1991).

determining reporting obligations are different from those it uses to decide whether purchases and sales should be matched for the purpose of requiring the disgorgement of short-swing profits. Once 10 percent beneficial holder status is determined, section 16's reporting and short-swing profit provisions apply only to securities in which the insider has a direct or indirect pecuniary interest.

Rule 16a-2(a)(2)[27] begins by setting forth the basic rule that for reporting purposes beneficial ownership hinges on the direct or indirect pecuniary interest in the shares, and that interest may be the result of "any contract, arrangement, understanding, relationship, or otherwise." This includes the opportunity to participate, directly or indirectly, in any profit attributable to transactions in the shares in question. The rule then goes on to list examples of "indirect pecuniary interest" that trigger section 16. Securities held by immediate family members sharing the same household are included. A general partner's proportional interest in securities held by a general or limited partnership is similarly included. In contrast, a shareholder does not have a pecuniary interest in the portfolio securities held by a corporation, limited partnership, or similar entity, as long as he is not a controlling shareholder of the entity and neither has nor shares investment control over the entity's portfolio securities.

Because of the breadth of the beneficial ownership rules, section 16 problems arise when X joins with Y and Z to sell their Alpha shares for Beta shares pursuant to a lock up agreement imposed by Beta whereby for a period of two years they were barred from disposing of the shares. Though X's interest in the Beta shares was less than 2.5 percent, the combined Beta holdings of the three constituted 18 percent of Beta's outstanding shares. While the shares were subject to the agreement, X individually engaged in a number of trades in Beta shares. The Second Circuit,[28] rejecting the view that beneficial ownership by a group required proof of an intent to acquire control, remanded the case for further findings whether X, Y, and Z had combined for the common objective of "acquiring" or "holding" shares as provided by the beneficial ownership rule that is applicable to groups.[29] If so, Section 16(b) liability would arise from X's trades.

The question of who is an "officer" or "director" may also lead to a fact inquiry insofar as those terms include persons performing similar functions.[30] An analysis of

---

Courts refer to the rules that the SEC has adopted for Section 13(d) for guidance in resolving who is a beneficial owner. *See* Morales v. Freund, 163 F.3d 763 (2d Cir. 1999).

[27] 17 C.F.R. §240.16a-2(a)(2) (2002).

[28] *See* Morales v. Quintel Entertainment, Inc., 249 F.3d 115 (2d cir. 2001).

[29] Rule 13d-5, 17 C.F.R. §240.13d-5 (2002). *See generally* General Aircraft Corp. v. Lampert, 556 F.2d 90 (1st Cir. 1977) (finding a group for section 13d-3 purposes).

For a more restrained approach to the role under section 16(b) of membership in a group, *see* Rosenberg v. XM Ventures and Matient Corp., 274 F.3d 137 (3d Cir. 2001) (must have owned shares before becoming member of the group; group membership and subsequent trading is insufficient for liability); Rosen v. Brookhaven Capital Management Co., 113 F. Supp. 2d 615 (S.D.N.Y. 2000) (investment professional fell within exemption in Rule 16a-1(a)(1) for shares held as representative capacity if shares acquired without intent to control issuer and the exemption is not lost by also being a member of a group that beneficially owned more the ten percent).

[30] The Ninth Circuit has held that where a company had 350 executive vice presidents, the title merely created an inference of "opportunities for confidential information." Merrill Lynch, Pierce,

A. Short-Swing Profits

the relevant cases reveals that when an employee, although denominated an officer, does not possess the type of executive power or decision-making authority likely to give him or her access to inside information, section 16(b) will not be held applicable.[31] This pragmatic analysis is supported by SEC rule-making that provides that section 16 applies to executive officers[32]—that is, those who are clothed with policymaking authority. The focus thus is not on a person's title but whether in discharging his or her duties the individual is likely to obtain information that would be helpful in avoiding the risks ordinarily associated with short-swing speculation.[33]

In *Foremost-McKesson, Inc. v. Provident Securities Company*,[34] the Supreme Court held that a 10 percent beneficial owner was not subject to the Act until after that status was achieved; thus the threshold purchase was not covered by 16(b). This test is met, however, when the holder of a security convertible into more than 10 percent of the outstanding common shares converts into the common and disposes of some of the common shares so acquired within six months of the conversion.[35] In contrast to the treatment of owners of more than ten percent, the difference in statutory language for officers and directors led the Second Circuit to apply a stricter rule, holding that officers and directors fall within section 16(b) if they have that status at the time of either purchase or sale.[36] As part of its massive rule-making initiatives in 1992, the SEC has clarified its position on this issue. Transactions by officers and directors prior to taking office do not have section 16 implications.[37] Transactions occurring within the six months after leaving office

---

Fenner & Smith, Inc. v. Livingston, 566 F.2d 1119, 1122 (9th Cir. 1978). The court went on to say that the defendant vice president was not subject to section 16(b) liability because he met the burden of proof "that the title was merely honorary and did not carry with it any of the executive responsibilities that might otherwise be assumed." *Id. See also, e.g.*, Pier 1 Imports of Ga., Inc. v. Wilson, 529 F. Supp. 239, 244 (N.D. Tex. 1981).

The current SEC rules take the position that section 16 should not be applied to individuals who are officers only in name. 17 C.F.R. §240.16a-1(f) (2002). In essence, the rules limit section 16 obligations to executive officers who are truly in policymaking positions. Merrill Lynch, Pierce, Fenner & Smith, Inc. v. Livingston, 566 F.2d 1119 (9th Cir. 1978) (title of "vice president" raises only an inference of 16(b) insider status); Colby v. Klune, 178 F.2d 872 (2d Cir. 1949) ("production manager" may be a 16(b) officer); Selas Corp. of Am. v. Voogd, 365 F. Supp. 1268 (E.D. Pa. 1973) ("executive vice president" subject to 16(b)); Lockheed Aircraft Corp. v. Campbell, 110 F. Supp. 282 (S.D. Cal. 1953) (assistant treasurer and assistant secretary not subject to 16(b)); Lockheed Aircraft Corp. v. Rathman, 106 F. Supp. 810 (S.D. Cal. 1952) (assistant treasurer not subject to 16(b)). *See generally* David E. Gardels, Comment, Section 16(b) of the Securities and Exchange Act of 1934: Is a Vice President an Officer?, 58 Neb. L. Rev. 733 (1979).

[31] Merrill Lynch, Pierce, Fenner & Smith, Inc. v. Livingston, 566 F.2d 1119, 1122 (9th Cir. 1978). *See also, e.g.*, Pier 1 Imports of Georgia, Inc. v. Wilson, 529 F. Supp. 239, 244 (N.D. Tex. 1981); Schimmel v. Goldman, 57 F.R.D. 481 (S.D.N.Y. 1973).

[32] Rule 16a-1(f) includes in the definition of "executive officer" the president, any vice president in charge of a principal unit or division, and the principal financial and accounting officers, as well as any other officer who performs a policymaking function. 17 C.F.R. §240.16a-1(f) (2002).

[33] Sec. Exch. Act Rel. No. 34-28869 [1990-1991 Transfer Binder] Fed. Sec. L. Rep. (CCH) ¶84,709 (Feb. 8, 1991), relying on Colby v. Klune, 178 F.2d 872, 873 (2d Cir. 1949).

[34] 423 U.S. 232 (1976).

[35] *See* Medtex Scientific, Inc. v. Morgan Capital LLC, 258 F.3d 763 (8th Cir. 2001).

[36] Adler v. Klawans, 267 F.2d 840 (2d Cir. 1959).

[37] 17 C.F.R. §240.16a-2(a) (2002).

may be matched against purchases or sales occurring while the officer or director was still in office.[38]

In 2002, Congress amended Section 16(a) to provide for trades to be disclosed within two days unless the SEC prescribes if it believes this time period "is not feasible."[39]

B.   THE ANTIFRAUD PROVISION OF THE SECURITIES EXCHANGE ACT

§12.09   Section 10(b) and Rule 10b-5 of the Securities Exchange Act of 1934

The 1929 stock market crash, and the fraudulent stock promotions that played a contributing role, provided the impetus for federal regulation. The Securities Act of 1933[1] and the Securities Exchange Act of 1934[2] were enacted to regulate the initial distribution of securities—day-to-day securities trading activities and the securities markets in general. While state general corporation laws are concerned with corporate chartering and the protection of the shareholders' proprietary interest, the federal and state securities laws are geared to investor protection.[3] The Securities Act of 1933 or "Truth in Securities" Act requires registration and full disclosure for all nonexempt securities distributions.[4] In contrast, the Securities Exchange Act of 1934 is directed at a range of securities market abuses as well as seeking full and fair disclosure in connection with trading in securities. Overall, the 1934 Act seeks to maintain the integrity of the securities markets by regulating exchanges[5] and broker-dealers.

The Exchange Act contains several provisions that are of importance to a corporate attorney who does not specialize in securities law. For example, as has been discussed in the preceding section, the Act provides that insider short-swing profits "shall inure to and be recoverable by the issuer."[6] The Act also regulates prac-

---

[38] 17 C.F.R. §240.16a-2(b) (2002).

[39] *See* Section 403 of the Sarbanes-Oxley Act, Pub. L. No. 107-204 (July 30, 2002), *amending* 15 U.S.C. §78p(a) (2000).

§12.09   [1] Act of May 27, 1933, ch. 38, tit. 1, 48 Stat. 881 (1933) (current version at 15 U.S.C. §§77a-77bbbb (2000).

[2] Act of June 6, 1934, ch. 404, 48 Stat. 881 (1933) (current version at 15 U.S.C. §§77a-78bb-1 (2000).

[3] Although some states had enacted securities acts as far back as 1911, these laws proved ineffective against much of the pervasive securities frauds. The scope of both the state and federal regulatory schemes is discussed in Chapter 27. Helpful treatises in this area include the multivolume work by Professors Loss and Seligman, Loss & Seligman, *supra* §12.08 note 6, and Thomas Lee Hazen, Treatise on the Law of Securities Regulation (4th ed. 2002).

[4] *Cf.* Milton H. Cohen, Truth in Securities Revisited, 79 Harv. L. Rev. 1340 (1966).

[5] 15 U.S.C. §§78f, 78k (2000).

[6] 15 U.S.C. §78p(b) (2000), discussed *supra* §12.08.

B. The Antifraud Provision of the Securities Exchange Act

tices with respect to the solicitation of proxies.[7] Section 10(b) of the Act[8] contains a general antifraud provision that renders unlawful manipulative and deceptive acts and practices in connection with the sale or purchase of a security. This section specifically empowers the SEC to promulgate rules in order to define the prohibited conduct. Rule 10b-5,[9] which was drawn under this authority, constitutes a catch-all antifraud provision. In addition to prohibiting fraudulent acts and practices in connection with the purchase of a security, this rule expressly renders it unlawful "to make any untrue statement of material fact or to omit to state a material fact" in connection with the purchase or sale of a security.[10] The rule's breadth is great, as it applies to *any* security, regardless of whether the security is subject to the Act's registration and reporting requirements.[11] Further, the rule applies to any transaction utilizing an instrumentality of interstate commerce, including the mails and even intrastate telephone conversations.[12]

By the terms of the statute, violations of Rule 10b-5 subject an offender to civil enforcement proceedings brought by the SEC as well as to criminal prosecution by the Justice Department. Nevertheless, the primary significance of the rule has been its availability for a private right of action by an injured purchaser or seller of a security.[13] Beginning with a 1946 federal district court decision,[14] the implied private right of action for violation of Rule 10b-5 grew from a "legislative acorn" into a "judicial oak."[15] The rule's reach grew rapidly, until the Supreme Court turned to its pruning shears in reshaping the remedy.[16]

Rule 10b-5's broad language has been applied in a wide variety of fact contexts. Picking up where section 16(b) leaves off, Rule 10b-5 has an impact on trading in securities based on inside information.[17] The rule can be used to regulate

---

[7] 15 U.S.C. §78n(a) (2000) and Reg. 14A promulgated thereunder, which are discussed *infra* §§13.20-13.23.

[8] 15 U.S.C. §78j(b) (2000).

[9] 17 C.F.R. §240-10b-5 (2002).

[10] *Id.* The rule was patterned after the 1933 Securities Act's antifraud provision. 15 U.S.C. §77h(d) (2000).

[11] *Compare, e.g.,* 15 U.S.C. §78p(a) (2000) (proxy regulation); *id.* §78m(d) (2000) (tender offer regulation), *with id.* §78p(b) (2000) (insider short-swing profits).

[12] *E.g.,* Dupuy v. Dupuy, 511 F.2d 641 (5th Cir. 1975).

[13] *See, e.g.,* 8 Loss & Seligman, *supra* §12.08 note 6, 3680-3726.

[14] Kardon v. National Gypsum Co., 69 F. Supp. 512 (E.D. Pa. 1946). Seventeen years later the Supreme Court recognized an implied remedy under Rule 14a-9's the antifraud provisions relating to shareholder suffrage and the proxy machinery. J.I. Case Co. v. Borak, 377 U.S. 426 (1954). *See also* Herman & McLean v. Huddleston, 459 U.S. 375, 380 (1983) (recognizing a private 10b-5 remedy). Although these two implied remedies are well established, subsequent Supreme Court pronouncements indicate that any additional implied remedies will have an uphill road. *See* Thomas L. Hazen, Treatise on the Law of Securities Regulation §12.1 (4d ed. 2002); Thomas L. Hazen, Implied Private Remedies Under Federal Statutes: Neither a Death Knell nor a Moratorium—Civil Rights, Securities Regulation and Beyond, 33 Vand. L. Rev. 1333 (1980).

[15] Blue Chip Stamps Co. v. Manor Drug Stores, 421 U.S. 723 (1975).

[16] Santa Fe Indus. v. Green, 430 U.S. 462 (1977) (deception requirement); Ernst & Ernst v. Hochfelder, 425 U.S. 185 (1976) (defendant must have acted with scienter); Blue Chip Stamps Co. v. Manor Drug Stores, 421 U.S. 723 (1975) (plaintiff must be a purchaser or seller of the security).

[17] *See* §12.08. This fills a significant void in the law of many states. *See* §12.07.

the flow of information to the investing public and in many instances to compel corporate disclosure of material facts.[18] The rule has also proved to be a weapon against certain types of corporate mismanagement.[19] This versatility is due to the breadth of the statute's and rule's language.[20] In addition to material misstatements or omissions reasonably calculated to affect an investor's decision in ordinary sales or purchases of securities,[21] Rule 10b-5 applies to a corporation's issuance of stock or bonds,[22] mergers and other organic changes,[23] a corporation's purchase or sale of its own or another company's securities,[24] and the sale of a controlling interest in a corporation.

Because the cause of action is implied, there was not, until 2002, any expressly provided statute of limitations. Earlier, the Supreme Court held that a limitations period is that which applies to the express causes of action under the securities laws.[25] As a result of the Court's action, the limitations period is the relatively short time of within one year of discovery of the fraud and in no case more than three years after the violation.[26] In 2002, the Congress extended the statute of limitations period to two years of discovery with a maximum length of five years of the commission of the violation.[27]

Federal jurisdiction over suits based on Rule 10b-5 is exclusive.[28] When, as is frequently the case, a particular set of facts gives rise to both a 10b-5 claim and a cause of action under state law, the aggrieved buyer or seller of securities is generally able to combine both in federal court under the doctrine of pendent or supplemental jurisdiction.[29] Note, however, that in most class actions, state securities fraud claims are preempted.[30]

---

[18] See §12.11.

[19] See §12.12.

[20] 17 C.F.R. §230.10b-5 (2002).

[21] Zweig v. Hearst Corp., 592 F.2d 1261 (9th Cir. 1979) (sustaining complaint against financial columnist for alleged material misinformation).

[22] Lanza v. Drexel & Co., 479 F.2d 1277 (2d Cir. 1973) (also imposing liability on collateral participants such as attorneys and accountants); Hooper v. Mountain States Sec. Corp., 282 F.2d 195 (5th Cir. 1960), cert. denied, 365 U.S. 814 (1961).

[23] E.g., Goldberg v. Meridor, 567 F.2d 209 (2d Cir. 1977), cert. denied, 434 U.S. 1069 (1978). Since these transactions also frequently involve shareholder approval, a concurrent remedy exists under Rule 14a-9 in 1934 Exchange Act, which applies to reporting companies. See TSC Indus. v. Northway, Inc., 426 U.S. 438 (1976).

[24] Superintendent of Ins. v. Bankers Life & Cas. Co., 404 U.S. 6 (1971) (sale of other issuers' securities); Mutual Shares v. Genesco, Inc., 384 F.2d 540 (2d Cir. 1967) (corporate purchase of its own shares).

[25] In Lampf, Pleva, Lipkind, Prupis & Petigrow v. Gilbertson, 501 U.S. 350 (1991), a sharply divided five-to-four decision ruled that the applicable statute of limitations is one year from discovery (or reasonable discovery) of the fraud but in no event more than three years after the transaction.

[26] See, e.g., Tregenza v. Great American Communications Co., 12 F.3d 717 (7th Cir. 1993).

[27] See section 804 of the Sarbanes-Oxley Act of 2002, Pub. L. No. 107-204 (July 20, 2002), amending 28 U.S.C. §1658.

[28] 15 U.S.C. §78aa (2000).

[29] See Lewis D. Lowenfels, Pendent Jurisdiction and the Federal Securities Acts, 67 Colum. L. Rev. 474 (1967); Note, The Evolution and Scope of the Doctrine of Pendent Jurisdiction in the Federal Courts, 62 Colum. L. Rev. 1018 (1962). The frequency of concurring federal and state claims is explained by the fact that claims of corporate mismanagement often give rise to a 10b-5 action as well.

[30] 15 U.S.C. §78bb(f) (2000).

B. The Antifraud Provision of the Securities Exchange Act

Four Supreme Court decisions have narrowed—but at the same time defined more clearly—important parameters of the 10b-5 implied private right of action. First, in order to sue for damages, the plaintiff must have been a purchaser or seller of a security.[31] Second, the defendant's misrepresentation must be committed with more than negligent oversight on the defendant's part; the defendant's misrepresentation must be committed with scienter.[32] Third, the conduct complained of must involve deception or manipulation.[33] And, in its most startling holding, the Supreme Court eliminated aiding and abetting liability in private actions under Rule 10b-5.[34] What follows is an examination of each of the elements of a Rule 10b-5 case.

§12.09.01   Materiality

In order for a misstatement or omission to be actionable under Rule 10b-5, it must be a material one. The Supreme Court has defined "materiality" in terms of the type of information that a reasonable investor would consider significant in making an investment decision.[35] The test of materiality is an objective one and not one that turns upon the unique information needs of the particular investor. When the misstated or omitted fact is contingent or speculative, such as a prediction, a forecast, or even an appraisal of the value of an asset, the standard definition of materiality must account not solely for the probability that the forecasted event or item will in fact occur. In such a case, the Supreme Court holds that there is to be a balancing of the probability of the event's occurrence and its expected magnitude to make the materiality determination.[36] In such an instance, even

[31] Blue Chip Stamps Co. v. Manor Drug Stores, 421 U.S. 723 (1975). *See* Birnbaum v. Newport Steel Corp., 193 F.2d 461 (2d Cir.), *cert. denied,* 343 U.S. 956 (1952); James D. Cox et al., Securities Regulations Cases and Materials (3d ed. 2001), at 730-739, 752-765. In a shareholder derivative suit the standing requirement is satisfied where the corporation is either a purchaser or a seller.

[32] Ernst & Ernst v. Hochfelder, 425 U.S. 185 (1976). At common law, scienter includes statements made with reckless disregard as to their truth or falsity as well as to intentional conduct. Derry v. Peek, 14 App. Cas. 337 (House of Lords 1889). The Supreme Court in *Hochfelder* specifically reserved the question of whether reckless conduct satisfies the 10b-5 scienter requirement (425 U.S. at 193-194, n.12); a majority of circuit courts of appeals have held that it does. *E.g.,* Nelson v. Serwold, 576 F.2d 1332 (9th Cir.), *cert. denied,* 439 U.S. 1039 (1978); Rolf v. Blyth, Eastman Dillon & Co., 570 F.2d 38 (2d Cir.), *cert. denied,* 439 U.S. 1039 (1978); Coleco Indus. v. Berman, 567 F.2d 569 (3d Cir. 1977), *cert. denied,* 439 U.S. 830 (1978); Sundstrand Corp. v. Sun Chem. Corp., 553 F.2d 1033, 1044 (7th Cir.), *cert. denied,* 434 U.S. 875 (1977).

[33] Santa Fe Indus. v. Green, 430 U.S. 462 (1977).

[34] Central Bank of Denver v. First Interstate Bank of Denver, 511 U.S. 164 (1994). Prior to its decision, each circuit, some for two or more decades had recognized aiding and abetting liability.

[35] The standard for materiality is the same for the antifraud provision as it is for other provisions of the securities laws, such as the proxy solicitations. The leading case for materiality is TSC Indus. v. Northway, Inc., 426 U.S. 438, 449 (1976) (decided under the proxy rules).

[36] *See* Basic, Inc. v. Levinson, 485 U.S. 224 (1988) (decided under Rule 10b-5 involving the denial of merger negotiations).

A related issue is the obligation of reporting companies on Form 10-Q and Form 10-K to address, within the "Management Discussion and Analysis" portion of those reports "trends, demands, commitments or events" that the issuer knows are "reasonably likely" to occur or will have a material

though an event might be accorded a low probability of occurrence, a very substantial magnitude should it occur can result in the item being deemed material.[37] Even though an opinion is not a "fact" as such, misrepresenting one's opinion, such as stating that "loan reserves are adequate," can violate Rule 10b-5 if the speaker is aware there is objective evidence that contradicts her opinion.[38] The Supreme Court holds that opinion statements can be materially misleading only when they are "objectively" false, i.e., when the plaintiff can establish by objective evidence that the opinion statement was false.[39] Hence, directors who opine that $40 is a "high" price commit fraud if they have before them evidence that the fair price is $60. However, no violation occurs if the directors have been advised that $40 is the fair price, but the directors' personal belief is that the shares' intrinsic value is higher.

The materiality of a particular item is determined within the "total mix" of information that is publicly available. Through the total mix lens a statement is assessed in light of the other information available to investors. As seen below, this invites defenses such as "truth on the market" and "bespeaks caution." As materiality questions are highly fact-specific, summary judgment is rarely appropriate.[40] Because of the breadth of the definition of materiality there are many categories of information that can, under the right set of circumstances, be deemed materiality. Broad categories of information courts have held material include past business failures of the promoters,[41] on-going criminal investigation of the firm's president,[42] and directors' concealment of a bribery and kickback scheme.[43]

Whether a fact is material is a joint question of law and fact and in theory is poorly suited for resolution on the pleadings. However, the courts with some regularity dismiss actions after concluding the alleged omission or misstatement was not material. Aside from their willingness to weigh the likely importance to the objectively qualified investor of an omitted or misstated item, there are several other heuristics that have developed that empower the court to determine the plaintiff has failed to allege a material misrepresentation. The first is the doctrine

---

impact on its financial condition or performance. *See, e.g.,* In the Matter of Caterpillar, Inc., Exchange Act. Rel. No. 30532 (Mar. 31, 1992) (violation found where failed to disclose that 23 percent of firm's net profits were derived from Brazilian subsidiary and those profits were the result of macroeconomic events unique to Brazil that could change due to the upcoming national elections).

[37] *See, e.g.,* Kronfeld v. Trans World Airlines, Inc., 832 F.2d 726 (2d Cir. 1987).

[38] *See, e.g.,* Shapiro v. U.J.B. Financial Corp., 964 F.2d 272 (3d Cir. 1992).

[39] *See* Virginia Bankshares, Inc. v. Sandberg, 501 U.S. 1083 (1991). In contrast, subjective falsehood arises when, for example, the evidence before the speaker is not inconsistent with the opinion expressed, such as the price is a "fair" price, but despite the information before the speaker the charge is that speaker did not honestly believe the price was fair.

[40] For examples of materiality in various contexts, *see* James D. Cox, et al., Securities Regulation Cases and Materials ch. 2 (3d ed. 2001); 2 Thomas L. Hazen, Treatise on the Law of Securities Regulation §12.9 (4th ed. 2002).

[41] *See, e.g.,* SEC v. Carriba Air, Inc., 681 F.2d 1318 (11th Cir. 1981).

[42] *See, e.g.,* SEC v. Electronics Warehouse, Inc., 689 F. Supp. 53 (D. Conn. 1988), *aff'd*, 891 F.2d 459 (2d Cir. 1989).

[43] *See, e.g.,* Weisberg v. Coastal States Gas Corp., 609 F.2d 650 (2d Cir. 1979). But absent evidence of self-dealing behavior, a leading case holds social character of directors' decisions are not material. *See* Gaines v. Houghton, 645 F.2d 761, 778 (9th Cir. 1982).

of "puffing." A puffing statement is a generalized statement of optimism that, in the court's eye, is not material to the investor because the investor would never attribute any importance to statements as "the business is proceeding well."[44] As Judge Richard Posner observed about statements that the quest for a buyer for the firm was going well (when in fact it was going badly): "*Everyone* knows that someone trying to sell something is going to look and talk on the bright side. You don't sell a product by bad mouthing it."[45]

A second tool for addressing whether a statement is materially misleading is the so-called truth-on-the-market defense. This defense arises when the court is persuaded that, even though the defendant's representations in isolation were materially misleading, they could not have misled investors in an efficient market because truthful information was publicly available. For example, a company, when touting the contribution its new product lines would make did not commit a material omission by failing to disclose that its established product lines were approaching obsolescence and, hence, would yield smaller and smaller profits; the court noted that the omitted information was set forth in numerous analysts' reports.[46]

The third tool is the "Bespeaks Caution" doctrine that applies only to forward looking statements, such as a forecast or prediction. Pursuant to this doctrine an erroneous forward looking statement is not materially misleading if accompanied by "meaningful cautionary language." In the leading case, *Kaufman v. Trump's Castle Funding*,[47] the prospectus for a bond offering to finance a casino-hotel in Atlantic City stated the firm "believes that funds generated from the operation of the Taj Mahal will be sufficient to cover all of its debt service (interest and principal). . . ." The firm went bankrupt before even the first payment was due. The court found that the forward looking statement was not misleading because the prospectus contained extensive description of a range of uncertainties the firm must overcome to remain solvent.[48] Not only is the Bespeaks Caution doctrine well established among the various federal circuits,[49] the doctrine is also now part of the statutory safe harbor for forward looking statements. The statutory safe harbor was added to the Securities Act[50] and Securities Exchange Act[51] in 1995 by the

---

[44] *See, e.g.*, In re Burlington Coat Factory Sec. Lit., 114 F.3d 1410 (3d Cir. 1997) (earnings will grow at a faster rate than sales); Lasker v. New York State Electric & Gas Co., 85 F.3d 55 (2d Cir. 1996) (observing that diversification will "lead to continued prosperity" when knew this would lead to lower profits).

[45] Eisenstadt v. Centel Corp., 113 F.3d 738, 745 (7th Cir. 1997).

[46] *See* In re Convergent Technology Sec. Lit., 948 F.2d 507, 513 (9th Cir. 1991). *See also* Phillips v. LCI International, Inc., 190 F.3d 609 (4th Cir. 1999); Wielgos v. Commonwealth Edison Co., 892 F.2d 509 (7th Cir. 1989) (optimistic forecasts regarding time and future cost to bring nuclear reactors on line not misleading because all its prior forecasts on this subject were equally optimistic); In re Apple Computer Sec. Litig., 886 F.2d 1109 (9th Cir. 1989).

[47] 7 F.3d 357 (3d Cir. 1993).

[48] *Id.*, at 362.

[49] *See, e.g.*, Romani v. Shearson Lehman Hutton, 929 F.2d 875 (1st Cir. 1991); I. Meyer Pincus & Assoc. v. Oppenheimer & Co., 936 F.2d 759 (2d Cir. 1991); Sinay v. Lamson & Sessions Co., 948 F.2d 1037 (6th Cir. 1991); In re Convergent Technologies Sec. Litig., 948 F.2d 507 (9th Cir. 1991).

[50] *See* Section 27A, 15 U.S.C. §77z-2 (2000).

[51] *See* Section 21E, 15 U.S.C. §78uu-1 (2000).

Private Securities Litigation Reform Act. These provisions each provide essentially two distinct safe harbors for forward looking statements (in addition, they each provide their own definition for what constitutes a forward looking statement). The first safe harbor essentially codifies the Bespeaks Caution doctrine since it provides a forward looking statement is not actionable if accompanied by meaningful cautionary language. The Conference Committee Report accompanying this provision clarifies that there can be meaningful cautionary language even though the cautionary statements do not include the particular factor that ultimately causes the forward looking statement not to come true.[52] Second, the Conference Report emphasizes that the cautionary statements "must convey substantive information about factors that realistically could cause results to differ materially from those projected," mere boilerplate is insufficient.[53] Neither the Bespeaks Caution doctrine nor the statutory safe harbor protect misrepresentations of historical fact—each applies only to protect forward looking statements.[54]

The second safe harbor arises if the plaintiff fails to prove that the forward looking statement was made with knowledge of its falsity. Juxtaposing this second safe harbor with the first reveals that the first safe harbor applies even if management knows the forward looking statement is false, provided they have surrounded the knowingly false forecast with meaningful cautionary language. Under the Bespeaks Caution doctrine courts, when it is clear the forecast was knowingly false, have either found that the cautionary language was deficient or that the defendants had committed material misrepresentations of fact, i.e., non-forward looking statements.[55] The statutory safe harbor does not apply to forward looking statements made in certain types of transactions, such as initial public offerings or tender offers, although the Bespeaks Caution doctrine would apply in those contexts.

§12.09.02   Scienter and Its Pleading

The Supreme Court has definitively held that the enabling language of Section 10(b) that authorizes the SEC to proscribe through rule making "deceptive or manipulative devices or contrivances" forecloses Section 10(b) and, hence, Rule 10b-5 from reaching conduct that involves no greater fault than mere negligence.[56] Though the Supreme Court has yet to speak on the subject, reckless dis-

---

[52] H.R. Conf. Rep. No. 369, 104th Cong., 2d Sess. 11 (1995).

[53] *Id.*

[54] In a case where the allegation was that a list of factors that would influence future operations was misleading, the court applied the statutory safe harbor even though the list was a mixture of forward looking statements and some statements that were not. *See* Harris v. IVAX Corp., 182 F.3d 799 (11th Cir. 1999).

[55] *See, e.g.,* Franklin High Yield v. County of Martin Minnesota, 152 F.3d 736 (8th Cir. 1998); Rubinstein v. Collins, 20 F.3d 160 (5th Cir. 1994); Kline v. First Western Gov't Sec. Inc., 24 F.3d 480 (3d Cir. 1994).

[56] This holding was first reached in Ernst & Ernst v. Hochfelder, 425 U.S. 185 (1976) for private actions and was soon applied to SEC enforcement actions in Aaron v. Securities and Exchange Commission, 446 U.S. 680 (1980). Though some believed that negligence was a standard of fault sometimes applied before

B. The Antifraud Provision of the Securities Exchange Act

regard of the truthfulness, as well as knowledge of the falsity, of the representation are widely recognized by the lower courts as permissible standards for fault, i.e., scienter, in both private and SEC actions under Rule 10b-5. Scienter under the "knowledge" formula does not require, as does the common law action of deceit, that the defendant have intended that the misrepresentation induced the plaintiff to trade. It is enough that the defendant was aware of the untruth and its likelihood of influencing investor behavior.[57] The area of the greatest uncertainty regarding possible future Supreme Court action is whether representations and statements made with reckless disregard of their truthfulness are actionable under Rule 10b-5. Presently all the circuits recognize reckless as a permissible standard of fault in some respect.[58] There are various formulations of what constitutes recklessness under Rule 10b-5. Recklessness falls obviously somewhere between intent and negligence. One court has explained its location as "a lesser form of intent [rather] than a merely greater degree of ordinary negligence."[59] Though a somewhat weaker version of recklessness is a standard of "carelessness approaching indifference" to the truth of the representation,[60] courts more frequently impose a somewhat higher hurdle of what could be called "severe recklessness."[61] However recklessness is defined, and even in a case not involving an allegation of recklessness, the true hurdle facing the plaintiff is that heightened pleading requirements that now apply to securities fraud actions.

The passage of the Private Securities Litigation Reform Act of 1995 (PSLRA) (amending the Securities Act and the Securities and Exchange Act) ended the liberal notice pleading requirements for securities litigation. To discourage what Congress believed was frequent baseless securities fraud litigation, the PSLRA requires that the private plaintiff's complaint not only continue in its other portions to meet the specificity requirements of Federal Rule of Civil Procedure 9(b), but also that the complaint "state with particularity facts giving rise to a *strong inference* that the defendant acted with the requisite state of mind."[62] Adding to the plaintiff's difficulties is that the PSLRA bars any discovery until the resolution of any pending motion to dismiss. Consequently, the plaintiff cannot use discovery, as she once could, to obtain the necessary information to amend her earlier complaint so as to meet the particularity requirements that would be in issue following the defendant's motion to dismiss. Not surprisingly, there is a wide variance among the circuits, and one can even find variances among the district court judges within a single circuit, on just what facts or circumstances give rise to a

---

Ernst & Ernst, a close examination of the pre-*Ernst & Ernst* cases suggest otherwise. *See* James D. Cox, *Ernst & Ernst v. Hochfelder*. A Critique and Evaluation, 28 Hastings L.J. 569 (1977).

[57] *See, e.g.*, AUSA Life Insurance Co. v. Ernst & Young, 206 F.3d 202 (2d Cir. 2000); SEC v. Falstaff Brewing Co., 629 F.2d 62, 76 (D.C. Cir. 1980).

[58] *See* Hollinger v. Titan Capital Corp., 914 F.2d 1564, 1568-70 (9th Cir. 1990).

[59] Sanders v. John Nuveen & Co., 554 F.2d 790, 793 (7th Cir. 1977).

[60] *See* Hoffman v. Estabrook & Co., 587 F.2d 509, 516 (1st Cir. 1978). Similarly, consider Kiernan v. Homeland, Inc., 611 F.2d 785, 788 (9th Cir. 1984) ("had reasonable grounds to believe material facts were misstated or omitted, but nonetheless failed to obtain or disclose such facts although they could have done so without extraordinary effort").

[61] Broad v. Rockwell International Corp., 642 F.2d 929, 961-62 (5th Cir. 1981).

[62] 15 U.S.C. §78u-4(b)(2) (2000) (emphasis added).

"strong inference." Indeed, following the PSLRA, the question of pleading scienter is the single most litigated issue in a Rule 10b-5 case. Many courts believe that the template for what constitutes a "strong inference" was the pre-PSLRA Second Circuit decision in *In re Time Warner Securities Litigation*,[63] where a majority of the panel held that scienter was plead with particularity by facts supporting a "motive or opportunity" to commit fraud on the part of the company's officers. In *Time Warner* such facts were found in the managers' likely desire to prop up the price of the company's shares to facilitate a public offering of the securities. The Conference Report accompanying the PSLRA expressly states it did not intend to codify the Second Circuit's case law, although the new standard was there stated to have been based in part on the Second Circuit's standard.[64] Other courts, following what can be seen as an intermediate approach, though finding that motive and opportunity relevant, considered other facts of the particular case.[65] By far the most demanding standard is that first recognized in *In re Silicon Graphics*,[66] which rejects the motive and opportunity approach and requires the plaintiff to plead a strong inference of deliberate recklessness or fraudulent intent.

§12.09.03 Standing—The Purchaser or Seller Requirement

The SEC's standing to sue under the antifraud provision is never in serious doubt since under Section 21(d)(1)[67] the agency is authorized to initiate an enforcement action in the federal district court and can proceed internally pursuant to its cease and desist powers under Section 21C of the Exchange Act.[68] Private investors seeking a monetary recovery must, however, be either a purchaser or seller of a security in connection with the fraud alleged to have been committed by the defendant. Once known as the *Birnbaum* doctrine,[69] a reference to the leading case first enshrining it within the Rule 10b-5 jurisprudence, it was not until three decades after *Birnbaum* was decided that the Supreme Court in *Blue*

[63] 9 F.3d 259 (2d Cir. 1993).

[64] S. 1260, H.R. Conf. Rep. No. 105-803, 104th Cong., 1st Sess. at 41. For an excellent review of the legislative history on this topic, *see* Joseph A. Grundfest & A.C. Pritchard, Statutes with Multiple Personality Disorders: The Value of Ambiguity in Statutory Design and Interpretation, 54 Stan. L. Rev. 627, 650-665 (2002).

[65] Greebel v. FTP Software, Inc., 194 F.3d 185 (1st Cir. 1999). *Accord* In re Comshare, Inc. Sec. Litig., 183 F.3d 542, 551 (6th Cir. 1999); Bryant v. Avado Brands, Inc., 187 F.3d 1271, 1282-1283 (11th Cir. 1999).

[66] 183 F.3d 970, 979 (9th Cir. 1999). However, showing continuing divisions among panels within the same circuit, a later panel held that the more demanding pleading standard of *Silicon Graphics* applied only to motions to dismiss and not motions for summary judgment. *See* Howard v. Everex Sys., Inc., 228 F.3d 1057 (9th Cir. 2000). *Contra* Geffon v. Micrion Corp., 249 F.3d 29 (1st Cir. 2001).

[67] 15 U.S.C. §78u(d)(1) (2000).

[68] 15 U.S.C. §78u-3(2000).

[69] *See* Birnbaum v. Newport Steel Corp., 193 F.2d 461 (2d Cir), *cert. denied*, 343 U.S. 956 (1952).

B. The Antifraud Provision of the Securities Exchange Act

Chip Stamps v. Manor Drug Stores[70] affirmed the practice that had been uniformly followed in the circuits. *Blue Chip Stamps* above all other cases denotes the change in attitude toward private securities suits from the earlier more liberal approaches of the Warren Court. It was not just that *Blue Chip Stamps* opted for a technical standing requirement that signaled a new balance within what was then the Burger Court, but it was the Court's reasons for opting for the technical rule. The Court was not guided by what it thought were logical inferences to be drawn from legislative history. Rather the basis for its mandating a purchaser-seller requirement was its belief of the need for a rule that would insulate companies and their officers from what the court described as "vexatious litigation."[71]

The purchaser-seller requirement is by far the most rigid fixture of Rule 10b-5 litigation. This requires an executed purchase or sale, not merely a speculative opportunity to trade.[72] Even where the defendant's successful intent to prevent the plaintiff from selling by purposefully misrepresenting material facts is beyond peradventure, suit to recover for the losses suffered is barred, even if the sale occurs later after the true facts are known.[73] The sale that is in connection with the fraud does not have to arise by volition so long as the losses are causally related to the sale. Thus, when control of a company was acquired by fraud practiced upon all its shareholders and thereafter the remaining stockholders are cashed out in a squeeze-out merger, the so-called forced seller doctrine applies to confer standing.[74] Somewhat related to the forced seller is the "aborted purchaser-seller." This arises when the defendant's fraud aborts a formal plan involving the sale or exchange of shares.[75] Following the lead of a leading pre-*Blue Chip Stamps* case,[76] most courts that have been called upon to decide the matter have held that the plaintiff seeking injunctive relief need not be a purchaser or seller of shares.[77] There seems to be little cause to deny standing for prospective injunctive relief to a plaintiff who has neither purchased nor sold if the plaintiff sustains the burden

---

[70] 421 U.S. 723 (1975).

[71] 421 U.S. at 743.

[72] Kagan v. Edison Brothers Stores, Inc., 907 F.2d 690 (7th Cir. 1990), held that an oral agreement to sell that was secured by fraud is not a sale, since the oral agreement was not enforceable. However, the Supreme Court in Wharf (Holdings) Ltd. v. United Int'l Holdings, 532 U.S. 588 (2001), held that the Exchange Act's language applies to "any contract for the purchase or sale of a security" so that even the purchaser of an *oral* option has standing to sue under Rule 10b-5.

[73] *See* Gurley v. Documation, Inc., 674 F.2d 253 (4th Cir. 1982).

[74] The leading case for this doctrine is Vine v. Beneficial Finance Co., 374 F.2d 627 (2d Cir), *cert. denied*, 389 U.S. 970 (1967). For post *Blue Chip Stamps* decisions recognizing the doctrine, *see* 7547 Corp. v. Parsley Dev. Part. L.P., 38 F.3d 211 (5th Cir. 1994) (however, proof that there was a substantial change in the rights, privileges, or preferences of the plaintiff's securities is needed to establish a sale); Alley v. Miramon, 614 F.2d 1372 (5th Cir. 1980); Kahn v. Lynch Communication Sys. Inc., 638 A.2d 1110 (Del. 1994) (W.D. Wash. 1990) (facts similar to *Vine*).

[75] *See* Mosher v. Kane, 784 F.2d 1385 (9th Cir. 1986); Pittsburgh Terminal Corp. v. B & O. RR. Co., 680 F.2d 933 (3d Cir. 1982) (conversion option was undercut by board of directors setting date of record as the same date as the date of declaration of an extraordinary and substantial dividend).

[76] *See* Mutual Shares Corp. v. Genesco, 384 F.2d 540 (2d Cir. 1967).

[77] *Compare* Tully v. Mott Supermarkets, Inc., 540 F.2d 187 (3d Cir. 1976) (upholding injunctive action by a non seller/purchaser) *with* Cowin v. Bresler, 741 F.2d 410 (D.C. Cir. 1984) (strictly applying *Blue Chip Stamps'* reasoning to deny standing to non-trading plaintiff).

of proving that, if equitable relief is not awarded, the defendant's violation likely will cause the plaintiff to suffer a loss through the purchase or sale of a security.

§12.09.04   "In Connection With"

Not only must there be a purchase or sale of a security, but Rule 10b-5, reflecting the operative language of Section 10(b), itself requires that the violation, i.e., the deception, must be "in connection with" the purchase or sale of a security. The language does not, however, require that the defendant be engaged in a security transaction. Thus, companies that release false financial information into a marketplace are liable under Rule 10b-5, even though the company itself does not purchase or sell securities.[78] Correlatively, there is no need to prove in a private suit that the plaintiff is in privity of contract through his purchase or sale with the defendants. Indeed, the in connection with requirement is satisfied even if the target of the fraud is someone other than the purchasing or selling plaintiff.[79] Consequently, untruthful statements about a company's products, certainly in the technology sector where investors can be expected to accord product features on a level akin to earnings per share, can subject such announcements to Rule 10b-5 exposure.[80]

Just what are the permissible bounds of a statement being "in connection with" has been repeatedly muddied by the Supreme Court. In its initial foray into this area, the question was whether a company officer that engineers the board's approval to dispose of bonds its owns violated Rule 10b-5 when the officer's secret intent was to embezzle the proceeds of the resulting sale. One might question on these facts just where the deception was—e.g., the failure to disclose to the board the officer's secret intent—as well as whether the deception required must be one that relates to the inherent value of the security to be sold (as contrasted with the motive for the sale). Instead, Justice Douglas said that the fraud need simply "touch" a securities transaction to satisfy the in connection with requirement.[81] The guidance provided by the Supreme Court has not improved with time. In its decision, *The Wharf (Holdings) Ltd. v. United International Holdings*,[82] the court held the in connection with requirement was met when the defendant did not disclose

---

[78] This point was expressly addressed in a landmark insider trading case, *see* Securities and Exchange Commission v. Texas Gulf Sulphur Co., 401 F.2d 833, 860 (2d Cir. 1968) (en banc), *cert. denied*, 394 U.S. 976 (1969) ("We do not believe that Congress intended that the proscriptions of the Act would not be violated unless the makers of a misleading statements also participated in pertinent securities transactions in connection therewith. . . .").

[79] *See, e.g.*, In re Ames Dept. Store Stock Litig., 991 F.2d 953 (2d Cir. 1993); Heit v. Weitzen, 402 F.2d 909 (2d Cir. 1968).

[80] *See generally* Robert A. Prentice and John H. Langmore, Beware of Vaporware: Product Hype and the Securities Fraud Liability of High Tech Companies, 8 Harv. J. L. & Tech. 1 (1994).

[81] *See* Superintendent of Insurance v. Bankers Life & Casualty Co., 404 U.S. 6, 10 (1971). *See generally* James D. Cox, Fraud Is in the Eye of the Beholder: Rule 10b-5's Application to Corporate Mismanagement, 47 N.Y.U. L. Rev. 674 (1972).

[82] 532 U.S. 588 (2001).

its intention not to honor an oral option that was granted as part of a transaction. The court reasoned that "even were it the case that the Act covers only misrepresentations likely to affect the value of securities, Wharf's secret reservation was such a misrepresentation" because the defendant's secret intent rendered the option valueless. Thus, the Court gives little insight as to just what determines whether the fraud is "in connection with" the purchase or sale of a security. We might believe from the above quote that *Wharf Ltd.* does wish for the deception to relate to the value of the security transaction to the plaintiff. But in *Bankers Life* there was no misstatement of the value the company would receive for the bonds; the defendant simply failed to disclose his intent to misappropriate the proceeds of that sale. The Court's most recent decision, *SEC v. Zandford*,[83] on this subject returns to the defendant who engineers a security transaction for the purpose of misappropriating the proceeds. What is different from *Bankers Life* in *Zandford* is that the defendant had sole discretion over purchases and sales of the investor's brokerage account. Thus, as a technical matter the investor's judgment was never directly impacted by the defendant's misconduct because the investor had committed that task to the defendant by establishing a discretionary account. The court held that the in connection with requirement was met by allegations that sales were undertaken for the purpose of yielding proceeds that could then be misappropriated. The court did not focus on interdicting the customer's investment judgment. Instead it held there clear was a "scheme to defraud" and that its execution coincided with a securities transaction. Just what constitutes a scheme to defraud would, in light of *Zandford*, appear to include any undisclosed plan to transfer assets from an investor to the defendant. The in connection with requirement is then met if a security transaction is at the heart of that scheme.

§12.09.05   Causal Relationship and Damages

Causation is an element of a Rule 10b-5 action. Many courts have divided causation into two subparts: transaction causation and loss causation. Transaction causation requires a showing that but for the violations in question, the transaction would not have occurred (at least in the form that it took).[84] Loss causation requires a showing of a causal nexus between the transaction and the plaintiff's loss.[85]

As is the case with any fraud claim, the plaintiff must be able to establish damages. In most Rule 10b-5 litigation, the appropriate measure of damages is the out-

---

[83] 122 S. Ct. 1899 (2002).

[84] Reliance may well affect one's decision to trade or the price at which the plaintiff would have traded had the true facts been known. It can include other steps as well. For example, even if the plaintiff had taken some steps to protect himself in the event of an IPO, had the true facts been disclosed he might well have sought even greater protection. *See* Castellano v. Young & Rucican, Inc., 257 F.3d 171 (2d Cir. 2001).

[85] Loss causation is a separate element from transaction causation, and the two cannot be collapsed into each other. AUSA Life Ins. Co. v. Ernst and Young, 206 F.3d 202, 216 (2d Cir. 2000).

of-pocket loss proximately caused by the material misstatement or omission. On occasion, disgorgement of ill-gotten profits or benefit of the bargain might be a more appropriate measure of damages. Other forms of equitable relief are also available to private parties in Rule 10b-5 cases, including rescission.[86]

Inquiry into transaction causation in many instances occurs by inquiring whether the plaintiff relied upon the deception. When this occurs the plaintiff must not only prove that the misstated or omitted fact would have assumed actual significance in the deliberations of the reasonable investors under circumstances similar to those that the plaintiff operated within (this of course is the materiality element), but also that the misstated or omitted fact assumed such significance for the plaintiff that it caused the plaintiff to purchase (or to sell, as the case may be) which the plaintiff would not have done had the defendant not misrepresented the facts.[87] This approach gets tricky, if not ethereal, if the plaintiff is required to prove reliance upon a material fact that was omitted. In such a case, the plaintiff is assisted by the holding of *Affiliated Ute Citizens v. United States*,[88] whose facts are narrower than the language the court used to express its holding; in a non-disclosure case (i.e., pure omission case) reliance can be presumed from a showing that the omitted fact was material.[89] The actual facts of the case suggest the holding might be narrower. The investors were native Americans who depended upon the defendant bank to sell their securities. All dealings were face-to-face and the bank failed on each trade to disclose that the shares were being resold at a higher price. Thus, the case is not simply an omission case, but one involving a clear fiduciary relationship between the bank and the plaintiffs. This should make it an easier case to conclude reliance *in fact* by the plaintiffs on the bank to deal fairly.

Due to the influence of *Affiliated Ute*, it is common in face-to-face transactions as well as even open market purchases for the plaintiff to enjoy the presumption of his reliance when the defendant has committed only an omission.[90] The presumption, however, can be rebutted.[91] Courts adhering strictly to the unique facts of *Affiliated Ute* where there was a fiduciary relationship between the plaintiff and defendant accord this presumption only when there is a preexisting relationship between the plaintiff and defendant.[92] In cases of misstatements or a combination of misstatements and omissions, proof of reliance by the plaintiff is required.[93]

[86] *See, e.g.*, Ambassador Hotel Co. Ltd v.Wei-Chuan Inv., 189 F.3d 1017 (9th Cir. 1999) (rescission measure of damages awarded to contractor for hotel who agreed to receive payment in shares whose value the defendant misrepresented).

[87] *See* List v. Fashion Park, Inc., 340 F.2d 457 (2d Cir. 1965).

[88] 406 U.S. 128 (1972).

[89] *Id.* at 153.

[90] *See, e.g.*, Rowe v. Maremont Corp., 850 F.2d 1226 (7th Cir. 1988); Rifkin v. Crow, 574 F.2d 256 (5th Cir. 1978).

[91] *See, e.g.*, Moody v. Bache & Co., 570 F.2d 523 (5th Cir. 1978) (omitted facts occurred many months before the challenged securities transactions which the court believed were not influenced by the earlier misrepresentations).

[92] *See, e.g.*, Cavalier Carpets, Inc. v. Caylor, 746 F.2d 749 (11th Cir. 1984) (court denied the presumption to a plaintiff who carried out his own investigation).

[93] *See, e.g.*, Cox v. Collins, 7 F.3d 394 (4th Cir. 1993).

B. The Antifraud Provision of the Securities Exchange Act

The major exception to proving the investor's reliance upon the defendant's misrepresentation is the "fraud on the market" theory that was upheld by the Supreme Court in *Basic Inc. v. Levinson*.[94] The theory relieves the plaintiff of proving reliance upon the particular false announcement or representation that is the focus of her claim.

> The fraud on the market theory is based on the hypothesis that, in an open and developed securities market, the price of a company's stock is determined by the available information regarding the company and its business. . . . Misleading statements will therefore defraud purchasers of stock even if the purchasers do not directly rely on the misstatements. . . . The causal connection between the defendant's fraud and the plaintiff's purchase of stock in such a case is no less significant than in a case of direct reliance on misrepresentations.[95]

The theory applies only for securities trading that occurs in a market believed to be efficient.[96] Thus, face-to-face trades, exchanges with the corporation and the like are not transactions whose plaintiffs are the beneficiaries of the fraud on the market theory.[97] Just what is an efficient market is rarely litigated, though courts appear to recognize all trading on the New York Stock Exchange as well as larger capitalized companies traded on Nasdaq are covered by the theory.[98] An obvious consequence of the theory is that it facilitates class action certification because when the theory applies there is no inquiry into each class member's reliance. If there were, this would likely render class certification unlikely since common questions of law and fact are not likely to predominate if reliance were required to be established by each class member. This is not to suggest that reliance is not a theoretical impossibility. Even *Basic Inc.* acknowledged that "a plaintiff who believed that Basic's statements were false and that Basic was indeed engaged in merger discussions, and who consequently believed that Basic was artificially underpriced, but sold his shares nevertheless because of an unrelated concern. . . could not be said to have relied on the integrity of the price he knew had been manipulated."[99] We might well question why even this plaintiff should not be permitted to recover. To be sure, the plaintiff hypothesized by the Supreme Court did not rely. But note that because of the defendant's misstatements (denying on three occasions that it was engaged in merger negotiations) did adversely affect

---

[94] 485 U.S. 224 (1988).

[95] Peil v. Speiser, 806 F.2d 1154, 1160-1161 (3d Cir. 1986), quoted in Basic Inc. v. Levinson, 485 U.S. at 229.

[96] *See, e.g.*, Freeman v. Laventhol & Horwath, 915 F.2d 193 (6th Cir. 1990).

[97] *See, e.g.*, Feinman v. Dean Witter Reynolds, Inc., 84 F.3d 539 (2d Cir. 1996) (broker-customer disputes are not subject to fraud on market theory).

[98] *See, e.g.*, Binder v. Gillespie, 172 F.3d 649 (9th Cir. 1999) (plaintiff failed to show what factors would persuade court that over-the-counter stock was traded in an efficient market); Miller v. NTN Communications, Inc. [1999 Transfer Binder], Fed. Sec. L. Rep. (CCH) ¶90,514 (S.D. Cal. 1999) (small number of analysts following stock does not remove security from benefits of fraud on the market theory).

[99] 485 U.S. at 249. *See also* Cadiz Land Co. v. Waste Management Inc. [2000 Transfer Binder], Fed. Sec. L. Rep. (CCH) ¶91,203 (9th Cir. 2000) (preferred shares were disposed of to permit plaintiff to engage in an acquisition and not in reliance on integrity of market).

the price at which the hypothetical plaintiff sold her shares. Why should the defendant not compensate that plaintiff for the losses causally related to its lies as much as the plaintiff whose decision to sell the shares was based on whim or perhaps the chance throwing of darts? It seems that to require reliance in such cases ignores the role of reliance—to establish a causal nexus between the defendant's violation and the plaintiff's loss. In an efficient market that nexus would appear established by proof that the market price of the shares would have been higher or lower but for the defendant's violation. In an efficient market, investors are to be seen as price takers and, in cases such as *Basic Inc.*, the price so taken is one affected by the defendant's violation.

The issue of reliance can arise by the defendant placing in issue that the plaintiff's reliance upon the defendant's false representation was unreasonable. The essence of this argument is that the plaintiff's recover should be barred when with modest effort the plaintiff could have discovered the untruth and thereafter protected himself by either not going forward with the transaction or negotiating a better price. For example, a sophisticated investor was not able to recover from the broker selling it hybrid securities without disclosing the serious risks inherent in the instrument; the court reasoned that given the investor's sophistication a non-reckless investor would have sought advice from knowledgeable advisors.[100] Thus, the sophisticated investor is under some obligation to protect himself from the unscrupulous promoter.[101] However, the courts appear to require some greater departure on the plaintiff's part than the absence of reasonable care, thus placing the plaintiff on a footing equal to the scienter standard by which the fault of defendants is determined.[102]

A special causation issue arises in mergers and recapitalizations that are accompanied by a material misrepresentation and the parties responsible for the deception control sufficient voting power to assure approval of the merger or recapitalization. As will be seen in a later section, the sine qua non of Rule 10b-5 violation is the presence of a material misrepresentation.[103] Without any deception there can be no violation of Rule 10b-5.[104] We might therefore conclude that in such a situation, because the transaction can be effected without the approval

---

[100] *See* Banca Cremi S.A. v. Alex Brown & Sons, 132 F.3d 1017 (4th Cir. 1997). But when the investors are not as sophisticated, the suit was permitted to proceed even though oral misrepresentations made to the investors were contradicted by warnings in the private placement brochure. *See* Myers v. Finkle, 950 F.2d 165 (4th Cir. 1991).

[101] *See, e.g.,* Royal American Managers, Inc. v. IRC Holding Co., 885 F.2d 1011 (2d Cir. 1989) (one sophisticated in the industry could not recover from seller's attorney who falsely represented that government approval was not necessary to dispose of less than half the interest in the reinsurance business); Kennedy v. Josephthal & Co., 814 F.2d 798 (1st Cir. 1987) (false representations were blatantly inconsistent with representations in the offering brochure); Zobrist v. Coal X Inc., 708 F.2d 1511 (10th Cir. 1983) (same).

[102] *See, e.g.,* Mallis v. Bankers Trust Co., 615 F.2d 68 (2d Cir. 1980) (J. Friendly); Goodman v. Epstein, 582 F.2d 388 (7th Cir. 1978); Holdsworth v. Strong, 545 F.2d 687 (10th Cir. 1976). But some cases still have the ring of ordinary care barring the plaintiff. *See, e.g.,* Davidson v. Wilson, 973 F.2d 1391 (8th Cir. 1992); Sharp v. Coopers & Lybrand, 649 F.2d 175 (3d Cir. 1981).

[103] *See* §12.12.

[104] *See* Santa Fe Ind. v. Green, 430 U.S. 462 (1977).

of any minority stockholder, there could be no violation of Rule 10b-5. This is true, provided that the state law does not accord the minority an appraisal remedy in the event they should dissent from the transaction.[105] When there is an appraisal remedy, the minority have two alternative investment decisions to consider, each with a different financial outcome. One choice is to accept what is offered in the transaction being supported by the majority. The other choice is to vote against the transaction and pursue their appraisal remedy. This choice is very much an investment decision, being a decision essentially in which forum to dispose of one's shares and at what price. Thus the courts have consistently recognized that the availability of an appraisal remedy resuscitates what would otherwise have been a moribund Rule 10b-5 cause of action.[106]

§12.09.06 Primary Participants, Aiders and Abettors, and Control Persons

As discussed above, through the mid-1970s, the Supreme Court acquiesced in the circuit and district courts' expansive view of Rule 10b-5. That trend has not continued. For example, in *Central Bank of Denver v. First Interstate Bank of Denver*, by a five-to-four decision the Court held that there is no implied right of action to redress aiding and abetting a Rule 10b-5 violation.[107] The Court's holding is limited to private rights of action. After *Central Bank*, there no longer is liability in private suits for aiding and abetting. One must be a primary participant, the scope of which is discussed below, or fall within one of the now narrower instances (i.e., vicarious liability or control person liability, discussed below) for secondary liability. Aiding and abetting may still be charged in SEC injunctive and other enforcement actions as well as in criminal prosecutions.[108]

Central Bank reinforces the narrow approach the Supreme Court has taken in recent years in its interpretation of the scope of the implied causes of action under the federal securities laws. In the course of its opinion, the Court took a literal

---

[105] *See* Virginia Bankshares Inc. v. Sandberg, 503 U.S. 1083 (1991) (though the minority were invited to vote on the cash out merger and their approval was no doubt affected by material misstatements, causation was lacking under the proxy rules because their approval was without meaning since the defendants controlled 85 percent of the voting rights and there was not appraisal remedy provided by state law).

[106] *See, e.g.*, Wilson v. Great American Ind, Inc., 979 F.2d 924 (2d Cir. 1992); Howing Company v. Nationwide Corp., 972 F.2d 700 (6th Cir. 1992). *See generally* Harvey Gelb, Implied Private Actions Under SEC Rules 14a-9 and 10b-5: The Impact of Virginia Bankshares Inc. v. Sandberg, 76 Marq. L. Rev. 363 (1993).

[107] Central Bank of Denver v. First Interstate Bank of Denver, 511 U.S. 164 (1994).

[108] Following *Central Bank*, Congress removed any doubt regarding the SEC's authority to prosecute aiders and abettors by adding Section 20(f), 15 U.S.C. §78t, to the Securities Exchange Act empowering the SEC to prosecute those who "knowingly provides substantial assistance" to another committing a violation. For an analysis of why *Central Bank*'s reasoning should not extend to SEC enforcement actions, *see* James D. Cox, Just Deserts for Accountants and Attorneys After *Bank of Denver*, 38 Ariz. L. Rev. 519, 536-540 (1996).

approach and stressed the importance of looking to the wording of the statute as the primary source of statutory interpretation (including the implication of a private remedy).[109] The most salient part of *Central Bank*'s holding is its holding that Section 10(b) and Rule 10b-5 proscribe only "the *making*" of a material misstatement (or omission) or the *commission* of a manipulative act."[110] Thus, to be a primary participant there must be evidence that the defendant *made* a misrepresentation or *committed* a manipulative act. The better view is that principals are bound by the misrepresentations their agents make with apparent authority.[111]

After *Central Bank* two divergent approaches have developed to address whether a defendant can be held to have *made* the misrepresentation that is the gravamen of the case. The most liberal of the two approaches is the substantial factor test which inquires whether the defendant has been a substantial participant in making the false representation. Under this approach, one who drafts, edits, and reviews the document containing the misrepresentation is liable as primary participants.[112] A far more restrictive approach is the so-called bright-line test whereby it is not sufficient for primary participant liability that the defendant have a substantial or even central role in preparing the false statement. Under the bright-line test, no one is a primary participant unless the misrepresentation can be attributed or otherwise identified with having been made by that defendant by the plaintiff. The source of this requirement is the reasoning of *Central Bank* that to permit recovery against one who has merely assisted in making the misrepresentation would allow the plaintiff to circumvent Rule 10b-5's reliance requirement.[113]

Section 20(a) of the Exchange Act[114] imposes secondary liability upon those who are deemed control persons of the primary violator. Most circuits apply a two-prong test to determine whether a person is a control person subject to Section 20(a) liability. First, the defendant must have actually exercised general control over the operations or activities of the primary participant. Second, the control person must have had the power or the ability—even if not exercised—to control the specific transaction or activity that gave rise to the violation.[115] Thus, outside

---

[109] *Cf.* Musick, Peeler & Garrett v. Employers Ins. of Wausau, 113 S. Ct. 2085 (1993), holding that there is an implied right to contribution among joint defendants. In the *Central Bank* case, the Court distinguished the *Musick* decision on the basis that the securities laws contain an express statement of controlling personal and joint and several liability, which is in contrast to the absence of a general aiding and abetting provision.

[110] 511 U.S. at 177.

[111] *See* In re Atlantic Financial Management, Inc., 784 F.2d 29 (1st Cir. 1985) (J. Breyer); Centennial Technologies Litigation, 52 F. Supp. 178 (D. Mass. 1999). *Contra* Converse v. Norwood Venture Corp. [1998 Transfer Binder], Fed. Sec. L. Rep. (CCH) ¶90,121 (S.D.N.Y. 1997). The fear that all such agency concepts are swept aside by the wooden character of *Central Bank* is reflected by the dissent. *See* Central Bank of Denver v. First Interstate Bank of Denver, 511 U.S. 164, 200 n.12 (1994).

[112] *See, e.g.*, Rubin v. Schottenstein, Zox & Dunn, 143 F.3d 263 (6th Cir. 1998) (attorney who commits misrepresentation while speaking to investors); Anixter v. Home-Stake Production Co., 77 F.3d 1215 (10th Cir. 1996) (accountant who prepares false financial statements).

[113] 511 U.S. at 180.

[114] 15 U.S.C. §78t(a) (2000).

[115] The leading case is Metge v. Baehler, 762 F.2d 621, 630-31 (8th Cir. 1985).

directors who serve on the audit committee and in that capacity approved accounting practices are control persons with respect to recognizing sales prematurely.[116] However, other outside directors would not be so held, unless involved in the review or release of the misleading information.[117]

Controlling person liability is not absolute. Section 20(a) provides the control person is liable to the same extent as the primary participant, "unless the controlling person acted in good faith and did not directly or indirectly induce the act or acts constituting the violation or cause of action." Note that this arises defensively so that the control person must prove both items. Since most control persons are able to establish that they did not induce the violation, the larger number of litigated cases turn on whether the control person has established her "good faith" defense. Good faith is an elastic expression capable of mandating in some instances only the absence of knowledge. In other contexts good faith implicates the absence of recklessness,[118] and still others good faith calls for the imposition of reasonable procedures to deter and detect misconduct by the controlled party.[119] A minority of the circuits essentially duplicate the good faith inquiry by making it part of the plaintiff's case to establish that a defendant is amenable to being a control person. The adherents of this minority view take the position that Congress intended to impose liability not solely upon a control person, but that the control person must in some meaningful sense have been a culpable participant in the violation either by being an actor in the violation or intended his acquiescence or passivity to further the violation.[120]

Quite separate from controlling person liability is vicarious liability premised upon the doctrine of respondeat superior. It is quite easy to understand that control person liablity is not the exclusive form of vicarious responsibility. Recall that respondeat superior liability is the means for holding the master responsible for torts committed by the servant within the scope of the servant's employment. Under respondeat superior liability it is the employing organization that is liable. Whereas, under control person liability, responsibility can be imposed upon the supervisor of the primary participant, even though the supervisor is not the employing organization. Courts have therefore held that respondeat superior and

---

[116] *See* In re Gupta Securities Litig. [1995 Transfer Binder], Fed. Sec. L. Rep. (CCH) ¶98,689 (N.D. Cal. 1995); Jacobs v. Coopers & Lybrand LLP [1999 Transfer Binder], Fed. Sec. L. Rep. (CCH) ¶90,443 (S.D.N.Y. 1999).

[117] *See* Domarko v. Hemodynamics, Inc., 848 F. Supp. 1335 (W.D. Mich. 1993) (excusing outside directors from liability but not director who served as firm's general counsel and had reviewed the misleading announcment).

[118] *See, e.g.*, Donohoe v. Consolidated Operating & Production Corp., 30 F.3d 907 (7th Cir. 1994) (substantial stockholders and directors met defense by background check of rogue officer and mandating procedures designed to prevent fraud).

[119] Classically this is the case for brokerage houses. *See, e.g.*, Harrison v. Dean Witter Reynolds, Inc., 79 F.3d 609 (7th Cir. 1996); Paul F. Newton & Co. v. Texas Commerce Bank, 630 F.2d 1111 (5th Cir. 1980); Marbury Management, Inc. v. Kohn, 629 F.2d 705 (2d Cir. 1980).

[120] *See* Boguslavaky v. Kaplan, 159 F.3d 715, 720 (2d Cir. 1998); Sharp v. Coopers & Lybrand, 649 F.2d 175, 185 (3d Cir. 1981).

control person liability coexist, i.e., that control person liability is not the exclusive means to reach the employer.[121] There is some cause for pause, however, that the narrow construction given to the securities laws by the Supreme Court, especially in *Central Bank*, may someday find its impact on the availability of respondeat superior liability. Such a result would indeed twist Congress's intent in providing control person liability. Its intent in crafting into the securities laws control person liability was to expand the scope of liability not to constrict it.[122]

§12.09.07   Statutory Restraints on Private Actions via PSLRA and SLUSA

The 103rd Congress bestowed a unique honor on securities fraud actions by enacting the Private Securities Litigation Reform Act of 1995[123] and thereby accorded *securities* class actions their own procedural rules. To date, no other area of private suit has earned its own set of special procedural rules, or more accurately, impediments to the private litigant. At the core of the PSLRA was tweaking the incentives that surround the initiation, prosecution, and settlement of securities class actions. Overall the concern was the relative lack of restraint that Congress believed characterized class action litigation.

An important contribution of the PSLRA to securities class actions is its embrace of the "lead plaintiff," which the Act provides presumptively is the class member with the "largest financial" loss.[124] The lead plaintiff is authorized to make recommendations to the court regarding the selection and dismissal of the suit's counsel. Congress's obvious intent is to harness to the class action's oversight the economic self-interest of such a large claimant.[125] After the PSLRA, being the first lawyer to file a complaint no longer provides a leg up to becoming lead coun-

---

[121] *See, e.g.*, Hollinger v. Titan Capital Corp., 914 F.2d 1564 (9th Cir. 1990) (en banc); Commerford v. Olson, 794 F.2d 1319 (8th Cir. 1986); In re Atlantic Financial Management, Inc., 784 F.2d 29 (1st Cir. 1986); Kerbs v. Fall River Ind., Inc., 502 F.2d 731 (10th Cir. 1974). The Third Circuit takes a somewhat different approach, recognizing respondeat superior liability for organizations that have a high duty to supervise their employees. *See* Sharp v. Coopers & Lybrand, 649 F.2d 175 (3d Cir. 1981).

[122] *See generally* Robert A. Prentice, Conceiving the Inconceivable and Judicially Implementing the Preposterous: The Premature Demise of Respondeat Superior Liability Under Section 10(b), 58 Ohio St. L. J. 1325 (1997). For a post *Central Bank* decision recognizing respondeat superior liability, *see* AT&T v. Winback and Conserve Program, Inc., 42 F.3d 1421 (3d Cir. 1994).

[123] Pub. L. No. 104-67, 109 Stat. 737 (codified in scattered sections in 15 U.S.C. (2000) [hereinafter PSLRA].

[124] Exchange Act Section 21D(a)(3)(B)(iii)(bb), 15 U.S.C. §78u-4 (2000). For provisions parallel to those described here for Exchange Act based suits that are applicable to suits brought under the Securities Act of 1933, *see* Section 27, 15 U.S.C. §77z-1 (2000).

At least one court imposes additional requirements for one to be a lead plaintiff, *see* Berger v. Compaq Computer Corp., 257 F.3d 475, 482-83 (5th Cir. 2001) (lead plaintiff must "possess a sufficient level of knowledge and understanding to be capable of 'controlling' or 'prosecuting' the litigation").

[125] For a study documenting that such self-interest abounds, and how the lead plaintiff provision could be imposed even had Congress not mandated it, *see* Elliott J. Weiss & John S. Beckerman, Let the Money Do the Monitoring: How Institutional Investors Can Reduce Agency Costs in Securities Class Actions, 104 Yale L.J. 2053 (1995).

B. The Antifraud Provision of the Securities Exchange Act

sel. The evidence to date suggests that securities class actions still are lawyer driven, albeit not of the magnitude as before the PSLRA. A good deal of effort is spent by the lawyers wooing investors with large losses, particularly financial institutions, to petition the court to be a lead plaintiff (all with the understanding that if selected as lead plaintiff the requesting investor would then retain the law firm that recruited the investor).[126] Among the issues posed by the lead plaintiff are whether an aggregation of individual investors who in combination have a larger loss than a single institutional investor is the preferable choice[127] and whether the selection of a lead plaintiff prevents the use of an auction to choose counsel for the class action.[128]

As seen above,[129] the PSLRA introduced something of a "double whammy" by tightening the pleading requirement beyond the standard particularity requirement and barring any discovery until the exhaustion of the defendant's motion to dismiss. The plaintiff "with respect to each act or omission alleged to" be a violation "must plead with particularity facts giving rise to a strong inference that the defendant acted with the required state of mind" to be liable.[130] And, the misrepresentation must be pled with particularity as well as setting forth the facts that support any allegation of misrepresentation that is based upon information or belief.[131] Discovery is not available to assist the plaintiff in satisfying meeting the tightened pleading requirement.[132] The intent of the discovery bar is to revoke the former license the plaintiff's counsel had to conduct a "fishing expedition" into the defendants' files solely by leveling bald accusations of fraud in the complaint.

The PSLRA mandates that the notice of settlement provided class members set forth an estimate of the average recoverable amount per share.[133] A further provision to chasten any bold class action counsel willing to push a questionable case is the PSLRA's mandating that the trial judge at the conclusion of each case make a finding whether the litigants have complied with Rule 11.[134] If so, then appropriate sanctions are to be imposed upon the violating party. Outside of securities litigation, Rule 11 sanctions arise customarily by a motion of one of the parties. The new provision introduced by the PSLRA avoids the possibility of the plaintiff's and defendant's counsel agreeing as part of the settlement that neither will raise Rule 11 sanctions.

Many substantive changes were also introduced by the PSLRA. There is a safe harbor for forward looking statements,[135] a provision for proportionate liability

---

[126] *See, e.g.,* In re Razorfish, Inc. Sec. Litig., 143 F. Supp. 2d 304 (S.D.N.Y. 2001).

[127] *See* A. Chris Heck, Comment, Conflict and Aggregation: Appointing Institutional Investors as Sole Lead Plaintiffs Under the PSLRA, 66 U. Chi. L. Rev. 1199 (1999). For an extreme case permitted such aggregation, *see* Netsky v. Capstead Mortgage Corp., 2000 U.S. Dist. Lexis 9941 (N.D. Tex. 2000) (group of 1,155 investors to produce a collective loss of $1.26 million).

[128] *See* In re Cendant Corp. Litig., 264 F.3d 201 (3d Cir. 2001).

[129] §12.09.02.

[130] Exchange Act Section 21D(b)(2), 15 U.S.C. §78u-4(b)(2) (2000).

[131] Exchange Act Section 21D(b)(1), 15 U.S.C. §78u-4(b)(1) (2000).

[132] Exchange Act Section 21D(b)(3), 15 U.S.C. §78u-4(b)(3) (2000).

[133] Exchange Act Section 21D(a)(7)(B), 15 U.S.C. §78u-4(a)(7)(B) (2000).

[134] Exchange Act Section 21D(c)(1), 15 U.S.C. §78u-4(c)(1) (2000).

[135] Exchange Act Section 21E, 15 U.S.C. §78u-5 (2000). Also this provision exists in the Securities Act Section 27A, 15 U.S.C. §77z-2 (2000).

that extends to contribution claims,[136] the elimination of securities claims from being a predicate act that satisfies RICO (unless there has been a prior criminal conviction),[137] and a statute of limitations for contribution claims.[138]

Soon after the PSLRA's passage, there was a noticeable increase in securities fraud filings in state courts. The concern arose that resourceful plaintiff's were, by filing their actions in state courts, circumventing the PSLRA's procedural and substantive provisions. Thus, the second shoe to drop in Congress's focus on securities litigation was the passage in 1998 of Securities Litigation Uniform Standards Act (SLUSA).[139] To counter the migration to the state courts, SLUSA preempts state court jurisdictions in *class actions* for certain "covered securities."[140] Class actions are defined as suits seeking damages on behalf of more than 50 persons.[141] Suits arising from misrepresentations made in acquisitions or involving a vote of the stockholders as well as by state pension funds or political subdivisions of the state is among the narrow set cases that are expressly exempted from SLUSA.[142] The most notable of its exclusions is the so-called Delaware carve-out that preserves the state court's jurisdiction to hear certain claims based upon fiduciary principles of the issuer's state of incorporation.[143]

§12.10   Rule 10b-5 and Insider Trading

Rule 10b-5 prohibits certain individuals—insiders, misappropriators, and tippees—from engaging in transactions in their company's stock if they do so on the basis of information not available to the investing public. This prohibition has been extended to tipping such information when doing so is a breach of a fiduciary duty.

As seen earlier in this chapter, common law rules pertaining to insider trading did not offer much protection against the trading of shares on the basis of confidential inside information not generally available to the investing public. Section 16(b) of the Exchange Act[1] somewhat fills a gap by providing prohibitions against insider short-swing speculative profits. Recall that Section 16(b) applies to a relatively limited number of situations because it requires both a purchase and a sale within six months and applies to equity securities of companies that are subject to

---

[136] Exchange Act Section 21D(f), 15 U.S.C. §78u-4(f) (2000).

[137] Racketeer Influence and Corrupt Organizations Act Section 1964(c), 18 U.S.C. §1964(c) (2000).

[138] Exchange Act Section 21D(f)(9), 15 U.S.C. §78u-4(f)(9) (2000).

[139] Exchange Act Section 28(f). 15 U.S.C. §78bb(f) (2000).

[140] Covered securities are defined in Section 18(b) of the Securities Act, 15 U.S.C. §77r(b) (2000), and include securities traded on the New York Stock Exchange, American Exchange, and Nasdaq, certain other exchanges that have been designated by the SEC, issued by a company subject to the periodic reporting requirements of the Exchange Act, as well as securities offered pursuant to certain exemptions from the registration requirements of the Securities Act.

[141] Exchange Act Section 28(f)(5)(B), 15 U.S.C. §78bb(f)(5)(B) (2000).

[142] Exchange Act Section 28(f)(3), 15 U.S.C. §78bb(f)(3) (2000).

[143] Exchange Act Section 28(f)3)(A)(i), 15 U.S.C. §78bb(f)(3)(i) (2000).

§12.10   [1] 15 U.S.C. §78p(b) (2000). *See supra* §12.08.

the 1934 Act's registration and reporting requirements and reaches only the trading of narrowly defined insiders.[2] Thus, insiders who on the basis of their confidential knowledge trade in securities that are not those of a reporting company, or who have not purchased and sold, or vice versa, within six months, or the person trading is not an officer, director, or an owner of more than 10 percent of a company that is subject to the jurisdictional reach of Section 16, can escape the prophylaxis provided by Section 16(b).

Origins of "Disclose or Abstain" Rule. The first step toward making Rule 10b-5 the major enforcement weapon for the regulation of insider trading occurred in 1961 in *In re Cady, Roberts & Co.,*[3] an SEC administrative proceeding. The directors of Curtiss-Wright Corporation decided to cut the company's regular dividend, but the decision was not immediately made public. Advance news of the development reached a stockbroker who had been purchasing the stock for his customers; he then liquidated the customers' holdings before the news of the dividend cut depressed the market price. The SEC disciplined the broker for having violated Rule 10b-5.

Seven years after the *Cady, Roberts* ruling, a highly significant Rule 10b-5 decision was handed down by the United States Court of Appeals for the Second Circuit in *Securities & Exchange Commission v. Texas Gulf Sulphur Company.*[4] In that case, TGS was exploring eastern Canada for possible mining sites. In March 1959, aerial surveys revealed that the Kidd-55 segment had good potential. In late October 1963, ground surveys proved equally optimistic and confirmed the desirability of drilling test holes. Within two weeks, samples from a 655-foot-deep test hole at K-55-1 provided visual evidence of copper and zinc. This was sufficient to convince TGS to acquire the land in question. TGS management decided to keep the test results quiet in order to facilitate an advantageous acquisition of the drill site.

About this time a number of TGS officers began acquiring stock on the open market at less than 18 dollars per share.[5] In early December, laboratory assays of the samples confirmed a high copper, zinc, and silver content. By March 27, 1964, TGS resumed drilling. On April 12, the company issued a pessimistic press release, purportedly to quell rumors, explaining that although the samples were encouraging "[t]he work done to date has not been sufficient to reach definite conclusions and any statement as to size and grade of one would be premature and possibly misleading."[6] At that point, TGS stock was trading at between $30⅛ and $32. On the very next day, continued drilling revealed that the previous optimism had been justified. Three days later, in an April 16 press release, the company made the facts public. TGS stock climbed to a high of $37 and by May 15 was selling at slightly more than $58; thus making the insiders a substantial profit.

---

[2] *See* §12.08.

[3] In re Cady, Roberts & Co., 40 S.E.C. 907 (1961).

[4] 401 F.2d 833 (2d Cir. 1968), *cert. denied,* 394 U.S. 976 (1969), s.c., 446 F.2d 1301 (2d Cir. 1971).

[5] This activity continued through April 1964 as the price slowly rose to $30. *See* 401 F.2d at 840, n.2.

[6] 401 F.2d at 845.

The foregoing facts raised a number of questions, including (1) the accountability of those insiders who profited from their pre-April 16 purchases; (2) the posture of the "tippees," who were not corporate officers but had advance notice of the events surrounding K-55-1; and (3) the corporation's responsibility for the misleading April 12 press release. The court ruled that the corporation violated Rule 10b-5 in negligently issuing the April 12 press release. That part of the holding, which is discussed elsewhere,[7] has been surpassed as by the Supreme Court's ruling that negligence is not sufficient to support a Rule 10b-5 claim.[8]

With regard to the insider trading activity, following the lead of the *Cady, Roberts* ruling, the Second Circuit in *SEC v. Texas Gulf Sulphur* ruled that once there were material facts known only to insiders, they and their tippees were barred by Rule 10b-5 from profiting from such information:

> Thus, anyone in possession of material inside information must either disclose it to the investing public, or, if he is disabled from disclosing it in order to protect a corporate confidence, or he chooses not to do so, must abstain from trading in or recommending the securities concerned while such inside information remains undisclosed.[9]

The court then determined the "materiality" by looking to the dramatic increase in insider stock acquisitions. The court reasoned that this provided strong circumstantial evidence of the time at which the reasonable investor would consider the information a substantial factor in making an investment decision.[10] This resolved the question only with regard to the trading insiders and did not necessarily bear upon the question of materiality insofar as it would affirmatively compel corporate disclosure.[11]

Texas Gulf Sulphur further held that the insiders' good faith was not a defense to an SEC injunctive action, although today it is clear that it must be shown that the defendants acted with scienter.[12] The question of whether a defendant acted with mere negligence or even recklessness rarely arises in insider trading cases since the conduct proscribed can hardly arise by inadvertence.[13] These are not instances, as are many cases involving false statements, where the defendant can lament, "whoops, I have traded on inside information."

[7] *See supra* §12.09.02.

[8] Ernst & Ernst v. Hochfelder, 425 U.S. 185 (1976).

[9] 401 F.2d at 848.

[10] Materiality is a question of fact depending on all of the surrounding circumstances, yet the courts have been unable to define the concept in a meaningful way. *Compare* TSC Indus. v. Northway, Inc., 426 U.S. 438 (1976), with Mills v. Electric Auto-Lite Co., 396 U.S. 375 (1970) *and* Gerstle v. Gamble-Skogmo, Inc., 478 F.2d 1281 (2d Cir. 1973) (all decided under the proxy rules). *See* Homer Kripke, Rule 10b-5 Liability and "Material Facts," 46 N.Y.U. L. Rev. 1061 (1971).

[11] *See* §12.11.

[12] Aaron v. Securities & Exch. Commn., 446 U.S.680 (1980) (scienter is required under Rule 10b-5 and section 10b-5 of the 1934 Act but is not an element of a violation of sections 17(a)(2), (3) of the 1933 Act). *See also, e.g.*, Ernst & Ernst v. Hochfelder, 425 U.S. 185 (1976); *supra* §12.08 note 12.

[13] For an early case prosecuted on the theory of negligent tipping, *see* SEC v. Bausch & Lomb, Inc., 565 F.2d 8 (2d Cir. 1976) (affirming decision not to issue injunction because isolated instance of poor judgment does not suggest there is likelihood the defendant will commit a future violation).

B. The Antifraud Provision of the Securities Exchange Act

In deciding when insiders could trade in the TGS stock, the court reasoned that the disclosure date was not conclusive, because the public needed time to digest and analyze the information once it was released. The court then extended these proscriptions to trading tippees—non-insiders who trade on the basis of advance notice—but it did not address the accountability of the non-trading tippers.[14]

Impact of **Chiarella** *and Misappropriation Theory.* Insider trading regulation took a momentary setback in *Chiarella v. United States.*[15] The defendant, Vincent Chiarella, a financial printer, worked on a number of tender offers and, using his ingenuity, discovered in advance the identity of the thinly disguised target companies. Armed with knowledge of the impending takeover attempt, the printer purchased stock in target companies with the comforting knowledge that the price would rise with the announcement of the tender offer. The Court overturned his criminal conviction, basing its decision on the absence of a fiduciary relationship between the defendant and any of the companies in which he invested. The Court noted that the purportedly injured sellers had not placed any reliance on the printer's activity and that the impersonal nature of the transactions precluded a 10b-5 violation.

Later the Supreme Court, in dicta, recognized that those not in the permanent employ of the corporation may nevertheless become "temporary insiders" because they have assumed a position of trust and confidence with respect to material information shared with them.[16]

Thus *Chiarella* limits Rule 10b-5's presumption of defendants who traded in the securities of corporations with whom the defendant has a fiduciary relationship. Significantly the court left open the question of what types of fiduciary or other relationships might suffice to establish a duty to disclose or abstain from trading. The potential limiting effect of *Chiarella* was shortlived; drawing on the view expressed by four justices in *Chiarella,* the lower courts have embraced the misappropriation theory as a basis to reach individuals, such as Vincent Chiarella, who breach a fiduciary relationship with one entity by using confidential information obtained from that entity to trade in the stock of another corporation.[17]

The misappropriation theory first expands Rule 10b-5 to situations in which a defendant can properly be said to be under a fraud-based duty to disclose or abstain from trading because of a fiduciary relationship not to use confidential information for private gain.

---

[14] *See* Astor v. Texas Gulf Sulphur Co., 306 F. Supp. 1333 (S.D.N.Y. 1969). This was not the first time the tipping issue surfaced. *See, e.g.,* Ross v. Licht, 263 F. Supp. 395 (S.D.N.Y. 1967); In re Cady. Roberts & Co., 40 S.E.C. 907 (1961).

[15] 445 U.S. 222 (1980).

[16] *See* Dirks v. SEC, 463 U.S. 646, 655 n.14 (1983).

[17] *See* SEC v. Materia, 745 F.2d 197 (2d Cir. 1984) (financial proofreader, facts similar to *Chiarella*); United States v. Newman, 664 F.2d 12 (2d Cir. 1981), *aff'd on remand,* 722 F.2d 729, *cert. denied,* 464 U.S. 863 (1983) (investment banker misappropriated information about his employer's clients). Lawyers and other law firm employees have similarly been held to have violated Rule 10b-5.

The misappropriation theory reached the Supreme Court in 1987.[18] The defendant was a financial columnist (writing the influential Wall Street Journal's "Heard on the Street" column) who had tipped his friends in advance as to the contents of upcoming columns that would affect the price of certain stocks. The Second Circuit had held that this information had been misappropriated from the defendant's employer, Dow Jones, and thus, under the disclose-or-abstain rule, the columnist and his friends had violated Rule 10b-5.[19] The Supreme Court granted certiorari and had the opportunity to finally resolve the issue; however, the Rule 10b-5 conviction was affirmed without opinion by an equally divided Supreme Court.[20] Since an affirmance by an equally divided Supreme Court does not contain any opinions, there is no indication whether the division was over a wholesale application of the misappropriation theory or on some other grounds.

Though many lower courts embraced the misappropriation theory to expand the reach of insider trading regulation beyond that proscribed in *Chiarella*, two circuits rejected the misappropriation theory.[21] The split between the circuits attracted the interest of the Supreme Court, which, in 1997, once again considered the viability of the misappropriation theory.[22] On this occasion, challenges to this basis of Rule 10b-5 liability were finally put to rest. In *United States v. O'Hagan*, the Court held that a Rule 10b-5 violation can be based on a breach of a duty to the sources of the information even when the violator is not an insider of the company whose securities are being traded. The necessary deception is present by virtue of the defendant failing to disclose her plans to trade in the securities, i.e., "feigning fidelity" to the source of the information.[23] Furthermore, this deception is "in connection with the purchase or sale of any security" even though it cannot be linked to identifiable purchasers or sellers.[24] In other words, the duty underlying the Rule 10b-5 violation need not be owed to a purchaser or seller of securities.

Problems abound in determining what constitutes a fiduciary relationship. Thus, in *United States v. Chestman*,[25] the Second Circuit, sitting en banc, held that the marital relationship was not itself a sufficient basis upon which the misappropriation theory would operate. In *Chestman*, the defendant learned from his wife, who did not otherwise swear him to preserve the information's confidentiality, certain material non-public information which later was the basis for trading

---

[18] Carpenter v. United States, 484 U.S. 19 (1987).

[19] United States v. Carpenter, 791 F.2d 1024 (2d Cir. 1986).

[20] Carpenter v. United States, 484 U.S. 19 (1987). Note that the decision to recognize the misappropriation theory also finds support in the legislative history of the 1988 Insider Trading and Securities Fraud Enforcement Act (ITSFEA), H.R. Rep. No. 100-910, 100th Cong. 2d Sess. 10-11 (1988).

[21] United States v. O'Hagan, 92 F.3d 612 (8th Cir. 1996), *rev'd*, 521 U.S. 642 (1997); United States v. Bryan, 58 F.3d 933 (4th Cir. 1995).

[22] United States v. O'Hagan, 521 U.S. 642 (1997).

[23] *Id.* at 655.

[24] *Id.* at 652.

[25] 704 F. Supp. 451 (S.D.N.Y. 1989), *rev'd*, 903 F.2d 75 (2d Cir. 1990), *reh'g en banc*, 947 F.2d 551 (2d Cir. 1991), *cert. denied*, 112 S. Ct. 1759 (1992).

B. The Antifraud Provision of the Securities Exchange Act

before that information became public.[26] Much needed guidance to the courts is now provided by Rule 10b5-2 which provides a nonexclusive definition of the types of relationships and circumstances that impose a duty of "trust and confidence for the purpose of the misappropriation theory."[27] Rule 10b5-2 provides that trust and confidence can arise by agreement or a history or practice of sharing confidences with reason to believe the confidentiality of the information is to be maintained. Also, information shared among certain family members is similarly deemed confidential, unless the opposite is proven that the person receiving the information did not know and could not reasonably expect that the source of the information expected confidentiality in light of the parties' past practices.

Tippers and Tippees. In *Dirks v. SEC,*[28] the Supreme Court underscored the importance of a preexisting fiduciary relationship when it held that outsiders may freely trade on an insider's selective disclosure (that is, a "tip") as long as the disclosure was not "improper." Secrist, a former officer of Equity Funding of America, informed Dirks, an investment analyst, that Equity Funding's assets were fraudulently overstated. In the course of aggressively investigating Secrist's tip, Dirks shared Secrist's revelation with five investment advisers, who caused their advisees to liquidate more than $16 million worth of Equity Funding stock. The Supreme Court held Dirks did not violate Rule 10b-5 because Secrist's disclosure was not improper. The Supreme Court offered an extremely narrow concept of what constitutes an "improper" tip: A disclosure is improper if the insider tips a relative or a friend, or expects to reap a pecuniary gain from the selective disclosure.[29] In reaching this conclusion, the Court demonstrated the pragmatic view that to have held otherwise would have had a chilling effect on the socially desirable activities of security analysts.[30]

The *Dirks* holding has wider significance than merely to protect analysts: The case restrains the scope of the disclose-or-abstain rule. First, it provides an

---

[26] Chestman learned of the information from Loeb, who learned of the information from his wife, who learned of it from other family members. The majority of the court held that marriage alone did not create a fiduciary relationship. For a different view of the marital relationship, *see* SEC v. Lenfest, 949 F. Supp. 341 (W.D. Pa. 1996) (spouse of director violated confidential relationship by trading on the basis of information obtained from her husband).

Another decision case showing the potential breadth of liability under this view is United States v. Willis, 737 F. Supp. 269 (S.D.N.Y. 1990). A former CEO of Shearson and former president of American Express was considering becoming CEO of BankAmerica. He discussed these plans with his wife, who in turn discussed them with her psychiatrist in the course of her treatment. The psychiatrist traded in the marketplace on the basis of this material nonpublic information and profited as a result. On the basis of the breach of the confidential and hence fiduciary relationship between the psychiatrist and his patient, the court held that the psychiatrist had violated Rule 10b-5.

[27] 17 C.F.R. §240.10b5-2 (2002).

[28] 463 U.S. 646 (1983).

[29] *Id.* 663-664. In SEC v. Warde, 151 F.3d 42 (2d Cir. 1998), the government won a significant victory with its successful prosecution of a tippee on the exclusive basis he received the information from a long-time friend; the friend served on the board of the corporation whose shares the defendant purchased and the friend received no tangible or specific benefit by virtue of making the tip.

[30] *Id.* at 662.

extremely narrow definition of what constitutes an *improper* tip. Second, even though a tip is improper, only those who are aware the disclosure was improper are subject to Rule 10b-5 liability if they trade or pass the tip on to another. Because of *Dirks*, the bystander who overhears another discussing material non-public information may freely trade, provided he is not a friend or relative, or conferred or could confer a pecuniary benefit upon the speaker.[31] But if the parties are not perfect strangers, it is easier to establish the selective disclosure was improper.[32] The tippee liability does not require proof that his tipper knew his tippee would trade; it is enough that the tippee knew that the selective disclosure to him was a breach of the tipper's duty to the employer.[33] When, however, tipping is prosecuted under Rule 14e-3 there is not the same requirement for the selective disclosure to constitute a breach of fiduciary obligation so that the inquiry instead is whether the tippee knew the information was material, non-public, and selectively disclosed after a substantial step had been undertaken toward a tender offer.[34] And, when the act of tipping is within the scope of, for example, the senior officer's employment, the employer can be liable.[35] In most instances, however, tipping and insider trading are outside the scope of one's employment and, hence, does not subject their employer to vicarious liability.[36]

The license that *Dirks* conferred upon analysts has been significantly confined by the SEC's adoption in late 2000 of Regulation FD.[37] In broad overview, Regulation FD (the acronym for "fair disclosure") greatly restricts the freedom public companies formerly enjoyed to make selective disclosures of material non-public information to market professionals or shareholders. The scope of its requirements is examined in a later section of this chapter.[38]

Possession versus Use. There has been ongoing debate as to whether a case for improper insider trading under Rule 10b-5 can be made by showing that the defendant traded while in *possession* of material non-public information or whether it must be established that he or she in fact *used* the information in making the trades in question. In a 1998 decision, the Eleventh Circuit adopted an "on

---

[31] The classic illustration involves a famous football coach who while attending his son's track meet overheard another proud parent discussing an upcoming "deal." *See* SEC v. Switzer, 590 F. Supp. 756 (W.D. Okla. 1984); SEC v. Platt, 565 F. Supp. 1244 (W.D. Okla. 1983). *See also* SEC v. Falbo, 14 F. Supp. 2d 508 (S.D.N.Y. 1998) (tippee prevailed by proving that he obtained information by eavesdropping and also alleging he did not know how extensive an access the tipper had).

[32] *See, e.g.,* United States v. Falcone, 257 F.3d 226 (2d Cir. 2001) (conspirators traded on advance knowledge of what companies would be discussed in forthcoming issues of Business Week).

[33] *See* United States v. Libera, 989 F.2d 596 (2d Cir. 1993). For a case deferring to the jury to make factual determinations such as whether the tippee knew the disclosure was improper, *see* SEC v. Thrasher, 152 F. Supp. 2d 291 (S.D.N.Y. 2001).

[34] *See* Securities and Exchange Commission v. Mayhew, 121 F.3d 44 (2d Cir. 1997); Securities and Exchange Commission v. Maio, 51 F.3d 623 (7th Cir. 1995); SEC v. Musella, 748 F. Supp. 1028 (S.D.N.Y. 1989).

[35] *See* SEC v. Geon Ind., Inc., 381 F. Supp. 1063 (S.D.N.Y. 1974), *modified*, 531 F.2d 39 (2d Cir. 1976).

[36] *See, e.g.,* Moss v. Morgan Stanley, Inc., 553 F. Supp. 1347 (S.D.N.Y.), *aff'd*, 719 F.2d 5 (2d Cir. 1983).

[37] Rule 100, 17 CFR §240.100 (2002).

[38] *See infra* §12.11.

B. The Antifraud Provision of the Securities Exchange Act

the basis" rather than "mere possession" test of liability.[39] The court went on to point out, however, that trades while in possession of such information can be used to create a "strong inference" that the defendant in fact used the information.[40] In contrast is the reasoning of Judge Richard Posner that proof that the defendant traded when he had knowledge of insider information should place upon him the burden of establishing that he did not trade on the basis of that information.[41] The SEC has addressed the split in the circuits in its Rule 10b5-1,[42] which essentially equates the meaning of "on the basis" to "in possession."[43] Rule 10b5-1, however, provides a safe harbor for trading when the aware of material non-public information if the trade is strictly pursuant to a binding written contract to purchase or sale that was entered into before the defendant became aware of the inside information.[44]

Insider trading is also proscribed under Rule 14e-3,[45] being among the many antifraud provisions promulgated by the SEC under the authority conferred on it by the Williams Act amendments to the Exchange Act. The validity of Rule 14e-3 was upheld in *United States v. O'Hagan*.[46] Its proscription of insider trading is triggered when "a susbstantial step or steps to commence . . . a tender offer" have been taken. This at least occurs when negotiations have commenced between the corporations.[47]

Government Enforcement Actions. Willful violations of the federal securities laws may give rise to a criminal prosecution by the Department of Justice, resulting in fines and/or imprisonment. Furthermore, violations may result in sanctions from the SEC. For example, the Commission may impose administrative sanctions: if the violator is a broker-dealer or other market professional, her license can be suspended or revoked. The SEC is authorized to seek either temporary or permanent injunctive relief in the courts "whenever it shall appear to the Commission that any person is engaged or is about to engage in any acts or practices which constitute or will constitute a violation."[48] More frequently, the SEC seeks some form of monetary recovery in addition to a prospective injunction against future violations.

---

[39] SEC v. Adler, 137 F.3d 1325 (11th Cir. 1998). *See also* United States v. Smith, 155 F.3d 1051 (9th Cir. 1998) (at least in a criminal proceeding, prosecution must prove defendant used inside information and not appropriate to infer such from proof the defendant was aware of the material non-public information). *See generally, e.g.,* Insider Trading, 30 Sec. Reg. & L. Rep. (BNA) 625 (April 24, 1998). *Contra* United States v. Teicher, 987 F.2d 112 (2d Cir. 1993) (the knowing possession standard comports with the notion that a fiduciary must hold that information in confidence).

[40] SEC v. Adler, 137 F.3d 1325, 1337 (11th Cir. 1998).

[41] *See* SEC v. Lipson, 278 F.3d 656 (7th Cir. 2002).

[42] 17 C.F.R. §240.10b5-1 (2002).

[43] Rule 10b5-1(b) provides that "on the basis" means "if the person making the purchase or sale was aware of the material nonpublic information when the person made the purchase or sale."

[44] *Id.* at (c).

[45] 17 C.F.R. §240.14e-3 (2000). *See* §24.05.01, *infra.*

[46] 521 U.S. 642 (1997).

[47] SEC v. Maio, 51 F.3d 623 (7th Cir. 1995).

[48] 15 U.S.C. §78t (2000).

In the wake of the Supreme Court decisions in *Chiarella*[49] and *Dirks*,[50] Congress enacted even stronger insider trading penalties, available for use by the SEC. The Insider Trading Sanctions Act of 1984 (ITSA) increased civil and criminal penalties for trading while in possession of material nonpublic information: The SEC is authorized to seek disgorgement of profits[51] and a civil penalty of up to three times the profits gained or the loss avoided by the defendant,[52] and the criminal penalty was increased from $10,000 to $100,000. However, while facially applicable to transactions involving misuse of non-public material information, ITSA does not define the scope of permissible conduct. Thus ITSA does not alter the availability of a cause of action, but merely the penalties that may be imposed.

ITSA has proven to be an effective enforcement weapon. Following its enactment, the SEC was increasingly vigorous in enforcing insider trading prohibitions and has reached some lucrative settlements.[53] The question arises whether actions under ITSA and criminal prosecutions based on the same transactions violate the constitutional prohibition against double jeopardy.[54] Beyond the increased penalties in ITSA, in October 1990, Congress enacted the Securities Enforcement Remedies and Penny Stock Reform Act, which, among other things, gave the SEC the power in an administrative proceeding to require disgorgement of illegal profits.

Private Rights of Action for Insider Trading. In a face-to-face transaction, an action will lie against someone who sells or purchases while in possession of material inside non-public information.[55] However, in an open-market context, standing to sue is more problematic and, therefore, at one time posed ticklish standing questions.[56] Congress stepped in to change this result. The Insider Trading and Securities Fraud Enforcement Act (ITSFEA) was enacted by Congress in 1988 to supplement any remedy that may exist under Rule 10b-5. The Act provides an

---

[49] *See supra* note 15.

[50] *See supra* note 28.

[51] On the measurement of the amount of profits to be disgorged, *see* SEC v. MacDonald, 699 F.2d 47 (1st Cir. 1983) (en banc) (need disgorge only profits up to the market's reaction to initial disclosure and not the later higher price reached by the security).

[52] Both disgorgement and treble profits can be recovered as the purpose of ITSA was not to reduce the scope of other relief the SEC may obtain. *See* SEC v. Lipson, 278 F.3d 656 (7th Cir. 2002).

[53] *See, e.g.*, SEC v. Certain Unknown Purchasers of Common Stock & Call Options of Santa Fe Intl. Corp. [1985-1986 Transfer Binder], Fed. Sec. L. Rep. (CCH) ¶92,484 (S.D.N.Y. 1986) (consent order to disgorge $7,800,000 in alleged insider trading profits); SEC v. Boesky [1986-1987 Transfer Binder], Fed. Sec. L. Rep. (CCH) ¶92,991 (S.D.N.Y. 1986) (settlement of $50,000,000 disgorgement and $50,000,000 penalty); SEC v. Kidder Peabody & Co., 19 Sec. Reg. & L. Rep. (BNA) 811 (S.D.N.Y. 1987) (settlement of more than $25,000,000).

[54] In United States v. Halper, 490 U.S. 435 (1989). Under *Halper*, a sanction is punishment if it is deemed to serve the traditional goals of "deterrence or retribution." This was disavowed in Hudson v. U.S., 522 U.S. 93 (1997).

[55] Affiliated Ute Citizens of Utah v. United States, 406 U.S. 128 (1972), *reh'g denied*, 407 U.S. 916 (1972). Causation was not a problem because the purchaser dealt directly with the seller. Further, the Court held that reliance on the nondisclosure could be presumed from the materiality of the information.

[56] Friedrich v. Bradford, 542 F.2d 307 (6th Cir. 1976), *cert. denied*, 429 U.S.1053 (1977).

express private right of action by contemporaneous traders against persons making improper use of material non-public information.[57] Damages in such an action are limited to the profit (or loss avoided) that is attributable to the defendant's illegal conduct, reduced to the extent that the SEC has secured disgorgement (as opposed to a penalty) under the 1984 ITSA legislation.

§12.11   Rule 10b-5 and the Duty to Disclose

Rule 10b-5 plays a major role in ensuring the flow of corporate information to the investing public. The 1934 Exchange Act imposes an affirmative disclosure requirement on corporations that are sufficiently large to fall within the Act's registration and reporting requirements.[1] These provisions require, inter alia, complete financial disclosure, descriptions of the company's operations and future plans, and detailing of management activities, as well as dealing with the more specialized problems of shareholder suffrage, tender offers, and insider trading.[2] Even beyond these express disclosure provisions, the broad prophylactic language of Rule 10b-5 has had a significant impact in the disclosure area.

The duty to not misstate material facts applies regardless of the medium or the intended audience of the misstatement. Thus, a document issued with regard to one type of securities, such as bonds, can have 10b-5 ramifications as to the common stock where the misstatements are material to both.[3] Similarly, statements made in connection with shareholder votes are subject to Rule 10b-5 scrutiny where there is a securities transaction, as is the case, for example, in a merger[4] or in the issuance of additional shares.[5] A purposeful understatement of profits so as not to run afoul of government contracting requirements exposes those releasing the depressed earnings report to liability under Rule 10b-5.[6] Furthermore, a suit exists for investors who purchase the company's shares based on bouncy overstatements regarding the capabilities of the company's new product.[7] The point is that information mediums are seamless so that information intended for one audience can be expected to be accessed by investors whose appetite is

---

[57] 15 U.S.C. §78t-1 (2000).

§12.11   [1] By virtue of section 12 of the Act, all securities listed on a national securties exchange as well as any class of equity securities of a company with more than $10 million in assets and more than 500 shareholders. 15 U.S.C. §78*l* (2000). The registration requirement in turn triggers corporate periodic reports (*e.g.,* 15 U.S.C. §78m, *o* (2000)), reporting requirements on insiders, (15 U.S.C. §78p(a) (2000)) as well as the Act's tender offer provisions and proxy regulation (15 U.S.C. §§78m(d), (e); 78n(a), (d), (e) (2000)).

[2] *See generally* Homer Kripke, The SEC and Corporate Disclosure: Regulation in Search of a Purpose (1979).

[3] Lanza v. Drexel, 479 F.2d 1277 (2d Cir. 1973).

[4] *E.g.,* Schlick v. Penn-Dixie Cement Corp., 507 F.2d 374 (2d Cir. 1974), *cert. denied,* 421 U.S. 976 (1975).

[5] *E.g.,* Hooper v. Mountain States Sec. Corp., 282 F.2d 195 (5th Cir. 1960), *cert. denied,* 365 U.S. 814 (1961).

[6] *See* Heit v. Weitzen, 402 F.2d 909 (2d Cir. 1968).

[7] *See, e.g.,* Stac Electronics Sec. Litig., 82 F.3d 480 (9th Cir. 1996).

insatiable for information bearing on the company's position, performance, and future.

The truly challenging issue under Rule 10b-5 and the securities laws generally arises in providing definitive guidance of when there is a duty to speak. That is, omissions, not misstatements, pose the greatest intellectual challenge under Rule 10b-5. Duty is an element in a Rule 10b-5 action only in the case of the omission of a material fact since a matter in issue is the defendant's obligation to disclose the omitted fact. Note here that the securities laws are quite selective in the instances when there is an express duty to speak. Corporations subject to the registration requirements of Section 12 of the Exchange Act[8] must periodically file reports with the SEC.[9] The Exchange Act does not, however, expressly require a corporation to report material information that is not otherwise required by the periodic reporting and shareholder information requirements. The reporting called for by the Exchange Act is periodic, as contrasted with continuous reporting, in part because of the great difficulty in defining when there should be a duty to speak. Hence, there is no affirmative duty to disclose the types of material developments and information mandated by the SEC's periodic disclosure requirements until the corporation's next quarterly or annual report is due. And, those disclosure requirements are relatively focused in terms of the precise types of information that is required to be disclosed. Furthermore, the listing requirements of the major stock exchanges expressly require corporations to make timely disclosure of all information that would be material to the reasonable investor, but nevertheless accord the issuer business discretion to withhold information when non-disclosure best serves the corporate interest.[10] Thus, the instances in which Rule 10b-5 imposes a duty to speak are fairly limited. The courts are particularly firm in holding that there is no duty to disclose internal projections or business strategies that may be pursued.[11]

Thus, the starting point in examining the duty to speak is a fairly broad principle that the issuer and others are under no duty to speak absent an independent basis for the duty to disclose.[12] This view is supported by the Supreme Court ruling in insider trading cases that the mere possession of confidential inside information is not sufficient to trigger the duty to disclose or abstain from trading.[13]

The most frequent instances of finding a breach of the duty to disclose material information is where the plaintiff alleges the defendant has committed a half-truth by withholding information that thus rendered what the defendant has

[8] 15 U.S.C. §78*l* (2000).

[9] 15 U.S.C. §78m (2000).

[10] N.Y.S.E. Company Manual, 3 Fed. Sec. L. Rep. (CCH) ¶23,121; American Stock Exchange Company Guide (CCH) ¶10,121; Sec. Exch. Act Rel. No. 34-8995 [1970-71 Transfer Binder], (CCH) ¶77,915 (Oct. 15, 1970).

[11] *See, e.g.,* San Leandro Emergency Medical Group Profit Sharing Plan v. Philip Morris Co., 75 F.3d 801 (2d Cir. 1996).

[12] *See, e.g.,* Murphy v. Sofamor Danek Group Inc., 123 F.3d 394 (6th Cir. 1997) (no duty to disclose products promoted illegally or that premiums charged for its products could not be sustained).

[13] Dirks v. SEC, 463 U.S. 646 (1983); Chiarella v. United States, 445 U.S. 222 (1980).

B. The Antifraud Provision of the Securities Exchange Act

disclosed materially misleading.[14] Disclosures made pursuant to the requirements of either the Securities Act of 1933 and the Exchange Act of 1934 not only require that there be disclosed the information set forth specifically in the SEC's disclosure guides, but expressly require that SEC registrant's include in their filings "such further material information . . . as may be necessary to make the required statement, in light of all of the circumstances . . . not misleading."[15] Entangled with the defendant's duty to avoid half-truths is the relative certainty of the information known to the defendant but not disclosed to the plaintiff. This is best illustrated by the issuer of whether the issuer must disclose adverse developments that the business is incurring during the fiscal quarter that it is offering its securities to the public.

Notwithstanding the absence of an affirmative duty to disclose, once a statement has been made, there may be a continuing duty to update and/or correct the information that was previously disseminated.[16] The duty to update refers to the situation in which an earlier statement was true when made, but subsequent facts have rendered the earlier statement materially misleading. In contrast, the duty to correct arises when the earlier statement was false when made, but the party making it did so innocently, i.e., without scienter, but later has knowledge (or is reckless) of the untruthfulness of the earlier statement. Both the duty to update and the duty to correct assume that the earlier-made statement is still influencing investor behavior. If the court is persuaded that the earlier representation is stale, being eclipsed by subsequent information reaching the plaintiff, there is no basis to believe investors are being harmed by the earlier information and, hence, there is no basis for either a duty to update or correct.

The duty to correct is not absolute because it is triggered only when failure to do so would make the statement made materially misleading.[17] Certainly there is no duty to correct rumors or forecasts that cannot be attributed to the issuer.[18] However, if management confirms the forecast to be made by an analyst or otherwise entangles the issuer with another's statements, there is a duty to correct on the part of the issuer.[19]

Public companies are placed in a difficult position when there are rumors about the company's securities, its fundamental condition, or possible takeover

---

[14] *See, e.g.,* Ansin v. River Oaks Furniture Inc., 105 F.3d 745 (1st Cir. 1997) (failure to disclose when repurchasing shares from some of its stockholders that it would engage in IPO was material omission); Stransky v. Cummins Engine Co., Inc., 51 F.3d 1329 (7th Cir. 1995) (announcement that cost of engines was falling misleading by nondisclosure that warranty costs were rising).

[15] Securities Act Rule 408, 17 C.F.R. §230.408 (2002). A similar requirement appears in Exchange Act Rule 12b-20, 17 C.F.R. §240.12b-20 (2002).

[16] *See, e.g.,* Backman v. Polaroid Corp., 910 F.2d 10 (1st Cir. 1990) (although not initially misleading, subsequent developments triggered a duty to correct overly optimistic predictions). For an opinion that is equivocal as to whether there is a legal obligation per se to update, *see* Stransky v. Cummins Engine Corp., 51 F.3d 1329 (7th Cir. 1995).

[17] Moss v. Healthcare Compare Corp., 75 F.3d 276 (7th Cir. 1996) (no duty to correct what is merely a tentative estimate); Backman v. Polaroid Corp., 910 F.2d 10 (1st Cir. 1990).

[18] *See, e.g.,* Elkind v. Liggett & Myers, Inc., 635 F.2d 156 (2d Cir. 1980).

[19] *See, e.g.,* In re Cypress Semiconductor Sec. Litig., 891 F. Supp. 1369 (N.D. Cal. 1995), *aff'd sub nom.* Eisenstadt v. Allen, 113 F.3d 1240 (9th Cir. 1997).

activity.[20] When approached by the press, market researchers, or securities analysts,[21] corporations are faced with a dilemma. They cannot issue a denial if to do so would be materially misleading. Thus, for example, the Supreme Court reaffirmed a materiality standard determined by those facts that a reasonable investor would deem significant in making an investment decision, thus precluding denials of existing merger negotiations.[22]

In such situations, issuers have two alternatives. The issuer can, of course, make full disclosure. Alternatively, the issuer can issue a "no comment" response if the response is given pursuant to an established no-comment policy. There are instances in which the "no comment" response is inappropriate. For example, the SEC has taken the position that if the company or its agents are responsible for leaks of sensitive information or market rumors, there is a duty to correct any misinformation.[23] It follows that public companies should manage their proprietary information, not only for insider trading reasons but also to prevent being forced into premature disclosures by the existence of market rumors due to leaked information. Caution dictates that public companies develop information policies, including the creation of an information ombudsman, as well as limit the issuer's personnel who are authorized to divulge information or respond to outside questions.

As a corollary to the absence of an affirmative duty to disclose, the mere possibility of an event occurring does not trigger a duty to predict or project information that is positive; yet the SEC has long taken the view that material information that is negative must be disclosed.[24] For example, item 303 of Regulation S-K (the SEC's general disclosure guide) requires periodic management discussion and analysis (MD&A) of financial condition operations. As part of this requirement, management is required to disclose and discuss negative trends and uncertainties.[25] The SEC has taken a vigorous enforcement stance on these disclosures.[26] The MD&A disclosures, of course, may also result in material misstatements or omissions that will form the basis of civil liability in a private action.[27]

---

[20] See Symposium, Affirmative Disclosure Obligations Under the Securities Laws, 46 Md. L. Rev. 907 (1987); John H. Matheson, Corporate Disclosure Obligations and the Parameters of Rule 10b-5: *Basic, Inc. v. Levinson* and Beyond, 14 J. Corp. L. 1 (1988).

[21] See, e.g., Helwig v. Vencor, Inc., 210 F.3d 612, 620-621 (6th Cir. 2000) (corporation cannot be held responsible for analysts' statements about its financial health unless corporation takes some affirmative action other than simply providing information to analysts).

[22] Basic, Inc. v. Levinson, 485 U.S. 224 (1988); *on remand*, 871 F.2d 562 (6th Cir. 1989).

[23] See In re Carnation Co., Sec. Exch. Act Rel. No. 34-22214 [1985-1986 Transfer Binder], Fed. Sec. L. Rep. (CCH) ¶83,801 (July 8, 1985).

[24] E.g., Starkman v. Marathon Oil Co., 772 F.2d 231 (6th Cir. 1985), *cert. denied*, 475 U.S. 1015 (1985).

[25] See Management Discussion and Analysis of Financial Condition, Sec. Act Rel. No. 33-6835 (SEC May 18, 1989).

[26] See In re Caterpillar, Inc., Exch. Act Rel. No. 34-30532, 6 Fed. Sec. L. Rep. (CCH) ¶73,829 (SEC March 31, 1992) (settlement order involving MD&A analysis and failure to adequately discuss the possible risk of lower earnings in the future). *Compare* Ferber v. Travelers Corp., 802 F. Supp. 698 (D. Conn. 1992) (finding adequate discussion in MD&A of "known trends" and "uncertainties" relating to problems with issuer's real estate portfolios).

[27] Cf. Steckman v. Hart Brewing Co., 143 F.3d 1293 (9th Cir. 1998) (obligation imposed by Item 303 gives rise to a duty that can be enforced in private suit under Sections 11 and 12(a)(2) of the Securi-

B. The Antifraud Provision of the Securities Exchange Act

The SEC has imposed pursuant to its Regulation FD[28] a duty on domestic companies that are subject to the Exchange Act's reporting requirements to assure that when it does make certain disclosures that they are not made selectively. In broad overview, Regulation FD greatly restricts the freedom public companies formerly enjoyed to make selective disclosures of material nonpublic information to securities market professionals or its shareholders.

§12.12   Rule 10b-5 and Control of Corporate Mismanagement

Rule 10b-5's implied private remedy has even played an important role in the regulation of internal corporate affairs,[1] due in large part to the expansive reading that has been given to the rule's "in connection with" requirement. Even in the face of a restrictive Supreme Court decision,[2] the federal mismanagement remedy continues to flourish.[3] However, as will be seen below, a remedy for corporate skullduggery exists under the antifraud provision only if accompanied by deception committed in connection with the purchase or sale of a security.

The plaintiff in *Santa Fe Industries* owned a minority interest in the Kirby Lumber Co., a 95 percent subsidiary of defendant Santa Fe. Utilizing the Delaware "short form" merger procedure,[4] Santa Fe "cashed out" the plaintiff—that is, forced him to surrender his shares for cash. The plaintiff sued under 10b-5, claiming that the merger was unfair due to the low valuation placed on his shares and, further, lacked any valid business purpose.[5] The Second Circuit upheld the complaint, but the Supreme Court reversed due to the plaintiff's failure to allege an act of deception deriving from a material misstatement or omission.[6] In so holding, the Court was limiting the 10b-5 action to fact settings more closely connected with or similar to the garden variety type fraud in a purchase or sale of a security.

---

ties Act) *with* Verifone Sec. Litig., 11 F.3d 865 (9th Cir. 1993) (Regulation S-K does not create independent duty under the antifraud provision).

[28] 17 C.F.R. §§243.100 et seq. (2002).

§12.12   [1] *See* James D. Cox, Fraud is in the Eyes of the Beholder: Rule 10b-5's Applications to Acts of Corporate Mismanagement, 47 N.Y.U. L. Rev. 674 (1972); Thomas L. Hazen, Corporate Mismanagement and the Federal Securities Acts Antifraud Provisions: A Familiar Path with Some New Detours, 20 B.C. L. Rev. 819 (1979).

[2] Santa Fe Indus. v. Green, 430 U.S. 462 (1977). *See also* Ernst & Ernst v. Hochfelder, 425 U.S. 185 (1976); Blue Chip Stamps Co. v. Manor Drug Stores, 421 U.S. 723 (1975).

[3] Healey v. Catalyst Recovery of Pa., Inc., 616 F.2d 641 (3d Cir. 1980).

[4] Del. Code Ann. tit. 8, §253 (2001) permits a simplified merger between a 90 percent owned subsidiary and its parent corporation, which eliminates the necessity for shareholder approval and does not give statutory appraisal rights to dissenting shareholders of the parent.

[5] Many courts have recognized a state law cause of action for this type of unfairness in "freeze-out," "squeeze-out" or "going private" transactions. *See, e.g.,* Bryan v. Rock Blevins Co., 490 F.2d 563 (5th Cir.), *cert. denied,* 419 U.S. 844 (1974).

[6] 430 U.S. at 470-471.

The Supreme Court in the *Santa Fe Industries* decision focused on the statutorily mandated element of deception. It thereby reinforced the basic thrust of the securities laws in requiring disclosure to investors, rather than in protecting shareholders' proprietary interests. The Court noted an emerging split of authority under common law and the various state corporate chartering statutes and expressed its unwillingness to "impose a stricter standard of fiduciary duty than that required by the law of some states."[7] The *Santa Fe* decision should not be viewed as the death knell for the champions of effective enforcement of the securities laws. In fact, a number of subsequent circuit court rulings have read the *Santa Fe* restriction as being relatively narrow. Moreover, deception can be found in the defendants' failure to disclose their misdeed to all of the directors when the directors approved the transaction.[8]

However, it is clear that, standing alone, a breach of fiduciary duty is not a securities law violation. The utility of Rule 10b-5 as a weapon against corporate mismanagement was further restricted by the Supreme Court. In *Virginia Bankshares, Inc. v. Sandberg*,[9] the Court ruled that a shareholder vote that was not mandated by state law and thus was not an essential cog in the merger machinery could not form the basis of a federal proxy claim. In *Sandberg*, minority shareholders of a corporation involved in a cash-out merger challenged a vote that was allegedly conducted through the use of misleading proxy solicitation materials. The proxies in question did not relate to a vote directly on the merger because management controlled 85 percent of the shares and the minority were not entitled to an appraisal remedy. A failure to secure the shareholder vote in question would not necessarily have prevented the challenged merger. In a five-to-four decision, the Supreme Court held that there could be no action under the federal proxy rules because the shareholder vote was not an essential link in the transactional chain. Had the plaintiff been afforded an appraisal remedy, they would then have a viable cause of action by alleging that the misrepresentation deprived the minority from voting against the merger so that they would then be able to pursue their appraisal remedy.[10]

---

[7] *Id.* at 479 n.16. *But see* Goldberg v. Meridor, 567 F.2d 209 (2d Cir. 1977), *cert. denied*, 434 U.S. 1069 (1978).

[8] *See* Estate of Soler v. Rodriquez, 63 F.3d 45, 54 (1st Cir. 1995) (two interested directors concealed from other directors that stock was being sold to them at too low a price).

[9] 501 U.S. 1080 (1991).

[10] *See, e.g.*, Wilson v. Great American Ind., Inc., 979 F.2d 924 (2d Cir. 1992); Howing Co. v. Nationwide Corp., 972 F.2d 700 (6th Cir. 1992), *cert. denied*, 507 U.S. 1004 (1993).

CHAPTER 13

Rights and Powers of Shareholders: Inspection Rights, Voting, and Proxies

A.   SHAREHOLDERS' RIGHTS

§13.01   The Nature of the Shareholders' Interest

A share of stock is primarily a profit-sharing contract, a unit of interest in the corporation based on a contribution to the corporate capital. Under their share contract and by virtue of their status as owners of shares, shareholders have three classes of rights against the corporation: (1) rights as to control and management, (2) proprietary rights, and (3) remedial and ancillary rights.[1]

The first class of shareholder rights includes: (a) voting rights for the election—and usually for the removal—of directors, in addition to the incidental right to the holding of annual and special meetings and due notice thereof; (b) voting rights as to the making of amendments to the charter and other fundamental changes in the corporate existence and setup; (c) voting rights as to the making and amending of bylaws, which regulate many matters, including the authority of directors and officers and their compensation; and (d) the right to have the corporation managed honestly and prudently for the benefit and profit of the shareholders within the scope of the authorized business.

The second class of shareholder rights, designated as proprietary rights, includes: (a) the right to participate ratably in dividend distributions when declared by the management; (b) the right to participate in the distribution of assets in total or partial liquidation; (c) the right to equality and honesty of treatment by the management and by majority shareholders in corporate transactions affecting share interests, such as new issues of shares or amendments of the articles; (d) the right to be registered as a shareholder on the corporate books, subject only to valid and authorized transfers of the shares; and (e) immunity from personal liability for corporate debts, subject to judicial limitations against abuse of this privilege.

---

§13.01   [1] Share rights, being in essence contract rights, are determined by the terms of the shares as described in the articles of incorporation in conjunction with provisions of the general corporation laws. The corporate attorney is thus given a wide range of choices in defining the scope of such rights. *See* Chapter 14, dealing with close corporations, and Chapters 16 and 17, dealing with the issuance of shares and the capital structure.

B.   Right to Information

Remedial rights of shareholders include: (a) the right to information and inspection of the corporate records; (b) the right to bring representative or derivative suits on corporate causes of action to prevent or remedy mismanagement and unauthorized acts and compel the corporation to enforce its rights; and (c) common law, equitable, and statutory remedies for infringement of individual rights.

B.   RIGHT TO INFORMATION

§13.02   Basis of Shareholders' Right to Information

A shareholder has a common law right to inspect corporate books and records, in person or by an agent, for a proper purpose in order to protect the shareholder's interest. Most states also provide shareholders a statutory right of inspection, which is generally viewed as supplementing rather than supplanting the common law right.[1] Many states permit reasonable charter and bylaw provisions regulating inspection.

The shareholder's right to ascertain how the affairs of the business are being conducted by the officers and directors has traditionally been founded on the ownership interest and the necessity of protecting that interest.[2] The common law right of inspection rests on the underlying rights of ownership of the corporate property.[3]

There has been much litigation over the proper scope of the shareholder's right to inspect corporate books, files, and records. Thus a statute authorizing inspection of "books and records of account" has been held not to authorize inspection of quarterly financial statements,[4] but the statute does reach recordations and contracts of on-going business transactions.[5] A court may limit the scope of a shareholder's inspection to those records that are necessary to protect the shareholder's interest in the corporation.[6]

§13.03   Proper Purposes for Inspection

Shareholders today generally have the right of inspection only for legitimate purposes related to their interest as investors. The common law privilege, however, is

---

§13.02   [1] *See* Scattered Corp. v. Chicago Stock Exch., Inc., 67 A.2d 874 (Del. Ch. 1994); Tucson Gas & Elec. Co. v. Schanz, 428 P.2d 686 (Ariz. Ct. App. 1967).

[2] Otis-Hidden Co. v. Scheirich, 219 S.W. 191 (Ky. 1920); Farmers' Loan & Trust Co. v. Pierson, 222 N.Y.S. 532 (Sup. Ct. 1927); Annot., 22 XIII-1 A.L.R. 24, 57 (1923).

[3] Varney v. Baker, 80 N.E. 524 (Mass. 1907) (equitable ownership).

[4] State ex rel. Jones v. Ralston Purina Co., 358 S.W.2d 772 (Mo. 1912); Bitters v. Milcut, Inc., 343 N.W.2d 418 (Wis. 1983).

[5] *See* Meyer v. Ford Indus., 538 P.2d 353 (Or. 1975) (reaches contracts, records, and correspondence).

[6] *See, e.g.*, Wells v. League of American Theatres & Producers, Inc., 706 N.Y.S.2d 599, 604 (Sup. Ct. 2000); Troccoli v. L & B Contract Indus., Inc., 687 N.Y.S.2d 400, 401 (App. Div. 1999).

not absolute, and the corporation may show in defense that the applicant is acting out of wrongful motives, or that the information sought is not germane for the state purpose.

An examination of modern decisions reveals that among the purposes held to justify an inspection demand are to ascertain (1) the financial condition of the company or the propriety of dividends;[1] (2) the value of shares for sale or investment;[2] (3) whether there has been mismanagement;[3] (4) to obtain, in anticipation of a shareholders' meeting, a mailing list of shareholders to solicit proxies or otherwise influence voting;[4] or (5) information in aid of litigation with the corporation or its officers involving corporate transactions.[5] A purpose is proper even though it yields no direct benefit to the corporation, but it should not be adverse to the corporation's interest.[6] Among the improper purposes that may justify management denial of a shareholder's claimed right of inspection are: (1) to obtain information as to business secrets or to aid a competitor;[7] (2) to secure business prospects or investment or advertising lists;[8] and (3) to find technical defects in corporation transactions in order to bring strike suits for purposes of blackmail or extortion.[9] In general, a demand is improper if it is motivated merely by idle curiosity or to annoy or harass management.[10]

The decisions place great emphasis on the shareholder's subjective purpose. For example, applying Delaware law, the Supreme Court of Minnesota in *Pillsbury v. Honeywell*,[11] upheld management's refusal to allow an antiwar activist shareholder to have access to the shareholder lists in order to communicate his antiwar beliefs. In so ruling, the court noted: "We do not mean to imply that a shareholder

§13.03   [1] Gregson v. Packings & Insulations Corp., 708 A.2d 533 (R.I. 1998) (even though financial statements not prepared, access to books granted to determine propriety of bonuses and extraordinary dividend).

[2] Friedman v. Altoona Pipe & Steel Supply Co., 460 F.2d 1212 (3d Cir. 1972); State ex rel. Waldman v. Miller-Wohl Co., 28 A.2d 148 (Del. 1942).

[3] Security First Corp. v. U.S. Die Casting and Dev. Co., 687 A.2d 563 (Del. 1997) (permitting inspection based on suspected mismanagement); Everett v. Hollywood Park, Inc., 1996 WL 32171 (Del. Ch. 1996) (permitting inspection for suspected waste and mismanagement).

[4] E. L. Bruce Co. v. State ex rel. Gilbert, 144 A.2d 533 (Del. 1958); Shamrock Assoc. v. Texas Am. Energy Corp., 517 A.2d 658 (Del. Ch. 1986) (proxy contestant permitted to inspect list of beneficial owners).

[5] Finance Co. of Am. v. Brock, 80 F.2d 713 (5th Cir. 1936); Compaq Computer Corp. v. Horton, 631 A.2d 1 (Del. 1993) (proper purpose where objective is to solicit other shareholders to join in conduct of derivative suit and share suit's expenses).

[6] COMPAQ Computer Corp. v. Horton, 631 A.2d 1 (Del. 1993) (focusing on whether stated purpose is related to the interests of the shareholder which should not be adverse to interests of the corporation).

[7] Morton v. Rogers, 514 P.2d 752 (Ariz. Ct. App. 1973); Keeneland Assoc. v. Pessin, 484 S.W.2d 849 (Ky. 1972).

[8] E. L. Bruce Co. v. State ex rel. Gilbert, 144 A.2d 533 (Del. 1958).

[9] State ex rel. Linihan v. United Brokerage Co., 101 A. 433 (Del. 1917); Shabshelowitz v. Fall River Gas Co., 588 N.E.2d 630 (Mass. 1992) (improper purpose to seek list to solicit existing shareholders to sell their shares to plaintiff); Brown v. E. H. Clement Co., 166 S.E. 515 (N.C. 1932).

[10] Carpenter v. Texas Air Corp., 1985 WL 11548 (Del. Ch. 1985); 5A William M. Fletcher, Cyclopedia of the Law of Private Corporations, §§2226.1, 2226.4 (1995).

[11] State ex rel. Pillsbury v. Honeywell, Inc., 191 N.W.2d 406 (Minn. 1971).

B. Right to Information

with a bona fide investment interest could not bring this suit if motivated by concern with the long- or short-term economic effects on Honeywell resulting from the production of war munitions."[12] Subsequently, the Delaware Chancery Court, in *Conservative Caucus v. Chevron Corp.*,[13] distinguished *Pillsbury* as a case where the petitioning shareholder had failed, in making his request for the stockholders' list, to establish any adverse consequences to the corporation from its continuing to manufacture armaments. *Conservative Caucus* granted the shareholder access to the stockholders' list to solicit their support for a proposal to discourage the corporation from continuing to do business in Angola. Delaware courts have indicated that a shareholder's motives in demanding books and records can be relevant. Thus, for example, where a shareholder's true purpose appeared to be for personal rather than corporate reasons, the inspection request should not be granted.[14]

The majority common law rule does not seem to place the burden on petitioners to show the propriety of examination, nor that the refusal by the officers or directors was wrongful.[15] Similarly, most modern statutes place the burden on the corporation.[16]

§13.04   Statutory Regulation of Inspection Rights

In most jurisdictions, the shareholders' right to inspect and examine the books and records of a corporation is not left entirely to the common law but is declared in whole or in part by statutes. Statutory provisions often define the right of inspection only of certain books, such as the stock ledger or list of shareholders. Under this type of statute, the right of inspection of other records, such as books of account, minutes of the meetings of directors and shareholders, and corporate documents, which may be of the greatest importance, are thus left to the common law.[1] Despite a former tendency to give shareholders by statute a more absolute

---

[12] *Id.* at 411. For an analogous case dealing with a socially conscious shareholder's proposal, *see* Medical Committee for Human Rights v. SEC, 432 F.2d 659 (D.C. Cir. 1970), *vacated as moot*, 404 U.S. 403 (1972).

[13] 525 A.2d 569 (Del. Ch. 1987). *See also* Credit Bureau of St. Paul, Inc. v. Credit Bureau Reports, Inc., 290 A.2d 689 (Del. Ch. 1972), *aff'd*, 290 A.2d 691 (Del. 1972) (criticizing *Pillsbury*).

[14] Berkowitz v. Legal Sea Foods, Inc., 1997 WL 153815 (Del. Ch. 1997) (the record indicated that plaintiff's true purpose was not his stated purpose but rather to pursue individual claims against his father and siblings).

[15] N V F Co. v. Sharon Steel Corp., 294 F. Supp. 1091 (W.D. Pa. 1969); Gilmore v. Emsco Derrick & Equip. Co., 70 P.2d 251 (Cal. Ct. App. 1937); Shaw v. Agri-mark, Inc., 663 A.2d 464 (Del. 1995) (mandamus action to enforce inspection requires only that stockholder identifies the corporation, alleges petitioner is owner of record, that proper demand made, and that corporation failed to comply with its duty).

[16] *E.g.*, Del. Code Ann. tit. 8, §220 (2001). *See, e.g.*, Bennett v. Mack's Supermarkets, Inc., 602 S.W.2d 143 (Ky. 1979). *Contra* Weigel v. J. W. O'Connor, 373 N.E.2d 421 (Ill. App. Ct. 1978); Crouse v. Rogers Park Apartments, Inc., 99 N.E.2d 404, 405-406 (Ill. App. Ct. 1951) (constituting Ill. Rev. Stat. §157.45).

§13.04   [1] Tucson Gas & Elec. Co. v. Schanz, 428 P.2d 686 (Ariz. Ct. App. 1967); Brentmore Estates, Inc. v. Hotel Barbizon, Inc., 33 N.Y.S.2d 331 (App. Div. 1942).

right of inspection than the qualified right existing at common law, the general trend of recent legislation and decisions is to adopt the common law rule and limit the inspection right to proper purposes reasonably related to the interests of the shareholder.[2] Under a statute that provides in general terms that the shareholders of all corporations shall "have the right of access to, inspection and examination of the books, records and papers of the corporation at all reasonable and proper times," it is generally held that inspection will not be allowed for purposes hostile to the interests of the corporation. Ulterior motives may thus be shown by a corporation as a matter of defense.

§13.05   Remedies If Inspection Is Denied

If the officers of a corporation wrongfully deny a shareholder the right to inspect its books or papers, the traditional remedy to enforce the shareholder's right was a common law proceeding known as mandamus.[1] Because mandamus was historically used to enforce public rights and duties, the petition was presented in the name of the state on the "relation" or complaint of the party beneficially interested.[2] In a number of states, the real party in interest was named as plaintiff, and the state was not mentioned even as a formal party.[3]

There is a conflict of authority whether a statute appearing to make the right of inspection absolute takes away a court's discretion to refuse the writ of mandamus where inspection is sought for an improper purpose. Most decisions favor the exercise of sound discretion to withhold the writ to protect the just interests of the corporation and the other shareholders against abuse.[4] This discretion is spoken of as inherent in the remedy of mandamus, but it is generally applied in giving equitable relief of a specific nature to avoid injustice and remit the suitor to other forms of relief. There are comparatively few reported cases in which the courts have enforced the right of inspection in equity by injunction. In some jurisdictions, it has been held, however, under statutory provisions or otherwise, espe-

---

[2] Berkowitz v. Legal Sea Foods, Inc., 1997 WL 153815 (Del. Ch. 1997) (inspection should be denied when the true purpose was not the stated purpose but rather to pursue individual claims against father and siblings).

§13.05 [1] Stern v. South Chester Tube Co., 390 U.S. 606 (1968) (construing Pennsylvania statute); Miles v. Bank of Heflin, 349 So. 2d 1072 (Ala. 1977); State v. Superior Oil Corp., 13 A.2d 453 (Del. 1940); State ex rel. Armour & Co. v. Gulf Sulphur Corp., 233 A.2d 457 (Del. Ch. 1967), aff'd, 231 A.2d 470 (Del. 1967); Hanrahan v. Puget Sound Power & Light Co., 126 N.E.2d 499 (Mass. 1955). But see Fed. R. Civ. P. 81(b) (abolishing the remedy in this context).

[2] E.g., State ex rel. Foster v. Standard Oil Co. of Kan., 18 A.2d 235, 240 (Del. 1941).

[3] See, e.g., People v. Pacheco, 29 Cal. 210 (1865); J. High, Extraordinary Legal Remedies 340 (1884).

[4] In re DeVengoecha, 91 A. 314 (N.J. Sup. Ct. 1914) (mandamus denied due to petitioner's hostile motive). See, e.g., Day & Co. v. Booth, 123 A. 557 (Me. 1924); Comment, 30 Mich. L. Rev. 769 (1932). See also Former MBCA §52 (1969), which preserves the equitable remedy; but see Model Business Corp. Act §16.04, which mentions court action only under the statute.

cially when ancillary to other equitable relief, that enforcement by an injunction (that is, a mandatory injunction or specific performance) is available.[5]

Modern corporation statutes specifically set forth remedies for enforcing inspection rights. Thus the Delaware statute states that if a corporation does not grant inspection within five business days of a demand, the shareholder may commence an action in the Court of Chancery to enforce the demand.[6] The Model Business Corporation Act as revised in 1984 provides that a court of the county in which the corporation's principal office is located (or, if none in the state, its registered office) may summarily order inspection and copying of the records.[7]

§13.06 Accessing Corporate Reports, Financial Statements, and NOBO List

The notes to the Uniform Business Corporation Act,[1] a predecessor of the Model Act, suggested that each state require detailed annual reports of a corporation's financial condition for the information of shareholders, creditors, and the investing public. This was a response to complaints about the inadequacy of financial statements and reports issued by leading corporations.[2] The great burden and expense to an individual shareholder of exercising the right of inspection of corporate books and records, not to mention bringing suit to enforce that right, make this a poor method of getting needed information. Although the response of state legislatures was not favorable, the federal securities laws filled the need with respect to publicly held corporations.

The Securities Exchange Act of 1934 requires registration and periodic reporting by publicly held companies.[3] Further, the SEC's proxy regulations under that Act require that proxy statements be mailed to shareholders in connection with the solicitation of proxies. These proxy statements must include much financial information as to proposed corporate changes and proceedings. The making of reports and the rendition of financial statements by corporations, however, are generally held not to be substitutes for the shareholders' right of inspection and

---

[5] Otis-Hidden Co. v. Scheirich, 219 S.W. 191 (Ky. 1920); Huyler v. Cragin Cattle Co., 2 A. 274 (N.J. Ch. 1885); Flowers v. Rotary Printing Co., 31 N.E.2d 251 (Ohio Ct. App. 1940); Klein v. Scranton Life Ins. Co., 11 A.2d 770 (Pa. Super. Ct. 1940). Cf. Henderson v. Brown, 20 F. Supp. 522 (W.D. La. 1937) (awarding both mandamus and an injunction).

[6] Del. Code Ann. tit. 8, §220(c) (2001).

[7] Model Business Corp. Act §16.04(a),(b) (1984).

§13.06 [1] The Uniform Act was approved by the American Bar Association at its July 1928 meeting. The annual report requirement is imposed by the latest revision of the Model Act. Model Business Corp. Act §§16h.20-16.22 (1984).

[2] William Zebina Ripley, Main Street and Wall Street 209 (1929); Adolf A. Berle, Publicity of Accounts, 25 Mich. L. Rev. 827 (1927).

[3] The Public Utility Holding Company Act of 1935 (15 U.S.C. §§79 et seq. (2000)) requires similar reports. See generally Thomas L. Hazen, Treatise on the Law of Securities Regulation ch. 9 (4th ed. 2002). In general, complying with the SEC requirements is no small task. See Homer Kripke, The SEC and Corporate Disclosure: Regulation in Search of a Purpose (1979).

are no excuse for management's refusal to permit a shareholder to examine corporate books and records.[4]

An important constraint on the utility of obtaining a list of the stockholders for a public corporation is that in most instances the list does not identify who votes the shares. The stockholders' list identifies only the names and addresses of the stockholders of record. Most stock in public corporations is held not in the name of the owner of the shares but in the name of the brokerage house where the owner maintains an account. Holding shares in the brokerage house's "street name" greatly facilitates purchases and sales of securities because the owner of the shares does not have to endorse the shares and deliver them to the broker before selling the shares. Indeed, most ownership in public companies is not represented by a certificate but appear only as an electronic entry in the share registry. This is, in part, because holding shares via street names facilitates trading in the shares of public corporations. On purchasing shares investors do not take delivery of any share certificates, but receive only a statement that the shares they have purchased are held in a trust depositary that maintains its own records regarding the identity of the owners of the shares that are on deposit with the trust depositary. The dominant trust depositary in the United States is CEDE & Co.

An examination of the list of stockholders for a public corporation, such as IBM Corporation, will show that a substantial portion of the shares is recorded in the name of CEDE & Co. Separately, CEDE makes available to the corporations whose shares are on deposit with it a list of the brokerage firms holding stock in the CEDE name. This is called the "CEDE breakdown" list. This document, however, does not reveal the names and addresses of customers for whom the broker holds the shares in its street name. The SEC requires brokers to ask each customer who holds stock in a street name if she objects to her name and address being disclosed to the corporation in which she has invested. Those who do not object are then identified to the corporation on the NOBO (non-objecting beneficial owners) list. Thus, it is through the NOBO list that one can determine who the beneficial shareholders are for some of the outstanding shares held in street names (i.e., those in the hands of non-objecting shareholders).

Given the pervasiveness of holding public shares in street names and, hence, the importance of the NOBO list, the question arises whether a shareholder seeking inspection of the list of shareholders is also entitled to the NOBO list. The courts have been unwilling to build upon the principles that underlie the general rights of stockholders to access to company records and their power to communicate with their fellow stockholders by conferring upon the stockholders the power to compel the corporation to acquire a NOBO list. Most courts that have engaged

---

[4] Kerkorian v. Western Air Lines, Inc., 253 A.2d 221, 225 (Del. Ch.), aff'd, 254 A.2d 240 (Del. 1969); White v. Coeur D'Alene Big Creek Mining Co., 55 P.2d 720 (Idaho 1936); Feick v. Hill Bread Co., 103 A. 813 (N.J. Sup. Ct. 1918), aff'd, 105 A. 725 (N.J. 1919); Moore v. Rock Creek Oil Co., 59 S.W.2d 815 (Tex. Comm'n App. 1933). But cf. State ex rel. Cochran v. Penn-Beaver Oil Co., 143 A. 257 (Del. 1926); State ex rel. Miller v. Loft, Inc., 156 A. 170 (Del. 1931). See Wood, Walker & Co. v. Evans, 300 F. Supp. 171 (D. Colo. 1969), aff'd, 461 F.2d 852 (10th Cir. 1972) (federal proxy regulation does not have preemptive effect).

this subject conclude that the requesting shareholder can obtain the NOBO list only if such list is already in the corporation's possession,[5] but the shareholder cannot compel the corporation to obtain or otherwise prepare a NOBO list.[6]

§13.07   Directors' Right of Inspection

By both case law[1] and statute,[2] the right of a director to inspect corporate books and records is more extensive than that of a shareholder.[3] The director's right has often been said to be absolute and unqualified.[4] It has been held that the right may not be denied on the ground that the director is hostile to the corporation and that his only object is to promote a claim against it; if the hostility goes to the extent of justifying his removal from office, that remedy is to be followed.[5] Even a claim the documents are protected by the attorney-client privilege is not an absolute bar to the director's access.[6]

Inspection should be denied, however, when necessary to prevent abuse by the director or his representative.[7] It has been declared that directors must act in good faith and therefore may not exercise their right of examination for purposes that conflict with their fiduciary obligations.[8] The duties of their positions require

[5] Shamrock Assoc. v. Texas Am. Energy Corp., 517 A.2d 658 (Del. Ch. 1986).

[6] Luxottica Group S.p.a. v. U.S. Shoe Corp., 919 F. Supp. 1091 (S.D. Ohio 1995); RB Assoc. of N.J., L.P.v. Gillette Co., 1988 WL 27731 (Del. Ch. 1988); Nu Med Home Health Care, Inc. v. Hospital Staffing Service, Inc., 664 So. 2d 353 (Fla. Dist. Ct. App. 1995); Parsons v. Jefferson-Pilot Corp., 426 S.E. 2d 685 (N.C. 1993). *Contra* Sadler v. NCR Corp., 928 F.2d 48 (2d Cir. 1991) (construing N.Y.B.C.L. §1315 (McKinney 1986) to hold that a corporation can be required to compile a NOBO list). In 1998, as part of its amendment of the Model Business Corporation Act to recognize that inspected information may be provided electronically, the commentary was changed to opine that a corporation "generally is not required to generate" a NOBO list but to provide one only "to the extent such information is in the corporation's possession." Former MBCA §16.03 Official Comment, reprinted in Proposed Changes in the Model Business Corporation Act, 53 Bus. Law. 815, 822 (1998).

§13.07 [1] *See, e.g.,* Cohen v. Cocoline Prods., Inc., 127 N.E.2d 906 (N.Y. 1955). *See* William C. McLaughlin, Director's Right to Inspect the Corporate Books and Records—Absolute or Otherwise, 22 Bus. Law. 413 (1967).

[2] *E.g.,* Cal. Corp. Code §1602 (West 1990).

[3] Kortum v. Webasto Sunroofs Inc., 769 A.2d 113 (Del. Ch. 2000). *Cf.* Lewis v. Pennsylvania Bar Ass'n, 701 A.2d 551 (Pa. 1997) (members' inspection rights are narrower than those given to directors).

[4] *See, e.g.,* Kortum v. Webasto Sunroofs, Inc., 769 A.2d 113 (Del. Ch. 2000) (prima facie showing of entitlement to documents made by allegation requesting party is a director); State ex rel. Gundaker v. Davis, 932 S.W.2d 885 (Mo. Ct. App. 1996) (enforcing unqualified right of director to gain access to books and records).

[5] Wilkins v. M. Ascher Silk Corp., 201 N.Y.S. 739 (App. Div. 1923), *aff'd,* 143 N.E. 748 (N.Y. 1924).

[6] *See* Kosachuk v. Harper, 2000 Del. Ch. Lexis 176 (Del. Ch. Dec. 9, 2000); Intrieri v. Avatgex Corp., 1998 WL 326608 (Del. Ch. 1998).

[7] *See, e.g.,* Kortum v. Webasto Sunroofs Inc.,769 A.2d 113 (Del Ch. 2000) (reasonable limits may be imposed if proven director's agent's interests conflict with those of the corporation and the corporation failed to meet its burden of proving that the director or agent has such a conflict; the court was satisfied that the director was not competing with the corporation *when* the request was made).

[8] State ex rel. Farber v. Seiberling Rubber Co., 168 A.2d 310 (Del. 1961); Chappel v. Applied Control Systems, Inc., 39 Pa. D. & C. 4th 168 (Com. Pl. 1998) (access would be denied if established requesting director was employee of competitor).

directors to keep themselves informed of the business and to be familiar with the affairs of the company.[9] Inspection by a shareholder is primarily for the purpose of protecting her individual interests. Inspection by a director is with a view to enabling him to perform his duties intelligently.

In making an examination of corporate records, a director, like the shareholder, is entitled to expert assistance in order to exercise the privilege effectively and may use attorneys and accountants to help. Wrongful denial of the request allows the director to the sanction provided by law.[10]

C. SHAREHOLDERS' MEETINGS AND VOTING

§13.08 Shareholder Act at Meetings or by Written Consent

The stockholders' meeting is an important feature of corporate law, but we might well question whether the ritual of a meeting where owners physically come together is a relic of the past. Certainly in the public company we might even question whether the annual meeting has the same importance as it did in the past in terms of providing a medium for management to sense the concerns of the firm's owners. The growing concentration of institutional holders combined with their increasing activism outside the annual meeting context support the view that the annual meeting is not necessary for such companies to assure interaction between owners and managers. Also, the sheer number of individual investors in many public companies renders the annual meeting setting a weak medium. As the number of owners increases, the collective action problem becomes an ever increasing obstacle to an effective exercise of their judgment. As seen later in this chapter,[1] the Internet is now being harnessed to corporate governance mechanisms so that the day of the virtual meeting may well not be far away.

As is the case with directors,[2] according to traditional doctrine, a majority of the shareholders have no power to vote or act for the corporation except at a meeting, duly called on proper notice, at which a quorum is present. Absent statutory authorization, written or oral consent to a corporate act by the shareholders or members individually, even though a majority may agree, is not binding on the corporation.[3]

---

[9] *See, e.g.,* Kelley v. Heritage Nat'l Bank, 897 S.W.2d 96 (Mo. Ct. App. 1995) (director's inspection rights based on necessity for knowledge to discharge duties and, therefore, *former* director's access was denied).

[10] *See, e.g.,* McGowan v. Empress Entertainment Inc., 791 A.2d 1 (Del. Ch. 2000) (equitable to permit recovery of attorneys fees upon showing of bad faith denial of request).

§13.08 [1] *See* §13.12.

[2] *See* §9.07.

[3] De La Vergne Refrigerating Mach. Co. v. German Sav. Inst., 175 U.S. 40 (1899); Sellers v. Greer, 50 N.E. 246 (Ill. 1898); Stott v. Stott, 242 N.W. 747 (Mich. 1932); Ambler v. Smith, 262 N.Y.S. 208 (App. Div. 1932); Kelly v. Galloway, 68 P.2d 474 (Or. 1937); 1 Model Business Corp. Act Ann. §7.04 comment (3d ed. 1994).

C. Shareholders' Meetings and Voting

Most modern statutes authorize shareholder action to be taken or approved without a meeting by the written consents of shareholders holding shares with voting power.[4] The Model Business Corporation Act provides for action without a meeting only on unanimous written consent;[5] however, the statutes vary in their requirements from state to state.[6] For example, Delaware permits a majority of the shareholders to act by consent.[7] A provision common to statutes authorizing action outside a meeting via the consent of less than all the stockholders is a requirement of prompt notice to all the non-consenting shareholders.[8] Consents are analogous to proxies and are revocable.[9]

§13.09 Annual and Special Meetings

Each shareholder has a right to have an annual meeting called and held to elect directors.[1] Modern statutes expressly confer this right.[2] A statutory, charter, or bylaw provision stating that a meeting shall be held every year for the election of directors confers a right on each individual shareholder to have an annual meeting called and held at the time specified or at some later reasonable time.[3] Indeed, statutes commonly provide stockholders with a procedure to compel an annual meeting to be convened when a certain number of months have elapsed since the last annual meeting.[4]

[4] Cal. Corp. Code §603(a) (West Supp. 2002); Del. Code Ann. tit. 8, §§228, 275(c) (2001); Mass. Ann. Laws ch. 156B, §43 (Law. Co-Op 1979); N.J. Stat. Ann., §14A:5-6 (West Supp. 2002) (does not apply to mergers); N.Y. Bus. Corp. Law §615 (McKinney 1986); Tex. Bus. Corp. Act Ann., art 9.10 (Supp. 2002).

[5] Model Business Corp. Act §7.04(a); Former Model Business Corp. Act §145 (1969).

[6] Cal. Corp. Code §603(a) (West Supp. 2002) (authorizes action by consent of as many shareholders as would be needed to pass the action at a meeting unless the articles of incorporation provide otherwise).

[7] Del. Stat. Ann. tit. 8 §228 (2001). See also Ark. Code Ann. §4-27-704 (Michie 2001); Fla. Stat. Ann. §607.0704 (West 2001); Wis. Stat. Ann. §180.0704 (West 2002).

[8] See Cal. Corp. Code §603 (West Supp. 2002); Del. Code Ann. tit. 8, §228 (2001); Ill. Comp. Stat. Ann. ch. 805, ¶5/7.10 (West 1993).

[9] Calumet Indus. v. MacClure, 464 F. Supp. 19 (N.D. Ill. 1978). But see Hoschett v. TSI Intl. Software Ltd., 683 A.2d 43, 44 (Del. Ch. 1996) (annual meeting requirement is not satisfied by using shareholder written consents to elect directors).

§13.09 [1] See, e.g., Saxon Indus. v. NKFW, 488 A.2d 1298 (Del. 1984).

[2] Former Model Business Corp. Act §28 (1969) (the right is not absolute in that the shareholder cannot demand that the meeting be held on the bylaw date because the statute gives a 13-month period); Model Business Corp. Act §7.01 (1984) (no express 13-month period).

[3] See, e.g., Morris v. Thomason, 672 So. 2d 433 (La. Ct. App. 1996) (directors could not be elected at a special meeting when articles call for their election at annual meeting).

[4] Some states acccord a shareholder the right to compel an annual meeting if no meeting has been held within 18 months. Thus, the annual meeting requirement means a right to have meetings every 18 months rather than every 12 months. Hilton Hotels Corp. v. ITT Corp., 962 F. Supp. 1309 (D. Nev. 1997) (applying Nevada law). Once the statutory grounds for requiring a meeting are established, the right to an order mandating a meeting is "virtually absolute." Speiser v. Baker, 525 A.2d 1001 (Del. Ch. 1987) (plaintiff's complicity in early failures to convene a meetings not enough to bar relief).

The time and place for a regular annual meeting of the shareholders are usually fixed in the bylaws. In a few jurisdictions, if the charter or bylaws fix the place, the day, and the hour at which regular meetings shall be held, no further notice may be legally necessary.[5] However, under most modern statutes, notice must be given within a minimum and a maximum number of days before the meeting to every registered shareholder entitled to vote.[6] The notice must specify the time and place of the meeting, but there is no requirement that it elaborate on the purpose of the meeting unless the articles of incorporation require otherwise.[7]

In the absence of an express provision in the charter or bylaws, special meetings may be called by the board of directors whenever deemed necessary or on demand of the shareholders or a certain percentage of them.[8] Once granted by statute, the shareholders' right to call a special meeting presumably cannot be abridged or altered unless permitted by statute.[9] Statutes generally confer a right upon 10 percent of the shareholders to convene a special meeting.[10] The Model Act now permits the articles of incorporation to fix a lower percentage as well as a higher percentage, but not to exceed 25 percent.[11] The shareholders' right to call a special meeting provides an important check on the powers of the directors.[12] However, the requested meeting must be for a matter that is a proper subject for stockholder action.[13]

§13.10   The Time, Place, and Notice of the Meeting

Charter or bylaw provisions authorizing corporate meetings at a certain time are not intended to prevent meetings at other times on proper notice.[1] The matter of

---

[5] This used to be the prevailing view. 1 Model Business Corp. Act Ann. 2d §29 comment (1971).

[6] Model Business Corp. Act §7.05 (no fewer than ten, nor more than sixty days before the meeting); Former Model Business Corp. Act §29 (1069) (no less than ten nor more than sixty days before the meeting).

[7] Model Business Corp. Act §7.05(b).

[8] "Special meetings of the shareholders may be called by the board of directors, the holders of not less than one-tenth of all the shares entitled to vote at the meeting, or such other persons as may be authorized in the articles of incorporation or the bylaws." Model Business Corp. Act §7.02.

[9] The Model Act as enacted in most states permits the call of a special meeting by holders of 10 percent of the votes entitled to be cast. In 1995, the Model Act was amended to permit the articles of incorporation to provide for a lower percentage or a higher percentage up to 25 percent (Model Business Corp. Act §7.02(a)(2)).

[10] E.g., Model Business Corp. Act §7.02(a)(2) (1995).

[11] Id.

[12] See, e.g., Cullen v. Milligan, 575 N.E.2d 123 (Ohio 1991) (proper to call a meeting for shareholders to consider an offer to acquire company's assets as well as to fill vacancies on the board).

[13] See, e.g., Siegman v. Palomar Medical Technologies, Inc., 1998 Del Ch. Lexis 22 (Feb. 2, 1998) (denying request for meeting to approve settlement of litigation on terms proposed by the petitioner).

§13.10   [1] In re Hammond, 139 F. 898 (S.D.N.Y. 1905); Scanlan v. Snow, 2 App. D.C. 137 (1894); People v. Town of Fairbury, 51 Ill. 149 (1869); Beardsley v. Johnson, 24 N.E. 380 (N.Y. 1890), aff'd, 1 N.Y.S. 608 (Sup. Ct. 1888).

C. Shareholders' Meetings and Voting

notice is now governed by statute, although statutes permit deviation by the articles of incorporation or bylaws.[2] Proper notice includes mention of the time and place. As against absent shareholders or members, a meeting is not legal if held before the day or hour specified in the notice of the meeting.[3] And when the hour for a meeting is fixed by the notice, the meeting should be opened at that hour or within a reasonable time thereafter.[4] As against shareholders who are not present and who do not consent, a meeting held at a different place from that specified in the notice of the meeting is a nullity.[5]

Generally, there is no geographical restriction on the location at which a shareholders' meeting may be held, provided proper notice is given. Virtually all state corporation statutes permit meetings outside the state, at least if the articles or bylaws so provide.[6] Delaware allows shareholder meetings by means of remote communication if the directors so choose.[7] Meetings outside the state may be binding on the participants even if unauthorized.[8]

Insufficient notice, which deprives any shareholders of the opportunity to attend, argue, and vote on proposed measures renders action taken at a shareholders' meeting voidable at the instance of those who did not participate.[9] If all the shareholders who did not receive notice attend a meeting and participate, this constitutes a waiver of notice, and neither they nor the corporation can question the validity of a corporate act authorized at the meeting.[10] Mere attendance for the purpose of objecting to notice does not constitute waiver of notice.[11] The minutes of a shareholders' meeting should show the proper notice, provide proof of mailing or otherwise that gives notice, or show a waiver of notice either in the minutes themselves or in attached exhibits to which reference is made in the minutes.

Most state statutes authorize shareholders to waive any required notice. Such a waiver must be in writing and can be executed at anytime, and the meeting is not invalid because of the lack of notice if all shareholders entitled to notice but

---

[2] For a case intimating that notice may even arise by custom, see State ex rel. East Cleveland Democratic Club, Inc. v. Bibb, 470 N.E.2d 257 (Ohio Ct. App. 1984).

[3] People v. Albany & Susquehanna R.R., 55 Barb. 344 (1869), aff'd, 5 Lans. 25, 57 N.Y. 161 (1874). But shareholders who are present and take part cannot complain. Hussey v. Gallagher, 61 Ga. 86 (1878). More generally, a special meeting without notice is invalid. See Louisiana Weekly Pub. Co. v. First Nat'l Bank, 475 So. 2d 1126 (La. App. 1985).

[4] South School Dist. v. Blakeslee, 13 Conn. 227 (1837); State v. Bonnell, 35 Ohio St. 10 (1879).

[5] Miller v. English, 21 N.J.L. 317 (1848); American Primitive Socy. v. Pilling, 24 N.J.L. 653 (1855).

[6] E.g., Del. Code Ann. tit. 8, §211 (2001); Model Business Corp. Act §7.01(b); Former MBCA §28 (1969).

[7] Del. Code Ann. tit. 8, §211(a) (2001).

[8] Handley v. Stutz, 139 U.S. 417 (1891); Missouri Lead Mining & Smelting Co. v. Reinhard, 21 S.W. 488 (Mo. 1893); Heath v. Silverthorn Lead Mining & Smelting Co., 39 Wis. 146 (1875); but see Ellsworth v. National Home & Town Blders., 164 P. 14 (Cal. Ct. App. 1917); Franco-Texan Land Co. v. Laigle, 59 Tex. 339 (1883).

[9] J.M. Clayton v. Martin, 339 S.E.2d 280 (Ga. Ct. App. 1985); Berger v. Amana Society, 111 N.W.2d 753 (Iowa 1962).

[10] Lofland v. Di Sabatino, 1991 WL 138505 (Del. Ch. July 25, 1991); Ski Roundtop, Inc. v. Hall, 658 P.2d 1071 (Mont. 1983).

[11] Darvin v. Belmont Indus., Inc., 199 N.W.2d 542 (Mich. Ct. App. 1972); Block v. Magee, 537 N.Y.S.2d 215 (Sup. Ct. App. Div. 1989).

who did not receive it either execute a written waiver or attend and participate in the meeting.[12] To be effective the waiver must be executed by the holder of record, not by the share's beneficial owner.[13]

Notice is given to the shareholders of record. Statutes authorize the board of directors or the bylaws to fix a record date for the purpose of determining who is entitled to notice of and to vote at the meeting.[14]

§13.11   Quorum and Voting at Shareholders' Meetings

Nearly all states require the corporation to make available for inspection a list of shareholders entitled to vote.[1] Most states further specify the number of days preceding the meeting that the list must be available for inspection.

At common law, absent a provision to the contrary in statute, charter, or bylaw, a quorum was met by any number of shareholders, provided there were at least two and any required notice of the meeting had been given.[2] However, generally by express provision of the statute, charter, or bylaws, a majority of the shares entitled to vote (or sometimes less if so provided in the charter or bylaws) must be present in person or by proxy to constitute a quorum for the transaction of business; if there are less than the number of shares so present required for a quorum the meeting is not validly convened.[3] The articles of incorporation and corporate statute must be closely examined not only to determine what classes of shares are entitled to vote, but also whether the voting power is equal among all shares of the same class. Considering the contractual nature of the corporation, the articles of incorporation can impose voting restrictions provided they do not conflict with the provisions of the state law. Thus, a provision placing a ceiling on the total number of votes any stockholder could cast, regardless that otherwise her shareholdings would entitle her to a greater vote, was upheld as a permissible variation from the typical one-share one-vote principle.[4] In the typical setting, each share entitled to vote has one voting right. However, many corporations are adopting "tenure voting" whereby holders of shares have greater voting rights the longer they have owned their shares.[5]

[12] See Cal. Corp. Code §601 (West 1990); Ill. Comp. Stat. Ann., ch. 805, ¶5/7.20 (West 1993); N.Y. Bus. Corp. Law §606 (McKinney 1986); Model Business Corp. Act §7.06.

[13] Gim v. Jan Chin, Inc., 362 A.2d 143 (R.I. 1976).

[14] See, e.g., Ark. Code Ann. §4-27-707 (Michie 2001); Del. Code Ann. tit 8, §213 (2001); N.Y. Bus. Corp. Law §604 (McKinney 1986); Model Business Corp. Act §7.07 (no greater than 70 days before meeting).

§13.11   [1] See, e.g., Del. Code Ann. tit. 8, §219 (2001); Ill. Comp. Stat. Ann. ch. 805, ¶5/7.30 (West 1993); N.J. Stat. Ann. §14A:5-8 (West Supp. 2002); Model Business Corp. Act §7.20.

[2] Sylvania & G. R.R. v. Hoge, 59 S.E. 806 (Ga. 1907); Morrill v. Little Falls Mfg. Co., 55 N.W. 547, 549 (Minn. 1893) ("[I]t is immaterial whether the number present is only one or more than one").

[3] Former Model Business Corp. Act §32 (1969) ("Unless otherwise provided in the articles of incorporation, a majority of the shares entitled to vote . . . shall constitute a quorum at a meeting of shareholders, but in no event shall a quorum consist of less than one-third . . ."); Model Business Corp. Act §7.25 (1984) (same).

[4] See Providence & Worcester Co. v. Baker, 378 A.2d 121 (Del. 1977).

[5] See, e.g., Williams v. Geier, 671 A.2d 1368 (Del. 1996).

C. Shareholders' Meetings and Voting

The applicable corporate statute, articles of incorporation, and bylaws should be read carefully to determine whether a separate quorum determination is required for each item coming before the stockholders, especially when a corporation has more than one class of stock and the meeting's agenda includes a matter that requires the approval of more than one class of stock. A similar close reading is called for to determine if a greater than majority vote is required. States following the Model Business Corporation Act require a separate quorum determination be made for each matter to be acted on at the meeting.[6]

Most courts have held that where a quorum is once present at a shareholders' meeting, the quorum is not broken by the subsequent withdrawal of some of the shareholders, whether present in person or by their proxies.[7] Some courts, however, have held to the contrary, ruling that a withdrawal that leaves the number of shareholders present or represented below the required number destroys the quorum and precludes any further action except a motion to adjourn.[8]

A validly convened meeting can be adjourned to a later date. Many state statutes expressly deal with the question of whether notice of the date and place of the adjourned meeting must be given. Their treatment of this issue varies widely. Some require no notice of the adjourned meeting so long as it is held within a certain number of days;[9] others require notice if a new record date is set.[10] The statutes further condition avoiding the need for any new notice of the adjourned meeting on the new meeting's time and location being announced at the meeting that is being adjourned.

When a quorum is present, the vote of a majority of those present is sufficient to elect directors or to decide any questions, although it need not be a majority of all the shareholders or members, nor a majority of the voting power.[11] By the weight of authority, a plurality of the votes actually cast will be decisive, although some of the shareholders or members who are present may abstain and the majority of the votes cast may not be a majority of the persons present or stock represented.[12] A bylaw or charter provision requiring the affirmative vote of a majority of the shareholders at a corporate meeting means a majority in interest (that is,

---

[6] Model Business Corp. Act §7.25(a).

[7] Testa v. Jarvis, 1994 WL 30517, 19 Del. J. Corp. L. 1321 (Del. Ch. Jan. 12, 1994); Duffy v. Loft, Inc., 151 A. 223 (Del. Ch.), aff'd, 152 A. 849 (Del. 1930).

[8] Testa v. Jarvis, 1994 WL 30517 (Del. Ch. Jan. 12, 1992) (withdrawal from meeting of one of two 50 percent holders is tantamount to adjournment); Levisa Oil Corp. v. Quigley, 234 S.E.2d (Va. 1977) (construing bylaw).

[9] See Me. Rev. Stat. Ann. tit. 13-A, §604 (West 1981) (30 days); Cal. Corp. Code §601 (West 1990) (45 days).

[10] See Del. Code Ann. tit. 8, §222 (2001); Fla. Stat. Ann. §607.0705 (West 2001); Wash. Rev. Code Ann. §23 B.07.050 (1994).

[11] Hill v. Town, 138 N.W. 334 (Mich. 1912); In re Rapid Transit Ferry Co., 44 N.Y.S. 539 (App. Div. 1897); Commonwealth v. Vandergrift, 81 A. 153 (Pa. 1911).

[12] Inhabitants of First Parish in Sudbury v. Stearns, 38 Mass. (21 Pick.) 148 (1838); In re Martin v. Chute, 24 N.W. 353 (Minn. 1885); Columbia Bottom Levee Co. v. Meier, 39 Mo. 53 (1866). But see Commonwealth v. Wickersham, 66 Pa. 134 (1870).

one vote per share) rather than a majority in number only.[13] These rules are codified in most state corporation statutes, which also generally permit higher voting requirements if specified in the articles.[14] A few statutes still require an extraordinary majority—that is, two-thirds—for approval of charter amendments, mergers, and other organic changes.[15] Also, there may be statutory, charter, or bylaw requirements for class voting by different classes of shares.[16]

§13.12 Stockholders' Meetings in a Digital Age

The states are slowly, but at a quickening rate, adapting to the digital age by amending various provisions of their corporate statutes to authorize the use of the Internet, Email, etc. in connection with stockholders' meeting. The most advanced statute in terms of liberating functions such as notice, voting, and even deliberations from the traditional format for stockholders' meeting is contained in the Delaware statute, which was amended in July 2001 to permit Delaware corporations to take advantage of advances in communications technology.[1] What sets this statute apart from the important steps taken by other states reviewed below is that the board of directors of a Delaware corporation now has discretion to hold the stockholders' meeting solely "by means of remote communication."[2] Several states authorize shareholders to participate in meetings by whatever medium so long as each can hear and communicate with others.[3] This provision would appear broad enough to permit webcasts of meetings.

A common corporate provision permits notice of the forthcoming stockholders' meeting to be imparted electronically.[4] However, the statute may condi-

---

[13] Weinburgh v. Union Street-Ry. Adv. Co., 37 A. 1026 (N.J. Ch. 1897). *See also* Bank of Los Banos v. Jordan, 139 P. 691 (Cal. 1914). The Delaware court has upheld an arrangement one vote per 20 shares for all additional shares of a single holder. Providence & Worcester Co. v. Baker, 378 A.2d 121 (Del. 1977). *See also* Annot., 3 A.L.R.3d 1204 (1981).

[14] Model Business Corp. Act §7.01(b); Former Model Business Corp. Act §32 (1969). Extraordinary voting and quorum requirements are frequent control devices in the closely held enterprise. 1 F. Hodge O'Neal and Robert B. Thompson, O'Neal's Close Corporations §4.12 (3d ed. 1998).

[15] *E.g.*, Neb. Rev. Stat. Ann. §§21-2057, 2072 (Michie 1999).

[16] *See* Elliot Assoc., L.P. v. Avatex Corp., 715 A.2d 843 (Del. 1998) (class vote when rights adversely affected by "merger, consolidation or otherwise" arises when firm is acquired).

§13.12 [1] Delaware also provides a sweeping definition of what constitutes "electronic transmission." *See* Del. Code Ann. tit. 8. §232(c) (2001) (defining to cover any form of communication that does not directly involve the physical transmission of paper, so long as a record of the communication is such that it can be retained, retrieved, and reviewed by its recipient and as long as the recipient can reproduce the communication in paper form by automated process).

[2] Del. Code Ann. tit. 8 §211(a) (2001). This is conditioned upon the board implementing reasonable measures to verify that those present and voting are either stockholders or hold valid proxies of a stockholder, that all stockholders have a reasonable opportunity to participate and vote, and that participants have an opportunity substantially concurrently to read or hear the proceedings.

[3] *See, e.g.*, Ariz. Rev. Stat. Ann. §§10-822(a) & 10-708 (West 1996).

[4] *See, e.g.*, Conn. Gen. Stat. Ann. §33-603(a) (West Supp. 2002) ("Notice by electronic transmission is written notice if it is accomplished in a manner that is suitable for retention, retrieval and reproduction. . . .").

C. Shareholders' Meetings and Voting

tion the effectiveness of such delivery upon the shareholder first consenting to delivery of notice in this form.[5] This would appear to permit email messages to stockholders, but it would be no more appropriate to treat merely placing an announcement on the company's website as notice, as it would have been in a paper-based society to impart notice by a classified advertisement. In contrast to the authorization for notice to be given electronically are the tradition bounded statutes that call for notice to be "written or printed"[6] and to be delivered "personally or by mail."[7]

A clear majority of the states permit proxies to be executed and transmitted electronically. Though there is broad authorization for the electronic execution and transmission of proxies, this is somewhat qualified by the need for determining the validity of the authorization.[8] There are also provisions for actions without a meeting, a parallel to the written consent procedures discussed earlier,[9] to occur electronically.[10]

In 2001, the SEC approved changes in the NYSE listing requirements that now permit proxy materials to be delivered by electronic means. Such delivery requires the prior consent of the stockholder, which itself can be conveyed by email. With the proper consent in hand, the company can forward the proxy materials by email attachment or simply notify the holder by email that the material is posted on the company's website.[11]

§13.13   Conduct of Shareholders' Meetings

Section 7.08 of the Model Act[1] envisions a strong, but fair, chair. The meetings' decorum and overall order can be assured as well by attention to the rules of parliamentary procedure, although those not versed in the technical niceties of the rules may well prefer the informality of a fair-minded chair.[2]

[5] See Del. Code Ann. tit. 8 §232 (2001).
[6] See, e.g., Ala. Code §10-2B-7.05(a) (Michie 1999); Kan. Stat. Ann. §17-6512(a) (1995); Minn. Stat. Ann. §302A.135(3) (West 2001).
[7] See, e.g., Alaska Stat. §10.06.410 (Michie 2000); Me. Rev. Stat. Ann. tit. 13-A §604(1) (West 1981); R.I. Gen. Laws §7-1.1-21 (1999).
[8] See, e.g., Ariz. Rev. Stat. Ann. §10-722(c)(2) (West Supp. 2001); Colo. Rev. Stat. §7-107-402(2) (2001); Fla. Stat. Ann. §607.0722(2) (West Supp. 2002); Mich. Comp. L. Ann. §450.1421 (West Supp. 2001); Nev. Rev. Stat. Ann. §78.355(2)(b) (1999); N.Y. Bus. Corp. L. §609 (McKinney Supp. 2002); N.C. Gen. Stat. Ann. §55-7-22(b) (West Supp. 2001); Va. Code Ann. §13.1-663(1) (Michie 1999); Wis. Stat. Ann. §180.0722(2)(b)(1) (West Supp. 2002).
[9] See §13.08.
[10] See Del. Code Ann. tit. 8 §228(d) (2001) (authorizing electronically executed written consents).
[11] See NYSE Company Manual §402.04 approved in Securities Exchange Act Release No. 44133 (Mar. 29, 2001).
§13.13 [1] Model Business Corp. Act §7.08 (1995). Committee on Corporate Laws, Changes in the Model Business Corporation Act—Amendments Pertaining to Shareholder Meetings and Voting, 51 Bus. Law. 209 (1995).
[2] See A.B.A. Corporate Governance Committee, Handbook for the Conduct of Meetings (2001) (calling for parliamentary procedures to be replaced by a strong concentration of authority in a chair who must operate pursuant a fairness standard).

A leading decision of the New York Court of Appeals[3] illustrates how shareholders, by making their wishes known and commencing removal proceedings against some of the directors, can bring pressure to bear on the directors to change their decisions. The corporation's charter provided for a board of eleven directors. Class A shareholders elected nine of the directors and the common shareholders elected two. The Class A holders instituted a mandamus proceeding to compel the corporation's president to call a meeting of Class A holders, as a bylaw required him to do whenever a specified percentage of the shareholders so requested. Among the purposes advanced in the request were: (1) to vote on a resolution endorsing the administration of a former president, who had been removed by the directors, and to demand that the former president be reinstated; (2) to hear charges against four of the directors, vote on their removal, and select their successors; and (3) to vote on a proposal to amend the charter or bylaws to provide that vacancies on the board arising from the removal of a director or resignation of a director against whom charges were pending would be filled by the class of shareholders that the removed or resigned director had represented. The president opposed calling the meeting on the ground that no proper purpose had been stated. The court, however, held that all of the purposes were proper and affirmed the order compelling the president to call the meeting. While the shareholders could not directly reinstate the former president, the court noted that they were privileged to express themselves and thereby bring shareholder sentiments forcefully to the attention of the directors, who would be standing for election at the next annual shareholders meeting. The court went on to say that shareholders who elect directors have the inherent power to remove them for cause.[4]

In an interesting Delaware case,[5] two factions of shareholders, one led by Tomlinson and the other by Vogel, the corporation's president, were fighting for control of the corporation. As a result of a compromise agreement, each faction designated six directors of the thirteen-person board, and the two factions jointly appointed a thirteenth or neutral director. Friction continued, however, and the neutral director, two Vogel directors, and one Tomlinson director resigned, leaving only five Tomlinson directors and four Vogel directors on the board. At a special directors' meeting, which only the five Tomlinson directors attended, the Tomlinson directors attempted to elect two new directors and thereby gain control of the board. The court, however, invalidated the purported election, holding

---

[3] Auer v. Dressel, 118 N.E.2d 590 (N.Y. 1954), noted in Joe G. Davis, Note, Corporations—Stockholders' Right to Remove Directors, 7 Baylor L. Rev. 313 (1955).

[4] The fact that the corporation's certificate of incorporation empowered the board to remove a director for cause does not itself deprive the stockholders of their power to remove directors. 118 N.E.2d at 592-593. The court also held that Class A shareholders could amend the bylaws to empower Class A shareholders to elect successors for Class A directors so removed.

[5] Campbell v. Loew's, Inc., 134 A.2d 852 (Del. Ch. 1957). For the background of this case from the viewpoint of the attorney representing the faction of shareholders headed by the corporation's president, see Louis Nizer, My Life in Court ch. 6 (1961).

the meeting invalid for want of a quorum.[6] In the meantime, Vogel, acting in his capacity as president, had called a shareholders meeting for the following purposes: (1) to fill director vacancies; (2) to amend the bylaws to increase the number on the board from 13 to 19 and the quorum from seven to ten; (3) to remove two of the Tomlinson directors; and (4) to fill the newly created positions and the vacancies that would result from the removal of the two Tomlinson directors.

The Chancellor refused to enjoin the meeting, holding that the bylaws gave the president power to call a shareholder meeting even though a majority of the incumbent directors opposed the meeting;[7] that the bylaws so interpreted did not impinge on the statute giving management powers to the board of directors as long as only matters appropriate for shareholder action were considered at the meeting; that the president, without board approval, could propose a bylaw amendment to enlarge the board; that the shareholders have the power to remove directors for cause even though the corporation has cumulative voting in director elections; that under the bylaws the shareholders had the power to fill "vacancies" on the board; and that shareholders have the inherent right between their annual meetings to fill newly created directorships.[8]

In many states, the provision of the corporation statute that details the procedure for amending the charter indicates that before shareholders can vote on an amendment, the directors must adopt a resolution setting forth the proposed amendment and directing that it be submitted to a vote at a meeting of the shareholders.[9] No provision is made in these states for a shareholder-initiated amendment of the charter. In a distinct minority of states, the statutory procedure for amending the charter seems to provide leeway for shareholder amendment without director approval,[10] and in a few instances shareholders appear to have successfully utilized a charter amendment to increase the number of directors over the opposition of a majority of the board.[11]

---

[6] See Tomlinson v. Loew's, Inc., 134 A.2d 518 (Del. Ch.), *aff'd,* 135 A.2d 136 (Del. 1957).

[7] *See also* Republic Corp. v. Carter, 253 N.Y.S.2d 280 (App. Div.), *aff'd,* 204 N.E.2d 206 (N.Y. 1964).

[8] The chancellor's opinion covered many other matters, including procedures and rules governing the solicitation of proxies in a contest between factions of shareholders and in a proceeding to remove directors.

[9] *See, e.g.,* Del. Code Ann. tit. 8, §242(c) (2001) (specifying that every amendment "shall be made and effected" in the manner described); MBCA §§10.02, 10.03 (1984); Former MBCA §59 (1969).

[10] *See, e.g.,* Mass. Ann. Laws ch. 156, §42 (Law. Co-Op. 1996) (amendment may be authorized by a vote of two-thirds of each class of outstanding stock entitled to vote, or by a larger vote as provided in the charter).

[11] *See* Republic Corp. v. Carter, 253 N.Y.S.2d 280 (App. Div.), *aff'd,* 204 N.E.2d 206 (N.Y. 1964). However, a charter amendment does not appear necessary to increase the number of directors in view of N.Y. Bus. Corp. Law §702(b) (McKinney 1986), which authorizes an increase by amendment of the bylaws or by board or shareholder action under a bylaw adopted by the shareholders. *See also* Auer v. Dressel, 118 N.E.2d 590 (N.Y. 1954) (decided under an earlier statute).

§13.14   *Shares Entitled to Vote*

The general rule is that all legal owners of voting shares in a stock corporation and all members of a non-stock corporation have a right to be present and vote at all corporate meetings.[1]

In the interest of certainty as to voting rights and of the right and duty as to notice of meetings, corporations are universally permitted by statute and charter provisions to look to the corporate records of registered shareholders to determine who is a shareholder entitled to vote, to notice of meetings, to dividends, and to other rights of shareholders.[2] The practice of closing the transfer books for a period of 40 days, more or less, before a meeting is frequently authorized in order to give ample time to make up voting lists of shareholders. In recent years, however, instead of this crude expedient of closing the books against recording transfers, statutes and bylaws have authorized the alternative method of fixing record dates for voting, dividends, and other purposes, so that stock transfers may be continually entered into the books. Those who are registered on the books on the record date remain the shareholders of record for the given purpose, although they may cease to be owners after the record date and before the activity takes place.[3] The former Model Act, which was typical of modern statutes, permitted the closing of the transfer books at the corporation's discretion for not less than 10 nor more than 50 days or the fixing of the record date by bylaw or directors' resolution to be not less than 10 nor more than 50 days before the meeting.[4] The Revised Model Act extends the maximum to 70 days.[5]

The right to vote is an incident of stock ownership except insofar as the corporation needs protection by its records against incurring liability to adverse claimants.[6] In some states, the books are prima facie evidence of the right to vote.[7] Other statutes have provided that the transfer of stock is conclusive evidence of the right to vote as to inspectors of the election, but such statutes are not conclusive on the courts as to share ownership, and rival claimants may litigate their

---

§13.14 [1] In re Giant Portland Cement Co., 21 A.2d 697, 701 (Del. Ch. 1941); Taylor v. Griswold, 14 N.J.L. 222 (1834); Stokes v. Continental Trust Co., 78 N.E. 1090 (N.Y. 1906); Commonwealth v. Dalzell, 25 A. 535 (Pa. 1893).

[2] Bryano v. Western Pac. Ry., 35 A.2d 909 (Del. Ch. 1944); In re Chilson, 168 A. 82 (Del. Ch. 1933); People v. Robinson, 1 P. 156 (Cal. 1883). An unrecorded transferee and the transferor may work out their rights between themselves. One way to deal with the unrecorded transferee is through an irrevocable proxy given by the transferor.

[3] See, e.g., Mariner LDC v. Stone Container Corp., 729 A.2d 267, 273 (Del. Ch. 1998) (preferred shares not entitled to vote on acquisition though the articles of incorporation were amended to accord preferred full voting rights prior to merger because the date of record was set before the amendment).

[4] Former Model Business Corp. Act §30 (1969). See Del. Code Ann. tit. 8, §213 (2001) (no more than 60 days in advance).

[5] Model Business Corp. Act §7.07 (1984).

[6] In re Algonquin Elec. Co., 61 F.2d 779 (2d Cir. 1932); Dennistoun v. Davis, 229 N.W. 353 (Minn. 1930).

[7] Bernheim v. Louisville Property Co., 221 F. 273 (W.D. Ky. 1914) (Kentucky law); Commonwealth v. Patterson, 27 A. 998 (Pa. 1893).

rights.[8] The unregistered or equitable owner of shares has the right to compel the holder of the naked legal title to give her a proxy to vote or to vote at her direction.[9] Over three-fourths of the state statutes provide that redeemable shares lose their voting rights once notice of redemption of the shares is given.[10]

Most statutes provide that a shareholder who has pledged shares has the right to vote until the shares have been transferred to the name of the pledgee.[11] The person whose name appears on the books of a corporation (or otherwise is designated as the absolute owner of stock) clearly has the right to vote those shares, even though he in fact may hold the shares as trustee. The Model Act provides that the trustee is entitled to vote as long as the shares are registered in her name.[12] An executor or administrator has the right to vote shares belonging to the estate even though they stand on the books of the corporation in the decedent's name.[13]

If shares are owned by two or more persons jointly, the right to vote is in them jointly, and they must agree in order to vote the shares.[14] This rule of joint action applies to stock held by several executors or trustees unless there is a provision for majority vote on disagreement.[15] Depending on the statutory authority, fractional shares of stock may or may not be used as the basis of voting, cumulatively or otherwise.[16]

---

[8] Lawrence v. I. N. Parlier Estate Co., 100 P.2d 765 (1940); Ginn v. Jan Chin, Inc., 362 A.2d 143 (R.I. 1976).

[9] CIR v. Southern Bell Tel. & Tel. Co., 102 F.2d 397, 402 (6th Cir. 1939); In re Canal Constr. Co., 182 A. 545 (Del. Ch. 1936); Ginn v. Jan Chin, Inc., 362 A.2d 143 (R.I. 1976).

[10] See, e.g., Ariz. Rev. Stat. Ann. §10-721 (West 1996); Conn. Gen. Stat. Ann. §33-705 (West 1997); R.I. Gen. Laws §7-1.1-31 (1999); Model Bus. Corp. Act. §7.71 (1984).

However, shares that are subject to redemption by virtue of an agreement are not subject to this kind of voting restriction where the statute contemplates the redemption privilege is to be set forth in the articles of incorporation. See Morrison v. Madhaska Bottling Co., 39 F.3d 839 (8th Cir. 1994).

[11] See Former Model Business Corp. Act §33 (1969). Cf. Model Business Corp. Act §§7.21, 7.24 (1984).

This was the general rule in the absence of a statute. Lawrence v. I. N. Parlier Estate Co., 100 P.2d 765 (Cal. 1940); In re Schirmer's Will, 248 N.Y.S. 497, 505 (App. Div. 1931); State ex rel. Reed v. Smith, 14 P. 814, 15 P. 137 (dissenting opinion) (on petition for rehearing) (Or. 1887); Seward v. American Hardware Co., 171 S.E. 650, 661 (Va. 1933). See Note, 29 Cal. L. Rev. 424 (1941).

[12] Model Business Corp. Act §7.24(b)(5); Former Model Business Corp. Act §33 (1969).

[13] Ibid. See Billings v. Marshall Furnace Co., 177 N.W. 222 (Mich. 1920); Annot., 14 A.L.R. 1057 (1938). The same is true with regard to a receiver if the shares are registered in her name or if authority to vote is contained in the applicable court order. Former Model Business Corp. Act §33 (1969).

[14] Sellers v. Joseph Bancroft & Sons Co., 17 A.2d 831 (Del. Ch. 1941); Tornga v. Michigan Gas & Elec. Co., 144 N.W.2d 640 (Mich. Ct. App. 1966); Clowes v. Miller, 47 A. 345 (N.J. Ch. 1900); Annot., 134 A.L.R. 989 (1941). But see Levine v. Randolph Corp., 188 A.2d 59 (Conn. 1963).

[15] People ex rel. Courtney v. Botts, 34 N.E.2d 403 (Ill. 1941); Townsend v. Winburn, 177 N.Y.S. 757 (Sup. Ct. 1919); Tunis v. Hestonville, M. & F.P. Ry., 24 A. 88 (Pa. 1892); Highland v. Empire Nat'l Bank, 172 S.E. 544, 548 (W. Va. 1933).

[16] Commonwealth ex rel. Cartwright v. Cartwright, 40 A.2d 30 (Pa. 1944) (decided under Pennsylvania statute: Pa. Stat. Ann. tit. 15, §1608 (1967)), noted in 43 Mich. L. Rev. 986 (1945); 93 U. Pa. L. Rev. 321 (1945). See Model Business Corp. Act §6.04(c) (1984).

§13.15   Power to Vote Treasury Shares and Shares Held by a Subsidiary

Shares of its own stock acquired by a corporation are no longer outstanding and are denominated "treasury shares" unless subject to cancellation.[1] Since shares are contracts with the corporation, on surrender to the corporation they can have only a potential or fictitious existence and cannot have voting rights.[2] Shares acquired by the corporation that issued them cannot be voted even when they are held in the name of a trustee[3] or have been pledged by the corporation.[4] It does not violate this principle to permit the parent corporation's directors to constitute a majority of the subsidiary's board, even though this has the indirect effect of allowing individuals who are directors of the subsidiary to decide how to vote the shares issued by the subsidiary.[5] Moreover, the shares held by the issuer as trustee for another can be voted by the issuer in its capacity as trustee.[6]

Shares of a parent company's stock purchased by a wholly-owned subsidiary do not *ipso facto* become treasury shares,[7] but shares of a parent corporation held by its subsidiary should be treated as equivalent to treasury shares at least as far as voting rights are concerned.[8] Otherwise, such shares could be voted by the directors of the parent corporation to continue themselves in office almost as freely as treasury shares could be so voted. The Model Act and most state corporation statutes impose a voting disability on shares a subsidiary holds in its parent.[9]

§13.16   Cumulative Voting

Cumulative voting is the privilege of multiplying the number of shares held by the number of directors to be elected and casting the product for a single candidate or distributing the product among two or more candidates. With cumulative voting, shareholders can distribute their votes among some of the vacancies to be filled instead of using "straight voting"—that is, casting votes according to the

---

§13.15   [1] Former Model Business Corp. Act §2(h) (1969). Recent amendments to the Model Act abolish the concept of Treasury shares. *See* §§21.07-21.08. A corporation's acquisition of its own shares is discussed in Chapter 21.

[2] Atterbury v. Consolidated Coppermines Corp., 20 A.2d 743, 747 (Del. Ch. 1941); Tapper v. Boston Chamber of Commerce, 126 N.E. 464 (Mass. 1920). *See* Model Business Corp. Act §7.21(d) (1984); Former Model Business Corp. Act §33 (1969).

[3] Tapper v. Boston Chamber of Commerce, 126 N.E. 464 (Mass. 1920); American Ry.-Frog Co. v. Haven, 101 Mass. 398 (1869). *See* Lawrence v. I. N. Parlier Estate Co., 100 P.2d 765 (Cal. 1940).

[4] Granite Brick Co. v. Titus, 226 F. 557 (4th Cir. 1915); Brewster v. Hartley, 37 Cal. 15 (1869); Thomas v. International Silver Co., 73 A. 833 (N.J. Ch. 1907). *But cf.* Vail v. Hamilton, 85 N.Y. 453 (1881).

[5] State ex rel. Washington Ind., Inc. v. Shacklett, 512 S.W.2d 284 (Tenn. 1974).

[6] *See* Graves v. Security Trust Co., 369 S.W.2d 114 (Ky. 1963).

[7] Golden State Theater & Realty Corp. v. C.I.R., 125 F.2d 641, 642-643 (9th Cir. 1942).

[8] Speiser v. Baker, 525 A.2d 1001 (Del. Ch. 1987) (subsidiary barred from voting shares of its parent though parent owned less than majority of the subsidiary's shares).

[9] *See* Model Bus. Corp. Act §7.21(b) (1984).

number of shares held for each vacancy. If five vacancies are to be filled, each share of stock may be voted five times for one individual to fill one position, instead of casting one vote per share for each of the five positions. In other words, a person or persons holding 100 shares may cast 500 votes in favor of one candidate or may distribute the votes in favor of one or more persons for the five vacancies.

The aim of cumulative voting is to allow a minority to secure representation on the board of directors.[1] Without cumulative voting, holders of a bare majority of the shares may elect the full board and thus control the corporation without any representatives of other interests being present at board meetings.

Under cumulative voting, unwary majority shareholders, if they spread their votes over too many offices, may find that a vigilant minority has deprived the majority of control. If there are 1,000 shares outstanding and ten directors to be elected, and one person holds 600 shares, he should be able to elect the majority of the directors. If, however, he casts 600 votes straight for each one of ten candidates, and if the 400 minority shareholders cumulate their 4,000 votes on six candidates, the minority will elect six directors and the majority will elect only four.[2] To be safe under a cumulative system, where there is a substantial block of minority shares, majority shareholders must often abandon the attempt to elect a complete board and must cumulate their votes on such a portion of the members of the board as the number of their shares bears to the total number of shares that will be voted at the election. Thus each group, majority and minority, should ascertain the portion that the number of shares it holds bears to the number of shares it expects to be voted at the election, and then vote its shares cumulatively for that portion of the number of directors to be elected.[3] If after casting his vote a shareholder sees he has made a mistake, he may recall his ballot and change his vote before the presiding officer finally announces the result of the voting.[4]

---

§13.16   [1] Maddock v. Vorclone Corp., 147 A. 255 (Del. Ch. 1929); Williams, Cumulative Voting for Directors ch. 2 (1951); 1 F. Hodge O'Neal & Robert B. Thompson, O'Neal's Close Corporations §3.178 (3d ed. 1998); Chapter 14; Harlowe E. Bowes & Ledlie A. DeBow, Cumulative Voting at Elections of Directors of Corporations, 21 Minn. L. Rev. 351, 353 (1937); Whitney Campbell, The Origin and Growth of Voting for Directors, 10 Bus. Law. 3 (1955).

[2] Dulin v. Pacific Wood & Coal Co., 35 P. 1045 (Cal.), *aff'd per curiam,* 37 P. 207 (Cal. 1894); Schwartz v. State, 56 N.E. 201 (Ohio 1900); Pierce v. Commonwealth, 104 Pa. 150 (1883).

[3] The following algebraic formula is sometimes used to determine how many votes of those present is sufficient under cumulative voting to elect a specified number of directors:

$$x = \frac{a \times b}{c + 1} + 1$$

with *a* representing the number of directors it desires to elect, *b* the number of shares present and voting, *c* the total number of vacancies to be filled, and *x* the number of shares necessary to achieve the desired objective. For an example of what can happen when a majority shareholder fails to anticipate the effects of cumulative voting, see Stancil v. Bruce Stancil Refrigeration, Inc., 344 S.E.2d 789 (N.C. Ct. App. 1986).

[4] Zierath Combination Drill Co. v. Croake, 131 P. 335 (Cal. Ct. App. 1913); Zachary v. Milin, 293 N.W. 770, 772 (Mich. 1940); Washington State Labor Council v. Federated Am. Ins. Co., 474 P.2d 98 (Wash. 1970); State ex rel. David v. Dailey 158 P.2d 330 (Wash. 1945).

For cumulative voting to work, all the directors to be elected in a given year must be voted for at one time; each director position cannot be voted on separately.[5] The more directors there are to be elected, the smaller the minority needed to secure a representative. Where the directors are classified, with only one-half or one-third to be elected annually, the benefits to the minority of cumulative voting are greatly diminished.[6] For example, if there are five directors to be chosen and one-fifth of the shares are voted for one nominee, that nominee is practically assured of getting a place on the board, while if only three directors are to be chosen, one-third of the shares would be required for the same assurance.

Constitutional or statutory provisions in some states establish mandatory cumulative voting for all corporations[7]—that is, the privilege of cumulating their votes is granted to the shareholders irrespective of authorization in the charter or bylaws. In most jurisdictions, however, cumulative voting is only permissive and does not exist unless affirmatively authorized by provision in the charter or, sometimes, the bylaws.[8] It has been suggested that the majority shareholders should not have the power to withdraw the privilege of cumulative voting by amendment of the charter or otherwise.[9] If the privilege of cumulative voting is to be granted at all for protection of the minority, it should be made mandatory, not merely permissive at the option of the incorporators or the majority group.

Some states have a constitutional or statutory provision making cumulative voting for directors mandatory and also a statute permitting the staggered election of directors—that is, the classification of directors and the election of each class in a different year—say, for a three-year term. The question of the validity of staggered elections where cumulative voting is mandatory has led to conflicting answers. A Pennsylvania case[10] held that a *constitutional* cumulative voting requirement did not prohibit the classification of directors and the staggering of elec-

---

[5] Wright v. Central Cal. Colony Water Co., 8 P. 70 (Cal. 1885).

[6] Reducing the number of directors to be voted for reduces the chances of minority representation. Accordingly, some corporations, in an attempt to dilute minority representation, have staggered the terms of directors. *See, e.g.*, McDonough v. Copeland Refrigeration Corp., 277 F. Supp. 6 (E.D. Mich. 1967); Janney v. Philadelphia Transp. Co., 128 A.2d 76 (Pa. 1956).

[7] Some states have repealed constitutional provisions for mandatory cumulative voting and replaced them with statutes permitting limitation or elimination of cumulative voting. *E.g.*, Ill. Comp. Stat. Ann. ch. 805, §5/7.40 (West Supp. 2002).

[8] Maddock v. Vorclone Corp., 147 A. 255 (Del. Ch. 1929); Chappell v. Standard Scale & Sup. Corp., 138 A. 74 (Del. Ch.), *rev'd on other grounds*, 141 A. 191 (1928); In re Brophy, 179 A. 128 (N.J. Sup. Ct. 1935). *See* In re American Fibre Chair Seat Corp., 193 N.E. 253 (N.Y. 1934) (informal amendment). For a case holding that the mandatory cumulative voting laws of one state be imposed on a foreign corporation transacting most of its business in that state, *see* Wilson v. Louisiana-Pacific Resources, Inc., 187 Cal. Rptr. 852 (Ct. App. 1983).

[9] *See* Maddock v. Vorclone Corp., 147 A. 255 (Del. Ch. 1929) (unfair exercise of right of amendment by majority but no fraud shown); Bowes & DeBow, *supra* note 1, at 369.

[10] Janney v. Philadelphia Transp. Co., 128 A.2d 76 (Pa. 1956). *See* Stockholders Comm. for Better Management v. Erie Tech. Prods., Inc., 248 F. Supp. 380 (W.D. Pa. 1965). The constitutional provision has since been repealed and replaced by statutory discretionary cumulative voting.

tions, but in Illinois the staggered election was held to be unconstitutional.[11] Questions may also arise as to the validity of shareholder voting agreements in the face of mandatory cumulative voting.[12]

§13.17   Interference with the Stockholders' Franchise

Sometimes, when their control is threatened by an outsider, directors manipulate the timing of a stockholders' meeting to gain a strategic advantage. For example, in a leading Delaware case, *Schnell v. Chris-Craft Industries, Inc.,*[1] the directors, who were engaged in a proxy contest, advanced the date of the stockholders' meeting from the date initially established for the meeting. The directors acted in response to the on-going proxy campaign by an insurgent group and the effect of advancing the date was to reduce considerably the time the insurgents would have to persuade other stockholders to grant their proxies to the insurgents and not management. The court enjoined the convening of the meeting on the ground that the directors acted solely to obstruct the legitimate efforts of dissident shareholders to oust the board.[2] It was not until later, in *Blasius Industries v. Atlas Corp.,*[3] that the approach taken in *Schnell* became fully articulated such that it is now an important principle of corporate law. At a time that Blasius Industries was soliciting written consents to expand Atlas's board and fill the newly created seats with nominees who would support a recapitalization plan, Atlas's board quickly met and added three additional board members. The effect of this was to prevent Blasius's on-going efforts to result in it obtaining a majority of the board seats. Chancellor Allen concluded that the board's actions were taken in good faith and were undertaken in the the reasonable belief that the recapitalization plan would not be in the best interests of Atlas or its stockholders. However, he reasoned that good faith alone does not justify the board intentionally interfering with the exercise of the stockholders' franchise. Placing the matter within principal-agent context, where the agent is deemed to act inequitably when taking steps to frustrate the principal's control of the agent, *Blasius* thus placed upon management the burden of proving a "compelling justification" for acts taken to thwart the exercise of stockholder franchise. *Blasius* is about the validity of directorial power and not an abstract affirmation of shareholder voting rights.

Later Delaware decisions emphasize that in *Schnell* the directors altered the date of a stockholders' meeting that had already been scheduled and that in *Blasius* the procurement of written consents had commenced were pivotal considerations for determining whether directors' actions are judged by the "compelling

---

[11] Wolfson v. Avery, 126 N.E.2d 701 (Ill. 1955). *See generally* W. Edward Sell & Lloyd H. Fuge, Impact of Classified Corporate Directors and the Constitutional Right of Cumulative Voting, 17 U. Pitt. L. Rev. 151 (1956).

[12] *See* 1 F. Hodge O'Neal & Robert B. Thompson, O'Neal's Close Corporations §§3.17 (3d ed. 1998).

§13.17   [1] 285 A.2d 437 (Del. 1971).

[2] *Id. See also* In re Unexcelled, Inc., 281 N.Y.S.2d 473 (App. Div. 1967) (board may set annual meeting at different dates sometimes less than 12 months apart such that incumbent directors' term is less than one year).

[3] 564 A.2d 651 (Del. Ch. 1988) (Chancellor Wm. Allen).

justification" standard:[4] whether the directors are obstructing the *on-going* exercise of the shareholder franchise.[5] This doctrine is not limited to when there is an on-going contest for control.[6] That is, directors and officers bear a substantial burden of justifying conduct that impedes the *existing* efforts and activities of the shareholders to participate in the corporation's governance. Where the directors' and officers' actions are clearly defensive, but do not interfere with any on-going exercise of the stockholder franchise, their acts are judged by the standard customarily applied to defensive maneuvers. Thus, *Schnell* and *Blasius* do not deprive management of acting strategically, even in the face of on-going efforts to unseat them.[7] The distinction made in the cases serves the justifiable purpose of subjecting to extremely rigorous review those board actions that are taken in order to thwart the efforts of aroused shareholders. We might well question why *Schnell* and *Blasius* should be limited to thwarting the stockholders when engaged in the exercise of their governance rights. Indeed, some flexibility in the doctrine's application appears from time to time. For example, management may well take such steps as calling the meeting where an item known to be controversial will be discussed and purposefully give such short notice as to effectively foreclose any pos-

---

[4] *See also, e.g.*, IBS Fin. Corp. v. Seidman & Associates, LLC, 136 F.3d 940 (3d Cir. 1998) (*Blasius* standard is not limited to cases involving a battle for corporate control; directors' reduction of size of board, in advance of annual meeting, was allegedly designed to disenfranchise certain shareholders and thus was not valid without showing a compelling justification). In Williams v. Geier, 671 A.2d 1368, 1376 (Del. 1996), the court observed:

> *Blasius'* burden of demonstrating a "compelling justification" is quite onerous and therefore is applied rarely. . . . [T]he application of the "compelling justification" standard set forth in *Blasius* is appropriate only where the "'primary purpose' of the board's action [is] to interfere with or impede exercise of the shareholder franchise," and the stockholders are not given a "full and fair opportunity to vote."

(quoting from Stroud v. Grace, 606 A.2d 75, 92 (Del. 1992)).

[5] Stroud v. Grace, 606 A.2d 75 (Del. 1992); Stahl v. Apple Bancorp., 579 A.2d 1115 (Del. Ch. 1990) (*Blasius* in applicable where meeting date had not previously been set). *See also* Shoen v. AMERCO, 885 F. Supp. 1332 (D. Nev. 1994) (advancing meeting date violated Blasius); IBS Fin. Corp. v. Seidman and Assocs., LLC, 136 F.3d 940 (3d Cir. 1998) (corporation enjoined from reducing size of board of directors from seven to six on the eve of an annual meeting at which a shareholder committee was seeking representation on the board); Hilton Hotels Corp. v. ITT Corp., 978 F. Supp. 1342 (D. Nev. 1997) (injunction against proposal to stagger board terms without a shareholder vote, on the eve of the annual meeting, that was part of a comprehensive reorganization plan to thwart hostile takeover).

[6] *See, e.g.*, IBS Financial Corp. v. Seidman & Assoc. LLC, 136 F.3d 940 (3d Cir. 1998); State of Wisconsin Inv. Bd. V. Peerless Systems Corp., 2000 WL 1805376 (Del. Ch. Dec. 4, 2000) (applied when issue was modification to stock option plan and management adjourned meeting so as to secure necessary votes to approve plan).

[7] *See, e.g.*, Glazier v. Zapata Corp., 658 A.2d 176 (Del. 1993) (in face of takeover issuing shares to supporter of management); Wyser-Pratte v. Smith, 1997 WL 153806 (Del. Ch. 1997) (upholding directors' fixing record date for special meeting when set within permissible statutory period but at a date that placed insurgent group at a disadvantage); Dolgoff v. Projectavision, Inc., 1996 WL 91945 (Del. Ch. Feb. 29, 1996) (advancing date of annual meeting for purpose of shortening time director would otherwise serve not inequitable); State ex rel. KelCor, Inc. v. Nooney Realty Trusts, Inc., 966 S.W.2d 399 (Mo. Ct. App. 1998) (upholding delay in meeting date on grounds that 13 percent may not be able to attend earlier date which could give rise to expense of reconvening another meeting).

sible opposition from mounting a proxy contest. In this situation, and it would seem others, the fundamental principle should be not whether the opposition is currently taking steps to exercise their shareholder franchise, but whether management has taken steps that prevent such steps from even being commenced. Such an approach does get into difficult factual and problematic factual inquiries. For this reason, having a bright-line test of whether the insurgents are then engaged in steps to oppose management or its position is useful. But it seems that exceptions to this standard can be made where on its face the steps taken by management clearly thwart any possibility of opposition exercising their shareholder franchise.[8]

§13.18   Vote-Buying and Coercion

Vote-buying[1] and coercion are two separate but related concepts. Each involves a shareholder voting for or against a matter for reasons other than its intrinsic merits. In vote-buying, a shareholder is enticed with extra benefits that the shareholder would not have received otherwise. Wrongful coercion is where shareholders are threatened through statements that the controlling stockholder, directors, or others will take action that may harm the stockholders' interest.

For the past two decades, vote-buying has been a matter litigated exclusively in Delaware and without success by the party invoking the argument as the foil to prevent the implementation of a transaction requiring stockholder approval. At one time the mere presence of any consideration bestowed for a stockholder's vote was invalid. The rationale for this result was twofold. First, the courts believed that each stockholder owed his fellow stockholders a fiduciary duty when voting to exercise his own independent judgment.[2] This view no longer prevails; only controlling stockholders are held to have a fiduciary duty to other stockholders.[3] Second, during corporate law's formative years analogies to other contexts were made, some analogies, of course, being stronger references than others. Thus, courts reasoned that just as vote-buying by politicians was harmful, so it should be for the purchase of the stockholder's vote.[4]

In 1982, Delaware put an end to vote-buying being per se void. *Schreiber v. Carney*[5] arose in the context of a corporate restructuring of Texas International Airlines that required approval of each class of its outstanding securities. One of the

---

[8] *See, e.g.,* Linton v. Everett, 1997 WL 441189 (Del. Ch. July 31, 1997) (after failing to convene stockholders' meeting for three years, called meeting with only 30 days' notice which, in granting injunction, court reasoned effectively prevented opposition slate being put forth).

§13.18   [1] On the subject of vote buying, *see* Douglas R. Cole, E-Proxies for Sale? Corporate Vote-Buying in the Internet Age, 76 Wash. L. Rev. 793 (2001); Richard L. Hasen, Vote Buying, 88 Cal. L. Rev. 1323 (2000); Thomas J. Andre, Jr., A Preliminary Inquiry Into The Utility of Vote Buying in the Market for Corporate Control, 63 So. Cal. L. Rev. 533 (1990); Robert C. Clark, Vote Buying and Corporate Law, 29 Case W. Res. L. Rev. 776 (1979).

[2] *See, e.g.,* Cone's Ex'rs v. Russell, 21 A. 847, 849 (N.J. Ch. 1891).

[3] *See, e.g.,* Priddy v. Edelman, 883 F.2d 438, 445 (6th Cir. 1989) Waters v. Double L, Inc., 769 P.2d 582, 583-584 (Idaho 1999).

[4] For early cases expressing this view, see Andre, *supra* note 1 at 542, n.26.

[5] 447 A.2d 17 (Del. Ch. 1982).

three outstanding classes of shares was convertible preferred shares and a majority of those shares were held by Jet Capital, who also held warrants covering 800,000 Texas International common shares. Jet Capital was not favorable to the restructuring because upon its occurrence it would incur a substantial tax liability with respect to the warrants. To secure its approval, Texas International agreed to lend $3.4 million to Jet Capital to enable it to exercise the warrants. In a derivative suit challenging this arrangement on the grounds of unlawful vote-buying, the Delaware Chancery Court voiced a more tolerant approach to vote-buying, reasoning that the despite its unsavory connotation, vote-buying "is simply a voting agreement supported by consideration personal to the stockholder."[6] Instead of being void per se, the court set forth the following two-part approach:

> [V]oting agreements in whatever form . . . should not be considered to be illegal
> *per se* unless the object or purpose is to defraud or in some way disenfranchise the
> other stockholders. That is not to say, however, that vote-buying for some laudable
> purpose is automatically free from challenge. Because vote-buying is so easily sus-
> ceptible of abuse it must be viewed as a voidable transaction subject to a test of
> intrinsic fairness.[7]

In *Schreiber*, the court found no harm to the other stockholders because the entire purpose of the restructuring was to benefit the other stockholders and the arrangement with Jet Capital was necessary to secure for them the advantages provided by the restructuring. Moreover, the court concluded the loan transaction was intrinsically fair because it was subsequently ratified by the stockholders. After *Schreiber* vote-buying arrangements have with great regularity been upheld.[8]

At one time, many state statutes proscribed vote-buying. Today, remnants of the former hostility to vote-buying can be found among a few corporate statutes that prohibit vote-buying.[9]

Coercion claims have arisen in but a few cases. The leading decision finding coercion is *Lacos Land Co. v. Arden Group, Inc.*,[10] where the CEO threatened to block any future beneficial corporate transactions unless the stockholders approved a corporate restructuring. The restructuring before the stockholders would effectively confer control of the company upon the CEO because he received super voting shares called for by the restructuring. In contrast, the other stockholders would receive shares with diminished dividend rights and limited transferability. Because of the CEO's threat, the court found the shareholders were being coerced to approve the transactions.[11] It accordingly issued a preliminary injunction against the restructuring. However, in another case involving

---

[6] *Id.* at 23.

[7] *Id.* at 25-26.

[8] *See, e.g.,* Polk v. Good, 507 A.2d 531 (Del. 1986); In re *ICX* Communications, Inc. Shareholder Litig, 1999/WL 1009174 (Del. Ch. Oct. 27, 1997); Kass v. Eastern Airlines, Inc., 1986 WL 13008 (Del. Ch. Nov. 14, 1986).

[9] *See* N.Y. Bus. Corp. L. §609(e) (McKinney 1986); Mont. Code Ann. §35-1-525(9) (2001).

[10] 517 A.2d 271 (Del. Ch. 1986).

[11] *Id.* at 278-279.

tenured voting, the court found stockholder approval was not obtained by coercion, despite the proxy statement's disclosure that even absent the sought after two-thirds stockholder approval the arrangement would be carried out with the effect that the shares would be delisted by the NYSE for failure to obtain the two-thirds approval required by the NYSE's listing requirements. The court, somewhat unrealistically, saw this as not a threat, but merely disclosing all the facts necessary for the stockholders to be informed.[12] Thus, what constitutes coercion is not only a factual inquiry, but one for which at least the Delaware Chancery Court appears to have a fairly high level of tolerance of the type of pressure minority stockholders can withstand and still act independently of that pressure. It remains to be seen whether other courts will be more willing to find coercion than has Delaware.

D.   STATE REGULATION OF THE PROXY MACHINERY

§13.19   The Nature of a Proxy

A "proxy" is the authority given by one shareholder to another to vote her shares at a shareholders' meeting. The term is also used to refer to the instrument or paper that is evidence of the authority of the agent, as well as to the agent or proxy holder who is authorized to vote.[1] The proxy holder is an agent whose authority may be general or limited. Being an agent, the proxy holder is thus, in the eye of the law, a fiduciary.[2] As the Delaware court has said: "A person acting as proxy for another is but the latter's agent and owes to the latter the duty of acting in strict accord with those requirements of a fiduciary relationship which inhere in the conception of agency."[3]

It was accordingly held in that case that the proxy holder, as agent, could not bind his principal by an act done with an interest adverse to that of the shareholder, such as the proxy holder's ratification of an issue of stock to himself for an illegal consideration.[4]

---

[12] *Id.* at 1382-1383. *See also* Brazen v. Bell Atlantic Corp., 695 A.2d 43 (Del. 1997) (presence of a $550 million penalty payable to its merger partner if the stockholders did not approve the merger was not deemed coercive where represented only 2 percent of firm's market capitalization).

§13.19   [1] *E.g.*, Eliason v. Englehart, 733 A.2d 944, 946 (Del. 1999); Duffy v. Loft, Inc., 151 A. 223 (Del. Ch. 1930).

[2] *See* Preston v. Allison, 650 A.2d 646 (Del. 1994) (trustee of ESOP breached fiduciary obligations to plan participants by voting shares counter to participants' wishes); In re Ideal Mutual Ins. Co., 190 N.Y.S.2d 887 (Sup. Ct.), *aff'd*, 190 N.Y.S.2d 895 (N.Y. App. Div. 1959) (setting aside election of directors when proxy holder voted for slate different than that initially contemplated by proxy giver and holder).

[3] Rice & Hutchins, Inc. v. Triplex Shoe Co., 147 A. 317, 322 (Del. Ch. 1929), *aff'd*, 152 A. 342 (Del. 1930).

[4] Rice & Hutchins, Inc. v. Triplex Shoe Co., 147 A. 317 (Del. Ch. 1929), *aff'd*, 152 A. 342 (Del. 1930).

At common law, all votes at shareholders' meetings had to be given in person; there was no right to vote by proxy.[5] This is still the rule for directors' meetings. However, as a result of statutory provision, charter, or bylaw provision, the shareholders' privilege of voting by proxy is universal in stock corporations.[6] When the right is given by statute or charter, a shareholder cannot be deprived of it, nor can it be unreasonably restricted by a bylaw.[7]

A general unrestricted proxy or authorization to attend and vote at an annual meeting, "with all the powers the undersigned would possess if personally present," gives a general discretionary power of attorney to vote for directors and on all ordinary matters that may properly come before a regular meeting, even though specific mention of them is not made in the notice of the meeting.[8] Courts distinguish sharply between what business may be transacted at a regular meeting without notice of specified purposes and what may be transacted at a special meeting.[9] A general proxy is no authority to vote for a fundamental change in the corporate charter or for dissolution or a transfer of all of the property to another corporation, or other unusual transactions, at least where the shareholder has not received proper statutory notice.[10]

A limited proxy may restrict the authority to vote to specified matters only and may direct the manner in which the vote shall be cast.[11] Shares represented by proxy are deemed "present" at a meeting, even though the proxy is granted for the express purpose to "withhold approval" of the slate of diretors being put forth by management (when there is no opposing slate of nominees).[12] Failure of proxy holders to produce and file the written evidence of authority will not prevent the votes being counted to make up a quorum to organize a meeting.

There must be satisfactory proof that a proxy has been executed, which minimally requires written evidence of the proxy holder's authority,[13] but courts have recognized proxies executed by a rubber stamp facsimile of the owner's signa-

---

[5] Taylor v. Griswold, 14 N.J.L. 222 (1834); Pohl v. Rhode Island Food Dealers Ass'n, 7 A.2d 267 (R.I. 1939).

[6] 5 William Fletcher, Cyclopedia of Corporations §2050 (rev. ed. 1996). *See* Model Business Corp. Act §7.22(a) (1984). Former Model Business Corp. Act §33 (1969).

[7] People's Home Sav. Bank v. Superior Court, 38 P. 452 (Cal. 1894).

[8] McClean v. Bradley, 282 F. 1011 (N.D. Ohio 1922), *aff'd,* 299 F. 379 (6th Cir. 1924); Gow v. Consolidated Coppermines Corp., 165 A. 136, 143 (Del. Ch. 1933); Note, 33 Ill. L. Rev. 914, 917-918 (1939). In 1995, the Comments to the Model Act were amended to provide that in publicly held corporations, discretionary proxy authority may be exercised only in compliance with SEC Rule 14a-4(c)(1).

[9] *See* §13.09.

[10] Raible v. Puerto Rico Ind. Dev. Co., 392 F.2d 424 (1st Cir. 1968) (reducing par value with the effect of reducing foreclosure costs to pledge).

[11] Bache v. Central Leather Co., 81 A. 571 (N.J. Ch. 1911); State ex rel. Lally v. Cadigan, 174 P. 965 (Wash. 1918); Note, 33 Ill. L. Rev. 914, 917 (1939).

[12] *See* North Fork Bancorp., Inc. v. Dime Bancorp., Inc., 2000 Del. Ch. Lexis 155 (Nov. 8, 2000). However, the shares are not deemed "present" for a matter when the proxy holder has no power to vote the shares on that matter. *See* Berlin v. Emerald Partners, 552 A.2d 482 (Del. 1989).

[13] *See* Dynamics Corp of Am. v. CTS Corp., 643 F. Supp. 215 (N.D. Ill. 1986); Eliason v. Englehart, 773 A.2d 944, 946 (Del. Ch. 1999).

ture[14] as well as by only the owner's initials.[15] Keeping up with technological advances, proxies can be given by electronic transmission and also by telephone so long as certain procedures are followed.[16]

§13.20   Revocation, Duration, and Termination of Proxies

A proxy, like an agency in general, is revocable unless "coupled with an interest." Most state statutes provide a proxy's duration cannot extend beyond 11 months, unless the proxy provides a longer period.[1] One who has given a proxy or power of attorney to another to vote her shares may revoke the agency at any time if it is not coupled with an interest, even though it is expressly declared to be irrevocable or a consideration for the appointment is stated.[2] It was formerly against the general policy of the law governing corporate control that an irrevocable power of voting, or of directing the vote of stock, should be created even by contract of the shareholder.[3]

Revocation of a proxy need not be made by formal notice in writing to the corporation unless so required by statute. Revocation may be expressed to the proxy holder or to the election judges or may be indicated by a subsequent proxy to another or by sale of the shares.[4] Appearing and asserting the right to vote at a meeting revokes a proxy previously given.[5] Thus a proxy may be revoked orally or by conduct. Just like any other agency, a proxy is terminated by the death of the principal or of the agent or by the loss of capacity by either party, unless this rule is changed by statute.[6]

---

[14] Schutt v. Climax Molybedenum Co., 154 A.2d 221 (Del. Ch. 1959).

[15] Atterbury v. Consolidated Coppermines Corp., 20 A.2d 743 (Del. Ch. 1941). *See also* Viele v. Devaney, 679 A.2d 993 (Del. Ch. 1996) (proxy validly executed by signature "Raymond E. Stefans" though shares registered "R.E. Stefans"). *See* Model Business Corp. Act §7.24 Official Comment (1995). *See* Committee on Corporate Laws, Changes in the Model Business Corporation Act— Amendments Pertaining to Shareholder Meetings and Voting, 51 Bus. Law. 209 (1995).

[16] Model Business Corp. Act §7.22(b) (1995).

§13.20   [1] *See, e.g.,* Ill. Comp. Stat. Ann. ch. 805, §5/7.50 (West Supp. 2002); Mo. Ann. Stat. §351.245 (West 2001); N.Y. Bus. Corp. L. §609 (McKinney Supp. 2002); Model Bus. Corp. Act. §7.22 (c) (1984).

[2] In re Chilson, 168 A. 82 (Del. Ch. 1933); Schmidt v. Mitchell, 41 S.W. 929 (Ky. 1897); Stein v. Capital Outdoor Advertising, Inc., 159 S.E.2d 351 (N.C. 1968). *See also* In re Schwartz & Gray, 72 A. 70 (N.J. 1909); Commonwealth v. Patterson, 27 A. 998 (Pa. 1893); Note, 33 Ill. L. Rev. 914, 919 (1939).

[3] *See* §13.26.

[4] Concord Fin. Group, Inc. v. Tri-State Motor Transit Co., 567 A.2d 1 (Del. Ch. 1989) (proxies having same date of execution, the proxy with the later postmark was counted).

[5] *See* State ex rel. Breger v. Rusche, 39 N.E.2d 433 (Ind. 1942); In re Manacher, 133 N.Y.S.2d 265 (Sup. Ct.), *aff'd mem.,* 131 N.Y.S.2d 914 (App. Div. 1954) (the mere presence of a shareholder is no reason for refusing to permit a vote by a proxy holder); In re Estate of Croonberg, 988 P.2d 41, 46 n.1 (Wyo. 1999).

[6] Note, 44 Harv. L. Rev. 265 (1930); Restatement (Second) of Agency, §§120-123 (1988). *See, e.g.,* Minn. Stat. Ann. §302A.449(4) (West Supp. 2002); Ohio Rev. Code Ann. §1701.48(E) (West 1994).

Even though it is not so stated, a proxy has generally been viewed as irrevocable when it is "coupled with an interest" in the shares.[7] What constitutes a sufficient interest in the shares to make a power to vote them irrevocable is an unsettled question.[8] According to the conventional view, the interest must be either (1) a charge, lien, or some property right in the shares themselves; or (2) a security interest given to protect the proxy holder for money advanced or obligations incurred.[9] Under this view, a "recognizable property or financial interest in the stock in respect of which the voting power is to be exercised," which renders the proxy irrevocable, is said to be distinguishable from "an interest in the corporation generally" and from "an interest in the bare voting power or the results to be accomplished by the use of it," neither of which has that effect.[10]

The more recent liberal view holds that the proxy is also irrevocable when the interest protected is in the corporation for which the shares are held as additional security.[11] It seems that modern courts usually find an interest where the proxy is given for the protection of a right of the proxy holder or a third person or to ensure the performance of a duty. Under either view, payment to the shares' owner as compensation for being allowed to vote the owner's shares violates the common law rule against vote-selling such that the arrangement confers no authority on the proxy holder.[12] More recently, the Delaware courts have shifted from viewing vote-buying as *per se* invalid, to being *voidable*, subject to a test for intrinsic fairness.[13] Thus, consideration paid by a corporation that was approved by its outside directors as being in the best interests of the corporation was not invalid.[14] An irrevocable proxy is not terminated by revocation or by death of the creator of the proxy or by his loss of capacity.

A number of states have either tried by statute to avoid the ambiguous term "coupled with an interest" by specifying the circumstances in which a proxy can be made irrevocable and the procedure for making it irrevocable, as in New York,[15] or have tried to broaden, clarify, or define the term. For example, the Delaware statute attempts to broaden the term by stating that: "A duly executed proxy shall be irrevocable if it states that it is irrevocable and if, and only as long as, it is coupled with an interest sufficient in law to support an irrevocable power. A proxy may be made irrevocable regardless of whether the interest with which it is cou-

---

[7] Mobile & O. R.R. v. Nicholas, 12 So. 723, 731 (Ala. 1893); Smith v. San Francisco & N.P. Ry., 47 P. 582 (Cal. 1897); Chapman v. Bates, 47 A. 638 (N.J. 1900).

[8] Abercrombie v. Davies, 123 A.2d 893, 906-907 (Del. Ch. 1956), *rev'd on other grounds*, 130 A.2d 338 (Del. 1957); In re Chilson, 168 A. 82 (Del. Ch. 1933).

[9] *See* Calumet Ind., Inc. v. MacClure, 464 F. Supp. 19 (N.D. Ill. 1978); In re Chilson, 168 A. 82, 85-86 (Del. Ch. 1933).

[10] *See* In re Chilson, 168 A. 82, 86 (Del. Ch. 1933). *Cf.* Smith v. Biggs Boiler Works Co., 82 A.2d 372 (Del. Ch. 1951).

[11] *See* Diebler v. Charles H. Elliot Co., 81 A.2d 577 (Pa. 1951).

[12] *See* Chew v. Inverness Management Corp. 352 A.2d 426 (Del. Ch. 1976).

[13] *See generally* Robert C. Clark, Vote Buying and Corporate Law, 29 Case W. Res. L. Rev. 776 (1979).

[14] Schreiber v. Carney, 447 A.2d 17 (Del. Ch. 1982).

[15] N.Y. Bus. Corp. Law §609(f), (g) (McKinney 1986).

pled is an interest in the stock itself or an interest in the corporation generally."[16] The Model Business Corporation Act more comprehensively defines "coupled with an interest."[17] Under that act, an appointment made irrevocable is revoked when the interest with which it is coupled is extinguished.[18]

Management customarily solicits proxies seeking authority to vote not only on matters that management knows will arise at the meeting, but also discretionary authority to vote the shares on any other matter that may be proposed at the meeting. In the time between soliciting or even obtaining proxies and the meeting, management may become aware of a matter a stockholder intends to propose for stockholder action at the meeting. Under state law this does not by itself revoke the proxy obtained by management. However, the SEC's position, which applies to companies that are covered by the Securities Exchange Act's proxy rules, is that management cannot exercise its discretionary authority if after obtaining the proxy it learns that a matter will be proposed for stockholder action at the meeting and the proponent intends to solicit proxies in support of that proposal from the holders of at least a majority of the shares.[19]

§13.21 The Proxy Voting System

The presence in person or by proxy of holders of a majority of a corporation's shares is generally required to constitute a quorum.[1] It is accordingly of great importance that shareholders unable to attend in person appoint suitable agents to represent them so that elections can be held and other necessary business transacted. As a New Jersey court said of a large steel corporation, "[i]t would be stupid indeed to assume that the 80,000 stockholders may possibly attend the meeting in person."[2] It has similarly been observed: "[I]n the larger corporations the stockholders' meeting is now only a necessary formality; that stockholders' expression can only be had by the statutory device of proxy. As a result, within limitations, realistically the solicitation of proxies is today the stockholders' meeting."[3] In other words, the proxy system is usually a species of absentee voting by mail for the slate of directors and the proposals suggested by the management.

Management has a great advantage in the solicitation of proxies because it is lawful for the directors to send out blank proxies printed at the expense of the

[16] Del. Code Ann. tit. 8, §212(c) (2001). *See* Eliason v. Englehart, 733 A.2d 944, 947 (Del. 1999) (because statute requires a statement it is irrevocable, the word "irrevocable" must appear somewhere in the granting of the proxy and not sufficient that this is expressed in the acknowledgment which appears after the proxy giver's signature).

[17] Model Business Corp. Act §7.22(d) (1984).

[18] Model Business Corp. Act §7.22(f) (1984).

[19] *See* Idaho Power Co., SEC No-Action Letter, Fed. Sec. L. Rep. (CCH) ¶77,224 (Mar. 13, 1996) (interpreting Rule 14a-4(c)(1)).

§13.21 [1] *See* §13.11.

[2] Berendt v. Bethlehem Steel Corp., 154 A. 321, 322 (N.J. Ch. 1931).

[3] Sheldon E. Bernstein & Henry G. Fischer, The Regulation of the Solicitation of Proxies: Some Reflections on Corporate Democracy, 7 U. Chi. L. Rev. 226, 227 (1940).

company and to provide postage paid for by the company, at least if it is not purely a personal contest. The ordinary holder of a relatively small number of shares has practically no alternative, other than not voting at all, to delegating his vote to a proxy committee of persons whom he does not know, over whom he has no control, and as to whose intended action he is very poorly informed, except as these matters are regulated by the federal rules on proxy solicitation.

Although proxy contests are usually limited to closely held businesses, there have been a number of bitterly fought proxy fights in publicly held corporations,[4] in large part due to Securities and Exchange Commission regulation of shareholder suffrage.[5] Notwithstanding the resultant increased emphasis on fairness in shareholder suffrage, the success of groups opposing incumbent management and its policies unless within the context of a takeover attempt has not been great when measured in terms of victories at the ballot box.[6] The primary reasons for the continued success of incumbent management are its control of the proxy machinery and shareholder inertia in voting.

§13.22   *Proxy Contest Expenses*

In addition to having control of the voting process, management's ability to use company funds during a proxy contest assures its success in most cases. Through its board of directors a corporation may spend reasonable sums in a contested election where the expenditures further the intelligent exercise of judgment by the shareholders.[1] In a contest over policy, as distinguished from purely personal struggles for power, the board may authorize reasonable corporate expenditures to support policies that the directors believe in good faith to be in the corporation's best interest.[2] On the other hand, it has been held that shareholders may vote to reimburse successful insurgents for their expenses.[3] The decisions suggest that in the case of both incumbent management and successful insurgents reimbursement is properly limited to actual,

---

[4] *See generally* Randall S. Thomas & Catherine Dixon, Aranow & Einhorn, Proxy Contests for Corporate Control (3d ed. 2001); Hazen, *supra* §13.10 note 3, §§10.03-10.5; Louis Loss & Joel Seligman, 6 Securities Regulation 1922-1933 (1990). For control battles within the closely held context, *see* §13.24, Chapter 14.

[5] *See* §§13.19-13.22.

[6] *See* Lewis S. Black, Jr., Shareholder Democracy and Corporate Governance, 5 Sec. Reg. L.J. 291 (1978); Donald E. Schwartz, The Public-Interest Proxy Contest: Reflections on Campaign GM, 69 Mich. L. Rev. 419 (1971).

§13.22   [1] In practice this enables management to perpetuate itself and control the corporation. *See* William Fletcher, Cyclopedia of Corporations §2052.3 (rev. ed. 1996).

[2] Levin v. Metro-Goldwyn Mayer, Inc., 264 F. Supp. 797 (S.D.N.Y. 1967); Rosenfield v. Fairchild Eng. & Airplane Corp., 128 N.E.2d 291 (N.Y. 1955).

[3] Steinberg v. Adams, 90 F. Supp. 694 (S.D.N.Y. 1950), noted in 36 Cornell L.Q. 558 (1951); 49 Mich. L. Rev. 605 (1951); 61 Yale L. J. 229 (1952); Rosenfeld v. Fairchild Eng. & Airplane Corp., 128 N.E.2d 291 (N.Y. 1955).

reasonable bona fide expenditures and, with regard to insurgents, only on approval of the shareholders.[4] It is frequently said that expenses solely in the interest of the incumbents' perpetuation in office are not properly paid for by the corporation. In most contests for corporate control, however, it is impossible to sever questions of policy from personality because questions of policy usually are inexorably intertwined with personalities. Thus the courts have had difficulty drawing a line between the two.

At first blush it may seem unjustified to tilt the playing field so heavily in favor of the incumbents by permitting them to use corporate funds and other resources in the proxy contest while requiring the insurgents to finance their own efforts. But consider the results if the rules were otherwise.[5] If incumbents had to defend their present control of the board with their own funds, such a defense likely would not be forthcoming. Individuals certainly would be less likely to serve as directors if they thought doing so would require substantial expenditures of their own funds to seek or retain the position. Also, the idea of being easily opposed in an election is not one warmly greeted by those likely to quest a directorship in a public corporation. Certainly any change in the existing rules on reimbursement of proxy context expenses would lead to more proxy contests, as insurgents would not have to worry about the incumbents "playing with other peoples money" as occurs presently. At the same time, there is a serious risk that insurgents who are willing to spend their own funds to gain control of the corporation can be expected to seek some financial benefits from the corporation if they successfully gain control of the board of directors. That is, changes in the existing rules regarding proxy contest expenses may lead to undesirable self-dealing transactions by incumbents and insurgents to recoup the cost of securing their positions. The present rules are far more transparent than what would otherwise occur. Finally, the present rules avoid problematic inquiries regarding when unsuccessful incumbents should be reimbursed.

E.   FEDERAL REGULATION OF PROXIES

§13.23   Section 14 of the Securities Exchange Act of 1934—An Overview

Nondisclosure of needed information and other abuses foisted on the corporate election system led to federal regulation of proxy solicitation.[1] Section 14(a) of the

---

[4] Grodestsky v. McCrory Corp., 267 N.Y.S.2d 356 (Sup. Ct. 1966), *aff'd*, 276 N.Y.S.2d 841 (App. Div. 1966).

[5] *See* Lucian A. Bebchuck & Marcel M. Kahan, A Framework for Analyzing Legal Policy Towards Proxy Contests, 78 Cal. L. Rev. 1071 (1990).

§13.23   [1] Thomas Lee Hazen, Treatise on the Law of Securities Regulation ch. 14 (4th ed. 2002).

Securities Exchange Act of 1934[2] declares it unlawful to solicit any proxy or consent or authorization from the holder of any security subject to the act's registration and reporting provisions[3] in violation of such rules as may be prescribed by the Securities and Exchange Commission. Pursuant to this authority, the SEC has promulgated extensive requirements regarding the disclosures that must be made in connection with the solicitation of proxies.[4]

With rare exceptions the only way in which shareholders in a large corporation with shares widely diffused can participate in the election of directors and in voting on fundamental changes in the corporate structure is by the use of proxies. Thus to participate effectively, shareholders must be informed by the management, or by others soliciting proxies, about the director candidates and measures for which their authorization is solicited. The general purpose of the federal proxy rules is to require that security holders be provided with sufficient information bearing upon and explanation of the matters on which the persons to whom they give proxies are authorized to cast their votes, so that they may know what they are authorizing. Under the proxy rules, shareholders are also afforded an opportunity to limit the authorization and indicate disapproval as well as approval of management proposals—that is, to specify whether their proxies shall be voted for or against each proposal submitted. To avoid the problem of managers coupling unpopular proposals with so-called "sweeteners," the proxy rules now prohibit a group of related proposals to be bundled as a single resolution.[5] This change avoids the problem of stockholders having their natural choice distorted by an artful coupling of value-decreasing proposals with a change that shareholders desire.[6]

The fundamental requirement of the proxy rules is disclosure of accurate and adequate information by those who solicit a proxy, consent, or authorization. The rules and Schedule 14A must be consulted to determine what information is required for each different item requiring shareholder action, such as election of directors, a plan of remuneration of directors and officers, an amendment of the charter or bylaws, a proposal for merger, consolidation, or sale of assets, or modifications of the corporation's securities.[7] An area of concern is corporate governance in publicly held corporations; the Securities Exchange Commission has responded with detailed disclosure requirements concerning the activities of

---

[2] 15 U.S.C. §78n(a) (2000).

[3] This includes any security traded on a national exchange as well as any class of equity security with more than 500 shareholders where the issuer has more than $10 million in assets. Rule 12g-1, 17 C.F.R. §240.12g-1 (2002). *See also* §12(g), 15 U.S.C. §78*l*(g) (2000).

[4] *See, e.g.*, Schedule 14A, 17 C.F.R. §240.14a-101 (2002).

[5] 17 C.F.R. §240.14a-4 (2002). The standing of shareholders to privately enforce Rule 14a-4's proscription of the impermissible grouping of voting items was recognized in Koppel v. 4987 Corp., 167 F.3d 125 (2d Cir. 1999).

[6] *See* Lucian Bebchuk, Limiting Contractual Freedom in Corporate Law: The Desirable Constraint on Charter Amendments, 102 Harv. L. Rev. 1820, 1836-1830 (1989).

[7] The Commission specifies in great detail the types of information, both financial and otherwise, that must be disclosed. General Rules & Regulations, Securities Exchange Act of 1934, 17 C.F.R. §§240.14a-1 *et seq.* (2002).

E. Federal Regulation of Proxies

directors, including the composition and functioning of the various committees of the board as well as the directors' individual attendance records.[8]

If fraud or noncompliance with the rules occurs, that constitutes grounds for an injunction against using the proxies and holding the meeting until the proxies have been resolicited.[9] Nothing in Section 14 makes action taken at any meeting invalid, even though the action is taken pursuant to proxies obtained in violation of the rules. The only express remedy the Securities and Exchange Commission has for violations of the proxy rules is to seek injunctive relief before the meeting or to give the matter to the Justice Department for criminal proceedings after the meeting.[10] However, as is the case with SEC Rule 10b-5,[11] the most powerful impact of section 14(a) and, in particular, Rule 14a-9, is the antifraud provision, since it provides an implied cause of action available to the corporation or an aggrieved shareholder.[12]

The formal proxy solicitation material to be used in a solicitation must be filed with the Commission for inspection at least ten days before the beginning of the solicitation. All other proxy material, such as letters, advertisements, and supplementary material, need not be filed in advance. The material filed is examined by the Commission. On request, informal suggestions may be made by the Commission in advance of the filing date. In many instances, corporations have been required to issue corrected proxies and statements, and meetings have had to be postponed. Full disclosure requirements, of course, have a discouraging effect on the presentation of unfair proposals to the shareholders.

Under the federal proxy rules, if a security holder wishes to solicit proxies himself, he may require that the management mail to those who are solicited by the management a form of proxy and other material furnished by the applicant/security holder, provided the applicant makes provision for expenses in connection with the mailing. Thus management is required to cooperate in mailing solicitation literature of dissident groups, and shareholders are given a medium of communication with fellow investors. Provision is also made in the proxy rules for a shareholder who desires to present proposals at the annual shareholders' meeting to have her proposal submitted and explained in a management proxy solicitation if she gives timely notice to management of her intention to present the proposal at the meeting.[13]

---

[8] A director's track record, including remuneration and potential conflicts of interest, is relevant to the shareholder's election decision. Berkman v. Rust Craft Greeting Cards, Inc., 454 F. Supp. 787, 789 (S.D.N.Y. 1978). Similarly, all material facts surrounding a director's transactions with the corporation must be disclosed. Maldonado v. Flynn, 597 F.2d 789 (2d Cir. 1979).

[9] 15 U.S.C. §78n, 78u (2000). *See* Thomas L. Hazen, Administrative Enforcement: An Evaluation of the Securities and Exchange Commission's Use of Injunctions and Other Enforcement Methods, 31 Hast. L.J. 427 (1979).

[10] *See* Thomas L. Hazen, Administrative Enforcement: An Evaluation of the Securities Exchange Commission's Use of Injunctions and Other Enforcement Methods, 31 Hast. L.J. 427 (1979).

[11] 17 C.F.R. §240.10b-5 (2002). *See* §12.08.

[12] J. I. Case Co. v. Borak, 377 U.S. 426 (1964). *See infra* §13.26.

[13] 17 C.F.R. §240.14a-8 (2002). Management's duty on such a request gives rise to difficult problems. *See infra* §13.25.

§13.24   Definition of "Solicitation" and "Proxy"

The vast majority of the Securities Exchange Act's disclosure provisions are directed toward requiring full information in the marketplace so that informed and intelligent investment decisions can be made. In contrast, in its concern for shareholder suffrage, section 14(a)'s proxy regulation approaches very closely the fine line separating proxy regulation from the chartering function of the state's general corporation laws.[1] The basic rationale for federal involvement in the internal affairs of large corporations through the Exchange Act's reporting and disclosure requirements is that informing the marketplace of significant corporate developments is necessary to investor confidence and protection. The SEC, although lacking authority to weigh in directly on corporate governance issues,[2] nevertheless does so discretely through its disclosure requirements.

To begin with, the Commission has laid down a broad definition of "proxy solicitation."[3] "Solicitation" includes all communications directed to shareholders that are reasonably calculated to affect a voting decision. The regulation has been extended to cover many kinds of communications that are not garden variety vote solicitations. For example, in the course of a merger between two railroads, management's open letter to the Interstate Commerce Commission extolling the virtues of the proposed transaction and urging its administrative approval was held to be subject to the SEC's filing and disclosure requirements, because the shareholder vote had not yet been taken and the letter contained statements that were likely to influence a voting decision.[4]

The courts continue to adhere to the early standard that a communication that itself does not request the giving of any authorization is nevertheless a proxy solicitation when it is "part of a 'continuous plan' intended to end in solicitation and to prepare the way for success."[5] Thus a letter asking several other stockholders to join the request to access the company's list of stockholders was deemed a proxy solicitation because the letter's author intended to use the list in his campaign to solicit proxies. Moreover, a letter to the stockholders that discussed recent activities at the corporation can be deemed a proxy solicitation because the definition includes communications that are designed to discourage stockholders from giving a proxy to someone else.[6]

Sometimes the expansive definition of "proxy solicitation" collides with the First Amendment. In *Long Island Lighting Company v. Barbash,*[7] Long Island Lighting Co. (LILCO) was embroiled in a proxy contest over its mishandling of the

---

§13.24   [1] *See* Thomas L. Hazen, Corporate Chartering and the Securities Markets: Shareholder Suffrage, Corporate Responsibility and Managerial Accountability, 1978 Wis. L. Rev. 391.

[2] Business Roundtable v. SEC, 905 F.2d 406, 410-12 (D.C. Cir. 1990).

[3] General Rules & Regulations, Securities Exchange Act of 1934, 17 C.F.R. §240.14a-1 (2002).

[4] *See* Union Pac. R.R. v. Chicago & N.W. Ry., 226 F. Supp. 400 (N.D. Ill. 1964).

[5] Studebaker Corp. v. Gitlin, 360 F.2d 692, 696 (2d Cir. 1966), citing SEC v. Okin, 132 F.2d 784 (2d Cir. 1943).

[6] *See* Sargent v. Genesco, Inc., 492 F.2d 750 (5th Cir. 1974). *See also* Brown v. Chicago, Rock Island & Peoria R.R., 328 F.2d 122 (7th Cir. 1964).

[7] 779 F.2d 793 (2d Cir. 1985).

E. Federal Regulation of Proxies

design and construction of the Shoreham Nuclear Power Plant. LILCO sued a citizens' group over advertisements it had placed calling for LILCO to be replaced by a Long Island power authority. Even though the ads made no reference to the on-going proxy contest, LILCO argued that the ads were subject to proxy rules. The district court dismissed the suit, reasoning that otherwise the proxy rules would violate the citizens' group's First Amendment rights.[8] In a divided opinion, the Second Circuit reversed, holding that the proxy rules could apply to communications appearing in the general media and reasoning that it was premature for the court to reach the First Amendment issue. In a strong dissent, Judge Winter argued that the proxy rules should be interpreted to not apply to newspaper advertisements so as to avoid a serious First Amendment issue.[9]

In 1992, the SEC amended the proxy rules to reduce in important ways the earlier restrictions on stockholders to communicate among themselves.[10] New Rule 14a-2(b)(1) broadly (but somewhat ambiguously) exempts from the filing and format requirements communications with stockholders by a person who himself is not seeking proxies and who does not have a "substantial interest" in the subject matter. This exemption is not available to certain classes of individuals, such as officers, directors, director nominees, or one who has in a Williams Act filing disclosed a possible intent to control the issuer. Moreover, a communication by a holder of more than $5 million of the company's stock must file the communication within three days of its use. A further relaxation appears in new Rule 14a-1(l)(2)(iv), which permits holders to announce how they will vote on any matter. A further innovation allows proxy contestants to solicit proxies for less than a full slate of dissident nominees—that is, the dissident can seek proxies for some of its nominees as well as some of the incumbent management's nominees. The function of allowing such "short slates" is to facilitate minority representation on the board.[11]

Overall, the 1992 proxy rule amendments go a long way toward answering the criticism that the former proxy rules prevented institutions and other sophisticated investors from effectively coordinating their actions to improve the performance and governance of their portfolio companies.[12] Under the new rules, investors can more easily coordinate their actions to maximize their influence at the stockholders' meeting because they are no longer subject to the costly and burdensome prefiling and format requirements. However, their communications continue to be subject to Rule 14a-9's prohibition against misleading communications in connection with a proxy solicitation. However, in late 1999 the SEC did relax the pre-filing obligations of management with respect to announcements

---

[8] Long Island Lighting Co. v. Barbash, 625 F. Supp. 221, 222 (S.D.N.Y. 1985).

[9] In Securities & Exch. Comm'n v. Wall St. Pub. Inst., 851 F.2d 365 (D.C. Cir. 1988), *cert. denied,* 489 U.S. 1066 (1989), a case under other provisions of the securities laws, the court held that the long-established powers to regulate the securities industry support the reasonableness of the interference with the defendant's speech.

[10] *See* Exchange Act Rel. No. 31326 (Oct. 16, 1992).

[11] *See* Capital Real Estate Investors Tax Exempt Fund Ltd. Partnership v. Schwartzberg, 917 F. Supp. 1050, 1061 (S.D.N.Y. 1996).

[12] *See* Bernard Black, Shareholder Passivity Reexamined, 89 Mich. L. Rev. 520 (1990).

related to acquisitions, even though the announcement contained deal related information. Under new Rule 14a-12 the company (or those acting on its behalf) can release announcements related to an acquisition without first filing the information or deliver a proxy statement, provided there is not then a request for a proxy.[13]

The filing and disclosure requirements are not applicable solely to incumbent management; under Rule 14a-11, insurgent shareholders are subject to the same rigors.[14] Shareholders who run afoul of the proxy rules may be subjected to the same consequences as management, even including disenfranchisement with regard to the vote in question.[15]

The Securities Exchange Act also provides for SEC regulation of broker-dealer involvement in the proxy process, including the problem of voting or giving proxies for securities held for investors by stock brokerage firms "in street names."[16] Further, the Act requires management disclosure prior to an annual meeting even if management does not solicit proxies.[17] Additionally, the SEC rules governing the solicitation of proxies from security holders of registered public utility holding companies and their subsidiaries[18] are even more far reaching than the disclosure requirements applicable under section 14 of the Exchange Act to ordinary business corporations.

§13.25   *Shareholder Proposals Under the Proxy Rules*

Shareholders have made frequent use of Rule 14a-8, which requires management to submit appropriate shareholder proposals to the shareholders for a vote. Among the proposals based on economic or business considerations that shareholders have asked management to submit for consideration at shareholder meetings are the following: (1) to inaugurate a system of cumulative voting for directors; (2) to place a ceiling on the amount of compensation the corporation can pay to any one executive or to the officers as a group; (3) to move the location of shareholders' meetings to a place more convenient for shareholders or to provide for the rotation of meeting places; (4) to send to the shareholders a post-meeting report on each annual meeting; and (5) to provide for the shareholders to select the company's independent public auditors.[1]

---

[13] 17 C.F.R. §240.14a-12 (2002).

[14] *See* Levin v. Metro-Goldwyn-Mayer, Inc., 264 F. Supp. 797 (S.D.N.Y. 1967). Shareholder proposals are discussed *infra* §13.25.

[15] *See* Committee for New Management of Butler Aviation v. Widmark, 335 F. Supp. 146 (E.D.N.Y. 1971).

[16] Section 14(b) of the Exchange Act, 15 U.S.C. §78n(b) (2000). *See, e.g.*, S.E.C., Street Name Study (1976).

[17] 15 U.S.C. §78n(c) (2000).

[18] Section 12(e) of the Public Utility Holding Company Act of 1935, 15 U.S.C. §79(k) *et seq.*

§13.25   [1] Interestingly, proposals that attempt to curtail or limit capital expenditures can be omitted on the basis that they concern ordinary business operations. *See, e.g.*, Grimes v. Centerior Energy Corp., 909 F.2d 529 (D.C. Cir. 1990). However, a proposal requiring shareholder approval of all expenditures in excess of $500,000 that are not part of the ordinary business could not be omitted. Storage Technology Corp., SEC No-Action Letter, Fed. Sec. L. Rep. (CCH) ¶77,537 (March 18, 1999).

E. Federal Regulation of Proxies

"Public interest" and "public responsibility" groups have also resorted to Rule 14a-8 to bring social and political issues before the shareholders at annual meetings and thus give those issues publicity.[2] Among commonly recurring proposals of the recent past have been the following: to terminate a corporation's business activities in South Africa (when apartheid was practiced); to prohibit a corporation from participating in the Arab boycott of Israel; to prohibit a corporation from making political contributions here or abroad; to terminate a corporation's manufacture or sale of armaments or other war materials; and to terminate a corporation's sponsorship of television programs featuring violence or sex. Each proxy solicitation season has its "in" topics.

Although shareholders submitting proposals opposed by management seldom get a substantial vote at the annual meeting, managements have often modified corporate policies or practices to obtain the withdrawal of a shareholder proposal or simply to remove irritants to good shareholder relations. For example, corporations have now virtually abandoned the practice of holding shareholders' meetings at places inconvenient for large numbers of shareholders, and a growing number of corporations provide shareholders with detailed post-meeting reports on annual meetings. In some instances, however, management will rule a proposal not appropriate for shareholder action or otherwise improper under the proxy rules and thus excludible from the proxy materials. Although the ultimate question of a proposal's propriety for shareholder action is often a matter of state law, it is a violation of Rule 14a-8 not to include a proper proposal in the proxy materials. Under the most recent version of the rule, a shareholder must be the beneficial owner for at least one year of at least 1 percent or of $2,000 in market value of the securities entitled to vote. The shareholder may submit no more than one proposal with a supporting statement; there is a maximum 500-word limit.[3]

In a Commission enforcement action under the shareholder proposal rules,[4] the Court of Appeals, Third Circuit, required management to include in its proxy materials a shareholder proposal (1) to amend the corporate bylaws to provide for independent public auditors, (2) to require notice of all proposed bylaw amendments, and (3) to require that a report of the annual shareholders' meeting be sent to shareholders. In contrast, a federal district court has upheld management's decision to exclude a shareholder's resolution that the company intensify its offshore drilling efforts.[5] The court pointed to the standard statutory mandate that the directors manage the business and affairs of a corporation and then upheld the Commission's finding that the proposal "related to . . . the ordinary business" and "was made 'primarily for the purpose of promoting a general economic or political cause.'"[6] It

---

[2] Labor unions have become more active in shareholder issues. *See, e.g.,* Stewart J. Schwab & Randall S. Thomas, Realigning Corporate Governance: Shareholder Activism by Labor Unions, 96 Mich. L. Rev. 1018 (1998); Randall S. Thomas & Kenneth J. Martin, Should Labor Be Allowed to Make Shareholder Proposals?, 73 Wash. L. Rev. 41 (1998).

[3] General Rules & Regulations, Securities Exchange Act of 1934, 17 C.F.R. §240.14a-8(b)(1) (2002).

[4] SEC v. Transamerica Corp., 163 F.2d 511 (3d Cir. 1947), *cert. denied,* 332 U.S. 847 (1948). *See, e.g.,* Bayless Manning, Book Review, 67 Yale L.J. 1477, 1490 (1958).

[5] Broks v. Standard Oil Co., 308 F. Supp. 810 (S.D.N.Y. 1969).

[6] *Id.* at 814.

would appear that any proposal that deals with the *timing* of an act the corporation is already committed to is likely to be deemed as related to "ordinary business."[7]

A leading case on a social and political shareholder proposal is *Medical Committee for Human Rights v. Securities and Exchange Commission.*[8] The proposal was to amend the corporation's charter to forbid it to make napalm without several limitations on its use. The Commission had allowed management to exclude the proposal. The Court of Appeals, D.C. Circuit, remanded the case to the Commission to reconsider the shareholder's claim within the proper limits of the Commission's discretionary powers, as delineated by the court. The company thereafter voluntarily included the proposal in its proxy statement, and the proposal received less than 3 percent of the votes.[9]

From the inception of the shareholder proposal rule, a frequently invoked basis for management to exclude a shareholder proposal is on the grounds, now embodied in subsection (i)(7) of Rule 14a-8, which authorizes exclusion of proposals "relating to the company's ordinary business operations."[10] Where ordinary business operations cease and fundamental corporate policy issues that affect the character of the enterprise begin is difficult to discern. For example, in one decision, the Court of Appeals for the District of Columbia reasoned that capital expenditures may reach such a level that they no longer merely involve "ordinary business."[11]

Since 1976 the SEC's position has been that a proposal could be excluded whenever it involves business matters "that are mundane in nature and do not involve any substantial policy or other considerations."[12] Under this standard, the SEC consistently held that proposals concerning equal employment opportunities could not be excluded on the basis that they involve ordinary business because they involve important policy questions and were not, under its 1976 interpretative guidelines, merely mundane.[13] In 1992, in the *Cracker Barrel* no-action letter,[14] the SEC retreated from the special treatment accorded proposals involving equal employment opportunities, so that the mere fact that a proposal is tied to a social issue no longer protected it from being omitted if the proposal otherwise focuses on the conduct of ordinary business.[15] Not surprisingly, its retreat stirred a great deal of controversy. Thus, in 1997, the SEC announced it was considering revert-

---

[7] *See* Roosevelt v. E. I. du Pont de Nemours & Co., 958 F.2d 416 (D.C. Cir. 1992).

[8] 432 F.2d 659 (D.C. Cir. 1970), *vacated as moot*, 404 U.S. 403 (1972).

[9] Under the current shareholder proposal rule, a proposal is excludable if it has been submitted within the prior five years and received less than 3 percent of the vote. Rule 14a-8(i)(12), 17 C.F.R. §240.14a-8(i)(12) (2002).

[10] The current version is found in rule 14a-8(i)(7), 17 C.F.R. §240-14a-8(i)(7) (2002).

[11] Grimes v. Centerior Energy Corp., 909 F.2d 529 (D.C. Cir. 1990).

[12] Adoption of Amendments Relating to Proposals by Security Holders, Exchange Act Rel. No. 12,999, 41 Fed. Reg. 52,994, 52,998 (Dec. 3, 1976).

[13] For a review of the SEC's course after 1976, *see* Amalgamated Clothing & Textile Workers v. Wal-Mart Stores, Inc., 821 F. Supp. 877 (S.D.N.Y. 1993).

[14] Cracker Barrel Old Country Stores, Inc. No-Action Letter, 1992 SEC No-Act. LEXIS 984 at *43 (Oct. 13, 1992).

[15] Cracker Barrel Old Country Stores, Inc. No-Action Letter, 1992 SEC No-Act. LEXIS 984 at *43 (Oct. 13, 1992). The SEC's power to make this interpretative change was upheld in New York City Employees' Retirement Sys. v. SEC, 45 F.3d 7 (2d Cir. 1995).

ing to its prior practice of reviewing each employment-related proposal to determine if it relates to the ordinary business of the company or to more far-reaching social issues, in which case it would not be excludable from management's proxy statement.[16] In 1998, the Commission officially announced this change in position and the reversal of the position that had been taken in the controversial *Cracker Barrel* no-action letter.[17]

§13.26 *Implied Private Action Under Rule 14a-9*

The first time that the Supreme Court gave its imprimatur to an implied cause of action under the securities acts was with regard to Rule 14a-9's antifraud limitations on the use of the proxy machinery.[1] *J. I. Case Company v. Borak*[2] involved a shareholder's claim of misleading statements in management's solicitation of shareholder support for a proposed merger.[3] The Court relied on the legislative history supporting section 14(a) as requiring basic standards of honesty and the necessity of management's affording at least certain minimum intra-corporate rights to shareholders.[4] While there is a serious question concerning the Supreme Court's continued willingness to imply additional private remedies, under the federal securities laws the Rule 14a-9 implied private cause of action, like the implied cause of action under Rule 10b-5, can no longer be questioned.[5]

There have been both pre-[6] and post-[7] *Hochfelder*[8] decisions that have upheld a negligence standard in a Rule 14a-9 action, notwithstanding the more stringent scienter requirements of Rule 10b-5.[9] In those circuits that require more than

[16] Amendments to Rules on Shareholder Proposals, Sec. Exch. Act Rel. No. 34-39093, 62 Fed. Reg. 50682-01 (SEC Sept. 26, 1997).

[17] Amendments to Rules on Shareholder Proposals, Sec. Exch. Act Rel. No. 34-40018, 1998 WL 254809 (SEC May 21, 1998).

§13.26 [1] The implied remedy under rule 10b-5 is discussed *supra* §§12.08-12.11.

[2] 377 U.S. 426 (1964).

[3] Mergers and other methods of corporate fusion have provided fertile grounds for proxy-related claims; *e.g.*, TSC Indus. v. Northway, Inc., 426 U.S. 438 (1976); Mills v. Electric Auto-Lite Co., 396 U.S. 375 (1970). *See* Chapter 27.

[4] "The section stemmed from the congressional belief that '[f]air corporate suffrage is an important right that should attach to every security bought on a public exchange.'" H.R. Rep. No. 1383, 73rd Cong., 2d Sess. 13, quoted with approval in 377 U.S. at 431.

[5] *See* Thomas Lee Hazen, Treatise on the Law of Securities Regulation §12.1 (4th ed. 2002).

[6] Gerstle v. Gamble-Skogmo, Inc., 478 F.2d 1281 (2d Cir. 1973).

[7] Herskowitz v. Nutri/Sys., Inc., 857 F.2d 179 (3d Cir. 1988), *cert. denied*, 489 U.S. 1054; Shidler v. All Am. Life & Fin. Corp., 775 F.2d 917, 927 (8th Cir. 1988); Gould v. American-Haw. Steamship Co., 535 F.2d 761 (3d Cir. 1976). *Contra*, Adams v. Standard Knitting Mills, 623 F.2d 422 (6th Cir. 1980) (scienter standard to be applied to issuer's accountants). *See generally* Thomas Lee Hazen, Treatise on the Law of Securities Regulation §§10.3, 12.8 (4th ed. 2002).

[8] 425 U.S. 185 (1976).

[9] The no-scienter approach to actions under section 14(a) seems mandated by the Supreme Court's ruling that scienter is not an element of a claim under section 17(a)(2) or (a)(3) of the 1933 Act, Aaron v. SEC, 446 U.S. 680 (1980). *See* Thomas L. Hazen, The Supreme Court and the Securities Laws: Has the Pendulum Slowed?, 30 Emory L. Rev. 3, 24-27 (1981).

mere negligence or the complaint alleges knowledge or recklessness in committing the misrepresentation in the proxy materials, the tightened pleading requirement introduced by the Private Securities Litigation Reform Act of 1995, discussed earlier,[10] applies.[11]

In addition to applying only to solicitation of proxies by Exchange Act reporting issuers,[12] section 14(a) necessarily applies only to issues that are brought before the shareholders for a shareholder vote. State corporation statutes all contain a mandate to the effect that the business of the corporation is managed by the board of directors or under the supervision of the board,[13] a mandate that excludes a large number of mismanagement cases from the Rule 14a-9 remedy.

Overlap with Rule 10b-5. Most of the important proxy cases have arisen within the context of organic corporate changes, such as mergers or consolidations, that require a shareholder vote.[14] Since such corporate reorganizations generally provide for an exchange or other disposition of the stockholders' shares, Rule 10b-5's proscriptions also apply. It is quite common, therefore, for aggrieved shareholders to seek relief under both rules.[15] Because the Rule 14a-9 remedy has different standing and, perhaps, fault requirements, this implied remedy may give relief where a Rule 10b-5 claim will fail. Also, because mergers and organic corporate changes frequently result in statutory appraisal rights for dissenting shareholders,[16] and because such changes are often challenged as being in breach of state fiduciary principles, actions under these rules bring the relationship between federal and state law issues into sharp focus.

Materiality. The dominant concern in any action under Rule 14a-9 is whether the proxy solicitation contained a *material* omission or misstatement of fact. A fact's materiality is a mixed question of law and fact that arises in pretrial motions as well as at trial. *TSC Industries, Inc. v. Northway, Inc.*[17] is the leading case on the standard to be applied in deciding whether an omission or misstatement is material:

> An omitted fact is material if there is a substantial likelihood that a reasonable shareholder would consider it important in deciding how to vote. This standard is fully consistent with *Mills*' general description of materiality as a requirement that "the defect have a significant propensity to affect the voting

---

[10] *See* §12.09.

[11] *See* Fanni v. Northrop Grumman Corp., 23 Fed. Appx. 782 (9th Cir. 2001). The tightened pleading requirement should not apply to a complaint that does not "sound in fraud." *See, e.g.,* In re Cendant Corp. Litigation, 60 F. Supp. 2d 354 (D.N.J. 1999). *Contra* In re McKesson HBOC, Inc. Sec. Litig., 126 F. Supp. 2d 1248 (N.D. Cal. 2000).

[12] *See* 15 U.S.C. §78*l* (2000).

[13] Model Business Corp. Act §8.01(b) (1984); *see supra* §§9.01-9.02.

[14] *See, e.g.,* TSC Indus. v. Northway, Inc., 426 U.S. 438 (1976).

[15] *See, e.g.,* Schlick v. Penn-Dixie Cement Co., 507 F.2d 374 (2d Cir. 1974), *cert. denied,* 421 U.S. 976 (1975); *supra* §12.08.

[16] Model Business Corp. Act §§13.02, 1320-13.26 (1984). *See* §§22.19-22.22.

[17] 426 U.S. 438 (1976).

process." It does not require proof of a substantial likelihood that disclosure of the omitted fact would have caused the reasonable investor to change his vote. What the standard does contemplate is a showing of a substantial likelihood that, under all the circumstances, the omitted fact would have assumed actual significance in the deliberations of the reasonable shareholder. Put another way, there must be a substantial likelihood that the disclosure of the omitted fact would have been viewed by the reasonable investor as having significantly altered the "total mix" of information made available.[18]

Subsequent Supreme Court decisions refined without limiting this standard of materiality. Thus, in *Basic, Inc. v. Levinson*,[19] the court held that the standard for determining materiality for soft information, such as financial forecasts, appraisals, and future financial expenditures, that "materiality will depend at any given time upon a balancing of both the indicated probability that the event will occur and the anticipated magnitude of the event in light of the totality of the company activity."[20] Under this sliding scale standard, an event with a low probability of occurrence can nevertheless still be material if its occurrence will have a significant impact on the company's net worth or profits. Thus, in *Basic, Inc.*, false denials that the company was engaged in merger negotiations were material because on the merger the value of the company's shares would increase dramatically.

Contrary to a literal reading of both Rule 14a-9 and *TSC Industries*, the Supreme Court held in *Virginia Bankshares, Inc. v. Sandberg*[21] that opinion statements can be the bases of a materiality claim under Rule 14a-9. In *Virginia Bankshares*, management's proxy statement described the merger's terms as providing the stockholders with a "high" value and elsewhere described the price as "fair." The court held that opinion statements could be materially misleading and just as harmful as misrepresentations of fact. However, *Virginia Bankshares* held that more must be alleged than that the defendant misrepresented their motives, true intentions, or beliefs; otherwise vexatious litigation would arise. The Supreme Court thus conditioned that any suit for materially misleading opinion statements must bear on the substance of the transaction for which approval was sought. This additional requirement was satisfied in *Virginia Bankshares* because the plaintiff alleged the merger's terms were unfair.[22]

---

[18] *Id.* at 449. The reference is to Mills v. Electric Auto-Lite Co., 396 U.S. 375 (1970), a case not requiring the court to resolve whether an omission was material where the court in dicta stated a fact is material if it "*might* have been considered important" and contradicted itself by stating materiality required "a significant propensity to affect investors." The lower court in TSC Indus., 512 F.2d 324 (7th Cir. 1975), invoked the "might" standard and granted the plaintiff's summary judgment. The Supreme Court, of course, held summary judgment was not appropriate under the above quoted test. On the general topic of the materiality standard for the securities laws, *see* §12.08.

[19] 485 U.S. 224 (1988).

[20] *Id.* at 238, *quoting with approval* SEC v. Texas Gulf Sulphur Co., 401 F.2d 833, 849 (2d Cir. 1968) (en banc), *cert. denied*, 394 U.S. 976 (1969).

[21] 501 U.S. 1083 (1991).

[22] Indeed, the basis for alleging that the directors misrepresented their opinion statements was that the directors were in possession of at least one report that placed the firm's value at $18 per share higher than the price being paid in the merger and that the offering price would provide no premium for the shares if the assets were determined at their appraised value.

It should be apparent that the standard of materiality makes it especially difficult for many matters to be resolved on the basis of pretrial motions. In its breadth the standard is not necessarily pernicious or unwieldy; it simply defies mathematical predictability. Adding to the uncertainty is the statement in *TSC Industries* that the materiality of an item is to be determined by the "total mix" of information made available. This invites consideration of whether an omission, or even a misstatement, is corrected because the correct information is otherwise in the public domain. In particular, the "total mix" criterion invites consideration of the impact of the efficient market hypothesis, which holds that information that is publicly available will be quickly impounded into the pricing of a security. Thus companies whose stock or investors operate in relatively information-rich environments and that are followed by sophisticated traders may well argue that any omission in their proxy statement or otherwise is not a material omission because information available from alternative sources is available and known to investors.

At the same time, there is reason to believe that the context in which the disclosure issue arises is very important in setting forth the parameters of what is the total mix of information. Consider *United Paperworkers International Union v. International Paper Company,*[23] where the proponent of a shareholder proposal calling for the company to adhere to certain strict environmental disclosures complained that management's response urging shareholders to vote against the proposal was materially misleading because it failed to disclose that the company had been convicted of numerous environmental violations and generally had a bad environmental record. The company argued that these matters were all disclosed in its annual report and Form 10-K filed with the SEC and as such were all part of the total mix of information before the shareholders. The Second Circuit held these matters should have been disclosed in the proxy statement and that their omission was a material one not corrected by the information being in other reports that were available to the stockholders.

International Paper appears to take the sensible position that when shareholder attention is riveted on a specific document, such as a proxy statement, it is unreasonable to expect stockholders to search through other sources to evaluate the credibility of arguments contained in that document. One can expect, however, that investors considering whether to purchase or sell a company's securities can be more resourceful in considering the merits of that decision, or at least that its publicly available information will be accessed by some market intermediaries whose trading will drive the security's price to a level appropriate in light of such information. Whereas no such arbitrage behavior is possible in the context of proxy voting.

Another troubling question is the social, criminal, and ethical background of directors. On this question, the courts generally have been unwilling to apply the broad tenets of *TSC Industries* to require directors to disclose their prior ethical or legal lapses. For example, several courts have held that the proxy statement in

---

[23] 999 F.2d 51 (2d Cir. 1993). *See also* Chambers v. Briggs & Stratton Corp., 863 F. Supp. 900, 904 (E.D. Wis. 1994) (duty of management in their own solicitation materials to identify and briefly describe an opposing nominee to the board of directors).

which the directors are seeking reelection does not have to disclose that the directors standing for reelection acquiesced in management's making foreign bribes.[24] Directors also need not disclose that they had willfully acted to thwart the labor laws.[25] One must approach such restrictive opinions with caution, viewing them largely as decisions in which expediency is preferred over the indeterminacy of opening disclosure inquiries to a wide range of social issues.[26] Certainly one can well imagine a wide range of business issues for which advance knowledge of the individual director's social, ethical, or philosophical proclivities would be highly relevant to evaluating that director's ability to serve the stockholders' interests. Though it may keep the size of proxy statements from growing any larger than their present bulk, and this in turn may save a few forests, there is a weak artificiality in holding that proxy statements need not disclose the directors' countenancing the illegal conduct of others or that the directors do not themselves commit the corporation to live within the bounds of the law.

Causation. Questions of causation are especially difficult in the context of misleading proxy solicitations. Therefore, in one case, the failure to disclose details of earlier discussions with a possible merger partner, though concluded by the court to be material, were nonetheless not believed to rise to the level of materiality as to have had a causal impact on the vote of the stockholders.[27] For most issues, the proxy solicitation involves a collective, rather than an individual, decision. Stockholders decide as a group whether to amend the articles, to elect a director, or to merge with another company. Structural decisions, such as the merger or sale of a company, frequently allow dissenters a right to have their shares appraised, so in this regard the decision has both a collective and an individual character. In either case, the causation question is whether the particular omission or misstatement must be shown to have misled the individual stockholder or group of stockholders.

At the same time, it must be recognized that because the decisions are collective decisions and all stockholders are generally bound by the will of a majority, each stockholder's interest is impacted by a misrepresentation that causes her fellow stockholders to approve or forgo a transaction to the extent that transaction impacts the company. Causation is further complicated by the *TSC Industries* standard of materiality, quoted above, which holds that a fact is material without proof "of a substantial likelihood that disclosure of the omitted fact would have caused the reasonable investor to change his vote."[28] Thus a fact is material even though it does not have a dispositive impact on how the individual stockholder votes.

The Supreme Court has treated causation questions in Rule 14a-9 actions somewhat ambiguously. In *Mills v. Electric Auto-Lite Company,*[29] the court stated "a

---

[24] *See, e.g.,* Gaines v. Haughton, 645 F.2d 761 (9th Cir. 1981), *cert. denied,* 454 U.S. 1145 (1982); Weisberg v. Coastal States Gas Corp., 609 F.2d 650 (2d Cir. 1979), *cert. denied,* 445 U.S. 951 (1980).

[25] *See* Amalgamated Clothing & Textile Workers v. J. P. Stevens & Co., 475 F. Supp. 328 (S.D.N.Y. 1979), *vacated as moot per curiam,* 638 F.2d 7 (2d Cir. 1980).

[26] *See* Gaines v. Haughton, 645 F.2d 761, 778 (9th Cir. 1981), *cert. denied,* 454 U.S. 1145 (1982).

[27] *See* Minzer v. Keegan, 218 F.3d 144 (2d Cir. 2000).

[28] TSC Indus. v. Northway, Inc., 426 U.S. 438, 449 (1976).

[29] 396 U.S. 375 (1970).

sufficient causal relationship between the violation and the injury . . . [is shown, if] he proves that the proxy solicitation itself, rather than the particular defect in the solicitation materials, was an essential link in the accomplishment of the transaction."[30] *Mills*'s loose proscription that the proxy solicitation itself be an essential link takes on some meaning from the facts of that particular case. In *Mills* the Seventh Circuit held that because it was not practicable to ascertain how a defect in the proxy statement influenced each stockholder's voting decision, the court would use the fairness of the transaction as a surrogate for causation. That is, if the transaction was unfair, the court would award relief to the stockholders in the belief that the misleading proxy statement duped them into approving an unfair merger. The Supreme Court rejected this approach, on the sound reasoning that mere evidence of a transaction's fairness does not assure shareholder support. This may strike some as a curious behavioral conclusion, but it rests on the understanding that fairness is a range of values, not a specific point. Thus a merger's terms may be within a range of fairness, but at the low end of the range such that informed stockholders may well vote against the transaction in the belief they should receive a price in the higher range of fairness.

Many have interpreted *Mills* as merely recognizing a rebuttable presumption of reliance by all the stockholders so that the defendant was faced with the nearly impossible burden of proving that the particular defect did not have a causal impact on how the stockholders voted.[31] Overall, the courts responded to *Mills* by according causation a most liberal interpretation, with the effect that a finding of materiality also satisfied causation.[32]

One major requirement of causation is that the alleged omission or misstatement in the proxy statement must pertain to a transaction for which stockholder approval was sought. This is the so-called transaction-causation requirement that is sometimes used in the courts' language.[33] To illustrate, consider the court's treatment of numerous cases brought in the 1970s alleging the board of directors failed to disclose in the proxy statement in which they sought election that they had acquiesced in foreign bribery payments carried out by management. With great consistency the courts dismissed Rule 14a-9 actions seeking to hold the directors liable for the bribery payments. The courts ruled that because the bribery payments were not submitted to the stockholders for their approval, transaction causation was lacking—that is, there was no causal relationship between the failure to disclose in the proxy statement the directors' misbehavior and the bribes themselves.[34] There is a more direct link between the nondisclosure of the

[30] *Id.* at 385.
[31] *See* Note, Causation and Liability in Private Actions for Proxy Violations, 80 Yale L.J. 107 (1970).
[32] *See* Mosher v. Kane, 784 F.2d 1385 (9th Cir. 1986) (causation established where defective proxy statement caused bankruptcy court not to approve the transactions such that stockholders never had opportunity to vote); Cowin v. Bresler, 741 F.2d 410 (D.C. Cir. 1984); Cole v. Schenley Indus., 563 F.2d 35, 39-40 (2d Cir. 1977).
[33] *See* Rosenbaum v. Klein, 547 F. Supp. 586 (E.D. Pa. 1982). At least one case has found transaction causation where no stockholder approval was sought. *See* Mosher v. Kane, 784 F.2d 1385 (9th Cir. 1986).
[34] *See, e.g.,* Abbey v. Control Data Corp., 603 F.2d 724 (8th Cir. 1979); Gaines v. Haughton, 645 F.2d 761 (9th Cir. 1981).

directors' acquiescence in foreign bribery and their own election. As seen above, the plaintiffs tended to be unsuccessful in those actions because the courts were unwilling to extend the scope of materiality to include the directors' acquiescence in foreign bribery. Generally, therefore, Rule 14a-9 does not provide recovery for damages suffered by the corporation as a consequence of the directors' decisions, even though the directors obtained their election through a misleading proxy statement.[35]

More recently, life has been breathed into the causation area by the Supreme Court's decision in *Virginia Bankshares, Inc. v. Sandberg.*[36] The Court held that causation was not established when the First American Bank of Virginia (Bank) was merged into a wholly owned subsidiary of First American Bankshares, Inc. (FABI), who also owned 85 percent of Bank's shares. The approval of the minority Bank stockholders was solicited by an allegedly misleading proxy statement; state law did not require the approval of the minority stockholders and did not extend an appraisal remedy to dissenters. The plaintiff argued causation was present because, had the proxy statement disclosed the merger's unfairness, it would have been possible for the plaintiff to obtain equitable relief based on a breach of the defendants' state-law-based fiduciary duties.[37] The plaintiff's argument was that certain nondisclosures are material and also establish causation because they are "sue facts," which, if disclosed, would have armed the plaintiff with a state-law-based cause of action to enjoin the transaction.

Justice Souter's opinion in *Virginia Bankshares* rejects the "sue facts" approach to causation. He reasoned that because the plaintiff possessed enough information to allege in his Rule 14a-9 action that the proxy statement failed to disclose the unfairness of the transaction that the plaintiff therefore possessed enough information when he filed his Rule 14a-9 action to have instead sought the relief he alleged was available to him under state fiduciary principles. Justice Souter therefore concluded that the proxy statement did not prevent the plaintiff from seeking such relief as was available under state law. *Virginia Bankshares* thus demonstrates the type of Catch 22 situation that plaintiffs face if they seek to protect themselves under Rule 14a-9 by alleging the nondisclosure prevented the plaintiff from obtaining protection under state law.

Certainly the result would have been different in *Virginia Bankshares* if the misleading proxy statement had prevented the minority stockholders from pursuing their appraisal remedy, a course of action that is predicated on stockholders voting against the merger.[38] Also, *Virginia Bankshares* does not appear to affect the causation inquiry where the defendant does not hold enough shares to approve

---

[35] *See, e.g.,* General Elec. Co. v. Cathcart, 980 F.2d 927 (3d Cir. 1992).

[36] 501 U.S. 1083 (1991).

[37] This approach builds on the reasoning of Judge Friendly in Goldberg v. Meridor, 567 F.2d 209 (2d Cir. 1977), *cert. denied,* 434 U.S. 1069 (1978).

[38] *Compare* Wilson v. Great Amer. Indus., 979 F.2d 924 (2d Cir. 1992) (antifraud provision applied when misrepresentation alleged to deprive pursuit of appraisal remedy); Howing Co. v. Nationwide Corp., 972 F.2d 700 (6th Cir. 1992) (same) *with* Grace v. Rosenstock, 228 F.3d 40 (2d Cir. 2000) (suit dismissed where only loss alleged was deprivation of information that would have shamed management such that the transaction would not have been pursued).

the transactions, as was the case with FABI, which owned 85 percent of Bank's voting shares. Indeed, post-*Virginia Bankshares* decisions continue to hold that the individual Rule 14a-9 plaintiff need not prove either that she relied on the misrepresentation or even exercised her proxy.[39] In sum, *Virginia Bankshares* appears to sharpen somewhat the causation area by holding that potential injunctive relief under state law cannot serve as a bridge between the violation and the harm suffered as a consequence of the transaction. Lower courts have applied *Virginia Bankshares* reasoning to actions under the antifraud provision section 10(b) and under Rule 10b-5.[40]

Remedies. A panoply of remedies is available in Rule 14a-9 actions. The Supreme Court in *Mills* conditioned damages being available to the extent that the transaction's unfairness can be established.[41] On remand, the lower court reviewed the terms of the merger and concluded they were fair, so no damages were awarded.[42] Injunctive relief is especially appropriate where matters have not been pursued so far as to be beyond the prospective relief of a court of equity. Rescission is possible but is inappropriate where the rights of third parties or excessive transaction costs will be incurred.

F.   CORPORATE CONTROL DEVICES

§13.27   *Various Voting Control Devices*

The operation of the proxy system has led to almost universal "management control" and a situation in which "ownership of corporate shares without appreciable ownership has become a natural phenomenon of our economic system."[1] Various devices have been used to obtain control of publicly held corporations with their valuable patronage for little or no investment. On the other hand, many of these same devices have proved to be useful and legitimate tools in meeting the special needs of close corporations and the desires of the owners of such corporations.[2]

The principal control devices by which groups may seek to gain or retain control of corporations by a combination of voting power or otherwise are as follows: (1) voting agreements entered into by a group of shareholders to assure their voting control; (2) voting trusts; (3) pyramiding, the use of holding companies or a series of holding companies to hold controlling shares of their subsidiaries;

[39] *See, e.g.,* Stahl v. Gibraltar Fin. Corp., 967 F.2d 335 (9th Cir. 1992).

[40] *See, e.g.,* Scattergood v. Perelman, 945 F.2d 618 (3d Cir. 1991).

[41] Mills v. Electric Auto-Lite Co., 396 U.S. 375 (1970).

[42] Mills v. Electric Auto-Lite Co., 552 F.2d 1239 (7th Cir. 1977).

§13.27   [1] Detroit Edison Co. v. SEC, 119 F.2d 730, 739 (6th Cir. 1941); Adolf A. Berle & Gardiner C. Means, The Modern Corporation and Private Property 72-80, 84-90 (rev. ed. 1968). *See* §2.07. This state of affairs is not without its supporters; *e.g.,* Robert Hessen, In Defense of the Corporation (1979).

[2] *See* Chapter 14.

(4) classification of common shares into voting and nonvoting, with the voting power vested in a small class of "management stock"; (5) management contracts, often with a parent or affiliated corporation; and (6) classification of directors, with staggered elections of only some of the directors each year. Another device is to provide for per capita rather than per share voting.[3]

Difficult policy questions arise as to how far the law should permit the use of devices that tend to divest the shareholders, who after all are the contributors of capital and the risk-takers, of any chance to share in control. How should these mechanisms by which some seek to obtain the management and patronage of vast aggregations of capital be limited and regulated? How, if at all, should the legal norms vary with the number of shareholders?[4]

§13.28   Nonvoting Shares and Voting-Only Shares

Preferred shares are frequently given only contingent rights to vote for directors and on other matters in the event of nonpayment of dividends for a specified period.[1] Under most statutes a corporation may issue nonvoting common stock.[2] The common stock may thus be divided into Class A nonvoting and Class B voting shares. Frequently in such cases the Class A shares will be widely sold to the public and Class B, the voting shares, will be closely held by promoters or managers. It is argued that vesting such control in the active promoters and managers so that no other group can dislodge them is for the benefit of the enterprise. But it may be questioned whether such an arrangement does not deprive investors in the nonvoting shares of potential participation in control, which should be their means of self-defense.[3] At least in close corporations, however, controlling shareholders, while perhaps not fiduciaries to the same extent as directors, are not free to exercise control for their own selfish interests and to oppress or defraud holders of minority or nonvoting shares who have no voice in the selection of management. And notwithstanding their denomination as nonvoting or conditional voting stock, holders of preferred as well as nonvoting common shares are entitled under most modern corporation statutes to vote for organic changes that directly affect their ownership interests.[4]

Control arrangements may also take the form of the corporation issuing shares that have voting rights with few or no accompanying financial interests in the company. For example, in *Lehrman v. Cohen*,[5] the Lehrman and Cohen families each held a separate class of stock that enabled each family to elect two directors. A third class of stock with no equity in the company but the power to elect

---

[3] Sagusa, Inc. v. Magellan Petroleum Corp., 1993 WL 512487, 19 Del. J. Corp. L. 1304 (Del. Ch. 1993), *aff'd without opinion*, 650 A.2d 1306 (Del. 1994) (upholding per capita voting).

[4] *See* Chapter 14.

§13.28   [1] *See* §18.04. Unless there is the privilege of class voting and the right to elect a majority of the board, such contingent voting provides only illusory protection.

[2] *E.g.*, Del. Code Ann., tit. 8, §151(a) (2001); Model Business Corp. Act §6.01(c)(1) (1984).

[3] William Zebina Ripley, Main Street and Wall Street 86 (1929).

[4] Model Business Corp. Act §10.04(d) (1984).

[5] 222 A.2d 800 (Del. 1966).

the fifth director was issued to the firm's attorney. The arrangement was intended to avoid deadlocks at the board meetings but was challenged when Cohen was replaced as president by the attorney. The validity of the "voting-only" class of shares was challenged. The Delaware Supreme Court held that the arrangement was not a voting trust subject to a ten-year limit because the shares' holder exercised all voting power; the arrangement was not an unlawful delegation of directors' powers; and public policy was not violated by shares having no proprietary interest.

The latter is most important in those states following the Model Business Corporation Act, which defines "shares" as embodying a "proprietary" interest in the firm. At least one other court has upheld the validity of issuing shares that have only voting rights.[6] Overall, the courts are well advised to sustain the validity of shares with unique features where they appear intended to fulfill the special desires of the owners and there is no evidence of fraud or overreaching conduct in their issuance.

§13.29   The Voting Trust—Its Use and Abuse

The normal method of delegating voting power is by a proxy, which, as noted earlier, is generally freely revocable unless coupled with an interest. It has been said that the voting trust was developed as a device to achieve irrevocable proxies.

To meet business needs, adroit lawyers invented the voting trust to give what is in essence a joint irrevocable proxy for a term of years the protective coloring of a trust, thus enabling the trustees to vote as owners rather than as mere agents.[1] In most jurisdictions, the voting trust has met the formal objections to an irrevocable proxy and, subject to certain formalities and limitations on duration, is now validated by statute.[2]

Modern statutes provide broad validation of the voting trust.[3] These statutes typically state that the trust agreement must be in writing and filed with the corporation; they also usually limit the duration of the voting trust, most often to ten years.[4] The voting-trust formalities are considered mandatory,[5] and courts have invalidated voting trusts that exceed the statutory duration[6] as well as for other

---

[6] See Stroh v. Blackhawk Holding Corp., 272 N.E.2d 1 (Ill. 1971).

§13.29   [1] See generally Norman D. Lattin, Corporations 384-385 (2d ed. 1971); Henry W. Ballantine, Voting Trusts, Their Abuses and Regulation, 21 Tex. L. Rev. 139 (1942); Note, 42 N.Y.U. L. Rev. 348 (1967).

[2] E.g., Del. Code Ann., tit. 8, §218 (2001); N.Y. Bus. Corp. Law §621 (McKinney 1986); Model Business Corp. Act §§7.30, 7.31 (1984). See Thomas W. Watkins, Development of Voting Trust Legislation, 35 U. Det. L.J. 595 (1958). Ironically, the voting trust can be a more dangerous abdication of shareholder safeguards than an irrevocable proxy.

[3] Model Business Corp. Act §§7.30, 7.31 (1984).

[4] See 1 F. Hodge O'Neal & Robert B. Thompson, O'Neal's Close Corporations §§5.15-5.19 (3d ed. 1998); John J. Woloszyn, A Practical Guide to Voting Trusts, 4 U. Balt. L. Rev. 245 (1975).

[5] Smith v. Biggs Boiler Works Co., 82 A.2d 372 (Del. Ch. 1951).

[6] Perry v. Missouri-Kansas Pipe Line Co., 191 A. 823 (Del. Ch. 1937); Christopher v. Richardson, 147 A.2d 375 (Pa. 1959).

types of noncompliance with the statute.[7] The modern attitude is to uphold arrangements that do not comply with all the requirements of the state voting-trust statute as long as the arrangement does not otherwise violate public policy.[8] Most statutes today are not intended to invalidate all other voting agreements, and in 1969 the Model Act was amended to reflect this.[9]

§13.30   Voting Trusts—Scope of Trustee's Powers

One object of forming a voting trust is to ensure permanency of tenure for the directors and to take from the shareholders the power to change management. Such an arrangement sometimes is a response to some special business need, and good reason can be shown for this drastic change in the rights of the shareholders, who by law and by the corporation's charter have the right to vote on the selection of directors and on fundamental corporate changes.[1] Obviously it is not a legitimate function of a voting trust to capture the voting power of the shareholders for those who propose to use it in their own selfish interest[2] or for purposes hostile to the corporation or its shareholders.[3] A voting trust offers to promoters of a corporation the temptation of seizing and retaining dictatorial control over the investments of others with little or no investment and keeping all the patronage and perquisites of control.[4]

The following are among the purposes usually regarded as legitimate for voting trusts: (1) to aid in reorganization plans and adjustments with creditors in bankruptcy or financial difficulty; (2) to assist financing, to procure loans, and to protect bondholders and preferred shareholders; (3) to accomplish some definite plan or policy for the benefit of the company and to assure stability and continuity of management for this purpose; (4) to prevent rival concerns or competitors from gaining control; (5) to apportion representation and protect minority interests by putting the selection of directors in impartial hands; and (6) as a device in

[7] Abercrombie v. Davies, 130 A.2d 338 (Del. 1957). In re Morse, 160 N.E. 374, 376 (N.Y. 1928): "No voting trust not within the terms of the statute is legal, and any such trust, so long as its purpose is legitimate, coming within its terms, is legal."

[8] See Oceanic Exploration Co. v. Grynberg, 428 A.2d 1 (Del. Super. Ct. 1981) (public policy offended only if noncomplying arrangement was mechanism to secretly acquire control).

[9] 1 Model Business Corp. Act Ann. §34 comment (2d ed. 1971). See Schrieber v. Carney, 447 A.2d 17, 25-26 (Del. Ch. 1982); Oceanic Exploration Co. v. Grynberg, 428 A.2d 1 (Del. Super. Ct. 1981).

§13.30   [1] A familiar example is that found within the closely held corporation. See infra Chapter 14.

[2] See Sanchez v. Guerro, 2000 U.S. Dist. Lexis 3616 (N.D. Cal.) (reformation of trust appropriate if purpose is no longer to provide stability to company's operations but to perpetuate control of trustee).

[3] See Warehime v. Warehime, 761 A.2d 1138 (Pa. 2000). See also Clarke v. Central Railroad & Banking Co., 50 F. 338, 346 (S.D. Ga. 1892); Bankers' Fire & Marine Ins. Co. v. Sloss, 155 So. 371, 373, 378 (Ala. 1934); People ex rel. Arkansas Valley Sugar Beet & Irrigated Land Co. v. Burke, 212 P. 837, 841 (Colo. 1923); Grogan v. Grogan, 315 S.W.2d 34 (Tex. Civ. App. 1958), writ of error denied, 322 S.W.2d 514 (Tex. 1959).

[4] See Report of the Securities & Exchange Commission on Investment Trusts and Investment Companies, Part III, ch. V, at 1913 (1940).

connection with mergers, consolidations, or purchases of a business to assure that the predecessors or constituents, though in the minority, may have representation.[5]

The trustee of a voting trust is a fiduciary to the beneficiaries of the trust. The voting of the trusts shares to support a transaction in which the trustee has a direct financial interest calls for close scrutiny of the transaction and the trustee's motives.[6]

Warehime v. Warehime[7] presents an interesting illustration of the scope of the voting trustee's powers to vote the trust shares in a manner that advances his interests. John, CEO of HFC, became the sole trustee of two voting trusts established by his father. The shares held by the two trusts represented a majority of the voting power and among their beneficiaries were John and his two siblings. The siblings chafed under John's stewardship of the firm, but bided their time until the trusts' ten-year term expired. In the meantime, John wielded his power to eliminate cumulative voting and installed non-family members on the board. On the eve of the trust's termination, the shares were voted in approval of creating a new class of preferred that would be held by the company's 401(k) plan. The shares would enjoy super voting rights in the event (surely to occur) that John and his siblings could not concur on who was to be elected to the board. The plan's trustees were the company's independent directors (the appointees of John) and a majority of them were to decide how the preferred shares were to be voted if they were to be entitled to vote. John's siblings cried foul, alleging quite properly that the arrangement had the effect of extending John's control of the company. The court relied heavily upon the trial court's finding that John acted consistent with his fiduciary duty of good faith as trustee in approving the recapitalization which served the ends of the corporation and its stockholders by providing stable governance and a means to resolve intracorporate disputes. Though not emphasized by the Pennsylvania Supreme Court, a significant consideration in John's strategy was placing the role of Solomon with the company's independent directors. The dissenters gave short shrift to this factor and instead saw John's deeds as nothing less than the trustee engaging in self-dealing. Notable in the court's disposition was that it took a broader view of the trustee's obligations; the majority assessed John's actions not solely by their impact on the trust's beneficiaries, but by their impact on the corporation and its shareholders. The majority justified this broader view because of the trust agreement's broad authority that the trustee was to exercise his best judgment and act in good faith.

§13.31   The Voting Trust in Operation

The voting trust involves a more complete and formal surrender of the shareholder's legal rights and remedies than any other control device. Voting-trust pro-

---

[5] Seward v. American Hardware Co., 171 S.E. 650, 659-660 (Va. 1932).

[6] *See, e.g.*, Regnery v. Myers, 679 N.E.2d 74 (Ill. Ct. App. 1997) (trustee breached obligation by voting trust's shares to approve company's issuance of shares to him at less than their fair market value; also breach by his co-conspirators). The burden of proof in such a case is on the plaintiff. *See* In re Estate of Halas, 568 N.E.2d 170 (Ill. Ct. App. 1991) (breach made out by establishing dishonesty, bad faith, or abuse of discretion).

[7] 761 A.2d 1138 (Pa. 2000).

cedures commonly require that the shares' ownership be transferred to the voting trustee, that there be a formal voting-trust agreement signed by the shareholders creating the trust, and that a copy of that agreement must be filed with the corporation's principal officer.[1] The failure to comply with these provisions at one time led to the arrangement being viewed as invalid.[2] More recent decisions have upheld arrangements under state voting-trust statutes when there was less than literal compliance with the statute.[3]

The beneficial owners may cease to be recognized as shareholders of record and may be deprived not only of any right to vote but also of any right of inspection, notice, or information from the corporation or any voice in fundamental changes, such as mergers and consolidations, sales of entire assets, increase and reduction of capital, and bylaw and charter amendments that may adversely affect them. There is ordinarily no justification for such a complete stripping of the shareholders of all the safeguards provided by law for their protection. Persons who have put their shares in a voting trust—that is, the holders of voting-trust certificates—are often spoken of as "equitable owners" of shares of stock. They become in effect equitable tenants in common in the mass of shares transferred to the trustees, with a contract right to receive dividends and retransfer of the shares on termination of the trust. The remedies of the holder of a voting-trust certificate are primarily against the trustees to cancel the trust for fraud, to remove the trustees if guilty of misconduct or for conflicting interests, or to sue for an accounting for secret profits.[4] Voting trustees are subject to the usual fiduciary principles of a trust.[5]

A voting-trust certificate is a profit-sharing security or contract issued by the trustees as a kind of association or holding company, of which the "charter" is the voting agreement. Since voting-trust certificates in effect represent shares in such an association, the transfer thereof can result in a taxable event.[6] Under both state[7] and federal[8] securities legislation, voting-trust certificates are securities and thus are subject to those acts' antifraud and registration provisions.

---

§13.31   [1] Cal. Corp. Code §§706, 711 (West 1990); Del. Code Ann. tit. 8, §218(a), (b) (2001); N.Y. Bus. Corp. Law §621 (McKinney 1986). *See* Model Business Corp. Act §7.30; Former Model Business Corp. Act §34 (1969).

[2] *See* Abercrombie v. Davies, 130 A.2d 338 (Del. 1957). *But see* Del. Code Ann. tit. 8, §218(c) (2001) (inviting enforcement of voting agreements generally according to their terms). *See also, e.g.,* State v. Keystone Life Ins. Co., 93 So. 2d 565 (La. 1957).

[3] *See* Reserve Life Ins. Co. v. Provident Life Ins. Co., 499 F.2d 715 (8th Cir. 1974) (omitted address of trustee); Oceanic Exploration Co. v. Grynberg, 428 A.2d 1 (Del. Super. Ct. 1981) (agreement would be struck down as illegal voting trust only if noncomplying arrangement offended public policy as a mechanism to secretly acquire control).

[4] Overfield v. Pennroad Corp., 42 F. Supp. 586, 607-611 (E.D. Pa. 1941); Moore v. Bowes, 64 P.2d 423 (Cal. 1937); Perrine v. Pennroad Corp., 171 A. 733 (Del. Ch. 1934).

[5] Brown v. McLanahan, 148 F.2d 703 (4th Cir. 1945). *See also* Tankersley v. Albright, 514 F.2d 956 (7th Cir. 1975).

[6] Orpheum Bldg. Co. v. Anglim, 127 F.2d 478, 484 (9th Cir. 1942).

[7] *See, e.g.,* Uniform Securities Act §401(1) (1956).

[8] 15 U.S.C. §§77b(a)(1); 78c(a)(10) (2000).

CHAPTER 14

Close Corporations

A.   INTRODUCTION TO THE NEEDS AND SPECIAL TREATMENT OF CLOSE CORPORATIONS

§14.01   Close Corporations: Definitions and Distinctive Needs

"Close corporation" (or "closely held corporation") is defined in a number of ways. The term is often used to refer to a corporation with only a few shareholders to distinguish a corporation of that kind from a publicly held company. A popular definition describes a close corporation as one whose shares are not generally traded in the securities markets.[1] "Close corporation" frequently connotes an incorporated business in which the owners consider themselves partners and make decisions and conduct their business affairs as though they were partners. Further, the principal shareholders in a close corporation are generally active in management. Summing up the characteristics of a close corporation, a Massachusetts court commented that such a corporation is typified by: "(1) a small number of stockholders; (2) no ready market for the corporate stock; and (3) substantial majority stockholder participation in the management, direction and operations of the corporations."[2]

A number of states have enacted special legislation to define and govern the close corporation. In Delaware and several other states, for example, this special statutory regulation states that a close corporation's charter must provide that (1) its stock shall be held by not more than a specified number of persons; (2) its stock is subject to transfer restrictions; and (3) it shall not engage in public offerings of its stock.[3] In a few states, the special close corporation statute defines "close corporation" simply as any corporation that elects close corporation status for purposes of the statute.[4] As discussed throughout this chapter, courts recognize the special needs of close corporations even in the absence of statute. This special treatment applies even if a corporation elects not to incorporate under a state's special close corporation statute. However, there is authority in Delaware that corporations desiring to be treated as close corporations must elect to do so under the Delaware Close Corporation Act.[5]

A person taking a minority position in a close corporation may desire and therefore bargain for protection against the power of those holding a majority of a corporation's voting stock to make decisions that will prejudice minority interests. Participants may use some kind of contractual arrangement to set up a con-

---

§14.01   [1] Elvin R. Latty, The Close Corporation and the New North Carolina Business Corporation Act, 34 N.C. L. Rev. 432, 439 (1956).

[2] Donahue v. Rodd Electrotype Co., 328 N.E.2d 505, 511 (Mass. 1975).

[3] Del. Code Ann. tit. 8, §342(a)(1)-(3) (2001) (30 nominal shareholders); Ill. Ann. Stat. ch. 805, §5/2A.10 (Smith-Hurd 1993).

[4] See, e.g., Md. Code Ann., Corps. & Assns. §4-101 (Michie 1999).

[5] Nixon v. Blackwell, 626 A.2d 1366 (Del. 1993).

trol pattern for the corporation that differs from the traditional corporation control structure. The arrangement may take the form of a pre-incorporation agreement among the participants, a shareholders' agreement after the corporation has been organized, a voting trust, special charter and bylaw provisions, irrevocable proxies, or employment contracts between the corporation and the shareholder-employees of the corporation. Most of these arrangements and the laws applicable to them are discussed briefly in the sections that follow.

§14.02 Close Corporation Statutes—Scheme, Pitfalls, and Objectives

A substantial number of states have enacted special close corporation statutes or have added to their general corporation statute separate supplements or divisions that apply only to close corporations.[1] This special legislation varies from state to state in both format and substance. In most states with special close corporation legislation, a corporation must meet stated requirements to qualify as a close corporation and must elect close corporation status for the special rules to apply.[2]

In some states, the special close corporation statute gives the organizer greater flexibility in molding the corporation's control pattern than the general corporation statute does. For example, in a state in which the general corporation statute contemplates that a corporation will have a board of directors, the close corporation statute may permit the elimination of a corporation's board of directors and the substitution of direct management by the shareholders.[3] Further, special close corporation legislation may provide broader or additional remedies for conflicts among shareholders than is provided by the general corporation statute.

Some close corporation statutes seem to sanction, if not encourage, informal operation of a close corporation and to disregard the usual corporate ritual. Several provide that failure by a close corporation to observe the usual corporate formalities shall not be used by a court as a basis for disregarding the corporation's separate entity and imposing liability on the shareholders for the corporation's obligations.[4] Maryland legislation states that an annual shareholders' meeting need not be held unless requested by a shareholder.[5] The Wisconsin statute provides that provisions required by law to be set forth in a corporation's bylaws can be stated with equal effect in the corporation's articles of incorporation or in a shareholders' agreement.[6]

Corporations electing to be close corporations under the typical close corporation statute must include in their articles a statement that the corporation is

---

§14.02 [1] F. Hodge O'Neal & Robert B. Thompson, Close Corporations: Law and Practice §§1.15, 1.16 (3d ed. 1998).

[2] See, e.g., Cal. Corp. Code §158(a),(b) (West 1990); Del. Code Ann. tit. 8, §§343, 344 (2001).

[3] See, e.g., Del. Corp. Code Ann. tit. 8, §351 (2001). Cf. Model Business. Corp. Act §8.01 (1984), which permits any corporation with 50 shareholders or less to dispense with the board.

[4] See Cal. Corp. Code §300(e) (West 1990); Wis. Stat. Ann. §180.1835 (West 1992).

[5] Md. Code Ann., Corps. & Assns. §4-402 (Michie 1999).

[6] Wis. Stat. Ann. §180.1825 (West 1992).

a close corporation.[7] If the election is made after shares have been issued, an amendment to the articles of incorporation adding or deleting the provision must obtain the approval of a supermajority of the stockholders.[8] States sometimes require the articles of incorporation to state that the shares of the electing close corporation will be held by no greater number than the number stated in the articles, which can be no greater than a number specified in the statute.[9] A transfer of shares that causes the corporation to exceed the limit stated in its articles of incorporation terminates the entity's status as a close corporation. In some states, the corporation is granted a short statutory period of grace in which to take corrective action, such as amending the articles to increase within the statutory limits the number of shareholders specified or reducing the number of shareholders by purchase.[10]

The overall objective of electing close corporation status is more than likely to invoke the statutory imprimatur for the close corporation participants to organize the governance of their business and their own participation in a manner different from what customarily follows from being a corporation. The foremost consideration in this regard is the so-called shareholders' agreement that is authorized by most close corporation statutes. Of those states that authorize shareholder agreements, most follow the style first enacted in North Carolina by setting forth various bases on which the agreement cannot be attacked. For example, the Delaware statute provides:

> No written agreement among the stockholders of a close corporation . . . shall be invalid on the ground that it is an attempt by the parties to the agreement or by the stockholders of the corporation to treat the corporation as if it were a partnership or to arrange relations among the stockholders or between the stockholders and the corporation in a manner that would be appropriate only among partners.[11]

On reflection, authorization that takes the form, as does the above Delaware provision, of negating the types of arguments that can be raised against the agreement is a very curious form of legislative authorization. Viewed historically, the statute can be seen as a strong legislative statement rejecting an early line of cases, discussed elsewhere in this chapter, that more often than not invalidated shareholder agreements on the grounds captured today in the statute. But the statute appears to invite the resourceful lawyer to identify a basis not already negated in the statute as the missile to sink the shareholders' agreement. In contrast, the

---

[7] *See, e.g.,* Cal. Corp. Code §158(a) (West 1990); Del. Stat. Ann. tit. 8, §343 (2001); Md. Code Ann., Corps. & Assns. §4-201 (Michie 1999); Tex. Bus. Corp. Act Ann. art. 12.11 (Supp. 2002); Model Statutory Close Corp. Supp. §3(a).

[8] *See, e.g.,* Cal. Corp. Code §158(b), (c) (West Supp. 2002) (unanimous vote to add and two-thirds approval to remove); Del. Stat. Ann. tit. 8, §§344 & 346 (2001) (two-thirds vote to elect or terminate election).

[9] *See, e.g.,* Cal. Corp. Code §158(a) (West 1990) (35 holders); Del. Stat. Ann. tit. 8, §342 (2001) (30 persons).

[10] *See, e.g.,* Del. Stat. Ann. tit. 8, §348 (2001) (30 days).

[11] Del. Code Ann., tit. 8, §354 (2001). *See also* Cal. Corp. Code §300(b) (West 1990); N.Y. Bus. Corp. Law §620(b) (McKinney Supp. 2002).

Texas close corporation provisions provide a nonexclusive list of many broad topics that may validly be included in a shareholders' agreement.[12]

In sum, close corporation statutes vary widely not simply in the approach each takes toward meeting the unique needs of close corporations but also in the legislature's perception of what areas of the close corporation merit special treatment. This is especially surprising in light of the fact that a perusal of the literature reflects very little disagreement as to how the position of a stockholder in a close corporation differs from that of a stockholder in a public corporation. Though there appears to be no disagreement on this fundamental point, the wide variance among corporate statutes bears testament to great differences among policy-makers on the appropriate legislative response to meeting the needs of close corporation participants.

B. SHAREHOLDER AGREEMENTS IN CLOSE CORPORATIONS

§14.03 Shareholders' Agreements: Contents

Participants in close corporations frequently enter into agreements among themselves to provide protection to minority shareholders against the principle of majority rule or to tailor the corporate structure to the participants' particular desires and the needs of the enterprise.[1] Minority shareholders often seek agreements that will provide them with representation on the board of directors or will otherwise give them input in the management of the corporation. Although board membership may give the minority access to information on some decisions being made for the corporation, membership alone provides the minority with very little protection against the power vested in the majority by the principle of majority rule. Consequently, the minority may bargain for power to veto some or all corporate decisions or for some other effective participation in corporate affairs. The majority may agree to share their power with the minority in order to encourage potential shareholders to invest in the enterprise, bring into the enterprise valuable patents or know-how, or provide needed executives or scientifically skilled employees as key members of the company.

Shareholders who hold a majority of a corporation's shares sometimes enter into an agreement among themselves with a vastly different objective, usually to guarantee that they will continue to act jointly in making corporate decisions. Shareholders' agreements to which minority shareholders are parties typically

---

[12] Tex. Bus. Corp. Act Ann. art. 12.32-12.35 (Supp. 2002). *See also* Md. Code Ann., Corps. & Assns. §4-401(a) (McKinney Supp. 1999); Model Statutory Close Corp. Supp. §20.

§14.03 [1] *See* F. Hodge O'Neal & Robert B. Thompson, Close Corporations: Law and Practice ch. 5 (3d ed. 1998). *See also* Statutory Needs of Close Corporations—An Empirical Study: Special Close Corporation Legislation or Flexible General Corporation Law?, 10 J. Corp. L. 849, 904 (1985).

cover selection of the members of the board of directors, the naming of corporate officers, employment of shareholders and their salaries, and the amount of time each participant is to devote to the business.[2]

§14.04   Forms and Execution of Shareholders' Agreements

A shareholders' agreement may take a number of forms. In a simple shareholders' pooling agreement, the parties agree to vote their shares in the manner set forth in the agreement. The shareholders retain title to their shares and the right to vote them; however, they are contractually bound to vote pursuant to a pre-arranged plan.[1] A pooling agreement is to be distinguished from a shareholders' management agreement, in which the parties attempt to control corporate decisions that otherwise would be made by the board of directors, such as determining corporate policy, selecting officers, fixing salaries, and declaring dividends.[2]

More frequently, the objective of a shareholders' agreement is to restrict the freedom of its parties or to arrange their economic rights in a manner different than would follow their proportionate share ownership. For example, in *Wasserman v. Rosengarden*[3] the shareholders' agreement among the minority 20 percent owner and the husband and wife who owned the remaining shares, among other features, assured the minority holder an equal share in profits with the other two holders.[4] The court held that, absent any fraud or apparent injury to public policy, the agreement was valid.

A shareholders' agreement is frequently the document that imposes restrictions on the transfer of shares or even contains covenants not to compete. As would be expected, covenants not to compete are subjected to close scrutiny on policy grounds, and transfer restrictions are subjected to a lower level of review, being upheld in the absence of fraud, duress, or undue influence.[5] A shareholders' agreement can also be the device that accords rights on nonshareholders, such as giving a creditor veto power over board financial decisions.[6]

---

[2] *See* Sternheimer v. Sternheimer, 155 S.E.2d 41 (Va. 1967) (failure to include provision dealing with amount of time participants are to work for corporation and extent to which outside part-time activities are allowed can lead to dissension and litigation).

§14.04   [1] 5 William M. Fletcher, Cyclopedia of the Law of Private Corporations, §2064 (rev. perm. ed. 1987).

[2] Annot., Validity and Effect of Agreement Controlling the Vote of Corporate Stock, 45 A.L.R.2d 799 (1956, Later Case Service 1980 & Supp. 1985).

[3] 406 N.E.2d 131 (Ill. App. Ct. 1980).

[4] Likewise, a shareholders' agreement can be used to provide a pre-established salary to a party. *See* Roos v. Aloi, 487 N.Y.S.2d 637 (Sup. Ct. 1985).

[5] *See, e.g.,* Shortridge v. Platis, 458 N.E.2d 301 (Ind. Ct. App. 1984); Mayeaux v. Ellsworth, Scheznaydre & Crosby, 470 So. 2d 887 (La. Ct. App. 1985) (agreement enforceable according to its terms in absence of some absurd or evidently unintended result); In re Gusman, 577 N.Y.S.2d 667 (App. Div. 1991).

[6] *See* Westland Capitol Corp. v. Lucht Engg., Inc., 308 N.W.2d 709 (Minn. 1981) (venture capitalists granted power to overrule capital expenditures in excess of $25,000).

B. Shareholder Agreements in Close Corporations

Many state statutes prescribe specific requirements for shareholders' agreements authorized under their close corporation statutes. For example, California defines "shareholders' agreement" as a written agreement signed by all the shareholders.[7] Several state statutes include authorization for shareholder agreements for those corporations that have duly qualified as close corporations. It is a question of legislative intent whether an agreement that does not comply strictly with such requirements should be held invalid on its face. It would appear wiser to view the statute as merely a safe harbor for such agreements, but not the exclusive means for enforceable agreements to arise.

For example, in a leading case, *Zion v. Kurtz,*[8] the sole stockholders of a Delaware corporation agreed that no business or activities of the corporation would be conducted without the consent of the minority stockholder. The defendant in that action argued, in part, that the agreement was invalid because, although several provisions of the Delaware statute authorized the agreement entered into between the parties, that authorization applied only to a corporation that had taken the steps required under Delaware law to formally be a close corporation. The corporation in question had not taken the formalities required to qualify as a close corporation.[9] The New York Court of Appeals held the agreement was valid, reasoning that despite the agreement's noncompliance with the statute's formal requirements, the agreement's substance did not offend Delaware public policy in view of the fact that all the stockholders were signatories to the agreement.

The approach taken in *Zion* is consistent with the cases that have upheld even oral agreements among the shareholders,[10] as well as arrangements that failed to strictly comply with the statutory requirements for that type of provision.[11] Decisions such as *Zion* run the risk of robbing statutory provisions of their significance. One approach may be to view statutory provisions authorizing special arrangements within qualifying close corporations as safe harbors where questions of public policy and affronts to the statutory scheme have been resolved by the legislature; noncomplying agreements would, as in *Zion,* still be scrutinized on these factors and perhaps others.

The Delaware Supreme Court in *Nixon v. Blackwell*[12] expressed less flexibility for its close corporation provisions than the New York court did in *Zion.* The specific issue before the Delaware court was whether non-employee-shareholders could require the corporation to purchase their shares because the shares held by

---

[7] Cal. Corp. Code §186 (West 1990).

[8] 405 N.E.2d 681 (N.Y. 1980). For a holding similar to *Zion, see* Ramos v. Estrada, 10 Cal. Rptr. 833 (Cal. Ct. App. 1992).

[9] Among the requirements not satisfied was a statement in the articles of incorporation designating the corporation as a close corporation and stating its shares could not be held by a greater number than a stated number of individuals. *See* Del. Code Ann. tit. 8, §342 (2001).

[10] *See* Wasserman v. Rosengarden, 406 N.E.2d 131 (Ill. App. Ct. 1980).

[11] *See, e.g.,* Adler v. Svingos, 436 N.Y.S.2d 719 (App. Div. 1981); R. H. Sanders Corp. v. Haves, 541 S.W.2d 262 (Tex. Ct. App. 1976). *Contra* Gazda v. Kolinski, 458 N.Y.S.2d 387 (App. Div. 1982) (agreement that salaries could be increased only with unanimous shareholder approval was valid only if placed in articles of incorporation).

[12] 626 A.2d 1366 (Del. 1993).

certain employee-shareholders had been purchased. In ruling against the petitioning minority shareholders, the Delaware Supreme Court expressed its unwillingness to create special ad hoc rules for the participants of a small corporation that had not followed the formal procedures to qualify as a close corporation under Subchapter 14 of the Delaware General Corporation Law. Failing to so qualify, the court concluded a corporation is not governed by Delaware's close corporation provisions. Taken literally, it would appear that Delaware would not, as *Zion* concluded, permit the participants in a small corporation to arrange their affairs in a manner that is appropriate only for a "statutory close corporation" if the corporation has not met the technical statutory requirements to be a "close corporation." *Nixon* can be viewed as treating Delaware's close corporation provisions as exclusive safe harbors for agreements that otherwise are impermissible arrangements for corporations. So viewed, only by meeting the statutory requirements to qualify as a close corporation can the corporation's participants invoke the certainty and protection of Delaware's close corporation provisions.

§14.05 Validity of Shareholders' Agreements Attacked Because They Limit the Board of Directors' Discretion or Authority

In the past courts looked with much distrust on shareholders' agreements and often condemned not only dishonest schemes but also any agreement that might conceivably have been injurious to noncontracting shareholders or corporate creditors. Indeed, in some instances courts were overly strict and rejected shareholders' agreements that served a useful purpose and were in the best interest of the corporation and all shareholders and creditors. They applied their concepts of public policy unrealistically, oblivious to the fact that a party to a shareholders' agreement who sets up the illegality of the agreement as a defense often does so simply to escape an honest bargain that has become burdensome.

Most modern statutes provide that shareholders' agreements may stipulate the manner in which the parties will vote their shares,[1] but this does not preclude attacks based on violation of other statutory norms. A common basis for attacking shareholders' control agreements is that they are incompatible with the statutory scheme of corporate management and operation.[2] The statutory section providing that the business of a corporation shall be managed by (or under the supervision of) its board of directors is frequently used to attack the validity of a shareholders' agreement if the agreement purports to control matters within the traditional powers of the directors.[3]

§14.05 [1] See Model Business Corp. Act §§7.30, 7.31 (1984); Former Model Business Corp. Act §34 (1969).

[2] See Benintendi v. Kenton Hotel, Inc., 60 N.E.2d 829 (N.Y. 1945) (invalidating bylaws).

[3] See, e.g., Conn. Gen. Stat. Ann. §33-735(b) (1997); Pa. Stat. Ann. tit. 15, §1721 (Supp. 2002).

B. Shareholder Agreements in Close Corporations

Shareholders' agreements that tend to control directors' actions have often been held invalid even though the agreements were made in good faith and actually were beneficial to the company and its shareholders.[4] Numerous early decisions held that shareholders' agreements, especially agreements by less than all of a corporation's shareholders that restricted the discretion of the directors were invalid as contrary to public policy.[5] The courts reasoned that since the corporation statute provided that the business of a corporation shall be managed by or under the direction of its board of directors, the directors' power of control existed for the benefit of all the shareholders, and they could not bargain away in advance the free exercise of director discretion. Thus shareholders' agreements calling for the election of "sterilized" or dummy directors who would place or maintain designated persons in the corporation's employment were generally held void.

The New York Court of Appeals invalidated a unanimous shareholders' agreement giving broad management powers to designated shareholders because it would "sterilize" the board.[6] The same court refused to enforce a unanimous shareholders' agreement providing that a designated person would serve as president of the company for ten years and not be subject to discharge by the board.[7] The current New York statute is more liberal in sanctioning arrangements that deprive directors of traditional powers, provided those arrangements are placed in the corporation's certificate of incorporation.[8] Further, in a sharply divided four-to-three decision,[9] a New York court, applying Delaware law, upheld an agreement giving a minority shareholder a veto over corporate decisions, even though the agreement was not included in the company's charter or bylaws.

The courts' liberal approach toward agreements restricting director discretion can be traced to *Clark v. Dodge*.[10] In exchange for Clark's agreement to disclose a secret formula that would be promoted through their corporation, Dodge agreed to vote as a director to select Clark as the company's general manager and to approve a salary or dividends paid to Clark equal to one-fourth of the company's net income. Several critical points must be observed regarding the facts of *Clark v. Dodge*. First, the agreement restricted the discretion of Dodge as a director on the specific issues of who would be the company's general manager and what

---

[4] *E.g.*, McQuade v. Stoneham, 189 N.E. 234 (N.Y. 1934), *reh'g denied*, 191 N.E. 514 (N.Y. 1934).

[5] West v. Camden, 135 U.S. 507 (1890); Manson v. Curtis, 119 N.E. 559 (N.Y. 1918); Withers v. Edmunds, 62 S.W. 795 (Tex. Civ. App. 1901); 15 Samuel Williston, Treatise on the Law of Contracts, §§1736, 1737 (Walter H. E. Jaeger ed., 3d ed. 1972).

[6] Long Park, Inc. v. Trenton-New Brunswick Theatres Co., 77 N.E.2d 633 (N.Y. 1948).

[7] Fells v. Katz, 175 N.E. 516 (N.Y. 1931). Some recent decisions purport to follow Fells v. Katz but have emphasized that good cause must be shown to discharge an employee covered by agreement. *See* Napoli v. Carrano, 486 N.Y.S.2d 339 (App. Div. 1985); Dubin v. Michnick, 438 N.Y.S.2d 920 (Sup. Ct. 1981), *modified*, 447 N.Y.S.2d 472 (App. Div. 1982); Puro v. Puro, 393 N.Y.S.2d 633 (Sup. Ct. 1976).

[8] Weber v. Sidney, 244 N.Y.S.2d 228 (App. Div. 1963), *aff'd*, 200 N.E.2d 867 (N.Y. 1964); N.Y. Bus. Corp. Law, §620(b) (McKinney Supp. 2002).

[9] Zion v. Kurtz, 405 N.E.2d 681 (N.Y. 1980). *See also* Richard A. Kaplan, Note, Close Corporation Shareholders' Agreements and the Signal of *Zion v. Kurtz:* Frustration of the Statutory Notice Requirement, 46 Alb. L. Rev. 198 (1981).

[10] 199 N.E. 641 (N.Y. 1936).

compensation the general manager would receive. It was on this point that Dodge later argued that his agreement with Clark was void as against public policy because it removed his discretion as a director to select another as president or to approve a different compensation arrangement for Clark. Second, the action was in equity because Clark wanted specific enforcement of the contract, not damages for its breach. Equity jurisdiction was available because damages could not be determined; Clark's compensation was premised on one-fourth of the net income to be derived by the promotion of his secret process. The profits of such a promotion could only be determined through enforcement of the agreement; hence, damages at law were not adequate. Third, the essence of the agreement was to provide assurance that the secret process could be successfully promoted through the efforts of Clark. This is the reason Clark demanded an agreement that he have unspecified tenure as the company's general manager. Finally, Dodge was obligated to vote for Clark as general manager only so long as he was "efficient and competent."

The New York court in *Clark v. Dodge* departed from precedent and upheld the agreement. The court was influenced not only by the fact that all the stockholders signed the agreement, but also that its limitation on the directors' discretion was limited to specific areas, namely the selection of the general manager and his compensation. Thus, there were many other areas where the directors' discretion was unrestrained by the agreement (e.g., selection of other officers, authority to borrow funds, or approval of corporate expenditures and budgets). In its now classic expression, *Clark* reasoned that rather than an attempt to "sterilize the board of directors" by wholesale removal of its discretion, the agreement before it only "slightly impinged" on the board's discretion. Moreover, the court was impressed that the agreement was among the sole shareholders of the corporation and persuaded that creditors were not harmed by the agreement because there was an *implied* condition of good faith that any payments to Clark would be after making reasonable and adequate provision for creditors. *Clark v. Dodge* thus established a fairly consistent line of case upholding, certainly among the signatories of the agreement, contracts that removed discretion from directors in specific areas, provided enforcement poses no threat to the interest of other stockholders or creditors.[11]

The continuing trend has been toward an increasing statutory and judicial acceptance of shareholders' management agreements.[12] Some courts have upheld shareholders' agreements depriving directors of some managerial powers if they concluded that the agreements took from the directors only relatively unimportant powers and thus impinged only slightly on the statutory norm of director management.

The typical shareholders' management agreement in a close corporation gives minority holders a voice in control and management of the corporation and assures them of employment by the corporation. Such an agreement is now usually held valid, at least if all shareholders are parties and the agreement is not

---

[11] *See, e.g.*, Galler v. Galler, 203 N.E.2d 577 (Ill. 1964) (upholding agreement providing for election of certain persons to specified offices for a period of years).

[12] *See, e.g.*, Galler v. Galler, 203 N.E.2d 577, 585 (Ill. 1964).

detrimental to prospective shareholders.[13] More recently, courts appear not to emphasize the quantum of discretion removed from the directors by the agreement but instead emphasize the freedom of the stockholders to mold the relationship they prefer through private contractual arrangements, the absence of any harm or fraud on nonsignatories, and the trend toward upholding special arrangements in close corporations.[14] It appears that, whereas courts formerly began their scrutiny with a jealous eye toward the norms and policies believed to be embodied in the local corporate statute, the approach today invariably is contractual. Today, it appears that any limits on the scope or validity of shareholders' agreements are imposed only when there is a clear conflict with the governing corporate statute[15] and, more particularly, if there is any fraud in the agreement's execution or operation.[16]

§14.06 Shareholders' Reciprocal Pooling Agreements Controlling Voting for Directors

Agreements to vote for specified persons as directors or to vote as the holders of a majority of the shares in a pool may direct are valid and binding if they do not contemplate limiting the discretion of the directors or the committing of any fraud, oppression, or wrong against other shareholders. The validity of voting agreements therefore depends on their purposes, effects, and tendencies.

Courts consider a variety of factors when determining the validity of a shareholders' agreement. Among those factors are the following: (1) the purpose or object of the agreement, (2) the statutes in force in the particular jurisdiction in which the agreement is made, (3) the conceptions of public policy prevailing in the courts of the jurisdiction regarding the separation of voting power from the beneficial ownership of shares, (4) the situation of the corporation and the shareholders at the time the agreement was made, (5) whether or not all of the shareholders in the corporation are parties to the agreement, (6) whether the contracting shareholders are also directors or expect to be at the time of the performance of the contract, (7) the length of time during which the agreement will control the shareholders' right to vote their shares, (8) whether the person challenging the validity of the agreement is a party to it or is a creditor or shareholder not party to the agreement, (9) whether the person challenging the agreement is simply trying to "welch" on his undertaking, (10) whether or not there is consideration, other than the mutual promises of the parties to support the undertakings, to vote in accordance with the terms of the agreement, (11) how long the

---

[13] See Glazer v. Glazer, 374 F.2d 390 (5th Cir.), cert. denied, 389 U.S. 831 (1967).

[14] See, e.g., Wasserman v. Rosengarden, 406 N.E.2d 131 (Ill. App. Ct. 1980); Westland Capitol Corp. v. Lucht Engg., Inc., 308 N.W.2d 709 (Minn. 1981); Roos v. Aloi, 487 N.Y.S.2d 637 (Sup. Ct. 1985); Adler v. Svingos, 436 N.Y.S.2d 719 (App. Div. 1981); R. H. Sanders Corp. v. Haves, 541 S.W.2d 262 (Tex. Ct. App. 1976).

[15] See, e.g., Gazda v. Kolinski, 458 N.Y.S.2d 387 (App. Div. 1982).

[16] See Miller v. Miller, 700 S.W.2d 941 (Tex. Ct. App. 1985).

contract has been in operation and the extent to which action has been taken or positions have changed in reliance on it, and (12) the kind of corporation whose stock is subject to the voting arrangement.[1]

Although most modern statutes declare that voting agreements are enforceable according to their terms,[2] this declaration is far from an unlimited validation of all shareholders' agreements. For example, in a famous Delaware case,[3] the two contracting parties, Mrs. Ringling and Mrs. Haley, who between them had sufficient shares to elect five of the seven directors, agreed to act jointly in exercising their voting rights and, in the event of disagreement, to vote in accordance with the decision of an arbitrator. After a disagreement between the two and a decision by the arbitrator as to how the shares of the two were to be voted, Mrs. Haley disregarded the arbitrator's decision and voted her shares contrary to his directions. The Court of Chancery ordered that a new election be held before a master and that effect be given to the agreement. On appeal, however, the Delaware Supreme Court modified the decree by ordering that Mrs. Haley's votes be rejected but that the other votes cast at the shareholders' meeting be counted. The result was that only six directors (instead of seven) were elected, three by Mrs. Ringling and three by Mr. North, the third shareholder. Although this decision of the Delaware Supreme Court frustrated the objective of the agreement, perhaps the decision was justified in a technical sense as a recognition of the rights of Mr. North, who was not a party to the agreement and who had cast his votes properly at a regular shareholders' meeting.

In a subsequent decision,[4] since repudiated by statute, the Delaware court invalidated a pooling agreement on the ground that it was in effect a voting trust that failed to comply with statutory formalities. The court pointed out that the agreement provided for deposit of the parties' stock with irrevocable stock powers conferring on a group of fiduciaries exclusive voting powers over the pooled stock. The court distinguished the *Ringling* agreement, pointing out that it did not create a proxy empowering someone to vote another's shares.[5] In response to this decision, the Delaware legislature enacted a provision stating that the voting trust statute "shall not be deemed to invalidate any voting or other agreement among stockholders or any irrevocable proxy which is not otherwise illegal."[6] In states that do not have this explicit legislative declaration, the Delaware court's reasoning remains a factor to be considered in drafting pooling agreements.[7]

A shareholders' agreement containing a valid irrevocable proxy has the same effect functionally as an ordinary shareholders' pooling agreement that the courts will specifically enforce; it follows that considerations governing the validity of the

---

§14.06   [1] F. Hodge O'Neal & Robert B. Thompson, Close Corporations: Law and Practice §5.08 (3d ed. 1998).

[2] *See* Model Business Corp. Act §7.31 (1984); Former Model Business Corp. Act §34 (1969).

[3] Ringling Bros.-Barnum & Bailey Combined Shows, Inc. v. Ringling, 53 A.2d 441 (Del. 1947), *modifying* 49 A.2d 603 (Del. Ch. 1946).

[4] Abercrombie v. Davies, 130 A.2d 338 (Del. 1957), *remanded,* 131 A.2d 822 (Del. Ch. 1957).

[5] 130 A.2d at 346.

[6] Del. Code Ann. tit. 8, §218(d) (2001).

[7] *See* DeFelice v. Garon, 395 So. 2d 658 (La. 1980).

two should be the same. In either instance, if the agreement has a legitimate business purpose, it should be given effect in accordance with the intentions of the parties.[8]

§14.07   Use of Charter or Bylaw Provisions in Lieu of Shareholders' Agreements

Objectives sought in shareholders' agreements can sometimes be achieved by using special charter or bylaw provisions. For example, charter or bylaw clauses imposing an extraordinarily high quorum or voting requirement for shareholder and director action have frequently been employed to allocate control within a close corporation. Such provisions have the effect of giving minority shareholders a veto power over corporate decisions.[1]

In a leading vintage New York case,[2] the court invalidated as contrary to the statutory scheme of corporate governance bylaws requiring: (1) the unanimous vote of the shareholders for shareholder action; (2) the unanimous vote of the shareholders to elect the directors; and (3) the unanimous vote of directors for board of directors action. The court upheld a fourth bylaw requiring the unanimous vote of the shareholders to amend the bylaws. The decision was legislatively repudiated by a statute authorizing the placing of high vote requirements for shareholder or director action in a corporation's charter (but, note, not in its bylaws).[3] Further, almost all states now permit a corporation to insert in its charter a provision setting a high vote for shareholder and director action,[4] and some states permit high vote requirements to be placed in either the charter or the bylaws.[5] In addition, some courts hold that a charter or bylaw provision unanimously adopted by the shareholders may be treated as a contract among the shareholders and thus enforceable as long as there are no new nonapproving shareholders.[6] Even though high vote requirements are clearly permitted, their tendency to lead to deadlock has led some courts to construe them strictly so as to minimize their restrictive effect.[7]

Other special charter and bylaw provisions can be used to depart from the traditional corporate management pattern or to grant protection to minority

---

[8] F. Hodge O'Neal & Robert B. Thompson, Close Corporations: Law and Practice §5.13 (3d ed. 1998); Henry W. Ballantine, Voting Trusts, Their Abuses and Regulation, 21 Tex. L. Rev. 139, 142 (1942).

§14.07 [1] *See* 1 F. Hodge O'Neal & Robert B. Thompson, Close Corporations: Law and Practice ch. 4 (3d ed. 1998) for guidance on the planning and drafting of veto arrangements.

[2] Benintendi v. Kenton Hotel, Inc., 60 N.E.2d 829 (N.Y. 1945).

[3] N.Y. Bus. Corp. Law §616 (McKinney Supp. 2002). *See* Sutton v. Sutton, 614 N.Y.S.2d 369 (1994).

[4] *See, e.g.,* Cal. Corp. Code §§204 (West 1990), 602 (West Supp. 2002); Ill. Ann. Stat. ch. 805, §§5/7.60, 5/8.15 (Smith-Hurd 1993).

[5] *See, e.g.,* Del. Code Ann. tit. 8, §141(b), 216 (2001); Model Business Corp. Act §8.24(c) (1984).

[6] *E.g.,* E. K. Buck Retail Stores v. Harkert, 62 N.W.2d 288 (Neb. 1954).

[7] *See* Blount v. Taft, 246 S.E.2d 763 (N.C. 1978) (finding that bylaws calling for across the board unanimity could be repealed or amended by a simple majority in conformance with the statutory norm).

shareholders. Among special provisions that may be found useful in particular circumstances are the following: clauses requiring cumulative voting for directors; clauses abolishing the board of directors or restricting its powers; clauses authorizing or prohibiting informal operation of the corporation; clauses strengthening shareholders' rights to inspect corporate books and records; clauses controlling dividends and other distributions to shareholders; clauses defining shareholders' preemptive rights; clauses dealing with deadlocks among shareholders and directors; clauses imposing restrictions on the transfer of shares; clauses requiring shareholder approval of officer compensation; clauses giving a shareholder power to dissolve the corporation; clauses prohibiting corporate loans to officers or directors; and clauses providing for arbitration or some other method for resolving disputes among the shareholders.

C. RESTRICTIONS ON THE TRANSFER OF SHARES

§14.08 Restrictions on the Transferability of Shares; Reasons for Restrictions; Types of Restrictions

In the absence of valid restrictions on their transferability, corporate shares are freely transferable, and the corporation may not refuse to accept a bona fide transferee as a shareholder.[1] In publicly held corporations, free transferability of shares is a valuable attribute in that it encourages contributions to corporate capital by a multitude of investors. In closely held corporations, on the other hand, the participants usually do not want shares to be freely transferable. Considerable latitude is allowed the participants in imposing share transfer restrictions; restrictions will usually be sustained unless palpably unreasonable under the circumstances.[2] Restrictions may be imposed by the articles of incorporation, the bylaws, or a shareholders' agreement.

Participants in a close corporation may want to restrict the transferability of shares for a number of reasons. Because of the close working relationship that often exists among owners and managers, they may want to retain power to select future associates and thus be able to exclude persons who will not be congenial or will not fit into the management team. Further, the participants may desire to restrict the transferability of shares to prevent their purchase by competitors or other persons unfriendly to the corporation.[3] They may also impose transfer restrictions to prevent any one shareholder from gaining absolute control of the

---

§14.08 [1] Mark S. Rhodes, Transfer of Stock §5:1 (6th ed. 1985); 12 William Fletcher, Cyclopedia of Corporations §5452.

[2] Goldberg v. United Parcel Serv., 605 F. Supp. 588 (E.D.N.Y. 1985); Hamel v. White Wave, Inc., 689 P.2d 709, 711 (Colo. Ct. App. 1984).

[3] This can be a useful device to prevent competitors from acquiring control of a corporation. *See* Joseph E. Seagram & Sons, Inc. v. Conoco, Inc., 519 F. Supp. 506 (D.C. Del. 1981); Bechtold v. Coleman Realty Co., 79 A.2d 661 (Pa. 1951), noted in 25 Temp. L.Q. 213 (1951), 100 U. Pa. L. Rev. 133 (1951).

C. Restrictions on the Transfer of Shares

corporation by purchasing colleagues' stock. Another reason for restricting the transferability of shares is to preserve the corporation's eligibility to elect the tax status provided by Subchapter S of the Internal Revenue Code[4] or its eligibility to elect to be governed by special close corporation legislation in a number of states requiring close corporations to restrict the transfer of their stock.

There are many different types of share transfer restrictions.[5] The most widely used is the so-called first-option or refusal,[6] which grants the corporation or the other shareholders a right to purchase shares at a set price or at the price offered by a third party, respectively, if a holder decides to sell or otherwise transfer her shares.[7] Other types of transfer restrictions are as follows: (1) absolute prohibitions against transfer; (2) prohibitions against transfer to designated classes of persons, such as competitors;[8] (3) limitation of transfers to stated classes of persons—for example, descendants of the corporation's founders or residents of a designated American state; (4) "consent restraints" that prohibit the disposition of stock without approval of the corporation's directors or shareholders or a stated percentage of one of those groups;[9] and (5) options giving the corporation or the other shareholders the right to purchase the shares of a holder on his death or disability,[10] on the termination of his employment with the corporation,[11] or on the occurrence of some other event. Somewhat related functionally to restrictions on the transfer of stock are buyout agreements, whereby the shareholder agrees to sell stock, and the corporation or the other shareholders agree to buy it, on the occurrence of a stated contingency, such as the shareholder's death or retirement. Such an agreement stipulates a transfer price or sets out a formula for determining price.[12] Mention should also be made of charter provisions that empower the corporation to redeem ("call") a holder's stock either generally at the corporation's option or on termination of the holder's employment with the corporation.[13] Courts have often been called on to pass on the validity of transfer

---

[4] By preventing transfer to a shareholder who does not qualify under Subchapter S or who will refuse to consent to the corporation's election of Subchapter S. *See* I.R.C. §§1371-1373 (1988). Restrictions on the transfer of stock are also useful in implementing exemption from the 1933 Securities Act's registration provisions. *See* 15 U.S.C. §§77b(a)(11), 77d(1), (2) (2000).

[5] *See* 12 William Fletcher, Cyclopedia of Corporations §5461.1; 2 F. Hodge O'Neal & Robert B. Thompson, Close Corporations: Law and Practice §7.05 (3d ed. 1998); William H. Painter, Corporate and Tax Aspects of Closely Held Corporations, §3.1 (2d ed. 1981 & Supp. 1985).

[6] *See, e.g.,* Hall v. Tennessee Dressed Beef Co., 957 S.W.2d 536 (Tenn. 1997) (implying notice requirement from right of first refusal).

[7] *See, e.g.,* Tribune Publishing Co. v. Commissioner, 731 F.2d 1401 (9th Cir. 1984).

[8] *See, e.g.,* Martin v. Villa Roma, Inc., 182 Cal. Rptr. 382 (Ct. App. 1982).

[9] *See* Ogden v. Culpepper, 474 So. 2d 1346 (La. Ct. App. 1985); Hill v. Warner, Berman & Spitz, 484 A.2d 344 (N.J. Super. Ct. 1984).

[10] *See* In re Dissolution of Penepent Corp., 96 N.Y.2d 186, 192, 726 N.Y.S.2d 345, 750 N.E.2d 47, 50 (2001).

[11] *See, e.g.,* Stephenson v. Drever, 947 P.2d 1301 (Cal. 1997).

[12] *See* Helms v. Duckworth, 249 F.2d 482 (D.C. Cir. 1957); Horne v. Drachman, 280 S.E.2d 338 (Ga. 1981).

[13] Hamel v. White Wave, Inc., 689 P.2d 709 (Colo. Ct. App. 1984); Groves v. Rosemound Improvement Ass'n, 413 So. 2d 925 (La. Ct. App. 1982). The right to purchase may be given to the other shareholders rather than the corporation. *See* Galler v. Galler, 203 N.E.2d 577, 579 (Ill. 1964).

restrictions against a claim that the restrictions constitute unreasonable restraints on the alienation of property.

§14.09   Legal Limits on the Use of Transfer Restrictions

Courts have always looked with disfavor on absolute stock transfer restrictions unlimited in time, regardless of whether they are included in a corporation's articles or bylaws, or in a shareholders' agreement.[1] The courts have, however, generally upheld restraints that they consider reasonable in light of all the circumstances.[2] In passing on the validity of transfer restrictions, the courts have considered a number of factors, including the following: the corporation's size, the extent of the restraint on the holder's power to alienate the shares, the length of time the restriction is to remain in effect, and whether the restriction is conducive to the attainment of corporate objectives and otherwise promotes the corporation's best interests. Generally, courts are more willing to recognize the validity of stock transfer restrictions in close corporations than in publicly held enterprises. However, there are limits on the enforceability of clearly unreasonable restrictions.[3]

The validity of transfer restrictions has frequently been challenged where a great disparity exists between the transfer price provided in the restrictions and the value of the shares. A few courts have held that a restriction, such as a first-option provision, which requires the transfer of shares for considerably less than their value, is an unreasonable restraint on alienation and is thus invalid.[4] Shareholders are not likely to sell their shares if they must first offer them to the corporation or other shareholders at a price that is far below their fair value. Thus a large gap between the option price in a first-option arrangement and the current value of shares may for practical purposes effectively create what is virtually an absolute restraint on alienation.[5] Nevertheless, the great majority of the courts have not invalidated transfer restrictions on the basis that they required the transfer of shares at a price below their value. Even when the value of shares has appeared to be ten, twenty, or even a thousand times greater than the transfer price, courts have sustained the restrictions.[6]

In many cases, the transfer price was not purposely set low initially; instead it fell below the shares' real value as the company prospered and the value of its

---

§14.09   [1] See Hill v. Warner, Berman & Spitz, 484 A.2d 344 (N.J. Super. Ct. 1984).

[2] See, e.g., Groves v. Prickett, 420 F.2d 1119, 1122 (9th Cir. 1970).

[3] See, e.g., Man O War Restaurants, Inc. v. Martin, 932 S.W.2d 366 (Ky. 1996) (provision in employment contract requiring employee to sell stock back to the corporation for the price originally paid was voided based on the court's strong public policy against forfeiture).

[4] B & H Warehouse, Inc. v. Atlas Van Lines, Inc., 490 F.2d 818 (5th Cir. 1974).

[5] Cf. Man O War Restaurants, Inc. v. Martin, 932 S.W.2d 366 (Ky. 1996) (provision in employment contract requiring employee to sell stock back to the corporation for the price originally paid was voided based on the court's strong public policy against forfeiture).

[6] See, e.g., Helms v. Duckworth, 249 F.2d 482 (D.C. Cir. 1957) (upholding agreement whereby deceased shareholder's estate received only $10 per share for stock worth $80 per share).

C. Restrictions on the Transfer of Shares

shares increased. Even when the transfer price is not fixed in the restriction but is to be determined by formula, the formula price often does not reflect share value accurately for any significant period of time after the restriction is imposed.[7] In upholding these restrictions, the courts have sometimes pointed out that the transfer price was fair and equitable at the time it was adopted.[8] In many cases, however, courts have upheld restrictions where a disparity between value and transfer price existed at the time the restriction was imposed.[9]

In the early cases some courts held that "consent restraints"—that is, restrictions that prohibit transfers unless approved by the directors or other shareholders—were invalid as contrary to public policy and as imposing undue restraints on alienation of property.[10] Many modern courts, however, uphold consent restraints.[11] In a few jurisdictions, however, the validity of consent restraints is still questionable because early decisions have not been overruled.[12]

Since the 1960s most states have enacted legislation governing the validity of stock transfer restrictions. The wording and the substance of the legislation varies from state to state. The Delaware statute provides that stock transfer restrictions or restrictions on the amount of securities that may be owned by any person or group may be imposed either by a corporation's certificate of incorporation, its bylaws, or an agreement among its security holders or among such holders and the corporation, but that a restriction will not be binding with respect to securities issued before adoption of the restriction unless the holders of the securities are parties to an agreement or voted in favor of the restriction.[13]

In addition, the special close corporation section of the Delaware statute, which requires that all of a close corporation's issued stock of all classes be subjected to one or more of the permitted restrictions,[14] provides that if a transfer restriction is held to be unauthorized, "the corporation shall nevertheless have an option, for a period of 30 days after the judgment setting aside the restriction becomes final, to acquire the restricted security at a price which is agreed upon by the parties, or if no agreement is reached as to price, then at the fair value as determined by the Court of Chancery."[15]

---

[7] See Note, Stock Transfer Restriction Enforced Despite Nominal Price Term, 16 Stan. L. Rev. 449, 452 (1964).

[8] Cutter Lab., Inc. v. Twining, 34 Cal. Rptr. 317 (Ct. App. 1963); In re Estate of Weinsaft, 647 S.W.2d 179 (Mo. App. 1983); Jones v. Harris, 388 P.2d 539 (Wash. 1964).

[9] E.g., In re Estate of Mather, 189 A.2d 586 (Pa. 1963).

[10] E.g., McNulta v. Corn Belt Bank, 45 N.E. 954, 959 (Ill. 1896) ("[B]y-law is illegal and void . . . because it seeks to keep the future action of the shareholders . . . in subjection to the will of the . . . directors.").

[11] E.g., Schaffer v. Below, 278 F.2d 619 (3d Cir. 1960) (transfer of shares in violation of consent restraint passed equitable title but not legal title to transferee); People ex rel. Rudaitis v. Galskis, 233 Ill. App. 414 (1924) (restraint on transfer held reasonable and valid).

[12] See, e.g., Minstar Acquiring Corp. v. AMF, Inc., 621 F. Supp. 1252 (S.D.N.Y. 1985) (plan that provided for nontransferability of rights and adopted in face of hostile tender offer, stricken as unreasonable restraint on alienability).

[13] Del. Code Ann. tit. 8, §202(b) (2001).

[14] Id. at §342(a)(2).

[15] Id. at §349.

Similarly, the Revised Model Business Corporation Act provides that a corporation's articles of incorporation or bylaws or an agreement among shareholders or between shareholders and the corporation may impose restrictions on the transfer of shares but that a restriction does not affect shares issued before the restriction was adopted unless the holders of the shares are parties to the restriction agreement or vote in favor of the restriction.[16] The Model Statutory Close Corporation Supplement to the Model Business Corporation Act states that an interest in shares of a statutory close corporation—that is, shares of a corporation that has adopted the status made available by the supplement, "may not be voluntarily or involuntarily transferred, by operation of law or otherwise, except to the extent permitted by the articles of incorporation . . . ."[17] However, the supplement provides a rather extensive list of exceptions to this prohibition.[18]

The Revised Model Business Corporation Act[19] and the general corporation statutes in a number of states require that restrictions be noted conspicuously on the front or back of a share certificate.[20] Unless the restriction is stated, both the Model Business Corporation Act and the Uniform Commercial Code provide that the restriction is not enforceable against a transferee without knowledge.[21]

A further source of caution is the narrow construction courts frequently give to the terms of the transfer restriction. For example, the provision that "no stock in the corporation may be issued, transferred, sold or hypothecated to any person who is not a blood descendant" was held not to reach a testamentary disposition outside the family.[22] Courts frequently appear to manifest bare tolerance of transfer restrictions by strictly construing their scope.[23] The failure of a shareholder to abide by the terms of a valid transfer restriction has been treated as a breach of that shareholder's fiduciary duty.[24]

---

[16] Model Business Corp. Act §6.27(a) (1984).

[17] Model Statutory Close Corp. Supp. §11(a).

[18] *Id.* at §§11(b), 12. *See also id.* §13 (attempted share transfer in breach of prohibition), §14 (compulsory purchase of shares after death of shareholder).

[19] Model Business Corp. Act §6.27(b) (1984).

[20] *See* Ling & Co. v. Trinity Sav. & Loan Ass'n, 482 S.W.2d 841 (Tex. 1972) (general reference in small type on back of certificate to existence of share restriction in articles not conspicuous but may have placed holder on notice).

[21] Model Business Corp. Act §6.27(b) (1984); U.C.C. §8-204 (1991). The corporation and its transfer agent were held liable in Dean Witter Reynolds, Inc. v. Selectronics, Inc., 594 N.Y.S.2d 174 (N.Y. Sup. Ct. App. Div. 1993), for failing to place a restriction on shares required because they had been issued pursuant to an exemption from registration under the securities laws. The shares had been pledged as collateral for a loan and the pledgor sued the corporation and its transfer agent when it was barred from disposing of the shares.

[22] *See* In re Estate of Martin, 490 P.2d 15 (Ariz. Ct. App. 1971).

[23] *See, e.g.,* In re Estate of Riggs, 540 P.2d 361 (Colo. Ct. App. 1975) (generally worded right of first refusal does not reach testamentary dispositions).

[24] *See* Yiannatsis v. Stephanis, 653 A.2d 275 (Del. 1995).

D. DISSOLUTION AND OTHER REMEDIES FOR DISSENSION

§14.10   Dissension in the Close Corporation

Dissension among the owners of a close corporation has a heavy impact on the enterprise. Because of the participants' intimately close working relationship, in most close corporations, once dissatisfaction or distrust has developed, intracorporate friction is likely to continue to grow. Dissatisfied shareholders of a publicly held corporation have a ready market for their shares, whereas an interest in a closely held corporation does not have a readily available market, at least if the interest is not a controlling one. The marketability of a minority interest in a close corporation is further narrowed if the corporation is racked by dissension. Even if a buyer can be found for a minority interest, the price may be sharply discounted.[1] Furthermore, the existence of transfer restrictions may enable an antagonistic associate to thwart an unhappy shareholder's sale of close corporation shares. Dissension and the inability of unhappy shareholders to get out sometimes results in serious and continuing strife among the shareholders and managers[2] and may result in extensive litigation and serious harm to the corporation and the shareholders.[3]

Deadlocks among the shareholders and in the directorates of closely held corporations may occur because of the way voting shares and positions on the board are distributed.[4] Shares are sometimes divided equally among two or more

---

§14.10   [1] The New Jersey Supreme Court has addressed the issue of whether to apply a marketability discount when a court orders a shareholder to sell his or her stock, concluding that the court must take into account what is fair and equitable. More specifically, a marketability discount cannot be used by the controlling or oppressing shareholders to benefit themselves to the detriment of the minority or oppressed shareholders. Lawson Mardon Wheaton, Inc. v. Smith, 734 A.2d 738, 752 (N.J. 1999); Balsamides v. Protameen Chems., Inc., 734 A.2d 721, 738 (N.J. 1999). In *Lawson* the court declined to apply a marketability discount, since no extraordinary circumstances existed. However, in *Balsamides,* a case in which the oppressing shareholder was ordered to sell his shares to the oppressed shareholder, the court found that a 35 percent marketability discount was appropriate. Otherwise, the remaining (oppressed) shareholder would be forced to absorb the full reduction for lack of marketability if he sold the company at a future date. Balsamides v. Protameen Chems., Inc., 734 A.2d 721, 735-736 (N.J. 1999). The court noted that an oppressing shareholder who has instigated the problems should not benefit at the expense of the oppressed, and that ordering a buyout at an undiscounted price under these circumstances would penalize the oppressed shareholder. *Id.* at 738. *Accord* Advanced Communication Design, Inc. v. Follett, 601 N.W.2d 707, 711 (Minn. Ct. App. 1999) (citing *Lawson* and *Balsamides* and holding that marketability discount could not be applied to minority shareholder's shares when sale resulted in buyer becoming sole owner of corporation). For a general discussion of marketability discounts in valuing closely held businesses, *see* Mukesh Bajaj, David J. Denis, Stephen P. Ferris & Atulya Sarin, Fair Value and Marketability Discounts, 27 J. Corp. L. 89 (2001).

[2] *See, e.g.,* Hall v. John S. Isaacs & Sons Farms, Inc., 163 A.2d 288 (Del. 1960). *See* Carlos L. Israels, The Sacred Cow of Corporate Existence: Problems of Deadlock and Dissolution, 19 U. Chi. L. Rev. 778, 781 (1952); Note, 1972 Duke L.J. 653; Comment, 58 Neb. L. Rev. 791 (1979).

[3] *See, e.g.,* In re Radom & Neidorff, Inc., 119 N.E.2d 563 (N.Y. 1954); In re Weiss, 301 N.Y.S.2d 839 (App. Div. 1969).

[4] A "deadlocked" corporation is one that, because of decision or indecision of the shareholders, cannot perform its corporate powers. However, a minority shareholder's mere disagreement with

shareholders or groups of shareholders. And it is not unusual for a close corporation to have an even number of directors; thus a deadlock of directors is likely to occur. Further, in an effort to protect themselves against the power generally vested in shareholders and directors to determine corporate policy by simple majority vote, minority shareholders often bargain for and obtain a veto over corporate policies and decisions.[5] Such a veto power increases the risk of corporate paralysis.[6] As one Virginia court eloquently stated, "A recalcitrant . . . shareholder may embalm his corporation and hold it helpless . . . in a state of suspended animation."[7]

Despite the frequency of dissension and deadlock in close corporations, in some states neither legislatures nor courts have provided satisfactory solutions. Therefore, during the organization of a close corporation, counsel must anticipate such problems and may need to provide special contractual arrangements to resolve them. These arrangements usually are set up in the corporation's charter or bylaws or in a shareholders' agreement. They typically take one or more of the following forms: (a) provisions for the buyout of the interests of aggrieved shareholders, (b) the creation of special dissolution rights and procedures, or (c) undertakings to arbitrate disputes. Further possibilities to consider to avoid locking unhappy shareholders into a corporation for an indefinite period of time are: (d) limiting the life of the corporation rather than giving it perpetual existence, (e) setting up a voting trust that gives trustees the power to vote for dissolution, and, where legal, (f) issuing stock that is convertible into notes or debentures.

§14.11 Dissolution for Deadlock

Among the several bases for involuntary dissolution, most corporate statutes include deadlock within the board of directors or among the shareholders. Section 14.30(2) of the Model Business Corporation Act is representative of the position taken by most of the states:

> (i) the directors are deadlocked in the management of the corporate affairs, the shareholders are unable to break the deadlock, and irreparable injury to the corporation is threatened or being suffered, or the business and affairs of the corporation can no longer be conducted to the advantage of the shareholders generally, because of the deadlock; . . .[1]

In fact, the various statutory expressions are but imprecise attempts to capture the true basis on which courts appear to order dissolution under their provi-

---

management's decision or dislike of another shareholder does not create a deadlock. Woodward v. Andersen, 627 N.W.2d 742, 751-752 (Neb. 2001).

[5] Roach v. Bynum, 403 So. 2d 187, 192 (Ala. 1981).

[6] Veto arrangements are popular. In most jurisdictions, a valid way of setting up effective veto arrangements is available. *See, e.g.,* Zion v. Kurtz, 405 N.E.2d 681 (N.Y. 1980).

[7] Kaplan v. Block, 31 S.E.2d 893, 896-897 (Va. 1944).

§14.11 [1] Model Business Corp. Act §14.30(2)(i)(iii) (1984).

sions—namely, that irreconcilable differences exist between the contesting owners. Deadlock is truly a phenomenon of the closely held corporation; it would not long exist within the public corporation. Thus, when equal owners of a corporation are divided over whether the sole corporate asset should be sold or developed, there is little room for compromise. It is ironic that the remedy available in such a case, an order of dissolution, leads to the very result that the shareholder seeking the asset's sale has sought.[2] It is on such facts that some jurisdictions permit shareholders owning 50 percent of the shares to petition for voluntary dissolution.[3] Essentially, what is required is proof that the differences between the shareholders are such that it is no longer reasonable to expect that they will be able to resolve their differences.[4] Acrimony is not required, though it may be present.[5]

Thus statutory requirements such as "irreparable harm" or that the corporation is "unable to conduct business to the shareholders' advantage" are somewhat irrelevant to the courts' inquiry. Courts instead emphasize the deep divisions between the shareholders, the length of those divisions, and the unlikelihood of the division being corrected.[6] Courts do not inquire as to whether a business is going badly or is not expanding. Certainly the latter inquiry is at best problematic. Just how successful would a business be if cohesion existed among its managers and owners? Thus one can find more to commend in those statutes that authorize dissolution merely on proof of deadlock, believing this is harm enough.

§14.12 Oppression; Protecting Reasonable Expectations

When dissension or deadlock occurs in a corporation, the shareholders can voluntarily dissolve the enterprise, but voluntary dissolution requires the affirmative vote of holders of a majority of the shares in some jurisdictions and a two-thirds vote in others.[1] At one time the courts generally held that unless authority is conferred by statute, courts of equity had no authority over the suit of a minority

---

[2] *See* Gilligham v. Swan Falls Land & Cattle Co., 683 P.2d 895 (Idaho Ct. App. 1984).

[3] *See* In re Security Fin. Co., 317 P.2d 1 (Cal. 1957) (court will grant voluntary dissolution where 50 percent shareholder sought to put end to conflict, but court will exercise its equitable powers if necessary to protect interests of other shareholders).

[4] *See* Behrens Co. v. B. D. Rawls, 518 So. 2d 945 (Fla. Dist. Ct. App. 1987).

[5] *See* In re Hedberg-Friedheim & Co., 47 N.W.2d 424 (Minn. 1951) (director-owner constructed partition around desk to avoid conversation with fellow director-owners).

[6] *See* Behrens Co. v. B. D. Rawls, 518 So. 2d 945 (Fla. Dist. Ct. App. 1987); Kolbaum v. K. & K. Chevrolet, Inc., 244 N.W.2d 173 (Neb. 1976). For an older view refusing to order dissolution because the corporation was profitable although there were deep divisions between the equal shareholders, *see* In re Radom & Neidorff, Inc., 119 N.E.2d 563 (N.Y. 1954). The law has since been changed so that the result in *Radom & Neidorff* would not occur today. *See* N.Y. Bus. Corp. L. §§1102 (McKinney 1996), 1104 & 1111 (McKinney Supp. 2002).

§14.12 [1] *E.g.*, Model Business Corp. Act §14.02(e) (1984) (majority); Del. Code Ann. tit. 8, §275(b) (2001) (majority); N.Y. Bus. Corp. Law §1001 (McKinney Supp. 2002) (two-thirds vote); N.C. Gen. Stat. §55-14-02 (2001) (majority). Voluntary dissolution is discussed in Chapter 26.

shareholder to order dissolution of a solvent corporation or to appoint a receiver to distribute its assets and liquidate its affairs.[2] A number of courts, however, recognized that, in the absence of other adequate remedy, there are circumstances under which a court of equity should afford relief to shareholders against fraud and gross mismanagement by appointing a receiver and winding up a solvent corporation.[3] Such relief may be appropriate in instances of deadlock among the shareholders and directors, failure of corporate purpose, or gross mismanagement by those in control of the corporation.[4]

In many states modern corporation statutes now expressly give the courts power to dissolve a corporation in a suit by a minority shareholder if the directors and majority shareholders are guilty of fraud, gross mismanagement, or oppression of minority shareholders, or if such dissension exists among the shareholders that the corporate business cannot be carried on or it appears that a winding up of the corporate affairs is necessary to protect the rights of the complaining shareholder.[5] The corporation statutes vary greatly from state to state both on the kinds of situations that trigger a court's power to dissolve and in the percentage of shares a person must hold to be entitled to petition for dissolution. In some states the statutory grounds for involuntary dissolution are rather narrow and specific, such as a deadlock in the board of directors that the shareholders cannot break; in other states the grounds for involuntary dissolution are stated in broad terms, such as for "just or sufficient cause" or "where reasonably necessary for the protection of shareholders."[6]

Public corporations are rarely dissolved involuntarily. The remedy of involuntary dissolution thrives within close corporations, being not merely a mechanism to remedying hopeless deadlocks but also an important avenue for remedying oppressive misconduct by the majority stockholders. Whereas the oppressed minority in a public corporation protect themselves through private actions seeking damages or equitable relief, oppressed shareholders in a close corporation frequently file an action seeking the corporation's dissolution as a means to salvage their investment in the venture. It is therefore safe to say that over the past two decades there has been an extensive and significant melding of fiduciary standards to state involuntary dissolution statutes such that it is difficult to isolate the doctrine of fiduciary obligation in close corporations from involuntary dissolution. Difficult though it be to so isolate the two areas, the

[2] *See* Grocery Supply, Inc. v. McKinley Park Serv., Inc., 128 F. Supp. 594 (D.C. Alaska 1955); Wall & Beaver St. Corp. v. Munson Line, Inc., 58 F. Supp. 101, 108 (D. Md. 1943).

[3] *See* Ross v. American Banana Co., 43 So. 817 (Ala. 1907); Noble v. Gadsden Land & Improv. Co., 31 So. 856 (Ala. 1901); Bowen v. Bowen-Romer Flour Mills Corp., 217 P. 301 (Kan. 1923), *later appeal,* 266 P. 65 (Kan. 1928); Miner v. Belle Isle Ice Co., 53 N.W. 218 (Mich. 1892); Thwing v. Miowa Co., 158 N.W. 820 (Minn.), *modified,* 159 N.W. 564 (Minn. 1916).

[4] Tower Hill-Connellsville Coke Co. v. Piedmont Coal Co., 64 F.2d 817 (4th Cir.), *cert. denied,* 290 U.S. 675 (1933).

[5] *See, e.g.,* Cal. Corp. Code §1800 (West 1990); Del. Code Ann. tit. 8, §226 (2001); N.Y. Bus. Corp. Law §1104 (McKinney 1986); Former Model Business Corp. Act §97 (1969); Model Business Corp. Act §§14.30, 14.31 (1984).

[6] *See, e.g.,* Lowder v. All Star Mills, Inc., 330 S.E.2d 649, 655 (N.C. Ct. App. 1985) (court has power to liquidate an action by shareholder when "reasonably necessary for the protection of the rights or interests of the complaining shareholder").

D. Dissolution and Other Remedies for Dissension

materials in this chapter will nevertheless make an attempt at doing so. The material in the balance of this section focuses almost entirely on how the courts have used the "reasonable expectations" of the shareholders to guide the court in deciding whether grounds for invoking the state's dissolution statute have been established.

In the typical case, the "reasonable expectation" doctrine emerges in a suit by the minority shareholder seeking a close corporation's dissolution under a statute that authorizes involuntary dissolution when those in control of the company have acted in an oppressive manner,[7] or dissolution is necessary to protect the rights or interests of the petitioning stockholder or stockholders generally. Frequently, the specific dissolution provision is limited to close corporations or corporations with a small number of stockholders.[8] In broad overview, the courts that have embraced the talisman of the shareholder's reasonable expectations consider conduct that defeats those expectations as being oppressive or as grounds for concluding dissolution is necessary for the protection of that shareholder.

To be protectable, expectations should be part of an understanding, explicit or implicit, between the participants in the corporation.[9] In a leading case, the North Carolina Supreme Court in *Meiselman v. Meiselman*[10] held that reasonable expectations should be determined on a case-by-case basis, using the full history of the relationship in question—from inception through any later developments.[11] *Meiselman* also required that the expectations must be compared with and known to the other stockholders, so privately held expectations are not reasonable.[12] Furthermore, a minority shareholder's reasonable expectations must be balanced against what is reasonably believed to be in the best interests of the corporation.[13]

Meiselman was a dispute between two brothers: One brother held a majority of the stock and was in control of the corporation; the other brother, because he had fallen from grace with the family, had only a minority interest in the company. After the controlling stockholder had removed his brother from his employment position with the company, the removed brother sought the firm's dissolution on the grounds that "liquidation is reasonably necessary for the protection of the

---

[7] Professor Thompson reports that 37 states base relief on oppression or language that can be similarly interpreted. *See* Robert B. Thompson, The Shareholder Cause of Action for Oppression, 48 Bus. Law. 699, 709 n.70 (1993).

[8] *See* N.J. Stat. Ann. §14A-12(7) (West Supp. 2002) (25 or fewer stockholders); N.Y. Bus. Corp. Law §1104-a (McKinney Supp. 2002) (shares are not publicly traded); Model Statutory Close Corp. Supp. §§40, 43 (fewer than 50 stockholders, and articles of incorporation state corporation is a close corporation).

[9] *See* Longwell v. Custom Benefit Programs Midwest, Inc., 627 N.W.2d 396, 399-400 (S.D. 2001) (reasonable expectations should be analyzed in light of the entire history of the parties' relationship; the court must balance the minority shareholder's reasonable expectations against the corporation's ability to exercise its business judgment).

[10] 307 S.E.2d 551 (N.C. 1983).

[11] *Id.* at 563. *See also, e.g.*, Royals v. Piedmont Electric Repair Co., 529 S.E.2d 515 (N.C. App. 2000).

[12] 307 S.E.2d at 563.

[13] *See, e.g.*, Willis v. Bydalek, 997 S.W.2d 798 (Tex. App. 1999) (wrongful lockout did not establish oppression).

rights or interests of the complaining shareholder."[14] The court concluded that dissolution or other equitable relief was appropriate under the "rights or interests" language of the statute when:

> [The plaintiff] . . . (1) had one or more substantial reasonable expectations known or assumed by the other participants; (2) the expectation has been frustrated; (3) the frustration was without fault of the plaintiff and was in large part beyond his control; and (4) under all the circumstances of the case plaintiff is entitled to some form of equitable relief.[15]

Meiselman is the most liberal decision yet to define "reasonable expectations." The Meiselman brothers inherited their shares from their father, so their expectations were not those of co-founders of a business enterprise; theirs were expectations formed after the company was in operation. In extending *Meiselman* to its logical conclusion, reasonable expectations are evolutionary, not static. Also, the protectable expectations depend upon the surrounding circumstances. Thus, for example, continued employment by the corporation is not a protectable expectation of all minority shareholders who are also employees.[16] It therefore follows that not every termination of a shareholder's employment will be a breach of fiduciary duty.[17]

Using less sweeping language than that of *Meiselman,* the New York Court of Appeals in *In re Kemp & Beatley*,[18] acting under a statute that authorized dissolution for "illegal, oppressive or fraudulent" conduct, stated that oppression exists "when the majority conduct substantially defeats expectations that, objectively viewed, were both reasonable under the circumstances and were central to the petitioner's decision to join the venture."[19] The court held that an investor in a close corporation may reasonably expect to participate in the active management of the firm as well as to receive a fair return.[20] *Kemp & Beatley* held that dissolution was the only way that the two petitioners, who had been officers and shareholders in the firm for 35 and 42 years, could expect a reasonable return on their investment when, after one of them had resigned and the other had been fired, the firm changed its policies so that significant distributions from earnings were no longer based on stock ownership but on the basis of services to the corporation. In

---

[14] N.C. Gen. Stat. §55-125(a) (1955), since replaced by N.C. Gen. Stat. §55-14-30 (2001).

[15] 307 S.E.2d at 564. After remand for reconsideration of the facts in light of the court's reasonable expectation standard, the case was settled.

[16] *See, e.g.,* Harrison v. Netcentric Corp., 744 N.E.2d 622 (Mass. 2001) (applying Delaware law, upholding termination of minority shareholder as employee).

[17] *Id.*; Crowder Construction Co. v. Kiser, 517 S.E.2d 178 (N.C. App. 1999).

[18] 473 N.E.2d 1173 (N.Y. 1984).

[19] *Id.* at 1179. *See also, e.g.,* Landstrom v. Shaver, 561 N.W.2d 1, 7 (S.D. 1997), noted in 43 S.D. L. Rev. 218 (1998) ("The question has been resolved by considering oppressive actions to refer to conduct that substantially defeats the 'reasonable expectations' held by minority shareholders in committing their capital to the particular enterprise").

[20] 473 N.E.2d at 1178. *See also, e.g.,* Muellenberg v. Bikon Corp., 669 A.2d 1382 (N.J. 1996) (minority shareholder had protectable expectation that limited other two shareholders' ability to exercise control to freeze out the minority shareholder; court ordered the unusual remedy of a minority buy-out of the majority).

another case, the New Jersey Supreme Court held that reasonable expectations can be nonmonetary,[21] but required a stronger showing that the expectations include employment of persons other than the petitioning shareholder.[22]

The breadth of the reasonable-expectations standard is that, within the close corporation, participation in management—and certainly the receipt of a salary—are the rewards shareholders customarily seek when investing in a close corporation. This therefore conditions the power of the majority to sever the minority stockholder from the firm's payroll on there being either an adequate return to the owners through dividends or just cause for the employee's termination.[23] Even just cause for terminating an employee-owner may not be sufficient to avoid a court's intervention, as illustrated by *Gimpel v. Bolstein*,[24] where, even though the court refused to protect the salaried position of a co-owner who had engaged in embezzlement, the court nevertheless required the majority to devise some means to provide a financial return commensurate with the petitioning stockholder's investment in the firm. The protection of minority shareholders' interests are not limited to the closely held corporation principles discussed herein. Protectable expectations may exist on the simple basis of an enforceable agreement, even if not in writing.[25]

§14.13 Policy Questions Surrounding Dissolution and Alternative Remedies

Today, the remedy most frequently resulting from a court's finding that the state's dissolution statute was satisfied is an order requiring a buyout of the petitioner's shares or some other affirmative relief. There is statutory authority for courts ordering a buyout in many states, but courts have ordered buyouts in the absence of express statutory authorization.[1] The better view is for the courts to consider they have a full panoply of remedies available once the grounds proscribed in the state dissolution statute have been established. The severity of the petitioner's grievance as well as the relative rights of other stockholders and the corporation

---

[21] *See* Brenner v. Berkowitz, 634 A.2d 1019, 1029 (N.J. 1993) (nexus between alleged misconduct and the interest the plaintiff has in the corporation must be alleged).

[22] *Id.* at 1033-1034.

[23] *See, e.g.*, O'Donnel v. Marine Repair Serv., Inc., 530 F. Supp. 1199 (S.D.N.Y. 1982); In re Wiedy's Furniture Clearance Center Co., 487 N.Y.S.2d 901 (App. Div. 1985); Topper v. Park Sheraton Pharmacy, Inc., 433 N.Y.S.2d 359 (Sup. Ct. 1980). *See* Musto v. Vidas, 658 A.2d 1305, 1311 (N.J. Super. App. Div. 1995) (though buyout of the minority interest by the majority was justified and consistent with the "majoritarian principle" that underlies much of corporate law, the minority shareholder was entitled to have his salary continued for a few years as this was part of his original expectation in joining the firm).

[24] 477 N.Y.S.2d 1014 (1984).

[25] *See, e.g.*, Penley v. Penley, 332 S.E.2d 51, 64 (N.C. 1985) (protecting interests based on contract principles).

§14.13 [1] *See, e.g.*, Sauer v. Moffitt, 363 N.W.2d 269 (Iowa Ct. App. 1984); Maddox v. Norman, 669 P.2d 230 (Mont. 1983).

itself should guide the court in considering what relief is appropriate under the circumstances.[2] It is in this light that the Model Statutory Close Corporation Supplement sets forth nine types of relief (in addition to ordering dissolution or a buyout) that the court may order when it finds the bases for dissolution have been established.[3] In addition to court-ordered buyouts, the statutes of some states extend to the corporation or to the nonpetitioning stockholders a mechanism to avoid dissolution by purchasing the petitioning stockholder's shares at their "fair value."[4] The statutes providing this escape from an order of dissolution customarily provide procedures for a neutral party to determine a fair price for the petitioner's shares when the parties cannot reach an agreement.

The commentators are divided on the question of whether a liberal construction of a state dissolution statute is economically efficient. In a classic article, Professors Hetherington and Dooley[5] argue that minority stockholders in close corporations should have a right to require the majority to purchase their shares. They reason that equipping the minority with a "put" for their shares would serve as a low-cost protection against oppression as well as an incentive by the majority to exercise their control so as to maintain the minority's confidence.[6] Professor Hillman voices concern that allowing too easy an exit from the firm not only adds to the enterprise's instability but also is not likely to give sufficient consideration to the costs and burdens this approach visits upon the majority in finding the funds to acquire the minority's shares.[7]

---

[2] *See, e.g.*, Sauer v. Moffitt, 363 N.W.2d 269 (Iowa Ct. App. 1984) (partial liquidation and exemplary damages awarded instead of dissolution); In re Trocino, 482 N.Y.S.2d 670 (Sup. Ct. 1984) (dissolution appropriate when all other remedies inadequate).

[3] Model Statutory Close Corp. Supp. §41. The types of relief so ordered are:

(1) the performance, prohibition, alteration, or setting aside of any action of the corporation or of its shareholders, directors, or officers of or any other party to the proceedings;
(2) the cancellation or alteration of any provision in the corporation's articles of incorporation or bylaws;
(3) the removal from office of any director or officer;
(4) the appointment of any individual as a director or officer;
(5) an accounting with respect to any matter in dispute;
(6) the appointment of a custodian to manage the business and affairs of the corporation;
(7) the appointment of a provisional director (who has all the rights, powers, and duties of a duly elected director) to serve for the term and under the conditions prescribed by the court;
(8) the payment of dividends;
(9) the award of damages to any aggrieved party.

[4] *See, e.g.*, Cal. Corp. Code §2000 (West 1990); N.Y. Bus. Corp. Law §1118 (McKinney 2002).

[5] John A. C. Hetherington & Michael P. Dooley, Illiquidity and Exploitation: A Proposed Statutory Solution to the Remaining Close Corporation Problem, 63 Va. L. Rev. 1 (1977).

[6] *Id.* at 47-48.

[7] *See* Robert Hillman, The Dissatisfied Participant in the Solvent Business Venture: A Consideration of the Relative Performance of Partnerships and Close Corporations, 67 Minn. L. Rev. 1, 77-81 (1983). *See also* Frank Easterbrook & Daniel Fischel, Close Corporations and Agency Costs, 38 Stan. L. Rev. 271, 290 (1986).

D. Dissolution and Other Remedies for Dissension

The opposite positions taken by these commentators capture nicely the policy question that courts face in considering their approach to a petition asking the court to provide a means for the minority to exit the corporation with their investment. Consideration of the parties' expectations does not address the concerns that dissolution may be inefficient because of its impact on the resources of the majority and quite likely ultimately the corporation. The reasonable-expectations analysis only provides assurance that dissolution or another remedy is not inconsistent with the parties' probable intentions had they been prescient and contracted *ex ante* a solution for the problem that prompted the minority to seek dissolution. In this way, the reasonable-expectations standard may well be the quintessential illustration of the position taken by many economists that the corporation is but a nexus of contracts, so that the role of a court in response to a dissolution petition is to carry out the probable intent of the parties. This view not only is the embodiment of the reasonable-expectation standard but commends as well the panoply of other possible remedies, discussed above, that courts may substitute in place of ordering the corporation's dissolution or a buyout of the minority.

The current willingness of courts to protect the minority's expectations or to shield a stockholder from unfair treatment in a close corporation is a dramatic change from the position courts took on such matters not that many years ago, when dissolution or ordering a buyout were seen as drastic remedies. For example, in applying a former New York statute that required a showing that dissolution would be beneficial to the shareholders and not injurious to the public,[8] the New York Court of Appeals denied dissolution of a deadlocked corporation that was still operating profitably.[9] In repudiation of this result, New York amended its statute to provide that "dissolution is not to be denied merely because it is found that the corporate business has been or could be conducted at a profit."[10] The amended statute further provides an important consideration in deciding whether to dissolve by providing that in a dissolution proceeding brought by directors or shareholders "the benefit to the shareholders of a dissolution is of paramount importance."[11] The court's consideration of the benefit to the shareholders is included within the reasonable-expectations standard that is now followed in New York such that dissolution is appropriate even for a profitable firm.

Where authorized by statute, court appointment of a provisional director is considered less severe than dissolution or receivership and thus has been held to be appropriate where appointment of a receiver or involuntary dissolution would

[8] N.Y. Gen. Corp. Law §§103, 106, 109 (Thompson's 1939).

[9] In re Radom & Neidorff, Inc., 119 N.E.2d 563 (N.Y. 1954), *motion denied*, 120 N.E.2d 865 (N.Y. 1954), noted 68 Harv. L. Rev. 714 (1955). A corporation's profitability has been given weight by other courts. *See, e.g.*, Baker v. Commercial Body Builders, Inc., 507 P.2d 387 (Or. 1973).

[10] N.Y. Bus. Corp. Law §1111(b)(3) (McKinney 1986).

[11] *Id.* For a discussion of amendments to the New York act that have put it "more in harmony" with the Model Business Corporation Act, *see* Michael A. Schaeftler, Corporations, 31 Syracuse L. Rev. 129, 133-138 (1980).

not be.[12] In states not having statutes authorizing judicial appointment of a provisional director, insertion of a provision in the corporation's charter can achieve the functional equivalent of a statutory provisional director. For example, a corporation's charter can be amended to create a separate class of stock with no proprietary rights but with power to elect a director in the event the board becomes deadlocked; that class of shares can then be issued for nominal consideration to an impartial person, enabling that person to elect a deadlock-breaking director.[13] Another device is a charter provision for arbitration in the event of deadlock or dissension; this device can be useful as long as the dispute in question is arbitrable under the applicable state law.

The advantage of arbitration over litigation as a method of dispute settlement in a close corporation is that it is quicker and less expensive. Most objections to arbitration of intracorporate disputes are based on the supposed unfitness of the arbitral process for formulating corporate policy and making managerial decisions. Before deciding to use arbitration in a close corporation, the lawyer should carefully search the statues and judicial decisions of the state of incorporation for corporate norms that would either invalidate arbitration agreements in the particular business situation involved or would otherwise nullify their effectiveness.[14] Further, the lawyer should examine the state arbitration statute and applicable common law principles of the forums in which litigation may arise to determine the proper limits of arbitration.[15]

§14.14   Custodians' Resolution of Shareholder Deadlocks and Disputes

The terms "custodian" and "receiver" are frequently used interchangeably. A custodian is appointed when there is a stockholder or director deadlock or other extreme situation for which an extraordinary mechanism is needed to resolve the situation; a receiver is appointed only when the corporation is insolvent or is being liquidated.[1] The Delaware statute[2] and case law have greatly influenced the efforts of other states that include within their corporate statutes authority for the court to appoint a custodian as a means to resolve internal corporate disputes.

---

[12] In re Jamison Steel Corp., 322 P.2d 246 (Cal. Ct. App. 1958).

[13] Lehrman v. Cohen, 222 A.2d 800 (Del. 1966) (the Delaware court approved the issuance of such stock). *Cf.* Stroh v. Blackhawk Holding Corp., 272 N.E.2d 1 (Ill. 1971) (validating class of stock that had no proprietary rights—i.e., rights to dividends or assets on dissolution; its sole attribute was voting rights).

[14] *See* Ringling v. Ringling Bros.-Barnum & Bailey Combined Shows, 49 A.2d 603, 607 (Del. Ch. 1946), *modified*, 53 A.2d 441 (Del. 1947); Blum Folding Paper Box Co. v. Friedlander, 261 N.E.2d 382 (N.Y. 1970).

[15] *See* Meacham v. Jamestown, F & C. R.R., 105 N.E. 653 (N.Y. 1914).

§14.14   [1] *See* Andreae v. Andreae [1991-1992 Transfer Binder], Fed. Sec. L. Rep. (CCH) ¶96,571 at 92,652 (Del. Ch. 1992).

[2] Del. Code Ann. tit. 8, §226 (2001).

D. Dissolution and Other Remedies for Dissension

The Delaware statute authorizes the appointment of a custodian[3] in three distinct instances. First, in section 226(a)(1),[4] a custodian may be appointed if at any meeting held for the election of directors a division of the stockholders prevents the election of successors to the current directors whose terms have expired. There is no requirement under the Delaware statute either that the division among the shareholders necessarily must be equal or that they must have failed for more than one successive annual meeting.

The second basis for obtaining a custodian's appointment is provided in section 226(a)(2)[5] and arises when the business is suffering or is threatened with irreparable harm stemming from a division of the directors respecting the management of the corporation's affairs such that a vote required for action by the board of directors cannot be obtained and the stockholders are unable by voting to bring an end to the division among the directors.

Section 226(a)(3)[6] authorizes a custodian's appointment when the corporation has abandoned its business. In interpreting this provision, the court must walk a line between exercising its role of enforcing the state's statute, intended for the protection of the shareholders' interests, and deferring to the judgment of a board of directors resisting the appointment of a custodian.[7]

It is also within the court's equitable powers to appoint a custodian when those in control of the corporation have engaged in fraud or gross management or have otherwise created a condition of imminent danger of great loss to the corporation that otherwise can be avoided.[8]

§14.15 Fiduciary Duties in the Close Corporation

As the preceding sections of this chapter illustrate, both the legislatures and the courts have recognized the unique needs of the close corporation. In allowing special control devices, such as high vote requirements for shareholder and director action and shareholders' agreements that control action within the traditional province of the board of directors, the law has increasingly recognized the so-

---

[3] The same bases apply as well to the appointment of a receiver, subject to the qualification, *supra* note 1, that a receiver's charge is to preside over either an insolvent corporation or a solvent corporation's liquidation.

[4] Del. Code Ann. tit. 8, §226(a)(1) (2001).

[5] Del. Code Ann. tit. 8, §226(a)(2) (2001). *See, e.g.,* Niehenke v. Right O Way Transp., Inc., 1995 WL 767348 (Del. Ch. 1995) (appointing custodian in the face of deadlock in two-shareholder corporation).

[6] Del. Code Ann. tit. 8, §226(a)(3) (2001).

[7] *E.g.,* Francotyp-Postalia AG & Co. v. On Target Technology, Inc., 1998 WL 928382, 24 Del. J. Corp. L. 649 (Del. Ch. 1998) (refusing to appoint custodian).

[8] *See* Hall v. John S. Issacs & Sons Farms, Inc., 163 A.2d 288 (Del. 1960); Tansey v. Oil Producing Royalties, Inc., 133 A.2d 141 (Del. 1957) (strong showing of fraud or gross mismanagement is required); Andreae v. Andreae [1991-1992 Transfer Binder], Fed. Sec. L. Rep. (CCH) ¶96,571 at 92,652 (Del. Ch. 1992).

called "incorporated partnership."[1] A concurrent development has been the recognition of partnership-like fiduciary obligations running between the participants in close corporations.[2] The fiduciary duty exists among the close corporation's stockholders, and in appropriate cases continues even though the minority stockholder has been frozen out of his position as an officer of the corporation.[3]

That corporate directors and officers owe a fiduciary duty to their corporation is, of course, well established. Some early decisions[4] and even an occasional modern decision[5] treat this duty as running only to the corporation, not to its shareholders. Most decisions and some statutes, however, affirm that this duty is owed to the corporation's shareholders as well as to the corporation itself.[6] Further, most modern courts have accepted the principle that the controlling shareholders as well as the directors and officers owe a fiduciary duty to other shareholders—to public shareholders in a publicly held corporation and to minority shareholders in a close corporation.[7]

A landmark decision recognizing high fiduciary duties among shareholders in a close corporation was *Donahue v. Rodd Electrotype Co.*[8] In that case, a corporation's founder and his sons, to whom he had given some shares, caused the corporation to purchase a portion of the founder's remaining shares without giving the minority shareholder an opportunity to sell her shares to the corporation at the same price per share. The Supreme Judicial Court of Massachusetts analogized the relationship among close corporation owners to that of partners and held that the corporation's purchase from the founder had to be rescinded or the minority shareholder had to be given an opportunity to sell her shares to the corporation at the same price per share, since the strict partnership standard of "utmost good faith and loyalty" applies in a close corporation, in contrast to the "less stringent standard of fiduciary duty that applies to larger corporate structures."[9]

---

§14.15   [1] *See* William L. Cary, How Illinois Corporation May Enjoy Partnership Advantages: Planning for the Closely Held Firm, 48 Nw. U. L. Rev. 427 (1953).

[2] *See, e.g.,* Hollis v. Hill, 232 F.3d 460 (5th Cir. 2000).

[3] *See* Rexford Rand Corp. v. Ancel, 58 F.3d 1215, 1221 (7th Cir. 1995) (minority shareholder who two years earlier had been frozen out of the corporation breached duty by acquiring corporation's name after the corporation had been administratively dissolved). *But see* Advanced Communication Design, Inc. v. Follett, 601 N.W.2d 707, 711 (Minn. Ct. App. 1999) (minority shareholder did not have fiduciary duty to fellow shareholder, since they never operated as equals, or to corporation, since he was never a director and in no sense controlled the corporation).

[4] Carpenter v. Danforth, 52 Barb. 581 (N.Y. Sup. Ct. 1868); Robert S. Stevens, Corporations §150 (2d ed. 1949).

[5] *See, e.g.,* Lochhead v. Alacano, 662 F. Supp. 230 (D. Utah 1987) (applying Utah law); State Teachers Retirement Bd. v. Fluor Corp., 566 F. Supp. 939 (S.D.N.Y. 1982) (citing four decisions from mid-1800s).

[6] *See, e.g.,* Junker v. Crory, 650 F.2d 1349 (5th Cir. 1981); Berman v. Gerber Prods. Co., 454 F. Supp. 1310 (W.D. Mich. 1978).

[7] *See, e.g.,* Mardel Sec., Inc. v. Alexandria Gazette Corp., 320 F.2d 890 (4th Cir. 1963).

[8] 328 N.E.2d 505 (Mass. 1975), noted in 61 Cornell L. Rev. 986 (1976); 89 Harv. L. Rev. 423 (1975).

[9] 328 N.E.2d at 515. The approach taken by the court in *Donahue* is a logical extension of the landmark decision in Meinhard v. Salmon, 164 N.E. 545 (N.Y. 1928), in which Chief Judge Cardozo explained: "Joint adventurers, like copartners, owe to one another . . . the duty of the finest loyalty. . . . [They are] held to something stricter than the morals of the market place. Not honesty alone, but the punctilio of an honor the most sensitive, is then the standard of behavior." *Id.* at 546.

D. Dissolution and Other Remedies for Dissension

In yet another important decision, *Wilkes v. Springside Nursing Home, Inc.*,[10] the Supreme Judicial Court of Massachusetts applied the same strict fiduciary standard in protecting a minority shareholder against arbitrary elimination from the board of directors and discharge from company employment. In that case, the four equal owners of a nursing home had from the inception of the corporation been employed by the home and had participated in management and policy decisions as directors, each receiving the same amount of compensation. After a dispute the other three shareholders, in their capacity as majority members of the board of directors, terminated Wilkes's salary, and at the next annual meeting of shareholders the three failed to reelect Wilkes to the board. The court held that the removal of Wilkes from the board and from employment with the corporation breached fiduciary duties the other shareholders owed Wilkes.[11]

Not all jurisdictions, however, embrace the view that participants in a close corporation are subject to "heightened fiduciary responsibilities" or that those responsibilities are necessarily founded on a liberal construction of their reasonable expectations. The Delaware Supreme Court in *Nixon v. Blackwell*[12] reasoned that it was inappropriate to fashion ad hoc rules according minority shareholders rights not provided them by statute and which were not otherwise contracted for by the shareholders. Subsequently, in *Riblet Products Corp. v. Nagy*[13] the Delaware court rejected the right of the minority shareholder/employee that had been recognized in Massachusetts in the *Wilkes* decision.[14]

---

[10] 353 N.E.2d 657 (Mass. 1976).

On occasion courts have recognized a fiduciary duty running from the minority to the majority. For example, in A.W. Chesterton Co. v. Chesterton, 128 F.3d 1 (1st Cir. 1997), the court held that a disgruntled minority shareholder's transfer of stock that would destroy the corporation's Subchapter S tax status would be a breach of fiduciary duty to the majority shareholder.

[11] *Cf.* Merola v. Exergen Corp., 668 N.E.2d 351 (Mass. 1996) (notwithstanding fiduciary duty of majority, minority shareholder did not have an expectation of continued employment).

[12] Nixon v. Blackwell, 626 A.2d 1366, 1379 (Del. 1993). *Accord,* Riblet Products Corp. v. Nagy, 683 A.2d 37 (Del. 1996); Ueltzhoffer v. Ueltzhoffer, 1991 WL 271584, 17 Del. J. Corp. L. 1297 (Del. Ch. 1991), aff'd, 618 A.2d 90 (Del. 1992); Olsen v. Seifert, 1998 WL 1181710 (Mass. Super. 1998).

[13] 683 A.2d 37 (Del. 1996).

[14] *See also, e.g.,* Harrison v. NetCentric Corp., 744 N.E.2d 622, 627 (Mass. 2001).

CHAPTER 15

The Derivative Suit

A. CHARACTERISTICS OF THE DERIVATIVE SUIT

§15.01   Nature and Basis of Derivative Action

An almost necessary consequence of a wrong to a corporation is some impairment of the value of each shareholder's stock interest. As a general rule, however, shareholders are considered to have no direct individual right of action for corporation wrongs that impair the value of their investment. Injuries to the corporation such as those resulting from negligence, mismanagement, or fraud of its directors or officers normally are not dealt with as wrongs to the whole group of shareholders in their corporate capacity but rather as a violation of the corporation itself, which can be redressed in a suit by or on behalf of the corporation.[1]

The evolution of a proper method of redress by way of a shareholder's suit for corporate wrongs has been a tortuous one, with many troublesome problems. The famous English decision of *Foss v. Harbottle*[2] gave a somewhat grudging recognition to a remedy. A basis of equitable relief was found in the absence of any adequate remedy other than a suit instituted by individual shareholders asking protection of those rights to which the shareholders as a group in their corporate capacity were entitled. But the English court was exceedingly strict in laying down the conditions precedent to bringing such a suit, in that it required a suing shareholder to make prior demands for action both on the directors and on all the shareholders. These restrictions have been carried forward into current American law. Originally recognized by the courts in most states as well as in federal courts, the derivative suit today is regulated by statute or by court rules.[3]

We may question why certain types of misconduct must be redressed only by or through the corporation when the ultimate impact of the misconduct is visited, albeit indirectly, upon the corporation's owners. Would it not make far better sense to allow individual stockholders to seek their own recoveries? Individual suits by shareholders would not result in wasteful multiplicity of suits because the initiating stockholder could use modern class action procedures to sue on behalf of all stockholders.

There are at least three sound reasons that continue to support the continuing distinction between direct and derivative actions. To permit shareholders to sue separately whenever the value of their shares is diminished by a wrong to the corporation would conflict with (1) the separate-corporate-entity concept, (2) the prior rights of creditors, and (3) the duty of management to sue for the protection of all concerned. Further, it would result in confusion in ascertaining the

---

§15.01   [1] Dodge v. Woolsey, 59 U.S. (18 How.) 331 (1855); Stevens v. Lowder, 643 F.2d 1078 (5th Cir. 1981), *reh'g denied,* 652 F.2d 1001 (1981); EMI Ltd. V. Bennett, 738 F.2d 994 (9th Cir. 1984); Sparling v. Hoffman Constr. Co., 864 F.2d 635 (9th Cir. 1988).

[2] Eng. Rep. 189, 203 (Ch. 1843). *See* Hitchens v. Congreve, 38 Eng. Rep. 917, 922 (1828).

[3] *E.g.,* Fed. R. Civ. P. 23.1; N.Y. Bus. Corp. Law §627 (McKinney 1986). *Compare* Fed. R. Civ. P. 23, dealing with class actions.

A. Characteristics of the Derivative Suit

effect of partial recoveries by individuals on the damages recoverable by the corporation for the same wrongful act.[4] A single action by the corporation, or by a shareholder in a derivative suit on its behalf, at least in theory obtains redress for all the shareholders and also protects the priorities of creditors, who may be unable to collect their claims if corporate assets are recovered by the shareholders individually.

The derivative suit plaintiff is self-selected; without election or appointment he presents himself as spokesman for the corporate interest. Because the plaintiff usually has no significant financial interest in the corporation, the possible harmful economic effects of prosecuting the suit cannot be expected to guide his decision to litigate. The derivative suit plaintiff has a fiduciary relationship to the other stockholders of the corporation,[5] yet such a person is not a worthy candidate to decide by himself whether the corporate interest is served by suing on a contract the corporation has entered, a tort allegedly committed to the corporation's property, or any other matter whose initial impact was on the corporation. These are the types of decisions for which the discretionary judgment of the board of directors or its delegates are readily called into play.

As will be seen in succeeding sections, a faint aura of legitimacy accrues to the plaintiff's authority to represent the corporate interest when the demand requirement is excused or otherwise satisfied because the board of directors, due to its own failings or misconduct, is incapacitated from carrying out an independent assessment of the corporate interest served by the suit. To be sure, that aura is not nearly as bright as it would be had the corporation's board of directors, after an assessment from the corporation's perspective of the costs and benefits, crisply resolved to pursue the cause of action. Nevertheless, within the narrow band of factual settings in which the corporate cause of action is today allowed to proceed at the instance of the derivative suit plaintiff, there is a highly recognizable legitimacy to the right of the plaintiff and her lawyer, under the watchful eye of the derivative suit court, to vindicate the corporation's injury.

Various theories have been suggested to explain the ground on which an individual shareholder may be allowed to sue on a corporate right of action. One theory merely explains the suit as an exceptional procedure to give a remedy for a corporate wrong affecting the shareholders indirectly that would otherwise escape redress due, among other things, to concealment by director—or officer—wrongdoers.[6] It has also been said that "[t]he right of the stockholder to sue exists because of special injury to him for which otherwise he is without redress."[7]

---

[4] See Brooks v. Land Drilling Co., 564 F. Supp. 1518 (D. Colo. 1983); General Rubber Co. v. Benedict, 109 N.E. 96 (N.Y. 1915); Note, 2 U. Chi. L. Rev. 317 (1935).

[5] See Seeburg-Commonwealth Litig. [1974-1975 Transfer Binder], Fed. Sec. L. Rep. (CCH) & 94,969 (S.D.N.Y. 1975).

[6] General Elec. Co. v. Bucyrus-Erie Co., 563 F. Sup. 970 (D.N.Y. 1983); In re Longhorn Sec. Litig., 573 Supp. 255 (D. Okla. 1983); Foss v. Harbottle, 67 Eng. Rep. 189, 203 (Ch. 1843); Burland v. Earle [1902] A.C. 83, 93.

[7] Home Fire Ins. Co. v. Barber, 93 N.W. 1024, 1029 (Neb. 1903).

The idea that the plaintiff sues because of the special indirect damage to the plaintiff as a shareholder caused by the wrong to the corporation is not an adequate explanation of the basis of the derivative suit. It is more aptly said that "the plaintiff does not sue in his own right, but in that of the corporation."[8] Hence the terms "representative" or "derivative" suit.

A further view, recognized by a number of courts, analyzes the shareholder's suit as in effect a combination of two causes of action—that is, a proceeding having a dual nature. The individual shareholders may be regarded as having a right in equity to compel the assertion of a corporate right of action against the directors or other wrongdoers when the management wrongfully refuses to act. The proceeding may be viewed as a "propulsive" one, to accomplish in one proceeding (1) the enforcement of the obligation owed by the corporation to the plaintiff and to all its shareholders to enforce its claims and (2) the enforcement of the corporation's rights of action against the wrongdoers. The wrongdoers are joined as parties-defendant in order that the corporate duty and right of action may be enforced for the benefit of all in one proceeding.[9] The corporation is the beneficiary of any recovery in the suit.

A shareholder's derivative suit should not be confused with a class suit, in which shareholders having *individual* rights and causes of action against the corporation are represented by a member of the class of shareholders having the rights and causes of action; the transactions and the questions of law and fact involved in the suit are common to all members of the class. In other words, a class action is used for direct shareholder claims against the corporation.

Plaintiffs in a direct suit based on violations of their individual rights—as opposed to a derivative suit—seek redress of an injury peculiar to themselves as shareholders or a class of shareholders, not an injury to the corporation.[10] The suit is brought to enforce a personal cause of action arising from acts independent of wrongful conduct against the corporation; the plaintiff must demonstrate injury in an individual capacity.

A shareholder class action is simply an action on behalf of persons whose individual claims are identical or substantially similar but who are so numerous that their joining in a single action is impractical. This type of action is a practical and inexpensive way for numerous claimants, especially ones with small claims, to obtain relief by pooling their claims into one lawsuit brought by one or a few individuals for and on behalf of the entire group. A direct class action is thus available to corporate shareholders whenever their common injury is not derivative through injury to the corporate entity. As is pointed out in the next section, diffi-

---

[8] Ross v. Bernhard, 396 U.S. 531, 539 (1970).

[9] Hawes v. Oakland, 104 U.S. 450, 452 (1882); Liddy v. Urbanek, 707 F.2d 1222 (11th Cir. 1983); Rose Hall, Ltd. v. Chase Manhattan Overseas Banking Corp., 576 F. Supp. 107 (D. Del. Ch. 1983).

[10] "It is only where the injury sustained to one's stock is peculiar to himself alone, and does not fall alike upon other stockholders, that one can recover as an individual." 12B William M. Fletcher, Cyclopedia of Corporations §5913 (2000). Otherwise stated, "[f]or a shareholder to obtain a personal right of action there must be relations between him and the tort-feasor independent of those which the shareholder derives through his interest in the corporate assets and business." Green v. Victor Talking Mach. Co., 24 F.2d 378, 381 (2d Cir.), *cert. denied*, 278 U.S. 602 (1928).

cult questions may arise as to the categorization of a particular claim as direct or derivative.

Shareholder derivative suits are the principal remedy by which defrauded minority shareholders may call directors, officers, promoters, and controlling shareholders to account for mismanagement, diversion of assets, and fraudulent manipulation of corporate affairs. In some cases, however, in which a corporate injury results from wrongdoing, an individual right of action may also arise, and a shareholder may be permitted to sue and recover directly and individually for the loss she suffers.[11] For example, a shareholder who is injured by wrongdoing in connection with her initial purchase of stock may have a direct claim against the wrongdoers. Thus, many suits brought under common law rules or the securities acts for fraud in connection with the sale or purchase of securities will be direct, with the class action available where there is an injury common to a number of securities holders or former holders.[12] But, at least conceptually, claims for individual losses and the impairment in the value of shares due to corporate mismanagement are improper allegations in a derivative suit based on a corporate right of action.

§15.02   *Distinguishing the Shareholder's Individual Suit from the Derivative Suit*

As a rule, the shareholder's judicial remedy for mismanagement or other wrongful acts of directors, officers, or third parties is by a derivative or representative suit on behalf of the corporation. This result reflects not only the practical assessment that the misconduct's initial impact is on the corporation itself, with any stockholder harm being consequential to that impact, but also that the duty breached is one owed directly to the corporation such that it is the corporation's right that is violated by the breaching conduct.[1] The characterization of a particular cause of action as derivative or direct (which in appropriate cases may be brought as a class action) brings significant procedural differences, which are explored in succeeding sections. Because of these differences, the initial characterization of a suit can be of critical significance.

---

[11] Where a choice exists on whether to frame a complaint as a class action or a derivative suit, suing on behalf of a class avoids the restrictions to which derivative suits are subject and allows other shareholders to intervene in the litigation and share expenses. Prerequisites to maintaining class actions do exist. *See* Fed. R. Civ. P. 23. One drawback to a class action proceeding is that each named representative may be required to meet the federal jurisdictional amount requirement, whereas in a derivative action damage sustained by the corporation, rather than by the individual plaintiff, is the test. Zahn v. International Paper Co., 414 U.S. 291 (1973) (jurisdictional amount requirement in class action unsatisfied). *See generally* 7A Charles Alan Wright, Arthur R. Miller & Mary Kay Kane, Federal Practice and Procedure §§1756, 1759 (2001).

[12] For general discussions of class actions, *see* John C. Coffee, Jr., Rethinking the Class Action: A Policy Primer on Reform, 62 Ind. L.J. 625 (1987).

§15.02   [1] *See* Flynn v. Merrick, 881 F.2d 446 (7th Cir. 1989); Citibank N.A. v. Data Lease Fin. Corp., 828 F.2d 686 (11th Cir. 1987); Kramer v. Western Pac. Indus. 546 A.2d 348 (Del. 1988).

The basic distinction between a derivative and a direct action hinges on whether the aggrieved shareholder is claiming an injury to the corporation or the infringement of some right personal to her, although based on her status as a shareholder or otherwise—for example, as an employee. Thus, for example, a suit claiming mismanagement by the officers or directors has been described as a "classic derivative suit," as contrasted with an action to compel inspection of the corporate books, which is the plaintiff's individual claim against the corporation as the "real defendant."[2] On the other hand, the directors' gross negligence in approving the selling price of the company gives rise to an individual cause of action.[3] Thus it can be seen that in many instances shareholder suits are not so easily classified as either individual or derivative.

In distinguishing between individual suits and derivative actions, it is helpful to identify some of the underlying policy rationales. Requiring an injury to the corporation to be vindicated either in a suit brought by the corporation itself or in a derivative suit avoids multitudinous litigation that would result from individual shareholder suits.[4] However, the availability of class action treatment would appear a more direct manner to address this concern. A further policy rationale is that, because recoveries in derivative actions generally accrue to the corporation, the derivative suit thus provides a mechanism that assures that the fruits of the derivative suit are channeled so that the relative rights and interests of corporate creditors[5] and *all* shareholders[6] are preserved. This may well argue that the derivative suit mechanism is a necessary prophylaxis for the benefit of creditors. Nevertheless, one may question whether the courts could not appropriately tailor shareholder-based recoveries so as to prevent any fraud or harm to creditors.

Perhaps the true rationale for continuing to distinguish the derivative suit from the class action individual-based suit is the availability of a prescreening device on this form of representative suit. That is, as seen earlier, there is a genuine malaise over whether representative suits (that is, class actions and derivative suits) are socially desirable; this concern arises because empirical evidence is consistent with the hypothesis that representative suits are socially destructive because they sometimes (or to their harshest critics, frequently) seek to extort a settlement from the defendants or the corporation. For derivative suits, the corporation has, through the demand requirement,[7] a mechanism that prescreens harmful derivative suits. No such prescreening device is available for class actions. Thus one potential purpose of continuing to distinguish between individual and derivative

---

[2] *See* Kramer v. Western Pac. Indus., 546 A.2d 348 (Del. 1988).

[3] *See, e.g.,* Smith v. Van Gorkom, 488 A.2d 858 (Del. 1985).

[4] Watson v. Button, 235 F.2d 235, 237 (9th Cir. 1956); Sutter v. General Petroleum Corp., 170 P.2d 989 (Cal. 1946).

[5] Corporate creditors will be protected because the recovery will go into the corporate treasury, and creditors will have the first claim on the corporation's assets in case of its liquidation or bankruptcy. Watson v. Button, 235 F. 2d 235, 237 (9th Cir. 1956).

[6] Derivative actions protect all shareholders because a recovery by the corporation will raise the value of each share equally. *Id.*

[7] *See infra* §§15.05 and 15.06.

A. Characteristics of the Derivative Suit

actions is that the courts can accommodate the corporation's interest in having the corporate voice heard on the desirability of the suit being initiated and prosecuted.

Courts frequently have great difficulty in classifying a plaintiff's claim as individual or derivative. For example, there has been a conflict as to the proper classification of a suit to compel dividends. In a federal case applying Pennsylvania law, the court held such a suit to be direct and individual, reasoning that because "[t]he right to dividends is an incident of [stock] ownership," the shareholder has been injured directly, and recovery "will benefit only the shareholders."[8] In contrast, a New York court held, over a strong dissent, that a suit to compel dividends must be brought derivatively because it is grounded on a duty owed by the directors to the corporation, but the New York rule has since been changed by statute.[9] It is possible to justify both views.

On the one hand, an action to compel dividends should be considered an individual action when the complaint is that the majority or management has withheld dividends for the purpose of driving the minority stockholders from the corporation. On the other hand, the suit is properly a derivative action when the complaint is that by failing to declare dividends the corporation risks being subject to punitive excess retained-earnings taxes or that the retained earnings will otherwise be used improvidently.[10] Another sometimes litigated question is the proper classification of a shareholder suit to enforce a shareholder's preemptive rights to a new issuance of shares. Under the better view the action is direct, as it is based on the shareholder's contractual claim against the corporation.[11]

A source of the inconsistency among the courts on their treatment of suits as individual or derivative is a misunderstanding of the effect the court should accord the fact that a class of shareholders has been similarly harmed. Some courts have reasoned that a derivative action is the only basis for a shareholder to complain unless the shareholder has suffered a loss or other injury different from that of the other minority stockholders.[12] This is erroneous. As Justice Traynor so clearly stated in *Jones v. H. F. Ahmanson & Company*,[13]

> The individual wrong necessary to support a suit by a shareholder need not be unique to the plaintiff. The same injury may affect a substantial number of

---

[8] Knapp v. Bankers Sec. Corp., 230 F.2d 717-722 (3d Cir. 1956). This is the preferable view.

[9] Gordon v. Elliman, 119 N.E.2d 331 (N.Y. 1954); N.Y. Bus. Corp. Law §626(a) (McKinney 1986) (adding "in its favor" to statute is intended to overrule *Gordon*). *See* Eisenberg v. Flying Tiger Line, Inc., 451 F.2d 267 (2d Cir. 1971).

[10] *See* Maul v. Kirkman, 637 A.2d 928 (N.J. Super. App. Div. 1994).

[11] Shaw v. Empire Sav. & Loan Ass'n, 9 Cal. Rptr. 204 (Ct. App. 1960); Waters v. Horace Waters & Co., 94 N.E. 602 (N.Y. 1911). *Cf.* Elster v. American Airlines Inc., 100 A.2d 219 (Del. Ch. 1953) (suit to enjoin exercise of stock options held derivative where vice was corporate waste).

[12] *See, e.g.,* Grace Brothers Ltd. v. Farley Ind., Inc., 450 S.E.2d 814 (Ga. 1994) (barring direct claim by minority stockholders who complained of unfair treatment in a cash-out merger).

[13] 460 P.2d 464 (Cal. 1969).

shareholders. If the injury is not incidental to an injury to the corporation, an individual cause of action exists.[14]

The difference between individual and derivative actions can be illustrated by examples. The following actions have been held to be individual (direct) actions:

(1) A claim founded on a contract between the corporation and the shareholder as an individual.[15]
(2) A claim based on false and misleading proxy solicitation.[16]
(3) An action to compel dissolution of the corporation.[17] However, dissolution may also be sought in a derivative suit.[18]
(4) A suit against directors for fraud in the sale or purchase of the individual shareholder's stock.[19]
(5) A claim founded in tort for injury directly upon the shareholder's person or property.[20]
(6) An action against a director for disseminating false reports about the validity or value of shareholder's stock that harms the shareholder in his individual capacity as an investor.[21]
(7) A claim against a voting trustee for a breach of her obligations.[22]
(8) An action to protect the shareholder's relative voting power.[23]
(9) A suit to protect a shareholder's inspection rights.[24]
(10) A suit against takeover maneuvers, such as adopting poison pill or issuing stock for the purpose of wrongfully perpetuating or shifting control.[25]

---

[14] *Id.* 460 P.2d at 470-471. *See also* Strougo v. Bassini, 282 F.3d 162, 173 (2d Cir. 2002):

> An inquiry that asks only whether shareholders have suffered "undifferentiated harm" rather than whether the shareholders have suffered injury distinct from any potential injury to the corporation, could lead to situations in which shareholders are improperly left with an injury without legal recourse. There may be acts that injure shareholders equally but do not injure the corporation at all; indeed they might be seen as benefiting the company in the sense that they might increase its assets.

[15] *See, e.g.,* Buschmann v. Professional Men's Ass'n, 405 F.2d 659 (7th Cir. 1969).

[16] *See* Mills v. Electric Auto-Lite Co., 396 U.S. 375 (1970); Yamamoto v. Omiya, 564 F.2d 1319 (9th Cir. 1977). However, both cases left open the possibility that a derivative action may also have been appropriate.

[17] Fontheim v. Walker, 141 N.W.S. 2d 62 (Sup. Ct. 1955).

[18] *See, e.g.,* Gottfried v. Gottfried, 50 N.Y.S.2d 951 (Sup. Ct. 1944). *See infra* note 35.

[19] *See, e.g.,* Siegel v. Engelmann, N.Y.S.2d 193 193 (Sup. Ct. 1955); Von Au v. Mangenheimer, 110 N.Y.S. 629 (App. Div. 1908), *aff'd,* 89 N.E. 1114 (N.Y. 1909).

[20] *See, e.g.,* Gieselmann v. Stegeman, 443 S.W.2d 127 (Mo. 1969).

[21] *See, e.g.,* Grogan v. Garner, 806 F.2d 829 (8th Cir. 1986); Dowling v. Narragansett Capital Corp., 735 F. Supp. 1105 (D.R.I. 1990).

[22] *See, e.g.,* Lurie v. Rupe, 201 N.E.2d 158 (Ill. App. Ct. 1964), *cert. denied,* 380 U.S. 964 (1965); Eisner v. Davis, 109 N.Y.S.2d 504 (Sup. Ct. 1951), *aff'd,* 112 N.Y.S.2d 672 (App. Div. 1952).

[23] *See, e.g.,* Lochhead v. Alacano, 697 F. Supp. 406 (D. Utah 1988); Lipton v. News Int'l, 514 A.2d 1075 (Del. 1986).

[24] *See, e.g.,* Smith v. Flynn, 155 So. 2d 497 (Ala. 1963); Gieselmann v. Stegeman, 443 S.W.2d 127 (Mo. 1969).

[25] *See, e.g.,* In re Gaylord Container Corp. Shareholders Litigation, 747 A.2d 71 (Del. Ch. 1999); Alexander v. Atlanta & W.P. R.R., 38 S.E. 772 (Ga. 1901); Fox v. Kansas Farmers' Union Royalty Co., 139 P.2d 815 (Kan. 1943).

A. Characteristics of the Derivative Suit

(11) An action to enjoin a threatened *ultra vires* act.[26]

(12) An action to compel payment of a declared dividend.[27]

(13) An action to vindicate a wrong to the individual shareholder, although the same wrongful act may also create a separate corporate cause of action.[28]

(14) A suit against the only other shareholder(s) for injuring the corporation's business where a judgment in a derivative suit would benefit the wrongdoer.[29]

(15) Suit alleging board abdicated its powers to the CEO.[30]

(16) A suit alleging directors breached fiduciary duty when negotiating to sell company.[31]

(17) Suit based on oppressive action designed to force the minority shareholder(s) from the corporation or other coercive action directed at the minority.[32]

The following claims have been held to be derivative:

(1) An action seeking recovery due to managerial misconduct, producing a proportionate decline in the company's shares, such as the waste of corporate assets or usurpation of corporate opportunities.[33]

(2) An action against the purchaser of corporate assets seeking rescission of the sale.[34]

(3) An action under section 10(b) of the Securities Exchange Act of 1934 and SEC Rule 10b-5, where the corporation has purchased or sold securities and the individual shareholder is precluded from relief because he is neither a purchaser nor seller of securities.[35]

(4) An action to recover for injuries to corporate assets caused by fraud or by third parties.[36]

(5) An action to recover damages for an *ultra vires* act.[37]

(6) A suit to compel the directors to dissolve the corporation due to director misconduct.[38]

---

[26] *See, e.g.*, Independence Lead Mines Co. v. Kingsbury, 175 F.2d 983 (9th Cir.), *cert. denied*, 338 U.S. 900 (1949).

[27] *Id.*

[28] *See, e.g.*, Snyder v. Epstein, 290 F. Supp. 652 (E.D. Wis. 1968); O'Hare v. Marine Elec. Co., 39 Cal. Rptr. 799 (Ct. App. 1964); Stinnett v. Paramount-Famous Lasky Corp., 37 S.W. 2d 145 (Tex. App. Comm'n 1931).

[29] *See, e.g.*, Fischer v. Fischer, No. 16864, 1999 Del. Ch. Lexis 217 (Nov. 9, 1999).

[30] Grimes v. Donald, 673 A.2d 1207, 1213 (Del. 1996).

[31] Parnes v. Bally Entertainment Corp., 722 A.2d 1243 (Del. 1999).

[32] Strougo v. Bassini, 282 F.3d 162 (2d Cir. 2002).

[33] *See, e.g.*, Kramer v. Western Pac. Indus., 546 A.2d 348 (Del. 1988).

[34] *See, e.g.*, Bassett v. Battle, 1 N.Y.S.2d 869 (App. Div. 1938).

[35] *See, e.g.*, Ray v. Karris, 780 F.2d 636, 641 (7th Cir. 1985); Bailey v. Meister Brau, Inc., 320 F. Supp. 539 (N.D. Ill. 1970).

[36] *See, e.g.*, Green v. Victor Talking Mach. Co., 24 F.2d 378 (2d Cir.) (misappropriation of corporate assets).

[37] *See, e.g.*, Lee Moving & Storage, Inc. v. Bourgeois, 343 So. 2d 1192 (La. Ct. App. 1977) (with good faith and due diligence).

[38] *See, e.g.*, Wood v. Akridge, 36 P.2d 804 (Utah 1934); H F.2d 378 (9th Cir. 1928), *cert. denied*, 278 U.S. 602 (1929); Parks v. Multimedia Technologies, Inc., 520 S.E.2d 517, 523 (Ga. Ct. App. 1999).

(7) An action on a contract between the corporation and a third party.[39]

(8) Managerial decisions designed to thwart a takeover and thereby deprive the stockholders of an opportunity to dispose of their shares at a premium.[40]

(9) Breach of fiduciary duty during a merger transaction.[41]

There are situations in which a claim can be framed either as a derivative or as a direct claim.[42]

In voluntary corporate dissolution, where corporate affairs are being wound up or the process of liquidation is completed, the weight of judicial authority allows shareholders to sue the directors individually for wrongs they committed during corporate existence or for abuse of their authority in winding up the corporation.[43] Today, this matter is generally covered by statute. Even in states in which the general corporation statute does not prolong corporate existence after dissolution for winding-up purposes, the winding-up should be treated as continuing the same concern, as is the case in partnership dissolution. Corporate assets and claims should be administered for the benefit of all concerned, just as they should have been administered before the formal dissolution that terminated the authority of the directors to continue the business.[44]

Several modern cases hold that the individual-derivative distinction assumes relevancy in the close corporation only when there is a justifiable concern that creditors may be harmed if any recovery resulting from the suit does not go to the corporation. Cases have frequently held that in suits between two co-owners of a close corporation that the suit need not be maintained as a derivative suit, even though the suit is premised on conduct that in other contexts would involve only a corporate cause of action.[45] This result appears correct, especially where the record supports the view that creditors are unlikely to be prejudiced should the recovery bypass the corporation. In the tightly held close corporation, where only two or maybe three or four shareholders exist, it is difficult to attribute a *persona* to the corporation when the issue is whose cause of action is being vindicated. Clearly there is no basis to believe there is a true independent voice that can speak through the demand requirement as to the suit's probable impact on the corporation's interests. The American Law Institute encourages such flexibility by rec-

[39] *See* Boothe v. Baker Indus., 262 F. Supp. 168 (D. Del. 1966).

[40] *See, e.g.,* Nowling v. Aero Serv. Int'l, 752 F. Supp. 1304 (E.D. La. 1990); Newell Co. v. Vermont Am. Corp., 725 F. Supp. 351 (N.D. Ill. 1989).

[41] *See, e.g.,* Friedman v. Mohasco Corp., 929 F.2d 77 (2d Cir. 1991); In re First Interstate Bancorp Litig., 729 A.2d 851 (Del. Ch. 1998).

[42] *See* Boothe v. Baker Indus., 262 F. Supp. 268 (D. Del. 1966) (where right of action existed as to both derivative and nonderivative causes, adjudication of state court nonderivative class action held bar to federal derivative suit).

[43] Moore v. Occupational Safety & Health Rev. Comm'n, 591 F.2d 991 (4th Cir. 1979); Donsco, Inc. v. Casper Corp., 587 F.2d 602 (3d Cir. 1978).

[44] George D. Hornstein, Voluntary Dissolution, 51 Yale L.J. 64, 80 (1941). Dissolution and winding up are discussed in Chapter 26.

[45] *See, e.g.,* Byelik v. Vivadelli, 79 F. Supp. 2d 610 (E.D. Va. 1999) (reaching result believed Virginia courts would reach); Caswell v. Jordan, 362 S.E.2d 769 Ga. Ct. App. 1987).

ommending that the court exercise such discretion where "it finds that to do so will not (i) unfairly expose the corporation or the defendants to a multiplicity of actions, (ii) materially prejudice the interests of creditors of the corporation, or (iii) interfere with a fair distribution of the recovery among all interested persons."[46]

§15.03   Individual Recovery in Derivative Suits

As a general rule, recovery in derivative suits inures to the corporation, with the proceeds becoming a part of the corporate assets.[1] In some situations, however, the shareholder-plaintiff in a derivative suit on a corporate right of action may recover individual damages in lieu of a corporate recovery. For example, where only few stockholders are injured by the breach, there is no fear that creditors may be disadvantaged if recovery does not go to the corporation, and the wrongdoers are still in control of the corporation, recovery may go directly to the shareholder or shareholders who complain.[2] If a corporate recovery will not cure the injury or if granting equitable relief to the corporation by way of rescission would unsettle and disturb significant interests of innocent third parties, the court should be able to give relief according to the needs of the case.

Accordingly, where special circumstances exist,[3] courts have allowed direct pro rata recovery by the shareholders.[4] Courts have decreed individual pro rata recovery in order to facilitate the distribution of corporate funds in a variety of situations: (1) where the corporation is in the process of liquidation, (2) where the wrongdoers retain substantial control of the corporation and corporate recovery would return the funds to their control,[5] (3) where the defendants sell control of the corporation for an unlawful premium and the court seeks to prevent a windfall to purchasers of the wrongdoers' shares,[6] (4) where a majority of the corporation's shares are held by persons who could not bring the derivative suit because of their personal involvement in, or ratification of, the wrongdoing,[7]

---

[46] ALI, 2 Principles of Corporate Governance: Analysis and Recommendations §7.01(d) (1994). For a decision adopting the ALI's approach, *see* Barth v. Barth, 659 N.E.2d 559 (Ind. 1995); *contra* Wessin v. Archives Corp., 592 N.W.2d 460 (Minn. 1999). *See also* Warden v. McLelland, 288 F.3d 105 (3d Cir. 2002) (inviting district court *on remand* to consider whether Pennsylvania would, following decision in Cuker v. Mikalauskas, 692 A.2d 1042 (Pa. 1997), and adopt other features of the ALI, such as section 7.01(d)).

§15.03   [1] *See* Keenan v. Eshelman, 2 A.2d 904 (Del. 1938); Wolf v. Rand, 685 N.Y.S.2d 708 (N.Y. App. Div. 1999); Outen v. MICAL, 454 S.E.2d 883 (N.C. Ct. App. 1995).

[2] *See, e.g.*, James v. Microwave Communications Inc., 385 F. Supp. 7598 (N.D. Ill. 1974).

[3] *E.g.*, Pcrlman v. Feldmann, 219 F.2d 173 (2d Cir.), *cert. denied*, 349 U.S. 952 (1955); Atkinson v. Marquart, 541 P.2d 556 (Ariz. 1975).

[4] *See* Note, 56 Harv. L. Rev. 1314 (1956).

[5] *See, e.g.*, Atkinson v. Marquart, 541 P.2d 556 (Ariz. 1975); Gabhart v. Gabhart, 370 N.E.2d 345 (Ind. 1977) (injured corporation merged into corporation controlled by those responsible for harm).

[6] *E.g.*, Perlman v. Feldmann, 219 F.2d 173 (2d Cir.), *cert. denied*, 349 U.S. 952 (1955).

[7] *Id.*

and (5) where a pro rata recovery fairly resolves the varying equities among differently situated stockholders.[8]

It is difficult to formulate hard and fast rules as to when direct shareholder recovery is appropriate in a derivative suit. Generally, direct recovery is granted where it is the most effective means of dealing with inequities that would otherwise result.[9]

B.   THE DEMAND REQUIREMENT

§15.04   Necessity of Demand on the Shareholders

The authority to sue for corporate injuries is vested primarily in corporate management.[1] For a shareholder to show a right to sue on behalf of the corporation, he must allege with some particularity in his complaint that he has exhausted his remedies within the corporation by making a demand on the directors or other officers to sue, or he must allege sufficient reason for not doing so.[2] At one time the requirement that a shareholder exhaust her intracorporate remedies meant that it was insufficient for a shareholder merely to make a demand on the directors that they institute suit; he must also make a similar demand upon the shareholders as a body. Where this requirement applies, the would-be plaintiff must attempt to convene a shareholders' meeting in order that a majority of the shareholders, if not implicated in the wrong, may vote on the question of bringing suit, ratifying the acts complained of, or perhaps electing other directors who will properly represent the corporation in the proposed law suit.[3] It is rare today to find a demand on the shareholders required, in part because most derivative suits allege misconduct that cannot be ratified by a majority vote of the stockholders.[4] However, the derivative suit plaintiff must take care to plead the basis for excusing the demand or otherwise incur the likelihood of dismissal in those jurisdictions that have not abolished this requirement.[5]

An application to the shareholders and the calling of a shareholders' meeting is an exceedingly unreasonable requirement, certainly if the conduct that is

---

[8] *See, e.g.*, Raskin v. Frebank Co., 121 Cal. Rptr. 348 (Ct. App. 1975).

[9] *See, e.g.*, Gabhart v. Gabhart, 370 N.E.2d 345 (Ind. 1977) (allowing individual recovery by former shareholder of merged corporation whose means of redress cut off by merger).

§15.04   [1] *See infra* §15.05 for discussion of the directors' exercise of discretion not to sue.

[2] *E.g.*, Hawes v. Oakland, 104 U.S. 450, 460-461 (1882); Smith v. Sperling, 354 U.S. 91 (1957); Lewis v. Curtis, 671 F.2d 779 (3d Cir. 1982); Clark v. Lomas & Nettleton Fin. Corp., 625 F.2d 49 (5th Cir. 1980), *cert. denied*, 450 U.S. 1029 (1981).

[3] *See* Strougo v. Scudder, Stevens & Clark, Inc., 964 F. Supp. 783 (S.D.N.Y. 1997) (invoking these considerations as a basis for believing a demand on the shareholders is futile in a suit against the directors alleged to have diluted the value of shares in a closed-end mutual fund).

[4] *See, e.g.*, Wolgin v. Simon, 722 F.2d 389 (8th Cir. 1984) (requiring demand on the stockholders because misconduct alleged was self-dealing and waste in warding off a takeover which did not fall within the general exception to the requirement); Gibbs v. Macari, 1997 WL 1261225 (Mass. Super. Nov. 21, 1997) (dismissing suit for failure to allege basis to excuse a demand); McLeese v. J.C. Nichols Co, 842 S.W.2d 115 (Mo. Ct. App. 1992) (same).

[5] *See, e.g.*, McLeese v. J.C. Nichols Co., 842 S.W.2d 115 (Mo. Ct. App. 1992).

B.   The Demand Requirement

the focus of the derivative suit can only be ratified by all the stockholders.[6] But the burdens of making such a demand in a public corporation, regardless of the nature of the underlying complaint, are so substantial that it is difficult to understand how the social benefits of making a demand can justify the burdens of this requirement. At best, it erects a needless barrier to legitimate shareholder derivative suits, which are already expensive and burdensome. The requirement is based on a policy of protecting the majority and preventing a large corporation from being unduly vexed by suits brought by shareholders with small holdings whose motives may be hostile to the corporation and who may have made no effort to ascertain the opinion or will of the majority.[7] In general it seems impractical to require, as a condition precedent to bringing a derivative suit, calling a shareholders' meeting or making a demand on many scattered shareholders, in view of the difficulty, expense, delay, and small benefit to be gained thereby.[8] Where an abuse of process is at issue, a refusal by the directors to sue ought to be sufficient to establish a default by the corporation in enforcing its rights, without an additional application to the shareholders. That is, the demand requirement and the special litigation committee are far more effective filters of unwise or harmful derivative suits than we can expect to flow from mandating a demand on the stockholders.[9] Today, the necessity that a demand be made on the shareholders is largely of historical significance.[10] Most modern decisions readily excuse making a demand or the governing statute eliminates the requirement.[11] Only rarely do the courts fail to excuse the demand and condition the derivative suit's continuation on this requirement being satisfied.[12] The American Law Institute's proposals

[6] This is the central reasoning of the leading modern case. *See* Mayer v. Adams, 141 A.2d 458 (Del. 1958). For an extreme case requiring such a demand, *see* Unigroup, Inc. v. O'Rourke Storage & Transfer Co., 834 F. Supp. 1171 (E.D. Mo. 1993) (dismissing derivative suit *counterclaim* alleging wasteful bonuses were paid to executives).

[7] Foss v. Harbottle, 67 Eng. Rep. 189 (Ch. 1843). *See also, e.g.,* Yates Ranch Oil & Royalties, Inc. v. Jones, 100 F.2d 419 (5th Cir. 1938); Claman v. Robertson, 128 N.E.2d 429 (Ohio 1955).

[8] *See* Elgin v. Alfa Corp., 598 So. 2d 807 (Ala. 1992) (though demand is ordinarily required it was excused for this mutual insurance company with numerous members); New Crawford Valley. Ltd. v. Benedict, 847 P.2d 642 (Colo. Ct. App. 1993) (excusing demand because cost prohibitive in a corporation with 8,000 stockholders); Slutzker v. Rieber, 28 A.2d 525 (N.J. Ch. 1942).

[9] *See infra* §§15.05-15.06.

[10] Foss v. Harbottle, 67 Eng. Rep. 189 (Ch. 1843); Hawes v. Oakland, 104 U.S. 450 (1882); Fed. R. Civ. P. 23.1.

[11] *See, e.g.,* Cal. Corp. Code §800 (West 1990); N.Y. Bus. Corp. Law §626 (McKinney 1986). Jacobs v. Adams, 601 F.2d 176 (5th Cir. 1979) (holding Florida has abolished necessity of demand on shareholders).

[12] *See* Wolgin v. Simon, 722 F.2d 389 (8th Cir. 1984) (applying Missouri law); Bell v. Arnold, 487 P.2d 545 (Colo. 1971); Gibbs v. Macari, 1997 WL 1261225 (Mass. Super. Nov. 21, 1997); S. Solomont & Sons Trust, Inc. v. New England Theatres Operating Corp., 93 N.E.2d 241 (Mass. 1950); McLeese v. J.C. Nichols Co., 842 S.W.2d 115 (Mo. Ct. App. 1992); Claman v. Robertson, 128 N.E.2d 429 (Ohio 1955). *See generally* Deborah A. DeMott, Demand in Derivative Actions: Problems of Interpretation and Function, 19 U.C. Davis L. Rev. 461, 474-484 (1986); Annot., 48 A.L.R.3d 595 (1973).

Fed. R. Civ. P. 23.1 requires shareholder demand "if necessary." *See* 7C Charles Alan Wright, Arthur R. Miller & Mary Kay Kane, Federal Practice and Procedure §1832 (2d ed. 1986). *See also* Note, 73 Harv. L. Rev. 746 (1960).

for derivative suits dispense with the requirement of a demand on the share-holders.[13] As a general rule, informed collective shareholder consideration of the proposed litigation is not feasible. Massachusetts, which continues to be a tenacious adherent to the necessity of a demand on the shareholders, empha-sizes (and, in the American Law Institute's view, overstates) the value of the col-lective judgment of the stockholders, even in cases where the misconduct cannot be ratified by the stockholders.[14] Nonetheless, even Massachusetts rec-ognizes exceptions to the demand requirement when demand would be futile because the other shareholders are interested, or when the very large number of shareholders involved would make demand a pointless or impossibly burden-some act.[15]

Federal Rule of Civil Procedure 23.1 provides that the plaintiff's complaint must set forth her efforts to obtain action from the stockholders "if necessary." As such, the demand on the stockholders becomes a question in the first instance of substantive state law, save where making a demand would prove inconsistent with federal policy underlying any federal question raised in the derivative suit.[16] As noted above, where state law continues to embody a demand on the shareholders, modern decisions have been most willing to excuse the requirement on one of several possible bases, such as the alleged misconduct being of the type that can-not be approved by a majority vote of the stockholders,[17] or that the defendant holds a majority or controlling block of the voting power,[18] or there is such a large number of stockholders that the plaintiff would incur unreasonable expenses, burdens, and delays in fulfilling the requirement.[19]

§15.05   The Demand on the Directors Requirement

The derivative suit complaint must plead with particularity the efforts the plaintiff has made to seek the board of directors to prosecute the cause of action the plain-tiff seeks to initiate or set forth the reasons for not seeking such action by the

---

See Mayer v. Adams, 141 A.2d 458 (Del. 1958); Continental Sec. Co. v. Belmont, 99 N.E. 138 (N.Y. 1912). See also Cal. Corp. Code §800(b)(2) (West 1990); N.Y. Bus. Corp. Law §626(c) (McKinney 1986); N.C. Bus. Corp. Act §55-7-42(b) (2000).

[13] ALI, 2 Principles of Corporate Governance, supra §15.02 note 46, §7.03(c).

[14] See S. Solomont & Sons Trust, Inc. v. New England Theatres Operating Corp., 93 N.E.2d 241, 247-248 (Mass. 1950). See also Pomeranz v. Clark, 101 F. Supp. 341 (D. Mass. 1951).

[15] Harhen v. Brown, 730 N.E.2d 859, 868 (Mass. 2000) (insurance company had seven million other policyholders).

[16] See Burks v. Lasker, 441 U.S. 471 (1979).

[17] See, e.g., Mayer v. Adams, 141 A.2d 458 (Del. 1958). Contra, S. Solomont & Sons Trust, Inc. v. New England Theatres Operating Corp., 93 N.E.2d 241 (Mass. 1950).

[18] See, e.g., Gottesman v. General Motors Corp., 268 F.2d 194 (2d Cir. 1959); Heilbrunn v. Hanover Equities Corp., 259 F. Supp. 936 (S.D.N.Y. 1966); Pupecki v. James Madison Corp., 382 N.E.2d 1030 (Mass. 1978).

[19] See, e.g., Weiss v. Sunasco Inc., 316 F. Supp. 1197 (E.D. Pa. 1970). Contra Bell v. Arnold, 487 P.2d 545 (Colo. 1971).

B. The Demand Requirement

board of directors.[1] This is the demand requirement and is the single most challenging hurdle that lies in the path of the derivative suit plaintiff. The requirement of a demand on the directors dates back to the leading Supreme Court case of *Hawes v. Oakland.*[2] It is codified in the Federal Rules of Civil Procedure[3] and is followed in most states.[4] In general, the directors have discretion to refuse to sue if they decide in good faith not to do so and do not exceed the scope of the business judgment rule. In a leading Supreme Court case,[5] Justice Brandeis declared:

> Whether or not a corporation shall seek to enforce in the courts a cause of action for damages is, like other business questions, ordinarily a matter of internal management and is left to the discretion of the directors, in the absence of instructions by vote of the stockholders. Courts interfere seldom to control such discretion intra vires the corporation, except where the directors are guilty of misconduct equivalent to a breach of trust, or where they stand in a dual relation which prevents an unprejudiced exercise of judgment; and, as a rule, only after application to the stockholders, unless it appears that there was no opportunity for such application, that application would be futile (as where wrongdoers control the corporation), or that the delay involved would defeat recovery.

Even if the directors believe that the corporation has a good cause of action for an injury committed by officers or third parties, that fact does not necessarily make it incumbent on them to bring suit. If in the honest and impartial opinion of the directors the best interests of the company are served by not bringing suit, the directors' decision not to sue is a bar to a shareholder's bringing a derivative suit. In making the decision whether to enforce a corporate cause of action, management generally invokes a cost-benefit analysis. Courts have often said that the question of whether to sue is within the directors' discretion, and that if they act in good faith, their refusal is binding.[6]

There is good reason to argue that the directors' response to a demand should not carry the same presumptive weight as courts accord directors' judgment in traditional business matters. The considerations that justify the overwhelming deference that courts accord directors' decisions in normal commercial transactions do not justify the same deference when a committee of the directors recommends dismissal of a derivative suit or the board collectively rejects a demand for suit.[7] For example, if a court is asked to upset a directors' decision to

---

§15.05 [1] *See, e.g.,* Fed. R. Civ. P. 23.1; Cal. Corp. Code §800 (West 1990); Del. Ch. Ct. R. 23.1; N.Y. Bus. Corp. Law §626(c) (McKinney 1986); Model Bus. Corp. Act §7.42 (1990).

[2] 104 U.S. 450 (1882).

[3] Fed. R. Civ. P. 23.1.

[4] *See, e.g.,* Cal. Corp. Code §800(b)(2) (West 1990); Del. Ch. Ct. R. 23.1; N.Y. Bus. Corp. Law §626(c) (McKinney 1986).

[5] United Copper Sec. Co. v. Amalgamated Copper Co., 244 U.S. 261, 264 (1917).

[6] Burks v. Lasker, 441 U.S. 471 (1979); United Copper Sec. Co. v. Amalgamated Co., 244 U.S. 261 (1917); Abbey v. Control Data Corp., 603 F.2d 724 (8th Cir. 1979), *cert. denied,* 444 U.S. 1019 (1980). Auerbach v. Bennett, 393 N.E.2d 994 (N.Y. 1979).

[7] *See* Victor Brudney, The Independent Director—Heavenly City or Potempkin Village?, 95 Harv. L. Rev. 597, 630-631 (1982); John C. Coffee, Jr. & Donald E. Schwartz, The Survival of the Derivative Suit: An Explanation and a Proposal for Legislative Reform, 81 Colum. L. Rev. 280-283 (1981).

acquire Blackacre for allegedly too high a price, the court must weigh that prayer with a healthy respect for the idea that, if it does set aside the directors' judgment, the directors will be liable for the consequential damages of their decision. In contrast, if the court should rule against the directors or a committee of the directors, there is no causal relationship between the directors' decision (that the suit not be pursued) and any harm to the corporation. That is, the directors cannot be held liable for any losses that can be attributed to the court's decision not to dismiss the derivative suit as suggested by the directors. Therefore, the court need not temper its scrutiny of the directors' recommendation in order to spare those directors of personal liability for having reached an improper result. Moreover, the directors' judgment that the suit should be dismissed is not peculiarly within their business expertise. For truly business decisions, courts wisely defer to the managerial, financial, manufacturing, and planning expertise of directors. This indeed is the wisdom of the business judgment rule. But director expertise in evaluating the merits and impact of a suit would appear to be no better, and likely could be a good deal less, than that of a derivative suit court. Courts thus can justifiably be less deferential in the demand-on-director area than they are when asked to review the decisions of directors in other contexts.

The demand requirement gives the board of directors the opportunity to assume control of the decision to litigate.[8] Once a demand is made, the response of the board of directors must be within a reasonable time; if not so forthcoming, the demand required is deemed satisfied.[9] If the directors accede to the shareholder's demands, the corporation supplants the derivative plaintiff for the purpose of enforcing its corporate rights. If the directors refuse to sue despite a proper demand, a few courts have stated that the shareholder is not automatically entitled to pursue the derivative claim.[10] Most courts hold that, if an independent board decides in good faith against the demand (that is, rejects the demand), the directors' refusal to sue falls within the business judgment rule, and the suit must be dismissed.[11] The standard of review of a dismissal recommendation in a demand required case is the same whether the recommendation is proffered by the board or a committee of the board.[12] Only in rare cases will a derivative suit be

---

[8] *See* Brody v. Chemical Bank, 517 F.2d 932, 934 (2d Cir. 1975). Instances are rare, however, when directors respond favorably to a demand.

[9] Lewis v. Sporck, 646 F. Supp. 574 (N.D. Cal. 1986) (three-month delay assured that board had sufficient time); Rubin v. Posner, 701 F. Supp. 1041 (D. Del. 1988) (30 days sufficient where no complex issues posed).

[10] *See* Papilsky v. Berndt, 503 F.2d 554, 556 (2d Cir. 1974), *cert. denied*, 419 U.S. 1048 (1975) (dicta).

[11] *See, e.g.*, Atkins v. Hibernia Corp., 182 F.3d 320, 324 (5th Cir. 1999); Cramer v. General Tel. & Elec. Corp., 582 F.2d 259 (3d Cir. 1978). The plaintiff may, however, be granted leave to amend the complaint. *See* Abramowitz v. Posner, 513 F. Supp. 120, 125 (S.D.N.Y. 1981), *aff'd*, 672 F.2d 1025 (2d Cir. 1982).

[12] *See* Allied Ready Mix Co., Inc. v. Allen, 994 S.W.2d 4 (Ky. Ct. App. 1998); Harhen v. Brown, 730 N.E.2d 859 (Mass. 2000); In re PSE & G Shareholder Litigation, 718 A.2d 254 (N.J. Super. Ct. Ch. Div. 1998). For a criticism of this result, *see* Harry G. Hutchison, Presumptive Business Judgment, Substantive Good Faith, Litigation Control: Vindicating Socioeconomic Meaning of *Harhen v. Brown*, 26 J. Corp. L. 285 (2001).

B. The Demand Requirement

allowed to proceed after the board of directors has rejected the demand.[13] In essence, the inquiry into whether the board lacks the capacity to make the decision not to sue is much like the inquiry into whether the demand should be excused because it would be futile.[14] Because instances are rare when the board of directors approves of the action *and* does not authorize the corporation's counsel to take over the suit, most derivative suits arise where the plaintiff has successfully pleaded facts that excuse any demand on the board of directors.[15] (Common bases for excusing a demand on the board of directors are discussed below.) A plaintiff who has made a demand on the board of directors cannot reverse course and seek to proceed with the suit on the ground that the demand should have been excused.[16]

The demand requirement centralizes in the board of directors a necessary and unique perspective on whether the suit is in the corporation's best interests. Thus the demand requirement protects directors from harassment by litigious shareholders contesting matters clearly within the directors' discretion[17] and helps curtail strike suits by shareholders making reckless charges for personal gain rather than corporate benefit.[18] Shareholders must allege with particularity the efforts made to obtain the action they desire from directors,[19] and the demand must be timely in order to afford the directors a reasonable opportunity to act.[20] Some courts have adopted a permissive view as to the excuse of the demand requirement, viewing the demand requirement as consistent with the flexible standards of modern notice pleading.[21] This in fact is the position taken by the American Law Institute in its proposals for derivative suits in its adoption of the so-called universal demand approach.[22] Others have taken a much stricter view, which characterizes excuse of prior demand as "an exceptional rule of pleading, serving a special purpose. . . ."[23] The wide divergence in the decisions whether to excuse a demand on the board of directors indicates that to a considerable extent the necessity for a demand lies within the sound discretion of the court.[24] The role to accord demand and, more particularly, how easily a demand on the board of directors will be excused, is linked to the degree of deference the legislature or

---

[13] *See* Ashwander v. Tennessee Valley Auth., 297 U.S. 288 (1936); Stepak v. Addison, 20 F.3d 398 (11th Cir. 1994); Galef v. Alexander, 615 F.2d 51, 59-61 (2d Cir. 1980).

[14] Grimes v. DSC Communications Corp., 724 A.2d 561 (Del. Ch. 1998).

[15] *See* Daniel R. Fischel, The Demand and Standing Requirements in Stockholder Derivative Actions, 44 U. Chi. L. Rev. 168 (1976).

[16] *See* Spiegel v. Buntrock, 571 A.2d 767 (Del. 1990) (the making of demand concedes board's independence); Allied Ready Mix Co., Inc. v. Allen, 994 S.W.2d 4 (Ky. Ct. App. 1998).

[17] Barr v. Wackman, 329 N.E.2d 180, 186 (N.Y. 1975).

[18] *Id.* Fischel, *supra* note 15, at 172.

[19] Fed. R. Civ. P. 23.1.

[20] Bartlett v. New York, N.H. & H.R. Co., 109 N.E. 452, 454 (Mass. 1915).

[21] Liboff v. Wolfson, 437 F.2d 121, 122 (5th Cir. 1971); deHaas v. Empire Petroleum Co., 435 F.2d 1223, 1228 (10th Cir. 1970).

[22] *See* ALI 2 Principles of Corporate Governance, *supra* §15.02 note 46, §7.03.

[23] In re Kauffman Mut. Fund Actions, 479 F.2d 257, 263 (1st Cir.), *cert. denied*, 414 U.S. 857 (1973).

[24] Kusner v. First Pa. Corp., 395 F. Supp. 276 (E.D. Pa. 1975), *rev'd in part*, 531 F.2d 1234 (3d Cir. 1976); Nussbacher v. Continental Ill. Nat'l Bank & Trust Co., 518 F.2d 873 (7th Cir. 1975), *cert. denied*, 424 U.S. 928 (1976).

court wishes to accord the board's rejection of any demand made on it. That is, if the board of directors' perspective on the derivative suit's continuation is accorded great deference in all cases, excusing a demand becomes the vehicle for *ex ante* determining the instances in which the board's judgment is not entitled to such deference, perhaps on the ground that the directors are not independent. On the other hand, if the court is prepared to evaluate the board of directors' rejection of a demand made on it, considering such matters as the reasonableness and independence of the directors, there is much less reason for broad grounds for excusing a demand. This essentially is the reasoning of the American Law Institute, which embraces a "universal demand requirement."[25] Although universal demand has been statutorily adopted in many states, courts have been slow to depart from their customary formulations of the demand requirement, or more particularly, when the requirement may be excused on the basis of futility.

In *Kamen v. Kemper Financial Services, Inc.,*[26] the Seventh Circuit held in a derivative action brought under the Investment Company Act of 1940 that a universal demand requirement that abolishes the futility exception should apply to federal question litigation and dismissed the derivative suit for failure to make a demand on the board of directors. The Supreme Court reversed, reasoning that unless a federal statute provides otherwise, federal courts should use state law in determining the necessity of a demand unless to do so would be inconsistent with the policies underlying the federal statute on which the derivative suit is based. The choice of state law was based on the view that "the function of the demand doctrine in delimiting the respective powers of the individual shareholder and of the directors to control corporate litigation clearly is a matter of 'substance' and not 'procedure.'"[27] Thus, to the extent that states differ in their bases for excusing demand, those differences become reflected in federal-question derivative suit litigation unless the specific federal statute should require otherwise. For example, it is inconsistent with federal policies to require a demand in a suit brought on behalf of a mutual fund company where the clear intent of Congress was that such an action is individual, not derivative, although the action would be characterized otherwise under state law.[28] Such an inconsistency is not found with respect to derivative actions brought under the antifraud provisions of the federal securities laws.[29]

Whether a demand is excused for futility is determined at the time the complaint is filed.[30] The courts express in various ways their overall standard for finding futility, but the unique facts of the individual case and the judicial philosophy of the court appear to dominate the outcome more than the general standard that

---

[25] ALI, 2 Principles of Corporate Governance, *supra* §15.02 note 46, §7.03 (demand is excused "only if the plaintiff makes a specific showing that irreparable injury to the corporation would otherwise result").

[26] 500 U.S. 90 (1991).

[27] *Id.* at 96-97.

[28] *See* Daily Income Fund, Inc. v. Fox, 464 U.S. 523 (1984).

[29] *See, e.g.,* Lewis v. Anderson, 615 F.2d 778, 784 (9th Cir. 1979).

[30] Brody v. Chemical Bank, 482 F.2d 1111 (2d Cir. 1973); Brick v. Dominion Mortgage & Realty Trust, 442 F. Supp. 283, 295 (W.D.N.Y. 1977); Drage v. Procter & Gamble, 694 N.E.2d 479, 483 (Ohio Ct. App. 1997).

B. The Demand Requirement

is to guide any finding of futility.[31] When a complaint alleges with particularity that a majority of the board has engaged in fraud, self-dealing, or solely out of self-interest, most courts excuse the demand on the theory that it would be futile, because directors cannot be expected to sue themselves in order to enforce corporate rights.[32]

In the leading New York decision, *Marx v. Akers*,[33] the court stated that demand should be excused when:

> (1) . . . a complaint alleges with particularity that a majority of the board of directors is interested in the challenged transaction. Director interest may either be self-interest in the transaction at issue . . . or a loss of independence because a director . . . is controlled by a self-interested director. (2) . . . a complaint alleges with particularity that the board of directors did not fully inform themselves about the challenged transaction to the extent reasonably appropriate under the circumstances. (3) . . . a complaint alleges with particularity that the challenged transaction was so egregious on its face that it could not have been the product of sound business judgment of the directors.[34]

Though the court in *Marx* concluded that a demand on the board was excused under the first ground with respect to the board establishing its own compensation, the court dismissed the claim because a bare allegation of self-interest failed to establish a cause of action in light of the legislature having expressly authorized boards of directors of New York corporations to fix their own compensation. The court reasoned that the only possible basis for excusing a demand on the facts alleged would be the third ground, namely, that the compensation was excessive on its face. Even though compensation was increased from $20,000 to $55,000 with no apparent change in responsibilities or performance, the change was not deemed excessive on its face.[35]

The leading Delaware case on demand futility is *Aronson v. Lewis*[36] which holds that a demand is excused for futility under one of two alternate standards:

---

[31] The most intricate of the standards is that of Delaware, which holds that a demand is excused for futility under one of two alternate standards: "(1) whether threshold presumptions of director disinterest or independence are rebutted by well-pleaded facts; and, if not, (2) whether the complaint pleads particularized facts sufficient to create a reasonable doubt that the challenged transaction was the product of a valid exercise of business judgment." Levine v. Smith, 591 A.2d 194, 207 (Del. 1991). *See also* In re PSE & G Shareholder Litig., 2002 WL 1610282 (N.J. July 23, 2002) (adopting *Aronson's* two-prong inquiry approach; albeit going to some lengths to stress that the approach is one that is less deferential than arises in the standard business judgment rule inquiry).

[32] Nussbacher v. Continental Ill. Nat'l Bank & Trust. Co., 518 F.2d 873, 877 (7th Cir. 1975), *cert. denied*, 424 U.S. 928 (1976).

[33] 666 N.E.2d 1034 (N.Y. 1996).

[34] *Id.* at 1040-1041.

[35] *Id.* at 1043. *See also* Cooper v. USCO Power Equip. Corp., 655 So. 2d 972, 975 (Ala. 1995) (demand not excused by mere allegation that directors breached their fiduciary duty to the corporation and were related to one another).

[36] 473 A.2d 805 (Del. 1984). *See also* Silver v. Allard, 16 F. Supp. 2d 966 (N.D. Ill. 1998) (recognizing that Illinois applies *Aronson*); The Oakland Raiders v. Nat'l Football League, 93 Cal. App. 4th 572 (Cal. Ct. App. 2001) (applying *Aronson*); In re PSE & G Shareholder Litig., 2002 WL 1610282 (N.J. July 23, 2002) (adopting *Aronson's* two-prong inquiry approach; albeit going to some lengths to stress that the approach is one that is less deferential than arises in the standard business judgment rule inquiry).

(1) whether a reasonable doubt as to the director's disinterest or independence is raised by well-pleaded facts; and, if not, (2) whether the complaint pleads particularized facts sufficient to create a reasonable doubt that the challenged transaction was the product of a valid exercise of business judgment.[37]

Where the defendant is alleged to control a majority of the board, demand is generally excused on grounds of futility only if such control is alleged with sufficient particularity that on the facts so pleaded it is futile to believe a majority of the directors could act independently in the matter.[38] Unsupported allegations that the directors are controlled by the alleged wrongdoers are insufficient to excuse the demand.[39] The most liberal decision to date is *De Hass v. Empire Petroleum Company*,[40] where two of five directors were clearly under the defendant's control and demand was excused on finding that the remaining directors were elected by the defendant notwithstanding that on prior occasions those directors had voted against positions favored by the defendant.

In contrast, the Delaware Supreme Court refused to excuse a demand where the defendant who received an allegedly excessive compensation arrangement and interest-free loans owned 47 percent of the shares and his co-defendants who approved those transactions owned an additional 10 percent.[41] The Delaware Supreme Court reasoned that mere proof of majority of the voting powers does not excuse a demand absent further specific allegations that demonstrate "that through personal or other relationships the directors are beholden to the controlling person."[42]

A demand is not required if the directors have made clear that they are opposed to bringing the suit.[43] The most difficult questions for excusing a demand arise when the plaintiff alleges a demand on the board would be futile because the directors have approved the transaction that is the focus of the derivative suit and are thus themselves named as defendants for either having approved the transaction with gross negligence or in bad faith. This is distinguished from the case where the plaintiff pleads that a majority of the directors are financially interested in the transaction that is the subject of the derivative suit. In a case such as financial interest, the demand is easier to excuse than when the basis for arguing futility is based solely on the directors' earlier approval of the suspect transac-

---

[37] *Id.* at 814. *See also* Levine v. Smith, 591 A.2d 194, 207 (Del. 1991) (rephrasing *Aronson*, which is captured in the above text).

[38] *E.g.*, Delaware & Hudson Co. v. Albany & S. R.R., 213 U.S. 435 (1909); Doctor v. Harrington, 196 U.S. 579 (1905); Cathedral Estates, Inc. v. Taft Realty Corp., 228 F.2d 85, 88 (2d Cir. 1955); Country Nat'l Bank v. Mayer, 788 F. Supp. 1136 (E.D. Cal. 1992).

[39] *E.g.*, Kaster v. Modification Sys., 731 F.2d 1014 (2d Cir. 1984).

[40] 286 F. Supp. 809 (D. Colo. 1968), *aff'd*, 435 F.2d 1223 (10th Cir. 1970), criticized in Fischel, *supra* note 15, at 168, 174.

[41] *See* Aronson v. Lewis, 473 A.2d 805 (Del. 1984).

[42] *Id.* at 815. Allegations that the Commissioner of the National Football League, who was the defendant in the derivative suit, exercised influence over many of the members of the league was similarly dismissed. *See* The Oakland Raiders v. Nat'l Football League, 93 Cal. App. 4th 572 (Cal. Ct. App. 2001).

[43] Nussbacher v. Continental Ill. Nat'l Bank & Trust Co., 518 F.2d 873 (7th Cir. 1975), *cert. denied*, 424 U.S. 928 (1976).

tion or that the demand asks the directors to approve a suit against themselves. In a leading case, the court reasoned that "[i]t does not follow . . . that a director who merely made an erroneous business judgment in connection with what was plainly a corporate act will 'refuse to do [his] duty in behalf of the corporation if [he] were asked to do so.' "[44] The clear majority rule will not excuse a demand on the board of directors on a bare allegation that a majority of the board of directors has acquiesced or approved the transaction that is the subject of the derivative suit. The plaintiff must also plead facts that fairly support the conclusion that, by so approving, the directors engaged in a wasteful or purposeful departure from their fiduciary obligations to the corporation.[45] There is sometimes a tendency to attribute to the foregoing bases for excusing a demand a talisman-like effect so that the presence or absence of some mechanical showing resolves the necessity of the plaintiff making a demand. It would appear far better to consider from the totality of the pleadings whether it is likely that the directors can be expected to render a detached evaluation of the suit; this question, not solely the substantive violations alleged, should be the focus of the inquiry.[46]

There are now developing several nontraditional bases for excusing a demand. A special excuse can arise in the close corporation where the plaintiff is but one of two directors.[47] Also, if the board of directors responds to the suit by appointing a special litigation committee that has the sole authority to evaluate whether to pursue the litigation, the court can conclude that the board has conceded its disqualification to entertain a demand.[48]

As the foregoing indicates, courts are not willing to lightly excuse the demand requirement. In fact, as noted by a recent federal decision, there has been a trend toward strengthening the demand requirement.[49] Furthermore, there appears to be a strong movement at the state level toward a universal demand requirement; a good many states have modified their statutes to adopt the universal demand requirement put forth in the Model Act.[50] This shift is noted

---

[44] In re Kauffman Mut. Fund Actions, 479 F.2d 257 (1st Cir. 1973), quoting Bartlett v. New York, N.H. & H. R. Co., 109 N.E. 452, 455 (Mass. 1915).

[45] See, e.g., RCM Sec. Fund Inc. v. Stanton, 928 F.2d 1318 (2d Cir. 1991).

[46] See Lewis v. Curtis, 671 F.2d 779 (3d Cir.), cert. denied, 459 U.S. 880 (1982).

[47] See Collie v. Becknell, 762 P.2d 727 (Colo. Ct. App. 1988). But see Norman v. Nash Johnson & Sons' Farms, Inc., 537 S.E.2d 248 (N.C. Ct. App. 2000) (finding no basis in 1995 amendment adopting universal demand to recognize a close corporation exception). Cf. Wessin v. Archives Corp., 592 N.W.2d 460 (Minn. 1999) (refusing to follow ALI approach, which treats suits involving small number of owners of close corporation as direct suits).

[48] See Peller v. Southern Co., 911 F.2d 1532 (11th Cir. 1990) (the court intimates different result may occur if corporation filed motion to dismiss for failure to make demand and after filing that motion established special litigation committee); Seminaris v. Landa, 662 A.2d 1350 (Del. Ch. 1995), relying on Spiegel v. Buntrock, 571 A.2d 767 (Del. 1990).

[49] Boland v. Engle, 113 F.3d 706 (7th Cir. 1997).

[50] Approximately twenty states have statutorily imposed a universal demand requirement. See, e.g., Conn. Gen. Stat. §33-722; Fla. Stat. ch. 607.07401(2); Ga. Code Ann. §14-2-742; Mich. Comp. Laws §450.1493a; Miss. Code Ann. §79-4-7.42; Mont. Code Ann. §35-1-543; Neb. Rev. Stat. §212072; N.H. Rev. Stat. Ann. §293-A:7.42; N.C. Gen. Stat. §55-7-42; Va. Code Ann. §13.1672.1; Wis. Stat. §180.0742.

by the Seventh Circuit, which observed that the American Law Institute's Corporate Governance principles have prompted a trend of "both the case law and academic commentary moving strongly in that direction as well."[51]

§15.06   Special Litigation Committees[1]

A practice that began in the 1970s has been for the board of directors to delegate the decision of whether to sue on a corporate claim to an independent committee of directors, sometimes with special counsel appointed to assist the committee.[2] Today, it is becoming a common practice for the corporation, either in a demand required or a demand excused case, to establish a committee of independent directors to assess whether continuance of a suit against directors or officers is in the best interests of the corporation.[3] Such committees generally have concluded that continuation of the suit would not promote the best interests of the corporation. Occasionally, a committee will propose a settlement of the action to the derivative suit court.[4] The judicial decisions are in conflict regarding the appropriate standard for reviewing a recommendation of a special litigation committee and a distinct minority of the cases have held such committee action does not merit the attention of the court.

The special litigation committee was created by a melding of the business judgment rule, the demand requirement, and statutory authority for the delegation of board powers. It was intended to provide an efficient means of judging the corporate interest served by a derivative suit when the full board is otherwise disabled by self-interest from gaining the court's attention. The defendant board members' ability to handpick the members of the special litigation committee and defendants' perfect record before these committees, however, have provoked questions about both a committee's ability to render an unbiased assessment of the suit's impact on the corporate interest and the broader issue of whether directors can be impartial in any context when judging their colleagues' actions. The standards for review of the special litigation committee recommendations are

---

[51] Boland v. Engle, 113 F.3d 706, 712-713 (7th Cir. 1997) (relying on Kamen v. Kemper Fin. Servs., Inc., 939 F.2d 458, 461-463 (7th Cir. 1991); Cuker v. Mikalauskas, 692 A.2d 1042 (Pa. 1997), *on remand*, 35 Pa. D.&C. 87 (1998).

§15.06   [1] This section is a current adaptation of James D. Cox & Harry L. Munsinger, Bias in the Boardroom: Psychological Foundations and Legal Implications of Corporate Cohesion, 48 Law & Contemp. Probs. 83, 114-129 (1985).

[2] Lewis v. Anderson, 615 F.2d 778 (9th Cir. 1979), *cert. denied*, 449 U.S. 869 (1980).

The practices regarding special litigation committees described in this section are applied with equal force in the partnership setting. *See* Hirsch v. Jones Intercable, Inc., 984 P.2d 629 (Colo. 1999).

[3] *See, e.g.*, Gaines v. Haughton, 645 F.2d 761 (9th Cir. 1981), *cert. denied*, 454 U.S. 1145 (1982) (committee's determination that not in best interests of corporation to pursue derivative action required dismissal of stockholder's claims); Lewis v. Anderson, 615 F.2d 778, 780 (9th Cir. 1979), *cert. denied*, 449 U.S. 869 (1980); Abbey v. Control Data Corp., 603 F.2d 724, 727 (8th Cir. 1979), *cert. denied*, 444 U.S. 1019 (1980).

[4] *See, e.g.*, Carlton Investors v. TLC Beatrice Int'l Holdings, Inc., 1997 WL 305829 (Del. Ch. 1997).

B. The Demand Requirement

evolving, and there continues to be a good deal of uncertainty surrounding these standards in many leading cases.

Presuming Impartiality. The most skeptical judicial response to the charge that directors are afflicted by structural bias is *Auerbach v. Bennett*,[5] which holds that it is inappropriate for a court to evaluate a special litigation committee's weighing of the legal, ethical, commercial, public relations, or fiscal grounds that support its recommendation that a derivative suit be dismissed.[6] In this way, *Auerbach* effectively confines judicial review to two narrow areas that have traditionally been open to attack by the plaintiff under the business judgment rule: the directors' independence and good faith.[7] These two areas permit plaintiff challenges to the adequacy and appropriateness of the committee's procedures; the substantive bases for the committee's recommendation, however, are shielded by the business judgment rule and according to *Auerbach* are removed from judicial scrutiny.[8]

Auerbach and its progeny[9] are important, not only for the limitations they impose on judicial review of the committee's recommendation but also because they stand as unwavering testimonials to a wide application of the business judgment rule and to the courts' belief that directors are devoted primarily to the corporate interest. Courts persuaded by *Auerbach*'s articulation of the limited judicial review necessary in special litigation committee cases have in effect announced a substantial presumption that the committee has acted properly, so that its recommendation can be overturned only in extreme situations.[10]

Questioning the Appointive Process. In contrast to *Auerbach, Miller v. Register & Tribune Syndicate, Inc.*[11] expressed the fear that even the most finely tuned adversarial inquiry could not clearly distinguish rationally drawn conclusions from collegial bias. The issue in *Miller* was whether a committee whose members were all nominated to the board after the derivative suit's commencement could cause that suit's dismissal. The Iowa Supreme Court held that it could not.[12] The *Miller* court's approach nevertheless singled out a specific situation in which committee recommendations were disallowed:

> We believe that the potential for structural bias on the part of a litigation committee appointed by directors who are parties to derivative actions is sufficiently

[5] 393 N.E.2d 994 (N.Y. 1979).

[6] *Id.* at 1002.

[7] *Id.* at 996.

[8] *See id.*

[9] For other jurisdictions following *Auerbach, see, e.g.,* Curtis v. Nevens, 31 P.3d 146 (Colo. 2001); Drilling v. Berman, 589 N.W.2d 503, 506-507 (Minn. Ct. App. 1999) (interpreting statute as embracing *Auerbach*-type limited review standard).

[10] Hasan v. CleveTrust Realty Investors, 548 F. Supp. 1146, 1149 (N.D. Ohio 1982). *But see* Drilling v. Berman, 589 N.W.2d 503 (Minn. Ct. App. 1999) (distinguishing *Hasan* as case where committee's independence was in doubt and that finding "Other courts invoking the *Auerbach* approach still evaluate the overall adequacy of the committee's investigation as a litmus of its "good faith."

[11] 336 N.W.2d 709 (Iowa 1983). *See also* Alford v. Shaw, 324 S.E.2d 878 (N.C. Ct. App. 1985).

[12] 336 N.W.2d 709.

great and sufficiently difficult of precise proof in an individual case to require the adoption of a prophylactic rule. We conclude that we should prevent the potential for structural bias in some cases by effectively limiting the powers of such directors in all cases.[13]

Dispatching Skepticism Through Judicial Review. A leading case concerning the review standards for special litigation committee recommendations is *Zapata Corp. v. Maldonado,*[14] which clearly expresses its concern for the directors' potential bias:

> [N]otwithstanding our conviction that Delaware law entrusts the corporate power to a properly authorized committee, we must be mindful that directors are passing judgment on fellow directors in the same corporation and fellow directors, in this instance, who designated them to serve both as directors and committee members. The question naturally arises whether a "there but for the grace of God go I" empathy may not play a role. And the further question arises whether inquiry as to independence, good faith and reasonable investigation is sufficient safeguard against abuse, perhaps subconscious abuse.[15]

While recognizing a serious threat of director bias, *Zapata* did not include *Miller*'s sweeping solution. The *Zapata* court reasoned that judicial review of a committee's recommendation should not eviscerate the valuable role the directors' judgments of a suit's worth can play in derivative suit litigation. The court charted what it believed to be a middle course between allowing committee recommendations so much deference that the derivative suit is mortally wounded, on the one hand, and being so skeptical of the committee that the corporation is totally unable to rid itself of a harmful suit, on the other. Into this breach, the Delaware Supreme Court placed a two-step test.

Under *Zapata*'s first step, the court evaluates the committee members' independence, good faith, and bases for their recommendation.[16] *Zapata* reinforced these requirements by demanding a detailed report of the committee's investigation procedures and findings, by placing the burden of establishing these factors on the committee, and by subjecting the committee's reasoning to close scrutiny.[17] This scrutiny represents the court's most sweeping response to the threat of structural bias. In its second step, *Zapata* invited the reviewing court to exercise its independent judgment in determining whether the corporate interest is served by the derivative suit's continuance.[18] This discretion is to be exercised only in limited instances, however.

---

[13] *Id.* at 718.

[14] 430 A.2d 779 (Del. 1981).

[15] *Id.* at 787. Zapata has been used in suits arising within limited partnerships. *See* Katell v. Morgan Stanley Group, Inc. [1995 Transfer Binder], Fed. Sec. L. Rep. (CCH) ¶98,861 (Del. Ch. 1995).

[16] *Id.* at 788-789.

[17] *See id.*

[18] *Id.* at 789. One court has referred to *Zapata*'s second step as invoking an "imprecise smell test." *See* Strougo v. Padegs, 27 F. Supp. 2d 442, 490 (S.D.N.Y. 1998).

For the view that statutory provisions, such as the Model Act, that prescribe the criteria for a committee recommendation to give rise to dismissal of the derivative suit necessarily preclude resort to Zapata's second step, *see* Cutshall v. Barker, 773 N.E.2d 973, 970 (Ind. Ct. App. 2000).

B. The Demand Requirement

The criteria *Zapata* proposed unfortunately are quite vague, so that achieving *Zapata*'s objectives primarily depends on the reviewing court's general concern for structural bias. *Zapata* offers no insight into the meaning of any of the first-level standards. Potentially the standards of independence, good faith, and reasonable bases could be interpreted and applied to generate more penetrating inquiry into the committee's actions than the inquiry likely to result using the standards of *Auerbach*.

The syntax of *Zapata*'s two-step analysis suggests that greater deference be accorded a committee's recommendation in the first step than in the second step. As seen above, the court's independent judgment, exercised at the second step, is reserved for nonfrivolous cases. Frivolity no doubt is in the eye of the beholder. To be sure, it is neither necessary nor appropriate under *Zapata* for a court to exercise its own independent judgment in step two when it concurs in the committee's assessment that the suit lacks merit. Unanswered in *Zapata*, however, is how deeply the court should probe the committee's report at step one, in making its threshold determination of the suit's merits, before it can advance to the second-step analysis. The Delaware Supreme Court's concern that directors retain some power to deflect a wasteful derivative action[19] suggests an approach in which deference is extended to the committee's opinion on the merits, except when a prima facie case can be established solely on the basis of the committee's report showing that the committee's dismissal recommendation is grounded on weak considerations such as the suit's incidental costs exceeding its benefits.[20] *Zapata* may well envision that the committee's view of the suit's merits should enjoy the same level of deference that courts extend to director judgments in other areas in which directors are, under the reasonable basis criterion, free to select from among several reasonably supported alternatives.[21]

The Independence and Good Faith Inquiries. Independence, whether for considering whether a demand should be required or whether a recommendation of a special litigation committee or, for that matter, the board of directors in a demand required case, should cause the suit's dismissal, turns on the ultimate question whether the opining directors have a relationship with the individual defendant or the suit itself that would reasonably be expected to affect the directors' judgment with respect to the litigation.[22] The threshold requirement for the

---

[19] 430 A.2d at 786-787.

[20] *See, e.g.*, Abramowitz v. Posner, 513 F. Supp. 120, 123-124, 131-132 (S.D.N.Y. 1981), *aff'd*, 672 F.2d 1025 (2d Cir. 1982); *see also* Lewis v. Anderson, 615 F.2d 778 (9th Cir. 1979), *cert. denied*, 449 U.S. 869 (1980).

[21] *E.g.*, in Elfenbein v. American Fin. Corp., 487 F. Supp. 619 (S.D.N.Y. 1980), the court held that the directors of a parent corporation had a reasonable basis for their exercise of warrants in a subsidiary corporation because they relied on counsel's opinion that the exercise presented no perils under the tax laws, even though two other experts disagreed.

[22] *See* Einhorn v. Culea, 235 N.W.2d 78, 98 (Wis. 2000) (listing the following factors to be considered: whether the director has potential liability in the underlying action including being a defendant therein; director's participation or approval or receipt of benefits from the challenged transaction; director's past or present business dealings with individual defendant; director's family, personal, or social relationships with defendant; director's past or present financial relations with the corporation; number of members of the committee; and roles of corporate counsel and independent counsel);

independence of committee members is that they are not themselves defendants in the derivative suit.[23] A committee does not lack independence solely because its members were appointed by the defendants.[24] There is little doubt that the number of committee members is a factor to consider in evaluating its independence from the defendants,[25] specifically that single-person committees raise interesting flags.[26]

Independence has successfully been questioned on a showing that the committee member has a material financial relationship with the corporation.[27] A committee was found to lack independence where just prior to its formation all the directors, including those later appointed to the committee, voted to resist the derivative suit.[28] And, in a case that appears to have all possible indicia of what does not make a committee independent, *Lewis v. Fuqua,*[29] the sole member of the committee

> . . . was a member of the board of directors of Fuqua Industries at the time the challenged actions took place; he is one of the defendants in this suit; he has had numerous political and financial dealings with J. B. Fuqua who is the chief executive officer of Fuqua Industries and who allegedly controls the Board; he is President of Duke University which is a recent recipient of a $10 million pledge from Fuqua Industries and J. B. Fuqua; and J. B. Fuqua has, in the past, made several contributions to Duke University and is a Trustee of the University.

Moreover, the committee's recommendation lacks the force of an independent body where it is purely advisory to the full board of directors most of whose members are defendants in the derivative action.[30]

An important consideration, indeed it can be regarded as a separate requirement, for the committee's independence is that the committee be advised by

---

Kaplan v. Wyatt, 499 A.2d 1184, 1189 (Del. 1989) (when decisions are reached on the merits and not "by extraneous considerations or influences"). Statutes sometimes provide their own prescription of what constitutes a "disinterested" director. *See, e.g.,* Cutshall v. Barker, 733 N.E.2d 973 (Ind. Ct. App. 2000) (construing Ind. Code §23-1-32-4(d)). The approach taken under the Model Act is to identify separate relationships which "by itself" would not cause a director not to be "independent." *See* MBCA §7.44(c) (1990).

[23] *See, e.g.,* Gaines v. Haughton, 645 F.2d 761 (9th Cir. 1981), *cert. denied,* 424 U.S. 1145 (1982); Abbey v. Control Data Corp., 603 F.2d 724, 727 (8th Cir. 1979), *cert. denied,* 444 U.S. 1017 (1980).

[24] *See, e.g.,* Strougo v. Padegs, 27 F. Supp. 2d 442 (S.D.N.Y. 1998); Peller v. The Southern Co., 707 F. Supp. 525 (N.D. Ga. 1998).

[25] *See* Houle v. Low, 556 N.E.2d 51, 59 (Mass. 1990).

[26] *See* Hasan v. CleveTrust Realty Investors, 729 F.2d 372 (6th Cir. 1984); Lewis v. Fuqua, 502 A.2d 962, 967 (Del. Ch. 1985) ("If a single member committee is to be used, the member should be like Caesar's wife, be above reproach.").

[27] *See* Hasan v. CleveTrust Realty Investors, 729 F.2d 372 (6th Cir. 1984) (single person committee who owned 25 percent of firm that received substantial fees from corporation managed by derivative suit defendant and also owned 2 percent of real estate partnership with defendant).

[28] *See* Swenson v. Thibaut, 250 S.E.2d 279 (N.C. Ct. App. 1978).

[29] 502 A.2d 962, 966-967 (Del. Ch. 1985).

[30] Par Pharmaceutical Inc. Derivative Litig., 750 F. Supp. 641 (S.D.N.Y. 1990).

B. The Demand Requirement

counsel with no historical relationship with the firm.[31] Underlying this requirement is concern that the committee's independent judgment may be compromised whenever the committee's chief legal advisor has a long-standing professional representation of the firm that in no small part depends upon personal relations with the derivative suit defendants. There also is concern that dual representation of the committee and former and on-going representation of the corporation may seriously compromise the confidentiality requirements of the attorney-client relationship.[32]

Auerbach provides a useful definition of the "good faith" requirement, stating "proof . . . that the investigation has been so restricted in scope, so shallow in execution, or otherwise so *pro forma* or halfhearted as to constitute a pretext or sham . . . would raise questions of good faith. . . ."[33] Thus, a thoughtful, systematic and probing investigation of the facts and report of the findings and conclusions significantly bolster the belief the committee has acted in good faith.[34] Investigations, however, need not be with the formalities of a court proceeding so that stenographic records or testimony under oath are not required to establish the committee's good faith inquiry.[35] The committee's reliance on its independent counsel to perform most of the investigation and the avenues of inquiry that the committee reasonably explained for not exploring is not a basis for finding that its inquiry was so flawed as to constitute a bad faith investigation.[36] A classic illustration of how a committee's report serves to document the absence of good faith is *Hasan v. Clevetrust Realty Investors*,[37] even though the report is 122 pages in length. The derivative suit complaint arose out of greenmail payments made to each of two companies that had acquired a significant percentage of the derivative suit corporation's shares. Reasoning that the committee's failure to interview the personnel of either company was so pertinent to whether the purchase price was fair and was motivated by management's fears for their jobs, the court held that the committee's report was not prepared in good faith. Other cases have also established a lack of good faith based on the superficial quality of the underlying

---

[31] In re Perrigo Co., 128 F.3d 430 (6th Cir. 1997); Bell Atlantic Corp. v. Bolger, 2 F.3d 1304 (3d Cir. 1993); Musheno v. Gensemer, 897 F. Supp. 833 (M.D. Pa. 1995); In re Oracle Sec. Litigation, 829 F. Supp. 1176 (N.D. Cal. 1993); In re Par Pharmaceutical Inc. Derivative Litig., 750 F. Supp. 641 (S.D.N.Y. 1990). *See also* Einhorn v. Culea, 612 N.W.2d 78 (Wis. 2000) (emphasizing important consideration in assessing committee's independence is counsel that previously did not represent the firm). However, the committee's independence was not compromised when counsel that was first retained after the initiation of the suit might thereafter represent both the committee and the corporation. *See* Cutshall v. Barker, 733 N.E.2d 973 (Ind. Ct. App. 2000).

[32] *See* Musheno v. Gensemer, 897 F. Supp. 833, 838 (M.D. Pa. 1995).

[33] Auerbach v. Bennett, 419 N.Y.S.2d 920, 929 (N.Y. 1979).

[34] For excellent descriptions of steps committees have taken, *see* Strougo v. Padegs, 27 F. Supp. 2d 442, 451-453 (S.D.N.Y. 1998); Johnson v. Hui, 811 F. Supp. 479, 489 (N.D. Cal. 1991); Rosengarten v. Buckley, 613 F. Supp. 1493, 1503 (D. Md. 1985); Cutshall v. Barker, 733 N.E.2d 973 (Ind. Ct. App. 2000); Drilling v. Berman, 589 N.W.2d 503, 509 (Minn. Ct. App. 1999).

[35] *Id.*

[36] *See, e.g.,* Maldonado v. Flynn, 485 F. Supp. 274, 284 (S.D.N.Y. 1980); Rosengarten v. International Tel. & Tel., 466 F. Supp. 817 (S.D.N.Y. 1979).

[37] 729 F.2d 372 (6th Cir. 1984).

report[38] or that the committee had taken action inconsistent with the report's facts.[39]

"Valuing" the Suit. Significantly, post-*Zapata* decisions fail to recognize the discretionary aspect of *Zapata*'s second step. Courts purporting to follow *Zapata* have instead interpreted the case to require the exercise of independent business judgment in *all* cases.[40] The most insightful application of this interpretation of *Zapata* was by the Second Circuit in *Joy v. North*,[41] which offered the following description of the reviewing court's function:

> [T]he burden is on the moving party, as in motions for summary judgment generally, to demonstrate that the action is more likely than not to be against the interests of the corporation. . . . [T]he function of the court's review is to determine the balance of probabilities as to likely future benefit to the corporation, not to render a decision on the merits, fashion the appropriate legal principles or resolve issues of credibility. Where the legal rule is unclear and the likely evidence in conflict, the court need only weigh the uncertainties, not resolve them. The court's function is thus not unlike a lawyer's determining what a case is "worth" for purposes of settlement.[42]

The approach advocated in *Joy* is light years beyond the uncritical evaluation embraced in *Auerbach*. Minimally, the *Joy* approach is a more fully textured description of the review process initially proposed in *Zapata*. Moreover, *Joy* is the rare instance in which a court has refused to follow a committee's recommendation to dismiss a derivative action on the substance of the committee's report.[43]

---

[38] *See, e.g.,* Holmstrom v. Coastal Indus. [1984 Transfer Binder], Fed. Sec. L. Rep. (CCH) ¶91,486 (N.D. Ohio 1984); Electra Inv. Trust PLC v. Crews, 1999 Del. Ch. Lexis 36 (Del. Ch. 1999).

[39] *See* Watts v. Des Moines Register & Tribune, 525 F. Supp. 1311, 1329-1330 (S.D. Iowa 1981) (special counsel opined that five of the pled causes of action should be pursued).

[40] *See, e.g.,* Joy v. North, 692 F.2d 880, 888-889 (2d Cir. 1982), *cert. denied,* 460 U.S. 1051 (1983); Maldonado v. Flynn, 671 F.2d 729, 732 (2d Cir. 1982); Abella v. Universal Leaf Tobacco Co., 546 F. Supp. 795, 801 (E.D. Va. 1982); Watts v. Des Moines Register & Tribune, 525 F. Supp. 1311, 1329 (S.D. Iowa 1981). In both *Watts* and *Maldonado,* the two earliest post-*Zapata* cases, the courts, even though satisfied that the committees acted in good faith and were independent, did not grant their recommendations that the suits be dismissed because each committee failed to offer an adequate explanation of its reasoning. The result in each case, however, turned on unique procedural configurations, not on the court's actual exercise of an independent business judgment. Delaware continues, however, to view the second-step analysis as being a matter of discretion. Kaplan v. Wyatt, 484 A.2d 501, 508-509 (Del. Ch. 1984).

[41] 692 F.2d 880 (2d Cir. 1982), *cert. denied,* 460 U.S. 1051 (1983).

[42] *Id.* at 892. For other cases following this methodology, *see* Stougo v. Padegs, 27 F. Supp. 2d 442 (S.D.N.Y. 1998); Skoglund v. Brady, 541 N.W.2d 17 (Minn. Ct. App. 1995).

[43] One other case has rejected the committee's recommendation because of substantive considerations in the committee's report. *See* Holmstrom v. Coastal Indus. [1984 Transfer Binder], Fed. Sec. L. Rep. (CCH) ¶91,486 (N.D. Ohio 1984). Another case delayed any action in response to a committee's report until the committee further developed its reasons for recommending dismissal. Watts v. Des Moines Register & Tribune, 525 F. Supp. 1311, 1327-1329 (S.D. Iowa 1981). And three other cases have rejected the committee's recommendation because its independence and good faith were doubted. Hasan v. CleveTrust Realty Investors, 729 F.2d 372, 379 (6th Cir. 1984); Miller v. Register & Tribune Syndicate, 336 N.W.2d 709, 718 (Iowa 1983); Swenson v. Thibaut, 250 S.E.2d 279, 298 (N.C. Ct. App. 1978).

B. The Demand Requirement

The complaint in *Joy* arose from loans made by Citytrust Bankcorp, Inc. to Katz, a developer in precarious financial condition. The loans ultimately exceeded the maximum limit permitted to a single borrower by the National Bank Act.[44] Katz's default caused Citytrust to absorb a certain loss of more than $5 million.[45] The special litigation committee was established nearly two years after the derivative suit was commenced. The committee, after nine months, recommended dismissal of the derivative suit against the 23 "outside" defendants, concluding that there was "no reasonable possibility" they would be held liable.[46] As for the remaining seven "inside" defendants, who were senior officers of Citytrust and therefore deeply involved in approving the Katz loans, the committee's recommendation was equivocal. The committee reasoned that there was a possibility that the inside defendants had acted negligently and recommended that settlement negotiations be undertaken with the inside defendants. The committee nevertheless cautioned that its recommendation that settlement negotiations were appropriate did not necessarily imply that the committee believed continued litigation against the inside defendants served the corporate interest.[47]

The *Joy* court's review of the committee's dismissal recommendation nicely frames the dilemma that a special litigation committee poses to a court responding to a recommendation that a derivative suit be dismissed. The court was forced to choose between accepting the committee's evaluation of law and facts, which possibly was contaminated in some indeterminate amount by the directors' bias, or pursuing a final resolution of the legal and factual uncertainties through costly litigation of the claim. The special litigation committee's potential contribution toward shortening the course of wasteful litigation is exemplified by cases such as *Joy*, where the suit's outcome is problematic at the pretrial stage. This situation arises when, on the one hand, the conclusions to be drawn from the facts—such as the defendants' involvement in the alleged wrongdoing or the existence of a business purpose that would exonerate them—remain uncertain even after pretrial investigation or, on the other hand, when the applicable legal duties and defenses are still evolving and are therefore indefinite.[48] When neither the facts nor the law are disputed, however, the special litigation committee adds little to the defendants' arsenal for ridding themselves of a wasteful derivative suit during the pretrial stage. The more conventional pretrial motion for summary judgment (aided by uncontroverted affidavits) or motion to dismiss are available to dispose of a suit.

***The American Law Institute, The Model Act, and* Alford v. Shaw.** The American Law Institute in its corporate governance project joins the ranks of

---

[44] 12 U.S.C. §84 (2000).

[45] 692 F.2d at 895.

[46] *Id.* at 884.

[47] *Id.*

[48] This is an insight overlooked by the Delaware Chancery Court. Chancellor Brown in Kaplan v. Wyatt, 484 A.2d 501 (Del. Ch. 1984), observed that special litigation committees are wasteful because they contribute toward "litigation within litigation." *Id.* at 511.

commentators[49] (and a few courts[50]) who have counseled that the same review standards should apply to demand-required cases as are applied to committee recommendations in demand-excused cases. The ALI carries forward the demand-on-directors requirement[51] and severely limits the bases for excusing these demands.[52] However, later provisions[53] reduce the operational effects of making a demand. The purpose of demand is no longer to provide the target toward which the defendant's colleagues direct their shared beliefs that the suit is not in the corporation's best interest; under the proposal, the response to the suit occurs through a recommendation proffered independently of the demand. The recommendation is made by a committee of directors chosen by the board[54] or, on the corporation's request, by a committee of nondirectors chosen by the court.[55] The Reporters have thereby tailored the demand requirement's effects so that the act of making a demand serves as a means for corrective action or as a step toward the corporation's assuming control over the suit.[56] The American Law Institute therefore embraces "universal demand." This is now the approach taken by the Model Business Corporation Act. On this point the ALI's and Model Act's approaches appear infinitely sound. Certainly there is no suggestion in the materials reviewed earlier that structural bias is less robust when the so-called independent directors constitute a majority of the board (so that under contemporary standards a demand is required and a lower level of review occurs) than when only a minority of the board is considered independent (so that demand is excused).

The centerpiece of the American Law Institute and Model Act approaches is the prescreening of suits through an independent board or special litigation committee.[57] The review court's focus is upon the "good faith" of the recommending body and whether it has caried out a "reasonable inquiry."[58] Under the Model Act, the assignment of the burden of proof on these matters rests upon whether a majority of the board's directors are independent. If, when a demand is made, a majority of the board is independent the plaintiff bears the burden of proof.[59] If the board lacks an independent majority, the burden of proof is upon those seeking the suit's dismissal to establish their good faith and reasonable inquiry.[60]

[49] *See, e.g.,* James D. Cox, Searching for the Corporation's Voice in Derivative Suit Litigation: A Critique of Zapata and the ALI Project, 1982 Duke L.J. 959, 1009-1010.

[50] *See, e.g.,* Alford v. Shaw, 358 S.E.2d 323 (N.C. 1987). *See generally* James D. Cox, Heroes in the Law: Alford v. Shaw, 66 N.C. L. Rev. 565 (1988).

[51] ALI, 2 Principles of Corporate Governance, *supra* §15.03 note 46, §7.03(a). The Pennsylvania Supreme Court has unqualifiedly accepted the proposals of the ALI as the law for Pennsylvania. *See* Cuker v. Mikalauskas, 692 A.2d 1042 (Pa. 1997). *See also* In re PSE & G Shareholder Litigation, 718 A.2d 254 (N.J. Super. Ct. Ch. Div. 1998) (adopting approach of *Cuker* and *Alford*).

[52] ALI, 2 Principles of Corporate Governance, *supra,* §15.03 note 46, §7.03(b) ("specific showing that irreparable injury to the corporation would otherwise result").

[53] *Id.* §§7.07-7.10.

[54] *Id.* §§7.07, 7.08.

[55] *Id.* §7.12.

[56] *Id.* at 53-55.

[57] *Id.* §§7.07, 7.08

[58] *See* NBCA §744(a) (1984).

[59] *See id.* §7.44(e).

[60] *See id.*

B. The Demand Requirement

The North Carolina Supreme Court in *Alford v. Shaw*[61] took a position similar to the Model Act. It held that the level of judicial scrutiny does not depend on the limited consideration of whether the case is a demand-required or demand-excused case. Courts following the approach of *Alford v. Shaw* consider a wide range of considerations relevant to the committee's independence and good faith, whether it be a demand-required or demand-excused case.[62] This does not overlook whether there is a critical mass of directors who are not implicated in the conduct or transaction that is the basis of the derivative suit; such evidence is but a factor in weighing the deference the court is to accord the directors' or committee's dismissal recommendation.

Federalism and the Special Litigation Committee. The Supreme Court in *Burks v. Lasker*[63] held that in federal question litigation, when confronted with a dismissal recommended by a special litigation committee, the federal district court must follow a two-stage analysis. The first inquiry is to determine the extent to which the committee has the power under state law to cause the derivative suit to be dismissed. If the committee has such power under the facts before the court, the court must determine, second, whether dismissal of the suit would be inconsistent with the policy underlying the federal cause of action. Where Congress has addressed the directors' discretionary powers to terminate a derivative suit with such particularity that it would be inconsistent with Congress's obvious intent to permit the directors to deflect the derivative suit, the Court reasoned that dismissal would be inappropriate.[64] The courts have consistently held that *Burks* does not bar a dismissal at the recommendation of a special litigation committee under the antifraud provisions of the federal securities laws.[65]

§15.07   Standing to Bring a Derivative Suit

In order to maintain a derivative suit to redress or prevent injuries to the corporation, the plaintiff must be either an owner of shares or have some beneficial interest therein when the suit is brought.[1] As a general rule, the plaintiff must continue to be a stockholder throughout the life of the suit so that the plaintiff stands to benefit derivatively by the relief given; if the plaintiff ceases to be a shareholder by reason of a transfer of shares, he loses standing to complain.[2] The purpose of

---

[61] 358 S.E.2d 323 (N.C. 1987). *See* Cox, *supra* note 50.

[62] *See* Lewis v. Boyd, 838 S.E.2d 215 (Tenn. Ct. App. 1992); Houle v. Low, 556 N.E.2d 51 (Mass. 1990); In re PSE & G Shareholder Litig., 718 A.2d 254, 260-261 (N.J. Super. Ch. Div. 1998).

[63] 441 U.S. 471, 480 (1979).

[64] 441 U.S. at 484.

[65] *See, e.g.*, Lewis v. Anderson, 615 F.2d 778 (9th Cir. 1979).

§15.07   [1] A distinct minority of the states require the derivative suit plaintiff to be an "owner of record." *See* W. Va. Code Ann. §31-1-103 (Michie 2001). Formerly this was the case in other states as well.

Standing is extended even to equitable holders. *See* Mullen v. Sweetwater Dev. Corp., 619 F. Supp. 809, 817 (D. Colo. 1985).

[2] *See, e.g.*, Lewis v. Chiles, 719 F.2d 1044 (9th Cir. 1983).

the rule is to align the plaintiff's economic interests with the corporate interest to be advanced by the diligent prosecution of the suit.[3] But as is true with any rule whose rigid enforcement can lead to unfair or inequitable results, notable exceptions to this continuous-ownership requirement are recognized in many jurisdictions.[4]

A creditor has no proprietary interest and thus cannot maintain a derivative suit.[5] The authorities are split on whether holders of debentures convertible into stock may bring a derivative suit.[6] The standing of holders of American Depositary Receipts to bring a derivative can be affected by provisions of the deposit agreement.[7] With the exception of the rare corporate statute that provides otherwise, directors and officers who cannot satisfy the share-ownership requirement do not have standing to bring a derivative suit solely because of their capacity as directors or officers.[8] A derivative suit may, however, be brought by a deceased shareholder's administrator or executor having the title to shares in such capacity, by the beneficial owner of shares if a trustee refuses to sue and is made a party defendant,[9] by a pledgee of shares,[10] or by a pledgor of shares, such as a margin customer of a stockbroker holding the stock in the street name for the customer's account.[11]

Under the federal rules[12] and most state statutes,[13] the plaintiff in a shareholder's derivative suit must have been a shareholder of record, a holder of voting trust certificates, or a beneficial owner *at the time of the transaction* that is the subject of the suit. This requirement is also met if the suit's plaintiff acquired her shares by operation of law from one who held the shares at the time of the trans-

---

[3] *See* Schupack v. Covelli, 498 F. Supp. 704 (W.D. Pa. 1980) (only party with present interest in corporation will adequately represent corporation's interests in derivative action).

[4] Brown v. Brown, 731 A.2d 1212 (N.J. Super. App. Div. 1999).

[5] *See, e.g.,* Darrow v. Southdown, Inc., 574 F.2d 1333 (5th Cir. 1978); Dodge v. First Wis. Trust Co., 394 F. Supp. 1124 (E.D. Wis. 1975). Highly critical analysis of denying creditors standing to bring derivative suits appears in Morey McDaniel, Bondholders and Corporate Governance, 41 Bus. Law. 413 (1986); Note, Creditors' Derivative Suits on Behalf of Solvent Corporations, 88 Yale L.J. 1299 (1979).

[6] *Compare* Kunser v. First Pa. Corp., 395 F. Supp. 276 (E.D. Pa. 1975), *aff'd in part and rev'd in part on other grounds,* 531 F.2d 1234 (3d Cir. 1976); Simon v. Cogan, 549 A.2d 300 (Del. 1988) (denying standing to convertible debenture holders), and Harff v. Kerkorian, 324 A.2d 215 (Del. Ch. 1974), *aff'd in part and rev'd in part on other grounds,* 347 A.2d 133 (Del. 1975) (denying convertible bondholders standing to bring a derivative action), *with* Hoff v. Sprayregan, 52 F.R.D. 243 (S.D.N.Y. 1971).

[7] Batchelder v. Kawamoto, 147 F.3d 915 (9th Cir. 1998) (standing denied because deposit agreement provided holders' rights would be determined according to Japanese law, which does not treat holders of ADR's as shareholders).

[8] Wright v. Floyd, 86 N.E. 971 (Ind. Ct. App. 1909). *But see* Cal. Corp. Code §9142(2)&(3) (West 1990) (allowing officers and directors of a nonprofit corporation to sue for corporate injury); N.Y. Bus. Corp. Law §720(b) (McKinney 1986).

[9] Cal. Corp. Code §800 (West 1990); N.Y. Bus. Corp. Law §626(a) (McKinney 1986); MBCA §7.40 (1981).

[10] Green v. Hedenberg, 42 N.E. 851 (Ill. 1896). *See also* Weinhaus v. Gale, 237 F.2d 197 (7th Cir. 1956).

[11] Braasch v. Goldschmidt, 199 A.2d 760 (Del. Ch. 1964).

[12] Fed. R. Civ. P. 23.1.

[13] Del. Code Ann. tit. 8, §317 (2001); N.Y. Bus. Corp. Law §626(b) (McKinney 1986).

B. The Demand Requirement

action giving rise to the derivative suit complaint. This requirement is commonly referred to as the "contemporaneous ownership" rule. Where it exists,[14] the contemporaneous ownership rule bars suit by those who acquired their shares or beneficial ownership *after* the misconduct that is the subject of the derivative suit.[15] The rule harmonizes with the basic standing principle that a plaintiff must have sustained a real injury in order to have the right to sue.[16] Most modern courts also agree that a justification for the contemporaneous ownership rule is the prevention of strike suits and speculative litigation.[17] The more dominant rationale for the contemporaneous ownership rule is the prevention of unjust enrichment. As has been seen, any monetary recovery obtained through a derivative suit flows to the corporation, except in those rare cases in which the court orders a pro rata recovery. With the suit's fruits flowing to the corporation, all of its shareholders are the true beneficiaries of the recovery in a derivative suit with each shareholder indirectly reaping a benefit proportionate to his ownership of the firm.[18] In a publicly traded corporation ownership is constantly changing such that there is inherent in any derivative suit a distinct windfall to shareholders who become such after the misconduct that is redressed in the derivative suit. This occurs because shares purchased subsequent to a significant injurious transaction are likely to reflect a decreased market value because of the transaction. A subsequent purchaser normally receives value equal to the purchase price. Therefore, any recovery by the corporation that benefits a subsequent purchaser arguably constitutes unjust enrichment of the purchaser.[19]

This concern, however, does not apply where the value of the stock does not reflect the consequences of the harmful activity until some time after a purchaser has acquired the shares. Thus on close examination, any strong concern for unjust enrichment most certainly should in most cases doom the derivative suit for publicly traded corporations. Simply put, some level of unjust enrichment is inevitable. One may therefore question just how strong a public policy is served by continuing to embrace the contemporaneous ownership requirement for derivative suit litigation involving public corporations.

Some weakening of the support for the contemporaneous ownership rule appears in statutes that have relaxed the requirement considerably.[20] The proposals of the American Law Institute adopt the novel approach of conditioning a suit

---

[14] The requirement appears in Fed. R. Civ. P. 23.1 and exists in a majority of the states either by statute, case law, or court rule. *See generally* 12B Fletcher, *supra* §15.01 note 10, §5981 (perm. ed. 2000).

[15] *See, e.g.*, International Broadcasting Corp. v. Turner, 734 F. Supp. 383 (D. Minn. 1990); Centrella v. Morris, 597 P.2d 958 (Wyo. 1970).

[16] This reasoning comes from Home Fire Ins. Co. v. Barber, 93 N.W. 1024, 1029 (Neb. 1903) (one who does not own stock at the time of mismanagement is not injured unless the effects continue and are injurious to him), which is generally credited with giving impetus to the force with which the doctrine is applied today.

[17] Gottesman v. General Motors Corp., 28 F.R.D. 325, 326 (S.D.N.Y. 1961); Phillips v. Bradford, 62 F.R.D. 681, 685 (S.D.N.Y. 1974); Lawson v. Baltimore Paint & Chem. Corp., 347 F. Supp. 967, 974 (D. Md. 1972).

[18] Bangor Punta Operations v. Bangor & Aroostock R.R., 417 U.S. 703 (1974); Home Fire Ins. Co. v. Barber, 93 N.W. 1024, 1033 (Neb. 1903).

[19] *See* Bangor Punta Operations Co. v. Aroostock R.R., 417 U.S. 703 (1978).

[20] *See e.g.*, Cal. Corp. Code §800(b)(1) (West 1990).

on the plaintiff's having become a stockholder "before the material facts relating to the alleged wrong were publicly disclosed or were known by, or specifically communicated to, the holder."[21] In so placing the cutoff for a holder's standing to sue derivatively, the American Law Institute embraces a more realistic test of when the share prices are likely to reflect the impact of the misconduct. Those becoming stockholders after the public becomes aware or the shareholders are aware of the misconduct are more likely to derive a windfall as a consequence of the suit than one who purchased shares subsequent to misconduct that became known only after that purchase.

Problems arise in identifying the time of the wrongful transaction for purposes of the contemporaneous ownership rule. If the alleged wrong is a single act, the critical date is of course easy to identify. When the acts complained of occurred over a period of time, however, many courts have adopted a rule that for a plaintiff to maintain a derivative suit for harmful activity that commenced before her acquisition of shares, the harmful activity must continue to endanger corporate assets thereafter.[22] Whether a court will grant standing to a derivative plaintiff on a "continuing wrong" theory depends on how the court perceives or interprets what constitutes a "transaction."[23] In fact, there appears to be no strong disagreement that the continuing wrong theory is a necessary dimension of the contemporaneous ownership rule, but the courts vary widely in their interpretation of what a continuing wrong is. Thus Delaware has split on whether the wrong is continuing when, on the one hand, the plaintiff purchased before shares were issued but after the resolution authorizing their issuance,[24] and, on the other hand, when the plaintiff purchased after stock option plans were issued to officers but before the options' exercise,[25] when in each case the complaint was that the shares were being issued for insufficient or no consideration. Statutes in several states embrace the continuing wrong theory by conditioning a suit on the plaintiff having been a stockholder at the time of the transaction "or any part thereof."[26]

The plaintiff must be a shareholder at the time of the suit,[27] and most courts take the position that a plaintiff's ownership must have been uninterrupted during the interim period between the complained of transaction and the bringing of the suit[28] and must continue through the life of the suit.[29] This "continuing ownership" requirement poses serious problems when the misconduct that is the focus of the derivative suit occurred in connection with the corporation's acquisi-

---

[21] ALI, 2 Principles of Corporate Governance, *supra* §15.02 note 46, §7.02(a)(1).

[22] *See, e.g.,* Bateson v. Magna Oil Corp., 414 F.2d 128, 130 (5th Cir. 1969), *cert. denied,* 397 U.S. 911 (1970); Palmer v. Morris, 316 F.2d 649, 650 (5th Cir. 1963).

[23] *See, e.g.,* Goldie v. Yaker, 432 P.2d 841, 843-844 (N.M. 1967). *See generally* 7A Wright, Miller & Kane, *supra* §15.04 note 12, §1828 at 65 (2d ed. 1986).

[24] Maclary v. Pleasant Hills, Inc., 109 A.2d 830 (Del. Ch. 1954) (continuing-wrong theory applies).

[25] Elster v. American Airlines, Inc., 100 A.2d 219 (Del. Ch. 1953). *See also* 7547 Partners v. Beck, 682 A.2d 160 (Del. 1996).

[26] *See, e.g.,* Cal. Corp. Code §800(b)(1) (West 1990); Wis. Stat. Ann. §180 (West 1992).

[27] Schilling v. Belcher, 582 F.2d 995, 999 (5th Cir. 1978).

[28] McNeil v. S. GolfInvs. of Ga., Inc., 492 S.E.2d 283 (Ga. Ct. App. 1997).

[29] *See* Schilling v. Belcher, 582 F.2d 995, 999 (5th Cir. 1978).

B. The Demand Requirement

tion by another entity. For example, assume that the plaintiff was the owner of Beta Company shares just prior to Beta's acquisition by Alpha Company. If Alpha acquired Beta on terms that provide only cash for the Beta stockholders, the plaintiff no longer is a continuing owner of shares. If Alpha exchanged its shares for Beta shares, plaintiff is a shareholder but not a continuing holder of Beta shares.

The courts are badly divided on whether former shareholders of a corporation that does not survive after an acquisition have standing to maintain a derivative suit on behalf of the non-surviving corporation. A cash-out merger that occurs for no apparent purpose other than to deny the plaintiff standing to maintain a derivative suit was held not to cause the suit's dismissal, absent an independent good faith judgment that the suit harmed the corporate interest.[30] Moreover, the consummated acquisition does not adversely affect the shareholder's individual causes for fraud or unfairness.[31] The American Law Institute proposals provided a reasonable response to cutting the alternative of terminating the derivative suit abruptly on the company's acquisition:

> A holder . . . has standing to commence and maintain a derivative suit action if the holder . . . (2) continues to hold the equity security until the time of judgment, unless the failure to do so is the result of corporate action in which the holder did not acquiesce, and either (A) the derivative action was commenced prior to the corporate action terminating the holder's status, or (B) the court finds that such holder is better able to represent the interests of the shareholder than any other holder who has brought suit.[32]

The contemporaneous ownership rule appeared before the Supreme Court's decision in *Erie Railroad Company v. Tompkins*.[33] The Federal Rules of Civil Procedure now clearly govern procedural matters in diversity jurisdiction cases, but a number of important substantive issues are governed by state law.[34] For example, whether a suit based on state law is derivative or direct is a state law issue,[35] as is the question of who is a qualified shareholder[36] to bring and maintain a derivative suit. However, it is uncertain whether determining the time of the complained-of transaction for contemporaneous-ownership-rule purposes is a matter of substance or procedure.[37] Thus far, only the Ninth Circuit has definitively ruled on the question, holding that the contemporaneous ownership requirement is procedural, so that it applies in diversity actions.[38] In contrast, the requirement that

---

[30] *See* Merritt v. Colonial Foods, Inc., 505 A.2d 757 (Del. 1986); Slade v. EnderVelt, 571 N.Y.S.2d 452 (App. Div. 1991).

[31] *See, e.g.,* Cede & Co. v. Technicolor, Inc., 542 A.2d 1182, 1188 (Del. 1988).

[32] ALI, 2 Principles of Corporate Governance, *supra* §15.02 note 46, §7.02(a)(2). *See* Demoulas v. Demoulas Super Markets, Inc., 677 N.E.2d 159, 169 (Mass. 1997).

[33] 308 U.S. 64 (1938).

[34] *Id.*

[35] *See* Gadd v. Pearson, 351 F. Supp. 895 (M.D. Fla. 1972).

[36] Kauffman v. Dreyfus Fund, Inc., 434 F.2d 727 (3d Cir. 1970), *cert. denied,* 401 U.S. 974 (1971).

[37] *See also* Bangor Punta Operations v. Bangor & Aroostock R.R., 417 U.S. 703 (1974); Pioche Mines Consol., Inc. v. Dolman, 333 F.2d 257 (9th Cir. 1954); Kriendler v. Marx, 85 F.R.D. 612, 614 (N.D. Ill. 1979).

[38] Kona Enters. Inc. v. Estate of Bishop, 179 F.3d 767 (9th Cir. 1999).

the derivative suit plaintiff continue to own shares in the corporation is treated as a matter of state substantive law.[39]

§15.08   Double Derivative Suits

A parent corporation as a shareholder of a subsidiary can bring a derivative action to redress injury to the subsidiary.[1] In turn, a shareholder of a parent company can maintain a "double derivative" suit to enforce a cause of action in favor of a subsidiary company if the directors of both companies have refused after due request to institute an action in the name of either camp.[2] The parent company has a duty to use its control of the subsidiary to compel the subsidiary to sue to right wrongs done to it, and a shareholder of the parent may in effect compel specific performance of this duty in a double derivative suit.[3] A necessary predicate to a double derivative suit is that the parent has not less than operating control of the subsidiary.[4] It is still an open question whether a shareholder in a corporation that holds less than a controlling interest in a company against which a wrong has been committed is entitled to sue on a double derivative basis,[5] although one court has answered the question affirmatively.[6]

C.   SPECIAL PROCEDURAL AND SUBSTANTIVE ISSUES IN DERIVATIVE SUIT LITIGATION

§15.09   The Plaintiff as an Adequate Representative

The plaintiff in a derivative suit must fairly and adequately represent similarly situated shareholders.[1] Properly interpreted, this means that the plaintiff must be representative of the shareholders who have been injured. The better view is the defendant has the burden of proving the plaintiff is an inadequate representative.[2]

---

[39] *See* Susman v. Lincoln Am. Corp., 587 F.2d 866, 871 (7th Cir. 1978).

§15.08 [1] Fed. R. Civ. Proc. 23.1. *See generally* 7A Wright, Miller & Kane, *supra* §15.04 note 12, §1821.

[2] An individual shareholder can sue derivatively on a corporation's behalf to enforce its right to enforce the subsidiary's right. *See* Puzatu v. National Ins. Co. of Washington, 400 A.2d 313 (D.C. Ct. App. 1979). A double derivative action cannot be maintained unless plaintiff demonstrates that the corporation against which the wrong was committed is a subsidiary of the corporation in which plaintiff is a shareholder. Kennedy v. Nicastro, 517 F. Supp. 1157 (N.D. Ill. 1981).

[3] *See* Saltzman v. Birrel, 78 F. Supp. 778 (S.D.N.Y. 1955); Kaufman v. Wolfson, 151 N.Y.S.2d 530 (App. Div. 1956).

[4] *See* Brown v. Tenney, 532 N.E.2d 230 (Ill. 1988).

[5] William H. Painter, Double Derivative Suits and Other Remedies with Regard to Damaged Securities, 36 Ind. L.J. 143, 152 (1961).

[6] Isner v. Aldrich, 254 F. Supp. 696 (D. Del. 1966).

§15.09 [1] Fed. R. Civ. P. 23.1.

[2] *See, e.g.,* Smallwood v. Pearl Brewing Co., 489 F.2d 579, 582 (5th Cir.), *cert. denied,* 419 U.S. 873 (1974); Riggin v. Rea Riggin & Sons, Inc., 738 N.E.2d 292, 303-304 (Ind. Ct. App. 2000).

C. Special Procedural and Substantive Issues in Derivative Suit Litigation

To meet the fair and adequate representation requirement, a plaintiff must have the same interests as the other shareholders and must be free of interests that conflict with theirs.[3] A plaintiff in a derivative action must also show that he will pursue the claim vigorously and competently.[4] The most frequent basis for finding that a plaintiff is not an adequate representative is when the transparent purpose of the derivative suit is to enable the plaintiff to gain leverage in his personal claims or transactions with the defendants or the corporation.[5] The right to initiate a derivative suit is not defeated by the fact that the plaintiff-shareholder owns only a few shares of stock in the corporation so that her injury is comparatively trivial and her benefit (through an increase in the value of stock held) from the sought-after recovery will be slight. Theoretically a minority shareholder has the same right as the largest shareholder to insist that the corporation's assets not be wrongfully diverted from the objectives for which it was created.[6] At the same time, the smallness of the plaintiff's holdings may well confirm the court's belief that the plaintiff is seeking to serve a distinct and private agenda through the derivative suit.[7] This concern has prompted some courts to appoint a "lead plaintiff" using the criteria applied in securities law class actions by which the most adequate plaintiff is the shareholder with the largest holdings.[8]

The courts are badly divided as to whether the bidder for control of a corporation is an adequate representative for a suit brought against the incumbent management for misdeeds they allegedly committed in seeking to thwart the bidder's attempt to obtain control.[9] In this area the courts are presented with the tough choice between a bidder who seeks to serve its private agenda through the successful prosecution of the derivative suit and a plaintiff who can surely be expected to be tenacious in pursuing whatever causes of action the corporation has.

§15.10 Bona Fide Purchasers of "Tainted" Shares

One of the most significant decisions in the development of the derivative suit is *Home Fire Insurance Company v. Barber,*[1] which, ironically, was not a derivative suit.

---

[3] *See, e.g.,* Davis v. Comed, Inc., 619 F.2d 588 (6th Cir. 1980) (providing six factors bearing on adequacy).

[4] Barrett v. Southern Conn. Gas Co., 172 Conn. 362, 373, 374 A.2d 1051, 1057 (Conn. 1977).

[5] *See, e.g.,* Zarowitz v. BankAmerica Corp., 866 F.2d 1164 (9th Cir. 1989).

[6] In the close corporation, it quite likely that the derivative suit is the only effective discipline that the small holder has against the much larger owner-defendant. *See* Halsted Video, Inc. v. Guttilo, 115 F.R.D. 177 (N.D. Ill. 1987) (20 percent owner of close corporation is adequate representative in suit against other owner, who holds 80 percent interest).

[7] *See* Blum v. Morgan Guar. Trust Co., 539 F.2d 1388 (5th Cir. 1976).

[8] *See* In re Conseco, Inc. Sec. Litig., 120 F. Supp. 2d 729 (S.D. Ind. 2000) (appointing fund to lead derivative suit).

[9] *Compare* Torchmark Corp. v. Bixby, 708 F. Supp. 1070 (W.D. Mo. 1988); Baron v. Strawbridge & Clothier, 646 F. Supp. 690 (E.D. Pa. 1986) *with* Airline Pilots Ass'n Int'l v. UAL Corp., 717 F. Supp. 575 (N.D. Ill. 1989), *aff'd,* 897 F.2d 1394 (7th Cir. 1990); A. Copeland Enter. v. Guste, 706 F. Supp. 1283 (W.D. Tex. 1989).

§15.10   [1] 93 N.W. 1024 (Neb. 1903).

In *Home Fire Insurance,* Commissioner Roscoe Pound held that a corporation whose sole shareholder acquired his shares from the defendant at an admittedly fair price could not sue that former controlling stockholder for misconduct committed during the years of his control. *Home Fire Insurance* thus established the "vicarious incapacity" principle, under which the corporation is barred from suing for misconduct when its sole or substantial stockholder acquired his shares from those responsible for the misconduct that is the subject of the suit. Such shares are sometimes referred to as "tainted" shares. Courts frequently reach the result by piercing the plaintiff-corporation's veil to identify the real party of interest.[2] But, as seen earlier, veil-piercing is but a mechanism to reach a result believed socially desirable on some other basis; it is rarely a sole justification.

Today the courts emphasize that the objective served by the vicarious-incapacity principle is to avoid the unjust enrichment that otherwise would occur if the holder of tainted shares were allowed to recover from his seller for misconduct that did not cause the current controlling stockholder any economic loss.[3] However, the bar extends to a wider range of issues than preventing the new holder of control from obtaining a windfall. As a general rule, a person who purchases shares in a corporation knowing that the transferor is estopped by laches, participation, or acquiescence to complain of misapplication of funds or other illegal transactions is in precisely the same position as the transferor and is also estopped.[4] One court has even reasoned that one who purchases control knowing or having reason to know that the seller has mistreated the corporation "is not a *bona fide* purchaser without notice of those facts; therefore the purchaser may not maintain the action."[5] The weight of authority is that a transferee of tainted shares is in the same position as the transferor with respect to suing on transactions that occurred before the transfer, even if the transferee is a purchaser without notice.[6] The high water mark of the vicarious-incapacity principle is *Jannes v. Microwave Communications, Inc.,*[7] where the court partially disallowed a derivative suit because the defendant had acquired 90 percent of the corporation's stock after the alleged wrongs had been committed; thus any recovery on behalf of the corporation would, absent a pro rata recovery,[8] have largely redounded to the benefit of the defendant. A somewhat related concept, discussed later,[9] is whether the plaintiff's

[2] *See* Bangor Punta Operations, Inc. v. Bangor & Aroostock R.R., 417 U.S. 703, 716 (1974).

[3] *See, e.g.,* Bangor Punta Operations, Inc. v. Bangor & Aroostock R.R., 417 U.S. 703, 716-717 (1974); National Union Elec. Corp. v. Matsushita Elec. Corp., 498 F. Supp. 991, 999 n.9 (E.D. Pa. 1980); Courtland Manor, Inc. v. Leeds, 347 A.2d 144 (Del. Ch. 1975); Capitol Wine & Spirit Corp. v. Pokrass, 98 N.Y.S.2d 291, 292 (N.Y. App. Div. 1950), *aff'd*, 98 N.E.2d 704 (N.Y. 1951); Damerow Ford Co. v. Bradshaw, 876 P.2d 788 (Or. Ct. App. 1994); Advanced Business Comm. v. Myers, 695 S.W.2d 601 (Tex. App. Ct. 1985).

[4] *See* Blum v. Morgan Guar. Trust Co., 539 F.2d 1388 (5th Cir. 1976); Parson v. Joseph, 8 So. 788 (Ala. 1891); 148 A.L.R. 1100 (1944).

[5] Damerow Ford Co. v. Bradshaw, 876 P.2d 788, 794 (Or. Ct. App. 1994).

[6] *See* Bangor Punta Operations v. Bangor & Aroostock R.R., 417 U.S. 703 (1974); In re REA Express, Inc., 412 F. Supp. 1239 (E.D. Pa. 1976); Damerow Ford Co. v. Bradshaw, 876 P.2d 78 (Or. Ct. App. 1994).

[7] 385 F. Supp. 759 (N.D. Ill. 1974).

[8] *See supra* §15.03.

[9] *See infra* §15.12.

knowledge of the earlier wrongdoing constitutes either laches or acquiescence such that the plaintiff is barred from initiating a derivative suit. The courts' adoption of the vicarious incapacity principle and its allied extensions says much about the dominance of the compensation objective over the possible deterrence value of the derivative suit.[10]

The most significant impact of *Home Fire Insurance* is not its effect on those few cases where the corporation seeks to recover from its former controlling stockholder after a change in ownership. The lasting effects of *Home Fire Insurance* are evident in the wide adoption of the contemporaneous ownership rule, discussed earlier.[11] As seen earlier, concerns about unjust enrichment underlie the continuing force the contemporaneous ownership rule enjoys with the courts and legislatures such that even the few instances of its rigid application being relaxed are guided by a comparative assessment of the unjust enrichment that otherwise will arise.[12]

§15.11   Security-for-Expense Statutes

In 1944 the New York legislature, with a view to controlling abuses of derivative suits, took the drastic step of adopting a statute requiring plaintiffs in such suits to give security for the prospective litigation expenses of defendants.[1] Under the current version of the New York statute, a court can require a security deposit unless a plaintiff represents 5 percent of a class of shares or the value of plaintiff's shares exceeds $50,000.[2] The Model Business Corporation Act's security-for-expense provision[3] was deleted from the act in 1982.[4] The current Model Business Corporation Act does not contain a security-for-expense provision but does authorize the court to require the plaintiff to "pay any of the defendant's reasonable expenses . . . if it finds that the proceeding was commenced or maintained without reasonable cause or for an improper purpose."[5]

The primary purpose of such a provision is to reduce strike suits.[6] If plaintiff fails to post security as ordered by the court, the result is dismissal of the derivative suit.[7] Courts generally conduct a fairly close review of the pleadings and any

---

[10] *See* Damerow Ford Co. v. Bradshaw, 876 P.2d 788 (Or. Ct. App. 1994).

[11] *See* discussion *supra* §15.07.

[12] *See* text *supra* §15.07 following note 15.

§15.11   [1] N.Y. Gen. Corp. Law §61b, now N.Y. Bus. Corp. Law §627 (McKinney 1986).

[2] N.Y. Bus. Corp. Law §627 (McKinney 1986).

[3] MBCA §49 (1969) (unless plaintiff's shares represent 5 percent of the class or have $25,000 in value).

[4] *See* Report of the Committee on Corporate Laws, Proposed Revisions of the Model Business Corporation Act Affecting Actions by Shareholders, 37 Bus. Law. 261, 265-266 (1981).

[5] MBCA Ann. §7.46(2) (Supp. 1992).

[6] Former MBCA §49 Comment (1969). The other purposes are to protect the other shareholders who otherwise would have to bear the expense of an unfounded action and to prevent attorneys who sued only in order to obtain substantial attorneys fees. *Id.*

[7] *See, e.g.*, Haberman v. Tobin, 626 F.2d 1101 (2d Cir. 1980).

supporting affidavits before requiring the plaintiff to post security. As applied to ordinary investors, the security-for-costs requirement is oppressive, and, as a practical matter, it denies the only civil remedy that ordinary shareholders have for breach of fiduciary duties by those entrusted with the management and direction of their corporations. Many writers have vigorously attacked the requirement;[8] others have supported it.[9]

On the whole, security-for-expense statutes have not been a major impediment to the initiation and continuation of derivative suits. Within a decade of its enactment, the New York security-for-expense statute had already proven largely ineffective.[10] Such statutes are rendered impotent by their common exception for suits brought by a plaintiff or plaintiffs who own at least a stated percentage—for example, 5 percent—or stock with a minimum market value. If the original plaintiff does not meet these criteria, he may obtain a stay after a motion for security is made, during which time the plaintiff may procure a list of the stockholders and solicit their participation as plaintiffs in order to satisfy the minimum ownership requirement.[11] Board members, preferring not to have the corporation's dirty linen further aired in such a public manner, frequently prefer not to invoke the statute. Moreover, the plaintiff with a keen eye may skillfully avoid the security-for-expense statute by selecting a forum based on the forum's applicable choice-of-law rules.

For suits in federal court in which jurisdiction is based on diversity of citizenship, the security for expense requirement is considered substantive.[12] However, the federal court abides by the choice-of-law rule of the forum state in deciding whether to apply the security-for-expense statute of the corporation's domicile. Thus, in a leading case the federal court refused to require the plaintiff to post security, although the corporation's domicile would have so required because, under the forum state's choice-of-law rule, the federal court viewed the security-for-expense statute as procedural, not substantive.[13] Similar results should occur if suit is brought in a state other than the state of incorporation and the forum state does not treat security-for-expense statutes as procedural. Suits based on federal issues, such as those brought under the federal securities acts, do not

[8] See, e.g., Henry W. Ballantine, Abuses of Shareholders' Derivative Suits: How Far Is California's New "Security for Expenses" Act Sound Regulation, 37 Cal. L. Rev. 399 (1949); Daniel J. Dykstra, The Revival of the Derivative Suit, 116 U. Pa. L. Rev. 74 (1967); George D. Hornstein, The Death Knell of Shareholders' Derivative Suits in New York, 32 Cal. L. Rev. 123 (1944).

[9] See, e.g., Ralph M. Carson, Further Phases of Derivative Actions Against Directors, 29 Cornell L.Q. 431, 454-460 (1944); Maximilian Koessler, The Stockholders' Suits: A Comparative View, 46 Colum. L. Rev. 238, 240-241 (1946).

[10] See Note, Security for Expenses Legislation—Summary, Analysis, and Critique, 52 Colum. L. Rev. 267, 281 (1952).

[11] See, e.g., Baker v. McFadden Pub., Inc., 90 N.E.2d 870 (N.Y. 1950); Sivin v. Schwartz, 254 N.Y.S.2d 914 (App. Div. 1964); Auerbach v. Shafstor, Inc., 229 N.Y.S.2d 927 (Sup. Ct. 1962), aff'd, 240 N.Y.S.2d 146 (App. Div. 1963).

[12] Cohen v. Beneficial Indus. Loan Co., 337 U.S. 541 (1949).

[13] See Berkwitz v. Humphrey, 130 F. Supp. 142 (N.D. Ohio 1955). See generally James Wm. Moore, 5 Moore's Federal Practice ¶¶23,01-23,34 (Mathew Bender 3d ed. 1997).

have to meet the forum state's security-for-expense requirement,[14] although that requirement continues to apply to pendent state claims.[15]

§15.12   Statute of Limitations, Laches, and Acquiescence as Defenses

The dual aspect of a shareholder's derivative suit—(1) enforcement in equity of a shareholder's right to have the corporation sue on its claims and (2) enforcement in the same proceedings of the basic or underlying corporate right of action against the alleged wrongdoers, which right of action may be legal or equitable—creates questions as to the applicable period of limitations for bringing the suit. The time limit for commencing suit is not necessarily governed by the statute of limitations on equitable proceedings generally, as the shareholder can enforce only such claims as the corporation itself could assert. Accordingly, the general rule has been that the period of limitations is the one that would be applicable to the action if it were brought by the corporation.[1]

In derivative suits courts now generally apply the limitations period applicable to the underlying cause of action.[2] Where the cause of action is for damages in tort or contract, the appropriate legal period of limitations applies.[3] Because the limitations period varies under state statutes depending on the character of the underlying cause of action, courts must classify the action before determining the applicable limitations period. If a state has a statute of limitations expressly applicable to derivative suits, however, the limitations period so provided applies.[4] As many federal laws do not contain an express statute of limitations, the courts at one time in applying those federal laws used an analogous provision under state law, but this practice was overruled recently by the Supreme Court and in 2002 Congress acted to extend the limitations period for securities actions.[5]

The statute of limitations begins to run on the date the cause of action accrues. There invariably is a question whether the running of the statute of limitations should be tolled. Statutes of limitations are statutes of repose intended both to promote judicial economy and to allow individuals to plan for the future free of an indefinite threat of litigation. At the same time, there is obvious unfairness in barring the plaintiff when there is no reasonable basis to believe she could

---

[14] *See* McClure v. Borne Chem. Co., 292 F.2d 824 (3d Cir. 1961).

[15] *See* Haberman v. Tobin, 480 F. Supp. 425 (S.D.N.Y. 1979), *aff'd*, 626 F.2d 1101 (1980).

§15.12   [1] *See* Backus-Brooks Co. v. Northern Pac. Ry., 21 F.2d 4 (8th Cir. 1927); Felsenheld v. Bloch Bros. Tobacco Co., 192 S.E. 545 (1937). *See generally* Note, Statute of Limitations and Shareholder Derivative Actions, 56 Colum. L. Rev. 106 (1956).

[2] *See, e.g.*, Teren v. Howard, 322 F.2d 949, 954 (9th Cir. 1963).

[3] *See, e.g.*, Hughes v. Reed, 46 F.2d 435 (10th Cir. 1931); Kalamanash v. Smith, 51 N.E.2d 681 (N.Y. 1928); Robertson v. Davis, 90 S.W.2d 746 (1936).

[4] *See, e.g.*, N.Y. Civ. Prac. Law §213.8 (McKinney 1990).

[5] Lampf, Pleva, Lipkind, Prupis & Pettigrew v. Gilbertson, 501 U.S. 350 (1991). Pub. L. No. 107-204 (July 30, 2002) (Sarbanes-Oxley Act of 2002) in section 804 amends 28 U.S.C. 1658 to extend the limitations to two years of discovery but not longer than five years of violation.

have asserted those rights. Hence, the doctrine of tolling applies. Courts therefore regularly toll the statute for the period during which the defendant has fraudulently concealed her wrongdoing.[6]

In other contexts, courts apply the so-called discovery rule, under which the statute of limitations commences to run when the plaintiff knows or should have reason to know of the wrong.[7] Because the derivative suit redresses a wrong committed against the corporation, and the wrongdoers are usually corporate officers or directors or those in control of the corporation, knowledge is a tricky concept in the context of the derivative suit.

In addition to facing a possible bar to the action under the applicable statute of limitations, since the derivative suit is procedurally equitable the plaintiff is also open to the equitable defense of laches.[8] When successfully invoked by the defendant, laches bars an action because of special facts surrounding the delay in the suit's initiation, even though the delay did not push beyond the limitations period provided at law.

> The equitable defense of laches was based on the theory that upon a person's acquiring knowledge of a wrong affecting his rights, any unreasonable delay in asserting an equitable remedy will bar such form of relief. Further, laches . . . unlike the statute of limitations at law, is not predicated upon the mere passage of time but rather calls for a showing that if the claim sought to be tardily enforced will result in an inequity because of an intervening change in conditions prejudicial to the party raising the defense, then it should be barred.[9]

The three requirements for laches are inexcusable delay, the plaintiff having knowledge of the misconduct, and a bona fide change in position causing prejudice to the party raising the defense.[10] Prompt suit after notice of the misconduct deprives the defense of laches of its most important element, unreasonable delay in prosecuting the action.[11] The plaintiff's acquiescence can also be the basis of barring her initiation of the suit. Laches and acquiescence are related but distinct concepts:

---

[6] See, e.g., Rieff v. Evans, 630 N.W.2d 278 (Iowa 2001) (plaintiff has burden of proving either defendant's affirmative concealment or existence of fiduciary relationship to the plaintiff and failure to disclose information underlying the wrongdoing).

[7] See Abbott v. McNeff, 171 F. Supp. 2d 935, 940 (D. Minn. 2001) (numerous bases to conclude that plaintiff was suspicious of the defendant's dealings from the early days of their relationship); Telxon Corp. v. Bogomolny, 792 A.2d 964 (Del. Ch. 2001) (statute tolled until proxy statement disclosed facts regarding option that is the focus of the suit); Poffenberger v. Risser, 431 A.2d 677 (Md. 1981); Mellon Service Co. v. Touche Ross & Co., 17 S.W.3d 432 (Tex. Ct. App. 2000).

[8] See Yokochi v. Yoshimoto, 353 P.2d 820 (Haw. 1960) (burden of proving plaintiff barred by laches is on defendant). For the view that the personal involvement or misbehavior of the plaintiff should not itself be disabling in view that the suit is on behalf of the corporation and not the plaintiff, see Kullgren v. Navy Gas & Supply Co., 149 P.2d 653 (Colo. 1944).

[9] Skouras v. Admiralty Enter., 386 A.2d 674 (Del. Ch. 1978).

[10] See, e.g., Herald Co. v. Seawell, 472 F.2d 1081, 1099 (10th Cir. 1972); Norris v. Osburn, 254 S.E.2d 860 (Ga. 1979); Dowry v. Dowry, 590 N.E.2d 612 (Ind. Ct. App. 1992); Rogers v. Ricane Enter., 772 S.W.2d 76 (Tex. 1989).

[11] See Squaw Mtn. Cattle Co. v. Bowen, 804 P.2d 1292 (Wyo. 1991).

C. Special Procedural and Substantive Issues in Derivative Suit Litigation

> Acquiescence is a doctrine springing from the rule that he who seeks equity must do equity. Acquiescence and laches are not correlative terms because they relate to different times within the same spectrum. Laches relates to delay after the act is done, while acquiescence relates to inaction during the time the act is being performed. Laches implies passive assent while acquiescence imports active assent.[12]

Thus a plaintiff is deemed to acquiesce in the misconduct by intentionally failing to complain about a proposed repurchase of shares for an employee stock benefit plan which the plaintiff later challenged as an impermissible defensive maneuver.[13] Acquiescence is far more likely to occur within a small or closely held corporation because it is easier to establish, somewhat objectively, that the plaintiff forbore with full knowledge of the underlying facts.[14] But forbearance should not too easily be attributed to the plaintiff; for example, the court wisely concluded that the mere failure to attend the meeting at which the details of the transaction were discussed did not bar the non-attending plaintiff from initiating an action challenging the transaction.[15] Quite apart from the defense of acquiescence is the bar against plaintiffs who purchased their stock with knowledge of earlier or even continuing misconduct from bringing suit for that misconduct.[16] It remains to be seen whether written agreements entered into by shareholders waiving their right to initiate a derivative suit over matters related to the corporation's formation or otherwise will be accorded the same effect as such agreements have had in the partnership or LLC context.[17]

§15.13 Derivative Suits and the Right to a Jury Trial

Many courts earlier held that a jury trial is unavailable in derivative suits because of the equitable nature of that kind of action.[1] However, in *Ross v. Bernhard*[2] the

---

[12] Herald Co. v. Seawell, 472 F.2d 1081, 1099 (10th Cir. 1972).

[13] *See* Herald Co. v. Seawell, 472 F.2d 1081, 1099 (10th Cir. 1972); Matthews v. Tele-Systems, Inc., 525 S.E.2d 413 (Ga. Ct. App. 2000).

[14] *See, e.g.,* Swafford v. Berry, 382 P.2d 999 (Colo. 1963); Tagarelli v. McCormick, 614 So. 2d 11 (Fl. Ct. App. 1993).

[15] *See* Shapiro v. Greenfield, 764 A.2d 270, 284 (Md. Ct. App. 2000).

[16] *See* Blum v. Morgan Guar. Trust Co., 539 F.2d 1388 (5th Cir. 1976); P.J. Acquisition Corp. v. Skoglund, 453 N.W. 2d 1 (Minn. 1990).

[17] *See* Elf Atochem North America, Inc. v. Jaffari, 727 A.2d 286 (Del. 1999) (upholding agreement in LLC that waived rights by members to initiate derivative suits for matters related to the operating agreement).

§15.13 [1] *See, e.g.,* Cohen v. Beneficial Indus. Loan Corp., 337 U.S. 541 (1949); Koster v. Lumberman's Mut. Casualty Co., 330 U.S. 518 (1947); Meyer v. Fleming, 327 U.S. 161 (1946); Hawes v. Oakland, 104 U.S. 450 (1882). Note, The Right to a Jury Trial in a Stockholders Derivative Action, 74 Yale L.J. 725 (1965).

[2] 396 U.S. 531 (1970). The Supreme Court has not decided whether the Sixth Amendment assures a jury trial in criminal proceedings. *See generally* Alan L. Adlestein, A Corporation's Right to a Jury Trial under the Sixth Amendment, 27 U.C. Davis L. Rev. 375 (1994).

U.S. Supreme Court ruled that the Seventh Amendment to the Constitution guarantees the right to a jury if the underlying basis of the claim would have been recognized in an action at law. On a somewhat related issue, the Supreme Court has held that the right to a jury trial does not preclude application of collateral estoppel where the first suit was in equity without a right to a jury.[3]

§15.14 Control and Settlement of a Derivative Suit

A shareholder's authority to enforce a corporation's cause of action arises from the failure of the official managers to act on its behalf.[1] Assuming the shareholder is a proper representative, the plaintiff does not have absolute control of the litigation but instead has a stewardship function that is exercised under the watchful eye of the derivative suit court to assure that the action's continuation, dismissal, or settlement is in the best interests of the corporation. Thus in a leading case, *Saylor v. Lindsay*,[2] over the objections of the plaintiff, the court approved a settlement supported by his attorney and the defendants. The Federal Rules of Civil Procedure fully reflect the court's role in protecting the corporation's interests with respect to the derivative suit:

> The derivative action may not be maintained if it appears that the plaintiff does not fairly and adequately represent the interests of the shareholders or members similarly situated in enforcing the right of the corporation or association. The action shall not be dismissed or compromised without the approval of the court, and notice of the proposed dismissal or compromise shall be given to shareholders or members in such manner as the court directs.[3]

The question of representation is crucial in safeguarding the interests of all shareholders as well as the corporation.

The final authority to determine whether the action shall be dismissed is the court,[4] and a paramount consideration is the strength of the plaintiff's case relative to the settlement's terms.[5] Under both statutory and judicially imposed court supervision, the scope of judicial control is not limited to achieving fairness to the

---

[3] Parklane Hosiery Co. v. Shore, 439 U.S. 322 (1979).

§15.14 [1] *See* §15.01.

[2] 456 F.2d 896 (2d Cir. 1972) ("[A] contrary view would place too much power in a wishful thinker or a spite monger to thwart a result that is in the best interests of the corporation and its stockholders.").

[3] Fed. R. Civ. P. 23.1.

[4] Whitten v. Dabney, 154 P.2d 312, 316 (Cal. 1944); Clarke v. Greenberg, 71 N.E.2d 443 (N.Y. 1947); Goodwin v. Castleton, 144 P.2d 725 (Wash. 1944). It is said to be the right and duty of the court to protect the interests of the corporation and the absent shareholders by exercising supervision over the conduct of the suit by the fiduciary plaintiff. *See* In re Walt Disney Co. Derivative Litig., 1997 WL 118402, at *3 (Del. Ch. Mar. 13, 1997) (denial of voluntary dismissal of suit requested so that a parallel action initiated in California could be pursued more efficiently).

[5] *See, e.g.,* In re Traffic Executive Ass'n E. R.R., 627 F.2d 631 (2d Cir. 1980). For a more extensive check list (13 items), see Desimone v. Industrial Bio-Test Labs., Inc., 83 F.R.D. 615, 618-619 (S.D.N.Y. 1979).

particular plaintiff; it extends to the interests of other shareholders, to the corporation as an entity, and to the effect of a settlement on other pending actions. Thus courts frequently consider the continuing costs to the corporation if the suit continues,[6] but a court will have a difficult time accepting a settlement of a viable cause of action when the only tangible benefit to the corporation is avoidance of further costs to the corporation and inconvenience to its employees.[7] The courts, however, rarely provide a close analysis of the costs and benefits of the settlement's terms;[8] they content themselves with broad incantations sounding in fairness to all the interests before them:

> In examining the settlement, the Chancellor need not try the case. Indeed, he is not required to decide any of the issues on the merits. . . . Instead, he . . . exercises a form of business judgment to determine the overall reasonableness of the settlement. . . . [O]ur review is more limited than that of the Court of Chancery. It is not our function to determine the intrinsic fairness of the settlement or to exercise our own business judgment respecting its merits. We limit ourselves to the question of an abuse of discretion by the trial court in exercising its business judgment.[9]

In discharging their responsibility to review settlements, a court relies on the record and documents—including depositions, interrogatories, and affidavits—already before it as well as any documents filed in support or in opposition to the settlement. A court can convene a hearing on the settlement.[10]

---

[6] *See* Shlensky v. Dorsey, 574 F.2d 131, 147 (3d Cir. 1978); Newman v. Stein, 464 F.2d 689, 692 (2d Cir. 1972); Schreiber v. Jacobs, 128 F. Supp. 44 (E.D. Mich. 1955).

[7] *See* In re Pittsburgh & Lake Erie R.R. Sec. & Antitrust Litig., 543 F.2d 1058 (3d Cir. 1976) (district court's approval of such a settlement reversed).

[8] For a critique of the internal inconsistencies of settlement review criteria and lack of adequate factual basis to undertake a meaningful review, *see* Note, When Should Courts Allow the Settlement of Duty-of-Loyalty Derivative Suits, 109 Harv. L. Rev. 1084 (1996); *see also* Note, The Need for Findings of Fact and Conclusions of Law in the Approval of Proposed Settlements of Shareholders' Derivative Actions, Greenspun v. Bogan, 492 F.2d 375 (1st Cir. 1974), 36 Ohio St. L.J. 163 (1975). For a contrast to the approach with the close analysis that accompanies most reviews of dismissal requests made on the basis of a special litigation committee, *see* Joy v. North, 692 F.2d 880 (2d Cir. 1982).

[9] Polk v. Good, 507 A.2d 531, 536 (Del. 1986). At least in the federal courts, appellate review is not nearly as circumscribed as that stated in Polk for the Delaware Supreme Court. *See* In re Pittsburgh & Lake Erie R.R. Sec. & Antitrust Litig., 543 F.2d 1058, 1070 (3d Cir. 1976).

One study found that during a 2½-year period, "of the 98 corporate and class action suits in which the . . . [Delaware Court of Chancery] held settlement hearings, more than 95 percent . . . were approved as submitted, and approximately two-thirds of the attorneys' fee petitions were granted in full." Carolyn Berger & Darla Pomeroy, Settlement Fever, Business Law Today 7 (Sept.-Oct. 1992).

[10] In a most interesting case, In re Cellular Communications Int'l Shareholders Litig. 752 A.2d 1185 (Del. Ch. 2000), the Delaware Chancery court refused to approve the settlement of a class action complaining that the price of $65.75 per share offered by the defendant-acquiring firm was too low. Subsequently the bidder voluntarily raised its offer to $80 and the plaintiffs moved for the class action to approve a settlement based upon this amount. Vice Chancellor Stephen Lamb reasoned that, since the plaintiffs had consistently sought a price greater than the $80 figure that the acquirer had voluntarily offered, there was no basis to believe that there was a contract-like arrangement to support an enforceable settlement. He therefore believed the appropriate result was to dismiss the suit as moot without further notice of the action.

In considering its role in reviewing the proposed settlement the court should take a sobering view of the inherent weaknesses of the suit's participants' incentives to serve the corporation's interests.[11] Simply put, each party lacks a strong economic incentive that can be expected to guide his actions so as to avoid either adopting an overly aggressive litigation strategy or becoming so passive that the resulting settlement is woefully inadequate in light of the suit's intrinsic worth. For example, as seen earlier, the derivative suit plaintiff is not required to have a substantial ownership interest as a condition to bringing suit. Lacking a substantial ownership interest, the plaintiff bears little of the consequences of a suit that produces tangible adverse effects to the corporation. Thus the adverse impact of an ill-advised suit cannot be expected to rein in a maverick plaintiff. The problem is heightened by the practice prevalent in America of such suits being pursued on a contingency fee basis. The engine that drives the derivative suit generally is the derivative suit's counsel, whose strongest weapon against the defendants' usual army of lawyers is that the plaintiffs' attorneys' participation occurs at a lower unit cost than does that of the defendants.[12] This difference between the two sets of lawyers generally allows the derivative suit's counsel somewhat longer staying power, for they need not match the defense counsels' expenditure dollar for dollar. Moreover, the derivative suit attorneys have the great benefit of diversification, so that the riskiness of any particular suit is judged by them in light of the portfolio of suits being prosecuted out of their offices; on the other hand, the individual defendant focuses only on the risks posed to him by the single suit. Thus the derivative suit counsel can be somewhat less risk-averse with respect to litigation strategies than can the individual defendants.

The defendants also enjoy an advantage, however, for they can "play" with other people's money, thanks to the scope of insurance policies and liberal indemnification arrangements, discussed later.[13] Settlement may not totally remove the mud the derivative suit has tossed in the defendants' direction, but it does provide the means for minimizing the defendants' losses, because settlement amounts are carefully tailored to fall within existing insurance and indemnification arrangements.

Thus the carefully drafted settlement arrangement can hold the defendants harmless. While such a settlement earns the gratitude of the defendants for their lawyers, why should derivative suit counsel let the defendants off so easy? The answer lies in the juncture between how the fee for derivative suit counsel is established and the economic principle of diminishing marginal returns. As will be seen later, courts frequently award derivative suit counsel fees based on the time they have invested in the case rather than on a set percentage of the fee recovered.[14] Under this method, the derivative suit counsel, not being neutral to risk, can see that by rejecting a settlement and continuing to pursue the action exposes

---

[11] See John C. Coffee, Jr., Understanding the Plaintiff's Attorney: The Implications of Economic Theory for Private Enforcement of Law Through Class and Derivative Actions, 86 Colum. L. Rev. 669, 671-677 (1986).

[12] Id. at 701-704.

[13] See infra §15.19.

[14] See infra §15.18.

herself to risk of ultimately recovering nothing or substantially less than the prof-fered settlement, which risk is not adequately compensated by the marginal expected value of continuing the suit. In sum, the gains of continuing the suit, being on a diminishing basis, do not adequately reward the derivative suit counsel for continuing to aggressively pursue the case.

A further wrinkle to this scenario is that derivative suit counsel obtains a fee award even though no monetary recovery results from the successful prosecution of the suit; therefore defendant's counsel, rather than proposing a cash settle-ment, most frequently minimizes the drain from the defendants—or the insur-ance company that stands behind the defendants—by proposing a nonpecuniary recovery.[15] That is, defense counsel, wishing to contain damages, can fulfill this objective by a settlement that ironically places the major financial burden on the corporation itself. This makes possible results such as *In re General Tire & Rubber Company Securities Litigation*[16] where a suit with damages clearly exceeding $100 million was settled on terms that secured for the derivative suit counsel $500,000. The only benefit to the corporation was its undertaking to include two outside directors on its board for two years.[17]

§15.15 The Corporation as a Passive Party in Derivative Suits; Defenses

The corporation for whose benefit a derivative suit is brought must be joined as a party defendant.[1] Not only is the corporation an indispensable party, but the suit will be dismissed if the corporation is not served with process as if it were an actual defendant or if it does not voluntarily appear by counsel.[2]

The corporation is commonly referred to as a "nominal" defendant.[3] In gen-eral, it is required to adopt a neutral or passive role, with only a limited power to defend itself while the shareholder plaintiff—its volunteer representative—con-ducts for the corporation's benefit the litigation that its management has failed or refused to bring. The corporation need not file an answer to the complaint or take any steps in the proceedings. It cannot assume the status of a co-plaintiff—the

[15] *See* Roberta Romano, The Shareholder Suit: Litigation Without Foundation?, 7 J.L. Econ. & Organ. 55, 61 (1991) (only 21 percent of derivative suit settlements produced a cash payment to the corporation or its stockholders).

[16] 726 F.2d 1075, 1088 (6th Cir. 1984).

[17] *Id.* 1079. *See also* Lewis v. Anderson, 81 F.R.D. 436, 439 (S.D.N.Y. 1979) (defendants agreed to comply with company policy for which they were already subject); Cannon v. Texas Gulf Sulphur Co., 55 F.R.D. 308, 317 (S.D.N.Y. 1972) (defendants agreed not to obtain indemnification, which under governing law was quite doubtful). *See generally* John C. Coffee, Jr., The Unfaithful Champion: The Plaintiff as Monitor in Shareholder Litigation, 1985 Law & Contemp. Probs. 5-9.

§15.15 [1] *See* Kilburn v. Young, 536 S.E.2d 769 (Ga. Ct. App. 2000) (granting the plaintiff a rea-sonable time to join in the suit the absent corporation).

[2] *See, e.g.,* Ross v. Bernhard, 396 U.S. 531 (1970); Bogart v. Southern Pac. Co., 228 U.S. 137 (1913).

[3] *See, e.g.,* Miller v. American Tel. & Tel. Co., 394 F. Supp. 58 (E.D. Pa. 1975), *aff'd mem.*, 530 F.2d 964 (3d Cir. 1976).

complaining shareholder has the right to control the litigation.[4] If the defendants are corporate directors and officers and control corporate funds, they may well be tempted to exercise their corporate powers to aid their defense. However, apart from reimbursements and advances under indemnification statutes and agreements,[5] it is improper to use corporate funds to give financial aid or to assist in the defense of directors, officers, or other defendants in a derivative suit brought on the corporation's behalf.[6] The plaintiff shareholder is entitled to an opportunity to prosecute the suit without having the resources of the corporation turned against him.

How far the corporation may go in raising defenses to protect its own interests is not entirely settled. The corporation may appear specially to object to service of process or to lack of jurisdiction, and it may resist the appointment of a receiver.[7] Whether the corporate defendant may raise a particular defense depends on the nature of the defense and the interest that the defense is designed to protect.[8] The corporation is allowed to defend when its interests are brought into issue by the suit.[9] Potential defenses can be divided into three groups. First, there are conventional defenses that defeat the corporate right of recovery and are designed to protect the real defendants from liability. The corporation may not assert this type of defense in a derivative suit[10] unless it is a real defendant as to an issue in the litigation.[11] Second are conventional defenses such as laches and ratification. As these defenses are usually designed to protect the alleged wrongdoers, the corporate defendant as a general rule is not allowed to assert these defenses. Third, there are certain defenses that are peculiar to a derivative suit, such as failure to make demand on the board of directors and the necessity for plaintiff to show contemporaneous ownership. These defenses are designed to protect the corporate interest and are therefore ordinarily available to the corporate defendant.

§15.16   The Role of Counsel in a Derivative Suit

The individual defendants in derivative litigation frequently seek representation by counsel who also represent the corporation.[1] Questions arise as to the ability of

---

[4] Otis & Co. v. Pennsylvania R.R., 57 F. Supp. 680, 682 (E.D. Pa. 1944), *aff'd,* 155 F.2d 522 (3d Cir. 1946), *citing* Groel v. United Elec. Co. of N.J., 61 A. 1061, 1064-1065 (N.J. 1905).

[5] *See infra* §15.19.

[6] Meyers v. Smith, 251 N.W. 20 (Minn. 1933).

[7] Otis & Co. v. Pennsylvania R.R., 57 F. Supp. 680, 682 (E.D. Pa. 1944), *aff'd per curiam,* 155 F.2d 522 (3d Cir. 1946).

[8] Foust v. Transamerica Corp., 391 F. Supp. 312 (N.D. Cal. 1975).

[9] *See, e.g.,* Otis & Co. v. Pennsylvania R.R., 57 F. Supp. 680 (E.D. Pa. 1944), *aff'd,* 155 F.2d 522 (3d Cir. 1946).

[10] *See, e.g.,* Kartub v. Optical Fashions, Inc., 158 F. Supp. 757 (S.D.N.Y. 1958).

[11] *See* Otis & Co. v. Pennsylvania R.R., 57 F. Supp. 680 (E.D. Pa. 1944), *aff'd,* 155 F.2d 522 (3d Cir. 1946).

§15.16   [1] *See* Westinghouse Elec. Corp. v. Kerr-McGee Corp., 580 F.2d 1311 (7th Cir. 1978); Fund of Funds, Ltd. v. Arthur Anderson & Co., 567 F.2d 225 (2d Cir. 1977); Joel G. Chefitz, Note, Attorney's Conflict of Interests: Representation of Interest Adverse to That of Former Client, 55 B.U. L. Rev. 61 (1975).

C. Special Procedural and Substantive Issues in Derivative Suit Litigation

counsel to represent both the corporate and individual defendants. The corporation's true interest in a derivative suit is as a real party plaintiff.[2] Thus where common counsel simultaneously represents the alleged wrongdoers and the corporation, conflicts of interest may arise.[3] Disqualification of counsel will be ordered where sufficient conflict exists.[4] Courts have held, however, that no conflict exists where the charge is that directors have breached their duty of care in the discharge of their office; the courts reason that this is an attack on the corporation's decisions, and there is no substantial conflict in such a case.[5] Separate attorneys for individual defendants and the corporations are generally desirable. Also, in the special litigation committee context, the courts customarily assess the committee's "good faith" by considering whether it was represented by counsel who was independent from the officers or directors who are the focus of the derivative suit; hence, counsel that has not historically represented the corporation (and hence developed rapport, and perhaps even economic dependence on the suit's defendants) is called for in such instances.[6]

§15.17 The Attorney-Client Privilege in Derivative Suits

Although a corporation, just as any other client, is entitled to the attorney-client privilege,[1] sensitive questions arise if the corporation attempts to assert the privilege in a derivative suit or other action that is initiated by one of its shareholders against the corporation or even its directors or officers.[2] In the leading case of *Garner v. Wolfinbarger*,[3] the court ruled that on a showing of "good cause" that the plaintiff in a derivative suit may discover relevant facts and documents that would otherwise be covered by the privilege.[4] The court commented:

---

[2] *See* §15.01.

[3] *See* Murphy v. Washington Am. League Baseball Club, Inc., 324 F.2d 394 (D.C. Cir. 1963).

[4] Messing v. F.D.I., Inc., 439 F. Supp. 776 (D.N.J. 1977); Cannon v. U.S. Acoustics Corp., 398 F. Supp. 209 (N.D. Ill. 1975), *aff'd in part*, 532 F.2d 1118 (7th Cir. 1976).

[5] *See, e.g.*, Bell Atlantic Corp. v. Bolger, 2 F.3d 1304 (3d Cir. 1993).

[6] *See, e.g.*, Einhorn v. Culea, 612 N.W.2d 78 (Wis. 2000); Drilling v. Berman, 589 N.W.2d 503, 509 (Minn. Ct. App. 1999).

§15.17 [1] For a classic description of the attorney-client privilege, *see* United States v. United Shoe Mach. Corp., 89 F. Supp. 357, 358-359 (D. Mass. 1950).

[2] *See generally* Note, Attorney-Client Privilege for Corporate Clients: The Control Group Test, 84 Harv. L. Rev. 424, 425 (1970) (hereinafter Note, Attorney-Client Privilege for Corporate Clients).

[3] 280 F. Supp. 1018 (N.D. Ala. 1968), *vacated and remanded*, 430 F.2d 1093 (5th Cir. 1970), *cert. denied*, 401 U.S. 974 (1971), *on remand*, 56 F.R.D. 499 (N.D. Ala. 1972). For the view that *Garner*'s holding is inconsistent with reasoning used by the Supreme Court in *Upjohn*, discussed below, and Jaffee v. Redmond, 518 U.S. 1 (1996), which recognizes the patient-psychiatrist privilege, *see* Is the *Garner* Qualification of the Corporate Attorney-Client Privilege Viable After Jaffee v. Redmond?, 55 Bus. Law. 243 (1999).

[4] 430 F.2d at 1103-1104. Grimes v. LCC International Inc., 1999 WL 252381 (Del. Ch. 1999) (attorney-client privilege applies to documents prepared by general counsel unless good cause is shown). *See also* In re Perrigo Co., 128 F.3d 430 (6th Cir. 1997) (Privilege covering litigation committee's report waived due to derivative suit plaintiff's substantial need for access to the report in order to

[I]t must be borne in mind that management does not manage for itself and that the beneficiaries of its actions are the shareholders. . . . Management judgment must stand on its merits, not behind an ironclad veil of secrecy which under the circumstances preserves it from being questioned by those for whom it is, at least in part, exercised.[5]

Among the "indicia" that the court stated bear on whether good cause exists are the following:

the number of shareholders [requesting the information] and the percentage of stock they represent; the bona fides of the shareholders; the nature of the shareholders' claim and whether it is obviously colorable; the apparent necessity or desirability of the shareholders having the information and the availability of it from other sources; whether, if the shareholders' claim is of wrongful action by the corporation, it is of action criminal, or illegal but not criminal, or of doubtful legality; whether the communication is of advice concerning the litigation itself; the extent to which the communication is identified versus the extent to which the shareholders are blindly fishing; and the risk of revelation of trade secrets or other information in whose confidentiality the corporation has an interest for independent reasons.[6]

Garner's "need for information" criterion, where adopted, appears to embody no greater showing than the normal standards for relevance.[7]

The most important limitation on *Garner* is the minority view that *Garner* does not apply when the plaintiff seeks a recovery for themselves rather than on behalf of the corporation.[8] In contrast, the majority view is that the individual nature of the suit is but one of the factors to consider in determining whether good cause has been shown.[9] Some courts have extended *Garner*'s "flexible approach" to permit shareholders in a subsidiary company to discover documents prepared by lawyers for the parent company.[10] Finding *Garner*'s good-cause standard vague and unworkable, some courts have rejected its holding.[11] There is little doubt that as a consequence of *Garner* and its progeny, clients who are aware of *Garner*'s holding are likely to be much less forthcoming in their communications with the corporation's lawyers.[12] And, although *Garner* is invoked in cases involving the derivative

---

respond to committee's dismissal recommendation. However, waiver was partial so that trial court erred in ordering report's release to public.); In re Subpoena Duces Tecum Served on Wilkie Farr & Gallagher, No. M8-85 (JSM), 1997 U.S. Dist. LEXIS 2927 (S.D.N.Y. March 14, 1997) (privilege waived when counsel's investigation report shared with outside auditors); Natta v. Zlentz, 18 F.2d 633, 634-635 (7th Cir. 1969); Deutsch v. Cogan, 580 A.2d 100 (Del. Ch. 1990).

[5] 430 F.2d at 1104.

[6] *Id.*

[7] *See* Herbert E. Milstein, Attorney-Client Privilege and Work Product Doctrine Corporate Applications A-29 (B.N.A. Corporate Practice Series No. 22, 2d ed. 1994).

[8] *See* Weil v. Investments/Indicators, Research & Management, 647 F.2d 18 (9th Cir. 1981) (*Garner* does not apply to individual fraud action against corporation).

[9] *See* Fausek v. White, 965 F.2d 126 (6th Cir. 1992).

[10] *See* Cohen v. Uniroyal, Inc., 80 F.R.D. 480 (E.D. Pa. 1978).

[11] Shirvana v. Capital Inv. Corp., 12 F.R.D. 389 (D. Conn. 1986).

[12] *See* Leo Herzel, The Attorney-Client Privilege: A Pragmatic Approach, 6 Del. J. Corp. L. 443 (1981).

suit plaintiff's discovery of documents, evidence, etc. produced by a special litigation committee, the essential guiding principle in addressing such a request is not *Garner* but the bases upon which the plaintiff can challenge the dismissal recommendation of a special litigation committee.[13]

At one time the question of whether the attorney-client privilege attached at all to a communication between a corporation's attorney and an employee or director of the corporation depended on whether the representative communicating with the attorney was within the corporation's "control group"—that is, whether the representative was sufficiently advanced in the corporate hierarchy to have relevant decision-making authority and whether the representative was acting within the scope of his employment.[14] The attorney-client privilege applies to some, but not all, the communications of the general counsel who also has several other corporate roles; the privilege applies to communications that were created solely in the person's capacity as counsel.[15] An alternative to the control group test is the "subject matter" test, which did not confine the attorney-client privilege to such a narrow a set of individuals as occurs under the control group test. Under the subject matter test, communications are within the attorney-client privilege if they are made at the direction of a supervisor and pertain to the subject matter for which the attorney's advice was sought.[16] The control group test has since been restricted if not totally rejected with respect to matters before the federal courts by the Supreme Court in *Upjohn Company v. United States*.[17]

In *Upjohn*, the Court reasoned:

> The control group test adopted by the court below thus frustrates the very purpose of the privilege by discouraging the communication of relevant information by employees of the client to attorneys seeking to render legal advice to the client corporation. . . .
>
> The narrow scope given the attorney-client privilege by the court below not only makes it difficult for corporate attorneys to formulate sound advice when their client is faced with a specific legal problem but also threatens to limit the valuable efforts of corporate counsel to ensure their client's compliance with the law. . . . The test adopted below is difficult to apply in practice. . . . [I]f the purpose of the attorney-client privilege is to be served, the attorney and client must be able to predict with some degree of certainty whether particular discussions will be protected. An uncertain privilege, or one which purports to be certain but results in widely varying applications by the courts, is little better than no privilege at all.[18]

---

[13] *See* Carlton Investors v. TLC Beatrice, Inc., 1997 WL 38130 (Del. Ch. 1997) (deposing the committee's counsel denied); Weiser v. Grace, 683 N.Y.S.2d 781 (N.Y. Sup. Ct. 1998) (reviewing committee's counsel's interview summaries to protect matters related to mental impressions, conclusions, opinions or legal theories).

[14] *See* Diversified Indus. v. Meredith, 572 F.2d 596 (8th Cir. 1978); Harper & Row Publishers, Inc. v. Decker, 423 F.2d 487 (7th Cir. 1970), *aff'd by an equally divided court*, 400 U.S. 348 (1971).

[15] *See* Grimes v. LLC International Inc., 1999 WL 252381 (Del. Ch. 1999).

[16] *See, e.g.*, Harper & Row Publishers, Inc. v. Decker, 423 F.2d 487, 491-492 (7th Cir. 1970), *aff'd per curiam by an equally divided court*, 400 U.S. 348 (1971).

[17] Upjohn v. United States, 449 U.S. 383 (1981).

[18] 449 U.S. at 392-393.

Thus, after *Upjohn* the position of the communicating employee is not determinative of whether that communication is within the privilege. Questions related to control and the control group, however, should continue to be germane to the issue of whether the communicating employee was "at the direction" of a superior.[19] Thus a district manager's communication to in-house counsel was not within the privilege because there was no evidence that anyone in a supervisory capacity had directed the manager to speak with counsel.[20] Moreover, state courts are not bound by *Upjohn*, which decided the scope of section 501 of the Federal Rules of Evidence, and some states continue to prefer the control person test.[21]

§15.18   *Award of Attorneys' Fees and Expenses of Suit*

As a general proposition, unless there is express statutory authority, courts will not award attorneys' fees to either party to litigation, regardless of the litigation's outcome.[1] A well-recognized exception to this common law rule is the "common fund" or "substantial benefit" doctrine, by which a court may award attorneys' fees where litigation results in a substantial benefit to a number of persons in whose interest the suit was maintained.[2] Under this exception, a liberal allowance for counsel fees and expenses may be made to a successful plaintiff in a derivative action if the corporation and, derivatively, the other shareholders receive benefits from the suit.[3] The rationale underlying this doctrine is that the plaintiff's efforts have conferred a benefit on the corporation for which the corporation would otherwise have had to pay, and fairness requires that the plaintiff be reimbursed the necessary expenses of conferring that benefit.[4]

The earliest cases recognizing a right to reimbursement involved litigation that had produced or preserved a "common fund,"[5] but later decisions clearly indicated that a court could order a corporation to reimburse the derivative suit

---

[19] *Upjohn* emphasizes at different points that the lower level employees were complying with the directions of their superiors and those superiors were seeking information for the purpose of obtaining legal advice. *See* 449 U.S. at 394.

[20] Independent Petrochem. Corp. v. Aetna Casualty & Sur. Co., 654 F. Supp. 1334 (D.D.C. 1986).

[21] *See* Consolidation Coal Co. v. Bucyrus-Erie Co., 432 N.E.2d 250 (Ill. 1982).

§15.18   [1] *See, e.g.*, Alyeska Pipeline Serv. Co. v. Wilderness Socy., 421 U.S. 240 (1973); Schlensky v. Dorsey, 574 F.2d 131 (3d Cir. 1978). *See* Alexander Hammond, Stringent New Standards for Awards of Attorney Fees, 32 Bus. Law. 523 (1977).

[2] *See, e.g.*, Trustees v. Greenough, 105 U.S. 527 (1882); Barton v. Drummond Co., 636 F.2d 978 (5th Cir. 1981); Nemeroff v. Abelson, 620 F.2d 339 (2d Cir. 1980).

[3] *See, e.g.*, Mills v. Electric Auto-Lite Co., 396 U.S. 375 (1970).

[4] *See, e.g.*, Bailey v. Meister Brau, Inc., 535 F.2d 982 (7th Cir. 1976); Jones v. Uris Sales Corp., 373 F.2d 644 (2d Cir. 1967).

[5] The common fund approach has been upheld even where the defendant and the plaintiff are the only two shareholders. *See* De Fontaine v. Passalino, 584 N.E.2d 933 (Ill. App. Ct. 1991).

plaintiff's attorneys' fees and expenses of plaintiffs irrespective of whether an actual recovery had been attained in the corporation's favor as long as a "substantial benefit"[6] was conferred as a consequence of the suit.[7] Thus nonpecuniary corporate benefits,[8] such as the cancellation of a disadvantageous contract or transaction, have been held a sufficient basis for allowing counsel fees and expenses.[9]

The plaintiff in a derivative suit has been held entitled to an award of counsel fees where a settlement resulted in replacement of directors and officers.[10] Similarly, an award of counsel fees has been based on protection of the corporate name[11] or the obtaining of a restraining order preventing corporate mismanagement.[12] In a most unusual case, the Delaware Supreme Court held there is no class action or derivative suit prerequisite to an award of attorneys' fees under the common benefit exception.[13] It therefore awarded a fee, even though the *individual* suit arising out of a misleading proxy solicitation was voluntarily dismissed because the corporation had taken action to correct the misrepresentations in its proxy statement. An award of attorneys' fees against a corporation was denied, however, where no corporate fund is established and no assets preserved, and the resulting benefit is to only one class of shareholders as opposed to the corporation;[14] fees were also denied when the purported benefit required the company to include in all vendor contracts an undertaking not to discriminate against vendors on the

---

[6] "Substantial benefit" has been defined in a leading case as: "[O]ne that accomplishes a result which corrects or prevents an abuse which would be prejudicial to the rights and interests of the corporation or affect the enjoyment of protection of an essential right to the shareholder's interest." Bosch v. Meeker Coop. Light & Power Ass'n, 101 N.W.2d 423, 427 (Minn. 1960).

[7] *See, e.g.,* Mills v. Electric Auto-Lite Co., 396 U.S. 375 (1970); Denney v. Phillips & Buttorff, 331 F.2d 249 (6th Cir.), *cert. denied,* 379 U.S. 831 (1964); Berger v. Amana Socy., 135 N.W.2d 618 (Iowa 1965).

[8] *But see* Rosenbaum v. Allister, 64 F.3d 1439 (10th Cir. 1995) (reducing attorneys' fees because, among other considerations, the nonpecuniary benefits were negligible).

[9] *See, e.g.,* Mencher v. Sachs, 164 A.2d 320 (Del. Ch. 1960).

[10] Granada Inv., Inc. v. DWG Corp., 961 F.2d 1577 (6th Cir. 1992); Fletcher v. A.J. Indus., 72 Cal. Rptr. 146 (Ct. App. 1968). *Compare* Chrysler Corp. v. Dann, 223 A.2d 384 (Del. 1966), *aff'g* 215 A.2d 709 (Del. Ch. 1965) (changes in management were held insufficient to support a fee award, but new management incentive plan adopted in settlement of derivative suit was proper basis for $450,000 fee award). *See also* Amalgamated Clothing & Textile Workers Union v. Wal-Mart Stores, Inc., 54 F.3d 69 (2d Cir. 1995); In re Chicago & Northwest Transp. Co. Shareholders Litig. [1995 Transfer Binder], Fed. Sec. L. Rep. (CCH) ¶98,823 (Del. Ch. 1995) (fees awarded where suit caused supplemental proxy statement setting forth three additional facts that may have been a material omission in earlier proxy statement).

[11] *See, e.g.,* Taussig v. Wellington Fund, Inc., 313 F.2d 472 (3d Cir.), *cert. denied,* 374 U.S. 806 (1963).

[12] *See, e.g.,* Modern Optics, Inc. v. Buck, 336 S.W.2d 857 (Tex. Civ. App. 1960). *See also* Blau v. Rayette-Fabrege, Inc., 389 F.2d 469 (2d Cir. 1968) (reasonable attorney-investigation fees allowed where shareholder demand resulted in direct action by corporation); Gilson v. Chock Full O'Nuts Corp., 331 F.2d 107 (2d Cir. 1964) (same).

[13] *See* Tandycrafts, Inc. v. Initio Partners, 562 A.2d 1162 (Del. 1989).

[14] *See, e.g.,* Missouri Pac. R.R. v. Slayton, 407 F.2d 1078 (8th Cir.), *cert. denied,* 395 U.S. 937 (1969); Simpson v. Spellman, 522 S.W.2d 615 (Mo. Ct. App. 1975); Leggett v. Missouri State Life Ins. Co., 342 S.W.2d 833 (Mo. 1966).

basis of race when there was no evidence it had so discriminated and the law forbid such discrimination.[15] Further, it has been held that mere declaratory relief regarding the rights of preferred and common shares may not constitute a sufficient corporate benefit to support an award of fees.[16]

Until 1973, fee awards were computed as a percentage of any fund, with the precise percentage being within the reasonable discretion of the trial court. In that year, the Third Circuit set forth new award guidelines, commonly known as the "lodestar" approach.[17] Under the lodestar approach, the trial court multiplies the number of hours it deems reasonably to have been spent by the plaintiff's counsel by an hourly rate[18] that the court believes appropriate for litigation of the type that is conducted on a *non*-contingent fee basis. This calculation produces the lodestar figure. Next, the figure may be adjusted up or down (rarely is it down) by what is commonly referred to as the "multiplier" to reflect various factors, such as the quality of counsel's advocacy, the relative risk of the suit proving successful, and the like.[19] Though the lodestar approach was developed initially for class actions, it is frequently used in derivative suits on sound justification that each is a representative suit.[20]

Critics of the lodestar method argue that fee awards that emphasize the number of hours devoted to a case not only run the risk of rewarding inefficiency and a luxurious practice of the law[21] but also focus on a factor that discourages early acceptance by plaintiff's counsel of reasonable settlement offers and does not

---

[15] Kaplan v. Rand, 192 F.3d 60 (2d Cir. 1999).

[16] Bank of Am. Nat'l Trust & Sav. Ass'n v. West End Chem. Co., 100 P.2d 318 (Cal. Ct. App. 1940). *See also* Bird v. Lida, Inc., 681 A.2d 399 (Del. Ch. 1996). *But see* Edward B. Rock, Saints and Sinners: How Does Delaware Corporate Law Work?, 44 UCLA L. Rev. 1009, 1098 (1997).

[17] *See* Lindy Bros. v. American Radiator & Stan. Sanitary Corp., 487 F.2d 161 (3d Cir. 1973), *appeal following remand,* 540 F.2d 102 (3d Cir. 1976).

[18] Courts are divided on whether to apply the attorney's customary hourly rate or the market rate prevailing in the forum's community for litigation. *See* Copeland v. Marshall, 641 F.2d 880 (D.C. Cir. 1980) (en banc).

[19] *See* Johnson v. Georgia Highway Express, Inc., 488 F.2d 714, 717-718 (5th Cir. 1974), adopting the following 12-factor method for determining the multiplier:

> (1) the time and labor required;
> (2) the novelty and difficulty of the questions involved;
> (3) the skill requisite to perform the legal service properly;
> (4) the preclusion of other employment by the attorney due to acceptance of the case;
> (5) the customary fee;
> (6) whether the fee is fixed or contingent;
> (7) time limitations imposed by the client or the circumstances;
> (8) the amount involved and the results obtained;
> (9) the experience, reputation, and ability of the attorneys;
> (10) the undesirability of the case;
> (11) the nature and length of the professional relationship with the client;
> (12) awards in similar cases.

[20] *See* Powers v. Eichen, 229 F.3d 1249 (9th Cir. 2000) (whether lodestar or percentage-of-the-fund approach is used for awarding fees in derivative suit is within discretion of trial court); Harman v. Lyphomed, Inc., 945 F.2d 969, 975 (7th Cir. 1991) (same).

[21] *See* Blank v. Talley Indus., 390 F. Supp. 1, 5 (S.D.N.Y. 1975).

C. Special Procedural and Substantive Issues in Derivative Suit Litigation

directly link the size of any pecuniary recovery with the rewards for the action's advocate. The latter consideration has been frequently identified as leading to the increasing frequency of derivative suit litigation, yielding only nonpecuniary benefits to the corporation.[22] Moreover, the lodestar method imposes greater burdens on the trial court than does the percentage-of-the-fund approach because of the wider range of factors that go into calculating both the lodestar and the multiplier. The most significant criticism of the lodestar method comes from the body that created it, the Third Circuit Task Force Report,[23] which describes the lodestar method as a "cumbersome, enervating, and often surrealistic process of preparing and evaluating fee petitions."[24] The Task Force recommended that all fee awards in common fund cases be determined on a percentage-of-the-fund approach.[25] The Task Force noted that using the percentage-of-the-fund approach removes the incentives to unnecessarily increase hours, encourages prompt early settlements, reduces time-consuming paperwork for both counsel and the court, and provides a degree of predictability to fee awards.[26] The Private Securties Litigation Reform Act of 1995 added to the securities laws a provision that fees awarded to class counsel "shall not exceed a reasonable percentage of the amount of any damages . . . actually paid to the class" has been interpreted not to foreclose the use of the lodestar method.[27] The Act also introduced a procedure for selecting a lead plaintiff in securities class actions and when that is done the retainer agreement entered into between the lead plaintiff and class counsel is entitled to great deference.[28]

What appears to be the clear trend in light of these conflicting arguments is a view that neither method—percentage of recovery or lodestar—is without flaws. No doubt a blunt application of the percentage-of-the-fund approach does over-compensate attorneys in those instances where for many reasons unrelated to the skill of counsel a large settlement is proposed and accepted early in the litigation process. At the same time, the lodestar method discourages the attorney from continuing to pursue aggressively a tough case or pecuniary benefits because the hours logged in the case produce at least a normal profit for her efforts so long as some benefit is conferred as a consequence of the suit. Furthermore, there is abundant evidence that the lodestar method does not result in fee awards that are out of line with the percentage-of-the-fund approach.[29] By joining the two methods, certainly under the watchful and skeptical eye of the court, much can be

---

[22] *See* Coffee, *supra* §15.14 note 11, at 720-728.

[23] Court Awarded Attorney Fees: Report of the Third Circuit Task Force (1985), *reprinted in* 108 F.R.D. 237 (1985) (headed by Professor Arthur Miller).

[24] *Id.* at 258.

[25] *Id.*

[26] *Id.*

[27] *See* Powers v. Eichen, 229 F.3d 1249 (9th Cir. 2000).

[28] *See* In re Cendant Litigation, 264 F.3d 201 (3d Cir. 2001).

[29] Robert T. Mowrey, Attorney Fees in Securities Class Action and Derivative Suits, 3 J. Corp. L. 267 (1978).

done to assure that the right discipline and incentives are applied to the representative suit's counsel.[30]

For the reasons discussed above, the initial enthusiasm for the lodestar approach has given way to several sobering considerations that question whether it improves the incentives approach over the percentage-of-the-fund approach. Not surprisingly, the circuit and state courts are divided on which method to use. There are at least three distinct camps: One group of courts, although acknowledging the weaknesses of the lodestar approach, continues to use that method;[31] courts that reject the lodestar method for the percentage-of-the-fund approach;[32] and courts that find either method acceptable as long as the resulting fee is reasonable.[33]

The proposal of the American Law Institute does not choose between these conflicting positions; the proposal does, however, require that "in no event should the attorney's fee award exceed a reasonable proportion of the value of the relief (including nonpecuniary relief) obtained by the plaintiff for the corporation."[34] So conditioning the fee awarded should force the courts to reduce the frequency with which large fees are awarded in derivative suits that yield nonpecuniary benefits of doubtful value.

§15.19   Indemnification and Insurance for Directors and Officers

When an officer or director is named as a defendant in a lawsuit charging misconduct in office, is he entitled to indemnification for expenses if the defense is successful? Further, may he be reimbursed for his costs even in the event that the plaintiff prevails? All states have indemnification statutes.[1] The former Model Business Corporation Act[2] as well as the current Model Business Corporation Act[3]

---

[30] See In re Safety Components, Inc. Litig., 166 F. Supp. 2d 72 (D.N.J. 2001) (excellent illustration of using both methods and factors within each method to award fees); Mashburn v. National Healthcare, Inc., 684 F. Supp. 679 (M.D. Ala. 1988) (using the two methods to justify a multiplier of 3.1 to support fee based on percentage-of-the-fund approach).

[31] See, e.g., Longden v. Sunderman, 979 F.2d 1095 (5th Cir. 1992); Weinberger v. Great Northern Nekoosa Corp., 925 F.2d 518 (1st Cir. 1991).

[32] Swedish Hosp. Corp. v. Shala, 1 F.3d 1261 (D.C. Cir. 1993); Camden I Condominium Assoc., Inc. v. Dunkle, 946 F.2d 768, 774 (11th Cir. 1991).

[33] Powers v. Eichen, 229 F.3d 1249 (9th Cir. 2000); Harman v. Lyphomed, Inc., 945 F.2d 969 (7th Cir. 1991).

[34] See ALI, 2 Principles of Corporate Governance, supra §15.02 note 46, §717.

§15.19   [1] See Model Business Corp. Act §8.50 (1984) (hereinafter MBCA).

[2] See Former MBCA §5 (1969), which was patterned after the Delaware indemnification provisions, see Del. Code Ann. tit. 8, §145 (2001).

[3] MBCA Ann. §§8.50-8.58. The MBCA reflects the changes made in the Model Business Corporation Act in 1980. See Changes in the Model Business Corporation Act Affecting Indemnification of Corporate Personnel, 34 Bus. Law. 1595 (1979). Further liberalization is now being proposed for the MBCA. See Changes in the Model Business Corporation Act—Amendments Pertaining to Indemnification and Advance for Expenses, 49 Bus. Law. 741 (1994). Among the more significant changes proposed for the act are:

have greatly influenced the overall structure and philosophy of state indemnification statutes. Approximately one-half the state indemnity provisions are substantially similar to the 1969 version of the former Model Business Corporation Act,[4] and all but a handful of the remaining states pattern their indemnification statutes after the current Model Business Corporation Act.[5] The major difference between the two model acts is that the current Model Business Corporation Act makes its provisions the exclusive means for indemnifying directors, empowers the court to approve indemnification in certain instances, precludes indemnification when the defendant receives an improper personal benefit, and requires notice to the shareholders when directors are indemnified.[6] Important variations exist among the states regardless of which particular initiative that state chose as the model for its own indemnification provision.

Both at common law and by statute, the indemnification rules that apply to derivative suits differ from those applicable to suits brought against officers, directors, or corporate agents (outsiders) by third parties. It is well established agency law that, subject to illegality and in the absence of an agreement to the contrary, a principal is bound to indemnify his agent for "expenses of defending actions by third parties brought because of the agent's authorized conduct. . . ."[7]

An important threshold consideration is the breadth of corporate personnel covered by the state's corporate indemnity statute. For example, the Delaware and New York statutes apply to the "director and officers,"[8] whereas a few states extend their statutes to others, such as employees, agents, or other representatives of the corporation.[9]

---

(1) altering procedures for advancing expenses and authorizing indemnification;

(2) allowing the court to advance expenses;

(3) clarifying when an officer may be indemnified and obtain advances for her expenses; and

(4) authorizing charter provisions to allow indemnification to the same extent that directors may now obtain immunity from liability through a charter provision. *Id.* at 742.

[4] MBCA Ann. §8.50 note on statutory comparison (3d ed. 1994).

[5] *Id.* The few states that have chosen not to follow either of the model acts are California, Cal. Corp. Code §317 (West 1990); Mass. Ann. Laws ch. 56B, §67 (Law. Co-op 1996); Minnesota, Minn. Stat. Ann. §302A.521 (Supp. 2002); New Jersey, N.J. Stat. Ann. §§14A:2-7 & 14A:3-5 (Supp. 2002); New York, N.Y. Bus. Corp. Law §§721-726 (McKinney Supp. 2002); and North Dakota, N.D. Cent. Code §10-19.1-91 (2001).

[6] *See* Changes in the Model Business Corporation Act Affecting Indemnification of Corporate Personnel, 34 Bus. Law. 1595 (1979).

[7] Restatement (Second) of the Law of Agency §439(d) (1958). This right may also arise under labor statutes, *see* Jacobus v. Krambo Corp., 93 Cal. Rptr. 425 (Cal. Ct. App. 2000) (relying on a provision of the California labor code).

[8] Del. Code Ann. tit. 8, §145(a)(b) (2001); N.Y. Bus. Corp. Law §722(a)(b) (McKinney Supp. 2002).

[9] *See, e.g.,* Conn. Bus. Corp. Act. §33-777 (West Supp. 2002); Mass. Gen. Laws Ann. ch. 156B §67 (Law. Co-op 1996); Wyo. Stat. §17-16-857 (2001). As to the meaning of agent under such a statute, *see, e.g.,* APSB Bancorp. V. Thornton Grant, 1994 Cal. App. LEXIS 709 (Cal. Ct. App. 1994) (CPA not subject to company's control so not deemed an agent); Channel Lumber Co. v. Porter Simon, 93 Cal. Rptr. 2d 482 (Cal. Ct. App. 2000) (outside counsel not agent within scope of statute).

Most statutes provide for indemnification as a matter of right "to the extent" the director or officer is "successful" in his defense and, subject to varying standards and limitations, authorize permissive (that is, discretionary with a body such as the independent directors, independent counsel, or the court) indemnification in other cases. The "to the extent . . . successful" language thus overrules those common law decisions that followed the *New York Dock Company* decision denying the successful director indemnification.[10] In determining whether there has been success, it is important whether the statute envisions a decision on the suit's merits or whether a prejudicial dismissal on procedural grounds entitles the corporate official to indemnification. The statute's inclusion of language such as "on the merits *or otherwise*"[11] obviously invites a broad construction of the meaning of "success." Indemnification as a matter of right may also arise by virtue of supplementary indemnification provisions in the employee's contract with the corporation or by virtue of the bylaws of the corporation that are authorized in most states.[12]

In a leading case, *Merritt-Chapman & Scott v. Wolfson*,[13] the Delaware Supreme Court held that the directors were successful within the meaning of the Delaware indemnification statute for their expenses related to the criminal counts, which were dropped as a result of their plea bargaining, entered into after their convictions were reversed on appeal. The defendants pled guilty to a single count that was not dropped as a result of their plea bargain. To avoid requiring partial indemnification of the defendant's expenses under facts such as those of *Merritt-Chapman & Scott*, the current Model Business Corporation Act requires that the defendant have been "wholly successful."[14] A defendant is wholly successful "only if the entire proceeding is disposed of on a basis which involves a finding of nonliability."[15] Courts have also held that a dismissal because of the statute of limitations is deemed a successful defense.[16]

---

[10] 16 N.Y.S. 844 (Sup. Ct. 1944).

[11] *See, e.g.,* Del. Code Ann. tit. 8, §145(c) (2001). Even though California's statute does not include the "or otherwise" language, indemnification has been awarded when the action against former officers was dismissed by virtue of mutual releases between the corporation and the officers. *See* Wilshire-Doheny Assoc, Ltd. v. Shapiro, 100 Cal. Rptr. 478 (Cal. Ct. App. 2000) (interpreting "success on the merits"). However, a voluntary dismissal with a right to refile is not "success on the merits." *See* Groth Bros. Oldsmobile, Inc. v. Gallagher, 118 Cal. Rptr. 2d 405 (Cal. Ct. App. 2002).

[12] VonFeldt v. Steel Fin. Corp., 714 A.2d 79 (Del. 1998) (individual elected to serve on subsidiary corporation's board of directors is covered by provision of parent company's bylaws that extends indemnification as a matter of right to one who perform a function "at the request" of the parent). On the topic of supplementary indemnification rights, *see infra* text accompanying note 43.

[13] 321 A.2d 138 (Del. 1974). *See also* Waltuch v. Conticommodity Services, Inc., 88 F.3d 87 (2d Cir. 1996).

[14] MBCA §8.52 (1984).

[15] MBCA Ann. §8.52 official comment (3d ed. 1994). It would appear to satisfy the "wholly successful" requirement to require partial indemnification where the defendant prevails in many but not all the causes of action brought against him in a civil proceeding. *See* MCI Telecommunications Corp. v. Wanzer, 1990 WL 161198 (Del. 1990). Similarly, the defendant is wholly successful where the settlement payment by other defendants causes the suit against the defendant seeking indemnification to be dropped. *See* B & B Inv. Club v. Kleinert's, Inc., 472 F. Supp. 787, 791 (E.D. Pa. 1979).

[16] *See* Dornan v. Humphrey, 106 N.Y.S.2d 142 (Sup. Ct. 1951), *modified on other grounds,* 112 N.Y.S.2d 585 (App. Div. 1952).

C. Special Procedural and Substantive Issues in Derivative Suit Litigation

The policy choices within indemnity statutes become more numerous in the case of the unsuccessful corporate officer or director. It is at this point that the greatest variation in approaches and language appears among the state statutes. The former Model Business Corporation Act,[17] following the architecture of the Delaware statute,[18] treats separately indemnification arising from actions by or on behalf of the corporation and all other types of actions. The concern that drives treatment of actions that are by or on behalf of the corporation as separate from others is that of the circularity of otherwise allowing the director or officer to be reimbursed for a recovery that the derivative suit obtained on behalf of the corporation. To allow indemnification for actions by or on behalf of the corporation mocks the therapeutic purposes of the suit because it will be the corporation, not the real defendant, who will be the worse off as a consequence of the suit. The current Model Business Corporation Act takes a different path by barring indemnification in actions by or on behalf of the corporation where the request arises from any proceeding in which the director has received an improper personal benefit or in any proceeding by or on behalf of the corporation in which she has been adjudged liable.[19]

The former Model Business Corporation Act and the Delaware statute distinguish between actions by or on behalf of the corporation and all other actions in that indemnification is allowed for the former only for the defendant's reasonable expenses, but not for any resulting settlement or judgment.[20] Similarly, the current Model Business Corporation Act allows indemnification of the defendant's expenses but not for any amount paid as a fine, judgment, or settlement, provided a court orders such indemnification on a finding that he is "reasonably and fairly entitled to indemnification."[21]

The unsuccessful corporate director or officer is not entitled to indemnification as a matter of right; she must persuade a designated decision-maker to exercise her discretion to indemnify the director or officer. Statutes generally confine the decision-maker to a body of independent directors, independent counsel, or a court.[22] The route the statute lays out for the decision-maker, however, is not a two-way street. There appears in the statute no restraint on the decision-maker refusing to indemnify the unsuccessful director or officer. That is, the petitioner who seeks indemnification for her unsuccessful defense is not entitled to indemnification as a matter of right; the indemnification authorized by the statute for the unsuccessful defendant is permissive.

---

[17] See Former MBCA §5(a)(b) (1969).

[18] See Del. Code Ann. tit. 8, §145(a)(b) (2001).

[19] MBCA §8.51(d) (1984). The same procedures apply for officers, except the Model Business Corporation Act allows broader indemnification for officers to occur via contractual agreements. See Id. at §8.56.

[20] See Del. Code Ann. tit. 8, §145(b) (2001); former MBCA §5(b) (1969). See also TLC Beatrice Int'l Holdings Inc. v. CIGNA Ins. Co., 1999 U.S. Dist. Lexis 605 (S.D.N.Y. 1999).

[21] MBCA §8.54(2) (1984). But see N.C. Gen. Stat. §55 8 57 (2000) (authorizing more expansive indemnification by optional provisions in articles or bylaws or otherwise by agreement).

[22] Del. Code Ann. tit. 8, §145(d) (2001); MBCA §§8.54 & 8.55 (1984); former MBCA §5(b)(d) (1969).

Moreover, the decision-maker cannot indemnify the unsuccessful defendant unless satisfied that the defendant's conduct meets the standards set forth in the statute. Indemnification provided without meeting the standards is improper, and the amounts can be recovered by the corporation.[23] The most frequent standards to be satisfied are that the defendant "acted in good faith and in a manner he reasonably believed to be or not opposed to the best interests of the corporation."[24] The New York Court of Appeals interpreted good faith to require that the officer or director acted for a purpose she reasonably believed to be in the best interests of the corporation.[25] The standard was not met by an officer who engaged in racial discrimination.[26] Good faith can also be interpreted more broadly to be violated by an intentional violation of the law. Thus, in an interesting bribery case, this standard for indemnification was not satisfied, even though the bribe was made to advance what the defendant genuinely believed was his employer's interest, because the defendant was believed not to have acted in good faith because he consciously violated the law.[27] And, steps taken by executives to prevent federal regulators from exercising control over the company, even though undertaken for what the executives believed furthered the interests of the company, were nonetheless deemed in bad faith because they sought to undermine the government's regulatory authority.[28] Under statutes that condition reimbursement on whether the executive was "adjudged liable" one court applying this standard upheld indemnification, even though the jury found that the officer had breached his fiduciary duty; since the breach produced no damages the court held that the officer had not been adjudged liable.[29]

When the defendant in an earlier proceeding was found to have breached a fiduciary duty to the corporation and now seeks indemnification, generally the court is the sole decision-maker applying these standards,[30] and the court is under the additional obligation to find that the defendant is "fairly and reasonably entitled to indemnification."[31] Thus, in a decision that makes good sense but no doubt is not politically correct, the court found indemnification of directors was in order

[23] *See* Behrstock v. Ace Hose & Rubber Co., 496 N.E.2d 1024 (1986); B & B. Inv. Club v. Kleinert's, Inc., 472 F. Supp. 787 (E.D. Pa. 1979).

[24] *See, e.g.,* Cal. Corp. Code §317(b) (West 1990); Del. Code Ann. tit. 8, §145(a)(b) (2001); N.Y. Bus. Corp. Law §722(a)(c) (McKinney 1986); MBCA §8.51(a) (1984); former MBCA §5(a)(b) (1969). (McKinney 1986 & Supp. 1994); MBCA §8.54(2) (1984); former MBCA §5(b) (1969).

[25] *See, e.g.,* Biondi v. Beekman Hill House Apartment Corp., 731 N.E.2d 577, 581 (N.Y. 2000) (key to indemnification is director's good faith toward corporation, and mere judgment against director is not dispositive of this issue; in this case, however, director's willful racial discrimination was not in corporation's best interest).

[26] *Id.* at 581.

[27] *See* Associated Milk Producers, Inc. v. Parr, 528 F. Supp. 7, 8 (E.D. Ark. 1979).

[28] *See* In re Landmark Land Co. of Caronlina, Inc., 76 F.3d 553 (4th Cir. 1996); Pilpiak v. Keyes, 729 N.Y.S.2d 99 (N.Y. App. Div. 2001) (violates public policy to indemnify executive expenses incurred in unsuccessful defense of grand larceny).

[29] *See* Waskel v. Guaranty Nat'l Corp., 23 P.3d 1214 (Colo. App. Ct. 2000).

[30] *See* MBCA §§8.51(d)(1), 8.54(2) (1984).

[31] *See, e.g.,* Cal. Corp. Code §317(c)(1) (West 1990); Del. Code Ann. tit. 8, §145(b) (2001); N.Y. Bus. Corp. Law §722(c).

C. Special Procedural and Substantive Issues in Derivative Suit Litigation

where the defendant directors of an all-male club sought indemnification for their continued defense of what they believed the desirable policy for the club.[32] An additional standard is applicable when the defendant seeks indemnification after an unsuccessful defense in a criminal proceeding; the decision-maker must also determine that the defendant "had no reasonable cause to believe his conduct was unlawful."[33]

Most indemnification statutes authorize the corporation to advance expenses to its officers or directors. Advances are especially important when any applicable insurance coverage does not include litigation expenses or, if such coverage exists, the policy has a fairly large deductible before the insurance carrier becomes obligated to assume the defense costs. Even though corporation's power to advance expenses is not unrestrained by the statute, the propriety of making such advances should not depend on the merits of the claim against the officer or director.[34] For example, the Model Business Corporation Act requires:

(1) the director furnish the corporation a written affirmation of his good faith belief that he has met the standard of conduct described in section 8.51;
(2) the director furnishes the corporation a written undertaking, executed personally or on his behalf, to repay the advance if it is ultimately determined that he did not meet the standard of conduct; and
(3) a determination is made that the facts then known to those making the determination would not preclude indemnification under this chapter.[35]

A key policy issue for any legislative body is whether the state indemnity statute should be exclusive. It is over this question that the greatest variation appears among the states. The strong current follows the position of Delaware, whose statute provides:

The indemnification and advance of expenses provided by, or granted pursuant to, the other subsections of this section shall not be deemed exclusive of any other rights to which those seeking indemnification or advancement of expenses may

---

[32] *See* Cross v. Midtown Club, Inc., 365 A.2d 1227 (Conn. Super. Ct. 1976).

[33] *See, e.g.,* Cal. Corp. Code §317(b) (West 1990) ("had no reasonable cause to believe the conduct of the person was unlawful"); Del. Code Ann. tit. 8, §145(a) (2001); N.Y. Bus. Corp. Law §722(a) (McKinney 1986 & Supp. 1994); MBCA §5(a) (1969); MBCA §8.51(a)(3) (1984); former MBCA §5(a) (1969).

[34] *See* Ridder v. Cityfed Fin. Corp., 47 F.3d 85, 87 (3d Cir. 1995) (interpreting Delaware law); Citadel Holding Corp. v. Roven, 603 A.2d 818, 826 (Del. 1992). *Cf.* Murphree v. Federal Ins. Co., 707 So. 2d 523 (Miss. 1997) (though indicted for embezzlement, advances were covered by contract and should be made).

[35] MBCA §8.53 (1984). The statute must of course be read closely, because while some that authorize advances are permissive, others require such an advance unless the corporation provides otherwise in its articles of incorporation, bylaws, or contract with its personnel. *See* Barry v. Barry, 28 F.3d 848 (8th Cir. 1994). In any case, the authority of the board of directors to advance costs does not depend on the merits of the claim asserted. *See, e.g.,* Ridder v. Cityfed Fin. Corp., 47 F.3d 85, 87 (3d Cir. 1995); Neal v. Neumann Medical Center, 667 A.2d 479 (Pa. Commw. Ct. 1995). And where the bylaws provide for such an advance, the director, officer, or employee can enforce that right and recover her costs to obtain the advance. *See* Mitrano v. Total Pharm. Care, Inc., 75 F.3d 72, 74 (1st Cir. 1996).

be entitled under any bylaw, agreement, vote of the stockholders or disinterested directors or otherwise, both as to action in his official capacity and as to action in another capacity while holding such office.[36]

One court has held that the corporation does not have carte blanche authority in drafting such an extra-statutory indemnification. In *Waltuch v. Conticommodity Services*,[37] the court held that the above quoted provision of the Delaware statute could not authorize indemnification in instances that violate the substantive standards, e.g., "good faith" set forth in the statutory provision circumscribing the corporation's power to indemnify unsuccessful directors and officers. Therefore, the above non-exclusive provision did not permit indemnification of an officer who knowingly violated the law, even though such was called for by his private contract with the corporation. This leaves the above quoted provision authorizing deviations from non-substantive statutory provisions, such as who the decision maker can be and, for example, requiring advances of expenses for which there is no substantive standard.[38] At the same time, mandatory indemnification for successful executives provided by statute is not to be reduced by technical requirements found in supplementary bylaw or contractual indemnification arrangements.[39] Some states permit additional indemnification arrangements, provided they are authorized in the articles of incorporation or bylaws.[40] Many other state indemnity statutes expressly state that their provisions are exclusive.[41]

With the virtual universal acceptance by courts and legislature of at least a limited right to indemnification, the next legal development was liability insurance for corporate officers and directors. The typical directors' and officers' (D&O) policy has two distinct parts.[42] The first part provides coverage to reim-

---

[36] Del. Code Ann. tit. 8, §145 (f) (2001).

[37] 88 F.3d 87 (2d Cir. 1996). Where indemnification would not be inconsistent with public policy, as it would have been in *Waltuch*, the supplementary indemnification rights in a company's contract with the officer or bylaws may provide him with indemnification rights greater than those that exist under the statute. *See, e.g.,* VonFeldt v. Steel Fin. Corp., 714 A.2d 79 (Del. 1998).

[38] *See* Owens Corning v. National Union Fire Ins. Co., 257 F.3d 484 (6th Cir. 2001) (recognizing authority under above quoted Delaware provision to set forth a presumption of good faith action); Citadel Holding Corp. v. Roven, 603 A.2d 818, 826 (Del. 1992) (ordering advancement of sums to meet all reasonable costs to defend suit alleging malfeasance); Neal v. Neuman Med. Center, 667 A.2d 479 (Pa. Comm. Ct. 1995) (upholding mandatory advancement of fees provision of bylaws as not inconsistent with statutory restrictions on indemnification).

[39] *See* Chaimson v. Healthtrust, Inc., 735 A.2d 922 (Del. Ch. 1998) (indemnification ordered even though officer had not complied with provision of indemnity contract that required officer to be represented by counsel approved by corporation).

[40] *See, e.g.,* Cal. Corp. Code. §317(g) (West 1990) (authorized in articles of incorporation); N.Y. Bus. Corp. Law §721 (McKinney Supp. 2002) (authorized either in articles of incorporation or bylaws).

[41] *See, e.g.,* N.Y. Bus. Corp. Law §721 (McKinney 1986). *See also* MBCA §§8.56(3), 8.58 (1984) (exclusive as to directors but not as to officers).

[42] Insurance carriers also offer "entity" policies, especially for securities related matters, which provide insurance to the company even though the suit does not name any director or officer. When through the entity coverage the corporation becomes the insured under the D&O coverage, and the corporation enters bankruptcy when claims are to be dispersed from the policy, an issue can arise regarding what portion of the policy belongs to the bankrupt estate. Another variation is a "pre-deter-

burse the corporation for its costs in indemnifying its directors and officers. The second part extends coverage directly to the individual officer or director for which indemnification from the corporation is not available or forthcoming. The latter is sometimes referred to as "Side A" or "last resort" coverage; it comes into effect only when the corporation cannot or will not indemnify the officer or director. Such a denial of indemnification is most frequently the result of a change of control. The standard D&O policy rarely requires the insurer to defend the officer or director and operates on a claims-made basis—that is, the policy covers only those actions brought during the period of the policy.[43] However, if the policyholder gives proper notice to the insurer of a transaction or event that could give rise to a claim at some future date, the claim if made will be covered by the policy even if outside the stated policy period. A 5 percent deductible is not uncommon among policies, and the policies generally exclude from their coverage fines and penalties arising from criminal actions as well as reimbursements for liability arising in civil actions for dishonesty or where the officer or director has personally gained as a consequence of her breach.[44] The standard policy covers non-intentional violations and customarily has many other exclusions, most of which are items likely to be covered by a different type of corporate policy, such as its general liability policy (for the D&O exclusions for libel, slander, environmental liabilities, and other forms of property damage).[45] The key provisions of the policy's coverage are its definition of "wrongful act" and its numerous exclusions. It is standard for the policy to prohibit covered executives from incurring defense costs without the consent of the insurer.

The Model Act empowers a corporation to purchase insurance for any director, officer, employee, or agent for any liability arising out of their corporate capacity "whether or not the corporation would have the power to indemnify or advance expenses to him against the same liability. . . ."[46] Some states, such as New York,[47] place statutory limits on the type of insurance that corporations may provide directors and officers, and, despite the broad language of the Model Act, decisions such as *Waltuch* remind us that liability insurance for gross misconduct may be void as against public policy. This however is largely a theoretical proposition because insurers exclude from their coverage intentional conduct of the type that poses such public policy considerations.

---

mined allocation option" which provides no coverage to the company unless the officers or directors are also named in the suit.

[43] *See, e.g.,* Foster v. Summit Medical Systems, Inc., 610 N.W.2d 350 (Minn. Ct. App. 2000).

[44] *See* International Ins. Co. v. Johns, 874 F.2d 1447 (11th Cir. 1989) (settlement returning to corporation amounts received as "golden parachutes" not within exclusion for "personal gains" where court concluded golden parachute arrangement was protected by business judgment rule).

[45] *See, e.g.,* Cincinnati Ins. Co. v. Irwin Co., 2000 Ohio App. LEXIS 6045 (Ohio Ct. App. Dec. 22, 2000) (upholding denial of claim by officers who engaged in inside trading).

[46] *See* MBCA §8.57 (1984). *See also* Cal. Corp. Code §317(i) (West 1990) (with extensive provisions dealing with propriety of such insurance carrier being affiliated with the corporation); Del. Code Ann. tit. 8, §145(g) (2001); former MBCA §5(g) (1969).

[47] *See* N.Y. Bus. Corp. Law §726(b) (McKinney Supp. 2002).

CHAPTER 16

Issuance of Shares

A. SHARE SUBSCRIPTIONS AND UNDERWRITING

§16.01 *Nature and Form of Subscription Agreements*

One may become a shareholder either by (1) subscription contract with the corporation for the issue of new shares; (2) purchase from the corporation of treasury shares—that is, shares already issued and reacquired by the corporation; or

(3) transfer from an existing holder of outstanding shares, with the new owner being substituted in the place of the transferor.[1] Share subscribers are persons who have agreed to take and pay for the original unissued shares of a corporation, formed or to be formed. A subscription differs from a contract of sale, a subscription being a contract for the corporation to issue or create new shares, as contrasted with an agreement by a stockholder for the transfer of title to issued shares or shares to be issued.[2]

Unless the corporate statute or charter requires otherwise, a subscription can be oral or written, as long as it is sufficiently definite to satisfy the requirements for a valid contract. This minimally requires evidence of an agreement to purchase a given number of shares in the corporation at a specified price.[3] The states are split as to whether a subscription for stock must be in writing and signed by the subscriber to be enforceable. Approximately one half of the states follow the scheme of the current Model Business Corporation Act or its predecessor by not requiring that the subscription be in writing to be enforceable.[4] Even in jurisdictions that do require a written contract, the subscriber's conduct may estop him from raising the absence of a written agreement as a defense.[5] And in one case, the court interpreted the statute's requirement of a written agreement as affording a defense only to the subscriber; the corporation could have had an unwritten agreement enforced against it by the subscriber.[6] However, courts frequently have held a subscription for stock subject to the statute of frauds, like an agreement for the sale of goods, wares, merchandise, or choses in action.[7]

§16.02   Pre-Incorporation Subscriptions—Revocability

The subscriber's power to revoke a stock subscription today is circumscribed by state corporation statutes, which generally render pre-incorporation subscriptions irrevocable for a certain period of time, most frequently six months, unless oth-

---

§16.01   [1] Corporate capital structure and the various types of ownership interests are discussed in Chapter 18.

[2] See Zukowski v. Dunton, 650 F.2d 30 (4th Cir. 1981); Penley v. Penley, 332 S.E.2d 51 (N.C. 1985); Sprague v. Straub, 451 P.2d 49, 52 (Or. 1969).

[3] Klapmeier v. Flagg, 677 F.2d 781 (9th Cir. 1982); White County Guar. Sav. & Loan Ass'n v. Searcy Fed. Sav. & Loan Ass'n, 410 S.W.2d 760, 763 (Ark. 1967).

[4] See Bielinski v. Miller, 382 A.2d 357 (NH 1978); Byrd v. Tidewater Power Co., 172 S.E.2d 183 (NC 1934); A written subscription agreement, however, may be required by statute. Model Bus. Corp. Act §6.20 (1984).

[5] See Duncan v. Brookview House, Inc., 205 S.E.2d 707 (S.C. 1974).

[6] Putman v. Williams, 652 F.2d 497 (5th Cir. 1981). See also Beck v. Motler, 384 N.Y.S.2d 397 (App. Div. 1973).

[7] See Cooper v. Vitraco, Inc., 320 F. Supp. 239 (D.V.I. 1970) (decided under U.C.C. §8-319); Spencer v. McGuffin, 130 N.E. 407 (Ind. 1921).

erwise agreed or unless all other subscribers agree to the release.[1] In the absence of a statute, courts have sometimes found it difficult to determine the legal principles applicable to pre-incorporation subscriptions.

§16.03   Liability on Unpaid Subscriptions to Corporations and Creditors

Under modern statutes, a corporation's board of directors may determine the payment terms of pre-incorporation subscriptions if the subscription agreement does not specify them.[1] A subscriber's default creates a debt due to the corporation, which may be accordingly collected.

Unless liability is imposed by statute, neither subscribers nor shareholders are directly accountable to the corporation's creditors.[2] The subscriber's liability is to the corporation and is pursued by its representatives.[3] In the absence of receivership or bankruptcy proceedings, the usual remedies available to corporate creditors to reach the indebtedness of shareholders for partly paid shares is a creditors' bill in equity or garnishment, in which creditors must show they have exhausted their remedies at law or are excused from doing so.[4]

§16.04   The Underwriting Services of Investment Bankers

It is important for business lawyers to understand the nature of the underwriting arrangements commonly used by issuers and investment bankers in bringing out and distributing issues of corporate securities.[1] However, lawyers should also be aware that securities may be "distributed" to the investing public directly by the management of a going corporation or by the promoters of a new enterprise without the aid of investment bankers or the use of an underwriting agreement. Small concerns often cannot afford underwriting by investment bankers and must rely on corporate officers and agents to sell securities. Large concerns are sometimes able to place large issues of high-grade securities directly with life insurance companies, pension funds, or other institutional investors. In direct private financing,

---

§16.02   [1] *See, e.g.*, Ala. Code 1975 §10-2B-6.20 (Michie 1999); Col. Rev. Stat. Ann. §7-106-201 (West 1986 & Supp. 2002); Geo. Code Ann. §14-2-620 (Michie 1994); 805 Ill. Comp. Stat. Ann. 5/6.20 (West 1993 & Supp. 2002); N.Y. Bus. Corp. L. §503(a) (McKinney 1986 & Supp. 2002); Former MBCA §17 (1969).

§16.03   [1] *See, e.g.*, MBCA §6.20 (1984); Former MBCA §17 (1969).

[2] Thompson Houston Elec. Co. v. Murray, 37 A. 443 (N.J. Sup. Ct. 1897); Annot., 7 A.L.R. 100 (1920). *See* Patterson v. Lynde, 106 U.S. 619 (1882).

[3] Kerosec v. Yirga, 230 N.E.2d 587 (Ill. App. Ct. 1967).

[4] *See* Denniston & Co., Inc. v. Jackson, 468 So. 2d 170 (Ala. Civ. App. 1985); Stewart v. Ahern, 32 F.2d 864 (9th Cir. 1929); Spencer v. Anderson, 222 P. 355, 358 (Cal. 1924).

§16.04   [1] *See generally* 1 Thomas Lee Hazen, Treatise on the Law of Securities Regulation §2.1 (4th ed. 2002).

underwriting commissions are saved, as are other expenses such as registration under the securities laws.[2]

The methods for raising corporate capital can be divided into ten basic categories. A corporation—or any other enterprise, for that matter—theoretically at least can raise capital *without an investment banker* by (1) a direct offering of securities to the public or a limited group of people, (2) a direct offering to existing security holders (sometimes called a "rights offering"), (3) a direct private placement, (4) public sealed bidding, or (5) bank loans, mortgage loans, equipment loans, and "lease-backs." The five basic methods *using the services of an investment banker* are (6) a negotiated, underwritten public offering of securities, (7) an underwritten public offering through sealed bids, (8) an underwritten offering to existing security holders, (9) an offering to existing security holders with the investment banker acting as agent, and (10) private placement with the investment banker acting as agent for the issuer. Financial realities and business exigencies frequently limit the actual choices.

"Origination" by underwriters of securities refers to the many steps an investment banker undertakes in preparation for a client company's public offering of securities. These steps include investigating the affairs and needs of would-be issuers, selecting companies that offer good investment opportunities, devising the types and terms of securities to be offered, negotiating with an issuer the spread or discount between the price the underwriters pay the issuer for the securities and the price at which they will be offered to the public or some other arrangement for compensating the underwriters, and arranging for associated underwriters and broker-dealers. "Distribution" involves the managing of selling syndicates, advertising the securities, and presenting them to investors.[3] Largely because of the federal securities laws, there are extraordinarily high due diligence standards for all participants in the distribution process, including underwriters and professionals such as lawyers and accountants.[4]

The relationship between underwriter and issuer generally begins many months before the public offering is commenced. The managing underwriter provides a wide range of services to the issuer preparatory to the offering, including advice on the type and amount of security to be offered, the offering's timing, and the steps the issuer should take to put its financial and operational status in as favorable a light as possible prior to the offering.

An interesting dimension of underwriting is the matching of underwriter reputation with the relative riskiness of the issuer. The risks of a firm commitment

---

[2] *See* William M. Prifti, Securities: Public and Private Offerings §§1.10-1.13 (2000); Eli Shapiro & Charles R. Wolf, The Role of Private Placements in Corporate Finance (1972).

[3] At one time, underwriters also had the job of "stabilizing" a soft market, but today such activity is severely restricted by SEC regulation. *See* 17 C.F.R. §§240.10b-6, 10b-7 (2002).

[4] *See* Section 11(b)(3), 15 U.S.C. §77k(b)(3) (2000). Feit v. Leasco Data Processing Equip. Corp., 332 F. Supp. 544 (E.D.N.Y. 1971); Escott v. Barchris Constr. Co., 283 F. Supp. 643 (S.D.N.Y. 1968); 1 Hazen, *supra* note 1, §§7.03, 7.10; Carlos L. Israels, Checklist for Underwriters' Investigation, 18 Bus. Law. 90 (1962).

A. Share Subscriptions and Underwriting

underwriting are that investor demand for the security will be weak so that the underwriter's capital is tied up in the offering. Moreover, its reputation is damaged by having misjudged the marketability of that issuer's securities. It is not surprising, therefore, that lower-risk issuers tend to attract more established, higher-reputation underwriters.[5]

Underwriters' services may be valuable to both issuers and investors. Large investment banking firms have prestige and direct access to the best dealers and customers. Leading underwriters develop a clientele that has faith in the underwriter's investigation, judgment, and responsibility. Thus, by using the services of underwriters, an issuing company may obtain needed funds promptly and save on the terms at which the securities are offered, such as the rate of interest on bonds or debentures or the dividend rate on preferred stock.

Investment bankers frequently establish special relationships with a corporation issuing securities. They may, for example, obtain representation on the corporation's board of directors or acquire control of the corporation by requiring the corporation's shareholders to put their shares into a voting trust with trustees the underwriters select. Underwriters' charges may cover origination costs, compensation for the underwriting risk and syndicate management, and selling compensation. Some underwriters have at times taken advantage of their influence to obtain an undue "spread" between the wholesale price that they pay the issuer and the retail price at which they sell the issue to the public.[6]

Section 11(a)(5) of the federal Securities Act of 1933 imposes responsibility on underwriters for nondisclosure of their arrangements with the issuer and also for misrepresentations in the registration statement or prospectus.[7] The registration statement filed with the Securities and Exchange Commission under the Securities Act must contain information as to the nature of the underwriting arrangements, including a list of all underwriters, as defined in the Act, together with the amount of the issue that each has underwritten. The Securities Act also requires disclosure of underwriting commissions. These disclosure requirements are imposed on participants in the underwriting, including dealers and members of selling syndicates who participate in distributing the securities, unless their compensation is limited to the customary seller's commission. Sections 11 and 12 of the Securities Act thus impose liability on various classes of persons taking part in underwriting and distributing securities in channels of interstate commerce or

---

[5] See Michael P. Dooley, The Effects of Civil Liability on Investment Banking and the New Issues Markets, 58 Va. L. Rev. 776, 785-787 (1972).

[6] See Ferdinand Pecora, Wall Street Under Oath, ch. 10 (1939); John F. Meck, Jr. & William L. Cary, Regulation of Corporate Finance and Management Under the Public Utility Holding Company Act of 1935, 52 Harv. L. Rev. 216, 238-242 (1938). One response to this practice was the SEC rule under the Public Utility Holding Company Act that imposed the requirement of public invitation of proposals for the purchase or underwriting of securities by registered holding companies and their subsidiaries. See Moran Stanley & Co. v. SEC, 126 F.2d 325 (2d Cir. 1942); Comment, Competitive Bidding in the Sale of Public Utility Bonds, 50 Yale L.J. 1071, 1077 (1941); 7 S.E.C. Ann. Rep. 98-102 (1941).

[7] 15 U.S.C. §77k(a)(5) (2000). See authorities cited supra note 4.

by the mail.[8] "Underwriter" is a term of art under the Securities Act, and the verbiage of the definition is awkward and vexatious.[9] In substance "underwriter" includes any person who purchases from an issuer, or sells for an issuer, with a view toward the distribution of any security, or anyone who participates directly or indirectly in any such undertaking.[10]

Investment banking firms that act as underwriters are open to various conflicts of interest. For example, a firm's research department may be biased by the firm's desire to retain its investment banking clients. In bullish markets when new issues flourish there is the potential for underwriters manipulating the distribution process to gain advantage for themselves or for favored clients.[11] In 2002, the New York Attorney General, working with other state regulators, secured massive settlements against investment banking firms for various sales practices including those relating to their underwriting activities.

B.   THE ISSUANCE OF SHARES

§16.05   The Nature of Shares and Share Certificates

A share of stock is a profit-sharing contract, one of a series of units of interest and participation, authorized by the corporate charter, by which capital is obtained in consideration of a proportional right to participate in profits and growth through dividends and other distributions.[1] All subscribers and purchasers of stock make themselves parties to a contract—the corporate charter—which in a broad sense includes not only the articles of incorporation but also the applicable corporation laws as well.[2] The charter contract usually gives the shareholder a vote in the selection of directors, in the adoption of bylaws, and in the making of fundamental changes in the corporate structure. It gives a proportional right to participate in the distribution of assets on dissolution and winding up after payment of debts, as

---

[8] Ernest L. Folk, Civil Liabilities Under the Federal Securities Acts: The *Bar Chris* Case, 55 Va. L. Rev. 1 (1969); James C. Freund & Henry S. Hacker, Cutting Up the Humble Pie: A Practical Approach to Apportioning Litigation Risks Among Underwriters, 48 St. John's L. Rev. 461 (1974); Note, Section 11 of the Securities Act: The Unresolved Dilemma of Participating Underwriters, 40 Fordham L. Rev. 869 (1972). *See infra* §27.06.

[9] 15 U.S.C. §77b(11) (2000).

[10] *See, e.g.,* Harden v. Raffensperger, Hughes & Co., Inc., 65 F.3d 1392 (7th Cir. 1995). 1 Hazen, *supra* note 1, §4.24; SEC v. Chinese Consol. Benev. Ass'n, 120 F.2d 738 (2d Cir. 1941); Ira Haupt & Co., 23 S.E.C. 589 (1946); Reiter-Foster Oil Corp., 6 S.E.C. 1028 (1940).

[11] *See generally* 1 Thomas Lee Hazen, Treatise on the Law of Securities Regulation §6.3.

§16.05 [1] DRW Builders, Inc. v. Richardson, 679 N.E.2d 902 (Ind. Ct. App. 1997) ("share of stock" defined as instrument conferring proportional part in certain rights in management and profits of a corporation); McGahan v. United Engr. Corp., 180 A. 195, 199 (N.J. Ch. 1935); United States Radiator Corp. v. State, 101 N.E. 783 (N.Y. 1913); William D. Ford, Share Characteristics Under the New Corporation Statutes, 23 Law & Contemp. Probs. 264 (1958).

[2] Garey v. St. Joe Mining Co., 91 P. 369, 371 (Utah 1907).

well as certain auxiliary or remedial rights. The share contract is a property right—namely, a fractional interest in the corporate enterprise that includes an indirect interest in its property and earnings, subject to its liabilities.

A certificate for shares certifies that one is a holder or owner of a certain number of shares of stock in the corporation. It is ordinarily documentary evidence of the holder's ownership of shares and a convenient instrument for the transfer of title. The one-time paper crunch on Wall Street has been a major impetus behind the recent move to recognize uncertificated shares.[3] A certificate of stock is in "street name" when it has been issued in the name of an individual or firm and endorsed in blank so that it can be negotiated without further endorsement.[4]

§16.06   Issuance, Creation, or Allotment of Shares

Shares of stock are contracts created by mutual assent of the corporation and its shareholders. The shares must first be "authorized" by appropriate provisions in the corporation's charter, which detail the rights attaching to ownership.[1] Once shares are authorized, the power to issue them lies with the board of directors.[2] When shares are sold by the corporation, they are "issued," and those shares are thereafter referred to as "authorized *and* issued." As long as they are not reacquired by the corporation—that is, they remain in the hands of shareholders—they are also "outstanding" (that is, "authorized, issued, and outstanding"); shares that are "authorized, issued, but *not* outstanding" are shares that were previously issued by the corporation but subsequent to their issuance have been reacquired by the corporation. Such shares are more commonly referred to as "treasury shares" or "treasury stock."

The word "issue" is generally employed to indicate the making of a share contract—that is, a transaction by which the directors create new shares and a person becomes the owner of the shares. Share ownership can result either from subscription to an original issue of shares by the corporation or from the transfer of shares from a prior owner and the substitution of the transferee in the place of the prior owner. A corporation usually may resell treasury shares—that is, shares that have already been issued and have been reacquired by the corporation but not retired. Such a resale has the same market impact as the issue or creation of new shares, although the transaction generally gives rise to a different accounting treatment by the corporation.

"Issue" is often associated with the execution and delivery of a share certificate, but the issue of the shares is not dependent on delivery. To become shareholders, in the sense of becoming owners of shares, subscribers need not receive

---

[3] *See* MBCA §6.26 (1984); Former MBCA §23 (1969). U.C.C. Art. 8 (2002 revision).

[4] *See* R. Baruch and Co. v. Springer, 184 A.2d 206 (D.C. App. Ct. 1962).

§16.06   [1] MBCA §6.01 (1984); Former MBCA §§15, 54(d) (1969).

[2] *See, e.g.,* MBCA §6.21 (1984); Former MBCA §18 (1969). Issuance without board approval is void. *See* Foster v. Blackwell, 747 So. 2d 1203 (La. Ct. App. 1999).

a certificate.[3] However, until the subscriber becomes a holder of record, she ordinarily has no right to vote, to receive notice of shareholders' meetings, and to inspect corporate books; she also has no right against the corporation to participate in dividends.[4]

§16.07   *Flexibility in Terms of Preferred Shares*

As with common stock, the rights, preferences, and restrictions of any class of preferred shares generally are fixed in the charte, i.e., articles of incorporation.[1] The financing of an enterprise may go on year after year, as business expands or the needs for capital arise. New issues of securities may be made from time to time; and, if preferred shares are issued, it may be necessary to meet changing market conditions by variations over time in the dividend rate and other terms of the preferred share contract. Thus the rights, privileges, and restrictions of a series of preferred shares issued at an earlier time quite probably are inappropriate for a contemporary issuance of additional shares. Absent flexible corporate enabling statutes, the serial nature of preferred stock issuances, each with the need for their rights, privileges, and restrictions to meet prevailing market conditions that are different from those of earlier issuances, would necessitate serial amendments to the articles of incorporation to authorize each new series of preferred shares. To avoid the expense and delay of such serial charter amendments, most modern corporation statutes permit a corporation's articles of incorporation to authorize the board of directors to fix the dividend rate, liquidation price, voting rights, and other terms of a class or a series within a class as the board of directors believes in the best interests of the corporation.[2] The board of directors' discretion must be exercised within the limits, if any, set forth in the enabling provision of the articles of incorporation, and the articles must set forth the number of shares of the class of shares over which the board of directors has such authority. Such shares are sometimes referred to as "blank stock" preferred shares. Absent such broad authorization, the board of directors lacks authority to so fix the terms of preferred shares.[3]

"Blank stock" preferred assumed a new role beginning with the takeover frenzy of the 1980s as a potentially powerful takeover defensive weapon. Boards of directors seized upon such blank stock authorization as the mechanism to issue "rights" that would confer upon their holders financial or voting rights whose exercise would thwart any hostile takeover of the corporation. The devices are popularly known as "poison pills."

---

[3] Golden v. Oahe Enters., Inc., 240 N.W.2d 102 (S.D. 1976) (once corporate stock is paid for, it is issued regardless of whether share certificate is executed and delivered).

[4] *See* §16.02. *But cf.* Bielinski v. Miller, 382 A.2d 357 (N.H. 1978).

§16.07   [1] *See, e.g.,* MBCA §6.01 (1984).

[2] *E.g.,* MBCA §6.02 (1984).

[3] Laster v. Waggoner, 581 A.2d 1127 (Del. 1990).

B. The Issuance of Shares

Most statutes permit enabling charter provisions authorizing the directors to subdivide classes of preferred shares into series. A series of shares is a subclass or subdivision of a class.

§16.08   Significance of Par Value

"Par value" is a rapidly vanishing feature of corporate law.[1] In broad overview, par value was at one time believed a workable approach toward assuring that the full price was paid for a corporation's shares and that a financial cushion existed for the benefit of creditors against improvident dividend payments and share repurchases. As will be discussed later, the protections that were believed to arise from the shares' par value were largely illusionary because they could be easily circumvented by, among other approaches, the use of shares having a very low par value or even shares without any par value. California began what has become an accelerating trend within corporate statutes to accord no legal significance to a share's par value.[2] Delaware and New York are two important corporate domiciles whose corporate statutes continue to embrace this otherwise outmoded approach toward creditor protection.[3]

What is the significance of the "par value" of shares? "Par value" clearly is not intended to reflect the true value of the shares, as their value will constantly fluctuate.[4] It is not a "value" in any sense. Traditionally, the primary function of par was to fix a minimum subscription or original issue price for the shares.[5] It indicates the amount that the original subscribers are supposed to contribute to capital as the basis of the privilege of profit-sharing with limited liability. Par value does not restrict the price of resales of outstanding shares among investors.[6] The aggregate par value of issued shares gives the basis for computing the minimum amount of the corporation's "legal capital." Difficulty can arise when a going concern, after making its original offering of shares, needs to raise more capital by subsequent share issues because the shares cannot be issued for less than par. Unless the corporation has been successful at keeping the market price of the shares above the par value, it cannot market additional shares. To avoid this trap, the practice developed to set an arbitrarily selected low par, for example, $1 per

§16.08 [1] *See* Venture Stores, Inc. v. Ryan, 678 N.E.2d 300, 303 (Ill. Ct. App. 1997) ("Today the concept of par value is an anachronism.").

[2] *See* Cal. Corp. Code §202(d) (1990) (legislative committee comment).

[3] *See* Del. Code. Ann., tit. 8, §§102(a)(4), 153 (2001); N.Y. Bus. Corp. L. §402(a)(4) (McKinney 1986).

[4] *See* Dewing, *supra* §16.04 note 5.

[5] Former MBCA §18 (1969) ("Shares having a par value may be issued for such consideration expressed in dollars, not less than the par value thereof, as shall be fixed from time to time by the board of directors."). In 1980 the Model Business Corporation Act was revised to eliminate the concept of par, but many states will probably be slow to adopt this radical change. *But see* Ill. Ann. Stat. ch. 805, ¶5/9.10 (West 1993 & Supp. 2002); Minn. Stat. Ann. §302A.551 (West 1985 & Cum. Supp. 2002).

[6] *See, e.g.,* Torres v. Speiser, 701 N.Y.S.2d 360 (N.Y. App. Div. 2000).

share, with the amount so specified being much below the actual issue price. Though it has been argued that par value can provide a useful method for checking the directors' discretion to issue new shares at a low price and thereby dilute the interest of existing shareholders, clearly the increasing trend today is that par is "outmoded" and "vestigial."[7]

Even in the absence of a statute setting par as the minimum issue price, it has long been the general rule that directors may not fix the issue price at less than par or give a discount from par value.[8] The hardships created by such a rigid approach resulted in the Supreme Court's providing some flexibility in *Handley v. Stutz*,[9] which held that a going concern in need of funds to continue in business may issue additional shares at the best available price free from liability to creditors, even though that price is below the shares' par value. Thus in the absence of a statute, there generally is no shareholders' liability where an operating corporation issues new shares in good faith at the best price that can be obtained, although far less than par, whether in payment of debts or to raise money for the continuance of its business.[10]

§16.09   Sale of Treasury Shares at Less Than Par

Shares that once were issued as fully paid and have then been reacquired by the corporation and not retired are called "treasury" shares.[1] Such shares are treated as still having the status of "issued" shares for purposes of resale, although they no longer have dividend or voting rights.[2] It has generally been held that the corporation may reissue and sell these treasury shares for less than their par value.[3] Treasury shares are not truly assets to be sold, but merely represent the power to reissue the shares, which is distinguished from the power to create shares by subscription upon original issue.[4] The reason given for this distinction is that the corporation has already received a capital contribution for treasury shares and has thereby created for the corporation a stated capital "liability" with respect to the shares so issued, which was not eliminated upon the corporation's reacquisition of

---

[7] William L. Cary & Melvin A. Eisenberg, Corporations Cases & Materials 918 (abridged 6th ed. 1988). California and the 1980 revisions to the Model Business Corporation Act, which have been adopted in Minnesota and Illinois, do away with par value. Cal. Gen. Stat. §500 (West Supp. 1990 & Supp. 2002); MBCA §6.40 (1984).

[8] Rickerson Roller-Mill Co. v. Farrell Foundry & Mach. Co., 75 F. 554 (6th Cir. 1896); Utica Fire Alarm Tel. Co. v. Waggoner Watchman Clock Co., 132 N.W. 502, 505 (Mich. 1911).

[9] 139 U.S. 417 (1891).

[10] Clark v. Bever, 139 U.S. 96 (1891); Fogg v. Blair, 139 U.S. 118 (1891).

§16.09   [1] The 1980 revisions to the Model Act abolish treasury shares. Former MBCA §6 (1980); MBCA §6.31 (1984).

[2] Former MBCA §2(h) (1969). *See id.* §18, which provides that treasury shares may be issued at a price fixed by the board without regard to par.

[3] Borg v. International Silver Co., 11 F.2d 147, 152 (2d Cir. 1925).

[4] *See* Borg v. International Silver Co., 11 F.2d 147 (2d Cir. 1925); Americar, Inc. v. Crowley, 282 So. 2d 674 (Fla. Ct. App. 1973) (Carroll, J. dissenting).

the shares. Upon their subsequent reissue, these shares do not increase the corporation's stated capital.

§16.10   No-Par Shares; Advantages, Issue Price

New York[1] initiated the movement to authorize the use of shares without par value. No-par shares have since been authorized in nearly every state.[2] The comparative advantages of using no-par and par value shares should be weighed in drafting the stock clauses of a corporation's charter.[3]

The number of no-par shares that may be issued must be specified in the articles of incorporation, or the shares will be void.[4] The great feature of no-par shares is price flexibility in that they require no fixed minimum capital contribution, although the same kind of quality of consideration is required as for par value shares. No-par shares may be issued from time to time at different prices, yet the subscribers and holders of the same class and series of shares will be entitled to participate equally share-for-share in the distribution of dividends and assets. The issue price of no-par shares may ordinarily be fixed by the directors.[5]

§16.11   Kinds of Consideration That Validate Payment for Shares

A corporation is not limited to a cash payment for its shares; it may receive payment in property or services if they are of a kind recognized as capable of valuation and are properly valued.[1] Most state statutes set forth the types of consideration the corporation can receive for its shares if the shares are to be "fully paid and nonassessable."[2] The types of consideration commonly authorized are money and real and personal property, including intangible property, as well as services rendered. These traditional forms of eligible types of consideration exclude executory forms of consideration, such as promissory notes or a promise of future services. A minority of the states follow the scheme of the Model Business Corporation Act and allow promissory notes and future services as well as the traditional types of consideration.[3]

§16.10   [1] N.Y. Stock Corp. Law §12 (1912).

[2] *E.g.*, Del. Code Ann., tit. 8, §153 (2001). *See* Former MBCA Ann. §§15, 18 (Supp. 1971, 1977).

[3] Floyd Franklin Burtchett, Corporation Finance, 81-84 (4th ed. 1964).

[4] Triplex Shoe Co. v. Hutchins, 152 A. 342 (Del. 1930).

[5] *See, e.g.*, Del. Code Ann., tit. 8, §153(a)(b) (2001).

§16.11   [1] *E.g.*, West v. Sirian Lamp Co., 44 A.2d 658 (Del. Ch. 1945); Former MBCA §19 (1969); MBCA §6.21 (1984). *See* Adolf A. Berle & Gardiner C. Means, The Modern Corporation and Private Property 222-224 (1967 rev. ed.).

[2] *See, e.g.*, Ariz. Rev. Stat. §10-621(B) (West 1996 & Supp. 2001); Colo. Rev. Stat. §7-106-202(2) (West 2001); Del. Code Ann., tit. 8 §152 (2001); N.Y. Bus. Corp. L. §504(a) (McKinney 1986 & Supp. 2002).

[3] Following the modern trend, New York amended its statute in 1998 to authorize future services, N.Y. Bus. Corp. L. §504(b) (McKinney 1986 & Supp. 2002) (Historical and Statutory Notes); MBCA

The difference separating the states adhering to the traditional restrictive forms of valid types of consideration from those following the current Model Business Corporation Act is the choice between embracing prophylactic protections for creditors on the one hand and accommodating commercial practices on the other. The commentary for the current Model Business Corporation Act makes clear that the over-arching view is "that only business judgment should determine what kind of property should be obtained for shares. . . ."[4] Perhaps the biggest question to be raised is whether future service is, from a creditor's perspective, appropriate consideration. For example, if the corporation becomes insolvent before the services are performed, the unperformed obligation hardly enriches the bankrupt company's estate. In most cases, the services to be exchanged for shares have a special value to that corporation, but their value to others is doubtful. In addition, services, particularly those that are promised by the promoters at the corporation's formation, are easily overvalued, and thus a ban may well be justified solely as a necessary prophylaxis for promoter misconduct. Hence, the bar can be seen as a prophylaxis for possible stock watering. Nevertheless, it cannot be overlooked that an important cornerstone to a young company's future is harnessing the creative entrepreneurial talents of key individuals through providing them an ownership interest in the firm proportionate to their prospective contributions. In any case, many creative solutions are available to circumvent the statutory bar to issuing stock for future services.[5] Similarly, there are many means to circumvent the bar to issuing stock for a promissory note,[6] and creditors have the ability to enforce the promissory note, which may well be marketable. The potential for circumvention and the related transaction costs challenges rather than supports the continued vitality of the bar to future services or a promissory note as eligible forms of consideration.

Courts are reasonably liberal in their construction of the statutory prescription of eligible forms of consideration. Thus, for example, shares issued for the goodwill of another corporation have been upheld.[7] For an item to constitute "property" as contemplated by the statute, it must have intrinsic worth and not be illusory, such as having value only upon the occurrence of a substantial condition precedent.[8] Much the same result has been reached by holding that the evidence of the value of such items is insufficient.[9] The overall objective of restricting the issuance of shares to certain types of consideration is to protect creditors by assuring that the corporation receives something having intrinsic worth and also to

---

§6.21(b) (1984). For a decision holding that the New York amendment does not apply retroactively, *see* Carr v. Marietta Corp., 211 F.3d 724 (2d Cir. 2000).

   [4] MBCA §6.21, Official Comment (1984).

   [5] *See* David R. Herwitz, Allocation of Stock Between Services and Capital in the Organization of a Close Corporation, 75 Harv. L. Rev. 1098 (1962).

   [6] *E.g.*, Guardian State Bank v. Humphrey, 762 P.2d 1084 (Utah 1988).

   [7] Eastern Okla. Television Co. v. Ameco, Inc., 437 F.2d 138 (10th Cir. 1971).

   [8] *See, e.g.*, Scully v. Automobile Fin. Co., 109 A.2d 49 (Del. 1919).

   [9] *See* Gillett v. Chicago Title & Trust Co., 82 N.E. 891 (Ill. 1907) (rights to unwritten play and prospective patents on scene-shifting devices in payment of $1,999,600 of fully paid stock).

B. The Issuance of Shares

shield the other stockholders from dilution.[10] The restrictions on the type of consideration shares can be issued for does not apply to treasury shares.[11]

Among the kinds of consideration that have been questioned as valid are promoters' services rendered before incorporation,[12] agreements by promoters, directors, or others to render future services,[13] services in marketing or underwriting securities,[14] services that do not benefit the issuing corporation,[15] future profits,[16] making a loan where shares are issued as a bonus to induce the loan,[17] making a loan in consideration for a pledge of unissued shares as security for the loan,[18] and promissory notes of subscribers.[19] The note of a subscriber has sometimes been viewed as only another promise to pay for the shares; therefore the shares may not be considered as fully paid although the promise itself is binding.[20] In a leading case,[21] it was held that services to be rendered in the future cannot be a valid consideration for the issue of shares as fully paid and nonassessable under the Delaware constitution calling for "labor done." This does not mean, however, that shares may not be issued in consideration of specified services to be rendered in the future as long as the certificates for the shares are not marked as fully paid but are treated as representing partly paid shares issued on credit.[22]

§16.12 Valuation of Consideration for Shares

At one time, a few jurisdictions adhered to what was known as the "strict value rule." According to this rule, payment for shares in property or services was satisfaction as against creditors only to the extent of the true value of the consideration, notwithstanding the good faith of the directors in fixing the value of the property or services.[1] This attempt to allow review of the directors' determination of value has been abandoned in the jurisdictions that had once adhered to it.[2]

---

[10] *See* H. J. Cohn Furn. (No. 2) Co. v. Texas Western Fin. Corp., 544 F.2d 886 (5th Cir. 1977).

[11] *See, e.g.,* Public Inv., Ltd. v. Bandeirante Corp., 740 F.2d 1222 (D.C. Cir. 1984); Ogden v. Culpepper, 474 So. 2d 1346 (La. Ct. App. 1985) (dicta).

[12] Lofland v. Cahall, 118 A. 1 (Del. 1922).

[13] Frasier v. Transwestern Land Corp., 316 N.W.2d 612 (Neb. 1982).

[14] Ludlam v. Riverhead Bond & Mortgage Corp., 278 N.Y.S. 487 (N.Y. App. Div. 1935).

[15] Clark v. Cowart, 445 So. 2d 884 (Ala. 1984).

[16] *See* Norton v. Digital Applications, Inc., 305 A.2d 656 (Del. Ch. 1973).

[17] Hopper v. Brodie, 106 A. 700 (Md. 1919).

[18] *See* McAndrews v. Idawa Gold Mining Co., 210 N.W. 514 (N.D. 1926).

[19] Sohland v. Baker, 141 A. 277, 284 (Del. 1927); Kirk v. Kirk's Auto Elec., Inc., 728 S.W.2d 529 (Ky. 1987); Capoferri v. Day, 523 S.W.2d 547 (Mo. Ct. App. 1975).

[20] Jacobs v. Frontier Tractor & Equip., Inc., 712 P.2d 493 (Colo. Ct. App. 1985).

[21] Scully v. Automobile Fin. Co., 174, 109 A. 49 (1919). *Accord,* Maclary v. Pleasant Hills, Inc., 109 A.2d 830 (Del. Ch. 1954). *But see* Petrishen v. Westmoreland Fin. Corp., 147 A.2d 392 (Pa. 1959).

[22] Norton v. Digital Applications, Inc., 305 A.2d 656 (Del. Ch. 1973); Del. Code tit. 8, §§152, 156 (2001). *See* MBCA §6.21(C) (1984).

§16.12 [1] Wm. E. Dee Co. v. Proviso Coal Co., 125 N.E. 24, 26 (Ill. 1919).

[2] *See* Clinton Mining & Mineral Co. v. Jamison, 256 F. 577 (3d Cir. 1919).

Modern statutes and decisions have established the "good faith rule," under which the judgment of the board of directors, shareholders, or incorporators as to the value of property or services a corporation receives for shares is conclusive unless fraud or intentional over-valuation is shown by the creditor.[3] Statutes frequently express the standard as being "in the absence of fraud" or "absence of *actual* fraud."[4] There are some variations, however, in what amounts to fraud. According to some courts, there must be actual fraud or dishonesty on the part of the directors in order to render the subscriber (or his transferee with notice) liable to creditors for the difference between the actual value paid and the par value or issue price of the shares subscribed.[5] Under this approach, mere proof of excessive valuation does not alone overturn the presumption that normally accompanies decisions of the board of directors.[6] On the other hand, according to other courts and statutes, an actual fraudulent intent is not necessary. "Constructive fraud" is found if the over-valuation is deliberate or intentional, and such intention can be inferred from the surrounding circumstances.[7] Most courts hold that a conscious and intentional over-valuation is fraudulent as a matter of law rather than merely evidence of fraud.[8] Other courts have indicated that a gross over-valuation can amount to "equitable fraud."[9] A conscious or deliberate overvaluation is easier to prove than dishonesty or an intent to deceive creditors. Some courts follow what may be called "a reasonable judgment rule" and regard a determination of value by the directors as fraudulent if the directors fail to make a reasonable investigation to determine the elements of value.[10]

"Fraud" is an elastic concept. Lack of good faith or inequitable conduct on the part of the directors may more readily be found where dilution of the holdings of other shareholders by an unfairly low issue price is involved than where liability to creditors is concerned. The shareholders' interest to be protected against unfair dilution of their shareholdings by discrimination in the issue price of a solvent corporation's shares is stronger than a creditor's claim to enforce a precise capital contribution by shareholders of an insolvent corporation. A leading Delaware case held that even disinterested shareholder approval of the issuance of options to each of the company's directors does not insulate the transaction

---

[3] *See, e.g.*, Arkota Ind., Inc. v. Naekel, 623 S.W.2d 194 (Ark. 1981); First Nat'l Bank of Council Bluffs v. One Craig Place, Ltd., 303 N.W.2d 688 (Iowa 1981).

[4] Former MBCA §119 (1969). *See* Del. Code Ann. tit. 8, §152 (West 2001) ("in the absence of actual fraud").

[5] *See* Diamond State Brewery, Inc. v. De La Rigaudiere, 17 A.2d 313 (Del. Ch. 1941).

[6] *See* Pipelife Corp. v. Bedford, 145 A.2d 206 (Del. Ch. 1958).

[7] Coit v. North Carolina Gold Amalgamating Co., 119 U.S. 343 (1886); Bowers v. Rio Grande Inv. Co., 431 P.2d 478, 480 (Colo. 1967). *See* Del. Code Ann. tit 8, §152 (2001).

[8] Elyton Land Co. v. Birmingham Warehouse & Elev. Co., 9 So. 129, 135 (Ala. 1891); Kaye v. Merz, 198 P. 1047 (Cal. 1921); Scully v. Automobile Fin. Co., 109 A. 49 (Del. Ch. 1919); Tooker v. National Sugar Refining Co., 84 A. 10, 15 (N.J. 1912).

[9] *But cf.* Santa Fe Indus. v. Green, 430 U.S. 462, 467-468 (1977), *rev'g* 533 F.2d 1283 (2d Cir. 1976), *rev'g* 391 F. Supp. 849 (S.D.N.Y. 1975) (equitable fraud is not sufficient to satisfy SEC Rule 10b-5's deception requirement).

[10] Pinnacle Consultants, Ltd. v. Leucadia Nat'l Corp., 101 F.3d 900, 905 (2d Cir. 1996) (directors' reasonably determined that officers had produced a dramatic turnaround in the company's performance such that being rewarded for their past efforts by issuing warrants was justified).

B.   The Issuance of Shares

from closer scrutiny when the magnitude of the option's value to each director is significant.[11]

There is a great need for careful and impartial valuation, especially where there is a potential conflict of interest. It is proper practice for the board of directors, by resolution entered in its minutes, to state its appraisal, after careful investigation, of the fair dollar value of services or property for which shares with or without par value are being used. An over-valuation without reasonable and impartial investigation into the elements of present value is evidence of lack of good faith. In many situations the board should seek an independent appraisal.

A determination in dollars of the value of the property or consideration received by the corporation is necessary for accounting purposes in stating the cost or value of its assets and in making up balance sheets showing the corporation's financial condition.[12] It is also necessary to designate what part of consideration received for shares is to be attributed to stated capital and what amount, if any, is to be attributed to paid-in surplus, particularly in connection with the issue of shares without par value. However, the absence of such a designation should not prevent the shares from being issued, assuming an eligible form of consideration was exchanged for the shares.[13]

Those states following the Model Business Corporation Act's treatment of the issuance of shares, whereby only the *adequacy* of any consideration is determined by the board of directors,[14] do not require that the directors assign a set value to any non-cash consideration received for the shares when the shares are issued. Under this approach the directors can, if they wish, be more reflective and deliberate and can value the non-cash consideration at some later date. A precise value must at some time be assigned to the non-cash consideration because the corporation's accounting records demand that all assets be recorded in dollars on the company's books at their cost. By requiring the board of directors to pass only on the adequacy of the consideration exchanged for shares before the shares are issued, the Model Business Corporation Act separates the legal consequences of the board's issuance of shares from the accounting questions. Such separation should make successful challenges to the issuance of shares less likely. Moreover, requiring a determination only of adequacy of consideration is consistent with the overall deregulatory and facilitating philosophy of the Model Business Corporation Act.

---

[11] *See* Lewis v. Vogelstein, 699 A.2d 327 (Del. Ch. 1997). *Compare* Zupnick v. Goizueta, 698 A.2d 384 (Del. Ch. 1997) (lucrative options issued in reward for past services upheld because independent board believed the executive's services were extraordinary).

[12] Garber v. Excel Mold, Inc., 397 N.E.2d 296 (Ind. Ct. App. 1979); Knickerbocker Improvement Co. v. Board of Assessors, 65 A. 913, 915 (N.J. 1907).

[13] *See* Bissias v. Koulovatos, 761 A.2d 47, 49 (Me. 2000) (statute regulating issuance of no-par shares stated the consideration would "be fixed from time to time by the board" interpreted to require only that the "consideration be given for the shares and for such consideration to have a value").

[14] Section 6.21(c) of the Model Business Corporation Act provides simply that before the shares are issued "the board of directors must determine that the consideration received or to be received for shares" is adequate.

§16.13   Equitable Limitations for Pricing Shares

Directors have a fiduciary duty to fix a reasonable price for issues of shares, both with and without par value. Timing can be a crucial factor in applying the equitable yardstick of reasonableness. If a newly formed corporation issues no-par or low-par shares to its promoters or others, there is ordinarily no legal restriction on the *amount* of consideration the corporation can receive for the shares, as long as there is some lawful consideration. However, insiders have a heavy burden of establishing the fairness of the transactions when they issue shares to themselves at a significant discount from the price available to outsiders.[1] If the corporation has been in business for some time and has demonstrated its earning capacity, the price at which additional shares are issued will have a direct effect on the interests of existing shareholders. Too low a price will dilute the interest of the holders of outstanding shares and unfairly impair the values underlying their holdings. Ideally, if new shares are not offered to the existing shareholders, the shares should be issued at a fair price, based on market conditions and the value of the corporation's assets and prospective earnings—subject, however, to a reasonable range of business discretion. As a practical matter, new offerings to the public are frequently priced at a discount as a means of attracting investors and reducing any exposure of underwriters to liability.

Differences in the prices at which shares, either par or no-par, are issued must be justified by showing fairness in light of the circumstances. Shares of the same class may be issued for different amounts of consideration at the same time if the discrimination in price is justified by adequate business reasons and is not a matter of favoritism.[2]

Disputes regarding the price at which shares are to be sold rarely arise within companies whose shares are publicly traded. For such firms, the shares' market price provides a powerful benchmark for assessing the board of directors' decision; a rational business purpose is needed to justify offering the shares below their current market value. As stated in a leading case, *Bodell v. General Gas & Electric Corporation*:[3]

> Notwithstanding . . . the absolute terms in which the power of the directors of this corporation to fix the price at which its unissued stock may be sold is expressed, equity will nevertheless by analogy to that reasoning which underlies the doctrine of preemptive right interfere to protect existing stockholders from an unjustified impairment of the values underlying their present holdings.

Bodell related to a question of discrimination regarding the issue price of Class A shares as between two different classes of common shares, Class A and Class B, which were closely related. The Class A shares were in reality a species of participating preferred stock, for they were entitled to a priority over Class B to

---

§16.13   [1] *See* Schwartz v. Marien, 335 N.E.2d 334 (N.Y. 1975).

[2] Bodell v. General Gas & Elec. Corp., 132 A. 442 (Del. Ch. 1926), *aff'd*, 15 Del. Ch. 420, 140 A. 264 (Del. 1927).

[3] 132 A. 442 (Del. Ch. 1926), *aff'd*, 140 A. 264 (1927). *See also* Atlantic Refining Co. v. Hodgman, 13 F.2d 781 (3d Cir. 1926), *rev'g* 300 F. 590 (D. Del. 1924), *cert. denied*, 273 U.S. 731 (1926).

annual noncumulative dividends of $1.50 per share and to a $25 per-share liquidation preference. After the Class B common had received equal dividends per
share, both classes were to share equally in dividends and in distributions of assets
subject to the class A's $25 liquidation preference. The directors announced a pol-
icy to enhance the attractiveness of Class A shares by giving the privilege of applying yearly dividends thereon toward the purchase of additional Class A shares with
a stated purchase price of $25 per share. As a result of this arrangement, the com-
pany was able to issue additional Class A shares at $45 and higher. Against a chal-
lenge to this arrangement by a holder of Class B shares, the court held that the
directors' discretion would not be interfered with except for fraud, such as
improper motive, personal gain, arbitrary discrimination, or conscious disregard
of the interests of the corporation and the rights of other shareholders. Because
the directors articulated a reasonable basis for their decision of making the Class
A shares more attractive to investors at a time that the corporation needed to raise
cash for expansion, a basis further supported by the high price the Class A shares
enjoyed in the market, the court dismissed the action.

On closer analysis, the court may have applied the wrong type of analysis to
the dispute in *Bodell*. The arrangement allowed the holder of Class A shares to
apply his $1.50 annual dividend toward the purchase of additional Class A shares
at a set price of $25. The practical effect of the directors' decisions was to augment
the annual dividend with an additional return in the form of a bargain purchase
of additional Class A shares. For every sixteen and two-thirds Class A shares
owned, a shareholder received a dividend of $25 ($16^{2}/_{3} \times \$1.50$), plus the gain in
the amount that the stated purchase price of additional shares was exceeded by
the then fair market value of Class A shares. Thus, if the Class A shares had a fair
market value of $45, the holder of Class A shares received a yearly benefit of $45
for every sixteen and two-thirds Class A shares owned, or approximately $2.70 per
Class A share. Without doubt, the arrangement was fair and useful to the corporation, because it clearly stimulated investor interest in the Class A shares at a time
when the corporation was aggressively issuing Class A shares to outside investors.
But the board of directors could have produced the same effect by raising the dividends on the Class A shares from $1.50 to $2.70 per share. But to have done so
would have violated the terms of the Class B shares that were to participate fully
with the Class A shares after each class of common received its $1.50 per share div-
idend. Thus the question in *Bodell* was not solely that of whether the directors
exercised their discretion fairly and in the best interests of the corporation. The
court needed to more fully consider the relative rights of the two classes of common shares in light of a transaction that effectively increased the economic return
for one class in the face of contractual arrangements that envisioned that economic returns would be shared equally.[4]

A more frequent basis of complaint in the public corporation is that the
board of directors has issued the shares to entrench the incumbent management

---

[4] William L. Cary & Melvin A. Eisenberg, Corporations Cases & Materials 1101-1102 (5th ed. unabr.
1980); 1 E. Merrick Dodd, Jr. & Ralph J. Baker, Cases on Business Associations 961, 1013 n.27, 1274-
1275 (1940). *See* §16.12.

team. When this is established, appropriate equitable relief is provided, generally to cancel shares that were issued or to enjoin their pending issuance.[5] But the courts will not intrude when a bona fide business purpose supports the shares' issuance, even though a necessary effect of issuing more shares is to entrench management.[6] Moreover, the decision to place a substantial percentage of the stock in "friendly" hands does not itself condemn the shares' issuance where the board of directors after reasonable investigation determines in good faith that such a defensive maneuver is a reasonable response to the threat the hostile bid for control poses to the corporation or its stockholders.[7] The relative freedom of the board of directors to deflect an unwanted suitor is discussed in Chapter 23.

Equitable challenges to the corporation issuing more shares frequently arises in the close corporation, where delicate balances of power and economic participation can be swiftly upset by a board resolution selling shares to one faction of stockholders. The complaint in this setting is invariably that the shares are being sold for less than their fair value or to dilute substantially the plaintiff's ownership interest, or both. As for the concern that the shares have not been fairly priced by the board of directors, the courts emphasize a variety of considerations in determining the fair value of shares in the individual case.[8] For example, a substantial departure from the shares' book value—a highly conservative benchmark, given that book value assumes that the firm's assets have no greater worth than their historical cost less any recorded depreciation or amortization—removes the pricing decision from the business judgment rule.[9] More frequently yet, equitable relief is awarded in the close corporation when the transparent purpose of issuing additional shares is to substantially dilute the plaintiff's voting power.[10] However, a business purpose for issuing the shares and no effort to exclude the plaintiff from purchasing them insulates the shares' issuance from equitable attack.[11]

§16.14   The Shareholders' Preemptive Right

The directors' power to issue shares is subject to a common law fiduciary duty not to impair the ratable rights and interests of existing shareholders. The recognition

---

[5] *See, e.g.,* Klaus v. Hi-Shear Corp., 528 F.2d 225 (9th Cir. 1975); Phillips v. Insituform of N. Am., 1987 WL16285 (Del. Ch. 1987); Condec Corp. v. Launkenheimer Co., 230 A.2d 769 (Del. Ch. 1967).

[6] *See* Empire of Carolina, Inc. v. Deltona Corp., 514 A.2d 1091, 1097 (Del. 1986) (finding bona fide purpose though did also have effect of entrenching management); Cummings v. United Artists Theatre Cir., Inc., 204 A.2d 795 (Md. 1964); Goldberg v. Goldberg, 527 N.Y.S.2d 451, 452 (N.Y. App. Div. 1988) (presence of bona fide business purpose justifies departure from equal treatment of shareholders).

[7] *See* Hearald v. Seawell, 472 F.2d 1081 (10th Cir. 1972).

[8] *See* Direct Media/DMI, Inc. v. Rubin, 654 N.Y.S.2d 986 (N.Y. Sup. 1997); Maguire v. Osborne, 130 A.2d 157 (Pa. 1957).

[9] *See, e.g.,* Hyman v. Velsicol Corp., 97 N.E.2d 122 (Ill. 1951); Katzowitz v. Sidler, 249 N.E.2d 359 (N.Y. 1969).

[10] *See, e.g.,* Gregory v. Correction Connection, Inc., 1991 LEXIS 3659 (E.D. Pa. 1991); Savin Bus. Mach. Corp. v. Rapifax Corp., 305 A.2d 469 (Del. Ch. 1977).

[11] *E.g.,* Herbik v. Rand, 732 S.W.2d 232 (Mo. Ct. App. 1987).

B. The Issuance of Shares

of preemptive rights to an offer of an opportunity to subscribe ratably for new issues arose from an attempt by the courts to create a prophylaxis to unfairness and abusive dilution of existing shares.

Originally, the preemptive right was recognized by the courts as mandatory, but now every state by statute allows the corporate charter to limit or deny the common law preemptive right or eliminates the preemptive right unless it is affirmatively granted by corporate charter. By express statutory provision in many states a corporation's article of incorporation may contain provisions limiting or denying preemptive rights.[1] Some such statutes merely refer to the ability to limit or deny the right in a corporation's articles of incorporation, whereas in other states the statute details the scope of the right in the absence of a defining, limiting, or denying provision in the articles.[2] Most frequently, states provide that there are no preemptive rights unless granted in the corporation's articles of incorporation.[3] And even though provided in the articles of incorporation, preemptive rights can be removed through the amendment process.[4] Since preemptive rights are now effectively permissive, drafters of corporate charters should keep in mind the various factors to be weighed as well as the necessity for making clear the extent of any preemptive right.

Preemptive rights aim to safeguard holders against unfairness in the issue of shares, particularly against two possible wrongs: (1) the manipulation of voting control of the corporation by the issuance of shares to one faction of shareholders to the exclusion of other shareholders, and (2) the issue of shares at an inadequate price to favored persons, thereby diluting the proportionate interest of other shareholders to dividends and to corporate assets on dissolution.[5] As the Minnesota high court earlier said, "If a corporation, either through the officers, directors or majority stockholders, may dispose of new stock to whomsoever it will, at whatever price it may fix, then it has the power to diminish the value of each share of old stock, by letting the parties have equal interest in the surplus, and in the goodwill or value of the established business."[6]

---

§16.14 [1] *See* Alaska Stat. §10.06.210 (Michie 2000); Minn. Stat. Ann. §302A.413 (West 1985 & Supp. 2002); MBCA Ann. §10.01 (3d ed. 1995).

[2] *E.g.,* Fla. Stat. Ann. §607.0202 (West 2001); N.H. Rev. Stat. Ann. §293-A:6.30 (1999); N.Y. Bus. Corp. Law §622 (McKinney 1986); Former MBCA §26A (1980).

[3] Ariz. Rev. Stat. §10-630 (West 1996); Cal. Corp. Code §204 (West 1990); Conn. Gen. Stat. Ann. §§33-683 (West 1997); Del. Code Ann., tit. 8, §102(b)(3) (2001). *Compare* MBCA §6.30 (1984), which also denies the right in the face of silence but which defines the extent of the right when the charter merely provides that there shall be preemptive rights. In 1997, New York amended its statute to eliminate the presumption of preemptive rights for corporations formed after 1997. *See* N.Y. Bus. Corp. L. §622(b)(2) (McKinney 1986 & Supp. 1998).

[4] *See* L. I. Minor Co. v. Perkins, 268 So. 2d 637 (Ga. 1980); Seattle Trust & Sav. Bank v. McCarthy, 617 P.2d 1023 (Wash. 1980).

[5] *See* Katzowitz v. Sidler, 249 N.E.2d 359, 363 (N.Y. 1969). *See also* Joseph W. Bartlett & Kevin R. Garlitz, Fiduciary Duties In Burnout/Cramdown Financings, 20 J. Corp. L. 593 (1995).

[6] Jones v. Morrison, 16 N.W. 854, 861 (Minn. 1883). *See also, e.g.,* Stokes v. Continental Trust Co., 78 N.E. 1090 (N.Y. 1906); Albrecht, McGuire & Co. v. General Plastics, Inc., 9 N.Y.S.2d 415 (App. Div. 1939), *aff'd,* 21 N.E.2d 887 (N.Y. 1939).

The preemptive rights doctrine, however, has never been adequate to cover all situations and, further, has been subject to numerous limitations and exceptions based on practical convenience. Equitable relief remains available to protect against wrongful dilution of financial or voting rights, even though the plaintiff possessed a preemptive right that if exercised would have protected her from the dilution that otherwise occurred.[7] The courts have wisely allowed minority stockholders to choose between invoking self-help through exercising their preemptive right and seeking the protective remedies of a court of equity. The mere availability of a preemptive right should not foreclose other avenues of protection that are available in cases when a preemptive right is not provided. The prophylactic of a preemptive right is available only if the stockholder exercises her right to acquire more of the company's shares. Because the shareholder either may not then have the funds to purchase the shares or could well believe that her monies are better invested elsewhere, the theoretical protection believed to be provided by a preemptive right can, in many cases, elude the minority stockholder. Hence, a full panoply of remedies of a court of equity should be available, even though the plaintiff is also armed with a preemptive right that theoretically if exercised would avoid the dilution that is at the heart of her prayer for equitable action.

In all jurisdictions, preemptive rights can be denied in a corporation's articles of incorporation; even when not denied, they apply, according to most courts, only to an issue of newly authorized shares and do not extend to a new issue of originally or previously authorized shares, at least not where the issue does not raise funds to expand the business.[8] A few courts, however, have held that preemptive rights extend to original shares that are issued long after the creation of the corporation and a material time after the original offering of shares has come to an end.[9] The latter is the better view because the availability of such an important prophylaxis should not depend on the fortuity of whether less than all the originally authorized shares were issued. This view is even more compelling when the parties have expressly provided for preemptive rights in the articles of incorporation, as they have thereby expressed a desire for affirmative protection against dilution.

The preemptive right is most frequently granted to the holders of common shares.[10] In the absence of a provision in a corporation's articles of incorporation granting holders of a class of stock preemptive rights in issues of another class, it is doubtful to what extent a holder of shares of one class has a preemptive right to

---

[7] See Schwartz v. Marien, 335 N.E.2d 334 (N.Y. 1975); Katzowitz v. Sidler, 249 N.E.2d 359 (N.Y. 1969). Contra Koos v. Central Ohio Cellular, Inc., 641 N.E.2d 265 (Ohio Ct. App. 1994) (since all shareholders had an opportunity to acquire shares being sold for below their fair market value no breach of a fiduciary duty occurred).

[8] Yasik v. Wachtel, 17 A.2d 309 (Del. Ch. 1941), noted in 40 Mich. L. Rev. 115 (1941); Dunlay v. Avenue M Garage & Repair Co., 170 N.E. 917 (N.Y. 1930); Annot., 52 A.L.R. 220 (1928); Annot., 138 A.L.R. 527 (1942). But see Tully v. Mott Supermarkets, Inc., 337 F. Supp. 834 (D.N.J. 1972).

[9] Titus v. Paul State Bank, 179 P. 514 (Idaho 1919); Dunlay v. Avenue M Garage & Repair Co., Inc., 170 N.E. 917 (N.Y. 1930).

[10] More specifically, the registered owner of the shares is entitled to exercise the preemptive right such that the owner-pledgor of shares may exercise preemptive rights with respect to shares he has pledged to secure a loan. See Peri-Gil Corp. v. Sutton, 442 P.2d 35 (Nev. 1968).

B. The Issuance of Shares

an issue of the shares of another class. The cases are in conflict. Should a preemptive right to new issues of common always be given to the holders of preferred shares or only if the preferred shares currently carry voting rights equal to the common shares? Certainly, if preferred is nonvoting and nonparticipating in dividends, there is no basis for dilution of their interest. If preferred shareholders have full voting rights but no participating rights as dividends, or vice versa, the resolution of whether the preferred has a preemptive right is more problematic and should, in the absence of express contractual provisions, turn on the likely intent of the parties.

As the share structure of a corporation becomes more complex, it is very difficult, if not impossible, to grant preemptive rights to a class of preferred shares without some change in the relative rights of other classes.[11] In the absence of a charter provision to the contrary, some jurisdictions limit preemptive rights to holders of shares of the same class as those being issued.[12] Confusion and uncertainty about such matters in a particular jurisdiction may make it desirable to waive or clarify preemptive rights by specific provision in the articles of incorporation.

States adopting the approach taken in the Model Business Corporation Act provide a great deal of certainty to the question of whether the holders of one class of stock have a preemptive right to acquire shares of another class of stock. Under the Model Business Corporation Act, holders of nonvoting shares of one class do not have a preemptive right to acquire shares of another class, regardless of any other preferences those shares may have, unless the articles of incorporation otherwise provide. Moreover, the holders of shares of a class with general voting rights but no preference as to distributions of assets do not have a preemptive right to acquire shares of a class that does have a preference to asset distributions. The twin objectives, therefore, of the Model Business Corporation Act-type of definition of "preemptive rights" are to shield holders from dilution of their voting rights and their economic rights.

The preemptive right ordinarily does not extend to shares issued as consideration for property or services, shares issued to discharge a bona fide debt, or shares issued in a merger.[13] The reasons for these exemptions relate to matters of commercial necessity, practical convenience, and the need for directors to be able to issue shares to accomplish corporate purposes.

Preemptive rights do not ordinarily extend to the reissue or resale of treasury shares.[14] This exception is also based on practical grounds, as treasury shares are usually sold from time to time and not reissued in large amounts. The directors' duty of good faith and fairness, however, applies to a corporation's sale of treasury shares and also to other issues of shares in which no preemptive right is recognized.[15]

---

[11] *See* Russell v. American Gas & Elec. Co., 136 N.Y.S. 602 (App. Div. 1912).

[12] *E.g.,* MBCA §6.30(b)(5) (1984).

[13] Rogers v. First Nat'l Bank of St. George, 410 F.2d 579 (4th Cir. 1969); Kelly v. Englehart Corp., 2001 WL 855600 (Iowa Ct. App. 2001) (stock for stock no preemptive right unless provided otherwise in articles of incorporation); MBCA §6.30(b)(3)(iv) (1984).

[14] Borg v. International Silver Co., 11 F.2d 147 (2d Cir. 1925). *But see, e.g.,* Schwartz v. Marien, 335 N.E.2d 334 (N.Y. 1975) (breach of fiduciary duty in connection with issuance of treasury shares).

[15] Schwab v. Schwab-Wilson Mach. Corp., 55 P.2d 1268 (Cal. Ct. App. 1936).

Preemptive rights generally do not apply to a corporation's issuance of shares under an employee stock option or employee stock purchase plan. If in a particular state preemptive rights do apply to shares issued under such a plan, or if that matter is in question, waiver of preemptive rights may have to be submitted to the shareholders, or the corporation's articles of incorporation may have to be amended.[16] The value of the employees' right to purchase under such a plan should, of course, have some reasonable relation to the value of the services rendered or to be rendered by the employees.[17]

When a corporation is issuing shares, market conditions may not allow for delay that would result from honoring preemptive rights by offering shares to all the shareholders. In such a situation, the requirement of a preemptive rights offering may harm the shareholders more than it helps them.[18] Thus the conclusion of many courts is that preemptive rights do not apply to shares that are part of those originally authorized. In any event, the existence of a preemptive right can impose a serious timing problem on the corporation's needs to raise capital because any preemptive right postpones sales to outsiders until existing stockholders have been approached. Thus a company that anticipates a future need to raise funds from new investors is well advised to consider removing preemptive rights as a predicate to that offering.

Preemptive rights do not make sense in a public-issue corporation. In fact, their presence can severely hamper future financing. Accordingly, the charters of public companies typically eliminate such rights if the statutes of their domiciles do not do so. If preemptive rights are abrogated or waived, the directors still must not discriminate unfairly in the issue of shares; differences in the issue price of the shares may be made only in the exercise of fair business judgment for the benefit of the corporation.[19] In a close corporation, however, in the interest of preserving the original shareholders' proportionate preemptive rights, they often should not only be retained but also should be extended to cover many of the share-issue transactions that are generally excepted from the rights.[20]

It is thus clear that regardless of preemptive rights, a corporation's directors must observe their fiduciary responsibilities in issuing new shares; otherwise the shares may be subject to cancellation.[21] In the issuance of shares, however, the directors have the latitude, including pricing, given by the business judgment

---

[16] *See, e.g.*, Schwartz v. Custom Printing Co., 926 S.W.2d 490 (Mo. Ct. App. 1996). MBCA §6.30(b)(3) (1984) (not requiring shareholder approval of the plan).

[17] Dickenson v. Auto Ctr. Mfg. Co., 639 F.2d 250 (5th Cir. 1981); Holthusen v. Edward G. Budd Mfg. Co., 52 F. Supp. 125, 130 (D. Pa. 1943), s.c., 53 F. Supp. 488 (Pa. 1943).

[18] Venner v. American Tel. & Tel. Co., 181 N.Y.S. 45, 47 (Sup. Ct. 1920); Henry S. Drinker, Jr., The Preemptive Right of Shareholders to Subscribe to New Shares, 43 Harvard C. Rev. 615 (1930).

[19] Hodgman v. Atlantic Refining Co., 13 F.2d 781 (3d Cir. 1926); Bodell v. General Gas & Elec. Corp., 15 Del. Ch. 420, 140 A. 264 (Del. 1927); Schwartz v. Marien, 335 N.E.2d 334 (N.Y. 1975).

[20] *See* Fuller v. Krough, 113 N.W.2d 25, 32 (Wis. 1962); F. Hodge O'Neal, Molding the Corporate Form to Particular Business Practices: Optional Charter Clauses, 10 Vand. L. Rev. 1, 41 (1956); 1 F. Hodge O'Neal & Robert B. Thompson, O'Neal's Close Corporations §3.39 (3d ed. 1987 & Supp. 2002).

[21] *See, e.g.*, Mason Shoe Mfg. Co. v. Firstar Bank Eau Claire, N.A., 579 N.W.2d 789 (Wis. Ct. App. 1998).

B. The Issuance of Shares

rule.[22] Even though there is some division in the courts as to whether a shareholder suit based on an alleged violation of preemptive rights is direct or derivative,[23] the better view is that the preemptive right, as a right of the individual stockholder, should give rise to a direct cause of action.

Even though a shareholder has a preemptive right to acquire a proportionate amount of a new issue, the board of directors generally fixes a specific date beyond which shareholders can no longer exercise their right to acquire the shares. A shareholder who does not exercise his right within the time so designated is deemed to have waived his right, and the board of directors may offer to anyone else the shares not acquired. When no time is so set, the shareholders' acquiescence by failure to complain is treated as a waiver of her preemptive rights.[24] The better view, however, is that there is no waiver if material facts are misrepresented, the offer's terms are significantly altered, or other unfairness occurs in connection with the stockholder's decision to forgo her preemptive rights.[25]

§16.15   The Theory Behind the Legal Capital Concept

The merger of law and accounting is nowhere more evident than in the statutory regulation of the corporation's power to make distributions to its shareholders. The focus of such regulation is threefold: (1) first and foremost, the protection of creditors against unreasonable diminution in the debtor corporation's assets through asset distributions to its shareholders; (2) if there are more than two classes of shares outstanding, the protection of classes having the senior economic rights from erosion of those rights as a result of corporate distributions to the junior shareholders; and (3) the protection of all shareholders from improvident distributions that impair the corporation's power to carry on its business. The bulwark of such protection centers on the concept of "legal capital," the synonyms for which being "stated capital," "capital stock," and "paid-up capital."

Whereas the economist and the accountant both define "capital" as the assets of the business, "capital" in the legal sense is the *amount* the business's proprietors agree to invest in the corporation. Under early corporate statutes, capital was measured by the aggregate par value of the issued shares. Recall that par value is an arbitrary figure, unrelated to a share's intrinsic value, that is fixed in the corporation's charter. The legal significance of par value to a purchaser or subscriber of corporate shares is that it establishes the minimum amount that must be paid for the shares. If less than par value is paid, the corporation and its creditors may recover the deficiency.

---

[22] *See* Schwartz v. Marien, 335 N.E.2d 334 (N.Y. 1975); Katzowitz v. Sidler, 249 N.E.2d 359 (N.Y. 1969).
Many of the same issues are involved in organic corporate questions and the requirement of fundamental fairness. *See* Chapters 23 and 25.
[23] *See* Bellows v. Porter, 201 F.2d 429 (8th Cir. 1953); Hyman v. Velsicol Corp., 97 N.E.2d 122 (Ill. App. Ct. 1951); Maguire v. Osborne, 130 A.2d 157 (Pa. 1957).
[24] *See, e.g.*, Rejsa v. Beeman, 1997 WL 526320 (Minn. Ct. App. 1997).
[25] *See* Gord v. Iowana Farms Milk Co., 60 N.W.2d 820 (Iowa 1953); Naquin v. Air Engineered Sys. & Serv., Inc., 423 So. 2d 713 (La. Ct. App. 1982).

§16.16   Legal Capital of Par and No-Par Shares

A corporation's legal or stated capital (or, to use an older designation, "capital stock") is established or increased on the issue of shares.[1] Legal capital fixes the margin of net assets or value that must be retained in the business and restricts the distribution of assets to the shareholders. If the shares a corporation issues are par value shares, its legal capital is generally an amount equal to the aggregate par value of the issued shares. When shares without par value were introduced, a different definition of "legal capital" became necessary. Modern corporation acts avoid the use of the old term "capital stock," with its variable meanings, and many statutes substitute the term "stated capital."[2] This latter term is no doubt derived from the practice of specifying what part of the subscription price for low-par or no-par shares is to be attributed to capital and what part to paid-in surplus. Under such a statute, if a corporation's shares are without par value, its stated capital is the aggregate amount of the consideration paid or agreed to be paid that is not allotted to paid-in surplus.[3]

The Concept of Legal Capital. The old terms "capital stock" and "capital" have various meanings and express different concepts in different contexts. As a New York court said in an important dividend case,

> Capital means one thing to an economist, or perhaps more accurately different things to different economists, and it has still different meanings to accountants and to business men. It means different things in different statutes. . . . To determine its meaning in this statute it thus is essential . . . to consider the history of the statute and what our courts have said respecting the statute's predecessors.[4]

Legal capital is an amount that measures the margin of net assets or value that is to be retained in the business as against withdrawals in favor of the shareholders.[5] Legal capital is an amount, a limitation—not the actual corporation assets or property.[6] Corporations under such a regime were permitted to distribute as dividends or as repurchases of their shares the amount by which their assets exceed the sum of the firm's liabilities and legal capital. That is, firms paying dividends or repurchasing their shares are not at liberty to do so to the point that their assets equal their liabilities. Additional sums must be retained in the enterprise—namely, the amount of assets retained within the business following the payment of a dividend or repurchase of shares must not be less than the sum of the firms' liabilities *and* its legal capital. Thus legal capital is the margin of safety prescribed by corporate statutes for the benefit of the firm's creditors.

---

§16.16   [1] *See, e.g.*, Witherbee v. Bowles, 95 N.E. 27 (N.Y. 1911).
[2] *See* Del. Code Ann., tit.8, §154 (2001).
[3] *Id.*
[4] Randall v. Bailey, 23 N.Y.S.2d 173, 179 (Sup. Ct. 1940).
[5] Randall v. Bailey, 23 N.Y.S.2d 173, 179 (Sup. Ct. 1940), *aff'd*, 288 N.Y. 280, 43 N.E.2d 43 (N.Y. 1942).
[6] Crocker v. Waltham Watch Co., 53 N.E.2d 230, 237, 238 (Mass. 1942).

B. The Issuance of Shares

The "trust fund doctrine" that is at the core of the corporate statutes' embrace of the concept of legal capital is primarily a rule against the wrongful withdrawal of assets that should be retained by the corporation for the protection of creditors. There is in fact no true trust fund at all, but only a legal prohibition against withdrawals of corporate assets that reduce the margin of safety for creditors. The margin so identified, however, has no intrinsic relationship to the variables that subject creditors to improper risks or prejudice some of the shareholders themselves.[7] The amount of a corporation's legal capital is an artificial figure, being the product of the number of outstanding shares and their par value or, if any shares are without par value, an amount up to the value of the consideration received for the shares allocated to legal capital by the board of directors. The corporation's legal capital is entered on the liability side of its balance sheet and is deducted from the corporation's net worth (assets minus liabilities) in ascertaining what can be paid to shareholders in dividends or other distributions.

Relation of Issued Shares to Stated Capital. Properly regarded, the relation of stated capital to issued shares is only historical. Under the former version of the Model Act, "stated capital" means (1) the aggregate par value of all issued shares; (2) the amount of consideration fixed for no par stock that is so allocated by the directors; and (3) such amount that the directors have transferred from the surplus accounts "minus all reductions from such sum as have been effected in a manner permitted by law."[8]

Most states do not require that all consideration received for no-par shares be counted in fixing the amount of the legal capital margin. Many states permit the board of directors to allocate to paid-in surplus an unlimited portion of the consideration received on the issue of no-par shares, thus weakening any requirement to establish an adequate stated capital.[9]

Although still in force in most jurisdictions, this system has been criticized as archaic.[10] In a forward-looking statute, California was the first state to abandon the relationship between par and stated capital.[11] It was followed thereafter by the current Model Business Corporation Act.[12] The current Model Business Corporation Act continues the trend by removing any legal significance to par value and thereby premises the regulation of distributions to stockholders[13] on key financial relationships by requiring that no distribution reduce the firm's assets below its

---

[7] McDonald v. Williams, 174 U.S. 397 (1899); Wood v. City Nat'l Bank, 24 F.2d 661 (2d Cir. 1928); Bartlett v. Smith, 160 A. 440 (Md. 1932).

[8] Former MBCA §2(j) (1969).

[9] *E.g.,* Former MBCA §21 (1969); Del. Code Ann. tit. 8, §154 (2001); N.Y. Bus. Corp. Law §506 (McKinney 1986).

[10] *See* George D. Gibson, *Surplus, So What?*, 17 Bus. Law. 476 (1962).

[11] Cal. Corp. Code §500 (West 1990). The act goes on to eliminate surplus and stated capital as the bases for dividend distributions.

[12] *See* Committee on Corporate Laws, Changes in the Model Business Corporation Act—Amendments to Financial Provisions, 34 Bus. Law. 1567 (1979).

[13] The Revised Model Business Corporation Act subjects both dividends and share repurchases to the same regulatory treatment through its definition of "distribution." *See* MBCA §§1.40(6) & 6.40 (1984).

liabilities or render the corporation unable to pay its debts as they mature in the ordinary course of business.[14]

The distinguishing feature of the current Model Business Corporation Act from the impairment-of-capital approach is that the latter required that the assets remaining after the distribution equal not only the firm's liabilities but also its stated capital—that is, the aggregate par value of issued shares. California's modern provision provides somewhat greater protection to creditors than does the present Model Business Corporation Act because it requires that the assets remaining after the distribution equal at least $1\frac{1}{4}$ times the firm's liabilities.[15] The regulation of dividend and share repurchases is discussed in Chapters 20 and 21, where the issues posed by the modern statutes are examined further.

---

[14] MBCA §6.40(c)(1), (2) (1984).

[15] Cal. Corp. Code §500(b)(1) (West 1990). California is also more conservative than the Model Business Corporation Act by requiring assets be measured pursuant to generally accepted accounting principles, *see id.* at §114, whereas the Model Act permits assets "on a fair valuation or other method that is reasonable in the circumstances." MBCA §6.40(d) (1984).

CHAPTER 17

Liability for Watered, Bonus, and Underpaid Shares

§17.01   Varieties of Watered Stock

"Watered stock" refers to shares issued as fully paid when in fact the consideration agreed to and accepted by the corporation's directors is something known to be much less than the par value of the shares or lawful subscription price. The term is frequently used to cover bonus shares as well as discount shares and those issued for property or services at an overvaluation.

If shares have been issued by a corporation as paid in full when in fact the subscriber has not paid or agreed to pay the full par value or lawful issue price, in either money, property, or services, the shares are said to be watered to the extent to which they have not been, or are not agreed to be, fully paid.[1] There are various ways in which underpaid or watered shares may come into being. They may be issued gratuitously without any consideration passing to the corporation.[2] They

---

§17.01   [1] *See* E. Merrick Dodd, Jr., Stock Watering (1933).
[2] *See, e.g.,* Andrews v. Chase, 49 P.2d 938, 941 (1935), *reh'g denied,* 57 P.2d 702 (1936).

may be issued for cash at a discount below par value,[3] or in exchange for property, labor, or services that are known to be worth less than the par value.[4]

Shares may also be issued as a "bonus" or inducement to the purchaser of bonds or preferred shares. Bonus shares are legitimate when viewed as further consideration for the purchase price that has to be apportioned between them and the other securities.[5] It is often difficult to allocate or apportion the credit where bonus stock has been issued. The word "bonus" implies a gift or gratuity and is sometimes used in the sense of shares issued without any consideration.

Another variety of watered stock may be issued in the guise of a stock dividend. In such a case the stock is issued to existing shareholders as shares that represent a transfer of surplus to capital when in fact there is insufficient surplus to justify their issuance.[6]

The sections that follow consider the legal implications of and potential liabilities arising out of watered or over-capitalized shares.

§17.02   Evils and Abuses of Stock Watering

Flagrant stock watering was common in the promotion and financing of corporations in the latter part of the nineteenth and the early years of the twentieth centuries. The evils of stock watering consist primarily of injuries to the corporation, innocent shareholders, and creditors perpetrated by promoters and those in control by depriving the corporation of needed capital and of the corporation's opportunity to market its securities to its own advantage, thus hurting its business prospects and financial responsibility. Existing and future shareholders are injured due to dilution of the proportionate interests of those who pay full value for their shares.[1] Present and future creditors are injured when the corporation is deprived of the assets to be contributed by all the shareholders as a substitute for individual liability for corporate debts. Stock watering involves fictitious capitalization and is deceptive both to the corporate management in declaring dividends and to those who deal with the corporation or purchase its securities. Watered stock is invariably accompanied by misleading corporate accounts and financial statements, particularly by an overstatement of the value of assets received for the shares in order to conceal a capital deficit resulting from overvaluation and underpayment of purported capital contributions.

Three developments have significantly reduced the frequency of suits under state corporate statutes for watered stock liability. First, the advent of low-par and

---

[3] *See, e.g.*, Harman v. Himes, 77 F.2d 375 (D.C. Cir. 1935); Christensen v. Eno, 12 N.E. 648 (N.Y. 1887). *See also* Scovill v. Thayer, 105 U.S. 143, 154 (1882).

[4] *E.g.*, Elyton Land Co. v. Birmingham Warehouse & Elevator Co., 9 So. 129 (Ala. 1890).

[5] In re Associated Oil Co., 289 F. 693 (6th Cir. 1923).

[6] Whitlock v. Alexander, 76 S.E. 538 (N.C. 1912). Dividend restrictions based on the corporate balance sheet are discussed in §§20.05-20.13.

§17.02 [1] Bodell v. General Gas & Elec. Co., 132 A. 442 (Del. Ch. 1926), *aff'd*, 140 A. 264 (Del. 1927).

no-par stock has to a large extent eliminated watered stock problems in the strict definitional sense. By eliminating par value, the present Model Business Corporations Act also does away with watered stock in its strictest meaning.[2] Finally, the prophylactic effects of state blue sky laws and remedial benefits available under the antifraud provisions, section 10(b) and Rule 10b-5, of the Securities Exchange Act of 1934, have largely supplanted the regulatory impact of state corporate statutes for watered stock, at least with respect to protecting the corporation and later-purchasing shareholders. The discussion that follows closely examines the remedies the corporation and its creditors have for watered stock.

§17.03   *Contract and Trust Fund Theories*

The liability of shareholders to or for the benefit of creditors on watered or fictitiously paid-up shares has rested on various theories. Some courts look to the artificial "trust fund" theory, while others rely on fraud or holding out. A few jurisdictions base liability to creditors on a common law or statutory obligation to pay for the par value of the shares. The trust fund theory merely describes the rule that the legal obligation to pay par, imposed by common law or by statute, runs to the corporation and may not be released by any agreement with the corporation or by any fictitious or simulated payment, even though accepted by the directors as payment in full. The theory generally is regarded as having originated with Judge Story's 1824 opinion in *Wood v. Dummer,*[1] which was a case not of watered stock liability but of shareholder liability to creditors to restore dividends paid out by an insolvent bank as a distribution of capital.

Under the trust fund theory in its original form, however, the implication of the promise seems to have been based on the policy that the obligation to pay the par value of shares arises from the privilege of exemption from individual liability and that the release from full payment is an evasion of the law as against all creditors.[2] Thus unless the fraud theory is accepted, the creditors' right of action against the holder of watered stock is considered to be an equitable right to reach an asset of the corporation, as in the case of shares issued on credit. The shareholders' liability is thus a legal obligation to the corporation to make a capital contribution required as one of the conditions of doing business with limited liability for the protection of all creditors.[3]

---

[2] However, the same evils can be accomplished by the issuance of shares at a grossly overvalued price.

§17.03   [1] 30 Fed. Cas. 435 (C.C.D. Me. 1824) (No. 17944). *See* Edward H. Warren, Safeguarding the Rights of Creditors, 36 Harv. L. Rev. 509, 544-546 (1923).

[2] Scovill v. Thayer, 105 U.S. 143, 154 (1882); Sawyer v. Hoag, 84 U.S. (17 Wall.) 610, 620 (1873).

[3] It has been said that "where stock of a corporation is issued without being fully paid up, the amount remaining unpaid is, so far as the creditors are concerned, deemed to be money due to the corporation from the stockholders." R. H. Herron Co. v. Shaw, 133 P. 488, 489 (Cal. 1913).

§17.04   The Fraud or Holding-Out Theory

The prevailing theory of liability on bonus or watered shares has been founded in tort against the creditors rather than in an obligation to the corporation. The wrong to creditors is fraud and deceit by the directors, participated in by the shareholders, in falsely representing that the par value has been paid or agreed to be paid in full.[1] Under the early form of this theory, subsequent creditors without notice were presumed to have been deceived by this misrepresentation.[2]

The leading case of *Hospes v. Northwestern Manufacturing & Car Company*[3] severely criticized the trust fund theory as a basis of shareholders' liability on watered stock and placed this liability on the ground of fraud, actual or constructive. The "fraud" consists of a supposed representation to creditors as to the amount of capital contributed or subscribed by the shareholders.[4] The creditors are presumed to have extended credit to the corporation in reliance on the consideration received or to be received for the shares in accordance with legal requirements.[5]

The constructive fraud doctrine, as formulated in the *Hospes* case and followed by many courts, is even less sound and practical as a basis for shareholders' liability than the original trust fund doctrine. The economic reality is that prudent creditors do not look to the capital stock as indicia of creditworthiness.[6] The true victims of the fraud are more likely to be the public subscribers and shareholders with little or no complicity in any misrepresentation to creditors.[7]

In its more recent application, some courts came to recognize the deficiencies of the fraud or holding-out theory. For example, in *Bing Crosby Minute Maid Corporation v. Eaton*,[8] the California Supreme Court ruled that under the fraud theory the creditor's *actual* reliance on the misstated capital is a "prerequisite to the liability of a holder of the watered stock."[9] This narrower view of shareholder liability comports with current business practice and avoids the hardships of both the trust fund theory and presumption of reliance under a holding-out analysis.[10]

---

§17.04   [1] Hirschfield v. McKinley, 78 F.2d 124 (9th Cir. 1935), *cert. denied,* 297 U.S. 703 (1936); Spencer v. Anderson, 222 P. 355 (Cal. 1924).

[2] *But see* Bing Crosby Minute Maid Corp. v. Eaton, 297 P.2d 5 (Cal. 1956).

[3] 50 N.W. 1117 (Minn. 1892). *See* Henry W. Ballantine, Stockholders' Liability in Minnesota, 7 Minn. L. Rev. 86-89 (1922).

[4] Rhode v. Dock-Hop Co., 194 P. 11, 16 (Cal. 1920).

[5] *E.g.,* R. H. Herron Co. v. Shaw, 133 P. 488 (Cal. 1913) (public policy requires that reliance by creditor not be element of watered stock claim). *See* William L. Cary & Ralph Jackson Baker, Cases and Materials on Corporations 811 (3d ed. 1959) ("Shareholders have rarely been successful in overcoming this presumption [of reliance] except by proof that the creditors had actual knowledge of the facts of the transaction." Such knowledge is an affirmative defense that must be pleaded and proven by the shareholders.). *But see* Bing Crosby Minute Maid Corp. v. Eaton, 297 P.2d 5 (Cal. 1956).

[6] *See* Norman D. Lattin, Corporations 475 (2d ed. 1971). *See also, e.g.,* Harry George Guthmann & Herbert Dougall, Corporate Financial Policy 437 (1954).

[7] Dodd, *supra* §17.01 note 1, at 299, 311-312.

[8] 297 P.2d 5 (Cal. 1956).

[9] *Id.* at 9.

[10] The *Hospes* rule was subsequently overruled by statute. Minn. Bus. Corp. Act of 1933 114 (IV), (V).

Under the fraud theory, only those creditors who have relied, or who can fairly be presumed possibly to have relied, on the professed amount of capital contributions will be recognized as having a claim against guilty holders of watered stock. In other words, the shareholders' liability is limited to subsequent creditors without notice of the watering. No prior creditors or subsequent creditors with notice can complain. The soundness of the distinction between claims and equities of prior and subsequent creditors is very doubtful where no requirement exists for a creditor to prove reliance. The practical justification, if any, is that of a more or less arbitrary limitation of liability of shareholders, thus avoiding hardship in certain cases.[11]

§17.05   The Statutory Obligation Doctrine

Beginning about the middle of the nineteenth century, the evils of stock watering had become so aggravated as to lead many states to adopt constitutional and statutory provisions prohibiting the practice.

The most specific and important type of statute provides that a shareholder shall be liable to creditors, either directly or through the corporation, "to the amount of their stock subscribed and unpaid, and no more" or words to that effect. For example, the pre-1980 Model Business Corporation Act requires that par value stock not be issued for less than par[1] and that no shareholder liability to creditors or the corporation arises "other than the obligation to pay to the corporation the full consideration for which such shares were issued or to be issued."[2] Although they are rather vague and general, these statutory declarations of duty to pay the amount due give the courts an opportunity to make liability on watered stock a legal obligation to pay in full the amount of consideration for which the shares were required to be issued.[3]

This construction has been followed by the courts of New Jersey and Delaware, which place shareholders' liability on watered stock on neither the contract theory nor the "trust fund" or "holding out" theory, but on a statutory obligation that the law requires be made good for the benefit of creditors of insolvent companies, without discrimination between prior and subsequent creditors, or between creditors who had notice and those who had no notice.[4] In most other jurisdictions, however, these constitutional and statutory provisions have usually been rendered nugatory, being construed as merely declaratory of the fraud

---

[11] 2 Garrard Glenn, Fraudulent Conveyances & Preferences §§608, 1060-1062 (1940); Comment, 47 Yale L.J. 1178, 1179, 1185 (1938).

§17.05   [1] *See* Former MBCA §18 (1969).

[2] *Id.* §25. Subsequent versions similarly limit shareholders' liability. MBCA §6.22 (1984); former MBCA §25 (1969).

[3] *See* Henry W. Ballantine & Graham L. Sterling, California Corporation Laws 171 (1949).

[4] DuPont v. Ball, 106 A. 39 (Del. 1918), *aff'g* John W. Cooney Co. v. Arlington Hotel Co., 101 A. 879 (Del. Ch. 1917); Easton Nat'l Bank v. American Tile & Brick Co., 64 A. 917 (N.J. 1906); Del. Code Ann. tit. 8, §162 (2001); N.J. Stat. Ann. §14A:5-30 (West 1969).

theory developed by the courts and subject to the arbitrary limitations of that theory.[5]

§17.06   Liability of Transferees of Watered Stock

Bona fide transferees of watered stock will not be liable unless they may be regarded as having constructive notice of the fictitious payment. When combined with the serious difficulty of proving deliberate or fraudulent overvaluation of shares issued for property or services, this rule has made judicial remedies limited if not ineffectual.

According to the better view, the holder of watered or fictitiously paid-up stock cannot escape liability to creditors by transferring the shares to an irresponsible person, an insolvent corporation or person, or to a bona fide purchaser.[1] In some states the transferor remains liable even though the transferee is solvent and took the shares with notice.[2]

§17.07   Creditors', Receivers', and Trustees' Remedies

Creditors generally must proceed by a creditors' bill in equity to enforce the liability of shareholders on bonus and watered stock unless there is statutory direct liability.[1] Two exceptions to the general requirement of special statutory authorization for direct liability have emerged: first, when the corporation ceases to do business and is insolvent;[2] and, second, when the officers or directors who are also shareholders act in their corporate capacity to perpetrate the fraud on the creditors.[3]

The more recent exception to the general requirement of special statutory authorization is to allow creditors to sue directly the directors or officers, or shareholders who intentionally perpetrate the fraud of watering the stock even in the absence of statute.[4] For example, a 1967 Massachusetts case[5] recognized direct shareholder liability to creditors where the shareholders/directors transferred

[5] In re Associated Oil Co., 289 F. 693, 695-696 (6th Cir. 1923) (South Dakota statute); Bing Crosby Minute Maid Corp. v. Eaton, 297 P.2d 5 (Cal. 1956); Smith v. Mississippi Livestock Producers Ass'n, 188 So. 2d 758, 764 (Miss. 1966).

§17.06   [1] See Palmer v. Scheftel, 186 N.Y.S. 84 (N.Y. App. Div. 1921), aff'd, 142 N.E. 263 (N.Y. 1923) (transferor remains liable because transferee without notice escapes liability).

[2] See Graham v. Fleissner's Exr., 153 A. 526, 529 (N.J. 1931); Wolcott v. Waldstein, 97 A. 951 (N.J. Ch. 1916).

§17.07   [1] E.g., Eskimo Pie Corp. v. Whitelawn Dairies, Inc., 266 F. Supp. 79 (S.D.N.Y. 1967).

[2] Providence State Bank v. Bohannon, 426 F. Supp. 886 (E.D. Mo. 1977); Sherman v. S. K. D. Oil Co., 197 P. 799 (Cal. 1921).

[3] See Hoover v. Galbraith, 498 P.2d 981 (Cal. 1972).

[4] Mitchell Co. v. Fitzgerald, 231 N.E.2d 373 (Mass. 1967); Hoover v. Galbraith, 498 P.2d 981 (Cal. 1972). Cf. Sutton v. Reagan & Gee, 405 S.W.2d 828 (Tex. Civ. App. 1966).

[5] Mitchell v. Fitzgerald, 231 N.E.2d 373 (Mass. 1967).

no assets in consideration for the corporate stock. All of the shareholders/directors/officers of this closely held corporation had known of the fraud. The court held that, because the corporation was formed for an illegal purpose (to defraud creditors), equity dictated that the creditors be permitted to sue directly as individual creditors.[6]

This ruling of the Massachusetts Supreme Judicial Court seems to be the better policy, particularly when the corporation is closely held. Many courts simply pierce the corporate veil.[7] To require a first suit against the insolvent corporation is time-consuming and unnecessarily increases the creditor's expenses.

Whether the liability on watered stock will be enforced for the benefit of the corporation's creditors by either receivers or trustees in bankruptcy or individual creditors will depend on the law of the state of incorporation.[8] In many states, shareholders' liability on watered, bonus, discount, or subscription shares is recognized as an equitable asset of the corporation held for the benefit of creditors.[9] Conversely, under a fraud rationale, shareholders' liability on watered stock is to the creditors directly and only subsequent creditors may recover because they are presumed to have relied on the misrepresentations.[10] Some courts have ruled that shareholder liability on watered stock is not an asset to the corporation, and its trustee or receiver cannot sue for the benefit of the corporation's creditors.[11]

§17.08   *Creditors Against Holders of Watered No-Par Stock*

A primary advantage to no-par stock[1] is the freedom from any requirement of a fixed minimum capital contribution. Some have questioned whether no-par shares may not pose a serious danger of fraud on existing and possibly on future shareholders as well as on the corporation because there is no statutory restraint on their issuing price.[2] Adequacy of corporate capital is, of course, equally important, whether par value or no-par shares are used. No-par shares involve a relaxation of the requirements as to the establishment of an adequate stated capital and the legal safeguards protecting creditors;[3] a similar effect can be accomplished through the use of low-par shares. As contrasted with that on no-par

---

[6] *Id.* at 376.

[7] *See* §§7.04-7.05.

[8] Harrigan v. Bergdoll, 270 U.S. (1925).

[9] In re Gribbin Supply Co., 371 F. Supp. 664 (N.D. Tex. 1974); Geigy Co. v. Wilfling, 149 A. 609 (R.I. 1930); Fulton v. Abramson, 369 S.W.2d 815 (Tex. Civ. App. 1963); Guaranty Trust Co. v. Satterwhite, 97 P.2d 1005 (Wash. 1940).

[10] Union Guardian Trust Co. v. Barlum, 259 N.W. 297 (Mich. 1935); Grand Rapids Trust Co. v. Nichols, 165 N.W. 667 (Mich. 1917). *Cf.* Sutton v. Reagan & Gee, 405 S.W.2d 828 (Tex. Civ. App. 1966).

[11] Union Guardian Trust Co. v. Barlum, 259 N.W. 297 (Mich. 1935); Dysart v. Flemister, 140 S.W.2d 350 (Tex. Civ. App. 1940); Thomason v. Miller, 4 S.W.2d 668 (Tex. Civ. App. 1928).

§17.08   [1] *See* §16.10.

[2] *See* Carlos L. Israels, Problems of Par and No-Par Shares: A Reappraisal, 47 Colum. L. Rev. 1279, 1289-1300 (1947).

[3] *See* Russell Carpenter Larcom, The Delaware Corporation 102-103 (1937).

shares, the liability to creditors of holders of watered par value shares finds its true ground of support either in the contract of the subscriber to pay a definite price in money value for his shares or on a legal or a statutory obligation to pay up to their par value, notwithstanding a corporate release or acceptance of a fictitious equivalent.[4] Par value shares have a minimum issue price in dollars fixed by the charter, which cannot be released as against creditors. With no-par shares this money standard of value may be eliminated, and the price may be fixed in specified property or services or any medium that constitutes valid consideration. If, however, the consideration for no-par shares is fixed in money at, say, $20 per share and only $10 is paid in and this is accepted by the corporation as full payment, the subscriber or holder with notice is liable for the balance in event of insolvency, if the balance is needed to pay creditors. A holder with notice of no-par shares will thus be liable for the unpaid balance of the consideration fixed in money if this is paid in property or services at a consciously inflated valuation, as in case of par value shares.

In *G. Loewus & Company v. Highland Queen Packing Company*,[5] the proprietors of a business sold it to the corporation for shares of no-par stock. The agreement stated, "It is understood that the said shares of stock shall be issued at the price of $20 per share and representing a total value of $6000." It was alleged by the receiver that the assets and good will of the business turned over were worth only $1,500. The receiver of the corporation sought an assessment against the subscribers on the ground that the no-par shares were not fully paid and that the prices of the shares had been fixed at $20 per share. The New Jersey court held that the only consideration actually agreed to be given was the transfer of business and that the statement of a price of $20 per share was not intended to fix the consideration to be paid. The duty of the subscribers to pay for the shares was accordingly fully satisfied, and they were not liable for the underpayment. The *Loewus* opinion thus evidences a judicial propensity against recognizing an evasion of the subscriber's obligation to pay for no-par shares.

§17.09   Cancellation and Assessment of Diluted or Watered Shares

A few courts hold that shares issued for less than their par value or for an ineligible type of consideration are void, not merely voidable.[1] This result stands on their head the principles on which the violations are based. Why should the holder of watered shares be able to raise her own breach of the state corporate statute so as to avoid liability to creditors of a now insolvent corporation? Or why should a holder who has not given the statutorily prescribed amount or type of consideration but who has enjoyed all the rights of stock ownership, including voting and

---

[4] *See* Israels, *supra* note 2, at 1289-1300.

[5] 6 A.2d 545 (N.J. Ch. 1939).

§17.09   [1] *See, e.g.*, Foster v. Blackwell, 747 So. 2d 1203 (La. Ct. App. 1999); Frankowski v. Palermo, 363 N.Y.S.2d 159 (App. Div. 1975). *See also* §§16.11, 16.12.

dividends, not be required to pay fully for those shares when her nonpayment has been discovered? Most courts that have reflected on questions such as these reach the wise conclusion that by treating shares issued for overvalued consideration, as consideration, or an ineligible type of consideration as voidable, the court can thereby more fully address the equities of the individual case.[2]

Thus the equities cry out in favor of allowing creditors to recover for watered shares when the corporation is insolvent; an unfair result would arise if the shares' issuance was treated as a void act.[3] And, as a general rule, in disputes among shareholders, the equities call for treating invalidly issued shares as void.[4] However, where the other stockholders acquiesce in the illegal issuance or otherwise have lulled the shares' holder into believing he enjoyed the full rights of stock ownership, there is a type of waiver of the statutory protections such that it would be inequitable to cancel those shares, even though they were illegally issued.[5] When the courts hold that the shares issued for less than their par value or for an ineligible type of consideration are void, they are divided as to whether to void all the shares[6] or only those in excess of the amount of shares for which the full par value was received.[7] Similar considerations arise when the complaint is that the issuance of the shares entailed a breach of fiduciary obligation by their recipient.[8] Cancellation may be decreed for only such part of the shares obtained by the promoters as represents an illegal profit, leaving the taker with such number of shares as can be regarded as paid for at a fair price.

[2] *See, e.g.,* Murray v. Murray Labs., Inc., 270 S.W. 927 (Ark. 1954); Warren v. Warren, 460 A.2d 526 (Del. 1983); Finch v. Warrior Cement Corp., 141 A.2d 54, 62 (Del. Ch. 1928); Byrne v. Lord, 1996 WL 361503 (Del. Ch. 1996).

[3] *See* Belt v. Belt, 679 P.2d 1144, 1148 (Idaho Ct. App. 1984) (as between shareholder who has not paid par value and innocent creditor, shareholder cannot escape liability by arguing shares are invalidly issued).

[4] *See* Belt v. Belt, 679 P.2d 1144, 1148 (Idaho Ct. App. 1984); Frasier v. Trans-Western Land Corp., 316 N.W.2d 612 (Neb. 1982).

[5] Frasier v. Trans-Western Land Corp., 316 N.W.2d 612, 616-617 (Neb. 1982).

[6] *See* Frankowski v. Palermo, 363 N.Y.S.2d 159 (App. Div. 1975).

[7] *See* Belt v. Belt, 679 P.2d 1144, 1149 (Idaho Ct. App. 1984).

[8] *See, e.g.,* Bowers v. Rio Grande Inv. Co., 431 P.2d 478 (Colo. 1967); Warren v. Warren, 460 A.2d 526, (Del. 1983).

CHAPTER 18

Capital Structure, Preferences, and Classes of Securities

A. INTRODUCTION OF SENIOR SECURITIES

§18.01   *Choices in Debt and Equity Financing*

The "capitalization," financial structure, or permanent financing of a corporation is based on the issuance of capital securities. Permanent financing includes not only common stock but also senior securities, which can be (1) an equity interest by way of preferred stock or (2) bonds and debentures, which are the long-term or funded debts. Debt obligations are issued against the corporation's actual or prospective earning power even more than against its assets. The power to issue bonds and other debt obligations is not dependent, as stock issues are, on express authorization by the corporate charter. Debt financing thus provides more flexibility because there generally is no need for prior shareholder approval.

A sound and well-balanced capital structure must be carefully planned. The choice between stocks and bonds of different varieties depends on many considerations, including whether the business has an established earnings record, the ratio of property to its obligations, the rate of return that must be paid, probable marketability and attractiveness to investors, advantages under federal and state tax laws, and the effect on the future credit and ability of the corporation to survive business cycles.[1]

The tax laws encourage debt financing by treating interest payments, but not dividends on stock, as deductible from corporate gross income.[2] In order to safeguard against abuse due to thin equity financing, payments on the debt instruments may be treated for tax purposes as disguised dividends.[3] Similarly, too high a debt-to-equity ratio may lead a bankruptcy court to classify debt as stock for the purposes of subordinating claims of shareholder/creditors to those of other creditors.[4]

Attorneys are frequently asked to assist in evaluating the financial soundness of a firm's capital structure. The choice among different kinds of securities should be determined by the organizer and managers, considering the inducements needed to attract different types of investors and the control of management. They must further adequately anticipate the corporation's future financial needs.[5] Questions that inevitably arise include: (1) How can the company raise money at the lowest cost? (2) What are the tax advantages of different forms of securities? (3) How can control be reserved to the organizers without requiring them to invest too large an amount in the corporation? (4) To what extent can the company meet fixed financial charges when its income is fluctuating? (5) How can the company best ensure its credit for future financing to meet expansion and growth?

Preferred shares, which are frequently viewed as a hybrid of debt and equity, may be advisable as an alternative to pure debt because payment of dividends is not a mandatory fixed charge and non-payment will not entail foreclosure or receivership. In addition to the ability to pass on payments without being in

---

§18.01   [1] For a close treatment of the subject of the considering of the choices available for financing the firm, *see, e.g.,* James C. Van Horne, Financial Management and Policy 285-295 (11th Ed. 1998); Douglas R. Emery & John D. Finnerty, Corporate Financial Management 463-494 (1997); J. Fred Weston, Scott Besley, & Eugene F. Brigham, Essentials of Managerial Finance 710-715, 727-736 (11th ed. 1996).

[2] I.R.C. §§163, 301 (2000). A slight tax advantage of stock dividends accrues to the shareholder by way of the $100 dividend exclusion, which does not apply to bond interest. I.R.C. §116(a) (1988).

[3] I.R.C. §385 (2000).

[4] *See* Costello v. Fazio, 256 F.2d 903 (9th Cir. 1958). The issue here is analogous to the "deep rock" doctrine, which has been used to subordinate shareholder salary claims. *See* Pepper v. Litton, 308 U.S. 295 (1939).

[5] *See generally* authorities cited *supra* note 1.

default, there is usually no maturity date for retirement of preferred shares, and the redemption provision, if any, is normally an option in favor of the corporation. In the absence of a prohibitory covenant, the corporation has the power to borrow money by issuing notes or bonds that take priority over the preferred shares. Preferred shares may be desirable because they tend to attract a type of investor different from those who invest in pure debt instruments. Special features, such as the right of conversion into a different type of security, further expand the alternative vehicles for raising capital.

The issuance of senior securities such as bonds and preferred shares may be attractive to the issuer for various reasons. First, senior securities create "leverage" for the common shares—that is, a greater chance of possible gain to the common on the total capital investment. Second, senior securities represent money invested for a limited return on the basis of a stable income to the investor; therefore, they have no claim on capital appreciation or increased corporate income. Third, preferred shares facilitate retention of voting control by the initial or current investors, as all senior securities usually have at most only contingent voting rights. This reduces the amount of investment necessary to obtain voting control by way of either initial investment or subsequent acquisition. Fourth, preferred shares and bonds can be used to tap the reservoir of savings of those who seek to avoid the risks of common stocks.

§18.02 Bonds and Debt Financing

Bonds or debentures are essentially promissory notes with more elaborate provisions than ordinary commercial loans. They are generally long-term, but in times of fluctuating interest rates shorter-term instruments are not uncommon. Despite its existence as a corporate debt, the longer-term instrument has led to the view of bondholders as "joint heirs in the corporate fortunes—participants in the success or failure who have been given preferential rights in the common hazard."[1]

There are two parts to every bond issue: (1) the trust indenture and (2) the separate bonds. In broad overview, the trust indenture has two distinct parts: The first part sets forth all the obligations and restrictions on the bonds' issuer; the second part not only sets forth the bondholders' rights on default of the conditions set forth in the first part but also, by tracking the standards embodied in the Trust Indenture Act of 1939, sets forth the relationship between the indenture trustee and the bondholders.[2] There are also provisions related to amendment of the indenture as well as protection of any conversion privilege.

The bond is the only writing that the bondholder ordinarily sees. Bonds and debentures may be described as a series of instruments or notes representing units of indebtedness, yet regarded as but parts of one entire debt. The rights of all the bondholders are governed by an underlying trust, deed, mortgage, or indenture

---

§18.02 [1] Arthur S. Dewing, The Financial Policy of Corporations 236 (5th ed. 1953).
[2] *See* Model Simplified Indenture, 38 Bus. Law. 741 (1983).

between the corporation and a trustee, who is the representative of all the different bondholders. Within this framework the remedies of an individual bondholder are limited.[3] The indenture or mortgage, has grown to be an extraordinarily complicated and elaborate legal instrument.

The Trust Indenture Act of 1939[4] today applies to corporate debt obligations where the aggregate issue price is $10 million or greater.[5] The focus of the Act is on providing "an effective and independent trustee." Further, the relationship of the trustee to the bondholders has been subject to various classifications:[6] (1) as fiduciary;[7] (2) as founded in principal-agent law,[8] and (3) based on the contract rights, as defined in the indenture agreement.[9]

§18.03   Types of Bonds[1]

Open and Closed Mortgage Bonds. A serious error in corporate financing can be the failure to consider future needs for additional capital. The best framed bond mortgages make liberal provision for the increase of indebtedness by future borrowing under the same mortgage, the increase to be made under careful safeguards and restrictions. Such mortgages are known as "open-end" mortgages or bond issues and vary in the degree of openness. A closed bond issue is one in which no more bonds can be issued under a mortgage or deed of trust.

---

[3] Joseph C. Kennedy & Robert I. Landau, Corporate Trust Administration and Management 238-244 (4th ed. 1992). *See also* Yakov Amihud, Kenneth Garbade, & Marcel Kahan, A New Governance Structure for Corporate Bonds, 51 Stan. L. Rev. 447 (1999) (reviewing weaknesses of present system which addresses poorly the bondholders' collective action problem and sets forth the model of the "supertrustee").

[4] 15 U.S.C. §§77aaa *et seq.* (2000).

[5] The legislation authorizes the Securities and Exchange Commission to set the dollar level by exercising its rulemaking authority. *See* General Rules and Regulations of the SEC Rule 4a-3, 17 C.F.R. §260.4a-3 (2002).

[6] John P. Campbell & Robert Zack, Put a Bullet in the Poor Beast, His Leg Is Broken and His Use Is Past, 32 Bus. Law. 1705, 1723 n.56 (1977).

[7] York v. Guaranty Trust Co., 143 F.2d 503, 512 (2d Cir. 1944), *rev'd on other grounds,* 326 U.S. 99 (1945).

[8] *E.g.,* First Trust Co. v. Carlsen, 261 N.W. 333, 337 (Neb. 1935).

[9] *E.g.,* Hazzard v. Chase Nat'l Bank, 287 N.Y.S. 541 (Sup. Ct. 1936).

§18.03 [1] For a review of the technical features of bonds and their financial significance, *see* Frank J. Fabozzi, Bond Markets, Analysis and Strategies 143-163, 340-345, 389-394 (4th ed. 2000); James C. Van Horne, Financial Management and Policy 53742 (11th ed. 1998); Richard A. Brealey & Stewart C. Myers, Principles of Corporate Finance 357-361, 680-692 (5th ed. 1996); Frank J. Fabozzi, T. Dessa & Michael G. Ferri, Overview of the Types and Features of Fixed Income Securities in The Handbook of Fixed Income Securities ch. 1 (4th ed. 1995) (hereinafter Handbook of Fixed Income Securities); Frank J. Fabozzi, Richard S. Wilson, Harry C. Sauvain & John C. Ritchie, Jr., Corporate Bonds in Handbook of Fixed Income Securities *supra* ch. 10; Eugene F. Brigham & Louis C. Gapenski, Intermediate Financial Management ch. 13 (3d ed. 1990).

A. Introduction of Senior Securities

Redemption Privilege/Obligation. Frequently bonds and preferred stock contain redemption and/or conversion provisions.[2] When a redemption feature is included, the borrower almost invariably reserves the option to call or redeem bonds or debentures on any interest-paying date prior to their maturity after giving appropriate notice to the bondholders. Without provision for redemption the debtor corporation would have no right to prepay the bonds, which it may wish to do to free itself of high interest payments or restrictions of the mortgage or indenture. A small premium is usually provided in the redemption or prepayment price; although it is not as large a premium as that commonly given for the redemption of preferred stock, it adds to the value and marketability of the bonds.

Conversion Privilege. In order to make a security attractive, corporations often confer upon bond or debenture holders the privilege of exchanging their securities for a predetermined number of shares of stock.[3] This is known as a right or privilege of conversion. The bond indenture will then provide: (1) the kind of security into which the bond may be converted; (2) the ratio of conversion — that is, the number of shares that may be called for in exchange; (3) the period or time limits during which the conversion right extends; and (4) protection against dilution and capital adjustments.[4] It is most common to make both bonds and preferred shares convertible into common shares, although in some instances bonds have been made convertible into preferred shares.[5] Bonds and debentures are frequently issued with a stock purchase warrant giving the option to purchase a certain number of shares at a designated price; this is somewhat similar in its effect to the privilege of conversion.[6] Unlike the conversion privilege, warrants can be marketed separately from the accompanying debenture. In either case, the option or conversion privilege will be adjusted in case of capital changes, split-ups, or dilution of the stock as to which option is to be exercised.[7]

Sinking Funds. Corporations frequently provide a sinking fund for the purchase or retirement of its bonds, thus increasing their security and salability.

---

[2] *See generally* William A. Klein, C. David Anderson, & Kathleen G. McGuinness, The Call Provision of Corporate Bonds: A Standard Form in Need of Change, 18 J. Corp. L. 653 (1993).

[3] *See generally* James C. Van Horne & John M. Waschowicz, Jr., Fundamentals of Financial Management 586-597 (10th ed. 1998); Richard A. Brealey & Stewart C. Myers, Principles of Corporate Finance chs. 18 & 22 (5th ed. 1996).

[4] For thoughtful analyses of the standard anti-dilution clause, *see* Broad v. Rockwell Int'l Corp., 642 F.2d 929 (5th Cir. 1981) (en banc); Stephen I. Glover, Solving Antidilution Problems, 51 Bus. Law. 1221 (1996); Stanley A. Kaplan, Piercing the Corporate Boilerplate: Anti-Dilution Clauses in Convertible Securities, 33 U. Chi. L. Rev. 1 (1965).

For a survey of practices in drafting anti-dilution clauses within a sample of indentures, *see* Marcel Kahan, 2 Stan. J. L. Bus. & Fin. 147 (1995).

[5] *See, e.g.,* Augusta Trust Co. v. Augusta H. & G. R.R., 187 A. 1 (Me. 1936).

[6] *See* Henry B. Reiling, Warrants in Bond-Warrant Units: A Survey and Assessment, 70 Mich. L. Rev. 1411 (1972).

[7] George S. Hills, Convertible Securities — Legal Aspects and Draftsmanship, 19 Col. L. Rev. 1 (1930).

There are various types of sinking funds.[8] Payments for debenture sinking funds, which may be conditioned on net earnings, typically must be made to a sinking fund agent, who frequently is the trustee under the indenture. Default in sinking fund payments may be grounds for acceleration of the bonds' maturity. Serial bonds are made to mature from time to time, so there is a gradual retirement of part of the bonds without payment of a premium.[9] It is more common, however, to provide for an annual sinking fund to be applied solely to the purchase or to the call and retirement of bonds.[10] Such periodic purchases support the price of outstanding bonds and provide some additional liquidity for their holders. Further, if the bond market is depressed so that the price has fallen below face value, the issuer's ultimate financial burden in retiring the indebtedness is reduced, and, during the time that the bonds continue to be outstanding, the redemption of other bonds supports their value by reducing the company's future financial burdens so there is less risk associated with the payment of their interest and principal. It is common for the indenture to provide that the trustee select by lot the bonds to be retired out of the sinking fund.

The sinking fund may be funded so that a designated amount is set aside and invested, usually by a third party. This is generally the case with bonds. Alternatively, as is frequently the case with preferred stock, the sinking fund may be unfunded, with no funds set aside but with appropriate restrictions placed on "surplus" in the corporate balance sheet. This provides far less financial protection than that guaranteed by the funded sinking fund.[11]

Income Bonds. Income bonds, which are not normally issued except during a corporate reorganization, are obligations that call for interest payments only to the extent that income is earned annually or within specified interest periods. Such interest payments ordinarily are not made cumulative. Income bonds remove the menace of fixed charges and depend for their return on the success of the business.[12] In this respect they are very similar to non-cumulative preferred shares. The indenture should define carefully the method for determining the periodic net earnings from which interest is to be paid.

Rights of Bondholders. Some states recognize that under certain circumstances bondholders may become concerned with the management of the corporation and accordingly provide that the bondholders be given inspection rights and voting rights.[13] Ordinarily these rights are contingent and are triggered by default in

---

[8] Brigham & Gapenski, Financial Management: Theory and Practice 625-628 (6th ed. 1991); 1 Dewing, *supra* §18.02 note 1, ch. 8; Note, Sinking Funds, 24 Va. L. Rev. 293 (1937).

[9] Floyd Franklin Burtchett & Clifford M. Hicks, Corporation Finance, Policy and Management 186-195 (4th ed. 1964).

[10] *See id.* ch. 10.

[11] The chief protection provided by unfunded sinking funds is the restriction on dividend distribution and share repurchases.

[12] *See* Warner Bros. Pictures, Inc. v. Lawton-Byrne-Bruner Ins. Agency Co., 79 F.2d 804, 816, 818 (8th Cir. 1935); J. W. Hansen, Legal and Business Aspects of Income Bonds, 11 Temple L.Q. 330, 352 (1937).

[13] *E.g.,* Del. Code tit. 8, §221 (2001).

interest payments or by earnings falling below a certain relation to interest requirements.[14] Conditional voting rights make bonds look more like shares of stock, and it is questionable whether in the absence of a statute such protections can be put into the indenture agreement or articles of incorporation. Voting protection for bondholders, particularly in reorganization, is sometimes provided through a voting trust for common shares.

§18.04   Classes of Stock

The ideal financial structure would appear to be the simplest: one class of common shares. In large enterprises, however, especially railroads and public utilities, a reasonable amount of short-term borrowings and of long-term or funded debts is usually included in the capitalization of the firm. Bonded debt has unfortunately often become over-extended, without sufficient basis in existing or foreseeable earnings to give debts a safe margin of protection. This over-extension frequently results in receivership and reorganization. In close corporations, classification of securities is frequently a good device for tailoring control arrangements and participation in profits to the particular desires of the participants.[1]

The law does not limit the various classes, varieties, or combinations of preferred shares that may be authorized, as long as the distinction between debt and shares is observed.[2] The organizers and managers of a corporation may wish to subdivide and classify the units of participation in the corporate income, assets, and control. A corporation may thus issue such varieties of preferred shares as the prospects and needs of the enterprise may call for and as the tastes of the investing public may absorb. These classes of shares may differ as to priority of claim on dividends, as to limited or participating dividend rights, as to conversion rights, voting rights, amounts payable on redemption, dissolution, or liquidation, and in protection against dilution and changes of capital structure. A security's precise financial features are driven not only by the prevailing conditions in the market but also by the risk and return objectives of the security's issuer and the various market participants, who can be expected as prospective holders to parcel different components of the security's features among themselves.[3]

---

[14] See Tooley v. Robinson Springs Corp., 660 A.2d 293, 295-296 (Vt. 1995) (receipt of late payment does not bar holders from exercising their rights that are provided for default, but will bar them from seeking interest on the late payment).

§18.04   [1] See James C. Van Horne, Financial Management and Policy 543-546 (11th ed. 1998); Ronald L. Gallatin, "Preferred Stock I: Concepts and Categories" in Corporate and Municipal Securities, 3 Library of Investment Banking 467-506 (Kahn ed. 1990) (hereinafter Library of Investment Banking); Richard S. Wilson & Harry C. Sauvain, Preferred Stock II: Non-convertible Preferred Stock, Library of Investment Banking 507-529.

[2] See Model Business Corp. Act §6.01 Official Comment (1984) (hereinafter MBCA).

[3] See generally Henry Hu, New Financial Products, the Modern Process of Financial Innovation, and the Puzzle of Shareholder Welfare, 69 Texas L. Rev. 1273 (1991). Directors must often resolve conflicts among classes of stock. Value allocation decisions by boards are generally protected by the business judgment rule. The fact that the directors own more of one class than another does not

Corporations sometimes issue more than one class of "common stock," one being given full voting power and the other either being nonvoting or having only a fractional vote for each share. If the distinction between classes of common stock is not in voting rights but in priority of amount of participation in earnings or assets, the class that has priority is in effect a participating preferred stock as against the other class.[4]

Preferred shares have been called "compromise securities" because they occupy an intermediate position between common shares and debts. It is this intermediate position that causes some to believe they have greater risks than either the common or bondholders.[5] They usually have a specified limited rate of return or dividend and a specified limited redemption and liquidation price. This creates "leverage" because of the greater possible gain to the common shareholders on the total capital invested and the lesser investment necessary to obtain voting control.

§18.05   The Preferred Share Contract

Preferred stock is distinctive because of its relationship to common stock. As the highest New York court has declared, "Whatever preferential rights and privileges may thus be granted to a stockholder, the law regards them as contractual. 'The certificate of stock is the muniment of the shareholder's title, and evidence of his right. It expresses the contract between the corporation and his co-stockholders and himself. . . .' "[1] As such, the traditional rules of construction and interpretation apply to determine the rights of the preferred shareholders as set forth in their contract with the corporation.[2]

It is not generally true, however, that the certificate of stock is the authoritative source, evidence, or expression of the preferred share contract.[3] The contract is made with the individual shareholders when they agree to become owners of shares and make themselves parties to the charter contract, not necessarily when a certificate of ownership is issued.[4] In many states all the terms of the preferred share contract must be set forth in the articles of incorporation or charter and cannot be added to or changed by the bylaws, stock certificates, or corporate resolutions.[5] This promotes certainty of information as to the terms of the contract from an authoritative document that is a matter of public record.

---

necessarily implicate the directors' good faith or loyalty. Solomon v. Armstrong, 747 A.2d 1098, 1118, 1123 (Del. Ch. 1999), *aff'd*, 746 A.2d 277 (Del. 2000).

[4] *See, e.g.,* Bodell v. General Gas & Elec. Corp., 140 A. 264 (Del. 1927).

[5] *See* Lawrence E. Mitchell, The Puzzling Paradox of Preferred Stock (And Why We Should Care About It), 51 Bus. Law. 443, 449-454 (1996).

§18.05 [1] Strout v. Cross, Austin & Ireland Lumber Co., 28 N.E.2d 890, 893 (N.Y. 1940), quoting Kent v. Quicksilver Mining Co. 78 N.Y. 159, 180 (1879).

[2] *See* Swoskin v. Rollins, 634 F.2d 285 (5th Cir. 1981). *See also, e.g.,* Elliott Associates, L.P. v. Avatex, 715 A.2d 843 (Del. 1998); Waggoner v. Laster, 581 A.2d 1127 (Del. 1990).

[3] The older view was otherwise. *See* Ericksen v. Winnebago Indus., 342 F. Supp. 1190 (D. Minn. 1972) (applying former Iowa statute that did not require redemption to be set forth in the articles of incorporation).

[4] *See supra* §§16.01, 16.02 for discussion of the role played by pre-incorporation share subscriptions.

A. Introduction of Senior Securities

The preferred holders' rights are, therefore, largely those provided in the articles of incorporation as augmented by provisions of the state corporate statute. However, in isolated instances preferred holders successful invoke fiduciary principles to protect their interests. Thus, in *Jackson National Life Ins. Co. v. Kennedy*,[6] the Delaware Chancery court held that preferred stockholders could proceed with claims that the director and controlling shareholder breached a fiduciary duty of candor by failing to disclose certain material facts involved with the forthcoming sale of a significant product line, even though no vote by the stockholders was called for to approve the sale.[7] Furthermore, the court applied a line of Delaware authority holding that directors owe a fiduciary duty to common and preferred stockholders when dividing the consideration received in a merger or other extraordinary transaction.[8]

§18.06   Flexibility Through a "Blank Stock" Authorization

The rigidity that results from having the dividend rate and certain other preferences on classes or series of preferred shares fixed in the charter is relaxed in several states by permission to authorize the board of directors to set the terms of new series of classes of preferred shares or even to create different classes from time to time. A series is a subdivision of a class. These "blank stock" statutes enable the directors to vary the terms as to dividend rates and certain other rights of new series or classes according to what the condition of the financial market and that of the corporation may seem to require for ready sale. Blank stock can thus provide advantages similar to bonds with regard to flexibility of terms.

B.   PREFERRED STOCK: FINANCIAL FEATURES AND EQUITABLE PROTECTION OF RIGHTS

§18.07   Cumulative Dividends

If preferred shares are either expressly or impliedly "cumulative" and dividends are not paid in any year or dividend period, the arrears must be made up in

---

[5] *See, e.g.,* Judah v. Delaware Trust Co., 378 A.2d 624, 628 (Del. 1977); Gaskill v. Gladys Belle Oil Co., 146 A. 337 (Del. Ch. 1929).

Under most modern statutes the articles can authorize the directors to divide designated classes of stock into series with different share attributes, in which cases the appropriate resolution must be on public file. *See, e.g.,* MBCA §6.02 (1984).

[6] 741 A.2d 377 (Del. Ch. 1999).

[7] *Id.* at 390-391. The case would be even stronger if a shareholder vote were required, *see* Gilmartin v. Adobe Resources Corp., 1992 WL 71510 (Del. Ch., Apr. 6, 1992).

[8] *Id.* at 391. The court relied upon In re FLS Holdings, Inc. Shareholder Litig., 1993 WL 104562 (Del. Ch. Apr. 2, 1993), *aff'd,* 628 A.2d 84 (Del. 1993) (unpublished opinion).

subsequent years, whether earned or not, before any dividends can be declared or paid on common shares.[1] Sometimes dividends on preferred shares are in express terms made to depend on the profits of each particular year, so the holders of the shares will not be entitled to any dividends for a particular year if there are not enough profits in that year to pay them, or they will be entitled only insofar as there were profits. These shares are known as "cumulative if earned," and in the absence of sufficient profits the dividends are non-cumulative and are not made up out of the profits of subsequent years.[2]

Unless a contrary intention appears, dividends on preferred shares have generally been held to be impliedly cumulative.[3] Careful draftsmanship should not leave questions open for judicial interpretation.

§18.08   Non-Cumulative Preferred Shares

The great advantage of non-cumulative preferred shares is that they avoid an undue accumulation of dividend arrearages, particularly for years in which dividends are not earned. Non-cumulative shares are frequently employed in reorganizations, when it is necessary to limit dividend rights and the investors must take what the enterprise can carry,[1] but the non-cumulative shares may not be listed on the New York Stock Exchange.[2]

The principal types of non-cumulative preferred share contracts may be divided into three general groups, subject to internal variation: (1) the discretionary dividend type; (2) cumulative if earned, or "mandatory" dividend type; and (3) "dividend credit" type.[3]

Discretionary Dividend Type. An example of a non-cumulative preferred share contract held to be of the discretionary dividend type is found in a leading

---

§18.07   [1] Bank of Am. Nat'l Trust & Sav. Ass'n v. West End Chem. Co., 100 P.2d 318 (Cal. Ct. App. 1940).

For example, suppose a Company for three years (including the current year) has made no profits and declared no dividends on either the preferred or common shares. During the past year it has accumulated profits, and its directors now propose to declare the regular annual dividend of 7 percent on the cumulative preferred shares and a dividend of 8 percent on the common. The cumulative preferred shareholders are entitled to the dividends for the three years in which none were paid them before anything can be paid on the common shares.

[2] Wabash Ry. v. Barclay, 280 U.S. 197 (1930).

[3] *E.g.,* Arizona Power Co. v. Stuart, 212 F.2d 535 (9th Cir. 1954); Hazel Atlas Glass Co. v. Van Dyke & Reeves, Inc., 8 F.2d 716, 720 (2d Cir.), *cert. denied,* 269 U.S. 570 (1925) (dictum); Garrett v. Edge Moor Iron Co., 194 A. 15 (Del. Ch. 1937), *aff'd sub nom.* Pennsylvania Co. for Ins. on Lives & Granting Annuities v. Cox, 199 A. 671 (Del. 1938).

§18.08   [1] See New York, L. E. & W. R.R. v. Nickals, 119 U.S. 296 (1886). *Cf.* 1 Dewing, *supra* §18.02 note 1, at 138 (late nineteenth century railroad reorganizations commonly employed non-cumulative shares).

[2] NYSE Listed Company Manual §A15, ¶281.

[3] *See* W. H. S. Stevens, Rights of Non-Cumulative Preferred Stockholders, 34 Colum. L. Rev. 1439 (1934).

B.   Preferred Stock: Financial Features and Equitable Protection of Rights

Supreme Court case holding that even if there are net profits, the preferred stockholder's right to dividends thereon in any year depends on the judgment and discretion of the directors.[4] The dividend right for any particular fiscal year is gone if the directors, without abuse of discretion, withhold a dividend declaration for that year.[5]

The shareholders' protection under such a discretionary non-cumulative contract lies in equitable relief against abuse of discretion rather than in any ability to enforce a series of supposed contract claims.[6] The mere showing that annual profits, accumulated profits, or earned surplus existed from which a dividend might lawfully have been declared is not sufficient to establish a breach of duty on the part of the directors in failing to declare it. No wrong is done unless the withholding of the dividend would be oppressive, fraudulent, or unfairly discriminatory.[7]

Cumulative-if-Earned or "Mandatory Dividend" Type.[8] A non-cumulative preferred share contract may be made a kind of hybrid "cumulative non-cumulative" type by providing in the articles of incorporation that all back dividends, if earned, must be paid ahead of any common stock dividends.[9] A preferred stock provision mandating dividends up to a certain amount so long as there are profits, net earnings, or net income invariably pose important interpretative questions as to the meaning of these expressions. To the extent that terms conditioning the right to dividends have particular significance in the discipline of accounting, as do the terms "profits," "net earnings," and "net income," it is customary to abide by generally accepted accounting principles in applying such terms to a particular situation.[10]

Dividend Credit Rule. The highest court of New Jersey affirmed by an equally divided vote[11] the decision of the Court of Chancery, which had interpreted a non-cumulative provision to be cumulative if earned. A later New Jersey decision explained: "[W]here non-cumulative preferred stock has not been allotted the full

---

[4] Wabash Ry. v. Barclay, 280 U.S. 197 (1930).

[5] *Accord,* Guttmann v. Illinois Cent. R.R., 189 F.2d 927 (2d Cir.), *cert. denied,* 342 U.S. 867 (1951); Joslin v. Boston & M. R.R., 175 N.E. 156 (Mass. 1931), noted in 29 Mich. L. Rev. 1077 (1931). *Contra,* Sanders v. Cuba R.R., 120 A.2d 849 (N.J. 1956).

[6] *See generally* Adolf A. Berle & Gardiner C. Means, The Modern Corporation and Private Property 172-178, 231-232 (rev. ed. 1967).

[7] *E.g.,* Levin v. Mississippi River Corp., 59 F.R.D. 353 (S.D.N.Y.), *aff'd,* 486 F.2d 1398 (2d Cir.), *cert. denied,* 414 U.S. 1112 (1973); Moskowitz v. Bantrell, 190 A.2d 749 (Del. 1963).

[8] "Mandatory dividend" is a misnomer because, although dividends may accrue if earned, they do not vest and thus become a debt until declared by the board of directors who, except in the most egregious case, have discretion to retain the earnings for the corporation.

[9] Wood v. Lary 17 N.Y. (Hun.) 550 (1888), *aff'd,* 26 N.E. 838 (N.Y. 1891); Burk v. Ottowa Gas & Electric Co., 123 P. 857 (Kan. 1912).

[10] *See* Kern v. Chicago & E. Ill. R.R., 285 N.E.2d 501 (Ill. App. Ct. 1972); Koppel v. Middle States Petroleum Corp., 96 N.Y.S.2d 38, 42 (Sup. Ct. 1950).

[11] Day v. United States Cast Iron Pipe & Foundry Co., 126 A. 302 (N.J. 1924, *aff'g* 123 A. 546 (N.J. Ch.); Comment, Corporations—Non-Cumulative Preferred Stock—Necessity of Making Up Unpaid Preferred Dividends Before Paying Any Common Dividend, 38 Harv. L. Rev. 686 (1925).

dividend to which it is entitled in any one year and the corporation for that year has earned more than the dividend paid to the preferred stockholders, the preferred stock is entitled to have allotted to it such withheld earnings to the extent of its priority before dividends are paid to common stockholders."[12] At one time it appeared that the New Jersey rule was being eroded;[13] however, it has been reaffirmed in subsequent decisions[14] and perhaps even strengthened.[15]

In general, preferences depend not on any statute or rule of law but on the provisions in the preferred share contract. The New Jersey cases are best interpreted as not holding that the bare word "non-cumulative" necessarily means that dividends are cumulative to the extent earned in each fiscal year.[16] Just as cumulative-if-earned dividends can be established in other states by express charter provision, an equally clear clause in a New Jersey charter can create preferred shares with strictly non-cumulative dividends.[17]

§18.09   Participation of Preferred Shares Beyond Their Preference

By express provision, preferred shares may participate in dividend distributions beyond their fixed dividend priority. One or two courts adopted the view that preferred shares are entitled to participate equally with the common shares in any distribution of profits after the common shares have received in the same year a dividend at the same rate as that stipulated as a preference for the preferred, unless the share contract provides to the contrary.[1] It seems reasonable to infer that in consideration of preferential rights, the preferred shareholders agree to accept priority in dividends at a fixed rate in lieu of further participation with the common. This is the understanding of the investing public, especially in view of the fact that participating preferred stock is an unusual type of security having a special feature that should be specified and defined.

---

[12] Cintas v. American Car & Foundry Co., 25 A.2d 418, 422 (N.J. Ch. 1942), aff'd, 28 A.2d 531 (N.J. 1942).

[13] 12 William M. Fletcher, Cyclopedia of the Law of Private Corporations §5447.2 (rev. ed. 1996).

[14] Sanders v. Cuba R.R., 120 A.2d 849 (N.J. 1956); Leeds & Lippincott Co. v. Nevius, 144 A.2d (N.J. Super. Ct. 1958), modified on other grounds, 153 A.2d 45 (N.J. 1959).

[15] Cf. Carlos L. Israels, The Corporate Triangle—Some Comparative Aspects of the New Jersey, New York and Delaware Statutes, 23 Rutgers L. Rev. 615, 627 (1969) (recent statutory amendments left rule in intact, thus missing "an opportunity to bring the law and modern corporate finance into a more realistic relationship").

[16] The dividend-credit rule will imply cumulative-if-earned dividends for non-cumulative preferred shares only where the certificate of incorporation is silent or is so general as to leave adequate room for construction of the contractual arrangements between the parties. Leeds & Lippincott Co. v. Nevius, 144 A.2d 4 (N.J. Super. Ct. 1958), modified, 153 A.2d 45 (N.J. 1959).

[17] E.g., Leeds & Lippincott Co. v. Nevius, 144 A.2d 4 (N.J. Super. Ct. 1958), modified, 153 A.2d 45 (N.J. 1959).

§18.09   [1] Niles v. Ludlow Valve Mfg. Co., 202 F. 141 (2d Cir. 1913); Tennant v. Epstein, 189 N.E. 864 (Ill. 1934).

B. Preferred Stock: Financial Features and Equitable Protection of Rights

§18.10   *Preference on Liquidation*

When a corporation's assets are distributed among its shareholders as part of dissolution and winding up, the holders of preferred shares have the same, and no greater, right to share proportionately in the net assets as do the holders of common shares unless the holders of preferred shares have a contractual preference.[1] Usually, however, preferred shares contain provisions for not only a dividend preference but also a stated preference in liquidation or winding up. This liquidation preference most often includes a right to receive any arrears of cumulative dividends in priority to any distribution of assets to the common shareholders.[2] It has generally been held that a liquidation preference including accrued dividends is valid, whether or not there are accumulated earnings or surplus available for dividends.[3]

By the prevailing view, merger or consolidation of a corporation with another is not such a "dissolution" or "liquidation" as to entitle the holder of preferred shares to payment of the liquidation price or preference, unless it is clearly so specified.[4]

§18.11   *Voting Rights of Preferred*

In most instances, the participation in corporate governance by preferred stockholders is much the same as for bondholders: they are much like children, to be seen but not heard. Thus the preferred's contract provides for a periodic return through dividends that is either cumulative or non-cumulative, and perhaps a preference on the firm's liquidation. And, like bondholders, rarely do preferred stockholders enjoy voting rights in the election of directors or most other matters requiring a shareholder vote. Under the typical preferred stock arrangement, any voting rights of preferred stockholders arise in those limited situations where the state corporate statute requires the approval of the preferred when an amendment to the articles of incorporation will change or adversely affect the preferred shares.[1] The precise language of the articles of incorporation frequently generally determines whether the preferred get a vote. Thus, in one case the Delaware Supreme Court held the preferred had a right to vote on a recapitalization that was accomplished via a consolidation because the articles provided for a vote when the preferred shares' rights were adversely affected by "amendment" "whether by merger, consolidation or otherwise."[2] However, when the articles more generally provide for a class vote of the preferred by action "to amend" the

---

§18.10   [1] Continental Ins. Co. v. United States, 259 U.S. 156, 181 (1922). *See* Otis & Co. v. SEC, 323 U.S. 624, 634, 645 (1945); Lloyd v. Pennsylvania Elec. Vehicle Co., 72 A. 16 (N.J. 1909).

[2] *But see* Wouk v. Merin, 128 N.Y.S.2d 727 (App. Div. 1954).

[3] Fawkes v. Farm Lands Inv. Co., 297 P. 47 (Cal. Ct. App. 1931).

[4] *See, e.g.*, Rothschild Int'l Corp. v. Liggett Group, Inc., 474 A.2d 133 (Del. 1984).

§18.11   [1] *See infra* §25.04.

[2] *See* Elliott Assoc. v. Avatex Corp., 715 A.2d 843 (Del. 1998).

articles so as to "to alter or change" the rights of the preferred, a merger changing such rights was held not to fall within this provision because the change occurred by virtue of the merger and not by an amendment so that there is no vote by the preferred is required.[3] With their voting rights so narrowly circumscribed, the preferred shareholder generally lacks a means within the traditional corporate governance mechanisms to, for example, assure that their dividends are regularly paid or that the board of directors does not pursue policies that are likely to harm the future returns of the preferred shareholders. To be sure, there is some economic coercion on the directors when the preferred dividends are cumulative because any arrearages delay dividends to the common stockholders who have elected the board of directors. However, the law is replete with cases in which, after many years of failing to pay the preferred their cumulative dividend, the company undergoes a recapitalization that removes the dividend arrearage and allows future participation by the common on a level more favorable than if the preferred dividends had first been satisfied.[4]

A potentially potent force in the hands of the preferred holders is a provision in their contract granting the preferred the right to vote in the election of directors, and perhaps on other matters, if the corporation fails to pay the preferred dividend. Such contingent voting rights, when provided, usually arise only after a certain number of quarterly dividends have not been fully satisfied—for example, four quarters. The listing requirements of the New York Stock Exchange mandate contingent voting rights for preferred shares.[5] The drafter should carefully consider whether such contingent voting rights should extend to the power to elect the entire board of directors or a majority of the board,[6] or merely provide minority representation on the board. In *Baron v. Allied Artist Pictures Corporation,*[7] the preferred shareholders obtained control of the board after their contingent voting rights were triggered by successive nonpayments of dividends. The preferred's representatives restored the company to profitability, but because the preferred dividends had not been paid, control over the board had not been restored to the common. The common shareholders sued, arguing unsuccessfully that the mission of the directors elected by the preferred was to extinguish the dividend arrearages so that the control over the board could be returned to the common shareholders. While recognizing that the directors had a fiduciary duty to see that the preferred's dividends were brought up to date, the court nevertheless ruled

---

[3] *See* Warner Comm. Inc. v. Chris-Craft Ind., Inc., 583 A.2d 962 (Del. Ch. 1989).

[4] *See, e.g.,* Goldman v. Postal Tel., Inc., 52 F. Supp. 763 (D. Del. 1943). The common may also seek to take advantage of the depressed preferred share prices due to the nonpayment of preferred dividends. *See* Eisenberg v. Chicago Milwaukee Corp., 537 A.2d 1051 (Del. Ch. 1987) (after 1987 market crash, issuer launched tender offer to purchase preferred for which dividends had not been paid for many years).

[5] *See* NYSE Listed Company Manual §313.00(e)(C) (at least six quarterly dividends, but the power need only extend ability to elected two directors; also recommending same rights for unlisted preferred). *See also* American Stock Exchange Guide Original Listing Requirement §124 (listing will not be favorably regarded without such protection).

[6] This is the requirement for companies subject to the Public Utility Holding Company Act §§6 and 7, PUHCA Rel. No. 13,106, 5 Fed. Sec. L. Rep. (CCH) ¶36,691.

[7] 337 A.2d 653 (Del. Ch. 1975).

against the common, holding there was no evidence of bad faith in the current directors' stewardship of the firm.[8]

Some have argued that corporations lack the power to issue shares that have only voting rights. The reasoning behind this argument is that implicit in the meaning and status of "shares" is a proprietary interest. In the only reported decision on this point, the court held that preferred shares are valid even though they carry only voting rights.[9]

§18.12   The Redemption Provision: Voluntary or Compulsory for the Corporation

Corporations frequently reserve the option to redeem preferred shares at a certain redemption price in order to facilitate future financing. Where such a right exists, the board of directors must exercise the power to redeem in a manner consistent with the terms set forth in the articles of incorporation.[1] In closely held corporations, redemption provisions, like options to repurchase, may be used to keep control of the corporation's stock among a limited number of shareholders.[2] The corporation's right to redeem is generally discretionary with the corporation's board of directors.

Repurchase is subject to the requirement that full disclosure of all material facts be made to the stockholders as well as to the equitable consideration that the repurchase not be coercive. In *Eisenberg v. Chicago Milwaukee Corporation*,[3] just after the October 1987[4] stock market collapse (which drove the preferred shares to $41), the board of directors sought to purchase at $55 per share preferred shares whose redemption price was $100. The Delaware Chancery Court enjoined the issuer's tender offer because the directors failed to disclose that they stood to gain by the repurchase as common stockholders because the elimination of the preferred would remove an impediment to their receipt of dividends. Also, the court emphasized that the board's action was coercive because they announced their intention to have the preferred shares delisted from the stock exchange.

Since a corporation's power to redeem shares at a set price is part of the preferred share contract, complaints that a redemption price is unfair vis-à-vis the shares' market value should be unsuccessful. The exercise is subject to the standard requirements of the business judgment rule.

---

[8] There was evidence that payment of the preferred's dividends were delayed due to a deficiency owed the IRS.

[9] Stroh v. Blackhawk Holding Corp., 272 N.E.2d 1 (Ill. 1971).

§18.12   [1] *See generally* White v. Investors' Management Corp., 888 F.2d 1036 (4th Cir. 1989). Absent a redemption provision in the articles or some extrinsic document, the entity is not bound to repurchase its shares. Colaluca v. Climaco, Climaco, Seminatore, Lefkowitz & Garofoli Co. L.P.A., 648 N.E.2d 1341, 1342 (Ohio 1995).

[2] Some states, however, do not permit redemption of common shares.

[3] 537 A.2d 1051 (Del. Ch. 1987).

[4] *See also* Kahn v. United States Sugar Corp., 1985 WL 4449 (Del. Ch. 1985); Cottle v. Standard Brands Paint Co. [1990 Transfer Binder], Fed. Sec. L. Rep. (CCH) ¶95,306 (Del. Ch. 1990).

Compulsory redemption provisions and repurchase contracts are sometimes included in preferred share contracts and subscription agreements in order to make shares more attractive to timid investors.[5] Under such contracts the corporation is required to redeem or repurchase its preferred shares at a fixed date or at the option of the owner (essentially granting her a "put" option with respect to the shares), thus giving the shareholders a right to demand a return of their initial investment. Serious harm may result from redemption or repurchase of shares under such contracts. If allowed without restriction, redemptions may injure creditors and other shareholders by depriving the corporation of needed capital.[6]

§18.13   The Redemption or Sinking Fund for Retirement of Preferred Shares

A redemption fund, often loosely termed a "sinking fund," may be provided for the purchase or retirement of preferred shares; it is thus similar to a sinking fund used for the gradual or partial retirement of bonds. As with bonds, the sinking fund may consist of a separate account where funds are actually deposited or, as is more commonly the case with preferred shares, it may be unfunded, with balance sheet entries reflecting appropriate restrictions on the surplus accounts. The redemption fund may be accumulated by setting aside specified installments either based on a percentage of the net annual profits, payable out of net assets in excess of capital, based on a periodic small flat percentage of the par value of the preferred shares concerned that are outstanding, or derived from some other source.

§18.14   Convertible Shares and Warrants

Preferred shares and bonds may be issued with a conversion privilege or with warrants.[1] The conversion privilege confers upon the holder the option of exchang-

---

[5] *E.g.*, Schulte v. Boulevard Gardens Land Co., 129 P. 582 (Cal. 1913); Grace Sec. Corp. v. Roberts, 164 S.E. 700 (Va. 1932). *See, e.g.*, Del. Code Ann. tit. 8, §151(b) (2001).

[6] In the words of the Supreme Court, "[s]tock which has no retirement provisions is the backbone of a corporate structure." Ecker v. Western Pac. R.R., 318 U.S. 448, 477 (1943).

§18.14 [1] *See generally* Richard T. McDermott, Legal Aspects of Corporate Finance §§502-506 (3d ed. 2000); George W. Dent, Jr., The Role of Convertible Securities in Corporate Finance, 21 Iowa J. Corp. L. 241 (1996) (examining various theories advanced to explain use of convertible securities, concluding that reasons vary from case to case); William W. Bratton, The Economics and Jurisprudence of Convertible Bonds, 1984 Wis. L. Rev. 667. On the financial considerations that surround convertible securities, *see* Frank J. Fabozzi, Bond Markets, Analysis and Strategies 143-163, 340-345, 389-394 (4th ed. 2000); James C. Van Horne & John M. Waschowicz, Jr., Fundamentals of Financial Management 424-447, 586-597 (10th ed. 1998); Richard A. Brealey & Stewart C. Myers, Principles of Corporate Finance chs. 18 & 22 (5th ed. 1996).

B.   Preferred Stock: Financial Features and Equitable Protection of Rights

ing fixed or limited income securities for shares of common stock at a designated price or prices and within a specified period.[2] A warrant is an option to purchase shares. Corporations issuing convertible shares or bonds or giving stock purchase warrants must be ready to issue the shares and meet the demands of holders who exercise their options at any period within the time frame specified in the contract.[3] The holder of a convertible security does not become the holder of the security acquired through conversion, and that security is not deemed outstanding, until the conversion occurs.[4]

Warrants may be issued accompanying shares of stock or bonds giving the holder the option to subscribe for or to purchase shares of common stock at a stipulated price or prices per share, usually within a limited time. Warrants may be inseparable from the securities with which they are issued. More commonly, however, warrants are separable and are frequently traded on the stock exchanges. Standing alone, a warrant is not an equity interest; the holder's rights are wholly contractual and may expire on dissolution, consolidation, or by lapse of time.[5] Warrants are sometimes issued to shareholders and general creditors in the reorganization of a bankrupt corporation for otherwise unsatisfied claims.[6]

The financial distinction between convertible bonds and warrants is practically nonexistent if one assumes that warrants are issued in connection with their holder's purchase of a senior security, whether that senior security be a bond or preferred stock. The practical distinction between a convertible security and a warrant is that the latter is a separate security, detachable from the senior security that the initial holder was required to purchase in order to obtain the warrants. The warrant also carries with it an exercise price, thus requiring that fresh cash be paid as consideration for the underlying security, whereas the consideration for the underlying security acquired through conversion is the security converted into the underlying security. The value of the warrant and the value of the conversion feature of the senior security are each dependent on the value of the underlying security—that is, the security that can be acquired on exercise of the warrant or conversion of the senior security.

It is commonly stated that warrants and convertible securities are a form of "delayed equity financing." Absent the corporation's right to redeem, the warrant and conversion feature portend the day when their holder will exercise the warrant or convert and thereby acquire the underlying common stock. Obviously, that

---

[2] Warrants occasionally have no expiration date; they are then considered perpetual.

[3] Marony v. Wheeling & L. E. R.R., 33 F.2d 916 (S.D.N.Y. 1929); Hills, *supra* §18.03 note 7, at 12. In Swiss Bank Corp. v. Dresser Industries, Inc., 141 F.3d 689 (7th Cir. 1998), the court held that when the expiration date for the exercise of a warrant falls on a state holiday, Good Friday, the expiration date is not extended to the following weekday.

[4] *See* Nerken v. Standard Oil Co., 810 F.2d 1230 (D.C. Cir. 1987).

[5] Helvering v. Southwest Consol. Corp., 315 U.S. 194 (1941). However, they do qualify as "equity securities" under the federal securities laws.

[6] Ecker v. Western Pac. R.R., 318 U.S. 448, 476 (1943) (dictum); 1 Dewing, *supra* §18.02 note 1, at 267-268.

option is exercised only when the market value of the common shares is materially greater than the exercise price of the warrant or that portion of the bond's value not attributed to its conversion feature (at some point, the principal determinant of a convertible bond's value is the common shares that can be acquired on conversion). The preceding only elaborates on the reasons a warrant or conversion feature, when included in the bundle of rights investors acquire on the issuance of senior securities, is seen as a "sweetener" to the offered financial package. So viewed, one may question whether a warrant or conversion feature truly reduces the cost of raising capital (that is, the benefits referred to in the above excerpt) or merely postpones the full costs of financing until the warrant or the conversion feature is exercised.[7]

§18.15   Implied Conditions of Good Faith

The principle is well established that any protection bondholders and preferred stockholders enjoy arises from the four corners of their contract with the corporation (that is, indenture or terms set forth in the articles of incorporation). There are, however, rare instances in when the preferred can invoke the protection of a fiduciary obligation. For example, in *Jackson National Life Insurance Co. v. Kennedy*,[1] the Delaware Chancery court held that preferred stockholders could proceed with claims that the director and controlling shareholder breached a fiduciary duty of candor by failing to disclose certain material facts involved with the forthcoming sale of a significant product line, even though no vote by the stockholders was called for to approve the sale.[2] Furthermore, the court applied a line of Delaware authority holding that directors owe a fiduciary duty to common and preferred stockholders when dividing the consideration received in a merger or other extraordinary transaction.[3] But in most instances, there are no fiduciary obligations that accompany their relationship to the corporation.[4] By far the greatest problems with this classic contract-law approach have arisen when the bond or preferred share enjoys a conversion privilege that places their holder but a step away from full equity ownership. It is with respect to such securities that critics of the classic contract-law treatment of senior securities holders' rights make their strongest case, by emphasizing not only that it is nearly impossible to contract around every possible contingency but that in light of that impossibility there

---

[7] *See generally* George W. Dent, Jr., The Role of Convertible Securities in Corporate Finance, 21 Iowa J. Corp. L. 241 (1996); William Klein, The Convertible Bond: A Peculiar Package, 123 U. Pa. L. Rev. 547 (1975).

§18.15   [1] 741 A.2d 377 (Del. Ch. 1999).

[2] *Id.* at 390-391. The case would be even stronger if a shareholder vote were required, *see* Gilmartin v. Adobe Resources Corp., 1992 WL 71510 (Del. Ch., Apr. 6, 1992).

[3] *Id.* at 391. The court relied upon In re FLS Holdings, Inc. Shareholder Litig., 1993 WL 104562 (Del. Ch. Apr. 2, 1993), *aff'd*, 628 A.2d 84 (Del. 1993) (unpublished opinion).

[4] *See, e.g.,* Broad v. Rockwell Int'l Corp., 642 F.2d 929, 958-959 (5th Cir.) (en banc) (applying New York law), *cert. denied*, 454 U.S. 965 (1981).

B.   Preferred Stock: Financial Features and Equitable Protection of Rights

quite likely is purchased within the contract some rough semblance of fair treatment.[5]

> The characterization of the naked conversion privilege as a fragile option, while perfectly felicitous, is by no means inevitable. One can with equal felicity characterize the premium paid for the conversion privilege at original issue as an "equity" investment in the issuer and go on from there to require corporate law treatment of dilutent and destructive issuer actions.[6]

Following the developments that have touched modern contract law,[7] gaps in the indenture or preferred stock contract have sometimes been filled, however, by attributing to their contract an implied condition of good faith and fair dealing.[8]

A leading case for invoking an implied condition of good faith and fair dealing is *Van Gemert v. Boeing Company,*[9] involving convertible debentures whose terms required the company to give notice, and provided that such notice could be published in a newspaper, before exercising its option to redeem them. The court concluded that because the debentures did not specify the kind of notice that would be provided, the debenture holders were entitled to expect reasonable

---

[5] The leading critic of rigidly applying classic construction techniques is Professor William W. Bratton. *See* William W. Bratton, Corporate Debt Relationships: Legal Theory in a Time of Restructuring, 1989 Duke L.J. 92; William W. Bratton, The Interpretation of Contracts Governing Corporate Debt Relationships, 5 Cardozo L. Rev. 371 (1984). *See also* Victor Brudney, Corporate Bondholders and Debtor Opportunism: In Bad Times and Good, 105 Harv. L. Rev. 1821, 1870-1875 (1992) (arguing courts should interpret bond contracts to place the risk of unusual or not reasonably foreseeable debtor behavior on the debtor rather than the public bondholders); Marcel Kahan, The Qualified Case Against Mandatory Terms in Bonds, 89 Nw. U. L. Rev. 565, 613-620 (1995) (concluding that mandatory indenture terms or fiduciary obligations to bondholders will prove inefficient); Mark E. Van Der Weide, Against Fiduciary Duties to Corporate Stakeholders, 21 Del. J. Corp. L. 27 (1996) (analysis contrasts different position of equity and bondholders to conclude that extending fiduciary obligations to bondholders will decrease social wealth); Lawrence E. Mitchell, The Puzzling Paradox of Preferred Stock (And Why We Should Care About It), 51 Bus. Law. 443 (1996) (managerial opportunism vis-à-vis preferred shareholders should be addressed on an interim basis by protecting preferred shareholders' legitimate expectations); Larry Ribstein, Takeover Defenses and the Corporate Contract, 78 Geo. L.J. 71 (1989); Morrey McDaniel, Bondholders and Stockholders, 13 J. Corp. L. 205 (1988).

A thoughtful commentary on the unimportant role that courts have assumed and are likely to have in facilitating efficient contracting with respect to bond indentures, *see* Frederick W. Lambert, Path Dependent Inefficiency in the Corporate Contract: The Uncertain Case With Less Certain Implications, 23 Del. J. Corp. L. 1077 (1998).

[6] William W. Bratton, The Economics and Jurisprudence of Convertible Bonds, 1984 Wis. L. Rev. 683-684.

[7] *See generally* Robert S. Summers, The General Duty of Good Faith—Its Recognition and Conceptualization, 67 Cornell L. Rev. 810 (1982); Steven J. Burton, Breach of Contract and the Common Law Duty to Perform in Good Faith, 94 Harv. L. Rev. 369 (1980).

[8] *See* Rossdeutcher v. Viacom, Inc., 768 A.2d 8 (Del. 2001) (applying New York law to hold there was implied duty of good faith and fair dealing not to manipulate stock price so as to reduce the firm's liability to holders of rights that had variable value depending on how well the post-acquisition price of the firm performed); Merrill v. Crothall-American, Inc., 606 A.2d 96, 101 (Del. 1992) ("At common law the duty of fair dealing and good faith was deemed impliedly to be a part of contracts of every kind.").

[9] 520 F.2d 1373 (2d Cir.), *cert. denied,* 423 U.S. 947 (1975).

notice of the redemption call. The court held that fair and reasonable notice was not provided by the company to redeem its indentures, even though notice was published in the newspapers.[10]

Judicial restraint is very much a two-way street and can also work against the issuer and its fellow stockholders. *Reiss v. Financial Performance Corporation,*[11] concerned whether the exercise price of warrants should be adjusted upward following the corporation undertaking a one-for-five reverse stock split. On three different occasions the firm had issued warrants allowing their holder to acquire common shares at $.10 per share. Only for one of the three earlier transactions was there a provision adjusting the exercise price in the event of a reverse stock split. The corporation asked the court to imply such a provision for the other two warrant transactions so as to avoid their holders reaping a windfall. The Court of Appeals of New York held the parties rights must be determined from their contract and, since the contracts were not ambiguous, it refused to imply a provision as requested by the warrants' issuer.

---

[10] *Contra* Lohnes v. Level 3 Communications, Inc., 272 F.3d 49 (1st Cir. 2001) (warrant holders not entitled to personal notice of a forthcoming stock split that would erode the value of outstanding warrants).

[11] 764 N.E.2d 958 (N.Y. 2001).

CHAPTER 19

Accounting Statements and Dividend Law

§19.01   The Importance of Accounting to Corporate Law

There is a close interplay between accounting and many corporate transactions. For example, in the preceding chapter it was emphasized that accounting principles play a pivotal role in interpreting bond indentures and the preferred stock's contract when those provisions use expressions that have accounting significance. The connection is equally direct in the case of the states' regulation of corporate distributions, a point examined in the next two chapters. Therefore, because of the frequent interplay between corporate law and accounting, a solid understanding is necessary of the major conventions that underlie accounting principles as well as of the important financial statements produced through the accounting process.[1] This chapter reviews the major conventions on which

---

§19.01   [1] Proper accounting often depends on legal concepts. *See* Miguel de Capriles, Modern Financial Accounting (Pt. I), 37 N.Y.U. L. Rev. 1001 (1962), (Pt. II) 38 N.Y.U. L. Rev. 1 (1963); William P. Hackney, The Financial Provision of the Model Business Corporation Act, 70 Harv. L. Rev. 1357 (1957); Homer Kripke, A Case Study in the Relationship of Law and Accounting: Uniform Accounts 57 Harv. L. Rev. 433, 435, 693 (1944).

In addition to the foregoing authorities, helpful secondary sources include Lawrence A. Cunningham, Introductory Accounting and Finance (3d ed. 2002); David R. Herwitz & Matthew J. Barrett,

accounting principles are premised and provides an introduction to the two principal accounting statements: the balance sheet and the income statement.

On certain topics, such as valuation, depreciation, and depletion, the law impliedly adopts what may be termed "good accounting practice" or, as it is commonly and professionally designated, "generally accepted accounting principles" (GAAP). It should be noted, however, that the courts have the final say in interpreting corporation acts and on legal questions, as between conflicting accounting opinions, and tend to follow what will further the legal objective in view.

There have been recent departures from the traditional legal capital system in California and from the 1980 revisions to the Model Act, which were carried forward in the Revised Model Business Corporation Act in 1984. California expressly adopts GAAP and thus places the courts in the somewhat unusual position of final arbiter of proper accounting methods.[2]

§19.02   Major Conventions of Accounting

Nearly all generally accepted accounting principles are anchored in a set of major tenets, more commonly referred to as "accounting conventions. These conventions are briefly set forth below.

The Separate-Entity Assumption. Just as corporate law distinguishes the corporate entity from its owners, accounting statements reflect the performance and financial position of a distinct entity. Thus the financial statements of a corporation report its assets and income, not those of its stockholders; and this is also true for a partnership and its partners. To be sure, there are principles for presenting the performance and position of companies that are affiliated, known as consolidated financial statements, discussed below, but the overarching principle is that financial reports are developed from the viewpoint of a specific entity.

Cost Convention. The bedrock of accounting principles is that each purchase of assets, services, or expenses, as well as liabilities and owners' equity, is recorded at an item's historical cost (in contrast to the item's fair market value). Thus a building that was acquired ten years earlier is today depreciated on the basis of the cost of acquiring it ten years earlier, even though the building's current fair market value is much above its cost. Similarly, the building is reported on the balance sheet at its historical cost, less depreciation.

Accounting for Lawyers (2d ed. 1997); Ted J. Fiflis, Accounting Issues for Lawyers, Teaching Materials (4th ed. 1991); James D. Cox, Financial Information, Accounting and the Law (1980).

[2] This may cause more problems than the dual system of legal and general accounting principles poses because lawyers and judges are often ill equipped to deal with accounting technology. The 1980 revision of MBCA §45 adopts a reasonableness test as to accounting practices—that is, reasonable under the circumstances. The comments to the Act at 34 Bus. Law. 1867, 1884, state that the statute *does not* constitute a statutory enactment of GAAP. The statute, however, would permit the use of GAAP as a general rule.

To be sure, difficult questions sometimes arise in measuring an item's cost. For example, when stock is issued for Blackacre, there is a need to record a future value for the capital stock account as well as for Blackacre. In this situation the fair market value of Blackacre, assumed to be $500,000, is the cost for Blackacre and is also reported in the capital stock account to reflect what was received for the shares. From that point forward, however, Blackacre continues to be reported at $500,000, its cost, even though the land greatly appreciates in value. But the cost convention is not a two-way street. Should there be a material and permanent decline in an asset's market value, accounting requires the asset's carrying amount be reduced to its new, and lower, value. Thus accounting embodies a highly conservative view of the world in which purchases and assets are recorded at cost and any declines are recognized, but upward appreciation in value is not. Hence the old saying among accountants, "anticipate no gain and recognize all losses."

Constant-Dollar Assumption. Financial reports reflect measurements in a given type of currency, usually that of the company's principal domicile. Whether inflation is moderate or high, the true purchasing power of that unit of measurement is reduced over time. Nevertheless, financial reports are prepared on the assumption of a stable monetary unit or, alternatively expressed, that any changes in the monetary unit are not significant. At one time generally accepted accounting practice (GAAP) required public reporting companies to present information in the footnotes of the financial statements reflecting the effects of inflation; however, the recent modest rate of inflation has caused that requirement to be suspended.

Continuity Assumption. Statements are prepared based on the assumption the business will have a continuous existence. This is frequently referred to as the "going-concern assumption." Thus expenditures for such items as future insurance coverage, a new piece of machinery, and inventory are not charged against revenues as an expense if these assets are believed to contribute to the operations in future years. That is, by assuming an indefinite life for the business, the accountant can assign present expenditures to future years on the basis estimates regarding when a purchased item is likely to contribute to operations. If a going concern were not assumed, then all expenditures would be "expensed" in the year the item was purchased.

Discrete Reporting of Time-Periods. Even though a business is assumed to have an indefinite life, accounting reports provide periodic measurements of the firm's performance and financial position. Such periods are called fiscal periods and may be a quarter, a year (calendar year or fiscal year), or sometimes even longer. This requires discrete judgments as to what precise time-period revenues are to be reported and their matching expenses are to be identified. Such decisions are not always clear, and judgment calls invariably arise. Nevertheless, a cornerstone of financial reporting is the need for periodic information regarding the firm's health and operations, even though these reports must be understood not to present a perfectly accurate picture of the firm; perfect accuracy of the firm's overall performance and financial position can be known only when the firm terminates its existence and liquidates. But the users of financial information cannot wait until that day. Hence the assumption that the firm's performance can be divided into defined fiscal periods and reported on.

Realization Principle. A further manifestation of accounting conservatism is the realization principle, which is concerned with the timing of when revenue can be recognized. "Recognized" refers to when the financial statements can report an item's disposition as a sale among its revenues. Simply stated, revenue is not recognized until it is earned. With few exceptions, revenue is not realized until the goods that are sold have been transferred to their purchaser or the services that were acquired have been provided. Thus the primary test of revenue recognition is the completion of the seller's performance; in the case of goods, when title to the goods is transferred.[1]

Matching Principle. If statements were prepared solely on a cash basis, there would be no need for a matching principle. In using a cash basis, expenses are reported as liabilities are incurred or as cash is expended, and sales are recognized when payment in cash occurs. Most business records are not on a cash basis but on an accrual basis, under which the realization principle guides when revenue is reported and the matching principle determines when expenses are recognized. Under the matching principle, accounting decisions essentially entail a two-step process. First, revenues are determined pursuant to the realization principle. Thus goods shipped to customers on account are recorded as sales, even though the customer's cash payment has not yet been received. The important difference, therefore, between the cash and accrual basis of reporting is that the latter allows revenue recognition even though cash has not been received. The second step is *matching* the revenues to be recognized in the fiscal period with all the expenses incurred to produce those revenues. This process requires numerous judgments and estimates as to the connection between realized revenues and their related expenses.

The Consistency Principle. This principle calls for the consistent use of the same method or standard in recording and reporting transactions over successive periods. The consistent use of the same assumptions, approach, and reporting method assures comparability over time. Nevertheless, GAAP does permit assumptions, estimates, and principles to change, provided there is sufficient collateral disclosure.[2]

§19.03 The Balance Sheet

The balance sheet sets forth a company's cumulative financial position as of a specific date. Thus the balance sheet reports on the composition of the company's

---

§19.02 [1] *See generally* Lanny G. Chasteen, Richard E. Flaherty & Melvin C. O'Connor, Intermediate Accounting 329-361 (6th ed. 1998).

[2] *See* AICPA APB Opinion No. 20, Accounting Changes (Aug. 1971).

assets, liabilities, and owners' equity at a fixed point in time, whereas the income statement reports the company's operations over a period of time. In separately stating the amount and composition of all the company's assets, and also reporting the totals of its liabilities and owners' equity, the balance sheet follows the established accounting equation where

$$\text{Total Assets} = \text{Total Liabilities} + \text{Total Owners' Equity}$$

As will be seen, the balance sheet is the basic financial report for dividend purposes; most important, it indicates whether, pursuant to an older regulatory pattern, a corporation has sufficient "surplus," or, pursuant to statutes patterned after the current Model Business Corporation Act, its assets are sufficient in light of the firm's liabilities, so that there is a basis for dividends or other distributions to shareholders.

The balance sheet may appear to be inferior to the income statement, the other major financial statement, but when the two are read in tandem, the relationship between them becomes manifest. More specifically, the amount of net income reported on the income statement, together with the amount of dividends, explains the change in net surplus (retained earnings) from the beginning to the end of the accounting period. The balance sheet lists the assets, liabilities, capital, and surplus in two sections or groups: one on the left side—a classified list of the assets with their book values (generally reflecting historical cost less depreciation), the other on the right side—a classified list of the liabilities, capital, and surplus (or shareholders' equity) and their amounts. A vertical arrangement with assets placed at the top may also be used. The capital represented by the different classes of shares and the different kinds of surplus are entered along with the true liabilities on the right side of the balance sheet. The difference between the assets and the liabilities to creditors is sometimes called the net assets or net worth of the enterprise.[1] It is more frequently referred to as the "equity" of the shareholders— their proprietary interest—and indicates the "book value" of the shares.[2] If the value of the assets is less than the sum of the amount of the liabilities plus the legal or stated capital, then there is a capital deficit. If the value of the assets, at a proper

---

§19.03   [1] For a typical statutory definition of net assets, *see* former MBCA §2(i) (1969). The convenient term "net worth," which indicates the value of the net assets, was at one time widely used but is now almost never found in published balance sheets or accounting publications. The reason for this is that capital and surplus usually do not truly represent the excess of going-concern value of the business over liabilities to outsiders or creditors. This is due to the methods of valuation of fixed assets, which are listed at historical cost, and the fact that balance sheets do not purport to show the true value of intangibles, such as good will, patents, and trade secrets and processes. Lenders, courts, and corporate managements often rely on balance sheets as some evidence of net worth, although they do not purport to show the present realizable value of the net assets.

[2] The objectives of financial reporting, as set forth in Financial Accounting Standards Board (FASB) Concepts Statement No. 1, do not require accounting information to directly measure the value of the business enterprise. That is, balance sheets are not intended to reflect enterprise market value. This value estimation is the role of investment analysis, not accounting. Accounting provides information useful for the analysis.

valuation, is less than the liabilities to creditors properly estimated, then the corporation is insolvent, at least in the bankruptcy sense.[3]

§19.04   Classification of Assets on the Balance Sheet

Assets are stated at their acquisition cost, less any changes due to depreciation, depletion, or amortization. Owners' equity reports not only the amount invested in the company but also cumulative increases arising from profitable operations (retained earnings) or decreases due to a net loss from operations. These terms are defined according to generally accepted accounting principles.

In addition to being broadly grouped into assets, liabilities, and stockholders' (owners') equity, the balance sheet's individual items are classified into subcategories according to an underlying characteristic. The most basic subcategories are the following:

Assets	Liabilities	Stockholders' Equity
Current Assets	Current Liabilities	Capital Stock
Fixed Assets	Long-Term Liabilities	Capital in Excess of Par Value
Other Assets	Deferred Credits[1]	Retained Earnings

The above classifications are not exclusive. For example, a parent company's investment in a subsidiary will appear on its unconsolidated balance sheet as "Investments" and appears after Fixed Assets and before Other Assets. Also, over time a highly ambiguous fourth category has developed between Liabilities and Stockholders' Equity, entitled "Deferred Income" or "Deferred Credits." Deferred income refers to advance payments for goods that have not yet been shipped or for services to be provided by the company in the future. In such cases, the *recognition* of revenue is held not yet to have been *realized* because of such non-shipment of goods or non-provision of services. Thus the receipt of revenues in connection with a transaction for which realization has not occurred because of the tenets of the realization convention are reported on the balance sheet as deferred income. Deferred credits most frequently arise because many items or transactions are reported differently in determining taxable income than in determining net income on the company's financial statement. The cumulative differences between the tax expense reported on the company's financial statement

---

[3] "Insolvency" as defined in the federal Bankruptcy Code is the excess of liabilities over assets valued at fair value. 11 U.S.C. §101(31) (2000). This is in contrast to defining "insolvency" in terms of the inability to pay debts as they become due.

§19.04   [1] The term "credit" has its own, indeed arbitrary, meaning in accounting. It is not synonymous with a benefit or privilege owned by the company. "Credit" refers merely to an entry that appears on the right-hand side of an account, the left side being the debit side.

and the tax liability actually determined on its tax return are reported as deferred tax credits.

Current Assets. Current assets include cash in banks and on hand, accounts receivable, notes receivable, and marketable securities that are readily converted into cash. The current-assets category also includes less liquid assets, such as inventories, finished goods, work in process, raw materials, and factory supplies that may soon be salable. The standard definition of items suitable for inclusion within "current assets" covers items reasonably expected to be converted into cash or consumed within one year or one operating cycle, whichever is longer.[2] The true significance of current assets is their ability to be converted into cash during normal operations. Assets within this category are the first, if not principal, source for satisfying a company's liabilities and other cash needs in the short run. "Working capital" usually refers to the net current assets—that is, the excess of current assets over current liabilities available for use in the business operations.[3] Entries are generally listed at historical cost.

Inventories include goods held for sale, goods in production, or goods that are consumed in the ordinary course of business. Because inventories are constantly being replenished, some assumptions are made regarding the order of their replacement. Common methods used are LIFO (last in, first out) and FIFO (first in, first out). While the latter no doubt reflects the physical flow of most goods, the former more nearly matches cost with actual operations if one sees the act of replenishing inventory as the cost of the goods that gave rise to the need to replenish the inventory.

The basis of valuation for securities and inventories, however, is frequently indicated "at the lower of cost or market" or "cost or market, whichever is lower." Special provision is generally made for slow and doubtful accounts to reflect their actual or discounted worth. The assets are ordinarily listed in the general order in which they may be turned into cash or, as it is often expressed, in the order of their "liquidity."

An entity's financial status for immediate credit purposes is not indicated merely by the proportion that exists between the total assets and the total liabilities but even more so by the current ratio between them. "The current ratio" represents the proportion of the current assets to the current liabilities—that is, between the more immediate liabilities to be met and the various kinds of assets that will be available for meeting them. Even though total assets far exceed the liabilities, forced liquidation may occur if these assets are "frozen,"—that is, are not a kind that may be relied upon to raise needed cash. Working capital and the current ratio thus provide a better indication of a corporation's financial liquidity. It is not, however, *per se* unlawful to declare a dividend when there is a sufficient

---

[2] The operating cycle is the combined time, on average, to acquire, process, and sell inventory, plus the time necessary to realize cash from any sales made on credit.

[3] That is, if all of the current assets were converted into cash at their book value and all of the current liabilities paid at their book value, working capital would be the amount of cash remaining.

surplus of assets over liabilities, although there may not be sufficient cash or liquid assets on hand, and borrowing to pay the dividends may be necessary.[4]

Fixed Assets. Fixed assets comprise those that are held indefinitely for the purpose of conducting the business, as contrasted with those that are intended for sale. Assets within this category contribute to future operations through their use or consumption during a longer time period than one year or operating cycle. They may be tangible or intangible property interests owned by the business and include land, buildings, machinery, and equipment as well as goodwill, patents, trade secrets, and other intangible assets. Overvaluation of tangible or intangible assets has frequently been the cause for skepticism as to whether such assets' fair market value can ever be reliably determined.[5]

Fixed asset value, as represented on the balance sheet according to GAAP, is not customarily based on a fair market appraisal or realizable value of the asset. Rather, the value is a record of the original cost of the asset, less the estimated depreciation that has accrued to date.[6] In this respect, the balance sheet is largely an historical record, because fixed asset valuations are often greater than any recorded amounts. As a result, the capital and surplus accounts, as far as being dependent on the historical cost of the fixed assets or even on their present appraisal, are usually of little significance as bearing on the ability to pay either debts or dividends. Current assets as opposed to fixed assets are the liquid resources. These assets are customarily (and conservatively) stated on the basis of cost or market, whichever is lower. Generally, the basis of all asset values should be, and is, disclosed more clearly in footnotes to the balance sheet than in its corpus. The Securities and Exchange Commission has formulated extensive policies as to the necessary accounting and valuation bases so as not to make these public disclosures misleading. These standards of reporting are provided by the accounting profession.[7] These recognize that historical cost can no longer be the sole basis of valuation for all purposes.

Deferred Charges and Prepaid Expenses. This special class of debits, seemingly of relatively minor importance, might best not be designated as assets. By definition, a "deferred charge" is an expenditure for a service that will contribute to the generation of revenues in the future. Prepaid expenses, as the name implies, more closely resemble operating expenses but are temporarily designated as assets, until

[4] Steele v. Locke Cotton Mills Co., 58 S.E.2d 620 (N.C. 1950). *See generally* Gabriel A. D. Preinreich, The Nature of Dividends (reprinted ed. 1978).

[5] Randall v. Bailey, 23 N.Y.S.2d 173, 177 (Sup. Ct. 1940), *aff'd,* 43 N.E.2d 43 (N.Y. 1942).

[6] William W. Pyle, Fundamental Accounting Principles 29 (13th ed. 1993) (former authors, William W. Pyle & John Arch White).

[7] The FASB, in its Statement of Financial Accounting Standards No. 33, requires large public enterprises to file supplemental reports with their financial statements to provide, among other information, the increase or decrease in the current costs of inventory and plant and equipment. SEC Accounting Series Release No. 287 adopts the same position. *See* 6 Fed. Sec. L. Rep. (CCH) ¶1172, 309. *See generally* Douglas W. Hawes, Symposium on Accounting and the Federal Securities Laws, 28 Vand. L. Rev. 1 (1975).

they are consumed by the business. Examples of prepaid expenses are prepaid premiums for insurance covering the protection one or more years in advance, and rent paid in advance. These two examples represent expenses that are not charged against income for the period in which incurred but instead set up as prepayments, to be amortized (or "expensed") as they are used up. In contrast, deferred charges may be described as long-term prepaid expenses. One example is the unamortized debt on bond discount plus the expense of the bond issue. Likewise, legitimate organizational costs may be regarded as creating intangible assets for a going concern, from which the earning capacity of the business will benefit over long periods. Therefore these too are designated as deferred charges and are also amortized periodically.

§19.05   Classification of Liabilities

Liabilities are customarily designated as current or long-term. Current liabilities are those debts and obligations that are reasonably expected to be paid during the upcoming year or operating cycle. Liabilities that do not qualify as current liabilities appear under the heading Long-Term Liabilities and include such items as mortgages payable and bonds payable. Each class of bonds or debentures should be shown on the balance sheet at the face value of the bonds outstanding, with the maturity date and interest rate included. Any discount or premium on the issuance of the bond should also be shown, but in a separate or "contra" account. These contra accounts are customarily amortized using the straight line or the interest rate method, based on the valuation period and the actual and effective interest rates. The two accounts—the face value and the contra entries—are netted to show the amount owing on the account. Furthermore, serial maturities of long-term liabilities should be transferred to the current liability group within the last year before maturity because these amounts then become current.

Current liabilities are usually sub-classified into three or four accounts, such as accounts payable, notes payable, dividends payable, accrued liabilities, and taxes payable. Customarily, debts maturing within a year are current liabilities, although in rare cases, such as when a business's operating cycle is longer than one calendar year, its current liabilities may not mature within that period.

A demand of any sort against a corporation, even though contingent, unliquidated, or disputed, such as a damage claim or a guaranty of another's obligation, is still characterized as a liability. The accountant thus has a difficult task in estimating the nature and amount of contingent liabilities. Once they are recognized, the accountant must choose between determining whether to make the disclosure in the balance sheet itself or in the accompanying footnotes. This choice is necessary because contingent liabilities not sufficiently certain to be estimable are usually reflected in footnotes to the financial statement, rather than specifically in a balance sheet account. Nevertheless, where possible, a reserve against contingencies should be provided if there is a substantial likelihood of such contingent liabilities accruing. Despite their separate treatment, notes to balance sheets, especially qualifications in the accountant's certification to the financial statement with regard to them, must be read with care, as they too can be a basis for the accountant's liability for malpractice or negligence in performing the audit function.

§19.06   Stockholders' Equity Accounts

The various classes of shares of stock are all listed in the corporation's balance sheet. The balance sheet displays information as to the number or amount of par value of shares authorized and the number and amount of shares outstanding as well as those shares that have been repurchased and are thus carried on the books as treasury shares. The rights, privileges, and preferences of each class of stock are also presented in summary fashion. In the case of corporations whose shares have a par value, the "capital stock" entry usually sets forth the aggregate par value of the shares authorized and also of those issued and outstanding, each class of shares being shown separately if more than one exists. In the case of no-par shares, the stated capital figure usually represents the aggregate capital contributions of all the issued shares.

Shares of stock outstanding are usually represented at their aggregate par value if they have such, or otherwise at their stated value. Reflecting par value in the capital stock account is more or less mechanical and traditional, for it has little or no reliability as a record of the amount of actual investment of the shareholders in the business. The directors may allocate a larger part of the paid-in capital to stated capital rather than account for it as capital surplus. The customary capital stock entry corresponds more closely to the important concept of stated or legal capital.[1] Therefore once an amount is designated as legal capital, it acts as a limitation to the capital margin. Thus legal capital limits distributions, rather than representing a figure of any independent financial significance.[2] All corporation laws, except California's and those of states adopting the current Model Business Corporation Act,[3] still adhere to the legal-capital basis of accounting and thus requires a working knowledge thereof on the part of corporate counsel.

Accumulated but undistributed profits are reported in earned surplus/retained earnings. A word about the choice of parlance with this item. "Earned surplus" is the term used in the older varieties of corporate statutes; however, the accounting profession eschews using "surplus" correctly seeing it as an ambiguous expression poorly understood by investors. The accounting profession thus

---

§19.06   [1] Legal capital is computed as the number of shares outstanding multiplied by their par value, stated value, or issue price (for no-par shares). The amount of legal capital is properly recorded in the capital stock account. Amounts received in excess of legal capital should be recorded in other appropriately designated accounts.

[2] *See generally* Case v. New York Cent. R.R., 232 N.Y.S.2d 702 (Sup. Ct. 1962), *rev'd*, 243 N.Y.S.2d 620, 19 A.D.2d 383 (App. Div. 1963), *rev'd*, 204 N.E.2d 643 (N.Y. 1965); Robert A. Kessler, Business Associations, 15 Syracuse L. Rev. 235, 247 (1964). *See also* Current Issues on the Legality of Dividends from a Law and Accounting Perspective: A Task Force Report, 39 Bus. Law. 289 (1983).

[3] Cal. Gen. Corp. Law §§501 *et seq.* (West 1990); Changes in the Model Business Corporation Act— Amendments to Financial Provisions, 34 Bus. Law. 1867 (1979) adopted 35 Bus. Law. 1365 (1980).

prefers the expression "retained earnings." The amount recorded in earned surplus/retained earnings represents the sum of all profits since the company was formed, less any losses or dividends paid to its shareholders since its formation. Sometimes this account is restricted or appropriated to meet future contingencies or expenditures. The effect of such a restriction (frequently referred to as a "reserve") is to reduce the company's future ability to purchase its shares or declare dividends, since both those acts depend on the amount of *unrestricted* earned surplus or retained earnings.

Losses from operations are recorded as reductions in earned surplus (retained earnings) and, should the losses exceed such accumulated earnings, a deficit will thus appear in earned surplus (retained earnings). In no case will the deficit appear other than in the Stockholders' Equity section of the balance sheet. When earned surplus (retained earnings) has a negative balance, it effectively reduces pro tanto the balance for stockholders' equity.

§19.07   The Income or Profit and Loss Statement

The mission of the income statement is to report the net income or loss for a given fiscal period, such as a quarter or year. In broad overview, it reports the revenues realized less the expenses incurred to produce those revenues plus any other gains or losses during that reporting period. Because the accountant assumes the business will have an infinite life, the task of accounting is to provide reliable measurements within discrete fiscal periods of the firm's performance. As a result of dividing reported operations into successive fiscal periods, it becomes necessary to employ a variety of assumptions, estimates, and judgments in the allocation of revenues and expenses among successive fiscal periods. In combination, these decisions introduce a good deal of uncertainty as to the accuracy of what is actually captured on the financial statements.

The income statement usually reflects "earnings from operations" or "profit from operations" in a general format. The income statement may particularize as to the gross sales and net sales or other revenue, as well as "nonrecurring" income, after deducting the cost of sales and operations, administrative and general expenses, maintenance and repairs, and provision for taxes, depreciation, depletion, amortization, and unusual expenses and losses. The income statement is concerned with the earning results and realized gain or loss for an accounting period. Because it best bears on the financial performance of the firm over a recent fiscal period it is viewed by many as the most important financial statement. In the income statement, the cost of goods sold, including selling, administrative, and general expenses, are subtracted from sales, thus bearing a net income (or loss) figure. Depreciation, depletion, and amortization taken during the year are also subtracted as normal operating costs or expenses of the business. In a manufacturing operation, such charges become imbedded in the cost of the goods manufactured during the fiscal period. Thus the depreciation of an asset, such as the machinery in the company's plant, is first allocated to the products manufactured during that fiscal period. As recorded, it becomes part of the asset "inventory." It is only when the manufactured product is sold that depreciation is effectively charged against revenues, such charge being imbedded in the cost of goods sold for that fiscal period.

As seen earlier, a major accounting convention is that revenues or income is recognized when earned—whether or not received in cash—and expenses are recognized when incurred—whether or not paid in cash.[1] Most businesses and substantially all corporations use the accrual method of ascertaining income or profit and loss instead of the simpler but less informative cash basis. "Accrual accounting" is a system that matches expenses with revenues but does not require the actual receipt of cash as a precondition for revenue recognition.

Depreciation in the Income Statement. As described above, there can be no profits recognized until all expenses, depletions, and depreciation have been deducted. No one would think of computing the profits of a factory by omitting from the cost of the goods sold the value of the fuel consumed in manufacturing. Likewise, the value of the machinery is consumed in the manufacturing process just as truly as is the fuel. Depreciation reflects this decrease in value due to the "wear and tear" of machinery. Depreciation is an inevitable element of operating cost and must therefore be reckoned in determining profits. The federal income tax laws have done much to improve accounting practice in this respect. Depreciation is thus to be treated as an operating expense, or equivalent entry, that is deductible from current or operating revenue before obtaining the net operating income.

Direct Charges of Certain Losses to Surplus. A serious question is whether unusual losses on items not connected with ordinary operations of the period and extraordinary non-recurring charges are to be included in the annual profit-and-loss statement or whether they should be shown elsewhere. An increase in assets due to the additional investment of funds is not entered in the income account. A question also arises as to whether certain losses that have undoubtedly diminished the net value of the corporation should be reflected in the income statement or instead are to be treated as deductions from earned surplus. At one time, an extraordinary loss, say by earthquake or fire, was sometimes accounted for as a loss of earned or paid-in surplus rather than as a deduction from the profits of the period.[2] The accounting profession has greatly restricted such extraordinary items from bypassing the income statement.[3] Today, extraordinary gains and losses are separately reported in the income statement, not in the statement of earned surplus. The income statement is then reconciled with a surplus statement commonly

---

§19.07   [1] The major objective of accounting is the determination of periodic net income by matching appropriate costs against revenues. The timely recognition of income and related expenses reflects this objective, which is called the "matching principle." *See* §19.02.

[2] The effect of an extraordinary item, if material, should be classified separately in the income statement. The Accounting Principles Board, in APB Opinion No. 30 (Oct. 1973), provides, as an authoritative guide, that "extraordinary items" refer to events or transactions that are *both* unusual and infrequent in occurrence. APB Opinion No. 30, AICPA, Professional Standards §§2010.16, 2012.10. *See* David F. Hawkins, Corporate Financial Reporting 248 (rev. ed. 1977).

[3] *See* APB Opinion No. 30, Reporting Results of Operations (June 1973).

termed the "statement of retained earnings." This statement shows the opening and closing balance of the earned surplus (retained earnings) account and the changes that occurred throughout the fiscal year such as by the payment of dividends or the repurchase of shares. Moreover, the income statement should be reconciled with the balance sheet regarding the increase or decrease of earned surplus shown thereon by reason of unusual sources of gain or loss. An income report for a particular year, like a single balance sheet, should not be relied on to show earning capacity but should be compared with those of preceding years to ascertain the trend of earnings.

Explanatory Comments. Balance sheets and income statements often seem needlessly cryptic and obscure. Supplementary explanatory comments as to the different classes of assets and liabilities, reserves, and surplus are often supplied for the enlightenment of shareholders and investors in connection with the technical financial exhibits. Generally accepted accounting practice mandates the use of footnotes, parenthetical notes, and discussion statements to explain the figures shown on financial statements, especially with regard to foreign investments, contingent liabilities (such as pending lawsuits), bases of valuation, and investments in subsidiary companies.[4] Certain important qualifications, warnings, explanations, or even disclaimers may be called for in the accountant's comments and certificate. This statement, called the auditor's report, consists of a concise report by the auditor or public accountant expressing an opinion on the statement and the representations it contains, and how far the auditor assumes responsibility for its fairness of presentation. Such matters as changes in accounting practice and unusual accounting methods should be disclosed clearly and prominently.

§19.08   Consolidated Financial Statements

Where, as often happens, a group of affiliated companies make up one large business enterprise conducted by a parent or holding company, with one or more subsidiaries and affiliates, annual reports generally include consolidated financial statements. The consolidated statements are really an economic concept, valid only as to the creditors and shareholders of the parent corporation. The statements and the financial status of the enterprises, or system as a whole, operate as though they were a single entity.[1] This method does not purport to represent the statements of one particular entity; it is simply a device used for reporting purposes.

A consolidated balance sheet eliminates the parent company's investment in each of its associated companies; the actual assets and liabilities of such companies being substituted therefor. Thus the statement includes assets that legally do not belong to the parent corporation but are instead the property of affiliated corporations. Any minority interest in affiliated companies—that is, the shares held by

---

[4] *See* SEC Regulation S-X, Rule 3-16, 17 C.F.R. §210.3-16 (2002).
§19.08   [1] *See* David R. Herwitz & Mathew J. Barrett, Accounting for Lawyers 115 (1997).

non-affiliates—must be shown on the right-hand side of the balance sheet, because such outstanding shares, in the public's hands, have an equity interest in the assets of their respective companies. Although the parent company may have an equity interest of only four-fifths of the net assets of its subsidiary companies, the entire complex of assets of all the companies is used in the artificial, consolidated enterprise. As a general rule, consolidated statements will not include a subsidiary unless it is more than 50 percent owned. As noted above, the fact that there is a divided interest in these assets is accounted for by exhibiting on the right-hand side of the balance sheet the portion of the value of the net assets to be allocated to the holdings of the minority or outside shareholders.

Additional modification is necessary in the consolidated balance sheet with regard to intercompany relations where an asset of one of the associated corporations consists of a liability of another member of the group. For financial reporting purposes, the effects of intercorporate transactions must be removed from all consolidated financial statements. Intercompany receivables and payables are also eliminated and should not appear in the consolidated statement. As for liabilities, the consolidated balance sheet shows the combined amounts owing from the parent company and the associated companies to outsiders or public holders. This assures that gain or loss is recognized in consolidated statements only when a member of the consolidated entity has transactions with entities that are not members of the group.

By taking the above-mentioned measures, the consolidated balance sheet thus summarizes the total assets of a group of companies and indicates the parent company's pro rata portion of the cash, inventory, and other assets of the consolidated entities. A consolidated balance sheet thus aims to cut through the artificial legal subdivision of a group of companies and presents the actual assets and liabilities of the entire economic unit. Through this format, consolidated statements provide a comprehensive view of the situation of the combined business as a whole.

CHAPTER 20

Dividend Distributions: Rights, Restrictions, and Liabilities

A. RIGHTS TO DIVIDENDS

§20.01 Declaration and Payment of Dividends

A dividend is properly declared by formal resolution of the board of directors specifying the amount, the time of payment, and the "record date," and fixing the date for ascertaining the shareholders of record. Most dividends are distributed to shareholders in the form of cash. Distributions may also be made in property or in the corporation's own shares. Regardless of the method of declaration or payment, the distribution of dividends among shareholders of the same class must be without discrimination and pro rata unless it is otherwise agreed by all.[1]

§20.02 Directors' Refusal to Declare Dividends

A corporation may have a surplus or accumulated profits legally available for dividends, but the right of the shareholders to the making of any distribution is dependent on the exercise of the directors' good faith discretion with regard to financial advisability at the time.[1] An abuse of this discretion may call for equitable relief.

There are two dangers of abuse of the directors' discretion in declaring or withholding dividends. One is a policy of wastefulness or prodigality—improvident distributions that are injurious to present or future creditors and investors reduce working capital and weaken the corporation as a going concern. The converse abuse is undue accumulation beyond the reasonable needs of the business—the arbitrary refusal to pay shareholders a fair return on their investment when it clearly would be possible and wise to divide accumulated profits. Investors purchasing shares in a business often expect to obtain a return in the form of more or less regular dividends according to the corporation's ability to pay. The management's desire for expansion and more compensation instead of dividends in some cases may defeat the shareholders' just expectations.[2] The law has been concerned primarily with restraining dividend distributions that are dangerous to the rights of corporate creditors.

Directors are the judges of the financial and business situation and what dividends shareholders can have, and when. But as judges they are by no means always fair, unbiased, or impartial. Management and shareholders, particularly in modern large-scale corporations, often have conflicting interests. Because the shareholders may own only a few shares, it may be more profitable for the direc-

---

§20.01 [1] Stout v. Oates, 234 S.W.2d 506 (Ark. 1950); Perata v. Oakland Scavenger Co., 244 P.2d 940 (Cal. Ct. App. 1952).

§20.02 [1] An obvious justification is that the corporation does not satisfy the minimum statutory requirements for the payment of dividends. See, e.g., Jones v. Jones, 637 N.Y.S.2d 83 (N.Y. Sup. Ct. App. Div. 1996).

[2] Miller v. Magline, Inc., 256 N.W.2d 761 (Mich. Ct. App. 1977); Patton v. Nicholas, 279 S.W.2d 848 (Tex. 1955).

A. Rights to Dividends

tors, and the officers who influence them, to expand the investment and divert the flow of income to fixed salaries and "incentive" compensation by profit-sharing contracts and bonuses rather than to distribute a large share of the profits to those whom they represent.[3] The directors have wide discretion as to the proper amount of compensation for executive officers, but it may be judicially reviewed. Their discretion does not extend to wasteful diversion of income that fails to leave a fair return to the shareholders.

Many may have the false belief that judicial review of the board's dividend policy is a simple inquiry that calls for little more than reviewing the company's most recent financial statements to ascertain whether operations are sufficient to justify a modest return on the shareholder's investment. This perspective on the question ignores the role that earnings play in the ongoing financial planning of the corporation.

The major source of funds for business expansion is the accumulated but undistributed profits of the business. The board of directors' decision to expand the business opens a host of questions as to how the expansion should be financed—by issuance of equity, by debt, or from undistributed earnings. Even though a school of financial theory counsels that the firm's value is not impacted by whichever of these choices occurs,[4] this "irrelevancy principle" can be seen as placing more emphasis on intangible considerations that are best commended to the board of directors unless an abuse of discretion is otherwise demonstrated. Thus the courts hesitate to substitute their judgment on complicated questions of business policy for that of the elected managers of the business and have limited the scope of judicial review that they are willing to undertake.

It is accordingly a well-settled doctrine that whether or not dividends shall be paid, and the amount of the distribution at any time, is primarily to be determined in the good faith discretion of the directors.[5] Courts examine directors' decisions regarding dividends through the lens of the business judgment rule. In fact the rhetoric of the cases suggest a slightly more deferential standard, stating the court will not intrude upon the decision to not declare dividends absent "fraud or gross abuse of discretion."[6] In sum, dividend declarations are like other matters within the discretion of the board of directors for which director judgments are presumptively valid. The mere fact that a corporation reports a substantial surplus or large profits out of which a dividend might lawfully be declared is not of itself sufficient ground to compel the directors to make a dividend.[7] Directors are given a great deal of discretion to use corporate resources to expand the business, to

---

[3] Adolf A. Berle & Gardiner C. Means, The Modern Corporation and Private Property 112-116 (rev. ed. 1968).

[4] The seminal work on this topic is Franco Modigliani & Merton Miller, The Cost of Capital, Corporation Finance and the Theory of Investment, 48 Amer. Econ. Rev. 261 (1958).

[5] In re Reading Co., 711 F.2d 509 (3d Cir. 1983); Gabelli & Co. v. Liggett Group, Inc., 479 A.2d 276 (Del. 1984); Sinclair Oil Corp. v. Levien, 280 A.2d 717 (Del. 1971) (minority shareholder's complaint of excessive dividends); Berwald v. Mission Dev. Co., 185 A.2d 480 (Del. 1962).

[6] See, e.g., Baron v. Allied Artists Pictures Corp., 337 A.2d 653, 659 (Del. Ch. 1975); Cashman v. Petrie, 201 N.E.2d 24, 25-26 (N.Y. 1964).

[7] In re Estate of Butterfield, 341 N.W.2d 453 (Mich. 1983).

increase executive compensation by bonuses and profit-sharing contracts, and to establish various reserves if they consider it to be in the interests of the corporation to do so. Thus many reasonable bases have successfully been advanced to justify the directors' decision not to declare dividends: the seasonable nature of the business,[8] new equipment and the possible relocation of a plant,[9] the repurchase of outstanding shares,[10] expansion of business and a contingency for increased competition,[11] and to buffer the corporation against the possible loss of a major account.[12]

However, it is generally supposed that the end and purpose of a business corporation is to do business and earn profits for its shareholders rather than for its management. Ordinarily, it is not the corporate purpose to go on year after year accumulating a surplus indefinitely without prospects of dividends, or to pay out all income in extravagant compensation. Earnings that clearly warrant dividends may not be withheld or diverted fraudulently or for adverse personal motives; in clear and extreme cases of abuse of managerial discretion, a court of equity will give relief.[13]

Dodge v. Ford Motor Company[14] is the classic case of a court compelling distribution of an excessive accumulated surplus.[15] Two minority shareholders[16] holding one-tenth of the issued shares sued to compel the distribution of an extra dividend of not less than three-fourths of the available surplus. Henry Ford, who controlled the directors, had stated that the greater part of the profits should be put back into expanding the business in order to increase employment and sell more cars at a lower price per car. The court said, "A business corporation is organized and carried on primarily for the profit of the stockholders. . . . The discretion of the directors is to be exercised in the choice of means to attain that end, and does not extend to a change in the end itself, to the reduction of profits, or to the non-distribution of profits among stockholders in order to devote them to other purposes."[17]

In most cases where dividends have been compelled, it has been shown that the directors willfully abused their discretion by withholding distributions because

---

[8] Iwasaki v. Iwasaki Bros., 649 P.2d 598 (Or. 1982).

[9] In re Reading Co., 711 F.2d 509 (Pa. 1983); Zidell v. Zidell, Inc., 560 P.2d 1086 (Or. 1977).

[10] Kohn v. Birmingham Realty Co., 352 So. 2d 834 (Ala. 1977).

[11] Gay v. Gay's Super Markets, Inc., 343 A.2d 577 (Me. 1975).

[12] Coduti v. Hellwig, 469 N.E.2d 220 (Ill. 1984).

[13] Channon v. H. Channon Co., 218 Ill. App. 397 (1920); Cole Real Estate Corp. v. Peoples Bank & Trust Co., 310 N.E.2d 275 (Ind. Ct. App. 1974); Dodge v. Ford Motor Co., 170 N.W. 668 (Mich. 1919); Miller v. Magline, Inc., 256 N.W.2d 761 (Mich. Ct. Appls. 1977) (compelling dividend and retaining jurisdiction).

[14] 170 N.W. 668 (Mich. 1919).

[15] It appeared that on July 31, 1916, the defendant, a close corporation, had a surplus of almost $112,000,000, that it could expect a net annual income of at least $60,000,000 a year, and that it had cash on hand and municipal bonds amounting to virtually $54,000,000.

[16] "After this case, Ford acquired the dissenters' stock. The Dodge brothers used these funds in developing the rival firm that bore their name . . . although the firm later passed under the control of Walter Chrysler." Detlev F. Vagts, Basic Corporation Law 110 (2d ed. 1979).

[17] 170 N.W. at 684. The Michigan Supreme Court affirmed the lower court's decree requiring the distribution of 50 percent of the accumulated cash surplus as dividends. It reversed the lower court's injunctions, which would have effectively limited Ford's expansion program, however.

of an adverse interest, a wrongful purpose, or bad faith. In one case, dividends had not been declared in more than 20 years, even though the firm was profitable and its majority stockholder had awarded herself with an excessive salary and had misappropriated the company's assets.[18] More frequently the prevailing minority stockholder is able to link the nonpayment of dividends to a larger scheme to drive the minority out of the corporation.[19]

By far the greatest success plaintiffs have had in challenging the nonpayment of dividends has been within closely held corporations. It would appear that personal hostility is more visible and thus easier to establish in the close corporation. It is also much easier to refute the business justifications advanced for nonpayment in a close corporation. The authority of the directors is usually said to be absolute as long as they act in the exercise of honest judgment. If the refusal to make a distribution of profits is shown to be clearly unjust even though no fraud or intent to harm the shareholders appears, some courts have indicated that relief should be given and that the minority shareholders should not wait indefinitely while profits are needlessly accumulated.[20] It should be noted that the limitation on the discretion of directors of close corporations may not apply to large corporations with listed stock and a ready market that reflects capital appreciation.

§20.03 Rescission or Revocation of Dividend Declarations

A director's resolution declaring a cash dividend probably does not become immediately binding and irrevocable until an announcement to the shareholders or to the public. A leading Massachusetts case held that a directors' vote authorizing a dividend may be revoked if it has not been made public or communicated to the shareholders.[1]

It has been asserted that directors ought to have power, in the exercise of their sound discretion and in the absence of estoppel, to countermand payment of a declared dividend.[2] There are plausible arguments for this view in case of a serious mistake as to business prospects or the destruction of the corporation's plant by fire, earthquake, or other disaster soon after the passage of the resolution. But the arguments against the directors' power to rescind dividends after

---

[18] *See* Cole Real Estate Corp. v. Peoples Bank & Trust Co., 310 N.E.2d 275 (Ind. Ct. App. 1974).

[19] *See, e.g.,* Fischer v. Stealville Community Banc-Shares, 713 S.W.2d 850 (Mo. Ct. App. 1986).

[20] Stevens v. United States Steel Corp., 59 A. 905, 907 (N.J. Ch. 1905); Tefft v. Schaefer, 239 P. 837, 840 (Wash. 1925).

§20.03 [1] Ford v. Easthampton Rubber Thread Co., 32 N.E. 1036 (Mass. 1893).

[2] Robert S. Stevens, Handbook on the Law of Private Corporations 459-461 (2d ed. 1949). *See* Note, Corporations—Declaration of Dividends—Stockholders as Creditors, 28 Mich. L. Rev. 914 (1930).

notice of the declaration seem conclusive.[3] It has thus become established that a cash or property dividend, once announced, cannot be revoked.[4]

§20.04   Right to Dividends Declared Prior to Transfer of Shares

In general, any dividend already declared when shares are transferred belongs to the transferor and does not pass by the transfer, and the fact that the dividend is made payable at a future date does not alter the rule. Frequently this problem is solved by the directors' declaration fixing a record date in order to determine who is entitled to the distribution.

The shareholders' right to a corporate distribution becomes fixed by the dividend declaration in the absence of a record date.[1] This general rule, which is codified in many states,[2] is based on the theory that a dividend declaration automatically makes the corporation a debtor to the shareholder.[3] The right or debt thus does not pass on transfer of the shares. Accordingly, when dividends are made payable at a future date, usually for the convenience of the corporation, a transfer between the date of declaration and the date of payment will not affect the transferor's right to the dividends. The dividends will be payable to the owner at the time of declaration rather than at the time of payment.[4] Dividends declared subsequent to the transfer of ownership belong to the transferee.[5] A share of stock has been compared to a fruit tree: the seller may retain any fallen fruit (declared dividends) on sale of the tree but may not shake the tree to recover more fruit after the sale.[6] If the transferor of the stock receives dividends that were declared after the transfer, he is liable to the transferee for them, whether or not the transfer was recorded or registered with the corporation;[7] however, the corporation is not liable to a transferee without notice.[8]

---

[3] The shareholders' right to a declared dividend may be based on more than a promise implied from the directors' resolution. As proprietors of the business, shareholders may be entitled to a distribution of accumulated profits. E.g., Dodge v. Ford Motor Co., 170 N.W. 668 (Mich. 1919); Miller v. Magline, Inc., 256 N.W.2d 761 (Mich. Ct. App. 1977); supra §20.02.

[4] See Comment, Is a Declaration of Subscription "Rights" Revocable? 39 Yale L.J. 1163, 1166-1173 (1930). A possible change in position of some shareholder or purchaser in reliance on the declaration is thus sufficient without any proof of actual reliance.

§20.04   [1] Ford v. Ford Mfg. Co., 222 Ill. App. 76 (1921); Nutter v. Andrews, 142 N.E. 67 (Mass. 1923); Munro v. Mullen, 121 A.2d 312 (N.H. 1956).

[2] See MBCA §6.40 (1984); Former MBCA §30 (1969).

[3] Caleb & Co. v. E. I. du Pont de Nemours & Co., 615 F. Supp. 96 (S.D.N.Y. 1985); Ford v. Ford Mfg. Co., 222 Ill. App. 76 (1921).

[4] Id.; Western Sec. Co. v. Silver King Consol. Mining Co., 192 P. 664 (Utah 1920). But see Smith v. Taecker, 24 P.2d 182 (Cal. Ct. App. 1933).

[5] See Caleb & Co. v. E. I. du Pont de Nemours & Co., 615 F. Supp. 96 (S.D.N.Y. 1985); Wilcom v. Wilcom, 502 A.2d 1076 (Md. 1986).

[6] DeGendre v. Kent, L.R. 4 Eq. 283 (1865).

[7] Smith v. Taecher, 24 P.2d 182 (Cal. Ct. App. 1933); Richter & Co. v. Light, 116 A. 600 (Conn. 1922); Herzfeld & Stern v. Friedus, 330 N.Y.S.2d 479 (Sup. Ct. App. Term 1971).

[8] Richter & Co. v. Light, 116 A. 600 (Conn. 1922); Turnbull v. Longacre Bank, 163 N.E. 135 (N.Y. 1928); Lunt v. Genessee Valley Trust Co., 297 N.Y.S. 27 (City Ct. 1937); Cooper v. Citizens Nat'l Bank, 267 S.W.2d 848 (Tex. 1954).

B. RESTRICTIONS ON DIVIDEND DISTRIBUTIONS

§20.05 The Purpose of Dividend Restrictions

A difficult and complex branch of corporation law deals with legal capital requirements and the limitations on distributions to shareholders. The rule against capital impairment has long been the fundamental restriction on dividends. Historically, statutes have attempted to provide for the establishment, contribution, and maintenance of some margin of asset values over liabilities for the protection of creditors. But because these statutes did not keep up with changes in generally accepted accounting practices and the insights of modern finance, legal capital has become a dated dividend restriction. One mitigating factor has been the addition of an insolvency test in most statutes.

§20.06 The Various Dividend Limitations

Every state statutorily restricts the directors' authority to make dividend distributions based on the corporation's financial condition. These statutes contain one or more of the following restrictions:

(1) A prohibition of dividends when the corporation is insolvent or that would render it insolvent.

(2) The requirement that a general surplus exists from which dividends may be paid and that consists of the value of the net assets or net worth of the corporation over the stated or legal capital margin, determined from the balance sheet and usually excluding any unrealized appreciation of fixed assets.

(3) The requirement that an earned surplus exists, which devises its value from accumulated earnings or profits.[1] All legal-capital statutes permit dividends from capital surplus but the availability of capital surplus has been restricted by several acts to preferred shares.

(4) As an alternative to surplus, the existence of current earnings usually measured for the year in which the dividend is declared or in the preceding year will permit "nimble dividends" in a few states, regardless of impairment of capital.

(5) A certain ratio of certain assets to current liabilities, or assets to liabilities, such as 1¼ to 1, may be required to be left after a distribution of dividends in order to avoid impairment of debt-paying ability and working capital position.[2]

---

§20.06 [1] In order to comport with GAAP the California statute speaks in terms of "retained earnings." Cal. Gen. Corp. Law §500(a) (West 1990).

[2] This is the alternative approach, as compared with the use of retained earnings in California. Cal. Gen. Corp. Law §500(b) (West 1990).

(6) An exception to the general dividend restrictions permits a "wasting asset corporation," although not formed for the liquidation of specific property, to distribute the proceeds derived from the consumption of wasting assets without deduction for their depletion or exhaustion.[3] This in effect permits liquidating dividends or a distribution of capital, which may be dangerous to creditors and preferred shareholders.

In addition to the foregoing legal capital restrictions, there is the new balance-sheet approach and "distribution" restrictions adopted in the 1980 amendments to the former Model Business Corporation Act, and these are carried forward in the current Model Business Corporation Act.[4] They prohibit a distribution if, after giving effect to such distribution, the corporation's total assets would be less than its total liabilities plus the maximum amount required for the payment of any liquidation preferences. Nearly one half the states have patterned their statutes after the model acts, and the remaining states continue to adhere to some form of legal capital restriction.

As will be seen in the next chapter, statutory restrictions on the purchase by a corporation of its own shares are often similar to, or at least related to, those on dividend distributions, because both transactions involve the withdrawal of corporate assets in favor of shareholders.[5]

Dividend restrictions also appear in loan agreements as creditors frequently resort to private contracting for protection to supplement the minimum level provided by corporate statutes and fraudulent transfer acts. Where such a provision exists, the limits found in the agreement entered into with a single creditor is much like rain—its benefits fall upon all the corporation's creditors since the debtor's reduced discretion to make distributions to its stockholders has the effect of conserving assets that are available to all of its creditors.[6] Because of the frequency of detailed loan agreements among public companies it is safe to say that the ultimate restriction on distributions to stockholders by public companies is that found in their loan agreements and not corporate statutes or fraudulent transfer provisions.

§20.07   The Capital Impairment Limitation

The oldest and still prevalent dividend restriction limits dividends to the extent that there is sufficient surplus, which is defined in the statutes as the amount net

---

[3] See §20.12.

[4] MBCA §§2(i), 45(b) (1980); MBCA §§1.40(b), 6.40 (1984). The text to the 1980 amendments to the Model Business Corporation Act is reported in 34 Bus. Law. 1867-1889 (1979).

[5] See, e.g., Cal. Gen. Corp. Law §166 (West 1990). See generally Chapter 21.

[6] For an analysis of whether state-imposed dividend restrictions reflect efficient contracting by creditors, see John Armour, Share Capital and Creditor Protection: Efficient Rules for a Modern Company Law, 63 Mod. L. Rev. 355 (2000).

B.   Restrictions on Dividend Distributions

assets or net worth is in excess of the legal capital.[1] The laws of Delaware, New York, and a number of other states permit dividends out of surplus of any and all varieties, whether earned or capital surplus.[2] Unlike the pre-1980 Model Business Corporation Act,[3] these states do not draw distinctions between an "earned surplus" and the different kinds of "capital surplus" that may be derived from paid-in surplus or from reduction surplus arising on the reduction of the legal capital. The pre-1980 Model Business Corporation Act distinguishes among different types of surplus, with the result that dividends and share repurchases premised on available earned surplus have much fewer limitations than those premised on other forms of surplus (for example, capital surplus). The pre-1980 Model Business Corporation Act's definitional section divides "surplus" into two components and treats them dissimilarly in important ways. Section 45(a) of the act authorizes dividends in cash or property to the extent of unreserved and unrestricted earned surplus. Because it arises almost invariably from shareholder's investment in the enterprise,[4] capital surplus is burdened with most of the restrictions that surround stated capital. Capital surplus does, however, have some uses accorded earned surplus. For example, even though distributions to the shareholders from capital surplus are allowed, such distributions are conditioned on there being express authorization in the corporation's charter for utilization of capital surplus or approval of a majority of the shares of each outstanding class of stock.[5] Use of capital surplus is prohibited if the corporation's net assets following the distribution are less than the aggregate liquidation preference of a senior class of stock. The prohibition also applies whenever there are any unpaid dividends for any class of stock having a preferential right to dividends. None of these limitations arise when dividends are based on earned surplus. All distributions, whether from earned surplus or capital surplus, must not under the equity test render the corporation insolvent—that is, unable to satisfy its obligations as they mature.

Until the adoption of the current provisions of the Model Business Corporation Act, discussed below, there were few exceptions[6] to the view that unrealized appreciation in value of fixed assets could not be counted in the computation of a surplus as a basis for cash or property dividends.[7] Historically,

§20.07   [1] Del. Code Ann. tit. 8, §§170(a), 173, 154 (2001); N.Y. Bus. Corp. Law §510 (McKinney Supp. 2002).

[2] Id.

[3] This was the case prior to the 1980 Model Business Corporation Act amendments. Former MBCA §45(a) (1969). See §20.08.

[4] Other sources of capital surplus are transfers from earned surplus to capital surplus on approval of the board of directors, Former MBCA §70 (1969), by a reduction in stated capital, id., or issuances of shares as part of an exchange or conversion of outstanding shares. Id. §§18, 19.

[5] Former MBCA §16 (1969).

[6] Randall v. Bailey, 43 N.E.2d 43 (N.Y. 1942), aff'g 23 N.Y.S.2d 173 (Sup. Ct. 1940). See Thomas A. Reynolds, Note, Cash Dividends Payable from Unrealized Appreciation of Fixed Assets—A Reconsideration of Randall v. Bailey, 20 U. Pitt. L. Rev. 632 (1959).

[7] Klang v. Smith's Food & Drug Centers, 702 A.2d 150, 154 (Del. 1997) (directors have the power to use fair value of assets to determine the firm's surplus); Morris v. Standard Gas & Elec. Co., 63 A.2d 577 (Del. Ch. 1949); Woodson v. Lee, 389 P.2d 196 (N.M. 1963).

dividend regulation rested on certain metrics focused on the firm's balance sheet. Since assets under generally accepted accounting principles (GAAP) are recorded at their historical cost, less any depreciation, amortization, or depletion, this approach naturally led to view that unrealized asset appreciation was necessarily foreclosed as a basis of dividends. The presumed intent of the legislature in adopting regulation dependent upon the balance sheet is that the legislature intended the statutory tests to incorporate GAAP for defining the terms used in the statute, that is, terms which historically have significance within the field of accounting should carry forward their meaning from that field. An assumed connection between dividend regulation and GAAP should be powerful because the purposes that underlie GAAP's conservatism and dividend regulation are identical.[8] GAAP's adherence to historical cost and strict rules for the realization of gains and income are based on a number of factors, including: the lack of relevance of market or replacement costs to a fixed asset that is not intended to be sold, the difficulties of valuation, the loss of comparability of financial statements of corporations using different valuation methods, problems of application in depreciation accounting that is intended only to charge asset costs against operations, and the possibilities of employing unrealized appreciation as a purely fictitious basis for dividends.

The leading case for recognizing unrealized gains as a source for dividends is *Randall v. Bailey*,[9] which was decided under an impairment-of-capital statute that permitted dividends as long as "the *value* of its assets remaining after the payment of such dividend, or after such distribution of assets . . . shall be at least equal to the aggregate amount of its debts and liabilities including capital or capital stock as the case may be."[10] When *Randall* was decided not only did practice vary widely among accountants with respect to what was required to recognize income—that is, the realization convention as we understand it today was not then widely practiced[11]—but also courts were far more willing to exercise their judgment as to the meaning of "significant accounting terms."[12] These distinctions, did not, however, enter the Delaware Supreme Court's thinking in *Klang v. Smith's Food and Drug Centers*,[13] when the court permitted unrealized appreciation in assets to meet the state's impairment of capital test:

> The General Assembly enacted the statute to prevent boards from draining corporations of assets to the detriment of creditors and the long-term health of the corporation. That a corporation has not yet realized or reflected on its balance sheet the appreciation of assets is irrelevant to this concern. Regardless of what a balance sheet that has not been updated may show, an actual, though unrealized

---

[8] *See* Current Issues on the Legality of Dividends from a Law and Accounting Perspective, 39 Bus. Law. 289, 292-300 (1983).

[9] 23 N.Y.S.2d 173 (Sup. Ct. 1940), *aff'd*, 43 N.E.2d 43 (N.Y. 1942).

[10] N.Y. Stock Corp. Law §58, enacted in 1923 (emphasis added).

[11] *See* James D. Cox, Financial Information, Accounting and the Law 257 (1980). *See also* §19.02.

[12] *See* Cox, *supra* note 9, at 694-695.

[13] 702 A.2d 150 (Del. 1997).

appreciation reflects real economic value that the corporation may borrow against or that creditors may claim or levy upon. Allowing corporations to revalue assets and liabilities to reflect current realities complies with the statute and serves well the policies behind this statute.[14]

As examined below, the policy referred to by the Delaware Supreme Court may not be well served by permitting unrealized appreciation to be the source of dividend distributions.

Sound policy supports allowing firms to distribute true economic gains to their owners. Such gains are those that are not needed to replace the facilities and resources either committed or already consumed within the company's current business.[15] If the land on which the company's plant is built increases in value, that is not a true economic gain that can be distributed to the shareholders—any sale of the land or a parcel of it would possibly necessitate an equal expenditure to replace the land so that operations can continue. Thus pure holding gains are rarely a true advance in a company's fortunes if those gains are associated with an asset without which the business cannot operate. However persuasive such arguments are, they are moot in the face of the clear language of the present Model Business Corporation Act:

> The board of directors may base a determination that a distribution is not prohibited . . . either on financial statements prepared on the basis of accounting practices and principles that are reasonable in the circumstances or on a *fair valuation* or other method reasonable in the circumstances.[16]

The official comment to this section expressly states "the statute authorizes departures from historical cost accounting and sanctions the use of appraisal and current value methods to determine the amount available for distributions." There appears little likelihood that the relaxed method of determining distributable dividends under such a provision will occur within a public corporation where dividend practices, particularly for companies in financial distress, have historically been conservative and have been muffled by external lending agreements. But the freedom permitted by the current Model Business Corporation Act is likely to be irresistible within a close corporation, where the rush to grab the assets within a failing company is all too well documented. Certainly one must ponder whether the very meaning of the standards embodied in statutes intended for the protection of creditors should ever be commended to those whose interests are adverse to creditors.

---

[14] *Id.* at 154.

[15] This indeed is the notion within the accounting movement calling for current-value accounting. *See* C. Morley Carscallen & Kenneth P. Johnson, Financial Reporting Under Changing Values: An Introduction to Current Value Accounting 16-20 (AMA 1977).

[16] MBCA §6.40(d) (1984) (emphasis added). This is the interpretation the Delaware Supreme Court has applied to the Delaware statute. *See* Klang v. Smith's Food & Drug Centers, 702 A.2d 150 (Del. 1997). For an earlier decision on this point, see Morris v. Standard Gas & Electric Co., 63 A.2d 577 (Del. 1949).

§20.08   The Earned-Surplus Test

Following the pre-1980 Model Business Corporation Act,[1] many states restricted dividend distributions to earned surplus except in special cases, such as when expressly authorized in the articles of incorporation, when stockholders vote to use capital surplus, when distributions are used to pay cumulative dividends on preferred shares, or when distributions are made from a wasting asset corporation.[2] The role of GAAP in the construction of earned surplus is not clear under the Model Business Corporation Act or, for that matter, under most other statutes.[3] It is generally believed that the earned-surplus test looks to realized gains and accumulated but undistributed profits as the normal basis of dividends on common shares.[4] Similarly, as an alternative test in California, distributions are permitted to the extent of "retained earnings"; thus the current accounting terminology is substituted for the old.[5]

Earned surplus is generally a far more conservative limitation on common share dividends, and on share purchases also, than surplus generally because it links such distributions directly to the financial performance of the company. But even earned surplus may be based in large part on fixed, unmarketable, and frozen assets, such as investments in machinery or real estate. The ability to pay dividends, as distinct from the legal right to pay dividends, depends largely on the liquidity of the financial position—that is, on the so-called current ratio and the sufficiency of working capital to keep the business going. While the existence of the required surplus over capital may satisfy the statutory prohibition, it is the duty of directors to take many other factors into account in the exercise of prudent management.[6]

The earned-surplus restriction is often coupled with prohibitions against capital impairment and payments that would render the corporation insolvent.[7]

---

§20.08   [1] Former MBCA §§45, 46 (1969).

[2] *See* §20.12.

[3] The commentators in varying respects argue that the Model Business Corporation Act permits some departure from generally accepted accounting principles. *See* Ray Garrett, Capital and Surplus Under the New Corporation Statutes, 23 Law & Contemp. Probs. 239, 259 (1958) (unrealized gains can be recognized); William P. Hackney, The Financial Provisions of the Model Business Corporation Act, 70 Harv. L. Rev. 1377-1383 (1957) (unrealized appreciation can increase capital surplus, and that earned surplus may be even less than permitted by accountants because of need to recognize effects of inflation); George Seward, Earned Surplus—Its Meaning and Use in the Model Business Corporation Act, 38 Va. L. Rev. 435, 440-443 (1952) (inclusion of all "gains" within definition permits revaluation of assets to recognize unrealized appreciation).

[4] Former MBCA §2(1) (1969). *See* Commissioner v. Filoon, 38 N.E.2d 693 (Mass. 1941); Hackney, *supra* note 3; George Seward, Earned Surplus—Its Meaning and Use in the Model Business Corporation Act, 38 Va. L. Rev., at 435-443.

[5] Cal. Gen. Corp. Law §500(a) (West 1990).

[6] *See* John A. Brittain, Corporate Dividend Policy (1966); David F. Scott, Jr. & C. Wayne Shepherd, Corporate Dividend Policy: Some Legal & Financial Aspects, 123 Am. Bus. L.J. 199 (1975).

[7] Former MBCA §45 (1969). The insolvency test is also used new or in conjunction with other dividend tests in state statutes. *See* Cal. Gen. Corp. Law §501 (West 1990); Mass. Ann. Laws ch. 156B, §61 (Supp. 2002); N.Y. Bus. Corp. Law §510(a) (McKinney Supp. 2002).

B. Restrictions on Dividend Distributions

§20.09   Capital Surplus as a Source of "Distributions" to Shareholders

In many states, including Delaware and New York, capital surplus is available equally with earned surplus for dividends on all kinds of shares.[1] This can create a danger to preferred shareholders and creditors because directors are given the authority by many corporation acts to attribute substantially all of the consideration received on the issue of no- or low-par shares, either common or preferred, to paid-in surplus rather than to capital. A dividend paid out of paid-in surplus would then leave an inadequate capital margin for creditor and preferred shareholder protection. Conceivably, dividends could even be paid to common shareholders out of paid-in surplus received from the issue of the preferred shares and thus divert part of the investment of the senior shares to the holders of the junior shares. Any abuse of this discretion by the directors, however, is properly subject to equitable limitations.[2]

Dividends from paid-in surplus and from capital reduction surplus are a return on capital akin to a partial liquidating distribution, because they represent a distribution of part of the price invested by the original share-subscribers in the business, and, as such, they are not taxable as dividend income, but are treated as a capital return.[3] Most statutes require notice to the shareholders of the extent to which the dividend represents capital surplus.[4] It is surprising that only a few states have required that capital surplus be available for dividends only in the absence of an earned surplus.[5]

The former Model Business Corporation Act, like other "earned surplus" statutes, permits "distributions from capital surplus" under certain circumstances.[6] In addition to the insolvency limitation, such distributions must be authorized either in the charter or by a majority shareholder vote on a class basis, including nonvoting shares. This authorization is not necessary, however, in the case of distributions in discharge of cumulative dividend rights, provided there is no earned surplus. Distributions out of capital surplus may not be made in a manner prejudicial to preferred shareholders.[7]

---

§20.09   [1] Del. Code Ann. tit. 8, §§154, 170(a) (2001); N.Y. Bus. Corp. Law §510 (McKinney Supp. 2002); MBCA Ann. 3d §640 Statutory Comparison ¶1(c) (Supp. 1993).

[2] Adolf A. Berle, Investors and the Revised Delaware Corporation Act, 29 Colum. L. Rev. 563, 573-575 (1929).

[3] I.R.C. §§316, 301(c)(2) (2000). Corporate distributions are "dividends" and are part of taxable income under IRC §316 to the extent the corporation has accumulated "earnings and profits" since February 28, 1913, or earnings or profits during the taxable year.

[4] A number of state statutes require notice to shareholders of the source of the distribution if not from earned surplus or if from capital surplus. See, e.g., N.Y. Bus. Corp. Law §501(c) (McKinney 1986). See AICPA, Accounting Research and Terminology Bulletins No. 43 ch. 7a (1961). Notice to shareholders is important for federal tax purposes. Cf. Former MBCA §46(c) (1969) (requiring such notice).

[5] See Ark. Code Ann. §4-26-619(B) (Michie 2001).

[6] Former MBCA §46 (1969).

[7] All cumulative arrearages must have been paid, and the distribution cannot reduce the next assets below the aggregate liquidation preference. Id. at §46(e), (d) (1969).

California, in its departure from "legal capital" concepts, does not limit dividends solely to "retained earnings" but in effect allows distributions from capital surplus through a balance-sheet test, which requires that after giving effect to a distribution, total assets be at least equal to 1¼ of the total liabilities, and current assets be at least equal to current liabilities.[8] Note that the effect of this standard is to effectively require that corporations relying on this standard (in contrast to the "retained earnings" standard) cannot have a ratio of liabilities to equity greater than four to one. The 1980 amendments to the Model Business Corporation Act were even more unconventional. They allow any distribution that meets the insolvency test and that does not reduce the corporation's total assets below the sum of maximum liquidation preferences payable and liabilities after giving effect to the distribution.[9] These amendments were carried forward into the present Model Act.

§20.10 The Insolvency Limitation

At one time insolvency was the only statutory restriction on dividends in some jurisdictions.[1] Today virtually all statutes have some form of balance-sheet test in addition to an insolvency limitation.[2] Only Massachusetts, Minnesota, and North Dakota have the insolvency test as their exclusive requirement.[3]

There are two rival definitions of "insolvency": (1) The commercial or equity test of an inability to meet debts and obligations promptly as they fall due;[4] and (2) the bankruptcy or "balance sheet" test, an excess of the amount of liabilities over the total value of the assets.[5] It is not always clear in dividend statutes which of the two possible meanings of "insolvency" should be taken. The rule against impairment of capital should take care of the question of the total assets at least

---

[8] Cal. Gen. Corp. Law §500 (West 1990). However, id. §§502 and 503 protect preferred shareholders. California also has an insolvency test. Cal. Gen. Corp. Law §501 (West 1990). See §20.13.

[9] Former MBCA §45 (1980); MBCA §6.40 (1984); Ill. Comp. Stat. Ann. ch. 805, §5/9.10 (West 1993); Minn. Stat. Ann. §302A.551 (West 1985 & Supp. 2002); Mont. Code Ann. §35-1-712 (2002); N.M. Stat. Ann. §53-11-44 (Michie 2001); Wash. Rev. Code Ann. §23B-06-400 (Supp. 2002).

§20.10 [1] E.g., The Business Corporation Law ch. 434, §35, 1903 Mass. Acts 418, 435 (1903) (current version of Mass. Gen. Laws Ann. ch. 156B, §61 (West Supp. 1994); An Act on Corporations, ch. 77, §21, 1892 Miss. Laws §§269, 276 (1892); Act of Dec. 2, 1871, ch. 80, art. III §28, 1871 Tex. Gen. Laws (2d Sess.) §§66, 71 (1871); Act of Feb. 17, 1939, ch. 62, §28-131, 1939 Wyo. Sess. Laws §§66, 71 (1871).

[2] E.g., Former MBCA §43 (1969). See MBCA Ann. 3d §6.40 Statutory Comparison ¶1(a) (3d ed. 1994). This limitation also applies to distributions out of capital surplus as well as to redemptions and other share repurchases. See Chapter 21.

[3] Mass. Gen. Laws Ann. ch. 156B, §61 (West Supp. 2002); Minn. Stat. Ann. §§51, 302A (West 1985 & Supp. 2002); N.D. Cent. Code §10-19.1-92.1.

[4] See Larrimer v. Feeney, 192 A.2d 351 (Pa. 1963); Meyer v. General Am. Corp., 569 P.2d 1094 (Utah 1977); Cal. Gen. Corp. Law §501 (West 1990); N.Y. Bus. Corp. Law §102(a)(8) (McKinney 1986); Former MBCA §2(n).

[5] See Tukmorkin v. Galloy, 127 F. Supp. 94 (S.D.N.Y. 1954); Prismo Universal Corp. v. City of Little Rock, 472 S.W.2d 92 (Ark. 1971); Saperstein v. Holland, McGill & Pasker, 496 P.2d 896 (Utah 1972).

equaling the liabilities,[6] but, if the insolvency limitation is to have any additional force or effect, it should be drawn so as to cover some objective test of reasonable grounds for believing that the corporation will not be rendered unable to pay its debts and liabilities, both long- and short-term, as they fall due.[7] Probably the most prevalent interpretation of prohibitions against insolvency in dividend statutes is the equity test.

The equity solvency test should be seen as setting forth a context within which traditional manners of inquiry occur as to whether the directors' decision is protected by the business judgment rule.[8] Within this context, a host of considerations are appropriate:

> [I]n determining whether the equity insolvency test has been met, certain judgments and assumptions as to the future course of the corporation's business are customarily justified, absent clear evidence to the contrary. These include the likelihood that (a) based on existing and contemplated demand for the corporation's products or services, it will be able to generate funds over a period of time sufficient to satisfy its existing and reasonably anticipated obligations as they mature, and (b) indebtedness which matures in the near-term will be refinanced where, on the basis of the corporation's financial condition and future prospects and the general availability of credit to business similarly situated, it is reasonable to assume that such refinancing may be accomplished. To the extent the corporation may be subject to asserted or unasserted contingent liabilities, reasonable judgments as to the likelihood, amount, and the time of any recovery against the corporation, after giving consideration to the extent to which the corporation is insured or otherwise protected against loss, may be utilized.[9]

§20.11   Nimble Dividends

Some state statutes allow dividends from the net profits or net earnings of the preceding year or other recent specified period in the absence of any surplus and in spite of a capital deficit.[1] These provisions providing for "nimble dividends"[2] have been criticized as being unduly lax. The privilege may be justified, however, on the

---

[6] Since rules against capital impairment operate on the theory that dividends will be paid out of the excess of net assets over liabilities and stated capital, such a rule requires the total assets to exceed total liabilities.

[7] See 1 Garrard Glenn, Fraudulent Conveyances and Preferences §32 (rev. ed. 1940) (hereinafter Fraudulent Conveyances).

[8] This linkage is expressly made in the present Model Business Corporation Act by premising director liability for unlawful distributions only if the director "did not perform his duties in compliance with section 8.30," which codifies the business judgment rule. MBCA §8.33(a) (1984).

[9] MBCA 6.40 Comment 2 (1984).

§20.11   [1] A number have since been repealed. Some require basically that the capital representing classes of stock having a liquidation preference not be impaired. See Del. Code Ann. tit. 8, §170(a) (2001); Kan. Stat. Ann. §17-6420 (1995).

[2] The phrase "nimble dividends" was coined by Professor Baker (see Recent Cases, Corporations—Dividends—Virginia Statute Construed to Allow Dividends from Current Profits Despite Capital Deficit, 62 Harv. L. Rev. 130 (1948)), meaning in essence that directors must be nimble in declaring dividends before the earnings are transferred to offset deficits.

ground that the surplus limitation at times becomes unreasonably strict and arbitrary, as it may permit dividends when they are inexpedient and forbid them when their distribution would be financially sound. The purpose of the law is to establish some minimum test of whether the financial condition of a corporation permits a distribution with a view to the safety of creditors and the investment of the shareholders.

§20.12 *"Wasting Asset" Corporations*

A controversial[1] provision in many states permits corporations solely or principally engaged in the exploitation of "wasting assets" to distribute the net proceeds derived from exploitation of their holdings, such as mines, oil wells, patents, and leaseholds, without allowance or deduction for depletion.[2] There may be a vague limitation of making sufficient provision for creditors and the liquidation priorities of preferred shareholders. Such statutes are often accompanied by a requirement of notice that liquidation dividends are being paid without allowance for depletion. The pre-1980 version of the Model Business Corporation Act imposes such limitations in addition to applying them only to corporations engaged principally in the exploration of natural resources.[3] The Act also limits such distributions to depletion reserves and requires authorization in the charter. As a result of the 1980 amendments eliminating legal capital, the wasting asset provision has been deleted.[4] Even in the absence of an express statute, some courts have permitted wasting-asset distributions.[5]

If a corporation is organized to exploit, liquidate, and distribute the proceeds of a particular mineral reserve, estate, or specific lot of assets, the corporation may be described as a "liquidating corporation," which may be excused by statute from making any reserve for depletion or replacement of the assets liquidated. But if the purpose of a corporation that is engaged in the oil or mining or similar business is a continuing one and not the exhaustion and liquidation of a particular property, then, as to keeping its capital intact there is no reason for treating such corporation as different from any other continuing concern, such as a manufacturing corporation.[6]

There is no justification for treating such corporations differently, and such provisions should be repealed. Moreover, there is little evidence that creditors are

---

§20.12 [1] *See* Charles G. Carpenter, A Critical Evaluation of the Wasting Asset Distribution, 25 Bus. Law. 1733 (1970).

[2] *E.g.*, Del. Code Ann. tit. 8, §170(b) (2001). *See* C. C. Williams, Dividends from Wasting Asset Corporations, 43 W. Va. L.Q. (1936).

[3] Former MBCA §45(b) (1969).

[4] MBCA §45 (1980); MBCA §6.40 (1984); Ill. Rev. Stat. ch. 805, §5/9.10 (West 1993); Minn. Stat. Ann. §302A.551 (West 1985 & Supp. 2002); Mont. Code Ann. §35-1-712 (2002); N.M. Stat. Ann. §53-11-44 (Michie Supp. 2001); Wash. Rev. Code Ann. §23B.06.400 (West Supp. 2002).

[5] *See* Excelsior Water & Mining Co. v. Pierce, 27 P. 44 (Cal. 1891). *See* 2 Harold Marsh, Marsh's California Corporation Law §13.3 (1981).

[6] Henry W. Ballantine & George S. Hills, Corporate Capital and Restrictions Upon Dividends Under Modern Corporation Laws, 23 Cal. L. Rev. 251 (1935).

deserving of less protection for wasting-asset corporations than for other types of corporations. It would therefore appear to be more consistent to settle on a useful prophylactic standard that would work, on average, for all types of corporations.

§20.13 The Innovations of the California Statute and the Model Business Corporation Act

Very few parts of the corporate mechanism are more complicated, unworkable, or incomprehensible than the system of legal-capital requirements, with its various attempted restrictions on unsafe distributions of assets to the shareholders.

The prevalent limitations as to capital and surplus rest on vague financial standards that are difficult to ascertain and to apply. The margin of safety measured by the legal capital is an arbitrary limit, established on the issue of shares, that has no relation to the kind of business being conducted, the liquidity of assets, the net current asset position, and the ability to meet or refinance obligations as they fall due.[1]

In discarding long-outmoded legal-capital concepts and adopting GAAP, California took an important step in improving the law's regulation of dividend distributions. An alternative new approach to dividend restrictions is embodied in the previously mentioned 1980 amendments to the Model Business Corporation Act, which are carried forward into the present Model Business Corporation Act.[2]

The current version of the Model Business Corporation Act follows California's lead in jettisoning most of the traditional legal-capital concepts. The treasury share enigma is abolished,[3] and both share repurchases and dividends are covered under the concept of "distributions" to shareholders.[4] Also, the equity insolvency test is retained as a basic restriction.[5] The Model Business Corporation Act diverges significantly from California and other current statutory approaches in rejecting a restriction based on earnings.[6] In lieu of retained earnings or earned surplus, the Model Business Corporation Act uses a simpler and more flexible balance-sheet test. The new provision prohibits distributions if, after the distribution, a corporation's total assets are less than its total liabilities plus liquidation preferences, if any.[7] The Model Business Corporation Act further declines dependency

---

§20.13 [1] The earning power of a corporation, its ability to pay debts and dividends, may not depend on the amount of its net assets.

[2] The text of the 1980 amendments and The Report of the Committee on Corporate Laws may be found in 34 Bus. Law. 1867-1889 (1979).

[3] MBCA §6.40 (and comments) (1984); Cal. Gen. Corp. Law §510 (West 1990). For treasury shares, *see infra* §§21.07-21.08.

[4] MBCA §1.40 (6) (1984); Cal. Gen. Corp. Law §166 (West 1990). For share repurchases, *see* Chapter 21.

[5] MBCA §45(a) (1980); MBCA §6.40 (1984); Cal. Gen. Corp. Law §501 (West 1990); *supra* §20.10.

[6] Both the earned-surplus test (Former MBCA §45 (1969) and California's retained-earnings test (Cal. Gen. Corp. Law §500(a) (West 1990)) are based on the concept of paying dividends based on the corporation's earnings or profits rather than on money (capital) paid into the company by the sale of shares.

[7] Former MBCA §45(b) (1969); RMBCA §6.40 (1984). *Cf.* N.C. Gen. Stat. §55-6-40(c)(2) (2001).

on GAAP by placing the method for valuation of assets and liabilities within the directors' discretion, subject to a standard of reasonableness under the circumstances.[8]

§20.14 The Issue of Shares as Stock Dividends and Stock Splits

The term "stock dividend" is an unfortunate misnomer. It is a dividend only in the sense that the corporation has made a pro rata distribution among a class of its stockholders. However, it is unlike the other kinds of dividends discussed in this chapter because the corporation is not distributing any of its assets to its shareholders, and in turn its shareholders receive only additional shares to represent their same proportionate ownership interest. The declaration of dividends in new shares is a kind of psychological, constructive, or symbolic benefit that is sometimes used in order to keep investors satisfied with the retention of profits in the business or for purposes of stock market manipulation by those in control. The customary dividend statutes, discussed in the preceding sections, and the surplus and capital impairment limits do not apply to stock dividends. As explained in a leading case,[1] "a stock dividend does not distribute property, but simply dilutes the shares as they existed before. . . ." It is in no sense a distribution of surplus.

Neither stock dividends nor stock split-ups themselves increase or decrease the assets or earnings of the corporation. Nevertheless, these two events are treated quite differently by the accounting profession. As will be seen in the next section, surplus equal to the market value of the shares distributed must be capitalized for stock dividends but not for stock split-ups. What distinguishes the two is not the name assigned to the distribution by the board of directors, but whether a material reduction in the shares' market value is likely to accompany the distribution.[2] Investors associate both events with positive news about the corporation, so that rarely is the market value of the corporation's outstanding shares less after the declaration date of either a stock dividend or stock split than before the declaration.[3]

---

[8] Former MBCA §45 (1969). Directors may make asset and liability determinations from financial statements based on accounting practices and principles that are reasonable under the circumstances. *See* Former MBCA §45 Comment (1969). In many cases the reasonableness standard may require use of GAAP.

§20.14 [1] Williams v. Western Union Tel. Co., 57 N.Y.S. 446, 453 (N.Y. 1883). *See* City Bank Farmers' Trust Co. v. Ernst, 189 N.E. 241 (N.Y. 1934); Ballantine & Hills, *supra* §20.12 note 6, at 255-258.

[2] AICPA, Accounting Research Bulletin No. 43 ch. 7, Stock Dividends and Stock Split-Ups ¶11 (1953) (hereinafter AICPA, Bulletin No. 43).

[3] *See, e.g.,* Mark S. Grinblatt, Ronald W. Masulis, & Sheridan Titman, The Valuation of Stock Splits and Stock Dividends, 13 J. Fin. Econ. 461 (1984); Eugene A. Fama, Lawrence Fisher, Michael C. Jenson, & Richard Roll, The Adjustment of Stock Prices to New Information, 10 Int'l Econ. Rev. 1 (1969). For the view that the signal to investors is sharper, i.e., there is a more positive stock price change, when the distribution of shares is required by corporate statute to give rise to a reduction in the future dividend capacity of the firm, i.e., reduction in surplus, *see* Craig A. Peterson & Norman W. Hawker, Does Corporate Law Matter? Legal Capital Restrictions on Stock Distributions, 175 (1997).

B. Restrictions on Dividend Distributions

A corporation's distribution of shares held by it in another corporation is properly referred to, not as a stock dividend, but as a property dividend, an actual distribution of corporate assets[4]—and, as such, is subject to the normal restrictions on cash and property dividends. The ordinary stock dividend—that is, the issuance of new shares, is very different in effect from a distribution of other property or of such shares to a different class. A stock dividend does not give the common shareholders any new or different interest in the corporation than they had before; it simply divides the holdings of each shareholder into a larger number of share units, with each stockholder maintaining the same proportionate interest in the corporation.[5]

A share or stock "split-up" is simply a division of outstanding shares by amendment of the articles of incorporation into a greater number of share units, like changing a five dollar bill into five "ones." It is the reverse of a share consolidation or "reverse stock split."[6] A share split-up does not, however, make any representations as to any accumulation of earnings or other surplus or involve any increase of the legal capital[7] as occurs with a stock dividend. In the case of a stock split, the per share par value or stated capital is decreased in the same proportion as the amount of the stock split. Share split-ups may be used for the legitimate purpose of reducing the market value of share units, which may otherwise be too high for general convenience in trading.

Under generally accepted accounting principles, the distinction between a stock dividend and a stock split is whether a material decline in the price of the shares is likely to occur on their distribution. When such a decline is not expected, the distribution is deemed a stock dividend, and surplus must be capitalized, as discussed in the next section, in an amount equal to the aggregate fair market value of the distributed shares. Under accounting standards, a distribution of less than 20 or 25 percent may not produce such an effect.[8] Stock splits are distributions where a material decline in the shares' market value is likely to occur. However, when characterizing a distribution with regard to allocation in trusts between principal and income, some courts have disregarded the dilution effect and instead have looked to the accounting entries made on the corporate balance sheet.[9]

---

[4] Peabody v. Eisner, 247 U.S. 347 (1918); City Bank Farmers' Trust Co. v. Ernst, 189 N.E. 241 (N.Y. 1934). Such distributions are frequently used to "spin off" undesired assets in the form of subsidiary's shares. *See* Rockefeller v. United States, 257 U.S. 176 (1921); Stephenson v. Plastics Corp. of Am., 150 N.W.2d 668 (Minn. 1967); Stanley Siegel, When Corporations Divide: A Statutory & Financial Analysis, 79 Harv. L. Rev. 534, 535, 546-548 (1966).

[5] Eisner v. Macomber, 252 U.S. 189 (1920); Gibbons v. Mahon, 136 U.S. 549 (1890). *See* Note, Share Dividends—Their Validity & Desirability, 97 U. Pa. L. Rev. 691, 693-694 (1949).

[6] *See* State ex rel. Radio Corp. of Am. v. Benson, 128 A. 107 (Del. 1924); Teschner v. Chicago Title & Trust Co., 322 N.E.2d 54 (Ill. 1974); Paul H. Dykstra, The Reverse Stock Split—That Other Means of Going Private, 53 Chi-Kent L. Rev. 1 (1976).

[7] In re Trust Estate of Pew, 158 A.2d 552 (Pa. 1960); In re Ree's Estate, 311 P.2d 438 (Or. 1957); Former MBCA §45(c) (1969).

[8] AICPA, Bulletin No. 43, *supra* note 2. *See also* AICPA, Accounting Research and Terminology Bulletin No. 53 (1961).

[9] *See, e.g.,* Sole v. Granger, 174 F.2d 407 (3d Cir. 1949); In re Fosdick, 152 N.E.2d 228 (N.Y. 1958). *But see* In re Strong's Will, 96 N.Y.S.2d 75 (Surr. Ct.), *aff'd,* 101 N.Y.S.2d 1021 (App. Div. 1950). It

§20.15   Capitalization of Surplus for Stock Dividends and Stock Splits

The principal limitation on the issue of the typical stock dividend is a peculiar one—the capitalizing of surplus. Capitalization of surplus refers to the accounting transfer from one of the surplus accounts to the capital stock (stated capital) account. The requirement for such a transfer arises from the commands of the state corporation statute, the listing requirement of the American or New York Stock Exchange, if applicable, and the demands of generally accepted accounting principles. This is more than a mere bookkeeping entry. It decreases surplus and increases the legal-capital margin, which limits dividend distributions. When a share dividend is charged against earned surplus, it has been said that this in effect is the same as a distribution of accumulated profits to the shareholders and a compulsory subscription for shares or reinvestment by them of the amount received in the corporation.[1] The increase of legal capital due to a decrease of surplus restricts the directors' authority to declare dividends payable in cash or property.

By far the least demanding of these is that of the corporation statute that requires that an amount of surplus not less than the aggregate par value of shares distributed as a stock dividend be capitalized.[2] When the shares issued as a dividend are without par value, there is no convenient measure of the amount of surplus to be transferred to capital. Many states leave the amount almost wholly to the directors' discretion.[3]

As seen in the preceding section, there is great concern that investors may misinterpret the true economic effects of a stock dividend. Thus, generally accepted accounting principles require capitalization of surplus equal to the aggregate *fair market value* of the distributed shares in those instances in which a material decline in the per share market value is not believed to accompany the stock dividend's distribution.[4] Since share dividends are usually issued to evidence retention of earnings for reinvestment by the corporation, surplus is transferred and capitalized to give some assurance that such earnings will be retained by the

---

should be noted that the purpose for the distinction between the treatment of stock dividends and stock splits for corporation law purposes may be different from that in trust allocation problems. Unfortunately, this problem of distinguishing usually arises in case law only with regard to trust allocation. *See* Annot., 81 A.L.R.3d 876 (1977) on the trust allocation rules.

§20.15   [1] Trefry v. Putnam, 116 N.E. 904, 911 (Mass. 1917); Commissioner v. Filoon, 38 N.E.2d 693, 700 (Mass. 1941).

[2] MBCA §45(d) (1969). *But see* Cal. Gen. Corp. Law §166 (West 1990); MBCA §1.40(6) (1984) and Former MBCA §2(i) (1969) which exclude stock dividends and splits from "distributions" to which their dividend restrictions apply.

[3] *E.g.*, Del. Code Ann. tit. 8, §173 (2001); N.Y. Bus. Corp. Law §511(a)(2) (McKinney Supp. 2002); MBCA §45(d)(2) (1969). Even in the absence of any express statutory requirements as to share dividends, it is generally recognized that a dividend of shares having a par value, being a new issuance of shares, increases the legal capital by an amount at least equal to the par value of the shares issued.

[4] AICPA, Bulletin No. 43, *supra* §20.14 note 2.

corporation and to prevent misleading investors.[5] It would seem that the padding of the accounts by estimates and conjectures, by reappraising of fixed assets, and by writing up of inventories in order to make a revaluation of surplus for share dividends is undue laxity, which may give a deceptive representation of corporate prosperity to shareholders and to the investing public.[6] GAAP requires transferring earned surplus to the category of permanent capitalization (i.e., "capital stock" and "capital surplus") an amount equal to the fair market value of the additional shares when a material adjustment in market prices is not likely to follow a stock dividend.[7]

Even though California and the Model Business Corporation Act exclude stock splits and stock dividends from the definition of "distributions,"[8] accounting standards still apply, so retained earnings must still be reduced if the states are to comply with generally accepted accounting standards and a material decline in the shares' market value is not likely to accompany the distribution.

C.   LIABILITIES OF DIRECTORS AND SHAREHOLDERS

§20.16   Directors' Liability for Unlawful Dividends

The primary responsibility for protecting capital and keeping dividend distributions within statutory limits rests on the directors by whose authority such distributions are made. Directors' liability is the principal sanction or means of enforcement of dividend restrictions, supplemented by the less effective liability of shareholders and by injunction suits at the instance of shareholders.[1]

Most instances in which directors are held liable for illegal dividends can best be described euphemistically as "bankruptcy planning," through which corporate assets have been purposely deflected by cunning insiders to themselves without satisfying or making provision for outstanding obligations and while the corporation is either insolvent or is winding up its affairs.[2] Absent clear proof that the insiders were aware of their company's financial distress, or otherwise flaunted the

---

[5] See AICPA, Bulletin No. 43.

[6] See supra §20.07.

[7] See ARB No. 43, ch. 7, Stock Dividends and Stock Split-Ups (AICPA 1953) (suggesting capitalization when the number of shares to be distributed is less than 20-25 percent of the shares outstanding before the stock dividend is declared).

[8] Cal. Gen. Corp. Law §166 (West 1990); Former MBCA §2(i) (1969).

§20.16   [1] In most jurisdictions remedies to recover illegal dividends from shareholders are limited to cases of insolvency or knowledge of impropriety. See §20.17.

[2] See, e.g., Retirement Benefit Plan of Graphic Arts Int'l Union Local 20-B v. Standard Bindery Co., 654 F. Supp. 770 (E.D. Mich. 1986); Tomorrow Inv., Inc. v. Friedman, 510 So. 2d 1095 (Fla. Dist. Ct. App. 1987); Hardwick-Morrison Co. v. Albertsson, 605 A.2d 529 (Vt. 1992); Commonwealth Transp. Commr. v. Matyiko, 481 S.E.2d 468 (Va. 1997).

statute's restrictions on distributions, director liability is highly unlikely.[3] Simply stated, the cases do not bear out the fear that directors will be hoisted on the petards of arcane principles and technical statutory requirements that so dominate the financial provisions of corporate statutes.[4]

Even in the absence of statutes expressly imposing liability, the directors are liable for participating in violations of the statutory restrictions that are directed to them.[5] All business corporation statutes contain express liability provisions making directors jointly and severally liable to the corporation[6] (or to its shareholders or its creditors) for payment of dividends in violation of statutory restrictions.[7] Drafting a satisfactory liability provision requires a delicate balancing between maintaining protection of creditors and avoiding harsh burdens on directors. One of the most interesting questions of construction and legislative policy is whether good faith and due care should be a defense. On the one hand, the legislature may consider that a drastic absolute liability is essential to prevent directors from declaring improper dividends and to give adequate protection to creditors and shareholders. On the other hand, there appears little reason to accord creditors greater protection and directors less protection in the area of illegal dividends than creditors enjoy derivatively in other areas of the directors' discretionary behavior. It would appear that the policy should protect directors whenever they act in good faith and with the reasonable care that the circumstances require. If greater protection is demanded, this should and does occur through the loan agreements that lenders so frequently require for their protection.

Many state statutes have sections on director liability similar to the Model Business Corporation Act. These sections make specific reference to the directors' general standard of care.[8] Accordingly, the business judgment rule is incorporated by reference, as is good faith reliance on counsel, public accountants, and officers or their financial statements and reports.[9] The Model Business Corporation Act

---

[3] See In re Elecs., Inc., 746 F.2d 915 (1st Cir. 1984) (no liability for insolvency within one and one-half years of payment to sole shareholder when evidence showed company was solvent immediately after payment made).

[4] See, e.g., Klang v. Smith's Food & Drug Centers, 702 A.2d 150, 156-157 (Del. 1997) (board resolution need not set forth amount of pre- and post-distribution surplus so that understatement of amount of liabilities does not give rise to directors' liability provided sufficient surplus in fact did exist).

[5] A statutory violation is not regarded as being negligence per se or even evidence of negligence, but willful or negligent violation must ordinarily be shown. Directors are not liable for mistakes or errors of judgment if they act in good faith or with due care, as usually shown by considering and checking balance sheets and relying reasonably on reports of subordinates. See Blythe v. Enslen, 95 So. 479 (Ala. 1922).

[6] Lerner v. Lerner Corp., 711 A.2d 233, 240-241 (Md. App. 1998) (shareholder lacks standing to complain of illegal dividend, the right of action belongs to the corporation).

[7] See MBCA Ann. §8.33 (3d ed. 1994). See also Commonwealth Transp. Commr. v. Matyiko, 481 S.E.2d 468 (Va. 1997); MBCA §8.33 (1984); Former MBCA §48 (1969).

[8] See MBCA §8.33 (1984); Former MBCA §48 (1969). See also, e.g., Cal. Gen. Corp. Law §316 (West 1990); Idaho Code §30-1-833 (Michie 1996); N.Y. Bus. Corp. Law §719 (McKinney 1986 & Supp. 2002).

[9] See Former MBCA §35, Comment (1969). See also, e.g., Cal. Gen. Corp. Law §309 (West 1990); Idaho Code §30-1-833 (Michie 1996); N.Y. Bus. Corp. Law §717 (McKinney Supp. 2002). See supra §10.04.

reflects the scheme of most state statutes on this subject. Liability is imposed on any director who "votes for or assents to" an unlawful distribution if it is established that he "did not perform his duties in compliance with section 8.30," the provision that codifies the business judgment rule.[10] Any director so held liable has a right of contribution from other directors who similarly breached their statutory duties[11] and from any shareholder for the amount she received knowing the distribution was in violation of the statute or the articles of incorporation.[12]

There is little basis for believing that statutory liability provisions relating to illegal distributions are the exclusive proscriptions for protecting creditors.[13]

§20.17 Shareholders' Liability to Return Illegal Dividends

It has already been pointed out that a dividend distribution in violation of statutory restrictions is primarily a wrong done by the directors who declare it.[1] The liability most frequently imposed by specific statutes is placed on the directors who declare the dividend rather than on the shareholders who receive it, although the directors may seek contribution against the shareholders who received the illegal dividend with knowledge.[2]

The clear trend among statutes is not to impose liability on shareholders unless it can be shown that the dividends were received with knowledge of the company's condition. This is the position taken in the present Model Business Corporation Act, which permits directors to obtain contribution "from each shareholder for the amount the shareholder accepted *knowing* the distribution was made in violation" of the statute.[3] There is no direct shareholder liability to the corporation provided within the Model Business Corporation Act. There is always a question, however, whether a state statute that sets forth rights against shareholders who receive unlawful distributions supplants the common law.[4]

[10] MBCA §8.33(a) (1984).
[11] MBCA §8.33(b) (1984).
[12] MBCA §8.33(c) (1984).
[13] A number of cases refute the exclusivity of statutory shareholder liability. *See, e.g.,* In re Kettle Fried Chicken of Am., Inc., 513 F.2d 807 (6th Cir. 1975); Reilly v. Segert, 201 N.E.2d 444 (Ill. 1964). Statutes may also leave open other possibilities of director liability. *See* Former MBCA §48 (1969): "In addition to any other liabilities imposed by law."
§20.17 [1] *See* §20.16.
[2] MBCA §8.33 (1984); MBCA §48 (1969).
[3] MBCA §8.33(b)(2) (1984) (emphasis added).
[4] *See* Reilly v. Segert, 201 N.E.2d 444 (Ill. 1964) (statute imposing liability on directors for unlawful distributions with a right of contribution from knowing shareholders does not preclude suit by receiver against shareholders).

CHAPTER 21

Purchase and Redemption by a Corporation of Its Own Shares

A. SHARE PURCHASES AND REDEMPTIONS

§21.01 American Rules on Share Repurchases

It is important to understand the financial difference between a corporation's purchase of its own shares and its purchase of shares issued by an independent enterprise. Shares in another entity are assets of possible value to creditors. On a surrender of a corporation's own shares, the purchase price is simply withdrawn from the issuer's business. Nothing of value to creditors takes its place except what is in reality an unissued share, which cannot profitably be reissued when there is a financial reversal.[1] Today all American jurisdictions permit a corporation to purchase its own shares, subject to various limitations such as impairment of capital.[2]

The main objection to share purchases does not spring from *ultra vires* or a lack of relation to the corporate objects and business. Purchases of its shares, like purchases of its bonds, may be regarded as an incident of adjusting its financial structure to the needs of the business.[3] Such powers are customarily conferred expressly by statute or charter provisions.[4] It is thus misleading to discuss the regulation of share purchases in terms of the *ultra vires* doctrine.

The underlying reason for limiting share purchases is the same as that of dividends. Safeguards should be imposed against a corporation's depletion of its assets and the impairment of its capital needed for the protection of creditors and other shareholders. This has sometimes been expressed in terms of the trust fund doctrine,[5] which has been used to protect creditors.[6]

Exceptions to a Restrictive Rule. There are certain situations that are considered to give little opportunity for abuse, in which the corporation is generally recognized to have the authority to purchase its own shares even out of capital. Exceptions include: the purchases of preferred shares subject to a redemption provision in the articles of incorporation; purchases to compensate dissenting shareholders under appraisal statutes; employee stock purchase plans that have an option or agreement to repurchase; and purchases pursuant to an authorized statutory method of reduction of legal capital.[7]

The Solvency Limitation. Many statutes also retain an insolvency test, however, along with the surplus or capital impairment tests.[8] As will be seen later in this chapter, the timing of these tests assumes special importance when shares are repurchased over a long period, perhaps on an installment basis. The courts are

---

§21.01   [1] Robinson v. Wangemann, 75 F.2d 756 (5th Cir. 1935). *See* Pace v. Pace Bros. Co., 59 P.2d 1 (Utah 1936); Arthur Nussbaum, Acquisition by a Corporation of Its Own Stock, 35 Colum. L. Rev. 971, 978-981 (1935).

[2] 1 Model Business Corp. Act Ann. §6.40, statutory comparison 1(b) (3d ed. 1994) (hereinafter MCBA Ann.).

[3] Weiss v. Samsonite Corp., 741 A.2d 366, 371-373 (Del. Ch. 1999) (noting that self-tender offer is conventional method of delivering to shareholders a return on their investment; self-tender offer to acquire 51 percent of corporation's common stock at a 33 percent premium was the functional equivalent of an extraordinary dividend).

[4] *See* Former Model Business Corp. Act §6 (1969) (Former MBCA); Hayman v. Morris, 36 N.Y.S.2d 756 (N.Y. Sup. Ct. 1972).

[5] In re Atlantic Printing Co., 60 F.2d 553 (D. Mass. 1921); Darnell-Love Lumber Co. v. Wiggs, 230 S.W. 391 (Tenn. 1921); Whittaker v. Weller, 111 P.2d 218 (Wash. 1941).

[6] In the classic English case, for example, more than one-fifth of the capital of the company had been withdrawn and the company had increased its bank borrowings by a wholesale policy of share-purchasing over a period of years. Trevor v. Whitworth 12 App. Cas. 409 (1887).

[7] *See* RFE Capital Partners, L.P. v. Weskar, Inc., 652 A.2d 1093 (Del. Super. Ct. 1994) (lender's option to "put" warrant to corporation held outside Delaware repurchase statute, which applied only to "capital stock").

[8] *See, e.g.,* Former MBCA §6 (1969); N.Y. Bus. Corp. Law §513 (McKinney 1986).

badly divided over whether the surplus and solvency tests are each applied to each installment payment or whether either of these tests should be applied only when the contract of purchase is entered into.

§21.02   The Dangers and Abuses of Dealing in the Corporation's Own Shares

The dangers and abuses incident to allowing a corporation, through its management, to make purchases and sales of its own shares are as follows:

(1) Stock repurchases make it possible for favored shareholders to withdraw current assets from the business and impair the capital and the financial responsibility on which creditors have a right to rely.

(2) Repurchases may be used to undermine the equity or margin of safety of preferred shares, to decrease assets, or to decrease surplus and thereby defeat the reasonable expectations of preferred shareholders as to dividend arrearages, future dividends, and liquidation preferences.

(3) Repurchases may be used with similar discriminatory effect against other common shareholders.

(4) Repurchases may be used to juggle the voting control of the corporation and to buy off bona fide opponents of the management. In the context of a takeover attempt, this practice is currently known as "greenmail."

(5) Repurchases may be used for speculation by the corporation or by its management and for manipulation of the market price of the corporation's stock.

In recognition of these and other dangers, state laws not only impose legal restrictions but also regulate the fairness of such transactions.[1] Additional protection is found under federal law, which imposes stringent disclosure requirements as a result of the 1968 Williams Act amendments to the Securities Exchange Act of 1934.[2]

§21.03   Statutory Restrictions on Repurchases of Shares

Dangers incident to the purchase by corporations of their own shares have led to statutory regulation of the practice. This was not always the case.[1] The repurchase of shares, like the distribution of dividends, is a method of distribution or withdrawal of assets, but the repurchase of shares is subject to even more abuse. What

---

§21.02   [1] See §21.06. But see Kohn v. Birmingham Realty Co., 352 So. 2d 834 (Ala. 1977)1.

[2] Pub. L. No. 90-439, 82 Stat. 454 (1968), codified at 15 U.S.C. §§78m(d)-(c), 78 n(d)-(f) (2000). See §24.01. There has been increasing concern over the use of greenmail as a defense to repel hostile takeover attempts. Both the SEC and Congress have considered new legislation. See 2 Thomas L. Hazen, Treatise on the Law of Securities Regulation §11.20 (3d ed. 1995).

§21.03   [1] Loveland & Co. v. Doernbecher Mfg. Co., 39 P.2d 668, 676 (Or. 1934).

is needed is the imposition of carefully drawn statutory regulations as to the conditions and reasons for which the purchase of shares may be made, the source or basis of permissible withdrawals for payment, the status of the shares after they are reacquired, the effect of later resale, reissue, or retirement of the shares, the accounting practices to be followed on their purchase or reissue, and the liability of directors and shareholders for improper purchases.

Under the pre-1980 Model Business Corporation Act, share repurchases were generally limited to the extent of unrestricted earned surplus or unrestricted capital surplus if specifically authorized by the articles or a majority shareholder vote.[2] The earlier version of the Model Business Corporation Act exempts certain repurchase transactions, such as elimination of fractional shares and retirement of redeemable shares.[3] There is also an insolvency limitation similar to that affecting cash or property dividends.[4] The Act further imposes liability on directors who vote for such illegal share purchases.[5] The 1980 amendments to the Model Business Corporation Act's financial provisions, carried forward to the present Model Business Corporation Act, treat share purchases as a form of distribution to shareholders and apply the same limitations to share purchases as to dividends.[6] As seen in the preceding chapter, the new limitations on distributions after the 1980 amendments do away with traditional legal-capital concepts and are much less restrictive than the former earned-surplus test.[7] California's general corporation statute was the first to use this preferable approach of treating share purchases as a distribution.[8] Because the California statute and since 1980 the Model Business Corporation Act provide that repurchased shares are restored to the status of authorized but unissued shares, they have each thereby prevented such shares from being reported as treasury shares.[9]

Some state corporation laws expressly authorize corporations to purchase their own shares "out of surplus."[10] The same limitation may be expressed by a prohibition against purchases that cause an impairment of capital.[11]

---

[2] Former MBCA §6 (1969). Most states have adopted similar provisions.

[3] *Id.* The former Model Business Corporation Act also appears to exempt transactions compromising indebtedness and payment of dissenting shareholders. *Id.* On redemption of redeemable shares, *see* §18.12.

[4] Former MBCA §6 (1969). *See* §20.10.

[5] Former MBCA §48(b) (1969). *See* §§21.09-21.10.

[6] *See* Model Business Corp. Act §6.40 (1984) (hereinafter MBCA); Former MBCA §§2(i), 6, 45 (1980). For the text and comments of the 1980 amendments to the Model Business Corporation Act, *see* ABA Committee on Corporate Laws, Changes in the Model Business Corporation Act—Amendments to Financial Provisions, 34 Bus. Law. 1867 (1979).

[7] The more restrictive earned-surplus test had become a trademark of the Model Business Corporation Act. These amendments present a radical departure to a total-assets-exceed-total-liabilities-plus-liquidation-preferences balance-sheet test. The Model Business Corporation Act does retain a basic insolvency test.

[8] *See* Cal. Corp. Code §166 (West Supp. 2002).

[9] Cal. Corp. Code §510(a) (West 1990); Former MBCA §6 (1969).

[10] La. Rev. Stat. Ann. §12:55(B) (West Supp. 2002); N.Y. Bus. Corp. Law §513 (McKinney Supp. 2002).

[11] *See* Del. Code Ann. tit. 8, §160 (2001). *See* American Heritage Inv. Corp. v. Illinois Nat'l Bank, 386 N.E. 905 (1979).

A. Share Purchases and Redemptions

These "earned surplus" statutes may allow purchases out of capital surplus when approved in the articles of incorporation or by a majority of the shareholders.[12] Many states allow a corporation to purchase or redeem its redeemable preferred shares out of capital as well as out of surplus—subject, however, to a provision that the capital shall not be impaired as to other preferred shares having priority or equality as to liquidation rights.[13] A general insolvency limitation is often added to these statutes. All such statutes invite inquiry into the extent to which generally accepted accounting principles (GAAP) will guide the statute's application with respect to terms that have accounting significance. As seen earlier, some states expressly incorporate GAAP into their statutes,[14] whereas the present Model Business Corporation Act, following the 1980 amendments to the Model Business Corporation Act, allows "fair valuation or other method that is reasonable in the circumstances,"[15] a result that has occasionally been reached by the courts.[16]

The Delaware Supreme Court in *Klang v. Smith's Food and Drug Centers*[17] provides a sweeping embrace of the authority of the board of directors to resort to unrealized appreciation in assets as a source for the repurchase of shares:

> The General Assembly enacted the statute to prevent boards from draining corporations of assets to the detriment of creditors and the long-term health of the corporation. That a corporation has not yet realized or reflected on its balance sheet the appreciation of assets is irrelevant to this concern. Regardless of what a balance sheet that has not been updated may show, an actual, though unrealized appreciation reflects real economic value that the corporation may borrow against or that creditors may claim or levy upon. Allowing corporations to revalue assets and liabilities to reflect current realities complies with the statute and serves well the policies behind this statute.[18]

This interpretation essentially brings the law of Delaware into line with the discretion the board of directors enjoys under the current Model Business Corporation Act to resort to unrealized gains as a source for distributions to shareholders. One should approach these developments with a healthy appreciation of the risks of allowing such discretion. Corporate law has historically restricted the ability of directors to make distributions to shareholders out of fear that if unrestricted the directors may prefer the interests of shareholders over the pressing rights of creditors. The historical limitations, albeit artificial, nevertheless were guided by metrics that were objective and certainly not within the control of the board of

---

[12] *See* Former MBCA §6 (1969).

[13] *See* Former MBCA §66 (1969). The 1980 amendments to the Model Business Corporation Act deleted this section. ABA Committee on Corporate Laws, *supra* note 6, at 1875.

[14] *See* Cal. Corp. Code §114 (West 1990).

[15] MBCA §6.40(d) (1984).

[16] *See* Klang v. Smith's Food & Drug Centers, 702 A.2d 150, 154 (Del. 1997); Bishop v. Prosser-Grandview Broadcaster, Inc., 472 P.2d 560 (Wash. Ct. App. 1970) ("conservative use of unrealized appreciation" is permissible).

[17] 702 A.2d 150 (Del. 1997).

[18] *Id.* at 154.

directors. *Klang* and the Model Act weaken such objectivity for the regulation of distributions to shareholders. Also, unrealized gains may well not be true economic profits. True gains are those that are amounts that are not necessary to continue to operate the business at its present state. Thus, the fact that the company's asset in Manhattan has appreciated greatly in value does not mean that the full amount of the appreciation is economic profit. If the parcel's location is central to the company's continued vitality—a vendor of Broadway show tickets—it is not entirely correct to believe the property could be sold, the gains realized, and the historical cost of the property reinvested in New Jersey so that the company can continue its business.

§21.04   Executory and Installment Contracts to Repurchase

Particular problems arise with regard to shares' purchase contracts that are executory in nature or where payment by the corporation is delayed by an installment agreement or by the issuance of a debt obligation. There may be important reasons for a corporation to repurchase some of its shares when it has insufficient funds to do so. Repurchase agreements are also common in close corporations,[1] but the commercial purpose for such repurchases may arise when the corporation lacks sufficient cash with which to make the repurchase.[2] A frequent response to these problems is for the corporation to purchase the shares in exchange for an installment note.[3]

Making installment payments to former shareholders when the corporation is insolvent is problematic in many states whose statutes or court decisions have not yet defined the moment when the statutory restrictions are to apply to the transaction. The question is whether, when applying the statutory restrictions to an installment repurchase of shares, the transaction should be treated as a single purchase, so that the restrictions are applied at the moment the contract is entered into, or whether the installment repurchase should be treated as a series of successive purchases, so that the statutory restrictions are to be satisfied as to each payment. At a time when states had only a solvency test, the highly influential decision of *Robinson v. Wangemann*[4] held that the state's solvency test should be applied at the moment of payment, not when the parties entered into the installment contract. This so-called insolvency cutoff rule has been widely followed where the question is the timing of a solvency test.[5]

---

§21.04   [1] *See* 2 F. Hodge O'Neal & Robert B. Thompson, 1 Close Corporations §§7.10, 7.11 (3d ed. 1998).

[2] In case of death or disability, the funding problem can be handled with key man insurance.

[3] *See* In re Envirodyne Indus. Inc., 79 F.3d 579 (7th Cir. 1996) (unsecured claims of nontendering cashed-out shareholders of corporation subordinated under Bankruptcy Act Section 510(c)).

[4] 75 F.2d 756 (5th Cir. 1935). Earlier another court addressed this problem with the same effect. *See* In re Fechheimer Fishel Co., 212 F.357 (2d Cir.), *cert. denied*, 234 U.S. 760 (1914).

[5] McConnell v. Estate of Butler, 402 F.2d 362 (9th Cir. 1968); Buggs v. Fleming, 66 F.2d 859 (4th Cir. 1933).

A. Share Purchases and Redemptions

Given the insolvency cutoff rule, with its emphasis on the time of payment and the gradual proliferation of statutory surplus tests for share repurchases, an issue arises as to whether statutory surplus tests should be applied at the time of the purchase or at the time of the actual payments. In *Mountain State Steel Foundry v. Commissioner,*[6] a tax case, the court held that the surplus test must be met only at the time of payment, not when the repurchase agreement was made. This is the so-called surplus cutoff rule. Thus, under the approach taken in *Mountain State,* an installment note for the repurchase of stock was valid even if the corporation did not have sufficient surplus to cover the repurchase at the time the note was given.[7] This surplus cutoff rule, requiring that statutory balance-sheet tests be met at the time of payment, has been accepted in many cases.[8] The cases adopting a surplus cutoff rule, according to one commentator, are the result of an unfortunate failure to "perceive any distinction between the insolvency cutoff rule and a surplus cutoff rule."[9] Even under the stricter surplus cutoff rule, however, where there are no creditors to be protected, a former shareholder may obtain specific enforcement of a note even if it forces the corporation into liquidation.[10]

Not all decisions have followed the surplus cutoff rule. An influential Texas decision relied on a supposed statutory distinction between "payment" and "purchase" in order to enforce a note executed at a time when there was sufficient surplus, although the corporation was insolvent at the time of payment.[11] The bifurcation of the two tests—solvency and surplus—so that the surplus test is applied at the outset and the solvency test is applied to each payment has been followed in the more recent decisions to consider the question.[12] While New Jersey was one of the few states that rejected the insolvency cutoff rule,[13] a subsequent New Jersey decision[14] imposed a surplus cutoff rule. This decision was later overruled by statute,[15] and that statute has been replaced by a provision patterned after the current Model Business Corporation Act, which applies the statutory tests to each payment only if the corporation did not earlier issue a note or other

---

[6] Mountain State Steel Foundries, Inc. v. Commissioner, 284 F.2d 737 (4th Cir. 1960).

[7] *See also* Christie v. Fifth Madison Corp., 123 N.Y.S.2d 795 (Sup. Ct. 1953); Rainford v. Rytting, 451 P.2d 769 (Utah 1969). *Contra,* McConnell v. Estate of Butler, 402 F.2d 362 (9th Cir. 1968).

[8] In re National Tile & Terrazzo Co., 537 F.2d 329 (9th Cir. 1976); McConnell v. Estate of Butler, 402 F.2d 362 (9th Cir. 1968); In re Trimble Co., 339 F.2d 838 (3d Cir. 1964).

[9] David Herwitz, Installment Repurchase of Stock Limitations, 79 Harv. L. Rev. 303, 326 (1965).

[10] Schneider v. Foster-Thronburg Hardware Co., 33 F. Supp. 271 (S.D. W. Va. 1940); Westerfield Bonte Co. v. Burnett, 195 S.W. 477 (Ky. 1917). *See also* Palmar Millinery Co. v. Spar, 487 F.2d 503 (2d Cir. 1973); In re Trimble Co., 339 F.2d 838 (3d Cir. 1964); Anderson v. K. 6 Moore, Inc., 376 N.E.2d 1238, 1242 (Mass. App. Ct. 1978), *cert. denied,* 439 U.S. 1116 (1979).

[11] Williams v. Nevelow, 513 S.W.2d 535 (Tex. 1974).

[12] *See, e.g.,* Walsh v. Paterna, 537 F.2d 329 (9th Cir. 1976); Tracy v. Perkins-Tracy Printing Co., 153 N.W.2d 241 (Minn. 1967); Niemark v. Mel Kramer Sales, Inc., 306 N.W.2d 278 (Wis. 1981).

[13] Wolff v. Heidritter Lumber Co., 163 A. 140 (N.J. Ch. 1932). *Accord,* Scriggins v. Thomas Dalby Co., 195 N.E. 749 (Mass. 1935).

[14] Kleinberg v. Schwartz, 208 A.2d 803 (N.J. Super. Ct. App. Div.), *aff'd on opinion below,* 214 A.2d 313 (N.J. 1965).

[15] New Jersey Business Corp. Act, ch. 350, §14A:7-16(6), 1968 N.J. Laws 1011, 1078 (repealed 1988).

evidence of indebtedness to acquire shares.[16] Delaware has also statutorily rejected a surplus cutoff rule.[17]

The pre-1980 Model Business Corporation Act, which is similar to the statute that was before the Texas court, speaks in terms of purchases out of surplus and then provides that "no purchase or payment" may be made that would render the corporation insolvent.[18] One commentator has suggested that this language creates a "well-nigh irresistible" inference that the surplus test not be applied at payment.[19] Beginning with the 1980 amendments, the Model Business Corporation Act supplants the surplus test with a requirement that the assets following the distribution not be less than the firm's liabilities and also maintain the solvency test.[20] The statute now applies its own timing standard for the application of both these tests, under which the tests would appear to be applied when the contract to repurchase is entered into, assuming that is the moment when the corporation issues the note embodying its obligation to pay for the shares.[21]

While the surplus cutoff rule certainly protects creditors, it results in the disservice of rendering uncertain the enforceability of bona fide repurchase arrangements should there be insufficient surplus when a later payment is required. To continue to apply both the solvency and the surplus tests to later payments places the withdrawing shareholders in a very difficult position—these shareholders lack the political or equitable powers of stockholders who can protect their future return and also lack the full rights of creditor status. To the extent that the prime concern is the protection of creditors, requiring adequate notice of the corporation's outstanding obligation to make future installment payments would appear to be ample protection. Any creditor unsatisfied with the situation can either demand subordination of the installment obligation or forgo lending money to the corporation.

Some courts have also held that former shareholders may enforce the debt despite insolvency or lack of surplus where there is an underlying lien.[22] One may wonder why the underlying debt that secures a lien should ever achieve greater dignity because of its existence than the debt it secures. Another view holds that a note given as partial consideration to repurchase shares when the corporation was insolvent is illegal, so that the corporation is not obligated to honor the note.[23]

§21.05   Redemption and Purchase of Callable Shares

"Repurchase of shares" is a generic term that includes the narrower concept of redemption pursuant to a contractual right embodied in the share contract and

---

[16] N.J. Business Corp. Act, ch. 350, §14A.7-14.1(4) (Supp. 2002).

[17] Del. Code Ann. tit. 8, §160(a)(1) (2001).

[18] Former MBCA §6 (1969).

[19] Herwitz, *supra* note 9, at 323.

[20] MBCA §45 (1980). *See also* MBCA §6.40 (1984).

[21] MBCA §45 (1980).

[22] In re National Tile & Terrazzo Co., 537 F.2d 329 (9th Cir. 1976); Tracy v. Perkins-Tracy Printing Co., 153 N.W.2d 241 (Minn. 1967). *See also* In re Hamman-McFarland Lumber Co., 629 F.2d 569 (9th Cir. 1980). *Cf.* In re Flying Mailman Serv., Inc., 539 F.2d 866 (2d Cir. 1976).

[23] *See* Field v. Haupert, 647 P.2d 952 (Or. Ct. App. 1982).

A. Share Purchases and Redemptions

the articles of incorporation. In many cases it is significant which type of repurchase is involved.

Preferred shares may be made subject not only to redemption that is optional with the corporation but also to compulsory redemption or resale. There are serious objections to compulsory redemption provisions. The normal redemption provision is an option in favor of the corporation to call in and retire preferred shares at a specified redemption price, usually at a premium over the issue price. Procedures exercising redemption rights, such as notice to the shareholders and some method of selection by lot, pro rata or otherwise, are usually provided in the charter to prevent discrimination for or against other holders if the entire class of shares is not called.[1] Such provisions have been held by some courts not to preclude a corporation from making independent share repurchases without making a pro rata redemption.[2] Even apart from a pro rata requirement, there are, of course, equitable limitations on both repurchases and redemptions.[3]

The option to redeem is exercised by the board of directors. A resolution adopted in accordance with the charter provisions calling certain shares for redemption creates a contract and, unless expressly conditional, the board's action may not be rescinded or modified.[4]

Traditionally, common shares may not be made redeemable at the option of the corporation.[5] "Stock which has no retirement provisions is the backbone of a corporate structure."[6] The chief function of the provision for redemption in stock or bonds is to facilitate the retirement of senior securities for the benefit of the holders of common shares and to make possible the reduction of capital or refinancing at a lower rate of return on new senior securities by paying off and terminating the old shares that call for a higher dividend. The rule against redeemable common stock must be kept in mind when drafting repurchase agreements.[7] Modern corporation acts make a distinction between the purchase of

---

§21.05 [1] Richard M. Buxbaum, Preferred Stock—Law and Draftsmanship, 42 Cal. L. Rev. 243, 265-266 (1954).

[2] Snyder v. Memco Engg. & Mfg. Co., 257 N.Y.S.2d 213 (App. Div. 1965); *contra* General Inv. Co. v. American Hide & Leather Co., 129 A. 244 (N.J. Ch. 1925). *See also* decisions requiring pro rata redemptions by corporations with such charter provisions, State ex rel. Waldman v. Miller-Wohl Co., 28 A.2d 148 (Del. 1942); Petty v. Penntech Papers, Inc., 347 A.2d 140 (Del. Ch. 1975).

[3] *See* §21.06.

[4] Taylor v. Axton-Fisher Tobacco Co., 173 S.W.2d 377 (Ky. 1934), noted in Recent Decisions, Corporations—Power of Directors to Rescind or Modify Action Calling Stock for Redemption, 42 Mich. L. Rev. 530 (1943). *See* Fox v. Johnson & Wimsatt, Inc., 127 F.2d 729 (D.C. Cir. 1942). The transaction involved in the *Taylor* case gave rise to a landmark decision concerning fiduciary duties in connection with redemption. *See* Zahn v. Transamerica Corp., 162 F.2d 36 (3d Cir. 1947), discussed *infra* §21.06.

[5] Starring v. American Hair & Felt Co., 191 A.887 (Del. Ch.), *aff'd mem.*, 2 A.2d 249 (Del. 1937); N.Y. Bus. Corp. Law §512(c) (McKinney 1986). *See* MBCA §15 (1969); Note, Unqualified Redemption of Common Stock: A Question of Public Policy, 50 Nw. U. L. Rev. 558 (1955).

[6] Ecker v. Western Pac. R.R., 318 U.S. 448 (1943).

[7] *See* In re West Waterway Lumber Co., 367 P.2d 807 (Wash. 1962) (upholding bylaw requiring sale to corporation on leaving the business). Callable common stock has its greatest value in the close corporation context. However, it still retains a number of disadvantages. *See* Note, Callable Common Stock, 68 Harv. L. Rev. 1240 (1955).

common shares and the exercise of the right to purchase of callable or redeemable preferred shares.[8] The former is subject to the standard requirement that the purchase can be made to the extent of unrestricted surplus, whereas the acquisition of redeemable shares can rely on the stated capital of the shares to be redeemed, with any additional amount coming from unrestricted surplus. Thus, the stated capital of redeemable shares is of a somewhat temporary character. If shares are redeemed out of capital, this reduces pro tanto the surplus thereafter available for dividends on the common.

Redemptions are subject of course to the general restriction in favor of the priority of creditors and may not be made when a corporation is insolvent or when the redemption would result in insolvency or inability to meet debts and liabilities as they accrue.[9] Many modern acts also take into account the liquidation preferences of shares to remain outstanding.[10] A charter provision may protect the dividend rights of preferred shareholders—for example, by providing that dividends shall be paid "before any sum shall be paid or set apart for the purchase or redemption of any stock now or hereafter authorized."[11]

§21.06 Fiduciary Limitations on Share Repurchases

Share repurchases are subject to abuse to the extent that they provide a facade for an unfair distribution of corporate assets. In a leading Massachusetts case[1] the majority shareholders caused the directors to repurchase a portion of their holdings at a premium. The court held that the fiduciary duties between shareholders in close corporations demanded equal treatment and a right of the minority to participate on a pro rata basis. Similarly, in a Georgia case[2] it was held that the corporate right to purchase its own shares is not absolute but is conditioned on good faith. "Good faith is not just a question of what is proper for the corporation. It also requires that the stockholders be treated fairly and that their investments be protected."[3] However, it has been held that the directors may authorize repurchase at a premium in order to protect the corporation against an outside

---

[8] *Compare* Former MBCA §6 (1969) *with id.* §66 (1969). Section 6(d) expressly exempts redemptions from the legal capital limits on share repurchases.

[9] Hurley v. Boston R. H. Co., 54 N.E.2d 183 (Mass. 1944); Mueller v. Kreauter & Co., 25 A.2d 874 (N.J. Ch. 1942). Former MBCA §66 (1969) makes this explicit. Most states have a similar provision. *But see* McCreery v. RSA Management, Inc., 287 S.E.2d 203 (Ga. 1982) (purchase by insolvent corporation pursuant to power to acquire shares at book value does not violate statute when shares have negative book value, so their acquisition does not require transfer of assets).

[10] *See* Former MBCA §66 (1969).

[11] *See* Peterson v. New England Furn. & Carpet Co., 299 N.W. 208 (Minn. 1941).

§21.06 [1] Donahue v. Rodd Electrotype Co., 328 N.E.2d 505 (Mass. 1975).

[2] Comolli v. Comolli, 246 S.E.2d 278 (Ga. 1978).

[3] *Id.* at 280. The court invalidated a corporate purchase of a deceased brother's shares with borrowed funds in order to perpetuate the control of one of the two surviving brothers, who could not afford to buy the entire holding. The shares had never been offered to the other brother.

A. Share Purchases and Redemptions

takeover attempt.[4] The Delaware court reached this conclusion by relying on the business judgment rule in the face of a claim that the directors were wasting corporate assets in order to perpetuate their control.[5] This practice, known as "greenmail," is discussed in Chapter 12. Greenmail is a subset of a wide range of concerns that arise when the incumbent management through the board of directors causes the corporation to make a defensive purchase of shares as a step toward thwarting a shift in control.[6] Both privately negotiated repurchases[7] and the redemption of a class of shares held by one stockholder[8] have been upheld when used to remove dissident shareholders. Frequently a corporation will purchase its own shares as a first step in a going-private scheme, a problem that is taken up later.[9]

The right to redeem shares may be balanced with the shareholder's conversion rights. In *Zahn v. Transamerica Corporation*,[10] for example, the Third Circuit invalidated a purported redemption on the grounds that it unfairly denied holders their right to convert and participate with the common shareholders in a distribution of assets. The decision may in fact have been based on inadequate notice and disclosure rather than on any duty of fair dealing.[11] The general question of fairness in corporate reorganizations, recapitalization, mergers, and other transactions is treated in a later section,[12] but these principles nevertheless apply to repurchases and redemptions.

At one time it appeared that SEC Rule 10b-5 had a significant role to play in regulating the fairness of share purchases by a corporation. However, the Supreme Court decision in *Santa Fe Industries, Inc. v. Green*[13] imposed a deception

---

[4] Cheff v. Mathes, 199 A.2d 548 (Del. 1964). *Cf.* Strassburger v. Earley, 752 A.2d 557, 572-573 (Del. Ch. 2000) (it is improper to cause the corporation to repurchase its stock for the sole or primary purpose of maintaining the board or management in control).

[5] *See* Kors v. Cary, 158 A.2d 136 (Del. Ch. 1960) (upholding corporate repurchase of shares from unsuccessful takeover attempt). *See also* Kaplan v. Goldsamt, 380 A.2d 556 (Del. Ch. 1977); Petty v. Penntech Papers, Inc., 347 A.2d 140 (Del. 1975). *But see* Bennett v. Propp, 187 A.2d 405 (Del. Ch. 1962) (where directors were unable to show exercise of independent judgment). *See* Note, Corporations.

[6] *See generally* Robert Gordon & Lewis Kornhauser, Takeover Defense Tactics: A Comment on Two Models, 96 Yale L.J. 295 (1986) (allowing incumbents discretion to acquire issuer's shares greatly skews balance of power in their favor); Michael Bradley & Michael Rosenzweig, Defensive Stock Repurchases, 99 Harv. L. Rev. 1378 (1986) (issuer self-tenders create wealth by stimulating auction, but open market purchases may lead to favoritism and can also be coercive).

[7] Martin v. American Potash & Chem. Corp., 92 A.2d 295 (Del. 1952).

[8] Hendricks v. Mill Engg. & Supply Co., 413 P.2d 811 (Wash. 1966). *See also* Strassburger v. Earley, 752 A.2d 557, 572 (Del. Ch. 2000) (corporation may repurchase shares of particular stockholders selectively, without offering to repurchase shares of all stockholders).

[9] *See* §23.04.

[10] 162 F.2d 36 (3d Cir. 1947). *See also* Judah v. Delaware Trust Co., 378 A.2d 624 (Del. 1977).

[11] *See* Van Gemert v. Boeing Co., 520 F.2d 1373 (2d Cir. 1975); Speed v. Transamerica Corp., 135 F. Supp. 176 (D. Del. 1955), *aff'd as modified*, 235 F.2d 369 (3d Cir. 1956). Disclosure obligations clearly attach to corporate repurchases. *See* David E. Wanis, Securities Law: McCormick v. Fund American Companies: Altering the Total Mix of Information Made Available During Disclosure in Corporate Repurchases of Stock, 25 Golden Gate U.L. Rev. 167 (1995). *See also* SEC Rule 13e-3's requirements for going-private transactions.

[12] *See* §§23.01-23.03, 25.05, 26.03.

[13] 430 U.S. 462 (1977); Blue Chip Stamps v. Manor Drug Stores, 421 U.S. 723 (1975) (imposing a purchaser/seller standing requirement).

requirement for 10b-5 and held that a showing of unfairness, even tantamount to equitable fraud, did not give rise to a federal remedy. Accordingly, any 10b-5 remedy would be dependent on some sort of nondisclosure or misrepresentation in connection with the share repurchase or redemption.[14]

The Williams Act amendments to the Securities Exchange Act of 1934[15] impose various substantive and disclosure requirements on tender offerors and issuers repurchasing their own shares. The term "tender offer" is not defined in the act. The term includes many share repurchases that are essentially tender offers by the issuer,[16] in light of the expansive interpretations by the SEC and the courts.[17] Although expressly excluded from most of the Williams Act's disclosure, filing, and substantive provisions,[18] the issuer is subject to section 14(e)'s[19] general antifraud provisions,[20] and section 13(e) expressly empowers the SEC to regulate share repurchases by SEC reporting companies.[21] Pursuant to its authority under this provision, the Commission has promulgated a going-private rule[22] as well as a general disclosure requirement for issuer tender offers.[23] An important provision prohibits the issuer from making any purchases of its shares after someone other than the issuer has commenced a tender offer unless certain detailed disclosures are made by the issuer.[24]

B.   STATUS OF TREASURY SHARES

§21.07   *The Peculiar Status of Treasury Shares*

Treasury shares carry neither voting rights[1] nor rights to dividends or other distributions.[2] Their existence as "issued shares" is a pure fiction, a figure of speech to explain certain special rules and privileges as to their reissue. A share of stock is simply a unit of interest in the corporate enterprise arising from a contract.[3]

---

[14] *See* Thomas L. Hazen, Corporate Mismanagement and the Federal Securities Act's Antifraud Provisions: A Familiar Path With Some New Detours, 20 B.C. L. Rev. 819 (1979).

[15] Pub. L. No. 90-439, 82 Stat. 454 (1968), *codified at* 15 U.S.C. §§78m(d)-(e), 78n(d)(f) (1988). The tender offer provisions are discussed *infra* §§24.01-24.05.

[16] 2 Thomas Lee Hazen, Treatise on The Law of Securities Regulation §11.3 (4th ed. 2002).

[17] *See* Wellman v. Dickinson, 475 F. Supp. 783 (S.D.N.Y. 1979), s.c., 497 F. Supp. 824 (S.D.N.Y. 1980).

[18] 15 U.S.C. §§78m(d)(6)(C), 78n(d)(8)(B) (2000).

[19] 15 U.S.C. §78n(e) (2000).

[20] Since subsection 14(d) contains a specific issuer exclusion and 14(e) contains no exclusion, 14(e) logically should extend to all tender offers, even those by an issuer. *See* Broder v. Dane, 384 F. Supp. 1312 (S.D.N.Y. 1974) (issuer in an attempt to go "private" was enjoined under 14(e) for failure to disclose a material fact).

[21] 15 U.S.C. §78m(e) (2000).

[22] Rule 13e-3, 17 C.F.R. §240.13e-3 (2002).

[23] Rule 13e-4, 17 C.F.R. §240.13e-4 (2002).

[24] Rule 13e-1, 17 C.F.R. §240.13e-4 (2002).

§21.07   [1] Former MBCA §33 (1969).

[2] *See, e.g.,* Nev. Rev. Stat. §78.283(2) (1994).

[3] *See* §16.05.

B. Status of Treasury Shares

When holders of a share surrender their rights to the corporation, it is obvious that the contract is in reality terminated. In cases where the presence, vote, or assent of the majority of the shareholders is required, it must be understood to mean shares that are issued and outstanding and that may be voted.[4] If shares in corporation A are purchased or held by corporation B, which is controlled or dominated by corporation A, the prevailing view is that such shares should not be regarded as treasury shares of the parent. Treasury stock is in essence authorized stock that may be reissued as fully paid without some of the restrictions on an original issue of shares as to consideration and as to preemptive rights, if any.

Due to the fictional nature of treasury shares, the current Model Business Corporation Act, following the 1980 amendments to the Model Business Corporation Act and the California statute, has abolished the need to recognize treasury stock. Under these provisions[5] all reacquired shares, whether by way of redemption or other purchase, are restored to the status of authorized but unissued unless the articles prohibit their reissue, in which case their repurchase results in an automatic amendment to the articles of incorporation reducing the number of authorized shares.

§21.08 The Reissue or Retirement of Treasury Shares

When treasury shares are reissued and sold by the corporation, the shares are issued to the new purchaser, and the corporation is viewed as an intermediate transferee between the former and new shareholders. In reality the old share contract has been extinguished and the new shares are new units of interest created in their place.

Retirement and Cancellation. Outside of California and states that have patterned their financial provisions after the Model Business Corporation Act, a corporation usually has the option on reacquisition of shares to treat them as treasury shares or to retire or cancel them.[1] Treasury shares are carried on the books as authorized and still issued but not outstanding.[2] When retired or cancelled, the shares usually retain the status of authorized but unissued shares.[3] Sometimes the terms "retired" or "cancelled" may be used in the articles of incorporation to mean that once a share is reacquired it may never be reissued. Such a permanent "retirement" results in an automatic reduction in the number of shares authorized by the articles of incorporation. This is common under provisions in the articles in connection with the redemption of preferred shares. To avoid confusion, such

---

[4] Former MBCA §33 (1969). *See* Annot., 90 A.L.R. 315, 318 (1934).

[5] Cal. Corp. Code §510 (West 1990). *See* Committee on Corporate Laws, *supra* §21.03 note 6, at 1869, 1878.

§21.08 [1] Former MBCA §§67, 68 (1969). *See also* N.Y. Bus. Corp. Law §515(b), (e) (McKinney 1986); 15 Pa. Cons. Stat. §1552 (1994).

[2] Former MBCA §2(h) (1969).

[3] Former MBCA §§67, 68 (1969).

provisions in the articles of incorporation should be drafted to expressly prohibit reissue and require reduction of authorized shares where that is desired.[4]

C.   REMEDIES FOR IMPROPER SHARE PURCHASES

§21.09   Recovery by Corporation for Unlawful Share Purchases

There appears little reason in theory to distinguish unlawful share repurchases from unlawful dividends when considering whether innocent shareholders should escape liability. In both cases the danger is the wrongful transfer of assets from the corporation that erodes the creditors' estate. The non-pro-rata nature of a share repurchase raises questions of fairness to nonselling shareholders but does not especially suggest a greater threat to creditors unless the non-pro-rata repurchase is inherently consistent with a richer factual mosaic in which insiders purposely are transferring assets to themselves, such as at the brink of the company's insolvency. And even in this context there appears little gained in the analysis by distinguishing between the treatment of cunning insiders who sell their shares to the corporation and of those who merely pay themselves dividends. Thus, since the 1980 amendments, the former Model Business Corporation Act and the current Model Business Corporation Act impose liability only on guilty shareholders.[1]

Initially, shareholder liability for improper share repurchases was grounded primarily in common law, but today this liability is primarily statutory.[2] Corporation statutes either provide directly for shareholder liability or subject shareholders to the contribution rights of directors.[3] Either form of liability is usually limited to those shareholders acting with knowledge of the impropriety.[4]

In the case of improper share purchases the directors are liable for causing a corporation to repurchase shares in violation of statutory legal capital requirements.[5] Director liability for improper distributions is usually governed by statutes

---

[4] The former Model Business Corp. Act §67 (1969) enables corporations to reduce authorized shares on redemption or repurchase through a provision in the articles. It specifies that reacquired shares have the status of authorized but unissued shares unless an article's provision prohibits reissue.

§21.09   [1] MBCA §8.33 (1984); MBCA §48 (1980).

[2] There continues to be a question as to whether such statutes are exclusive. See In re Kettle Fried Chicken of Am., Inc., 513 F.2d 807 (6th Cir. 1975) (court refused to conclude that Delaware general corporation statute §174's proscription of director liability for unlawful distributions with no reference to shareholder liability exempted shareholders from liability); Reilly v. Segert, 201 N.E.2d 444 (Ill. 1964).

[3] Cf. Cal. Code §506(a) (West 1990) (direct shareholder liability) with Former MBCA §48(d) (1969) (contribution to directors).

[4] See, e.g., Palmer v. Justice, 322 F. Supp. 892 (N.D. Tex.), aff'd per curiam, 451 F.2d 371 (5th Cir. 1971).

[5] See MBCA §8.33 (1984); Former MBCA §48(b) (1969).

C. Remedies for Improper Share Purchases

and is enforced through director liability provisions based on the directors' breach of the duty of care to the corporation.[6] There is some conflict of authority as to whether recovery from directors may be had only for the benefit of existing creditors or also for subsequent creditors. The trend, however, seems to be to allow recovery even to subsequent creditors without notice.[7]

§21.10 Right of Recovery by Creditors from Selling Shareholders

The standing of creditors to pursue unlawful share repurchases is no different from their standing to pursue unlawful dividends.[1] When the corporation is insolvent, creditors are usually represented by a receiver or trustee in bankruptcy. However, the individual creditor may bring an action for the improper payments. In this case, rather than suing the shareholder on the creditor's original claim, the creditor usually secures a judgment against the corporation first and then follows the assets of the corporation to the selling shareholders.[2]

---

[6] See Former MBCA §§48(b) (1969).

[7] For cases stating that recovery may be had for the benefit of subsequent creditors, see, e.g., Coleman v. Tepel, 230 F. 63 (3d Cir. 1916); Hansen v. California Bank, 61 P.2d 794 (Cal. Ct. App. 1936); Kleinberg v. Schwartz, 208 A.2d 803 (N.J. Super. Ct. App. Div.), aff'd on opinion below, 214 A.2d 313 (N.J. 1965).

§21.10 [1] See §§20.16-20.17.

[2] See 15A William M. Fletcher, Fletcher Cyclopedia of the Law of Private Corporations §§7417, 7419, 7585 (2000).

CHAPTER 22

Corporate Combinations

A.   INTRODUCTION TO MERGERS AND ACQUISITIONS

§22.01   Corporate Combinations Overview

The history of American business bears out that corporations transform themselves not solely by growth within but, more important, by acquisition—be they the acquired or the acquirer. This chapter examines the regulatory climate through which corporations acquire other corporations, sell all or substantially all their assets, or acquire the shares of another corporation. In this area the law threads a course between, on the one hand, freeing the entrepreneurial spirit that can mobilize resources to a new and, one hopes, more productive use and, on the other hand, being solicitous of the shareholders' desires not only to participate in that decision but also to protect their interests in the corporation.

The most basic form of acquisition of assets occurs in the simple buy-sell context, where one corporation for a mutually agreed upon price sells assets to another corporation. Not all asset sales merit the attention of state corporate statutes; as will be seen, only sales of all or substantially all the assets outside the ordinary course of business are singled out for special treatment under most corporate statutes. Alternatively, the acquirer and the acquired corporations may choose to merge so that their assets and liabilities are thereafter automatically combined by operation of law. Sometimes the merger of two corporations is structured so that neither corporation survives, but instead, pursuant to their plan of merger, a third corporation is created into which the assets and liabilities of the combining corporations will thereafter exist. This form of acquisition is known as a consolidation. A few state statutes continue to recognize this infrequent form of combination.

Sales of assets, mergers, and consolidations present three different methods of corporate fusion, each with its own financial and legal considerations. A fourth method of corporate combination is a share exchange, whereby all the outstanding shares of an approving class of stock are acquired by another corporation. A variation of this form is the purchase of shares of another corporation (called the "target" corporation). Such purchases can occur either through open market purchases or by a solicitation of the shareholders to sell, generally referred to as a "tender offer." Unlike the other methods of corporate fusion, the tender offer commits to the individual shareholders of the target corporation the decision whether to part with their shares. In contrast, the combination that is consummated by a sale of corporate assets, a merger, or a consolidation is authorized by complex statutory procedures, and generally requires shareholder approval by a set percentage of the class voting by each class of shares affected by the class.[1]

---

§22.01   [1] Model Business Corporation Act §§71, 72, 72-A, 73, 79 (1969) (hereinafter Former Model Bus. Corp. Act); Revised Model Business Corporation Act §§11.02, 11.03, 11.04, 12.02 (1984) (hereinafter Model Bus. Corp. Act) (the revised Act has deleted the section on consolidation).

A. Introduction to Mergers and Acquisitions

Any method of corporate combination or other fundamental change can work to the substantial prejudice of minority shareholders.[2] Accordingly, both the legislatures and the courts have recognized the need to protect the minority against abuse. The most prevalent mechanism to protect those who oppose the acquisition is the statutory appraisal remedy. This procedure allows dissenting shareholders to receive in cash the fair value of their shares, as determined through an independent appraisal.[3] As will be seen, the so-called dissenters' right is cumbersome and does not always protect the minority's interests. Further, the appraisal remedy does not apply to all types of acquisitions. There has been a serious conflict as to the availability of a judicial remedy for unfairness when dissenters' rights were available. The trend of recent decisions is to allow for judicial scrutiny of alleged unfair acquisitions in exceptional cases independent of any statutory remedy.[4]

The federal securities laws have substantial impact on the law relating to corporate combinations. Many methods of corporate combination involve shareholders exchanging their shares either for another class of shares, for shares of another corporation, or for cash. In each case the antifraud provisions of SEC Rule 10b-5 come into play, as is equally true when the corporation rather than the individual shareholder acquires or issues securities.[5] Whenever the issuance of securities is involved, the registration provisions of the Securities Act of 1933 must be considered.[6] Moreover, the federal proxy rules indirectly protect against abuse or ill-planned acquisitions by heightening the disclosure[7] and hence accountability that management is subject to when carrying out acquisitions involving publicly traded corporations subject to section 14(a) of the Securities Exchange Act of 1934.[8] Finally, significant regulatory protection occurs through the 1968 Williams Act amendments to the Securities Exchange Act of 1934 and subsequent state legislation that regulate tender offers and open market purchases of corporate shares.[9]

---

[2] *See* F. Hodge O'Neal & Robert B. Thompson, O'Neal's Oppression of Minority Shareholders ch. 5 (1985); Nelson Ferebee Taylor, Evolution of Corporate Combination Law: Policy Issues and Constitutional Questions, 76 N.C.L. Rev. 687 (1998).

[3] Former Model Bus. Corp. Act §§80, 81 (1969); Model Bus. Corp. Act §§13.02, 13.03, 13.20-13.26 (1984). *See* §§22.18-22.22.

[4] Weinberger v. UOP, Inc., 457 A.2d 701 (Del. 1983) (indicating appraisal remedy is exclusive in absence of fraud). *But see* Rabkin v. Phillip A. Hunt Chem. Corp., 498 A.2d 1099 (Del. 1985) (interpreting *Weinberger* as allowing for remedies other than appraisal when specific acts of unfairness are alleged).

[5] 17 C.F.R. §240.10b-5 (2002). *See* §§12.08-12.11. The strict liability of section 16(b) of the Exchange Act (15 U.S.C. §78p(b) (2000)) also may be a factor. *See* §12.06. *See generally* Thomas Lee Hazen, Treatise on the Law of Securities Regulation chs. 12, 13 (4th ed. 2002).

[6] 15 U.S.C. §§77(f), 77(g) (2000). *See generally* 1 Hazen, *supra* note 5, chs. 2-7.

[7] *Cf.* Skeen v. Jo-Ann Stores, Inc., 750 A.2d 1170 (Del. 2000) (rejecting enhanced disclosure requirement under state corporate law).

[8] *See* §13.23.

[9] 15 U.S.C. §§78m(d), 78m(e), 78n(d); 78n(f) (2000).

§22.02   Comparison of Methods of Combination or Reorganization

Although the three traditional methods of reorganization—merger, consolidation, and sale-purchase of assets—are distinct, they have a number of similarities. The essential steps to consolidate or merge[1] are as follows:

(1) A consolidation or merger always involves a transfer of the assets and business of one or more corporations to another corporation in exchange for its securities, cash, or other consideration.[2] A merger results in a transfer of the assets to one of the constituent corporations that absorbs the other. With a consolidation a new consolidated corporation is created into which each constituent corporation transfers its assets and liabilities. In each case, the transfer is made by operation of law—that is, by force of the statute operating on the agreement of the constituents to merge or consolidate.[3]

(2) A merger or consolidation entails the assumption of the debts and liabilities of the absorbed company or companies by operation of law.[4]

(3) A necessary effect of a merger or consolidation is the dissolution of the absorbed company or companies.[5] As will be seen, a sale of assets does not constitute a dissolution and does not necessarily call for the liquidation or dissolution of the seller.[6]

(4) A merger or consolidation involves a payment to the shareholders of the absorbed corporation in shares, debt, or cash or securities of the new or surviving corporation. Those who pursue their appraisal remedy can receive cash equal to the appraised value of their shares.

The principal differences between an acquisition by sale of assets and statutory merger or consolidation are:[7]

---

§22.02 [1] Merger and consolidation are two different forms of combination. In a merger, one corporation merges into another. In contrast, with a consolidation, the two combining companies consolidate into a third. Distinguished *infra* §22.08. Procedures for merger and consolidation are considered *infra* §22.11.

[2] *See, e.g.*, Shannon v. Samuel Langston Co., 379 F. Supp. 797 (W.D. Mich. 1974).

[3] Model Bus. Corp. Act §11.07 (1984); Former Model Bus. Corp. Act §76 (1969). For an interesting application of this principle, *see* Tekni-Plex Inc. v. Meyner and Landis, 664 N.E.2d 1258 (N.Y. 1996) (successor corporation possesses the attorney-client privilege with respect to pre-acquisition business operations of acquired company).

[4] *See* Good v. Lackawanna Leather Co., 233 A.2d 201, 208 (N.J. Super. Ct. Ch. Div. 1967); ASA Architects Inc. v. Schlegel, 665 N.E.2d 1083 (Ohio 1996).

[5] Knapp v. North Am. Rockwell Corp., 506 F.2d 361, 363 (3d Cir. 1974), *cert. denied*, 421 U.S. 965 (1975).

[6] Cleveland Worsted Mills Co. v. Consolidated Textile Corp., 292 F. 129 (3d Cir. 1923); Goldman v. Postal Tel., Inc., 52 F. Supp. 763, 771 (D. Del. 1943); Clarke Mem. College v. Monaghan Land Co., 257 A.2d 234 (Del. Ch. 1969).

[7] *See* George S. Hills, Consolidation of Corporations by Sale of Assets and Distributions of Shares, 19 Cal. L. Rev. 349, 351-352 (1931) (quoting from Henry W. Ballantine, Corporations (1927)).

A. Introduction to Mergers and Acquisitions

(1) In case of a sale by one corporation to another, the assets of the selling corporation are transferred by written instruments of conveyance, not by operation of law as occurs in a merger or consolidation.

(2) There are different statutory requirements as to the vote or consent of shareholders. As will be seen, the shareholders of both the successor or surviving corporation and those of the acquired corporation are generally entitled to vote and, if approved, those who dissent to the merger or consolidation are entitled to their appraisal remedy. In contrast, only the shareholders of the corporation selling its assets are entitled to vote on the transaction[8] because the purchasing corporation acts only through its board of directors.

(3) In a consolidation or merger, the method and basis of exchanging the shares of the constituent corporations for shares, debt, or cash of the successor corporation are set forth in the consolidation or merger agreement. This becomes binding on all parties except dissenting shareholders who elect to invoke their appraisal remedy. Thus, following approval there is a compulsory exchange of new shares for old. In contrast, authority distinct from the stockholders' approval of the sale must be involved to distribute the sales proceeds to the selling corporation's stockholders. Such authority arises after the stockholders have approved the corporation's dissolution. It is also possible, within the limitations of the local state statute, to distribute the sales proceeds through either a dividend or repurchase of shares. That is, neither the dissolution of the selling corporation nor the mechanism for distributing the sales proceeds to the selling corporation's shareholders is embodied in the state statutes that authorize corporations to sell all or substantially all their assets. Thus such a distribution pursuant to the plan is a separate transaction following the actual consummation of the sale itself.

(4) Unlike the rules for a merger or consolidation, the general rule for a sale of corporate assets is that the purchasing corporation is not liable for any of the liabilities of the seller.[9] As will be seen, exceptions to this generality abound. A purchaser of corporate assets will be found to have assumed the seller's liabilities in certain circumstances,[10] such as when (a) the purchaser expressly or impliedly has assumed the seller's obligations, (b) the transaction is determined to be a de facto merger, (c) the purchasing corporation is merely a continuation of the selling corporation, or (d) the transaction involved fraud.

---

[8] *See* §22.06, dealing with the de facto merger doctrine, involving cases where the purchase of assets is used to avoid statutory dissenters' appraisal rights. In Delaware even the shareholders of the selling corporation do not have statutory dissenters' rights. Del. Code Ann. tit. 8, §262 (2001).

[9] *E.g.*, Knapp v. North Am. Rockwell Corp., 506 F.2d 361 (3d Cir. 1974), *cert. denied*, 421 U.S. 965 (1975), noted in Note, 6 Seton Hall L. Rev. 477 (1975); Note, 49 Temple L.Q. 1014 (1976). *See supra* note 5.

[10] *See* §22.08; William L. Cary & Melvin A. Eisenberg, Cases & Materials on Corporations, 1148-1149 (6th unab. ed. 1988).

(5) A selling corporation is not dissolved by reason of a sale of its entire assets; this requires separate approval by the stockholders and can occur at the same meeting as their approval of the sale of the company's assets. Generally, after such a sale the corporation is liquidated pursuant to a vote approving its voluntary dissolution. A dissolution, however, is not the inevitable consequence of a sale, and the corporation may continue in the same or some new business or in a state of suspended animation.[11]

The ultimate choice of the form a corporate combination is to take is generally a function of legal considerations combined with business and financial realities. One point of primary importance in selecting a method of reorganization is to take advantage of those provisions of the federal tax code that make certain kinds of reorganization exchanges tax-free.[12]

B. SALE OF ASSETS

§22.03 *Purposes of Sale of Substantially All Assets*

The power to sell all of a corporation's assets can be a preliminary step to formal dissolution. Simply put, the authority to sell all its assets outside the regular course of business can be the means for the orderly cessation of business, whether going out of business was caused by financial distress or otherwise.

A purchase and sale of assets may be used not only as a method of expansion or acquisition of a business by another corporation, but also as a method of voluntary reorganization or recapitalization. In such cases a new corporation is organized for the purpose of acquiring the assets and business of the old, and these assets are then transferred to the purchaser in exchange for an issue of its securities to be distributed directly or indirectly to the shareholders of the selling corporation.[1]

§22.04 *Statutory Authorization of Sale of Assets*

Every jurisdiction has a statute expressly authorizing a corporation to sell, mortgage, or pledge, and to convey all or substantially all of its property rights with the

---

[11] Goldman v. Postal Tel., Inc., 52 F. Supp. 763, 771 (1943); McKenna v. Art Pearl Works, Inc., 310 A.2d 677 (Pa. Super. Ct. 1973); Levis v. Pittsburgh United Corp., 199 A. 332 (Pa. 1938). *See* Chapter 24.

[12] I.R.C. §368 (2000). 26 U.S.C.A. §368 (2000).

§22.03 [1] *E.g.,* United Milk Prods. Corp. v. Lovell, 75 F.2d 923 (6th Cir. 1935) (refunding of preferred shares by sale to new corporation formed just for that purpose).

B. Sale of Assets

vote or consent of its board of directors and a specified majority of its shareholders.[1] Under these statutes, the sale or transfer of all or substantially all of the corporate assets requires authorization by a majority of the board of directors and also the approval of at least a majority of the shareholders entitled to vote. Under most statutes, shareholder authorization can be given only after prior notice of the time, place, and purpose of the meeting at which the vote will be taken and after distribution of a complete and specific statement of the terms and conditions of the proposed sale to be considered.[2] In some jurisdictions, board approval may follow the shareholder action,[3] although generally the plan must first be adopted by the directors.[4] In a few jurisdictions a meeting is not necessary to obtain the shareholders' consent.[5] Under most statutes it is not required that there be final shareholder approval of the complete and final contract of sale;[6] shareholders are considered sufficiently protected if they approve the principal terms of the transaction and the nature and amount of the consideration to be received by the corporation upon the sale. Under the earlier version of the Model Business Corporation Act, even the fixing of consideration can be delegated to the board.[7] When the shareholder vote is subject to the federal proxy rules, there are more stringent requirements of specificity.[8]

Ordinarily class voting on proposals for the sale of assets is not required. It would seem, however, that a class vote is sound policy whenever the purpose of a sale is to carry out a recapitalization such that as a result of the transaction the relative rights, privileges, and preferences in the share contract will be altered. A class vote of the preferred shares would appear unnecessary when the sale is the prelude to a dissolution and liquidation of the company. In such a case, the entitlements and protection for the preferred shares should be those provided through their contract with the corporation—for example a vote on dissolution or a liquidation privilege.[9] If the purpose of the transaction is to dissolve and liquidate, the same rules as to voting should apply as in cases of dissolution.[10] The

---

§22.04   [1] Cal. Corp. Code §§152, 1001 (West 1990) (simple majority); Del. Code Ann. tit. 8, §271 (2001) (simple majority; no shareholder vote necessary for mortgage or pledge of assets, *id.* §272).

[2] *See, e.g.,* statutes cited *supra* note 1.

[3] *E.g.,* Cal. Corp. Code §§1001(a)(2), 1201(f) (West 2000).

[4] 3 Model Bus. Corp. Act Ann. §11.03 (3d ed. 1994).

[5] *E.g.,* Minn. Stat. Ann. §§302A.441, 302A.661 (2000) (requires unanimous consent). *Cf.* Del. Code Ann. tit. 8, §228 (2001) (generally allowing consent of a majority of shares without a meeting).

[6] *E.g.,* Cal. Corp. Code §1001(c) (Supp. 2002) ("Such sale . . . may be made upon such terms and conditions . . . as the board may deem in the best interests of the corporation"); Former Model Bus. Corp. Act §79(c) (1969) ("at such meeting the shareholders may authorize such sale . . . and may fix, or may authorize the board of directors to fix, any or all of the terms and conditions thereof and the consideration to be received. . . .").

[7] Former Model Bus. Corp. Act §79(c) (1969). The Revised Model Business Corporation Act requires the corporation to notify the shareholders of the consideration to be received. Model Bus. Corp. Act §12.02(d) (1984). Of course, the directors' discretion is constrained by considerations of fairness, *infra* §23.02, in addition to the specter of statutory appraisal rights, §§22.19, 22.20.

[8] SEC Schedule 14A, item 16.

[9] *See* Model Bus. Corp. Act §10.04 (1984); Former Model Bus. Corp. Act §60 (1969). The Model Business Corporation Act provides for class voting only if the transaction affects special rights of that class, which is generally not the case with a sale of corporate assets not followed by dissolution.

[10] *See* Chapter 26.

holders of common stock may well have the right to decide this question and to pay off the preferred shareholders in winding up if they so desire.

Today's statutes are not specific as to what constitutes "substantially all" of a corporation's assets. The statutory terminology negates the use of a hard and fast rule; one might use an 80 percent rule of thumb borrowed from the tax laws,[11] although courts have gone below this figure. For example, it has been held that stock in another company totaling more than 75 percent of the selling corporation's assets triggered the statutory requirement of shareholder approval prior to its disposition by the corporation.[12] The test has been said to be both quantitative and qualitative and thus depends on the entirety of circumstances surrounding the sale.

The vast majority of the states condition shareholder approval on both the sale being of "all or substantially all the assets" and the sale being "otherwise than in the usual and regular course of business."[13] Delaware is among those states that do not limit the scope of their statutes to sales outside the regular course of business, but in a leading case the Delaware Supreme Court applied such a limitation:

> If the sale is of assets quantitatively vital to the operation of the corporation *and* is out of the ordinary and substantially affects the existence and purpose of the corporation, then it is beyond the power of the Board of Directors.[14]

Thus the inquiry entails a dynamic interaction between a quantitative and qualitative standard. This approach has long been emphasized.[15] The comment to the Revised Model Business Corporation Act explains:

> The phrase "substantially all" is synonymous with "nearly all" and was added merely to make it clear that the statutory requirements could not be avoided by retention of some minimal or nominal residue of the original assets. A sale of all the corporate assets other than cash or cash equivalents is normally the sale of "all or substantially all" of the corporation's property. A sale of several distinct manufacturing lines while retaining one or more lines is normally not a sale of "all or substantially all" *even though the lines being sold are substantial business.* If the lines retained are viewed only as a temporary operation or as a pretext to avoid the "all or substantially all" requirements, however, the statutory requirements of chapter 12 [of the Model Business Corp. Act] must be complied with.[16]

---

[11] I.R.C. §322(b) (2000); 26 U.S.C. §332(b) (2000); Treas. Reg. §1.332-2. For a discussion of sales-of-assets statutes, *see* Stanley Siegel, When Corporations Divide: A Statutory and Financial Analysis, 79 Harv. L. Rev. 534, 534-545 (1966).

[12] *See* Philadelphia Nat'l Bank v. B. S. F. Co., 199 A.2d 557 (Del. Ch.), *rev'd on other grounds,* 204 A.2d 746 (Del. 1964). *See* Katz v. Bergman, 431 A.2d 1274 (Del. Ch. 1981) (sale of subsidiary that was parent's sole income-producing asset, was 51 percent of parent's total assets, and provided 45 percent of parent's net sales held to be sale of substantially all assets). *But cf.* Gimbel v. Signal Co., 316 A.2d 599 (Del. Ch.), *aff'd per curiam,* 316 A.2d 619 (Del. 1974) (41 percent of company's net worth not "substantially all").

[13] *See* Model Bus. Corp. Act §12.02(a) (1984).

[14] Gimbel v. Signal Co., 316 A.2d 599, 606 (Del. Ch.), *aff'd per curiam,* 316 A.2d 619 (Del. 1974).

[15] *See, e.g.,* Stiles v. Aluminum Prod. Co., 86 N.E.2d 887 (Ill. App. Ct. 1949) (assets sold were twice value of assets retained but were the essential operating assets as those retained were cash equivalents). *See generally* Siegel, *supra* note 11, 537-544.

[16] Model Bus. Corp. Act §12.01 Official Comment (1984) (emphasis added).

B. Sale of Assets

While the Model Business Corporation Act's comment may appear inconsistent with the statute's language, which has eliminated the "all or substantially all" standard and instead refers to a disposition that would leave the corporation without a "significant continuing business activity,"[17] the comment can best be seen as emphasizing the distinction made earlier between decisions that shift the company assets to new areas,[18] which decisions are committed to the discretion of the board of directors, and decisions that are a prelude to a structural change in the nature of investment, such as sales that are a prelude to liquidation, for which shareholder approval is necessary. Nevertheless, the comment and the statute are far from definitive in their content or scope.

Some courts have held that sales of real estate, even if the company's only asset, is not subject to a statute governing sale of assets.[19] The rationale here is that if the sale of real estate is a purpose for which the company was organized, such a sale is "in the ordinary course of business" and thus within the directors' purview.[20] The sale of property that is the core asset of a real estate investment corporation formed to manage the property's rental is not in the ordinary course of business.[21] There are no exceptions in such statutes for financial exigencies:[22] If the sale of assets is within the ordinary course of business, then no shareholder approval is required.[23]

§22.05 Sale of Assets for Securities

At one time there was a conflict as to whether in the absence of a statute a corporation could sell substantially all its assets in exchange for shares or other securities of the purchasing company. Today a corporation may exchange all or part of its assets for securities, but some statutes are silent as to what, other than shares of stock, constitutes legitimate consideration.[1] The statutory authority for these transactions is augmented by tax-free treatment where substantially all of the selling corporation's assets are exchanged solely for all or part of another corporation's voting stock.[2]

---

[17] Model Bus. Corp. Act §12.02(a) (1984).

[18] In this regard, the Model Act's Official Comment's use of "former" takes on added significance because it assumes the corporation's continuation.

[19] Roehner v. Gracie Manor, Inc., 160 N.E.2d 519 (N.Y. 1959). *Contra,* Boyer v. Legal Estates, Inc., 255 N.Y.S.2d 955 (Sup. Ct. 1964).

[20] Morris v. Washington Med. Ctr., Inc., 331 A.2d 132 (D.C. Ct. App. 1975).

[21] *See* Buyer v. Legal Estates, Inc., 255 N.Y.S.2d 955 (Sup. Ct. 1964). *See also* Naas v. Lucas, 739 P.2d 1051 (Or. Ct. App. 1987) (transfer of substantially all assets by president to satisfy bona fide debt not within ordinary course of business).

[22] Michigan Wolverines Student Co-Op., Inc. v. William Goodyear & Co., 22 N.W.2d 884 (Mich. 1946).

[23] Jeppi v. Brockman Holding Co., 206 P.2d 847 (Cal. 1949) (real estate); Santa Fe Hills Golf & Country Club v. Safehi Realty Co., 349 S.W.2d 27 (Mo. 1961) (five-year extension of lease).

§22.05 [1] Del. Code Ann. tit. 8, §271 (2001) ("money or other property, including shares of stock in and/or other securities . . .").

[2] I.R.C. §368(a)(1)(c) (1988).

§22.06   The De Facto Merger Doctrine

In a large majority of jurisdictions, with the important exceptions of Delaware and California, dissenting shareholders are given the right to be paid in cash for the appraised value of their shares in the event of a sale or exchange of all or substantially all of a corporation's assets not in the ordinary course of its business.[1] No showing of fraud, unfairness, or prejudice is required.[2] In Delaware this statutory remedy arises only in connection with statutory mergers and consolidations.[3] Whether or not the scope of appraisal statutes should be so extended is a question of policy depending on the jurisdiction's assessment of how well the appraisal remedy works and whether it does more harm than good.

In a state that does not grant dissenters' rights for sales of assets, there is a serious gap in the shareholder's protection because an effect the same as a merger can be achieved by a sale of assets.[4] For example, assume Corporation A sells its assets to Corporation B and as part of the deal B assumes A's obligations and A dissolves. Thereafter, Corporation A distributes the proceeds of the sale (the B securities) to its shareholders under its plan of dissolution. In reviewing these transactions some courts may determine that there has been a de facto merger, in which dissenters' rights under the merger statute are to be honored.[5] Two significant effects of so treating transactions so the procedural rights that accompany mergers apply are: The shareholders of the "purchasing" corporation will be entitled to vote on the transaction, and an appraisal remedy is available to all shareholders entitled to vote.

A far greater number of jurisdictions, including Delaware,[6] refuse to embrace the de facto merger doctrine. This refusal is based on the doctrine of "independent statutory significance" or equal dignity. This doctrine holds that each authorizing provision of the state's corporation statute is entitled to its own independent significance such that the substantive effects and procedural requirements of one provision are not to be harmonized with another provision under

---

§22.06   [1] *See* Former Model Bus. Corp. Act §80(a)(2) (1969). The Revised Model Business Corporation Act has replaced the "all or substantially all" and "usual and regular course of business" language with a standard defined by a disposition of assets that would leave the corporation without a "significant continuing business activity." Model Bus. Corp. Act §§12.02(a), 13.02(a)(3) (1984). *But see e.g.*, Del. Code Ann. tit. 8, §§253(d), 262 (2001). *Cf.* Cal. Corp. Code §1300 (West 1990, Supp. 2002).

[2] Homer v. Crown Cork & Seal Co., 141 A. 425, 434 (Md. 1928).

[3] Del. Code Ann. tit. 8, §262 (2001).

[4] *See* §22.09. Even in states granting dissenters' rights they can be eliminated by leaving some assets or by amending the charter to permit such sales in the ordinary course. *See* §22.20.

[5] *See generally* Ernest Folk, IV, De Facto Mergers in Delaware: *Hariton v. Arco Electronics, Inc.*, 49 Va. L. Rev. 1261 (1963); Marilyn Winthrop, Structuring a Corporate Acquisition to Avoid the De Facto Merger Doctrine, 6 Sec. Reg. L.J. 195 (1978); Jan Deutsch, The Form and Substance of a Merger: A Reading of Farris v. Glen Alden Corp., 20 Vill. L. Rev. 80 (1974).

[6] *See* Hariton v. Arco Elec., Inc. 188 A.2d 123 (Del. 1963), *aff'g* 182 A.2d 22 (Del. Ch. 1962); Heilbrunn v. Sun Chem. Corp., 150 A.2d 755 (Del. 1959), *aff'g* 146 A.2d 757 (Del. Ch. 1958); Graeser v. Phoenix Fin. Co., 254 N.W. 859 (Iowa 1934); Good v. Lackawanna Leather Co., 233 A.2d 201 (N.J. Super. Ct. Ch. Div. 1967).

B. Sale of Assets

which the same objective could have also been accomplished but pursuant to different procedural requirements. Thus, under the doctrine of independent statutory significance, if the formal requirements of the sale-of-assets statute are complied with, the transaction will be considered a sale rather than a merger, at least where the contract of sale does not call for dissolution and the selling corporation remains in existence long enough to receive the proceeds of the sale and distribute them to its shareholders.

The leading Delaware decision of *Hariton v. Arco Electronics, Inc.*[7] refused to apply the de facto merger doctrine to a sale of assets even though the sales contract contained an undertaking by the selling corporation to dissolve a new enterprise without the right to appraisal. The Supreme Court of Delaware, although conceding that a sale of assets coupled with a mandatory plan of dissolution and distribution achieves the same result as a merger, held that the transaction was legal. "This is so," said the court, "because the sale-of-assets statute and the merger statute are independent of each other. They are, so to speak, of equal dignity, and the framers of a reorganization may resort to either type of corporate mechanics to achieve the desired end."[8] In other words "the general theory of the Delaware Corporation Law [is] that action taken pursuant to the authority of the various sections of that law constitute acts of independent legal significance and their validity is not dependent on other sections of the Act."[9]

Several decisions in other jurisdictions have applied the de facto merger doctrine.[10] In the leading de facto merger case,[11] *Farris v. Glen Alden Corporation,* Glen Alden and List Industries, a holding company that had purchased large amounts of Glen Alden stock, entered into a "reorganization agreement," subject to shareholder approval in each company. Under the agreement, (1) Glen Alden was to acquire all List Industries assets; (2) Glen Alden was to increase its authorized stock and issue to List several million shares of Glen Alden stock, which in turn were to be distributed to the List shareholders—five shares of Glen Alden in exchange for six shares of List; (3) Glen Alden was to assume List's liabilities, including a $5 million note that List had given to purchase Glen Alden stock some years before, as well as existing stock options, incentive plans, and pension obligations; (4) Glen Alden's name was to be changed to "List Alden Corporation"; (5) the directors of both corporations were to become directors of List Alden, List directors would hold 11 of the 17 directorships on the new board, and the List interests would thus gain control of the new company; and (6) List was to be dissolved.

---

[7] 188 A.2d 123 (Del. 1963), *aff'g* 182 A.2d 22 (Del. Ch. 1962).

[8] 188 A.2d at 125.

[9] *Id.* at 124, quoting Langfelder v. Universal Labs., 68 F. Supp. 209, 211 n.5 (D. Del. 1946).

[10] *E.g.,* Shannon v. Samuel Langston Co., 379 F. Supp. 797 (W.D. Mich. 1974); Marks v. Autocar Co., 153 F. Supp. 768 (E.D. Pa. 1954) (Pennsylvania law); Pratt v. Ballman-Cummings Furn. Co., 549 S.W.2d 270 (Ark. 1977); Rath v. Rath Packing Co., 136 N.W.2d 410 (Iowa 1965); Farris v. Glen Alden Corp., 143 A.2d 25 (Pa. 1958).

[11] 143 A.2d 25 (Pa. 1958).

The Supreme Court of Pennsylvania held the transaction to be a de facto merger, so the plaintiff, a Glen Alden shareholder, was entitled to an appraisal remedy. The court concluded that whenever one corporation combines with another so as to lose its essential nature and alter the fundamental relationships of the shareholders among themselves and their relationships to the corporation, shareholders who do not wish to continue may treat their membership in the original corporation as terminated and may demand payment for the value of their shares. In *Glen Alden* the corporation in which the plaintiff originally held shares, a coal mining company, was to be transformed into a diversified holding company whose interests would range from motion picture theaters to textile companies. This transformation was most striking because the acquired company—List, a holding company—was the company that one would have expected to purchase the coal company. The assets of the enterprise in which the plaintiff was to be a shareholder doubled, and its debts increased sevenfold. Control of the new entity would have passed to the directors of List, and the plaintiff would suffer a serious financial loss as the book value of his shares would be reduced substantially.[12]

It has been suggested that the *Glen Alden* case must be taken in the context of its facts as an "upside-down" purchase in which the parties had purposely structured the transaction so that the smaller company acquired the larger.[13] Somewhat more visually, one can view Glen Alden's acquisition of List as a minnow swallowing a whale. The de facto merger doctrine has since been applied where there is no such disparity.[14] Two additional factors may have invited the court's belief that Glen Alden's shareholders needed some extra statutory protection. First, the acquisition was not at arm's length: List had secured through its substantial stock ownership in Glen Alden three nominees to the Glen Alden board of directors. Second, List's substantial ownership of Glen Alden stock was acquired with borrowed funds, so Glen Alden's assets could be used following the combination to satisfy the funds List had borrowed to acquire Glen Alden. When the assets of the acquired company are used by its acquirer to extinguish the debt the acquirer incurred to acquire control, the acquisition is frequently called a bootstrap acquisition. The Glen Alden-List combination was a bootstrap acquisition. The current Pennsylvania statute recognizes the right of appraisal in some situations for the

---

[12] From $38 to $21 per share. The court took the view that the statute denying dissenters' rights applied only to shareholders of a corporation that acquired the property or assets of another corporation, *without more;* and that whenever, as part of a combination between two corporations, one corporation dissolves, its liabilities are assumed by the survivor, its executives and directors take over the management and control of the survivor, and its shareholders acquire the majority of the survivor's stock, the transaction is a merger and not simply a purchase of assets or an acquisition of property. The court further commented that even if it were to be assumed that the transaction was a "sale of assets," the reality was that List was acquiring Glen Alden rather than Glen Alden acquiring List, and under Pennsylvania law a Glen Alden shareholder, as a shareholder in a company that in reality was selling its assets, had the right to receive the value of his shares.

[13] *See* Ernest Folk, IV, De Facto Mergers in Delaware: *Hariton v. Arco Electronics, Inc.,* 49 Va. L. Rev. 1261, 1267 (1963). A similar distinguishing point was the total change in nature of the business. *See* Heilbrunn v. Sun Chem. Corp., 150 A.2d 755 (Del. 1959), *aff'g* 146 A.2d 757 (Del. Ch. 1958).

[14] *E.g.,* Rath v. Rath Packing Co., 136 N.W.2d 410 (Iowa 1965).

shareholders of the purchasing corporation and thus would appear to preclude the de facto merger doctrine in other situations.[15]

It would be a mistake to believe that the only principle separating the competing approaches illustrated by *Hariton* and *Glen Alden* is a particular jurisdiction's obeisance to the doctrine of independent statutory existence. In a thorough consideration of this area, the late Professor Ernest Folk states that the result achieved in *Hariton* and its progeny rests on two hidden premises.[16] First, the judiciary's view of the vitality and usefulness of the appraisal remedy is argued to have an important bearing on whether a jurisdiction embraces the de facto merger doctrine. If the remedy is seen as socially harmful because it portends a drain of cash from the combining companies, the court is less likely to exercise its equitable powers to accord dissenting shareholders rights that arise in the analogous context of mergers. Similarly, the court may view skeptically the narrow band of transactions for which the legislature has prescribed an appraisal remedy for dissenting shareholders; recent events have shown that shareholders' expectations can be rapidly deflated through transactions and decisions that entail no statutorily prescribed vote or appraisal remedy whatever. In sum, the appraisal remedy can easily be seen as an arbitrary and unwelcome appendage of corporate law such that its expansion through the de facto merger doctrine is equally unwelcome. Second, the decision as to whether to apply the de facto merger doctrine directly confronts one of the most profound questions in corporate law—What is the nature of the shareholder's ownership interest?

> The basic premise implicitly adopted in *Hariton* may perhaps be stated more affirmatively. One does not invest in a unique corporate entity or even a particular business operation, but rather a continuous course of business which changes over a long period of time. Certainly the best investments are growth investments—investments in enterprises which change with time, technology, business opportunities, and altered demand. . . . Viewed this way, the fact that the change—for better or for worse—comes through marriage, whether by merger or assets sale, seems purely incidental. The fact that the corporate entity in which one invested disappears as a result of a merger or of a sale of assets coupled with dissolution is also beside the point. One's investment may gain immortality when it takes a new form, i.e., a share in a successor enterprise.[17]

It may well be that the de facto merger doctrine reaches the socially desirable result but through the wrong means. Almost any combination of two different companies will produce the effects emphasized in *Glen Alden* so that, unless courts are prepared to treat as mergers all combinations structured as a sale of assets, harmful uncertainty will accompany every such transaction. At the same time, the

---

[15] The Pennsylvania statute was amended to provide appraisal rights to the shareholders of the purchasing corporation when such transaction involves an issuance of a majority of the voting shares. 15 Pa. Cons. Stat. §2544 (1994). *See* Terry v. Penn Central Corp., 668 F.2d 188 (3d Cir. 1981).

[16] Ernest Folk, IV, De Facto Mergers in Delaware: *Hariton v. Arco Electronics, Inc.,* 49 Va. L. Rev. 1261, 1279-1281 (1963).

[17] *Id.* at 1280-1281.

parties have bona fide commercial reasons to structure a transaction as a sale of assets—for example, so that the purchaser can clearly identify the assets and liabilities it wishes to acquire and not acquire. Moreover, the parties may have selected the sale-of-assets procedure to reduce the transaction's cost that would arise if both corporations' shareholders had a right to vote and an appraisal remedy. In this light, the de facto merger doctrine challenges the legislative wisdom of providing for transactions very different procedural rights that can accomplish the same objective. Such a challenge appears to embrace an unduly adventuresome, if not mischievous, role for the courts. At the same time, disquiet arises whenever a statute allows important procedural protections to be bypassed at the option of those who are not intended to be the beneficiaries of such procedural protections. For this reason, some states have essentially codified the de facto merger doctrine by prescribing basic voting and appraisal rights regardless of the form the combination takes.[18]

The de facto merger doctrine is not limited to suits attempting to assert dissenters' rights. It may arise where creditors object to the failure of one corporation to assume liabilities along with the purchase of assets of another. This has been fertile ground for litigation with regard to attempts to avoid products liability damage awards.[19] The cases for successor liability have not been limited to product liability claims.[20] Further, the de facto merger doctrine is not limited to sales of assets: It may arise from other forms of corporate combination, such as a lease of all the productive assets or acquisition of a corporation's control block of stock[21] without merging or liquidating a subsidiary.

§22.07 Successor Corporation Liability

As was seen earlier, a distinguishing feature of a business combination carried out as a merger or consolidation is that by operation of law the surviving corporation is subject to all the liabilities of the acquired companies. In contrast, when the combination is structured as an asset or stock purchase-sale, absent special circumstances, the acquiring company is subject only to those liabilities it has agreed to assume. Traditionally, there were just four circumstances in which the selling corporation's creditors could successful proceed against a purchaser who had not so assumed the debt owed to that creditor:

> [T]here are four well recognized exemptions under which the purchasing corporation becomes liable for the debts and liabilities of the selling corporation.

---

[18] California was the leader in the movement to codify the de facto merger doctrine. *See* Cal. Corp. Code §§168, 1101, 1200 & 1300 (West 1990). Other states have recognized the doctrine as well. *See* N.J. Stat. Ann. §14A:10-12 (1998 supp.).

[19] *See* §22.07. *See also* Harry G. Henn & John R. Alexander, Effect of Corporate Dissolution on Products Liability Claims, 56 Cornell L. Rev. 865 (1971).

[20] *See, e.g.,* Fitzgerald v. Fahnestock & Co., 730 N.Y.S.2d 70 (N.Y. App. Div. 2001) (suit by former employee of acquired company).

[21] *See id.* (acquisition of stock).

B. Sale of Assets

> (1) Where the purchaser expressly or impliedly agrees to assume such debts; (2) where the transaction amounts to a consolidation or merger of the corporations; (3) where the purchasing corporation is merely a continuation of the selling corporation; and (4) where the transaction is entered into fraudulently in order to escape liability for such debts.[1]

This traditional approach continues to be the great weight of authority, despite the important inroads, discussed below, that modern tort law trends have made on the subject.[2] The most significant testing of the rigidity of these four exceptions has occurred, not surprisingly, in the context of product liability claims brought against corporations that acquired the assets of a company that during its previous life had produced a defective product, which defect did not cause a plaintiff-creditor's injury until after the acquisition.

The first exception referred to above involves little more than a straightforward interpretation of the contract of sale.[3] Buyers wishing to avoid unwanted or contingent liabilities need simply state that the buyer assumes no responsibility for any liabilities of any type or arising from any source, contingent or otherwise, beyond those expressly assumed within the contract.[4]

The de facto merger exception emphasizes the continuity of the acquired company's shareholders in the surviving enterprise. Thus this exception in its most orthodox application arises when stock, rather than cash, is the purchase consideration and the selling corporation dissolves shortly after the acquisition so that the stock is distributed to its shareholders.[5]

The third exception arises when the surviving company carries forward a common identity with the selling corporation in terms of its shareholders, management, name, place and nature of business, and employees.[6] It is simply old wine in a new bottle.

---

§22.07 [1] West Tex. Refinery & Dev. Co. v. Commissioner, 68 F.2d 77, 81 (10th Cir. 1933).

[2] *See, e.g.,* Dalton v. Peck, Stow & Wilcox Co., 739 F.2d 690 (1st Cir. 1984); Weaver v. Nash Int'l, Inc., 730 F.2d 547 (8th Cir. 1984); Bernard v. Kee Mfg. Co., 409 So. 2d 1047 (Fla. 1982). On the question of whether the successor corporation has a duty to warn its predecessor's customers of a product's defects, *see* Sherlock v. Quality Control Equip. Co., 79 F.3d 731 (8th Cir. 1996) (duty exists where successor has knowledge of dangerous condition and has regular contact with the purchasers of the defective product).

[3] *See, e.g.,* Keller v. Clark Equip. Co., 715 F.2d 1280 (8th Cir. 1983), *cert. denied,* 464 U.S. 1044 (1984); Piacente v. J.K. Funding, Inc., 706 N.Y.S.2d 198 (App. Div. 2000).

[4] Parker v. Western Dakota Insurors, Inc., 605 N.W.2d 181, 184-185 (S.D. 2000) (unambiguous contract with explicit provisions excluding any liability for debts and liabilities not enumerated in agreement weighs against finding of implied assumption).

[5] *See, e.g.,* R. C. McEntire & Co. v. Eastern Foods, Inc., 702 F.2d 471 (4th Cir. 1983), *cert. denied,* 464 U.S. 849 (1984).

[6] *See, e.g.,* Arnold Graphics Indus. v. Independent Agent Ctr., Inc., 775 F.2d 38 (2d Cir. 1985) (acquisition of all stock and transfer of all assets constituted a de facto merger; thus, judgment creditor could look to parent corporation for repayment of debts); Savage Arms, Inc. v. Western Auto Supply Co., 18 P.3d 49, 55 (Alaska 2000) (holding that "mere continuation" exception is available under Alaska law).

The fourth traditional exemption is but a specialized application of the law of fraudulent transfers. Thus, when the successor corporation acquires the predecessor's assets for nominal consideration and continues its operations under the same management, the court can easily conclude the transfer was a fraud on creditors.[7]

The most liberal approach to successor-corporation liability emphasizes the social policy that has driven developments for product liability generally, the question of who is in the best position to absorb the cost of the defect. The so-called product's-line exception has its genesis in *Ray v. Alad Corporation*,[8] where the California Supreme Court held that "a party which acquires a manufacturing business and continues the output of its line of products under the circumstances here presented assumes strict tort liability for defects in units of the same product line previously manufactured and distributed by the entity from which the business was acquired."[9] Two important jurisdictions, New Jersey and Pennsylvania, are among those to quickly adopt the product-line exception.[10] New York is among those states that adhere to the traditional rule[11] but break from its bonds where there is a breach of a duty to warn of a defect, such duty arising from statute, regulation, or negligence.[12]

Another non-traditional approach that is gaining judicial acceptance is the "continuity of enterprise" exception to limited liability, which, like the "mere con-

---

[7] *See, e.g.*, Lumbard v. Maglia, Inc., 621 F. Supp. 1529 (S.D.N.Y. 1985).

[8] 560 P.2d 3 (Cal. 1977).

[9] *Id.* at 11.

[10] *See* Lefever v. K.P. Hovnanian Enters., Inc., 734 A.2d 290, 292 (N.J. 1999) (applying product line exception when successor purchased assets at bankruptcy sale); Ramirez v. Amsted Indus., 431 A.2d 811 (N.J. 1981); Dawejko v. Jorgensen Steel Co., 434 A.2d 106 (Pa. Super. Ct. 1981) (Pennsylvania considers continuation of product line but one of many factors in the equation).

Under Michigan law, a corporate successor may be liable for its predecessor's defective products if the totality of the acquisition demonstrates a basic continuity of the predecessor's enterprise. Foster v. Cone-Blanchard Mach. Co., 597 N.W.2d 506, 509 (Mich. 1999). However, the "continuity of enterprise" doctrine applies only when the predecessor is no longer viable and capable of being sued. *Id.* at 511.

See also Huff v. Shopsmith, Inc., 786 So. 2d 383, 387-388 (Miss. 2001) (recognizing product line theory as viable; successor must produce the same product under a similar name, have acquired substantially all of the predecessor's assets, hold itself out as a mere continuation of the predecessor, and benefit from the predecessor's good will).

[11] *But see* Rothstein v. Tennessee Gas Pipeline Co., 696 N.Y.S.2d 528, 531 (App. Div. 1999) (noting that Appellate Division, Third Department has adopted product line exception; declining to decide issue for Second Department, since successor in this case purchased less than 20% of assets of predecessor, which continued as ongoing, viable business for ten years after transfer).

[12] *See, e.g.*, Rothstein v. Tennessee Gas Pipeline Co., 696 N.Y.S.2d 528, 531 (App. Div. 1999) (duty to warn may be imposed on successor corporation that maintains sufficient links to purchaser of products manufactured by its predecessor); Vergara v. Scripps Howard, Inc., 691 N.Y.S.2d 392, 395 (App. Div. 1999) (successor liability is premised on successor's superior knowledge of risk of personal injury; in this case, however, dangerous condition arose after product left manufacturer, due to its modification by plaintiff's employer); Radziul v. Hooper, Inc., 479 N.Y.S.2d 324 (Sup. Ct. 1984). *See also* Foster v. Cone-Blanchard Mach. Co., 597 N.W.2d 506, 512 (Mich. 1999) (successor's duty to warn predecessor's customer of predecessor's negligence requires special relationship between defendant and victim or defendant and third party who caused injury).

B. Sale of Assets

tinuation" exception, focuses on whether the totality of the transaction demonstrates a basic continuity of the predecessor enterprise. However, whereas the "mere continuation" doctrine requires that the two corporations have identical shareholders and directors, the "continuity of enterprise" analysis looks beyond that formal requirement and considers the substance of the underlying transaction—that is, whether the business has been transferred as a going concern. Under this limited exception, the successor corporation may be held liable for the obligations of its predecessor even though the sale of assets is for cash and there is not a complete identity of shareholders.[13]

Successor liability may also be imposed in the case of an acquisition of a target company's stock. Courts have indicated that successor liability will attach under the de facto merger doctrine when subsequent to the stock acquisition, the target company ceases to have an independent identity and the target's business can only be carried on through the acquiring corporation.[14]

Various federal statutes pose unique obligations for successor corporations. Significant successor liability arises under the "Superfund Law," Comprehensive Environmental Response, Compensation, and Liability Act (CERCLA),[15] which provides that owners as well as operators of property are liable for all costs in cleaning up a site, even though the generator of the waste was a prior owner.[16] Thus, by simply becoming an owner of property on which waste has been disposed of by others, the new owner can become a "responsible party" under CERCLA.[17] And continuity of the work force is an important factor under the labor laws, at least with respect to the successor corporation's obligation to bargain with the union that represented the acquired company's employees.[18]

[13] Savage Arms, Inc. v. Western Auto Supply Co., 18 P.3d 49, 55-56 (Alaska 2001) (adopting exception).

[14] *See* Fitzgerald v. Fahnestock & Co., 730 N.Y.S.2d 70 (N.Y. App. Div. 2001). The complaint alleged that the defendant acquired all of the target company's stock and the target's business was transferred to the acquiring corporation. The court reversed dismissal of a claim brought against the acquirer based on a judgment that had previously been obtained against the acquired company.

[15] 42 U.S.C. §9601 (2000). *See* Christopher B. Hood, Comment, Metaphors of Shareholder Liability under CERCLA, 10 J. Envtl. L. & Litig. 85 (1995). For other federal incursions on successor liability, *see* H. Lowell Brown, Successor Corporate Criminal Liability: The Emerging Federal Common Law, 49 Ark. L. Rev. 469 (1996).

[16] CERCLA, 42 U.S.C. §107 (2000).

[17] *See, e.g.,* New York v. Shore Realty Corp., 759 F.2d 1032 (2d Cir. 1985). *Cf.* United States v. Bestfoods, 524 U.S. 51 (1998) (if under applicable law there are grounds for piercing the corporate veil, then a parent corporation can be held liable for the CERCLA liability of its subsidiary); *see* §7.09.

[18] Fall River Dyeing & Finishing Corp. v. NLRB, 482 U.S. 27 (1987) (when majority of successor's employees had been employed by predecessor). More recently, the NLRB took an even broader approach, emphasizing the representations made by the successor of an "intention" to retain the acquired company's workforce. *See* Canteen Co., 317 NLRB No. 153, 317 NLRB 1052 (1995), *enf'd,* 103 F. 3d 1355 (7th Cir. 1997).

C.   MERGER AND CONSOLIDATION

§22.08   Merger and Consolidation Distinguished

A consolidation is the uniting or amalgamation of two or more existing corporations to form a new corporation.[1] The firm resulting from the union is called the "consolidated" corporation. A merger is a union effected by the absorbing of one or more existing corporations by another, which survives and continues the combined business.[2] The disappearing corporation is generally referred to as the "merged" corporation, with the other being the "surviving" corporation. The parties to a combination either by consolidation or merger are called the "constituent" corporations. The chief difference between mergers and consolidations is one of form; the procedure, legal effect, and end-product are the same.[3]

§22.09   Attributes and Advantages of Merger and Consolidation

Merger and consolidation are very complex proceedings involving several different transactions affecting many parties, all of which may be accomplished simultaneously by statute. Legislative authority is essential to authorize a true merger or consolidation.[1] These transactions are fundamental changes of the charter contract and the share contracts and also in the rights of creditors. Each constituent corporation must be authorized under the law of its domicile to enter into a union by merger or consolidation.[2] Each constituent corporation must comply with the procedure set forth by the statute of its state of incorporation.[3] A merger may be preferable to a consolidation in combining corporations because one of the corporations may have nonassignable leases, franchises, or employment contracts

---

§22.08   [1] *E.g.*, Metropolitan Edison Co. v. Commissioner, 98 F.2d 807, 810 (3d Cir.), *aff'd*, 306 U.S. 522 (1939); Former Model Bus. Corp. Act §72 (1969).

[2] *E.g.*, Alabama Power Co. v. McNinch, 94 F.2d 601, 610 (D.C. Cir. 1937); In re Cantor, 184 N.E. 474 (N.Y. 1933); Former Model Bus. Corp. Act §71 (1969); Richard Jennings & Richard M. Buxbaum, Corporations: Cases and Materials 1042(5th ed. 1979); Eldon Bisbee, Consolidation & Merger, 6 N.Y.U. L.Q. Rev. 404 (1929).

[3] Delaware retains the distinction between mergers and consolidations. Del. §264. In contrast, the Model Act has abolished consolidation as a separate form; the transaction can still be accomplished through a share exchange. Model Bus. Corp. Act §11.02. *Cf.* Former Model Bus. Corp. Act §§71, 72 (1969); *infra* §22.11.

§22.09   [1] *See* §22.11.

[2] *See* William B. Riker & Son Co. v. United Drug Co., 82 A. 930 (N.J. 1912).

[3] *E.g.*, Del. Code Ann. tit. 8, §252 (2001); N.Y. Bus. Corp. Law §907 (McKinney 1986, Supp. Supp. 2002); Former Model Bus. Corp. Act §73 (1969); Model Bus. Corp. Act §11.04 (1984). *See generally, e.g.*, Marshall L. Small, Corporate Combinations Under the New California General Corporation Law, 23 UCLA L. Rev. 1190 (1976).

that by their terms cannot pass to another entity. Another reason may be that one of the constituent corporations may have qualified to do business as a foreign corporation in a large number of other states and it would be burdensome to qualify a new corporation.[4]

As we have seen, the procedure of selling the entire assets and issuing shares in payment by the purchaser, followed by dissolution and winding up, is often preferable to either merger or consolidation.[5] A sale of assets is particularly helpful when the acquiring corporation is not interested in all of the business of the corporation to be acquired or where it wishes to make a selective assumption of liabilities—subject, of course, to the equitable rights of creditors.[6] Merger or consolidation can be used to acquire some part of the business when preceded or followed by a sale of assets to a third party. Another alternative is to place the unwanted assets in a subsidiary corporation and spin off the shares to the stockholders in the form of a dividend.[7]

The great advantage of a statutory merger or consolidation over combination by sale of assets is that it furnishes a short cut to accomplishing various transactions and may avoid difficulty, delay, and expense such as that attendant on a dissolution, winding up, and the distribution of securities to its shareholders by the selling corporation. By statute, all of the rights and liabilities of the transferor are assimilated into the transferee corporation.

Merger and consolidation are, in essence, the transfer of the property and business of one corporation to another in exchange for securities or cash issued by the purchaser to shareholders of the seller. Merger and consolidation involve the automatic (that is, by operation of law) assumption of all the debts and liabilities of the transferring corporations and a compulsory novation on the part of the creditors. As we have seen, in a combination by sale of assets there may not be a compulsory exchange or distribution of new shares for old or a compulsory substitution of a new debtor as to the debts and liabilities of the seller. In a sale of assets, sufficient funds must be reserved or adequate provision made to take care of the debts and liabilities of the seller; otherwise the transfer would be a fraudulent conveyance, which could be attacked by the creditors.

Merger and consolidation are also highly advantageous forms of reorganization because they bring the transaction of an exchange of property for shares within the class of tax-free reorganizations under the federal tax laws.[8]

---

[4] *See* Former Model Bus. Corp. Act §106 (1969); Note, 44 Fordham L. Rev. 1042 (1976); Note, 59 Yale L.J. 737 (1949).

[5] Norris Darrell, The Use of Reorganization Techniques in Corporate Acquisitions, 70 Harv. L. Rev. 1183 (1957); George S. Hills, Consolidation of Corporations by Sale of Assets and Distributions of Shares, 19 Cal. L. Rev. 349 (1931); *supra* §§22.02-22.03.

[6] *See* §22.03.

[7] *See* §§20.01, 20.06. Such two-step transactions, as well as the so-called triangular merger, are frequently used in tax-free reorganizations. *See* Darrell, *supra* note 5; Robert R. Tufts, The Taxable Merger, 7 J. Corp. Tax 342 (1981).

[8] *See* I.R.C. §368.

§22.10 Statutory Authority for Merger and Consolidation

Mergers and consolidations can be effected only under statutory authority.[1] The power of corporations to merge without unanimous shareholder approval does not exist without statutory authorization, so liability can arise for consequential damages from mergers consummated without complying with the applicable statutory requirements.[2] All jurisdictions have liberal provisions for merger, consolidation, sales of assets, and charter amendments, which on enactment were made applicable to existing corporations as well as to those to be formed.[3] In some jurisdictions constitutional doubts were raised as to the scope of the reserved power to authorize fundamental changes by majority shareholders in preexisting corporations.[4] Although the contrary has long been taken for granted by others, there still may be problems regarding the ability of legislatures to affect the internal rules of existing corporations.[5] The extent to which the authorization of such fundamental changes is dependent on provisions enabling objecting shareholders to demand payment of the fair value of their shares has also been questioned.[6]

§22.11 Procedures to Merge or Consolidate

Procedures Generally. The procedure to accomplish a merger is practically the same as that necessary to effect a consolidation. In general the essential steps in each involve: (1) the negotiation and approval of an agreement of merger or consolidation by the boards of directors of the constituent companies and the drafting of a formal agreement to combine in accordance with the applicable statute; (2) the submission of the agreement, either in full or in substance, to the shareholders for their approval by the specified majority vote after lawful notice of a shareholders' meeting; and (3) the execution of the formal agreement by the proper corporate officers, with the formal certificates of due authorization, and the filing of the agreement so duly certified with the secretary of state or other designated official.

§22.10 [1] *E.g.*, William B. Riker & Son Co. v. United Drug Co., 82 A. 930 (N.J. 1912); Colgate v. United States Leather Co., 72 A. 126 (N.J. 1909).

[2] Nelson v. All Am. Life & Fin. Corp., 889 F.2d 141 (8th Cir. 1989); Roddy v. Norco Local 4-750, 350 So. 2d 957 (La. 1978).

[3] This was highly desirable, if not necessary, for the sake of uniformity and the facilitation of business. *See, e.g.,* Brundage v. New Jersey Zinc Co., 226 A.2d 585 (N.J. 1967); Marshall L. Small, Corporate Combinations Under the New California General Corporation Law, 23 UCLA L. Rev. 1190 (1976).

[4] E. Merrick Dodd, Jr., Dissenting Stockholders and Amendments to Corporate Charters, 75 U. Pa. L. Rev. 585, 723, 735-737 (1927). *See* §25.03.

[5] *See* Nelson Ferebee Taylor, Evolution of Corporate Combination Law: Policy Issues and Constitutional Questions, 76 N.C. L. Rev. 687 (1998).

[6] *See* Nice Ball Bearing Co. v. Mortgage Bldg. & Loan Ass'n, 166 A. 239 (Pa. 1933); Lauman v. Lebanon Valley R.R., 30 Pa. 42 (1858).

C. Merger and Consolidation

Once a merger agreement is in place, it will create contractual obligations between the parties to the agreement. Merger agreements typically contain a "material adverse change" or "material adverse effect" provision allowing the contract to be avoided when material changes or effects are discovered after the merger agreement is made.[1] A noteworthy decision is *IBP Inc. v. Tyson Foods Inc.*[2] where the court held that a significant accounting restatement was not sufficient to trigger the material adverse change provision as an escape from the merger agreement. This and other decisions reveal that a generalized material adverse change provision will not always provide meaningful protection with respect to changed conditions. If the parties foresee specific contingencies, they would be well advised to enumerate them in the merger agreement as examples of what constitutes a material adverse change.

Voting Requirements. Most states now provide for majority approval by the shares entitled to vote,[3] although some adhere to the older practice of a two-thirds requirement.[4] Recent amendments to the Model Act if adopted by state legislatures would dilute the shareholders' power in reducing the required vote from a majority of those entitled to vote, to a plurality of those actually voting.[5]

In view of the fact that the interests of different classes of shares, particularly preferred and common, frequently conflict in a merger or a consolidation (they do as in the case of amendments to the articles of incorporation), a class vote is frequently accorded to each class of stock affected in a proscribed manner by the merger or consolidation. Jurisdictions following the scheme of the Revised Model Business Corporation Act define how the stock is "affected" broadly to include not only by any changes in the existing rights, privileges, and preferences of an outstanding class of stock but also by any dilution in their economic or voting rights through the issuance of additional shares of that class or of a class that will compete for assets with an outstanding class.[6] In contrast, a class vote is not provided in many states, such as Delaware, so that they grant inadequate protection to the holders of preferred shares.[7]

---

§22.11 [1] *E.g.*, Pine State Creamery Co. v. Land-O-Sun Dairies Inc., 201 F.3d 437 (4th Cir. 1999); Great Lakes Chemical Corp. v. Pharmacia Corp., 2001 WL 765187 (Del. Ch. June 29, 2001); Raskin v. Birmingham Steel Corp., 1990 WL 193326 (Del. Ch. 1990). *See generally* Dennis J. Block & Jonathan M. Hoff, Material Adverse Change Provisions in Merger Agreements, New York Law Journal (August 23, 2001). Courts generally do not interfere with an agreement based on factors extrinsic to the corporation. *See, e.g.,* Esplanade Oil & Gas Inc. v. Templeton Energy Income Corp., 889 F.2d 621 (5th Cir. 1989) (unexpected decline in price of oil did not trigger material adverse change provision in merger agreement); Pittsburgh Coke & Chemical Co. v. Bollo, 421 F. Supp. 908 (E.D.N.Y. 1976), *aff'd,* 560 F.2d 1089 (2d Cir. 1977).

[2] 2001 WL 675330 (Del. Ch. June 15, 2001).

[3] *E.g.*, Del. Code Ann. tit. 8, §251(c) (2001); Former Model Bus. Corp. Act §73 (1969); Model Bus. Corp. Act §11.03 (1984).

[4] Mass. Ann. Laws ch. 156, §46B(5) (Law. Co-op. 2000); N.Y. Bus. Corp. Law §903 (McKinney 1986 supp. 2002) (two-thirds of the outstanding shares for corporations incorporated before 1989).

[5] *See* Committee on Corporate Laws, Changes in the Model Business Corporation Act Pertaining to Appraisal Rights and to Fundamental Changes—Final Adoption 55 Bus. Law. 405 (1999).

[6] *See* Model Bus. Corp. Act §§11.04(f), 10.04 (1984).

[7] *See* SEC Report on Reorganization Committees Part VII 329, 376, 388, 397, 411, 530-536 (1938); Comment, 45 Yale L.J. 105, 113-114 (1935).

The modern trend among corporate statutes is to include a "small acquisition" exception to the right of shareholders to vote on mergers or consolidations. This exception removes mergers and consolidations from the necessity of any vote of the stockholders of the *surviving* corporation, provided the articles of incorporation are not amended to change their rights, privileges, or preferences, the number of shares each owns is not affected by the merger or consolidation, and the number of voting shares outstanding after the combination is not increased by more than 20 percent from the number of outstanding voting shares before the acquisition.[8] This exemption reflects the drafters' wisdom that some acquisitions are of such small impact to the corporation in terms of their dilutive effects that they should fall exclusively within the discretion of the board of directors to carry out. In a sense, in terms of the shareholders' involvement the transaction is treated no differently than if the board of directors had first sold common shares (not to exceed 20 percent of those already outstanding) for cash and used the cash to acquire another corporation.

The Agreement of Merger or Consolidation. The foundation of the merger or consolidation is an agreement negotiated and approved by the directors of each constituent corporation and approved by the requisite number of the outstanding shares. This agreement yields the "plan of merger" that is approved by the shareholders. In the case of consolidation, the agreement to consolidate or the articles of consolidation contemplates the articles of incorporation of the newly formed corporation. It should set forth matters required by statute to be stated in articles of incorporation. In the case of a merger, the agreement should state any matters as to which the articles of incorporation of the surviving corporation are to be amended. However, in a merger, separate procedures are required to carry out that amendment. In each case, the agreement should set forth the terms and conditions of the union and the mode of carrying it into effect, as well as the basis of converting the shares of the constituent corporations into shares of the consolidated or surviving corporation. Under the Delaware statute, once the agreement has been approved by the directors and officers, it is to be executed and filed publicly.[9] The Model Business Corporation Act requires the filing of "articles of merger or share exchange" with the secretary of state, which must include the articles of incorporation or any amendments thereto.[10] This document sets forth specific information regarding the shareholders' approval of the combination. The merger becomes effective on the effective date specified in the filed articles of merger or exchange.[11] In some states, the plan of merger itself is filed.[12] In some states a "certificate of merger" is filed with the proper state and/or county officials.[13]

---

[8] *See, e.g.,* Model Bus. Corp. Act §6.21(f), 11.04(g) (1984).

[9] Del. Code Ann. tit. 8, §251(c) (2001).

[10] Model Bus. Corp. Act §11.06 (1984); Former Model Bus. Corp. Act §74 (1969).

[11] Model Bus. Corp. Act §11.06(b) (1984).

[12] Cal. Corp. Code §1103 (West 1990, Supp. 2002); Del. Code Ann. tit. 8, §251(c) (2001); Kan. Stat. Ann. §17-6704(d) (2001).

[13] *E.g.,* Mass. Ann. Laws ch. 156 §§46F, ch. 156B §§78(d), 78(e), 84 (Law. Co-op. 1979 & Supp. 1994).

C. Merger and Consolidation

Distributions to Shareholders. Statutes commonly provide that the plan of merger submitted to the shareholders for approval must set forth the manner and basis for converting shares of each constituent corporation into shares of the surviving corporation's shares, the shares of a third corporation, or cash or other property.[14]

§22.12 "Short-Form" Mergers

Most states now provide for a simplified procedure in mergers of certain subsidiaries into the parent corporation or vice versa, or into another subsidiary.[1] Since the procedure is less complex than the normal statutory merger, such transactions are referred to as "short-form" mergers. Under these short-form merger statutes, no vote is required by the shareholders of either the surviving parent or the absorbed subsidiary, and the approval of the board of directors of the subsidiary is not required.[2] However, if the parent corporation is merged into the subsidiary, a vote of the parent shareholders will be required.[3] A significant result of the short-form procedure is the denial of dissenters' rights to the shareholders of the surviving parent, although such rights are given to the shareholders of the merged subsidiary.[4] Though the subsidiary's shareholders do not have an opportunity to dissent in a short-form merger, their avenue for appraisal is to give notice of their intent to seek appraisal after receiving notice of the parent's board's approval of the acquisition. In Delaware, California, and those states that have adopted the Model Business Corporation Act, the short-form merger is available for subsidiaries where 90 percent of the outstanding shares of each class are owned by the parent.[5] Some states impose a greater ownership requirement, although most have now adopted the 90 percent rule.[6] Some states require 95 percent ownership.[7]

The short-form merger can be the final step in a freeze-out or a going-private transaction, and the procedure has been condemned by some as not sufficiently protecting minority shareholders.[8] Another view is that the short-form merger

---

[14] *See* Auserehl v. Jamaica Builders' Supply Corp., 404 N.Y.S.2d 421 (App. Div. 1978) (no violation for failure to refer to manner in which ten shares in acquiring corporation are to be converted into same number of shares in surviving corporation).

§22.12 [1] *See* Former Model Bus. Corp. Act §75 (1969); Model Bus. Corp. Act §11.05 (1984); Comment, The Short Merger Statute, 32 U. Chi. L. Rev. 596 (1965).

[2] Cal. Corp. Code §1110 (1990, Supp. 1994); Del. Code Ann. tit. 8, §253 (2001).

[3] *See* Model Bus. Corp. Act §11.05 (1984). *But see* Del. Code Ann. tit. 8, §253(a) (2001).

[4] Del. Code Ann. tit. 8, §253(d) (2001); Former Model Bus. Corp. Act §80(c) (1969); Model Bus. Corp. Act §13.02(a)(1)(ii).

[5] Cal. Corp. Code §1110(b) (West 1990, Supp. 1994); Del. Code Ann. tit. 8, §253 (1983); Model Bus. Corp. Act §11.05 (1984); Former Model Bus. Corp. Act §75 (1969).

[6] N.Y. Bus. Corp. Law §905 (McKinney 1986, Supp. 2002), (formerly 95 percent, now 90 percent); Wis. Stat. Ann. §180.1104 (West 1992) (formerly 100 percent, now 90 percent).

[7] Neb. Rev. Stat. §21-2074 (2000).

[8] Comment, *supra* note 1.

statute avoids the hollow ritual of a 90-percent-plus owner convening a meeting to approve its decision to acquire the subsidiary; although the minority shareholders are disenfranchised, they still have their right to exit through the appraisal remedy.[9] And any business purpose required for ridding the organization of its minority shareholders is easily established.[10] The subsidiary's minority shareholders need not be given an opportunity to receive any interest in the surviving corporation.[11] Instead, they may be forced to accept cash payment as determined by the buy-out terms of a merger plan or, if they dissent, as determined by the statutory appraisal process.

§22.13   Triangular and Reverse Triangular Mergers

Generally speaking, there have been three traditional forms of corporate combinations: (1) merger or consolidation, (2) purchase or sale of assets,[1] and (3) acquisition of the stock of another corporation,[2] any of which may be entered into on a nontaxable basis. An ingenious variation that may also take advantage of the federal tax laws is the three-party or triangular merger.[3] There are three principal reasons for utilizing the triangular merger: (1) to avoid the automatic assumption of liabilities,[4] which can be particularly desirable when acquiring a high-risk enterprise; (2) to avoid a vote by the acquiring parent corporation's shareholders and their attendant appraisal rights; and (3) to continue the existence of the acquired corporation as a subsidiary of the parent acquiring corporation.[5] The triangular merger also avoids several disadvantages of a purchase of assets[6] and a straight stock acquisition of another company.[7]

---

[9] See Teschner v. Chicago Title & Trust Co., 322 N.E.2d 54 (Ill. 1974).

[10] See Cross v. Communications Channels, Inc., 456 N.Y.S.2d 971 (Sup. Ct. 1982) (avoids annual meetings, eliminates conflicts of interest involving inter-company transactions, and establishes a uniform set of goals).

[11] Stauffer v. Standard Brands, Inc., 187 A.2d 78 (Del. 1962); Coyne v. Park & Tilford Distillers Corp., 154 A.2d 893 (Del. 1959), noted in Note, 74 Harv. L. Rev. 412 (1960).

§22.13   [1] See §22.03.

[2] See §24.01.

[3] See generally Note, Three-Party Mergers: The Fourth Form of Corporate Acquisition, 57 Va. L. Rev. 1242 (1971).

[4] See In re Beck Indus., 479 F.2d 410 (2d Cir. 1973).

[5] With a merger or consolidation the acquired corporation disappears. Among the possible advantages of a continued existence are the opportunity to maintain ongoing agreements with prior creditors and the ability to retain existing labor contracts. Model Bus. Corp. Act §11.03 (1984) provides for an "exchange of shares" between two corporations that permits continuation of both parties to the merger. Former Model Bus. Corp. Act §72-A (1969); Model Bus. Corp. Act §11.03 (1984).

[6] Such advantages include (1) greater flexibility in the consideration to be paid without jeopardizing tax-free status because a qualifying purchase of assets must be solely for voting stock, I.R.C. §368(a)(1)(c) (1988); (2) avoidance of transfer-of-title problems; (3) there is no need to liquidate as a second step and the acquired corporation may remain in existence if desired; (4) the avoidance of a shareholder vote in those states requiring such for a purchase of assets.

[7] (1) There is greater freedom in the consideration for tax-free acquisitions; (2) the acquiring company is assured of complete control; (3) there is no need to worry about the various tender offer provisions of state and federal securities laws (see §24.01). However, with a triangular merger the

C. Merger and Consolidation

Straight Triangular Merger

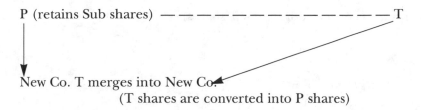

In the straight triangular merger, the acquiring corporation forms a subsidiary[8] for the purpose of merging with the target. A merger then occurs between the subsidiary and the target. Although standard merger law generally requires a vote of each merging corporation's shareholders, this is not a problem in the triangular merger because the subsidiary's shares are held exclusively by its parent (Acquiring Corporation), whose board of directors votes those shares. When Target merges into Subsidiary, Target's shareholders receive the stock of Acquiring Corporation. This can be accomplished by having capitalized Subsidiary with the parent's stock in exchange for the Subsidiary's shares. Alternatively, the stock can be issued directly by Acquiring Corporation to Target's shareholders. One possible pitfall is that the transactions must be structured to avoid the claim that the parent's shares have been issued for invalid consideration.[9] Statutes in most states now authorize the use of shares of another corporation as consideration for mergers. Since the parent is not a party to the merger no parent shareholder vote is required, assuming that there had already been authorized in the charter sufficient shares to be issued pursuant to the merger plan, because directors have the power to issue previously authorized shares.[10] As a bona fide parent-subsidiary structure, the subsidiary, not the parent, assumes the liabilities of the merged target company.

After the transaction described in the preceding paragraph, Acquiring Corporation owns 100 percent of Subsidiary, and Subsidiary has all the assets and liabilities of Target. If the parent corporation does not wish to continue Subsidiary's existence, it can use the short-form merger provision to merge Subsidiary into itself. In so structuring the transaction, the parent corporation's shareholders never have an opportunity to vote on its acquisition of Target. Thus the triangular merger is a straightforward mechanism to avoid the acquiring corporation's shareholders having a direct vote, and, for that matter, an appraisal remedy, in an acquisition of another company.

---

shareholders of the acquired company will be given dissenters' rights, but this is equally true of cleanup mergers that frequently follow tender offers.

[8] The subsidiary may also be referred to as a "phantom corporation," which has led to the alternative appellation "phantom merger." *See, e.g.,* Marcou v. Federal Trust Co., 268 A.2d 629 (Me. 1970); Charles J. Lynch, A Concern for the Interests of Minority Shareholders Under Modern Corporation Laws, 3 J. Corp. L. 19, 33 (1977).

[9] *See* §16.11.

[10] *See* §16.06; Equity Group Holdings v. DMG, Inc., 576 F. Supp. 1197 (S.D. Fla. Dec. 16, 1983), noted in 55 Corp. Rep. Bull. (P-H) ¶8.4 (Apr. 10, 1984).

Reverse Triangular Merger

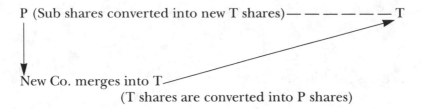

P (Sub shares converted into new T shares)— — — — — —T

New Co. merges into T

(T shares are converted into P shares)

A variation on the above procedure is the reverse triangular merger. In the reverse transaction, Subsidiary is merged with Target, so Target survives and becomes a subsidiary of the original parent. The advantage to the reverse method is that it allows the acquired company to continue to exist, unlike in a traditional two-party merger or consolidation. The continued existence of the target avoids the necessity of negotiating new labor contracts and making formal transfers of the target's property.[11] Additionally, the target's continued existence may be required by the terms of outstanding bonds or other types of agreements it has with creditors. The triangular and reverse triangular methods of combination are not limited to mergers; they can also be used for a purchase-of-assets acquisition.

§22.14 Statutory Share Exchange

It sometimes is desirable to structure an acquisition so that the acquired company continues as a separate, albeit wholly owned, subsidiary of the acquiring company or a holding company, rather than ceasing to exist. Ideally suited for this objective is the "share exchange," a procedure now authorized in numerous states that have patterned their own enactments after the Revised Model Business Corporation Act.[1] Following board of director and shareholder approval by each corporation, the shares of the acquired corporation are exchanged for cash or stock of the acquiring corporation or a third corporation. The agreement between the corporations can provide that only designated classes of stock of the acquired company will be exchanged, so that following a share exchange some classes of the acquired corporation are unaffected. In any case, following the share exchange, all the shares of one or more classes of stock are acquired by the acquiring corporation, and the existence of the acquired corporation continues.

---

[11] *Cf.* PPG Indus. v. Guardian Indus. Corp., 597 F.2d 1090 (6th Cir.), *cert. denied,* 444 U.S. 930 (1979) (surviving company could not avoid patent infringement under license granted to acquired company that permitted "transfers" only by consent). *But see* Dodier Realty & Inv. Co. v. St. Louis Nat'l Baseball Club, Inc., 238 S.W.2d 321 (Mo. 1951) (merger is transfer by operation of law and "nonassignment" provision in lease therefore not affected).

§22.14   [1] *See* Model Bus. Corp. Act §11.03 (1984).

C. Merger and Consolidation

§22.15   Rights of Creditors of Constituent Companies

Absent contractual provisions to the contrary, the creditors of a corporation cannot prevent its consolidation or merger with another corporation even if the new debtor corporation is not as satisfactory to them as the old.[1] Accordingly, it is not uncommon to find express restrictions, such as consent requirements, in credit agreements as well as in debt indentures and preferred-share contracts.[2] In general, the only recourse of the creditors of the constituent corporations is to sue the united corporation directly or to pursue the assets of the constituents into the hands of the new corporation under a theory of fraudulent conveyance.[3]

§22.16   Leveraged Buyouts as Fraudulent Conveyances

Fraudulent conveyance provisions trace their roots to the sixteenth century. Their proscriptions remain nearly as simple today as they were then, whether they appear in the state's version of the Uniform Fraudulent Conveyance Act,[1] the Uniform Fraudulent Transfer Act,[2] or the Bankruptcy Act's own version of this avoidance provision.[3] It is in their simplicity that these provisions raise highly troubling questions in the complex leveraged buyout (LBO) transaction.[4]

Leveraged buyouts can take many forms. A most common form involves creating a thinly capitalized corporation to purchase the corporation that is to be acquired. The funds for the purchase are borrowed by the newly formed corporation, usually through bridge loans from a syndicate of financial institutions. The loan's proceeds are used to purchase the shares of the acquired corporation. Upon the merger of the acquired corporation and the newly formed corporation, the acquired corporation's assets can be used to satisfy the loan. Thereafter the

---

§22.15   [1] Western Air Lines, Inc. v. Allegheny Airlines, Inc., 313 A.2d 145, 153 (Del. Ch. 1973); Cole v. National Cash Credit Ass'n, 156 A. 183 (Del. Ch. 1931). *See* Comment, 45 Yale L.J. 105, 122-123 (1935).

[2] *See* §§18.02, 18.03. Similarly, noncompliance with statutory requirements for shareholder approval of a sale of assets outside the ordinary course of business is not a defect creditors can raise. *See* Phillips Petroleum Co. v. Rock Creek Mining Co., 449 F.2d 664 (9th Cir. 1971); McDermott v. Bear Film Co., 33 Cal. Rptr. 486 (Ct. App. 1963).

[3] *See, e.g.,* Cameron v. United Traction Co., 73 N.Y.S. 981 (App. Div. 1902); Del. Code Ann. tit. 8, §259(a) (2001); N.Y. Bus. Corp. Law §906(b)(3) (1986); Former Model Bus. Corp. Act §76(e) (1969); Model Bus. Corp. Act §11.07(a)(4) (1984); Annot., 149 A.L.R. 787, 799 (1944); *infra* §22.16. *Cf.* In re Resorts International, Inc., 181 F.3d 505 (3d Cir. 1999) (payment made by debtor-corporation to shareholder pursuant to leverage buyout was a "settlement payment" under statute restricting bankruptcy trustee's power to avoid transfers qualifying as settlement payments, and thus was not avoidable as a fraudulent conveyance).

§22.16   [1] 7A U.L.A. 427 (1985).

[2] 7A U.L.A. 639 (1985).

[3] 11 U.S.C. §548 (2000).

[4] For the view that public policy should exclude LBOs from fraudulent conveyance laws, *see* Douglas G. Baird & Thomas H. Jackson, Fraudulent Conveyance Law and Its Proper Domain, 38 Vand. L. Rev. 829 (1985).

two corporations are combined, permanent financing is arranged, and the earnings and assets of the acquired corporation are used to meet these financial obligations. It is when all the various steps are collapsed together that the issue of the acquisition constituting a fraudulent conveyance arises.[5] In considering a collapse of the various steps of the LBO, courts frequently emphasize the interdependence of the various steps.[6]

§22.17   Accounting for Corporate Combinations

§22.17.01   Purchase and Pooling Methods: The Demise of the Pooling Method

For the longest time, there were two alternative methods of accounting for corporate mergers and other forms of combination: the purchase method and the "pooling-of-interest" approach.[1] As discussed more fully below, the purchase method requires a revaluation of the acquired company's assets based on the purchase price in connection with the merger. In contrast, the pooling method simply consolidated the existing balance sheets of the constituent companies.

In 1999, the Federal Accounting Standards Board voted unanimously to abandon the use of the pooling method of accounting for corporate mergers.[2] FASB chairman Jenkins explained that "the purchase method of accounting gives investors a better idea of the initial cost of a transaction and the investment's performance over time than does the pooling-of-interest method."[3] There then ensued many months of intense lobbying to deflect the FASB from its position or to prevent an absolute bar to this popular method for accounting for company acquisitions. All such efforts were to no avail as the FASB ultimately adopted FASB

---

[5] *See* Raymond J. Blackwood, Applying Fraudulent Conveyance Law to Leveraged Buyouts, 42 Duke L.J. 340 (1992).

[6] *See* Moody v. Security Pac. Bus. Credit, Inc., 127 B.R. 958 (Bankr. W.D. Pa. 1991). In Wieboldt Stores, Inc. v. Schottenstein, 94 B.R. 488, 503 (N.D. Ill. 1988), the court also considered the relative knowledge of the likely financial burdens the transaction would impose on the target corporation in deciding whether to collapse the steps so that the steps were collapsed as to the insiders but not as to outside shareholders.

§22.17 [1] *See generally* Victor Brudney & William W. Bratton, Cases and Materials on Corporate Finance Appendix A-10-A-36 (3d ed. 1993); Abraham J. Briloff & Calvin Engler, Accountancy and the Merger Movement: A Symbiotic Relationship, 5 J. Corp. L. 81 (1979); Miguel DeCapriles & John M. Brown, Accounting for Business Combinations Under the New California Corporations Code, 29 Hast. L.J. 851 (1978); William P. Hackney, Accounting for Mergers and Acquisitions Under the New Jersey Business Corporation Act, 23 Rutgers L. Rev. 689 (1969); L. P. Scriggins, Business Combinations—Developments in Combining Techniques and Constraints in Accounting Rule, 27 Bus. Law. 1245 (1972); Note, 23 Stan. L. Rev. 330 (1971); Note, 1972 Wis. L. Rev. 200.

[2] *See* FASB to Bar Pooling Method for Mergers; Trade Groups Unhappy, 31 Sec. Reg. & L. Rep. (BNA) 543 (April 23, 1999).

[3] *Id.*

Statement 141 that bars the pooling method of accounting for acquisitions completed after June 30, 2001.[4]

In broad overview, under the "purchase method" the acquired companies' assets are listed at their fair market value as determined by the consideration paid by the acquiring company. Because the purchase price will reflect the going-concern value rather than the liquidation or replacement value of the assets, under the purchase method it is necessary to list goodwill as an asset of the surviving corporation. Overvaluation of goodwill can give rise to fraud claims against directors.[5] Under generally accepted accounting practices (GAAP) goodwill must be amortized so that it is charged to earnings on a periodic basis.[6] Under the pooling-of-interests method of accounting, the assets of the constituent companies are pooled and are listed at their pre-combination book values; the constituents' retained earnings are similarly combined.

D. REMEDIES OF DISSENTING SHAREHOLDERS

§22.18   *Alternative Remedies of Dissenting Shareholders*

Shareholders in constituent corporations are put to a statutory election in merger and consolidation proceedings, and sometimes asset sales and recapitalizations, to take the securities specified in the agreement or withdraw from the enterprise and obtain payment in money for the appraised value of their shares by following the strict statutory appraisal procedure.[1] Dissenters cannot simply retain the old securities and assert any rights under them; if they fail to demand appraisal they are bound by the lawful action of the majority, just as if they had consented to the action taken.[2] In recent years, however, the exclusivity of statutory dissenters' rights has been subject to some isolated erosion, but generally the appraisal remedy displaces other state law remedies, discussed next, except in the case of fraud or illegality.[3] Denial or loss of statutory dissenters' rights is considered to be an injury to the shareholders' property (i.e., their stock) for statute of limitations purposes.[4]

---

[4] Pooling-of-interest accounting, however, can still be used for combinations of companies that are under the common control.

[5] *See, e.g.,* Williams v. Bartell, 225 N.Y.S.2d 351 (App. Div. 1962) (Bergan, J. dissenting) (amount of goodwill lowered as a result of SEC letter of consent).

[6] *See* APB Opinion No. 17 (1970).

§22.18   [1] Porges v. Vadsco Sales Corp., 32 A.2d 148, 1150 (Del. Ch. 1943). *See* §22.19 for discussion of the statutory appraisal right. As to the exclusivity of the rights, *see* §22.22.

[2] National Supply Co. v. Leland Stanford Jr. Univ., 134 F.2d 689 (9th Cir.), *cert. denied,* 320 U.S. 773 (1943); Beechwood Sec. Corp. v. Associated Oil Co., 104 F.2d 537 (9th Cir. 1939).

[3] Umstead v. Durham Hosiery Mills, Inc., 578 F. Supp. 342 (M.D.N.C. 1984). *But see* Weinberger v. UOP, Inc., 457 A.2d 701 (Del. 1983) (indicating that appraisal remedy is exclusive in absence of fraud).

[4] Willard v. Moneta Bldg. Supply, Inc., 551 S.E.2d 596, 599-600 (Va. 2001).

Injunction. Prior to the consummation of a merger, consolidation, or sale of assets, a dissenting shareholder may sue to enjoin its completion either on the ground of lack of authority or compliance with a statute or on the ground of fraud or abuse of power.[5] Similarly, an injunction will lie to prevent violations of the securities laws' disclosure provisions.[6] Dissenting shareholders may lose their right to equitable relief by injunction by laches—that is, by failing to bring suit with the utmost promptitude before the rights of third persons have intervened.[7] Another limitation on injunctive relief is the maxim that equity is not available if an adequate remedy at law exists.[8]

Rescission. Suits are sometimes brought for rescission of a completed merger or consolidation or sale of assets. Theoretically such a transaction may be voidable on the ground that it is unauthorized or procured by fraud or abuse of power. But as a practical matter the only relief granted in such suits is an award of pecuniary compensation or a cash settlement to redress the injury to the dissenting shareholder for loss of his investment. This is on the ground that the task of readjusting the rights and interests of the constituent corporations, the creditors, and perhaps the thousands of shareholders and investors concerned is so insurmountable as to make any attempt to do so, upon a rescission, utterly fantastic.[9] As an early Alabama court reasoned, "It would be a painful travesty upon justice if a court of equity, in order to conserve the rights of a few stockholders in one of the parent companies, should destroy the property rights of innocent stockholders in the new company."[10] A suit for rescission, therefore, is usually in practical effect treated as simply a suit for the value of the shareholder's interest as fixed by a judicial, non-statutory appraisal.[11]

Individual Shareholder Action for Damages. Where, in voting to dissolve, merge, consolidate, or sell substantially all corporate assets, the majority have exceeded their lawful powers, have failed to comply with statutory conditions, or have been guilty of abuse of powers, objecting shareholders frequently were allowed to sue and recover for the value of their holdings on the theory that their equitable interest in the corporation had been misappropriated, "converted" or

---

[5] *E.g.,* Bryan v. Brock & Blevins Co., 490 F.2d 563 (5th Cir. 1974); Young v. Valhi, Inc., 382 A.2d 1372 (Del. Ch. 1978); Kamp v. Angel, 381 A.2d 241 (Del. Ch. 1977); Berkowitz v. Power/Mate Corp., 342 A.2d 566 (N.J. Super. Ct. Ch. Div. 1975).

[6] Bryan v. Brock & Blevins Co., 343 F. Supp. 1062 (N.D. Ga. 1972), *aff'd on other grounds,* 490 F.2d 563 (5th Cir.), *cert. denied,* 419 U.S. 844 (1974).

[7] Federal United Corp. v. Havender, 11 A.2d 331 (Del. 1940); Peterson v. New England Furn. & Carpet Co., 299 N.W. 208, 211 (Minn. 1941).

[8] Dan B. Dobbs, Law of Remedies §2.5 (2d ed. 1993); Henry Lace McClintock, Principles of Equity §21, 22 (2d ed. 1948).

[9] McMillan v. Intercargo Corp., 768 A.2d 492, 500 (Del. Ch. 2000) (completed merger cannot be unwound once "the metaphorical merger eggs have been scrambled").

[10] Alabama Fidelity Mortgage & Bond Co. v. Dubberly, 73 So. 911, 915 (Ala. 1916).

[11] *See, e.g.,* Jones v. Missouri-Edison Elec. Co., 144 F. 765, 778-781 (8th Cir. 1906), 199 F.64 (8th Cir. 1912), *cert. denied,* 229 U.S. 615 (1913); Weinberger v. UOP, Inc., 457 A.2d 701 (Del. 1983).

destroyed by the wrongful or inequitable action of the corporation.[12] Because the purchase, merger, or transfer under such circumstances is illegal or wrongful, the purchaser or successor may be held personally accountable to the dissenting shareholder for the value of the shares or of his proportional interest either on the ground of participation therein or on the ground that the successor is subject to the liabilities of the predecessor.[13] An individual shareholder's direct right of action to recover for the destruction of the value of his shares, often explained on the artificial theory of conversion, is an exception to the general rule that a shareholder cannot recover damages payable to himself personally for what is primarily a wrong done against the corporation in the absence of some wrong peculiar to him.[14]

Direct Actions Under the Securities Laws. Under SEC Rule 10b-5 defrauded purchasers or sellers may sue for damages resulting from misrepresentation or nondisclosure that resulted in their being deceived.[15] Similarly, a business combination consummated through a misleading proxy statement gives rise to individual recoveries under Rule 14a-9 of the Exchange Act, and various express liabilities exist for the purchaser of new securities that may be issued pursuant to the place of merger, consolidation, or sale of assets.[16]

Statutory Dissenters' Rights. The foregoing remedies for dissenting shareholders are available through the courts. These remedies are supplemented and in many cases replaced by the statutory appraisal remedy. As discussed in the sections that follow, statutory appraisal rights have been adopted in every state although they vary in scope, application, and the extent to which they are the exclusive remedy available to dissenting shareholders.

§22.19   The Statutory Appraisal Remedy

Every state has adopted "appraisal" statutes, which give dissenting shareholders a right to demand payment of the fair value of their shares. The statutes vary broadly in their coverage. The right is given in case of certain fundamental changes, such as merger or consolidation, and often in case of sale of the entire assets, and sometimes in case of amendments that change the rights of a certain

---

[12] Parnes v. Bally Entertainment Corp., 722 A.2d 1243, 1245 (Del. 1999) (permitting direct suit by shareholder challenging merger); Lebold v. Inland Steel Co., 125 F.2d 369 (7th Cir. 1941), *modified,* 136 F.2d 876 (7th Cir. 1943) (wrongful dissolution and appropriation of business by majority shareholders).

[13] American Seating Co. v. Bullard, 290 F. 896, 900 (6th Cir. 1923); Equitable Trust Co. v. Columbia Nat'l Bank, 142 S.E. 811 (S.C. 1928); International & G.N. R.R. v. Bremond, 53 Tex. 96, 119 (1880) (unauthorized consolidation; laches as to conversion different from laches as to injunction).

[14] Comment, 23 Cal. L. Rev. 174, 178-179 (1935); Comment, 38 Yale L.J. 964 (1929). *See* §15.02.

[15] 17 C.F.R. §240.10b-5 (2002). *See* §§12.08-12.10.

[16] Securities Act 1933, §§11, 12(a)(1), 12(a)(2), 15 U.S.C. §§77k, 78l(a)(1), 78l(a)(2) (2000); Junker v. Crory, 650 F.2d 1349 (5th Cir. 1981) (action for damages alleging violation of §12(2) in merger transaction).

class of outstanding shares and some other changes.[1] There is a widely adopted but debatable exception for a corporation whose shares are publicly traded.[2]

The expansion of commerce in the nineteenth century created a need for bigger and more complex corporations. The rule of unanimity impeded corporate growth because any shareholder could prevent a corporate combination if he did not agree. Because of the importance of contract and property rights, courts held grave doubts regarding the constitutionality of permitting corporate actions over the protest of any single shareholder. It is from these concerns that the appraisal remedy was born.[3]

In 1858, Pennsylvania authorized the merger of two railroads, which a dissenting shareholder sought to enjoin. In the ensuing case, *Lauman v. Lebanon Valley Railroad,*[4] the court, fearing that the merger would be unconstitutional if the shareholder was forced to accept shares in another corporation, held that the Pennsylvania legislature must have meant to provide dissenters with an appraisal remedy. The court enjoined the merger but only until security was given for the appraised value of the plaintiff's shares. There appears to be no basis for the court inferring the legislature intended to provide such relief to dissenters. The Pennsylvania legislature took the court's hint and passed the first appraisal statute (limited albeit to railroads), and the corporate landscape has never been the same since.

The justification for the appraisal remedy has other foundations today. The principle is well ingrained that the majority may combine their corporation with another and alter existing rights among shareholders without fear of serious constitutional challenge. At the same time, it is rarely the remedy of other than the "wine and cheese" crowd, for seldom is appraisal sought by investors whose holdings are less than $100,000, and few appraisal proceedings in fact occur.[5] The more visible benefit of appraisal is that it does provide a safety valve through which dissenters' unhappiness can be ventilated without interrupting the acquisition. A more ethereal, but no less important, rationale is that the existence of an appraisal remedy complements other monitoring mechanisms for self-dealing or ineptitude on the part of the board of directors.[6] Certainly the directors will be less sanguine

---

§22.19   [1] In re Marcus, 74 N.E.2d 228 (N.Y. 1947) (enlarging the voting rights of one class of stock to the detriment of another gives rise to appraisal rights); In re Kinney, 18 N.E.2d 645 (N.Y. 1939) (reduction of stated capital). *But see* Tilley v. Kickoff Publishing Co., 454 F.2d 1288 (6th Cir. 1972) (recapitalization does not grant appraisal rights); Glens Falls Ins. Co. v. National Bd. of Fire Underwriters Bldg. Corp., 314 N.Y.S.2d 80 (N.Y. Sup. Ct. 1971) (denial of redemption rights gives no appraisal).

[2] *See, e.g.,* Del. Code Ann. tit. 8, §262(b)(1) (2001). *See* Note, A Reconsideration of the Stock Market Exception to the Dissenting Shareholder's Right of Appraisal, 74 Mich. L. Rev. 1023 (1976).

[3] *See generally* Elliott Weiss, The Law of Take Out Mergers: A Historical Perspective, 56 N.Y.U. L. Rev. 624, 624-630 (1981).

[4] 30 Pa. 42 (1858).

[5] *See* Joel Seligman, Reappraising the Appraisal Remedy, 52 Geo. Wash. L. Rev. 829, 829 n.3, 830 n.5 (1984).

[6] *See generally* Hideki Kanda & Saul Levmore, The Appraisal Remedy and the Goals of Corporate Law, 32 UCLA L. Rev. 429 (1985); Daniel Fischel, The Appraisal Remedy in Corporate Law, 1983 Am. B. Found. Res. J. 875, 877-881.

D. Remedies of Dissenting Shareholders

about a proposal they submit to the shareholders for approval if they believe there is an efficient mechanism for shareholders to realize an alternatively determined value for their shares than that being recommended by the board of directors. So viewed, an important consideration is whether the procedures for exercising the appraisal remedy as well as the substantive guidelines for determining fair value are indeed efficient and have the right social balance.[7]

It is important to consider the policy and purpose of the statutory remedy. As seen above, the impetus for creating the appraisal remedy was to remove possible doubt about the constitutionality of statutes authorizing fundamental changes as to existing corporations and the contract rights of shareholders.[8] In part, the purpose of these provisions has been to give dissenters a simple and direct remedy not only where there is a harmful change in the share contract but also where they simply do not desire to accept shares in a different corporation or shares different from those they purchased. As Professor Lattin put it, the purpose has been "[t]o placate the dissenting minority and, at the same time, to facilitate the carrying out of changes of a desirable and extreme sort."[9]

While in theory the ostensible purpose of the statutory appraisal remedy is to protect the minority and afford them a way out in case of fundamental changes, in reality it appears that the purpose is even more to aid and protect the majority. The proceeding by dissenting shareholders for the appraisal of their shares does not delay or prevent the completion of the consolidation, merger, sale of assets for securities, or recapitalization by amendment; the change takes place subject to a collateral proceeding to value the shares of the dissenting shareholders. However, appraisal proceedings do burden the constituent corporations, who may be more inclined to offer a generous exchange in an effort to avoid exercise of the appraisal remedy.

Those who have drafted and sponsored many of these statutes have been careful to avoid possible undue interference and obstruction by minority shareholders acting in bad faith and thus have made as little concession to the dissenters as possible. Those who wish to avail themselves of the statutory remedy must act with exceeding quickness in order to meet the stringent conditions precedent. Simply stated, most appraisal statutes contain multiple steps, each with a specific and short time period within which dissenters must comply to preserve and perfect their right of appraisal. For example, under the Model Business Corporation Act, if a shareholder vote is required for the fundamental change, the shareholders must give written notice of their intent to dissent prior to the vote

---

[7] Thus, among the objectives of the recently completed American Law Institute project was to reduce the procedural entanglements of seeking appraisal, allowing common counsel to be used in those proceedings, and providing a means for earlier payment of dissenters while not disturbing the strong presumption of propriety in non-self-dealing situations. *See* ALI Principles of Corporate Governance: Analysis and Recommendations §§7.21-7.25 (1994).

[8] *See* Lauman v. Lebanon Valley R.R., 30 Pa. 42 (1858). As noted earlier, this doubt has proved to be unfounded.

[9] Norman D. Lattin, Remedies of Dissenting Stockholders Under Appraisal Statutes, 45 Harv. L. Rev. 233, 237 (1931).

and then must refrain from voting in favor of the plan.[10] After the vote the dissenting shareholders will be informed of the procedures to be followed and must again make a written demand for payment of the fair value of their shares. The statutes vary greatly on the technical procedures to be followed. Under the Delaware Act, after the vote the corporation must within 10 days give notice of the right to dissent, and thereafter the shareholders have 20 days within which they must make a written demand.[11] Under the Model Business Corporation Act there is no time limit on the corporation's post-approval notice. The shareholders must be given at least 30 days.[12]

In most states, shares are not qualified for appraisal unless they have actually voted against the combination or, in some states, have at least abstained.[13] Accordingly, a shareholder not attending the meeting in person or by proxy cannot receive an appraisal regardless of how difficult or useless it may have been for him to comply with this voting requirement.[14] Statutes differ as to the status of dissenting shareholders after demand for payment. Under some acts, on demand for payment, they cease to have any interest in the shares or right to dividends[15] or other rights of shareholders.[16] Under other statutes, the rights cease only after payment of the appraised price.[17]

Under the Model Business Corporation Act, a shareholder who has perfected his rights to appraisal loses all rights as a shareholder, unless he withdraws from the appraisal process.[18] The shareholder is thereafter entitled to be paid the amount the corporation believes is the fair value of his shares.[19] And the shareholder can continue to press his claim in a formal appraisal proceeding for any additional amounts above paid by the corporation that the shareholder argues is necessary to raise the total payment to the shares' fair value.[20] Both the share-

---

[10] Model Bus. Corp. Act §13.21 (1984); Former Model Bus. Corp. Act §81(c) (1969). An excellent review of the Revised Model Business Corporation Act appears in Harry F. Johnson & Paul Bartlett, Jr., Is a Fistful of Dollars the Answer? A Critical Look at Dissenters' Rights Under the Revised Model Business Corporation Act, 12 J.L. & Com. 211 (1993).

[11] Del. Code Ann. tit. 8, §262(d)(2) (2001). Material misrepresentations in the notice of the right to appraisal are actionable. Nebel v. Southwest Bancorp, Inc., 1995 WL 405750 (Del. Ch. 1995) (corporation erroneously including another state's appraisal statute was required to provide a "quasi appraisal"; ordering rescission of the merger would go far beyond the statutory purpose of the Delaware appraisal remedy).

[12] Model Bus. Corp. Act §13.21(a) (1984); Former Model Bus. Corp. Act §81(b), 81(c) (1969). See Willard v. Moneta Bldg. Supply, Inc., 551 S.E.2d 596, 599-600 (Va. 2001) (corporation's failure to give proper notice constitutes injury to shareholder's property for statute of limitations purposes).

[13] Del. Code Ann. tit. 8, §262(b) (2001). See also Pinnacle Consultants, Ltd. v. Leucadia Nat'l Corp., 727 N.E.2d 543, 547 (N.Y. 2000) (shareholder who abstains from voting on merger is not necessarily estopped from later bringing suit, especially when predetermined number of affirmative votes is required to approve merger, in which case abstention is equivalent of negative vote).

[14] Former Model Bus. Corp. Act §81(d) (1969); Model Bus. Corp. Act §13.22(b) (1984) (corporation has 10 days; shareholders at least 30 and no more than 60).

[15] E.g., Mass. Ann. Laws ch. 156, §46 (Law. Co-op. 1979).

[16] See Baugh v. Citizens & S. Nat'l Bank, 281 S.E.2d 531 (Ga. 1981) (lost standing to enjoin merger).

[17] See Johnson v. C. Brigham Co., 136 A. 456 (Me. 1927) (under prior Maine statute requiring specific negative vote); Abbot v. Waltham Watch. Co., 156 N.E. 897, 902 (Mass. 1927).

[18] Model Bus. Corp. Act §13.23 (1984).

[19] Model Bus. Corp. Act §13.24 (1984).

[20] Model Bus. Corp. Act §13.26(a) (1984).

D. Remedies of Dissenting Shareholders

holder and the corporation have obligations with respect to initiating formal appraisal proceedings under the Revised Model Business Corporation Act. The shareholder must, among other requirements, demand payment of his estimate of the shares' fair value within 30 days,[21] and the corporation must within 60 days of that demand initiate the proceeding or be obligated to pay the shareholder the full amount sought.[22]

In an appraisal proceeding, evidence of value must be taken and a record must be kept.[23] An appraiser's report must usually be filed with the clerk of court, and the parties may take exception to the report.[24] After a hearing as to the exceptions, argument on the report, and the consideration of evidence, the court will confirm, modify, or reject the report.[25]

The expenses of an appraisal proceeding are a factor of serious importance, as they involve appraisers' fees, attorneys' fees, and fees for expert accountants and witnesses before the appraisers. This may be an undue burden on the dissenter, but it may also allow a shareholder acting in bad faith to cause the corporations to spend substantial sums.[26] Only a few statutes make adequate provision for attorneys' fees and other expenses of the petitioner.[27]

§22.20   Scope of Statutory Appraisal Rights[1]

Though it is well recognized that dissenters' rights only arise in those transactions specifically proscribed in the statute,[2] courts sometimes invoke the remedy by

---

[21] Model Bus. Corp. Act §13.26 (1984).

[22] Model Bus. Corp. Act §13.30(a) (1984). *See also* Waters v. Double L., Inc., 755 P.2d 1294 (Idaho App. 1987), *aff'd*, 769 P.2d 582 (1989). Somewhat related is the position that once notice is given of an intent to pursue appraisal, the shareholder cannot withdraw some of his shares for that process. *See* Lightman v. Recognition Equip., Inc., 295 A.2d 771 (Del. Ch. 1972).

[23] Model Bus. Corp. Act §13.30 (1984); Former Model Bus. Corp. Act §81(h) (1969).

[24] *See* Note, Rights of Dissenting Stockholders Pending Statutory Appraisal Proceedings, 21 Va. L. Rev. 825 (1935).

[25] *See* Francis I. du Pont & Co. v. Universal City Studios Inc., 312 A.2d 344 (Del. Ch. 1973), *aff'd*, 334 A.2d 216 (Del. 1975); In re Valuation of Common Stock of Libby, McNeill & Libby, 406 A.2d 54, 63 (Me. 1979); Piemonte v. New Boston Garden Corp., 387 N.E.2d 1145 (Mass. 1979); Warren E. Banks, Measuring the Value of Corporate Stock, 11 Cal. W. L. Rev. 1 (1974); Note, Valuation of Dissenters' Stock Under Appraisal Statutes, 79 Harv. L. Rev. 1453 (1966).

[26] *See* Dimmonk v. Reichhold Chem., Inc., 360 N.E.2d 1079 (N.Y. 1977) (ten-year proceeding produced an increase in value of $13,000 after expenses of $50,000).

[27] *See, e.g.,* Hernando Bank v. Huff, 609 F. Supp. 1124 (N.D. Miss. 1985), *aff'd*, 796 F.2d 803 (5th Cir. 1981) (expense assigned to corporation because appraisal yielded significant increase in amount to be paid by corporation); Francis I. du Pont & Co. v. Universal City Studios Inc., 334 A.2d 216 (Del. 1975); In re Delaware Racing Ass'n, 213 A.2d 203 (Del. 1965); In re Valuation of Common Stock of Libby, McNeill & Libby, 406 A.2d 54 (Me. 1979); Piemonte v. New Boston Garden Corp., 387 N.E.2d 1145 (Mass. 1979).

§22.20   [1] Model Bus. Corp. Act §13.02(a) (1984); Former Model Bus. Corp. Act §80(b)(2) (1969).

[2] *See* Valando v. Data Boutique, Ltd., 323 N.Y.S.2d 608 (Sup. Ct. 1971). At least one court has held that when the specific terms of a share of stock provide its value in the event of a merger, the appraisal remedy is not available for that class of stock. *See* In the Matter of the Appraisal of Ford Holdings, Inc. Preferred Stock, 698 A.2d 973 (Del. Ch. 1997).

analogy to the type of transactions covered by the statute. Thus, in *Moreley Brothers v. Clark*,[3] the court held a shareholder was entitled to appraisal when the corporation's issuance of new shares reduced the present stockholder's interest from 100 percent to 19.9 percent.[4] Correlatively, a transaction that formally is of the type specified in the state's appraisal statute substantively may not involve the type of change that appraisal was intended to apply. For example, a merger carried out to reincorporate under the laws of another state was held not to be within the type of merger transaction proscribed in the state appraisal statute.[5] Such a judicial gloss, though perhaps reaching the "right" result, creates a good deal of uncertainty when planning unorthodox transactions. A wise approach would be to apply appraisal statutes literally when considering the scope of this legislatively created remedy.

Serious gaps exist in the statutory protection for minority shareholders against fundamental corporate actions that may be prejudicial to their interests.[6] In some states, including Delaware, appraisal rights do not attach to sales of assets or charter amendments; thus this remedy is limited to mergers or consolidations.[7] In most states a corporation's sale of all or substantially all of its assets "not made in the usual and regular course of its business" triggers statutory dissenters' rights.[8] However, even with a sale of assets, dissenters' rights possibly can be avoided if some substantial asset—for example, a tract of real property—is left in the selling corporation.[9] Most statutes do not give dissenters' rights to shareholders of the purchaser of assets, and, subject to the infrequently applied de facto merger doctrine,[10] a transaction can thus be structured to avoid the statutory remedy.[11]

Appraisal rights extend to charter amendments under both the former Model Business Corporation Act and the Revised Model Business Corporation Act.[12] There are no states in which dissolution per se triggers dissenters' rights, although in some states a sale of all or substantially all assets in a dissolution proceeding will invoke the statutory right.[13] Under the Revised Model Business Corporation Act, appraisal rights also apply to a planned exchange of shares to which the corporation is a party if the shareholder is entitled to vote on the exchange.[14]

---

[3] 361 N.W.2d 763 (Mich. Ct. App. 1984).

[4] *See also* Orchard v. Covelli, 590 F. Supp. 1548 (W.D. Pa. 1984) (statute not exclusive and will protect minority in close corporation from oppression).

[5] China Prod. of N. Am., Inc. v. Manewals, 850 P.2d 565 (Wash. Ct. App. 1993).

[6] F. Hodge O'Neal & Robert B. Thompson, O'Neal's Oppression of Minority Shareholders §§5:28-5:29 (1985).

[7] Del. Code Ann. tit. 8, §262 (2001); Kan. Stat. Ann. §17-6712 (1988). A number of states deny dissenters' rights to shareholders in a surviving parent corporation that used a short form procedure to merge with a subsidiary. *See* §22.12.

[8] *E.g.*, 805 Ill. Comp. Stat. 5/11.60 (1993). *See* Dreiseszun v. FLM Indus., 577 S.W.2d 902 (Mo. Ct. App. 1979); King v. Southwestern Cotton Oil Co., 585 P.2d 385 (Okla. 1978).

[9] There is surprisingly little authority on what constitutes "substantially all."

[10] *See* §22.06. *See, e.g.,* Pratt v. Ballman-Cummings Furn. Co., 495 S.W.2d 509 (Ark. 1973).

[11] For another avoidance device *see* the discussion of triangular mergers *supra* §22.13.

[12] *E.g.*, N.Y. Bus. Corp. Law §806(b)(6) (McKinney 1986); Former Model Bus. Corp. Act §80(a)(4) (1969); Model Bus. Corp. Act §13.02(a)(4), (5) (1984). *See* §25.13.

[13] Florsheim v. Twenty-five Thirty-two Broadway Corp., 432 S.W.2d 245 (Mo. 1968).

[14] Model Bus. Corp. Act §13.02(a)(2) (1984).

D. Remedies of Dissenting Shareholders

Many states that have control-share anti-takeover provisions in their corporate statutes provide a remedy similar to the more traditional appraisal remedy. These provisions require a person making a "control share" acquisition to purchase the shares of any requesting shareholder. A "control-share acquisition" is variously defined but generally refers to one whose ownership interest reaches 20-25 percent and whose purchase has not been approved by the incumbent board of directors.[15]

The Corporate Governance Project of the American Law Institute contains sweeping recommendations as to the instances to which an appraisal remedy should be applied.[16] While the Corporate Governance Project covers mergers, consolidations, exchanges of shares, sales of assets, and amendments to the articles, a broad policy of the provision is not to necessarily condition the remedy's existence on the particular transaction requiring the particular shareholder's approval. This is something of a double-edged principle. Appraisal is not required, even though shareholders are required to approve the transaction, if a body of shareholders will not own less than 60 percent of the combined enterprise[17] and accords shareholders an appraisal remedy in a combination accomplished without their approval if they emerge from the transaction owning less than the 60 percent figure.[18] Because the scope of the appraisal remedy is predominantly a matter of state statutory law, the operative effect of this portion of the American Law Institute's treatment of the appraisal remedy is largely to influence the drafters of corporate statutes. However, where ambiguity exists under local statutes, the American Law Institute's treatment could be highly influential.

The Model Business Corporation Act[19] and some states now deny appraisal rights to holders of shares registered on a national securities exchange.[20] In Delaware, for example, where appraisal rights attach only to merger and consolidation, the statute now excludes transactions where shares of any class or series are either listed on a national exchange or held by more than 2,000 stockholders.[21]

In addition to the substantive limitations on the scope of the appraisal remedy, the risk of considerable expense as well as the procedural difficulties in pursuing the remedy further decrease its effectiveness in protecting minority shareholders. Even if a dissenting shareholder proceeds promptly and in compliance with all procedural requirements, the price to be received for his shares is unpredictable, whether or not the shares are publicly traded.

Further, federal tax laws discourage shareholders from exercising their right to have the dissenter's shares purchased. If the dissenter's rights are invoked, the

---

[15] *See, e.g.,* Me. Rev. Stat. Ann. tit. 13A, §910 (Supp. 1994) (more than 25 percent of the shares); 15 Pa. Cons. Stat. Ann. §2541-2548 (1994) (20 percent of the shares).

[16] *See* ALI Principles of Corporate Governance: Analysis and Recommendations §7.21 (1994).

[17] *Id.* §7.21(a).

[18] *See id.* Comment c, at 302-304. *See, e.g.,* Morley Bros. v. Clark, 361 N.W.2d 763 (Mich. Ct. Appl. 1984).

[19] Model Bus. Corp. Act §13.02(b) (1984).

[20] Note, A Reconsideration of the Stock Market Exception to the Dissenting Shareholder's Right of Appraisal, 74 Mich. L. Rev. 1023 (1976).

[21] Del. Code Ann. tit. 8, §262(b) (2001).

shareholders receive cash for their shares, and there is a tax on whatever capital gain is realized.[22] If by going along with a merger or other fundamental change the shareholders receive stock or securities, they may be able to avoid recognition of gain on the exchange.[23]

§22.21 Valuation of Shares in Appraisal Proceedings

The most difficult task in obtaining relief under appraisal statutes is establishing the fair value of the dissenting shares. The statutes use a variety of terms to describe what the dissenting share is worth. These include "value," "fair value," "fair cash value," or "fair market value." These different expressions in effect mean the same thing.[1] The use of the word "fair" indicates that market quotations for a particular day or even the average over a period of time is not conclusive as to the valuation of the shares.[2] Legislatures and the courts have not been able to establish any definite measure or standard of value. The Model Business Corporation Act simply provides that fair value should be determined "using customary and current valuation concepts and techniques generally employed for similar businesses in the context of the transaction requiring appraisal."[3] Although varying terms are used, the vague general standard leaves it up to the appraisers to fix a fair price as between the parties. The appraiser is expected to consider all the elements and factors, both positive and negative, that would be considered by practical and experienced business people in estimating the value of the shares as an investment. The process must take into account not only the liquidating value of the corporation's net assets but also the future prospects and earning power of the corporation as a continuing enterprise.[4] The appraisal, whether by an appraiser or the court, must be reasonable and fair.[5]

---

[22] I.R.C. §1001 (1988).

[23] I.R.C. §354(a)(1) (1988). See also I.R.C. §356 (1988).

§22.21 [1] But see Swope v. Siegel-Robert, Inc., 243 F.3d 486, 492 (8th Cir. 2001) (applying Missouri law; "fair value" in minority stock appraisal cases is not the equivalent of "fair market value" since dissenting shareholders do not have access to willing and ready buyers on an open market, but instead are unwilling sellers with no bargaining power); Lawson Mardon Wheaton, Inc. v. Smith, 734 A.2d 738, 746 (N.J. 1999) ("fair value" is not synonymous with "fair market value"; fair value is broader and more flexible test applied when appraised shares are not readily marketable); Balsamides v. Protameen Chems., Inc., 734 A.2d 721, 733 (N.J. 1999) (same).

[2] See, e.g., Bell v. Kirby Lumber Corp., 395 A.2d 730 (Del. Ch. 1978), aff'd in part and rev'd in part, 413 A.2d 137 (Del. 1980).

[3] Model Bus. Corp. Act §13.01(4)(ii) (1984).

[4] For a discussion of the various factors to be considered, see Robert B. Thompson, Exit, Liquidity, and Majority Rule: Appraisal's Role in Corporate Law, 84 Geo. L.J. 1 (1995). For an insightful and thorough examination of the many issues that can arise in the appraisal process, see Barry M. Wertheimer, The Shareholders' Appraisal Remedy and How Courts Determine Fair Value, 47 Duke L. J. 613 (1998). See also, e.g., In re 75,629 Shares of Common Stock, 725 A.2d 927 (Vt. 1999) (court properly ignored tax consequences that would accompany liquidation; also it was proper to ignore valuation in stock transfer restriction that did not expressly apply to appraisal context).

[5] See Gonsalves v. Straight Arrow Publishers, 701 A.2d 357, 361 (Del. 1997).

D. Remedies of Dissenting Shareholders

More important than the adjectives used to express the value that dissenters are to receive are the assumptions regarding the context in which such value is to be realized. One can assume the value of the firm based on its piecemeal liquidation, assuming that the firm is to go out of business and that there will be no purchaser of its assets as an operating economic unit. This assumption in most cases will produce the most conservative valuation of the firm because it does not permit consideration of the synergies the assets produce through their interaction as a going concern. This assumption is frequently referred to as the net asset value of the firm. If one values the corporation assuming it is a going concern, three different scenarios are possible: (1) the firm is auctioned off to the highest bidder; (2) the sale is at arm's length but without encouraging competing bids; or (3) the role of a third-party buyer is not considered[6] and the business is valued in light of its present income and risks. By far the most liberal valuation occurs under the assumption there is an auction; the more conservative ignores the impact of a third-party buyer on the intrinsic value of the firm.[7] By making the amount obtained through an arm's-length acquisition presumptive of fair value unless the dissenter proves otherwise by clear and convincing evidence, the American Law Institute discreetly reinforces the presumption of propriety that normally accompanies director actions not involving self-dealing. On the other hand, this presumption does not arise in self-dealing acquisitions, so these types of transactions can be put to something akin to a market test by measuring fair value in an auction setting.[8]

In arm's-length transactions, the American Law Institute recommends that the bargain struck is presumptively the shares' fair value, unless the dissenter proves otherwise by clear and convincing evidence.[9] And when the transaction is self-interested, the American Law Institute recommends those in control "match the highest realistic price that any other willing, able, and fully informed buyer would have paid. . . ."[10]

In determining the adequacy of particular appraisal prices, many courts, being influenced by the reasoning of earlier Delaware decisions, have used a weighted average of four values: (1) asset value, (2) market value, (3) earnings value, and (4) dividend value, with the relative weight to be decided according to all of the surrounding circumstances.[11] Where there is no ascertainable market value, the courts generally look to the other three factors.[12] The four factor analysis is generally known as the Delaware block method, which is a misnomer today because the Delaware Supreme Court has now discarded its strict adherence to a

---

[6] M.P.M. Enterprises, Inc. v. Gilbert, 731 A.2d 790 (Del. 1999).

[7] *See generally* Lucian Bebchuk & Marcel Kahan, Fairness Opinions: How Fair Are They and What Can Be Done About It?, 1989 Duke L.J. 27, 31-33.

[8] *See* ALI, Principles of Corporate Governance 319-324 (1994).

[9] *Id.,* §7.22(b).

[10] *Id.* at 316.

[11] *See, e.g.,* Bell v. Kirby Lumber Corp., 395 A.2d 730 (Del. Ch. 1978), *aff'd in part and rev'd in part,* 413 A.2d 137 (Del. 1980). In re Delaware Racing Ass'n, 213 A.2d 203 (Del. 1965).

For cases applying the Delaware block method, *see* In re Valuation of Common Stock of Libby, McNeil & Libby, 406 A.2d 54 (Me. 1979).

[12] *E.g.,* Foglesong v. Thurston Nat'l Life Ins. Co., 555 P.2d 606 (Okla. 1976).

weighted-average approach and has instituted a method of valuation based on all relevant factors.[13] In other words, Delaware will now accept as evidence "proof of value by any techniques or methods which are generally considered acceptable in the financial community and otherwise admissible in court."[14]

The determination of value is a factual one[15] and is thus done on a case-by-case basis. Certain principles, however, have been said to govern every valuation: (1) net asset value should not be heavily weighted, unless valuation is being made for liquidation, because the value of corporate assets bears little relation to the value of the stock;[16] (2) extraordinary gains, such as gains from a sale of fixed assets or "gains" achieved by changes in inventory accounting should not be considered, because these gains will not be repeated in the future, and therefore they are not indicative of future earnings potential;[17] (3) market value can be ignored or discounted[18] when shares are so thinly traded as to question the reliability of their market value.[19] In valuing shares of a closely held corporation, reference to comparable public corporations is sometimes appropriate when the comparative group has similar earnings and other financial relationships.[20]

With its decision in *Weinberger v. UOP, Inc.,*[21] Delaware broke free of the rigid adherence to the formulas of the Delaware block method[22] by holding that all relevant factors should be considered when appraising shares.[23] The underlying assumption in an appraisal valuation is that the dissenting shareholders would be willing to maintain their investment position had the merger not occurred. Con-

---

[13] Weinberger v. UOP, Inc., 457 A.2d 701 (Del. 1983).

[14] *Id.* at 713.

[15] Piemonte v. New Boston Garden Corp., 387 N.E.2d 1145 (Mass. 1979). The determination will stand if supported by substantial evidence. Kirtz v. Advanced Instruments, Inc., 581 S.W.2d 868 (Mo. Ct. App. 1979). Speculative sources of value, such as tax loss carryover or conditional offer to purchase the corporation, should not be considered. *Id.* at 870. For a discussion of fair value generally, *see* Rutherford B. Campbell, Jr., Fair Value and Fair Price in Corporate Acquisitions, 78 N.C.L. Rev. 101 (1999).

[16] *See* Hernando Bank v. Huff, 796 F.2d 803 (5th Cir. 1986); Miller Bros. Indus., Inc. v. Lazy River Inv. Co., 709 N.Y.S.2d 162, 165 (App. Div. 2000). The Delaware Supreme Court has held that a statutory appraisal can never be made solely on the basis of an actual liquidation net asset value, since the value of dissenting stock must be fixed on a going-concern basis. Paskill Corp. v. Alcoma Corp., 747 A.2d 549, 554 (Del. 2000).

[17] In re Valuation of Common Stock of Libby, McNeill & Libby, 406 A.2d 54 (Me. 1979).

[18] Munshower v. Kolbenhayer, 732 So. 2d 385 (Fla. Dist. App. 1999) (applying a 20 percent non-marketablity discount to shares in a closely held corporation).

[19] *See* Swope v. Siegel-Robert, Inc., 243 F.3d 486, 493 (8th Cir. 2001) (applying Missouri law; since fair market value is irrelevant in determining fair market value, market forces do not affect ultimate assessment of fair value in appraisal proceeding); Beerly v. Department of Treasury, 768 F.2d 942, 944-946 (7th Cir. 1985) (comptroller's method of appraising stock, i.e., computing adjusted book value, computing investment value, and averaging the two, was not arbitrary or capricious).

[20] *See* In re Radiology Assoc., Inc., 611 A.2d 485 (Del. Ch. 1991).

[21] 457 A.2d 701, 713 (Del. 1983).

[22] The rigidity of this method is best illustrated by Universal City Studios v. Francis I. duPont & Co., 334 A.2d 216 (Del. 1975), wherein the court mandated use of the five-year earnings average, though the trend line in earnings was steeply rising, countering this ultimate conservatism by imprecisely using lower discount rate with which to capitalize earnings.

[23] *Id.* This language now appears in the Delaware statute. *See* Del. Code Ann. tit. 8, §262(h) (2001).

sequently, the corporation must be valued as an operating entity.[24] This invites the use of modern financial valuation models used in business and finance to be used in appraisal proceedings. For example, a fairly widely used financial technique for valuing businesses is the "discounted cash flow technique," which was sometimes emasculated within the "earnings value" component of the Delaware block method. The discounted-cash technique, a variation on the method's application, is now well accepted in Delaware.[25]

The new Delaware appraisal method imposes some limits on what may be considered in arriving at a fair value. For example, the Delaware Supreme Court held that it was proper not to give any weight to "real world" offers for the target company shares.[26] The court pointed out that since the Delaware statute, as was the case with the Model Act, expressly provides that fair value shall be determined "exclusive of any element of value arising from the accomplishment or expectation of the merger."[27] According to the court, this means that synergies arising from an actual or expected transaction cannot be considered in determining fair value. The court explained that an arm's-length third-party offer is more likely to represent the synergistic value of the proposed acquisition rather than the fair value of the target company.[28]

The overall objective of the appraisal process is to determine the dissenter's proportionate value *of the firm,*[29] which is not the same as stating the value of her shares in the firm. In determining the value of the shares, the latter emphasis would consider such intangibles as whether the shares represent majority or minority interests in the firm. If minority shares, they are not nearly as valuable as majority shares because they lack the power to direct the company's operations. This is the so-called minority discount that some courts subtract from the dissenter's shares in determining their value. Some courts have employed a minority discount in valuing shares.[30] However, the great majority of the more recent decisions have emphasized that the appraisal statutes call for a value of the shareholder's proportionate interest in the firm, not simply their shares, so that it is

[24] Paskill Corp. v. Alcoma Corp., 747 A.2d 549, 553 (Del. 2000); M.G. Bancorporation, Inc. v. Le Beau, 737 A.2d 513, 525 (Del. 1999).

[25] *See* Cede & Co. v. Technicolor, Inc., C.A. No. 7129, 1990 WL 161084 (Del. Ch. Dec. 11, 1990). *See also* M.G. Bancorporation, Inc. v. Le Beau, 737 A.2d 513, 525 (Del. 1999) (approving "comparative acquisitions" approach).

[26] M.P.M. Enterprises Inc. v. Gilbert, 731 A.2d 790 (Del. 1999). Although the trial court admitted evidence of the offer, it decided not to give it any weight in the valuation process.

[27] *Id.* at 795; Del. Code Ann. Tit. 8 §262(h) (2001). Former Model Bus. Corp. Act §13.01(3) provided that fair value should be determined exclusive of "any appreciation or depreciation in anticipation of the corporate action unless exclusion would be inequitable." This language was eliminated in 1999. *See* Model Bus. Corp. Act §13.01(4) (revised definition of "fair value").

[28] 731 A.2d at 797.

[29] *See, e.g.,* Advanced Communication Design, Inc. v. Follett, 615 N.W.2d 285, 290 (Minn. 2000) ("fair value" means pro rata value of corporation's value as a going concern); First Western Bank Wall v. Olsen, 621 N.W.2d 611, 617 (S.D. 2001) ("fair value" means value of dissenters' shares as proportionate interest in going concern; appraisal proceeding should not focus on stock as a commodity).

[30] Offenbecher v. Baron Services, Inc., 2001 WL 527522 (Ala. Civ. App. 2001) (upholding lower court's application of 50 percent minority discount); English v. Artromick Intern., Inc., 2000 WL 1125637 (Ohio App. 2000) (permitting minority discount in suit challenging freeze-out).

inappropriate to deduct a minority discount.[31] The 1999 amendments to the Model Business Corporation Act follows the majority trend by taking the position that fair value is to be determined on a proportionate basis without considering a minority discount.[32]

Under many state statutes, the dissenting shareholder is not to be allowed a value enhanced by the prospective benefits of the merger, consolidation, or sale in which he refuses to participate.[33] Courts more recently have permitted post-transaction benefits to be included in determining the fair value of dissenter's shares.[34] It has been suggested, however, that fairness demands that the minority shareholders be compensated for their share of the synergism produced by the merger.[35] The synergistic formula was accepted by the Seventh Circuit in the context of determining fairness under the federal proxy rules and in upholding the terms of the merger.[36] However, it has been criticized by a number of commentators.[37] In 1999, the Delaware Supreme Court ruled that the appraisal statute prohibits considerations of synergies which would be created by the proposed business combination.[38]

§22.22   *Exclusivity of Statutory Appraisal Rights*

There has been a good deal of debate as to whether statutory provisions that permit dissenting shareholders to demand payment for their shares may or should be exclusive of other legal and equitable remedies by which minority shareholders seek to enjoin or attack changes such as merger or consolidation.[1] In some states

---

[31] *E.g.,* Swope v. Siegel-Robert, Inc., 243 F.3d 486, 495-496 (8th Cir. 2001) (applying Missouri law; minority status of stock is irrelevant in appraisal proceeding); Pueblo Bancorporation v. Lindoe, Inc., 2001 WL 921190 (Colo. App. 2001) (reversing trial court's use of minority discount); Cavalier Oil Corp. v. Harnett, 564 A.2d 1137 (Del. 1989); Blitch v. Peoples Bank, 540 S.E.2d 667 (Ga. App. 2000) (rejecting minority discount in appraisal); In re Valuation of Common Stock of McLoon Oil Co., 565 A.2d 997 (Me. 1989); Richton Bank & Trust Company v. Bowen, 798 So. 2d 1268 (Miss. 2001).

[32] Model Business Corporation Act §13.01(4).

[33] *See, e.g.,* Perlman v. Permonite Mfg. Co., 568 F. Supp. 232 (N.D. Ind. 1983) (Indiana law). *See also* Cede & Co. v. Technicolor, Inc., 684 A.2d 289 (Del. 1996).

[34] *See* M.P.M. Enterprises Inc. v. Gilbert, 731 A.2d 790 (Del. 1999).

[35] *See, e.g.,* Cawley v. SCM Corp., 530 N.E.2d 1264 (N.Y. 1988). In Cede & Co. v. Technicolor, Inc., 684 A.2d 289 (Del. 1996), the court explained that the statutory provision excluding "elements of value arising from the accomplishment or expectation of the merger" is to be narrowly construed. Accordingly, it was an error to exclude new business strategies implemented between the time of the merer agreement and the merger.

[36] Mills v. Electric Auto-Lite Co., 552 F.2d 1239 (7th Cir.), *cert. denied,* 434 U.S. 922 (1977).

[37] Victor Brudney & Marvin A. Chirelstein, Fair Shares in Corporate Mergers and Takeovers, 88 Harv. L. Rev. 297, 308-309 (1974); Simon Lorne, A Reappraisal of Fair Shares in Controlled Mergers, 126 U. Pa. L. Rev. 955 (1978).

[38] M.P.M. Enterprises, Inc. v. Gilbert, 731 A.2d 790 (Del. 1999).

§22.22 [1] *See generally* Steven D. Gardner, A Step Forward: Exclusivity of the Statutory Appraisal Remedy for Minority Shareholders Dissenting from Going-Private Merger Transactions, 53 Ohio St. L. Rev. 239 (1992); Hideki Kanda & Saul Levmore, The Appraisal Remedy and the Goals of Corporate Law, 32 UCLA L. Rev. 429 (1985); Robert Thompson, Squeeze-Out Mergers and the "New" Appraisal Remedy, 62 Wash. L.Q. 415 (1984); Daniel Fischel, The Appraisal Remedy in Corporate Law, 1983 Am. B. Found. Res. J. 875, 877-881.

the appraisal statutes are silent as to what effect the statutory right of appraisal has on the availability of other remedies.[2] In a few states, the statute expressly provides that appraisal is the exclusive remedy,[3] but this flat restriction is usually tempered by either other statutory language or judicial interpretation.[4]

In 1983, the Delaware Supreme Court indicated that in the absence of fraud or illegality, the appraisal remedy will be exclusive.[5] Material nondisclosures in connection with the transaction will preclude the exclusivity of the statutory appraisal remedy.[6] The Delaware Supreme Court has not elaborated on what types of unlawful conduct other than fraud will avoid the exclusivity of the statutory appraisal remedy. The court has merely stated that direct judicial review of a transaction may be found when the plaintiff establishes fraud or other misconduct.[7]

The meaning of "fraud," "illegality," and other such types of misconduct that prevent the appraisal statute from being the shareholder's exclusive recourse is fairly much decided on a case-by-case basis. The courts are fairly consistent in refusing to allow an exception to the appraisal statute when the sole complaint is that the merger does not offer a fair price for the dissenter's shares.[8] A bare allegation that the merger freezes the minority out of the corporation is generally not successful in overcoming the exclusivity of the appraisal remedy.[9] In some jurisdictions, the appraisal remedy is exclusive, even though the plaintiff charges that the majority was engaged in self-dealing and thereby sought to acquire the company at an unfair price.[10] The better view is to at least permit equitable relief in such a situation.[11] Appraisal does not foreclose complaints that the merger never

[2] E.g., Del. Code Ann. tit. 8, §262 (2001); Mass. Gen. Laws Ann. ch. 156, §§46, 46E (Law. Co.-op. 1979).

[3] E.g., Conn. Gen. Stat. Ann. §33-373(f) (West 1987). See In re Jones & Laughlin Steel Corp., 398 A.2d 186 (Pa. Super. Ct. 1979), aff'd, 412 A.2d 1099 (Pa. 1980).

[4] See Miller v. Steinback, 268 F. Supp. 255, 270 (S.D.N.Y. 1967) (former Pennsylvania statute's exclusivity limited to "good faith" and transactions that are not "sham or subterfuge"); Weckler v. Valley City Mills Co., 93 F. Supp. 444 (W.D. Mich. 1950), aff'd per curiam, 188 F.2d 367 (6th Cir. 1951) (former Michigan statute with exclusivity clause embodied implied term of good faith); Rabkin v. Phillip A. Hunt Chem. Corp., 480 A.2d 655 (Del. Ch. 1984); rev'd, 498 A.2d 1099 (Del. 1985).

[5] Weinberger v. UOP, Inc., 457 A.2d 701 (Del. 1983).

[6] E.g., Nagy v. Bistricer, 770 A.2d 43 (Del. Ch. 2000).

[7] Rabkin v. Philip A. Hunt Chemical Corp., 498 A.2d 1099, 1105 (1985) ("While a plaintiff's mere allegation of 'unfair dealing', without more, cannot survive a motion to dismiss, averments containing 'specific acts of fraud, misrepresentation, or other items of misconduct' must be carefully examined"; quoting from Weinberger).

[8] See, e.g., Theodore Trust U/A v. Smadbeck, 717 N.Y.S.2d 7, 7-8 (N.Y. App. Div. 2000) (action for damages alone may not be maintained by shareholders seeking redress for undervaluation of their stock in merger context); Werner v. Alexander, 502 S.E.2d 897 (N.C. App. Ct. 1998) (appraisal remedy is exclusive when only complaint essentially surrounds the price).

[9] See Kademian v. Ladish Co., 792 F.2d 614, 630 (7th Cir. 1986); Teschner v. Chicago Title & Trust Co., 322 N.E.2d 54 (Ill. 1974); Yeager v. Paul Seminon Co., 691 S.W.2d 227, 229 (Ky. Ct. App. 1985). But see Mullen v. Academy Ins. Co., 705 F.2d 971 (8th Cir.), cert. denied, 464 U.S. 827 (1983) (New Jersey statute not intended to foreclose complaint that freeze-out was breach of majority's fiduciary duty).

[10] Walter J. Schloss Ass'n v. Arkwin Indus., 460 N.E.2d 1090, 1108 (N.Y. 1984). See also Steinberg v. Amplica, Inc., 729 P.2d 683 (Cal. 1986), modified, 43 Cal. 3d 516 (Sup. Ct. 1987).

[11] See Walter J. Schloss Ass'n v. Arkwin Indus., 460 N.E.2d 1090 (N.Y. 1984) (appraisal exclusive if shareholder seeks damages but not for equitable protection against freeze-out); Theodore Trust U/A

secured the necessary approvals,[12] other procedural improprieties,[13] the corporation's failure to initiate dissenters' rights proceedings,[14] or for misconduct before the merger.[15] Finally, in *Cede & Co. v. Technicolor, Inc.*[16] the Delaware Supreme Court held that a shareholder who had begun an appraisal proceeding and thereafter, before that proceeding's conclusion, learned of fraud in the merger, could join in one proceeding the fraud and the appraisal actions so that if fraud were indeed proven appraisal would be moot; otherwise, appraisal could be pursued.

Many courts have invoked this rule despite the availability of appraisal where the parties controlling the transaction have misled the complaining shareholder or appraiser by fraudulent misrepresentations[17] concerning the value of the shares,[18] or have not complied with the procedural requirements for a merger or other fundamental corporate change.[19] One question that arises under the statutes making appraisal the exclusive remedy unless the conduct is "unlawful or fraudulent,"[20] and in decisions by courts phrasing the rule in terms of "fraud or illegality"[21] is whether a breach of fiduciary duty will be sufficient to overcome appraisal's exclusivity. Some courts have held that it is.[22] Other courts have held that a claim based only on a breach of fiduciary duty (without claims of self-dealing, waste, or fraud) will not avoid the appraisal remedy's exclusivity.[23]

Whatever the local position is as to the exclusivity of the appraisal remedy, the existence of an appraisal remedy does not bar any available action under the federal securities laws for deception. Thus inadequate disclosures during proxy solicitation have often resulted in challenges to the legitimacy of mergers and other

---

v. Smadbeck, 717 N.Y.S.2d 7, 7-8 (N.Y. App. Div. 2000) (action in equity is permissible to challenge fraudulent or illegal corporate activity).

[12] *See* Shindler v. All Am. Life & Fin. Corp., 775 F.2d 917 (8th Cir. 1985).

[13] Rabkin v. Phillip A. Hunt Chem. Corp., 498 A.2d 1099 (Del. 1985) (second step of acquisition purposely delayed to avoid paying higher consideration promised in first stage if merger completed within one year).

[14] Galligan v. Galligan, 741 N.E.2d 1217, 1225-1226 (Ind. 2001) (shareholders may proceed with separate claim against persons responsible for breach of fiduciary duty to initiate dissenters' rights proceedings).

[15] *See* Kandemian v. Ladish Co., 792 F.2d 614 (7th Cir. 1986).

[16] 542 A.2d 1182 (Del. 1988).

[17] Victor Broadcasting Co. v. Mahurin, 365 S.W.2d 265, 270 (Ark. 1963).

[18] Cole v. Wells, 113 N.E. 189 (Mass. 1916). *See also* Farnsworth v. Massey, 365 S.W.2d 1 (Tex. 1963), William v. Bartell, 225 N.Y.S.2d 351 (App. Div. 1962).

[19] *E.g.,* Starrett Corp. v. Fifth Ave. & Twenty-ninth St. Corp., 1 F. Supp. 868 (S.D.N.Y. 1932). *See also* Johnson v. Spartanburg Fair Ass'n, 41 S.E.2d 599 (S.C. 1947) (shareholder votes had not been validly cast).

[20] See N.Y. Bus. Corp. Law §623(k) (McKinney 1986); Model Bus. Corp. Act §13.02(d) (1984).

[21] *E.g.,* Weinberger v. UOP, Inc., 457 A.2d 701 (Del. 1983).

[22] *E.g.,* M&W, Inc. v. Pacific Guardian Life Insurance Co., 1998 WL 32685 (Haw. App. Ct. 1998) (depublished opinion), affirmed without opinion, 966 P.2d 1098 (Haw. 1998) (the court refused to follow the *Weinberger* decision because earlier Hawaii precedent following pre-*Weinberger* Delaware law was still binding).

[23] *See, e.g.,* Moon v. Moon Enterprises, Inc., 65 Ark. App. 246, 986 S.W.2d 134 (1999) (shareholder's failure to make written demand for payment under appraisal statute waived claim and precluded claim for breach of fiduciary duty in connection with challenged sale).

corporate combinations.[24] For example, undervaluation of a constituent company's assets,[25] failure to disclose the control of one constituent company by the other,[26] and the inflated value of the shares to be received[27] have all given rise to such suits. Courts also give relief to complaining shareholders where the parties controlling the transaction have deceived the shareholders as to the substantive fairness of a plan of merger or consolidation and thus have induced them not to invoke the right of appraisal.[28]

---

[24] *See, e.g.,* Emerald Partners v. Berlin, 726 A.2d 1215 (1999) (claims of misleading proxy solicitation in addition to unfairness in allegedly self-dealing merger).

[25] Gerstle v. Gamble-Skogmo, Inc., 478 F.2d 1281 (2d Cir. 1973).

[26] TSC Indus. v. Northway, Inc., 426 U.S. 438 (1976); Mills v. Electric Auto-Lite Co., 396 U.S. 375 (1970), *on remand,* 552 F.2d 1239 (7th Cir.), *cert. denied,* 434 U.S. 922 (1977).

[27] Schlick v. Penn-Dixie Cement Corp., 507 F.2d 374 (2d Cir. 1974).

[28] *See* Wilson v. Great American Indus., 979 F.2d 924 (2d Cir. 1992). This would also trigger remedies under the federal securities laws. *See* §§12.09, 13.23.

CHAPTER 23

Equitable Limits on Acquisitions and Defensive Maneuvers

§23.01 Fiduciary Obligations in Acquisition Transactions

The classic paradigm for an acquisition is two or more corporations combining in an arm's-length transaction. Shareholder approval follows the negotiation and approval of the plan of merger by the board of directors of the constituent corporations. When shareholder approval is required—that is, it is not avoided through the "small acquisition" exception discussed earlier—the desirability of the transaction is judged by the collective judgment of the shareholders and their board of directors. A major consideration is the full and fair disclosure of all material facts of the acquisition. When the parties are dealing at arm's length, there is little justification for judicial scrutiny, any more than for the business decisions of the board of directors or officers generally. This is not to suggest that mistakes, errors in judgment, or bad results do not flow from acquisitions; they most certainly do. The law's caution here mirrors the concerns examined in Chapter 10 that capitalism works best when it is Adam Smith's invisible hand, not causes of action, that guide the deployment of resources. That is, the preeminent force in placing resources to their highest use is not judicial intervention but the judgment of the firm's managers and its shareholders. Although courts will review the fairness of arm's-length acquisitions, the shareholder-plaintiff bears the substantial burden of proving "such gross disparity as will raise an inference of improper motives or reckless indifference to or intentional disregard of stockholders' interests."[1] Under such a standard, the plaintiff is rarely successful.[2]

But not all acquisitions fit within the orthodox mold of corporations dealing at arm's length. There has long been a history of judicial review of combinations between affiliated corporations, most particularly when the subsidiary is acquired by its parent. In the 1980s two additional acquisition forms became more prevalent—the merger freeze-out and the management buyout. In the freeze-out a majority stockholder initiates a transaction that eliminates the minority's continuing equity participation, generally by the terms of the merger forcing the minority to receive cash for their shares. The frequency of merger freeze-outs is enhanced by modern statutes, which today not only condition an acquisition's approval on a majority vote but also authorize the plan of merger to provide that cash or any other property can be exchanged for shares. Thus modern statutes authorize transactions that eliminate the minority, which classically, at least, were authorized only by short-form merger statutes.

The merger freeze-out poses a question that classic self-dealing acquisitions do not pose. While both freeze-outs and self-dealing acquisitions invoke concerns that the terms offered the minority are the product of self-interested negotiations, the merger freeze-out raises the additional concern as to whether, and in what contexts, the majority is able to exercise its power to terminate the minority's continuing participation in the firm. The management buyout (MBO) also eliminates the shareholders from the corporation. The transaction is part of a larger objective: to take the company private and for its present management to have a larger stake in its future operations and success. The MBO varies from other types of self-interested acquisitions because in the MBO those initiating the transaction and emerging as part of the control group previously did not have a controlling shareholder interest in the corporation. They nevertheless are not dealing with the corporation or its shareholders at arm's length unless, as discussed later, active steps are taken to interject an independent negotiator into the transaction.

The fount of the majority's fiduciary obligations in acquisitions is *Sterling v. Mayflower Hotel Corporation*,[3] where the court imposed an "entire fairness" standard on the majority:

> Hilton as a majority stockholder of Mayflower and the Hilton directors as its nominees occupy, in relation to the minority, a fiduciary position in dealing with Mayflower's property. Since they stand on both sides of the transaction, they bear

---

§23.01   [1] Baron v. Pressed Metals of Am., Inc., 123 A.2d 848 (Del. 1956); Wittman v. Crooke, 707 A.2d 422 (Md. Ct. App. 1997).

[2] One instance of such success is Gimbel v. Signal Co., 316 A.2d 599 (Del. Ch.), *aff'd per curiam*, 316 A.2d 619 (Del. 1974).

[3] 93 A.2d 107 (Del. 1952).

the burden of establishing its entire fairness, and it must pass the test of careful scrutiny by the courts.[4]

Sterling then embraced the give-get formula for measuring fairness, reasoning that "the test of fairness which we think [is] the correct one [is] that upon a merger the minority stockholder shall receive the substantial equivalent in value of what he had before."[5] The Delaware Supreme Court, and other courts,[6] now recognize that the minority should also participate proportionally in any nonspeculative gains generated by the acquisition.[7]

The procedural context in which the transaction is formulated, proposed, and approved has assumed increasing importance. For example, the Delaware Supreme Court has distinguished between "fair dealing" and "fair price" such that it more readily concludes the appraisal remedy is exclusive as to the latter but not necessarily as to the former.[8] "Fair dealing" is defined to include questions regarding the acquisition's timing, how it was initiated, structured, and negotiated, and the approvals of the directors and stockholders obtained.[9] In essence, fair dealing examines whether the transaction is the product of overreaching misbehavior by which those in a fiduciary relationship to the target corporation use their power to deprive the target corporation of fair and independent representation in the acquisition.[10] For example, in *Weinberger v. UOP, Inc.*[11] the parent corporation was

---

[4] *Id.* at 109-110. *See also* McMullin v. Beran, 765 A.2d 910 (Del. 2000); T. Rowe Price Discovery Fund, L.P. v. Rubin, 770 A.2d 536 (Del. Ch. 2000).

[5] 93 A.2d at 114.

[6] *See, e.g.,* Mills v. Electric Auto-Lite Co., 552 F.2d 1239 (7th Cir.), *cert. denied,* 434 U.S. 922 (1977); Cawley v. SCM Corp., 530 N.E.2d 1264 (N.Y. 1988).

[7] *See* Weinberger v. UOP, Inc., 457 A. 701 (Del. 1983).

[8] *See* Rabkin v. Philip A. Hunt Chem. Corp., 498 A.2d 1099 (Del. 1985).

In Cede & Co. v. Technicolor, Inc., 542 A.2d 1182 (Del. 1988), the court explained the exclusivity of the appraisal remedy in terms that appear to again distinguish between fair dealing and fair price. The court emphasized the Delaware appraisal remedy relief against the corporation; that relief is the value of the dissenter's shares. By contrast, fraud is a more expansive remedy, being available against parties other than the corporation and providing relief that is more encompassing than the intrinsic value of the shares. The court thus permitted both types of action to be maintained in the same suit, recognizing that appraisal may not provide complete relief for unfair dealing or fraud. Thus it would appear that in Delaware the exclusivity of the appraisal remedy turns not only on whether appraisal can address the injury alleged but also on whether the focus of that relief is someone other than the corporation. *See also, e.g.,* Emerald Partners v. Berlin, 726 A.2d 1215 (Del. 1999) (self-dealing merger permitted an entire fairness analysis of transaction); Parnes v. Bally Entertainment Corp., 722 A.2d 1243 (Del. 1999) (allegations that chairman and controlling stockholder favored his interests over interests of other shareholders in stock-for-stock merger stated a claim for relief).

[9] *See* Weinberger v. UOP, Inc., 457 A.2d 701, 711 (Del. 1983).

[10] *See* Parnes v. Bally Entertainment Corp., 722 A.2d 1243 (Del. 1999) (allegations that chairman and controlling stockholder favored his interests over interests of other shareholders tainted entire process such that if established fair dealing part of "entire fairness" standard would not have been satisfied); McMullin v. Beran, 765 A.2d 910 (Del. 2000) (directors who approved unfair merger at the insistence of the controlling stockholder and did not adequately inform themselves will be deemed to have breached their fiduciary duty).

[11] 457 A.2d 701 (Del. 1983). For a decision expressing great reluctance to sanction the acquiring or successor company for fraud or breach of fiduciary duty committed by the acquired company's

found to violate the requirement of fair dealing because two of its officers also sat on the subsidiary's board of directors and prepared a report of the subsidiary's value using the subsidiary's information, but did not share that report with their fellow subsidiary directors. Had they done so, their fellow directors would have learned that a 14 percent increase in the purchase price would have had minimal effect on the expected return the parent expected to garner from the acquisition.

These problems are circumvented by interjecting an independent negotiating committee between the parent and the target corporation.[12] A further means to clothe the controlled corporation with an independent voice is by conditioning the transaction's consummation on the approval of a majority of the disinterested shares. In *Weinberger* this avenue was unsuccessful, however, because the proxy statement failed to disclose all the material facts. It withheld, for example, the contents of the earlier described report.[13] However, the burden of proving the acquisition's entire fairness does not shift if the procedures followed are not truly independent. Thus, in *Kahn v. Tremont Corp.,*[14] the Delaware Supreme Court held that the creation of a special negotiating committee to approve the sale of the company to its controlling stockholder did not change the burden of proving entire fairness where the most active member of the committee enjoyed longstanding commercial ties to the controlling stockholder and the other two committee members were not active in the committee's deliberations. Furthermore, the committee's advisors were also not seen as being independent since they were indirectly tainted because they were selected on the recommendation of the committee's chair who the court concluded was not himself independent.

§23.02 Equitable Limitations on the Power of Sale or Merger

A controlling shareholder or parent corporation that dominates and controls another corporation is not as a matter of law precluded from purchasing the entire property and assets of the controlled corporation, either when the assets of a going concern are sold or when the corporation is being wound up. However, such a purchase by a controlling person or the company's managers implicates the same concerns examined in Chapter 10 regarding self-dealing such that close or rigorous judicial scrutiny occurs.[1]

The template most commonly followed for addressing the minority holder's complaint that the merger of the firm with its controlling stockholder (or an

directors in their approval of its acquisition, *see* Arnold v. Society for Savings Bancorp, Inc., 678 A.2d 533 (Del. 1996).

[12] *See* Rosenblatt v. Getty Oil Co., 493 A.2d 929, 937-939 (Del. 1985).

[13] 457 A.2d at 712.

[14] 694 A.2d 422 (Del. 1997). *See also* Kohls v. Duthie, 765 A.2d 1274 (Del. Ch. 2000).

§23.02 [1] Abelow v. Symonds, 173 A.2d 167 (Del. Ch. 1961) (sale of subsidiary's assets to parent required hearing to determine fairness of selling price).

entity under the controlling stockholder's influence) is *Weinberger v. UOP, Inc.*[2] The *Weinberger* court held that when the appraisal remedy is not exclusive,[3] the reviewing court should "carefully scrutinize the board's actions to ascertain whether the board instituted measures to ensure a fair process, and whether the board achieved a fair price for the disinterested stockholder minority."[4] This formula is more frequently stated as the "entire fairness" inquiry with fairness thus having two distinct components: fair dealings and fair price. The court undertakes a unified assessment that involves balancing the process followed and the price received by the minority.[5] Just as we saw earlier in Chapter 10, when there is a self-dealing acquisition it is inappropriate to apply the presumption of propriety that accompanies the business judgment rule. When there is a self-dealing acquisition the controller party has the burden of proving entire fairness.

In assessing the fairness of the process, the court will consider:

> [T]he board's composition and independence, the timing, structure and negotiation of the transaction; how the board and shareholder approval were obtained; and the extent to which the board and the shareholders were accurately informed about the transaction.[6]

Important considerations here are the presence of an independent committee to represent the interest of the minority holders in negotiating the transaction, the approval of a majority of the minority shares after full disclosure of all material facts, and the use of independent advisors for the outside directors considering the transaction.[7] Thus, fair dealing was not satisfied when the financial consultant to the independent directors had close ties to the law firm that customarily represented the controlling stockholder.[8] Fair dealing does not require, however, that the shareholders be provided with financial data needed to make an independent judgment.[9] The ratifying vote of a fully informed majority of the minority shifts

---

[2] 457 A.2d 701 (Del. 1983). *See also* Lerner v. Lerner Corp., 750 A.2d 709 (Md. Ct. App. 2000).

[3] On the exclusivity of the appraisal remedy, *see* §22.22.

[4] Lerner v. Lerner Corp., 750 A.2d 709, 711 (Md. Ct. App. 2000).

[5] *See* Cinerama, Inc. v. Technicolor, Inc., 663 A.2d 1156, 1179 (Del. 1995).

[6] Ryan v. Tad's Enterprises, Inc., 709 A.2d 682, 690 (Del. Ch. 1996).

[7] *See* Kahn v. Lynch Communication Systems, Inc., 669 A.2d 79, 84 (Del. 1995); Cinerama, Inc. v. Technicolor, Inc., 663 A.2d 1156, 1172 (Del. 1995). For a case emphasizing the importance of an independent negotiating committee in refusing to grant a request for a preliminary injunction against a MBO, *see* Kohls v. Duthie, 765 A.2d 1274, 1285 (Del. Ch. 2000).

[8] *See* Ryan v. Tad's Enterprises, Inc., 709 A.2d 682, 693 (Del. Ch. 1996). Similarly, when the transaction is not the product of the directors' independent judgment, but instead their obeisance to the wishes of the controlling stockholder, there is a breach of the directors' fiduciary duty of loyalty. *See* McMullin v. Beran, 765 A.2d 910 (Del. 2000).

[9] *See, e.g.,* McMullin v. Beran, 765 A.2d 910 (Del. 2000); Skeen v. Jo-Ann Stores, Inc., 750 A.2d 1170 (Del. 2000) (denying request that there be disclosure of, among other facts, the range of values determined by the firm's investment banker and the reason the board decided to sell the company). However, the controlling stockholder's and board of director's fiduciary obligation of full and fair disclosure, *see* §10.15, provides a good deal of shelter to the minority stockholders. *See, e.g.,* Arnold v. Society for Savings Bancorp, Inc., 650 A.2d 1270 (Del. 1994) (proxy statement misleading by failing to disclose that one of the company's subsidiaries had been subject to auction bid that exceeded the total value of the merger the shareholders were now asked to approve); Nagy v. Bistricer, 770 A.2d

the burden of proving fairness; such ratification has limited benefits to the defendant because the transaction still is subject to scrutiny under the entire fairness standard, albeit the burden shifts to the plaintiff to prove the transaction was not entirely fair.[10] There is no effective ratification if the vote is the product of coercion.[11] Fair price has been defined as meaning the amount a reasonable seller "would regard in the range of fair value."[12]

Though Delaware has pioneered in making law for the protection of minority shareholders frozen out via a merger, it has recently qualified the scope of the entire fairness review standard. In *Glassman v. Unocal Exploration Corporation*,[13] the court held that the parent company that exercises its right under the short-form merger provision[14] to rid itself of the minority shareholders in the subsidiary does not have to establish the entire fairness for its actions. In such a case the exclusive remedy to the minority, absent fraud or illegality, is the appraisal remedy.[15] The court believed that the legislative intent in providing a short-form merger procedure would be frustrated if the parent corporation were subject to the entire fairness review standard. Also, because the decision to accept a tender offer is an individual one, the entire fairness standard does not apply to a controlling stockholder's tender offer for the minority shares.[16]

§23.03   Merger Freeze-outs of Minority Shareholders

Abuses that may accompany a controlled merger or other conflict-of-interest transaction are magnified when the minority shareholder is cashed out and thus is not able to share in the profits of the surviving corporation. These cash-outs, also known as "squeeze-outs" or "freeze-outs," which are not new, have been accomplished in a variety of ways. The short-form merger[1] is the simplest of the

---

43, 61 (Del. Ch. 2000) (failure to disclose the salient facts regarding the merger in the notice of the merger was breach of fiduciary obligation and basis for granting plaintiff's motion for summary judgment). However, the disclosure breach, if in good faith, albeit grossly negligent, will not give rise to liability on the part of the directors if the corporation's articles of incorporation contain the standard immunity shield. *See* Arnold v. Society for Savings Bancorp Inc., 650 A.2d 1270, 1290 (Del. 1995) and liability for the acquiring company is difficult to establish either as wrongdoer itself or for vicarious responsibility. *See* Arnold v. Society for Savings Bancorp Inc., 678 A.2d 533 (Del. 1996). Hence, the real relief that may be possible is injunctive relief.

[10] *See* Kahn v. Lynch Communications Systems, Inc., 638 A.2d 1110 (Del. 1994).

[11] *See* Weiss v. Samsonite Corp., 741 A.2d 366 (Del. Ch. 1999).

[12] *Id.* For a case illustrating the failure to prove fair price, *see* Boyer v. Wilmington Materials, Inc., 754 A.2d 881 (Del. Ch. 1999). *But see* Barter v. Diodoardo, 771 A.2d 835 (Pa. Super. 2001) (negotiating to receive cash rather than a promissory note, as well as the privilege to continue to use the golf course, was deemed not to involve such fundamental unfairness such as to rise to a breach of fiduciary duty, but raised financial unfairness of the type that is best addressed through appraisal).

[13] 777 A.2d 242 (Del. 2001).

[14] Short-form mergers are discussed in §22.12.

[15] *Id.*

[16] *See* In re Siliconix, Inc. Shareholder Litig., 2000 Del. Ch. LEXIS 1583 (Del. Ch. 2001). But the presence of coercion in such an offer would be actionable, *see* Weiss v. Samsonite Corp., 741 A.2d 366 (Del. Ch. 1999).

§23.03   [1] *See* §22.12.

various statutory liberalizations and has led to an increase in the use of merger, consolidation, or sale of assets as a freeze-out technique.[2] This is a rapidly developing area in which there has been a great deal of judicial and scholarly energy directed toward the proper treatment of freeze-out transactions.[3] The cases recognizing a freeze-out remedy have focused on two factors: (1) the purpose of the transaction and (2) fairness to the minority shareholders. While some courts require a showing of no valid purpose as a threshold to scrutiny of the transaction's fairness,[4] older Delaware cases, at least in their language, put the burden of proving both on the defendants.[5] More recently, the Delaware Supreme Court has abandoned the business purpose requirement.[6]

The utility of the business purpose test appears to be its invitation to the court to review somewhat more widely the overall terms, objectives, and motivations surrounding the acquisition. There is little evidence that the business purpose test otherwise provides strong and predictable protection to the minority or ensures the majority against the unnecessary scrutiny of a fair transaction. It is important in this regard to stress that the emphasis of the business purpose test is on the purpose for the acquisition;[7] the business purpose test applied by the courts does not inquire as to why the acquisition's terms provide cash, rather than a continuing equity participation, to the acquired corporation.

The range of legitimate commercial purposes for an acquisition is so extensive that the business purpose test can reach only the most egregious types of misconduct.[8] On the other hand, if courts wish to recognize the right of shareholders to continue their participation in an enterprise, they would focus on the reasons for cashing the minority shareholders out of the corporation. Such a narrowed focus would likely reduce the frequency of merger freeze-outs. In one famous case, a freeze-out was justified by the objective of removing from the corporation an obstreperous minority shareholder who was blocking the majority's acceptance of a beneficial offer from a third party.[9] By either not requiring a business purpose

---

[2] Frequently this is accomplished by a two-step transaction where the acquiring corporation "locks up" control of the target by open-market purchases or by tender offer, and then has a clean-up merger to eliminate the minority.

[3] *E.g.*, Victor Brudney & Marvin Chirelstein, A Restatement of Corporate Freeze-Outs, 87 Yale L.J. 1354 (1978); Edward F. Greene, Corporate Freeze-out Mergers: A Proposed Analysis, 28 Stan. L. Rev. 487 (1976).

[4] *E.g.*, M & W Inc. v. Pacific Guardian Life Ins. Co., Ltd., No. 19276, 1998 WL 32685 (Haw. Ct. App. 1998); Gabhart v. Gabhart, 370 N.E.2d 345 (Ind. 1977); Bird v. Wirtz, 266 N.W.2d 166 (Minn. 1978) (temporary injunction); Alpert v. 28 Williams St. Corp., 473 N.E.2d 19 (N.Y. 1984) (upholding transaction as fair).

[5] Roland Int'l Corp. v. Najjar, 407 A.2d 1032 (Del. 1979); Tanzer v. International Gen. Indus., 379 A.2d 1121 (Del. 1977); Singer v. Magnavox, Inc., 380 A.2d 969 (Del. 1977).

[6] Weinberger v. UOP, Inc., 457 A.2d 701 (Del. 1983).

[7] *See, e.g.,* Coggins v. New England Patriots Football Club, Inc., 492 N.E.2d 1112 (Mass. 1986); Alpert v. 28 William St. Corp., 473 N.E.2d 19 (N.Y. 1984).

[8] *See generally* William Carney, Fundamental Corporate Changes, Minority Shareholders, and Business Purposes, 1980 A.B.F. Res. J. 69 (1980); Alan M. Terrell, Jr. & Alesia Ranney-Marinelli, What Constitutes a Valid Purpose for a Merger?, 51 Temp. L.Q. 852 (1978).

[9] *See* Matteson v. Ziebarth, 242 P.2d 1025 (Wash. 1952).

or focusing their inquiry on the more general purpose for the acquisition, the courts strongly embrace the concept of majoritarism within the American corporation, whereby the minority's interest can be terminated, albeit at a fair price, by the will of the majority. Any preoccupation with the fairness of the price offered the minority must confront the question of whether the appraisal remedy should be the minority's exclusive right to complain.[10]

An important consideration in evaluating the exclusivity of the appraisal remedy in the context of a self-interested acquisition is the procedural setting in which the relief is sought. Courts should be more willing to avoid the exclusivity of the appraisal remedy when the object of the action is a temporary or preliminary injunction. In this context, courts grant their relief when there is reason to believe purposeful manipulation of disclosure practices or operations has been carried out to artificially depress the price of the company's shares,[11] the transaction is purposely timed to deprive the minority of a higher price they would have received if the transaction's timing had been more neutrally determined,[12] or there appears to have been no independent determination by the board of directors of the fairness of the price offered to minority.[13] A recent Delaware Supreme Court decision provides discipline to the controlling shareholders in a merger freeze-out; the court held that shareholders who are frozen out in the second stage of a two-step acquisition are entitled in the appraisal process to a proportionate share of the gains arising from a business plan that was agreed to be followed after eliminating the minority in the second step of the acquisition.[14]

A management buyout (MBO) customarily takes the form of a purchase of the target corporation by a newly formed corporation largely with funds borrowed from financial institutions and the old management and their new partners holding a significant, if not exclusive, portion of the new company's equity. From a theoretical point, the MBO deals directly with the classic agency problem that arises from the separation of ownership and management. Managers become the sole or dominant owners after the MBO, so the firm's destiny is their own. Because they, not dispersed shareholders, reap the full benefits of the venture's upside potential, managers have powerful incentives to assure the venture's success.[15] On the

---

[10] *See* §22.27. Where the stockholders are not accorded an appraisal remedy, one court concluded they were entitled to equitable protection to assure they received fair value for their shares. *See* Stoneman v. United Nebraska Bank, 254 Neb. 477 (Neb. 1998).

[11] *See* Berkowitz v. Power/Mate Corp., 342 A.2d 566 (N.J. Ch. 1975).

[12] *See* Rabkin v. Philip A. Hunt Chem. Corp., 498 A.2d 1099 (Del. 1985).

[13] *See* Kahn v. Lynch Communication Sys., Inc., 638 A.2d 1110 (Del. 1994). Though the interested directors had the burden of proof, the court ultimately was satisfied that the merger price met the "intrinsic fairness" standard. Kahn v. Lynch Communication Systems, Inc., 669 A.2d 79 (Del. 1995). Thus, the standard formulation in Delaware today requires the interested directors bear the burden of proving "entire fairness." *See, e.g.,* Ryan v. Tad's Enterprises Inc., 709 A.2d 682 (Del. Ch. 1996).

[14] *See* Cede & Co. v. Technicolor, Inc., 684 A.2d 289 (Del. 1996). For a review of the implications of *Technicolor, see* Jesse A. Finkelstein & Russell C. Silberglied, *Technicolor IV:* Appraisal Valuation in a Two-Step Merger, 52 Bus. Law. 801 (1997).

[15] *See* Michael Jensen, Agency Costs of Free Cash Flow, Corporate Finance and Takeovers, 76 Amer. Econ. Rev. (Papers and Proceedings) 323 (1986); Robert Kaplan, The Effect of Leveraged Buyouts on Operations and Value, 24 J. Fin. Econ. 217 (1989).

other side of the social equation, questions abound when the managers are purchasing the corporation in such a setting.[16] First, there is the concern over the superior information advantage the managers have over the shareholders. Second, the stockholders' approval may not fully reflect their true sense of the fairness of the transaction when other offers or options have been constrained by the very managers proposing to purchase the firm. Third, there must be concern whether the price and terms of payment are the product of negotiations in the strictest sense of the meaning. Certainly, negotiations are difficult to imagine if the directors who recommend the proposal to the stockholders are also the purchasers.

Because the management buyout is the purest form of self-interested acquisition, it is subject to the closest scrutiny for fairness of the price, but more significantly for the process for approving the acquisition. There is no breach of fiduciary duty merely because the target corporation's assets and earnings will be used to purchase the firm's outstanding shares or because the managers gain from the transaction, absent proof they have reaped a unique advantage from their fiduciary position.[17] At the same time, what objective evidence exists that assures that the managers are offering a fair price? A convenient answer to this concern arises when there are competing offers. In this context the focus is to assure a free dynamic auction of control. Thus, in a leading MBO case, *Mills Acquisition Company v. Macmillan, Inc.,*[18] the Delaware Supreme Court struck down a lockup option granted to the MBO's financial partner because the corporation's directors, most of whom were participants in the MBO, were viewed as having skewed the results of the bidding competition through the lockup and several other actions they took. Other indicia of objective fairness are resorting to investment bankers' opinion letters[19] and constituting a group of independent directors to serve as a negotiating committee with the MBO group. If a duly constituted independent body of directors is not given the task of negotiating the acquisition with either the managers or the controlling stockholder, the burden of proving entire fairness of the acquisition falls on the interested party.[20]

Notwithstanding its subsequent rejection in Delaware, the business purpose test continues to be an issue in many other jurisdictions.[21] Further, the business

---

[16] *See generally* Richard Booth, Management Buyouts, Shareholder Welfare and the Limits of Fiduciary Duty, 60 N.Y.U. L. Rev. 630 (1985); Deborah A. DeMott, Puzzles and Parables: Defining Good Faith in the MBO Context, 23 Wake Forest L. Rev. 15 (1990); Thomas L. Hazen, Management Buyouts and Corporate Governance Paradigms, 25 Wake Forest L. Rev. 1 (1990).

[17] *See* Field v. Allyn, 457 A.2d 1089 (Del. Ch. 1983). *See also, e.g.,* DeMascole v. Tatro, 673 A.2d 57 (R.I. 1996) (the majority shareholder is not obligated to inform the minority of pending negotiations that would result in a sale of the company).

[18] 559 A.2d 1261 (Del. 1988). *See also* Edelman v. Fruehauf Corp., 798 F.2d 882 (6th Cir. 1986).

[19] *See* Lucian Bebchuk & Marcel Kahan, Fairness Opinions: How Fair Are They and What Can Be Done About It?, 1989 Duke L.J. 27. *See also* Comment, M. Breen Haire, The Responsibilities of Investment Bankers in Change-of-Control Transactions: *In re Daisy Systems Corp.,* 74 N.Y.U. L. Rev. 277 (1999).

[20] *See* Rosenblatt v. Getty Oil Co., 493 A.2d 929 (Del. 1985). The standard, however, remains "intrinsic fairness." Citron v. E. I. DuPont de Nemours & Co., 584 A.2d 490, 498-502 (Del. Ch. 1990).

[21] *E.g.,* Bryan v. Brock & Blevins Co., Inc., 490 F.2d 563 (5th Cir. 1974) (Georgia law); Gabhart v. Gabhart, 370 N.E.2d 345 (Ind. 1977); Bird v. Wirtz, 266 N.W. 2d 166 (Minn. 1978); Berkowitz v. Power/Mate Corp., 342 A.2d 566 (N.J. Super. Ct. 1975); People v. Concord Fabrics, Inc., 377 N.Y.S.2d

purpose test is not limited to mergers; it has also been applied, for example, where the directors issued additional shares to themselves to perpetuate their control.[22] Also, with developments in Rule 10b-5 mismanagement cases,[23] nondisclosure of conflicts of interest or any other facts that might give rise to a state law action will provide a federal remedy in freeze-out cases.

§23.04   Going-Private Transactions Under the Securities Laws

A very popular subspecies of the freeze-out merger is the going-private transaction.[1] This has been described as any organic corporate change, such as merger, reverse stock split, repurchase of shares, or recapitalization, that results in a publicly traded company being delisted or closely enough held so as no longer to be subject to the 1934 Exchange Act's reporting requirements.[2] There are various possible motives behind going private—for example, a company may decide that the burdens of SEC reporting are too expensive or it may be the final step in a takeover by another company. All of the fairness considerations applicable to any freeze-out transactions[3] necessarily apply with equal force to this special subspecies. In addition, there has been both SEC involvement and state law concern based on the fact that going-private transactions lessen the standards of corporate conduct.

Beyond the state law fiduciary standards for directors and controlling shareholders,[4] relief may be found under SEC Rule 10b-5,[5] the federal proxy rules if a shareholder vote is involved,[6] and section 14(e) of the 1934 Exchange Act, which deals with tender offers.[7] Issuer tender offers are specifically regulated under Rule 13e-4 of the Exchange Act.[8]

The SEC in Rule 13e-3 has promulgated extensive disclosure requirements and a special antifraud rule for going-private transactions.[9] In broad overview, Rule 13e-3 imposes special disclosure obligations on non-arm's-length mergers, recapitalizations, tender offers, and the like by the issuer or its affiliate that either

---

84 (App. Div. 1975). *See also,* M&W, Inc. v. Pacific Guardian Life Ins. Co. Ltd., No. 19276, 1998 WL 32685 (Haw. Ct. App. 1998) (damages awarded for lack of business purpose).

[22] Lichtenberger v. Long Island Mach. Sales Corp., 420 N.Y.S.2d 507 (App. Div. 1979).

[23] *See* §12.11.

§23.04   [1] *See* Lynch v. Vickers Energy Corp., 283 A.2d 278 (Del. 1977).

[2] S.E.C. Rule 13e-3, 17 C.F.R. §240.13e-3 (2002). *See* F. Hodge O'Neal & Robert B. Thompson, Oppression of Minority Shareholders §5:27 (2d ed. 1985).

[3] *See* §§23.01, 23.03.

[4] Bird v. Wirtz, 266 N.W.2d 166 (Minn. 1978); Berkowitz v. Power/Mate Corp., 342 A.2d 566 (N.J. Super. Ct. 1975). *See* Lynch v. Vickers Energy Corp., 429 A.2d 497 (Del. 1981).

[5] 17 C.F.R. §240.10b-5 (2002). *See* §12.11.

[6] *See* §13.23.

[7] 15 U.S.C. §78n(e) (2000). *See* §24.05.

[8] 17 C.F.R. §240.13e-4 (2002).

[9] 17 C.F.R. §240.13e-3 (2002). The filing, disclosure, and dissemination requirements apply to all regulated transactions, whereas the antifraud provision, Rule 13e-3b, reaches only those issuers that are reporting companies under section 12 of the Securities Exchange Act, 15 U.S.C. §78l (2000).

(1) will cause delisting by a securities exchange or NASDAQ of *any* class of the issuer's securities or (2) will reduce the number of its record stockholders below 300 so that it will be exempt from the registration and reporting requirements of the Securities Exchange Act.[10] Several exceptions to the going-private rule are provided, the most significant being (1) the second step of a pre-announced two-step acquisition, provided the consideration is at least equal to that offered in the earlier tender offer, the second step occurs within one year of the earlier tender offer, and the earlier tender offer fully disclosed the intention to undertake a second-step acquisition;[11] (2) the transaction provides that all the issuer's security holders receive only an equity security that has substantially the same rights as the equity security given up and is registered under the Securities Exchange Act;[12] and (3) issuer redemptions, calls, and other acquisitions pursuant to the rights established in the instruments (articles of incorporation) creating that class of security.[13] The term "affiliate" enjoys a fairly broad construction under the rule so that the issuer's combination with another company indirectly controlling the issuer can trigger the disclosures required by Rule 13e-3.[14]

If an exemption is not available, the issuer or its affiliate involved in a transaction subject to Rule 13e-3 must provide to each affected security holder of record the extensive disclosures required by the rule. This must be provided to the holders not later than 20 days prior to the purchase of the shares or the date when their consent or vote on such transaction will be sought.[15] The disclosure required by Rule 13e-3 is extensive. For example, Item 8(a) of Schedule 13E-3 requires the directors to express their opinion of the transaction's fairness to the frozen-out stockholders.[16] Further, Item 8(b) of Schedule 13E-3 requires a reasonably detailed discussion of the "material factors upon which the belief stated in Item 8(a) is based."[17] The full force of Rule 13e-3's disclosure demands appears in the Supreme Court's holding that opinion statements, such as those elicited by the going-private rule, can in appropriate circumstances be material misrepresentations that give rise to private recoveries.[18] Violations of Rule 13e-3's disclosure

---

[10] Rule 13e-3(a)(3), 17 C.F.R. §240.13e-3(a)(3) (2002).

[11] Rule 13e-3(g)(1), 17 C.F.R. §240.13e-3(g)(1) (2002).

[12] Rule 13e-3(g)(2), 17 C.F.R. §240.13e-3(g)(2) (2002). If the security given up was listed or traded on NASDAQ, the security received must also be listed or so traded for the exemption to apply. *See also* Rosenberg v. Nabors Indus., Inc., 2002 WL 1431820 (S.D. Tex. Jun. 14, 2002) (reincorporation from Delaware to Bermuda using a wholly owned subsidiary deemed to fall within the exception).

[13] Rule 13e-3(g)(4), 17 C.F.R. §240.13e-3(g)(4) (2002). Because of the administrative or judicial supervision of the transaction, two other exemptions apply to companies registered under the Public Utility Holding Company Act and to bankruptcy reorganizations. *See* Rule 13e-3(g)(3)(5), 17 C.F.R. §240.13(g)(3)(5) (2002).

[14] *See, e.g.,* Brewer v. Lincoln Int'l Corp., 148 F. Supp. 2d 792 (W.D. Ky. 2000) (agreement by acquiring company with person controlling 90 percent of the voting power that the latter would vote in favor of a step necessary for the acquisition to occur in exchange for ultimately receiving 50 percent of the acquiring company could make the acquiring company an affiliate).

[15] Rule 13e-3(f), 17 C.F.R. §240.13e-3(f) (2002).

[16] *See* 17 C.F.R. §240.13e-100 (Item 8(a)) (2002).

[17] *See id.* (Item 8(b)).

[18] *See* Virginia Bankshares, Inc. v. Sandberg, 501 U.S. 1083 (1991).

demands subject the violator not only to the full panoply of the SEC's enforcement remedies, but also to the private actions that are available under the rule for affected shareholders.[19]

§23.05   Defensive Tactics—Shark Repellant Provisions

In recent years tender offers[1] have become a popular alternative means of corporate acquisition. Tender offers are often not as time-consuming as proxy battles and, because they do not involve action by the target company, no dissenters' rights are involved. There are many different tender offer techniques,[2] which are often the first part of a multistep acquisition,[3] freeze-out, or going-private transaction. Tender offers may be consummated with the support of the target's management,[4] or can evolve into contested battles for corporate control.[5] Once a tender offer has been made, the target company's management must respond.[6] If management decides to go along amicably with the takeover, it will be bound to adhere to the fiduciary standards that apply to any controlled takeover.[7]

The defense against a takeover attempt is generally covered by the business judgment rule,[8] which allows management the use of reasonable corporate funds

---

[19] *See* Howing Co. v. Nationwide Corp., 826 F.2d 1470 (6th Cir. 1986), *cert. denied,* 486 U.S. 1059 (1988).

§23.05 [1] Although there is no statutory definition of "tender offer," both the courts and the SEC have taken an expansive approach to include certain privately negotiated control transfers and some open market purchases. *See, e.g.,* Wellman v. Dickinson, 475 F. Supp. 783 (S.D.N.Y. 1979) (privately negotiated "lock-up" of control).

[2] The techniques of tender offers are quite varied and have acquired very colorful names. For example:

> Saturday night special—No notice of the offer is given to the target management and the offer is held open only for a very short period.
>
> Classic bear hug—Notice is given to the target management, the offer is to buy shares at a specified price, and no announcement is made to the public.
>
> Strong bear hug—Notice to target management and an announcement to the public are given simultaneously, and the tender offeror is willing to negotiate the price of the offer for the corporation with the management.
>
> Super-strong bear hug—The same as a strong bear hug with the addition of the threat of reducing the offered price if opposed or delayed.
>
> Godfather offer—One that is too good to refuse.
>
> Block purchase—A large block of stock is purchased for use as a base in a subsequent tender offer.

[3] *See, e.g.,* Radol v. Thomas, 534 F. Supp. 1302 (S.D. Ohio 1982).

[4] *See, e.g.,* Smallwood v. Pearl Brewing Co., 489 F.2d 579 (5th Cir.), *cert. denied,* 419 U.S. 873 (1974).

[5] *See, e.g.,* Piper v. Chris-Craft Indus., 430 U.S. 1 (1977); Stephen A. Hochman & Oscar D. Folger, Deflecting Take-overs: Charter and By-Law Techniques, 34 Bus. Law. 537 (1979).

[6] *See* William H. Steinbrink, Management's Response to the Takeover Attempt, 28 Case W. Res. L. Rev. 882 (1978); Elliott Weiss, Tender Offers and Management Responsibility, 23 N.Y.L. Sch. L. Rev. 445 (1978).

[7] *See* §23.07; Marc I. Steinberg, Fiduciary Duties and Disclosure Obligations in Proxy and Tender Contests for Corporate Control, 30 Emory L.J. 169 (1981).

[8] *See* §10.01.

to defend its policies.[9] The business judgment rule does not apply, however, to decisions by directors who have a self-interest in the transaction. Often a charge is made that a takeover defense is motivated by the directors' desire to entrench themselves in office. Accordingly, as discussed in later sections,[10] the courts have to decide in which instances the directors will be insulated by the business judgment rule and in which instances their self-interest will limit their discretion to act.

Defensive tactics vary widely but can be placed in two categories: responsive or preventive. Some of the most popular responsive defensive tactics include arrangements and mergers with "white knights,"[11] the issuance of additional shares to dilute the tender offeror's holdings,[12] or the self-tender for shares from either the raider[13] or the other shareholders.[14] There is, of course, always a characterization issue whether a step taken by the board of directors or the company officers is a defensive maneuver.[15]

There are, of course, many other varieties and combinations of defensive tactics available to the target's management. A common feature of defensive maneuvers such as these is that they can be, and are, taken solely on the authority of the board of directors, without prior authorization or approval by the corporation's shareholders. The most frequently invoked measures are discussed in the next two sections.

A quite different type of defensive measure is the preventive measure, frequently called a "shark repellant" or "porcupine" provision. These measures place in the corporation's articles of incorporation or bylaws a provision or provisions designed not only to protect the corporation's shareholders from certain harmful effects that may accompany a shift in control but also to discourage attempts to make a hostile bid for control.

Three types of shark repellant or porcupine provisions have been identified.[16] The first type of amendment impedes the transfer of corporate control. This includes a staggering of directors' terms of office, which necessarily increases the time it will take to effect a turnover in management, the use of a classified

[9] Kaplan v. Goldsamt, 380 A.2d (Del. Ch. 1977); Cheff v. Mathes, 199 A.2d 548 (Del. 1964); Campbell v. Loews, Inc., 134 A.2d 852 (Del. Ch. 1957); Rosenfeld v. Fairchild Eng. & Airplane Corp., 128 N.E.2d 291 (N.Y. 1955).

[10] See §§23.06-23.07.

[11] See, e.g., Piper v. Chris-Craft Indus., 430 U.S. 1 (1977); Kern County Land Co. v. Occidental Petroleum Corp., 411 U.S. 582 (1973).

[12] A valid business purpose is required for the dilution. It is not allowable if merely a defensive tactic. See Norlin Corp. v. Rooney, Pace, Inc., 744 F.2d 255 (2d Cir. 1984).

[13] This is popularly known as submitting to "greenmail." See Cheff v. Mathes, 199 A.2d 548 (Del. 1964).

[14] The leading case upholding the self-tender for shares excluding the shares owned by the raider is Unocal Corp. v. Mesa Petroleum Co., 493 A.2d 946 (Del. 1985).

[15] See, e.g., Williams v. Geier, 671 A.2d 1368 (Del. 1996) (recapitalization that was supported by owners of more than 50 percent of the voting shares that had the effect of entrenching their control was not defensive maneuver).

[16] See Ronald G. Gilson, The Case Against Shark Repellant Amendments: Structural Limitations on The Enabling Concept, 34 Stan. L. Rev. 775 (1982).

board,[17] a provision that the removal of directors requires cause, the reservation to the board of the right to fill vacancies or add directors, the limitation of the use of consent and special meetings, and the setting of the date for shareholder meetings.[18] Management may further attempt to lock in these provisions by requiring a supermajority to further amend the charter or bylaws.[19]

The second type of amendment creates barriers to the second step in two-tiered transactions by requiring a supermajority for the authorization of a merger following a tender offer.[20] The percentage required is usually chosen as the average number of shareholders who regularly attend the meetings, so that near unanimity at the meetings is required.[21] Often management collectively controls enough stock to block the required supermajority.

The third type, the fair price amendment, is different from the first two in that, while it may deter a corporate raider, it operates mainly to benefit the shareholders rather than to preserve the management. A fair price amendment may be passed to waive the supermajority requirement for approval of a merger if the second-step buyout price is above a specified amount.[22] Another amendment of this type grants shareholders the right to have their shares redeemed at a certain price after a partial tender offer. This right of redemption is derived from the English Companies Act[23] and was apparently first used in the United States in 1978.[24] It deters tender offers because it removes control from them over how many shares they must purchase and it gives the target shareholders an incentive not to tender their shares at the initial offering.[25]

Much controversy remains over whether the use of various defensive tactics is legal, is within the power of the management at all, or is a breach of management's fiduciary obligations, and whether such use has a positive or negative impact on economic and public policy. Provisions are customarily examined under both the *Unocal* standard, discussed below,[26] and the *Blasius* standard, discussed earlier.[27]

---

[17] *See generally* Robert Daines, Do Classified Boards Affect Firm Value? Takeover Defenses After the Poison Pill, J. Fin. & Quant. Analysis (2002).

[18] *See* Mentor Graphics Corp. v. Quickturn Design Systems, Inc., 728 A.2d 25, 40-41 (Del. Ch. 1998) (upholding bylaw amendment providing that special meeting could not be convened in less than 90-100 days).

[19] *See* Chesapeake Corp. v. Shore, 771 A.2d 293, 343 (Del. Ch. 2000) (bylaw amendment required a 90 percent shareholder turnout for approval deemed to be preclusive, and if not preclusive, was unreasonable to the threat posed).

[20] Young v. Valhi, Inc., 382 A.2d 1372 (Del. Ch. 1978) (charter provision required approval of 80 percent of the issued and outstanding common shares in order to accomplish a merger with any offeror holding at least 5 percent of the corporation's stock).

[21] Gilson, *supra* note 16, at 784.

[22] *Id.* at 788.

[23] 11 & 12 Geo. 6, ch. 38, §209(2) (1948).

[24] Proxy of Rubbermaid, Inc., (Mar. 24, 1978), *reprinted in* 2 Martin Lipton & Erica H. Steinberger, Corporate Takeovers and Freeze-outs 400-447 (1979).

[25] *Id.* at 414-417.

[26] *See* §23.06.

[27] *See* §13.17.

§23.06   Defensive Maneuvers and the Business
Judgment Rule

There is now abundant evidence that defensive measures on average reduce shareholder welfare.[1] Until the mid-1980s, under the business judgment rule the prevailing approach upheld the directors' defensive maneuvers,[2] unless the plaintiff established that the primary motive behind management's defense was their own personal interest in retaining their jobs with the corporation.[3] Under this approach, defensive maneuvers of all types and magnitude were upheld on a showing that the bidder would likely operate the target company in a manner that diverged from the course followed or recommended by the incumbent management.[4] Because a bidder can always be expected to change at least some of the target company's operations if it successfully acquires control of the target, an approach that emphasizes solely the directors' motives for defending control strikes down defensive measures only when managers act in haste without developing an adequate record for their actions.[5] One can therefore conclude that a standard that arises only if the directors' primary motive is to save their jobs is an ineffective standard for protecting the interest of shareholders in receiving a valuable offer for their shares.

The most commonly used template for assessing defending control is *Unocal v. Mesa Petroleum Company*,[6] where the Delaware Supreme Court steered a course between the above two contending positions. In *Unocal* the court upheld Unocal's board of directors' decision to self-tender for its own shares in order to thwart a

---

§23.06   [1] For a close review of the empirical studies of the negative impact defensive measures have on share values and the overall wealth of shareholders and with the view that in assessing the data researchers must give close attention to how the defenses interact, *see* John C. Coates IV, Takeover Defenses in the Shadow of the Pill: A Critique of the Scientific Evidence, 79 Tex. L. Rev. 271 (2000).

For support for the view that competition for control, rather than permitting defensive maneuvers that are inherently anticompetitive, lead to successful bidders acquiring a larger percentage of the firm and, hence, reduces post acquisition moral hazard problems, *see* Mike Burkart, Denis Gromb, & Fausto Panunzi, Why Higher Takeover Premia Protect Minority Shareholders, 106 J. Pol. Econ. 172 (1998).

For a more positive view of the effects of defensive measures, *see* Assem Safiedine & Sheridan Titman, Leverage and Corporate Performance: Evidence fom Unsuccessful Takeovers, 54 J. Fin. 547 (1999) (firms that deflect takeover thereafter increase their leverage, reduce capital expenditures, sell assets, reduce employment, increase focus, and experience increased cash flows as well as improvements in their cash flows in the five years following being a target); Gerald T. Garvey & Gordon Hanka, Capital Structure and Corporate Control: The Effect of Antitakeover Statutes on Firm Leverage, 54 J. Fin. 519 (1999) (firms subject to state antitakeover statutes are less leveraged).

[2] The literature on defensive tactics is voluminous. *See generally* John C. Coates IV, Explaining Variations in Takeover Defenses: Blame the Lawyers, 89 Cal. L. Rev. 1301 (2001); Lucian A. Bebchuk & Alan Ferrell, Federalism and Corporate Law: The Race to Protect Managers from Takeovers, 95 Colum. L. Rev. 1168 (1999).

[3] *See, e.g.,* Johnson v. Trueblood, 629 F.2d 287, 292-293 (3d Cir. 1980).

[4] *See, e.g.,* Panter v. Marshall Field & Co., 646 F.2d 271 (7th Cir.), *cert. denied,* 454 U.S. 1092 (1981); Cheff v. Mathes, 199 A.2d 548 (Del. 1964); Kors v. Carey, 158 A.2d 136 (Del. 1964).

[5] *See* Bennett v. Propp, 187 A.2d 405 (Del. 1962).

[6] 493 A.2d 946 (Del. 1985).

takeover attempt by Mesa Petroleum. Mesa had commenced a front-end loaded two-tiered tender offer for 37 percent of Unocal's outstanding stock—that is, those accepting its offer would receive $54 in cash, and any shares not purchased were to be acquired in the second-stage cash-out merger for a bundle of securities purporting to be worth $54. Unocal's board, with the aid of their investment advisors, believed not only that $54 was an inadequate price, but also that action was necessary to protect the shareholders from a coercive offer. They therefore approved purchasing at $72 per share any Unocal shares not acquired by Mesa if Mesa acquired 50 million Unocal shares through its own tender offer.

After a review of earlier Delaware precedents, *Unocal* embraced a two-step process for judging defensive maneuvers. Under the first step, incumbents have the burden of proving they acted in good faith after reasonable investigation.[7] *Unocal* calls for the burden of proof to be placed on the target board of directors because of the "omnipresent specter that a board may be acting primarily in its own interests, rather than those of the corporation and its shareholders."[8] This level of the *Unocal* process invokes the same areas of concern historically examined under the business judgment rule, except for the location of the burden of proof.[9] Important in resolving this inquiry in favor of the Unocal board was their use of outside investment advisors, the fact that a majority of its directors were outside directors, and the deliberateness of the board's consideration of the issues posed by the Mesa bid.[10]

The second step of the *Unocal* test demands that the defensive measure "must be reasonable in relation to the threat posed."[11] This standard, interpreted literally, suggests courts are required to balance the particular defensive maneuver against the harm threatened by a particular bid. Such an approach necessarily invites more scrutiny of the directors' decisions than normally occurs when the court has already satisfied itself that the directors have acted in good faith after reasonable investigation. However, this step has been largely eroded in later decisions, discussed below.

At the opposite end of this interpretation of *Unocal* is the belief that the two steps in fact collapse into one, such that a board satisfying its burden of proving it acted in good faith after reasonable investigation can "just say no." In one of the most significant corporate decisions of the twentieth century, *Paramount Communications, Inc. v. Time, Inc.*,[12] the Delaware Supreme Court interpreted *Unocal*'s reasonable relationship standard as being much closer to the "just say no" approach than to one inviting acute assessments of the proportionality between the defensive maneuver and the perceived threat.

The seeds of *Paramount Communications* were planted in the quest by Time's board of directors for a strategic merger partner that, after several years of searching, had focused on Warner Communications. Time proposed a combination of

[7] *Id.* at 954.
[8] *Id.*
[9] *See* §§10.02; 10.09-10.12.
[10] *See* 493 A.2d at 952-956. Further evidence of the directors' independence is their holding a substantial share ownership in the company. *See* Unitrin, Inc. v. American General Corp., 651 A.2d 1361 (Del. 1995).
[11] 493 A.2d at 954.
[12] 571 A.2d 1140 (Del. 1989).

the two firms in which Warner would be acquired by Time in a stock-for-stock transaction that would have required a vote of the Time shareholders. Though Warner was structured as the seller, it was by far the larger entity; after the acquisition 62 percent of the combined companies would be held by the former Warner shareholders. Management succession was worked out so that the vitally important "Time culture" would be preserved. Just shortly after the boards' approvals, Paramount Communications announced an all-cash $175 per-share bid for Time. Because the amount that Paramount bid (which later was raised to $200 per share) was greatly in excess of the amount at which the market was valuing Time shares in light of its proposed acquisition of Warner, it was clear that Time shareholders would never approve its acquisition of Warner. Thus, after discussing alternative defenses to Paramount's bid, Time's board ultimately decided to alter the original agreement to provide that Time would pay cash to acquire Warner so that a vote of the Time shareholders would not be required. This change would require Time to borrow $7-10 billion to carry out the all-cash acquisition.

The Delaware Supreme Court deemed the alteration of the acquisition's consideration from stock to cash as a defensive maneuver that should be examined under *Unocal*.[13] In a major victory for target company directors, *Paramount* holds that the nature of the threat for which defensive measures can be crafted transcends questions of fair price or a coercive offer. For example, in *Paramount* the bid posed a threat to Time's preexisting long-range strategic plans as well as running the risk of confusing the shareholders' approval of a stock-for-stock transaction had that plan been submitted to the Time shareholders for their approval.

Thus *Paramount* reaffirms the board of directors as a presumptively infallible decision-maker regarding the long-term benefits of an incumbent board's strategic plan. The proxy machinery remains available to discipline through non-election those directors whose policies the shareholders believe do not maximize shareholder wealth. *Paramount* does not appear cleanly to authorize a "just say no" approach because the court reasoned that the reasonable-relationship standard is not violated merely because it made a bidder's acquisition more difficult—Paramount could still acquire Time but, following Time's acquisition of Warner, Paramount's acquisition would necessarily be much larger, but not impossible.[14] In this manner, it is possible to interpret *Paramount* as reasoning that the reasonable-relationship standard would be violated if the defensive maneuver would *preclude* any acquisition whatever of the target company or its successor. Thus a fair reading of *Paramount* is that it alters *Unocal* substantially by inquiring not as to whether on a careful weighing of the facts the defensive maneuver is disproportionate to the threat posed by the bidder or its offer, but whether the effect of the defensive maneuver is to preclude any takeover of the target at all.[15] This is a dramatic change in the court's role as initially set forth in *Unocal* and, as such, *Paramount* is correctly viewed as a watershed case.

---

[13] *Id.* at 1150.

[14] *Id.* at 1153.

[15] Hints of proportionality rather than the more demanding preclusive standard appears from time to time. *See* Chesapeake Corp. v. Shore, 771 A.2d 293, 342-343 (Del. Ch. 2000).

Even after *Paramount,* the *Unocal* test remains fairly open-ended such that results are determined on a case-by-case basis with little guidance evolving from such factually diverse inquiries. One likely consideration is whether the hostile bid is believed to be coercive. If not, courts appear less willing to uphold defensive steps.[16]

The *Unocal* enhanced duty standard does not apply in every instance that a corporation decides to reject an acquisition proposal. Thus, for example, a board that has no significant financial self-interest, can reject a takeover offer and still have the benefit of the business judgment rule.[17]

The Delaware court has since made it clear that even under the enhanced review standard of *Unocal,* a corporation's board has a wide range of discretion in reacting to hostile takeover attempts. Indeed, there is cause to doubt that little additional scrutiny is introduced through the second step of *Unocal.*[18] As seen in the above discussion of *Paramount,* a showing of preclusion has replaced the earlier proportionality test first embraced in *Unocal.* Moreover, in considering whether a board has acted improperly in refusing to redeem the corporation's poison pill so that a formal takeover of the firm can be considered by the stockholders, the Delaware courts have assumed that the theoretical possibility of a proxy contest renders the pill non-preclusive. Also, under *Unocal's* first step, though the burden of proof is on the target management a good deal of deference still is accorded its decision. Thus, in *Unitrin, Inc. v. American General Corp.,*[19] the court explained that, unless the defensive measures are "draconian" or outside a "range of reasonableness," the board's response should be upheld. A defensive measure is draconian when it is either coercive or preclusive.[20] As explained by the court in *Unitrin,* "[w]hen a corporation is not for sale, the board of directors is the defender of the metaphorical medieval corporate bastion and the protector of the corporation's shareholders."[21] A court should not substitute its judgment for that of the board of directors. The *Unitrin* court refused to compel the target company to redeem its poison pill absent proof that a proxy fight to unseat the target management "would be either mathematically impossible or realistically unattain-

---

[16] Two pre-*Paramount* decisions struck down defensive maneuvers where the hostile bid was not coercive because cash was offered for all the target shares. In AC Acquisitions Corp. v. Anderson, Clayton & Co., 519 A.2d 103 (Del. Ch. 1986), the target's partial self-tender offer at $60 barred in the face of a $56 hostile bid because it *precluded* the bidder's offer. The court reasoned the shareholders were entitled to choose between the two offers. *Id.* at 112-116. A potential distinguishing fact is that the target's investment banker could not opine that the outside offer was inadequate. *Id.* 108-110. *See also* Robert M. Bass Group, Inc. v. Evans, 552 A.2d 1227 (Del. Ch. 1988) (partial tender offer struck down under *Unocal* because it would not allow shareholders choice of two alternative transactions).

[17] Kahn v. MSB Bancorp, Inc., 1998 WL 409355 (Del. Ch. 1998), *affirmed,* 1999 WL 507085 (Del. 1999).

[18] *See generally* Mark J. Lowenstein, *Unocal* Revisited: No Tiger in the Tank, 27 J. Corp. L. 1 (2001).

[19] 651 A.2d 1361 (1995).

[20] "This court's choice of the term 'draconian' in *Unocal* was a recognition that the law affords boards of directors substantial latitude in defending the perimeter of the corporate bastion against perceived threats. . . . [D]epending upon the circumstances, the board may respond to a reasonably perceived threat by adopting individually or sometimes in combination: advance notice bylaws, supermajority voting provisions, shareholder rights plans, repurchase programs, etc." *Id.* at 1388 n.38.

[21] *Id.* at 1388.

Chapter 23. Limits on Acquisitions and Defensive Maneuvers

able."[22] Delaware courts place an especially high burden of proving fairness when the primary purpose of the board's defensive action is to interfere with the share-holders' voting franchise. In such a case, the defendants must present a "compelling justification" for the action.[23] As observed by the Delaware Supreme Court, this heightened standard of review "is quite onerous, and is therefore applied rarely."[24]

A central consideration in the *Unocal* analysis is the perceived "threat" posed by the unwanted suitor. In *Unocal* the threat was clearly present, because not only was the bidder a well-known greenmailer, but also its bid was coercive in that it was a front-end loaded two-tier offer that would leave any late-tendering or non-tendering shareholder with junk bonds. Post-*Unocal* decisions have greatly expanded the range of considerations that constitute a threat, applying the broad litmus of *Unitrin* whereby considerations short of a coercive bid are permissible threats if they fall within the "range of reasonableness" standard.[25]

There is some basis to conclude that courts outside of Delaware that invoke the *Unocal* standard accord directors less deference under the first step of *Unocal*.[26] Also, *Unocal* is not the only approach to assessing defensive maneuvers. Other judicial review standards for defensive maneuvers exist, but none is as widely adopted as *Unocal*. Some courts continue to emphasize the standards of good faith (that is, proper motive) and reasonable investigation, but clearly give the directors' defensive actions closer scrutiny than other challenges to their stewardship of the corporation's affairs.[27] Some courts require a compelling or independent business justification for the act that thwarts the bidder's attempt to gain control.[28] The American Law Institute's approach allows directors to take any step that "has the foreseeable effect of blocking an unsolicited tender offer" and then proceeds to provide that in considering whether the board's response is reasonable the "board may take into account all factors relevant to the best interests of the corporation and the shareholders," including "whether the offer, if successful, would threaten

---

[22] *Id.* at 1381 (Del. 1995).

[23] Blasius Indus. v. Atlas Corp., 564 A.2d 651 (1988).

[24] Williams v. Geier, 671 A.2d 1368, 1376 (Del. 1996).

[25] Unitrin v. American General Corp., 651 A.2d 1361, 1388 (Del. 1995).

[26] *See, e.g.,* Flake v. Hoskins, 55 F. Supp. 2d 1196, 1217 (D. Kan. 1999); Hilton Hotels Corp. v. ITT Corp., 978 F. Supp. 1342, 1347-1348 (D. Nev. 1997); AHI Metnall, L.P. by AHI Kan., Inc. v. J.C. Nichols Co., 891 F. Supp. 1352, 1356-1357 (W.D. Mo. 1995); Air Line Pilots Ass'n Int'l v. UAL Corp., 717 F. Supp. 575, 586-587 (N.D. Ill. 1989); Katz v. Chevron Corp., 27 Cal. Rptr. 2d 681 (Cal. Ct. App. 1994) (upholding defensive maneuvers engaged in by Delaware corporation as being "proportionate" but not invoking the lower "preclusive" standard); Hedberg v. Pantepec Int'l, Inc., 645 A.2d 543 (Conn. Ct. App. 1994) (though reversing trial court's finding that employment contract was not proportional, did so on basis of trial court's inaccurate reading of employment golden parachute contract).

[27] *See* Dynanics Corp. of Amer. V. WHX Corp., 967 F. Supp. 59 (D.C. Conn. 1997); NCR Corp. v. American Tel. & Tel. Co., 761 F. Supp. 475 (S.D. Ohio 1991); Buckhorn, Inc. v. Ropak Corp., 656 F. Supp. 209 (S.D. Ohio), *aff'd mem.*, 815 F.2d 76 (6th Cir. 1987).

[28] *See* Klaus v. Hi-Shear Corp., 528 F.2d 225 (9th Cir. 1975) (compelling business reason for transferring shares to ESOP); Norlin Corp. v. Rooney Pace Inc., 744 F.2d 255 (2d Cir. 1984) (independent justification to issue shares to subsidiary).

653

the corporation's essential economic prospects."[29] By placing the burden of proof on the person challenging the defensive maneuver, the American Law Institute embraces a less intrusive approach than occurs in Delaware and in most other states.[30] A further qualification and defensive maneuver arises when the directors must facilitate an auction for control.[31]

Although we might well conclude that there has been a weakening of the law's (most notably before the Delaware Supreme Court) moderating influence on management's tendency to deflect socially beneficial shifts in control, a more holistic view suggests that any weakness in the law may be counterbalanced by other developments. The move over the last decade to boards of directors that are more independent of the officers they monitor, the rise in stock and other incentive plans, and an increasingly more competitive product markets are each measures that are counter to the management entrenchment thesis. Such developments may account for why the level of takeover activity, while first declining in the years immediately following corporate law developments that tended to entrench managers, has returned to historically high levels.[32]

§23.07   Judicial Treatment of Specific Types of Defensive Maneuvers

Nowhere is the lawyer's creativity better documented than in the seemingly endless varieties of defensive maneuvers that have developed and continue to evolve. Moreover, the flexibility—or perhaps the indeterminacy—of the prevailing review standards (as seen in *Unocal*, discussed in the preceding section) becomes quite evident in examining how the very different features that distinguish defensive maneuvers from one another are treated under *Unocal*.

Poison Pills. The most common type of defensive measure is a shareholder rights plan, more commonly known as a "poison pill." The device begins with a corporation's distribution, generally in the form of dividend, of "rights" pro rata among its stockholders. A right entitles its holder to purchase stock or other security upon a certain triggering event. The precise triggering (or activating) event depends on the type of pill. As will be seen, in the "flip-over" variety of pill, the triggering event is a second-step transaction, such as a merger or asset purchase

---

[29] ALI, Principles of Corporate Governance: Analysis and Recommendations §6.02(a)(b) (1994). An important qualification is that non-shareholder interests may be considered "if to do so would not significantly disfavor the long-term interests of shareholders." *Id.* at §6.02(b)(2).

[30] *Id.* §6.02(c). An insightful critique of the undue conservatism of the ALI's approach appears in Elliott J. Weiss, Whose Rules Should Govern Takeovers: Delaware's, the ALI's, or Martin Lipton's?, 33 Ariz. L. Rev. 761 (1991).

[31] *See* §23.08.

[32] *See* Marcel Kahan & Edward B. Rock, How I learned to Stop Worrying and Love the Pill: Adaptive Responses to Takeover Law, 69 U. Chi. L. Rev. 871, 881-884 (2002).

by the bidder of the target corporation. In the "flip-in" variety of pill, the triggering event is usually a first-step transaction, such as the bidder launching a tender offer for, or completing the purchase of, a certain percentage of the corporation's stock—for example, 20 percent of its outstanding stock. The precise right that a holder has upon the triggering event's occurrence depends on the type of poison pill.

A flip-over poison pill allows the target company's shareholders to acquire the bidder's stock at a substantial discount, usually at half price (for example, the purchase of $200 worth of the bidder's common shares by paying only $100) if the two corporations merge. The flip-over pill becomes operative, therefore, when the bidder, after acquiring a substantial ownership interest in the target, merges the target into itself or another entity that it controls. The overall effect of the target shareholders' exercising their flip-over rights is to dilute substantially the value of the bidder's common shares. It is because of this possibility that the flip-over provision acts as a disincentive to unwanted suitors. Its primary benefit to the target shareholders is to protect them against an unfair, coercive second-step merger that forces them to give up their target shares for securities or cash of the bidder.

Another variety of poison pill is the "back-end" plan, under which the target corporation's board of directors designates a price deemed fair for the target shares. Thereafter, the target shareholders have a right to require the target corporation to acquire their shares at that price, provided the bidder has not already acquired the shares at that price. As with the flip-over pill, the primary objective of a back-end pill is to protect stockholders from a coercive second-step merger.

The flip-over pill is not operative, however, if the bidder does not merge with the target. Thus a flip-over provision can be avoided if the bidder operates the target as a controlled subsidiary. Even this arrangement does little to salve the unease that the target management may have for the unwanted bidder. Target management is not without mechanisms to discourage a nonmerging bidder—it may resort to a flip-in poison pill. A flip-in rights plan allows the holders to acquire stock or other securities of the target company at prices substantially below their market value. The triggering event for the flip-in pill is generally the bidder announcing a tender offer for a certain percentage of the target's shares and/or its purchase of a stated percentage of the target's shares. Because the amount specified is generally in the 20 to 30 percent range, the flip-in pill can be triggered even though control may not in fact be threatened.[1]

Consequently, if the rights are triggered and thereafter exercised by their holders, the cost of the acquisition to the bidder increases substantially as the value of its holdings is diluted by the ability of other holders to purchase additional shares of the target below their fair market value. The potency of poison

---

§23.07   [1] *See* Dynamics Corp. of Am. v. CTS Corp., 794 F.2d 250 (7th Cir. 1986), *rev'd on other grounds,* 481 U.S. 69 (1987) (invalidating flip-in pill where trigger was activated by bidder's purchase of 15 percent of the target shares, even though that bidder did not intend to seek control of bidder).

pills in dampening the appetite of would-be suitors of target corporations has been documented by several studies that reflect that negative stock effects accompany the adoption of poison pills.[2]

Poison pills have spawned a good deal of litigation regarding their validity under state statutes and the directors' fiduciary obligations with respect to a poison pill defense.[3] A common and necessary feature of any rights plan is that the bidder receives no rights and cannot acquire any rights from another.[4] That is, the dilutive effects vis-à-vis the bidder could easily be overcome by the bidder's purchase of the rights from their holders, if those rights could be so acquired. Thus rights plans commonly provide that the rights are not issued to the bidder and are not transferable. Some courts have invalidated rights plans because of their discriminatory treatment within the same class of shares.[5] Rights plans that do not include the bidder can have unanticipated and unwanted effects even if the rights are nontransferrable.[6]

The leading case applying *Unocal* to uphold the adoption of a poison pill plan is *Moran v. Household International, Inc.,*[7] where the Delaware Supreme Court reasoned that a flip-over provision was analogous to the antidilution provisions that customarily exist to protect holders of senior securities in mergers. With this predicate, the court then reasoned that a poison pill was a reasonable and proportional response to a threat of a harmful second-step coercive merger at a price unfair to the target shareholders. *Moran* emphasized that the rights were redeemable prior to their activation by the triggering event.

As *Moran* emphasized, the rights' redemption feature is a key element to their legal validity as a takeover defense and is central to understanding why poison pills are created in the first place.

Two pre-*Paramount Communications* decisions held that the target directors cannot refuse to redeem the pill in the face of an offer that is neither coercive nor unfair on its face.[8] An important feature of both these decisions was the non-coer-

---

[2] *See, e.g.,* Dosoung Choi, Sreenivas Kamma & Joseph Weintrop, The Delaware Courts, Poison Pills, and Shareholder Wealth, 5 J. L., Econ. & Org., 375 (1989); Gregg A. Jarrell, James A. Brickley, & Jeffrey N. Netter, Market for Corporate Control: Empirical Evidence Since 1980, 2 J. Econ. Persp. 49 (1988).

[3] *See* Gearhart Indus. v. Smith Int'l, Inc., 741 F.2d 707 (5th Cir. 1984) ("springing" feature of warrant was not manipulative under section 14(e)).

[4] The legality of such treatment was examined in §18.06.

[5] *See* Avon Prod., Inc. v. Chartwell Assoc. L.P., 907 F.2d 322 (2d Cir. 1990); Amalgamated Sugar Co. v. NL Indus., 644 F. Supp. 1229 (S.D.N.Y. 1986). Several state statutes now expressly authorize such discriminatory treatment. *See, e.g.,* Fla. Gen. Corp. Act §607.0624(2) (2001); N.J. Bus. Corp. Act §14A: 7-7(3) (Supp. 2002); N.Y. Bus. Corp. Law §505(c)(2)(i) (McKinney Supp. 2002).

[6] *See, e.g.,* Emeritus Corp. v. ARV Assisted Living, Inc., Case No. 793420 (Super Ct. Orange Cty. June 28, 1999) (defensive tactic that involved issuing shares to friendly investment group inadvertently triggered rights plan that hostile bidder could take advantage of).

[7] 500 A.2d 1346 (Del. 1985). *See also* Unitrin, Inc. v. American Gen. Corp., 651 A.2d 1361 (Del. 1995) ("reasonable relationship" standard does not require delicate calibration).

[8] Grand Metro. Public, Ltd. v. Pillsbury Co., 558 A.2d 1049 (Del. Ch. 1988) (restructuring response proposed by target management not clearly better than that of bidders because it would require long-term holdings to recoup predicted greater rewards than immediate cash all shares bid); City Capital Assocs. Ltd. P'ship v. Interco, Inc., 551 A.2d 787 (Del. Ch. 1988) (bidder's cash bid of $74 when compared with restructuring offer of management of cash and securities valued at $76 not clearly inadequate).

cive nature of the bidder's offer. On the other hand, there are a larger number of decisions that evidence the patience and deference courts accord the target board of directors' decision not to redeem the pill, at least to the extent of allowing the target board to devise or execute a plan for a greater return for the target shareholders.[9] *Paramount Communications'* deference to the target management being able to adhere to its preexisting strategic plan is consistent with the view that great deference is to be accorded decisions not to redeem a pill. Thus the traditional route of a proxy contest would be necessary to dislodge the recalcitrant board as a prelude to acquiring a controlling interest in a target firm.[10]

The most draconian form of the poison pill is the so-called "dead hand" poison pill, so named because its distinguishing feature is its continuing director provision which permits the rights to be redeemed only by the directors who were in office when the rights plan was put into place.[11] Thus, under a dead hand poison pill a new board of directors, whose members support the firm's acquisition, cannot redeem the rights that stand as an obstacle to the firm being acquired. On its face, such a continuing director provision conflicts directly with the well-established principle that contractual provisions that restrain the discretion of the board of directors are void as against public policy.[12] Emphasizing the strong public policy in the boards' power to manage the affairs of the corporation, the New York Supreme Court invalidated the dead hand poison pill of Irving Bank Co.[13] The Delaware Supreme Court invalidated what it described as a "no hand" or "delayed redemption provision" of a rights plan.[14] The delayed redemption provision provided that, if the shareholders replace a majority of the directors, the newly elected board could not redeem the rights for six months if the purpose or effect of the redemption were to facilitate a transaction with an "interested person." The court explained that such a provision by limiting the new directors' ability to redeem a poison pill could prevent them from authorizing a transaction that their fiduciary duty would otherwise require.[15] The Delaware Chancery Court struck down a "dead hand" poison pill,[16] since it would conflict with the Delaware statute imposing fiduciary duties on the new directors, because it violates the rule that the "shareholder vote has primacy in our system,"[17] and also because the dead hand poison pill is disproportionate and thus violates the Delaware Supreme

---

[9] *See, e.g.,* Dynamics Corp. of America v. WHX Corp., 967 F. Supp. 59 (D. Conn. 1997) (concluding the plaintiff-bidder continued to have the inferior offer so that pill need not be redeemed to preserve merger with another company offer greater premium); CRTF Corp. v. Federated Dept. Stores, Inc., 683 F. Supp. 422 (S.D.N.Y. 1988); BNS, Inc. v. Koppers Co., Inc., 683 F. Supp. 458 (D.C. Del. 1988).

[10] *See* Lyman Johnson & David Millon, The Case Beyond *Time,* 45 Bus. Law. 2105 (1990) (arguing that *Paramount* endorses the "just say no" defense).

[11] *See generally* Lese, Preventing Control From the Grave: A Proposal for Judicial Treatment of Dead Hand Provisions in Poison Pills, 96 Colum. L. Rev. 2175 (1996).

[12] *See* §§9.08, 14.05.

[13] *See* Bank of New York Co. v. Irving Bank Corp., 528 N.Y.S.2d 482 (N.Y. Sup. Ct. 1988).

[14] Quickturn Design Systems, Inc. v. Shapiro, 721 A.2d 1281 (Del. 1998).

[15] 721 A.2d at 1291-1292. Accord, Carmody v. Toll Bros., Inc., 723 A.2d 1180 (Del. Ch. 1998).

[16] Carmody v. Toll Bros., Inc., 723 A.2d 1180 (Del. Ch. 1998).

[17] Carmody v. Toll Bros., Inc., 723 A.2d 1180, 1195 (Del. Ch. 1998). *See* Blasius Indus. v. Atlas Corp., 564 A.2d 651 (Del. Ch. 1988).

Court's rulings in its *Unocal* and *Unitrin* decisions.[18] In contrast, two federal district courts have upheld dead hand pills under Georgia and Pennsylvania law.[19]

Poison pill rights plans have brought into question the relative power of shareholders and directors. Who has the final word in the adoption of poison pills—the shareholders or directors? The pill comes into existence by the fiat of the board of directors exercising its authority under the "blank stock" provision of the articles of incorporation.[20] Having the general authority to issue shares with such "rights, privileges and preferences" as the board believes is appropriate, no further approval from the stockholders is necessary for the rights to be issued.[21] In *International Brotherhood of Teamsters General Fund v. Fleming Companies,*[22] the Oklahoma Supreme Court upheld a shareholder adopted bylaw that restricted the board of directors' ability to adopt a rights plan. Among other things, the court noted that unlike some other states, Oklahoma does not have a statute specifically authorizing such rights plans, although it does have a statute authorizing stock options and rights generally. The absence of a statute specifically authorizing poison pill rights plans is a basis for distinguishing *Fleming* in those states having specific statutory authorization. According to the Oklahoma court in *Fleming*, the Delaware and Oklahoma statutes are similar. In a related development, the SEC indicated that in the absence of clear Delaware law on point, it was unable to conclude that the mandatory bylaw amendment was not a proper shareholder matter.[23]

Issuer Repurchases and Restructurings. One response that target management can make to a hostile bid believed to offer an inadequate amount for the target corporation's shares is to develop a plan that offers a greater amount. The simplest approach is for the target corporation to initiate its own tender offer for a certain percentage of its shares. This is unlikely to thwart the unwanted bid, however, as target shareholders would still be able to tender to the bidder the shares that were not acquired by the target in its self-tender offer. Thus all that a simply designed self-tender offer accomplishes is to reduce ultimately the number of shares the bidder must purchase to obtain control (that is, after the target corporation's self-tender, there are fewer outstanding shares, so control requires an absolute smaller number of shares to be held). To scuttle an unwanted offer a self-tender offer must be structured so as to coerce the shareholders to choose the issuer's offer over that of the outside bidder. Such an effect has been held to vio-

---

[18] Carmody v. Toll Bros., Inc., 723 A.2d 1180, 1194-1195 (Del. Ch. 1998). *See* Unitrin, Inc. v. American General Corp., 651 A.2d 1361, 1379 (Del. 1995), Unocal Corp. v. Mesa Petroleum Co., 493 A.2d 946 (Del. 1985), which are discussed *supra* §23.06.

[19] *See* AMP, Inc. v. Allied Signal, Inc., 1998 WL 778348 *8 (E.D. Pa. 1998) (unpublished case); Invacare Corp. v. Healthdyne Technologies, Inc., 968 F. Supp. 1578 (N.D. Ga. 1997).

[20] Blank stock authorizations are discussed in §18.06.

[21] *See* Leonard Loventhal Account v. Hilton Hotels Corp., 780 A.2d 245 (Del. 2001) (power recognized by *Moran* would be meaningless if rights plan required stockholder approval).

[22] International Brotherhood of Teamsters General Fund v. Fleming Companies, 975 P.2d 907 (Okla. 1999).

[23] General DataComm Industries, Inc. SEC No-Act LEXIS 1037 (SEC No-Action Letter Dec. 9, 1998). This was a reversal of the Commission's previous position.

late *Unocal* because of its coercive nature and because it likely will not be judged
to be reasonably related to the threat posed when the bidder's offer was for all the
outstanding shares.[24] Recall that the defensive maneuver upheld in *Unocal* was a
self-tender offer that excluded the shares of the hostile bidder; that offer was
upheld, however, because the bidder's offer posed the threat of a second-step
unfair cash-out merger of the target shares not acquired in its first-step tender
offer. A repurchase is also effective if it causes the insiders' percentage ownership
to increase such that they can veto any actions of the unwanted suitor.[25] When the
outside bid is for *all* the target shares, the target shareholders have the freedom
to compare that offer with what is offered by the target management. Thus there
appears no practical justification to protect the corporation or the shareholders
from the coercive features of target management's response.[26]

A means for the target to offer greater value than is being offered in the hostile tender offer is to undertake a restructuring of the corporation. Restructuring
includes a variety of ways by which a corporation can generate cash to distribute
pro rata among its stockholders by selling major divisions and by borrowing significant amounts of money with the effect of increasing the financial leverage
within its capital structure. After these steps are taken, the existing shareholders
are offered a package of securities (equity and debt) and cash that in combination
have a value greater than that offered by the hostile bid. Many successful restructurings are indistinguishable in their effects from a leverage buyout, as the target
corporation borrows to the full extent of is debt capacity, raising concerns for
future financial distress that may require additional asset disposals to reduce the
crushing burden of its newly incurred debt. Courts have been reluctant to enjoin
restructurings, viewing them as alternative means to maximize the value of the
firm for the benefit of its shareholders.[27]

Greenmail. Another form a defensive repurchase can take is "greenmail,"
whereby the target board of directors approves the corporation acquiring the target shares held by a raider at a premium above-market price so as to fend off a
takeover. For such a purchase to be protected by the business judgment rule, the
record must reveal a good faith reasonable belief of the target board of directors
that the corporate interest is served by the repurchase. In a few instances, the
courts have ruled favorably on pretrial motions brought by plaintiffs challenging
a greenmail transaction. A leading case is *Heckman v. Ahmanson,*[28] where the court

[24] *See* AC Acquisitions Corp. v. Anderson, Clayton & Co., 519 A.2d 103 (Del. Ch. 1986).

[25] *See* American Gen. Corp. v. Unitrin, Inc., 1994 LEXIS 187 (Del. Ch. 1994).

[26] This point was recognized in Shamrock Holdings, Inc. v. Polaroid Corp., 559 A.2d 278 (Del. Ch.
1989), but management's coercive self-tender offer was not enjoined because the court was persuaded that shareholders would have difficulty comparing the two choices before them because of
the indefiniteness of determining the future value of a significant patent infringement action the
issuer had against another major corporation. *But see* Unitrin, Inc. v. American Gen. Corp., 651 A.2d
1361 (Del. 1995) (repurchase of shares valid defense to inadequate bid for *all* target shares).

[27] *See* British Printing & Communication Corp. v. Harcourt Brace Jovanovich, Inc., 664 F. Supp.
1519 (S.D.N.Y. 1987); GAF Corp. v. Union Carbide Corp., 624 F. Supp. 1016 (S.D.N.Y. 1985).

[28] 214 Cal. Rptr. 177 (Ct. App. 1985).

preliminarily enjoined a greenmail payment by Walt Disney Productions Inc. that offered approximately a $60 million profit to the Steinberg Group. There was insufficient evidence that a corporate purpose was served by the repurchase, so the inference arose that the repurchase was guided only by the naked desire of the incumbents to retain their positions of control.[29]

In response to concern over greenmail, the Tax Reform Act of 1986 included provisions that disallow any deduction "for any amount paid or incurred by a corporation in connection with the redemption of its stock,"[30] and in 1987 Congress imposed a 50 percent excise tax on the gain or other income arising from a payment that is not made on the same terms to all shareholders.[31] The tax laws, therefore, provide a substantial disincentive for greenmail transactions.

Share Issuances and ESOPS. The most direct assault on a hostile bid is by the target board of directors issuing a substantial block of voting shares to a holder who can be depended on to support the incumbent management team.[32] In such a situation, the target board of directors has a heavy burden of proof either that its primary motive in approving the issuance of shares was not related to control of the corporation[33] or that the hostile bid posed a threat to the corporation or its shareholders. The most common form this defensive maneuver takes is the target corporation issuing shares to an employee stock ownership plan (ESOP). ESOPs are tax-favored devices[34] designed to provide retirement benefits for a corporation's employees through the collective stock ownership of their employer.

Challenges to ESOPs on the grounds that they are an invalid defensive maneuver have largely depended on whether the reviewing court is persuaded that the primary motive for transferring shares to the ESOP was to entrench management. Absent evidence that the corporate interest is in improving employee morale and productivity, an ESOP adopted in the heat of a takeover will most likely be enjoined.[35] To date, the most sympathetic reaction to an ESOP created in the heat of a takeover battle was that taken by the Delaware Chancery Court in

---

[29] For similar reasoning, *see* Lou v. Belzberg, 728 F. Supp. 1010 (S.D.N.Y. 1990); Feinberg Testamentary Trust v. Carter, 652 F. Supp. 1066 (S.D.N.Y. 1987).

[30] 26 U.S.C. §162 (2000).

[31] 26 U.S.C. §5881 (2000).

[32] *See, e.g.,* Unilever Acquisition Corp. v. Richardson-Vicks, Inc., 618 F. Supp. 407 (S.D.N.Y. 1985).

[33] *See, e.g.,* Klaus v. Hi-Shear Corp., 528 F.2d 225 (9th Cir. 1975).

[34] An employer can establish an ESOP in many ways, but the maximum tax advantages arise if the funds for the shares contributed to the ESOP are borrowed. The lender or employer can exclude from gross income 50 percent of the interest received from a loan to the employer or ESOP when the loan proceeds are used to acquire employer securities. In any case, employers are allowed to deduct the dividends paid on the ESOP shares when those dividends are distributed by the ESOP or the employer to the plan's participants. Finally, when an ESOP is created by the termination of a qualified plan, any excess assets that existed in the qualified plan that are transferred to the ESOP are exempt from the 10 percent excise tax that otherwise applies. *See generally* CCH Guide to Employee Benefits ¶¶271-277 (1986).

[35] *See, e.g.,* Norlin Corp. v. Rooney, Pace Inc., 744 F.2d 255 (2d Cir. 1984) (requires proof of a basis independent from threat posed by bidder for creation of ESOP); NCR Corp. v. American Tel. & Tel. Co., 761 F. Supp. 475 (S.D. Ohio 1991) (injunction granted on finding that entrenchment motive was primary motive).

Shamrock Holdings Inc. v. Polaroid Corporation,[36] where the court, applying the review standard of intrinsic fairness,[37] was persuaded that the ESOP was designed to improve employee productivity, that no substantial out-of-pocket costs were incurred by the corporation because funding came largely from the employees, and any immediate dilutive effects on share values would be recouped over time through expected gains in productivity.[38] Transfers of additional shares after a takeover bid to an ESOP created before that bid requires close consideration of whether the subsequent transfer of shares to the ESOP was part of the on-going strategy to improve employee productivity.[39] In contrast, an ESOP hastily initiated after the commencement of a hostile bid and approved without adequate information as to the ESOP's benefits to the company is outside the protection of the business judgment rule.[40]

> *Lock-up Options and Other Deal Protection Arrangements.* When confronted by two or more opposing bids for control, target management sometimes enters into an arrangement with one of the bidders that has the effect of conferring on that bidder a significant strategic advantage in the contest for control vis-à-vis the other bidders. These arrangements can take several forms, such as an option by the preferred bidder to acquire significant target assets at a favorable price (called a "lock-up option"), an agreement not to seek other bidders (called a "no-shop clause"), the payment of a significant fee if that bidder's offer does not result in the bidder obtaining control (called a "termination fee," "hello fee"or "goodbye fee"), or agreeing to share certain proprietary/inside information only with that bidder.[41] Because of their dampening effect on continued bidding for control, these arrangements are correctly characterized as defensive maneuvers and will be examined under *Unocal.* They also are more frequently examined under the special requirements of *Revlon,* discussed in the next section.

Termination fees can be examined either under contract law, where the question is whether it is an enforceable provision for liquidated damages or under corporate law. Under the former the first question is whether damages would be uncertain if the deal were not consummated. If so uncertain, the final test of the

---

[36] 559 A.2d 257 (Del. Ch. 1989).

[37] Because the directors did not themselves purport to judge their actions as defensive maneuvers such that their decision embraced the considerations demanded by *Unocal,* the court treated this as a standard conflict-of-interest case, whereby the directors have the burden of proving intrinsic fairness. *Id.* at 271.

[38] *Id.* at 272-273.

[39] *See* Danaher Corp. v. Chicago Pneumatic Tool Co., 633 F. Supp. 1066, 1071-1073 (S.D.N.Y. 1986).

[40] *Compare* NCR Corp. v. American Tel. and Tel. Co., 761 F. Supp. 475 (S.D. Ohio 1991) *with* Katz v. Chevron Corp., 27 Cal. Rptr. 2d 681 (Cal. Ct. App. 1994) (upholding creation of credit facility that acquired company's shares).

[41] There is extensive literature on lock-ups. *See* John C. Coates IV & Guhan Subramanian, A Buy-Side Model of Lockups: Theory and Evidence, Marcel Kahan & Michael Klausner, Lockups and the Market for Corporate Control, 48 Stan. L. Rev. 1539 (1996); David A. Skeel, Jr., A Reliance Damages Approach to Corporate Lockups, 90 Nw. U. L. Rev. 564 (1995); Steven M. Bainbridge, Exclusive Merger Agreements and Lock-Ups in Negotiated Acquisitions, 75 Minn. L. Rev. 239 (1994).

provisions validity is whether the amount so stated is reasonable.[42] From a corporate perspective the questions are examined under *Revlon* and/or *Unocal* being persuaded by such considerations as the provision being necessary to obtain the bid.[43] Fees of one to five percent of the transaction's value are believed reasonable.[44]

Another common provision requires a board to submit the merger proposal to its shareholders or bars the target management from actively pursuing other bidders. Each type of agreement inherently restricts the freedom of a board of directors and meets the historical reluctance of courts to uphold agreements that interfere with the directors' discretion. That is, the board of director's fiduciary obligation is paramount to any contractual obligation.[45] At the same time, the contractual requirements cannot simply be ignored under the guise that the directors are fiduciary.[46] Hence, there is an interesting dynamic that arises whereby the validity of the contractual restrictions is assessed in terms of whether ex ante entering into the contractual restrictions was pursuant to the directors' fiduciary responsibilities. In the leading case, *Paramount Communications, Inc. v. QVC Network, Inc.*,[47] the Delaware Supreme Court held that merger agreement terms that mandated directors act in a certain fashion or that the directors forbear were invalid. However, the case is distinctive because the merger posed a change of control such that the company had entered the *Revlon* moment, discussed below, and was not seen as the product of the board acting in a deliberate and open-minded manner. In *Ace Ltd. v. Capital Re Corp.*,[48] the Delaware Chancery court avoided invalidating such an agreement because the provision permitted the target board to escape the clause if there was an unsolicited superior bid and it was advised by counsel that not to consider the competing bid would constitute a breach of their fiduciary duties. The latter clause in *Capital Re* is known as a "fiduciary out" provision. A board that does not have such a contractual right to exit may nevertheless provide cover for itself if it develops second thoughts about the merger. Many state provisions permit the board to submit mergers to their shareholders without a board recommendation.[49] Thus, the board, having this statutory option, could

---

[42] *See* Brazen v. Bell Atlantic Corp., 695 A.2d 43, 48 (Del. 1997) (relying upon Lee Builders v. Wells, 103 A.2d 918 (Del. 1954)). This approach resulted in the *Brazen* court upholding a $500 million termination fee. *See also* Matador Capital Management Corp. v. BRC Holdings, Inc., 729 A.2d 280 (Del. Ch. 1998). In making its choice between examining the termination fee under contract law or corporate law, the *Brazen* court in choosing the former was heavily influenced by the parties having labeled the provision as "liquidated damages." 695 A.2d 47-48.

[43] *See* J.P. Stevens & Co. Shareholders Litigation, 542 A.2d 770 (Del. Ch. 1988).

[44] *See* Dennis J. Block & Jonathan M. Hoff, Protective Provisions, Fiduciary Outs in Merger Agreements, 224 N.Y.L.J. 5 (Aug. 24, 2000).

[45] *See* Paramount Communications v. QVC Network Inc., 637 A.2d 34 (1994).

[46] *See* Corwin v. deTrey, 16 Del. J. Corp. L. 267 (Del. Ch. 1989).

[47] 637 A.2d 34, 38-41 (Del. 1994).

[48] 747 A.2d 95 (Del. Ch. 1999). *See also* Cinema, Inc. v. Technicolor, Inc., 663 A.2d 1156, 1173 (Del. 1995). Agreements that permit the board to entertain unsolicited offers, including providing their bidders with information, is sometimes referred to as "window shop" provisions. *See* Samjens Partners I v. Burlington Ind., Inc., 663 F. Supp. 614 (S.D.N.Y. 1987).

[49] *See, e.g.,* Del. Code. Ann., tit. 8, §251(c) (2001); MBCA §11.04(b) (1999). *See* William T. Allen, Understanding Fiduciary Outs: The What and the Why of an Anomalous Concept, 55 Bus. Law. 658 (2000).

withhold its recommendations, make full disclosure of all the facts, and allow the shareholders then to decide whether to approve the acquisition. The crucial variables in determining the validity of such agreements are whether the agreement has the effect of terminating the "bidding process," whether the agreement was important in obtaining a bid from the present suitor or significantly improving its prior bid, and whether the target company has entered the *Revlon* moment, discussed below, because there is a prospective change of control. Standstill agreements entered into by parties exploring their possible combination also raise questions regarding the extent that the directors' discretion can be restrained.[50]

A unique defensive tactic is the acquisition of another business by the target company, creating a potential antitrust threat to impending tender offers.[51] A somewhat related strategy of imposing a regulatory obstacle in the suitor's path is to purchase assets of a type such that any change in their ownership requires prior governmental clearance. For example, the purchase of a radio station or some other heavily regulated business can tie up the takeover attempt in any administrative proceedings that may be needed to approve a change of ownership in the regulated business. Another type of asset acquisition that becomes a defensive maneuver is the "Pac-Man" defense, where the target company makes a tender offer for control of the original tender offeror.[52]

§23.08   The Directors' Role as Auctioneers— the "Revlon Moment"

A significant qualification of *Unocal* was announced by the Delaware Supreme Court in *Revlon Inc. v. MacAndrews & Forbes Holdings, Inc.*,[1] which arose from the competing efforts of Pantry Pride, Inc. and Forstmann Little & Company to acquire control of Revlon, Inc. Pantry Pride had begun its hostile bid at $47.50 per share and successively raised its bid as Revlon embraced a series of defensive maneuvers and soon authorized its investment banker to negotiate with other parties who might have been interested in acquiring Revlon. An interested bidder was found in Forstmann Little & Company, Revlon's white knight, but by then Pantry Pride had increased its offer to $50, then $53, and still higher, to $56.25 per share. After Pantry Pride's offer had reached $53 per share, Revlon's board considered a leverage buyout headed by Forstmann Little & Company that, among other features, would require the sale of two important Revlon divisions for approximately $1.2 billion. To assure that Forstmann Little would be the victor, Revlon's board

---

[50] *See* Crane Co. v. Coltec Ind., Inc., 171 F.3d 733 (2d Cir. 1999) (interpreting notice requirement of a standstill agreement).

[51] *See* Consolidated Gold Fields PLC v. Minorco, S.A., 871 F.2d 252 (2d Cir. 1989) (affirming the issuance of a preliminary injunction against tender offer on antitrust grounds); Panter v. Marshall Field & Co., 646 F.2d 271, 290-291 (7th Cir.), *cert. denied,* 454 U.S. 1092 (1981) (target department store chain acquired stores in areas where tender offeror national retail chain was already operating).

[52] *See* Martin Marietta Corp. v. Bendix Corp., 549 F. Supp. 623 (D. Md. 1982).

§23.08   [1] 506 A.2d 173 (Del. 1986).

granted it the option to acquire two other product lines for $100-175 million below their fair market value if another bidder acquired 40 percent of the outstanding Revlon shares. It was this feature that the Delaware Supreme Court, pursuant to the language of the court, set out below, held was inconsistent with the duties of directors under the facts to become "auctioneers." Citing *Unocal*, the court upheld the directors' various defensive actions taken in response to Pantry Pride's initial bid of $47.50 because the court was persuaded that the board had "acted in good faith, and on an informed basis, with reasonable grounds to believe that there existed a harmful threat to the corporate enterprise."[2]

> However, when Pantry Pride increased its offer to $50 per share, and then to $53, it became apparent to all that the break-up of the company was inevitable. The Revlon board's authorization permitting management to negotiate a merger or buyout with a third party was a recognition that the company was for sale. The duty of the board had thus changed from the preservation of Revlon as a corporate entity to the maximization of the company's value at a sale for the stockholders' benefit. This significantly altered the board's responsibilities under the *Unocal* standards. It no longer faced threats to corporate policy and effectiveness, or to the stockholders' interest, from a grossly inadequate bid. The whole question of defensive measures became moot. The directors' role changed from defenders of the corporate bastion to auctioneers charged with getting the best price for the stockholders at a sale of the company.[3]

Revlon should be seen as a qualification of *Unocal* rather than an alternative. It does not prohibit defensive maneuvers but requires that their reasonableness be measured not in terms of the threat to control but by the objective of obtaining the best offer for the target shareholders. Thus *Revlon* does not prohibit lock-up options when the directors have entered the "*Revlon* moment." The court stated "A lock-up is not per se illegal under Delaware law. . . . Such options can entice other bidders to enter a contest for control of the corporation, creating an auction for the company and maximizing shareholder profit."[4] Because the lock-up granted Forstmann Little did not result in a substantial improvement in its bid and did not attract a new bidder to the contest, the court viewed its only impact as bringing the intense bidding contest to a close for an insubstantial benefit to the target shareholders.[5]

Revlon can be seen as a natural extension of *Unocal* in the sense that both cases set standards for the target board of directors to act in their shareholders'

[2] *Id.* at 181.
[3] *Id.* at 182.
[4] *Id.* at 183.
[5] Not insignificantly, the court also observed that the Revlon directors were benefited personally by favoring Forstmann Little who promised to support the value of earlier issued bonds whose holders were suing the Revlon directors for their failure to support, as they had represented they would, the bond covenants that were designed to prevent an LBO's occurrence that would increase the risk of those bonds.

best interest. This view is supported by the body of commentators who believe that the legitimacy of defensive maneuvers is facilitating an auction.[6]

The mere commencement of a hostile bid does not trigger *Revlon* duties on the part of the target directors, even though that offer puts the target company into play.[7] Post-*Revlon* Delaware Supreme Court decisions have vaguely identified three alternative bases for applying *Revlon*'s auctioneering standard:[8]

(1) When the target initiates an active bidding process seeking to sell itself or effect a restructuring that will lead to the break-up of the company.[9]

(2) When the target abandons its long-term strategy and seeks an alternative plan that entails the break-up of the company.[10]

(3) Where the effect of the plan supported by the target board of directors is to bring about a change in control of the corporation.[11]

However, at least in Delaware, today it is reasonable to believe that *Revlon*'s impact is only felt in the "change of control" situation.

Revlon demands that the board's actions in favoring or disfavoring a particular bidder must have a reasonable relation to the advantage sought to be obtained.[12] The target board can enter into arrangements with one bidder that "tilt the playing field," provided doing so is in the shareholders' interest.[13] At the same time, there is no duty to seek additional bidders when a company is confronted by a hostile bid or is negotiating a friendly combination.[14] Traditional business judgment rule considerations regarding the director's independence and reasonable investigation continue to assume even greater significance when the target board has entered the *Revlon* moment.[15]

[6] *See, e.g.,* Ronald J. Gilson, A Structural Approach to Corporations: The Case Against Defensive Tactics in Tender Offers, 33 Stan. L. Rev. 819, 868-875 (1981); Louis Lowenstein, Toward an Auction Market for Corporate Control and the Demise of the Business Judgment Rule, 63 S. Cal. L. Rev. 65, 69 (1989).*But see* Frank H. Easterbrook & Daniel R. Fischel, The Proper Role of a Target Management in Responding to a Tender Offer, 94 Harv. L. Rev. 1161, 1175-1180 (1981); Alan Schwartz, Search Theory and the Tender Offer Auction, 2 J. L., Econ. & Org. 229 (1986).

[7] *See* Paramount Communications, Inc. v. Time Inc., 571 A.2d 1140, 1151 (Del. 1989). *See also, e.g.,* In re Santa Fe Pac. Corp. Shareholder Litig., 669 A.2d 59, 71 (Del. 1995) (*Revlon* not triggered by effecting a merger with a favored suitor though another corporation continued its bid for control).

[8] *See* Odyssey Partners, L.P. v. Fleming Companies, Inc., 735 A.2d 386 (Del. Ch. 1999).

[9] Flake v. Hoskins, 55 F. Supp. 2d 1196, 1215 (D. Kan. 1999); Paramount Communications, Inc. v. Time Inc., 571 A.2d 1140, 1151 (Del. 1989); Mills Acquisition Co. v. Macmillan, Inc., 559 A.2d 1261 (Del. 1989).

[10] 571 A.2d at 1151. This in fact was the situation in Revlon Inc. v. MacAndrews & Forbes Holding, Inc., 506 A.2d 173 (Del. 1986).

[11] Paramount Communications Inc. v. QVC Network Inc., 637 A.2d 34 (Del. 1994).

[12] *See, e.g.,* Black & Decker Corp. v. American Standard, Inc., 682 F. Supp. 772, 786 (D. Del. 1988); Mills Acquisition Co. v. Macmillan, Inc., 559 A.2d 1261 (Del. 1989).

[13] *See* West Point Pepperell, Inc. v. J. P. Stevens Co., 542 A.2d 770 (Del. Ch. 1988).

[14] *See* Barkan v. Amsted Indus., 567 A.2d 1279 (Del. 1989); Ivanhoe Partners v. Newmont Mining Corp., 535 A.2d 1344 (Del. 1987).

[15] *See, e.g.,* Hanson Trust PLC v. MLSCM Acquisition, Inc., 781 F.2d 264 (2d Cir. 1986); Mills Acquisition Co. v. Macmillan, Inc., 559 A.2d 1261 (Del. 1989); In re Pennaco Energy, Inc. Shareholder Litig., 787 A.2d 691 (Del. Ch. 2001.

The more limited discretion that directors have under *Revlon* compared with *Unocal* is illustrated by the very different treatment granted management's defensive maneuvers in two recent decisions, *Paramount Communications, Inc. v. QVC Network, Inc.*[16] and *Paramount Communications, Inc. v. Time, Inc.*[17] As seen earlier,[18] the Delaware Supreme Court in *Time, Inc.* upheld management's defensive maneuver under *Unocal* and refused to apply *Revlon* when Time's management, in response to a bid from Paramount Communications, altered the form of its combination with Warner Communications from the issuance of Time stock to the payment of cash for Warner shares. In contrast, *Revlon* was applied in *QVC Network, Inc.* when Paramount's own merger with Viacom, Inc. was threatened by a higher offer from QVC so that it entered into a no-shop agreement as well as an agreement granting Viacom a large termination fee and an option to purchase a significant number of Paramount shares at a substantial discount, all triggered if QVC acquired control of Paramount. In both cases the defensive maneuver did not make a hostile acquisition of the target corporation impossible; the particular defensive maneuvers merely made such an acquisition more expensive. However, by assessing the defensive maneuvers in *QVC Network, Inc.* under *Revlon,* the Delaware Supreme Court was able to conclude that the directors had prematurely terminated bidding, so their actions were inconsistent with their roles in obtaining the best offer for their shareholders. In contrast, the court reasoned in *Time, Inc.* that changing the acquisition from a stock-based to cash-based acquisition so as to avoid a stockholders' vote would avoid the threat that the higher bid made by Paramount for Time, Inc. posed to the Time shareholders who may not have fully comprehended the full value of the long-range strategy reflected in management's support of the Time-Warner combination. The only apparent variable that separates these two significant decisions is the court's application of *Revlon* in *QVC Network, Inc.*

A point worthy of emphasis in the contrasting results reached in *Time, Inc.* and *QVC Network, Inc.* is the basis for applying *Revlon* in one but not the other. In both cases the target shareholders would emerge from the management-supported combination owning a distinct minority of the combined company. However, the court concluded in *Time, Inc.* that such a change of control does not trigger *Revlon,* even though the former Warner Communication shareholders would own 62 percent of the combined company (hence, the former Time shareholders would own only 38 percent), because control would be held by a fluid aggregation of unaffiliated stockholders both before and after the acquisition.[19] In contrast, the transaction in *QVC Network, Inc.* resulted in control of the target corporation being held by a corporation controlled by a single individual.[20] The court clearly rejected the argument that some evidence of a break-up of the target firm was also necessary for *Revlon* to apply. A clear illustration of where there would be

---

[16] 637 A.2d 34 (Del. 1994).

[17] 571 A.2d 1140 (Del. 1989).

[18] *See* §23.06.

[19] Paramount Communications, Inc. v. QVC Network, Inc., 637 A.2d 34, 47 (Del. 1994).

[20] *Id.* at 48. *See also* In re Santa Fe Pac. Corp. Shareholder Litig., 669 A.2d 59, 71 (Del. 1995).

no change of control such that *Revlon* must be met is where the sale of the company is at the suggestion of that company's majority holder; in such an instance the courts reason it is unrealistic to believe that a meaningful auction would occur.[21] Hence, the focus is whether the directors acted reasonably and in good faith in securing a fair price for the company.

The crucial factor under *QVC* is thus whether there would be a transfer of control as a result of the challenged transfer.[22] Should such a control transfer be involved the result presumably would be the consumption of a control premium that would otherwise be potentially available to the complaining shareholders. In other words, had control of Paramount been transferred to Viacom which was controlled by a single shareholder, the former Paramount shareholders would no longer be able to enjoy any indicia of control of their corporation notwithstanding their ownership of Viacom shares. The following accurately captures the meaning of "change of control" as it has evolved in the case law:

> [A] board sells "control" and thus triggers *Revlon* duties . . . when it agrees to exchange a controlling stake in the company, either for cash or non-voting securities, or for voting shares in an acquirer with a controlling shareholder but not when it exchanges 100% of its voting shares for voting shares in a widely held acquirer, most commonly through a stock-for-stock merger. . . .
>
> The exchange of all of the target's voting shares for voting shares of another widely held company is *not* a sale of control, and thus does not trigger *Revlon*, on the logic that control of the target company was before, and control of the combined company remains afterward, in a "fluid aggregation of unaffiliated stockholders."[23]

Quite independent of *Revlon* is the more general question of whether directors can, consistent with their fiduciary duties, enter into an enforceable agreement with a bidder not to actively pursue or support competing offers. An early federal decision held that directors can at least bind themselves not to *accept* a competing merger offer until the shareholders have voted on an initial agreement.[24] The Nebraska Supreme Court held that directors were bound by the fiduciary duties to the shareholders to submit with a favorable recommendation a subsequent higher bid, even though they had agreed with an earlier bidder to support that offer.[25] Importantly, the Delaware Supreme Court has recently held that contractual provisions that bar the board of directors from actively pursuing another bidder must complement the directors' fiduciary obligations. Thus directors who have entered the *Revlon* moment cannot enter into a no-shop agreement if it is inconsistent with their likelihood of securing a better offer through the pursuit of other bidders and bids.[26]

---

[21] *See, e.g.*, McMullin v. Beran, 765 A.2d 910 (Del. Supr. 2000); Odyssey Partners, L.P. v. Fleming Companies, Inc., 735 A.2d 386 (Del. Ch. 1999).

[22] *See, e.g.*, Krim v. ProNet, Inc., 744 A.2d 523, 527-528 (Del. Ch. 1999).

[23] Bernard Black & Reinier Kraakman, Delaware's Takeover Law: The Uncertain Search For Hidden Value, 96 Nw. U. L. Rev. 521, 534-535 (2002).

[24] *See* Jewel Co. v. Pay Less Drug Stores Nw., 741 F.2d 1555 (9th Cir. 1984).

[25] *See* ConAgra, Inc. v. Cargill, Inc., 382 N.W.2d 576 (Neb. 1986).

[26] *See* Paramount Communications, Inc. v. QVC Network Inc., 637 A.2d 34 (Del. 1994).

CHAPTER 24

Federal and
State Takeover Laws*

---

*Portions of this chapter as it appeared in the first edition of this treatise were adapted from Thomas L. Hazen, Hornbook on the Law of Securities Regulation (2d ed. 1990). This chapter has been updated to reflect recent developments.

A.   THE WILLIAMS ACT AND THE ACQUISITION OF SHARES

§24.01   *Federal Regulation of Takeovers*

The vociferousness of contested takeover battles as well as the potential for abuse with negotiated or controlled offers has led to the federal regulation of tender offers, most notably through the 1968 Williams Act amendments to the Exchange Act.[1] The Williams Act provisions impose disclosure requirements on various persons in connection with tender offers and stock acquisitions. The required disclosures include identification of the entity launching the takeover attempt and a description of the purpose of the proposed action and related future plans. Disclosure is required of any person who acquires more than five percent of the outstanding shares of any class of equity security subject to the Act's reporting requirements.[2] This provision serves to prevent secret creeping acquisitions—that is, those in which the target company learns of the takeover attempt too late to take any action. At the same time, an overall effect of the Williams Act disclosure requirements as well as its many substantive rules regulating the conduct of tender offers is to increase the cost of a takeover, the premiums that are paid to target shareholders, and the uncertainty as to whether a bid for control will be successful.[3]

Under section 14(d), similar disclosure is required for "a tender offer for or request or invitation for tenders of" any equity security subject to the reporting requirements of the Exchange Act.[4] Disclosure and SEC filings must also be made by anyone resisting, opposing, or supporting any tender offer.[5] Section 14(e) of the Exchange Act is not limited to reporting companies; in effect it applies Rule 10b-5 standards to all conduct and statements in connection with a tender offer.[6]

Other rules and regulations that affect tender offers include SEC Rule 14e-5, which prohibits tender offerors from buying shares other than through the ten-

---

§24.01   [1] Pub. L. No. 90-439, §2, 82 Stat. 454 (1968) (codified at 15 U.S.C. §§78m(d)-(e), 78n(d)-(f) (1997 & Supp. 2002)). In the case of an exchange offer, as opposed to a cash tender offer, the new securities will be subject to the 1933 Act's registration requirements. 15 U.S.C. §§77f, g (1997 & Supp. 2002). *See* §27.07.

[2] 15 U.S.C. §78m(d) (1997). *See id.* §78m(e) (1997 & Supp. 2002), which prohibits misstatements, omissions, and fraud in connection with such SEC filings.

[3] *See* Gregg A. Jarrell & Michael Bradley, The Economic Effects of Federal and State Regulation of Cash Tender Offers, 23 J.L. & Econ. 371 (1980).

[4] 15 U.S.C. §78n(d) (1997). *See also id.* §78n(f) (1997), which requires disclosure of any agreement concerning management turnover.

[5] 15 U.S.C. §78n(d) (1997).

[6] 15 U.S.C. §78n(e) (1997). *See generally* 2 Thomas Lee Hazen, Treatise on the Law of Securities Regulation §§11. 6, 11. 10 (4th ed. 2002).

A. The Williams Act and the Acquisition of Shares

der offer itself,[7] and Rule 14e-4, which prohibits short tendering and hedged tendering during a tender offer.[8] Rules 14e-1[9] and 14e-2[10] govern the behavior of the tender offeror and the target management, respectively. Rule 14(e)-3 is a general prohibition of insider trading during a tender offer.[11]

While section 14(e) provides an express remedy only for the SEC or criminal enforcement,[12] the bulk of 14(e) litigation has arisen from implied private causes of action.[13] Section 14(e) is the preferred provision to proceed under, as it depends on the plaintiff's status as a target of some deceptive act in connection with a tender offer rather than on the narrower purchaser/seller requirement of Rule 10b-5.[14] There remains some question as to the requirement of scienter.[15] It seems clear, however, that section 14(e) does require detrimental reliance in order to establish a private remedy.[16]

In proceeding under 14(e), the plaintiff may be the tender offeror (but not a defeated tender offeror seeking damages),[17] the target management,[18] or shareholders of the target company.[19] There is no set definition of "manipulation," and there has been much controversy as to what is required for a 14(e) action. The Supreme Court examined this question in *Schreiber v. Burlington Northern, Inc.*, discussed below, and held that in order to state a cause of action there must be some element of non-disclosure, misrepresentation, or deception.[20] Accordingly, fully disclosed conduct that may be manipulative will not support an implied cause of action.

---

[7] 17 C.F.R. §240.14e-5 (2002).

[8] 17 C.F.R. §240.14e-4 (2002). These practices consist of tendering securities not owned or tendering securities subject to a put or call option.

[9] 17 C.F.R. §240.14e-1 (2002).

[10] 17 C.F.R. §240.14e-2 (2002).

[11] 17 C.F.R. §240.14e-3 (2002). The Supreme Court upheld the rule as a valid exercise of the SEC's rule-making power. United States v. O'Hagan, 117 S. Ct. 2199 (1997).

[12] Section 14(e) declares certain conduct unlawful but does not make any mention of a private remedy.

[13] It is clear that a defeated tender offeror cannot maintain an action for damages under section 14(e). Piper v. Chris-Craft Indus., Inc., 430 U.S. 1 (1977). However, most federal courts recognize an implied cause of action for target shareholders under section 14(e) only to prevent or offset damages incurred in the decision to tender shares during a tender offer.

[14] 15 U.S.C. §78n(e) (1997); 17 C.F.R. §240.10b-5 (2002).

[15] See §24.05; Schreiber v. Burlington N., Inc., 472 U.S. 1 (1985); Aaron v. SEC, 446 U.S. 680 (1980); Mobil Corp. v. Marathon Oil Co., 669 F.2d 366 (6th Cir. 1981), *cert. denied,* 455 U.S. 982 (1982).

[16] See Panter v. Marshall Field & Co., 646 F.2d 271 (7th Cir.), *cert. denied,* 454 U.S. 1092 (1981); Lewis v. McGraw, 619 F.2d 192 (2d Cir.), *cert. denied,* 449 U.S. 951 (1980); Smallwood v. Pearl Brewing Co., 489 F.2d 579 (5th Cir.), *cert. denied,* 419 U.S. 873 (1974).

[17] Piper v. Chris-Craft Indus., Inc., 430 U.S. 1 (1977).

[18] Rondeau v. Mosinee Paper Co., 422 U.S. 49 (1975); ICM Realty v. Cabot [1973-1974 Transfer Binder], Fed. Sec. L. Rep. (CCH) ¶94,585 at 96,048 (S.D.N.Y. June 6, 1974).

[19] Panter v. Marshall Field & Co., 646 F.2d 271, 287 (7th Cir.), *cert. denied,* 454 U.S. 1092 (1981); Lewis v. McGraw, 619 F.2d 192, 195 (2d Cir.), *cert. denied,* 449 U.S. 951 (1980).

[20] Schreiber v. Burlington Northern, Inc., 472 U.S. 1 (1985).

§24.02   Filing Requirements of Section 13(d)

Any person other than the issuer who acquires, directly or indirectly, beneficial ownership[1] of more than 5 percent of a class of equity security registered pursuant to section 12 of the 1934 Act[2] must file appropriate disclosures with the SEC within ten days after reaching the five percent threshold, pursuant to section 13(d)(1).[3] Somewhat similar disclosures are required of an issuer's purchases of its own shares (or through its affiliate) by virtue of section 13(e).[4]

Any person acquiring five percent of a class of equity securities must, within ten days after reaching the five percent threshold, file with the Commission six copies of a statement reflecting the information required by section 13(d)(1).[5] Under section 13(d)(1) the purchaser has a ten-day window between the crossing of the five percent threshold and the disclosure date. This gives the hostile bidder some important running space to acquire momentum toward acquiring control of the target company. There is no express limitation on the amount of securities that may be purchased prior to filing Schedule 13D. An SEC advisory group has recommended amending the rules to require filing in advance of the five percent purchase,[6] but no such change has taken place.

The appropriate filing under section 13(d)(1) is embodied in Schedule 13D.[7] Holders of less than 20 percent of the class of securities who certify that they do not have an intent to exercise control of the issuer (referred to as a "passive investor"), may use Schedule 13G in place of Schedule 13D.[8] Certain "qualified institutional investors" also may report their holdings on Schedule 13G regardless of whether their holdings are 20 percent or greater of a class of the issuer's securities, provided the institutional investor does not intend to control the issuer.[9]

---

§24.02   [1] Many questions arise as to who is a beneficial owner for the purposes of the Williams Act. For example, a nominee with voting power who may vote only at the instruction of third parties is not the beneficial owner of the shares in question and thus is not subject to the section 13(d) filing requirements. Calvary Holdings, Inc. v. Chandler, 948 F.2d 59 (1st Cir. 1991).

Rule 13d-3, 17 C.F.R. §240.13d-3 (2001), sets out the Commission's standards for determining who is a beneficial owner for purposes of the filings under section 13(d). *Compare* the 10 percent beneficial ownership threshold under section 16's insider trading provisions. 15 U.S.C. §78p (1997 & Supp. 2002). *See, e.g.,* Stichting Phillips Pensionbonds A & B [1987-1988 Transfer Binder], Fed. Sec. L. Rep. (CCH) ¶78,668 (SEC No-Action Letter Jan. 12, 1988) (foreign pension fund investing in regular course of its business and not with a view toward affecting control of target company qualified for Schedule 13G).

[2] Companies with securities listed on a national securities exchange must register by virtue of section 12(a). 15 U.S.C. §78l(a) (1997 & Supp. 2002). Section 12(g) and Rule 12g-1 impose registration requirements on issuers with more than $10 million in assets having a class of equity securities with 500 or more shareholders of record. 15 U.S.C. §78l(g) (1997 & Supp. 2002); 17 C.F.R. §240.12g-1 (2002).

[3] 15 U.S.C. §78m(d)(1) (1997). Section 12, 15 U.S.C. §78l (1997), is discussed *infra* §27.11.

[4] 15 U.S.C. §78m(e) (1997 & Supp. 2002); 17 C.F.R. §240.13e-3 (2002). *See* §23.04.

[5] 15 U.S.C.A. §78m(d)(1) (1997).

[6] *See* 15 Sec. Reg. & L. Rep. (BNA) 156 (June 17, 1983). Advancing the filing date lessens the surprise element and would give the target company's management additional time to prepare a response or defense. Defensive tactics are discussed *supra* §23.05-23.07.

[7] 17 C.F.R. §240.13d-1 (2002). Schedule 13D is found in 17 C.F.R. §240.13d-101 (2002).

[8] 17 C.F.R. §240.13d-1(c) (2001).

[9] 17 C.F.R. §240.13d-1(b) (2001). Qualified institutional investors are defined as registered broker dealers, banks, insurance companies, registered investment companies, registered investment advisers, employee benefit plans, parent holding companies, control persons, and savings associations. *Id.*

A. The Williams Act and the Acquisition of Shares

Passive investors must amend the Schedule 13G within forty-five days after the end of the calendar year to report any change in information on their previous report.[10] Moreover, amendments to Schedule 13G must occur "promptly" when the passive investor's holdings exceed ten percent of the class of securities and thereafter a prompt amendment is required to report an increase or decrease by more than five percent when the passive investor's holdings are greater than ten percent but less than twenty percent.[11] Finally, upon acquiring twenty percent or more, or upon a change of intent to control the issuer, the former passive investor is no longer considered passive and, therefore, must report the acquisition on Schedule 13D within 10 days and is subject to a "cooling off" period during which the investor is prohibited from voting any securities of the issuer until ten days after filing of a Schedule 13D.[12]

As discussed below, the failure to make a timely Schedule 13D filing may result in an injunction against future purchases, at least until the violation is cured.[13] The SEC has also obtained disgorgement of profits made on shares acquired during the period between when a filing should have been made and when the defendant filed its Williams Act disclosures.[14]

The long-form Schedule 13D requires the following disclosures.[15] Item One must contain a description of the security purchased and its issuer. Item Two elicits information regarding the beneficial owner, including the principal business of the person making the filing and whether the filer has been convicted within the past five years of criminal violations or has been the subject of a civil order arising out of a violation of the securities laws. Item Three requires detailed disclosures of the source and amount of funds or other consideration being used to acquire the securities.[16] Item Four requires a description of the purpose(s) of the transaction, including any plans the purchaser may have that likely will result in a reorganization or a business combination such as mergers, consolidations, sales or acquisition of substantial assets, tender offers, changes in dividend policies and the like.[17] The level of detail is generally less when the shares are acquired only for investment.[18] Item Five requires the person filing the Schedule 13D to provide detailed information regarding the number of the target company's securities owned by the filer and its affiliates. Item Six elicits descriptions of all contracts, arrangements, understandings, or relationships between the persons filing the Schedule 13D and any person with respect to the target company's securities.

---

[10] 17 C.F.R. §240.13d-2(b) (2001).

[11] 17 C.F.R. §240.13-2(d) (2001). Qualified institutional investors must file within ten days after the close of the month in which such change in ownership occurred. 17 C.F.R. §240.13d-2(c) (2001).

[12] 17 C.F.R. §§240.13d-1(e) (2)(i) & (f)(2)(i) (2001).

[13] See, e.g., SEC v. First City Fin. Corp., 890 F.2d 1215 (D.C. Cir. 1989) (enjoining future violations).

[14] E.g., SEC v. First City Fin. Corp., 890 F.2d 1215 (D.C. Cir. 1989).

[15] See 17 C.F.R. §240.13d-101 (2001); In re Phillips Petroleum Sec. Litig., 881 F.2d 1236 (3d Cir. 1989), on remand, 738 F. Supp. 825 (D. Del. 1990).

[16] See, e.g., SEC v. Levy, 706 F. Supp. 61 (D.D.C. 1989) (failure to disclose bank loans was in violation of section 13(d)(1)(B)).

[17] See, e.g., In re Phillips Petroleum Sec. Litig., 738 F. Supp. 825 (D. Del. 1990).

[18] In some such cases there may be an exemption from section 13(d)'s filing requirements. See 15 U.S.C. §§78m(d)(6), 78m(f) (1997).

In addition to the initial filings, the person acquiring the five percent threshold must make amendments reflecting any significant changes in the information contained in Schedule 13D or 13G.[19] In determining whether a change in circumstances necessitates an amendment, the general doctrine of materiality is applicable.[20] Under SEC Rule 13d-2(a)[21] a one percent or larger change in beneficial ownership is presumptively a material change.

The greatest interpretative problems in completing Schedule 13D arise with respect to Item 4, which requires a description of the control aspirations of the purchasers. For example, a purchaser's intent to acquire a twenty percent equity interest, thereby obtaining some representation on the target company's board, was held to create an obligation to disclose a plan to acquire control.[22] In considering such questions, the courts have applied Rule 12b-2(f)'s definition of "control"[23] to determine when a purchaser's objective is to affect control. In view of the overall objective of the Williams Act amendments to provide an early warning of a potential change in control, it is not surprising that disclosure of a control purpose is required even when the purchaser does not yet have a formalized concrete plan for exercising that control.[24]

By virtue of section 13(d)(3),[25] when two or more people combine their efforts, such as by forming a partnership, limited partnership, syndicate, or other group for the purpose of acquiring, holding, or disposing of a target company's securities, that group is deemed to be a "person" for the purposes of section 13(d).[26] Accordingly, a Schedule 13D must be filed when members of a group aggregately acquire five percent of a class of equity securities subject to the Exchange Act's reporting requirements. The Second Circuit has held that the determinative factor is whether a group has been established that holds the securities pursuant to an express or implied agreement, thus presenting the *potential* for a shift in control; no agreement to buy further securities is necessary.[27] Furthermore, it is not necessary that the agreement be in writing.[28] The Second Circuit has also held that the members' agreement to acquire control may be established by purchase of enough securities to reach the five percent threshold.[29]

---

[19] 15 U.S.C. §78m(d)(2) (1988); 17 C.F.R. §240.13d-2 (2001). Once a Schedule 13D has been filed, a sale of the stock so acquired must be disclosed promptly. In re Cooper Labs., Inc., 17 Sec. Reg. & L. Rep. (BNA) 1175 (SEC consent order June 26, 1985).

[20] *See* 17 C.F.R. §240.12b-2 (2001).

[21] 17 C.F.R. §240.13d-2(a) (2001).

[22] Dan River, Inc. v. Unitex Ltd., 624 F.2d 1216 (4th Cir. 1980), *cert. denied,* 449 U.S. 1101 (1981); Chromalloy Am. Corp. v. Sun Chem. Corp., 611 F.2d 240 (8th Cir. 1979).

[23] 17 C.F.R. §240.12b-2(f) (2001).

[24] Chevron Corp. v. Pennzoil Co., 974 F.2d 1156 (9th Cir. 1992) (triable issue of fact as to whether Schedule 13D was materially misleading in failing to adequately disclose intent to obtain board position and exert degree of management influence over target company).

[25] 15 U.S.C. §78m(d)(3) (1997).

[26] For a similar provision with regard to tender offers, *see* Section 14(d)(2), 15 U.S.C. §78n(d)(2) (1988); *infra* §24.04.

[27] GAF Corp. v. Milstein, 453 F.2d 709 (2d Cir. 1971), *cert. denied,* 406 U.S. 910 (1972).

[28] SEC v. Drexel Burnham Lambert Inc., 837 F. Supp. 587 (S.D.N.Y. 1993).

[29] Corenco Corp. v. Schiavone & Sons, Inc., 488 F.2d 207 (2d Cir. 1973).

On the other hand, discussions by various persons of the possibility of entering into an agreement do not alone establish the formation of a group.[30] The Seventh Circuit requires a greater showing of concerted activity to establish the formation of a group than does the Second Circuit. The Seventh Circuit requires the group to have an agreement not only to exert control but also to acquire additional shares also for the purpose of exerting control.[31] A group may be deemed to exist when parties agree to act in concert to purchase additional shares, regardless of the absence of a common plan with respect to the target corporation beyond the acquisition of additional shares.[32] Quite separate from section 13(d)(1) is the question of whether failure to disclose the existence of a group in Schedule 13D constitutes a material misstatement or omission. This depends on the facts of the case.

B.   THE REGULATION OF "TENDER OFFERS"

§24.03   Definition of "Tender Offer"

Whereas section 13(d)(1)'s filing requirements are aimed at creeping acquisitions and open-market or privately negotiated large block purchases,[1] section 14(d)(1)'s filing and disclosure provisions are called into play when there is a "tender offer." Although "tender offer" is not defined in the act, it is important in that it determines the applicability of section 14(d)(1)'s[2] filing requirements, section 14(e)'s[3] general antifraud proscriptions, and section 14(f)'s[4] disclosure requirements relating to new directors.

On more than one occasion Congress has considered and rejected[5] an objective definition of "tender offer," such as the one embodied in the proposed Federal Securities Code.[6] In contrast, most state tender-offer statutes contain objective

---

[30] Lane Bryant, Inc. v. Hatleigh Corp., 517 F. Supp. 1196 (S.D.N.Y. 1981).

[31] Bath Indus., Inc. v. Blot, 427 F.2d 97 (7th Cir. 1970) (enjoining group acquiring nearly 50 percent control from ousting incumbent management).

[32] Mid-Continent Bancshares, Inc. v. O'Brien [1982 Transfer Binder], Fed. Sec. L. Rep. (CCH) ¶98,734 (E.D. Mo. 1981).

§24.03   [1] 15 U.S.C. §78m(d) (1997). See §24.02.

[2] 15 U.S.C. §78n(d) (1997). See §24.04.

[3] 15 U.S.C. §78n(e) (1997). See §24.05.

[4] 15 U.S.C. §78n(f) (1997). See §24.06.

[5] See, e.g., Full Disclosure of Corporate Equity Ownership and in Corporate Takeover Bids, Hearings on S.510 Before the Subcomm. on Securities of the Senate Comm. on Banking and Currency, 90th Cong., 1st Sess. 131 (1967).

[6] The proposed code would have required an offer or solicitation directed toward more than 35 persons. See A.L.I. Fed. Sec. Code §292 (1979); id. §299.9(a) (Tent. Draft No. 1, 1972). The comments explain that although the present law has a "public connotation" of "tender offer," it is too vague and open-ended.

definitions.[7] The SEC has declined to use its broad rule-making power to promulgate objective standards[8] to determine the existence of tender offers.[9] This position was "premised upon the dynamic nature of [the] transactions [involved] and the need for the Williams Act to be interpreted flexibly."[10] Needless to say, the SEC preference for flexibility comes at the cost of sleeplessness for corporate planners, who quite naturally quest certainty for their client's acquisitions. The Commission's long-standing position is that the definition of "tender offer" "is not limited to the classical 'tender offer' where the person desiring to acquire shares makes a public invitation or a written offer to the shareholders to tender their shares. Nor is there a requirement that the shares be tendered through a depositary. The change in control may be effected by direct purchase from shareholders without a public or a written invitation for tenders having been made."[11] The essence of the SEC's position is that "tender offer" covers more than traditional takeover attempts involving public solicitation and may, under appropriate circumstances, include privately negotiated and open-market purchases.

In a widely cited decision, *Wellman v. Dickinson*,[12] the court adopted an eight-factor test to determine whether a tender offer exists. The eight factors can be summarized as follows:

(1) active and widespread solicitation of public shareholders;
(2) solicitation for a substantial percentage of the issuer's stock;
(3) whether the offer to purchase is made at a premium over prevailing market price;
(4) whether the terms of the offer are firm rather than negotiable;
(5) whether the offer is contingent on the tender of a fixed minimum number of shares;
(6) whether the offer is open only for a limited period of time;
(7) whether the offerees are subject to pressure to sell their stock; and
(8) the existence of public announcements of a purchasing program that precede or accompany a rapid accumulation of stock.[13]

These factors are simply broad guidelines.

Arguably, a series of control-related open-market purchases would fall within the "tender offer" definition as well. The cases, however, have taken a contrary

[7] *See generally* Report, State Takeover Statutes and the Williams Act, 32 Bus. Law. 187 (1976). The applicable state legislation is considered in §24.08.
[8] *See, e.g.,* Sec. Act Rel. No. 33-5731 [1976-1977 Transfer Binder], Fed. Sec. L. Rep. (CCH) ¶80,659 (SEC Aug. 2, 1976).
[9] The SEC quickly withdrew its 1979 proposed definition of "tender offer"; *see* Proposed Rule 14d1(b)(1) (1979).
[10] Sec. Exch. Act Rel. No. 34-16385 (Nov. 29, 1979).
[11] Cattlemen's Inv. Co. [1971-1972 Transfer Binder], Fed. Sec. L. Rep. (CCH) ¶78,775 at 81,627 (SEC Staff Reply, April 24, 1972).
[12] 475 F. Supp. 783, 823-824 (S.D.N.Y. 1979), *aff'd on other grounds,* 682 F.2d 355 (2d Cir. 1982), *cert. denied,* 460 U.S. 1069 (1983). *See also* SEC v. Carter Hawley Hale Stores, Inc., 760 F.2d 945 (9th Cir. 1985).
[13] The eight-factor test, which is not contained in any official SEC rule, has evolved over a period of time.

B. The Regulation of "Tender Offers"

view.[14] Thus a plan of successive open-market purchases was held not to be a tender offer where the aggregate number of shares so purchased fell short of the five percent threshold.[15] Even where the five percent threshold was exceeded, an attempt to exercise voting control after a series of open-market purchases was held insufficient to make the acquisition a tender offer.[16] Similarly, the purchase of twenty-five percent of a company's stock in a two-day period was held not to be a tender offer where only one of the *Wellman*'s eight factors was present.[17] The most compelling case to date for characterizing a series of open-market purchases as a tender offer is *Hanson Trust PLC v. SCM Corporation*,[18] where twenty-five percent of the target company's outstanding stock was acquired quickly through negotiated and market purchases after canceling its earlier publicly announced tender offer.[19] Such purchases are commonly referred to as "street sweeps."[20] The court in *Hanson Trust* reasoned that the price of the purchases was at the market price and that the privately negotiated purchases were accomplished without any pressure or secrecy.[21] A different result might have followed had the withdrawal of the tender offer been part of a plan designed to evade the protections of the Williams Act.[22]

A number of decisions have discussed whether privately negotiated transfers of a controlling block of shares can constitute a tender offer. The cases conflict, but most hold that privately negotiated transactions are susceptible to being categorized as tender offers even though most privately negotiated purchases will not fall within the definition of "tender offer." Any privately negotiated purchase that interferes with a shareholder's "unhurried investment decision" and "fair treatment of . . . investors"[23] defeats the protections of the Williams Act and most likely is a tender offer.[24]

---

[14] *See generally* David J. Segre, Open-Market and Privately Negotiated Purchase Programs and the Market for Corporate Control, 42 Bus. Law. 715 (1987).

[15] Gulf & W. Indus., Inc., v. Great Am. Atl. & Pac. Tea Co., 356 F. Supp. 1066 (S.D.N.Y. 1973), *aff'd*, 476 F.2d 687 (2d Cir. 1973).

[16] Water & Wall Assocs., Inc., v. American Consumer Indus., Inc. [1973 Transfer Binder], Fed. Sec. L. Rep. (CCH) ¶93,943 (D.N.J. 1973). *Accord*, SEC v. Carter Hawley Hale Stores, Inc., 760 F.2d 945 (9th Cir. 1985).

[17] Brascan, Ltd. v. Edper Equities, Ltd., 477 F. Supp. 773 (S.D.N.Y. 1979). The eight-factor test is set out in the text accompanying *supra* note 13.

[18] 774 F.2d 47 (2d Cir. 1985).

[19] These purchases were made within hours of the withdrawal of the tender offer.

[20] *See generally* Dale A. Oesterle, The Rise and Fall of Street Sweep Takeovers, 1989 Duke L.J. 202.

[21] 774 F.2d 47 (2d Cir. 1985). *Cf.* Wellman v. Dickinson, 475 F. Supp. 783 (S.D.N.Y. 1979), *aff'd on other grounds*, 682 F.2d 355 (2d Cir. 1982), *cert. denied*, 460 U.S. 1069 (1983).

[22] *Cf.* Field v. Trump, 850 F.2d 938 (2d Cir. 1988), *cert. denied*, 489 U.S. 1012 (1989), wherein the court found that a privately negotiated purchase sandwiched between the withdrawal of one tender offer and the initiation of a second, both at a lower price, was part of a single tender offer.

[23] Cattlemen's Inv. Co. v. Fears, 343 F. Supp. 1248, 1251 (W.D. Okla. 1972) (finding a tender offer to have occurred). *See also, e.g.*, In re G.L. Corp. [1979-1980 Transfer Binder], Fed. Sec. L. Rep. (CCH) ¶82,494 (1980) (offer for all-or-none purchase at premium may be tender offer). *See generally* Segre, *supra* note 14.

[24] Wellman v. Dickinson, 475 F. Supp. 783 (S.D.N.Y. 1979), *aff'd on other grounds*, 682 F.2d 355 (2d Cir. 1982), *cert. denied*, 460 U.S. 1069 (1983).

§24.04   The Williams Act Requirements for
Tender Offers

As discussed more fully below, section 14(d) and applicable SEC rules require filing with the SEC certain mandated disclosures at a tender offer's commencement.[1] In addition, there are certain substantive requirements in Regulations D and E for any tender offer subject to section 14(d)(1).

§24.04.01   Filing Requirements

Section 14(d)(1) of the Exchange Act[2] requires that all "tender offer material" for equity securities subject to the registration requirements of section 12 must be filed with the Commission and be accompanied by the appropriate disclosures.[3] Section 14(d)(1) requires disclosures of the type specified in Schedule 13D,[4] in addition to such other information as the SEC may require.[5] As is the case with a Schedule 13D filing for acquisition of five percent or more of a class of a target company's stock,[6] section 14(d)(1) filings must be updated to reflect material changes and developments.[7] Section 14(d)(1) does not apply to an issuer's acquisition of its own shares; those transactions are governed by section 13(e), not section 14(d)(1). However, the SEC's regulations for issuer tender offers are comparable to those in Regulation 14D's rules for third-party offers.[8]

Regulation 14D sets forth the Commission's filing and disclosure requirements under section 14(d)(1). Rule 14d-1[9] provides the basic definitions for covered tender offers and incorporates by reference all general definitions applicable under other provisions of the Exchange Act. Rule 14d-3 requires filing Schedule TO with both the SEC and the target company as well as with the exchange on which the target shares are listed and, if not listed, with the National Association of Securities Dealers (NASD). In addition to the long-form filing embodied in Schedule TO,[10] the tender offeror must file ten copies of all additional tender-

---

§24.04   [1] Filing requirements are not limited to the tender offeror but apply to anyone who is recommending in favor of or against a tender offer covered by the Act. *See* Schedule 14D-9.

[2] 15 U.S.C. §78n(d)(1) (1997).

[3] 15 U.S.C. §78n(d)(1) (1997).

[4] 15 U.S.C.A. §78m(d) (1997).

[5] *See* SEC Schedule TO and Rule 14d-1, 17 C.F.R. §§240.14d-100 (2002). Schedule TO was formerly Schedule 14D-1.

[6] 15 U.S.C. §78n(d) (1997). *Cf.* 15 U.S.C. §78m(d) (1997).

[7] 15 U.S.C. §78n(d) (1997). *Cf.* In re Revlon, Inc., Sec. Exch. Act Rel. No. 34-23320 [1986-1987 Transfer Binder], Fed. Sec. L. Rep. (CCH) ¶84,006 (SEC June 16, 1986) (finding violations of Rule 14d-4 due to failure to amend Schedule 14D-9 to reflect defensive merger negotiations).

[8] 15 U.S.C. §78m(e) (1997 & Supp. 2002). In 1986, the SEC amended Rules 13-4 and 14e-1 so as to subject issuer self-tenders to the same time periods and substantive regulation as third-party offers covered by section 14(d) and Regulation 14D.

[9] 17 C.F.R. §240.14d-1 (2001).

[10] 17 C.F.R. §240.14d-100 (2002).

offer materials with the Commission no later than the date on which it is first published or disseminated.[11] All documents used in the tender offer and the solicitation must thus be on file with the Commission prior to their use.[12] When the bidder's consideration includes non-exempt securities, the offer must be disseminated to the target shareholders through a prospectus, in compliance with the federal Securities Act of 1933.[13] In all other cases (that is, cash or exempt securities) the bidder has three alternative methods to disseminate its bid: the long-form publication, summary publication, and, using a list of stockholders, through a communication directly to the target shareholders.[14]

§24.04.02   Commencement of the Tender Offer

Rule 14d-2[15] provides that a tender offer begins at 12:01 a.m. on the day of the earliest of the following events: (1) the first publication of the long-form tender offer filed pursuant to Rule 14d-4(a)(1); (2) the first publication of a summary advertisement;[16] or (3) the first public announcement[17] of the tender offer, unless within five days of the announcement the "bidder"[18] makes a public announcement withdrawing the tender offer or complies with the disclosure and filing requirements of Rules 14d-3(a),[19] 14d-6,[20] and 14d-4,[21] all of which require public dissemination of the relevant information.[22]

§24.04.03   Schedule TO

All bidders must file Schedule TO. "Bidder" is defined as any person who makes a tender offer or on whose behalf a tender offer is made, except that an issuer seeking to acquire its own securities is not within the definition. Schedule TO

---

[11] 17 C.F.R. §240.14d-3(b) (2002).

[12] 17 C.F.R. §240.14d-3 (2001).

[13] In 1999 when the SEC eased its prefiling restrictions for exchange offers. *See* Regulation of Takeovers and Security Holder Communications, Sec. Act Rel. No. 33-7760, 1999 WL 969596 (SEC Oct. 22, 1999).

[14] *See* Rule 14d-4, 17 C.F.R. §240.14d-4 (2002).

[15] 17 C.F.R. §240.14d-2 (2002).

[16] Rule 14d-4(a)(2) allows summary publications for certain tender offers. 17 C.F.R. §240.14d-4(a)(2) (2001).

[17] Kahn v. Virginia Retirement Sys., 13 F.3d 110 (4th Cir. 1993) (joint press release announcing takeover agreement did not commence the tender offer).

[18] "The term 'bidder' means any person who makes a tender offer or on whose behalf a tender offer is made [except for a tender offer by the issuer]." 17 C.F.R. §240.14d-1(g)(2) (2002).

[19] 17 C.F.R. §240.14d-3(a) (2002) (filing and transmittal of tender offer statements).

[20] 17 C.F.R. §240.14d-6 (2002) (disclosure requirements with respect to tender offers).

[21] 17 C.F.R. §240.14d-4 (2002) (dissemination of tender offers).

[22] *Cf.* Weeden v. Continental Health Affiliates, Inc., 713 F. Supp. 396 (N.D. Ga. 1989) (filing of Schedule 13D coupled with public letter to target's board proposing a $6 per-share buyout was proposal to begin negotiations, not tender offer, and therefore did not implicate "five day" rule).

requires certain basic information regarding the bidder and the bid. For example, Schedule TO requires disclosure of the name of the bidder, the name of the target company, and the title of the class of securities being sought. It also requires that all "persons" reporting under the Schedule provide their names and addresses as well as disclosing whether or not they belong to a "group" within the meaning of section 14(d)(2).[23] But the disclosures demanded of the bidder are more extensive than mere background information. There must be disclosure of the source of funds to be used in connection with the tender offer and the identity and background of the person filing the document, including the disclosure of any criminal convictions or civil orders arising out of a securities violation within the past five years of the person presenting the tender offer. The tender-offer document must also disclose all contracts, transactions, or negotiations in the preceding three fiscal years between the bidder and the target company, its directors or its officers, the purpose of the tender offer, and the bidder's plans and proposals for the future with regard to the target company. The Schedule TO must divulge the bidder's current interest and holdings of securities of the target company as well as any contracts, arrangements, understandings, or relationships between the bidder and the target company. Present or proposed contracts, arrangements, understandings, or relationships between the bidder, its officers, directors, controlling persons, or subsidiaries and the target company or any of its officers, directors, controlling persons, or subsidiaries that are material to a stockholder's decision must be disclosed. Schedule TO must identify all persons retained or employed or compensated in connection with the tender offer. The bidder must also disclose extensive information regarding its financial position if the bidder's financial position is material to an investor's decision whether or not to tender shares in the target company.

Certain prospective information must be disclosed—such as any steps toward compliance, with necessary administrative approval for the offer, the possible impact of the antitrust laws, or the margin requirements,[24] as well as a summary of pending material legal proceedings.[25] When there have been material misstatements in a Schedule TO filing, they can be cured by subsequent correction, provided that adequate prominence is given to the curative changes.[26]

§24.04.04 The Bidders' Access to the Target Company's Shareholders

Rule 14d-5 spells out the target company's obligation to respond to requests for a shareholder list in connection with tender offers.[27] Briefly, if the bidder or

[23] 17 C.F.R. §240.14d-100 (2002).
[24] *See, e.g.,* Irving Bank Corp. v. Bank of N.Y. Co., 692 F. Supp. 163 (S.D.N.Y. 1988).
[25] *Cf.* Fry v. Trump, 681 F. Supp. 252 (D.N.J. 1988) (upholding section 14(a) claim based on failure to disclose 10 of 18 pending legal proceedings).
[26] *See, e.g.,* American Insured Mortgage Investors v. CRI, Inc. [1990-1991 Transfer Binder], Fed. Sec. L. Rep. (CCH) ¶95,730 (S.D. N.Y. 1990) (material changes had to be highlighted through the use of boldface and italic typeface).
[27] 17 C.F.R. §240.14d-5 (2002).

other person presents the request according to the rule's requirements, the target company's management must comply, but the reasonable cost of compliance can be charged to the bidder. Faced with such a request, the target company has two options. It may within three business days deliver the stockholder lists to the bidder making the request.[28] Alternatively, it can mail the bidder's materials, within three business days of receipt, to the target company's holders.[29] The SEC dictates the proper form for the bidder's written request.[30] Also, a bidder's request for such lists subjects the bidder to certain requirements, including the return of any lists furnished by the target company.[31]

§24.04.05   Withdrawal and Duration of Tender Offer

Rule 14d-7[32] provides that withdrawal rights may be exercised throughout the period that the tender offer remains open, which must be for at least twenty business days.[33] Any increase or decrease in the consideration offered under the tender offer requires that the tender offer's duration be extended for an additional ten business days from the date of change in consideration.[34] The rule also prescribes how the notice of withdrawal is to be given. The overall effect of the SEC's regulations respecting the duration of tender offers and providing withdrawal rights through the life of the tender offer is not only to remove pressure from the target shareholders to rush their acceptance of the bidder's offer but to create a climate within which competing bids may arise.

§24.04.06   Proration and "Best Price" Rules

Rule 14d-8[35] requires pro rata acceptance of shares tendered where the tender offer by its terms does not obligate the tender offeror to accept *all* shares

---

[28] 17 C.F.R. §240.14d-5(c) (2002).

[29] 17 C.F.R. §240.14d-5(b) (2002). The bidder is to be informed of the progress of any such mailing undertaken by the target company.

[30] 17 C.F.R. §240.14d-5(e) (2002).

[31] 17 C.F.R. §240.14d-5(f) (2002).

[32] 17 C.F.R. §240.14d-7 (2002). *See also* 17 C.F.R. §240.13e-4(f)(2)(i) (2002) (imposing same rule for issuer tender offers). *See* Exch. Act Rel. No. 34-23421 (July 11, 1986). The rule provides a longer withdrawal period than Congress specified in Section 14(d)(5) of the Act, 15 U.S.C. §78n(d)(5) (1997), which provides that all securities deposited pursuant to a tender offer may be withdrawn by or on behalf of the depositor at any time until the expiration of seven days after the first publication of the formal tender offer (or request or invitation) and at any time after 60 days from the date of the original tender offer or request for invitation unless a different period is provided for by SEC rules. *See* MacFadden Holdings, Inc. v. J. B. Acquisition Corp., 802 F.2d 62 (2d Cir. 1986) (adequate description of withdrawal rights where offer was contingent on FCC approval).

[33] 17 C.F.R. §240.14e-1 (2002).

[34] 17 C.F.R. §§240.13e-4(f)(1)(ii), 240.14e-1(b) (2002).

[35] 17 C.F.R. §240.14d-8 (2002).

tendered. This takes pressure off the target company's shareholders, who would otherwise have to make a quick decision were acceptance to be on a first-come basis. Proration occurs at the tender offer's close. Thus target shareholders can delay their acceptance of a bid until near its closing without fear they will be treated differently if the bidder's offer is oversubscribed. A tender offeror may not extend the proration period after expiration of the offer where the effect would be to alter the pro rata acceptance of the shares tendered.[36]

Section 14(d)(7) of the Securities Exchange Act[37] provides that whenever a bidder varies the terms of a tender offer or request before the expiration thereof by increasing the consideration offered to the holders of the securities sought, the bidder must pay to all persons tendering securities pursuant to their requests that same price, whether or not the securities were tendered prior to the variation of the tender offer's terms. This can be especially important if a series of transactions are integrated and held to be parts of a single tender offer.[38] This best price requirement is applicable to both issuer self-tenders and tender offers by third-party bidders.[39] The SEC "best price" requirement applies only to shares purchased during a single tender offer. As such, unlike state "fair price" statutes,[40] the SEC does not regulate two-tiered offers consummated in two distinct steps. The SEC best-price requirements do not prohibit different types of consideration, and the different consideration need not be substantially equivalent in value as long as the tender offer permits the security holders to elect among the types of consideration offered.[41]

When different types of consideration are offered, the tender offeror may limit the availability and offer it to tendering shareholders on a pro rata basis.[42] As is the case with the "all holders" requirements, discussed below, the Commission has given itself the power to grant exemptions from the operation of the best-price requirement.[43] As with the rules respecting the duration of tender offers and the withdrawal rights of tendering shareholders, the liberal proration rules and best-price rules shield the target shareholders from being pressured to tender their shares. In combination these rules contribute to an auction environment by making competing bids possible by assuring that the target shareholders are free within relative broad time periods to place their shares with the highest bidder. While this may well reduce the incentive for bidders to initiate a takeover, it is equally likely that the bidder that offers the high-

---

[36] Pryor v. United States Steel Corp., 794 F.2d 52 (2d Cir. 1986); Pryor v. USX Corp. [1991-1992 Transfer Binder], Fed. Sec. L. Rep. (CCH) ¶96,630 (S.D.N.Y. 1991).

[37] 15 U.S.C. §78n(d)(7) (1997).

[38] *See, e.g.,* Field v. Trump, 850 F.2d 938 (2d Cir. 1988), *cert. denied,* 489 U.S. 1012 (1989) (upholding complaint that withdrawal of first tender offer was a sham).

[39] 17 C.F.R. §§240.13e-4(f)(8)(ii), 240.14d-10(a)(2) (2002). *See, e.g.,* Field v. Trump, 850 F.2d 938 (2d Cir. 1988), *cert. denied* 516 U.S. 367 (1996).

[40] *E.g.,* Md. Code Ann., Corps. & Assns. §§3-602, 3-603 (1999 & Supp. 2001).

[41] 17 C.F.R. §§240.13e-4(f)(9), 240.14d-10(c) (2001).

[42] *Id.*

[43] 17 C.F.R. §§240.13e-4(g)(7), 240.14d-10(e) (2001).

est price, on average, is the company that can put the target corporation's assets to their highest use. To the extent that this leads to a better allocation of resources, the concomitant greater costs imposed by the Williams Act are not all that bad.

§24.04.07   The "All Holders" Requirement

A recent Delaware decision upheld a tender offer by an issuer that excluded a hostile tender offeror.[44] Since that decision, the SEC has adopted an "all holders" rule, so such an exclusion is now prohibited. Even though there is no explicit statutory requirement that a tender offer be made to all shareholders, the SEC takes the position that the "all holders" requirement is "necessary and appropriate" to implement the Williams Act.[45]

There is an exception in the "all holders" requirement for tender offers that exclude one or more shareholders in compliance with a constitutionally valid state statute.[46] In addition to reserving general exemptive power under the "all holders" rules,[47] the SEC has promulgated a specific but limited exemption for odd-lot tender offers by issuers. An "odd-lot offer" is one that is limited to security holders owning less than a specified number of shares under one hundred.[48]

§24.04.08   Exemptions from Regulation 14d; Mini Tender Offers

Section 14(d)(8) of the Act[49] exempts certain tender offers or requests for tenders from the scope of section 14(d)'s requirements. When the acquisition of the securities sought together with all other acquisitions by the same person of securities of the same class within the preceding twelve months does not exceed two percent of the outstanding securities of the class, section 14(d) does not apply.[50] Similarly, section 14(d) does not apply where the tender offeror is the issuer of the security.[51] The Securities Exchange Act also gives the SEC exemptive power by rule, regulation, or order from transactions "not entered into for the purpose of, and not having the effect of, changing or influencing

---

[44] Unocal Corp. v. Mesa Petroleum Co., 493 A.2d 946 (Del. 1985).

[45] See Sec. Exch. Act Rel. No. 34-23421 [1986-1987 Transfer Binder], Fed. Sec. L. Rep. (CCH) ¶81,016 (SEC July 11, 1986).

[46] 17 C.F.R. §§240.13e-4(f)(9)(ii), 240.14d-10(b)(2) (2002).

[47] 17 C.F.R. §§240.13e-4(f)(7), 240.14d-10(e) (2002).

[48] 17 C.F.R. §240.13e-4(h)(5) (2002). However, both the all-holders and best-price requirements apply to the terms of the odd-lot tender offer.

[49] 15 U.S.C. §78n(d)(8) (1997).

[50] 15 U.S.C. §78n(d)(8)(A) (1997).

[51] 15 U.S.C. §78n(d)(8)(B) (1997).

the control of the issuer or otherwise as not comprehended within the purposes of this subsection."[52]

Although not couched in terms of an exemption, section 14(d) provides that its provisions do not apply to tender offers when after completion of the offer, the bidder would hold less than five percent of a class of the target company's equity securities.[53] Tender offers falling below this threshold became known as mini tender offers. In the 1990s various fraudulent practice developed in connection with these largely unregulated mini tender offers, including offering to buy back stock at a price lower than the current market price.[54] In order to prevent the abuses of mini tender offers, the SEC issued guidelines that essentially require full disclosure with respect to mini tender offers.[55]

C.   OBTAINING COMPLIANCE AND ANTIFRAUD AND DIRECTOR TURNOVER PROVISIONS

§24.05   The Antifraud Provision—Section 14(e)

Section 14(e) of the Exchange Act[1] prohibits material misstatements, omissions, and fraudulent practices in connection with tender offers. The jurisdictional reach of this antifraud provision is broader than other provisions of the Williams Act because it applies to *any* tender offer in interstate commerce, regardless of whether the target company is subject to the Exchange Act's reporting requirements.[2] Whether a fact is material depends on whether a reasonable investor would consider it significant in making an investment decision.[3] Materiality is based on a highly factual inquiry and thus is difficult to predict. For example, it is not necessary to disclose preliminary merger discussions that may lead to a tender offer.[4] At the same time, a denial of such negotiations, even though they are at a very early stage, is not advisable in light of the Supreme Court's holding that whether a denial of preliminary merger negotiations is material is a question of fact.[5]

---

[52] 15 U.S.C. §78n(d)(8)(C) (1997).

[53] 15 U.S.C. §78n(d) (1997) section 14(d) covers "Tender offer by owner of more than five per centum of class of securities; exceptions").

[54] By labeling the offer a "tender offer," unwary investors were duped into tendering their shares and receiving less than they would have had they sold the shares on the market.

[55] *See* Commission Guidance on Mini-Tender Offers and Limited Partnership Tender Offers, Release No. 34-43069, 2000 WL 1050530 (SEC July 24, 2000).

§24.05   [1] 15 U.S.C. §78n(e) (1997). *See* James I. Junewicz, The Appropriate Limits of Section 14(e) of the Securities Exchange Act of 1934, 62 Tex. L. Rev. 1171 (1984).

[2] In contrast, the other provisions of the Williams Act are limited to securities of issuers subject to Section 12's registration requirements. 15 U.S.C. §78*l* (1997 & Supp. 2002).

[3] TSC Indus. v. Northway, Inc., 426 U.S. 438 (1976). *See* §13.32.

[4] Staffin v. Greenberg, 672 F.2d 1196 (3d Cir. 1982).

[5] Basic, Inc. v. Levinson, 485 U.S. 224 (1988).

C. Obtaining Compliance and Antifraud and Director Turnover Provisions

As in other areas of the securities laws, courts approach materiality determinations cautiously so as to preserve a healthy balance between the need of investors for information and the fact that too-demanding disclosure requirements ultimately will work against the interests of the corporation's shareholders.[6] Accordingly, subjective motivation behind fully disclosed transactions need not be spelled out as long as all material facts underlying the transaction are disclosed.[7]

The Supreme Court has held that there is no private remedy *for damages* in the hands of a competing tender offeror.[8] Lower courts have consistently recognized private actions for the target company or its shareholders for damages or such equitable relief as is appropriate under the circumstances.[9] The courts have also recognized the right of the bidder as well as a competing bidder to obtain injunctive relief.[10]

In an important decision, *Schreiber v. Burlington Northern, Inc.*,[11] the Supreme Court limited the thrust of section 14(e). Burlington Northern had made a hostile tender offer to purchase 25.1 million shares of El Paso Gas for $24 per share. After negotiations with El Paso management, the original offer was withdrawn, El Paso management was given "golden parachute" severance payments, and a new tender offer was made for 21 million shares from the public and 4.1 million shares from El Paso at $24 per share. It was claimed that a combination of El Paso management's golden parachutes and a decision to reduce the size of the offer to the public in order to infuse more cash into El Paso (presumably to pay for the golden parachutes) artificially affected the price of the El Paso stock and thus constituted manipulation. The source of the plaintiff's actual complaint was that because fewer shares would be purchased pursuant to the revised bid, as contrasted with the initial bid, the plaintiff would, under the proration rule, have fewer of her shares purchased. Rather than directly face the issue of defining "manipulative conduct," the Court held that "'manipulative' as used in §14(e) requires misrepresentation or nondisclosure."[12] The Court thus found section 14(e) was not violated because no omission or misstatement was alleged to have occurred in connection with the cancellation of the first tender offer.

A significant impact of *Schreiber* is it stopped a potential intrusion of federal law into the regulation of defensive maneuvers, an area historically regulated by state fiduciary duty law. Before *Schreiber* was decided, some lower courts held section 14(e) was violated by defensive measures when the tactic prevented further bidding so that the defensive measure could be seen as "locking" the target shares

---

[6] MacFadden Holdings, Inc. v. J. B. Acquisition Corp., 802 F.2d 62, 71 (2d Cir. 1986), *relying on* Data Probe Acquisitions Corp. v. Datatab, Inc., 722 F.2d 1, 5 (2d Cir. 1983), *cert. denied*, 465 U.S. 1052 (1984).

[7] Diamond v. Arend, 649 F. Supp. 408, 415-416 (S.D.N.Y. 1986).

[8] Piper v. Chris-Craft Indus., Inc., 430 U.S. 1 (1977).

[9] *See, e.g.*, Seaboard World Airlines, Inc. v. Tiger Int'l, 600 F.2d 355 (2d Cir. 1979) (recognizing the 14(e) remedy but finding no substantive violation).

[10] *See, e.g.*, Humana, Inc. v. American Medicorp., Inc., 445 F. Supp. 613 (S.D.N.Y. 1977). *Cf.* Rondeau v. Mosinee Paper Corp., 422 U.S. 49 (1975).

[11] 472 U.S. 1 (1985).

[12] 472 U.S. at 12.

into a price established by the defensive maneuver.[13] This controversially expansive holding had the potential of opening new frontiers for the federal regulation of tender offers, although it represented a minority view.[14] The *Schreiber* decision[15] made it clear that defensive tactics cannot violate section 14(e), even if manipulative, unless accompanied by a material mistatement or omission.

Unless the Court retrenches from its sweeping conclusion in *Schreiber,* it would appear that any rules promulgated under section 14(e) are at risk to the extent that they go beyond disclosure. This could result in a significant cutback on Regulation 14E and also would be a most questionable narrowing of the scope of the section. The statute expressly talks in terms of "manipulative" in addition to "fraudulent and deceptive conduct," and the Supreme Court cannot properly excise that term from the statute.

§24.05.01   Regulation 14E

The SEC has promulgated a series of rules under section 14(e), which appear as Rule 14E. Collectively they regulate certain conduct within tender offers regardless of whether the target corporation is subject to the reporting provisions of the Securities Exchange Act. Rule 14e-1[16] requires that any person making a tender offer must hold the offer open for at least twenty business days from the date on which it is first published. The *Schreiber* decision, discussed above, requires deception as an element of any section 14(e) violation. To the extent that the reasoning carries over to the SEC rule-making power, that decision casts a cloud over the validity of Rule 14e-1 because the rule regulates the duration of the offer and thus goes beyond mandating full disclosure.[17] It can, of course, be argued that the SEC's power to mandate a period during which the tender offer must remain open is justified because it gives investors and the market the time necessary to digest the information mandated by the Williams Act's affirmative disclosure requirements.[18]

Rule 14e-1(b) further provides that the tender offeror may not increase or decrease the terms of the offer, the type of consideration, or the dealer's soliciting fee unless the tender offer remains open for at least ten business days from the publication of the notice of such increase.[19] It also declares it to be an unlawful

---

[13] Mobil Corp. v. Marathon Oil Co., 669 F.2d 366 (6th Cir. 1981). *See, e.g.,* Elliot J. Weiss, Defensive Responses to Tender Offers and the Williams Act's Prohibition Against Manipulation, 35 Vand. L. Rev. 1087 (1982).

[14] *See, e.g.,* Radol v. Thomas, 772 F.2d 244 (6th Cir. 1985), *cert. denied,* 477 U.S. 903 (1986).

[15] *See supra* text at note 11.

[16] 17 C.F.R. §240.14e1(a) (2002).

[17] *But see* Polaroid Corp. v. Disney, 862 F.2d 987 (3d Cir. 1988), which upheld the SEC's "all-holders rule" (Rule 14d-10, 17 C.F.R. §240.14d-10 (2001)), reasoning that requiring the offer be made to all shareholders furthers the disclosure goals of the Williams Act.

[18] *Cf.* Polaroid Corp. v. Disney, 862 F.2d 987 (3d Cir. 1988).

[19] 17 C.F.R. §240.14e-1(b) (2002). *See also* 17 C.F.R. §240.13e-4(f)(1)(ii) (2002) (imposing same requirement for tender offers by issuers).

C. Obtaining Compliance and Antifraud and Director Turnover Provisions

practice for a tender offeror to fail to pay the consideration offered or to return the securities tendered promptly after either the withdrawal or termination of the tender offer.[20] Rule 14e-1(d)[21] makes it unlawful to extend the length of the tender offer without issuing a notice of such extension by press release or other public announcement, and the notice must give sufficient detail of the time period of the tender offer and its extension.

Whenever a tender offer is made for a target company's shares, the target company has ten business days from the first date on which the tender offer is published to respond.[22] Rule 14e-2[23] requires that the target company's management make one of the following responses within the ten-day period: (1) a recommendation of acceptance or rejection of the tender offer; (2) an expression of no opinion with a decision to remain neutral toward the offer; or (3) a statement that it is not able to take a position with respect to bidder's offer. The Rule 14e-2 statement must also include all reasons for the position taken, or the stance of neutrality, as well as any explanation of the inability to take a position. In setting forth its reasons, the target company's management is, of course, subject to all of the rules concerning materiality as well as to potential civil and criminal liabilities for material misstatements.

Rule 14e-3[24] prohibits insider trading during a tender offer.[25] The Rule 14e-3 prohibitions expressly apply not only to insiders of the target company but also to anyone else possessing nonpublic information of a pending tender offer. In 1997, the Supreme Court upheld the validity of Rule 14e-3 but left undecided the question of whether the SEC's rule-making authority is broader under section 14(e) than it is under section 10(b).[26]

An important anti-manipulation rule is Rule 14e-5 which prohibits a tender offeror from purchasing the target securities other than through the tender offer once the offer has commenced and until it is completed.[27] It has been held that violations of Rule 10b-13 (Rule 14e-5's predecessor) supported a private damage action,[28] but not all courts seem to agree.[29]

Rule 14e-4 prohibits short tendering[30]—the practice of tendering or guaranteeing securities not owned by the person making the tender or guarantee.[31]

[20] 17 C.F.R. §240.14e-1(c) (2002).
[21] 17 C.F.R. §240.14e-1(d) (2002).
[22] 17 C.F.R. §240.14e-2 (2002).
[23] *Id.*
[24] 17 C.F.R. §240.14e-3 (2001).
[25] *See supra* §12.09 for a discussion of insider trading generally.
[26] United States v. O'Hagan, 521 U.S. 642 (1997).
[27] 17 C.F.R. §240.14e-5 (2002).
[28] City Nat'l Bank v. American Commw. Fin. Corp., 801 F.2d 714 (4th Cir. 1986), *cert. denied,* 479 U.S. 1091 (1987).
[29] *E.g.,* Beaumont v. American Can Co., 797 F.2d 79 (2d Cir. 1986).
[30] 17 C.F.R. §240.14e-4 (2001).
[31] *See* Merrill Lynch, Pierce, Fenner & Smith, Inc. v. Bobker, 636 F. Supp. 444 (S.D.N.Y. 1986), *rev'd,* 808 F.2d 930 (2d Cir. 1986) (denying proration to shareholder who sold short while tendering).

§24.06   Director Turnover and Williams Act—
Section 14(f)

As is the case with any transfer of corporate control, tender offers will frequently result in a shift in corporate management.[1] Accordingly, it is not uncommon to find tender offers containing agreements relating to management turnover and the election of new directors. These control transfers can raise problems under state law relating to invalid control premiums and other breaches of fiduciary duty.[2] The Williams Act adds certain disclosure obligations when the bidder has arranged for at least a majority of the directorships to change. Under section 14(f) of the Exchange Act,[3] when in connection with a tender offer for equity securities subject to the Act's reporting requirements of section 14(d)(1) or a purchase of shares subject to section 13(d)(1) agreements arise concerning the designation of new directors who will be at least a majority of the target's board of directors and such change will occur otherwise than through a formal vote at a meeting of securities holders, extensive disclosure is required. Essentially, the information that must be disclosed is of a scale equal to that required in connection with a stockholders' meeting at which directors will be elected.[4] Contemplated management turnover, including any arrangement regarding the make-up of the majority of directors, also must be disclosed.[5] Thus, for example, where a stock purchase agreement permits the purchaser to designate a majority of the issuer's directors, section 14(f)'s disclosure obligation is triggered.[6] When the agreed upon shift in control occurs, a second filing obligation arises.[7]

§24.07   Remedies for Violations of Sections 13(d),
13(e), and 14(d)

Most of the litigation concerning the question of the existence of implied private rights of action under the Williams Act has arisen in the context of section 14(e)'s general antifraud proscriptions.[1] The courts recognize the existence of at least a limited implied remedy under section 14(e).[2] Since sections 13(d), 13(e), and 14(d) all apply to issuers subject to the Securities Exchange Act's registration and

---

§24.06   [1] *See* Thomas L. Hazen, Transfers of Corporate Control and Duties of Controlling Shareholders—Common Law, Tender Offers, Investment Companies and a Proposal for Reform, 125 U. Pa. L. Rev. 1023 (1977).

[2] This subject is discussed in Chapter 12.

[3] 15 U.S.C. §78n(f) (1997).

[4] Rule 14f-1 provides for specific disclosures in the event there is going to be a change in the majority of directors otherwise than at a shareholder meeting, in a transaction subject to either section 13(d) or section 14(d). 17 C.F.R. §240.14(f)-1 (2001).

[5] 15 U.S.C. §78n(f) (1997). *See* 17 C.F.R. §240.14f-1 (2001).

[6] Drobbin v. Nicolet Instrument Corp., 631 F. Supp. 860 (S.D.N.Y. 1986).

[7] *Id.*

§24.07   [1] 15 U.S.C. §78n(e) (1997). *See* §24.05.

[2] *See* §24.05.

reporting requirements[3] and involve mandatory filings with the Commission, there are a number of other remedies for material misstatements or omissions in these filings.

In *Rondeau v. Mosinee Paper Corporation*,[4] the defendant delayed filing his Schedule 13D more than four months after he acquired more than 5 percent of Mosinee Paper Corporation's stock. The Supreme Court reversed the Seventh Circuit's grant of an injunction, holding that such relief requires proof that the target company's shareholders have been irreparably harmed by the violation. The meaning of "irreparable harm" is an interesting question under the Williams Act, whose provisions ostensibly are designed to provide shareholders and investors sufficient information to enable them to make intelligent decisions when faced with a tender offer and at the same time not to tip the balance in favor of incumbent management in the battle for control.[5] Moreover, fashioning any restrospective, corrective equitable relief must be timed so as not to occur too late or it is like trying to unscramble the eggs.[6] At the same time, premature interference has the natural effect of altering the economic bargaining positions of the contestants, and these effects may well be irreversible.

Because time is of the essence in takeover battles, frequently the relief sought in an action under 13(d)(1), 13(e), or 14(d)(1) is for preliminary injunctive relief. Plaintiffs in such actions bear an especially high burden in light of the dual requirement that they prove both a substantial likelihood of success on the merits and irreparable injury if the preliminary injunction is not issued. Failure to meet either of these requirements will result in a denial of preliminary relief.[7] However, serious violations will warrant preliminary relief, because waiting until a full trial on the merits usually means that the challenged transaction will take place years before the case is resolved. As one court has put it, "[e]ffectively the only relief available to an issuer, under the prevailing view, is an order requiring the 5 percent owner to file a corrected 13D and perhaps enjoining further acquisitions pending the corrections."[8]

With regard to section 13(e) in general, it has been held a private remedy exists because the issuer's security holders constitute a class for whose special benefit the legislation was enacted.[9] The Sixth Circuit has recognized a private remedy for violation of section 13(e)'s going-private provisions that allegedly resulted in the loss of the plaintiff's state law appraisal remedy due to material misstatements or omissions.[10]

---

[3] 15 U.S.C. §§78*l*, 78n(a) (1997). *See* §27.12.

[4] 422 U.S. 49 (1975).

[5] *See* S. Rep. No. 550, 90th Cong., 1st Sess. 2-3 (1967); H.R. Rep. No. 1711, 90th Cong., 2d Sess. 4 (1968).

[6] Electronic Specialty Co. v. International Controls Corp., 409 F.2d 937, 947 (2d Cir. 1969).

[7] *See, e.g.,* Gelco Corp. v. Coniston Partners, 811 F.2d 414 (8th Cir. 1987) (once plaintiff fails to prove irreparable injury, there is no need to consider merits before denying preliminary injunction).

[8] Hubco, Inc. v. Rappaport, 628 F. Supp. 345, 354 (D.N.J. 1985).

[9] Howing Co. v. Nationwide Corp., 826 F.2d 1470 (6th Cir. 1987), *cert. denied,* 486 U.S. 1059 (1988) (implied private damage action); Fisher v. Plessey Co., 559 F. Supp. 442 (S.D.N.Y. 1983).

[10] Howing Co. v. Nationwide Corp., 972 F.2d 700 (6th Cir. 1992), *cert. denied,* 507 U.S. 1004 (1993) (decided under section 13(e)'s going-private rules).

D. STATE ANTI-TAKEOVER STATUTES

§24.08   State Regulation of Tender Offers

Approximately two-thirds of the states have statutes that regulate tender offers. In less than twenty years, the states have gone through three generations of takeover statutes.[1] Prior to the adoption of the Williams Act[2] in 1968, there was virtually no specialized regulation of tender offers at either the federal or state level. In most instances, the transparent intent behind state tender offer acts is to protect incumbent management and to preserve the payrolls of local companies that are potential takeover candidates. The statutes' effectiveness arise because they impose additional and substantial impediments to a takeover, thus inhibiting or at least slowing any transaction.[3]

Whereas the Williams Act can be seen as maintaining a level playing field between the bidder and the target corporation's shareholders, most state anti-takeover acts make no pretense of such evenhandedness. Hence they are collectively condemned under the rubric, "anti-takeover statutes." The discussion that follows is designed to present an overview of similarities within the three distinct types of state anti-takeover statutes. One must be mindful, however, that while general observations about broad categories of anti-takeover statutes are possible, important, albeit sometimes subtle, distinctions exist among the states in their implementation of such a common approach. In the words of one commentator, "State takeover acts are similar to snowflakes—if you think you have found identical ones, you are probably not looking closely enough."[4]

The various state statutes employ a wide range of jurisdictional provisions. However, because the Supreme Court declared unconstitutional an Illinois anti-takeover statute to the extent it extended its protection extraterritorially to target shareholders living outside of Illinois, the majority of the state acts base jurisdiction on the target company's incorporation within the state, or on the location within the state of the target company's principal place of business and/or substantial target company assets. Another important variation among the states is how they define "tender offer." The state statutes generally include precise but diverse statutory definitions, including the number of solicited target company shareholders required before the act applies.[5] For example, many states define a qualifying transaction in terms of the number of persons solicited. Some of the state statutes raise questions analogous to those raised under the Williams Act. For

---

§24.08   [1] *See* Thomas Lee Hazen, State Anti-Takeover Legislation: The Second and Third Generations, 23 Wake Forest L. Rev. 77 (1988).

[2] Pub. L. No. 90-439, 82 Stat. 454 (1968) (codified at 15 U.S.C. §§78*l*(i), 78m(d)-78m(e), 78n(d)-78n(f)) (1997). *See* §24.01.

[3] The most prominent example was the imposition of waiting periods between the filing and effective date of the tender offer. *See, e.g.,* Del. Code Ann. tit. 8, §203(a) (2001).

[4] Symposium, State Regulation of Tender Offers, 7 J. Corp. Law 603 (1982) (footnote omitted).

[5] *See, e.g.,* N.H. Rev. Stat. Ann. §421-A:2(VI)(a) (1998) ("'Takeover bid' does not include: (3) Any . . . offer to acquire an equity security, or the acquisition of such equity security pursuant to such offer . . . from not more than 25 persons . . .").

D. State Anti-Takeover Statutes

example, one state court has held that a series of open-market purchases does not constitute a tender offer.[6]

State anti-takeover laws have evolved through successive generations. Today, only the second and third generation statutes have survived constitutional challenges.

First Generation Anti-Takeover Statutes. Following the pattern of the state blue sky laws, many of the first generation anti-takeover statutes went beyond the disclosure philosophy of the Williams Act by giving the state administrator the power to review the merits of the tender offer's terms[7] or the adequacy of the bidder's disclosures.[8] The administrator was frequently empowered to hold hearings, which could be initiated by the administrator,[9] by the target company,[10] or by a certain percentage of the target company's shareholders.[11] Moreover, first generation statutes frequently imposed a waiting period of ten,[12] twenty,[13] or thirty days[14] between the filing of the tender offer and the date on which it was to become effective. After the SEC in 1979 adopted Rule 14d-2(b),[15] which establishes that a tender offer commences on publication of its terms, and because many substantive Williams Act regulations are then triggered by such commencement,[16] a conflict between state and federal law arose such that the SEC believed all such waiting periods were preempted.[17]

In *Edgar v. MITE Corporation,*[18] the Supreme Court declared the Illinois anti-takeover statute unconstitutional. The Illinois statute imposed a waiting period and provided for a hearing on the tender offer's terms. The court's majority believed the Illinois law violated the Commerce Clause because of the burdens it placed on interstate commerce in light of the state's interest in regulation:[19]

---

[6] Sheffield v. Consolidated Foods Corp., 276 S.E.2d 422 (N.C. 1981).

[7] *See* Kennecott Corp. v. Smith, 507 F. Supp. 1206 (D.N.J. 1981) (New Jersey takeover law frustrates the purpose of the Williams Act by substituting bureau chief's view of the offer for the informed judgment of shareholders).

[8] *E.g.,* La. Rev. Stat. §51:1501(E) (West 1987) (repealed); 70 Pa. Cons. Stat. §74(d) (Supp. 1993) (repealed).

[9] *E.g.,* Mo. Ann. Stat. §409.521 (West 2001).

[10] *E.g.,* 70 Pa. Cons. Stat. §74(d) (Supp. 1993) (repealed).

[11] *E.g.,* Conn. Gen. Stat. Ann. §366-44(a) (West 1996) (owners of "aggregate ten percent of the outstanding equity securities of the class involved in the tender offer" may petition the commissioner to schedule a hearing).

[12] *E.g.,* Id.

[13] *E.g.,* Del. Code Ann. tit. 8, §203(a)(1) (1983) (repealed); 70 Pa. Cons. Stat. §74(a) (Supp. 1993) (repealed).

[14] *E.g.,* N.C. Gen. Stat. §78B-4(a) (1985) (repealed).

[15] 17 C.F.R. §240.14d-2(b) (2001).

[16] *See* §§24.03, 24.04.

[17] *See* Sec. Act Rel. No. 6158 (SEC Nov. 29, 1979).

[18] 457 U.S. 624 (1982).

[19] The Illinois statute required the bidder to notify the secretary of state 20 business days before commencing its tender offer, and the secretary of state was empowered to convene a hearing in which case the tender offer could not proceed until the hearing's completion.

> While protecting local investors is plainly a legitimate state objective, the State has no legitimate interest in protecting nonresident shareholders. Insofar as the Illinois law burdens out-of-state transactions, there is nothing to be weighed in the balance to sustain the law.[20]

A plurality of the justices found the Illinois law also violated the Supremacy Clause in conflicting with the desire for evenhandedness embodied in the Williams Act. *Edgar v. MITE Corporation* was the death knell for first generation statutes.

Second Generation Anti-Takeover Statutes. Relying on some helpful language in *Edgar v. MITE Corporation*,[21] a number of states enacted second generation takeover statutes, which were designed to overcome the constitutional infirmities of the Illinois statute that was struck down in *MITE*. The basic thrust of many of these second generation statutes is to regulate tender offers through state law rules relating to corporate governance rather than through state securities laws and administrative regulations. That is, adhering to the traditional choice-of-law rule that questions regarding the internal affairs of a corporation are to be resolved according to the state of the company's incorporation, the second generation anti-takeover statutes introduce many corporate law requirements that operate to the serious disadvantage of the bidder for control. Ohio was the first state to adopt second generation legislation.[22] Many other states have since enacted second generation statutes.

A few second generation statutes are disclosure-oriented and are easily analogous to the states' historical administration of their blue sky laws.[23]

The most common and effective form of second generation anti-takeover statute is the "control share acquisition" statute. For example, the Ohio statute, which governs all forms of takeovers and is not limited to tender offers, applies to Ohio corporations having fifty or more shareholders and a principal place of business, principal offices, or substantial assets within the state.[24] The Ohio act then classifies takeover transactions by the percentage of shares owned by the acquiring person, with each control zone triggering the act's substantive requirements.[25] Acquiring persons must deliver to the target company a disclosure statement describing the proposed acquisition. The target company's board then has ten days to call a special shareholders' meeting, which must take place within fifty days. At that meeting the transaction requires approval of a majority of the disinterested shares not owned or controlled by the acquiring person or any affiliate.

In contrast to the "control share acquisition" type of statute is the "fair price" statute. For example, Maryland takes a more structural approach in regulating

---

[20] 457 U.S. at 644.

[21] 457 U.S. 624 (1982).

[22] Ohio Rev. Code Ann. §1701.832 (Baldwin 1986) (amended 1993).

[23] *See* Cardiff Acquisitions, Inc. v. Hatch, 751 F.2d 906 (8th Cir. 1984), *appeal after remand*, 751 F.2d 917 (8th Cir. 1984).

[24] Ohio Rev. Code Ann. §1701.831 (Baldwin Supp. 1993).

[25] For example, the Pennsylvania statute sets three control thresholds: 20 percent, 33⅓ percent, and 50 percent. 15 Pa. Cons. Stats. Ann. §2562 (West 1995 & Supp. 2002).

D. State Anti-Takeover Statutes

share acquisitions. The Maryland statute requires any takeover be approved by at least eighty percent of the shares and two-thirds of the disinterested shares unless all shareholders receive the best price paid by the acquiring person within a five-year period.[26] The best-price approach, patterned after fair price charter amendments adopted by many corporations, is designed to fend off two-tiered offers. The Maryland Act excludes "friendly" offers from its coverage. A number of states have adopted fair-price statutes, some of which vary the terms of the Maryland act. Another means by which fair price is determined is by the statute providing target shareholders an appraisal remedy in control acquisition transactions.[27]

Another form of statute within the second generation is the "constituency" or "stakeholder" statute,[28] which permits management to consider interests other than those of the shareholders in making decisions.[29] These statutes generally make it clear that although management may consider other interests, it does not have to. Still another approach taken in some of the second generation statutes is to give dissenters' rights to a wide variety of control transactions.

The Supreme Court in *CTS Corporation v. Dynamics Corporation of America*[30] upheld the constitutionality of Indiana's control share statute. Under the Indiana statute, voting rights are denied to shares held by anyone whose ownership exceeded twenty percent of the outstanding voting shares unless the "independent" target shareholders at a meeting to occur within fifty days of the threshold being crossed vote to grant voting rights to those shares. The bidder in *CTS Corporation* reasoned that the Indiana statute delayed the consummation of tender offers by fifty days, the length of time it needed to assure itself that it had indeed acquired voting control. Such delay, it was argued, conflicted with the Williams Act, which contemplates that tender offers need be of no greater duration than twenty business days. In an opinion whose language appears more often to support the bidder's than the target's position,[31] the Supreme Court swept the bidder's concerns aside. It first reasoned that the bidder was not disadvantaged because it could make its offer to purchase the shares conditional on later shareholder approval. Next, the Court advised that even if disadvantaged by a fifty-day delay, this delay was not unreasonable. Clearly a factor in the Court's reasoning is the spectre of having to cast aside the rich history of the "internal affairs" doctrine, which so clearly supports the state of a corporation's incorporation regulating its substantive affairs.[32]

---

[26] Md. Code Ann., Corps. & Assns. §§3-602, 3-603 (1999 & Supp. 2001).

[27] *E.g.*, 15 Pa. Cons. Stat. Ann. §§2545-2547 (West 1995).

[28] *E.g.*, Ind. Code Ann. §23-1-35-1(d) (Michie 1999 & Supp. 2002).

[29] *See* 21 Sec. Reg. & L. Rep. (BNA) 1501 (Oct. 6, 1989).

[30] 481 U.S. 69 (1987).

[31] *See generally* Donald C. Langevoort, The Supreme Court and the Politics of Corporate Takeovers: A Comment on *CTS Corp. v. Dynamics Corp. of America*, 101 Harv. L. Rev. 96 (1987).

[32] The Indiana statute applied to target corporations that (1) were incorporated in Indiana and (2) had their principal place of business or substantial assets within Indiana and a certain number of shareholders in Indiana. The latter two-point bases were not emphasized by the court, and logic would suggest that being incorporated within the state justifies applying its anti-takeover provisions.

Third Generation Anti-Takeover Statutes. Finding few limits in *CTS Corporation v. Dynamics Corporation of America,*[33] states have spawned a third generation of anti-takeover provisions even more draconian than their predecessors. A version of the third generation takeover statutes is modeled on the New York "freeze" statute,[34] also known as a business-combination statute. The idea behind such statutes is to delay any transaction that would complete the second step of a two-step acquisition where the first step was not agreed to by target company's management. Thus, for example, the New York statute prohibits a merger or other business acquisition within five years of the control acquisition date unless the transaction was approved by the target company's directors *prior* to the control acquisition date. Other states have followed the New York lead, including Delaware, which has a three-year-freeze statute.[35] The Delaware statute withstood early challenges to its constitutionality,[36] and the constitutionality of the Wisconsin freeze statute was upheld by the Seventh Circuit.[37] Statutes are still likely to fall victim of the Commerce Clause when they treat foreign bidders more harshly than local bidders.[38]

The varieties of third generation statutes continue to proliferate. In the spring of 1990, Pennsylvania adopted the most ambitious anti-takeover statute to date. In addition to adopting a control share statute, the Pennsylvania legislature enacted a provision requiring any person owning more than twenty percent of a company's voting shares to disgorge any profit realized within an eighteen month period.[39] The impact of this provision is to discourage suitors by locking them in as shareholders in the event that their takeover attempt is unsuccessful. Pennsylvania has taken yet another approach by expressly sanctioning use of poison pills as a defensive measure.[40] Also in 1990, Massachusetts enacted a statute that mandates dividing the directors into groups and staggering the election of directors.[41] A corporation's board by a majority vote may choose to opt out of the law, should the directors decide to have all directors elected annually. Shareholders can opt out of staggered elections only on a two-thirds vote.

---

[33] 481 U.S. 69 (1987).

[34] N.Y. Bus. Corp. Law §912 (McKinney Supp. 2002).

[35] Del. Code Ann. tit. 8, §203 (2001).

[36] *See* BNS, Inc. v. Koppers Co., 683 F. Supp. 458 (D. Del. 1988).

[37] Amanda Acquisition Corp. v. Universal Foods Corp., 877 F.2d 496 (7th Cir.), *cert. denied,* 493 U.S. 955 (1989).

[38] Campeau Corp. v. Federated Dept. Stores, 679 F. Supp. 735 (S.D. Ohio 1988).

[39] 15 Pa. Cons. Stat. Ann. §§2571-2576 (West 1999).

[40] *See* Pennsylvania Enacts Law Against Hostile Takeovers, 20 Sec. Reg. & L. Rep. (BNA) 502 (April 1, 1988).

[41] Mass. Gen. Laws. Ann. ch. 149, §184 (Law. Co-op. Supp. 1994).

CHAPTER 25

Amendments to the Corporate Charter

§25.01   Power to Authorize Fundamental Changes

Corporation statutes vest the management of corporate business in the board of directors. The board's authority extends to the making of contracts of any kind, incurring indebtedness, and authorizing any other act, unless otherwise limited by the articles of incorporation or by a provision in the state corporation statute.[1] Any statutory limitation on the board of directors' authority to carry out corporate business arises when the transaction is of a type for which the statute requires shareholder approval to be obtained. Shareholder approval is so required in those instances where the transaction poses a fundamental change in the corporation or the stockholders' economic or voting rights.[2] Fundamental corporate transactions are those characterized by their extraordinary nature as well as by the unusual changes they bring either to the corporate business or to the rights of its shareholders. It is because of their effects on the business and the shareholders that the

---

§25.01   [1] *See* Cal. Corp. Code §300 (West 1990); Model Business Corp. Act §§8.01, 8.02, 8.11, 8.30 (1984) (hereinafter MBCA); Model Business Corp. Act §35 (1969) (hereinafter Former MBCA). *See* §9.01.

[2] Under this traditional pattern of corporate governance, no direct power can be exercised by the shareholders unless by unanimous consent. *See* Manson v. Curtis, 119 N.E. 559 (N.Y. 1918); Continental Sec. Co. v. Belmont, 99 N.E. 138, 141 (N.Y. 1912).

authority to undertake such transactions is not commended solely to the discretion of the board of directors, but must be authorized by some specified vote or written consent of the shareholders.

While we may doubt that stockholders will diligently review and reflect on the significance of the transaction for which their approval is sought before they vote, there is no reason to believe fundamental transactions involve skills that are alien to the stockholder investor such that their involvement is harmful. Thus the concurrent approval of the shareholders is required to authorize a new class of stock or to increase the authorized number of shares of an existing class of stock;[3] to reduce the legal capital;[4] to convey, transfer, or lease all or substantially all the property of the corporation;[5] to amend the articles of incorporation;[6] to authorize a merger or consolidation with another corporation;[7] to dissolve the corporation voluntarily;[8] or to renew or extend the period of corporation's existence.[9] This chapter examines the power of the corporation as well as the procedures to amend the articles of incorporation.

To understand the formal procedures that accompany the process of amending the articles of incorporation invites a reconsideration of the earlier discussion that a corporation is but a "nexus of contracts."[10] This metaphor describes the unique contractual relationship that exists among the shareholders, the corporation, and the state of incorporation. At the heart of this contract are the corporation's articles of incorporation as well as the statute under which it is incorporated. By conceptualizing the shareholders' relationship with their corporation as contractual, with the terms of that contract set forth in both its articles of incorporation and the local corporate statute, a certain rigidity in that relationship appears. Thus, absent some authority in either the articles of incorporation or the laws of the governing state, an amendment of the articles of incorporation would appear to require the consent of all shareholders. This statement merely reflects the basic principle of contract law that the terms of any contract cannot be changed except by mutual consent.[11] Surely, in a long-term business relationship and within a dynamic commercial setting, corporate activity and shareholder interests cannot long survive if change in the rights of owners requires the approval of each affected owner. At the same time, one must have a healthy regard for the vulnerability of minority stockholders if their rights can

---

[3] *See* Chicago City Ry. v. Allerton, 85 U.S. (18 Wall.) 233 (1874); Hill v. Small, 183 S.E.2d 752 (Ga. 1971); but *cf.* 805 ILCS §5/10.15 (Smith-Hurd 1993) (directors may amend to split shares); MBCA §10.05(4) (1999).

[4] *E.g.,* W. Va. Code Ann. §31-1-115 (Michie 2001); Former MBCA §69 (1969) (the 1984 MBCA does not carry forward the approach in the former MBCA).

[5] *E.g.,* MBCA §12.02 (1984); Former MBCA §79 (1969).

[6] *E.g.,* Cal. Corp. Code §900 (West 1990); Del. Code Ann. tit. 8, §242 (2001).

[7] *E.g.,* MBCA §11.04 (1999); Former MBCA §73 (1969).

[8] *E.g.,* MBCA §14.02 (1984). Former MBCA §§83, 84 (1969).

[9] *E.g.,* Cal. Corp. Code §909 (West 1990); Ky. Rev. Stat. §217B.10-020(1) (Baldwin 1989); MBCA §10.05(l) (1999); Former MBCA §58(b) (1969). *See* Holekamp v. Holekamp Lumber Co., 340 S.W.2d 678 (Mo. 1960), *appeal dismissed,* 366 U.S. 715 (1961).

[10] *See* §§2.04, 2.05.

[11] *E.g.,* Allen v. Royale "16", Inc., 449 So. 2d 1365 (La. Ct. App. 1984) (any change in corporate charter must conform to corporation law).

be changed at the will of the majority. Hence, as statutes and doctrine have over the years become increasingly more permissive of amendments that alter the rights of shareholders on the approval of a majority of the shares, a question of growing importance is what equitable limitations or other protections should exist to shield the minority stockholders from unfair or coercive amendments of their rights, privileges, or preferences?

§25.02   Constitutional Limitations — The Dartmouth College Case

The Constitution declares that "[n]o State shall . . . pass any . . . Law impairing the Obligation of Contracts. . . ."[1] When the legislature of a state grants a charter to a private corporation, whether it be of a business or a charitable nature, the charter embodies a contract between the state and the corporation and later its shareholders. The leading case on the power of the state to authorize changes in the shareholders' contract with the corporation was decided by the United States Supreme Court in 1819 and is known as the *Dartmouth College* case.[2] Dartmouth College, a charitable corporation, had been created by a charter granted in 1769 by the governor of the colony acting in the name of King George III. The charter provided that the purpose of the institution was the instruction of Indian, English, and other youths. Management and control of the institution were entrusted to a self-perpetuating board of 12 trustees and their successors. In 1816, the New Hampshire legislature passed three special acts amending this charter. The newly enacted legislation changed the name of the corporation to Trustees of Dartmouth University and rearranged the control and administration of its affairs by increasing the number of trustees to 21 and created a board, to be appointed by the governor, of 25 overseers with power superior to the trustees.

The corporation brought an action attacking the charter amendments as void under the constitutional prohibition against impairment of the obligation of contracts. The state court upheld the legislation on the ground that the corporation was a public institution subject to the control of the legislature. The state court reasoned that the charter was not a contract within the meaning of the Constitution. The case was argued before the Supreme Court of the United States by Daniel Webster for the plaintiffs in error and William Wirt for the defendant in error. The Supreme Court reversed. The Court held that the corporation was a private entity founded and endowed by private means, that corporate charter was a contract within the meaning of the Constitution, and that the acts of the New Hampshire legislature impaired the contract and were void.

The *Dartmouth College* case clearly recognizes that the articles of incorporation and the corporation laws existing at the time of incorporation can therefore be regarded as a contract among the stockholders. Indeed, the reasoning of *Dartmouth College* captures nicely the threefold contract that is the embodiment of the

§25.02   [1] U.S. Const. art. I, §10, cl. 1.
[2] Trustees of Dartmouth College v. Woodward, 17 U.S. (4 Wheat) 518 (1819).

rights the shareholders hold in the corporation. The links in contract are: (1) between the state and the corporation, (2) between the corporation and the shareholders or members, and (3) among the shareholders themselves.[3]

§25.03   The Reservation of Power to Amend the Corporate Statute

In the *Dartmouth College* case, discussed in the previous section, Mr. Justice Story suggested that in granting a charter the state might reserve the power to amend or repeal the grant and thereby avoid the vested-rights problem. Since that decision, such statutory reservation has become universal.[1] Some states have a constitutional provision reserving such power,[2] but a statute or constitutional provision reserving the power to amend or repeal cannot amend or repeal the charter of a corporation that was created before the reservation[3] unless the corporation expressly or impliedly submits to it.[4] In states where existing corporations are subject to the reserved power to amend, a new statute or even a comprehensive new corporation code may apply to all corporations then existing as well as to those formed thereafter.[5]

The legislature's reserved power enters into and forms part of the charter contract of corporations created after its enactment. The reservation permits rearranging relative rights by amendment of the contract between the corporation and its shareholders or members[6] as well as changing the contract between the corporation and the state. The reserved power thus extends beyond mandatory changes made by amendment of the corporation laws. It also covers changes authorized by a specified majority of the shareholders, even if a particular class of shares suffers materially.[7]

The power reserved to the legislature to alter or amend the laws governing existing corporations is not unlimited.[8] Under the due process and contract clauses of state and federal constitutions, the power does not extend to contracts and property *acquired* under the charter; it extends only to rights that are governed by the charter. For example, the reserve clause may validly be relied on to authorize the elimination of dividends that are in arrears but not to authorize cancellation of dividends that have been declared but not paid. The reservation does

---

[3] *See* Staar Surgical Co. v. Waggoner, 588 A.2d 1130, 136 (Del. Ch. 1991) ("[A] corporate charter is both a contract between the State and the corporation, and the corporation and its shareholders. . . . The charter is also a contract among the shareholders themselves.").

§25.03   [1] *E.g.,* Cal. Corp. Code §900(a) (West 1990); Del. Code Ann. tit. 8, §394 (2001); MBCA §10.01(b) (1999); Former MBCA §58, 149 (1969).

[2] *E.g.,* N.Y. Const. art. 10, §1.

[3] Dodge v. Woolsey, 59 U.S. (18 How.) 331 (1855).

[4] *See* Golconda Mining Corp. v. Hecla Mining Co., 494 P.2d 1365 (1972).

[5] Barnett v. D. O. Martin Co., 11 S.E.2d 210 (Ga. 1940); Seattle Trust & Sav. Bank v. McCarthy, 617 P.2d 1023 (Wash. 1980).

[6] Adair v. Orrell's Mut. Burial Ass'n, 201 S.E.2d 905 (1974).

[7] Looker v. Maynard, 179 U.S. 46 (1900); Goldman v. Postal Tel., Inc., 52 F. Supp. 763 (D. Del. 1943).

[8] *See* Phillips Petroleum Co. v. Jenkins, 297 U.S. 629 (1936).

not authorize legislation depriving a corporation, its shareholders or its creditors of property rights without due process of law.[9]

§25.04   The Amendment Process

In most instances the amendment of the articles of incorporation requires the approval of both the board of directors and the shareholders entitled to vote. Many states follow the lead of the former Model Business Corporation Act and the current Model Business Corporation Act to permit certain types of amendments solely on the authority of the board of directors.[1] In most instances such authorization is confined to certain "housekeeping" changes, such as deleting the names or addresses of the initial directors, substituting the full expression "corporation" or "incorporated" for the abbreviated version, or vice versa, or to deleting the name or address of the initial registered agent. Some substantive changes are also authorized to be made solely on the authority of the board of directors, such as the power to extend the duration of the corporation if the corporation was formed at a time when a limited duration was required by law,[2] to change the par value of a class or series of shares,[3] or to create a series of shares within an authorized class.[4] In Illinois, a majority vote of the board of directors can authorize a stock split, provided that no class or series of shares is adversely affected.[5]

Subject to appropriate approval by the board of directors and the shareholders entitled to vote, all states expressly authorize amendments to the articles of incorporation if the provisions of the amendment could lawfully be contained in the original articles at the time the amendment is made.[6] However, the extent of the authority to amend the articles of incorporation depends on the wording of the governing provision in the corporation statutes. The most common state statutory approach is to provide a laundry list of amendments that are permissible;[7] other states provide a broad grant of power to amend the articles of incorporation.[8] Regardless of which statutory approach is taken, the power of amendment

---

[9] Superior Water, Light & Power Co. v. City of Superior, 263 U.S. 125, 137 (1923).

§25.04   [1] *See, e.g.,* Ga. Code Ann. §14-2-1002 (1994); Ind. Stat. Ann. §23-1-38-2 (Michie 1999); N.Y. Bus. Corp. Law §803(b) (McKinney 1986); N.C. Gen. Stat. §55-10-02 (2001); Wis. Stat. Ann. §180.1002 (West 2002); MBCA §§10.02, 10.03, & 10.05 (1999); Former MBCA §59(a) (1969).

[2] *See* MBCA §10.05(1) (1999).

[3] *See* Fla. Stat. Ann. §607.1002 (West 2001).

[4] *See* Wis. Stat. Ann. §180.1002 (West 2002).

[5] 805 ILCS §5/10.15(d) (West Supp. 2002).

[6] *See, e.g.,* Del. Code Ann. tit. 8, §242(a) (2001).

[7] *See, e.g.,* Del. Code Ann. tit. 8, §242(a) (2001).

[8] The official Comment to the Model Business Corporation Act Section 10.01 explains the permissive nature of the more general enabling language:

> The sole test for the validity of an amendment is whether the provision could lawfully have been included in (or in the case of a deletion, omitted from) the articles of incorporation as of the effective date of the amendment.

in most states generally requires approval by a vote of at least a majority of the shares eligible to vote;[9] a handful of states still require a two-thirds vote of the shareholders.[10]

The Model Business Corporation Act has a somewhat more intricate approach to determining the approval required to amend the articles of incorporation. In states adopting the Model Act's approach, the articles of incorporation are amended pursuant to a bare majority of the votes cast affirmatively or negatively at a stockholders' meeting at which a quorum is present; if the amendment is of the type that gives rise to a class vote the required approval (i.e., a majority of the votes cast provided a quorum of that group of shares is satisfied) of such class of shares must also be obtained.[11] The articles of incorporation may specify a greater quorum or voting requirement for resolutions to amend the articles of incorporation.

State statutes commonly require in specific types of amendments to the articles of incorporation that a class or series of shares is entitled to vote and the approval of a requisite percentage of the shares of that class or series must approve.[12] Such class voting is an important right to a class or series of shares. A class vote affords the possibility for a class affected by the amendment to veto the amendment. This power provides them with important bargaining power in assuring that any amendments of their rights, privileges, and preferences are not simply in the best interest of the corporation but are also in the economic interest of that class of shareholders. Some states have phrased their statutory provisions to grant a class vote only where the amendment would "adversely affect"[13] a class or series of shares,[14] and then proceed to enumerate a list of amendments that are deemed to adversely affect the rights of holders.[15] Delaware is distinctive in the brevity with which its statute proscribes amendments triggering a class vote.[16]

An appraisal remedy, also known as dissenters' rights, is a method an unhappy shareholder may use to mitigate any unfairness that arises in a fundamental change within the corporation. The appraisal remedy provides sharehold-

---

[9] See MBCA §§10.03, 10.05 (1999).

[10] See, e.g., 805 ILCS §5/10.20(c) (West 1993); Mass. Ann. Laws ch. 156B §71 (Law. Co-op. 1996).

[11] The actual means for accomplishing this result is a bit complex. MBCA §10.03(e) (1999) sets forth the requirement for shareholder approval and refers the reader to MBCA §10.04 (1999) to determine whether a class vote is required. The actual approval required, absent a charter provision calling for a greater requirement is the general shareholder voting requirements of MBCA §§7.25 & 7.26 (1999) . See MBCA §10.03 Official Comment (1999).

[12] The Model Business Corporation Act introduces new terminology by using "voting groups" in place of a class or series. See RMBCA §10.04 (1999).

[13] For a case considering whether a class is "adversely affected," see Dalton v. American Inv. Co., 490 A.2d 574 (Del. Ch. 1985) (not adversely affected by amendment switching from redemption by lot to redeeming via market and negotiated purchases 5% each year for 20 years).

[14] See, e.g., Mass. Gen. Laws Ann. ch. 156B, §71 (Law. Co-op. 1996); N.Y. Bus. Corp. Law §804(b) (McKinney 1986).

[15] See Mass. Gen. Laws Ann. ch. 156B §77(a)-(e) (Law. Co-op. 1996).

[16] Delaware provides a class vote only for amendments that (1) increase or decrease the aggregate number of authorized shares of the class, (2) increase or decrease the par value of the shares of the class, or (3) alter or change the powers, preferences, or special rights of the shares of the class. See Del. Code Ann. tit. 8, §242(b)(2) (2001).

ers with a right, subject to certain procedural preconditions, to dissent from certain types of changes and to obtain payment in cash for the fair value of their shares.

The Model Business Corporation Act grants appraisal rights when an amendment to the articles of incorporation with respect to a class or series of shares reduces the number of shares of a class or series owned by a shareholder to a fraction of a share if the corporation has the obligation or right to repurchase the fractional share.[17] As the Official Comment explains:

> The reasons for granting appraisal rights in this situation are similar to those granting such rights in cases of cash-out mergers, as both transactions could compel affected shareholders to accept cash for their investment in an amount established by the corporation. Appraisal is afforded only for those shareholders of a class or series whose interest is so affected.[18]

In addition, the Act grants appraisal rights in the event of any other amendment to the articles of incorporation to the extent provided by the articles, bylaws, or board resolution.[19]

§25.05 Equitable Limitations on Changes in Outstanding Shares

The problem of fairness in recapitalization has frequently been litigated in connection with charter amendments and other transactions undertaken to eliminate dividend arrearages on preferred shares.[1] The purpose for eliminating the preferred's accumulated dividends is not hard to understand. A board of directors that believes the corporation, after years of desuetude, has "turned the corner" toward continuing profitability may question whether honoring the preferred arrearages is necessarily the right choice. Recall that the board of directors is elected by the common shareholders and that the directors may themselves be the owners of common shares. Until the arrearages are paid or eliminated, dividends cannot be paid to the common stockholders. Hence their natural tendency is to reduce or eliminate the right to arrearages of dividends and any other features of the preferred share contract they believe is burdensome to the corporation. Additionally, substantial preferred arrearages cast a dark cloud over the ability of the corporation to attract new investors in its common stock because of the corporation's need to satisfy all accumulated dividends on the preferred before declaring dividends on its common shares. And new investors may be needed in this case because the new financial vigor of the corporation may be sustainable only with an expansion of its resources.

---

[17] MBCA §13.02(a)(4) (1999).
[18] MBCA §13.02 Official Comment (1999).
[19] MBCA §13.02(a)(5) (1999).
§25.05 [1] *See, e.g.,* State v. Bechtel, 31 N.W.2d 853 (Iowa 1948).

The courts are badly divided on the approach to be taken when considering whether a recapitalization should be enjoined on the basis of unfairness. Recall that the preferred are viewed in the same light as bondholders when they stand before the court; they are not residual claimants to the firm, the firm's obligations to them is provided by the terms of their contract, and, hence, the courts do not view either the preferred stockholders or bondholders as standing in a fiduciary relationship to the firm or its managers.[2] The least protective of the approaches requires evidence of fraud or bad faith before a court will enjoin a recapitalization.[3] More frequently the courts apply a fairness standard in assessing a recapitalization.[4] Few instances exist in which courts have used their equitable powers to protect the preferred shares' claim that the amendment of their rights was unfair or even fraudulent.

It is now generally understood that, in addition to securing the requisite shareholder approval after full disclosure of the material facts to the recapitalization, fairness demands only some reasonable compensation for the changes or sacrifices that an amendment visits upon the affected class. Thus the elimination of accrued dividends has been held fair because the preferred increased their equity interest in the corporation[5] or voting control shifted to the preferred.[6] In making these determinations one should initially be guided by the objective standard that, after the recapitalization, the preferreds' share of the firm's future value approximates their claim before the acquisition. This approach may be seen as placing too much weight on the economic feature of the shares and not giving sufficient attention to their other features, such as voting rights. Some courts therefore have applied rough estimates of fairness based on considering the shares' voting rights, liquidation rights, or future claims on dividends or earnings.[7] The far wiser approach is to view the economic rights of the parties on the assumption the firm will continue as an operating entity and to consider their positions primarily in financial terms. This assumption appears imminently reasonable because the very purpose of the recapitalization in most instances is to permit the firm to continue its operations, and the issues before everyone are predominantly how to share the future free cash flow of the business.

Thus proportionality should be informed in the first instance by the stockholders' relative shares in the firm's value before its recapitalization. This is at best a highly impressionistic beginning point, not only because valuing the firm and each class of stock's share of the firm is a highly subjective inquiry, but also because questions such as how voting rights are to be shared in a recapitalized

---

[2] See §18.15.

[3] See Aldridge v. Franco Wyoming Oil Co., 14 A.2d 380 (Del. 1940); McNulty v. W. & J. Sloane, 54 N.Y.S.2d 253 (Sup. Ct. 1945).

[4] See New Faunce v. Boost Co., 83 A.2d 649 (N.J. Super. Ct. 1951); State v. Bechtel, 31 N.W.2d 853 (Iowa 1948).

[5] See Hottenstein v. York Ice Mach. Corp., 136 F.2d 944 (3d Cir. 1943); McQuillen v. National Cash Register Co., 27 F. Supp. 639 (D. Md. 1946).

[6] See Porges v. Vadsco Sales Corp., 32 A.2d 148 (Del. Ch. 1943).

[7] See Page v. Whittenton Mfg. Co., 97 N.E. 1006 (Mass. 1912) (liquidation value); Page v. American & British Mfg. Co., 113 N.Y.S. 734 (App. Div. 1908).

firm do not lend themselves to quantification. Moreover, there should be some substantial room for bargaining differences between the two classes of stock so as to capture a host of intangible considerations that are not easily included in financial models. As such, equitable protections may be limited to those rare instances where the recapitalization plan appears as a transparent effort to reduce the influence or financial interest of the minority by a discrete block of shareholders who hold a majority of the shares.[8]

§25.06 The Debate over Power to "Opt Out" of State Laws

The modern trend continues to provide greater and greater freedom for corporations to amend their articles of incorporation. This trend moves hand in hand with the increasing tenor of corporate statutes to be enabling rather than regulatory. It remains to be seen whether this trend will continue, as some have argued it should, to permit corporations to amend their articles so as to "opt out" of certain types of regulatory provisions that normally apply. Several influential scholars have argued quite persuasively that corporations should be allowed to decide selectively what corporate regulatory provisions they wish not to have apply to that corporation.[1] Such an opt-out arrangement is a natural extension of the nexus-of-contracts view of corporations: if one accepts that a corporation is but the intersection of differing contractual relations, it is equally logical to accord the contracting parties freedom to arrange their rights and protections in a manner they believe appropriate, with little paternalism from the state. Not surprisingly, those who reject the nexus-of-contracts view strongly oppose the opt-out arrangement.[2] Any such opt-out arrangement appears to place a good deal of faith in the belief that the shareholders are fully informed as to the consequences of the choices placed before them and that they will respond effectively. In a large public corporation not only is the proxy mechanism poorly devised for such thoughtful participation but also the full ramifications of the proposal will be extremely hard to assess.[3] Nevertheless, the American Law Institute proposes an approach

---

[8] *See, e.g.,* Starr v. Engineering Contracting Co., 31 N.W.2d 313 (Neb. 1948).

§25.06 [1] *See, e.g.,* Frank Easterbrook & Daniel Fischel, The Corporate Contract in the Economic Structure of Corporate Law (1991); Richard Posner, Economic Analysis of the Law 393-397 (4th ed. 1992); Ralph Winter, State Law, Shareholder Protection, and the Theory of the Corporation, 6 J. Legal Stud. 251 (1977). For a thoughtful reply to Judge Easterbrook and Professor Fischel, *see* William W. Bratton, The Economic Structure of the Post-Contractual Corporation, 87 Nw. U. L. Rev. 180 (1992).

[2] *See, e.g.,* Victor Brudney, Corporate Governance, Agency Costs, and the Rhetoric of Contract, 85 Colum. L. Rev. 1403 (1985); Robert Clark, Agency Costs Versus Fiduciary Duties in Principals and Agents: The Structure of Business 55 (J. Pratt & R. Zeckhauser eds. 1985); John Coffee, No Exit? Opting Out, the Contractual Theory of the Corporation, and the Special Case of Remedies, 53 Brook. L. Rev. 919 (1988); Thomas L. Hazen, The Corporate Persona, Contract (and Market) Failure and Moral Values, 69 N.C. L. Rev. 273 (1991).

[3] *See generally* Lucian Bebchuk, Limiting Contractual Freedom in Corporate Law: The Desirable Constraints on Charter Amendments, 102 Harv. L. Rev. 1820 (1989).

akin to an opt-out choice by providing protection of directors and officers in limited circumstances against charges of self-dealing, of usurpation of corporate opportunity, or of competing with their corporation, when they have acted in accordance with valid standards of conduct embraced by the corporation in its bylaws or articles of incorporation.[4]

Perhaps the most visible and widely used opt-out provision is the director immunity shield whereby most state statutes authorize the articles of incorporation to include a provision that protects directors from liability for damages for grossly negligent acts.[5] The Model Business Corporation Act sets forth a variety of opt-out provisions, including an appraisal remedy for preferred shares when their rights are affected by amendment.[6]

---

[4] In ALI 1 Principles of Corporate Governance: Analysis and Recommendations §5.09 (1994), the ALI protects directors and officers who rely on a standard of the corporation for transactions involving dealings with their corporation, acquiring property for their personal benefit, and competing with their corporation. "Standard of the corporation" is defined as a rule of governance that appears either in the bylaws or the articles of incorporation whose validity is to be judged "by its consistency with corporate statutes, the principles of corporate law, and applicable rules of general law." *Id.* §1.36 Comment. When a corporation has taken advantage of a liability opt-out provision, the exculpatory defense is an affirmative defense that must be made by the defendants. Emerald Partners v. Berlin, 726 A.2d 1215, 1223-1224 (Del. 1999).

[5] Immunity shield provisions are discussed in §10.06.

[6] MBCA §13.02(c) (1984).

CHAPTER 26

Voluntary Dissolution, Administrative Dissolution, and Winding Up

§26.01   Voluntary Dissolution Versus Informal Liquidation

Dissolution of a corporation involves two legal steps: (1) the termination of the corporate existence, at least as far as the right to continue doing ordinary business is concerned, and (2) the winding up of affairs, payment of debts, and distribution of assets among the shareholders. Winding up may precede or follow the dissolution, depending on the jurisdiction's statutory procedures. For convenience in winding up, the corporate existence is usually continued either indefinitely or for some limited period in order to dispose of the assets and pay creditors.[1] This enables the directors to function as a board with title in the corporation rather than as trustees of liquidators. The pre-1984 Model Business Corporation Act provides a two-step process to dissolve. First, a statement of intent to dissolve that has

---

§26.01   [1] *See, e.g.,* Cal. Corp. Code §§1805, 1903, 2010 (West 1990); Del. Code Ann. tit. 8, §278 (2001).

been approved by the shareholders is filed with the secretary of state. Notice to known creditors must also be given before the second step is taken. Second, when the winding up process is completed, the articles of dissolution must be filed. The corporation is dissolved when a certificate of dissolution is issued.[2] The current Model Business Corporation Act and a clear majority of the states simplify the process by calling for only the articles of dissolution to be filed, and dissolution is effective as of the date the articles of dissolution are filed.[3]

A corporation's legal existence is terminated only when it is dissolved by legal authority, expires by limitation of its term of existence, or is dissolved by forfeiture.[4] Although it is not a formal dissolution, an informal liquidation may occur by sale of all the corporate assets, the abandonment of corporate activities, and the distribution of the corporation's property among the creditors and shareholders. This is sometimes referred to as a practical or de facto dissolution. However, a liquidation of assets does not terminate the corporate existence as a matter of law.

There may be reasons for retaining a corporation as a shell, such as for reactivation at a later date or for use in a corporate merger or consolidation. Unless such reasons exist, directors and shareholders should follow the proceedings prescribed by law for voluntary dissolution and winding up in order to protect creditors—otherwise the directors and shareholders risk liability due to unauthorized return of capital to the shareholders.[5] That is, absent dissolution, distributions to shareholders are lawful only to the extent that they do not exceed the regulatory limits for dividends or share repurchases.

§26.02   Statutory Authority for Voluntary Dissolution

Every American jurisdiction provides for the voluntary dissolution of a corporation when authorized by a specified majority vote.[1] The proposal to dissolve is usually to be made in the first instance by the directors. Most states require an authorization by the directors before the shareholders may vote,[2] and only a few states do not mandate director approval.[3] Upon the requisite stockholders' vote at a meeting held upon the prescribed notice to all shareholders without regard to class or voting restrictions, the dissolution can proceed without any confirmatory

[2] Former MBCA §§83, 84-87 (1969).

[3] MBCA §§14.03(b) & 14.06 (1984). The ease of voluntary dissolution has led one observer to suggest that it should replace the hostile takeover as a mechanism for replacing inefficient management. Park McGinty, Replacing Hostile Takeovers, 144 U. Pa. L. Rev. 983 (1996).

[4] In re Clark's Will, 178 N.E. 766 (N.Y. 1931); Levin v. Pittsburgh United Corp., 199 A. 332 (Pa. 1938).

[5] See Central Nat'l Bank v. Connecticut Mut. Life Ins. Co., 104 U.S. 54 (1881); Butler v. New Keystone Copper Co., 93 A. 380, 384 (Del. Ch. 1915); Darcy v. Brooklyn & N.Y. Ferry Co., 89 N.E. 461 (N.Y. 1909).

§26.02   [1] See 3 Model Business Corp. Act Ann. §14.02 at 14-14-14-16 (3d ed. 1994) (hereinafter MBCA Ann.). These statutes also give detailed procedures for the revocation of such proceedings prior to the final dissolution and winding-up. See MBCA §14.04 (1984); Former MBCA §§88, 91 (1969).

[2] E.g., Del. Code Ann. tit. 8, §275 (2001).

[3] E.g., Cal. Corp. Code §1900(a) (West 1990).

court action.[4] The number of stockholder votes required varies widely among the states,[5] with most requiring a majority of the shares entitled to vote. The corporation may, however, seek court supervision.[6] In some states, dissolution may be had upon the written assent of all or of a specified majority of the shares without a meeting.[7]

State statutes commonly authorize dissolution solely on the approval of the incorporators or the board of directors when the corporation either has not issued shares or has not commenced business.[8] Some jurisdictions so empower the incorporators or board of directors only if the corporation has not issued shares[9]; other states confer this power if the corporation has not commenced business, even though shares have been issued.[10] Both bases are embraced by the former Model Business Corporation Act and current Model Business Corporation Act.[11]

In most states only the voting shares have a voice as to dissolution under many corporation acts.[12] Filing of a certificate of dissolution and, in some states, the publication of notice are required steps. After the statement of intent to dissolve has been duly adopted and filed, notice thereof is generally required to be sent to all known creditors.[13] When a corporation has qualified to do business in several states, it must make appropriate filings for dissolution in each state.[14]

§26.03 Equitable Limitations on Voluntary Dissolution

In the case of a voluntary dissolution, as in the case of mergers, consolidations, and other fundamental changes, management and majority shareholders are given wide latitude. Nevertheless, as Justice Traynor observed in *In re Security Finance Company*,[1] a leading case, "[t]here is nothing sacred in the life of a corporation that transcends the interests of its shareholders, but because dissolution falls with such finality on those interests, above all corporate powers it is subject to

---

[4] *E.g.,* Del. Code Ann. tit. 8, §275 (2001); N.Y. Bus. Corp. Law §1001 (McKinney 1986); MBCA §14.03(b) (1984); Former MBCA §83 (1969).

[5] *See* Cal. Corp. Code §1900(a) (West 1990) (50 percent of the voting power); Del. Code Ann., tit. 8 §275 (2001) (majority of the shares entitled to vote).

[6] *See, e.g.,* MBCA §14.30(4) (1984); Former MBCA §87(c) (1969).

[7] *See, e.g.,* Del. Code Ann. tit. 8, §275(c) (2001); MBCA §7.04 (1984).

[8] *See, e.g.,* Del. Code Ann. tit. 8, §274 (2001).

[9] *See* Cal. Corp. Code §1900(b)(3) (West 1990).

[10] *See, e.g.,* Conn. Gen. Stat. Ann. §§33-880 & 33-882 (West 1997); 15 Pa. Cons. Stat. Ann. §1971 (West 1995).

[11] *See* MBCA §14.01 (1984): Former MBCA §82 (1969). *See also* Del. Code Ann. tit. 8, §274 (2001).

[12] *See, e.g.,* Del. Code Ann. tit. 8, §275 (2001).

[13] *See, e.g.,* Cal. Corp. Code §1903 (West 1990); Mass. Gen. Laws Ann. ch. 156B, §100 (Law. Co-op. 1996); N.Y. Bus. Corp. Law §1007 (McKinney 1986); MBCA §14.06(b) (1984); Former MBCA §87(a) (1969).

[14] *See* Cal. Corp. Code §§2112 & 2113 (West 1990).

§26.03   [1] 317 P.2d 1 (Cal. 1957).

equitable limitations."[2] In general, as we have seen,[3] courts refuse to review the motives of the majority or the fairness or expediency of these fundamental changes at the suit of minority shareholders. The courts' reserve reflects their belief that, absent a strong showing of improper motives or fraud, structural changes within the corporation involve questions of business policy and judgment on which the majority shareholders have the right of determination. Under many older cases there was little suggestion that the majority shareholders were fiduciaries. The courts held that the majority could act according to their own enlightened self-interest, which must be qualified, however, to the extent that the majority may act only after full disclosure and without any incident of independent wrongdoing.[4]

For voluntary dissolution most state statutes require the consent of the board of directors as well as a majority of the shareholders.[5] A few states provide appraisal rights for dissenting shareholders but only when the dissolution is accompanied by a sale of substantially all the assets.[6] When a shareholder in a close corporation initiates a voluntary dissolution, some courts will examine the circumstances to determine whether the decision to dissolve was made in good faith.[7] Thus, in *In re Security Finance Company*,[8] after repeated efforts to persuade the other owners of the business to either raise his salary or increase dividends, the holder of 50 percent of the shares petitioned the court to voluntarily dissolve the corporation, as authorized by the state's statute. Justice Traynor held the trial court properly granted the petition for judicial supervision of the company's voluntary dissolution. Even though recognizing that the petitioner as a major stockholder was under a duty to act in good faith in seeking the firm's voluntary dissolution, the court found this standard was more than satisfied under the facts because the petitioner acted to protect his own investment in seeking dissolution, and dissolution did not give him any unfair advantage.[9] An important consideration in *In re Security Finance Company* is that the assets of the dissolved company

[2] *Id.* at 5. Equitable limitations are especially implicated if the plan of dissolution discriminates between controlling and minority shareholders in the type of consideration each receives as a liquidating distribution.

[3] *See* §§22.22, 23.01.

[4] *See* Mansfield Hardwood Lumber Co. v. Johnson, 268 F.2d 317 (5th Cir.), *cert. denied*, 361 U.S. 885 (1959); Porterfield v. Gerstel, 222 F.2d 137 (5th Cir. 1955); Zahn v. Transamerica Corp., 162 F.2d 36 (3d Cir. 1947).

[5] *See, e.g.,* Cal. Corp. Code §1001 (West 1990) (majority of shares).

[6] *See* Fla. Stat. Ann. §607.1302 (West 2001); Mich. Comp. Laws §450.1762 (West 1990); MBCA §13.02(a)(3) (1984); Former MBCA §80(a)(2) (1969).

[7] *See* Kellogg v. Georgia-Pacific Paper Corp., 227 F. Supp. 719 (W.D. Ark. 1964) (majority cannot appropriate the business by freezing out the minority); In re Security Fin. Co., 317 P.2d 1 (Cal. 1957) (majority shareholders do not have an absolute right to dissolve a corporation; they have no right to defraud or freeze out minority shareholders; the dissolution must be in good faith). *Cf.* In re Radom & Neidorff, Inc., 119 N.E.2d 563 (N.Y. 1954) (shareholders—brother and sister—were hostile; brother filed for dissolution but court refused to grant involuntary dissolution because corporation was financially successful); Jackson v. Nicolai-Neppach Co., 348 P.2d 9 (Or. 1959) (refusing to allow involuntary dissolution because of deadlock; instead, judge suggested shareholders resolve their differences or buy each other out).

[8] 317 P.2d 1 (Cal. 1957).

[9] *Id.* at 6.

were to be sold to a third party, so that there was no argument either that dissolution was a means to freeze the other shareholders out of the corporation or that the price to be received through liquidation was unfair.[10] In contrast, dissolution is improperly granted if it is used as a mechanism to exclude the minority shareholders from participating in the business that will be continued by the petitioner.[11] On the other hand, courts are understandably much less likely to review the motives for voluntary dissolution of a publicly held corporation except in the case of freeze-outs or fraudulent transactions.[12]

If a majority of the shareholders vote to sell the assets and dissolve a prosperous corporation in order to turn over the assets and business to another corporation controlled by them, thereby excluding the minority or depriving them of the fair value of their investment, the minority shareholders may obtain equitable relief in the form of an injunction against their being unfairly frozen out of the corporation.[13] As was seen in the case of merger freeze-outs, the minority do not have an unqualified right to continue their participation in the corporation; however, the majority do not have carte blanche power to expel the minority. Each is conditioned frequently on the presence of the minority receiving the fair value of their shares. In many jurisdictions there is the further requirement of a bona fide business purpose for the transaction.[14] The court may alternatively award damages to the frozen-out minority based on their interest in the company before its dissolution.[15]

§26.04 Dissolution by Expiration of Stated Duration or Administrative Dissolution

A corporation may be dissolved upon expiration of a certain period of time or a specified event, if provided in the charter.[1] The corporation's right to exist as a *de jure* corporation ceases after that time unless it is extended or renewed by vote of the shareholders under legislative authority.[2] According to some authorities, there

---

[10] *Id.* at 3 (six offers for company's assets were obtained by petitioner).

[11] *See* Grato v. Grato, 639 A.2d 390, 397 (N.J. Super. Ct. App. Div. 1994) (quoting 19 Am. Jur. 2d Corporations §2752 (1986)).

[12] *See* Lebold v. Inland Steel Co., 125 F.2d 369 (7th Cir. 1941), *cert. denied,* 320 U.S. 787 (1943); Kellogg v. Georgia-Pacific Paper Corp., 227 F. Supp. 719 (D. Ark. 1964); Kirtz v. Grossman, 463 S.W.2d 541 (Mo. Ct. App. 1971).

[13] *See, e.g.,* Lebold v. Inland Steel Co., 125 F.2d 369 (7th Cir. 1941); Grato v. Grato, 639 A.2d 390 (N.J. Super. App. Div. 1994); Kavanaugh v. Kavanaugh Knitting Co., 123 N.E. 148 (N.Y. 1919). The same result applies to dissolution of a partnership. *See* Thibaut v. Thibaut, 607 So. 2d 587 (La. Ct. App. 1992), *writ denied,* 612 So. 2d 101 (La. 1993).

[14] *See* §23.03.

[15] *See* Grato v. Grato, 639 A.2d 390 (N.J. Super. App. Div. 1994) (dissolution had already occurred and defendants were already operating new company when plaintiff minority shareholders learned true purpose of earlier dissolution).

§26.04 [1] *See, e.g.,* Cal. Corp. Code §1800(b)(6) (West 1990). N.Y. Bus. Corp. Law §1002(a) (McKinney 1986). Such a provision is commonly required under statutes authorizing limited liability companies. *See* §1.10.

[2] *See, e.g.,* Mich. Comp. Laws Ann. §450.2815 (West 1990); *cf.* MBCA §10.02(1) (1984); Former MBCA §58(b) (1969).

may be an existence by estoppel or a *de facto* corporation by continuing corporate activities after the expiration of the charter.[3] By express statutory provision, the existence of a corporation, even when created for a limited time, is usually prolonged for the limited purpose of winding up business affairs, paying debts, distributing assets, and suing and being sued.[4]

A corporation may be dissolved administratively for failure to fulfill certain state requirements, such as nonpayment of state taxes and fees, failure to appoint or give timely notice of a change in its registered agent, or failure to file the mandated annual report with the secretary of state.[5] Most statutes require the state attorney general to bring an action to dissolve a corporation,[6] although under some statutes there is automatic dissolution.[7] Usually when a corporation becomes delinquent for failure to pay franchise or license taxes, it has its powers suspended but not forfeited. When corporate powers are suspended merely due to an administrative dissolution, the corporation's powers are reinstated on compliance with the state requirement that gave rise to the dissolution. Such reinstatement restores, usually retroactively, the corporation's power to sue.[8] This result reflects the incentive the legislature provides to ensure the payment of taxes and fees as well as filing of annual report information. As will be seen later, courts are divided on the question of whether such reinstatement relates back to the date of the corporation's dissolution.

§26.05   Grounds for Involuntary Dissolution

Action by Shareholders. The subject of involuntary dissolution in response to a petition by shareholders is examined in Chapter 14.[1] In broad overview, most corporation acts provide for involuntary dissolution in a suit by minority shareholders in some or all of the following four situations:[2] (1) when the directors are deadlocked, the shareholders cannot break the deadlock, and irreparable injury

---

[3] *See* §§6.03, 6.10, 6.04.

[4] *See, e.g.,* Cal. Corp. Code §§1805, 1903, 2010 (West 1990); Del. Code Ann. tit. 8, §278 (2001); N.J. Stat. Ann. §14A:12-9 (West Supp. 2002); N.Y. Bus. Corp. Law §1006 (McKinney 1986); Former MBCA §105 (1969).

[5] *See* 3 MBCA Ann. §14.20 at 14-81-14-84 (3d ed. 1994). *See also* James J. Cavanaugh, "Automatic" Forefeiture of Corporate Charters, 16 Bus. Law. 676 (1961).

[6] *See, e.g.,* MBCA §14.20 (1984).

[7] *See, e.g.,* Del. Code Ann. tit. 8, §510 (2001) (automatic if delay exceeds one year).

[8] *See* Scona, Inc. v. Green Willow Trust, 985 P.2d 1145 (Idaho 1999); Henderson-Smith Assoc., Inc. v. Nahamani Service Ctr., 752 N.E.2d 33 (Ill. Ct. App. 2001) (permitting reinstated company to maintain action on a cause of action that arose during the period of its administrative dissolution). *But see* South Mecklenburg Painting Contractors, Inc. v. The Cunnane Group, Inc., 517 S.E.2d 167 (N.C. Ct. App. 1999) (holding contract entered into when company was administratively dissolved was invalid and subsequent reinstatement did not affect the validity of the contract).

§26.05   [1] *See* §§14.11-14.13.

[2] *See, e.g.,* Cal. Corp. Code §1800 (West 1990); Del. Code Ann. tit. 8, §§226, 352 (2001). MBCA §14.30(2) (1984).

to the corporation is suffered or threatened; (2) when the directors, controlling managers, or majority shareholders are acting in an illegal, oppressive, or fraudulent manner; (3) when the shareholders are deadlocked and cannot elect directors; and (4) when corporate assets have been misapplied or wasted. The emphasis of such actions is the protection of the interests of the shareholders. The two categories of dissolution discussed below—dissolution by action of the state and dissolution by action of creditors—arise out of concern for the non-stockholder interests if the corporation's existence is not terminated. The final act of the dissolution process is filing the articles of dissolution with the state.[3]

Action by the State. Historically, the common law quo warranto action was available to the state, usually through its attorney general, to cause the forfeiture of a corporation's existence or to prevent the corporation from continuing its harmful activities.[4] Most jurisdictions have enacted quo warranto statutes that provide the method of forfeiting the charters of corporations for misuse or non-use of their powers, or based on other specified grounds.[5] However, in some states it is still a matter of common law.[6] In general, quo warranto is not an exclusive remedy, especially when more adequate remedies exist.[7]

Most states have adopted administrative mechanisms usually carried out within the secretary of state's office, by which the state can *administratively* dissolve corporations for the failure to meet requirements of this type.[8] The procedure generally commences with the secretary of state giving notice to the corporation of the particular defect that, if not corrected within a stated length of time—generally 60 days—will cause the corporation's administrative dissolution. Most state statutes provide that, even though a corporation has been administratively dissolved, its existence can be reinstated by curing the defect that gave rise to its dissolution, such as payment of past and current fees that are due the state.[9] The effect of administrative dissolution in most states is to suspend the corporation's powers, not terminate its existence outright. Such suspension bars any action on the corporation's behalf except as necessary to wind up its affairs.[10]

---

[3] *See* Multilist Service of Cape Giradeau, Missouri, Inc. v. Wilson, 14 S.W.3d 110 (Mo. Ct. App. 2000) (company was not voluntarily dissolved because had not filed its articles of dissolution although shareholder vote authorizing this step had occurred).

[4] *See* United States ex rel. Wisconsin v. First Fed. Sav. & Loan Ass'n, 248 F.2d 804 (7th Cir. 1957), *cert. denied,* 355 U.S. 957 (1958).

[5] *See, e.g.,* Cal. Civ. Proc. Code §803 (West 1980); N.Y. Bus. Corp. Law §1101 (McKinney 1986).

[6] Cleaver v. Roberts, 203 A.2d 63 (Del. 1964) (writ of quo warranto is common law remedy and may be prosecuted only in name of the state on relation of attorney general). Del. Code Ann. tit. 8, §283 (2001) is the statutory equivalent, but it does not abridge the common law remedy. Morford v. Trustees of Middletown Acad., 13 A.2d 168, 171 (Del. Ch. 1940).

[7] *See* Lapides v. Doner, 248 F. Supp. 883 (E.D. Mich. 1965).

[8] *See, e.g.,* Del. Code Ann., tit. 8, §510 (2001).

[9] *See, e.g.,* Iowa Code Ann. §490.1422 (West 1999) (within two years); R.I. Gen. Laws §7-1.1-88.1 (1999) (within five years); N.Y. Tax Laws §203-a(7) (McKinney Supp. 2002) (within 90 days); Wis. Stat. Ann. §180.1422 (1992) (no period specified after amendment in 1997 removing earlier two-year period).

[10] *See* Graham Inc. v. Mountain States Tel. & Tel. Co., 680 P.2d 1334 (Col. Ct. App. 1984).

Petition by Creditors. In a number of states, involuntary dissolution proceedings may be initiated by a creditor.[11] Under the former Model Business Corporation Act, for example, the action may be commenced by an unsatisfied judgment creditor after a fruitless attempt at execution or by any creditor where the corporation has admitted the debt in writing; in either case, the corporation's insolvency must be established.[12] In Delaware, when a corporation is insolvent, a creditor may petition for appointment of a receiver.[13] This provision is not to be confused with involuntary proceedings under the federal bankruptcy act, which may be brought by three or more creditors[14] and may culminate in liquidation or reorganization. Bankruptcy proceedings do not result in dissolution: that is a matter of state corporate law. In the absence of a formal proceeding, there is no automatic dissolution of the corporation even after liquidation and payment of all debts.[15] Such cases are especially appropriate for the court to exercise its authority to appoint a receiver to carry out the orderly liquidation of the company.[16]

§26.06 Winding Up and Statutory Continuation of Existence After Dissolution

The most important steps in connection with dissolution are the proceedings for liquidation and the winding up of corporate affairs. During the course of these proceedings, the assets will be collected and realized upon, the claims of creditors will be settled, and the remaining assets will be distributed to the shareholders. The statutes of most states proscribe the winding-up process only in a general way.[1] The most important questions are the rights of creditors, whether the title to the property remains in the corporation for winding-up purposes or passes automatically to the directors as trustees or to the shareholders subject to the power of the directors to make liquidating distributions.[2] It also is to be remembered that the directors of a corporation retain their fiduciary obligations during the winding-up process.[3]

Any analogy between the life and death of a natural person and the life and dissolution of a corporation is not compelling.[4] Under most state statutes, dissolution terminates the corporate existence for some purposes and continues it for

---

[11] *See, e.g.,* Ariz. Rev. Stat. Ann. §10-1430(c) (West 1996); Conn. Gen. Stat. Ann. §33-896 (West 1997).

[12] MBCA §14.30(3) (1984); Former MBCA §97(b) (1969).

[13] Del. Code Ann. tit. 8, §291 (2001).

[14] 11 U.S.C. §303(b)(1) (2000). Where there are fewer than 12 creditors, any one of them may institute involuntary bankruptcy proceedings. *Id.* §303(b)(2).

[15] *See* §26.02.

[16] *See, e.g.,* Lichtenstein v. Consolidated Services Group, Inc., 978 F. Supp. 1 (D. Me. 1997).

§26.06 [1] *See* MBCA §87(b) (1969).

[2] *See* 16A William M. Fletcher, Cyclopedia of the Law of Private Corporations §§8157-8162 (1995).

[3] *See, e.g.,* Addison D. Braendel, Winding Up a Delaware Corporation: Directors' Fiduciary Duties and Statutory Procedures, 26 Sec. Reg. L.J. 344 (1999).

[4] Such an analogy is sometimes applied. *See* United States v. Safeway Stores, Inc., 140 F.2d 834, 836, 840 (10th Cir. 1944).

other purposes that are germane to winding up its affairs.[5] The dissolution of a corporation, like that of a partnership, operates only with respect to future transactions. The corporation or partnership continues until all preexisting matters are terminated. The dissolution does not destroy the authority of a partner to act for his former associates and for creditors in winding up the business, as distinguished from carrying on the partnership's ordinary business.[6] Corporate agents have similar authority.

Today states commonly provide for continued existence of the corporation for winding-up purposes.[7] Absent such a statute, the common law prevails, and the directors at the time of dissolution are usually authorized to act as trustees and to sue and be sued as trustees on any claim of or against the corporation. In the eyes of the common law, the assets are a trust fund for creditors and shareholders, and a court of equity has the power to liquidate the assets.[8] Some statutes merely provide that dissolution "shall not take away or impair any remedy given against such corporation."[9] Such statutes fail to provide convenient machinery by which suits may be brought on behalf of the corporation and by which winding up and liquidation may be carried on other than by receivers.[10]

The issue sometimes arises concerning the liability of individuals who continue to act for the corporation after its dissolution. Statutes impose personal liability on those who continue to act on behalf of the corporation for purposes other than for winding up with knowledge that the firm has been administratively dissolved.[11]

§26.07   General Consequences of Dissolution

When a corporation is dissolved by expiration of the time specified in its charter, by a voluntary dissolution, by a judgment forfeiting its charter, or in any other manner, it ceases to exist unless there is some statutory provision continuing its existence. It no longer has the capacity or power to enter into contracts, to take, hold, or convey property, to sue or be sued, or to exercise any other power.[1] Debts due to or by the corporation are not extinguished. Even in the absence of a

---

[5] *See* Accurate Constr. Co. v. Washington, 378 A.2d 681 (D.C. 1977).

[6] Cotten v. Perishable Air Conditioners, 11 P.2d 603 (Cal. 1941); Uniform Partnership Act §30 (1969); 2 Alan A. Bromberg & Larry E. Ribstein, Law of Partnership §7.15 (Supp. 1999).

[7] *See, e.g.,* Cal. Corp. Code §2010 (West 1990). N.Y. Bus. Corp. Law §1005 (McKinney 1986).

[8] *See* Joseph Jude Norton, Relationship of Shareholders to Corporate Creditors Upon Dissolution: Nature and Implications of the "Trust Fund" Doctrine of Corporate Assets, 30 Bus. Law. 1061 (1975).

[9] *See, e.g.,* 805 ILCS §5/12.80 (West 1993); Former MBCA §105.

[10] *See, e.g.,* Harry G. Henn & John R. Alexander, Effect of Corporate Dissolution on Products Liability Claims, 56 Cornell L. Rev. 865, 879 (1971).

[11] *See, e.g.* Fla. Stat. Ann. §607.1421(4) (West 2001); Mo. Ann. Stat. §351.476.2(3) (West 2001). A similar provision is found in Model Act jurisdictions. *See* MBCA §2.04.

§26.07   [1] *See* Psychic Research & Dev. Inst., Inc. v. Gutbrodt, 415 A.2d 611 (Md. Ct. Spec. App. 1980) (corporation named as residual legatee whose charter was forfeited prior to testatrix's death could not be residual legatee even though charter was reinstated).

statute, a court of equity can enforce collection of debts due to a corporation for the benefit of creditors and shareholders and will satisfy debts due from the corporation out of its assets. The property of the corporation belongs to the shareholders, subject to the corporate debts and the powers of the liquidators.

§26.08   *Effect of Dissolution with Regard to Debts and Contracts*

Dissolution does not extinguish the interest or rights that stockholders have through their shares.[1] The dissolution of a corporation does not free its property from liability for payment of income taxes or any other debts.[2] Creditors may judicially enforce their claims in equity or by any other mode provided against corporate property as well as against those who receive the corporate assets. Under an older view, the property of a defunct corporation is regarded as a trust fund for its creditors and shareholders.

The liability of the distributing directors arises as a consequence of their breach of the fiduciary duty to the creditors. That duty is founded on their position as trustees for the benefit of the corporation's creditors. Today there is little evidence that the trust fund analysis guides the rights of creditors. The determining factor of director or shareholder liability is the state's survival statute.[3]

---

§26.08   [1] *See* Mallinga v. Harvey Family Medical Center, 688 N.E.2d 816 (Ill. Ct. App. 1997) (although the company was administratively dissolved, plaintiff continued to have economic rights in the company through shares subject to claims of creditors).

[2] *See* United States v. Glen Upton, Inc., 378 F. Supp. 1028 (W.D. Mo. 1974). See Rosemary Reger Schnall, Extending Protection to Foreseeable Future Claimants Through Delaware's Innovative Corporate Dissolution Scheme—In re Rego Co., 19 Del. J. Corp. L. 141 (1994).

[3] *See* Pacific Scene, Inc. v. Penasquitos, Inc., 758 P.2d 1182, 1185 (Cal. 1988) (en banc) ("the legislature has generally occupied the field with respect to the remedies available against former shareholders of dissolved corporations, thus preempting antecedent common law causes of action, and that of the trust fund theory"). The comment to the Model Business Corporation Act rejects the trust fund doctrine. *See* MBCA §14.05 Official Comment (1984).

CHAPTER 27

Investor Protection: State and Federal Securities Regulation

Chapter 27.   Investor Protection: State and Federal Securities Regulation

§27.01   Securities Regulation—Overview

State corporate laws are geared to the chartering function and for the most part do not concern themselves with investor protection.[1] The great problems caused by stock watering and other fraudulent promotional schemes at the turn of the century did not result in adequate common law safeguards. The courts' inability to prevent or redress these frauds led to the passage in 1911 of the first state securities regulatory scheme, or blue sky law.[2] Despite the growth of these statutes, frauds continued to flourish in the wake of the Great Crash of 1929. Congress realized that there was a gap in the protection investors needed and accordingly responded by enacting the Securities Act of 1933 and the Securities Exchange Act of 1934.[3] The importance of the state statutes has been dwarfed to a large extent by the impact of federal regulation. Yet, the state laws provide significant protection for investment schemes that are either small or essentially local in nature as well as supplementing federal law for more widely offered issues. The topic of securities regulation consumes several treatise volumes and thousands of pages in law reviews. What follows is but a general introduction and overview.

I.   STATE BLUE SKY LAWS

§27.02   History, Policy, and Purpose of State Securities Laws

The Kansas legislature in 1911 passed the first American securities act.[1] The law, popularly called a "blue sky law," attracted wide attention. Similar legislation has now been adopted in every state to protect investors against issuers having nothing behind their securities but water or blue sky.[2] As one court put it: "The name that is given to the law indicates the evil at which it is aimed, that is, 'speculative schemes which have no more basis than so many feet of "blue sky"'; or, as [it has been] stated, . . . 'to stop the sale of stock in fly-by-night concerns, visionary oil wells, distant gold mines, and other like fraudulent exploitations.' "[3]

---

§27.01   [1] *See* §2.05; Thomas L. Hazen, Corporate Chartering and the Securities Markets; Shareholder Suffrage, Corporate Responsibility and Managerial Accounting, 1978 Wis. L. Rev. 391-396.

[2] Kan. Laws 1911 ch. 133.

[3] 15 U.S.C. §§77a *et seq.,* 78a *et seq.* (2000). *See* §§27.05-27.13. *See generally* Thomas L. Hazen, Treatise on the Law of Securities Regulation (4th ed. 2002); Louis Loss & Joel Seligman, Securities Regulation (3d ed. 1989).

§27.02   [1] Kan. Laws 1911 ch. 133 ("an Act to provide for the regulation and supervision of investment companies and providing penalties for the violation thereof").

[2] For example, in State v. Whiteaker, 118 Or. 656, 247 P. 1077 (1926), the defendant claimed to have invented an electrical device that would extract gold from the waters of Mono Lake in California.

[3] Hall v. Geiger-Jones, 242 U.S. 539, 550 (1917).

It is the policy and purpose of this type of legislation to prevent unscrupulous dealers foisting on inexperienced persons unfair, spurious, and worthless securities, and further to provide some method of supervision and regulation of the marketplace.[4] Blue sky laws often give administrative officials great power over the activities of issuers, promoters, and dealers offering shares, bonds, and all types of securities and investment contracts of both incorporated and unincorporated companies for public sale. The laws thus regulate business trusts, partnerships, and individuals as well as corporations.

§27.03   *Preemption of State Registration Requirements*

Ever since the enactment of the Securities Act of 1933, Congress preserved the power of the states to regulate securities transactions notwithstanding the coverage of the federal securities laws. In 1996, however, Congress substantially reversed its position by expressly preempting the field with regard to most registration requirements. The National Securities Markets Improvement Act of 1996[1] took away from the states the power to impose registration and reporting requirements with regard to a large number of securities transactions. As amended by the 1996 legislation, Section 18 of the 1933 Act precludes the imposition of registration and reporting requirements in many securities transactions including securities listed on the New York Stock Exchange, the American Stock Exchange, or the NASD's National Market System.[2] The federal act, however, expressly preserves the states' right to require filing of documents solely for notice purpose,[3] which in effect preserves a state's ability to require registration by coordination with the federal registration. The preemption of state registration and reporting requirements is not limited to publicly traded securities.[4]

In summary, as a result of the 1996 federal amendments, most publicly offered securities that are registered federally cannot be regulated by the states beyond notice and/or coordinated filings. Most federally exempt transactions and securities are also preempted.[5] The preemption provisions create a pattern under which federally exempt transactions can result in state registration requirements only when the securities are offered to unsophisticated purchasers.

---

[4] As to the purposes of these acts, *see, e.g.*, SEC v. C. M. Joiner Leasing Corp., 320 U.S. 344, 353 (1943); State v. Hofacre, 206 Minn. 167, 173, 288 N.W. 13, 16 (1939).

§27.03   [1] 1 Pub. L. No. 104-290, 110 Stat. 3416 (1996).

[2] Section 18(b)(1)(A), 15 U.S.C. §77r(b)(1)(A) (2000). The Act gives the SEC rule-making power to expand the exemption to securities traded on other exchanges with listing standards similar to the exchanges listed in subsection (b)(1)(A).

[3] Section 18(c)(2), 15 U.S.C. §77r(c)(2) (2000).

[4] Section 18(b)(4), 15 U.S.C. §77r(b)(4) (2000).

[5] The primary federal exemptions that are not preempted are offerings subject to the intrastate exemption, the section 3(b) exemptions (most notably, Regulation A and Rules 504 and 505 of Regulation D). The federal exemptions are discussed *infra* §27.10.

§27.04 Preemption of State Securities Fraud
Class Actions

Federal preemption has continued. Congress largely eliminated the use of state courts for securities class actions when it enacted the Securities Litigation Uniform Standards Act of 1998, which mandates that class actions involving publicly traded securities be brought in federal court.[1] Class actions involving state securities law and common law class actions with regard to these securities are preempted. The Uniform Standards Act is not complete in its elimination of state court class actions since the Act preempts only those actions involving publicly traded securities. It is important to note further that the Uniform Standards Act applies only to class actions and thus not to individual or derivative suits. There also is an exclusion for actions brought in the state of incorporation involving certain corporate transactions.

The preemptive provisions apply only to "covered securities." Covered securities under the Uniform Standards Act are securities registered with the SEC and traded on the New York Stock Exchange, American Stock Exchange, the Nasdaq National Market, or other national markets designated by the Commission, as well as securities issued by investment companies registered under the Investment Company Act of 1940.[2] The preemption applies to any class action with more than 50 members involving misrepresentations, omissions, deception, or manipulation in connection with the purchase or sale of a covered security.[3] The Act does not preempt individual actions, derivative suits, or suits brought on behalf of 50 or fewer persons from being brought in state court. The Uniform Standards Act also preserves state court actions brought in the issuer's state of incorporation by shareholders challenging management's statements or recommendations in connection with corporate transactions or the exercise of appraisal rights.[4] Class actions by states or their political subdivisions, as well as class actions by state pension plans, are not subject to the Uniform Standard Act's preemptive effect.[5]

---

§27.04 [1] See, e.g., Thomas Lee Hazen, Treatise on the Law of Securities Regulation §§7.17[2], 12.15 [2] (4th ed. 2002).

[2] 15 U.S.C. §§77p(f)(3), 78bb(f)(5)(E); 1933 Act §16(f)(3). This definition in turn refers to section 18 of the Securities Act of 1933, 15 U.S.C. §77r, which preempts those securities from state registration requirements. Debt securities exempt under section 4(2) of the Investment Company Act are, however, excluded from the definition of covered securities. 15 U.S.C. §77p(f)(3); 1934 Act §28(f)(5)(E), 15 U.S.C. §78bb(f)(5)(E) (2000).

[3] 15 U.S.C. §78bb(f)(1) (a class action or constructive class action brought "by any private party alleging (1) an untrue statement or omission of a material fact in connection with the purchase or sale of a covered security, or (2) that the defendant employed any manipulative or deceptive device or contrivance in connection with the purchase or sale of a covered security"). Accord 15 U.S.C. §77p(b).

[4] 15 U.S.C. §§77p(d)(1), 78pp(f)(3)(A). This has been referred to as the "Delaware carve out," although it is not expressly limited to Delaware. It is designed to preserve remedies under Delaware law involving breaches of fiduciary duty and disclosure to existing shareholders in corporate transactions.

[5] 15 U.S.C. §§77p(d)(2), 78pp(f)(3)(B) (2000).

II.   FEDERAL PROTECTION OF INVESTORS

§27.05   The Origin and Scope of Federal
Securities Regulation

The collapse of the long boom in the stock market in October 1929, the grievous losses suffered by investors, and the lax financial and ethical standards exposed by subsequent public investigations called national attention to the urgent need for comprehensive regulation of the sale of securities and market manipulations by the strong arm of the federal government.[1] As an able New York lawyer wrote, "after the happenings of the 1920's, completely unregulated security markets seem unthinkable."[2] In the period between May 1933 and August 1940, a series of important federal statutes were enacted: (1) the Securities Act of 1933; (2) the Securities Exchange Act of 1934; (3) the Public Utility Holding Company Act of 1935; (4) the Commodity Exchange Act of 1936; (5) the Reorganization acts, Section 77B of the Bankruptcy Act (1934), revised in 1938 as Chapter X of the Chandler Act; (6) the Railroad Reorganization Act; (7) the Trust Indenture Act of 1939; (8) the Investment Company Act of 1940; and (9) the Investment Advisers Act of 1940.[3]

Congress enacted the Sarbanes-Oxley Act[4] in the wake of corporate scandals involving such companies as Enron and Worldcom. The Sarbanes-Oxley Act imposed corporate governance and accounting reforms. The Act focuses on a variety of issues including accounting and auditing reforms, the role of public corporations' audit committees, and increased accountability of executive officers and corporate attorneys.[5] In focusing on accounting problems, the Act created an

§27.05   [1] The staggering losses sustained by the investing public from the fraudulent creation, sale, and manipulation of securities were estimated in 1933 to have been $25 billion for the ten years preceding. Legislation (1933), 33 Colum. L. Rev. 1220, 1220 n.3 (1933).

[2] Arthur H. Dean, The Lawyer's Problems in the Registration of Securities; 4 Law & Contemp. Probs. 154, 189 (1937).

[3] 48 Stat. 74, 15 U.S.C. §§77a-77aa (2000) (Securities Act of 1933); 48 Stat. 881, 15 U.S.C. §§78a et seq. (2000) (Securities Exchange Act of 1934); 48 Stat. 912, 11 U.S.C. §207 (2000) (Bankruptcy Act §77B); 47 Stat. 1474, 11 U.S.C. §205 (2000) (Railroad Reorganization Act); 53 Stat. 1149, 15 U.S.C. §§77aaa et seq. (2000) (Trust Indenture Act of 1939); 49 Stat. 1491, 7 U.S.C. (generally disbursed through Chapter 1) (2000) (Commodity Exchange Act); 54 Stat. 79, 15 U.S.C. §§80a-1 et seq. and 80b-1 et seq. (1982) (Investment Company and Investment Advisers Acts of 1940).

The American Law Institute's Federal Securities Code would have recodified all of the securities laws while retaining the current thrust of federal legislation. A.L.I., Federal Securities Code (1979). See Symposium, The American Law Institute's Federal Securities Code, 30 Vand. L. Rev. 311 (1977); A.L.I. Proposed Federal Securities Code: A Program, 34 Bus. Law. 345 (1978). Because many of the proposed code's most significant changes have been adopted by the SEC, the proposed Code is no longer the focus of securities law reform.

[4] Sarbanes-Oxley Act of 2002, Pub. L. No. 107-204 (July 30, 2002). See Senate Report No. 107-205 (July 3, 2002).

[5] Sarbanes-Oxley Act of 2002, Pub. L. No. 107-204 §307 (July 30, 2002), which mandates SEC rule-making to define what constitutes proper representation by attorneys practicing before the SEC. The rules must require, inter alia; that once an attorney has evidence of serious corporate wrongdoing, he

accounting oversight board to oversee the accounting profession to police the self-regulatory system that previously existed.[6] The Act also addressed auditor independence requirements.[7] Another feature of the Sarbanes-Oxley Act is its increased criminalization of corporate conduct involving fraud with respect to publicly-held companies. Some of the more important provisions affecting public corporations are described below.

Title III of the Sarbanes-Oxley Act addressed various corporate governance concerns including the audit committee, requiring personal certifications of accuracy by the chief executive and chief financial officers of public companies.[8] The Act further prohibits loans to high ranking executives, subject to certain exceptions to be elaborated upon in SEC rulemaking. The Act also calls for enhanced financial disclosures by public companies.[9]

Titles VIII and IX of the Sarbanes Oxley Act[10] provide for enhanced criminal penalties for violations of the Act generally and in particular for frauds perpetrated upon shareholders of public companies. The Act provides protection to corporate whistle-blowers.[11] The Act also covers other areas, including heightened controls over securities analysts' conflicts of interest[12] and a sense of the Senate that federal corporate tax returns should be signed by a corporation's chief executive officer.[13]

A.   THE FEDERAL SECURITIES ACT OF 1933

§27.06   The Federal Securities Act of 1933—Overview

Section 2 of the 1933 Act sets forth the basic definitions.[1] The heart of the act is section 5,[2] which is designed to assure an informed market for investments. Section 5, absent an applicable exemption, prohibits the offer and sale of securities unless a registration statement has been filed with the Securities and Exchange Commission. Section 5 further requires the delivery of a prospectus to purchasers as well as to offerees. Section 3[3] exempts from the registration requirements a wide variety of securities, including securities issued by governmental bodies, banks, and insurance companies. Section 4[4] lists categories of transactions that are

---

or she must climb the corporate ladder, possibly to the audit committee and to the board of directors, until satisfied that the problem has been attended to.

[6] *Id.* at tit. I.

[7] *Id.* at tit. II.

[8] *Id.* at tit. III.

[9] *Id.* at tit. IV.

[10] *Id.* at tits. VIII, IX. *See also id.* tit. 11.

[11] *Id.* at §1107.

[12] *Id.* at §501.

[13] *Id.* at §1001.

§27.06   [1] 15 U.S.C. §77b (2000).

[2] 15 U.S.C. §77e (2000). *See* §27.07.

[3] 15 U.S.C. §77c (2000). *See* §27.10.

[4] 15 U.S.C. §77d (2000). *See* §27.10.

exempt from the registration and prospectus requirements.[5] Registration procedures are found in sections 6 and 8 of the act.[6] The disclosure requirements are broadly set forth in sections 7 and 10 and in Schedule A.[7] More detailed disclosure guidelines are found in the applicable SEC forms and regulations.[8] Section 11 provides a private right of action for investors who have purchased securities offered pursuant to a materially misleading registration statement.[9] Section 12 imposes civil liability on persons who sell securities in violation of section 5's registration and prospectus requirements as well as on anyone who sells a security using materially misleading statements.[10] Section 17 embodies general antifraud proscriptions in connection with the offer or sale of securities.[11] Section 19 gives the SEC broad rule-making power, and section 20 gives the Commission broad enforcement powers.[12]

§27.07   The Registration and Prospectus Requirements of the Securities Act of 1933

In the absence of a security or transaction exemption,[1] no security may be publicly offered or sold in interstate or foreign commerce or through the mails until it has been registered with the Securities and Exchange Commission. When new issues are distributed in a public offering by an issuer or underwriter, agent or dealer, complete information must be made publicly available for the benefit of original and subsequent purchasers. The 1933 Act thus closes the mails and other communications in interstate commerce to the sale, offering, or carriage for the purpose of sale or delivery of any security or any prospectus unless a registration statement is filed and is in effect as to such security.[2] Similarly, there can be neither offers to sell nor offers to buy prior to the filing of the registration statement.[3] After the registration statement has been filed, there is no longer any prohibition against offers to buy or oral offers to sell; however, all written offers to sell must

---

[5] *See also* section 28, which gives the SEC general exemptive authority through its rulemaking process. 15 U.S.C. §77z-3.

[6] 15 U.S.C. §§77f, 77h (2000).

[7] 15 U.S.C. §§77g, 77j, Schedule A (2000).

[8] *See* §27.07.

[9] 15 U.S.C. §77k (2000). *See* §27.11.

[10] 15 U.S.C. §77l (2000). *See* §27.11. Section 13 contains the statute of limitations applicable to remedies under sections 11 and 12. 15 U.S.C. §77m (2000).

[11] 15 U.S.C. §77q (2000)

[12] 15 U.S.C. §§77s, 77t (2000).

§27.07   [1] *See* 15 U.S.C. §§77c, 77d (2000).

[2] Sections 5(a), (b), 15 U.S.C. §77e(a), (b) (2000).

[3] Section 5(c), 15 U.S.C. §77e(c) (2000). There is some limited prefiling publicity that may be disseminated without violating the Act's gun-jumping prohibitions. *See* 17 C.F.R. §230.135 (2001).

conform to the Act's prospectus requirements.[4] Finally, no sales may be made until after the registration statement becomes effective.[5]

The first duty of counsel with reference to an issue of securities is to ascertain whether registration is required. The only way to avoid registration is by reliance on one of the Act's security or transaction exemptions. The lawyer must accordingly be able to answer the following questions:

(1) What constitutes a "security"?[6]
(2) What constitutes a sale or "offer to sell"?
(3) What securities and transactions are exempted?[7]

Section 5 of the 1933 Securities Act breaks down the registration process into three periods. These periods are based on the filing and effective date of the registration statement, which generally will be prepared by a team of lawyers, accountants, issuer's management, and underwriters.

The first is the "prefiling" period, starting months before the filing of the registration statement and lasting until the filing date. The second period, the "waiting" period, runs from the filing date until the effective date.[8] The last period, the "post-effective" period, begins at the effective date and is the first time that sales may take place.

Section 5 of the Act places various restrictions on the dissemination of information throughout the registration process. A violation of section 5 depends on use of the jurisdictional means—an instrumentality of interstate commerce. Section 5 limits the type of selling efforts that may be used. The scope of permissible selling efforts and the type of information that may be disseminated varies depending on whether one is operating during the prefiling period, waiting period, or post-effective period. In general, sections 5(a)(1) and 5(a)(2) are in effect in the prefiling and waiting periods, but not during the post-effective period. Section 5(b)(1) is in effect in the waiting period and post-effective period,

---

[4] 15 U.S.C. §77e(b) (2000). Section 2(10) defines "prospectus," and section 10 sets out the types of disclosures required. 15 U.S.C. §§77b(10), 77j (2000). After the filing of the last amendment to the registration statement, there is a 20-day waiting period until the effective date. 15 U.S.C. §77h (2000). No sales may be made during the waiting period. 15 U.S.C. §77e(a) (2000). The 20-day waiting period is subject to acceleration on application to the SEC. 15 U.S.C. §77h (2000).

[5] 15 U.S.C. §77e(a) (2000).

[6] See §27.09.

[7] See §27.10.

[8] The waiting period can be several months or longer. Pursuant to section 8 of the 1933 Act (15 U.S.C. §77h), the registration statement becomes effective 20 days from the date of the original filing or the filing of the most recent amendment, whichever is last. The 20-day period is misleading in terms of actual practice. The waiting period is usually much longer than the statutory 20 days for first-time issuers and for complicated offerings because of SEC review practices. Under section 8, the effective date of deficient registration statements can be delayed by a stop order or refusal order. Formal section 8 orders are the exception, as the SEC will generally respond to deficient registration statements with a letter of comment suggesting changes. The letter of comment will frequently be followed by a delaying amendment filed by the prospective issuer, which will put off the effective date until the deficiencies are corrected. When appropriate, the effective date can be accelerated (see SEC Rule 461; 17 C.F.R. §230.461 (2001)).

but not during the prefiling period. Section 5(b)(2) is in effect only in the post-effective period. Finally, section 5(c) is in effect only in the prefiling period.

Prefiling Period. Section 5(c) of the Act prohibits all offers to sell and buy prior to the filing of the registration statement. An offer to sell is any communication reasonably calculated to generate a buying interest.[9] It applies to oral as well as to written offers. A large body of public information concerning securities is generated by broker-dealers, investment advisers, and other financial analysts. Balanced against the desire to prevent "gun jumping," as expressed by the prohibitions of section 5(c), is the underlying purpose of federal securities regulation: affirmative disclosure. Therefore there are various exemptions from section 5(c)'s prohibitions in the prefiling period. For example, SEC Rules 137, 138, and 139 provide exemptions from gun-jumping prohibitions for certain broker-dealer recommendations in the case of securities of 1934 Act reporting companies.[10] These exemptions apply with equal force to the waiting and post-effective periods. These rules recognize the fact that many investment bankers have research analysts who are separate from the underwriting department. Accordingly, the rules permit the research department to continue with its regular business without violating the prohibitions of section 5 of the 1933 Act. The exemptions are conditioned on certain protections, including the requirements that the issuer of the recommended securities is sufficiently large and subject to the reporting requirements (which ensure that there is sufficient public information already available). At the same time, it is clear that any broker's or dealer's recommendation to purchase a security that does not fall within the parameters of these rules would violate section 5 — unless, of course, some other exemption could be found.

Section 2(a)(3)'s definition of the terms "sale" and "offer to sell" excludes preliminary negotiations and agreements between the issuer and the underwriter as well as among underwriters in privity with the issuer.[11] This exclusion permits the formation of the underwriting syndicate. However, generally only a letter of intent is signed at this stage; the final underwriting agreement is usually not executed until the eve of the offering. Although there may be prefiling activity

---

[9] See the SEC decision in Carl M. Loeb, Rhoades & Co., 38 S.E.C. 843 (1959). This case is generally considered the leading precedent for determining the scope of the definition of "offer to sell." In *Loeb*, the company at issue was planning to go public. It had made a preliminary agreement with a group of underwriters. The lead underwriter issued a press release providing many specific details about the forthcoming offering. The SEC, while recognizing that prefiling press releases may be a legitimate publicity device, ruled that this release was too explicit and was in fact designed to arouse buying interest, in violation of section 5(c). Subsequently, the SEC, recognizing the informational tensions at issue, amended one of its rules to address prefiling publicity by an issuer. *See* SEC Rule 135. There remains a question as to whether Rule 135, which speaks only of issuers releasing information, is the exclusive list of permissible information or whether the rule is simply a safe harbor.

[10] 17 C.F.R. §§230.137-139 (2001). Sections 13 and 15(d) of the 1934 Act provide for periodic reporting of issuers whose securities are traded on a national exchange, securities that have been subject to a 1933 Act registration, or issuers with more than $5 million in assets and more than 500 holders of a class of equity securities. Section 12, 15 U.S.C. §78l (2000).

[11] 15 U.S.C. §77b(a)(3) (2000).

designed to form the underwriting group, contacting too many potential under-writers or potential members of the retail "selling group" may be viewed as improperly preconditioning the market and therefore may result in a finding of illegally jumping the gun. The purpose of the section 2(a)(3) exclusion for under-writer negotiations and agreements is to balance the need for formation of the underwriting group against the desire not to have premature widespread genera-tion of a buying interest.

Section 5(a) of the 1933 Act prohibits sales prior to the effective date and thus operates during both the prefiling and waiting periods. Section 5(a)(1) pro-hibits the sale (or confirmation of a sale) prior to the effective date; section 5(a)(2) prohibits taking steps toward the sale or delivery of securities pursuant to a sale through instrumentalities of interstate commerce prior to the effective date.

Waiting Period. Section 5(c)'s prohibitions on offers to sell and buy no longer apply once the registration statement has been filed. However, section 5(a)'s pro-hibitions on sales continue through the waiting period. In addition, section 5(b) of the 1933 Act imposes prospectus requirements that have the effect of control-ling the types of written offers to sell that may be made during both the waiting and post-effective periods. Section 5(b)(1) provides that any prospectus must meet the requirements of section 10 of the 1933 Act.[12] Section 2(a)(10)[13] defines "prospectus" as any written or other permanent or widely disseminated offer to sell. For example, a telephone communication is not a prospectus, but a television or radio advertisement is. A written confirmation of a sale is expressly included in the statutory definition of "prospectus."[14]

The combination of these statutory provisions results in a limited variety of permissible written offers to sell that may be used during the waiting period (and post-effective period as well). While section 5 permits offers during the waiting period, section 2(a)(10) makes any offer in writing a prospectus, and section 5(b)(1) makes it unlawful to transmit any prospectus after the filing of the regis-tration statement unless the prospectus contains the information called for by sec-tion 10. This information may not be available until the underwriting agreements have been signed and the offering price set. The Act solves this problem by exempting from this path two types of written offering material: the "tombstone ad" and the preliminary, or "red herring," prospectus. Both are discussed below.

Because section 5(c) does not apply during the waiting period, offers to buy are permissible. However, an offer to buy that leads to a premature or otherwise illegal sale will violate section 5(a). By virtue of section 10(b), which permits cer-tain prospectuses during the waiting period, and section 2(a)(10), which excludes certain communications from the definition of "prospectus," there are four types of permissible waiting period offers to sell.

[12] 15 U.S.C. §77j (2000).
[13] 15 U.S.C. §77b(a)(10) (2000).
[14] Rule 10b-10 of the 1934 Act requires that all sales by broker-dealers be confirmed in writing. 17 C.F.R. §240.10b-10.

A. The Federal Securities Act of 1933

First, all oral communications are permitted, provided that no sale is consummated (lest there be a violation of section 5(a)).[15] Since an oral communication is not "permanent," it is excluded from the section 2(a)(10) definition of "prospectus."

Second, an "identifying statement" (one variety of which is known as a "tombstone ad"), as defined in section 2(a)(10)(b) and Rule 134, is permissible during the waiting period.[16] This is a relatively narrow category because the type of information that may be included is severely limited. Section 2(10)(b) expressly excludes these communications from the definition of "prospectus" as long as the requirements of Rule 134 are met. Inclusion of any information not specifically permitted by Rule 134 renders the rule unavailable and thus may result in a prospectus that fails to comply with section 10's requirements. This in turn can result in a violation of section 5.

Third, a preliminary (or "red herring") prospectus, as defined in Rule 430,[17] is permissible during the waiting period. The preliminary prospectus must contain the information required in a full-blown statutory prospectus, except that the price and some other terms may be omitted. Furthermore, there must be a legend explaining that it is a preliminary prospectus. This prospectus may be used only during the waiting period; it may not be used after the effective date.

Finally, a preliminary summary prospectus, as defined in Rule 431,[18] which, like the red herring prospectus, is a section 10(b) prospectus, may be used by certain experienced issuers during the waiting period. The summary prospectus may also be used after the effective date and, like the preliminary version, is available only for an issuer who is a 1934 Act registered reporting company. The Rule 431 prospectus must contain all of the information specified in the official SEC form accompanying the applicable registration statement form as well as a caption stating that a more complete prospectus will be available from designated broker-dealers. The summary prospectus may not include any information not permitted in the registration statement or in a tombstone ad, as spelled out in Rule 134(a). A Rule 431 summary prospectus satisfies only section 5(b)(1);[19] it does not satisfy section 5(b)(2).[20] Thus, when a Rule 431 summary prospectus is used, a full-blown (or statutory) section 10(a) prospectus must still be delivered to all purchasers. This necessarily increases the record-keeping and monitoring activities of the underwriters.

Post-Effective Period. Once the registration statement becomes effective, section 5(a)'s prohibitions cease to apply, and sales are permitted. Both of section 5(b)'s prospectus requirements apply. Subsection (b)(1) requires that all written or otherwise permanent offers to sell or confirmations of sales must be qualifying

[15] The only prohibition is on written offers to sell, thus any (including written) offers to buy are permissible, provided the sale is not consummated. Furthermore, while there are no section 5 implications, oral offers to sell are, of course, subject to the securities acts' general antifraud provisions.

[16] 15 U.S.C. §77b(2)(a)(10)(b) (2000); 17 C.F.R. §230.134 (2001).

[17] 17 C.F.R. §230.430 (2001).

[18] 17 C.F.R. §230.431 (2001).

[19] Section 5(b)(1) requires any written offer or confirmation to comply with section 10; a summary prospectus is valid for this purpose under section 10(b).

[20] Section 5(b)(2), which applies only during the post-effective period, requires every person who purchases a security in the offering to receive a section 10(a) "full-blown" prospectus prior to or with delivery of that security.

prospectuses (that is, a section 10(a) full-blown statutory prospectus or a qualifying section 10(b) prospectus). Section 5(b)(2) provides that no security may be delivered for sale unless accompanied or preceded by a statutory section 10(a) prospectus. In the case of securities held for a customer's account by a broker or other custodian, the customer must still receive the prospectus before delivery.

Under section 2(a)(10), "free writing" is permitted in the post-effective period. Thus supplemental sales information may be sent to prospective purchasers, provided that the information is preceded or accompanied by a prospectus that meets the requirements of section 10(a). In such a case, free writing is limited only by the antifraud provisions of the securities laws.[21]

Proposals for Reform. In 1998, the SEC issued a proposal which if adopted would totally revise the 1933 Act registration process.[22] The magnitude of these proposals led the Commission to dub the proposals "the aircraft carrier." The aircraft carrier proposals would overhaul the disclosures required in registered offerings, revise the current prospectus delivery rules, eliminate many of the restrictions on pre-offering communications, amend the rules dealing with integration of private and public offerings, and also significantly revise the periodic disclosure requirements. A few of the proposals have been adopted but none that have been adopted to date have radically altered the registration process.

§27.08 Aim of Disclosure

In the words of the SEC, "[t]he Securities Act, often referred to as the 'truth in securities' Act, was designed not only to provide investors with adequate information upon which to base their decisions to buy and sell securities, but also to protect legitimate business seeking to obtain capital through honest protestation against competition from crooked promoters and to prevent fraud in the sale of securities."[1] As former SEC Commissioner and Supreme Court Justice William O. Douglas pointed out, the effects of the Act are chiefly "(1) prevention of excesses and fraudulent transactions, which will be hampered and deterred merely by the requirement that their details be revealed; and (2) placing in the market during the early stages of the life of a security a body of facts which, operating indirectly through investment services and expert investors, will tend to produce more accurate appraisal of the worth of the security if it commands a broad enough market."[2]

[21] Other rules to look at include Rules 137, 138, and 139, which deal with broker-dealer recommendations of securities during the registration process.

[22] See Sec. Act Rel. No. 33-7314 (SEC July 30, 1996); Stephen J. Choi, Company Registration: Toward a Status-Based Antifraud Regime, 64 U. Chi. L. Rev. 567 (1997); Comment, Michael McDonough, Death in One Act: The Case for Company Registration, 24 Pepp. L. Rev. 563 (1997). See also, e.g., Dale Arthur Osterle, The Inexorable March Toward a Continuous Disclosure Requirement for Publicly Traded Corporations: "Are We There Yet?," 20 Cardozo L. Rev. 135 (1998).

§27.08 [1] 10 S.E.C. Ann. Rep. 14 (1944).

[2] William O. Douglas & George E. Bates, The Federal Securities Act of 1933, 43 Yale L.J. 171, 172 (1933).

A. The Federal Securities Act of 1933

The 1933 Act's basic philosophy is that an informed market will control the abuses that once existed.

§27.09 What Constitutes a Security Under Federal and State Law?

The federal securities laws provide jurisdiction, of course, over securities. But what is the definition of "security"? The term has been broadly defined by the statutes; section 2(a)(1) of the Securities Act of 1933 is representative.[1]

The administrative and judicial definition of "security" has developed primarily from the interpretation of the statutory phrase "investment contract." In struggling for an appropriate definition, courts have always been mindful that the bottom-line issue is whether the particular investment or instrument involved needs or demands the investor protection of the federal securities laws.[2]

The landmark case on the definition of "investment contract" is *SEC v. W. J. Howey Co.*[3] Under the test developed in that case, a contract, transaction, or scheme is an investment contract if "a person [1] invests his money [2] in a common enterprise[4] and [3] is led to expect profits [4] solely from the efforts of the promoter or a third party."[5]

Since the *Howey* decision, there has been substantial case law refining the four elements set forth by the Supreme Court.[6] For example, the requirement that profits be secured "solely" from the efforts of others has been refined so that the profits must come "primarily" or "substantially" from the efforts of others.[7] In determining if this test is satisfied, the focus is on the economic reality surrounding the investment package as a whole, not exclusively on any single factor. For example, in *Howey* the defendants claimed that orange trees were being sold. There was also an "optional" service agreement that could be purchased, whereby the promoters would handle all management of trees bought by the investor. The

---

§27.09 [1] 15 U.S.C. §77b(a)(1) (2000).

[2] *E.g.,* Marine Bank v. Weaver, 455 U.S. 551 (1982) (bank-issued certificate of deposit not a security subject to federal securities laws because it is already federally insured and purchasers therefore do not need that extra layer of protection the laws afford).

[3] 328 U.S. 293 (1946).

[4] Courts have developed the concept of "horizontal commonality" to describe the pooling of interests among investors. This is in contrast to "vertical commonality," where the promoter shares risk with the investor. Horizontal commonality clearly satisfies the *Howey* common enterprise requirement, but the courts are divided as to whether vertical commonality will suffice. *See, e.g.,* Revak v. SEC Realty Corp., 18 F.3d 81, 88 (2d Cir. 1994); SEC v. Continental Commodities Corp., 497 F.2d 516 (5th Cir. 1974); Schofield v. First Commodity Corp., 638 F. Supp. 4 (D. Mass. 1985), *aff'd,* 793 F.2d 28 (1st Cir. 1986).

[5] 328 U.S. at 298-299.

[6] For a detailed discussion *see* Thomas Lee Hazen, Treatise on the Law of Securities Regulation §1.6 (4th ed. 2002).

[7] *See, e.g.,* SEC v. Glenn W. Turner Enter., 474 F.2d 476 (9th Cir.), *cert. denied,* 414 U.S. 821 (1973) (pyramid sales arrangement is a security).

realities of the situation, however, revealed that what was being sold was an investment contract in the trees and their fruit. Buyers were not expected to come to the field and tend their own trees; in fact, that would have been nearly impossible. Based on the small size of the plots, only a common enterprise and the resultant economies of scale would make the plots economically feasible. Moreover, there was no physical access or right of access to the individual plots—as such, it was virtually impossible for any single buyer to manage his or her plot individually, or even use a competitor's services. Thus, although not tied by contract, as an economic reality the services offered by the promoters were tied to the property, creating a security.

Of course, the definition of "security" is not limited to investment contracts. For example, stock is explicitly included in the statutory definition. There is a strong presumption that stock is a security. Nevertheless, under the "economic reality" test, it has been held that some transfers of instruments called stock are not transfers of securities.

Both the 1933 and 1934 Acts provide that "any note" is a security. However, both the statutes themselves and the courts have modified the phrase so that it is not read literally. Special provisions deal with the applicability of the federal securities laws to short-term notes. Section 3(a)(3) of the Securities Act of 1933 exempts from registration (but not from liability imposed by antifraud provisions of the Act) any "note . . . aris[ing] out of a current transaction" with a maturity not exceeding nine months.[8] In contrast, section 3(a)(10) of the Securities Exchange Act of 1934 excludes (even from the antifraud provisions) such notes from the definition of "security."[9] In *Reves v. Ernst & Young*, the Supreme Court declared that the phrase "any note" "must be understood against the backdrop of what Congress was attempting to accomplish in enacting the Securities Acts."[10] In the *Reves* case, the Supreme Court adopted the "family resemblance" test for determining whether or not a note is a security. Using this approach, the starting point is a rebuttable presumption that the note is a security. Based on a number of factors, the courts have created a list of instruments that, although they are "notes," do not fall within the definition of "security."[11] The presumption that a note is a security may be rebutted by showing that the note in question fits in a category on the list, bears a strong "family resemblance" to a category on the list, or belongs to another category that should be on the list.

Another common form of investment is a partnership interest. Partnership interests can implicate the definition of "security." Since general partners ordinarily take an active part in the business, interests in a general partnership ordinarily will not be securities.[12] However, when partners are likely to be relying

---

[8] 15 U.S.C. §77c(3) (2000). The Act further exempts all renewals thereof that are likewise limited in time. *Id.*

[9] 15 U.S.C. §78c(a)(10) (2000).

[10] 494 U.S. 56, 63 (1990).

[11] *See, e.g.,* Chemical Bank v. Arthur Andersen & Co., 726 F.2d 930, 939 (2d Cir.), *cert. denied,* 469 U.S. 884 (1984); Exchange Nat'l Bank v. Touche Ross & Co., 544 F.2d 1126, 1137 (2d Cir. 1976).

[12] Holden v. Hagopian, 978 F.2d 1115 (9th Cir. 1992); Klaers v. St. Peter, 942 F.2d 535 (8th Cir. 1991); Matek v. Murat, 862 F.2d 720 (9th Cir. 1988); Rivanna Trawlers Unlimited v. Thompson Trawlers, Inc., 840 F.2d 236 (4th Cir. 1988).

substantially on the efforts of others, the interest may be a security.[13] It is for this reason that limited partnership interests (where investors cannot exercise control) will ordinarily be classified as securities.[14] In the case of the new form of doing business known as a limited liability company, if the enterprise is set up in such a way that the owners will be active participants, the securities laws are not likely to be implicated.[15] However, if the limited liability company is used as a passive investment for its members, then a security is likely to exist.[16]

As described more fully in the next section,[17] the 1933 Act sets forth exemptions from registration. These exemptions may be based on the type of security involved (generally covered by section 3 of the 1933 Act)[18] or on the type of transaction (generally covered by section 4 of the Act).[19] Exemptions are strictly construed, and the burden of proof falls on the person trying to establish the exemption.

§27.10   Securities and Transaction Exemptions Under Federal Law

It is to be recalled that section 5 of the 1933 Act applies to any offer or sale of any security unless an exemption exists.[1] Exemptions may be based on the type of security involved (generally covered by section 3 of the 1933 Act and various SEC rules promulgated thereunder)[2] or on the type of transaction (generally covered by section 4 of the Act and applicable rules). The exemptions granted are exemptions from registration, not from the antifraud provisions.

Section 3 of the 1933 Act[3] is designed to provide exemptions from section 5 because of the nature of the security involved. For example, section 3(a)(2) exempts bank securities, insurance policies, and government securities. Section 3(a)(11) contains an intrastate exemption for securities offered and sold exclusively within the issuer's state of incorporation.

---

[13] Koch v. Hankins, 928 F.2d 1471 (9th Cir. 1991).

[14] *See, e.g.,* Reeves v. Teuscher, 881 F.2d 1495 (9th Cir. 1989); SEC v. Interlink Data Network of Los Angeles [1993-1994 Transfer Binder], Fed. Sec. L. Rep. (CCH) ¶98,049 (C.D. Cal. 1993); Mitland Raleigh-Durham v. Myers [1993-1994 Transfer Binder], Fed. Sec. L. Rep. (CCH) ¶98,038 (S.D.N.Y. 1993). Limited partnerships are discussed in §1.08.

[15] See, *e.g.,* Great Lakes Chemical Corp. v. Monsanto Corp., 96 F. Supp. 2d 376 (D. Del. 2000) (interests in limited liability company were not securities).

[16] SEC v. Shreveport Wireless Cable Television Partnership, 1998 WL 892948 [1998 Transfer Binder], Fed. Sec. L. Rep. (CCH) ¶90,322 (D.D.C. 1998) (limited partnership and limited liability company interests would be securities where investors had no control over the enterprise).

[17] *See* §27.10.

[18] 15 U.S.C. §77c (2000). However, §§3(a)(9), 3(a)(10), 3(a)(11), 3(b), and 3(c) operate more like transaction exemptions (that is, later downstream resales may need a new exemption or else face registration).

[19] 15 U.S.C. §77d (2000).

§27.10   [1] *See* §27.07.

[2] 15 U.S.C. §77c (2000). However, as discussed *infra,* §§3(a)(9), 3(a)(10), 3(a)(11), 3(b), and 3(c) operate more like transaction exemptions (that is, later downstream resales may need a new exemption or else face registration).

[3] 5 U.S.C. §77l(c).

Section 3(b) of the 1933 Act empowers the SEC to provide additional small issues exemptions by promulgating appropriate rules. This section is not self-executing: It requires "enabling rules" developed and promulgated by the SEC. Thus, the SEC has the freedom to create the exemptions it believes necessary or appropriate in light of the agency's policy considerations. Currently, such exemptions arc limitcd to offcrings of $5 million or lcss. The cxemptions emanating from this provision can be found in Regulation A, Regulation B, Rules 504 and 505 of Regulation D, Regulation F, and Rule 701. The SEC proposed legislation that would raise section 3(b)'s ceiling[4] to $10 million, but in 1996, Congress gave the SEC broader, virtually unlimited exemptive authority via a new section 28 of the Act, making the raising of section 3(b)'s ceiling far less significant.[5]

Section 4 of the 1933 Act describes the types of transactions that are exempt from the registration requirements of section 5. Transaction exemptions rise and fall with both the form and substance of the transaction and the nature of the participants. These exemptions, once available, can be destroyed when purchasers under the exemption resell the securities. Downstream sales have the potential to eradicate an existing exemption.

Section 4(1) provides a transaction exemption for persons other than an issuer, underwriter, or dealer. "Issuer" and "dealer" are defined in the 1933 Act[6] and have been interpreted as in ordinary parlance, not as terms of art. "Underwriter," by contrast, has become a term of art subject to significant SEC and judicial construction.

Determining who is included in this definition has required substantial interpretation. Someone who is an essential cog in the distribution process is a statutory underwriter even if no remuneration is received.[7] It has been established that, by definition, underwriters include participants in relatively large transactions who may unwittingly become underwriters and thus subject to the proscriptions of section 5.[8] The Act's definition encompasses persons who purchase or otherwise obtain a large amount of securities directly from the issuer (or a control person) and who then resell the securities.[9]

---

[4] 15 U.S.C. §77c(b) (2000). In 1996, the Commission relied on section 3(b) for a new type of exemption based on an exemption from state blue sky registration. Rule 1001, 17 C.F.R. §230.1001, adopted in Sec. Act Rel. No. 33-7285, 1996 WL 225996 (SEC May 1, 1996) (exempting offerings up to $5 million that qualify for exemption under §25102(n) of the California Corporations Code). This new rule was added as Regulation CE ("coordinated exemptions") and may be a harbinger of similar exemptions in the future. However, to date, that has not proven to be the case.

[5] 15 U.S.C. §77z-3 (1996). The SEC invoked section 28 to lift the $5 million ceiling from the Rule 701 exemption.

[6] "Issuer" is defined in §2(a)(4) as "every person who issues or proposes to issue any security." "Dealer" is defined in §2(a)(12) as "any person who engages either for all or part of his time, directly or indirectly . . . in the business of offering, buying, selling, or otherwise dealing or trading in Securities issued by another person."

[7] *See, e.g.,* SEC v. Chinese Consol. Benevolent Assoc., 120 F.2d 738 (2d Cir.), *cert. denied,* 314 U.S. 618 (1941).

[8] *See, e.g.,* In the Matter of Ira Haupt & Co., 23 S.E.C. 589 (1946).

[9] *See, e.g.,* United States v. Wolfson, 405 F.2d 779 (2d Cir. 1968), *cert. denied,* 394 U.S. 946 (1969) (defendant purchased securities from issuer).

A. The Federal Securities Act of 1933

The need for predictability led to SEC promulgation of Rule 144, a safe-harbor rule. Rule 144 applies to all sales for control persons and other affiliates of the issuer,[10] and resales of restricted securities (generally restricted to preserve the original exemption) by anyone.

Section 4(2) exempts private placements and other "transactions by an issuer not involving any public offering."[11] This exemption was enacted to permit offerings by issuers for isolated sales to particularly sophisticated persons wherein there is no need for the Act's protections. Although the statutory language is somewhat vague, after years of SEC decisions, interpretive releases,[12] and judicial scrutiny, certain key factors have been isolated by the Supreme Court.[13] First, the number of offerees: although the Supreme Court expressly refused to adopt a "numbers test" as determinative, the number of offerees remains an important factor—the fewer the number, the greater likelihood that a section 4(2) exemption applies. Likewise, the size of the offering is a factor: the smaller the offering, the greater chance for an exemption. Second, access to information: each offeree should have access to the type of information that would be disclosed should the issuer be required to undertake a full-fledged registration. Third, the sophistication of investors: Each offeree should be sophisticated with respect to business and financial matters, as well as with respect to the particular investment being offered.[14] Fourth, the manner of the offering: it should be limited to those who have a privately expressed interest rather than be a general solicitation.

Section 4(3) provides an exemption from the prospectus delivery requirements for certain transactions by dealers.[15] This exemption is directed generally to the aftermarket, after primary distribution has occurred. Section 4(4) of the Act exempts unsolicited brokers' transactions.

Section 4(6) exempts offerings made solely to accredited investors where the aggregate amount of securities sold does not exceed the dollar limit of section 3(b) (currently $5 million). "Accredited investor" is defined in section 2(a)(15) of the 1933 Act.[16]

Under the authority of section 3(b) of the 1933 Act, the SEC promulgated Regulation A[17] to exempt certain "small issues." Regulation A is limited to issuers in the United States or Canada that are not investment companies, and it applies to issues with an aggregate offering price of $5 million or less within a one-year period. The Regulation A exemption contains "bad boy" disqualification provisions that render it unavailable in most cases if a participant in the offering has been subject to SEC disciplinary proceedings or has been convicted of a violation

---

[10] Rule 144(a)(1) defines "affiliate" as "a person that directly, or indirectly through one or more intermediaries, controls, or is controlled by, or is under common control with, such issuer." 17 C.F.R. §230.144(a)(1) (2001).

[11] 15 U.S.C. §77d(2) (2000).

[12] *See, e.g.,* Sec. Act Rel. No. 33-285 (Jan. 24, 1935); Sec. Act Release No. 33-5487 (Jan. 23, 1974).

[13] *See, e.g.,* SEC v. Ralston Purina Co., 346 U.S. 119 (1953).

[14] *See, e.g.,* Doran v. Petroleum Management Corp., 545 F.2d 893 (5th Cir. 1977).

[15] In this context, "dealer" is understood to include underwriters no longer acting as underwriters.

[16] 15 U.S.C. §77b(a)(15) (2000).

[17] Rules 251-264; 17 C.F.R. §§230.251-264 (2001).

of relevant laws in the last five years.[18] Regulation A is not a complete exemption, but rather is conditioned on what is comparable to a "mini" registration.

Regulation D[19] consists of three separate private offering and small offering exemptions: Rule 504, Rule 505, and Rule 506, a safe harbor. Rules 504 and 505 are section 3(b) exemptions, while Rule 506 is promulgated under section 4(2)'s nonpublic offering exemption. These three exemptions are all governed by Rules 501, 502, 503, 507, and 508. The exemptions are, of course, exemptions only from registration, not from the antifraud or civil liability sections of the federal securities laws; nor do the exemptions relieve the issuer of the necessity to comply with state securities laws. Regulation D exemptions are available only to the issuer of securities, not to affiliates or purchasers of securities that were initially acquired under Regulation D offerings.

Under Rule 504, which is an exemption promulgated under section 3(b), an issuer that is not an investment company or a 1934 Act reporting company may have an exemption for small offerings. There is a $1 million limit on the aggregate offering price. All securities offered within the past twelve months under a section 3(b) exemption and all securities offered in violation of section 5 within the past twelve months are included in calculating the aggregate offering price.[20] General solicitations of purchasers are permitted and no resale restrictions are required, but, as a practical matter, only if the offering is registered under applicable state securities law (or blue sky law) provisions.

Rule 505, which is also a section 3(b) exemption, exempts certain offerings up to $5 million by issuers that are not investment companies.[21] The offering must be limited to no more than 35 purchasers, but related purchasers and accredited investors do not count in that limit. No general solicitation is permitted. There are no limitations on the nature of the purchasers; however, there are informational requirements for any of the offerees who are not accredited. As with Regulation A offerings, Rule 505 offerings are subject to the "bad boy" disqualification provisions of Rule 262. Resales of the securities relying on this exemption are subject to restrictions.[22]

---

[18] For example, it is unavailable where the issuer, its predecessors, or affiliates are subject to a pending SEC proceeding or have within the preceding five years been subject to an SEC stop order, court securities injunction, or U.S. Post Office fraud order. Similarly, it is unavailable where any of the issuer's directors, officers, principal security holders, current promoters, or underwriters, or any affiliate of such underwriters has been convicted of any crime under the securities laws (not limited to federal securities laws) within the preceding five years or has been subject to an SEC or Post Office order. 17 C.F.R. §230.262 (2001). The SEC may waive the disqualification. *Id.*

[19] 17 C.F.R. §§230.501-509 (2001).

[20] This makes the planning, timing, and ordering of offerings very important. For example, an issuer cannot have a $500,000 Rule 504 offering following within one year of a $4.5 million Regulation A offering because Rule 504 puts a $1 million ceiling on §3(b) offerings within the preceding 12 months. On the other hand, an issuer can have a $500,000 Rule 504 offering followed by a $4.5 million Rule 505 offering because Rule 251 would permit it as within Rule 505's $5 million ceiling on §3(b) offerings within 12 months.

[21] The method of calculation is similar to Rule 504: include all securities offered within the past twelve months under a §3(b) exemption (that is, Regulation A or Rule 504), plus all securities offered in violation of §5 within the past 12 months.

[22] Rule 502(d) requires that resales be made in compliance with Rule 144. 17 C.F.R. §§230.144, 502(d) (2002).

A. The Federal Securities Act of 1933

Rule 506, the third exemption in Regulation D, is a safe harbor for a section 4(2) exemption.[23] There is no limit on the dollar amount of an offering under Rule 506. General solicitation of purchasers is not permitted, and the offering is limited to 35 unaccredited purchasers.[24] Moreover, all of the unaccredited purchasers must be knowledgeable, sophisticated, and able to evaluate and bear the risks of the prospective investment, or represented by such a person.[25] Additionally, the purchasers must have access to the information as required by Rule 502(b), and affirmative disclosure of such information must be made by the issuer if there are any unaccredited purchasers. Rule 506, like Rule 505, is subject to the limitations on resale imposed by Rule 502(d). Downstream sales are similarly governed by Rule 144.

The "integration" doctrine is to the SEC what the "step transaction" doctrine is to the IRS. It permits the telescoping of two or more purportedly separate transactions into one transaction. Under the integration doctrine, the SEC and the courts examine multiple offerings to determine whether they should be treated as a single, unitary transaction. The SEC has developed the following five-factor test[26] to determine whether the integration doctrine should be applied to two or more transactions:

(1) Are the sales part of a single plan of financing?
(2) Do the sales involve issuance of the same class of securities?
(3) Were the sales made at or about the same time?
(4) Is the same type of consideration received?
(5) Are the sales made for the same general purpose?

The Commission has not given much guidance on how these factors should be weighted. Accordingly, it would appear that in a particular case any one or more of the five factors could be determinative.

§27.11   Civil Liability for Violations of the Securities Act of 1933[1]

The 1933 Act creates private rights of action for both fraud-based violations and violations of the Act's registration provisions. The Act has three sections prohibiting fraud and misstatements. Sections 11[2] and 12(a)(2)[3] create remedies based on

---

[23] As such, Rule 506 is limited to the scope of the statutory section 4(2) exemption. However, this may change to the extent that the SEC invokes its general exemptive power under section 28 of the 1933 Act. 15 U.S.C. §77z-2 (2002).

[24] Closely related purchasers and accredited investors are excluded from the calculation of the number of purchasers.

[25] The former safe-harbor rule for §4(2), Rule 146, used to require this qualification for each offeree. Although this requirement is not specifically stated in Rule 506, disputes over whether a prohibited general solicitation has taken place frequently arise when this qualification is not met. *See, e.g.,* Doran v. Petroleum Mgmt. Corp., 545 F.2d 893 (5th Cir. 1977).

[26] *E.g.,* Sec. Act Rel. No. 33-4434 (Dec. 6, 1961).

§27.11 [1] *See* Thomas L. Hazen, Treatise on the Law of Securities Regulation ch. 7 (4th ed. 2002).
[2] 15 U.S.C. §77k.
[3] 15 U.S.C. §77*l*(a).

material misrepresentation.[4] Section 17 does not contain a private remedy but sets forth the Act's general antifraud provision[5] used primarily by the SEC and by the Department of Justice in criminal actions.

In addition to the antifraud provisions mentioned above, section 12(a)(1) of the 1933 Act creates a private right of action for violations of that Act's registration requirements.[6]

§27.11.01   Misrepresentations and Omissions in Registration Statements—Section 11

Section 11 imposes express civil liability on persons preparing and signing materially misleading registration statements.[7] Section 11 is the only liability provision limited to registered offerings. It imposes broader liability than other antifraud provisions because aggrieved purchasers need only show that they bought the security traceable to the offering, and there was a material misrepresentation in the registration statement. There is no requirement under section 11 that purchasers show that they relied on the misrepresentation.[8]

There are two standards of liability imposed by section 11. The first standard applies to the issuer, which is, generally, strictly liable once the plaintiffs have proved that they bought the stock and that there was a material misstatement in the registration statement. The only affirmative defenses for the issuer are (1) to show that the person acquiring the security knew of the untruth or omission in the registration statement at the time of the acquisition,[9] (2) lack of materiality, or (3) expiration of the statute of limitations.

The second standard of liability applies to nonissuers. For all persons other than the issuer,[10] section 11(b) provides three additional possible affirmative defenses. The first two defenses relate to someone who discovers the material misstatement or omission and takes appropriate steps to prevent the violation. Potential section 11 defendants may be relieved of liability by either (1) resigning or taking steps toward resignation, and informing the SEC and the issuer in writing that they have taken such action and disclaim all responsibility for the relevant sec-

---

[4] Most class actions based claiming fraud involving publicly traded securities must be brought in federal court.

[5] 15 U.S.C. §§77k, 77*l*(a)(2), 77q(a) (2000).

[6] 15 U.S.C. §77*l*(a)(1) (2000).

[7] 15 U.S.C. §77k (2000).

[8] *But cf.* the last clause of section 11(a) which requires a showing of reliance with respect to financial statements more than twelve months old.

[9] Reliance is not required, so an offer of proof that plaintiff never heard or read the misstatement is irrelevant.

[10] Persons liable include all signers of the registration statement (which must include the principal executive and financial officers, the issuer, and a majority of the directors), all directors (including people not yet directors but agreeing to be named as about to become directors), experts (e.g., the certifying accountant), and underwriters. *See* §§11(a)(1)-(5) for a list of these persons, 15 U.S.C. §77k(a) (2000).

tions of the registration statement; or (2) if the registration statement becomes effective without their knowledge, on becoming aware of the effectiveness they take appropriate steps toward resignation, inform the Commission as above, and give reasonable public notice that the registration statement became effective without their knowledge.

The third defense, contained in section 11(b)(3), is the most frequently used. This absolves defendants from liability if they had reasonable grounds for believing, and did in fact believe, that there was no omission or material misstatement. This accordingly insulates defendants from liability if after reasonable investigation, they have a reasonable basis to believe and did believe the registration statement was free of any material misstatement or omission when it became effective. As for any portion of a registration statement prepared on the authority of an expert, such as an accountant, others are liable only if they fail to establish they had no reasonable ground to believe and did not believe the registration statement contained a material misstatement or omission when it became effective.

Section 11(c) establishes the appropriate standard of care: "[T]he standard of reasonableness shall be that required of a prudent man in the management of his own property."[11] Thus this defense is often described as the "due diligence" (although that phrase does not appear in the statute) and "reasonable investigation" defense.

The courts have not articulated a bright-line test as to what satisfies the due diligence and reasonable investigation standard of care.[12] What has emerged, however, is a sliding scale of culpability depending on the defendant's knowledge, expertise, and status with regard to the issuer, its affiliates, or its underwriters, as well as the degree of the defendant's actual participation in the registration process and in the preparation of registration materials.[13]

§27.11.02 Liability of Sellers for Violations of Section 5 and Material Misstatements or Omissions in the Prospectus or Otherwise—Section 12

Section 12 of the 1933 Act[14] imposes liability in two contexts: when a person sells a security in violation of section 5,[15] or when a security is sold by means of a

---

[11] 15 U.S.C. §77k(c) (2000).

[12] See, e.g., Escott v. BarChris Constr. Corp., 283 F. Supp. 643 (S.D.N.Y. 1968); Feit v. Leaseco Data Processing Equip. Corp., 332 F. Supp. 544 (E.D.N.Y. 1971); In re Flight Transp. Corp. Sec. Litig., 593 F. Supp. 612 (D. Minn. 1984); Draney v. Wilson, Morton, Assaf & McElligott, 592 F. Supp. 9 (D. Ariz. 1984); In re Fortune Sys. Sec. Litig. [1987 Transfer Binder], Fed. Sec. L. Rep. (CCH) ¶93,390 (N.D. Cal. 1987).

[13] In an effort to clarify its position, the SEC promulgated Rule 176, which sets forth factors to be considered, reinforces the judicial sliding scale of culpability, and further provides for the necessity of a case-by-case, highly fact-specific analysis. 17 C.F.R. §230.176 (2001).

[14] 15 U.S.C. §77l (2000).

[15] This is the remedy set forth in section 12(a)(1). 15 U.S.C. §77l(a)(1) (2000).

prospectus or oral communication that contains a material misstatement or omission.[16] Unlike section 11, section 12 by its terms applies to any transaction, whether or not it is subject to the registration provisions of the 1933 Act. A major issue in many section 12 cases is whether the defendant is a permissible one—that is, a "seller" for purposes of section 12. Issuers and underwriters generally are not "sellers" within the meaning of section 12 unless they actively participate in the negotiations with the plaintiff/purchaser.[17] Similarly, an attorney's having worked on the offering circular will not make her a seller.[18] On the other hand, a broker who deals directly with the plaintiff is a seller under section 12.[19]

The Supreme Court has delineated two factors that should be considered in identifying a "seller" under section 12: (1) whether the defendant received direct remuneration or benefit as a result of the sale, and (2) whether the defendant's role in the solicitation and purchase was intended to benefit the seller (or owner) of the security.[20]

Civil Liability for Sales in Violation of Section 5—Section 12(a)(1). Anyone who offers or sells a security in violation of section 5 is liable in a civil action under section 12(a)(1) to the person "purchasing such security from him." In order to recover under this section, the plaintiff need only show that the defendant sold the security to him and that it was unregistered. The defendant then carries the burden of either showing that an exemption existed or establishing the in pari delicto (or equal fault) defense.

Liability of Sellers for Material Misstatements or Omissions—Section 12(a)(2). Section 12(a)(2) of the 1933 Act creates an express private remedy for a purchaser against the seller of a security for material misstatements or omissions in connection with the offer and sale. As is the case with section 12(a)(1), section 12(a)(2) is limited to the liability of sellers and thus imposes a privity requirement. Once the privity requirement is satisfied, the plaintiff must establish only that there was a material misstatement or omission in the prospectus or oral communication. There is no requirement that the plaintiff prove reliance; it will be presumed.[21] The plaintiff also need not have read the misstatement in question.[22] However, if the plaintiff knew of the untruth or omission, the section 12(a)(2) claim should be dismissed.[23] The defendant may also be absolved of liability if "he did not know, and in the exercise of reasonable care could not have known, of such untruth or

---

[16] Section 12(a)(2). 15 U.S.C. §77*l*(a)(2) (2000).

[17] *See* Foster v. Jesup & Lemont Sec. Co., 759 F.2d 838 (11th Cir. 1985). *See also* Pinter v. Dahl, 486 U.S. 622 (1988) (holding that to be a seller in an action under §12(a)(1), the defendant must have been both an immediate and direct seller; substantial participation alone will not suffice).

[18] *E.g.,* Abell v. Potomac Ins. Co., 858 F.2d 1104 (5th Cir. 1988), *cert. denied,* 492 U.S. 918 (1989); Stokes v. Lokken, 644 F.2d 779 (8th Cir. 1981).

[19] *E.g.,* Quincy Co-Operative Bank v. A. G. Edwards & Sons, Inc., 655 F. Supp. 78 (D. Mass. 1986).

[20] Pinter v. Dahl, 486 U.S. 622 (1988).

[21] Currie v. Cayman Resources Corp., 835 F.2d 780 (11th Cir. 1988).

[22] Sanders v. John Nuveen & Co., 619 F.2d 1222 (7th Cir. 1980), *cert. denied,* 450 U.S. 1005 (1981).

[23] *See* Mayer v. Oil Field Sys. Corp., 803 F.2d 749 (2d Cir. 1986).

omission."[24] The Supreme Court has limited the section 12(a)(2) actions to public offerings pursuant to an offering by prospectus.[25]

B. THE SECURITIES EXCHANGE ACT OF 1934

§27.12 The Securities Exchange Act of 1934

The Securities Act of 1933 is concerned primarily with securities' distributions while the Securities Exchange Act of 1934 is aimed at correcting trading abuses in outstanding securities, both on exchanges and in the over-the-counter markets.[1] The Exchange Act is thus concerned with securities' disclosure requirements, supervision and maintenance of the integrity of the marketplace, and the regulation of brokers, dealers, and other members of the securities industry. The 1934 Act also created the SEC and expanded greatly the administrative responsibilities that had been given to the Federal Trade Commission under the 1933 Securities Act.

The Securities Exchange Act of 1934 deals with a greater variety of subjects than the Securities Act of 1933. The Exchange Act provides for (1) the registration and supervision of national securities exchanges (section 6)[2]; (2) margin requirements, which govern the purchase of securities on credit, and restrictions on borrowing by members, brokers, and dealers (sections 7, 8)[3]; (3) prohibition of the manipulation of securities prices (sections 9, 10)[4]; (4) regulation of functions of brokers, members, and dealers (sections 11, 15(c))[5]; (5) registration requirements for securities trading on national exchanges, and reports of companies whose securities are listed (section 12)[6]—the registration and reporting provisions also extend to certain over-the-counter equity securities[7] and the reporting provisions for securities subject to registration under the 1933 Act[8]; (6) registration of over-the-counter brokers and dealers and supervision of their general trade practices (sections 15, 15A)[9]; (7) solicitation of proxies, consents, or authorizations as to securities registered on national securities exchanges (to be under

---

[24] 15 U.S.C. §77k(2) (2000).

[25] Gustafson v. Alloyd Corp., 513 U.S. 561 (1995).

§27.12 [1] *See* Thomas Lee Hazen, Treatise on the Law of Securities Regulation ch. 1 (4th ed. 2002).

[2] 15 U.S.C. §78f (Supp. 1993).

[3] 15 U.S.C. §78g, h (2000).

[4] 15 U.S.C. §§78i, j (1988 & Supp. 1993).

[5] 15 U.S.C. §§78k, 78o(c) (1988 & Supp. 1993). Jerry W. Markham & Thomas L. Hazen, Broker-Dealer Operations Under Securities and Commodities Law (2d ed. 2003).

[6] 15 U.S.C. §78l (2000). The Act also calls for registration of transfer agents. Section 17A(c), 15 U.S.C. §78q-1 (2002).

[7] Section 12(g)(1), as modified by Rule 12g-1 requires registration of any class of equity security with more than 500 shareholders where the issuer has more than $10 million in assets. 15 U.S.C. §78l(g)(1) (2000); 17 C.F.R. §240.12g-1 (2001).

[8] Section 15(d)(1). 15 U.S.C. §78o(d)(l) (2000).

[9] 15 U.S.C. §§78o, 78o-1 (1988 & Supp. 1993).

rules and regulations prescribed by the Commission) (section 14)[10]; (8) regulation of tender offers and other share acquisitions (sections 13, 14)[11]; (9) special rules for municipal securities dealers (section 15B)[12]; (10) recovery by the corporation of short-swing profits of directors, officers, and large shareholders in securities of their own companies to prevent unfair profits by insiders[13]; and (11) periodic and other reports by issuers subject to the Act (section 13).[14] The Commission has administrative power to expel or suspend members of exchanges whose conduct fails to conform to prescribed standards (section 19(3)). The Commission also has investigatory, adjudicatory, and prosecutorial functions with regard to violations of the Acts' various provisions.[15] Manipulative, deceptive, or fraudulent devices by brokers and dealers, such as the sale of securities in excess of prevalent market prices, are grounds for revocation of registration and license as broker or dealer and forfeiture of all undisclosed profits (section 15). Even beyond these administrative sanctions, the Act contains criminal penalties[16] and a broad spectrum of civil liability provisions.[17]

Issuers of securities are regulated by both the 1933 Act and the 1934 Act. The 1933 Act regulates distribution of securities; the 1934 Act deals with day-to-day trading. While most of the 1934 Act's regulation applies only to registered and/or reporting companies, two important provisions are not so limited: (1) the general antifraud provisions of section 10(b) and, in particular, SEC Rule 10b-5; and (2) the tender offer antifraud provision found in section 14(e).

There are two jurisdictional bases for regulation of securities and their issuers under the 1934 Act. First, some of the regulation is triggered by use of an instrumentality of interstate commerce.[18] The second basis for jurisdiction is found in the registration provisions of section 12 and the periodic reporting provisions of sections 13 and 15.

Section 12 of the 1934 Act requires registration of most publicly traded securities.[19] Under section 12(a), any security that is traded on a national exchange must be registered under the 1934 Act.[20] Section 12(a) thus covers exchange-traded equity securities (stock and securities convertible into stock), exchange-traded options (puts and calls),[21] and exchange-traded debt securities (bonds).

[10] 15 U.S.C. §78n (2000). See §§13.23-13.26.
[11] In particular Sections 13(d)-(e), 14(d)-(f). 15 U.S.C. §§78m(d)-(e), 78n(d)-(f). See Chapter 24.
[12] See Thomas Lee Hazen, Treatise on the Law of Securities Regulation §14.6 (4th ed. 2002).
[13] See §12.07.
[14] In particular, section 13(a), 15 U.S.C. §78m(a).
[15] See §27.05.
[16] 15 U.S.C. §§78o(a)-(c) (1988 & Supp. 1993).
[17] See §27.13.
[18] See, e.g., Rule 10b-5 and §14(e); 17 C.F.R. §240.10b-5 (2001); 15 U.S.C. §78n(e) (2000).
[19] Section 15(d) applies periodic reporting requirements to still others—namely, to those companies that had a public offering of securities that was registered under the Securities Act of 1933.
[20] The 1934 Act's registration requirement is set forth in 15 U.S.C. §78g (2000). It is quite different from 1933 Act registration; a corporation that has registered a class of securities under the 1934 Act will still have to register each particular offering of that class of securities under the 1933 Act.
[21] Options are included in the definition of equity securities because they are convertible into equity securities.

B. The Securities Exchange Act of 1934

The registration provisions of section 12 further apply to equity securities that are publicly traded in over-the-counter markets through the facilities of the National Association of Securities Dealers (NASD),[22] rather than on an exchange.

Section 12(g)(1) requires registration of certain equity securities that are not listed on a national securities exchange. Section 12(g)(1) applies on its face to companies with more than $1 million in assets that have a class of equity securities held by 500 or more persons. However, the SEC has narrowed the number of companies subject to 1934 Act registration. Rule 12g-1 exempts issuers if the company has less than $10 million in gross assets.[23] The registration and consequent periodic reporting obligations cease if on the last day of each of the issuer's last three fiscal years, the issuer (1) has had fewer than 300 shareholders of record of that class of securities or (2) has had assets not exceeding $5 million.[24] In such cases, the issuer may withdraw its registration.

Registration under the 1934 Act brings with it periodic disclosure obligations. Section 13 of the 1934 Act sets forth the periodic reporting requirements. The basic reports that must be filed with the SEC are (1) Form 10-K, an annual report; (2) Form 10-Q, a quarterly report; and (3) Form 8-K, an interim "current report." Form 8-K's interim reporting requirements are relatively limited, and, as a general rule, companies are not under an affirmative duty to disclose information until the next quarterly report. Section 13 periodic reporting requirements are not limited to companies that register securities. Section 15(d) of the 1934 Act also imposes the same periodic reporting requirements on companies who issue securities pursuant to a 1933 Act registration statement.[25]

§27.13 Civil Liability Under the Securities Exchange Act of 1934

The Securities Exchange Act of 1934 contains both express and implied private rights of action, although the three provisions that expressly create liability are

---

[22] The NASD operates the over-the-counter market, distinguished originally from the exchanges in two principal ways: (1) there is no central facility comparable to an exchange floor (although the NASD's introduction in 1971 of an electronic automated quotation system, NASDAQ and, more recently, its "national market system" have made this distinction less important); and (2) the function of a firm representing an individual buyer is different (in an exchange, the firm acts as a broker and the only dealer is the registered specialist in that stock; in the over-the-counter market, any number of firms may act as dealers or "market-makers" in a particular stock).

[23] 17 C.F.R. §240.12g-1 (2001). There is an exemption from 1934 Act registration for securities of foreign issuers, over-the-counter American depositary shares (ADSs), and American depositary receipts (ADRs) representing such securities. 1934 Act §12(g)(3) and Rule 12g3-2. The exemption depends on annually furnishing the SEC with all information that must be disclosed according to the laws of the issuer's domicile. This exemption was modified in 1983 and is no longer available for NASDAQ-listed securities; however, securities qualifying prior to that time retain their exempt status.

[24] Rule 12h-3, 17 C.F.R. §240.12h-3 (2001). To give an example of the numbers, there are approximately 3,000 exchange-listed securities (stocks and bonds, not options) and approximately 6,000 securities traded in the over-the-counter markets.

[25] 15 U.S.C. §78o(d). The 1933 Act registration requirements are discussed in §27.07.

much narrower than those in the Securities Act of 1933.[1] Section 9(e) of the Act confers a private remedy against one who has engaged willfully in market manipulation of securities subject to the Act's reporting requirements.[2] The Supreme Court has pointed out that "manipulation" is a term of art limited to specific types of market conduct designed to manipulate the price, such as artificial bids and wash sales, and thus does not extend to all cases where conduct has the deliberate intent to affect price.[3] Section 18(a) provides a private remedy to an investor defrauded by reliance on documents filed with the SEC.[4] Under the "eyeball" requirement, courts have limited the 18(a) remedy to plaintiffs who have viewed the actual filed document or a copy of it; thus section 18(a) does not apply to statements that are seen elsewhere.[5] There is no scienter requirement, but a defendant can prevail by proving good faith and lack of knowledge of the misstatement or omission. Under the better view, the section 18(a) remedy is not exclusive.[6] The third express remedy, under section 16(b), which was considered earlier, provides for disgorgement by insiders of short-swing profits on equity securities. Like the other two express remedies, section 16(b) is limited to reporting companies.[7]

The Supreme Court has recognized implied private remedy proxy antifraud prohibitions[8] and rule 10b-5's general antifraud provisions.[9] Although a competing tender offeror does not have standing to sue for damages,[10] a number of courts have recognized an implied remedy under section 14(e) relating to tender offers.[11]

Conduct Proscribed. As pointed out above, Rule 10b-5 represents delegated rule-making pursuant to statutory authority giving the SEC the power to prohibit the use of "manipulative or deceptive device[s] or contrivance[s]" "in connection with the purchase or sale of any security."[12] Since the rule represents law-making

§27.13   [1] *See* §27.11.

[2] 15 U.S.C. §78i(e). *See* Thomas L. Hazen, Treatise on the Law of Securities Regulation §12.1 (4th ed. 2002); Notes, 99 U. Pa. L. Rev. 651 (1951), 56 Yale L.J. 509 (1947).

[3] Santa Fe Indus. v. Green, 430 U.S. 462, 476-477 (1977); Ernst & Ernst v. Hochfelder, 425 U.S. 185, 199 (1976) (both interpreting Rule 10b-5 and section 10(b)); Crane Co. v. American-Standard, Inc., 603 F.2d 244 (2d Cir. 1979) (finding no "manipulation" as used in 9(a), (e)); SEC v. Resch-Cassin & Co., 362 F. Supp. 964 (S.D.N.Y. 1973) (interpreting 9(a)). *See also, e.g.,* Schreiber v. Burlington Northern, Inc., 472 U.S. 1 (1985).

[4] 15 U.S.C. §78r(a) (2000).

[5] *See* Heit v. Weitzen, 402 F.2d 909 (2d Cir. 1968), *cert. denied,* 395 U.S. 903 (1969); Jacobson v. Peat, Marwick, Mitchell & Co., 445 F. Supp. 518 (S.D.N.Y. 1977); Gross v. Diversified Mortgage Inv. [1977 Transfer Binder], Fed. Sec. L. Rep. (CCH) ¶96,170 (S.D.N.Y. 1977).

[6] *See* Herman & MacLean v. Huddleston, 459 U.S. 375 (1983).

[7] 15 U.S.C. §78p(b) (2000). *See* §12.07.

[8] *E.g.,* J. I. Case Co. v. Borak, 377 U.S. 426 (1964). *See* §13.26.

[9] *E.g.,* Herman & MacLean v. Huddleston, 459 U.S. 375 (1983); Superintendent of Ins. v. Bankers Life & Cas. Co., 404 U.S. 6 (1971).

[10] Piper v. Chris-Craft Indus., 430 U.S. 1 (1977). Most courts have held that even the bidder can sue for injunctive relief.

[11] *See* Chapter 24.

[12] 15 U.S.C. §78j(b) (2000).

delegated by the legislature, the rule can be only as broad as the delegating statutory provision. Accordingly, the terms of the statute place limits on the permissible scope of the rule. The rule itself has a sparse legislative history but has spawned a great deal of litigation. For example, the conduct prohibited by the rule must have been "deceptive."[13] This in turn has been interpreted to mean that the absence of full disclosure is the essence of the evil addressed. Additionally, the courts have read the deception requirement as limiting section 10(b) to fraudulent conduct. Rule 10b-5 is discussed in Chapter 12.[14]

---

[13] *E.g.,* Schreiber v. Burlington N., 472 U.S. 1 (1985); Santa Fe Indus. v. Green, 430 U.S. 462 (1977); Ernst & Ernst v. Hochfelder, 425 U.S. 185 (1976).

[14] *See* §§12.08-12.11.

Table of Cases

743

Table of Cases

Table of Cases

Index

Index

N

O

Index

Index

Index